Women's Lives

This cutting-edge and comprehensive fourth edition of *Women's Lives: A Psychological Perspective* integrates the most current research and social issues to explore the psychological diversity of girls and women varying in age, ethnicity, social class, nationality, sexual orientation, and ableness. Written in an engaging and accessible manner, its use of vignettes, quotes, and numerous pedagogical tools effectively fosters students' engagement, active learning, critical thinking, and social activism.

New information covered includes:

- neoliberal feminism, standpoint theory, mujerista psychology (Chapter 1)
- LGBT individuals and individuals with disabilities in media (Chapter 2)
- testosterone testing of female athletes, precarious manhood (Chapter 3)
- raising a gender nonconforming child, impact of social media on body image (Chapter 4)
- gender differences in narcissism and Big Five personality traits, women video-game designers (Chapter 5)
- asexuality, transgender individuals, sexual agency, "Viagra for women" controversy (Chapter 6)
- adoption of frozen embryos controversy (Chapter 7)
- intensive mothering, integrated motherhood, "living apart together," same-sex marriage (Chapter 8)
- single-sex schooling controversy (Chapter 9)
- combat roles opened to U.S. women, managerial derailment (Chapter 10)
- work-hours dilemmas of low-wage workers (Chapter 11)
- feminist health care model, health care for transgender individuals, Affordable Care Act (Chapter 12)
- feminist critique of CDC guidelines on women and drinking (Chapter 13)
- cyberharassment, gendertrolling, campus sexual assault (Chapter 14)
- transnational feminism, men and feminism (Chapter 15)

Women's Lives stands apart from other texts on the psychology of women because it embeds within each topical chapter a lifespan approach and robust coverage of the impact of social, cultural, and economic factors in shaping women's lives around the world. It provides extensive information on women with disabilities, middle-aged and older women, and women in transnational contexts.

Its up-to-date coverage reflects current scientific and social developments, including over 2,200 new references. This edition also adds several new boxed features for student engagement. *In the News* boxes present current, often controversial, news items to get students thinking critically about real-life applications of course topics. *Get Involved* boxes encourage students to actively participate in the research process. *What You Can Do* boxes give students applied activities to promote a more egalitarian society. *Learn About the Research* boxes expose students to a variety of research methods and highlight the importance of diversity in research samples by including studies of underrepresented groups.

Claire A. Etaugh, Caterpillar Professor of Psychology at Bradley University, has taught Psychology of Women for 35 years. Her research on gender has been published in several journals including *Psychology of Women Quarterly*, *Sex Roles*, *Developmental Psychology*, and *Journal of Marriage and Family*.

Judith S. Bridges, Professor Emerita of Psychology at the University of Connecticut, taught Psychology of Women courses for many years. Her research on women and gender has been published in *Psychology of Women Quarterly* and *Sex Roles*.

Fourth Edition

Women's Lives

A PSYCHOLOGICAL EXPLORATION

Claire A. Etaugh
Judith S. Bridges

Routledge
Taylor & Francis Group

NEW YORK AND LONDON

Fourth edition published 2018
by Routledge
711 Third Avenue, New York, NY 10017

and by Routledge
2 Park Square, Milton Park, Abingdon, Oxon, OX14 4RN

Routledge is an imprint of the Taylor & Francis Group, an informa business

First edition published by Pearson Education Inc., 2006
Third edition published by Pearson Education Inc., 2012

Library of Congress Cataloging-in-Publication Data
Names: Etaugh, Claire, author. | Bridges, Judith S., author.
Title: Women's lives : a psychological exploration / Claire A. Etaugh and
    Judith S. Bridges.
Description: 4th edition. | New York, NY : Routledge, 2017. | Includes
    bibliographical references and index. | Identifiers: LCCN 2017005839
    (print) | LCCN 2017022089 (ebook) | ISBN 9781138656666 (hb) |
    ISBN 9781138656697 (pb) | ISBN 9781315449401 (ebook) |
    ISBN 9781138656666 (hbk) | ISBN 9781138656697 (pbk)
Subjects: LCSH: Women—Psychology. | Women—North America—Social
    conditions.
Classification: LCC HQ1206 (ebook) | LCC HQ1206 .E883 2017 (print) |
    DDC 155.3/33—dc23
LC record available at https://lccn.loc.gov/2017005839

ISBN: 978-1-138-65666-6 (hbk)
ISBN: 978-1-138-65669-7 (pbk)
ISBN: 978-1-315-44940-1 (ebk)

Typeset in Adobe Garamond Pro
by Apex CoVantage, LLC

Visit the companion website/: www.routledge.com/cw/etaugh
Printed and bound by CPI Group (UK) Ltd, Croydon, CR0 4YY

To my grandchildren, Anthony and Isabel, who enrich my life and embody my hopes for the future.

—C.E.

To my grandsons Nick, Benjamin, and Devin, who reflect the promise of a more gender-neutral tomorrow.

—J.S.B.

CONTENTS

PREFACE

Over the last few decades, the burgeoning interest in psychology of women has been reflected in a rapidly expanding body of research and a growing number of college-level courses in the psychology of women or gender. The fourth edition of *Women's Lives: A Psychological Exploration* draws on this rich literature to present a broad range of experiences and issues of relevance to girls and women. Because it does not presuppose any background in psychology, this book can be used as the sole or primary text in introductory-level psychology of women courses and, with other books, in psychology of gender or interdisciplinary women's studies courses. Additionally, its presentation of both current and classical research and theory makes it a suitable choice, along with supplementary materials, for more advanced courses focused on the psychology of women or gender.

Every chapter in this textbook reflects substantial changes in this field during the past few years. We have made several changes based on the extremely helpful comments from reviewers and the many students and faculty who have used the two life span editions and the three topical editions of this book. This new topical revision includes the following highlights:

- Over 2,200 new references emphasize the latest research and theories, with more than half from 2015 to the present.
- *In the News,* a boxed feature in each chapter, presents current, and often controversial, news items to engage students in critically thinking about gender-related current events and to illustrate the real-life applications of course materials.
- *What You Can Do,* a boxed feature in each chapter, provides students with hands-on activities to both empower themselves and help promote a more egalitarian society.
- *Get Involved* is a set of activities in each chapter that promotes active student participation in research.
- Material highlighting the cultural, social, and economic forces that shape women's lives around the world (previously part of a boxed feature called *Explore Other Cultures*) is now integrated into the text, facilitating comparisons with women of other backgrounds, and making transnational issues a more integral and seamless part of the narrative.
- The unique life span approach of two previous chronological editions is embedded within topical chapters on sexuality, reproduction and childbearing, education and achievement, employment, physical health, mental health, and violence against girls and women.
- Coverage of the lives of women in the middle and later years and of women with disabilities is far more extensive than in any other textbook in the field.
- An updated list of Websites and an entirely new list of current books at the end of each chapter provides students with resources for additional study and research.
- Expanded use of vignettes and quotes from women add richness to the data and help students personally connect with the material.
- New and expanded coverage of many topics reflects scientific and social developments of the second decade of the new millennium.

These changes are broken down by chapter with key terms highlighted and include:

Chapter 1:
- Updated material on feminist research methods, including **standpoint theory**
- New discussion of **neoliberal feminism**
- New information on **mujerista psychology**
- Updated discussion of **social constructionism**
- New discussion of the relationship between power and **privilege**

Chapter 2:
- New section on portrayal of LGBT individuals in the media
- New section on portrayal of individuals with disabilities in the media

- Updated material on the depiction of older women in the media
- New discussion of **androcentrism** in language

Chapter 3:
- Updated coverage of multiple genders
- New material on the controversial testosterone testing of female athletes
- New discussion of **precarious manhood**

Chapter 4:
- New section on raising a gender nonconforming child
- New section on the trend toward gender-neutral clothing and toys
- Expanded material on body image in girls and women, including a new section on the influence of social media

Chapter 5:
- New section on gender-related differences in **narcissism**
- New section on gender-related differences in the **Big Five personality traits**
- Expanded section on factors affecting girls' and women's participation in STEM fields
- New section on women video game players and women in video game design

Chapter 6:
- New section on **asexual individuals**
- Expanded coverage of transgender individuals and gender identity
- New material on the concept of **sexual agency**
- New section on the controversy surrounding "Viagra for women"

Chapter 7:
- New section on the controversy regarding adoption of frozen embryos
- Updated trends in birthrates of teens and women over 35
- New information on assisted reproductive technologies and hormone replacement therapy

Chapter 8:
- New material on the effects of **intensive mothering**
- New material on the concept of **integrated motherhood**
- Expanded section on alternative couple arrangements such as **living apart together**
- Updated information on same-sex marriages in the U.S. and abroad

Chapter 9:
- New section on Malala Yousafzai, advocate for the education of girls in developing nations
- New material on the controversy surrounding the impact of single-sex schooling
- Updated information on the academic climate for women of color

Chapter 10:
- New material on opening of all U.S. combat roles to women
- Updated information on challenges for women in leadership roles, including **managerial derailment**
- New material on workplace issues for sexual minority women

Chapter 11:
- New section on shifting attitudes toward women's and men's work–family balance
- New material on the work-hours dilemmas of low-wage women workers

Chapter 12:
- New material on the **feminist health care model**
- New section on women and the Affordable Care Act
- New information on health care issues for transgender individuals

Chapter 13:
- New section on the feminist critique of new CDC guidelines on women and drinking
- Updated section on mental health issues of sexual minority women

Chapter 14:
- New section on cyberharassment and gendertrolling
- New material on **racialized sexual harassment**
- Expanded coverage of global violence against girls
- Expanded coverage of sexual assault on college campuses

Chapter 15:
- New and expanded coverage of transnational feminism
- Expanded coverage of men and feminism

SPECIAL FEATURES RELATED TO CONTENT AND ORGANIZATION

LIFE SPAN APPROACH EMBEDDED WITHIN TOPICAL CHAPTERS.   Virtually all textbooks on the psychology of women or psychology of gender use a topical approach and also include two or three chronological chapters. Typically, there is a chapter or two on childhood and adolescence and one on women in the middle and later years. Almost all coverage of midlife and older women is contained in that one chapter. The result is that many of the issues and experiences relating to women in midlife and beyond are barely touched on or simply are not covered at all. These older women remain relatively invisible.

Our approach is different. We have taken the unique life span approach of our two earlier chronologically focused texts and have embedded this approach within almost all chapters, including topical chapters on sexuality, reproduction and childbearing, education and achievement, employment, physical health, mental health, and violence against girls and women. Midlife and older women are discussed in all chapters except the one on infancy, childhood, and adolescence.

INTERSECTIONAL APPROACH THAT INTEGRATES WOMEN'S DIVERSE IDENTITIES.   The text provides extensive coverage of women of color, women in other cultures around the world, and sexual minority women. Although there is less information available, we have also included material on low-income women and women with disabilities whenever possible. We use an intersectional perspective that integrates women's diverse identities within each chapter rather than examining subgroups of women in separate chapters. We emphasize that women's identities are shaped not simply by adding the effects of their class, ethnicity, age, sexual orientation, physical ability, religion, and nationality, but by a complex combination of all these characteristics in which the whole is greater than the sum of its parts.

THOROUGH EXAMINATION OF BALANCING FAMILY AND WORK.   It is clear that the balancing of family and work has become a major issue facing families around the globe. We have devoted an entire chapter to this timely topic in order to thoroughly explore the theories, challenges, benefits, and solutions associated with this worldwide reality of the twenty-first century.

PEDAGOGICAL FEATURES

INTRODUCTORY OUTLINE.   Each chapter begins with an outline of the material, thus providing an organizational framework for reading the material.

OPENING VIGNETTES.   To grab students' attention and connect the material to real life, each chapter begins with one or two actual or hypothetical experiences illustrating one or more issues discussed in the chapter.

IN THE NEWS.   This new boxed feature presents current, and often controversial, news items designed to engage students in thinking critically about gender-related current events, and to illustrate the real-life applications of course materials.

WHAT YOU CAN DO.   This boxed feature provides students with experiential activities that help them to both empower themselves and promote a more egalitarian society.

WHAT DO YOU THINK?   The text includes critical-thinking questions in every chapter. The end-of-the-chapter questions foster skills in synthesis and evaluation by asking the student to apply course material or personal experiences to provocative issues from the chapter.

GET INVOLVED.   As a means of providing firsthand involvement in the material, each chapter contains a number of student activities. Some require collecting data on a small number of respondents and others focus solely on the student. Furthermore, each exercise is accompanied by critical-thinking questions that focus on explanations and implications of the activity's findings.

The active learning involved in these activities serves several purposes. First, it reinforces the material learned in the text. Second, those exercises that involve surveys of other people or analyses of societal artifacts introduce students to the research process, which, in turn, can stimulate interest in research, increase familiarity with a variety of assessment techniques, and provoke critical evaluation of research techniques. Third, the Get Involved activities demonstrate the relevance of the course material to students' experiences or to the experiences of important people in their lives.

LEARN ABOUT THE RESEARCH.   To stimulate students' interest in and appreciation of research as a source of knowledge about girls and women, each chapter has one or two boxed sections that focus on research. These Learn About the Research sections either highlight an interesting recent study or present an overview of recent findings in an intriguing research area. We expose students to a variety of research techniques (content analysis, interviews, questionnaires) without requiring that they have any background in psychological research methods. Furthermore, to highlight the importance of diversity in research samples, our selections include studies of underrepresented populations.

Following the research presentation are What Does It Mean? questions. These provoke more critical thinking by asking the student to consider a variety of issues related to the research, such as explanations and implications of the findings.

EXPLORE OTHER CULTURES.   In order to provide students with a deeper appreciation of women in a global context, each chapter features material that highlights the role of cultural, social, and economic factors in shaping women's lives around the world. In previous editions, this information was presented in separate boxes (Explore Other Cultures), but it is now integrated into the text in order to facilitate comparisons with women of other backgrounds and to make transnational issues a more integral and seamless part of the text.

KEY TERMS.   Terms in bold and definitions in italics within the text help students preview, understand, and review important concepts. These terms appear again at the end of each chapter, along with the page number on which the term appears.

SUMMARY.   The point-by-point end-of-the-chapter summary helps students synthesize the material.

IF YOU WANT TO KNOW MORE.   Recommended readings at the end of each chapter facilitate more extensive examination of the material. This edition includes completely updated lists of nearly 200 new and current recommended books to stimulate students to expand their knowledge.

WEBSITES.   An updated list of Websites at the end of each chapter provides students with additional resources.

WRITING STYLE

In order to engage the student and construct a nonhierarchical relationship between ourselves and the student, we use a nonpedantic first-person writing style. To reinforce this relationship in some of the opening vignettes and within the text, we have also presented our own experiences or those of our friends, families, and students.

SUPPLEMENTS

Routledge/Taylor & Francis is pleased to offer the following supplements to qualified adopters.

PowerPoint Presentation (0205866190). The PowerPoint presentation contains outlines of key topics for each text chapter, presented in a clear and visually attractive format.

ACKNOWLEDGMENTS

We owe a great deal to the many reviewers whose expert suggestions and insights were invaluable in the development of this book. Our sincere thanks to all of you who reviewed the text for the fourth edition.

It has been a pleasure to work with the publishing professionals at Routledge/Taylor & Francis. In particular, we acknowledge the invaluable support and assistance of Georgette Enriguez, our editor for this book. We also are deeply indebted to Brooke Engerman who cheerfully carried out the time-consuming tasks of recording over 2,200 new references and tracking down current Websites. We are grateful as well for the assistance of Robert Ray of the Chicago Public Library.

Thanks also to the students in our Psychology of Women courses who provided excellent editorial suggestions on earlier versions of the manuscript and for whom, ultimately, this book is written.

Finally, the book could not have been completed without the loving support of our families. Judith thanks her children, Rachel and Jason, and daughter-in-law, Nora, for providing support and inspiration throughout this project. Also, her deepest appreciation goes to her husband Barry, her life partner and best friend, for his unwavering patience, understanding, and encouragement. Claire's heartfelt thanks go to the women and men who have enriched her life and have been an endless source of encouragement and support: her late parents, Martha and Lou; siblings, Paula, Bonnie, and Howard; children, Andi and Adam; grandchildren, Anthony and Isabel; and "extended family" of friends, Peggy, Pat, Kathi, Barbara, Kevin, Pam, Suzanne, and John.

CHAPTER 1

Introduction to the Psychology of Women
History and Research

In 1965 when I (Judith) was applying to graduate schools, the chair of one psychology department informed me that my college grades met the criterion for male, but not female, admission into the program. That department (and others) had two sets of standards, and obviously, fewer women than men were admitted. When I look back at that time it is amazing to me to realize that I quietly accepted this pronouncement. I was disappointed but not outraged. I rejoiced at my acceptance by a comparable department but never thought to protest discriminatory admission policies (which were not unique to that department). A generation ago I did not identify this issue or any other gender inequality in institutional, legal, or interpersonal practices as a problem. However, over the last several decades my awareness and concern about these issues dramatically changed. Claire and I are deeply committed to gender equality in all areas of life and hope that this text will help illuminate both the progress women have made and the challenges that remain in the attainment of this important goal.

In this chapter we set the groundwork for the study of the psychology of women. We present major definitions, explore relevant history, examine research issues, and discuss the themes of the book. We begin with a look at the difference between sex and gender.

DEFINITIONS: SEX AND GENDER

Psychologists do not agree completely on the definitions of the words *sex* and *gender*. *Sex* is used to refer either to whether a person is female or male or to sexual behavior. This ambiguity of definition sometimes can cause confusion. For example, Claire offered a course several years ago entitled "The Psychology of Sex Differences." The course dealt with behavioral similarities and differences of females and males. After the first day of class, some students approached her with a puzzled look on their faces. The course title had led them to believe that the subject matter of the course was human sexuality.

The words *sex* and *gender* have often been used interchangeably to describe the differences in the behaviors of women and men. One example is the term *sex roles*, which is sometimes used to refer to culturally prescribed sets of behaviors for men and women. *Sex Roles* is even the name of a highly respected journal. Yet many psychologists believe that the term **gender roles** is more appropriate to describe the concept of *cultural beliefs applied to individuals on the basis of their socially assigned sex* (Magnusson & Mareck, 2012).

To avoid confusion, we will use the term **gender** to refer to *the meanings that societies and individuals give to female and male categories* (Wood & Eagly, 2015; Wood & Fixmer-Oraiz, 2017). We use the term **sex** to refer to *the classification of individuals as female or male based on their genetic makeup, anatomy, and reproductive functions*. Even this definition may be too simple: Recent research on intersex individuals indicates that there are more than two sexes (Feder, 2014; McCarthy & Gartner, 2014). See Chapter 3 for further discussion of that issue.

WOMEN AND MEN: SIMILAR OR DIFFERENT?

Scholars who study sex and gender issues usually take one of two approaches. Either they emphasize the similarities between women and men or they focus on the differences between them.

Similarities Approach

Those who adhere to the similarities viewpoint seek to show that *men and women are basically alike in their intellectual and social behaviors. Any differences that do occur are small and inconsistent, and produced by socialization, not biology* (Ball et al., 2013a; Blakemore et al., 2009). This approach, also called the **beta bias**, has its origins in the work of early twentieth-century women psychologists (Ball et al., 2013a). As we shall see later in the chapter, a number of these psychologists carried out research that challenged the prevailing belief that women are different from (and inferior to) men. Most feminist theory and research dealing with gender differences has retained this similarities approach (Zell et al., 2015).

Differences Approach

The differences viewpoint, also known as the **alpha bias**, *emphasizes the differences between women and men*. Historically, these differences have been thought to arise from *essential qualities within the individual that are rooted in biology* (Shapiro, 2015; Wood & Fixmer-Oraiz, 2017). This concept is known as **essentialism**.

The differences perspective has origins in both ancient Western and Eastern philosophies, which associate men with reason and civilization and women with emotion and nature (Goldenberg et al., 2013). As we have seen, early psychologists often equated women's differences from men with inferiority and "otherness." Men set the standard whereas women were seen as deviations from that standard (Etaugh, 2017). For example, Sigmund Freud stated that because women do not have a penis, they suffer from penis envy. Using the same logic, one could argue just as persuasively that men experience uterus envy because they cannot bear children. (Karen Horney [1926/1974], a psychoanalyst who challenged many of Freud's views, made this very proposal.)

Contemporary feminists regard female–male differences as arising from a culture's expectations of how individuals should behave. In other words, behavioral differences between the genders are not inborn but are socially constructed (Thompson & Armato, 2012). As we shall see at the end of this chapter, the social construction of gender is one of the three major themes of this book.

Some feminists have added still another twist to the differences approach. They embrace cultural feminism, a view that celebrates those positive qualities historically associated with women, such as a sense of human connection and concern for other people (Jordan, 2017; Kinser, 2010; Schuiling & Low, 2017). The theories of Nancy Chodorow (1994) and Carol Gilligan (1982, 2011) illustrate the cultural feminist approach. According to Chodorow, early childhood experiences forever set females and males down different paths in their development of identity, personality, and emotional needs. Girls develop an early attachment to their mother, whom they perceive as similar to themselves. This leads girls to develop relational skills and a desire for close emotional connections. Boys, on the other hand, reject their emotional attachment to their mother, who is perceived as dissimilar. Boys instead identify with male figures who are often more distant. In the process, they become more invested in separation and independence and develop a more abstract and impersonal style (Batalha & Reynolds, 2013). Gilligan (1982, 2011) also sees women's identity as based on connections and relationships to others. She believes that women reason and make moral judgments in a "different voice," a voice concerned with caring and responsibility. Men, on the other hand, are more concerned with abstract rights and justice. These different patterns of reasoning are equally valid and sophisticated, according to Gilligan. We shall discuss moral reasoning in females and males in greater detail in Chapter 5.

Regardless of one's approach to gender comparisons, the study of gender and the psychology of women is rooted in a feminist perspective. Therefore, let's now examine the meaning of feminism.

FEMINISM

A feminist is

someone who believes in equality in the workforce

a person who fights for women's rights

someone who protests about controversial issues, such as abortion or sexual harassment

a big, bra-burning, man-hating woman

(College students' view of feminism, from Houvouras & Carter, 2008, pp. 246–249)

Do any of these definitions reflect your own view of feminism? Although the term *feminism* is frequently used by the media, in opinion polls, and in casual conversation, people obviously differ in their conceptions of its meaning. There is even diversity among feminists. Although united in their belief that women are disadvantaged relative to men, feminists differ in their beliefs about the sources of this inequality and the ways to enhance women's status (Spade & Valentine, 2016; Wood & Fixmer-Oraiz, 2017). Let's examine five different types of feminism embraced by feminist scholars.

Liberal feminism is *the belief that women and men should have the same political, legal, economic, and educational rights and opportunities* (Kenschaft & Clark, 2016; Ryle, 2016). Liberal feminists advocate reform; their goals are to change attitudes and laws that are unfair to women and to equalize educational, employment, and political opportunities. For example, they seek the creation of an educational environment that encourages women's growth in all academic fields, removal of barriers to full participation and advancement in the workplace, and more political leadership positions for women. Liberal feminists stress the similarities between females and males and contend that gender differences are a function of unequal opportunities. For a different twist on liberal feminism, see In the News 1.1.

In contrast to liberal feminism, **cultural feminism** reflects *the belief that women and men are different and that women's special qualities, such as nurturance, concern about others, and cooperativeness, should be valued* (Higgins, 2016; Morton, 2013). Cultural feminists are concerned about destructive outcomes related to masculine traits, such as aggressiveness and lack of emotional expressiveness, and want to empower women by elevating the value attached to their interpersonal orientation.

Another type of feminism, **socialist feminism**, reflects *the attitude that gender inequality is rooted in economic inequality* (Kenschaft & Clark, 2016). Socialist feminists believe that various inequalities based on gender, ethnicity, and social class interact with one another and cannot be eliminated until the capitalistic structure of North American society is changed.

Radical feminism, on the other hand, is *the belief that gender inequality is based on male oppression of women* (Jensen, 2015; Kenschaft & Clark, 2016; Ryle, 2016). Radical feminists contend that **patriarchy**, *male control over and dominance of women*, has existed throughout history and must be eliminated to achieve gender equality. In other words, different from socialist feminists, radical feminists see men, rather than capitalism, as the source of women's oppression. Consequently, they are concerned not only about inequality in societal institutions, such as the workplace, but also about power differential in the family and other types of intimate relationships.

Many women of color have argued that the feminist movement is concerned primarily about issues that confront White women (Wright, 2014). Consequently, they often embrace **women of color feminism** (also known as womanism), which is *the belief that both **racism**, bias against people because of their ethnicity, and **classism**, bias based on social class, must be recognized as being as important as* **sexism**, *gender-based bias* (Gerbrandt & Kurtz, 2015; Harvey et al., 2013). A closely related concept, **mujerista psychology**, *advocates for the rights of Latina women* (Bryant-Davis & Comas-Diaz, 2016).

Clearly, there is no reason why a feminist perspective has to be limited to one viewpoint. Many individuals combine two or more into their personal definition of feminism. Now, perform the exercise in Get Involved 1.1 to more closely examine each of these types of feminism.

IN THE NEWS 1.1
Neoliberal Feminism

Neoliberal feminism emphasizes a woman's individual responsibility for achieving equity with men, while downplaying the role of cultural, social, and economic forces in producing inequalities between women and men. The emergence of neoliberal feminism in the United States is exemplified by the highly publicized book Lean In by Sheryl Sandberg (2013). Her book focuses on each woman's responsibility for overcoming obstacles, such as lack of confidence, that prevent her from getting ahead in the workplace (Valentine, 2015). Although Sandberg briefly mentions a few institutional barriers to women's success (e.g., the gender pay gap), her main argument is the neoliberal feminist view that individual women can rise to the top through their own efforts and by accepting full responsibility for their well-being (Annis, 2016). Some critics (see Rottenberg, 2013) are concerned that neoliberal feminism is displacing liberal feminism, which focuses on social justice, collective identity, basic rights, and shared efforts to change the social system.

HISTORY OF WOMEN IN PSYCHOLOGY

The first women in psychology faced a number of obstacles, especially in establishing their credentials, because many universities in the late 1800s and early 1900s did not welcome women who sought advanced degrees (Etaugh, 2017). Judith's experience described at the beginning of this chapter indicates that overt sexist policies toward women in psychology continued well into the twentieth century. Nevertheless, several women overcame the odds to become pioneers in the field.

GET INVOLVED 1.1
How Do People View Feminism?

Answer the following questions and then ask several female and male acquaintances to do the same. Save your own answers but do not refer back to them after completing this chapter.

First, indicate which of the following categories best characterizes your identity as a feminist:

1. consider myself a feminist and am currently involved in the women's movement
2. consider myself a feminist but am not involved in the women's movement
3. do not consider myself a feminist but agree with at least some of the objectives of feminism
4. do not consider myself a feminist and disagree with the objectives of feminism.

Second, on a scale from 1 (strongly disagree) to 6 (strongly agree), indicate the extent to which you disagree or agree with each of the following statements.

1. Women should be considered as seriously as men as candidates for the presidency of the United States.

2. Although women can be good leaders, men make better leaders.
3. A woman should have the same job opportunities as a man.
4. Men should respect women more than they currently do.
5. Many women in the workforce are taking jobs away from men who need the jobs more than women.
6. Doctors need to take women's health concerns more seriously.
7. Women have been treated unfairly on the basis of their gender throughout most of human history.
8. Women are already given equal opportunities with men in all important sectors of their lives.
9. Women in the United States are treated as second-class citizens.
10. Women can best overcome discrimination by doing the best they can at their jobs, not by wasting time with political activity.

WHAT DOES IT MEAN?

Before computing your scores for the 10 items, reverse the points for statements 2, 5, 8, and 10. That is, for a rating of 1 (strongly disagree), give 6 points, for a rating of 2, give 5 points, and so on. Then sum the points for all 10 items. Higher scores reflect greater agreement with feminist beliefs.

1. Are there differences in the feminist labels and/or feminist attitude scores between your female and male respondents?
2. For each respondent, including yourself, compare the feminist attitude score to the selected feminist category. Did you find that individuals who gave themselves a feminist label (i.e., placed themselves in category 1 or 2) generally agreed with the feminist statements and

obtained a score of 40 or higher? Similarly, did the individuals who did not label themselves as feminists (e.g., category 3 or 4) tend to disagree with the feminist statements and receive a score below 40? If there was no correspondence between the feminist identity label and the feminist beliefs, give possible reasons.

3. Do you think that individuals who vary in ethnicity and social class might hold different attitudes about feminism? If yes, explain.

Source: Putting the feminism into feminism scales: Introduction of a liberal feminist attitude and ideology, *Sex Roles*, 34, pp. 359–390, © 1996.

Margaret Floy Washburn was the first woman to receive a Ph.D. in psychology in America in 1894. It took another 40 years before doctorates in psychology were awarded to Black women: Inez Beverly Prosser and Ruth Winifred Howard (Ball et al., 2013b).

Women and the American Psychological Association

One year after the founding of the American Psychological Association (APA), in 1893, 2 of the 14 new members admitted were women: Mary Whiton Calkins and Christine Ladd-Franklin.

Suparna Rajaram (pictured) is the 2017–2018 president of the Association for Psychological Science (formerly the American Psychological Society). Since its founding in 1988, 13 other women have served as president.

Calkins went on to become the first woman president of the APA in 1905. Margaret Floy Washburn was elected the second woman president in 1921. It would be 51 years before the APA had another female leader (Chrisler, 2013).

Since the early 1970s, the number of women in APA leadership roles has increased notably and 15 women have become president (Azar, 2011). In 2013, women represented 58 percent of the APA members, and 61 percent of the board of directors, although only 31 percent of APA fellows, the most prestigious membership category, and only 27 percent of journal editors. A similar pattern is found in the other major U.S. psychological organization, the Association for Psychological Science (APS) (Etaugh & Geraghty, 2014).

Women's Contributions

Women have been relatively invisible in psychology; their contributions to the field have often been overlooked or ignored (Etaugh, 2017). Coverage of gender-related topics has also been limited.

Even when the works of women psychologists are cited, they may still be overlooked. There are two related reasons for this apparent invisibility of many women psychologists. First, the long-standing practice in psychology books and journal articles is to refer to authors by their last name and first initials only. Second, in the absence of gender-identifying information, people tend to assume that the important contributions included in psychology books and articles have been carried out by men (Etaugh, 2017). When Claire learned about the Ladd-Franklin theory of color vision in introductory psychology, she assumed that two men named Ladd and Franklin had developed the theory. Only later did she discover that it was the work of Christine Ladd-Franklin. Similarly, most people assume that it was *Harry* Harlow who established the importance of touch in the development of attachment. How many individuals know that his wife, psychologist Margaret Kuenne Harlow, was his research partner and a codeveloper of their groundbreaking theory? In order to make the contributions of women psychologists more visible in this book, we frequently use first names when identifying important researchers and theorists.

HISTORY OF THE PSYCHOLOGY OF WOMEN

Ignorance about women pervades academic disciplines in higher education, where the requirements for the degree seldom include thoughtful inquiry into the status of women as part of the human condition.

(Carolyn Sherif, cited in Denmark et al., 2000, p. 1)

How has the psychology of women developed as a field since Carolyn Sherif wrote this sentence about 35 years ago? Let us turn to a brief history of the feminist approach to the study of gender.

The Early Years

In the early years of psychology, gender studies as such did not exist (Etaugh, 2017). Not only were there few women psychologists, but also women's experiences were not deemed important enough to study. Concepts in psychology were based on the male experience. For example, as we shall see in Chapter 3, Sigmund Freud formulated his views of the Oedipus complex and penis envy from a male perspective but applied them to both genders. The same is true of Erik Erikson's notion of the development of identity during adolescence, as we shall see in Chapter 4.

In addition, early psychologists viewed women as different from and inferior to men (Etaugh, 2017). For example, to explain their premise that women are less intelligent than men and thus unfit for higher education, male psychologists claimed that women's brains were smaller than men's (Fine, 2017). This theory seemed to be discredited by the discovery that *relative* brain size—the weight of the brain relative to the weight of the body—is actually greater in women than in men. But stereotypes are not that easily erased. Scientists began comparing various segments of the brain in the two genders in an attempt to find the cause of women's purported inferior intelligence. No differences were found (Joel et al., 2015). Yet the search continued. In 1982, the prestigious journal *Science* published a study claiming that the corpus callosum (the connection between the two hemispheres of the brain) is larger in women than in men. The researchers stated that this difference might account for women's supposedly inferior spatial skills. (See Chapter 5 for a detailed discussion of this topic.) The study had many flaws, including the fact that only nine males' brains and five females' brains had been examined. Ruth Bleier, a neuroanatomist, and her colleagues did a study that corrected the flaws and used a much larger sample. They found no gender differences. Yet *Science* refused to publish their findings on the grounds that they were too "political" (Etaugh, 2017).

The first generation of women psychologists carried out research that challenged assumptions of female inferiority (Etaugh, 2017). Helen Thompson Woolley found little difference in the intellectual abilities of women and men. Leta Stetter Hollingworth tackled the prevailing notion that women's menstrual cycles were debilitating, rendering women unfit to hold positions of responsibility. She demonstrated that intellectual and sensory-motor skills did not systematically vary across the menstrual cycle. In addition, Karen Horney and Clara Thompson made important critiques of psychoanalytic theory during this period that stressed the social, cultural, and environmental factors in women's psychological development (Etaugh, 2017). Many of these ideas languished, however, because few women were able to obtain academic positions where they could study and teach about these topics.

The 1960s and 1970s

Several events of the 1960s signaled the beginning of the second wave of the feminist movement in the United States, including the publication of Betty Friedan's (1963) book *The Feminine Mystique*, the passage of the Equal Pay Act (see Chapters 10 and 15), and the formation of the National Organization for Women (NOW). In each case, the spotlight turned on glaring economic, social, and political inequities between women and men. The women's movement no doubt helped to serve as a catalyst for the emergence of psychology of women as a separate, legitimate field of study (Eagly et al., 2012).

During these years, the psychology of women emerged as a separate field of study. In 1969, the Association for Women in Psychology was founded, followed in 1973 by the APA Division (now Society) of the Psychology of Women. Several textbooks on the psychology of women were written, journals such as *Psychology of Women Quarterly* and *Sex Roles* were established, and college courses on the topic began to appear. Feminist theorists and researchers demonstrated the sexist bias of much psychology theory, research, and practice. They set about expanding knowledge about women and correcting erroneous misinformation from the past (Eagly & Riger 2014; Etaugh, 2017). Today, women make up more than two-thirds of the psychologists in the workforce. This percentage is very likely to increase because almost three out of four doctoral degrees in psychology are now awarded to women (Christidis et al., 2016; National Science Foundation, 2015a).

The Recent Years: Developments in Research and Theory

As we shall see in the next few pages, the application of feminist perspectives and principles has transformed the way women and gender have been studied in recent years. The transformation of the field has been documented thoroughly by Alice Eagly and her colleagues (2012). For one thing, the amount of published research has increased exponentially, with thousands of publications each year. These articles are not confined to journals that specialize in gender, but appear in psychology's core research journals. Study of the diversity of women's experiences has increased, more so in terms of race and ethnicity than in other areas. Research about women and gender has been influenced by the social and political climate of the times. As one example, the increase in work–family research is no doubt influenced by women's increased participation in the labor force during the past several decades.

Also in recent years, feminist scholars have developed an array of theoretical models. One such model is **standpoint theory**, which holds that *women and other groups see the world from their own subjective perspective, and that knowledge is not objective.* This view has given rise to the feminist experiential research model, which utilizes a variety of qualitative methods, such as field research and the interview. (We will discuss the latter method shortly.) (Etaugh, 2017) Another recent theoretical perspective is **social constructionism**. A key tenet of this view is that "facts" are created by communities and cultures. Thus, *social and cultural contexts influence what we know about the world.* The social construction of gender, as you will see shortly, is one of the themes of this textbook.

STUDYING THE PSYCHOLOGY OF WOMEN

With a basic understanding of the history of the psychology of women, we now turn to an examination of issues involved in performing psychological research. As you probably learned in introductory psychology, our understanding of human behavior stems from research conducted by psychologists and other scientists who use the scientific method to answer research questions. Although you might have learned that this method is value free, that it is not shaped by researchers' personal values, feminist scholars (Hesse-Biber, 2016) argue that values can influence every step of the research process. Let's turn now to a brief discussion of these steps to see how researchers' own ideas about human behavior can influence our understanding of the psychology of women.

Bias in Psychological Research

SELECTING THE RESEARCH TOPIC.   The first step in any scientific investigation is selecting the topic to examine. Just as your personal preferences lead you to choose one term paper topic over another, scientists' personal interests influence the topics they decide to investigate. Throughout the history of psychology, most psychologists have been males; thus, for many years, topics related to girls and women were rarely investigated. Since 1970, however, the increasing number of female psychologists and the growth of the psychology of women as a discipline have resulted in an explosion of research devoted to the psychology of woman and/or gender (Eagly et al., 2012). For example, an estimated 50–70 new scientific publications on sex differences appear each week (Ellis et al., 2008).

Another influence on topic selection is the researcher's assumptions about gender characteristics. For example, a psychologist who believes leadership is primarily a male trait is not likely to investigate the leadership styles of women. To give another example, aggressive behavior is typically associated with males. Consequently, relatively little is known about the relationship between aggressive behavior in girls and their adjustment in adulthood (Brennan & Shaw, 2013). Bias in topic selection is even more evident when one focuses on women of color. Not only are there relatively few psychologists of color but researchers, influenced by the biased assumption that people of color are deviant, deficient, and helpless, have examined ethnic minority women in relation to only a narrow range of topics, such as poverty and teen pregnancy (Cundiff, 2012; Erkut & García Coll, 2013). The tendency to treat women of color as helpless deviates reinforces a negative image of ethnic minority females and denies their full personhood as women with a wide breadth of concerns and experiences.

FORMULATING THE HYPOTHESIS. Once the topic is selected, the researcher generally formulates a hypothesis (a prediction) based on a particular theoretical perspective. Consequently, the researcher's orientation toward one theory or another has a major influence on the direction of the research. To better understand this effect, consider the link between two theories of rape and related research hypotheses. One theory proposes that rape has evolved through natural selection, which leads to the hypothesis that rape is present in nonhuman animals (Thornhill & Palmer, 2000). A very different theory contends that rape stems from a power imbalance between women and men (McPhail, 2010). One hypothesis stemming from this theory is that cultures with more gender inequality of power should have higher rates of rape than regions with less power imbalance (Turchik et al., 2016). As we see in the next section, these different hypotheses lead to very different kinds of research on rape.

Theoretical perspectives about ethnicity can similarly influence the hypotheses and direction of research. For example, many studies on women of color have been interpreted from a framework that views their behavior as deviant and problematic (Cundiff, 2012). Rather than examining strengths of women of color, this deviance perspective leads to research that focuses on ethnic minority women as powerless victims.

DESIGNING THE STUDY. Because the methods used to gather data stem from the underlying predictions, hypotheses based on disparate theories lead to different procedures. This, in turn, affects the type of knowledge researchers gain about the topic under investigation. Returning to our rape example, the hypothesis that rape is not unique to humans has led to investigations of forced copulation in nonhuman species (McKibbin et al., 2008), which would not be appropriate to the investigation of a power hypothesis. The prediction that rape is linked to the degree of gender inequality in society has led to studies of the relationship between a geographic area's rape rate and its occupational and educational gender inequality (Turchik et al., 2016). Each of these procedures provides very different kinds of information about rape that can lay the foundation for different attitudes about this form of violence (see Chapter 14). Examining specific aspects of research design will show us the ways bias can also affect the choice of procedures.

SELECTING RESEARCH PARTICIPANTS. One of the consistent problems in psychological research has been the use of samples that do not adequately represent the general population. A **sample** refers to *the individuals who are investigated in order to reach conclusions about the entire group of interest to the researcher* (i.e., the **population**). For example, a researcher might be interested in understanding the emotional experiences of first-time mothers in the first months following childbirth. It would be impossible, however, to assess the experiences of all new mothers (*population*). Instead, the investigator might seek 100 volunteers from among mothers who gave birth in any one of three hospitals in a specific geographical area (*sample*).

Unfortunately, research participants are not always representative of the larger population. Throughout most of the history of psychology, psychologists have focused primarily on young, White, middle-class, heterosexual, able-bodied males (Eagly & Riger, 2014; Etaugh, 2017). This procedure can lead to unfortunate and incorrect generalizations about excluded groups. It would be inappropriate, for example, to draw conclusions about women's leadership styles by examining male managers. Furthermore, focusing on selected groups can lead to the disregard of excluded groups.

A related issue is whether and how researchers specify the gender composition of their samples. One problem is that, until recently, a sizeable minority of authors in major psychology journals failed to mention the gender of their participants (Eagly & Riger, 2014). Therefore, the reader does not know whether the findings are applicable to both genders. Interestingly, the failure to report gender in the title of the article or to provide a rationale for sampling only one gender was more common in studies with male-only participants than in studies with female-only participants. Furthermore, discussions based on male participants were more likely to be written in general terms, whereas those based on only female participants were likely to be restricted to conclusions about females. These practices suggest that males are considered the norm, and results obtained from them generally applicable, whereas females are somehow "different." This principle, known as **male as normative**, means *that males are considered the standard against which all behavior is measured.* Even though more than 90 percent of papers in mainstream journals now report the gender of their research participants, fewer than 10 percent include gender in the hypotheses, analyses, or discussion of results (Cole, 2013).

Research samples have been limited in other ways as well. One problem is the relative invisibility of people of color, as members of minority groups continue to be underrepresented (Hall et al., 2016). A positive development is that many journals now require a description of the ethnicity of the sample even if it is restricted to White participants. Note, however, that specifying the ethnic composition of the sample does not mean that the researcher actually examined the relationship between the participant's ethnicity and the behavior under investigation. On a positive note, the growing recognition of the need to integrate findings related to ethnic, class, and cultural differences into mainstream theory, practice, and research has led in the past 25 years to an explosion of research on ethnicity and by ethnic minority women psychologists, including Thelma Bryant Davis, Jean Lau Chin, Fanny Cheung, Lillian Comas-Diaz, Oliva Espín, Cynthia de las Fuentes, Beverly Greene, Aída Hurtado, Gwendolyn Puryear Keita, Teresa LaFromboise, Carolyn Payton, Pamela Trotman Reid, Janis Sanchez-Hucles, and Melba Vasquez (Hurtado, 2010; "Revisiting Our Roots," 2010). Psychological research on immigrant women, however, still is unsystematic, and tends either to idealize or pathologize them (Yakushko & Consoli, 2014).

Samples have been restricted, additionally, in their socioeconomic status: Most participants have been middle class, and poor women, until recently, have been nearly invisible (Diemer et al., 2013; Liu, 2013; Lopez & Legan, 2016; Lott, 2012). As a result, problems that have a much greater impact on poor women than on middle-class women are rarely studied. For example, very little is known about the sexual harassment of low-income women by their landlords, even though this is unfortunately a common occurrence (Bullock et al., 2010; Perry-Jenkins & Claxton, 2009). In addition, most studies of employed women have focused on those in professional jobs. Moreover, when researchers do study poor and working-class individuals, they tend to focus on people of color, perpetuating a biased assumption about ethnicity and social class as well as limiting our understanding of both poor White women and middle-class women of color (Henderson & Tickamyer, 2009).

Pick up any psychology journal and you will see that many of the middle-class individuals who serve as research participants are college students. Because this group is restricted in age, education, and life experiences compared to the general population, numerous findings based on these samples cannot be generalized to other types of people (Tryon, 2017).

Other groups, such as lesbian, gay, bisexual, and transgender individuals and people with disabilities, are underrepresented in psychological research, and less research has focused on older women than on younger women or girls (Olkin, 2013; Quinlan et al., 2008; Stringer, 2016). What can explain researchers' narrow focus on White, middle-class, heterosexual, able-bodied, young individuals? One possibility is that psychologists are more interested in understanding the experiences of people like themselves, and the majority of investigators fit the characteristics of the typical participants. Another possibility is that psychologists might use these individuals in their research because it is easier to recruit them. These are the people most likely to be located within the situational contexts—such as academic or professional environments—inhabited by researchers (Quinlan et al., 2008). Also, due to cross-group mistrust and/or misunderstanding, it is sometimes more difficult for nonminority investigators to recruit minority individuals (Brewer et al., 2014; Cheng & Sue, 2016). Whatever the causes, the exclusion of certain groups of people from psychological examination not only devalues their experiences but can also lead to inaccurate conclusions about them based on faulty generalizations. To get firsthand knowledge about the extent of biased samples in recent psychological research, complete the exercise in Get Involved 1.2.

GET INVOLVED 1.2
Are Samples in Psychological Research Biased?

In this exercise you are to compare descriptions of samples published in journals oriented toward women or gender to mainstream psychological journals. At your campus library, select one recent issue of *Psychology of Women Quarterly* or *Sex Roles*. Also select a recent issue of one of the following: *Journal of Personality and Social Psychology*, *Developmental Psychology*, or *Journal of Consulting and Clinical Psychology*. For each article in these issues, read the brief section that describes the participants. This is found in the Method section of the article and is usually labeled Participants, Sample, or Subjects. As you read these sections, note the following information:

1. Is the gender of the participants specified? If yes, does the sample include females only, males only, or both?
2. Is the ethnicity of the participants specified? If yes, does the sample include predominantly or exclusively Whites, predominantly or exclusively individuals of another single ethnic group, or a balanced mixture of individuals from two or more ethnic groups?
3. Is the social class of the participants specified? If yes, is the sample predominantly or exclusively middle class, predominantly or exclusively working class or poor, or a mixture of social classes?
4. Are any other characteristics of the participants (e.g., sexual orientation, presence of a disability) given? If yes, specify.

After recording the information for each article from one journal, add up the number of articles that specified the gender of the sample, the number that specified ethnicity, and so on. Similarly, sum the articles that included both genders, those that included more than one ethnic group, and so forth. Follow the same procedure for the other journal.

WHAT DOES IT MEAN?

1. Which participant characteristic was described most frequently? Explain why.
2. Which participant characteristic was represented in the most balanced way? Explain why.
3. Which participant characteristic was specified least often? Explain why.
4. Did the two journals differ in their descriptions of their samples? If yes, explain.
5. What are the implications of your findings?

Source: Morgan (1996).

SELECTING THE MEASURES. Another step in the design of a study is the selection of procedures to measure the behaviors or characteristics under investigation. These procedures can determine the results that researchers find. For example, in their review of aggression in girls and boys, Jamie Ostrov and Stephanie Godleski (2010) note that different findings are obtained depending on how aggressive behavior is measured. Boys are more likely than girls to show physical aggression (e.g., pushing, hitting) whereas girls are more apt to show relational aggression (e.g., spreading malicious gossip). As you can see, relying on only one of these measures would have led to misleading conclusions.

ANALYZING AND INTERPRETING THE FINDINGS. Once the data have been collected, the researcher performs statistical analyses to discover whether the findings support the hypotheses. Although there are numerous types of statistical tests, they all provide information about the **statistical significance** of the results, which means that *the findings are not due to chance alone*. For example, in a study of college students' belief in rape myths (Girard & Senn, 2008), respondents rated the degree to which they agreed with 20 false statements often used to justify rape, such as "many women secretly desire to be raped." The rating scale for each item ranged from 1 (not agree) to 7 (strongly agree). Females had an average rating of 32.6 and males had a rating of 42.0. These numbers have no meaning in themselves. However, a statistical analysis applied to these data indicated that the difference of 9.4 between the male and female averages was not due to chance alone; males, more than females, believed in rape myths.

Once statistical tests have been applied to the data, the researcher must interpret the findings. Statistical analyses inform us only about the likelihood that the data could have been produced by chance alone. Now, the researchers must discuss explanations and implications of the findings. One type of bias occurring at this stage is interpreting the findings in a way that suggests a female weakness or inferiority. For example, studies have shown that females use more tentative speech than males do (see Chapter 5). They are more likely than men to say, "I *sort of* think she would be a good governor" or "She *seems* to be a strong candidate." Some researchers have suggested this is an indication of females' lack of confidence—an interpretation pointing to a female deficit (Petersen & Hyde, 2014). Another equally plausible and more positive interpretation is that females use more tentative speech as a means of encouraging other people to express their opinions (DeFrancisco et al., 2014). Susan Fiske, past president of the Association for Psychological Science, offers another example of how a trait can be labeled to suggest female inferiority. She cites the "field independence–field dependence" continuum. Men have been described as "field independent" (not being influenced by a surrounding context), considered a favorable attribute, whereas "field *de*pendence" was a deficit that women had (Fiske, 2010). What about being labeled field *sensitive*, clearly a more positive term, she asks?

A second problem related to the interpretation of findings is generalizing results based on one group to other groups. As discussed earlier in this chapter, psychologists frequently have examined narrowly defined samples, such as White, male, middle-class college students, and sometimes they have generalized their findings to other people, including females, people of color, and working-class individuals. Moreover, the experiences of White, middle-class women have been assumed to apply to all women, regardless of ethnicity and social class (Eagly & Riger, 2014).

A third bias in the interpretation of data has been the assumption that the presence of gender differences implies biological causes (Fine, 2013). For example, some researchers have assumed that the preponderance of men in the sciences is due to their higher levels of fetal testosterone, despite a lack of consistent supporting data (Fine, 2010; Valla & Ceci, 2011).

COMMUNICATING THE FINDINGS.

Publishing.   The primary way that psychologists communicate their research findings to others is by publishing their studies, usually in psychological journals. Unfortunately, editors and reviewers who make decisions about which studies are worthy of publication tend to favor those that report statistical significance over those that do not, the so-called "file-drawer effect" (Spellman, 2012). This publication bias can affect the body of our knowledge about gender. Studies that show a statistically significant gender difference are more likely to be published than those that do not and can lead to exaggerated conclusions about the differences between females and males (Christianson et al., 2012; Fine, 2017).

Another type of publication bias exists as well. Victoria Brescoll and Marianne LaFrance (2004) found that politically conservative newspapers were more likely than liberal newspapers to use biological explanations for gender differences. Moreover, readers tended to believe whatever bias was represented in these news stories. Let the reader beware!

Gender-Biased Language.   The language that researchers use in their research papers is another possible source of gender bias in the communication of findings. Gender-biased language, such as the use of the male pronoun to refer to both genders, can lead to serious misinterpretation. As is discussed in Chapter 2, male pronouns tend to be interpreted as males only, not as males and females (Eagly & Riger, 2014). Fortunately, although this practice was prevalent in the 1970s and 1980s, the *Publication Manual of the American Psychological Association* (American Psychological Association, 2010) now specifies that gender-biased language must be avoided. Research is now more likely to be reported using nonsexist language (Sechzer & Rabinowitz, 2008).

Another, more subtle type of biased language is the use of nonparallel terms when writing about comparable female and male behaviors, thus implying an essential difference between the genders. For example, much of the research on gender and employment refers to women who work outside the home as "employed mothers" but refers to men who work outside the home as simply "employed" (Gilbert, 1994). This distinction carries the implicit assumption that the primary role for women is motherhood whereas the primary role for men is the provider.

Conclusion.   Although it is unlikely that most researchers attempt to influence the research process in order to support their preconceived ideas about a topic, the biases they bring to the research endeavor can affect their choice of topic, hypotheses, research design, interpretation of findings, and communication about the study. Given that researchers have very human personal interests, values, and theoretical perspectives, they do not fit the image of the objective scientist (Eagly, 2013a).

Despite these inherent biases, we do not want to give the impression that psychological research is unduly value laden or that it provides no useful information about the psychology of women. Most researchers make a concerted attempt to be as unbiased as possible, and research from psychology and other social scientific disciplines has provided a rich body of knowledge about females' experiences. However, one must read these studies critically, with an understanding of their possible limitations—especially their failure to focus on the diversity of girls and women. For a look at doing gender research around the world, see the section on Cross-Cultural Research on Gender.

Feminist Research Methods

Traditional psychological research emphasizes objectivity, control, and quantitative measures as a means of understanding human behavior, and some feminist psychologists advocate adherence to this general methodology. Others, however, contend that more accurate representations of women's lives are achieved with qualitative procedures, such as women's accounts of their experiences (Brisolara et al., 2014; Crawford, 2013; Gergen et al., 2015; Hesse-Biber, 2016; Yost & Chmielewski, 2013). For example, a qualitative investigation of women's friendships might ask participants to describe, in their own words, the most important friendships they have had. In contrast, an objective measure might ask them to complete a questionnaire written by the researcher in which participants indicate how often they have experienced a variety of feelings and interactions in their most important friendships. Whereas the qualitative approach attempts to capture each participant's unique perspective, the quantitative approach compares participants' responses to a standard situation. Feminist research also aims not only to inform, but also to transform society (Kaestle, 2016). For a more detailed examination of principles of feminist research, look at Learn About the Research 1.1.

Cross-Cultural Research on Gender

Cross-cultural research has made important contributions to our understanding of gender development (Best & Thomas, 2004). Nevertheless, there are methodological pitfalls that need to be avoided in order to draw meaningful conclusions from such research. For one thing, most cross-cultural projects, especially those using surveys, require translation from the researchers' languages to one or more other languages. In such cases, a major challenge is to make sure that the translated version is as close to the original as possible. However, languages differ in sentence structure and grammatical rules, and seemingly identical words may have slightly different meanings. For example, in Russian and Arabic, the word "cousin" always specifies the cousin's sex, unlike in English (Shiraev & Levy, 2013). In addition, similar findings may have different meanings depending upon the culture being studied. For example, Judith Gibbons (2000) and her colleagues studied adolescents' drawings of the ideal woman. In a variety of cultures, many adolescents drew the ideal woman as working in an office. However, when the drawings were then presented to peers in the same culture for interpretation, adolescents gave responses that were both similar across cultures, but also culturally specific. For instance, in all countries studied, women working in offices were described as hardworking. However, Guatemalan adolescents also viewed them as working for the betterment of their families, Filipino teenagers described them as adventurous and sexy, and U.S. teens saw them as bored with the routine of office work.

Another formidable methodological challenge in cross-cultural research is the issue of sampling. In studying gender issues, samples are often drawn from a certain setting, such as colleges and

LEARN ABOUT THE RESEARCH 1.1
Principles of Feminist Research

Although feminists have a variety of opinions about the most effective methods for studying girls and women, they agree that such research should increase our understanding of females and help change the world for them (Hesse-Biber, 2016; Sprague, 2016). Thus, feminists, like all researchers, bring a set of values to the research process, values that can direct the nature and interpretation of the research. Claire and her colleague Judith Worell (Worell & Etaugh, 1994; 2012) have articulated a set of principles that are based on the values of feminist research. These are summarized as follows:

1. Challenging the traditional scientific method.
   a. Correcting bias in the research process.
   b. Expanding samples beyond White, middle-class participants.
   c. Acknowledging the legitimacy of both quantitative and qualitative methods.
2. Focusing on the experiences of women.
   a. Examining diverse categories of women.
   b. Investigating topics relevant to women's lives.

   c. Attending to women's strengths as well as their concerns.
3. Considering gender imbalances in power.
   a. Recognizing that women's subordinate status is a sign of power imbalance, not deficiency.
   b. Attempting to empower women.
4. Recognizing gender as an important category for investigation.
   a. Understanding that a person's gender can influence expectations about and responses to that person.
5. Recognizing the importance of language.
   a. Changing language to be inclusive of women.
   b. Understanding that language can both influence thought and be influenced by thought.
6. Promoting social change.
   a. Creating a science that benefits women.
   b. Guiding action that will lead to justice for women.

WHAT DOES IT MEAN?

1. Assume you are a feminist researcher interested in examining how women handle employment and family obligations. Using the feminist principles outlined earlier, describe the characteristics of the sample you might wish to study and the research methods you would use in collecting your data.
2. A hypothetical study of the educational expectations of White, Mexican American, and Vietnamese American eighth-grade

girls found that the White girls expect to complete more years of schooling than the other groups. The researcher concluded that Latina and Asian American girls have lower educational expectations than White girls. Critique this conclusion, using feminist research principles.

_____

Sources: Based on Worell and Etaugh (1994); Etaugh and Worell (2012).

---

universities, as a way to ensure equivalent samples. But college or university students do not reflect the population similarly in different countries because the proportion of the population attending university differs widely internationally.

Drawing Conclusions From Multiple Studies

Researchers use one of two procedures to draw conclusions about gender differences on the basis of large numbers of published studies. This section examines these two techniques.

NARRATIVE APPROACH.   The traditional way of examining psychological gender differences has been to sift through dozens or even hundreds of studies on a particular topic and to form an impression of the general trends in their results. The first major attempt to synthesize the research on gender differences in this narrative fashion was carried out by Eleanor Maccoby and Carol Nagy Jacklin in 1974. In this massive undertaking, they tallied the results of over 1,600 published and unpublished studies appearing in the 10 years prior to 1974. Gender differences were declared to exist when a large number of studies on a given topic found differences in the same direction. Although the contribution of this pioneering work is enormous, a major drawback is its use of a simple "voting" or "box-score" method, which gave each study the same weight regardless of sample size or magnitude of the reported difference (Schmidt & Hunter, 2014). In addition, the possibility of subtle biases is always present in any narrative review.

META-ANALYSIS.   A more sophisticated and objective technique of summarizing data has been developed in recent years. **Meta-analysis** is *a statistical method of integrating the results of several studies on the same topic*. It provides a measure of the magnitude, or size, of a given gender difference rather than simply counting the number of studies finding a difference (Zell et al., 2015).

Gender researchers using meta-analysis first locate all studies on the topic of interest. Then they do a statistical analysis of each study that measures the size of the difference between the average of the men's scores and the average of the women's scores. This difference is divided by the standard deviation of the two sets of scores. The standard deviation measures the variability or range of the scores. For example, scores ranging from 1 to 100 have high variability, whereas scores ranging from 50 to 53 show low variability. Dividing the difference between men's and women's scores by the standard deviation produces a d statistic. Finally, the researchers calculate the average of the d statistics from all the studies they located. The resulting d is called the **effect size**. *It indicates not only whether females or males score higher but also how large the difference is.* This is one of the major advantages of meta-analysis over the traditional narrative method of summarizing research (Hyde, 2014).

The value of d is large when the difference between means is large and the variability within each group is small. It is small when the difference between means is small and the variability within each group is large (Hyde, 2014). Generally a d of 0.20 is considered small, 0.50 is moderate, and 0.80 is large. However, these guidelines still do not settle the debate of whether a particular difference is *meaningful* or important. In cancer research, for example, even a very small effect size can have powerful consequences. Suppose a treatment was discovered that completely cured a small number of women with a highly lethal form of cancer. Although the effect size might be quite small, this discovery would be hailed as a major medical breakthrough. As we discuss later in the book, the effect sizes for some psychological gender differences are greater than those found in most psychological research whereas others are close to zero.

Now that we have explored the historical and methodological framework for understanding the psychology of women, we focus on the major themes that characterize this book.

THEMES IN THE TEXT

Science is not value free. As we have seen, the evolving belief about the importance of women has had a powerful impact on topics and methods of psychological research. Similarly, this text is not value neutral. It is firmly rooted in a feminist belief system, which contends (1) that the diversity of women's identities and experiences should be recognized and celebrated; (2) that men hold more power than women; and (3) that gender is shaped by social, cultural, and societal influences. These beliefs are shared by many feminist psychologists and are reflected throughout this book.

Theme 1: Intersectionality: The Diversity of Women's Identities and Experiences

As we saw in the discussion of research biases, minimal attention given to females throughout most of the history of psychology not only devalues women's experiences but also often leads to incorrectly generalizing men's experiences to include women. Similarly, a psychology of women restricted to White, middle-class, heterosexual, able-bodied, young females in North America minimizes the importance of women of color; poor and working-class women; lesbian, bisexual, and transgender women; women with disabilities; older women; and women in other cultures, and it can lead to the false conclusion that the experiences of the majority are applicable to all (Hobson, 2016; L. Rosenthal, 2016).

Consequently, this text examines the heterogeneity of females' experiences. We do so within a lens of **intersectionality**, which means that *people exist in a framework of multiple identities that interact with each other to determine an individual's experiences and that cannot be understood separately from each other because they are integral parts of a whole* (McCann & Kim, 2017). These identities include one's gender, ethnicity, class, sexual orientation, age, ableness, marital status, and nationality (Few-Demo, 2014; Hill Collins & Bilge 2016; May, 2015; Wallace, 2014). Intersectionality implies that to understand a woman's identity, you do not simply *add* one feature to another, as in woman + Black + heterosexual + middle-aged, but rather consider how these categories uniquely overlap (Marecek 2016, Sarno et al., 2015). As an example, compare two women born in New York City some years ago. One is Claire Etaugh, who is a White, college-educated, heterosexual, able-bodied psychology professor. The other is Audre Lorde, who was a Black, college-educated, lesbian, less able-bodied, renowned feminist writer and poet. To label both of us as educated, female New Yorkers is true, but ignores our very different life experiences shaped by the several intersecting identities that we did not share. In this text, the authors discuss both similarities and differences in the attitudes, emotions, relationships, goals, and behaviors of girls and women who have a diversity of backgrounds. For example, we explore interpersonal relationships of heterosexual and sexual minority women (Chapter 8); physical and mental health concerns of White women and women of color (Chapters 12 and 13); problems on campus and in the workplace faced by women with disabilities (Chapters 9 and 10); and health, employment, and interpersonal issues of older women (Chapters 8, 10, and 12). However, because most of the research to date on the psychology of women has been based on restricted samples, it is important to note that our presentation includes a disproportionate amount of information about young, middle-class, heterosexual, able-bodied, White women and girls living in the United States.

When referring to cultural variations among people, we use the term *ethnicity* rather than *race*. **Race** is *a biological concept that refers to physical characteristics of people*. However, experts disagree about what constitutes a single race, and there is considerable genetic variation among people designated as a single race. **Ethnicity**, on the other hand, refers to *variations in cultural background, nationality, history, religion, and/or language* (Hall et al., 2016), a term more closely associated with the variations in attitudes, behaviors, and roles that we discuss in this book.

Unfortunately, there are no universally acceptable labels that identify a person's ethnicity. Some terms are based on geographical origin as in *African American* and *Euro-American* whereas others are based on color, such as *Black* and *White*. Furthermore, each major ethnic category encompasses a diversity of ethnic subtypes. For example, Americans with Asian ancestry, regardless of their specific origin (e.g., China, Japan, Korea, Vietnam), are generally grouped into a single category of Asian Americans. Similarly, Whites from countries as diverse as Ireland, Germany, and Russia are combined into one ethnic group. Along the same lines, the label *Latina/o* refers to individuals from Mexico, Cuba, and Puerto Rico, and others of Hispanic origin (Robinson-Wood, 2017). With the hope that our usage does not inadvertently offend anyone, ethnic group labels used in this book are Asian American, Black, Latina/o, Native American, and White, recognizing that each of these broad ethnic categories actually encompasses a diversity of cultures.

Theme 2: Gender Differences in Power

In no known societies do women dominate men. . . . Men, on average, enjoy more power than women, on average, and this appears to have been true throughout human history.

(Pratto & Walker, 2004, p. 242)

Two interlocking ideas characterize our power theme. One is that the experiences of women in virtually all cultures are shaped by both **organizational power**, *the ability to use valuable resources to dominate and control others*, and **interpersonal power**, *the ability to influence one's partner within*

WHAT <u>YOU</u> CAN DO 1.1
Help Empower Girls and Women

One theme of this book is that men hold more power than women. Many national organizations that work to empower girls and women have local chapters, such as the NOW, the Girl Scouts, the YWCA (Young Women's Christian Association), and the American Association of University Women. Volunteer for one of these organizations in your community.

a specific relationship. The greater organizational power of males compared to that of females is evident in our discussion of numerous topics, including gender differences in salary (Chapter 10), the underrepresentation of women in high-status occupations (Chapter 10), and sexual harassment (Chapter 14). Additionally, gender differences in interpersonal power are clearly reflected in our discussions of interpersonal violence (Chapter 14), rape (Chapter 14), and the allocation of household responsibilities (Chapter 11).

Both of these power differentials reflect an undesirable imbalance in a form of power, called **power-over**, *a person's or group's control of another person or group*. This type of power is distinguished from **power-to**, *the empowerment of self and others to accomplish tasks* (Baker, 2015). Whereas the former is a negative type of power that restricts opportunities and choices of members of the less powerful group, the latter allows for personal growth for all. Thus, feminist psychologists want to eliminate the former and increase the latter (Denmark et al., 2015; Sen, 2017).

A second component of our theme of power differences is that many women experience more than one type of power imbalance. In addition to a gender difference in power, women can experience power inequities as a function of their ethnicity, social class, sexual orientation, age, and physical ability (Hawkesworth, 2016; Launius & Hassel, 2015). Furthermore, the effects of these imbalances are cumulative. For example, women of color experience greater discrimination in the workplace than do White women (Chapter 10). As bell hooks (1990) stated, "By calling attention to interlocking systems of domination—sex, race, and class—Black women and many other groups of women acknowledge the diversity and complexity of female experience, of our relationship to power and domination" (p. 187).

One consequence of gender differences in power is that women and women's issues receive less emphasis and visibility than men and men's issues. In this chapter, for example, we saw that women's contributions to psychology have often been overlooked. We examine other instances of this problem in our discussion of specific topics, such as the underrepresentation of females in the media (Chapter 2) and the exclusion of women from major studies of medical and health issues (Chapter 12). See What <u>You</u> Can Do 1.1 for ways you can help empower girls and women.

A term closely related to power is **privilege**, which is defined as *benefits, advantages, and power that accrue to members of a dominant group by virtue of their status in society*. Groups may be privileged without realizing, recognizing, or even wanting it. Dominant (i.e., privileged) groups are considered the norm, while marginalized groups are considered the "other" (Halley & Eshleman, 2016; Launius & Hassel, 2015). The *male dominance that characterizes virtually all societies* is referred to as **hegemonic masculinity** (Silvestri & Crowther-Dowey, 2016). In addition to males, what are some other groups that are privileged in Western societies?

Theme 3: Social Construction of Gender

As indicated at the beginning of this chapter, social scientists differentiate between sex, the biological aspects of femaleness and maleness, and gender, the nonbiological components. Our third theme is the **social construction of gender**, which points out that *the traits, behaviors, and roles that people associate with females and males are not inherent in one's sex; they are shaped by numerous interpersonal, cultural, and societal forces.* Even if some aspects of being a female or a male are biologically based, we live in a society that emphasizes gender, and our development as women and men—as well as our conceptions of what it means to be a female or a male—is significantly influenced by cultural and societal values (Eagly & Wood, 2013; Kenschaft & Clark, 2016; Ryle, 2015). We do not exist in a sterile laboratory; instead, we are continually affected by an interlocking set of expectations, pressures, and rewards that guide our development as women and men.

Furthermore, our experience and conceptions of femaleness and maleness cannot be viewed as separate from our ethnicity and social class (Rice, 2014) or from our sexual orientation and physical ability/disability (Launius & Hassel, 2015). Each of these identities is also socially constructed. Lesbians, for example, are affected not only by societal expectations about what women are like, but also by people's beliefs about and attitudes toward sexual minorities. To put it another way, studying women without looking at the intersections of their socially constructed multiple identities results in a limited and incomplete understanding of women's lives (Robinson-Wood, 2017).

The social construction of gender is discussed in relation to several topics in the text. For example, we examine theories that explain how children develop their ideas about gender (Chapter 3); explore the processes of instilling a child with expectations about what it means to be a girl or boy (Chapter 4); and look at social influences on gender in our discussion of gender differences in aggression (Chapter 5), friendship (Chapter 8), and the division of household labor (Chapter 11).

Summary

DEFINITIONS: SEX AND GENDER

- *Sex* refers to the classification of females and males based on biological factors. *Gender* refers to social expectations of roles and behaviors for females and males.

WOMEN AND MEN: SIMILAR OR DIFFERENT?

- The similarities approach (beta bias) argues that women and men are basically alike in their behaviors and that any differences are a product of socialization.
- The differences approach (alpha bias) emphasizes that women and men are different and that these differences are biologically based.

FEMINISM

- Liberal, cultural, socialist, radical, and women of color feminism all posit that women are disadvantaged relative to men. They differ in their assumptions about the sources of this inequality.

HISTORY OF WOMEN IN PSYCHOLOGY

- For many years, women attained few leadership positions and awards in the APA, but gains have been made in recent years.
- Women's contributions to psychology have often been overlooked or ignored, but that situation is improving.

HISTORY OF THE PSYCHOLOGY OF WOMEN

- In the early years of psychology, women were viewed as inferior to men and their experiences were rarely studied.
- Early women psychologists carried out research that challenged the assumptions of female inferiority.
- In the 1970s, the psychology of women emerged as a separate field of study.
- In recent years, research on diverse groups of women has increased and new theoretical models have been developed.

STUDYING THE PSYCHOLOGY OF WOMEN

- Psychological research is not value free. Throughout most of its history, psychology did not pay much attention to the experiences of girls and women in either the topics investigated or the participants studied.
- Since 1970, there has been an increase in research focus on females; however, most of this research has been carried out on White, middle-class, heterosexual, able-bodied women.
- Generalizing results based on one type of participant to other types of people can lead to inaccurate conclusions.
- The researcher's theoretical perspective influences the hypothesis examined in the research,

which in turn affects the type of information learned from the research.

- The measures used to study the research topic can influence the findings of the research.
- Due to publication bias, published studies are more likely to present gender differences than gender similarities.
- Very few studies use blatantly biased gender language, but a more subtle bias can be detected in the use of nonparallel terms for comparable female and male behaviors.
- Some feminists advocate the use of traditional objective, quantitative research methods, while others favor qualitative procedures.
- There are several principles that characterize most feminist research.
- The narrative approach and meta-analysis are two methods of integrating results of several studies on the same topic.

- Meta-analysis is a statistical method that provides a measure of the magnitude of a given difference, known as the effect size.

THEMES IN THE TEXT

- Three themes are prominent in this text.
- First, psychology must examine the intersecting identities and experiences of diverse groups of women.
- Second, the greater organizational and interpersonal power of men compared to women negatively shapes and limits women's experiences. Women of color, poor and working-class women, sexual minority women, and women with disabilities experience additional power inequities, with cumulative effects.
- Third, gender is socially constructed; it is shaped by social, cultural, and societal values.

Key Terms

gender roles *2*	racism *4*	intersectionality *16*
gender *2*	classism *4*	race *16*
sex *2*	sexism *4*	ethnicity *16*
beta bias *2*	mujerista psychology *4*	organizational
alpha bias *2*	standpoint theory *8*	power *16*
essentialism *2*	social constructionism *8*	interpersonal power *16*
liberal feminism *3*	sample *9*	power-over *17*
cultural feminism *4*	population *9*	power-to *17*
socialist feminism *4*	male as normative *10*	privilege *17*
radical feminism *4*	statistical significance *11*	hegemonic masculinity *17*
patriarchy *4*	meta-analysis *15*	social construction
women of color feminism *4*	effect size *15*	of gender *17*

What Do You Think?

1. Do you prefer the similarities approach or the differences approach to the study of gender issues? Why?
2. Which definition of *feminism* or combination of definitions best reflects your own view of feminism? Why?
3. Do you think it would be desirable for women and/or men if more people identified themselves as feminists? Explain your answer.

4. We noted a few experiences of women that are influenced by a gender imbalance in power, and we will cover other examples throughout the text. However, can you now identify any behaviors or concerns of women that you think are influenced by a power imbalance?

If You Want to Learn More

Brisolara, S., Seigart, D., & SenGupta, S. (Eds.). (2014). *Feminist evaluation and research: Theory and practice.* New York: Guilford.

Davidson, M. del G. (2017). *Black women, agency, and the new Black feminism.* New York: Routledge.

Davis, D. & Craven, C. (2016). *Feminist ethnography: Thinking through methodologies, challenges, and possibilities*. Lanham, MD: Rowman & Littlefield.

Disch, L. & Hawkesworth, M. (Eds.). (2016). *The Oxford handbook of feminist theory*. New York: Oxford University Press.

Harnois, C.E. (2013). *Feminist methods in survey research*. Los Angeles: Sage.

Hesse-Biber, S.N. (2013). *Feminist research practice: A primer*. Los Angeles: Sage.

Holgersson, U. (2017). *Class: Feminist and cultural perspectives*. New York: Routledge.

Jackson, S.A. (Ed.). (2014). *Routledge international handbook of race, class, and gender*. New York: Routledge.

Launius, C. & Hassel. H. (2015). *Threshold concepts in women's and gender studies: Ways of seeing, thinking, and knowing*. New York: Routledge.

McCann, C. & Kim, S. (2017). *Feminist theory reader: Local and global perspectives*. New York: Routledge.

Phellas, C.N. (2012). *Researching nonheterosexual sexuality*. New York: Routledge.

Roberts, T.-A., Curtin, N., & Duncan, L.E. (Eds.). (2016). *Feminist perspectives on building a better psychology of gender*. New York: Springer.

Rosenblum, K. & Travis, T.-M. (2015). *The meaning of difference: American constructions of race and ethnicity, sex and gender, social class, sexuality, and disability* (7th ed.). New York: McGraw Hill Education.

Rothenberg, P.S. (2016). *Race, class, and gender in the United States* (10th ed.). New York: Worth.

Sprague, J. (2016). *Feminist methodologies for critical researchers*. Lanham, MD: Rowman & Littlefield.

Tong, R.M. (2013). *Feminist thought: A more comprehensive introduction* (4th ed.). Boulder, CO: Westview.

Zinn, M.B. & Hondagneu-Sotelo, P. (2016). *Gender through the prism of difference* (5th ed.). New York: Oxford University Press.

Websites

Feminism

feminist.com
http://www.feminist.com/
https://femwoc.com

Cultural Representation of Gender

In September 1970, on the day I (Judith) began my academic career, there was a meeting of the faculty at my campus. As was the custom, the campus director introduced me and another new professor to the rest of the faculty and staff. His introduction of my male colleague was both unsurprising and appropriate; he identified him as "Dr. Lantry Brooks" and then provided his academic credentials. Although my educational background was also given, the director introduced me, quite awkwardly, as "Dr., Mrs. Judith Bridges."

What images of women's and men's roles does this dual title suggest? Is there a power difference implied by the different forms of address used for my male colleague and me?

Leap ahead to 2016. At that time, a colleague of Claire's went through a lengthy decision-making process about the surname she would use after her forthcoming marriage. She knew her fiancé was not going to change his name, and she considered taking his name, retaining her birth name, or hyphenating their names. She decided to hyphenate.

Does this colleague's decision have any effect on people's impressions of her? When students read her name in the course schedule, when she applies for grants, or when she is introduced to new acquaintances, does her hyphenated name suggest a different image than her alternative choices would have? Why do people associate different characteristics with different surname choices; that is, what social experiences help shape these images?

In this chapter, we explore these issues and similar ones as we examine stereotypes of females and males, the nature of sexism, and the representations of gender in the media and in language.

STEREOTYPES OF FEMALES AND MALES

Before we begin, think about your conception of the *typical* adult woman and the *typical* adult man. Then indicate your ideas in Get Involved 2.1.

The Content of Gender Stereotypes

The characteristics shown in Get Involved 2.1 reflect **gender stereotypes**, that is, *widely shared beliefs about the attributes of females and males*. These views are present in virtually all cultures that have been studied (Ruspini, 2011; Guimond et al., 2013). As this sample of traits indicates, *personality characteristics associated with women, such as sympathy, kindness, and warmth, reflect a concern about other people*. Social scientists call this cluster of attributes **communion**. *The group of instrumental traits associated with men, including achievement orientation and ambitiousness,* on the other hand, *reflects a concern about accomplishing tasks* and is called **agency** (Fuegen & Biernat, 2013; Wood & Eagly, 2015).

Consistent with the tendency to associate communal traits with females and agentic traits with males is people's tendency to expect different roles for women and men (Barretto & Ellemers, 2013; Beane et al., 2014). For example, although most women are employed, many individuals continue to expect that women will be the primary caregivers of both children and older parents and that men will be the primary providers (Donnelly et al., 2016). In addition, people perceive female family members (i.e., mothers, grandmothers, sisters, aunts) to be more communal toward them than male family members (Monin et al., 2008).

Interestingly, some of these stereotypes have remained relatively unchanged since the 1970s, especially those involving experiencing and expressing emotion and caring as more typical of women and those involving assertiveness, independence, and activity as more typical of men (Haines et al., 2016; Wood & Eagly, 2015). However, as women have gained status in Western culture in the last few decades, they have increasingly been viewed as having stereotypically masculine traits (Twenge, 2009). The typical woman is no longer considered to be less logical, direct, ambitious, or objective than the typical man or to have greater difficulty in making decisions or separating ideas from feelings. These traits constitute agentic characteristics having to do with competence and the capacity to be effective (Wood & Eagly, 2015).

You might have noted that the attributes comprising the male stereotype are more highly regarded in North American society and are more consistent with a powerful image and a higher status than those comprising the female cluster (Guimond et al., 2013). In Western culture, with its strong emphasis on the value of hard work and achievement, people tend to associate agentic qualities, such as ambition and independence, with power and prestige and to evaluate these traits more positively than communal attributes, such as gentleness and emotionality. In fact, highly competent and agentic women often are disliked, especially by men (Eagly, 2013). Thus, gender stereotypes are the first indication of the power imbalance discussed in Chapter 1.

Gender stereotypes are relevant to another theme, introduced in Chapter 1, the social construction of gender. Regardless of their accuracy, gender-related beliefs serve as lenses that guide one's expectations and interpretations of other people (Guimond, 2013). They can elicit stereotypic

GET INVOLVED 2.1
How Do You View Typical Females and Males?

Indicate which of the following characteristics reflect your conception of a *typical* adult woman and a *typical* adult man. Write *W* next to each characteristic you associate with women and *M* next to each characteristic you associate with men. If you think a particular trait is representative of both women and men, write both *W* and *M* next to that trait.

_____ achievement oriented		_____ emotional
_____ active		_____ gentle
_____ adventurous		_____ independent
_____ affectionate		_____ kind
_____ aggressive		_____ people oriented
_____ ambitious		_____ pleasant
_____ boastful		_____ rational
_____ charming		_____ softhearted
_____ daring		_____ sympathetic
_____ dominant		_____ warm

WHAT DOES IT MEAN?

Did your conceptions of a typical woman and a typical man match those reported by samples of university students from the United States and 28 other countries? These students described the typical woman with traits including affectionate, charming, emotional, gentle, kind, people oriented, softhearted, sympathetic, and warm; they described the typical man with characteristics such as achievement oriented, active, adventurous, ambitious, boastful, daring, independent, and rational.

1. If your impressions of the typical woman and the typical man did not agree with the descriptions reported by these samples of college students, give possible reasons.

2. What was the ethnic identity of the typical woman and man that you considered when performing this activity? If you thought about a White woman and man, do you think your conceptions would have varied had you been asked to specifically consider Blacks, Latinas/os, Asian Americans, or Native Americans? If yes, what are those differences and what can explain them?

3. Similarly, did you think of a middle-class woman and man? Would your impressions have varied had you thought about working-class or poor females and males? Explain any possible differences in gender stereotypes based on social class.

Sources: Based on De Lisi and Soundranayagam (1990) and Williams and Best (1990).

behaviors from others. For example, a high school teacher who believes that females are more nurturing than males might ask female students to volunteer in a day-care center run by the school. This activity would provide females but not males with the opportunity to develop their caregiving traits. Thus, the teacher's stereotype about the communal characteristics of girls and women might actually contribute to the construction of feminine traits in her female students.

The importance of gender stereotypes in the social construction of gender is also evident in the choices individuals make about their own behavior. For example, a gender stereotype that develops early is that males, more than females, have high-level intellectual ability (e.g., brilliance, genius). Girls as young as age 6 are less likely than boys to believe that members of their own gender are "really really smart," and they begin to avoid activities said to be for "really really smart" children (Bian et al., 2017). This gender stereotype may thus be steering girls into less ambitious career goals.

The traits we have examined thus far are those that North Americans see as *representative* of most women and men. However, these stereotypes differ from people's views of the *ideal* woman and man. Interestingly, both college students and faculty view the ideal woman and the ideal man as high in both agentic and communal traits.

The Perceiver's Ethnicity and Gender Stereotypes

When you performed Get Involved 2.1, did your selection of traits for females and males match those found in previous research? Possibly you indicated that some of these characteristics were reflective of both females and males or that some were more representative of the gender not usually associated with the stereotype. Although there is considerable consistency among people in their gender stereotypes, all individuals do not think alike.

In fact, there is evidence that people from different ethnic backgrounds vary in the degree to which they believe the ideal characteristics for females are different from the ideal traits for males, with Blacks less stereotypic in their views than Latinas/os or Whites (Carter et al., 2009; Hayes & Swim, 2013).

The Target's Characteristics and Gender Stereotypes

We have seen that people with diverse ethnic backgrounds differ somewhat in their perception of stereotypes of women and men. Now let's examine how these stereotypes vary as a function of the characteristics of the person who is the object, or target, of the stereotype. These characteristics include a woman's age, ethnicity, social class, sexual orientation, and ableness.

AGE.   One of the challenges facing older people in North America and many other parts of the world is the presence of stereotypes (mostly negative) that many people hold about older people (Levy et al., 2014; McHugh & Interligi, 2014; Vacha-Haase et al., 2014). Both children and adults express stereotyped views about older people, some positive (warm, kind, friendly, wise) and others negative (incompetent, inactive, unattractive, feeble, sick, cranky, forgetful, obstinate) (Chrisler et al., 2016; Lepianka, 2015; North & Fiske, 2015). Such negative stereotypes are part of a concept known as **ageism,** *a bias against older people.* Ageism resembles sexism and racism in that all are forms of prejudice that limit people who are the object of that prejudice. Unlike sexism and racism, however, everyone will confront ageism if they live long enough (Holstein, 2015; Nelson, 2016).

Ageism seems to be more strongly directed toward women than men. For centuries, unflattering terms have been used to describe middle-aged and older women: shrew, crazy old lady, crone, hag, wicked old witch, old maid, dreaded mother-in-law (Have you ever heard any jokes about fathers-in-law?) (American Psychological Association, 2007; Bugental & Hehman, 2007). Another example of negative attitudes toward older women is the double standard of aging that we will examine later in the chapter.

Psychologists seem to share society's negative views of older women (Baldwin & Garner, 2016). They are more likely to rate older women as less assertive, less willing to take risks, and less competent than younger women (American Psychological Association, 2007). Moreover, feminists are not free of ageism and have paid very little attention to older women (McHugh & Interligi, 2014). For example, even though textbooks on the psychology of women and psychology of gender note the invisibility of older women in the media, these texts themselves give only minimal coverage to midlife and older women (Etaugh et al., 2010). In addition, coverage of eating disorders and sexually transmitted infections in these textbooks focuses almost exclusively on younger women, even though these conditions affect women of all ages. Elder abuse also is ignored by most of the books.

Although aging women have traditionally been viewed less positively than aging men, there is some indication that attitudes toward older women may be improving. One positive sign is what psychologist Margaret Matlin (2001) calls the "Wise and Wonderful Movement." In the twenty-first century, more scholarly research is being devoted to how older women are contributing to the current climate of social change and how these positive developments can improve the lives of older women (Muhlbauer et al., 2015). In addition, there has been an explosion of books on women who discover themselves in middle or old age. The books present a positive picture of the challenges and opportunities for women in their later years. Three of these books, by Laura Hurd Clarke (2011), Martha Holstein (2015), and Lynne Segal (2013), are listed as recommended readings at the end of this chapter.

ETHNICITY.   Research has found that women are viewed differently according to their ethnicity. Latinas, for example, are described in relatively positive or neutral terms: pleasant, caring, family-oriented, and passive (Mindiola et al., 2002; Niemann et al., 1994). East Asian American women are often perceived as soft-spoken and subservient, but also as hard-working and highly educated, a "model minority" (Le & Dinh, 2015). South Asian American women are viewed as passive victims of oppressive families and cultures (Rice, 2014; Singh et al., 2017).

Black women tend to be viewed in terms of the cultural matriarchal stereotype: tough, direct, aggressive, dominant, and strong (Ashley, 2014; Helms, 2017). This somewhat negative stereotype indicates that individuals may overlook the harsh realities of racial and gender oppression in the lives of many Black women and may perceive Black women through a racist lens, a problem experienced by other ethnic minority women as well (Chisholm & Greene, 2008).

SOCIAL CLASS.   Studies have found that individuals of lower socioeconomic status are often characterized as unattractive, loud, dependent, lazy, stupid, uneducated, and promiscuous (Goodman et al., 2013; Loo et al., 2017; Lott, 2012). One study found that women from a poor, White community in Appalachia were perceived as dirty, uncouth, "white trash," and unfit mothers. Similarly, women who receive public aid are subjected to demeaning, hostile attitudes and treatment by workers in the welfare system (Lott, 2010).

SEXUAL ORIENTATION.   Lesbian, gay, bisexual, and transgender (LGBT) individuals experience widespread social stigmatization that either renders them invisible or causes them to be viewed as sick, immoral, or evil (Orel & Fruehauf, 2015; Robinson-Wood 2017). Moreover, many sexual minority individuals claim that the labels "masculine" and "feminine" represent efforts of the heterosexual community to pigeonhole LGBTs in traditional ways (Rathus et al., 2013).

ABLENESS.   People attribute more negative characteristics to women with disabilities than to able-bodied women. This bias against people because of their disability is known as **ableism** (Robinson-Wood, 2017). Women with disabilities, unlike able-bodied women, are frequently stereotyped as unattractive, asexual, unfit to reproduce, helpless, weak, and overly dependent (Fawcett, 2016; Nosek, 2010; Robinson-Wood, 2017).

In summary, we can see that gender stereotypes are not applied uniformly to all women. A woman's age, ethnicity, social class, sexual orientation, and ableness influence how she is perceived.

Stereotypes of Girls and Boys

We have seen that people have different expectations of the traits and behaviors of adult females and males. Now let's examine adults' gender-stereotypic expectations of children.

As early as the first few days of life, newborn girls and boys are perceived differently. Parents rate newborn daughters as finer featured, less strong, and more delicate than newborn sons, despite medical evidence of no physical differences between them (Karraker et al., 1995). Thus, it is apparent that adults hold gender stereotypes of the physical characteristics of children immediately after the child's birth.

Adults' gender stereotypes of children are not restricted to early infancy. When Canadian college students were asked to rate typical characteristics of 4- to 7-year-old girls and boys, they rated 24 out of 25 traits as being more typical for one gender than the other. Additionally, the traits seen as typical for girls versus boys reflected the communion–agency stereotypes evident in gender stereotypes of adults. For example, these students rated girls, compared to boys, as more gentle, sympathetic, and helpful around the house, and they rated boys as more self-reliant, dominant, and competitive than girls.

Bases for Gender Stereotypes

Our exploration of the origins of gender stereotypes focuses on two related issues: (1) the reasons why people stereotype on the basis of gender and (2) the reasons why these stereotypes center on communal traits for females and agentic attributes for males. In other words, we will consider explanations for both the *process* and the *content* of gender stereotyping.

SOCIAL CATEGORIZATION.   Because individuals are bombarded daily with diverse types of people, behaviors, situations, and so on, they simplify their social perceptions by *sorting individuals into categories*, a process called **social categorization** (Kang & Bodenhausen, 2015). They focus on the characteristics people share with other members of that category. As an example, in a hospital individuals might categorize the health professionals they encounter as doctors and nurses. Then, the differential set of characteristics they associate with physicians versus nurses serves as a behavior guide when they interact with them, enabling them to ask questions appropriate to their skills and knowledge.

Although individuals use a variety of cues for the sorting process, social categorization is frequently based on easily identified characteristics, such as ethnicity, age, and sex (Shutts, 2015; Zell et al., 2015). Sex is one of the most pervasive methods of categorizing people. The process of gender stereotyping begins with the categorization of individuals as females or males with the implicit assumption that the members of each sex share certain attributes. Then, when one meets a new individual, he/she attributes these gender characteristics to this person.

Although the social categorization and stereotyping processes help simplify a person's understanding of and interactions with other people, they can lead a person astray, because neither all females nor all males are alike. Individuals are most likely to rely on stereotypes when they have little differentiating information about the person. Once more details about a person are available, they use that information in addition to the person's gender to form their impressions and guide their interactions (Kite et al., 2008). For example, when evaluating an individual's level of ambition, people might make use of the person's gender if no other information were available. However, this information would be much less important if they knew the individual was the CEO of a major corporation.

SOCIAL ROLE THEORY.   Given that people divide others into gender categories and attribute similar characteristics to all members of a category, we turn now to the question of why people associate communion with females and agency with males. One possibility is that these stereotypes stem from people's observations of the behaviors individuals typically perform in their social roles. According to **social role theory** (Eagly, 2013a), *stereotypes of women and men stem from the association of women with the domestic role and men with the employee role*. Thus, because individuals have observed women primarily in the domestic role, they assume women have the nurturing traits characteristic of that role. Similarly, because more men than women have traditionally been seen in the employment role, people perceive men as having the agentic traits displayed in the workplace.

Support for this theory of gender stereotypes comes from studies that show the influence of a person's social role on the application of gender-related traits to her/him. For example, social roles can override gender when assigning communal or agentic characteristics to others. Specifically, when participants are asked to describe a woman and a man who are homemakers, they view them as equally communal. Similarly, when asked to describe a full-time female and male employee, they perceive both as agentic. In addition, women and men who are employed are viewed as more agentic than those who are not (Coleman & Franiuk, 2011), mothers are seen as more communal than non-mothers (Bridges et al., 2000; Etaugh & Poertner, 1992), and married women are perceived as more communal than unmarried women (Etaugh & Nekolny, 1990; Etaugh & Poertner, 1991). Clearly, when people are aware of an individual's social role, their stereotypes of the person are influenced by that role information.

The influence of social roles on gender stereotypes is evident even when people are asked to describe women and men in both the past and the future. When both college students and students after college were asked to rate the average woman and the average man in 1950, 1975, 2025, and 2050, they viewed females as becoming dramatically more masculine over time and males as becoming somewhat more feminine (Diekman & Eagly, 1997). What accounts for these perceptions? In support of social role theory, the researchers found that the decreasing degree of gender stereotyping was related to the belief that the occupational and domestic roles of women and men during this time period have become and will continue to become increasingly similar.

Keep in mind, however, the evidence presented earlier in this chapter—that stereotypes have remained relatively constant, at least since the 1970s. What can explain the discrepancy between the increased participation of women in the labor force and the consistency of gender stereotypes over time? Although more women are employed now than in the past, they are more likely than men to be employed in caregiving occupations, such as nursing and early childhood education. Also, regardless of their employment role, women still have the primary caregiving responsibility in their families. Although social roles are gradually changing, women remain the primary nurturers and men the primary providers around the world (Eagly, 2013). Consequently, it is not surprising that people's stereotypes of females and males have been resistant to change.

Recently, Alice Eagly and Wendy Wood (2013) proposed a biosocial constructionist model, which blends social role theory with biological processes. This biosocial model posits that biological specialization of the sexes (i.e., women's reproductive capabilities, men's speed and strength) made it more efficient for women and men in preindustrial societies to perform different activities. This gendered division of labor has given rise to gender role beliefs (i.e., social roles). These beliefs are maintained by socialization practices through which children learn what is considered acceptable behavior for each gender.

Stereotypes Based on Identity Labels

Recall the experience Judith described at the beginning of the chapter when she was introduced as "Dr., Mrs. Bridges." The fact that the campus director introduced her this way but did not present her male colleague as "Dr. Lantry Brooks who happens to be married" implies he believed that a woman's identity, more than a man's, is shaped by her marital role. Although his use of a dual title was unusual, his belief about a woman's identity is consistent with the long-standing cultural norm that a woman is defined in terms of her relationship to a man. Given that a woman's title of address can signify her marital role and that her marital status has been viewed as an important aspect of her identity, people might expect different stereotypes of women who use different titles for themselves. Consider the woman who chooses not to use the conventional "Miss" or "Mrs." labels that announce her marital status but instead identifies herself with the neutral "Ms." Kelly Malcolmson and Lisa Sinclair (2007) replicated older studies that had found that women who prefer the title Ms. are perceived as more agentic but less communal than traditionally titled women. Thus, the Ms. title remains a powerful cue eliciting a stereotype consistent with male gender-related traits and inconsistent with female gender-related traits. Other research by Carol Lawton and her colleagues (Lawton et al., 2003) found that *Ms.* was often defined as a title for unmarried women, especially by younger adults. Older unmarried women were more likely to prefer *Ms.* as their own title than were younger unmarried women, whereas married women overwhelmingly preferred the use of *Mrs.*

Given that people's impressions of a woman are influenced by her preferred title, a related question is whether these stereotypes vary according to another identity label, a woman's choice of surname after marriage. Similar to the preference for *Ms.* as a title of address, a woman's choice of a surname other than her husband's, such as her birth name or a hyphenated name, is a nontraditional practice that separates the woman's personal identity from her identity as a wife. Nowadays, about 20 percent of college-educated brides keep their birth surname, and another 10 percent hyphenate their name or use their birth surname as a middle name. Women are more likely to keep their name if they are older, not religious, have children from a previous marriage, or have an advanced degree and established career (Miller & Willis, 2015). Thus, it is not surprising that studies by Claire, Judith, and others (Etaugh et al., 1999; Etaugh & Conrad, 2004; Etaugh & Roe, 2002; Robnett et al., 2016) showed that college women and men view married women who use a nontraditional surname as more agentic and less communal than women who follow the patriarchal practice of taking their husbands' names after marriage.

Why do a woman's preferred title and surname influence the characteristics attributed to her? One possibility is that individuals have observed more women with nontraditional forms of address (i.e., title and/or surname) in the workplace than in the domestic role and, thus, attribute more agentic traits to her. Indeed we've just seen that married women who use nonconventional surnames are often highly educated and have prestigious occupations (Miller & Willis, 2015). Thus, consistent with social role theory (Eagly, 2013a), stereotypes of women who prefer nontraditional forms of address might be due to the belief that they are in nontraditional roles.

SEXISM: EXPERIENCES AND ATTITUDES

The definition of *sexism* as bias against people because of their gender can be directed at either females or males. However, because women have a power disadvantage relative to men, they are more likely to be targets of sexism (Becker et al., 2014). Therefore, our discussion focuses on the more specific definition of **sexism** as *stereotypes and/or discriminatory behaviors that serve to restrict women's roles and maintain male dominance*. For example, prescriptive stereotypes such as "women should be the primary caregivers" and "women are not competent to be police officers or university presidents" serve to shape women's role choices. *Violating these prescriptive gender stereotypes can result in social and economic reprisals*—a phenomenon referred to as the **backlash effect** (Williams & Tiedens, 2016). For example, a highly qualified female job applicant may be viewed as socially deficient, leading to hiring discrimination and ultimately the maintenance of male dominance in the culture at large.

Consider the real-life case of Ann Hopkins, a highly accomplished manager at Price Waterhouse, a prestigious accounting firm. In 1982, Hopkins was one of 88 candidates for partner and the only female candidate. At that time, she had more billable hours than any other contenders, had brought in $25 million worth of business, and was highly regarded by her clients. However, Ann Hopkins was turned down for the partnership. She was criticized for her "macho" style and was advised to "walk more femininely, talk more femininely, dress more femininely, wear makeup and jewelry" (Elsesser, 2015).

Hopkins filed a lawsuit, asserting that her promotion had been denied on the basis of her gender. Although she won this suit, her employer appealed the decision all the way up to the Supreme Court. The Court decided in Ann Hopkins's favor, concluding that gender-based stereotyping had played a role in the firm's refusal to promote her to partner. After this decision, Ann Hopkins did become a partner and was awarded financial compensation for her lost earnings.

Experiences With Sexism

Sadly, almost all girls and women experience sexism at one time or another (Bates, 2016; Szymanski & Moffitt, 2012). For example, a study of 600 teenage girls of varied socioeconomic and ethnic backgrounds (Leaper & Brown, 2008) found that half of the girls reported hearing discouraging, sexist comments about their abilities in science, math, or computer usage. Three-fourths had received disparaging comments about their athletic abilities and sports involvement. Male peers were the most common perpetrators of academic and athletic sexist remarks. Such disapproval may lead some girls to downplay their interests and competencies in sports or academic areas, which can ultimately diminish their later achievements in these areas. Even more troubling, perhaps, teachers were a frequent source of discouraging remarks about girls' academic abilities, as were fathers. (More about this in Chapter 5.)

The perception of sexism depends, in part, on a woman's interpretation (Dick, 2013). To one woman a joke that sexually degrades women is sexist, but to another woman that joke is simply funny. Women also differ from one another in the effect of sexist experiences on their psychological well-being. Experiencing sexist events is less distressing for women with high self-esteem and with higher levels of feminist identity (Szymanski & Moffitt, 2012). In a recent national poll (Perry Undem, 2017), 82 percent of U.S. women said that sexism is still a problem in society today, whereas men underestimated the sexism felt by the women in their lives.

Changes in Sexist Attitudes Over Time

Sexist attitudes are strongest in nations with greater gender inequality (Brandt, 2011). In the past few decades, however, the endorsement of traditional gender roles and overt sexism has decreased in many countries especially within North America and Europe (Jetten et al., 2013). The reduction in overt sexism likely is due, in part, to legislative actions (e.g., 1960s legislation prohibiting education and workplace discrimination on the basis of sex) and other social changes (e.g., the significant influx of married women into the workplace in the last few decades). However, some of the decline in overt sexism might reflect the decreased social acceptability of blatantly sexist views, rather than a real weakening of beliefs that serve to maintain traditional roles and power differences. Several theorists have suggested that more subtle types of sexism have emerged: modern sexism and ambivalent sexism.

Modern Sexism

Modern sexism (Barretto & Ellemers, 2013; Becker & Sibley, 2013) is based on the coexistence of conflicting attitudes. According to this perspective, some people hold egalitarian values but, at the same time, harbor negative feelings toward women. The resulting ideology is *characterized by the belief that gender discrimination is no longer a problem in society and is manifested by harmful treatment of women in ways that appear to be socially acceptable*. For example, a modern sexist might argue that policies that foster gender equality, such as affirmative action, should not be implemented (Hideg & Ferris, 2016). Thus, it is possible for a person to espouse sexist beliefs such as these but not appear to be prejudiced against women.

Do you know anyone who endorses modern sexism? See Get Involved 2.2 for examples of modern sexist beliefs.

Ambivalent Sexism

Generally, people consider sexism to comprise *negative* stereotypes about women, such as the beliefs that women are fragile, submissive, and less competent than men. And, of course, we can see how stereotypes such as these are detrimental to women. Interestingly, however, Peter Glick and Susan Fiske (2011) have proposed that sexism can be **ambivalent**, encompassing both **hostile sexism**, or *negative stereotypes of women*, and **benevolent sexism**, or *the seemingly positive view that idealizes women as pure objects of men's adoration and protection*.

Although hostile sexist beliefs are overtly demeaning, benevolent sexist views are usually accompanied by genuine affection, and the holder of these attitudes might be unaware of their implicit sexist bias. For example, a husband who shields his wife from the family's financial difficulties might be unaware of the biased assumptions implicit in his desire to protect her. According to Glick and Fiske (2011), hostile and benevolent sexism both imply that women are weak and best suited for traditional gender roles. Both serve to justify and maintain patriarchal social structures. Some aspects of benevolent sexism may appeal to some women. For example, beliefs that women are less physically strong or more emotionally sensitive allow women to not engage in distasteful activities ranging from taking out the garbage to fighting in wars. Moreover, some women may endorse benevolent sexism in order to avoid antagonizing their male partners (Expósito et al., 2010).

GET INVOLVED 2.2
Who Holds Modern Sexist Beliefs?

On a scale from 1 (strongly disagree) to 7 (strongly agree), indicate the extent to which you disagree or agree with each of the following statements. Also, ask several female and male acquaintances who vary in age to respond to these statements.

1. It is rare to see women treated in a sexist manner on television.

2. Society has reached the point where women and men have equal opportunities for achievement.

3. Over the past few years, the government and news media have been showing more concern about the treatment of women than is warranted by women's actual experiences.

4. Discrimination against women is no longer a problem in the United States.

5. Women's requests in terms of equality between the sexes are simply exaggerated.

6. Universities are wrong to admit women in costly programs such as medicine when, in fact, a large number will leave their jobs after a few years to raise their children.

7. Due to social pressures, firms frequently have to hire underqualified women.

WHAT DOES IT MEAN?

Sum the ratings you gave to these seven statements. Do the same for each of your respondents. Note that each statement reflects a sexist belief; therefore, the higher the score, the greater the sexism.

1. Are there differences between the views of your female and male respondents? Explain your finding.

2. Are there differences between the views of respondents who vary in age? Explain your finding.

3. Do you think it is possible that a person could endorse one or more of these beliefs but not be supportive of traditional roles and male dominance? Why or why not?

Sources: Based on Tougas et al. (1995).

However, research shows that benevolent sexism actually has a harmful effect on women's performances on cognitive tasks (Jones et al., 2014). In one study, patronizing statements read before task performance led to feelings of self-doubt and decreased self-esteem, which undermined performance. Hostile sexist statements did not have this negative effect (Dardenne et al., 2007). In addition, being put on a pedestal by a romantic partner may create stressful pressure on the idealized one to live up to unwanted or unrealistic standards, thus putting a strain on the relationship (Tomlinson et al., 2014).

 Ambivalent sexism is a global phenomenon. Peter Glick, Susan Fiske, and their colleagues (2000) measured ambivalent sexism in over 15,000 participants in 19 countries in Africa, the Americas, Asia, Australia, and Europe. Although both hostile and benevolent sexism were prevalent in all cultures, these attitudes were strongest in Africa and Latin America and weakest in Northern Europe and Australia. Without exception, men showed more hostile sexism than women. In contrast, women in about half the countries endorsed benevolent sexism as much as or even more than men did (Figure 2.1). What accounts for these cross-cultural differences? The key factor appears to be the degree to which gender inequality exists in the various nations. Gender inequality is measured by such things as women's (relative to men's) participation in a country's economy and political system, their life expectancy, educational level, and standard of living. In countries with the greatest gender inequality (i.e., in Africa and Latin America), both men's and women's sexism scores were highest. Furthermore, the more hostile sexism the men showed, the more likely women were to embrace benevolent sexism, even to the point of endorsing it more strongly than men. How can this be explained? One possibility is that the greater the threat of hostile sexism from a society's men, the stronger the incentive for women to adopt benevolent sexism's protective nature.

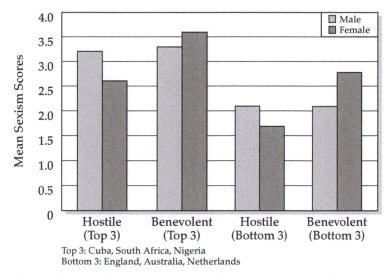

FIGURE 2.1   Hostile and Benevolent Sexism Across Countries: The Top Three in Gender Inequality Versus the Bottom Three

REPRESENTATION OF GENDER IN THE MEDIA

We have seen that North American adults have different conceptions of females and males. We turn now to the depiction of these stereotypes in the media. People are bombarded daily with differential images of females and males on television, in the movies, in books, and in magazines. Are these images consistent with gender stereotyping? Try the exercise in Get Involved 2.3 to examine television portrayals of gender.

Numerous investigations of the depiction of females and males in both electronic and print media have revealed several consistent patterns: the underrepresentation of females, the underrepresentation of specific groups of females, the portrayal of gender-based social roles, the depiction of female communion and male agency, and the emphasis on female attractiveness and sexuality. Our first task is to examine these patterns. Then we consider the effects of media images on gender stereotypes and attitudes.

Pattern 1: Underrepresentation of Females

As we have previously seen, women are perceived as less powerful and less important than men. This imbalance of power and value is reflected in the underrepresentation of females in media around the world. Moreover, the proportion of females has changed little since the 1990s. Currently, about 40 percent of characters on prime-time television shows for adults are female (Women's Media Center, 2014). Most children's television is even more unbalanced, with two or more male characters for every female (Kenschaft & Clark, 2016). Similarly, the percentage of female characters in television commercials (Das, 2011; Paek et al., 2011) and movies (Lauzen, 2015) ranges from approximately 20 to 45 percent. Among the 800 top films between 2007 and 2015, only 31 percent of speaking characters were women (Smith et al., 2016a). The underrepresentation of females is also mirrored in video games (Fox et al., 2015), Sunday morning news analysis shows (Women's Media Center, 2014), coloring books (Fitzpatrick & McPherson, 2010), and even cereal boxes (Black et al., 2009). The situation is even worse for the television coverage of women's sports, which has actually declined over the past 25 years. Currently, only 2 to 3 percent of sports news coverage focuses on women's events (Cooky et al., 2015).

This situation has improved in recent years in certain types of children's reading material. For example, picture books are now more likely to feature males and females equally in titles, as central characters, and in pictures (Etaugh et al., 2013). Children's school textbooks are less gender

GET INVOLVED 2.3
How Are Females and Males Portrayed on Prime-Time Television?

Watch five different prime-time shows and record the following information: (1) the number of major female and male characters; (2) the ethnicity of these characters; (3) the employment status and occupation, if employed, of each major female and male character; (4) the marital and parental status of these characters; (5) the approximate age of each of these characters (e.g., 20s, 30s); and (6) whether or not each character's physical appearance was mentioned or otherwise appeared to be an important characteristic of that person. After recording this information, examine commonalities and differences in the depiction of females and males and in the portrayal of different age groups. Also, if these shows featured women and/or men of color, compare portrayals of characters of varying ethnicities.

WHAT DOES IT MEAN?

1. Are your findings consistent with those presented in this chapter? If not, what might explain any differences you observed?

2. Do your findings indicate that members of each gender are depicted similarly, regardless of their ethnicity or age? If you found differences related to ethnicity or age, explain them.

3. Do you think that media images of gender, as described in this chapter and as shown by your analysis, help shape people's construction of gender? Explain your answer.

biased than they were 30 years ago, but male characters continue to outnumber female ones in basic readers and math materials (Piatek-Jimenez et al., 2014).

Pattern 2: Underrepresentation of Specific Groups of Females

ETHNICITY.   The invisibility of females is most evident when considering females in less powerful social categories. Women and girls of color, especially Latinas, Asian Americans, and Native peoples, are featured very infrequently in children's and adults' television shows and commercials (Baumann & Ho, 2014; Lemish, 2015), movies (Women's Media Center, 2014; Smith et al., 2015), and video games (Wohn, 2011). When they do appear, they are highly stereotyped (Gammage, 2016; Martin & Kazyak, 2009). For example, Latina characters are often shown in low-status occupations such as maids (Navarro, 2002). When they appear in top-grossing movies, they are more likely than other women to be dressed provocatively. Black women are often portrayed in a variety of negative roles, such as the promiscuous Jezebel, unmarried mother, or angry woman (Allison, 2016; Women's Media Center, 2014).

AGE.   Although older adults of both sexes are generally underrepresented in the media, this is especially true for women (Holstein, 2015; Lauzen, 2015; Smith et al., 2015). Joan Chrisler (2007) notes that the scarcity of images of women over 50 in the media conveys the message that women should either hide the signs of aging or stay hidden. The few older women who appear on television shows are portrayed less favorably than older men. They are often depicted as comic or eccentric figures, asexual, burdensome, dependent, interfering, gossipy, or downright villainous (Hant, 2011; Holstein, 2015). Whereas prime-time male characters aged 65 and older are depicted as active, middle-aged, mature adults, women of that age are more likely to be designated as elderly (Signorielli & Bacue, 1999). In the movies (Lauzen, 2015), female characters are younger than male characters, with most women under age 35. In fact, women over 40 are portrayed in only 20 percent of the roles in popular movies. Older women of color are rarely seen (Robinson et al., 2004).

Older women in popular films are portrayed as more unfriendly, unintelligent, unattractive, scary, or wicked (Hollis-Sawyer & Dykema-Engblade, 2016; Merry, 2016). In the popular animated

Disney films, for example, evil older women abound: the wicked queen in *Snow White and the Seven Dwarfs*, Cinderella's stepmother, Maleficent (*Sleeping Beauty*), Ursula (*The Little Mermaid*), Cruella DeVille (*101 Dalmatians*), the Red Queen (*Alice in Wonderland*), and Mother Gothel (*Tangled*). Attractive actresses such as Meryl Streep, Jessica Lange, and Diane Keaton are labeled "geezer babes"—and thus too old for romantic parts—whereas male actors many years their senior are portrayed as ageless heroes and are paired with young ingénues (Chrisler et al., 2016; Fairclough, 2014). In the top 100 films of 2015, fewer than 3 percent of actors with speaking roles were women age 60 or over, compared with more than 7 percent of men in that age group. Just three 60-plus women had a lead role (Smith et al., 2016b). Indeed, the careers of female actors peak at age 30, compared to age 46 for male actors. Hollywood's long-standing tendency to add years to actresses and subtract them from actors has led to some interesting—and biologically impossible—movie relationships. For example, 29-year-old Angelina Jolie played the mother of 28-year-old Colin Farrell in the 2004 film *Alexander* (Beumont, 2005).

Print media are no exception. In magazines targeting 40- and 50-year-old women, for example, most of the models are in their 20s and early 30s (Bessenoff & Del Priore, 2007). Readers of these magazines are bombarded with ads for antiaging products (Hurd Clarke, 2011). Those older women who do appear in the media are praised for their youthful appearance and for hiding the signs of aging. Ads for antiaging products send the message that older women are worthwhile only to the extent that they revert to middle-aged and even youthful norms of female beauty (Chrisler et al., 2016; Fairclough, 2014). In the words of Susan Bordo,

> *I'm 56. The magazines tell me that at this age, a woman can still be beautiful. But they don't mean me. They mean Cher, Goldie, Faye, Candace. Women whose jowls have disappeared as they've aged, whose eyes have become less droopy, lips grown plumper, foreheads smoother with the passing years. "Aging beautifully" used to mean wearing one's years with style, confidence, and vitality. Today, it means not appearing to age at all.*

(2004, p. 246)

In the present youth-oriented society, the prospect of getting older is generally not relished by either sex. For women, however, *the stigma of aging is much greater than it is for men*. This intersection of ageism and sexism creates a **double standard of aging** (Barrett & Naiman-Sessions, 2016). The same gray hair and wrinkles that enhance the perceived status and attractiveness of an older man diminish the attractiveness and desirability of an older woman (Pergament, 2013). Some researchers account for this by noting that a woman's most socially valued qualities—her ability to provide sex and bear children—are associated with the physical beauty and fertility of youth. As she ages, she is seen as less attractive because her years of social usefulness as childbearer are behind her. Men, on the other hand, are seen as possessing qualities—competence, autonomy, and power—that are not associated with youth but rather increase with age (Holstein, 2015; Wade & Ferree, 2015). Before going further, try Get Involved 2.4.

ABLENESS.   Few individuals with disabilities are shown in the media. For example, the percentage and number of television series regulars with disabilities in 2015 was less than 1 percent, a drop of 1.4 percent from the previous year. Similarly, only 2 percent of characters in the top 100 movies of 2015 were shown with a disability (Smith et al., 2016a). By comparison, the number of non-institutionalized individuals with visible disabilities in the United States is 12 percent (GLAAD, 2015–2016).

SEXUAL ORIENTATION AND IDENTITY.   Lesbian, gay, bisexual and transgender individuals have been another underrepresented group in the media. As recently as the early 1990s, there were few visible gay characters, and they were usually portrayed as unattractive, sad, suicidal, unstable, or psychopathic (GLAAD, 2015–2016). But as diverse sexual orientations and identities have become more

Older men are often portrayed as powerful and distinguished, but older women are perceived as losing their attractiveness.

accepted in recent years, sexual minority characters are increasingly being featured in mainstream television shows, films, and theater, although their numbers remain small (Smith et al., 2015). In 1997, the sitcom *Ellen* became the first prime-time television show to have an openly gay lead character. Shows such as *Will and Grace*, *Queer Eye for the Straight Guy*, *Queer as Folk* and *The L Word* were mainstream hits (DeFrancisco et al., 2014). See In The News 2.1 to see how LGBT individuals currently are portrayed in popular media.

Pattern 3: Portrayal of Gender-Based Social Roles

Females and males are portrayed differently in the media not only in terms of their numbers but also in relation to their social roles. Over the last few decades there has been an increase in the percentage of prime-time television shows that feature female characters who are employed and who hold powerful positions. One recent analysis found that prime-time women were 14 percent of corporate executives, 28 percent of high-level politicians, 30 percent of doctors/hospital managers, and 43 percent of investors/developers. The bad news is that only 45 percent of women were shown as employed (much lower than in real life), and that males still dominated high-level positions, and jobs in science (Smith et al., 2012). And although women lawyers, doctors, and executives appear on television, many of these depictions are unrealistic. For example, not all women in these professions are young, thin, and sexy (Smith et al., 2012)! And working-class employees such as Roseanne have almost vanished (Douglas, 2010).

On the other hand, consistent with the stereotypical association of men in the worker role and women in the family role, popular television shows (Matthes et al., 2016), commercials (Grau & Zotos, 2016; Grumbein & Goodman, 2013; Smith et al., 2012), movies (Lauzen, 2015), and children's readers (Etaugh et al., 2007) still show more men than women with jobs and more women than men in traditional family roles. In the movies, women are more likely than men to hold

GET INVOLVED 2.4
Media Advertisements and the Double Standard of Aging

Look through newspapers and magazines for advertisements that include middle-aged adults. Then answer the following questions:

1. Are there differences in the appearance of the women and the men?

WHAT DOES IT MEAN?

1. Do the advertisements show evidence of a double standard of aging?

2. What can advertisers do to minimize differences in the portrayal of middle-aged females and males?

2. Do females and males advertise different products?

3. In advertisements with two or more people, what is the role of the principal male or female in relationship to others?

3. How do media images of midlife adults help shape people's perceptions of middle-aged women and men?

IN THE NEWS 2.1
Current Portrayal of LGBT Individuals in Popular Media

Today, mainstream media are more likely than in the past to portray LGBT individuals as similar to heterosexuals in terms of appearance and interest, although largely asexual. In terms of numbers, 4 percent of the regular characters on 2016 prime-time programs were identified as lesbian, gay, or bisexual on series that premiered on Amazon, Zulu, and Netflix (GLAAD, 2015–2016). Shows such as *Transparent* and *Orange is the New Black* feature transgender characters. Comic books and graphic novels depict a growing number of individuals who identify as LGBT (Gustines, 2015). In 2014 and 2015, 18 percent of films from major studios contained LGBT characters. A few—*Carol, Dallas Buyers Club, The Danish Girl*—featured sympathetic portrayals of LGBT characters in lead roles (Buckley, 2015). But most LGBT characters had minor roles, and only 25 percent were people of color. Women were vastly underrepresented, with gay male characters outnumbering lesbians by a ratio of more than 3:1 (GLAAD, 2016). And older lesbians and bisexual women are rarely portrayed in the media (Traies, 2016).

powerless occupations, such as retail clerk, and they are rarely shown in leadership roles (Lauzen, 2015). Even in movies with a strong, successful, independent woman character, the woman's life is more constrained than the man's, and traditional cultural patterns triumph in the end (Ezzedeen, 2015). Sophisticated, successful, single career women, such as Ally McBeal and the four women of *Sex and the City*, expend considerable energy looking for Mr. Right (Dines, 2015). Thus, despite the presence of several positive employed-female role models on television and the fact that the majority of American married women are employed (Bureau of Labor Statistics, 2015), there is little depiction of women who successfully combine a career and marriage. The media send a message that successful women professionals cannot have rewarding home lives, if indeed they have any at all (Douglas, 2010). Even those news stories of women in power or political office, in contrast to stories of men, dwell on the women's physical appearance, clothing, and family life (Everbach, 2013).

In the leading teen magazine for girls, *Seventeen*, the world of work is dominated by powerful men, and fashion modeling is presented as the pinnacle of "women's work" (Massoni, 2004). Moreover, stereotyped depictions of women in both general interest and fashion magazine advertisements have decreased only slightly over the past 50 years (Lindner, 2004; Mager & Helgeson, 2011).

Despite the increasing participation of women in sports, female athletes continue to be under-represented in the media. Moreover, those who participate in socially acceptable feminine sports such as swimming, track, or gymnastics get more coverage than women who compete in more masculine team sports such as basketball or softball (Davis & Tuggle, 2012; Sherry et al., 2016). In the 2008 Olympics, women who competed in sports involving power or hard physical contact—discus throw, javelin throw, shot put, weightlifting, martial arts—received almost no television coverage (Davis & Tuggle, 2012). Moreover, the athleticism of female athletes tends to be underplayed. For example, female athletes are more likely than male athletes to be shown in passive and nonathletic poses (Sherry et al., 2016). In addition, sports announcers and writers highlight female athletes' femininity, minimize their athletic ability, and use comments that imply that female athletes are more vulnerable than their male counterparts ("Article on Body Image," 2015; Bruce, 2016).

Pattern 4: Depiction of Female Communion and Male Agency

Consistent with the depiction of females and males in different social roles, the communion stereotype for females and the agency stereotype for males are both evident in the media. Despite the growing body of movies and television shows featuring women fighting and committing mayhem—*Survivor, Fear Factor, Buffy the Vampire Slayer, Kill Bill, Charlie's Angels,* and *Terminator,* among others (Greenwood, 2007; Solomon, 2005)—boys and men are depicted as more active, assertive, aggressive, and powerful than females in a range of media (Lemish, 2015). These include adult films (Gilpatric, 2010), reality television shows (Grumbein & Goodman, 2013), children's programs (Lemish, 2015), print advertisements (Mager & Helgeson, 2011), toy commercials (Kahlenberg & Hein, 2010), Disney-Pixar films (Gillam & Wooden, 2011), children's literature (Basow, 2010a; Etaugh et al., 2003), and even coloring books (McPherson et al., 2007). Furthermore, consistent with their greater power, males are overrepresented as narrators in commercials that use voice-overs (e.g., Das, 2011; Matthes et al., 2016; Paek et al., 2011; Rodero et al., 2013), thus projecting an image of authority and expertise. In addition, men are two to three times more likely than women to be used as news sources both in newspapers and on television news (Desmond & Danilewicz, 2010).

On the other hand, the media portray females as communal, that is, oriented toward other people (Grumbein & Goodman, 2013; Lemish, 2015). Even when a woman is depicted as an action hero—such as Xena, the warrior princess—she is liked best when she embodies traditionally valued feminine traits such as nurturance, compassion, and using the mind over the sword (Calvert et al., 2001). Over half of the violent female action figures in contemporary American films are portrayed in a submissive role to the male hero and nearly half are romantically linked to him (Gilpatric, 2010). Similarly, even the most feisty of the more recent Disney "princesses," including Ariel, Belle, Jasmine, Mulan, Pocahontas, Rapunzel, and Tiana, are helpful, kind, obedient (or punished if they are not), and love-struck (England et al., 2011; Kenschaft & Clark, 2016; Nash, 2015).

Surprisingly, although the earliest Disney princesses (Cinderella, Snow White, Sleeping Beauty) were traditional, noncomplaining, and vulnerable, women spoke as much or more than men in these films. More recently, the princesses have become sassier, and even rebellious, but men speak most of the time in these movies: 68 percent in *Little Mermaid*; 71 percent in *Beauty and the Beast*; 90 percent in *Aladdin*; 77 percent in *Mulan* (she is counted as a woman even when playing a man); and 59 percent in *Frozen* (Fought & Eisenhauer, cited in Guo, 2016). One reason for this unexpected finding is that the newer films have larger, mostly male, casts, including male sidekicks.

Most mothers in children's literature are nurturers. Many are homemakers, whereas others are in traditional female nurturing occupations such as teaching, nursing, or social work (DeWitt et al., 2013; Lehr, 2001a). Similar gender messages even permeate Girl Scout and Boy Scout handbooks, with the former providing girls with more other-oriented activities, and the latter providing boys with more self-oriented activities (Denny, 2011). Ironically, women's communal nature is sometimes presented in a negative light. On the television show *Law and Order: Special Victims Unit*, for example, female criminals use relationships to harm others (Cuklanz & Moorti, 2015).

Pattern 5: Emphasis on Female Attractiveness and Sexuality

The media define females, more than males, by their looks and sexuality. For example, commercials show more women than men in suggestive clothing (Kenschaft & Clark, 2016). In addition, commercials, television shows, and movies portray women as more likely than men to receive comments about their appearance (Lauzen & Dozier, 2002; Smith et al., 2015). In pursuit of physical perfection, women routinely risk their health to undergo extensive plastic surgery on television reality shows such as *Extreme Makeover* (Grogan, 2017; Grumbein & Goodman, 2013).

Females in video games frequently are hypersexualized and scantily clad (Fox et al., 2015; Summers & Miller, 2014). The lyrics to popular music often contain explicit sexual references that are degrading to women (Hust et al., 2013; Lindsey, 2015). Moreover, music videos emphasize women's sexuality rather than their musical talent, featuring men performing and provocatively dressed, young women dancing suggestively (Aubrey & Frisby, 2011; Tiggeman et al., 2013, van Oosten et al., 2015). Although female sexuality is highlighted by the media, women often pay a heavy price if they actually engage in sexual activity. Two recent studies of women in the James Bond movies (Neuendorf et al., 2010) and in slasher horror films (Welsh, 2010) found that women who engaged in sexual behavior often were harmed or killed.

This emphasis on female appearance and sex appeal is apparent in print as well as in electronic media. Mainstream magazines targeted at teenagers and young women stress the importance of improving one's physical attractiveness through diet, exercise, fashion, and use of beauty products (Forster, 2015; Oliver, 2014). These magazines prey on women's insecurities to get them to buy the advertisers' wares (Whitefield-Madrano, 2016). Moreover, the depiction of women is more sexualized than that of men. Sexual imagery in women's magazine advertising has, in fact, increased in recent years (Graff, 2013; Reichert et al., 2012). Women are depicted as sex objects in two-thirds of the ads appearing in women's fashion magazines and in magazines for teen girls (Stankiewicz & Rosselli, 2008). Sexualized images of female athletes abound in sports magazines (Sherry et al., 2016). A typical example is a photograph showing four women members of the U.S. Olympic swim team standing naked behind a strategically draped American flag. Sports announcers and writers frequently refer to a female athlete's attractiveness, thus conveying to the audience that her looks are more salient than her athletic role ("Article on Body Image," 2015; Billings et al., 2014; Daniels & Lavoi, 2013).

Not only is a woman's attractiveness portrayed as highly important but that attractiveness is also depicted as overly thin (Bilefsky, 2016; Fikkan & Rothblum, 2012; Grogan, 2017). For example, most *Playboy* centerfold models are underweight, and approximately one-third are so thin that they meet the World Health Organization's standard for anorexia nervosa, a severe eating disorder (see Chapter 13). Magazines focusing on sports that emphasize thinness—gymnastics, ice skating, dancing—are more likely to feature overly thin cover models than are magazines dealing with sports such as running, tennis, and swimming (Ginsberg & Gray, 2006). In addition, Marla Eisenberg and her colleagues (2015) found that more than half of the episodes of popular television shows for adolescents contained weight-stigmatizing comments. On the show *America's Next Top Model*, dangerously underweight young women reaped praise for their looks, whereas normal-weight contestants at 5 feet 8 inches and 130 lbs were mocked as "plus-sized". Overweight women not only are underrepresented on television and considered less attractive, but are also less likely to interact with romantic partners (Fikkan & Rothblum, 2012).

Thus, the media still portray appearance and sexuality as two highly valued aspects of a woman's identity. More specifically, they present the message that it is White beauty that is valued. Black actresses and models who are depicted as physically desirable are likely to be light-skinned, straight haired, and to possess White facial features, thus informing the Black viewer that not just beauty but

At age 93, Bernice Perlman (Claire's aunt) embodies the timelessness of beauty.

White beauty is important (Scharrer, 2013; Wilder, 2015). Even popular children's fairy tales, such as Cinderella, Snow White, and Sleeping Beauty, highlight youthful feminine beauty, which often is associated with being White, virtuous, and economically privileged (Condis, 2015).

The media's portrayal of women's appearance does have some bright spots. In 2004, for example, Dove launched the "Dove Campaign for Real Beauty," a global effort intended to act as a catalyst for widening the definition and discussion of beauty. The campaign targeted the United States and Great Britain and featured billboard images of six women of various ages, sizes, types, and shapes (Olson, 2016). Each photograph showed a woman whose appearance challenges traditional stereotypes of beauty and asked viewers to judge her looks by casting votes and joining a discussion of beauty issues at the campaign's Website. For example, "Oversized? Outstanding?" were the choices next to Tabatha Roman, 34, a plus-size woman, and "Wrinkled? Wonderful?" appeared next to the photo of Irene Sinclair, 96.

More recently, the lingerie brand Aerie has featured women of various body sizes and shapes in its ads. And for the first time, *Sports Illustrated* put a plus-size model on the cover of its annual swimsuit issue (Olson, 2016). Still, the use of authentic-looking women to market products remains the exception.

Impact of Gender-Role Media Images

We have seen that the media portray a world more heavily populated by males than by females, a world in which males are more likely than females to have jobs and be active and assertive, and where beauty and romantic relationships are central to females' identity. Research shows that media not only reflect and transmit existing stereotypes but also have a socializing effect (Davis & Tuggle, 2012). For example, engagement with Disney Princess media and products is associated with more feminine gender-typed behavior (Coyne et al., 2016). A more troubling example is that exposure to sexualized media, such as music videos, is linked to increased misogynistic beliefs in adolescents (van Oosten et al., 2015), lowered body esteem, and decreased math self-confidence and performance (Grabe & Hyde, 2009; Pacilli et al., 2016). Thus, the media can play an important role in shaping people's construction of gender and in providing them with expectations of what females and males are like—their personality traits, social roles, and value to society. In addition, the very limited depiction of non-White or older females can reinforce perceptions of the powerlessness of these groups and communicate that their experiences are not important (Lemish, 2015).

Consider other types of media that might portray females and males stereotypically. See, for example, Learn About the Research 2.1 to find out about stereotypes in children's popular culture. Then read What <u>You</u> Can Do 2.1 to see how you can help to increase girls' and women's awareness of the effects of media.

LEARN ABOUT THE RESEARCH 2.1
Characters in Children's Popular Culture: How Gender-Stereotyped Are They?

We have seen that girls and boys are portrayed stereotypically in virtually all media. Sarah Murnen and her colleagues (2016) looked at the degree of gender-stereotyping in other cultural products aimed at children. Specifically, they examined popular Halloween costumes, valentines, dolls, and action figures. Female characters were much more likely than male characters to be shown with traditional feminine-typed characteristics such as decorative clothing and a friendly facial expression. They also were more likely to show hyper-feminine sexually submissive characteristics, such as revealing clothing. Male characters were much more likely to be depicted with traditional masculine attributes, such as functional clothing and moving bodies. They were often portrayed with hyper-masculine accessories, such as weapons and hands clenched into fists.

WHAT DOES IT MEAN?

1. Do the gender-stereotyped cultural products described above simply reflect cultural expectations or help to shape them? Explain your answer.

2. What are possible negative outcomes of encouraging hyper-femininity in girls and hyper-masculinity in boys?

3. When buying a Halloween costume, valentine, doll, or action figure for a child, do you look for something gender-stereotypic or nonstereotypic? Why?

WHAT <u>YOU</u> CAN DO 2.1
Increase Girls' and Women's Awareness of the Effects of Media

1. Contact About-Face (about-face.org), whose mission is to equip girls and women with tools to understand and resist harmful media messages that affect self-esteem and body image.

2. Contact the Girls, Women + Media Project (mediaandwomen.org), which works to increase awareness of how media represent and affect girls and women.

   After receiving information from either organization, make a presentation to a class, residence hall, sorority meeting, or Girl Scout troop.

REPRESENTATION OF GENDER IN THE ENGLISH LANGUAGE

The previous section demonstrated how communication via the mass media portrays different images of females and males. Now we examine the different ways females and males are depicted in the English language itself, and how this differential portrayal can shape conceptions of gender. *Language that unnecessarily differentiates between females and males or excludes and trivializes members of either sex* is called **sexist language**. Let's consider different types of sexist language.

Language Practices Based on the Assumption That Male Is Normative

Numerous language practices reflect the principle of **male as normative**; that is, *male behaviors, roles, and experiences are the standards (i.e., norms) for society.* Another name for this practice is **androcentrism**. You will recall from Chapter 1 that this view assumes that males are more important than females and that female behaviors, roles, and experiences deviate from the norm (Eagly & Riger, 2014; Hegarty et al., 2013; Kurtis & Adams, 2013). One indication of this assumption is

GET INVOLVED 2.5
Are Both Women and Men Persons?

Ask two acquaintances of each gender to help you with this activity. Tell them you are studying people's choices about grammatical structure; that is, you are examining students' selections of specific words in a sentence. Therefore, you would like them to fill in the blank in each of the following:

1. Debra Cook won the raffle at the charity fund-raising event. The event organizers will send the prize to this _____ in two weeks.

    person   woman

2. Dave Sherman moved to a new town and went to the Town Hall to register to vote. The registrar of voters gave this _____ the application form.

    person   man

WHAT DOES IT MEAN?

Examine the selections made by your respondents.

1. Did they select different terms depending on the gender of the person?
2. Were there any differences between the answers of the females and males?
3. Did these answers correspond to the findings of Hamilton, as discussed in this chapter?
4. What interpretation can you offer for your findings?

_____

Source: Hamilton (1991).

that adults tend to think of males as persons, as standard or normative individuals in society. For example, Mykol Hamilton (1991) found that college students were more apt to describe typical persons as males than as females and to refer to a male as a *person* but a female as a *woman*. Try Get Involved 2.5 and see if your findings match those reported by Hamilton. Even animals and inanimate objects tend to be conceived as male when their sex is unspecified (Maggio, 2015).

Now let's examine some of the language practices that reflect this belief of male as normative.

MASCULINE GENERIC LANGUAGE.   Consider the following situation:

> At the first session of a training program called "Reducing Man's Addictions," the program's director informed participants that they would be divided into small groups for discussion of the material and that each group should appoint a chairman to facilitate its discussion. Also, the director indicated that at the end of the training program each participant would have sufficient knowledge so that he could work at a drug rehabilitation center.

Describe your image of this event. Does the program deal with addiction problems of both women and men or men only? Will the chairs of the groups be men or women? What is the gender of the participants? Are these gender images clear?

Now substitute *woman's* for *man's*, *chairwoman* for *chairman*, and *she* for *he*. Ask yourself the same questions.

Regardless of your own interpretations of these two verbal descriptions, note that the latter was written using gender-specific (i.e., female) terms whereas the former was written in **masculine generic language**, which is *language that uses male terms but purports to be inclusive of females and males.* Both male pronouns, such as *he* and *his*, and male nouns, such as *chairman, freshman, businessman, man-hours, and forefathers*, are used not only in reference to males but also as inclusive of both genders (reflecting the assumption that male is standard).

Are these masculine generic terms interpreted as gender neutral; that is, are they as likely to elicit images of females as males? Research suggests they are not. Rather, these terms tend to be exclusionary, connoting just what they directly indicate, that is, men and boys (DeFrancisco et al.,

2014; Hegarty et al., 2013; Maggio, 2015; Sczesny et al., 2016). For example, in one study (Switzer, 1990), first- and seventh-grade children listened to the following story:

> Pretend that [teacher's name] told you that a new student is coming to be a part of your class. Tomorrow will be _____ first day. Describe how you think _____ will feel on the first day. (p. 74)

Students heard the story with one of the following pronouns inserted in the blanks: *he*, *he or she*, or *they*. The results showed that *he* is not assumed to mean both females and males. Its exclusionary interpretation was demonstrated by the finding that 93 percent of the children who heard the *he* story wrote that the student was a boy. On the other hand, when the pronouns were the inclusive *he or she* or *they*, the girls were more apt to write about a girl than a boy and the boys were more likely to write about a boy than a girl.

Given that male pronouns are evidently not gender neutral, it is not surprising that the use of male nouns as gender neutral similarly connotes male images. In one study (Gaucher et al., 2011), college students who read job advertisements that were constructed to include more masculine than feminine wording estimated that there were more men in these occupations. Women students found these jobs less appealing.

SPOTLIGHTING. **Spotlighting** refers to *the practice of emphasizing an individual's gender*, as in "*Female* professor receives prestigious grant" or, as in a headline about a treasurer for a youth baseball program who embezzled more than $300,000, "Grandma: Little League thief" (Pennington, 2016). Consistent with the male as normative perspective, this practice of highlighting a woman's gender reinforces the notion that males are the standard (Maggio, 2015). That is, although spotlighting does give recognition to specific females, it also conveys the message that these females are exceptions, who are often defined by their relationship to others.

One investigation of gendered spotlighting examined televised broadcasts of the 1989 women's and men's National Collegiate Athletic Association final four basketball tournaments (Messner et al., 1993). The researchers observed spotlighting an average of 26 times per game during the women's tournament with commentary such as ". . . is a legend in *women's* basketball" or "this NCAA *women's* semifinal is brought to you by . . ." (p. 125). However, there was no evidence of spotlighting during the men's games.

DIMINUTIVE SUFFIXES FOR FEMALE TERMS.   The English language sometimes differentiates genders by using a root word to designate a male and an added suffix to specify a female. This language feature, like others discussed in this section, is based on the assumption of the male as the standard. A suffix is needed to indicate the nonnormative exception, the female (Maggio, 2015). Examples of this include *actor/actress* and *poet/poetess*. In fact, according to Suzanne Romaine (1999), the only English words where the female term is the root word with a male suffix added are *widower* and *bridegroom*. Why do these words have female roots? Perhaps the term *widower* reflects the fact that women generally outlive men and *bridegroom* might be based on the traditional expectation that women's roles are linked to marriage and the family. Romaine (1999) contends that this practice of marking the female with a suffix added to the male root is one way the English language signifies that a woman is a "lesser man" (p. 140).

Negative Terms for Females

Another language practice that reflects the differential treatment of females and males is the greater number of negative terms depicting women than men.

PARALLEL TERMS.   There are numerous pairs of words in the English language in which the objective meanings of the female and male terms are comparable, but the female word has a negative connotation. Consider, for example, *bachelor* and *spinster* or *old maid*. All three refer to unmarried persons, but the female terms connote an undesirable state reflecting rejection and old age.

Another example is *master* versus *mistress*. Originally these referred to a man and woman in charge of a household, a usage that still pertains to *master*. *Mistress*, however, has developed a sexual connotation with negative overtones (DeFrancisco et al., 2014).

CHILDLIKE TERMS.   Have you ever heard the term *girl* in reference to an adult woman? Perhaps you have noted a male manager say something like the following to one of his associates: "I'll have my *girl* phone your *girl* to schedule a lunch meeting for us." Given that neither of the secretaries to whom he is referring is likely to be "a female child," the term *girl* is not appropriate. However, it is more common for people to refer to adult women as *girls* than to adult men as *boys* (DeFrancisco et al., 2014). For example, in televised coverage of the 2012 Olympic games, female athletes were often referred to as "girls" rather than women (Kian et al., 2013). One male television commentator at the 2016 Rio Olympics said of the gold-medal winning women's gymnastics team that "they might as well be standing around at the mall," reducing these world-class athletes to a group of flighty teenage girls (Dvorak, 2016).

Other childlike terms that are applied more to women than to men include *baby*, *babe*, and *sweetie*. Although these terms might be perceived as signs of affection in an intimate relationship, their use by nonintimates reflects the childlike quality of many terms used to identify women.

ANIMAL AND FOOD TERMS.   Researchers of the gender biases of language (DeFrancisco et al., 2014; Maggio, 2015) point to the heavy use of animal names and food products in reference to women as another example of the negative depiction of females. Examples of these include the animal labels *fox*, *chick*, *bitch*, and *cow*, and the food-related terms *honey*, *cookie*, *sweetie*, *dish*, and *feast for the eyes*.

SEXUALIZATION OF WOMEN.   As discussed earlier in this chapter, the media treat a woman's sexuality as an important aspect of her identity. American English also places a strong emphasis on a woman's sexuality. In one study (Grossman & Tucker, 1997), college students were asked to list all of the slang words they could think of for either a woman or a man. Although there was no difference in the number of terms associated with each gender, approximately 50 percent of the terms used for females were sexual (e.g., *slut*), whereas less than 25 percent of those used for males were. Furthermore, there are far more negative sexual terms for women than for men (DeFrancisco et al., 2014).

In Grossman and Tucker's study of slang, the terms used for women were more negative than those used for men. For example, among the most frequently listed terms were *bitch* and *slut* for women but *guy* and *dude* for men.

Significance of the Differential Treatment of Females and Males in Language

We have examined several indications that English depicts males as the societal standard and that many language conventions portray females in negative terms. Do these practices matter? According to many psychologists (Bou-Franch, 2016; Kurz & Donaghue, 2013; Maggio, 2015), they certainly do. Sexist language reinforces and perpetuates gender stereotypes and status differences between women and men. Even if we do not use sexist language, not speaking up when others use it condones this practice (Polk, 2016). Whether or not the speaker or writer intends harm, sexist language can have a negative effect on how girls and women perceive themselves (Bou-Franch, 2016).

The words of Jessica, a 25-year-old college senior, make this point vividly:

> *Using animal and food terms to refer to women is obviously degrading, and hazardous to a woman's self-esteem. If a woman hears herself being called a cow or bitch enough, she will believe that she is one. I didn't think it could happen if you were a strong person; I mean, I know I'm not a bitch, right? Wrong. After five years of hearing it from a significant other, I actually found myself calling myself these names aloud! It's powerful.*

Summary

STEREOTYPES OF FEMALES AND MALES

- Based on the tendency to sort others into gender categories, people assume that certain characteristics, behaviors, and roles are more representative of females and others of males. These are called gender stereotypes.
- Stereotypes vary according to the ethnicity of the person holding the stereotype and the age, ethnicity, social class, sexual orientation, and ableness of the target person.
- According to social role theory, because people associate females with the domestic role and males with the employment role, female stereotypes tend to center on communion and male stereotypes on agency.
- Women who choose to be called "Ms." or who use a nontraditional name after marriage are perceived as more agentic and less communal than women who prefer conventional titles of address.

SEXISM

- Large numbers of women have experienced either minor or major sexist incidents.
- Several different forms of sexism have been proposed by scholars. Modern sexism is a subtle form of sexism, based on egalitarian values combined with underlying negative feelings toward women. Ambivalent sexism includes both hostile and benevolent attitudes.

REPRESENTATION OF GENDER IN THE MEDIA

- Females are underrepresented in the media.
- Certain groups of women are particularly underrepresented, including ethnic minority women, older women, and sexual minority women.
- The stigma of aging is greater for women than men. This double standard is based on society's emphasis on youthful physical beauty for women.
- Although the media do depict women in occupational roles, television features few women who successfully combine family and work roles.
- Similarly, various media present messages consistent with the importance of the domestic role for women and the provider role for men.
- Many forms of media portray males as more agentic than females and show females as being relationship oriented.
- Media images emphasize the importance to females of physical attractiveness and sexuality.
- The media both reinforce and contribute to stereotypes of gender.

REPRESENTATION OF GENDER IN THE ENGLISH LANGUAGE

- Numerous English language practices, including using the masculine generic, spotlighting, and diminutive suffixes for female terms, are based on the assumption that the male is normative.
- Other practices that deprecate women include the use of parallel terms, childlike terms, animal and food terms, and sexual terms.
- The differential treatment of females and males in language both reflects and helps shape gender images.

Key Terms

gender stereotypes *22*
communion *22*
agency *22*
ageism *24*
ableism *25*
social categorization *26*
social role theory *26*

sexism *28*
backlash effect *28*
modern sexism *29*
ambivalent sexism *29*
hostile sexism *29*
benevolent sexism *29*
double standard of aging *33*

sexist language *39*
male as normative *39*
androcentrism *39*
masculine generic
    language *40*
spotlighting *41*

What Do You Think?

1. We have seen that women who use the title Ms. or who do not take their husbands' surnames after marriage are perceived as more agentic and less communal than women who use Miss or Mrs. or who take their husbands' names. One explanation for this is provided by social role theory. Can you think of any other possible explanations?

2. Consider the work by Glick and Fiske on ambivalent sexism.

   a. Do you agree that positive stereotypes of women can serve to maintain patriarchal roles and relationships? Why or why not?

   b. Do you believe that benevolent and hostile sexism are equally detrimental to women? Why or why not?

3. We have examined numerous sources of societal representations of gender, such as greeting cards, children's books, and television commercials. What other types of media might reflect gender stereotypes?

4. Which of the various language features that treat females and males differently do you think has the most detrimental effect on girls and women? Why?

5. Provide evidence, from the chapter or from your own experience, that language influences one's perceptions of gender.

If You Want to Learn More

Armstrong, C.L. (Ed.). (2013). *Media disparity: A gender battleground.* Lanham, MD: Lexington.

Bates, L. (2016). *Everyday sexism: The project that inspired a worldwide movement.* New York: St. Martin's Press.

Blue, M.G. (2017). *Girlhood on the Disney Channel: Branding, celebrity, and femininity.* New York: Routledge.

DeFrancisco, D.P., et al. (2014). *Gender in communication: A critical introduction.* Thousand Oaks, CA: Sage.

Dines, G. & Humez, J.M. (2015). *Gender, race and class in media* (4th ed.). Thousand Oaks, CA: Sage.

Gunter, B. (2014). *Media and the sexualization of childhood.* New York: Routledge.

Hedenborg, S. & Pfister, G. (Eds.). (2017). *Gender, media, sport.* New York: Routledge.

Hodgson, D. (2016). *The gender, culture, and power reader.* New York: Oxford University Press.

Holstein, M. (2015). *Women in late life: Critical perspectives on gender and age.* New York: Rowman & Littlefield.

Hurd Clarke, L. (2011). *Facing age: Women growing older in an anti-aging culture.* Lanham, MD: Rowman & Littlefield.

Krijnen, T. & Van Bauwel, S. (2015). *Gender and media: Representing, producing, consuming.* New York: Routledge.

Moseley, R., et al. (Eds.) (2017). *Television for women: New directions.* New York: Routledge.

Sales, N.J. (2016). *American girls: Social media and the secret lives of teenagers.* New York: Alfred A. Knopf.

Segal, L. (2013). *Out of time: The pleasure and perils of aging.* London: Verso.

Trier-Bienick, A. & Leavy, P. (Eds.). (2014). *Gender and pop culture: A text-reader.* Rotterdam: Sense.

Websites

The Media
Media Watch
http://www.mediawatch.com

Representation of Gender in Language
Gender-Neutral Language
http://dir.yahoo.com/society_and_culture/gender/gender_neutral_language/

CHAPTER 3

Gender Self-Concept and Gender Attitudes

Developmental Processes and Individual Differences

In 1965, soon after starting graduate school, Judith was discussing graduate student issues with her eight male classmates. During this conversation, much to her surprise and dismay, one of the men stated that she lacked femininity. When asked to explain, he said, "Judith is too highly achievement oriented to be feminine."

The comment by Judith's classmate suggests that, in his mind, people cannot combine female-stereotypic and male-stereotypic characteristics. Do you see problems with this type of thinking?

Now consider the lighthearted mockery of gender-expected behaviors shown by Judith's daughter and son-in-law during their wedding ceremony. On the one hand, the setting was traditional with the bride in a long white gown, the groom in a tuxedo, and an entourage of bridesmaids and ushers. On the other hand, inconsistent with traditional expectations, at the end of a beautiful and serious service, the officiator concluded with "Now you may kiss the groom!"

Do you know people who, like Judith's daughter and son-in-law, believe their behaviors should not be dictated by their gender? Do you know others who see value in separate roles for women and men?

In this chapter, we focus on issues like these as we examine the integration of gender into one's personal identity. After a brief look at the components of gender self-concept, we look at prenatal sex development and its influence on these gender concepts. Then we explore theoretical perspectives of gender learning and conclude with an examination of variations among people in their gender attitudes.

GENDER SELF-CONCEPT

One component of gender self-concept is **gender identity**: *one's self-definition as a female or male* (Wood & Eagly, 2015). This identity generally develops between the ages of 2 and 3. Most individuals establish *a gender identity in accordance with their external reproductive organs*. (In current terminology, these individuals are referred to as **cisgender**. "Cis" is Latin for "on this side of.") **Transgender** individuals, however, do not (see Chapter 6). They have a *gender identity inconsistent with their reproductive organs* ("Trans" is Latin for "on the other side of."). They firmly believe they were born with the body of the wrong sex and identify with the other sex (Brody, 2016a; Nagoshi et al., 2014).

Despite the usual consistency between anatomy and gender identity, there are variations in the degree to which people incorporate gender stereotypes into their own personalities and attitudes. As we saw in Chapter 2, there are numerous commonly held expectations about the appropriate traits and roles for females and males. However, these gender stereotypes reflect *beliefs* about individuals; they do not tell what anyone is *actually* like. Although these stereotypes are descriptive of some people, they are not representative of all. Instead, individuals differ in the extent to which their traits, behaviors, interests, and roles conform to those expected for their gender. Moreover, they differ in their **gender attitudes**, their *beliefs about the appropriate traits, interests, behaviors, and roles of females and males*.

Are various domains of an individual's gender self-concept associated with one another? Although most people's gender identity is consistent with their anatomy, that does not imply a connection between gender identity and gender-related attributes. A person can feel that she is a female but have masculine-typed traits, such as ambition and independence, or engage in occupations generally associated with men, such as construction worker or engineer. Furthermore, a person's gender-related attributes are not linked to her or his **sexual orientation**. *Preference for a same- or other-gender sexual partner* does not reflect the individual's gender-related traits, behaviors, interests, or roles (Zucker, 2001).

PRENATAL DEVELOPMENT

Our journey toward understanding the development of a personal sense of gender begins with an examination of **prenatal sex differentiation**, that is, *the biological processes that influence the making of one's physical sex*. The first step in this complex set of processes is the joining of the sex chromosomes in the fertilized egg, followed by several other events that collectively contribute to the determination of sex (see Table 3.1). As you can see, biological sex is multidimensional; it is defined by one's chromosomes, hormones, reproductive organs, and brain organization (Robinson-Wood, 2017).

Stages of Prenatal Sex Differentiation

The stages of prenatal sex differentiation begin with the sex chromosomes, followed by the development of the gonads and hormones, internal reproductive organs, external genitalia, and differentiation of the brain. Let us examine each of these steps in greater detail.

TABLE 3.1	Stages of Prenatal Sex Differentiation of Females and Males	
Stages	**Females**	**Males**
1. Chromosomes	XX	XY
2. Gonads and hormones	Ovaries (estrogens)	Testes (androgens)
3. Internal reproductive organs	Uterus, fallopian tubes, and upper vagina	Vas deferens, seminal vesicles, and prostate
4. External genitalia	Clitoris, labia, and vaginal opening	Penis and scrotum
5. Brain differentiation	Female differentiation of the hypothalamus	Male differentiation of the hypothalamus

CHROMOSOMES.   Sex differentiation begins with the combining of the sex chromosomes at conception. Normally individuals inherit 23 pairs of chromosomes from their parents. Twenty-two of these pairs contain genes that determine the general nature of the human species and the individual's specific characteristics (e.g., eye color), and one pair consists of the sex chromosomes, containing the genetic material that begins the process of sex differentiation. Genetic females have two X chromosomes, one received from each parent, and genetic males have one X chromosome received from their mother and one Y from their father (Bussey, 2013).

GONADS AND HORMONES.   Until the sixth week of development there are no anatomical differences between XX and XY embryos. In fact, all embryos contain the same undifferentiated tissue that will later develop along sexual lines (Robinson-Wood, 2017). However, during the sixth week, the SRY gene on the Y chromosome in XY embryos directs the previously undifferentiated gonadal tissue to develop into testes, the male sex glands (Henig, 2017). In XX embryos, gonadal development begins at approximately the twelfth week after conception; the previously undifferentiated gonadal tissue develops into ovaries, the female sex glands. Evidence suggests that the X chromosome might direct this development (Tobach, 2001).

   Once the gonads develop, the remaining process of sex differentiation is regulated by the sex hormones. Prenatal male differentiation requires the presence of the *male sex hormones*, collectively known as **androgens**. Until recently, it was believed that no gonadal hormones were necessary for female development and that differentiation of female sex organs would proceed in the absence of androgens. Now there is evidence that the *female sex hormones*, collectively known as **estrogens**, play a more active role in female development than previously believed (Jordan-Young, 2010).

INTERNAL REPRODUCTIVE ORGANS.   The female and male internal reproductive organs develop from the same previously undifferentiated tissue. Both XX and XY fetuses contain two sets of tissues, the Müllerian ducts and the Wolffian ducts. The **Müllerian ducts** are *the foundation for female structures*. The **Wolffian ducts** serve as *the basis for male internal reproductive structures*. In XX individuals, the Müllerian ducts differentiate into the uterus, fallopian tubes, and upper vagina and the Wolffian tissue degenerates. In XY development, two substances produced by the testes govern the process of developing male internal reproductive structures. **Testosterone**, *an androgen*, is needed to transform the Wolffian ducts into the male organs, including the vas deferens, seminal vesicles, and prostate; and the **Müllerian-inhibiting substance** is *necessary for the degeneration of the Müllerian ducts* (Robinson-Wood, 2017).

EXTERNAL GENITALIA.   Similar to the development of the internal reproductive structures, the external structures develop from previously undifferentiated tissue present in both XX and XY individuals. In XX fetuses, estrogen differentiates this tissue as the clitoris, labia, and vaginal opening. In XY development, testosterone transforms the tissue into the penis and the scrotum (Ryle, 2016).

BRAIN DIFFERENTIATION.   Sex differences in the brain are less observable and more controversial than sex differences in reproductive organs (Fine, 2017). Experimentation on animals and studies of humans whose prenatal exposure to androgens was abnormal for their genetic sex show that there is a critical period of time during which exposure to sex hormones can affect the hypothalamus and thus influence the threshold for subsequent behaviors. For example, in both animals and humans, this early exposure to androgens organizes the hypothalamus so that it becomes relatively insensitive to estrogen (Hines, 2010). The result is the elimination of the normal hormonal cyclical pattern associated with the menstrual cycle.

Although there are some differences in brain structure, however, research shows that brains do not fall into two classes, one typical of females and one typical of males. Rather, human brains are composed of unique "mosaics" of features, some of which are more common in females, some more common in males, and others common in both sexes (Joel et al., 2015).

Multiple Genders

All societies recognize female and male genders and roles, although there is considerable cross-cultural variability in how these roles are expressed. The United States and most Western nations formally recognize only two genders, and any variations from these are considered abnormal (Christmas, 2013; Rice, 2014; Nagoshi et al., 2014). The notion of sex as a binary construct has led to some questionable decisions about what makes a person a "man" or a "woman." Read In the News 3.1 to learn more. A number of non-Western cultures, however, recognize third and fourth genders. These are women and men who do not fit typical gender identities and roles. Often, these individuals are considered spiritually enlightened by having an alternative gender, and they may be respected and accepted (Sheppard & Mayo, 2013). The hijras of India are male-to-female transgender individuals who are viewed as a third gender embodying the spirits of both females and males. Frequently called upon to bless new babies, they dress as females, live in hijra communities, and some maintain a monogamous relationship with a man (Barry & Feit 2016; Choksi, 2013; Sheppard & Mayo, 2013). In Indonesia, transgender women known as "waria"—a combination of the words for woman and man—have been welcomed for centuries as entertainers and beauticians (Emont, 2015). Similarly, Polynesians recognize two-spirited people called "mahu," which means half-man, half-woman. These individuals include feminine men and masculine women, and they usually work in female-dominated occupations (Roughgarden, 2009). The muxes of Mexico are genetic males who dress as women or men, express themselves in a feminine manner, and often help their parents maintain the family household (Burnett, 2016). Many native North American societies recognize two-spirit individuals (DeMello, 2014; Meem et al., 2010; Sheppard & Mayo, 2013). Biological female two-spirits typically were found west of the Rockies among the Apache, Cheyenne, Mohave, Navajo, Tlingit, and Zuni. The "manly hearted woman," for example, wore men's clothes, led war parties, and was completely accepted in that role (Agonito, 2016). As native societies assimilated European beliefs, however, third- and fourth-gender roles often disappeared, changed, or came to be viewed negatively (Adams & Phillips, 2009).

Although recent efforts to be more flexible in recognizing additional gender categories have been controversial (Fausto–Sterling, 2012), Western cultures are, in fact, beginning to show acceptance of the idea that gender is not simply a binary construct. In 2013, Germany passed a law permitting children to be classified as neither female nor male when their genital characteristics were ambiguous. In 2014, Australia legally recognized a third "nonspecific" gender. Also in 2014, Facebook, in the United States, started offering 56 gender options, including "transperson" and "two-spirit" (Singer & Deschamps, 2017). Another related change is the movement to replace gendered language with gender-neutral language (for example, the pronoun "ze" in place of "he" and

IN THE NEWS 3.1
Too Much Testosterone to Compete as a Woman?

In 2014, the governing body for international track and field competitions (the IAAF) banned Indian sprinter Dutee Chand from women's races, claiming that her naturally high testosterone levels gave her an unfair advantage. To continue competing, she would have to lower her testosterone levels through surgery or drugs (Pieper, 2016). Yet studies find no evidence that successful athletes have higher testosterone levels than less successful ones. Moreover, other biological variables that do offer competitive advantages—such as increased aerobic capacity and number of fast-twitch muscle fibers—are not used to determine eligibility to compete. Chand challenged the ban, and in 2015, the IAAF suspended its hormone testing policy for two years, allowing Chand and other women with high testosterone to compete (Branch, 2015). While this is good news, Chand's case raises concerns about the ethics of forcing female athletes to undergo intrusive medical tests and face humiliating public scrutiny in order to compete (Montanoble & Olivesi, 2016). Should the sports world continue to insist that sex is a binary construct, even though science shows that the markers of biological sex exist on a continuum?

"she," and "hir" in place of "her" or "his"; Liben, 2016). The United Kingdom recently added the gender-neutral title MX to many government forms (Giang, 2015).

Intersexuality

The pattern of sex differentiation described earlier is the typical one that characterizes the prenatal development of most individuals. However, several variations can occur, and an examination of these can help one understand the role of the chromosomes and hormones in gender identity and gender-related attributes.

Intersexuality, *the intermingling of female and male sexual characteristics*, occurs in as many as 1.7 percent of births. In some cases, the baby has ambiguous genitalia that look like an enlarged clitoris or a mini-penis. In other cases, the external genitalia are at odds with the baby's gonads (Ryle, 2016). In Western nations, which recognize only two genders, the typical course of action has been early genital surgery, coupled with gender reassignment. But genital surgery can lead to loss of fertility, reduced sexual functioning, urinary difficulties, and psychological problems, without providing the individual with any firmer sense of gender identity or increased quality of life (Creighton et al., 2014). The Accord Alliance (formerly, the Intersex Society of North America), along with an increasing number of researchers, recommends that any surgery be postponed until adolescence, when the individual can make an informed choice (Creighton et al., 2014; Launius & Hassel, 2015). Let us take a closer look at some of the varieties of intersexuality.

TURNER SYNDROME.   **Turner syndrome** is *a condition in which the individual has a single X chromosome rather than a pair of sex chromosomes.* The missing chromosome could have been an X or a Y but is defective or lost. Because two chromosomes are necessary for the development of the gonads, the individual has neither ovaries nor testes. Externally, the genitalia are female and the individual is reared as a girl. Estrogen therapy at puberty enables girls with Turner syndrome to develop female secondary sex characteristics, such as breasts and pubic hair (Gould et al., 2013; National Institutes of Health, 2013a).

CONGENITAL ADRENAL HYPERPLASIA (CAH).   **Congenital adrenal hyperplasia** is *an inherited disorder in which the adrenal glands of a genetic female malfunction and produce abnormally high levels of androgens* (Halpern, 2012). Because this hormone is not produced until after the internal reproductive organs develop, these individuals have a uterus. However, the disorder causes either a partial or complete masculinization of the external genitals with the formation of an enlarged clitoris or a penis. Usually CAH is diagnosed at birth and the baby is reared as a girl, receiving some degree of surgical feminization of the genitals. Additionally, because this condition does not cease at birth, the individual generally needs hormonal therapy to prevent continued masculinization of her body (Hines, 2010).

ANDROGEN-INSENSITIVITY SYNDROME.   The **androgen-insensitivity syndrome** is *an inherited disorder in which the body of a genetic male cannot utilize androgen* (Halpern, 2012). Analogous to CAH, in which prenatal exposure to androgen masculinizes the external genitals of a genetic female, this inability of body tissue to respond to androgen feminizes the external genitals of a genetic male. Usually, the feminization of the external genitalia is complete and there is no suspicion that the baby is a genetic male. Similarly, the inability of the body to respond to androgen prevents the Wolffian ducts from differentiating into the internal male reproductive structures. However, because of the presence of the Müllerian-inhibiting substance, the Müllerian ducts do not develop into the internal female organs. Consequently, the individual has no internal reproductive organs.

5 ALPHA-REDUCTASE DEFICIENCY.   The **5 alpha-reductase deficiency** is *an inherited condition in a genetic male that prevents the prenatal differentiation of the external genital tissue into a penis* (Brinkmann, 2009). In other ways, prenatal development follows a male blueprint; testes and male internal reproductive organs develop. At birth, these genetic males appear to be girls and are labeled as such. However, the surge of testosterone at puberty causes a belated masculinization of the external genitals and the development of male secondary sex characteristics, such as a deepening voice and facial hair. Thus, these genetic males, generally raised as girls, now develop the body of a male. In the Dominican Republic, where certain communities have a high frequency of the disorder, it is known as *guevedoces*, or "eggs (i.e., testicles) at twelve" (Jordan-Young, 2010).

DEVELOPMENT OF INTERSEXUALITY.   The relative influence of prenatal and postnatal experiences on gender-related development has been the focus of considerable controversy. Studies of intersexuals have examined the role of prenatal hormones in the development of nonsexual gender-related attributes, gender identity, and sexual orientation, and have produced inconsistent findings. Some researchers contend that prenatal biological factors are highly influential, whereas others conclude that experiences after birth are more significant in shaping individuals' gender-related attributes.

First, let's examine the effects of prenatal hormones on gender-related interests and activities. On the one hand, higher levels of testosterone in pregnant women are related to more masculine-typed toy choices and activities in their young daughters (Hines, 2010). In addition, girls with CAH, who were exposed to androgens prenatally, show stronger-than-average preferences for boys' toys and activities and for boys as playmates (Jordan-Young, 2010; Leaper & Farkas, 2015). They report themselves to be more aggressive and less maternal. But most of the affected women are heterosexual, and their sexual identity and gender identity are almost always female.

Investigations on the effects of prenatal estrogen suggest that it might not be necessary for the development of female gender-related interests or role expectations. For example, girls with Turner syndrome, who lack prenatal estrogen, are similar to matched controls in their preferences for female playmates and female-style clothing, satisfaction with the female gender role, and interest in marriage and motherhood. Similarly, androgen-insensitive (XY) individuals raised as females tend to have female-related interests, although they too lack prenatal estrogen. Such individuals are generally romantically and sexually attracted to males. On tests of verbal and spatial skills, they also perform more like females than males (Lippa, 2005; Sybert & McCauley, 2004).

Turning to the development of gender identity, research similarly provides inconsistent findings. Some investigators have pointed to the importance of the gender of rearing, that is, experiences after birth, in gender identity (Zucker, 2008). Others, such as Milton Diamond (2009), contend that prenatal experiences predispose individuals toward a female or male identity. He further suggests that prenatal processes influence some intersexuals to switch from the gender of rearing to an identity with the other gender. One study, for example, examined genetic males with normal male hormones but who were born without a penis and subsequently underwent early sex-reassignment surgery and were raised as girls. Nearly half still developed male gender identity by adolescence (Reiner & Gearhart, 2004). Studies of individuals who have experienced the female-to-male body change caused by 5 alpha-reductase deficiency show similar results. In the Dominican Republic, for example, 16 of 18 who were raised as girls elected to reverse their gender identity at puberty and become males (Imperato-McGinley, 2002).

Finally, studies of intersexual individuals have led some researchers to contend that sexual orientation has its origins in prenatal development, suggesting that prenatal exposure to androgen may serve as one influence on sexual orientation (Halpern, 2012). However, based on their review of research on the topic, Amy Banks and Nanette Gartrell (1995) conclude that atypical prenatal hormone exposure is not related to increased same-gender sexual orientation.

What can researchers conclude about this controversial issue? Unfortunately, it is difficult to evaluate the relative contribution of biological and environmental factors because the relevant variables cannot be adequately controlled. For example, it is difficult to separate effects of the atypical exposure to prenatal hormones of CAH girls from the psychological and interpersonal reactions they might experience after birth. Both CAH girls and their parents are aware of these girls' masculinization, and this knowledge might serve as a powerful influence on the girls' gender-related self-concept and on their parents' treatment of them (Bussey, 2013). At this time, the most accurate conclusion to be drawn appears to be that gender is both a biological and a social phenomenon. The challenge for researchers is to examine how biological processes interact with social influences from the earliest years onward (Bussey, 2013; Fine, 2017).

THEORIES OF GENDER TYPING

Now we turn to an exploration of the major theories that attempt to explain *the acquisition of the traits, behaviors, and roles that are generally associated with one's gender*, a process known as **gender typing**. Although these theories propose different processes are involved in the learning of gender, only one (psychoanalytic theory) contends that the development of gender-related attributes is rooted in biological sex differences. The other perspectives share the assumption that gender traits, behaviors, and roles are socially constructed; that they develop from children's interactions with others; and that they are not inherent in humans' biology. Even psychoanalytic theory emphasizes the perceived significance of anatomical differences, rather than the effect of hormonal or other biological sex differences, on gender development. For a summary of the major theories of gender typing, see Table 3.2.

Psychoanalytic Theory

Psychoanalytic theory, developed by Sigmund Freud (1925/1989), proposes that *gender typing stems from children's awareness of anatomical differences between females and males combined with their strong inborn sexual urges*. According to this theory, during the so-called phallic stage of development (between ages 3 and 6) two experiences occur that have dramatic consequences for gender typing. The first is the child's discovery of the anatomical differences between females and males and the second is the child's love for the parent of the other gender.

The boy's sexual attraction for his mother, known as the **Oedipus complex**, is accompanied by a belief that his father is a rival for his mother's affections. The boy's growing awareness of the anatomical differences between males and females leads him to assume that females have been castrated, and that he, too, will be castrated by his powerful rival, his father. *The boy's fear of castration by his father*, called **castration anxiety**, induces him to give up his Oedipal feelings for his mother and *form a close emotional bond with his father*, called **identification**. Through this identification process, the boy adopts his father's masculine behaviors and traits and incorporates his father's values into his superego (the moral component of personality), thus developing a strong sense of morality.

The phallic stage follows a different course for the little girl. Her discovery of the anatomical distinction between females and males does not resolve the Oedipus complex, as in boys, but rather sets it in motion. Sometimes referred to as the Electra complex, the girl develops **penis envy**, *a desire to possess the male genitals*, and blames the mother for her "castrated" state. Her desire for

TABLE 3.2 Theories of Gender Typing

Theory	Major Theorist	Sources of Learning	Motive	Sequence of Events
Psychoanalytic theory	Sigmund Freud	Parents; emotional bond with same-sex parent is critical	Internal: reduce fear and anxiety; no reinforcement necessary	(Same-sex) parental attachment → identification (modeling) → gender identity
Social learning theory	Walter Mischel	Parents, larger social system provide models; child is relatively passive	External: reinforcements. Internal: Expected reinforcements. "I want rewards. I am rewarded for doing girl things. Therefore, I want to be a girl."	(Same-sex) parental attachment (due to rewards) → modeling (identification) → gender identity
Social cognitive theory	Albert Bandura	Parents, larger social system provide models; child is more active than in social learning theory in evaluating social standards; cognition plays a greater role	Similar to social learning theory	Similar to social learning theory
Cognitive developmental theory	Lawrence Kohlberg	Parents and larger social system interacting with child's cognitive system	Internal: desire for competence. "I am a girl. Therefore, I want to do girl things. Therefore, doing girl things is rewarding."	Gender identity → modeling (same-sex parent) → (same-sex) parental attachment
Gender schema theory	Sandra Bem	Parents and larger social system interacting with child's cognitive system. Society dictates that gender is an important schema, so child organizes information around this schema.	Similar to cognitive developmental theory	Because child learns that gender is an important schema, child develops gender identity. Sequence then proceeds as in cognitive developmental theory.

a penis is replaced by a desire for a child and she turns to her father to fulfill that wish. Because the girl does not fear castration (having already been castrated), the chief motive for resolving the Oedipus complex is absent. Later, realizing that she will never possess her father, the girl gives up her Oedipal feelings, identifies with her mother, and begins to acquire her mother's feminine traits and behaviors. However, her superego development is weak because it is not driven by the powerful motivator of castration anxiety.

EVALUATION. First, Freud's theory clearly is highly male-biased (i.e., androcentric; see Chapter 2) as shown by his use of the male term *phallic* to label the critical stage of gender development, his emphasis on the superiority of the male organ, and his assumption that females are doomed to feelings of inferiority because they lack a penis. For these reasons, psychoanalytic theory is not widely embraced by feminist scholars (Greene, 2015). Second, key psychoanalytic concepts, such as penis envy and castration anxiety, are conceptualized as unconscious; thus, they cannot be measured empirically. Third, Freud has been criticized for emphasizing the anatomical foundations of gender development to the virtual exclusion of societal influences. For Freud, gender is constructed from the presence or absence of a penis and not the societal value attached to males. Later psychoanalytic thinkers placed greater emphasis on the psychological and sociocultural aspects of gender development. Others, including Karen Horney, Clara Thompson, Nancy Chodorow, Jessica Benjamin, and Ellen Kaschak, have proposed psychoanalytic views that minimize the masculine orientation of Freud's theory (Bell, 2004; Halpern, 2012).

Social Learning Theory

Whereas psychoanalytic theory envisions the growing child as driven by inborn desires, **social learning theory** (Ryle, 2015) views *gender development as influenced by the social environment*. Based on learning theory principles, this perspective proposes that *children acquire behaviors associated with their gender because those behaviors are more likely to be imitated and to be associated with positive reinforcement*.

OBSERVATIONAL LEARNING.   One mechanism through which gender-related behaviors are acquired is **observational learning** (also called imitation or modeling); that is, *the acquisition of behaviors by observing role models*. Children are continually exposed to both real-life and media models who engage in gender-stereotypic behaviors. Children are more likely to imitate same-sex than other-sex models (Halpern, 2012). By observing these models, children learn which behaviors are considered appropriate for their gender. For example, 5-year-old Jenny sees her mother bake cookies and then pretends to bake in her play kitchen. And, because the nurses in her pediatrician's office are females, Jenny believes that only women can be nurses. Jenny also learns that it is important for women to be pretty because she sees women on television who are often concerned about their appearance.

REINFORCEMENT AND PUNISHMENT.   Social learning theory maintains that even though children may initially engage in both cross-gender and same-gender imitation, they are increasingly likely to perform gender-appropriate behaviors. The mechanisms that explain this phenomenon are reinforcement and punishment. If people expect a positive reinforcement (reward) for performing the behavior, children will likely engage in that behavior. Similarly, if children anticipate a negative consequence (punishment), they are not likely to perform that act. Thus, children learn, both through observing the consequences to models and through the consequences of their own behaviors, that girls are more likely to be rewarded for certain actions and boys for others. A girl playing "dress-up" might be praised for her beauty as she parades around wearing her mother's old dress and high heels. If her brother wears the same outfit, however, his parents might scold or ridicule him.

COGNITION.   A modification of social learning theory, known as **cognitive social learning theory**, states that *observational learning and rewards and punishments following behavior alone cannot account for gender typing; thought processes (cognitions) also play a role*. As children develop, they not only receive rewards and punishments from others but also begin to internalize standards about appropriate gender-related behavior (Bussey, 2013; Leaper, 2015). Thus, children initially engage in gender-appropriate behaviors because they anticipate rewards from others. Later, their internalized standards about gender-related behavior motivate them to engage in gender-appropriate activities in order to gain self-satisfaction and avoid self-censure. Thus, Pablo might refuse to play with his sister's dolls because doing so would violate his personal standard of appropriate behavior for boys.

EVALUATION.   Unlike psychoanalytic theory, the concepts of the social learning perspective are clear and observable. Numerous studies that have examined the theory's assumptions have provided support for some aspects of the theory and are inconclusive about others.

One assumption of social learning theory is that girls and boys receive encouragement and reinforcement for different behaviors. In support of this perspective, studies show that parents do treat their daughters and sons differently in regard to some behaviors. For example, parents buy their daughters and sons different types of toys, encourage different play activities, and assign them different chores (see Chapter 4).

According to social learning theory, the other process in gender typing is observational learning. Although children do imitate same-gender role models, observational learning is not restricted to the behaviors of individuals of the same gender as the child (Halpern, 2012). Other characteristics, such as a model's power, can influence the selection of role models.

Cognitive Developmental Theory

Cognitive developmental theory, originally formulated by Lawrence Kohlberg (1966), contends that *children are neither pushed by their biological desires nor pulled by external rewards and punishments. Instead, children are active learners, attempting to make sense of the social environment.* They actively search for patterns and rules that govern the functioning of females and males and then follow these in an attempt to best adapt to social demands.

By approximately 3 years of age, children can correctly label their own gender (that is, they have gender identity). However, they do not yet know that gender is unchangeable, that neither time nor behavioral and appearance modifications can alter one's gender. For example, Kohlberg (1966) reported that most 4-year-olds believe that a girl if wanted to could become a boy, if she engaged in boy-related activities or if she wore a boy's clothes.

This is because the young child relies on superficial physical characteristics, such as clothing or hair length to determine gender. Preschool children do not recognize that changes in an object's visible characteristics do not necessarily alter its fundamental nature.

Cognitive developmental theory contends that gender typing cannot take place until children develop the concept of **gender constancy**, *the belief that gender is permanent regardless of changes in age, behavior, or appearance*. Once children acquire that understanding, between the ages of 4 and 7, they seek out information about which behaviors are gender appropriate and which are not. To learn which behaviors are performed by females and which are performed by males, children actively observe parents and other role models. Then they engage in the gender-appropriate behaviors because behaving in a gender-consistent manner is, in itself, rewarding.

Cognitive developmental theory argues that rewards for gender-consistent behavior merely inform the child what is gender appropriate but do not serve to strengthen those behaviors, as in the social learning theory view. Rather, children engage in these behaviors because acting in a gender-consistent manner is, in itself, rewarding. Let's look at an example to clarify the distinction. Six-year-old Caitlin has been praised for helping her mother cook dinner. According to social learning theory, she then wants to cook again because she anticipates positive reinforcement from others (and possibly from herself) for cooking. Attaining gender constancy is not necessary, because her desire to cook stems from her expectation of reward, not because cooking is defined as a female activity. According to cognitive developmental theory, however, the praise given to Caitlin serves as information that cooking is a female activity. If she has attained gender constancy, she now wants to cook because behaving in a gender-consistent manner is, in itself, rewarding.

EVALUATION.   The concepts of cognitive developmental theory, like those of social learning theory, are clearly defined and easily measured and have generated considerable research. One key assumption of this perspective is that gender typing depends on an awareness of the unchangeability of gender. This assumption has received mixed support (Leaper & Farkas, 2014). Studies have shown that gender constancy precedes some, but not all, aspects of gender development (Bussey, 2013).

A second assumption of cognitive developmental theory, that children value same-gender activities once they attain gender constancy, receives considerable support. Numerous studies show that children value their own gender more highly than they value the other gender (e.g., Martin et al., 2016).

A major criticism of cognitive developmental theory is that it does not specify why children use gender as a classifying concept rather than other attributes such as race or eye color (Ryle, 2016).

Gender Schema Theory

Gender schema theory, proposed by Sandra Bem (1993), incorporates elements of cognitive developmental and social learning theories. Like the first, it proposes that *children develop an interrelated set of ideas, or schema, about gender that guides their social perceptions and actions.* However, unlike cognitive developmental theory, gender schema theory postulates that the use of gender as an organizing principle does not naturally stem from the minds of children. Similar to social learning theory, it assumes that *gender schema development stems from learning the gender norms and practices of society.*

The theory proposes that children form notions of the traits and roles associated with females and males on the basis of societal expectations. They then use this information to regulate their own behavior, and their self-esteem becomes contingent on their adherence to these gender schemas.

A significant difference between gender schema and cognitive developmental theories lies in the basis for gender schema development. Whereas Kohlberg (1966) assumes that the development of cognitive conceptualizations about gender is a natural process, Bem contends that children use gender to process social information because societal norms and practices emphasize its importance. Thus, children do not organize the social environment on the basis of physical attributes, such as handedness or hair color, because society does not give these characteristics the same significance it applies to gender. Bem argues that children cannot avoid noticing that different toys, activities, jobs, and chores are deemed acceptable for girls and boys by their parents, peers, and teachers. Elementary school teachers do not line up children separately by race because they do not want to emphasize race as a distinguishing characteristic. They often, however, group children by sex, thus increasing its perceived importance as a distinguishing characteristic. Indeed when preschool teachers make gender salient by doing such things as lining up children by gender and using gender-specific language (e.g., "I need a girl to hand out the markers"), children show increased gender stereotypes and decreased play with other-sex peers (Hilliard & Liben, 2010).

Bem (1998) claims that individuals vary in the degree to which they use gender schemas to understand and evaluate others and to guide their own behavior. According to Bem, people who have strong gender schemas consider a narrower range of activities as acceptable for individuals of each gender, including themselves. For example, boys have more powerful gender schemas than girls (Gelman et al., 2004). This finding is consistent with research showing that boys are more likely than girls to maintain gender boundaries (Leaper & Farkas, 2014).

Even within a given sex, some individuals have stronger, less flexible gender schemas than do others, perhaps due to individual differences in exposure to gender as an organizing characteristic. Consequently, Bem (1998) proposes several strategies parents can use to minimize the development of gender schemas and thus reduce the development of gender-stereotypic attitudes and behavior. Read What <u>You</u> Can Do 3.1 and share Bem's ideas with others. Also see Learn About the Research 15.1 on Why and How Should We Raise Feminist Children?

EVALUATION.   One strength of gender schema theory is that, unlike cognitive developmental theory, it explains why children structure their social perceptions around gender rather than other attributes. In addition, considerable research supports the theory (Batalha & Reynolds, 2013; Halpern, 2012). For example, one of the theory's assumptions is that gender schemas help individuals organize memories, thus facilitating the recollection of gender-consistent information. Consistent with this view, individuals remember material consistent with their own gender better than they remember material consistent with the other gender (Leaper & Farkas, 2014; Liben, 2016).

WHAT YOU CAN DO 3.1
Ways to Minimize Gender Schemas in Children

1. Eliminate gender stereotyping from your behavior. For example, share household duties instead of dividing them along gender lines.
2. Eliminate gender stereotyping from the choices you give your children. Offer toys, activities, and clothing associated with both females and males.
3. Define *femaleness* and *maleness* along anatomical and reproductive lines only, thus reducing your children's tendency to organize the social world according to gender. The following anecdote from Bem about her 4-year-old son Jeremy illustrates the limitations of a cultural definition of gender and the greater flexibility of a biological definition:

One day Jeremy decided to wear barrettes to school. Another little boy told Jeremy that he must be a girl because "only girls wear barrettes." After explaining to this child that "wearing barrettes doesn't matter" and that "being a boy means having a penis and testicles," Jeremy finally pulled down his pants to make his point more vividly. The other child was not impressed. He simply said, "Everybody has a penis; only girls wear barrettes." (1998, p. 109)

Source: Bem (1998).

GENDER-RELATED TRAITS

We have explored a variety of theories that explain gender typing. Now let's examine variations in individuals' conformity to stereotyped expectations about their gender.

The most commonly measured variation has been in the gender-related traits individuals ascribe to themselves, that is, in their personal identification with female-related and male-related characteristics. Historically, these two sets of traits were viewed as bipolar, that is, as opposite extremes of a single continuum. In the chapter opening vignette, Judith's classmate believed she could not be both feminine and achievement oriented, reflecting the bipolar view that a person cannot have characteristics stereotypically associated with both females and males.

In the 1970s, there was a change in this characterization of female-related and male-related traits. Psychologists began to conceptualize the two dimensions as independent, rather than opposite, of one another. Unlike a bipolar dimension, such as tall–short, in which it is impossible to be described by both traits, the new perspective posited that individuals can exhibit any combination of female-stereotypic and male-stereotypic characteristics. That is, a high degree of one does not imply a low degree of the other.

In 1974, Sandra Bem proposed that femininity and masculinity should be assessed independently and developed the Bem Sex Role Inventory (BSRI) to accomplish that goal. The BSRI includes one set of traits viewed as more desirable for females than for males and another set of items seen as more desirable for males than for females. Soon after, Janet Spence and Robert Helmreich (1978) developed and published the Personal Attributes Questionnaire (PAQ), which also has two separate dimensions to measure gender-related personality characteristics. On both instruments, the female-related scale comprises communal traits and the male-related scale reflects agentic traits (see Chapter 2); however, when used as measures of gender-related trait identification, they have typically been labeled "femininity" and "masculinity" (Wood & Eagly, 2015).

The BSRI and the PAQ evaluate femininity/expressiveness and masculinity/instrumentality as independent dimensions. Respondents receive a score on each dimension, and the combination of the two indicates which of four categories best describes their gender-related traits. These categories are (1) **femininity**, *a high score on the femininity/expressiveness scale and a low score on the scale for masculinity/instrumentality*; (2) **masculinity**, *a high score on the masculinity/instrumentality scale and a low score on the femininity/expressiveness scale*; (3) **androgyny** (derived from the ancient Greek words for male—*andro*—and female—*gyn*), *high scores on both scales*; and (4) **undifferentiation**, *low scores on both scales*. Any individual, regardless of gender, can be characterized by any of these categories.

To assess your own gender-related traits, try Get Involved 3.1.

Changes in Gender-Related Traits Over Time

College women and high school girls' . . . assertiveness . . . increased from 1931 to 1945, decreased from 1946 to 1967 and increased from 1968 to 1993. . . . Why did women's assertiveness scores switch twice over the century?

(Twenge, 2001, pp. 133, 141)

In the 1970s, studies showed that more female than male college students scored high on femininity, whereas more males than females scored high on masculinity and approximately one-third of both genders were androgynous (e.g., Spence & Helmreich, 1978). To determine whether there has been any change over time, Jean Twenge (1997b) performed a meta-analysis of femininity and masculinity scores based on samples from over 50 different college campuses since the 1970s. Interestingly, the most notable change found by Twenge was the dramatic increase in masculinity scores of women. Also, there was a significant increase in androgyny among women and a weaker increase among men. Other research (Harper & Schoeman, 2003; Spence & Buckner, 2000; Twenge, 2001) has found that women and men no longer differ on a number of items

---

GET INVOLVED 3.1
What Are Your Gender-Related Traits?

The following is a list of characteristics similar to those appearing on tests such the BSRI and the PAQ. Rate yourself on a scale from 1 (hardly ever applies to me) to 5 (almost always applies to me). Also ask a friend to rate you on these characteristics.

1.	Self-reliant	1 2 3 4 5
2.	Loving to children	1 2 3 4 5
3.	Gentle	1 2 3 4 5
4.	Assertive	1 2 3 4 5
5.	Helpful to others	1 2 3 4 5
6.	Kind	1 2 3 4 5
7.	Self-confident	1 2 3 4 5
8.	Competitive	1 2 3 4 5
9.	Warm	1 2 3 4 5
10.	Willing to take risks	1 2 3 4 5

WHAT DOES IT MEAN?

Add up your points for items 2, 3, 5, 6, and 9; this comprises your femininity/expressiveness score. Similarly, sum your points for items 1, 4, 7, 8, and 10; this comprises your masculinity/instrumentality score. Use the same procedure to score your friend's ratings of you.

1. Are your two scores similar to each other or is one much higher than the other? Does your pattern of scores reflect the gender-related trait category you think best describes you? Why or why not?

2. Is your pattern of scores similar to the pattern based on your friend's ratings? If not, describe the differences. Also, explain why your friend views your gender-related traits differently than the way you perceive them.

3. Although the PAQ and BSRI are widely used today, they were based on 1970s' perceptions of traits more typical of either females or males. Are there any characteristics presented here that no longer seem to be more representative of one gender than the other? Which ones?

long considered to be masculine. These include being active, independent, self-reliant, ambitious, assertive, acting as a leader, and defending one's beliefs. When compared to their own mothers, today's college women show more masculine-typed and less feminine-typed behaviors (Guastello & Guastello, 2003).

Jean Twenge, Janet Spence, and Camille Buckner suggest that these changes in gender-related traits may be accounted for by societal changes that have occurred in recent years. Girls have been encouraged to become more assertive, to stand up for their rights, to be independent, and to have high occupational goals. They have been given more opportunities to develop their agentic skills, especially in the educational, vocational, and sports arenas.

Similarly, women were expected to be self-sufficient during the Great Depression and World War II, in the early-to-middle years of the twentieth century, whereas passive domesticity was encouraged in the 1950s and early 1960s. These shifts in women's status and roles closely parallel the changes in women's assertiveness over the course of the century (Twenge, 2001).

Thus, today's young women are more likely than their counterparts in the 1970s to have witnessed or experienced roles that involve male-stereotypic characteristics. This could have contributed to the development of their greater masculinity and, in turn, their greater androgyny. So, consistent with the view that gender is socially constructed, changes in women's personal sense of gender seem to be related to their social experiences.

Gender-Related Traits and Psychological Adjustment

Once psychologists started to conceptualize gender-related traits as being more complex than a single dimension of femininity–masculinity, they began to examine the psychological well-being of individuals who varied in their pattern of gender-stereotypic traits. Some (see Vafael et al., 2016) hypothesized that because androgynous individuals are comfortable engaging in both feminine and masculine behaviors, they can adapt more adequately to various situational demands and should report greater well-being than nonandrogynous individuals. Research has supported this view (Bukowski et al., 2016; Pauletti et al., 2016). However, it appears that it is high masculinity, and not the specific combination of high masculinity and high femininity, that is strongly related to well-being and self-esteem (Priess et al., 2009; Wood & Eagly, 2015). Predictably, it is the positive aspects of masculinity (e.g., independence, mastery), not its negative components (e.g., aggressiveness, selfishness), that are linked with psychological health (Woodhill & Samuels, 2003).

What can explain the positive relationship between masculinity and psychological adjustment? As we saw in Chapter 2, masculine-typed traits are more highly valued in North America than feminine-typed traits. Therefore, people with masculine-typed traits perhaps feel better about their ability to function effectively. Derek Grimmell and Gary Stern (1992) found support for this explanation when they compared college students' BSRI self-ratings, their BSRI ratings of the ideal person, and their psychological well-being. The higher students' own masculinity was in relation to their perception of ideal masculinity, the higher their own self-esteem and the lower their anxiety and depression. Thus, it appears that the degree to which individuals feel they possess highly valued masculine traits is a good predictor of their psychological adjustment.

However, before we conclude that androgyny is not related to psychological well-being, let's consider a different conceptualization of androgyny. See Learn About the Research 3.1 for another approach to androgyny measurement and its psychological benefits.

Evaluation of the Concept of Androgyny

When the psychological measurement of androgyny was introduced in the 1970s, it was received enthusiastically by feminist scholars. It replaced the notion that psychological health required that females be feminine and males be masculine. By embodying socially desirable traits for both females and males, androgyny seemed to imply the absence of gender stereotyping. Furthermore, by incorporating both feminine and masculine behaviors, it appeared to broaden the scope of behaviors that can be used to handle different situations and, thus, lead to more flexible and adaptive behaviors.

LEARN ABOUT THE RESEARCH 3.1
A Real-Life Approach to Androgyny

We have seen that masculinity, and not the coexistence of masculinity and femininity, best predicts psychological adjustment. Jayne Stake, however, argues that the psychological benefits of androgyny are best demonstrated when communal and agentic behaviors are given in response to expectations demanded by specific life situations.

Stake focused on individuals' responses to job demands that required both communal and agentic behaviors. She wondered if people who use both types of behaviors in these situations experienced benefits compared to those who relied on one type or neither type. To study this, undergraduate students were individually asked to describe a work situation in which they were expected to behave with both "sensitivity and caring" (e.g., "Be sensitive to the needs of others," "Show others you care about them") and "mastery and independence" (e.g., "Always show that

you can handle things on your own—without the help of others," "Show you have technical know-how"). Then they were asked to describe the behaviors they used to cope with these dual expectations. These coping strategies were coded into one of the four categories generally used to classify gender-related traits. Students also indicated to what extent their well-being was affected by work situations that expected both types of behaviors.

The results showed that individuals who used androgynous responses to dual expectations in job situations experienced more rewards and fewer negative outcomes than those using other types of strategies. Thus, examining gender-related attributes as behavioral responses to specific situations and not just as general personality traits may be a fruitful approach to understanding the beneficial effects of various gender-related orientations.

WHAT DOES IT MEAN?

1. Stake examined expectations for communal and agentic behaviors in the workplace. What other situations might make simultaneous demands?
2. Identify a job experience you had where both types of demands were made. Describe

how you handled it and how you felt in this situation. Was your experience consistent with the results reported here?

_____

Source: Stake (1997).

Although androgyny continues to be viewed by feminist scholars as more positive than restrictions to either femininity or masculinity, several feminist criticisms have been leveled against this concept. One is that the notion of androgyny, similar to the bipolar differentiation of femininity–masculinity, is based on the division of gender into female-stereotypic and male-stereotypic characteristics (Rice, 2014). Rather than making traits *gender neutral*, androgyny involves the combination of *gender-specific* orientations. A second concern is that androgyny might be erecting unrealistic goals for individuals—the requirement that people be competent in both the communal and agentic domains. Third, according to Bem (1993), the concept of androgyny does not deal with masculinity and femininity in their unequal cultural context. It neither acknowledges nor attempts to eliminate the greater cultural value placed on male activities. Last, Bem is concerned that androgyny will not lead to the elimination of gender inequality, a goal that requires *societal* rather than *personal* change. That is, the mere existence of individuals with both feminine and masculine traits does not alter the patriarchal power structure in society.

GENDER ATTITUDES

Let's turn now to an examination of variations in gender attitudes. People differ in the degree to which they believe that gender should dictate females' and males' roles. Some individuals hold a **traditional gender attitude**, *the belief that females should engage in communal behaviors and roles and males should engage in agentic behaviors and roles.* They might believe, for example, that women should be the primary rearers of children whereas men should be the primary financial providers, or that women are better suited than men to nursing whereas men are better suited than women to corporate management. Others adhere to a **nontraditional or egalitarian gender attitude**, *the belief that behaviors and roles should not be gender specific.*

Individuals in Western industrialized nations tend to have less traditional beliefs about women's employment roles than they do about women's combined family and work roles (Anderson & Johnson, 2003; Treas & Widmer, 2000). For example, Judith Treas and Eric Widmer (2000) found that individuals in 23 developed nations overwhelmingly supported full-time employment for married women with no children. Mothers of preschoolers, however, were expected to stay home or work only part time. Let us now take a closer look at gender-role attitudes around the world.

 ## Gender Attitudes in Global Context

Deborah Best and her colleagues (Best, 2001; Best & Thomas, 2004) have conducted studies of the gender attitudes of university students in 14 different countries. Their research indicates that gender attitudes range from traditional to more egalitarian both across and within cultures. For example, the most egalitarian attitudes were found in northern European countries (England, Finland, Germany, the Netherlands). The United States was in the middle of the distribution, and the most traditional attitudes were found in Africa and in Asian countries (India, Japan, Malaysia, Nigeria, Pakistan). Other studies have found that Muslim nations in the Middle East and North Africa are the least likely of all nations to endorse gender equality. Across countries, women hold more egalitarian views than men. Within a given country, however, the gender attitudes of women and men correspond highly (Best & Thomas, 2004; Olson et al., 2007). Now go back to Chapter 2, and compare these results with those of Glick and Fiske (2000) on hostile and benevolent sexism across cultures.

Individual Differences in Gender-Related Attitudes

As we have seen, gender attitudes can vary from traditional to egalitarian. What demographic and personality characteristics are related to differences in gender attitudes?

GENDER. Not surprisingly, one characteristic is gender. Dozens of studies using mostly samples of Whites have shown that males have more traditional beliefs about the appropriate roles for women than females (Andre et al., 2013; Emmers-Sommer, 2014; Epstein & Ward, 2011). Similarly, Black men (Carter et al., 2009) and Asian men (Anderson & Johnson, 2003; Ui & Matsui, 2008) hold more traditional gender-role attitudes than their female counterparts.

ETHNICITY. Another demographic characteristic that is related to gender attitudes is ethnicity. As we saw in Chapter 2, Black women are less likely than White or Latina women to adhere to gender stereotypes. Correspondingly their attitudes about gender-related behaviors and roles also are less traditional. For example, Black women hold more egalitarian views about women's employment and political roles than White women do (Carter et al., 2009; Donnelly et al., 2016). Also, Black college women, compared to White college women, perceive less conflict in the combination of the provider and domestic roles (e.g., Bridges & Etaugh, 1996), a difference possibly due to Black women's longer history of combining work and family roles.

What about gender attitudes of Latinas? Traditionally, Latina/o families have been characterized as patriarchal, with a dominant, powerful husband/father and a submissive, self-sacrificing wife/mother. Thus, it is not surprising that Latina individuals have been found to hold more traditional views about women's employment and political roles than either Black or White persons (Cohn & Caumont, 2014). However, the views held by Latina women have become less traditional over time. For example, Donna Castañeda (2008) notes that second- and third-generation Latinas/os are less likely than first-generation women and men to believe that the husband should be the sole provider and decision maker within the family, and that females should do all of the housework and obey the husband's/father's demands. Thus, the degree of acculturation of Latina women and Latino men seems to be strongly related to their gender attitudes.

Research on Native Americans has focused on their actual gender-related behaviors and roles rather than on their attitudes and has shown great variations over time and across tribal groups. According to scholars such as Wendy Peters and her colleagues (2014) and Stephanie Sellers (2008), women's behaviors and roles in traditional Native American life included caregiving, spiritual continuation of their people, and transmission of cultural knowledge. Many Native American societies were characterized by complementary but equally powerful roles for some women and men (Deval, 2015). Other groups institutionalized alternative female roles. For example, within several Plains tribes, women's roles included masculine ones, such as the "warrior woman" and the "manly hearted woman" (aggressive and independent) in addition to the traditional role of the hard-working wife. Some tribes, such as the Hopi, Iroquois, Navajo, Pawnee, and Seminole, were matrilineal; women owned the material goods and passed these on to their daughters and sisters and played important economic, political, and spiritual roles (Robinson-Wood, 2017; Sellers, 2008; Weaver, 2009).

Scholars contend that colonization by Europeans and the increasing acculturation of Native Americans into the dominant White culture have contributed to a breakdown in complementary female–male roles and to an increase in male dominance and the subjugation of women in several Native American societies (Peters & Gray, 2014; Sellers, 2008; Weaver, 2009). However, in many tribes, women continue to have considerable political power because of their traditional roles of caretakers for the community and transmitters of the culture. Today, women increasingly are assuming positions of tribal leadership. For example, women head over 20 percent of tribal governments in California, the state with the highest Native population ("Woman Named Mohegan Tribal Chief," 2010). Two of the most influential recent female tribal leaders are Wilma Mankiller and Lynn Malerba. Mankiller, who died in 2010, was elected and served as the first woman principal chief of the Cherokee Nation, leading her people to increased economic independence and cultural renewal (Plec, 2011). Malerba was selected in 2010 as chief of the Mohegans, one of the best-known and most prosperous Native American Nations ("Woman Named Mohegan Tribal Chief," 2010). In order to learn more directly about the gender attitudes of women of different ethnicities, perform the interviews described in Get Involved 3.2.

GET INVOLVED 3.2
Ethnic Variations in Gender Attitudes

Interview two traditional-age college women of approximately the same age from each of two different ethnic groups. Ask the following questions:

1. Do you think there should be different roles for women and men in the family? In dating relationships? In the workplace? If your respondent answered "yes" to any of these, ask her to be specific.

2. How important is your future/current career to your personal identity?

3. Do you plan to marry and have children? If yes, do you anticipate any difficulty balancing your family and work roles?

4. Who do you think should be the primary provider in your family?

5. How do you think you and your spouse/partner will divide up the household and child care responsibilities?

WHAT DOES IT MEAN?

1. Although your sample is very small, did you observe any ethnic differences? Did these differences match those discussed in the text? If yes, show the connections. If no, explain why your results might differ from those reported in past research.

2. You interviewed women college students. Do you think your findings might have been different had your respondents been college graduates? Working-class or poor women without a college education? Explain your answers.

OTHER FACTORS.   Gender attitudes are also related to religious factors. Unaffiliated and Jewish individuals tend to have the least traditional gender beliefs and conservative Protestants the most, with mainline Protestants and Catholics somewhere in between (Cohn & Caumont, 2014; Davis & Greenstein, 2009). Moreover, the more strongly individuals embrace religion in their lives, the more traditional their gender attitudes are (Andre et al., 2013; Cohn & Caumont, 2014; Cunningham, 2008).

Other demographic characteristics related to gender attitudes are social class, political ideology, age, amount of education, academic performance, and college major. Specifically, nontraditional views about gender tend to be associated with attaining higher social and educational levels (Cohn & Caumont, 2014), having liberal political views (Fitzpatrick Bettencourt et al., 2011; Cichy et al., 2007), being a younger adult (Emmers-Sommer, 2014), being a senior in college as opposed to a first-year student (Bryant, 2003), having a high GPA (Bryant, 2003), and, for women, majoring in a male-dominated field (Karpiak et al., 2007).

In addition, gender attitudes are related to a personality characteristic known as authoritarianism, which is characterized by intolerance of ambiguity and is strongly related to prejudice toward members of perceived out-groups such as Blacks, Jews, sexual minorities, and people with disabilities. As you might guess, both women and men who are high in authoritarianism endorse traditional societal roles for women and men (Swim et al., 2010a, b). Traditional attitudes about gender are also associated with the belief that gender differences are caused by biological or religious (divine) causes as opposed to differences in socialization or opportunities (Neff & Terry-Schmitt, 2002).

Perceived Value of Female Versus Male Gender-Related Attributes

Given the greater power held by males in most societies, is it more advantageous to be a male than to be a female? Alternatively, are gender-related advantages and disadvantages equally distributed between the genders or, perhaps, balanced in favor of females? To examine this question, try the exercises in Get Involved 3.3.

When Arnie Cann and Elizabeth Vann (1995) asked college students to list advantages and disadvantages of being the other gender, they found that both women and men associated more advantages with being male. For example, they believed that females are under more pressure than males to focus on their appearance and that biological differences, such as pregnancy and menstruation, are disadvantageous to females. Interestingly, these students did not perceive males to have more social-role advantages than females. Although females were seen to be limited by workplace discrimination and the expectation to be subordinate in their relationships, males were viewed as hurt by the social pressure on them to be successful and to play a leadership role. Thus, these students seemed to be aware that the gender imbalance in power puts women at a disadvantage and that the social construction of the agentic, achievement-oriented male role establishes potentially difficult expectations for men.

Given the evidence that males are seen as having more advantages than females, it is not surprising that males who violate gender expectations are evaluated more negatively than females who do so (England, 2016; Leaper & Farkas, 2015). Scholars have proposed two possible explanations for this difference. The **social status hypothesis** contends that *because the male gender role is more highly valued than the female role is, a male is seen as lowering his social status by engaging in female-stereotypic behaviors, whereas a female performing male-stereotypic behaviors is perceived as raising her status* (England, 2016; Leaper & Farkas, 2015). Consequently, males who engage in cross-gender behaviors are viewed more negatively than are females who deviate from gender expectations. The social status hypothesis receives some support from the finding that people believe that occupations with higher prestige require skills associated with masculine characteristics and that these jobs should pay more than those requiring feminine characteristics (Kite, 2001). A concept similar to the social status hypothesis is that of **precarious manhood**. According to this view, found in many cultures worldwide, *manhood (unlike womanhood) is an achieved rather than an ascribed status that is difficult to earn but easy to lose.* (Bosson et al., 2013).

The other explanation of the more negative evaluation of male gender-role violation is the **sexual orientation hypothesis** (Kilianski, 2003; Kite 2001). This perspective argues that *cross-gender behavior in boys but not girls is considered a sign of actual or potential same-sex sexual orientation.* Several investigations have provided support for this perspective. For example, Emily Kane (2006)

GET INVOLVED 3.3
Would You Rather Be a Female or a Male?

Think about any advantages and/or disadvantages that would occur if you were the other gender. For each of the following two categories, list any advantages and/or disadvantages of being the other gender: (1) *social roles*, that is, opportunities that are not equally available to the two genders and/or behaviors that are considered more appropriate for one gender than the other; and (2) *physical differences*, for example, reproductive, size, or strength differences. Also, ask an other-gender friend to perform the same exercise. Discuss your answers with your friend.

WHAT DOES IT MEAN?

1. Did you imagine more advantages and/or disadvantages in one category than the other? If yes, how can you explain the pattern of perceived advantages and disadvantages?
2. Are your friend's perceptions of the advantages of being your gender consistent with your perceptions of the disadvantages of being your friend's gender? Why or why not?
3. Examine the number of advantages relative to disadvantages that you associated with being the other gender. Do the same for your friend's responses. Do you and/or your friend attach greater value to one gender or the other? If yes, explain.
4. If you or your friend perceive a relative advantage of one gender over the other, discuss some societal changes that would have to occur to reduce this discrepancy.

Source: Cann and Vann (1995).

---

found that parents of preschoolers accepted gender nonconformity in their daughters but not in their sons. Two-thirds expressed negative reactions to their sons' dressing up in feminine attire, wearing nail polish, or playing with Barbie dolls, and several expressed fears that such activity meant that the son either was gay or would be perceived as gay.

Summary

GENDER SELF-CONCEPT

- Gender self-concept includes gender identity and gender attitudes.

PRENATAL DEVELOPMENT

- Prenatal sex differentiation is a multistage process. The joining of the sex chromosomes at conception is followed by the differentiation of the gonads, the development of the internal and external reproductive organs, and the organization of the hypothalamus.
- After the gonads develop, the presence or absence of androgens influences the development of the reproductive organs and the brain.
- Estrogens appear to play a role in female development.

MULTIPLE GENDERS

- Many non-Western cultures recognize multiple genders. Western cultures typically recognize only two.

INTERSEXUALITY

- Some individuals experience variations in their prenatal development known as intersexuality.
- Turner syndrome is a chromosomal disorder in which the individual has a single X chromosome. These individuals are raised as girls and have female gender expectations, but no sex glands or prenatal estrogen.
- Genetic females with CAH are usually reared as girls, although they have a partial or complete masculinization of their external genitals.
- Genetic males with the androgen-insensitivity syndrome have feminized external genitals and are reared as girls.
- Genetic males with a 5 alpha-reductase deficiency experience a female-to-male body transformation at puberty.
- Studies of intersexuals provide mixed evidence regarding the relative influence of prenatal biological factors and the gender of rearing on nonsexual gender-related attributes, gender identity, and sexual orientation.

THEORIES OF GENDER TYPING

- Psychoanalytic theory proposes that gender typing stems from the child's identification with the same-gender parent, a process that occurs when the child resolves the Oedipus complex. For boys, the resolution stems from fear of castration by the father. For girls, it stems from the realization that she will never possess her father.
- Social learning theory proposes that children acquire gender behaviors via imitation of same-gender models and positive reinforcement of their own gender-consistent behaviors. Cognitive social learning theory stresses the added role of cognition.
- Cognitive developmental theory contends that once children attain gender constancy, they are motivated to behave in gender-appropriate ways. Thus, they actively seek out the rules that characterize female behavior and male behavior. They then engage in gender-consistent behaviors because it enables them to competently adjust to the social environment.
- Gender schema theory proposes that children develop an interrelated set of ideas about gender. They learn the societal norms and practices that signify the importance of gender. They then organize the social world on the basis of gender and guide their own actions accordingly.

GENDER-RELATED TRAITS

- On the basis of their gender-related traits, individuals can be categorized as feminine, masculine, androgynous, or undifferentiated.
- Research has shown an increase in masculinity and androgyny in women over time.
- Masculinity is related to psychological adjustment.
- Androgyny was once considered to be highly desirable, but recently feminist scholars have criticized it.

GENDER ATTITUDES

- Gender attitudes are multidimensional.
- College students have less traditional beliefs about the value of the employment role for women but more traditional views about the combination of women's employment and family roles.
- Across countries women hold more egalitarian gender attitudes than men.
- Among Whites, women are generally more nontraditional in their beliefs than men are.
- Among women, Blacks hold more traditional views about domestic responsibilities than Whites, but have more nontraditional views about the combination of women's employment and family roles.
- The roles of Latina/o women and men have become more egalitarian over time, but Latinas have more traditional views than Black and White women.
- The gender-related behaviors and roles of Native American women vary greatly across tribes and in several societies increased acculturation has been accompanied by greater male dominance.
- Traditional gender attitudes are linked to being older, more religious, less educated, of lower social class, politically conservative, and authoritarian.
- College women and men associate more advantages with being male than with being female.
- Males, compared to females, are more negatively evaluated for engaging in cross-gender behavior.

Key Terms

What Do You Think?

1. If you gave birth to an intersexual child, would you decide on surgical restructuring of the child's reproductive system and genitalia early in life, or would you wait until closer to puberty when your child could participate in the decision? Give reasons for your answer.

2. Evidence indicates that boys, more than girls, select role models who are powerful. Explain this finding.

3. As discussed in Chapter 2, it is possible that the media not only reflect gender stereotypes but also help shape them. Now that you are familiar with theories of gender typing, use one of these theories to explain how the media might contribute to an individual's acquisition of gender stereotypes.

4. Which gender-typing theory or theories best explain(s) the development of gender-related traits, behaviors, and roles? Explain. To help you develop your reasons, critically think about the evaluations presented in the text. Additionally, if you have had any contact with young children, try to provide anecdotal support for some of the theoretical concepts.

5. Discuss the advantages and disadvantages to girls/women and boys/men of gender-related trait identifications consistent with stereotypes, that is, femininity in females and masculinity in males. Can you think of the advantages and disadvantages of an androgynous identity?

6. There is some evidence that individuals who internalize their religious beliefs and attempt to live by them hold more traditional gender attitudes than individuals who do not. Consider possible explanations for this finding.

If You Want to Learn More

Amato, V. (2016). *Intersex narratives: Shifts in the representation of intersex lives in North American literature and pop culture.* Bielefeld, Germany: Transcript-Verlag.

Angello, M. & Bowman, A. (2016). *Raising the transgender child: A complete guide for parents, families, and caregivers.* Berkeley, CA: Seal Press.

Davis, G. (2015). *Contesting intersex: The dubious diagnosis.* New York: Hachette Books.

Fausto-Sterling, A. (2012). *Sex/gender: Biology in a social world.* New York: Routledge.

Feder, E.K. (2014). *Making sense of intersex: Changing ethical perspectives in biomedicine.* Bloomington, IN: Indiana University Press.

Jones, T. (2016). *Policy and gay, lesbian, bisexual, transgender, and intersex students.* New York: Springer.

Jordan-Young, R.M. (2011). *Brain storm: The flaws in the science of sex differences.* Cambridge, MA: Harvard University Press.

Nutt, A.E. (2016). *Becoming Nicole: The transformation of an American family.* New York: Penguin.

Swartz, W. (2015). *Two different worlds I've lived in: The true story of being intersex.* Author.

Van Lisdonk, J. (2014). *Living with intersex: DSD.* Amsterdam: Netherlands Institute of Social Research.

Villoria, H. (2017). *Born both: An intersex life.* New York: Hachette Books.

Yarhouse, M.A. (2015). *Understanding gender dysphoria: Navigating transgender issues in a changing culture.* Downers Grove, IL: InterVarsity Press.

Websites

Gender Identity

https://www.genderspectrum.org/quick-links/understanding-gender/

Women's Studies Links

http://dir.yahoo.com/health/diseases_and_conditions/intersexuality

4 CHAPTER

Infancy, Childhood, and Adolescence

I was 6 when I realized there were different expectations for boys and girls. My brother and I used to play dress up at home all the time. It was an Easter Sunday and I wanted to wear the tie and my brother wanted to wear the dress. My father got really mad and my mom told us that since we were going to church I had to wear the dress and my brother had to wear the suit. I had a fit about the hose itching and my father told me to get used to it because girls were supposed to dress like girls and boys like boys. (Traci, a 23-year-old college senior)

My mom wanted me to wear pink and my brother blue. At Christmas all of the granddaughters were given makeup and Barbie dolls whereas the boys were given GI Joe or hunting gear. My mother raised me to know how to cook, clean, budget, and do all of the work to take care of children and a household. However, my brother has never even washed a dish. (Jamie, a 20-year-old college junior)

Both my parents encouraged me to do well in school, but while my brother was signed up for karate lessons at the YMCA I was signed up for things like jazz dance. When I joined girls' football in high school, my mother cringed every time I left the house in a jersey or came back with a bloody lip. She kept telling me she would "never understand." I was teased constantly, mostly by boys. They told me I would never be good enough at football, but I kept my head high and ignored them. (Erika, a 20-year-old college junior)

An old nursery rhyme declares that little girls are made of "sugar and spice and everything nice," while little boys are made of "frogs and snails and puppy dogs' tails."

Are girls and boys really as different as the nursery rhyme suggests? Is there even a kernel of truth in these age-old stereotypes? And if so, what factors might be responsible? The childhood recollections of Traci, Jamie, and Erika indicate the important contributions made by family members. In this chapter, we focus on the development of girls in infancy, childhood, and adolescence and examine both similarities and differences between girls and boys during these years. We also explore factors that influence gender development, including the roles played by parents, siblings, schools, peers, and the media. We then look at the physical transformations of adolescence, examining puberty and individual differences in rates of physical maturation. Finally, we turn to psychosocial development in adolescence, exploring identity, self-esteem, gender intensification, and body image.

CHILDREN'S KNOWLEDGE AND BELIEFS ABOUT GENDER

Early childhood is a time when much of the social construction of gender takes place. Let's examine some of these processes more closely. For a summary of the major milestones of gender stereotyping and gender-role adoption, see Table 4.1.

Distinguishing Between Females and Males

"Is it a girl or a boy?" is typically the first question asked following a child's birth (unless of course, the parents chose to learn the answer from a sonogram months earlier!). From the moment babies enter the world, they are surrounded by abundant cues signifying gender. They are given gendered names and are outfitted in color-coded clothing, diapers, and blankets. It is not surprising that children learn to differentiate between females and males at an early age. Infants as young as 3–4 months of age can tell the difference between pictures of adult female and male faces, and 6-month-olds are able to distinguish between their voices. By the age of 12 months, children can match the face and voice of men and women (Shutts, 2015). Between the ages of 2 and 2½ years, they can accurately label pictures of girls and boys (Etaugh et al., 1989; Etaugh & Duits, 1990; Leaper & Farkas, 2014). Young children who learn to identify females and males early show more gender-typical preferences for toys and peers than children of the same age who do not make this distinction (Zosuls et al., 2014).

Gender Identity and Self-Perceptions

As we saw in Chapter 3, children develop gender identity between 2 and 3 years of age. By that time, they can accurately label their own gender and place a picture of themselves with other same-gender children (Leaper & Farkas, 2014; Leavell & Tamis-LaMonda, 2013). As children become more aware of their membership in a particular gender category, they begin to view their own gender more favorably than the other gender (Martin et al., 2016; Susskind et al., 2005). In one study of children in second through tenth grade, for example, girls believed that girls were nicer, harder workers, and less selfish than boys. Boys, on the other hand, felt that *they* were nicer, harder workers, and less selfish than girls (Etaugh et al., 1984).

Gender Stereotypes

In Chapter 2, we discussed how gender stereotypes are formed. This process begins early in life. Rudimentary knowledge about gender-typical objects and activities develops during the second year. Children as young as 24 months know that certain objects (e.g., ribbon, dress, purse) and activities (e.g., putting on makeup, rocking a baby, vacuuming) are associated with females and that other objects (e.g., gun, truck, screwdriver) and activities (e.g., fixing a car, shaving) are associated

Age	Gender Stereotyping and Gender-Role Adoption	Gender Identity
TABLE 4.1	**Milestones of Gender Typing**	
1–5 years	• "Gender-appropriate" toy preferences emerge. • Gender stereotyping of activities, occupations, and behaviors appears and expands. • Gender segregation in peer interaction emerges and strengthens. • Girls' preference for play in pairs, boys' for play in larger groups appears.	• Gender constancy develops in a three-stage sequence: gender labeling, gender stability, and gender consistency.
6–11 years	• Gender segregation reaches a peak. • Gender-stereotyped knowledge expands, especially for personality traits and achievement areas. • Gender stereotyping peaks between ages 5 and 7, then becomes more flexible.	• "Masculine" gender identity strengthens among boys; girls' gender identity becomes more androgynous.
12–18 years	• Gender-role conformity increases in early adolescence and then declines. • Gender segregation becomes less pronounced.	• Gender identity becomes more traditional in early adolescence ("gender intensification"), after which highly stereotypic self-perceptions decline.

Note: These milestones represent overall age trends. Individual differences exist in the precise age at which each milestone is attained and in the extent of gender typing.

Source: Adapted from Berk (2013).

with males (Bussey, 2013). By age 3, children also display knowledge of gender stereotypes for occupations (Leaper & Farkas, 2014). Gender-stereotyped knowledge of activities and occupations increases rapidly between ages 3 and 5 and is mastered by age 6 or 7 (Leaper & Farkas, 2014; Zosuls et al., 2008). For a closer look at how occupational stereotypes develop throughout childhood, read Learn About the Research 4.1.

In addition, preschoolers demonstrate a rudimentary awareness of gender stereotypes for personality traits. Traits such as "gets feelings hurt easily," "needs help," and "can't fix things" are applied to girls, whereas "hits people," "likes to win at playing games," "is not afraid of scary things," and "fixes things" are seen as characteristics of boys (Bauer et al., 1998; Leaper & Farkas, 2014). Preschoolers are also more likely to label an ambiguous emotional display by boys as anger, but as sadness when displayed by girls (Parmley & Cunningham, 2008). In general, knowledge of gender-typical personality traits emerges later than other stereotypical information (Bussey, 2013) and increases rapidly throughout elementary school (Best, 2010). But as early as age 6, children are aware that men generally have higher social status than women.

The gender stereotypes learned in the toddler and preschool years become quite rigid between 5 and 7 years of age. They then become more flexible until early adolescence when they begin to become more traditional again (Bussey, 2013; Halim, 2016; Leaper & Farkas, 2014). In one study (Alfieri et al., 1996), children 9 to 16 years old were given 12 trait-related terms, half of them feminine and half masculine, and were asked whether the items described males, females, or both. Gender-trait flexibility, indicated by choosing the "both" option, peaked at ages 11 and 12 and declined thereafter. Boys showed less flexibility than girls, particularly regarding masculine traits. Similarly, research by Elaine Blakemore (2003) and by Lisa Serbin and her colleagues (Serbin et al., 1993) has found that 11-year-olds know more about stereotypes than younger children

LEARN ABOUT THE RESEARCH 4.1
Gender Stereotypes About Occupations

The stereotype that certain occupations are more appropriate for one gender than the other emerges early in childhood (Butler, 2014). Even children as young as 2 and 3 years of age make a distinction between "women's jobs" and "men's jobs" (Betz, 2008). Not surprisingly, girls are more interested than boys in feminine-typed occupations, and boys are more interested than girls in masculine-typed occupations (Weisgram et al., 2010). However, girls generally are less rigid in their occupational stereotypes than boys and are more likely to have nonstereotyped career aspirations for themselves (Blakemore et al., 2009; Fulcher, 2005). For example, when ethnically diverse children from kindergarten through eighth grade are asked what they want to be when they grow up (Bobo et al., 1998; Etaugh & Liss, 1992), younger girls often choose traditional feminine occupations such as teacher and nurse, although a few list traditionally male occupations, such as doctor and pilot. Older girls, however, are more likely than younger ones to choose

a traditionally masculine career and are less likely to pick a feminine one. Boys, on the other hand, aspire to masculine careers at all ages and almost never choose a feminine occupation (Liben & Bigler, 2014). These results may stem from several factors: (a) By early childhood children view stereotypical feminine occupations less favorably than masculine occupations (Butler, 2014); (b) as early as first grade, children perceive that few feminine jobs are high in status (Teig & Susskind, 2008); and (c) children's occupational stereotypes are less restrictive for females who engage in counterstereotypic occupations (e.g., Mary, who is a doctor) than for males who engage in counterstereotypic occupations (e.g., Henry, who is a nurse) (Wilbourn & Kee, 2010). This is another example of evaluating males more negatively than females when they violate gender expectations (see Chapter 3). Interestingly, children of both sexes are more likely to have nontraditional occupational aspirations when their mothers hold nontraditional gender attitudes (Fulcher, 2011).

WHAT DOES IT MEAN?

1. Why are girls more flexible in their career aspirations than boys?

2. Why are male-dominated careers more attractive to both girls and boys than are female-dominated careers?

3. What are some ways that gender stereotypes about occupations can be reduced?

---

but are also more aware of gender-role exceptions, such as girls using tools and sports equipment and boys engaging in domestic chores. Although these older children retain the broad stereotypes, their increasing cognitive maturity allows them to recognize that gender roles are social conventions that can be modified (Halim, 2016; Leaper & Farkas, 2015).

To examine how gender stereotypes develop in other cultures, Deborah Best and John Williams (see Best, 2009; Best & Thomas, 2004) gave the Sex Stereotype Measure to 5-, 8-, and 11-year-olds in 25 countries. They found that stereotype learning in all countries accelerated during the early school years and was completed during adolescence and early adulthood. Girls and boys learned these stereotypes at the same rate. There was a tendency for male-typed traits to be learned somewhat earlier than female-typed traits. However, female-typed traits were learned earlier than male traits in Latin/Catholic cultures (Brazil, Chile, Portugal, Venezuela) where, according to Best and Williams, the female stereotype is more positive than the male stereotype. In predominantly Muslim countries, children learned the stereotypes at an earlier age than in non-Muslim countries, perhaps reflecting the greater divide between female and male roles in Muslim cultures.

GENDER-RELATED ACTIVITIES AND INTERESTS

We have seen that children acquire gender stereotypes at an early age. Are these stereotypes reflected in the interests children develop and the play activities they choose? Let's now examine this question.

Physical Performance and Sports

In the preschool and elementary school years, girls and boys are fairly similar in their motor skills. Boys are slightly stronger, and they can typically run faster, throw a ball farther, and jump higher (Mondschein et al., 2000). Their activity levels also tend to be greater, at least in some settings (Leaper & Farkas, 2014). Girls are better at tasks requiring overall flexibility, precise movement, and coordination of their arms and legs. This gives them an edge in activities such as jumping jacks, balancing on one foot, and gymnastics (Berk, 2013).

Gender differences in motor skills favoring boys become increasingly pronounced from childhood through adolescence (Blakemore et al., 2009). What might account for this change? It appears that childhood gender differences in motor skills (with the exception of throwing) are more likely a result of environmental factors, such as practice and gender role socialization, than biological ones (Blakemore et al., 2009). Boys receive more opportunities, encouragement, and support for participating in sports. So it is not surprising that by middle childhood, boys in most cultures spend more time than girls in vigorous, competitive, athletic activities, particularly in team sports (Dumith et al., 2011).

During puberty, hormonal changes increase muscle mass for boys and fat for girls, giving boys an advantage in strength, size, and power. But hormones are only part of the story. Social pressures on girls to act more feminine and less tomboyish intensify during adolescence, contributing to girls' declining interest and participation in athletic activities (Boiche et al., 2014; Dumith et al., 2011). This trend is troubling, given that involvement in sports is associated with a number of positive traits in girls and women, including higher self-esteem, better body image, enhanced sense of competence and control, reduced stress and depression, less risky sexual activity, lessened likelihood of smoking and substance abuse, better academic performance, and higher college graduation rates (Clarke & Ayres, 2014; Daniels & LaVoi, 2013; Milner & Braddock, 2016; National Coalition for Women and Girls in Education, 2012; Rauscher & Cooky, 2016; Varnes et al., 2015). Girls' sports participation has benefits that last well into adulthood, including greater likelihood of employment and healthier activity and weight levels (Kaestner & Xu, 2010). The good news is that the participation of girls and young women in sports has increased dramatically since the passage in 1972 of Title IX of the Education Amendments Act (Cooky et al., 2015). This federal legislation bars discrimination in all educational programs, including athletics. The number of girls and women in high school and college athletic programs is at least 10 times greater now than before Title IX. Currently, 42 percent of U.S. college athletes are women, with the percentage being highest in larger institutions (Sabo & Snyder, 2013). Canada has seen a similar rise in female student athletes (Hoeber, 2008). The bad news is that schools still spend disproportionately more money on recruiting, and operating expenses for men's sports and on the salaries of coaches (mostly White males) of men's teams (Cunningham, 2008; McBride & Parry, 2016). Moreover, since the passage of Title IX, the percentage of college women's teams coached by female head coaches has dropped from 90 percent to 43 percent (Women's Sports Foundation, 2016). Only 10 percent of Division I college programs have women as athletic directors (Lapchick, 2017). Furthermore, Black women have made fewer gains than White women, both as players and as coaches (Milner & Braddock, 2016; Lapchick, 2016).

Toys and Play

Gender differences in children's play activities and interests are more evident than they are in other areas such as personality qualities or attitudes (Leaper & Farkas, 2014). Girls and boys begin to differ in their preference for certain toys and play activities early in life, and at times these interests are quite intense (DeLoache et al., 2007). By the time they are 9 to 18 months old, girls prefer to play with dolls, cooking sets, dress-up clothes, and soft toys, whereas boys choose vehicles, sports equipment, and tools (Navarro, 2014). By 3 years of age, gender-typical toy choices are well established and these differences persist throughout childhood (Todd et al., 2016; Golombok et al., 2008; McHale et al., 2009). However, girls are more likely than boys to display neutral or cross-gender toy choices and activities (Goble et al., 2012; Weisgram et al., 2014). For example, girls are more likely to request transportation toys and sports equipment as gifts than boys are to ask for dolls (Etaugh & Liss, 1992).

Why are girls more likely to depart from the stereotype? In most cultures, masculine activities have greater prestige than feminine ones. Thus, according to the social status hypothesis (see Chapter 3), a girl who plays with "boys" toys will be viewed more positively than a boy who plays with "girls" toys, who will be seen as lowering his status. As we shall see later, girls who prefer boys' company and activities do, in fact, receive more peer and parental acceptance than boys who prefer the company and activities of girls (Carr, 2007). Moreover, children generally find boys' toys more interesting and appealing than girls' toys (Blakemore & Centers, 2005). You can do lots more fun and exciting things with Legos than with a tea set!

Because of their preferences, girls and boys experience very different play environments (Edwards et al., 2001). During the preschool and elementary school years, boys in a variety of cultures spend more time than girls in vigorous physical outdoor activities such as playing with large vehicles, climbing, exploratory play, sports, and **rough-and-tumble play**, which consists of *playful chasing, tumbling, hitting, and wrestling, often accompanied by laughter and screaming* (Byrd-Craven & Geary, 2013; Lancy, 2015; Hines, 2010). Boys are more likely to engage in competitive activities, to play in large groups that are organized around dominance, and to take more physical risks in their play (Schneider, 2016). Their fantasy play focuses on action and adventure themes (Leaper & Farkas, 2014). Girls' play preferences, on the other hand, include dolls, domestic play, reading, and arts and crafts. They also engage in more symbolic (i.e., "pretend") play than boys (Cote & Bornstein, 2009; McHale, Crouter, & Tucker, 2001). Girls' play is more sedentary, more cooperative and egalitarian, more socially competent, and more supervised and structured by adults. Also, girls are more likely than boys to play with a small group of children or just one other child (Blakemore et al., 2009; Poulin & Chan, 2010). To take a closer look at play patterns of girls and boys, try Get Involved 4.1.

Gender Segregation

Around 2 years of age, children begin to prefer playing with children of the same gender (Leaper & Bigler, 2013; Mehta & Strough, 2010). Gender segregation increases during childhood and is especially strong in middle childhood (Hart et al., 2015). It is found across cultures and settings (Lancy, 2015). Even when children choose seats in the lunchroom or get into line, they frequently arrange themselves in same-gender groups. Peer pressure can be a powerful motivator, as illustrated in Barrie Thorne's (1993) observation of second graders seating themselves in the lunchroom. One table was

---

GET INVOLVED 4.1
Play Patterns of Girls and Boys

Observe preschool-aged children in a day-care center or preschool during a free-play session. Keep a record of the following behaviors:

1. The toys that girls choose and those that boys choose.

2. The activities girls engage in and those that boys engage in.

3. How often (a) girls play with other girls; (b) boys play with other boys; and (c) girls and boys play with each other.

WHAT DOES IT MEAN?

1. Did boys and girls show different patterns of toy choice and activity preference? If so, describe these patterns. How do you account for any differences you observed?

2. Which toys in general were most in demand? Were these "girl" toys, "boy" toys, or gender-neutral toys?

3. Did boys prefer to play with same-gender peers more than girls did, was it the other way around, or were there no differences? How do you account for any differences you observed?

Girls' play is quieter, more symbolic, and more socially competent than is boys' play.

filling with both boys and girls, when a high-status second-grade boy walked by. He commented loudly, "Too many girls," and headed for another table. The boys at the first table picked up their trays and moved, leaving no boys at the first table, which had now been declared taboo. Children who cross the "gender boundary" are unpopular with their peers, although there are certain conditions under which contact with the other gender is permissible. Often these overtures involve playful teasing, pushing, and grabbing (Pellegrini, 2001).

Why do children play primarily with children of their own gender? Girls may avoid boys because they don't like the rough, aggressive, dominant play style of boys and because boys are unresponsive to their polite suggestions. Analogously, boys may avoid girls because girls are not responsive to their rough play (Martin et al., 2013). An alternative view is that rather than actively trying to avoid children of the other gender, children expect to and actually do prefer the company of their own gender because they share a preference for gender-typed activities and enjoy being with others like themselves (Andrews et al., 2016; Leaper & Brown, 2014; Pahlke et al., 2014).

INFLUENCES ON GENDER DEVELOPMENT

Socialization refers to *the process by which each generation passes along to children the knowledge, beliefs, and skills that constitute the culture of the social group.* Because societies prescribe somewhat different social roles for adult females and males, girls and boys are typically socialized differently in order to prepare them for the adult roles they will play (Bornstein et al., 2016; Tenenbaum & May, 2013). This is a restatement of the third theme of our book, namely, that much of gender is socially constructed. A variety of sources help shape the behaviors and interests of boys and girls. These include parents, siblings, teachers, peers, and the media. In Chapter 3, we briefly mentioned the role of these influences when we discussed theories of gender typing. In this section, we examine these factors in greater detail.

Parents

When I was 4 or 5, my father asked me what I wanted to be when I grew up.

ME: *I'll be a carpenter and make furniture.*
HIM: *Oh, no, Holly, girls can't be carpenters. Only boys* can.
ME: *Okay, then I'll be a fisherman.*
HIM: *No, girls can't be fishermen either. They aren't strong enough.*

(Holly, a 50-year-old middle school teacher)

Children's gender-typed views about themselves and others are closely linked to the gender self-concepts and attitudes of their parents (Croft et al., 2014; Leaper & Farkas, 2011). How do parents transmit their views on gender to their children? One of the most obvious ways is by providing their sons and daughters with distinctive clothing, room furnishings, and toys. Infant girls are likely to be dressed in a ruffled pink outfit (sometimes with a bow attached to wisps of hair), whereas baby boys typically wear blue (Bussey, 2013; Pomerleau et al., 1990). The bedrooms of infant and toddler girls contain dolls, dollhouses, and domestic items and are decorated in pastel colors, frills, and flowery patterns. Baby boys' rooms feature animal themes, sturdy furniture, blue bedding, and a variety of sports equipment, vehicles, military toys, and educational materials (Bornstein et al., 2016; Leavell & Tamis-LeMonda, 2013). Clearly, infants are too young to express their preference in these matters.

Could it be that infant girls and boys give off subtle cues that influence their parents' gender-typed behavior? Research suggests that this is not the case. For example, in some studies, adults are asked to play with an unfamiliar infant who has a girl's name and is dressed in girls' clothing. Other adults play with an infant who wears boys' clothes and has a boy's name. (In fact, it is actually the same baby, who is dressed and named according to whether it is introduced as one gender or another.) Adults who believe the child is a boy are more likely to offer "him" a football or hammer and to encourage physical activity. Those who think the baby is a girl are more apt to offer a doll (Etaugh & Rathus, 1995; Stern & Karraker, 1989).

Although there are very few sex differences in the physical and behavioral characteristics of infant girls and boys, parents perceive their babies in gender-stereotyped ways as soon as they are born. Compared to girls, infant boys are viewed as less emotional, more competent, larger, stronger, and more athletic (Bornstein, 2013). Both mothers and fathers play more roughly with their little boys than with their little girls, and fathers, in particular, roughhouse with their young sons (Bornstein, 2013; Leavell et al., 2012).

Moreover, parents in virtually all cultures expect their young children to adhere to traditional gender roles and they react negatively to those who do not do so. As we saw in Chapter 3, this is especially true for boys (Leaper & Farkas, 2014; Yu & Xie, 2010). For example, parents and other adults are less likely to purchase cross-gender toys than to purchase gender-typical toys for children, even when children request the cross-gender toy (Etaugh & Liss, 1992; Inman & Cardella, 2015; Karraker & Hartley, 2007). Boys are even less likely than girls to receive such toys (Fisher-Thompson et al., 1995). Parents, especially fathers, also tend to offer gender-typical toys to children during free play and are more supportive when children engage in gender-typical activities than in cross-gender activities (Leaper & Bigler, 2013). It is no wonder that more than one of Claire's male students has confided in her that as a child he longed to play with his sister's Barbies, but would do so only when no one else was home. Given that fathers treat children in more gender-typical ways than mothers do, it is not surprising that children's gender-typical activity preferences are more closely linked to their fathers' gender-related attitudes than to their mothers' (McHale et al., 1999).

One way in which parents foster gender stereotypes in their children is through conversation. Susan Gelman and her colleagues (Gelman et al., 2004) videotaped mothers and their daughters or sons (ages 2, 4, or 6) discussing a picture book that focused on gender. Although mothers rarely expressed gender stereotypes directly, they emphasized gender concepts indirectly. For example, they provided gender labels (e.g., "That's a policeman"), contrasted males and females (e.g., "Is that a girl job or a boy job?"), and gave approval to their children's stereotyped statements (e.g., "Ballet dancers are girls!").

Parents also shape their children's environment by assigning chores based on gender. In many cultures around the world, girls are more likely to be given domestic and child care tasks centered around the home, whereas boys typically are assigned outside chores such as yard work and taking out trash. In addition, girls are less likely to be paid than boys for doing their chores (Bornstein et al., 2016; Dotti Sani, 2016; Lancy, 2015; UNICEF, 2016b).

With the growing visibility and acceptability of individuals who do not conform to the gender binary, the experience of raising a gender nonconforming child has been receiving increased attention. For example, see Amy Ellis Nutt's book *Becoming Nicole: The Transformation of an American Family*. For a closer look at how parents raise gender-variant children, see Learn About the Research 4.2.

LEARN ABOUT THE RESEARCH 4.2
Raising a Gender Nonconforming Child

With the growing visibility and acceptability of individuals who do not conform to the gender binary, the experience of raising a gender nonconforming child has been receiving increased attention. For one example, see Amy Ellis Nutt's 2015 book *Becoming Nicole: The Transformation of an American Family*. Elizabeth Rahilly (2015) examined the strategies of 16 sets of mostly White middle-class parents who are raising gender-variant children, two-thirds of whom had been assigned as males at birth. She identified three critical practices used by these parents to accommodate their children's nonconformity: "gender hedging," "gender literacy," and "playing along." "Gender hedging" often was an early effort to curb the child's nonconformity while permitting small concessions (e.g., "A pink shirt is okay but not a dress."). "Gender literacy" involved finding an advocacy community that affirmed the child's nonconformity, and then sharing with the child a less binary view of gender. This included preparing children for bias (e.g., "Some people will be mean 'cause they don't understand boys can wear girly clothes.") and coaching their children on ways to explain their nonconformity to peers (e.g., "He tells them he's a boy who likes feminine things."). "Playing along" involved parents' honoring their children's request to not correct a stranger's misidentifying a child, as when someone in a store referred to a boy in girls' clothes as a "lovely little girl."

WHAT DOES IT MEAN?

1. Which of the three practices used by the parents do you think is most helpful in raising a gender nonconforming child? Why?

2. Can you think of other practices that could be employed?

Parents treat daughters and sons differently in other ways than encouraging activities or assigning chores. For example, mothers talk more to their daughters than to their sons as early as 6 months of age (Clearfield & Nelson, 2006). They also use warmer, more supportive speech with daughters than with sons (Gleason & Ely, 2002). Earlier, we saw that mothers also talk more about emotions with their daughters. Even in early childhood, mothers talk more to girls about relationships, the workings of reproductive bodies, and moral issues involving sexuality (Martin & Luke, 2010). Parents also emphasize prosocial behaviors and politeness more with their daughters than their sons (Butler, 2014), and act more warmly toward their daughters and discipline their sons more harshly (Bornstein et al., 2016). Furthermore, cross-cultural research in Argentina, Italy, and the United States shows that mothers are more emotionally involved with their toddler daughters than with their toddler sons, and that the daughters, in turn, are more responsive than the sons (Bornstein et al., 2008; Lovas, 2005).

In addition, parents control their daughters more than their sons, while granting their sons greater autonomy and greater opportunities to take risks (Butler, 2014; Leaper, 2013; Morrongiello & Hogg, 2004). For example, parents are more likely to make decisions for girls and to give them help even if it is not requested. Boys, on the other hand, are encouraged to make their own decisions and to solve problems on their own (Blakemore et al., 2009). Moreover, parents expect more risky behaviors from sons than from daughters, are more likely to tell daughters to be careful, and intervene less frequently to stop boys' injury-risk behavior in play settings (Morrongiello & Hogg, 2004; O'Neal et al., 2016).

Parents also respond differently to the emotions expressed by girls and boys. Starting in infancy, they are more likely to control the emotions of their sons. We have seen that parents talk more about emotions to daughters. They are also more tolerant of expressions of fear and sadness in their daughters, whereas they are more permissive of anger in their sons (Bornstein, 2013).

Parents not only directly instruct their children about gendered behaviors, but they also serve as role models of these behaviors (Blakemore et al., 2009; Tenenbaum & May, 2013). Take the case of maternal employment. More mothers work outside the home today than ever before.

Isabel or Isaac? Adults are more likely to offer a doll to "Isabel" and a football to "Isaac." (In fact, both babies are Claire's granddaughter, Isabel.)

Also, although to a lesser degree, more fathers are participating in child care and household chores (see Chapter 11). Not surprisingly, researchers have found that maternal employment is associated with less stereotyped gender-related concepts and preferences in their children (Davis & Greenstein, 2009; Schuette & Killen, 2009). Children also show less stereotyping in their activity preferences if their fathers are highly involved in sharing child care and housework and if their mothers frequently engage in traditional "masculine" household tasks such as washing the car and doing yard work (Etaugh & O'Brien, 2003; Murray & Steil, 2000).

Children growing up in single-parent homes tend to be less traditional in their gender stereotypes and activities than those from two-parent homes (Leaper, 2000). One reason for this is that a single parent engages in activities normally carried out by both parents, such as housework, child care, home repairs, and going to work. In addition, the absent parent is most often the father, who usually encourages children's adherence to gender norms more strongly than the mother does (Kane, 2006).

Siblings

The role of siblings in gender role socialization has received less attention than that of parents and peers. Yet siblings are the most frequent out-of-school companions for children through middle childhood (Dunn, 2014). Not surprisingly, siblings make significant positive contributions to each other's development (Farkas & Leaper, 2014; Leavell & Tamis-LeMonda, 2013). Consistent with social-learning predictions about the importance of role models (see Chapter 3), older siblings appear to play a role in the gender socialization of their younger siblings. For example, a recent meta-analyis (Farkas & Leaper, 2014) found that girls and boys with older brothers were more masculine gender-typed than children with older sisters.

School

Schools convey powerful messages to children about gender typing. For one thing, the school social structure is biased. Women hold most of the low-paying elementary school teaching positions, while men more often occupy the higher-paying high school teaching jobs. Additionally, men are more often in the leadership positions of principal and superintendent (Beane et al., 2014). This sends a clear signal that men hold more power than women, one of the themes of this book.

In the classroom, girls and boys are often treated unequally by their teachers (Beane et al., 2014). Teachers pay far less attention to girls than to boys across ethnicities and social classes (Butler, 2014; Leaper & Brown, 2014). This finding has been strikingly documented by Myra and David Sadker (1994; Sadker & Zittleman, 2009). The Sadkers found that teachers call on boys more often and give them more time to answer questions. Boys are more likely to be praised, corrected, helped, and criticized constructively, all of which promote student learning. Girls are more likely to receive a bland and ambiguous "okay" response. Black girls are the least likely to be given clear feedback. Teachers are more likely to accept calling out from boys, whereas girls are reprimanded for the same behavior. Boys are rewarded for being smart, but girls are rewarded for being neat, pretty, and compliant. In addition, teachers are likely to give girls the answer when they ask for help but tend to help boys use strategies to figure out the answer themselves (Kenschaft & Clark, 2016). Unfortunately, teachers are generally unaware that they are treating boys and girls differently. Later in the chapter, we will see how such unequal treatment may contribute to the declining self-esteem of adolescent girls.

African American girls may encounter unique educational perceptions and obstacles (Morris, 2016). One two-year study at a predominantly Black and Latina/o middle school found that Black girls performed well academically, but that teachers often questioned their manners and behavior. Many teachers perceived the Black girls as "loud and confrontational" and tried to mold them into displaying more "ladylike" behaviors, such as being quieter and more passive (Morris, 2007).

Peers

Children exert strong pressures on each other to engage in gender-appropriate behavior. As early as the preschool years, they modify their activity and toy preferences to conform to the patterns their peers reward. This seems especially true for boys who have many male friends (Ewing Lee & Troop-Gordon, 2011). The mere presence of other children inhibits gender-inappropriate play (Lott & Maluso, 2001). Children who show gender-typical behavior are accepted by their peers whereas acting in nonstereotypic ways can lead to peer victimization and social exclusion (Mulvey & Killen, 2015). Boys who display traditionally feminine activities are teased, rejected, and disliked by both boys and girls, whereas girls who engage in traditionally masculine activities generally are accepted by children of both sexes (Bussey, 2013; Leaper & Brown, 2014). Even the label given to boys who show cross-gender behavior—"sissy"—has negative overtones, whereas the term used for girls who display cross-gender behavior—"tomboy"—does not. It is thus not surprising that gender-atypical boys have more social adjustment problems than gender-atypical girls (Kreiger, 2005).

Media

We saw in Chapter 2 that females are underrepresented in the media and that females and males are portrayed in stereotyped ways. What is the impact of these media messages on children's gender-related learning? About 65 percent of young children (6 months to 8 years) watch television on a regular basis, 25 percent watch DVDs, 14 percent use a computer, 9 percent play console video games, and 8 percent use handheld game players, mobile phones, iPods, or iPads to access games, apps, and video (Calvert & Wartella, 2014). Children who are heavy television viewers have greater knowledge of gender stereotypes (Ward & Harrison, 2005). In these correlational studies, it is difficult to know the direction of influence. Television may cause children to develop stronger stereotypes. On the other hand, children with stronger stereotypes may choose to watch more television because it shows images that are consistent with their beliefs (Bussey, 2013). A third alternative is that both factors are involved.

Stronger evidence of the impact of television comes from experiments that examined whether television can undo or counter the stereotypic messages. Studies have found that exposure to characters who engage in nontraditional behaviors and roles (nurturing boys and girl auto mechanics, for example) reduces children's gender stereotypes about activities, domestic roles, and occupations (Ward & Harrison, 2005). In Chapter 5, we will look at the influence of gendered content in video games.

For a closer and more personal look at influences on gender role development, try the exercise in Get Involved 4.2.

Recently, some toymakers and major chain stores have cut back on marketing items only to girls or to boys and are promoting the concept of gender neutrality. To examine this trend in greater detail, see In the News 4.1.

GET INVOLVED 4.2
Influences on Gender Development

Describe your own gender socialization. Focus on specific things that were said, done, or modeled by (a) your parents and other family members; (b) your teachers; (c) your peers; and (d) television, books, and other media. Then ask two female friends and two male friends to do the same.

WHAT DOES IT MEAN?

Include your own responses when answering the following questions:

1. Did the females and the males you interviewed describe different kinds of socialization experiences? If so, what were they?

2. Identify aspects of your own socialization and that of your friends that are consistent with the material presented in the chapter.

3. When did you realize there were social expectations for your gender?

4. What happened in situations when you crossed gender lines?

5. How have your socialization experiences affected your current choices in activities, friends, major, career, and so on?

_____

Source: Based on Gilbert and Scher (1999).

IN THE NEWS 4.1
Blurred Lines: Gender Neutrality in Toys and Clothes

In 2015, Target and Amazon stopped labeling toys and other items as specifically for girls or boys. That same year, Disney Stores did away with "boy" and "girl" labels on Halloween costumes, backpacks, and other accessories. Mattel and DC Comics recently introduced DC Super Hero Girls, a line of comics, action figures, and videos (Tabuchi, 2015). What is going on here? Some see the trend as part of a wider movement to recognize a spectrum of gender identities, the culmination of the activism of parents, educators, and critics (Hains, 2014). Authors of recent popular parenting books have pushed for gender neutrality, pointing out research that shows the limiting effect on children of stereotyping toys, clothing, and costumes as appropriate for only one sex (Brown, 2014; Paoletti, 2013; Wardy, 2014). Not everyone favors the move toward gender neutrality, as you might imagine. What is your view on this issue?

PUBERTY

I think what is happening to me is so wonderful, and not only what can be seen on my body, but all that is taking place inside [. . .] Each time I have a period (and that has only been three times) I have the feeling that in spite of all the pain, discomfort, and mess, I have a sweet secret, and that is why, although it is nothing but a nuisance to me in a way, I always long for the time that I shall feel that secret within me again.

(Frank, 1995, pp. 158–159)

One of the most moving accounts of a young woman's entry into adolescence was written by Anne Frank, a Jewish girl who lived in Nazi-occupied Holland during World War II. Anne kept a diary during the two years she and her family hid from the Nazis in an attic. Anne wrote about her sudden physical growth, commenting on the shoes that no longer fit her and the undershirts that became "so small that they don't even cover my stomach" (Frank, 1995, p. 101). She also grew concerned about her appearance and asked her sister "if she thought I was very ugly" (p. 55). A few months before she and her family were discovered and sent to die in a concentration camp, Anne wrote the above entry about the "wonders that are happening to [my] body."

In this section, we will explore the physical transformations of adolescence. First we describe the events of puberty. We then discuss gender differences in these events. Finally, we examine individual differences in rates of physical maturation.

Events of Puberty

Puberty is the *period of life during which sexual organs mature and the ability to reproduce emerges.* Increasing levels of sex hormones stimulate the development of primary and secondary sex characteristics. **Primary sex characteristics**—in girls, the ovaries, fallopian tubes, uterus, and vagina—*are structures that make reproduction possible.* **Secondary sex characteristics** are *visible signs of sexual maturity that are not directly involved in reproduction,* such as breast development and the appearance of pubic and underarm hair (Donatelle, 2017; Rathus et al., 2013.

Most White girls begin to show the first signs of puberty (the budding of breasts) by the age of 10, and Black girls do so about a year earlier (Butts & Seifer, 2010). Other studies confirm that feelings of sexual attraction, one of the behavioral hallmarks of puberty, also first appear between the ages of 9 and 10 (Marano, 1997). However, some research shows that many girls start puberty far earlier than previously thought. For example, by the age of 8, more than 18 percent of White girls, 31 percent of Latina girls and 43 percent of Black girls have some breast development (Greenspan & Deardorff, 2014).

Menarche

Menarche, *the first menstrual period*, is a dramatic and meaningful event in women's lives, symbolizing the end of childhood and the start of adulthood. Many women have vivid memories of their first menstrual period and, even years later, can describe details of the experience. (If you, the reader, are female, can you?)

The average age of menarche in the United States is about 12.2 years for Black and Latina girls and 12.8 years for White girls, although it is quite normal for a girl to begin to menstruate any time between 8 and 17 (Butts & Seifer, 2010; Stubbs & Johnston-Robledo, 2013). *Over the past 150 years, the onset of puberty and the attainment of adult height and weight have occurred at progressively earlier ages in the United States and western Europe* (Villamor & Jansen, 2016). This **secular trend** is most likely a result of better nutrition and medical care. The onset of puberty seems to be triggered when individuals reach a certain body weight. Improved nutrition, health, and living conditions have led to the achievement of that weight at a younger age (Barnack-Tavlaris, 2015). The rise in obesity among American children may play a role as well, because girls with a high percentage of body fat in early childhood show earlier onset of puberty (Villamor & Jansen, 2016). Another more controversial hypothesis is that early puberty is triggered by consuming environmental chemicals (such as growth hormones in livestock) that mimic the effects of estrogen (Greenspan & Deardorff, 2014).

Environmental stress is also linked to an earlier onset of puberty. For example, girls exposed to childhood stress (e.g., father absence, harsh parenting, physical or sexual abuse) begin to menstruate earlier than other girls (Sung et al., 2016). One explanation for these findings is that stress may lead to overeating, which increases body weight, which then triggers the onset of puberty. Can you think of alternative explanations?

In many countries around the world, girls report mostly negative feelings about menarche (Bobel, 2010). In North America, girls have mixed feelings about the event with Black and Latina girls reporting more negative attitudes than White girls (Chrisler, 2008). On the one hand, menstruation is an eagerly awaited sign of growing up (Jackson & Falmagne, 2013; Stubbs & Johnston-Robledo, 2013; Newton, 2016). In the words of one adolescent girl, "It's a great feeling knowing that one day when you want to have a baby, that you can do it. To me that's just amazing" (Commonwealth Fund, 1997, p. 39). Still, some girls also believe that menstruation is embarrassing, frightening, or disgusting and worry about having an "accident" (Jackson & Falmagne, 2013; Natsuaki et al., 2014). "I was terribly worried about staining"; "It was gross. I felt very dirty" (Lee, 2008, pp. 615, 620).

Feminine hygiene advertisements reflect and reinforce these concerns by focusing on the discomfort and messiness of menstrual periods and the potential embarrassment of "showing" (Johnston-Robledo & Chrisler, 2013). Women are taught to conceal the fact that they are menstruating. Even within the family household, menstruation is often a sensitive topic that is not openly discussed (Johnston-Robledo & Chrisler, 2013). One of Claire's students shared the following experience: "When I started my period, I didn't tell a soul. I wrote down 'pads' on my parents' grocery list and they showed up in the bathroom closet. That was the extent of the 'birds and bees' talk in my family." Cultural pressure to hide menstrual cycles and marketing pitches for products that keep a woman clean and deodorized during her menstrual cycles send a clear message to women that their bodies are unacceptable in their natural state (Fahs, 2016). Moreover, with the recent availability of contraceptives that eliminate menstrual periods, ads for these drugs emphasize the debilitating effects of periods and the joys of menstrual suppression (Barnack-Tavlaris, 2015). Not surprisingly women who place a great deal of emphasis on their appearance and body image have more negative attitudes and emotions, including disgust and shame, toward their menstrual cycles.

A negative attitude toward menstruation before menarche is associated with greater menstrual discomfort (Barnack-Tavlaris, 2015). For example, girls whose mothers lead them to believe that menstruation will be uncomfortable or unpleasant later report more severe menstrual symptoms. Moreover, girls who begin to menstruate earlier than their peers, or who are otherwise unprepared and uninformed about pubertal changes, find menarche especially distressing (American Psychological

Association, 2002; Reid et al., 2008). Those with more supportive, helpful mothers and good preparation, on the other hand, hold more positive attitudes and are more satisfied with their bodies (Stubbs & Johnston-Robledo, 2013). When 14- and 15-year-old girls were asked what advice they would give to younger girls about menarche, they recommended emphasizing the normalcy of menstruation, providing practical information on handling menstrual periods, and discussing what menarche actually feels like (American Psychological Association, 2002). Today's mothers seem to be following this advice. In one study (Lee, 2008), for example, most college women recalled mothers who were supportive and helpful when they started menstruating. This finding may reflect the increasing openness in society about menstruation as well as the attitudes of a generation of mothers who have grown up with feminism (Lee, 2008).

Gender Differences in Puberty

Besides the obvious differences in secondary sex characteristics, girls and boys differ in other ways as they move through puberty. For one thing, girls begin and finish puberty about two years before boys, on average (Hollenstein & Lougheed, 2013). The **adolescent growth spurt**, *a rapid increase in height and weight*, also starts earlier in girls, at about age 9, whereas boys start their spurt at about age 11. The period of peak growth occurs at age 12 for girls and 14 for boys, on average, and then tapers off for two years or so. Boys grow more than girls during their spurt, adding an average of 12 inches to their height, whereas girls grow slightly over 11 inches. Boys also gain more weight than girls do during their growth spurt (Susman & Rogol, 2004).

Body shape changes in puberty as well. Girls gain twice as much fatty tissue as boys, largely in the breasts, hips, and buttocks, whereas boys gain almost twice as much muscle tissue as girls (DeRose & Brooks-Gunn, 2006). These changes produce the more rounded shape of women as compared to men. As the growth spurt begins to slow down, adolescents reach sexual maturity. In girls, the most obvious sign is menarche. We shall discuss other aspects of menstruation in Chapter 7.

Early and Late Maturation in Girls

> *I remember when I got my first period. It was the summer between fourth and fifth grades—I guess I was 10 . . . By sixth and seventh grades, I had this intense desire to hang out with older kids, usually older boys. I tried pot for the first time when I was 12. I could usually convince people I was 15 when I was in seventh grade and I started hanging out with other girls who looked older . . . Sometimes we would go off with older boys. Often we were drinking or smoking pot . . . Overall, I was pretty unhappy during the teen years; at times, I guess, depressed. I had a hard time fitting in at school even though I got good grades. I was always looking for a group where I belonged. It wasn't until college that I really found my niche.*
>
> (Graber & Brooks-Gunn, 2002, p. 35)

The timing of the events of puberty vary considerably from one girl to another (Greenspan & Deardorff, 2014), as shown in Table 4.3. Early-maturing girls may feel awkward and self-conscious because they begin the physical changes of puberty earlier than their peers. Boys may tease them about their height and developing breasts, which can lead to feelings of body shame and depression (Allison & Hyde, 2013; Skoog et al., 2015). In addition, because they look older than they actually are, others may place sexual and other expectations on them that are difficult to meet. No wonder that early maturers tend to have lower self-esteem, higher levels of depression and anxiety, and a poorer body image than girls who mature later (Graber, 2013; Mendle et al., 2016; Skoog & Stattin, 2014).

Early-maturing girls tend to associate with older peers. This may explain why they begin sexual activity at an earlier age and are more likely to engage in risky behavior such as smoking, drinking, substance abuse, and delinquent behavior (Beltz et al., 2014; Mendle, 2014; Moore et al., 2014). But not all early-maturing girls suffer negative consequences and for most, these behaviors do not last (Compitello, 2017). Those early maturers who have supportive parents and relatively few stressors in their lives are less apt to show problem behaviors (Skoog & Stattin, 2014).

Once early-maturing girls reach high school, they come into their own socially. They may serve as advisors to their late-maturing girlfriends on such increasingly important topics as makeup, dating, and sex. By late adolescence, early-maturing girls seem to be as well adjusted as other girls (Lien et al., 2010). By age 30, they appear to be more self-possessed and self-directed than their late-maturing peers. Perhaps learning to cope with the stresses of puberty at an early age prepares early-maturing girls to deal effectively with later stressful events (Weichold et al., 2003).

Late-maturing girls may have relatively low social status during the middle school and junior high school years. They look and are treated like "little girls" and are often excluded from boy–girl social activities. Late-maturing girls often are dissatisfied with their appearance and lack of popularity. By tenth grade, however, they are noticeably showing the physical signs of puberty. They often wind up more popular and more satisfied with their appearance than early-maturing girls. One reason for this may be that late maturers are more likely to develop the culturally valued slender body shape than early maturers, who tend to be somewhat heavier (Simmons & Blyth, 1987).

PSYCHOSOCIAL DEVELOPMENT IN ADOLESCENCE

How much do I like the kind of person I am? Well, I like some things about me, but I don't like others. I'm glad that I'm popular since it's really important to me to have friends. But in school I don't do as well as the really smart kids. That's OK, because if you're too smart you'll lose your friends. So being smart is just not that important. But what's really important to me is how I look. If I like the way I look, then I really like the kind of person I am. I've also changed. It started when I went to junior high school. I got really depressed. There was this one day when I hated the way I looked, and I didn't get invited to this really important party, and then I got an awful report card, so for a couple of days I thought it would be best to just end it all. I was letting my parents down, I wasn't good-looking anymore, and I wasn't that popular and things were never going to get better. I talked to Sheryl, my best friend, and that helped some.

(adapted from Harter, 1990, pp. 364–365)

This self-description from a 15-year-old girl illustrates some of the psychological characteristics of adolescent females. Notice how important physical appearance is to her self-esteem. Note also that she discloses her private thoughts to her best friend. Can you recall what was important to you at age 15?

Adolescence is a time of learning more about oneself and others. Two key issues are developing a sense of who you are and how you feel about yourself. Adherence to traditional gender roles often becomes stronger and girls begin to focus a great deal on their appearance. In this section, we explore four aspects of psychosocial development in the adolescent girl: identity formation, self-esteem, gender intensification, and body image.

Identity Formation

One of the most important tasks of adolescence is to develop a sense of **identity**, that is, *deciding who we are and what we want to make of our lives*. According to Erik Erikson (1968, 1980), adolescent identity formation involves commitment to a vocation and a philosophy of life. In order to do so, adolescents must **individuate**, that is, *see themselves as separate and unique*. Carol Gilligan (1982), Sally Archer (1992), Ruthellen Josselson (1996), and others maintain that this model describes the traditional identity development of males better than that of females. They believe that achieving identity for both female and male adolescents requires an interplay between separateness (meeting one's own needs) and connectedness (satisfying the needs of those one cares for) (Årseth et al., 2009).

Research supports the view that adolescent and young adult females and males take similar paths in their quest for identity (Beyers & Seiffge-Krenke, 2010; Carlsson et al., 2015). Elements of career choice, personal competence, and interpersonal relationships are central to the identity of both genders (Aronson, 2008; Giesbrecht, 1998). For one thing, adolescent girls' educational and career aspirations have increased in recent years and now parallel those of boys (Kleinfeld, 2009). In addition, an increasing number of teenagers (83 percent of females and 72 percent of males) say that having a good marriage and family life is extremely important to them as a life goal (Popenoe &

Whitehead, 1999). However, whereas most adolescent girls see interconnections between their career goals and family goals, most adolescent boys perceive no connection between the two. For example, young women place greater emphasis than young men do on flexible working hours that facilitate the coordination of employment and childrearing (see Chapter 11). Still, it appears that, nowadays, individual differences in identity development may be more important than gender differences (Klimstra et al., 2010; Waterman, 1999).

Studies conducted on the identity formation of ethnic minority adolescent girls have found that one key factor in this process is the family unit, often an extended kinship network, which is a highly valued part of life among Asian Americans, Blacks, Latinas/os, and Native Americans. Identity with the family and community seems to provide strength and resources for adolescent girls of color as they strive to integrate their ethnicity and their femaleness within a larger society that devalues both (Rhodes et al., 2007; Vasquez & de las Fuentes, 1999).

Self-Esteem

The two really blonde girls in our class dressed better than the rest of the girls, and I always felt like I couldn't compete with them. This feeling carried on throughout high school. Even though I felt like I was smarter than the boys, I didn't feel better because I didn't look nice enough to impress them. Basically, I grew up not really caring for boys and thinking that they were stupid, but that it was important to impress them by looking nice. I was so confused. I felt superior, but not. And I felt anxious around both males and females, but probably more anxious around males.

(Jamie, a 25-year-old college senior)

Self-esteem is *the sense of worth or value that people attach to themselves.* High self-esteem has long been associated with healthy psychological adjustment and good physical health (Zuckerman et al., 2016). Beginning in early adolescence, self-esteem diminishes for both genders, with girls showing lower self-esteem than boys. Two meta-analyses of over 1.1 million respondents (Kling et al., 1999; Zuckerman et al., 2016) shows that this gender gap becomes greatest in late adolescence, with a small-to-moderate effect size of 0.33 (see Chapter 1). This gender difference continues throughout adulthood, narrowing only in old age. Black girls have higher self-esteem than White, Latina, and Asian American girls during late adolescence (Erkut & García Coll, 2013; Hyde, 2014; Ridolfo et al., 2013). Compared to White adolescent girls, Black girls have more confidence in their physical attractiveness, sports ability, femininity, popularity, and social relations (Malanchuk & Eccles, 2006).

What causes girls' self-esteem to decline in adolescence and why do Black girls remain more self-confident than others? For one thing, focusing on one's physical appearance is closely linked to self-esteem (Bucchianeri et al., 2016; Impett et al., 2011). Girls are more dissatisfied with their appearance than boys, a difference that increases during adolescence (Evans et al., 2013). But Black girls, as we shall see, are less concerned about body shape and size than White girls, and physical appearance is less important to their sense of self-worth (Boroughs et al., 2010; Bucchianeri et al., 2016). Upon entering adolescence, for example, the self-esteem of obese Latina and White girls drops more than that of nonobese girls, but obese Black girls do not show this decline (Strauss, 2000).

In addition, we saw earlier in this chapter that schools shortchange girls in ways that undermine girls' perceptions of their competence and importance (Sadker & Zittleman, 2009). Black girls, however, seem less dependent on school achievement for their self-esteem. In fact, they are less accepted by their peers than are White girls when they do well in school (Fuller-Rowell & Doan, 2010). Black girls' view of themselves is more influenced by their community, family, and sense of ethnic identity (Abrams et al., 2016; Thomas et al., 2011). Black females are socialized early in life by their mothers and other female relatives and mentors to be strong, independent women who can cope with a society in which racism, sexism, and classism can be barriers to the development of a positive identity (Abrams et al., 2016; Comas-Diaz, 2013a; Ridolfo et al., 2013; Robinson-Woods, 2017).

Several theorists, including Carol Gilligan (2002) and scholars at the Stone Center (e.g., Jordan, 1997), maintain that as girls make the transition to adolescence, they become aware of growing up in a patriarchal society that devalues women and views the desirable stereotype of the "good woman" as being nice, pleasing to others, and unassertive. This places girls in conflict with their view of themselves as self-sufficient, independent, and outspoken. Many girls respond to this conflict by losing confidence in themselves and by suppressing their thoughts, opinions, and feelings, that is, by "losing their voice."

However, research by Susan Harter and her colleagues (Harter, 1998, 1999) found that adolescent boys and girls did not differ with respect to the loss of voice. About a third of young people of both genders said they disguised their true feelings and thoughts in dealing with certain categories of individuals, but a large majority of these females and males did not report doing so. Harter and her colleagues found that *gender role identity*, not gender itself, predicted the level of voice, a finding since confirmed by other researchers (e.g., Smolak & Munstertieger, 2002). Masculine and androgynous adolescents of both genders reported higher levels of voice and higher self-esteem than those with a feminine orientation. Although the feminine girls in Harter's study reported loss of voice in public contexts, such as school and group social situations, this did not occur with parents or close friends. Support, approval, and acceptance from parents and teachers appear critical to the development of high self-esteem and to the expression of one's thoughts and feelings (Harter, 1998).

See What You Can Do 4.1 to help girls "raise their voice" by empowering them to lead social change.

Gender Intensification

All through grade school, I had been very active in sports. Basketball was my favorite and I was really good at it. Basketball gave me self-esteem. When I was 13, I set my life's goal—to one day coach the Boston Celtics. I will never forget the reactions I got when I told people this. Everyone—my friends, my parents' friends, other adults—all said the same thing: A girl could never coach a professional men's team. Until then, it hadn't occurred to me that gender mattered. I just thought you needed talent and desire, which I had. I was totally heartbroken. Then I began to question whether women were as good as men in basketball. If not, why was I playing? I didn't ever again want people to tell me I couldn't do something because I was a girl. So I quit basketball and became a cheerleader. I didn't really want to, but I felt people wouldn't like me unless I became a "complete and total girl."

(Liz, a 21-year-old college senior)

Gender differences in value orientation become pronounced at the onset of adolescence. For example, a study by Kimberly Badger and her colleagues (1998) of geographically diverse American adolescents found that as early as sixth grade, girls were more likely than boys to place a high value on (1) compromising; (2) being kind and forgiving; (3) expressing feelings; (4) wanting to know what people are like inside; (5) enjoying people; (6) getting along with others; and (7) having friends, cooperating, and helping. In addition, early adolescent girls, compared to boys, are more agreeable, open, and conscientious (Klimstra et al., 2009). Early adolescence is also marked by an increase in the rigidity of gender-role stereotypes, although girls continue to remain more flexible than their male peers (Bartini, 2006; Basow, 2010b). This *increasing divergence in gender-related behaviors and attitudes of girls and boys that emerges in early adolescence* is known as **gender intensification**

WHAT YOU CAN DO 4.1
Empowering Girls to Lead Social Change

Girls for a Change (GFC; girlsforachange.org) is a national organization that empowers teen girls to create and lead social change by providing role models and leadership training. Become a volunteer or start a GFC team in your community.

(Priess & Lindberg, 2011). At this age, perceiving oneself to be a typical member of one's same-sex peer group is important to a sense of psychological well-being (Heinze & Horn, 2014).

Several factors contribute to the development of gender intensification. For one thing, the physical changes of puberty accentuate gender differences in appearance. Peers, parents, and other adults, especially those with traditional views of gender, apply increasing pressure on girls to display "feminine" behaviors (Carr, 2007; Raffaelli & Ontai, 2004), as illustrated poignantly by Liz's experience. This magnification of traditional gender expectations is stronger for girls than for boys, probably because girls have been given more latitude than boys have to display cross-gender behaviors in middle childhood (Crockett, 1991). In addition, when adolescents begin to date and enter romantic relationships, they may increase their gender-stereotypical behavior in order to enhance their appeal to the other gender. For example, girls become intensely interested in appearing physically attractive to boys and spend long hours focusing on their clothes, hairstyles, complexions, and weight (Hilbrecht et al., 2008). Furthermore, cognitive changes make adolescents more aware of gender expectations and more concerned about what others think of them (Crockett, 1991). The resulting adherence to a traditional construction of gender seems at least partly responsible for the gender differences in self-esteem, friendship patterns, dating behaviors, and cognitive skills that we discuss in this chapter and in Chapters 5 and 8.

Gender intensification starts to decrease by middle to late adolescence. Gender-related occupational stereotypes (see earlier in this chapter) become more flexible, and sexist attitudes (see Chapter 2) become less pronounced. Also, the understanding that gender-related traits, behaviors, and roles are culturally created and modifiable increases (Crockett, 1991).

Body Image

I was always heavier than other females my age, but was very healthy and athletic as a child and into high school. I played basketball, soccer, tennis, and softball. My weight was never an issue for me until I reached adolescence. I suddenly became very conscious of my weight. Boys in my class would make comments. It took me several years before I could become comfortable with my weight and grow to like my body.

(Becky, a 22-year-old senior)

The weight gain associated with puberty occurs within a cultural context that emphasizes a female beauty ideal of extreme thinness (Tiggemann et al., 2013). According to some feminist theorists (Murnen & Smolak, 2013; Rice, 2014), girls and women in Western culture internalize the masculine view of the body as a sexualized object to be looked at and evaluated, a process termed *self-objectification* (Heflick & Goldenberg, 2014). As girls internalize the "thin ideal" body image of Western society, which is unattainable for most women, they become intensely dissatisfied with their weight and shape (Karazsia et al., 2013). This is especially true for girls and women who conform strongly to traditional gender ideals (Calzo et al., 2016). Girls as young as age 3 already favor a thin body ideal (Harriger et al., 2010) and attribute more positive traits to a thin figure than a fat one (Spiel et al., 2012; Worobey & Worobey, 2014). Girls' body image starts to decrease in the early grade-school years, and substantial numbers of preteen girls show body dissatisfaction (Evans et al., 2013; Wertheim et al., 2009). By adolescence, girls are much more concerned with body weight and appearance than are males of the same age. They have a less positive body image, are less satisfied with their weight, and are more likely to be dieting and using laxatives (Dye, 2016; Calzo et al., 2016; Evans et al., 2013; Ingolfsdottir et al., 2014; Reilly et al., 2014; Strauss et al., 2015). American adolescent girls and women often view themselves as too heavy even at average weight levels, and many of them have a negative view of their overall appearance (Perrin et al., 2009). Body image concerns and disordered eating behaviors have been documented in females around the world. For example, a survey in Great Britain found that only 8 percent of the teenage girls responding were happy with their bodies. Even though 58 percent said they were of normal weight, two-thirds of the entire sample thought they needed to lose weight (Barton, 2005). Similarly, German teens described themselves as being too fat (Parker-Pope, 2008).

The importance of body image to adolescent females is indicated by the close association between teenage girls' body image and their self-esteem (Zeigler-Hill & Noser, 2015). The more negative their body image, the lower their self-esteem. For adolescent boys, however, evidence for a relationship is mixed (Dohnt & Tiggemann, 2006; Ricciardelli et al., 2009; Quick et al., 2013). Being overweight is associated with having a poorer self-image and greater body image dissatisfaction in girls as young as age 6 (Marks et al., 2015; Muhlig et al., 2015).

While body dissatisfaction among girls and women around the world has increased sharply over the last 50 or so years (Gerbasi et al., 2014), men's body image has remained relatively stable over time (Cash et al., 2004). What might account for this difference? The ideal American male body is muscular and powerful, but requires much less "body work" than the ideal American female body, which not only is slim and fit, but also "flawless" (i.e., no hairs, pores, or body odors), requiring nearly constant monitoring and managing (Spade & Valentine, 2016). We will discuss the unhealthy weight control behaviors known as eating disorders in Chapter 13.

A major factor contributing to the increase in poor body image is the increasing emphasis in Western culture on thinness as the ideal female body shape (Grogan, 2017; Record & Austin, 2015; Rohde et al., 2015). Studies of *Playboy* centerfolds, fashion models, and even cartoon characters have found that the average size and shape of the idealized woman has become thinner and more boyish over the last several decades (Kenschaft & Clark, 2016). Fifty years ago, the average *Playboy* centerfold model or Miss America had a body-mass index (BMI) that was 10 percent less than the average woman's, but today's have a BMI of 31 percent less and are dangerously underweight (Record & Austin, 2015). Magazines designed for women or girls are far more likely than magazines aimed at men or boys to focus on becoming slim, trim, and beautiful through diet, exercise, and cosmetic surgery (APA Task Force, 2007). So powerful is the cultural emphasis on slenderness in adolescent girls and young women that simply reading about or viewing media images of physically attractive women with idealized physiques is associated with diminished body image satisfaction, lower self-esteem, increased anger, anxiety, depressed mood, eating disorder symptoms, and approval of surgical body alteration (Fardouly et al., 2015; Hausenblas et al., 2013; Kaminski & Magee, 2013; Mischner et al., 2013; Pritchard & Cramblitt, 2014). Even girls as young as age 5 experience heightened body dissatisfaction after exposure to Barbie doll images (Jellinek et al., 2016). In addition, adolescent girls who read beauty and fashion magazines and articles about dieting are more likely to use unhealthy dieting methods (Utter et al., 2003; Van den Berg et al., 2007). In the words of one adolescent girl:

> There's such pressure. I look at movie stars and I'm like, "Oh, my God. She's so pretty. She's so thin. I want to look like that." I'm not a small person. I am never going to be like a size 2. I should be happy with what I am and just accept that. But inside I'm freaking out because I can't eat.

> (Commonwealth Fund, 1997, p. 67)

Recent research shows that exposure to teen magazines and television is related to body image concerns among so-called "tweenage" girls between ages 10 and 12 (Tiggemann & Slater, 2014b). But girls and young women are affected not only by these traditional media. Nowadays, they are spending more time on social networking sites (Fardouly & Vartanian, 2016; Perloff, 2014). Time spent on social media, such as Facebook, is at least as strongly related to body image and dieting behavior as exposure to either televised or print media (Holland & Tiggemann, 2016; Suchert et al., 2016).

Pressure from family and friends to be thin and to look good also can undermine girls' body images (Abraczinskas et al., 2012; Andrews et al., 2016; Hart et al., 2015; Wasylkiw & Williamson,

2013). Overweight teenagers are more likely than normal-weight children to be physically bullied by their peers, teased, or excluded from social activities (Fikkan & Rothblum, 2012; Kasardo & McHugh, 2015). Furthermore, girls whose peers tease them about their weight and pressure them to lose weight have more body dissatisfaction, engage in more disordered eating behaviors, and are more likely to become depressed (Forney et al., 2012; Mustillo, 2013). Even simply having conversations with peers about weight, shape, and size (known as "fat talk") lowers body satisfaction in girls (Compeau & Ambwani, 2013; Mills & Fuller-Tyszkewicz, 2016; Owen & Spencer, 2013; Sharpe et al., 2013). In addition, exposure to other girls of similar weight who are dieting increases dieting behavior in adolescent girls (Robert-McComb & Massey-Stokes, 2014). Within the family, parents (especially mothers) exert considerable influence on the body image of girls (Hart et al., 2015; Tatangelo et al., 2016; Thogersen-Ntoumani et al., 2016). Mothers are much more likely to identify and talk about weight as a problem with daughters than with sons (Berge et al., 2016). Teasing—especially by girls' fathers and brothers—is also a powerful influence on those who feel bad about their bodies (Eisenberg et al., 2003). Marla Eisenberg and her colleagues (2003) found that adolescents who were teased by family members or peers about their weight were more likely than other teenagers to be depressed and to think about or attempt suicide.

In their search for the "perfect look," more girls and young women are desiring and undergoing cosmetic surgery (Margraf et al., 2015). Girls are increasingly choosing breast augmentation, tummy tucks, liposuction, and even cosmetic genital surgery (American Society of Plastic Surgeons, 2015; Rabin, 2016). Preteen girls get manicures, pedicures, and facials, and use lipstick and nail polish (Murnen & Smolak, 2013; Tiggemann & Slater, 2014a; Turkewitz, 2015a).

Sexualization pervades a variety of products marketed to and worn by girls (Baker et al., 2016; Goodin et al., 2011). Items include push-up bras, string bikinis, revealing shorts, and low-cut tops. The Bratz and Monster High dolls that are highly popular among 8- to 11-year-old girls are even more sexualized in appearance than Barbie (Graff et al., 2012). Sexualization sends the message that one's value comes primarily from sexual appeal or behavior. Girls who have internalized this view have greater body shame and get lower grades in school (Baker et al., 2016). Can you think of ways to combat the sexualization of girls?

Black women, especially those with a strong cultural identity, are more satisfied with their bodies and are less concerned about weight loss and dieting than are White, Latina and Asian females (Capodilupo & Forsyth, 2014; deGuzman & Nishina, 2014; Dye, 2016; Quick et al., 2013; Watson et al., 2013). Standards of beauty and attractiveness in Black culture place less emphasis on thinness than in White culture (Chithambo & Huey, 2013; van Amsterdam, 2013). However, even though females of color may be more satisfied with their bodies than their White counterparts, they still have more body dissatisfaction and are more likely than males of color to be dieting (Dohm et al., 2010). Moreover, cosmetic surgery is gaining in popularity among Black, Latina, and Asian women. Both body dissatisfaction and eating disorders have been reported among Asian, Black, Latina, and Native American girls and women, and among the urban poor as well as the suburban middle class (Forbes & Frederick, 2008; Jennings et al., 2015; Kashubeck-West & Huang, 2013; Regan & Cachelin, 2006; Warren et al., 2010). The more that American ethnic minority women and non-Western women adopt the values of mainstream U.S. society, the more they may suffer from body dissatisfaction and eating disorders (Dohm et al., 2010; Swim et al., 2010a). Try Get Involved 4.3 for a closer look at the body images of Black and White women.

Lesbians are less preoccupied with weight and dieting and have higher levels of body self-esteem than heterosexual women and gay men, but they have still more weight concerns than heterosexual men (Alvy, 2013; Davids & Green, 2011; Engeln-Maddox et al., 2011; Wrench & Knapp, 2008). Why are lesbians more comfortable with their bodies? One explanation is that lesbian subculture may not be interested in the "male gaze" and therefore downplays or is more critical of the dominant cultural value placed on beauty for women (DeLamater & Koepsel, 2015; Hanley & McLaren, 2015; Jones & Malson, 2013; Markey & Markey, 2014; Watson et al., 2015).

GET INVOLVED 4.3
Perceptions of Actual and Desirable Physique

For this exercise, survey four young adult females, two Black and two White. Show each woman the following nine figure drawings and ask her the following questions:

1. Using the numbers under the figures, which represents your perception of *your current body?*

2. Which represents your perception of *your ideal body?*

3. Which is the body you feel *men find the most attractive?*

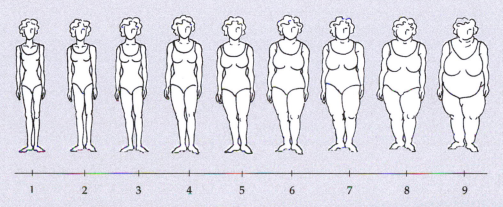

WHAT DOES IT MEAN?

1. How did the women's perceptions of their current body compare with their perception of their ideal body?

2. How did women's perceptions of their current body compare with what they feel men find most attractive?

3. Were there any differences in the perceptions of Black and White women?

Summary

CHILDREN'S KNOWLEDGE AND BELIEFS ABOUT GENDER

- Children are able to distinguish females and males as early as 3–4 months of age.
- By age 2 or 3, they can label their own gender and show some awareness of gender-typical objects, activities, and occupations.
- Awareness of gender stereotypes for personality traits emerges later in the preschool years.
- Stereotypes become more flexible after age 7.

GENDER-RELATED ACTIVITIES AND INTERESTS

- Preschool girls and boys are similar in their motor skills.

- Differences favoring boys become more pronounced in adolescence as a result of both environmental and biological factors.
- Participation in sports is associated with positive traits in females. Their participation has soared since the passage of Title IX.
- By age 3, gender differences in toy choices and activities are well established.
- Gender segregation, the preference for same-gender children, emerges by age 3 and increases during childhood.

INFLUENCES ON GENDER DEVELOPMENT

- Both parents, but fathers more than mothers, encourage gender-typical toys, play activities, and chore assignments for their children.

- Parents talk more to their daughters, give them less autonomy, and encourage their pro-social behaviors.
- Maternal employment is associated with less stereotyped gender-related concepts and preferences in sons and daughters.
- Older siblings influence the gender development of younger siblings.
- Boys receive more attention from teachers than girls do. They are more likely to be called on, praised, and criticized constructively.
- Girls are also shortchanged in school textbooks.
- Children exert strong pressures on each other to engage in gender-typical behavior.
- Boys are viewed more negatively than girls when they engage in cross-gender activity.
- Children who are heavy television viewers are more aware of gender stereotypes.
- Exposure to characters who show nontraditional behaviors reduces children's gender stereotypes.

PUBERTY

- During puberty, sexual organs mature and secondary sex characteristics appear.

- Menarche is a major event of puberty.
- Girls who mature early tend to adjust less easily than late-maturing girls.

PSYCHOSOCIAL DEVELOPMENT IN ADOLESCENCE

- Adolescent girls and boys show similar patterns of identity development, focusing on both occupational choices and interpersonal relationships.
- Girls begin to show lower self-esteem than boys in early adolescence, and the gender gap widens during adolescence. Explanations include girls' dissatisfaction with their physical appearance, shortchanging of girls in school, and girls' "losing their voice." Black girls have higher self-esteem than other girls.
- Early adolescents show an increasing divergence in gender-related behaviors and attitudes, known as gender intensification.
- Adolescent girls, compared to boys, have a more negative body image and are more likely to diet. Cultural pressures for slimness are partly responsible.

Key Terms

rough-and-tumble play *71*
socialization *72*
puberty *78*
primary sex characteristics *78*

secondary sex characteristics *78*
menarche *79*
secular trend *79*
adolescent growth spurt *80*

identity *81*
individuate *81*
self-esteem *82*
gender intensification *83*

What Do You Think?

1. Should parents attempt to raise their children in gender-neutral ways? If so, why? What would be the advantages? What would be the disadvantages? Incorporate material from Chapters 2 and 3 into your answers.
2. Why do you think teachers pay more attention to boys than to girls? What can be done to ensure more equal treatment of girls in the classroom?
3. In your opinion, why are boys who engage in feminine activities viewed more negatively than girls who engage in masculine activities?
4. Lois Gould (1990), in her fictional *X: A Fabulous Child's Story*, wrote about Baby X, whose gender was

concealed from everyone except its parents. This created considerable consternation among relatives and family friends. Why do you think that was?
5. The earlier onset of puberty in the United States and western Europe has not been accompanied by earlier gains in social and emotional development that would help children successfully manage their sexuality. What are the implications for individual adolescents and for society?
6. What actions can parents and teachers take to help enhance the self-esteem of adolescent girls?
7. How does the social construction of gender influence women's body images versus men's body images?

If You Want to Learn More

Bailey, J. (2016). *Sex, puberty, and all that stuff: A guide to growing up*. Hauppauge, NY: Barron's Educational Publishers.

Belgrave, F.Z. (2011). *African-American girls: Reframing perceptions and changing experiences*. New York: Springer.

Bryan, J. (2012). *From the dress-up corner to the senior prom: Navigating gender and sexual diversity*. Lanham, MD: Rowman & Littlefield.

Garcia, L. (2012). *Respect yourself, protect yourself: Latina girls and sexual identity*. New York: New York University Press.

Greene, S. (2015). *The psychological development of girls and women* (2nd ed.). New York: Routledge.

Greenspan, L. & Deardorff, J. (2014). *The new puberty: How to navigate early development in today's girls*. Emmaus, PA: Rodale.

Grogan, S. (2017). *Body image: Body dissatisfaction in men, women and children*. New York: Routledge.

Kilpatrick, H. & Joiner, W. (2012). *The drama years: Real girls talk about surviving middle school—bullies, brands, body image, and more*. New York: Free Press.

MacDonald, F. (2016). *Childhood and tween girl culture*. London, UK: Palgrave Macmillan.

Morris, M.W. (2016). *Pushout: The criminalization of Black girls in school*. New York: The New Press.

Richardson, N. & Locks, A. (2014). *Body studies: The basics*. New York: Routledge.

Wainwright, P.A. (2015). *Growing courageous girls: How to raise authentic, strong, and savvy girls in today's mixed-up culture*. Hanover, PA: Chaucer Press.

Wardy, M.A. & Newsom, S.S. (2014). *Redefining girly: How parents can fight the stereotyping and sexualizing of girlhood from birth to tween*. Chicago: Chicago Review Press.

Zurbriggen, E.L. & Roberts, T.-A. (Eds.). (2013). *The sexualization of girls and girlhood: Causes, consequences, and resistance*. New York: Oxford University Press.

Websites

Sports

Empowering Women in Sports
http://www.feminist.org/sports

http://www.girlpower.gov
http://www.girlsinc.org/
http://www.nedic.ca/

5 CHAPTER

Gender Comparisons
Social Behavior, Personality, Communication, and Cognition

In high school, I once struggled with some concepts in my advanced algebra class. My teacher did not help me much. He kept telling me not to worry about it; that I would not be using algebra in my future. I excelled in that class, and kept taking math courses, which surprised him. (Nathalie, a 22-year-old college senior)

GENDER-RELATED SOCIAL BEHAVIORS AND PERSONALITY TRAITS

In Chapter 2, we examined numerous gender stereotypes. How accurately do these stereotypes reflect actual differences in the social behaviors, personality characteristics, communication styles, and cognitive abilities of females and males? In this chapter, we review all four of these areas. As we shall see, some stereotypes have at least a grain (or more) of truth to them, whereas others are not supported by the evidence. Two cautionary notes: First, even when gender differences are found, they are typically small. Second, there is considerable overlap in the characteristics of females and males (Carothers & Reis, 2013; Zell et al., 2015).

For example, girls are generally more nurturant toward younger children than boys are, but some boys show greater nurturance than some girls.

Aggression

She talks about you.
You talk about her.
She glares at you.
You stare at her.
Is it a rumor, or is it the truth?
She lies to you, you lie right back.
You need a friend, but for sure not her.
She takes your guy.
You want him back.
Too much stress, too much pressure.
But I guess this is life.

(Kelsey, 12 years old)

Aggression is behavior that is intended to hurt someone, either physically or verbally. By age 2, boys show higher levels of physical aggression than girls, and during the preschool period, the differences become striking (Naerde et al., 2014; Russell et al., 2014). Boys continue to be more physically and verbally aggressive than girls into adulthood (Faris & Felmlee, 2011; Nivette et al., 2015; D.S. Richardson, 2014). The differences hold across socioeconomic groups and across cultures (Endendijk et al., 2016; Wölfer & Hewstone, 2015; Zell et al., 2015). Beginning in preschool, however, girls are somewhat more likely than boys to use **relational aggression**, which involves *harming others through nonphysical hurtful manipulation of their peer relationships*. For example, girls might exclude a peer from their play group, or spread malicious rumors and gossip about her, as illustrated in Kelsey's poem in the beginning of this section and in movies such as *Heathers* and *Mean Girls* (Hyde, 2014; Murray-Close et al., 2016). Moreover, girls are more likely than boys to perceive relationally aggressive acts as mean and hurtful and to be more distressed by such behaviors (Coyne et al., 2006; Crick et al., 2009). This gender difference in how children display aggression is so striking that even preschool children are aware of it (Giles & Heyman, 2005).

Interestingly, although aggression is typically associated with rejection by peers, girls who use relational aggression tend to be both popular and powerful within their peer group (Cillessen et al., 2014; Etekal & Ladd, 2015; Troop-Gordon & Ranney, 2014). What might account for this unexpected finding? According to Suzanna Rose and her colleagues (2004), strategic use of relational aggression may serve to maintain social dominance as well as to display superiority.

Both biological and environmental influences may contribute to gender differences in aggression (Constantinescu & Hines, 2012; Gavin & Porter, 2014). On the biological side, it has been noted that the gender difference emerges early and appears across most cultures. In addition, the sex hormone testosterone appears to play a role, at least in animal aggression. Research on the relationship between aggressive behavior and testosterone in humans, however, has produced mixed results (Stockley & Campbell, 2013). A meta-analysis by Angela Book and her colleagues (2001) yielded a weak, positive correlation between testosterone and aggressive behavior in humans. However, this correlation is difficult to interpret because the causal direction can go either way. That is, increasing testosterone levels can lead to aggression, but it is also the case that acting aggressively (such as winning a sports contest) leads to a rise in testosterone levels (Carre & Olmstead, 2015; McIntyre & Edwards, 2009). Jacquelyn White and Robin Kowalski (1994) suggest that studies showing a connection between aggression and testosterone may be unduly emphasized because they are consistent with the stereotype of the aggressive male and the submissive female.

Environmental factors are probably even more important than biological ones in producing gender differences in aggression. For one thing, parents are less tolerant of aggressive acting-out behaviors in girls (Blakemore et al., 2009; Chaplin et al., 2005). Consequently, girls expect more guilt, more peer and parental disapproval, and fewer material gains for aggression than boys do (Fischer & Evers, 2013). In addition, parents' encouragement of boys' rougher, dominance-oriented physical play and their use of gender-typical toys such as guns may serve to promote and maintain aggression. Also, parents use harsher physical control with boys than with girls which provides boys with a model for aggressive behavior (Endendijk et al., 2015). Furthermore, the rougher, dominance-oriented play of boys' groups may contribute to the maintenance of higher aggression levels in boys (Hines, 2010).

Prosocial Behavior

Prosocial behavior is *voluntary behavior intended to benefit someone else*. It includes helping, comforting and caring for others, sharing, and cooperating (Bussey, 2013). The stereotype is that females are more nurturant, supportive, and helpful than males (Frieze & Li, 2010). Are they?

Most studies of children have found gender differences in prosocial behavior favoring girls (Hei Li & Wong, 2016; Zosuls et al., 2014). For example, toddler girls under the age of 2 are more likely than boys to comfort someone in distress (Kiang et al., 2004). Girls also are kinder and help others more than boys do (Caprara et al., 2001; Eisenberg et al., 2009). This tendency of girls to be more prosocial has been found in a variety of cultures (Eisenberg et al., 2009).

Studies with adults, however, paint a different picture, with men helping more than women. This is partly because studies with adults frequently involve instrumental and chivalrous assistance, such as rescuing strangers, sometimes in potentially dangerous situations (e.g., helping to change a tire or picking up a hitchhiker). Women, on the other hand, are more likely to offer psychological support and help to friends and family members (Hyde, 2014; Wood & Eagly, 2010). Unfortunately, this aspect of helpfulness has largely been overlooked by researchers. In one extremely dangerous real-world situation—the rescuing of Jews during the Holocaust—women helped as often as men. They are also more likely to donate kidneys, volunteer for the Peace Corps, and serve as medical volunteers in dangerous settings (Wood & Eagly, 2010).

Gender differences in helping styles are consistent with stereotyped expectations for males and females. How do the differences arise? In many societies, girls are expected to be more nurturant, kind, and emotionally supportive than boys, and they are rewarded for these behaviors. Boys, meanwhile, are more often rewarded for helping behaviors that involve rescuing, risk taking, and chivalry (Hyde, 2014).

Influenceability

Females tend to be stereotyped as more easily influenced and more conforming than males. Is there any evidence to support this view? Again, the answer depends on several factors, such as the type of measure used and the gender composition of the group being studied (Carli, 2010). In the two major types of tasks used to measure one's tendency to be influenced participants indicate their position on a controversial topic. A different position supported by arguments is presented either by one other individual, or by a group of people, and the participant's position is again measured.

Alice Eagly and Linda Carli (1981) performed a meta-analysis on studies of both kinds of tasks and found that women were more easily influenced than men. But all differences were small. Females were influenced more when masculine topics, such as technology or sports, were used. The gender difference was also greater when the researchers were male.

Several factors may account for these findings. For one thing, females are socialized to yield to social influence whereas males are trained to do the influencing. Remember also that from an early age, females show more cooperation and less conflict in group settings. Accepting the views of others can be viewed as a mechanism for maintaining social harmony and avoiding conflict. In addition, consistent with the theme that females have less power than males, women are accorded a lower status than men in most societies. Individuals of lower status generally learn to conform to the wishes of higher-status individuals (Hogg, 2010).

Emotionality

In most societies, females are thought to be more emotional than males: more fearful, anxious, easily upset, and emotionally expressive. Males are viewed as more likely to express anger and pride and to hide or deny their emotions (Brody et al., 2016; Fischer & Evers, 2013; Hall, 2016; Shields, 2013). Even preschool children, when read stories in an emotionally ambiguous context, are more likely to perceive boys as angry and girls as sad (Parmley & Cunningham, 2008). Is there any truth to these stereotypes?

Preschool girls express less anger and more fearfulness than boys. They are also better at labeling emotions and understanding complex emotions such as pride (Bosacki & Moore, 2004). In elementary school, boys start to hide negative emotions such as sadness whereas girls begin to hide negative emotions, such as disappointment, that might hurt others' feelings. By adolescence, girls report more sadness, shyness, shame, and guilt, whereas boys deny experiencing these feelings. Girls and women also report more fear and anxiety than boys and men (Chaplin, 2015; Doey et al., 2014; Hyde, 2014). In addition, they report experiencing emotions more intensely and more readily (Blakemore et al., 2009). Note that these findings do not answer the question of whether females are actually more emotional than males or whether they simply are more likely to report their feelings.

Another aspect of emotionality is **empathy**, which involves *feeling the same emotion that someone else is feeling*. The stereotype is that women are more empathic than men. Are they in reality? The answer depends on how you measure empathy. When individuals are asked to report how they feel in certain situations (e.g., "Does seeing people cry upset you?"), females show more empathy than males (Bekker & van Assen, 2008; Eisenberg et al., 2006; Wentzel et al., 2007). However, when individuals' behaviors are observed unobtrusively or when their physiological reactions are measured, no gender differences in empathy are found (Eisenberg et al., 2006). These findings suggest that when people know what is being measured and can control their reactions, they may act in the socially acceptable gender-typical manner.

Socialization seems to be an important factor in the development of differences in emotionality (or in the willingness to report emotions). We saw in Chapter 4 that parents are more accepting of fear and sadness in girls and anger in boys. Mothers focus more on emotions when talking to their daughters than to their sons (Fivush et al., 2000; Aznar & Tenenbaum, 2015). In addition, parents put more pressure on sons to control their emotions, while encouraging their daughters to be emotionally expressive (Fischer & Evers, 2013). Parents also emphasize closer emotional relationships with daughters than with sons. As early as preschool, mothers and daughters are already closer emotionally than mothers and sons (Benenson et al., 1998).

A series of studies by Penelope Davis (1999) on adults' memories of childhood events provides an interesting illustration of the apparent social construction of gender differences in emotionality. She found that females and males did not differ either in the number of memories recalled or in how quickly they recalled them. However, females consistently recalled more childhood memories of events associated with emotion and were faster in accessing these memories.

Narcissism

Narcissism is defined as *a need for admiration and a relative lack of empathy*. It has been linked to a variety of outcomes, both negative and positive (Grijalva et al., 2015). Negative outcomes include the inability to maintain healthy long-term relationships, aggression when self-esteem is threatened, and unethical/exploitative behavior (e.g., academic dishonesty, white-collar crime). Positive outcomes associated with narcissism include high self-esteem, emotional stability, and leadership.

The widely held stereotype is that men are more narcissistic than women. A recent meta-analysis by Emily Grijalva and her colleagues (2015) confirms that this gender difference not only exists but is one of the more robust gender differences in the personality domain. They hypothesize that it is driven by men's heightened sense of entitlement and authority. Interestingly, although women have become more agentic over time, gender differences in narcissism have not decreased in the past 25 years, contrary to what one might expect (Grijalva et al., 2015).

The Big Five Personality Traits

The **Big Five personality traits** (**neuroticism**, **extraversion**, **openness to experience**, **agreeableness**, and **conscientiousness**) are viewed as *enduring patterns of thoughts, feelings, and behaviors*. Studies of gender differences in the Big Five from adolescence into late middle age have found the largest differences in agreeableness and neuroticism, with women showing more of both. Women score higher than men on the gregarious component of extraversion, while men score higher on the assertiveness component. Men also show more openness to experience. No gender differences are found in conscientiousness (Hyde, 2014; Lehmann et al., 2013).

Moral Reasoning

Are there gender differences in moral reasoning? The question has been hotly debated ever since Lawrence Kohlberg (Kohlberg & Puka, 1994) proposed that males show higher levels of moral reasoning than females. In his research, Kohlberg asked individuals to respond to moral dilemmas. In one dilemma, a druggist refuses to lower the price of an expensive drug that could save the life of a dying woman. Her husband, who cannot afford the drug, then steals it. Was he right or wrong in doing so, and why? Kohlberg reported that males' answers emphasized abstract justice and "law and order," which he believed to be more advanced than the emphasis on caring and concern for others expressed by females. As we saw in Chapter 1, Carol Gilligan (1982, 1994) argued that females' moral reasoning is just as advanced as that of males, but that females speak "in a different voice" that emphasizes personal connections rather than abstract legalities.

Research, however, generally fails to support Kohlberg's and Gilligan's view that there are gender differences in the underlying basis of moral reasoning (Turiel, 2006). For example, a meta-analysis of 113 studies by Sara Jaffee and Janet Hyde (2000) found only slight differences in the care orientation favoring females and in the justice orientation favoring males. In some studies, in fact, women are more likely than men to show both a care response *and* a justice response (Mainiero et al., 2008). In addition, extensive literature reviews (Gibbs et al., 2007; Walker, 2006) find no consistent gender differences in moral reasoning across a variety of cultures. And, among college students in the United States, women are more concerned with moral issues than are men (Skoe et al., 2002).

Moral reasoning appears to be more dependent on the context of the situation than on the gender of the individual (Turiel, 2006). For example, both women and men are more likely to use a care-based approach when interacting with a friend than with a stranger, or when interacting with a member of their in-group as opposed to someone outside their group (Fine, 2010).

COMMUNICATION STYLE

People believe that men have demanding voices, swear, are straight to the point, are forceful, and boastful. Women, on the other hand, are thought to talk a lot, speak politely and emotionally, enunciate clearly, use good grammar, talk about trivia, and gossip (Spade & Valentine, 2016). According to a popular book, women and men are so different in their communication styles that it is as if *Men Are From Mars, Women Are From Venus* (Gray, 1992). What does research tell us about differences between the communication styles of females and males?

Verbal Communication

Evidence supports a number of gender differences, and one of these is, indeed, the difference in talkativeness. Interestingly, however, the talking behavior of females and males is the opposite of the stereotype. In many situations studied by researchers, including online discussion groups, males talk more than females, more frequently, and for longer periods of time. Furthermore, this gender difference is apparent as early as the preschool years and continues throughout adulthood (Cameron, 2007; Carli, 2013; Gleason & Ely, 2002; Leaper & Ayers, 2007; Spade & Valentine, 2016).

Given the gender difference in talkativeness, one might expect that males also interrupt others more than females do. Research indicates that gender differences in the number of interruptions depend on the situations and also that women and men have different goals when they interrupt others (Gleason & Ely, 2002). One purpose of an interruption is *to show interest and affirm what the other is saying*—an **affiliative interruption**—for example, by saying "uh-huh." A second reason for interrupting is *to usurp the floor and control the conversation*—an **intrusive interruption**. This might be accomplished by taking over the conversation even though the previous speaker shows no signs of relinquishing the floor. It might not surprise you to learn that females are more likely to engage in affiliative interruption and males, in intrusive interruption (Athenstaedt et al., 2004; Carli, 2013; Eckert & McConnell-Ginet, 2003). These differences are consistent with both the social construction of females as other-directed and caring, and the gender inequality in power. Affiliative interruptions are one way to express an interest in other people, and females might have learned through their socialization that this was one means of showing concern about and reinforcing others. On the other hand, both intrusive interruptions and talkativeness are associated with the desire to maintain dominance and with the power to do so (Hancock & Rubin, 2014). More powerful individuals are seen as having the right to dominate the conversation and to usurp the floor. This connection between power and communication behavior is illustrated in a study by Elizabeth Cashdan (1998), who observed female and male college students in group discussions and asked them to rate their housemates on characteristics of power. The more powerful students were found to talk the most.

Gender differences have also been found in conversational style. Consistent with communal and agentic stereotypes, studies show that females use more emotional, polite, affiliative, soothing, and supportive speech, whereas males use more direct, goal-oriented, assertive, domineering, and abrupt speech (Carli, 2013; DeFrancisco et al., 2014; Leaper & Ayers, 2007). For example, women are more likely than men to refer to emotions and use intensive adverbs ("She is *really* friendly"), whereas men tend to use directives ("Think about this") and judgmental adjectives ("Working can be a drag") more than women do.

Another gender difference in conversational style is that females use speech that is sometimes referred to as more tentative or mitigating. Such speech may contain uncertainty verbs (e.g., "It *seems* that the class will be interesting"), hedges (e.g., "*I kind of feel* you should not be too upset about this"), tag questions ("It's hot in here, *don't you think*?"), and disclaimers of expertise ("*I may be wrong, but . . .*") (Hyde, 2014; Leaper & Robnett, 2011).

One explanation for this gender difference in speech is that females have lower self-esteem than males and, consequently, speak more tentatively (Petersen & Hyde, 2014). Another interpretation is that women's tentativeness results not from their uncertainty but from their lower status (Carli, 2013; DeFrancisco et al., 2014). Less powerful individuals are more likely to use more tentative speech, regardless of their own confidence in what they are saying, and, as we have noted throughout this text, women have less power than men.

Still another perspective on this gender difference in conversational style is that the language features used by women do not reflect tentativeness at all but instead are due to women's communal orientation—their desire to leave open the lines of communication and encourage the participation of others (Carli, 2013). Research has found that tag questions in fact serve a variety of functions depending on the situation. For example, in one study (Cameron, in LaFrance, 2001), both women and men in powerful roles used tag questions to generate talk from other participants. However, women and men in less powerful roles used them to seek reassurance for their opinions. This finding indicates that gender differences in verbal communication depend in part on the situation. For example, conversational style is generally more gender-stereotyped in same-sex groups than in mixed-sex groups (Athenstaedt et al., 2004; Leaper, 2004). In the latter groups, women and men tend to adjust their behaviors to each other. In addition, both women and men exhibit more communal speech (i.e., complimenting, verbally reinforcing, using more pleasant voices) when interacting with women than with men (Carli, 2013). Whatever the explanation for women's greater use of so-called tentative or mitigating speech, such speech makes people seem less credible, powerful, or persuasive (Carli, 2013). Can you think of how this perception might be problematic for women in leadership positions?

Another aspect of conversational style is the way people respond to a friend's troubles. Shari Michaud and Rebecca Warner (1997) found that women were more likely than men to offer sympathy in response to a friend's problems, whereas men were more likely to change the subject. In addition, women were more likely than men to appreciate receiving advice or sympathy, whereas men were more likely to resent it. On the other hand, research by Erina MacGeorge and her colleagues (2004) found only slight differences in the way women and men responded. Both sexes preferred to listen, sympathize, and give thoughtful advice. Men were only slightly more likely to give advice, and women were slightly more likely to provide support. Similarly, both women and men appreciated advice that was relevant to their problems and was given in a respectful, kind manner. MacGeorge and her colleagues concluded that women and men do not come from two different communication cultures but are instead from the same "planet." Do Get Involved 5.1 to see whether your findings support the view of Gray or MacGeorge.

Similar to conversational style, there are some differences in the actual content of females' and males' conversations. Women are more likely than men to talk about personal topics and social-emotional activities, whereas men are more likely to discuss impersonal topics and task-oriented activities (Newman et al., 2008). For example, Ruth Anne Clark (1998) asked college students to list all the topics discussed in a recent conversation with a same-gender close friend and to indicate the dominant topic. Not surprisingly, given the importance of romantic relationships to young adults, both females and males talked about the other gender. However, women's conversations were more likely than men's to be dominated by interpersonal issues whereas men were more likely to focus on sports and other leisure activities.

Nonverbal Communication

Consistent with the communal stereotype, people believe that females are more likely than males to engage in nonverbal behaviors that demonstrate interpersonal interest and warmth. Are these beliefs accurate? Considerable evidence shows that they are. For one thing, girls and women are more likely than boys and men to engage in mutual eye contact with another individual for longer periods of time, particularly if that individual is female (Ambady & Weisbuch, 2010; Hall, 2006). This gender difference in gazing behavior is not present at birth but appears as early as 13 weeks of age and continues through adulthood (Leeb & Rejeskind, 2004). Females also are more likely to smile, nod, lean forward,

GET INVOLVED 5.1
"Troubles Talk": Effects of Gender on Communication Styles

Give the following two-part survey to two female and two male traditional-aged college students.

PART I. Imagine your friend is upset because of having one of the PROBLEMS listed here. For each problem, indicate how likely you would be to make each of the listed RESPONSES.

PROBLEM A: *Your friend says "I'm upset because I may be breaking up with my dating partner."*
What do you do?

Offer sympathy	very unlikely	1	2	3	4	5	very likely
Change the subject	very unlikely	1	2	3	4	5	very likely

PROBLEM B: *Your friend says "I'm upset because I may fail a course." What do you do?*

Offer sympathy	very unlikely	1	2	3	4	5	very likely
Change the subject	very unlikely	1	2	3	4	5	very likely

PART II. Now imagine that you have each of the problems cited earlier. Indicate how you FEEL when your friend makes the indicated RESPONSES.

PROBLEM A: You tell your friend "I'm upset because I may be breaking up with my dating partner." Your friend offers SYMPATHY. How much do you feel the following?

Grateful	not at all	1	2	3	4	a lot
Resentful	not at all	1	2	3	4	a lot

PROBLEM B: You tell your friend "I'm upset because I may fail a course." Your friend gives ADVICE on solving the problem. How much do you feel the following?

Grateful	not at all	1	2	3	4	a lot
Resentful	not at all	1	2	3	4	a lot

Source: Adapted from Michaud and Warner (1997).

WHAT DOES IT MEAN?

For Part I, compare the scores of your female and male respondents on the "sympathy" scale of the two problems. Do the same for the "change the subject" scale. For Part II, compare the female and male respondents in terms of how grateful or resentful they are for receiving sympathy (Problem A), and how grateful or resentful they are for receiving advice (Problem B).

1. Did you find the same results as Michaud and Warner (1997) for Parts I and II of the survey? If not, give reasons.
2. As described in the chapter, John Gray theorizes that women and men come from two different cultures of communication, whereas Erina MacGeorge disagrees. Do your findings support the view of Gray or MacGeorge? Explain.
3. Your data, like those of Michaud and Warner (1997), were collected from traditional-aged college students. Do you think that middle-aged women and men would respond differently? (You would, of course, have to make the problems age-appropriate by, for example, substituting "spouse" for "dating partner," and "get a poor job performance evaluation" instead of "fail a course.") Explain your answer.

and approach others more closely (Fischer & LaFrance, 2015; Hall, 2006). Girls and women across cultures are also more sensitive to the meanings of nonverbal messages portrayed by others and more accurately interpret their emotions (Ambady & Weisbuch, 2010; Brody & Hall, 2008). In addition, research on interpersonal sensitivity indicates that females are better than males at initially getting to know the personality traits, emotional states, and behavioral tendencies of other people. They are also more accurate at recalling the appearance and behaviors of social targets (Hall & Schmid Mast, 2010).

One explanation for these gender differences is the differential socialization of females and males, with females receiving greater societal encouragement for being socially concerned (Fischer & Evers, 2013). Smiling and gazing communicate interest and involvement in another person. In addition, women's ability to accurately decipher other people's emotional states might stem from their greater interest in others and their more extensive experience with emotional communication.

A different explanation of females' superior sensitivity skills lies in their subordinate status within society. Less powerful individuals are good interpreters of the nonverbal cues of more powerful people (Keltner & Lerner, 2010; Kraus et al., 2010). This ability to decipher the nonverbal behavior of others allows lower-status individuals, including women, to anticipate the reactions of those in power and thus respond appropriately (Fischer & Evers, 2013; Kraus et al., 2010).

Touch is another form of nonverbal communication. Nancy Henley (1995) contended that there is an unwritten societal rule that high-status individuals can touch low-status individuals, but those of low status cannot touch those of high status. For example, it is more likely that the president of a corporation will pat a janitor on the back than the reverse. Henley concluded that because males have more power than females, there is more male-to-female touching than the reverse.

Studies show that males do show more touching associated with instrumental goals such as asserting power or showing sexual intent. On the other hand, women exhibit more touching in the form of hugs or other cues of social support (Hall, 2006). And in established heterosexual relationships, both women and men are found to initiate touch (DeFrancisco et al., 2014). Obviously, gender and status differences in touching are more complex than were originally believed.

GENDER COMPARISON OF COGNITIVE ABILITIES

Research into questions about sex differences and similarities in intelligence is fraught with political minefields and emotional rhetoric from all ends of the political spectrum. But research is the only way we can distinguish between those stereotypes that have some basis in fact and those that don't.

(Diane Halpern, president-elect of the American
Psychological Association, cited in Kersting, 2003)

Although females and males do not differ in general intelligence, they do vary in certain cognitive skills. Some differences emerge in childhood but others do not appear until adolescence (Ceci et al., 2014; Hines, 2010; Miller & Halpern, 2014). No doubt some of these differences have a bearing on the career choices made by females and males. Remember our cautionary notes from the beginning of this chapter. Gender differences, where they exist, are generally small. Females and males are much more alike in cognitive abilities than they are different. Even when there is a small average difference favoring one gender on a test of a particular cognitive skill, many individuals of the other gender will score well above the average. Also recall from Chapter 1 that the presence of a gender difference does not tell us anything about the causes of the difference. Finally, keep in mind that cognitive skills, like the social behaviors and personality traits we discussed earlier in this chapter, develop within a social context. As we shall see throughout this section, attitudes and expectations about the cognitive performance of females and males play an important role in socially constructing that performance.

Verbal Ability

Verbal abilities include a variety of language skills such as vocabulary, reading comprehension, writing, spelling, grammar, and word fluency. Females show superior performance on most verbal tasks, although the differences are small (Miller & Halpern, 2014; Hyde, 2014). Gender differences in verbal ability appear earlier than other cognitive gender differences. Girls are more vocal than boys during infancy, talk at an earlier age, produce longer utterances, have larger vocabularies, and are more fluent (Leaper & Smith, 2004; Stoner et al., 2005). They also are less likely to have developmental delays involving language (Sices et al., 2004).

Girls continue to show an edge in verbal skills throughout the grade-school years. Around the world, they achieve higher scores on tests of reading comprehension and are less likely to display reading problems such as reading disability (dyslexia) and reading below grade level (Mullis et al., 2012; U.S. Department of Education, 2011a, b). In adolescence, girls continue to outperform boys in reading, writing, verbal reasoning, language achievement, and speech production (OECD, 2015; U.S. Department of Education, 2011a, b; Voyer & Voyer, 2014).

Some researchers have suggested that gender differences in verbal skills and other cognitive abilities are becoming smaller (Hyde, 2014) but others conclude that these differences are remaining relatively stable or even increasing for some tasks (Miller & Halpern, 2014).

What might account for the greater verbal ability of girls? In Chapter 4, we saw that parents vocalize more to their infant daughters than to their infant sons (Clearfield & Nelson, 2006). This may lead to increased vocalization by female infants, which may in turn encourage parents to talk even more to their young daughters. Girls' early advantage with language may lead them to rely more on verbal approaches in their interactions with others, further enhancing their verbal ability. In addition, playing with stereotypically feminine toys such as dolls and stuffed animals may encourage pretend play and the development of verbal skills (Blakemore et al., 2009).

Parental expectations also may play a role in girls' superior verbal skills. Studies in Finland, Japan, Taiwan, and the United States find that as early as first grade, children and their mothers generally believe that girls are better than boys at language and reading (Butler, 2014; Lummis & Stevenson, 1990; Räty & Kasanen, 2010). In addition, girls whose mothers think that girls are better readers receive higher scores on reading comprehension and vocabulary than girls whose mothers think girls and boys read equally well.

Visual–Spatial Ability

Visual–spatial ability refers to skill in visualizing objects or shapes and in mentally rotating and manipulating them. Visual–spatial skills are used extensively in engineering, architecture, surgery, and navigation and in everyday activities such as doing jigsaw puzzles or reading maps (Tzuriel & Egozi, 2010).

TYPES OF VISUAL–SPATIAL ABILITY. Gender differences in visual–spatial ability are larger and more consistent than in other cognitive skills, with males outperforming females in many, although not all, areas (Halpern, 2012; Newcombe et al., 2013). The pattern of differences depends on the spatial ability being measured. For example, females consistently excel in remembering the spatial location of objects (Halpern, 2012). Three other facets of visual–spatial ability have been identified by Marcia Linn and Anne Petersen (1985). Tasks used to measure these three components are shown in Figure 5.1.

Mental rotation involves *the ability to rapidly manipulate two- or three-dimensional figures* (see Figure 5.1a). Meta-analyses (see Chapter 1) show that the largest gender difference in spatial skills occurs on tests of this ability, with an overall *d* value of 1.03 on timed tests and 0.51 with no time limits (Voyer, 2011). Boys begin to outperform girls as early as 3 to 5 months of age (Newcombe et al., 2013). The gender difference continues in childhood and increases into adulthood (Halpern, 2012; Zell et al., 2015).

Tests of **spatial perception** involve the *ability to locate the vertical or the horizontal while ignoring distracting information.* For example, individuals may be asked to identify a horizontal water line in a tilted bottle (see Figure 5.1b). Gender differences on spatial perception tests like this are smaller than those found on mental rotation tasks (overall *d* = 0.40) (Vasilyeva, 2010; Voyer et al., 1995). Boys begin to perform better than girls by age 9, and this difference gets larger during the adolescent and adult years (Hines, 2010).

Tasks measuring **spatial visualization** include *finding simple shapes hidden within larger, complex shapes* (see Figure 5.1c). Gender differences favoring males are much smaller or absent on these tasks (overall *d* = 0.20) (Voyer et al., 1995).

The size of gender differences on spatial visualization and spatial perception tasks has been decreasing over time (Feingold, 1993; Voyer et al., 1995). Differences on mental rotation tests, however, have remained stable (Halpern, 2012; Zell et al., 2015).

EXPLANATIONS OF GENDER DIFFERENCES. Several biological and environmental theories have been proposed to account for gender differences in visual–spatial abilities. Biological theories focus on genes, hormones, or the organization of the brain. According to one theory, visual–spatial ability is influenced by sex-linked recessive genes on the X chromosome. Research does not support this view, however (Newcombe, 2007).

Another biological theory is that sex hormone levels affect visual–spatial skills in either of two ways. One possibility is that hormones circulating in the bloodstream might directly affect visual–spatial performance (Halpern, 2012). Studies have shown that women with higher testosterone

a. **Mental Rotation**
Choose the responses that show the standard in a different orientation.

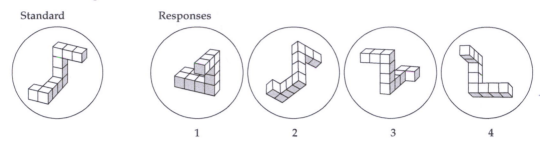

b. **Spatial Perception**
Pick the tilted bottle that has a horizontal water line.

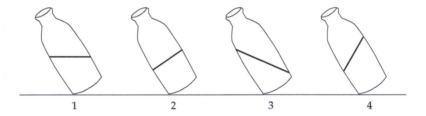

c. **Spatial Visualization**
Find the figure embedded in the complex shape below.

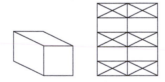

FIGURE 5.1 Types of spatial tasks. Large sex differences favoring males appear on mental rotation, and males also do better than females on spatial perception. In contrast, sex differences on spatial visualization are weak or nonexistent. *Source:* From "Emergence and Characterization of Sex Differences in Spatial Ability: A Meta-Analysis," M. C. Linn and A. C. Petersen, 1985, *Child Development, 56.* © The Society for Research in Child Development, Inc. Reprinted by permission.

levels achieve better spatial scores than women with lower testosterone levels, whereas the reverse is true in men (Puts et al., 2008). Keeping in mind that women's testosterone levels, on average, are lower than those of men, these findings suggest that the optimal level of testosterone for certain spatial skills is in the low male range (Hampson & Moffat, 2004). Other research, however, finds that actively circulating sex hormones do not affect spatial performance in adolescent girls and boys (Liben et al., 2002).

Another possibility is that prenatal sex hormones might irreversibly organize the brain to enhance certain spatial functions (Valla & Ceci, 2011). Evidence for this view comes from studies of girls with congenital adrenal hyperplasia (CAH) (see Chapter 3), which exposes them to high levels of prenatal androgens. At birth, the hormone imbalance is corrected and they are raised as girls. A meta-analysis found that CAH girls display better visual–spatial skills than unaffected girls (Miller & Halpern, 2014). Some psychologists (e.g., Jordan-Young, 2010), however, point out that parents' awareness of the possible masculinizing effects of androgens may influence their treatment of and expectations for their daughters. Additional evidence for the possible role of prenatal andro-gens is that women with male twins outperform women who have female twins on mental rotation tasks (Miller & Halpern, 2014). Can you think of an alternative explanation? (Hint: Think of the different sex-typed activities that girls with a boy twin versus a girl twin would experience.)

Some theorists have attributed gender differences in visual–spatial skills to differences in the lateralization of female and male brains. **Lateralization** refers to the *specialization of the cerebral hemispheres of the brain to perform different cognitive functions*. For most individuals, the left hemisphere is involved in language and mathematical computation, whereas the right hemisphere is more involved in processing visual and spatial information (Fine, 2010). Evidence is mixed on whether male brains are more completely lateralized or specialized than female brains (Halpern, 2012), but in any case, it is not clear that lateralization leads to better performance in visual–spatial or other cognitive skills (Newcombe, 2007).

Numerous environmental theories have been proposed to explain gender differences in visual–spatial skills (Hoffman et al., 2011). Most of these focus on the impact of cultural gender stereotypes, observational learning, and encouragement of gender-typed activities and interests on shaping the experiences and attitudes of females and males. Participation in spatial activities fosters the development of spatial abilities in both girls and boys (Hawes et al., 2015; Jirout & Newcombe, 2015; Levine et al., 2016), yet females engage in fewer spatial activities than males. Why is this? For one thing, gender-stereotyped "boys'" toys, such as blocks, Erector Sets, Legos, and model planes and cars, provide more practice with visual–spatial skills than gender-stereotyped "girls'" toys (Hawes et al., 2015; Jirout & Newcombe, 2015). In addition, boys are also encouraged more than girls to participate in sports, which often involves moving balls and other objects through space. Action video games, which are especially popular with boys, also develop spatial skills (Granic et al., 2014; Liben & Coyle, 2014; Uttal et al., 2013; Verdine et al., 2014). If experience enhances the development of visual–spatial skills, then appropriate training ought to improve these skills. Research indicates that it does, for both females and males. Some training procedures have reduced or eliminated gender differences (Ceci et al., 2014; Halpern, 2012; Tzuriel & Egozi, 2010; Uttal et al., 2013).

The stereotyping of visual–spatial activities as masculine also influences performance. Studies have found that females and males with more masculine self-concepts perform better on visual–spatial tasks than those with less masculine self-concepts (Reilly & Neumann, 2013). However, if females are led to believe they will do well on these tasks, their scores improve dramatically. For example, prior to giving high school students the mental rotations test, Angelica Moe (2009) told one group that men were better than women on the test, and told another group that women were better on the test. A control group received no gender information. Men performed better than women in the control and the "men are better" groups. But women in the "women are better" group outperformed all other women, and did just as well as men.

Mathematics Ability

Early studies of gender differences in mathematics performance found that girls and boys did equally well at understanding mathematical concepts at all ages but that boys did better than girls in problem solving, starting at age 15 (Xie et al., 2015). In studies that sampled from the general population, females showed a slight edge over males. However, in highly select samples (for instance, college students or mathematically precocious youth), differences in mathematics performance were larger and favored males.

Gender differences in mathematics performance have decreased since that time (Hyde, 2014; Miller & Halpern, 2014). One striking example is the change in the number of mathematically gifted girls and boys who score 700 on the math section of the SAT exam at age 13. Twenty-five years ago, there were 13 boys for every girl at that high level, achieved by only 1 out of every 10,000 students. Now, the ratio is only 2.4:1 (Miller & Halpern, 2014). In addition, gender differences in mathematics performance no longer exist among U.S. elementary or high school students and girls earn better grades in math than boys (Xie et al., 2015). The magnitude of the gender difference in mathematics is not the same in all cultures, however. Differences between cultures in mathematics performance are much greater than the sex differences in performance. In many countries, boys perform slightly better than girls, but results for individual countries, however, tell a different tale (Ceci et al., 2014). In recent studies, girls performed as well as boys in two of the three countries with the highest eighth-grade math scores (Chinese Taipei and Korea) and did better than boys in the third country (Singapore). Moreover, girls in all three countries scored much higher than boys in many other nations, including the United States (OECD, 2015).

Another indicator of the critical role of culture in fostering math talent in girls comes from research on the most difficult math competitions for young people, including the USA and International Mathematical Olympiads and the Putnam Competition. What is striking is that the majority of the top-scoring U.S. girls are immigrants or children of immigrants from countries where mathematics education is a priority for all children (Hyde & Mertz, 2009). Similarly, of the dozen top-ranked countries in the International Mathematical Olympiad, nearly all are in eastern Europe or Asia (e.g., Bulgaria, Korea, Romania, Ukraine) and many have several prize-winning girls on their teams (Andreescu et al., 2008; Hyde & Mertz, 2009). Once again, these are countries with rigorous math curricula and cultures that encourage both girls and boys to excel in math.

A related finding is that gender differences in math performance and attitudes are smaller in countries with greater gender equality. More specifically, girls perform better in countries where females have equal access to education and where more women have careers in scientific research (Eagly, 2013a; Miller & Halpern, 2014). Together, these results indicate the powerful role of culture in the social construction of mathematics achievement.

Let us now examine more closely some of the factors associated with women's math performance.

FACTORS ASSOCIATED WITH MATH PERFORMANCE.   The single best predictor of scores on mathematics achievement tests is the number of mathematics courses an individual has taken. High school girls are now as likely as boys to take advanced mathematics and advanced biology and chemistry courses (Ceci et al., 2014; Xie et al., 2015).

In college, however, some women avoid choosing math and science courses and careers even when they are gifted in mathematics (Di Bella & Crisp, 2016; Liben & Bigler, 2014). This is troubling, because mathematics is a critical factor in career development, paving the way to high-status and high-salary careers in the sciences, medicine, engineering, and business (Petersen & Hyde, 2014). Why, then, do many young women begin to avoid math and science in college?

One important clue is found in the attitudes and feelings that females and males develop toward mathematics. **Mathematics self-efficacy**, *one's beliefs concerning one's ability to successfully perform mathematical tasks*, is related to actual math performance (Williams & Williams, 2010; Xie et al., 2015). Researchers have found that males around the world have greater mathematics self-efficacy than females (Else-Quest et al., 2013; OECD, 2015; Spearman & Watt, 2013). Compared to males, females are more anxious about math and have less confidence in their ability to learn it, despite their equal or superior performance on tests and in the classroom (Hyde, 2014; Nix et al., 2015; Voyer & Voyer, 2014). This self-perception emerges as early as preschool, when girls begin to view math and science as part of the male domain, and it continues into adolescence and adulthood (del Rio & Strasser, 2013; Miller & Eagly, 2015; Sax et al., 2015a). The more that girls endorse this stereotype, and the lower their self-confidence in math, the poorer their math performance (Liben & Bigler, 2014), and the less interest they have in continuing math and science studies (Ellis et al., 2016; Kiefer & Sekaquaptewa, 2007). Adolescent girls are also less likely than adolescent boys to view mathematics and science as interesting and useful for their future careers (Cunningham et al., 2015; Petersen & Hyde, 2014; OECD, 2015). Keep in mind, however, that many girls and women have positive views about math. For a more detailed look at factors that are associated with women's perspectives on math, see Learn About the Research 5.1.

LEARN ABOUT THE RESEARCH 5.1
Factors Linked to Women's Perspectives on Math

Women's experiences with math and their attitudes toward it differ greatly. Debra Oswald and Richard Harvey (2003) set out to identify college women's differing perspectives on and experiences regarding math. They used a technique called the Q-method, which is considered a useful tool for feminist research (Hesse-Biber, 2016). In the first phase of the Q-method, women are interviewed about their thoughts, experiences, and attitudes regarding a topic, in this case, math. Researchers then select a large number of statements, called Q-sort items, and ask a new group of women to sort the items on a scale ranging from *strongly disagree* to *strongly agree*. Finally, participants with shared viewpoints are grouped together. Oswald and Harvey identified three groups of college women who differed in their experiences, attitudes, and awareness of stereotypes about math. Over half the women, labeled the "successfully encouraged" group, had high self-perceived math ability, found math to be personally relevant, and had positive attitudes toward it. They had been encouraged by parents and teachers and were relatively unaware of negative

stereotypes. About 20 percent of women were in the "mathematically aversive" group. They did not like math, had negative perceptions of their ability, and were somewhat aware of negative stereotypes about women and math. Although not directly discouraged in math, neither were they encouraged to pursue it. Nearly 20 percent of women belonged to the "stereotypically discouraged" group, consisting of women who were very aware of negative gender stereotypes regarding math, lacked parental and teacher support, and had negative experiences in math. These women were fairly neutral in their attitudes toward math and in their own math abilities.

This study clearly shows that a number of variables, including self-perceived ability, experience with math, encouragement (or discouragement), and degree of awareness of stereotypes, are key factors linked to women's perspectives on mathematics. The authors were encouraged that their largest group consisted of successfully encouraged women. They saw this as a possible indicator that women may become better represented in math-related fields in the future.

WHAT DOES IT MEAN?

1. The stereotypically discouraged group was keenly aware of gender stereotypes about math. Do you think these women might be experiencing *stereotype threat*? (See next section.) Explain your answer.
2. Do you think the results of this study would have been different if the participants had

been a group of noncollege women? Explain your answer.
3. Into which of the three groups would you place yourself? Explain your answer.

EXPLANATIONS OF GENDER DIFFERENCES. Several theories have been proposed to account for gender differences in math performance and attitudes. One viewpoint is that genetic, hormonal, and/or structural brain differences underlie gender differences in mathematical ability (Geary, 2007; Kimura, 2007). However, most research fails to support the notion that biology is the primary underlying cause of sex differences in quantitative ability (Ceci et al., 2014; Miller & Halpern, 2014).

Most researchers who study gender differences assert that whatever biological factors might exist are dwarfed by social forces that steer girls and young women away from mathematics. For starters, mathematics and science are stereotyped as male domains around the world (Tenenbaum & May, 2013). As early as first grade, parents in many countries believe that boys are better than girls in mathematics. These beliefs and expectations influence parents' perceptions and behaviors toward their children and also the children's own perceptions and behaviors (Hyde, 2014). For example, studies by Jacquelynne Eccles and her colleagues (e.g., Eccles et al., 2000; Simpkins et al., 2015 a, b) have found that parents with stronger stereotypes about the abilities of girls and boys in math, English, and sports had different expectations of their own daughters' and sons' abilities in these areas. These expectations, in turn, were linked to their children's performance and self-perceptions of competence regardless of their actual ability levels.

How are parents' expectations transmitted to their children? Among other things, parents provide different experiences for their daughters and sons. For example, they are more likely to buy their sons science-related toys and computer materials (Inman & Cardella, 2015; Simpkins et al., 2015a, b). (See Learn About the Research 5.2 for a discussion of gender, computers, and video games.) U.S. parents also discuss math and science concepts more often with sons than with daughters (Leaper & Brown, 2014). One study found that when parents take their young children to interactive science exhibits at museums, they are more likely to explain the science to their sons than to their daughters (Crowley et al., 2001). Similarly, both mothers and fathers are more likely to use scientific concepts and vocabulary when explaining a physics task to a son than to a daughter (Tenenbaum & May, 2013).

LEARN ABOUT THE RESEARCH 5.2
Gender, Computers, and Video Games

Girls and boys both like to play video games, but boys spend more time playing them (Grimes, 2015; Heeter, 2016). Why is this? One major reason is that girls find fewer games that appeal to them. For one thing, games have violent themes, many of which cause stress in girls who play then (Ferguson et al., 2016). The few females who appear in the games are often young, White, and hypersexualized (Fox, 2015; Grimes, 2015; Lynch et al., 2016). They are more likely than male characters to be shown partially nude or engaging in sexual behaviors (Summers & Miller, 2014). In addition, the females portrayed in video games are thinner than the average American woman, and those shown in games for children are thinner than those in games for adults (N. Martin et al., 2009). Playing video games that emphasize the female body in these ways lowers body esteem in young women players (Heeter, 2016), possibly decreasing the attractiveness of these games for them and thus their time commitment. Girls and women prefer educational, puzzle, and adventure-type games with female heroes to games with violence and sports themes (Gotlib, 2011; Heeter, 2016; Porter, 2015). Tween girls (10- to 12-year-olds) are especially attracted to games where they can interact, share content, and create avatars for role play (Kelly, 2012). In recent years, the number of games designed for girls has increased sharply (Grimes, 2015), but girls' games are as stereotyped as those designed for boys, featuring makeup, shopping, dressing up, cooking and boys (Kelly, 2012; Van Reijmersdal et al., 2013). One way to stimulate the creation of video games that are more appealing to female players is to encourage more women to enter the field of game design, but progress has been slow (See In the News 5.1.).

The gender gap in video game usage has important implications for girls' experience with computers because video games often provide a child's introduction to the computer. By the time children enter school, and well into adulthood, males have more positive attitudes toward computers than females and have greater confidence in their computer skills (Heeter, 2016; Misa, 2010). Although overall computer and Internet use rates for girls and boys are now about the same, boys are using computers to program, create Web pages, and solve problems, whereas girls dominate the blogosphere and social networking sites (Bennett & Yabroff, 2008; Pan, 2008).

How can girls' attitudes toward computing be improved? Here are some suggestions (Belec, 2015; Denner et al., 2013; Kelly et al., 2013; Master et al., 2016):

- Design more games that are gender-neutral and that portray female characters positively.
- Use computers throughout the school curriculum, including areas in which girls excel.
- Make efforts to combat girls' popular stereotype that computer work is masculine, "geeky", and antisocial.
- Encourage computer clubs and summer computer classes for girls.

WHAT DOES IT MEAN?

1. Why are most video games and educational software dominated by themes of violence and adventure?
2. What do you think accounts for gender differences in computer-related attitudes?
3. What can be done to minimize or eliminate these differences?

IN THE NEWS 5.1
Why Are So Few Women in Video Game Design?

The number of female video game players—both girls and women—has been growing. Currently, nearly half of all U.S women, compared to half of U.S. men, report playing video games (Duggan, 2015). Yet only 22 percent of digital game designers are women, and even that figure is a big increase from just a few years ago (Brownstein, 2015). Why are there relatively few women game designers? One key reason is online harassment of female game developers, which includes not just name-calling, but violent threats and rampant misogyny (Dougherty & Isaac, 2016; Harvey & Fisher, 2015). One prominent recipient of such threats has been Anita Sarkeesian, creator of Tropes vs. Women in Video Games, an online project dedicated to examining the stereotyped roles of women in many video games (for example, the damsel in distress and the murdered prostitute; Brownstein, 2015). It is not just female game designers who receive unwelcome online comments, however. Video game players who use a female name, voice, or avatar experience more sexually harassing and violent encounters than those who identify as a male agent (Heeter, 2016). What steps can be taken to combat such online harassment?

Children receive the same message in the math and science classroom, as illustrated in Nathalie's comments at the start of the chapter. High school math and science teachers believe boys to be higher achievers in these subjects than girls (Leaper & Brown, 2014). Teachers not only expect boys to do better but also overrate boys' math proficiency compared to similarly performing girls (Robinson-Cimpian et al., 2014). Because expectations often guide behavior, it is not surprising to find that math teachers spend more time instructing, interacting with, and giving feedback to boys than to girls (Blakemore et al., 2009). The long-lasting effects of such teacher biases can be substantial. In one study (Lavy & Sand, 2015), teachers overestimated boys' math abilities and underestimated those of girls, even though the girls had actually outperformed the boys in math. The boys who were thus encouraged went on to perform significantly better on later national exams in junior high and high school. The former president of Harvard University, Lawrence Summers, asserted a few years ago that women may be innately inferior to men in mathematics. These comments highlight the prejudice women scientists face at every stage of their careers. More recently, biochemistry Nobel Laureate Tim Hunt said at a national conference that the "trouble with girls" in laboratories is that "you fall in love with them, they fall in love with you, and when you criticize them, they cry" (Soper, 2015). And who knows how many young women are discouraged by such remarks from pursuing math and science careers in the first place? Recent research (Brown & Leaper, 2010; Cheryan et al., 2013; Robnett, 2016) indicates that negative stereotypes continue to discourage women from entering math and science careers and interfere with retention and advancement in these areas.

These prejudices provide another explanation for the poorer performance of females in math and in other masculine-stereotyped areas, such as visual–spatial tests, namely, the concept of **stereotype threat**. According to this view, developed by Claude Steele and his colleagues, *members of stereotyped groups (e.g., females and ethnic minorities) sometimes perform more poorly because they are anxious about whether their performance will confirm a negative stereotype held about the group's ability* (Betz et al., 2013; Petersen & Hyde, 2014; Spencer & Loge, 2016; Steele et al., 2002). Stereotype threat theory further predicts that performance suffers only when stereotype threat is activated but not when it is reduced or removed. To illustrate, researchers asked college students one of three questions before performing a mental rotation test, a task in which males usually excel (McGlone & Aronson, 2006). One group of students was asked about living in a single-sex or coed dorm, a question that activates gender stereotypes. A second group was asked why they chose to attend a selective private college. This primes students to focus on their intellectual talent. The control group was asked an irrelevant question about living in the northeastern United States. In the control group, men outperformed women on the mental rotation test, as in research discussed earlier in the chapter. In the group primed to focus on gender, the women did even worse, and the men did better. In the group cued to think about their status as students at a selective college, however, the gender gap closed dramatically. Women's scores increased but men's stayed the same, wiping out the gender difference in performance.

Similar results have been found in many academic settings, from elementary school through college, using various manipulations to either activate or minimize stereotype threat (Bagès et al., 2016; Boucher, 2015; Corbett & Hill, 2015; Flore & Wicherts, 2015; Petersen & Hyde, 2014; Picho et al., 2013; Shapiro et al., 2015; Tarampi et al., 2016; Zhang et al., 2013). The good news is that the pressures associated with negative stereotypes can be overcome by teaching students ways to reduce stereotype threat (Betz et al., 2013; Spencer & Loge, 2016). For example, Catherine Good and her colleagues (Good et al., 2003) assigned college students to mentor seventh graders in a low-income ethnically diverse school district. Some children were told that intelligence developed over time and that they could overcome challenges and achieve academic success. Others were given unrelated information about drug use. Girls given the positive message about their academic skills scored higher on a standardized math test than girls given the unrelated message. Similarly, minority and low-income students given the positive academic message did better on a standardized reading test than those in the unrelated message group.

GENDER EQUITY IN SCIENCE AND MATH EDUCATION.   In recent years, increasing emphasis has been given to establishing gender equity in the fields of science, mathematics, technology, and engineering education (Corbett & Hill, 2015). The National Science Foundation, the U.S. Committee on Women in Science, Engineering, and Medicine (CWSEM), and the AAUW Educational Foundation alone have funded hundreds of projects aimed at increasing the participation of girls and women in these fields (Di Bella & Crisp, 2016; Heaverlo et al., 2013; Valla & Williams, 2012). Many of the funded projects involve extracurricular activities such as field trips and museums; a large number include mentoring activities; and others provide workshops for teachers. In addition, the AAUW is working with the National Girls Collaborative Project to link over 1,500 projects that give girls positive science and math experiences (Britsch et al., 2010).

What are some things teachers can do to make the math and science classroom more "girl friendly"? Females respond more positively to math and science instruction if they are taught in a cooperative, student-centered manner, using small groups with high proportions of women, with an applied perspective and a hands-on approach rather than in the traditional competitive manner using a theoretical perspective and a book-learning approach (Corbett & Hill, 2015; Dasgupta et al., 2015). When the former practices are used, both girls and boys are more likely to continue taking courses in math and science and to consider future careers in these fields (Eccles & Roeser, 1999). In addition, having one or more faculty mentors, male or female, is a key factor in attracting high school and college women to science careers (Blackwell, 2010; Carrell et al., 2009). Exposure to female teachers may have a particularly powerful effect (Stearns et al., 2016).

See What You Can Do 5.1 for ways in which you can encourage girls' interest in math and science.

WHAT YOU CAN DO 5.1
Encouraging Girls in Math and Science

To encourage girls' interest and achievement in math and science, here are four things to share with educators and parents in your community and with the women and girls in your life.

1. **Teach children that intellectual skills, including spatial skills, are acquired.**
    Encourage children to play with construction toys, take things apart and put them back together, and work with their hands.
2. **Fight negative stereotypes about girls' math and science abilities.**
    Expose students to successful female role models in math and science.

3. **Help girls recognize their career-relevant skills.**
    Encourage girls to see their success in high school math and science as an indicator that they have the skills to succeed in science and engineering careers.
4. **Encourage high school girls to take calculus, physics, chemistry, and computer science.**
    These classes keep career options open.

Source: St. Rose (2010).

Summary

GENDER-RELATED SOCIAL BEHAVIORS AND PERSONALITY TRAITS

- Girls and boys are more alike than different in their social behaviors and personality traits. Gender differences, when found, are generally small.
- Boys are more physically aggressive than girls whereas girls are more likely to use relational aggression.
- Girls and boys are similar in prosocial behavior, but the few observed differences favor girls.
- Females are somewhat more easily influenced than males in certain situations.
- Girls are more likely than boys to express their emotions and report feeling empathy. Whether this reflects actual differences in emotionality or in the willingness to report feelings remains an open question.
- Men are more narcissistic than women.
- Women, compared to men, are more agreeable, neurotic, and gregarious but less assertive.
- Research does not support Kohlberg's and Gilligan's claim of gender differences in the underlying basis of moral reasoning. Both females and males show caring and justice concerns in resolving moral conflicts.

COMMUNICATION STYLE

- Gender differences in verbal communication include males' greater talkativeness and intrusive interruptions and females' greater affiliative interruptions and their use of speech characterized as tentative. When responding to friends' troubles, women are more likely than men to give support and less likely to give advice.
- Both college women and men like to talk to their friends about the other gender. However, women's conversations focus on interpersonal issues more than do men's.

- Females smile and gaze at their conversational partner more than males do. They are also better able to interpret nonverbal messages. These differences might reflect the communal socialization of females. Another possibility is that women's ability to understand others is an adaptive mechanism that stems from their lower societal status.
- Explanations for these gender differences focus on females' interpersonal orientation and the gender imbalance in power.

GENDER COMPARISON OF COGNITIVE ABILITIES

- Females and males do not differ in general intelligence but show some differences in certain cognitive skills.
- Girls have a slight advantage in verbal skills beginning in infancy. Girls outperform boys in reading, writing, and speech production and are less likely to have reading problems.
- On visual–spatial tests, gender differences favoring boys are greatest in mental rotation, less in spatial perception, and smaller or absent in spatial visualization.
- Girls are better than boys in mathematics computation skills and get better grades in mathematics courses. Boys are better at problem solving starting in mid-adolescence and perform better on standardized mathematics tests. These differences have been decreasing.
- Biological explanations for gender differences in cognitive skills focus on genetics, hormones, and brain structure or organization.
- Environmental explanations include differential socialization of girls and boys by parents and teachers, gender typing of activities as feminine or masculine, gender differences in attitudes toward various cognitive skills, and stereotype threat.

Key Terms

relational aggression *91*
prosocial behavior *92*
empathy *93*
narcissim *93*
Big Five personality traits *94*

affiliative interruption *95*
intrusive interruption *95*
mental rotation *99*
spatial perception *99*
spatial visualization *99*

lateralization *101*
mathematics self-efficacy *102*
stereotype threat *105*

What Do You Think?

1. Why do you think girls are more likely than boys to engage in relational aggression?
2. Adolescent girls report feeling more sadness, shame, and guilt than adolescent boys do. Do you think that females are actually more emotional than males or are simply more likely to report their feelings? Explain your answer.
3. Explanations for gender differences in verbal communication style focus on females' interpersonal orientation and the gender imbalance in power. Which of these explanations do you favor? Explain your answer.
4. What can parents do to maximize girls' potential for learning and liking math?

If You Want to Learn More

Abate, J. (2012). *Recoding gender: Women's changing participation in computing*. Cambridge, MA: MIT Press.

DeFrancisco, V.P. et al. (2014). *Gender in communication: A critical introduction*. Thousand Oaks, CA: Sage.

Fine, C. (2011). *Delusions of gender: How our minds, society, and neurosexism create differences*. New York: W.W. Norton.

Fine, C. (2017). *Testosterone rex: Myths of sex, science, and society*. New York: W.W. Norton.

Gavin, H. & Porter, T. (2014). *Female aggression*. New York: Wiley-Blackwell.

Halpern, D.F. (2012). *Sex differences in cognitive ability* (4th ed.). New York: Psychology Press.

Highsmith, J. & Broaster, S. (2016). *S.T.E.M. 4 girls: The urban girl's guide to the S.T.E.M. disciplines*. Milwaukee, WI: Empower Me Books.

Jordan-Young, R.M. (2011). *Brainstorm: The flaws in the science of sex differences*. Cambridge, MA: MIT Press.

Kilel, B. (2014). *Girls in STEM*. Frederick, MD: Zapphire.

Mosatche, H.S., Lawner, E., & Matloff-Nieves, S. (2016). *Breaking through!: Helping girls succeed in science, technology, engineering, and math*. Waco, TX: Prufrock Press.

Ruberg, W. & Steenburgh, K. (2011). *Sexed sentiments: Interdisciplinary perspectives on gender and emotion*. New York: Rodopi.

Shaw, A. (2014). *Gaming at the edge: Sexuality and gender at the margins of gamer culture*. Minneapolis, MN: University of Minnesota Press.

Websites

Association for Women in Mathematics
http://www.awm-math.org/

Engineer Girl!
http://engineergirl.org/

Girl Tech: Getting Girls Interested in Computers
http://math.rice.edu/~lanius/club/girls.html

Women in Engineering: ProActive Network
http://wepan.org/

CHAPTER 6

Sexuality

I don't want to be forced to take care of a child that I'm not ready for or get an STD . . . As for sex, it'll happen someday, but just not today. (a 17-year-old female high school senior; in Villarosa, 2003, p. D6)

We didn't have the choice of time when the kids were young. Now we have time during the day. We seldom make love at nighttime. Now we can choose. It might be 10 A.M. or 2 P.M.—whenever we're feeling turned on. (a 65-year-old woman; in Doress-Worters & Siegal, 1994, p. 85)

Did these opening vignettes surprise you? Both of them run counter to the popular stereotypes of the hormonally driven, sexually active teenager on the one hand and the sexually disinterested older woman on the other. In this chapter, we explore the fascinating diversity of women's sexuality throughout the life span, including sexual attitudes, behaviors, problems, and orientations.

SEXUALITY

We start with a discussion of women's sexual anatomy and sexual response. Then we look at sexual attitudes, behaviors, and problems.

Sexual Anatomy and Sexual Response

EXTERNAL FEMALE SEXUAL ANATOMY.   The *external female sexual organs* are collectively called the **vulva**. Women can get a clear view of their own vulva by squatting and looking into a hand mirror. The **mons pubis** (also *mons veneris*, mountain of Venus) is *a pad of fatty tissue covering the pubic bone*. During puberty, it becomes covered with coarse hair. The hair continues between the legs and around the anus, the opening of the large intestine. The *fatty hair-covered area between the legs forms flaps called* the **labia majora** (outer lips). They surround *soft hairless flaps of skin*, the **labia minora** (inner lips). Between the inner lips and the anus lies the perineum (Rathus et al., 2013). Spreading the inner lips apart reveals that they join at the upper end to form a fold of skin, or *hood*, over the **clitoris**. *This highly sensitive organ, whose only known function is sexual pleasure, consists of erectile tissue that swells during sexual stimulation* (somewhat like the penis). Although smaller than the penis, the clitoris has more than twice as many nerve fibers (Schulman, 2003). Right below the clitoris is the urethral opening, through which urine passes. Below that is the larger vaginal opening. The **vagina** is *the canal leading to the uterus*. The menstrual blood passes through it and it is the birth canal during childbirth (Rathus et al., 2013).

THE SEXUAL RESPONSE CYCLE.   Women and men respond similarly during the four phases of the **sexual response cycle**, *the physiological responses of individuals to sexual stimulation from any source* (sexual intercourse, masturbation, etc.) Here we discuss women's responses.

In the *excitement phase*, a major response is **vasocongestion**, *the swelling of genital tissues with blood*. Vasocongestion produces vaginal lubrication shortly after stimulation. The clitoris and labia swell with blood. The inner two-thirds of the vagina expand, the uterus elevates, the breasts enlarge, the nipples become erect, and the skin becomes flushed. Heart rate, breathing rate, and muscle tension increase.

During the *plateau phase*, the clitoris, now extremely sensitive, shortens and withdraws under the clitoral hood. *The low third of the vagina becomes engorged with blood, forming* the **orgasmic platform**. Heart rate, blood pressure, and breathing rate continue to rise.

In the *orgasmic phase*, the orgasmic platform, uterus, and anal sphincters contract strongly several times, at intervals of less than a second. These contractions constitute the orgasm.

During the *resolution phase*, the *body returns to its pre-arousal state* within 15 to 30 minutes. Blood is released from engorged areas; the clitoris, vagina, uterus, and labia return to normal size; and muscle tension dissipates. Heart rate and breathing rate return to pre-arousal levels.

MULTIPLE ORGASMS.   Alfred Kinsey and his colleagues (Kinsey et al., 1953) reported that 14 percent of the women they interviewed experienced multiple orgasms. Although a few studies have reported higher percentages, most report figures of about 5 percent, more in line with Kinsey's research ("Women Can Have," 2007). Unlike women, few men are physiologically capable of multiple orgasms. This is one of the major gender differences in sexual response, the other being that men but not women ejaculate during orgasm. Although having multiple orgasms can be a good thing, some women now feel that they are sexually inadequate if they don't. One orgasm can be quite satisfying, as can sex that does not culminate in orgasm.

ONE OR TWO KINDS OF ORGASM?   Freud (1938) proposed that there were two types of female orgasm: clitoral and vaginal. Clitoral orgasms were achieved through clitoral stimulation during masturbation. This form of orgasm, practiced by young girls, was considered immature and sexually inadequate in adult women. Women were expected to shift to vaginal orgasms, brought on by sexual intercourse (Torre, 2013). Research, however, has demonstrated that there is only one kind of orgasm, physiologically, whether it is brought on by clitoral or vaginal stimulation. Furthermore, the clitoris is indirectly stimulated even in vaginal intercourse. Although orgasms resulting from clitoral and vaginal stimulation are physiologically the same, there may be psychological or subjective differences (Rathus et al., 2013). For example, the context of sexual intercourse includes a partner to whom one may be emotionally attached, whereas masturbation is often (but not always) done without the presence of a partner. Sexual pleasure is also possible without orgasm. Expressing sexual feelings for another person involves a number of pleasurable activities, of which intercourse and orgasm may be only a part.

Sexual Attitudes

THE SEXUAL DOUBLE STANDARD.   Historically, women's sexuality was discouraged and denied, especially outside of marriage. The social construction of norms about female and male sexuality is nowhere seen more clearly than in this **sexual double standard**, *which allowed and even encouraged premarital sex for men, but not for women*. As premarital sex became more acceptable, the double standard has evolved into a belief that casual sexual activity is acceptable for men, but that women's sexual experiences should occur only in the context of a serious relationship (DeMello, 2014). As examples of the double standard, young women are judged more negatively than young men when they provide a condom for protection (Fassinger & Arseneau, 2008) or when they have a sexually transmitted infection (Smith et al., 2008). A related example is the growing incidence of "slut shaming" on the Internet, with women as the primary targets (Webb, 2015). Not surprisingly, men are more likely than women to endorse the sexual double standard (Sakaluk & Milhausen, 2012).

GENDER DIFFERENCES IN ATTITUDES.   Women generally have less permissive attitudes toward sexual behavior than men (Petersen & Hyde, 2010; Twenge et al., 2015). In a recent meta-analysis of research in several countries on sexual attitudes and behavior, Jennifer Petersen and Janet Hyde (2010) found that women reported more negative attitudes than men about casual sex. Women were somewhat more likely to feel anxious or guilty about sex and to emphasize relationships as a context for sex, and were less likely to endorse the double standard. No gender differences were found in attitudes toward masturbation, extramarital sex, and premarital sex when couples are committed or engaged. In general, gender differences in attitudes toward sexual behavior overall narrowed as people got older. These differences also diminished from the 1970s into the twenty-first century (Petersen & Hyde, 2010). A recent survey of Americans aged 18 and older found that although women continued to hold less permissive attitudes toward sex than men, attitudes of both groups have become more permissive. For example, in 2012, women were still less likely than men to say that premarital sex is not wrong (52 vs. 59 percent), but this represented a doubling of women's support for premarital sex compared to 40 years earlier (Twenge et al., 2015). Other studies show that men from countries around the world are more likely than women to rate sex as important and to report greater physical and emotional pleasure from it (Angier, 2007; Fisher, 2010).

ATTITUDES TOWARD WOMEN WITH DISABILITIES.   Girls and young women with disabilities may face particular challenges in developing a healthy sexuality (Altuntug et al., 2014; Hans, 2015). For one thing, a common stereotype is women with disabilities are asexual beings who have no sex life and who are unsuitable as romantic partners (Wade & Ferree, 2015; Yasuda & Hamilton, 2013). In addition, women with disabilities experience barriers to receiving adequate counseling on sexuality, birth control, pregnancy, and childbirth. Women with disabilities engage in less sexual activity and are less satisfied with their sex lives than able-bodied women (McRuer & Mollow, 2012; Nosek, 2010). Whereas able-bodied women often resent being treated as sex objects, some women with disabilities resent being treated as asexual objects (Bartlett, 2016). The view of women with disabilities as asexual is based on misconceptions about their sexual desires and abilities. Most individuals with disabilities have the same sexual desires as able-bodied persons. Their ability to perform sexually depends on their adjustment to the physical limitations of their disability and the availability of a helpful partner (Kattari, 2014; Siebers, 2012).

Sexual Behaviors

The recent National Survey of Sexual Health and Behavior (NSSHB), the most comprehensive study of sexuality in the United States, surveyed a representative sample of nearly 5,900 individuals from ages 14 to 94. The researchers found that both women and men engaged in diverse solo and partnered sexual activities. Masturbation, oral sex, and vaginal intercourse were prevalent in both sexes. The proportion of women and men engaging in these behaviors peaked in the 20s and decreased with age. Being in good health and having a partner were related to higher levels of sexual activity for both sexes (Herbenick et al., 2010a, b).

GENDER DIFFERENCES.   A number of gender differences in sexual activity were reported both in the NSSHB and in the recent meta-analysis by Petersen and Hyde (2010). Men, compared to women, had a higher incidence of intercourse and oral sex, more frequent intercourse, a greater number of partners, first intercourse at a younger age, and more extramarital sex. Women appear to be narrowing the adultery gap in recent years, however, with younger women being unfaithful to their spouses nearly as often as men (Parker-Pope, 2008).

Letitia Anne Peplau (2002) sums up these differences as indicating that men are more interested in sex than are women. She also contends that assertiveness and dominance are more closely linked to male sexuality than to female sexuality. For example, she notes that men tend to initiate sex in heterosexual relationships and that men are more likely than women to use intimidation or physical force to get an unwilling partner to engage in sex (see Chapter 14). Another gender difference proposed by Peplau (2002) and by Lisa Diamond (Diamond & Dickenson, 2012) is that women have greater sexual fluidity and plasticity, that is, their sexual beliefs and behaviors are more capable of being shaped and changed by cultural, social, and situational factors. For example, women are more likely than men to engage in sexual behavior that runs counter to their established pattern of sexual desire, that is, heterosexual women having sex with women and lesbians engaging in sex with men (England, 2016). Women's sexual attitudes and behaviors also seem to be affected more by their education level, religious views, and by the views of their culture than are men's attitudes and behaviors (Fassinger & Arseneau, 2008; Katz-Wise, 2015).

Although gender differences in sexuality are well documented, one must also keep in mind that there are tremendous variations in sexual expression among women of different ages, marital statuses, educational levels, religions, and races/ethnicities. Women who are younger, White, and well educated, and who have no religious affiliation have more varied sexual practices than other women. For example, they are more likely to have experienced oral and anal sex and to find these acts appealing (Laumann & Mahay, 2002).

Two limitations of research on sexual attitudes and behaviors must be kept in mind. One is the problem of volunteer bias. Many people refuse to participate in surveys of their sexual views and practices. Thus, samples are biased because they include the responses only of those individuals who are willing to discuss their intimate behavior. Such individuals tend to be more sexually permissive and to have more liberal attitudes toward sexuality than nonvolunteers. Therefore, survey results based on volunteer samples may not be representative of the population at large (Rathus et al., 2013).

A second problem is that all the results are based on self-reports, not on direct observations of behavior. It is possible that there are gender differences in reporting behaviors, but few, if any, differences in actual sexual behaviors or attitudes. Women may underreport their sexual experiences and men may exaggerate theirs (Jonason & Fisher, 2009). As a result of these two problems, one must take findings regarding gender differences in sexuality with a grain of salt.

Sexual Problems

What constitutes a sexual problem or dysfunction for women? How frequently do such problems occur? These issues are currently topics of vigorous debate among researchers. Some scholars have defined anything interfering with orgasm as a sexual problem. Others, however, argue that emphasizing orgasm reflects the male perspective that sex ends with ejaculation, whereas for many women, orgasm is not the goal or the most important part of sexual activity (Frith, 2013; Tiefer, 2014). In this section, we examine changing views of women's sexual problems.

Until recently, researchers who studied sexual problems typically employed the widely used system for classifying sexual dysfunction from the *Diagnostic and Statistical Manual of Mental Disorders IV* (*DSM-IV*) of the American Psychiatric Association (1994). Four categories are recognized in *DSM-IV*: sexual desire disorders, sexual arousal disorders, orgasmic disorders, and sexual pain disorders. Feminist scholars have criticized this categorization, as we shall see shortly, because it is overly genital and neglects issues of relationships and social context (Marecek & Gavey, 2013; Tiefer, 2014).

Large-scale studies using the *DSM-IV* categories to examine sexual problems in U.S. adults (Laumann et al., 1999, 2008a) have found that the most frequently reported sexual problem among women is *a lack of desire for sexual activity*, or **inhibited sexual desire**. About 25 percent of younger women and up to 40 percent of older women report having this problem. (Persons who have little interest in sex, but are not concerned by it, are not considered to have the disorder.) About one in seven younger women and over one in three older women report **sexual arousal disorder**, which involves *insufficient lubrication or a failure to be aroused*. In the recently adopted *DSM-V*, the two categories of low sexual desire and sexual arousal disorder have been replaced by one new category: Female Sexual Interest/Arousal Disorder (SI/AD; Holloway & Wylie, 2015; Spurgas, 2013). Nearly one in four younger women and one in three older women report **female orgasmic disorder**, defined as *experiencing the excitement phase of the sexual response cycle but not achieving orgasm*. (If a woman is satisfied with this situation, she is not considered to have an orgasmic disorder.) About 7 percent of younger woman and 18 percent of older women report **dyspareunia**, or *painful intercourse*. Often a physical condition, such as a sexually transmitted infection (STI), lack of lubrication, or a structural problem, is involved. Psychological factors such as anxiety about sex or prior sexual trauma may also be responsible (Buster, 2013). Another sexual pain disorder documented by Laumann and his colleagues is **vaginismus**, the *involuntary contraction of vaginal muscles*, making intercourse painful or impossible. Vaginismus is often caused by factors such as childhood sexual abuse, rape, a family upbringing that included negative attitudes toward sex, and a history of painful intercourse (Buster, 2013). In the new *DSM-V*, the two pain disorders have been merged into one category (Latif & Diamond, 2013).

Laumann and his colleagues (2008) also found that factors such as age, marital status, ethnicity, education, and economic status were related to the incidence of sexual dysfunction. For women, the prevalence of sexual problems declined until about age 60 and then leveled off, except for those who reported trouble lubricating. Men, on the other hand, had more problems with age, particularly erectile dysfunction and inability to achieve orgasm. Single, divorced, separated, and widowed individuals showed an elevated risk of sexual problems. Ethnicity also was associated with sexual problems. For example, among younger women, White women were more likely to report sexual pain, whereas Black women more often experienced low levels of desire and pleasure. Latinas, on the other hand, reported lower rates of sexual problems than other women.

Women and men with less education and lower income reported more sexual problems than more highly educated and affluent individuals. What might account for this social class difference in sexual problems? Poorer physical and mental health in individuals of lower social status may be a factor because diminished health is related to problems with sex (Hughes et al., 2015). Underlying physical conditions that can cause sexual dysfunction include diabetes, heart disease, neurological disorders, side effects of medications, alcoholism, drug abuse, and heavy smoking. Psychological causes of sexual problems include stress or anxiety from work, concern about poor sexual performance, marital discord, or depression. Some of these problems are all too common in the lives of poor women and men (Heiman, 2008). Unfortunately, the sociocultural predictors of sexual problems studied by Laumann and his associates have often been given little attention in the popular and professional media. Instead, media focus on the high incidence of physiological problems, and the need for drug companies to develop medical treatments, such as female Viagra, to treat women's sexual "illnesses" (Bergner, 2013; Spurgas, 2013). See In the News 6.1 for an update on this issue.

IN THE NEWS 6.1
Viagra for Women? Pros and Cons

In 2015, the U.S. Food and Drug Administration approved a controversial new drug, flibanserin (sold as Addyi), the first to treat low sexual desire in women (Joffe et al., 2016). Why is this drug controversial? On the one hand, some applaud the drug, calling it the woman's equivalent of Viagra, providing help for women with low sex drive (Gellad et al., 2015). On the other hand, critics note that the drug provides only modest benefits and has numerous side effects. Lenore Tiefer (see "A New View of Women's Sexual Problems," below) further argues that low sexual drive is mostly a psychological or relational problem, which is being inappropriately treated as a medical issue (McHugh, 2015). What is your view?

A NEW VIEW OF WOMEN'S SEXUAL PROBLEMS.   Recently, a group of therapists and sex researchers has developed a new view of women's sexual problems that focuses on the sociocultural, political, psychological, social, and relational bases of women's sexual problems (Cacchioni, 2015; Tiefer, 2014). These researchers define sexual problems as discontent or dissatisfaction with any emotional, physical, or relational aspect of sexual experiences that may arise in one or more of four interrelated aspects of women's sexual lives. This view focuses on the *prevention* of women's sexual problems through tackling the economic, political, and sociocultural root causes of the problems, and not on medical treatment alone (Tiefer, 2014).

LESBIAN, GAY, BISEXUAL, ASEXUAL, AND TRANSGENDER INDIVIDUALS

Before reading this section, try the exercise in Get Involved 6.1. Compare your findings with the information that follows.

GET INVOLVED 6.1
Attitudes Toward Lesbians

Ask two female and two male friends to complete the following exercise.

Our society views some groups of unmarried women as having higher social status or acceptability than other groups of unmarried women. Give each group below a social status score based on how you think these groups are viewed in society. Assign each group a score ranging from 1 to 100, with *high* scores indicating *high* status and *low* scores indicating *low* status.

Social Status Score

	Social Status Score
divorced heterosexual women	_____
never-married lesbians	_____
widowed heterosexual women	_____
never-married heterosexual women	_____

WHAT DOES IT MEAN?

1. In what ways are your female and male respondents' answers alike? In what ways are they different? Explain the differences and similarities.
2. How does the social status of lesbians compare to that of the three groups of heterosexual women?
3. How would you account for the differences in social status of these four groups of women?

_____

Source: Etaugh and Fulton (1995).

Sexual orientation consists of four components: sexual attraction, sexual arousal, sexual behavior, and sexual identity (J.M. Bailey et al., 2016). In the past, women's sexual orientation was divided into two categories: lesbian and heterosexual. Later, the bisexual category was added. Recently, a "mostly heterosexual" identity has been proposed to describe women who fall between homosexuality and heterosexuality (Vrangalova & Savin-Williams, 2014). Asexual and transgender categories are also fairly recent additions to the recognized spectrum of sexuality. A **lesbian** is a woman who is *emotionally and sexually attracted to other women*, a **gay man** is *attracted to other men*, a **bisexual** person is *attracted to both men and women* (Meem et al., 2010), and an **asexual** person is attracted to neither women nor men (Fischer & Seidman, 2016). A **transgender** person is an individual whose gender identity differs from the gender she or he was assigned at birth (Schilt & Westbrook, 2009). It is difficult to estimate the number of women who are lesbian, bisexual, asexual, or transgender because negative attitudes toward sexual minorities discourage some individuals from reporting this behavior. In addition, sexual identities of women may change over time. Whereas many gay men recall their same-sex attraction as beginning before puberty, many lesbians report not feeling same-sex attractions until adulthood (Diamond, 2008). In the NSSHB mentioned earlier, 7 percent of American women *identified* themselves as having a lesbian or bisexual sexual orientation; but twice that number reported *engaging in sexual behavior* with women during their lifetime (Herbenick et al., 2010b, c). However, a 10-year longitudinal study of lesbian and bisexual women found that two-thirds of the participants had changed sexual minority identities at least once in their lives and over one-third had done so more than once (Diamond, 2008). In addition, the comprehensive National Longitudinal Study of Adolescent Health found a great deal of fluidity in romantic attractions and relationships over an 18-month period. For example, of the 4 percent of girls who reported bisexual attraction at the beginning of the study, only one-fourth did so 18 months later; the majority of them later reported attraction to and relationships with males (Russell & Seif, 2002). Findings like these suggest that, as noted earlier in the chapter, female sexual orientation is more "fluid" than that of males, meaning that it is more sensitive to situational and contextual factors (Katz-Wise, 2015; Manley et al., 2015; Westwood, 2016).

Bisexual Individuals

Because most people view sexual orientation as consisting of two categories—heterosexual and homosexual—many bisexual individuals feel misunderstood or invisible (Allen & Roberto, 2016; Hayfield et al., 2014). Bisexual women and men are often viewed as going through a transitional stage between heterosexuality and homosexuality, denying their true sexuality, or avoiding commitment to a particular lifestyle or partner (Hoang, 2013). Furthermore, bisexuality is often criticized by both heterosexuals and lesbian/gay individuals as indicating promiscuity, indecisiveness, or immaturity (Diehl, 2013; Dodge et al., 2013; Kwon, 2013). The dilemmas faced by two of Claire's bisexual students were expressed this way:

Personally, I've experienced backlash from both the straight and LGBT communities. Generally, I'm viewed as being indecisive or as being in a phase which will inevitably lead to a choice between "fully" straight or lesbian. This is not as unexpected to me as the response from the LGBT community that I am not "gay enough" or that I am "straight-passing," and therefore do not belong to their community.

(Haley, age 21)

If I hear "The lesbian's dating a boy?!" one more time . . . So I met a boy and we've started dating, not a big deal to me but obviously to others. My main issue here is pigeon-holing. "I thought you were supposed to be gay," as if I have become a caricature of a human.

(Angelique, age 22)

Research shows that some individuals feel attracted to both sexes simultaneously and may carry on relationships with both men and women at the same time. This is more likely to occur in women than in men (Copen et al., 2016; Priebe & Svedin, 2013). Large-scale surveys have found that among women, bisexual attractions are much more common than same-sex attractions, whereas the opposite is true for men (J.M. Bailey et al., 2016; Burleson, 2016; Copen et al., 2016). Also, many bisexuals are more attracted to one gender than the other (Hoang, 2013).

Same-sex sexuality thus is a matter of degree for many women, who do not clearly fit into any one category. In the words of Susan:

> I'm in a physical/sexual sense 60 percent heterosexual and 40 percent gay . . . My sexual fantasies are often with a man but my romantic ones are with a woman . . . In the emotional realm I'm 30 percent heterosexual and 70 percent gay. I can't imagine spending my life with a guy! Sex wouldn't be enough. I want to take long trips with girls. I want to exchange lipstick colors and compare Hillary [Clinton] stories . . . I'm attracted to certain types of males, both the really femme girly boys and the really masculine studs . . . and the really feminine girls with powdered faces. The butch ones can be a Friday night fantasy. Don't think about writing down that I'm a lesbian, or even bisexual. I hate both words!
>
> (Savin-Williams, 2006, p. 316)

Asexual Individuals

Asexuality is defined as *a sexual orientation describing people who do not experience sexual attraction* (Cerankowski & Milks, 2014). Most scholars agree that asexuality is relatively rare, with evidence suggesting that 1 percent or less of the population identify as asexual (Stevenson, 2015). Cyber spaces such as the Asexual Visibility and Education Network (AVEN) provide a forum for discussing asexuality and a place for asexual individuals to develop a community (Kim, 2014).

Transgender Individuals

Transgender people (some refer to themselves as gender nonconforming) have a gender identity that does not match their sex assigned at birth, which is generally based on genital appearance. Estimates suggest that approximately 700,000 U.S. adults (fewer than 1 percent) are transgender (Schuster et al., 2016). While some transgender individuals choose to alter their bodies through surgery or hormonal therapy, many do not (Pew Research Center, 2013c). Visibility of transgender individuals and support for transgender rights have increased dramatically in recent years (Friedman, 2015; Sontag, 2015). As we saw in Chapter 2, media portrayals of LGBT individuals are becoming more numerous and more authentic. Yet, as we shall discover in Chapters 10, 12, and 14, transgender individuals still experience considerable discrimination. The highly publicized controversy over the right of transgender people to use bathroom and locker room facilities that match their gender identity rather than their assigned identity is but one example (Brody, 2016a; Stolberg et al., 2016).

Attitudes Toward Sexual Minorities

Heterosexism is *the view that heterosexuality is the norm and that homosexuality is abnormal.* Sexual minority individuals may themselves internalize heterosexist attitudes (Mason et al., 2015). This view often leads to **homophobia**, *negative reactions to homosexuality and irrational fear of LGBT individuals* (Reynolds & Singh, 2017). Attitudes toward transgender people are less favorable than those toward other sexual minorities (Norton & Herek, 2013). Such reactions are pervasive not only in American society (Herek & McLemore, 2013; Mustanski et al., 2014), but also in other parts of the world, as we shall see shortly. In a 2016 survey of American adults, for example, only one-third of individuals aged 70 and over supported gay rights, although on a positive note, 70 percent of young adults were supporters (Pew Research Center, 2016a). Similarly, although about one-half of older Americans oppose gay marriage, civil unions, and same-sex couples rearing children, only about one-fourth of young adults feel that way (Pew Research Center, 2013). For example, in a recent survey of first-year college students, 87 percent of women and 80 percent of men supported adoption of children by gays and lesbians (Eagan et al., 2013). Homophobic views are especially strong among males, political and religious conservatives, people with a high degree of religious commitment, those with less education, and individuals who hold traditional gender-role attitudes and authoritarian right-wing views. These individuals are less likely to have family members or friends who are openly gay or lesbian, and they are more likely to believe that a homosexual orientation is freely chosen (Cragun & Sumerau, 2015; Crawford et al., 2016; Frias-Navarro et al., 2015; Herek, 2015; Joslyn & Haider-Markel, 2016; Mitchell & DeZarn, 2014; Pew Research Center, 2013c; Pinsof & Haselton, 2016; Webb & Chonody, 2014).

Although heterosexual men are more negative than women toward gay men, there are small or no gender differences in attitudes toward lesbians (Petersen & Hyde, 2010; Webb & Chonody, 2014). This finding is consistent with the research we discussed in Chapters 3 and 4 showing that men who violate gender roles are judged more harshly than women who do so.

WOMEN OF COLOR.   Black individuals hold somewhat more negative attitudes toward sexual minorities than do Whites, Latina/os, and Asian Americans (Glass & Few-Demo, 2013; Le & Dinh, 2015; Pew Research Center, 2016a). Thus, lesbian, bisexual, and transgender women of color are confronted with the intersecting societal barriers of sexism, racism, and homophobia, placing them in "triple jeopardy" (Calabrese et al., 2015; Craig & Keane, 2014; DeBlaere et al., 2014). In some ethnic minority cultures, women who do not adhere to traditional gender roles or who are not subordinate to men are often ostracized or mistreated. For example, "two spirit" Native American women experience disproportionate levels of sexual and physical violence. At a time when transgender people are gaining visibility, transgender women of color are experiencing high rates of violence, including homicide (National Coalition of Anti-Violence Programs, 2016). Sexual minority women of color thus may be more reluctant to "come out," choosing to remain invisible rather than be rejected (Goldberg, 2017; Pastrana, 2015).

DISCRIMINATION.   Discrimination against sexual minorities is substantial and can take many forms (D'Haese et al., 2016; Herek, 2015; Spengler & Ægisdóttir, 2015). A meta-analysis of research on the experiences of LGB individuals in several nations found that 55 percent had experienced verbal harassment, 28 percent had been physically assaulted, and 27 percent had been sexually assaulted (Katz-Wise & Hyde, 2012). The most virulent form of homophobia is expressed in violent "hate crimes" often committed against gay and bisexual men by groups of young adult White males. One national study found that 84 percent of gay men had experienced verbal slurs, threats, or attacks compared with about 73 percent of lesbians and bisexual women and 47 percent of bisexual men (Pew Research Center, 2013; Smyth & Jenness, 2014). Sadly, homophobia and prejudice are daily experiences for many sexual minority students during the school day (Robinson & Espelage, 2013; Woodford et al., 2014). In one nationwide survey of more than 7,800 LGBT middle and high school students, nearly three in four were called names or threatened. Over one-third had been physically harassed and nearly one in five had been assaulted. More than half felt unsafe in school and nearly one-third missed at least a day of school because of feeling unsafe (Kosciw et al., 2014). Transgender individuals are even more likely than their lesbian, gay, and bisexual peers to experience harassment and assault (Fredriksen-Goldsen et al., 2014; Miller & Grollman, 2015; UNAIDS, 2014a).

Home may not be a safe haven either. Sexual minority teens and adults who "come out"—that is, declare their sexual orientation to others—may be rejected by their families (Mayer et al., 2014). In some cases, they are compelled to leave home and seek survival in the streets (Button & Worthen, 2014). Such experiences, not surprisingly, can lead to a reluctance to reveal one's sexual orientation (Gao, 2015) and to increased levels of emotional stress and psychological problems among harassed individuals (Martin-Storey, 2016). We shall explore some of these problems more fully in Chapter 13. Support from parents and peers can buffer the negative effects of victimization (Birkett et al., 2015). It is encouraging to note that nearly 60 percent of today's adults say they would not be upset to learn their child was gay, compared to fewer than 10 percent in 1985 (Gao, 2015). Despite the stress faced by many lesbian, gay, bisexual, and transgender youth, the good news is that most display strength and resiliency and are often involved in antihomophobia advocacy efforts (Hervick et al., 2014).

In July 2015, the U.S. Supreme Court ruled that same-sex marriage was legal in the United States. As of this writing, however, only 22 states, mostly on the East and West coasts and in the Northeast, bar discrimination on the basis of sexual orientation in employment, credit, housing, and public accommodation (Arendt & Buzzarell, 2017; Eckholm, 2015).

More than two-thirds of the 20 countries around the world that have legalized same-sex marriage are in western Europe. Many eastern European nations permit civil unions but ban same-sex marriage (Lipka, 2015). Let us now take a closer look at attitudes toward sexual minorities around the world.

 GLOBAL ATTITUDES TOWARD SEXUAL MINORITIES.   Sexual minorities are discriminated against in varying degrees by laws and social policies around the world (Bakirci, 2011; Rose & Hospital, 2015; Westwood, 2016). Same-gender sexual behavior is still illegal in dozens of countries, including much of Africa, the Middle East, and parts of Asia (Bailey et al., 2016). In these countries, homosexuality may be punishable with prison sentences, beatings, or death (Kasai & Rooney, 2012).

Canada, the U.S., and western European nations are the most accepting of sexual minorities, followed by the eastern European countries. Some nations that have decriminalized homosexuality (e.g., Brazil, China, Mexico) still have low tolerance of sexual minorities (Rose & Hospital, 2015). Thus, even where homosexuality is not illegal, sexual minorities often do not "come out" for fear of losing their children, jobs, and social status, or becoming the target of physical or verbal attack (Burn, 2011).

Lesbianism was acceptable in a number of Native American cultures before Western colonization. For instance, women from the Mohave, Maricopa, Cocopa, Klamath, and Kaska tribes could marry and make love with other women without stigma (Burn, 2011). However, contemporary attitudes of Native Americans, which have been influenced by the dominant American culture, may be less accepting (Rose & Hospital, 2015). Similarly, in the African country of Lesotho, it is not unusual for women to have romantic relationships with each other before and even during heterosexual marriage (Burn, 2011). However, these relationships occur less often in Lesotho women exposed to Western ideas.

See What You Can Do 6.1 for ways in which you can help support the rights of sexual minorities.

Explanations of Sexual Orientation

The origins of homosexuality are complex and controversial (Bailey et al., 2016; LeVay, 2011). A number of psychological and biological theories have been proposed. Psychoanalytic theorists blamed dysfunctional parents—the overbearing mother and the distant father—for children's homosexuality. Little evidence exists in support of this theory, however (J.M. Bailey et al., 2016). From a learning theory point of view, early positive sexual activity with members of one's own gender or negative sexual experiences with members of the other gender could lead to homosexuality. However, many lesbians and gay men are aware of their sexual orientation before they have engaged in any sexual activity. Nor is there any evidence to support the notion that one's sexual orientation is a matter of free choice (LeVay, 2011).

WHAT YOU CAN DO 6.1
Supporting Rights of Sexual Minorities

1. If your school has a gay–straight alliance, get involved. If not, start one. Ideas can be found at www.glsen.org.
2. Volunteer for Parents and Friends of Lesbians and Gays (PFLAG). For information, contact www.pflag.org.

3. Volunteer for the Trevor Project, www.thetrevorproject.org, a suicide prevention hotline that supports sexual minority youth.

_____

Source: Burn (2011).

Biological theories focus on genetic or hormonal factors. One recent study of over 400 gay brothers found that gay men shared similarities on the X chromosome and on chromosome 8 (Sanders et al., 2015). So, sexual orientation appears to be strongly influenced by genetics.

Is sexual orientation influenced by sex hormones? In adulthood, there is no link between levels of female and male sex hormones and sexual orientation (J.M. Bailey et al., 2016). *Prenatal* sex hormones may be a factor, however. Studies of intersexuality discussed in Chapter 3 pointed to the prenatal influence of androgen on the development of females' sexual orientation (Hines, 2010). For example, the finger-length patterns in lesbians resemble those of men more than those of heterosexual women (J.M. Bailey et al., 2016). This finding and others suggest that high levels of androgens (male sex hormones) during the prenatal period may partially masculinize certain physiological and anatomical characteristics of lesbians, including the brain structures responsible for sexual orientation (Hines, 2010; LeVay, 2011).

Most likely, complex interactions among biological, psychological, and environmental factors determine sexual orientation, and different causal mechanisms may operate for different individuals (Richards & Barker, 2013).

SEXUAL ACTIVITY DURING ADOLESCENCE

Why does it seem that all boys want is sex? (Brenda, age 14)

What happens when I have a boyfriend who wants to have sex and I don't? (Ruth, age 13)

Why is it that when a guy has sex with a girl, he is called a "stud," but the girl is considered a "slut"? (Veronica, age 13; all in Zager & Rubenstein, 2002)

Although most teenagers have their first sexual intercourse in their mid-to-late teens (Guttmacher Institute, 2016a), the experience is quite different for females and males. More women than men describe their first experience as unwanted and they are less likely to report physical pleasure and orgasm (Else-Quest, 2014; Guttmacher Institute, 2016a). Women are also more likely to indicate an emotional connection with their partners and partner pressure as reasons for their sexual initiation (Walsh et al., 2011). In fact, one out of 10 female teens reports that their first intercourse was non-voluntary (Hoffman, 2008), while three-fourths report it was with a committed partner (Rutter & Schwartz, 2012). Let's take a closer look at sexual activity during adolescence. We'll discuss teenage pregnancy in Chapter 7.

Frequency of Sexual Activity

Males become sexually active at younger ages than females. Among females, Black girls show the earliest onset of sexual activity and Asian Americans the latest. In addition, adolescent boys, compared to adolescent girls, have more sex (including same-sex behavior) and more sex partners (Kann, 2016). Rates of teenage sexuality reached near-record highs in the late 1980s, but have declined since the early 1990s. For example, the percentage of high school students who had intercourse decreased from 54 percent in 1991 to 46 percent in 2009 (Eaton et al., 2010). The decline has been most noticeable among Black youth (Sweeney & Raley, 2014). Efforts to educate young people about safe sex and about the risks of pregnancy and STIs such as AIDS have played a key role in reducing these numbers. Still, by the time they graduate from high school, nearly two-thirds of girls will have engaged in sex (Guttmacher Institute, 2014).

Two forms of sexual activity that are growing in popularity among college students and young adults are the "hook-up" and "friends with benefits." For a more detailed look at these sexual encounters, see Learn About the Research 6.1.

Another trend in teenage and young adult sexuality involves using the Internet and social media to interact with others (Temple-Smith et al., 2016). The term **cybersex** (also called online sexual activity) has several meanings but is often defined as a *social interaction between at least two persons who exchange computer messages for purposes of sexual arousal and satisfaction*

LEARN ABOUT THE RESEARCH 6.1
Hook-Ups and Friends With Benefits

Among both female and male college students and young adults, one increasingly common form of sexual activity is the **hook-up**, a *one-time casual unplanned sexual encounter that can range anywhere from kissing to intercourse* (Fielder, 2014; Monto & Carey, 2014). Another form of sexual intimacy is known as **friends with benefits**. In this arrangement, the *partners start out as friends and decide to periodically engage in sexual behavior but not become a couple* (Mongeau et al., 2013). About 70 percent of college students report hav-ing had a hook-up experience, usually after consuming alcohol (Armstrong et al., 2012; Garcia et al., 2012). Men are more likely than women to prefer hooking up to dating, while the reverse is true for women (Grieger, 2017), perhaps because women view hooking up as less likely to lead to a relationship (Owen et al., 2010; Regnerus & Uecker, 2011). Compared to men, women who hook up are more likely to report guilt, regret, psychological distress, and depression (Bersamin et al., 2014; Fielder, 2014; Harden, 2014).

WHAT DOES IT MEAN?

1. Discuss concerns that young people who have hook-ups or friends with benefits don't learn to build emotional intimacy before they get physically intimate and may fail to know how to connect with future partners on an intimate level. Are these concerns valid? Why or why not?
2. When, if at all, do you consider it to be acceptable to have a hook-up or a "friend with benefits"? What level of physical intimacy do you think is appropriate between people who don't have an emotional relationship?
3. Some feminists view hooking up as liberating or empowering, while others see it as exploitative and sexist (Gavey, 2012). What is your opinion?

(Döring, 2009). There are two feminist views of cybersex, quite different from each other. The victimization perspective focuses on how women and girls as individuals and as a group are harmed by online harassment and virtual rape. In contrast, the liberation perspective argues that cybersex benefits girls and women by allowing them to explore their sexuality freely and more safely (Döring, 2009; Eleuteri et al., 2014). Which view do you agree with, and why?

Factors Associated With Sexual Activity

Many factors affect the onset of sexual activity, the number of sexual partners, and the risk of becoming pregnant or causing a pregnancy. These include the effects of puberty, family, and peers, as well as individual characteristics (Hardin, 2014; Silk & Romero, 2014). As we noted in Chapter 4, early-maturing girls tend to initiate sexual activity sooner than other girls (Mendle, 2014; Moore et al., 2014). One likely reason for this is that the development of breasts, curves, and other secondary sex characteristics may attract sexual attention from males (Zabin & Cardona, 2002).

You may be surprised to learn that parents are the biggest influence on teenagers' decisions about whether to have sex and that friends are next (National Campaign to Prevent Teen Pregnancy, 2003). Parents, however, underestimate their own influence and believe that teenagers' friends play a more important role. Unfortunately, fewer than half of older teen women and just over one-fourth of men this age say that they have talked with a parent about birth control and how to say "no to sex" (Centers for Disease Control and Prevention, 2011). And although many teens look up sexual health information online, these Websites often contain inaccurate information (Guttmacher Institute, 2016a).

Teenagers who delay the onset of sexual activity, who have fewer partners, and who are at lower risk of pregnancy are close to their parents, see them as supportive, and communicate well with them (Kan et al., 2010; Kincaid et al., 2012; Parkes et al., 2011; Silk & Romero, 2014). Their parents are more likely to be married, better educated, have a higher income level, use firm, consistent discipline, and be aware of their teen's friends and activities (Manlove et al., 2009; Maness et al., 2016; Moilanen, 2015; Roche & Leventhal, 2009). Teenagers who begin sexual activity later and who have a lower pregnancy risk are also more apt to be religious, have better grades in school, higher educational aspirations, greater social maturity, and lower levels of alcohol, cigarette, and drug use; and, in the case of girls, are more apt to participate in sports (Carlson et al., 2014; Fortenberry, 2013; Guzmán & Stritto, 2012; Thomas & Lou, 2015).

An early onset of sexual activity, a greater number of partners, and increased risk of pregnancy are linked to having sexually active or pregnant siblings and peers, growing up in a single-parent home, having parents who are permissive about sex but do less monitoring of their teen's behavior, and being in a committed dating relationship (Almy et al., 2015; Carlson et al., 2014; Hawes et al., 2010; Hofferth & Goldscheider, 2010; McClelland & Tolman, 2014; Van de Bongardt et al., 2015; White & Warner, 2015). Girls who have sexual intercourse at an early age, as well as those who fail to use contraceptives, tend to be depressed and have low self-esteem, negative body image, and little sense of control over their lives (APA Task Force, 2007; Fortenberry, 2013; Rubin, Gold, et al., 2009). Sexual and physical abuse in childhood, which may contribute to these negative feelings about oneself, also increase the likelihood of both early sexual activity and early pregnancy (Australian Institute of Family Studies, 2013; Logsdon-Conradsen, 2011).

The Double Standard

Despite the relaxing of sexual prohibitions over the past few decades, the double standard of sexuality in society—acceptable for boys, but not girls—remains alive and well (Lefkowitz et al., 2013; Spade & Valentine, 2016). Parents may be willing to condone sexual experimentation in their sons ("Boys will be boys") but rarely sanction it in their daughters. Girls, more than boys, are encouraged to express their sexuality only within the context of a committed, socially approved relationship. In addition, teen girls who report having sex are less accepted by peers over time, whereas the same behavior in males is linked to *greater* peer acceptance (Kreager, Staff, et al., 2016). Consequently, it is not surprising to find that adolescent girls are more likely than adolescent boys to focus on the emotional aspect of sex and to consider affection a prerequisite for sexual intimacy (Walsh et al., 2011). Along the same lines, a recent meta-analysis of sexual attitudes and behaviors found that females were much less likely than males to endorse casual sex (Petersen & Hyde, 2010).

Some feminists note that navigating sexuality has become even more complex for young women today. They argue that young women are judged not only along the "virgin–slut" continuum, but also in terms of their degree of **sexual agency**, that is, *their level of personal responsibility and conscious choice* (Bay-Cheng, 2015; Tolman et al., 2015). These scholars ask if women are, on the one hand, encouraged to be proactive in their sexual behavior while being criticized for doing so on the other.

Sexual Desire

Girls and young women receive powerful societal messages that it is *their* responsibility to suppress desire and serve as sexual gatekeepers (Bay-Cheng, 2015). Perhaps for this reason, the sexual desire of teenage girls was rarely studied until recently. When Deborah Tolman (2002, 2012) interviewed adolescent, low-income girls of color and middle-income White girls, all reported feelings of powerful sexual desire. At the same time, the girls feared the potential of negative consequences of expressing these desires: pregnancy, STIs, losing respect and reputation, and limiting educational opportunities. The ethnic minority girls were more afraid of physical violation, and encountered stereotypes that they are oversexualized. White girls felt physically safer but faced a different troublesome stereotype, that of the "good girl" who is supposed to show no evidence of sexuality. Individual girls resolved these "dilemmas of desire" in different ways. Some suppressed their sexual desires, others avoided situations that could arouse sexual feelings, and still others arranged conditions in which they could safely express desire.

SEXUAL ACTIVITY IN MIDLIFE

A number of stereotypes exist about the sexuality of the midlife woman. She is often depicted in popular culture as either asexual or, if portrayed as sexually active and attractive, she may be viewed with derision, disgust, or labeled as a "cougar" (McHugh & Interligi, 2014; Ussher et al., 2015).

Sexual activity and satisfaction vary among midlife women just as they do among young women. Women who in their earlier years found sexual expression to be fulfilling typically continue to enjoy sex in their middle years and beyond. Other women, whose sexual desires were not strong earlier, may find that their interest diminishes further during middle age. In this section, we examine the sexuality of women in midlife.

Physical Changes

Most women experience a number of physical changes as they enter menopause, some of which may affect sexual activity. Decline in the production of estrogen is responsible for many of these changes. The vaginal walls become less elastic, thinner, and more easily irritated, causing pain and bleeding during intercourse. Decreases in vaginal lubrication can also lead to painful intercourse (Etaugh, 2013b; Yücel & Eroglu, 2013).

Various lubricants, along with topical estrogen therapy, can ease vaginal dryness (J. Simon et al., 2014). Paradoxically, one of the best remedies is to have more sex! Sexual activity increases blood flow to the vagina, which makes the tissues fuller, and also triggers lubrication (Brody, 2009). Signs of sexual arousal—clitoral, labial, and breast engorgement and nipple erection—become less intense in midlife, and sexual arousal is slower (Thomas & Thurston, 2016). Most menopausal women, however, experience little or no change in *subjective* arousal. Although the number and intensity of orgasmic contractions are reduced, few women either notice or complain about these changes. Furthermore, slower arousal time for both women and men may lengthen the time of pleasurable sexual activity (Etaugh, 2013b).

Patterns of Sexual Activity

Whereas some midlife women report a decline in sexual desire and the capacity for orgasm during these years, others report the opposite pattern (Buster, 2013; Fileborn et al., 2015; McCabe & Goldhammer, 2012; Ussher et al., 2015). Some women report an increased desire for nongenital sexual expression such as cuddling, hugging, and kissing (Block, 2008). The extent of sexual activity in middle-aged women is strongly influenced by past sexual enjoyment and experience. Years of sexual experience can more than make up for any decrease in physical responsiveness (Rathus et al., 2013). Women who have been sexually responsive during young adulthood are most likely to be sexually active as they get older (Etaugh, 2013b). Moreover, women with a positive body image report greater sexual desire and satisfaction (Woertman & van den Brink, 2012). In addition, both heterosexual and lesbian women who communicate openly with their partners and make changes in their sexual activities to adapt to menopausal changes are more likely than other women to report active and satisfying sex lives (Thomas et al., 2015; Winterich, 2003).

Many postmenopausal women find that their sexual interest and pleasure are heightened. Books such as *Sex and the seasoned woman* (Sheehy, 2007) and *Prime* sing the praises of the sexual passions of midlife women. What are some possible reasons for this renewed sexual interest? One is freedom from worries about pregnancy (Agronin, 2014). This factor may be especially relevant for older cohorts of women for whom highly effective birth control methods were unavailable during their childbearing years. Another reason is the decrease in caregiving and related activities (Fileborn et al., 2015). A third reason is the increase in marital satisfaction that often develops during the postparental ("empty nest") years (Etaugh, 2013b). Factors contributing to an active and satisfying sex life in partnered postmenopausal women include open sexual communication and setting the mood for sexual activity (Gillespie, 2016).

Sexual activity decreases only slightly and gradually for women in their 40s and 50s. Greater declines in activity and in sexual satisfaction may result from physical or psychological changes, however (Fisher, 2010; Hughes et al., 2015; Lindau & Gavrilova, 2010). Physical causes include various medical conditions, certain medications, and heavy drinking (Buster, 2013). Medical procedures such as mastectomy and hysterectomy do not impair sexual functioning. In fact, many women experience improved sexual function, including greater sexual desire, an increase in orgasms, and a drop in painful intercourse following a hysterectomy (Etaugh, 2013b). For those women who feel that their ability to enjoy sex after a hysterectomy is diminished, counseling can be helpful (Block, 2008). Similarly, mastectomy does not interfere with sexual responsiveness, but a woman may lose her sexual desire or her sense of being desired (Ussher et al., 2013). Talking with other women who have had a mastectomy often helps. One resource is the American Cancer Society's Reach to Recovery program (American Cancer Society, 2016b).

Sexual activity and contentment during middle age are more likely to diminish for individuals who have lost their partners (Thomas et al., 2014). For example, in a recent nationally representative study of sexuality in Americans aged 45 and over, only one in ten who had no partner, but six in ten of those with sexual partners, was satisfied with their sex lives (Fisher, 2010). Although about three-fourths of men of all ages have a sexual partner, only two-thirds of young and middle-aged women do. Among women aged 75 and over, only four in ten have a partner (Lindau & Gavrilova, 2010).

SEXUAL ACTIVITY IN LATER LIFE

Before reading this section, try Get Involved 6.2. See how your attitudes and those of your friends compare to the information in the chapter.

Sexual activity can be as gratifying in the later years as in the younger years (Kazer, 2013; Shifren et al., 2013). Unfortunately, as Get Involved 6.2 demonstrates, there are a number of myths and stereotypes about sexuality in later life. Most of today's older Americans grew up at a time when attitudes toward sexuality were more restrictive than they are today, particularly for women

---

GET INVOLVED 6.2
Attitudes Toward Sexuality in Later Life

On a scale from 1 (strongly disagree) to 7 (strongly agree), indicate the extent to which you disagree or agree with each of the following statements. Also, ask three female and three male acquaintances who vary in age to respond to these statements.

1. Older people lose their interest in sex and no longer engage in sexual activity.

2. Changes in hormone levels that occur during and after menopause cause women to find sex unsatisfying and unpleasant.

3. Women who are beyond the childbearing years lose their sexual desire and their sexual desirability.

4. In order to have a full and satisfying sex life, a woman must have a male partner.

5. Older women who still enjoy sex were probably nymphomaniacs when they were younger.

6. Older people with chronic illness or physical disabilities should cease sexual activity completely.

WHAT DOES IT MEAN?

Add up the ratings you gave to these six statements. Do the same for each of your respondents. Note that each statement reflects a myth based on folklore and misconceptions. Therefore, the higher the score, the more the respondent holds unfounded beliefs about sexuality in later life.

1. Are there differences between the views of your female and male respondents? Explain your answer.

2. Are there differences between the views of respondents who vary in age? Explain your answer.

3. In what way might society's attitudes toward aging and older people be related to the persistence of these myths about sexuality in later life? Explain your answer.

_____

Sources: Doress-Worters and Siegal (1994).

(Marshall, 2012). Unlike men, many women were taught that they should not enjoy sex and should not initiate it. This "double standard" of sexuality for women and men mentioned earlier in the chapter exists for adults of all ages. Older women also are subjected to the double standard of aging discussed in Chapter 2. Thus, compared to older men, women in their later years are perceived as sexually inactive and sexually unattractive (McHugh & Interligi, 2014; Lai & Hynie, 2011). Men tend to choose younger women or women who look young as their sexual partners and mates (Rathus et al., 2013). Many older women themselves are self-conscious about their aging bodies (Hillman, 2012; Thorpe et al., 2015). Let us examine older women's sexuality—the benefits of sexual activity in later life, sexual behaviors and the factors affecting them, and enhancement of sexual experience in the later years.

Benefits of Sexual Activity in Later Life

Sexual activity can have physical, psychological, and emotional benefits for older adults. The physical benefits include improving circulation, maintaining a greater range and motion of joints and limbs in arthritic persons, helping one sleep, and controlling weight gain (Etaugh, 2013b; Karraker & DeLamater, 2014; Syme, 2014). Sexual activity among older people has psychological and emotional benefits as well. It can improve one's sense of well-being, increase life satisfaction, enhance a woman's feeling of femininity and desirability, offer an outlet for emotions, and provide a shared pleasurable experience (DeLamater & Koepsel, 2015; Etaugh, 2013b; Ryan et al., 2013). In the later years, sexual activities other than intercourse—oral sex, manual stimulation, caressing—bring pleasure with or without orgasm (Rathus et al., 2013).

Sexual Behavior of Older People

Interest in sexual activity remains fairly high throughout adult life, especially for men, declining only gradually in the later years (Agronin, 2015; DeLamater & Koepsel, 2015; Fisher, 2010; Herbenick et al., 2010b). In a recent national survey, 40 percent of men but only 11 percent of women aged 75–85 reported still having sexual desires (Lindau & Gavrilova, 2010).

Still, some women find sex more satisfying and their attitudes toward sex more positive and open in later life (Trompeter et al., 2012). In one nationwide survey of Americans over age 60, 70 percent of sexually active women said they were as satisfied, or even more satisfied, with their sex lives than they were in their 40s (Etaugh, 2013b). Once grown children have left the nest, couples may experience a "second honeymoon" as marital satisfaction increases. (See the second vignette at the beginning of the chapter.)

In the earlier mentioned survey (Lindau & Gavrilova, 2010), over 80 percent of men aged 57–64, two-thirds of those aged 64–75, and 40 percent between age 75 and 85 had engaged in sexual behavior within the past year. Many of them had done so on a weekly basis. The corresponding figures for women were 60 percent, 40 percent, and 17 percent, respectively. Women at all ages were less likely than men to be sexually active, in part because more of them lacked a partner. In addition, good health is related to sexual interest and activity, and older women are less likely than men to report being in good or excellent health (Lindau & Gavrilova, 2010). Decreased sexual desire of one's partner is another reason for a decline in sexual activity among older people (DeLamater & Koepsel, 2015).

Factors Affecting Sexual Behavior

A number of both physical and psychological factors influence sexual behavior in older women.

PHYSICAL FACTORS.   The physical changes in the reproductive system that begin in midlife (see Chapter 7) become more pronounced in the later years, as estrogen levels continue to decline. Physical changes, illness, chronic disabilities, and medication can affect sexuality in later life (Karraker & DeLamater, 2014; Shifren et al., 2013). However, even the most serious conditions should not stop women and men from engaging in satisfying sexual activity. Heart disease, especially if one has had a heart attack, leads many older adults to give up sex, fearing it will cause another attack. But the risk of this is low (Rosman et al., 2014). Stroke rarely damages sexual function and it is unlikely that sexual exertion will cause another stroke. Arthritis, the most common chronic disability, causes joint pain that can limit sexual activity. Surgery and drugs can relieve the pain, but in some cases, medications decrease sexual desire. Exercise, rest, warm baths, and using pillows to cushion joints can be helpful ("Dont Accept," 2016). Medications such as certain antidepressants and tranquilizers can also reduce a woman's sexual desire. However, a physician can often prescribe a different medication without this side effect (Agronin, 2014).

PSYCHOSOCIAL FACTORS.   A person's attitudes toward sex-related physical changes can interfere with sexual activity more than the actual changes themselves. A major psychosocial constraint is the societal view that sexual desire in older adults, especially older women, is abnormal (Doll, 2013). As a result, older adults who want to fulfill their sexual desires may feel apprehensive and guilty. In addition, many older women feel unattractive and thus may avoid sexual activity with a partner or decide not to seek a new partner if they become widowed or divorced (Hillman, 2012).

Another constraint for residents of nursing homes is that the attitudes of nursing home staff are often not supportive of sexual behavior. Although more staff are respecting the wishes of their clients for sexual freedom and privacy (Agronin, 2015; Doll, 2013; Hu, 2016), some nursing home administrators feel that sexual activity on the part of residents "causes problems," even if the individuals are married. Sexual activity among LGBT couples is tolerated even less (DeLamater & Koepsel, 2015).

Enhancing Sexuality in Later Life

Sexual activity can be more rewarding for older adults if people come to realize that sexual expression is a normal part of life regardless of age. Sex counseling can help remove inhibitions restricting an older person's sexual behavior. Emphasizing the quality of the sexual relationship rather than performance can make sexual experiences more enjoyable for older people (Agronin, 2014). Those who are in supervised living arrangements need to be given opportunities to have private time together for intimate contact. Health care professionals should provide information and counseling to older people regarding the impact of both normal physical changes and medical conditions on sexual functioning, yet doctors rarely address sexual concerns in older adults, particularly in women (Baldiserra et al., 2012).

The many older women who are not in an ongoing physical relationship need to feel it is permissible to express their sexuality in whatever way is comfortable for them, whether it be enjoying their fantasies, engaging in masturbation, using a vibrator, or accepting an asexual lifestyle (Bowman, 2014; Etaugh, 2013b; Hillman, 2012). Although some older women are celibate because they lack the opportunity to meet partners, others choose to be celibate but still enjoy sensuous experiences:

> In Colette's novel, Break of Day, I discovered celibacy as a strategy for older women who too often see themselves as stripped of identity without a partner. Colette sees age fifty-five as the end of having lovers, but the beginning of an aloneness that is joyous and drenched in sensuality—particularly for the artist in all of us. It is a great gift to be one's self at last.
>
> (Marilyn Zuckerman, a poet in her 60s, in Doress-Worters & Siegal, 1994, p. 88)

Summary

SEXUALITY

- The external female organs (vulva) consist of the mons pubis, labia majora, labia minora, and clitoris.

- The four phases of the sexual response cycle are excitement, plateau, orgasm, and resolution.
- Women, more so than men, are capable of multiple orgasms.

- Orgasms resulting from clitoral and vaginal orgasm are physiologically the same.
- The sexual double standard condones casual sexual activity for men but not for women.
- Women have less permissive attitudes toward sexual behavior than men and emphasize relationships as a context for sex.
- Women are less likely than men to engage in most sexual behaviors.
- The four major types of sexual dysfunction are sexual desire disorders, sexual arousal disorders, orgasm disorders, and sexual pain disorders.
- The new view of women's sexual problems focuses on sociocultural, psychological, and relational factors.

LESBIAN, GAY, BISEXUAL, ASEXUAL, AND TRANSGENDER INDIVIDUALS

- Lesbians and gay men are attracted to same-sex persons; bisexuals are attracted to both sexes and asexual individuals are attracted to neither. The gender identity of transgender persons differs from the one assigned at birth.
- Sexual identities of some sexual minority individuals change over time.
- Homophobia is pervasive in American society. It is most commonly found in older, less educated, politically conservative males who hold traditional gender-related attitudes and fundamentalist religious beliefs.
- Complex interactions among genetic, hormonal, and environmental factors appear to determine sexual orientation.

SEXUAL ACTIVITY DURING ADOLESCENCE

- Rates of teenage sexuality have been decreasing.
- The onset of sexual activity is influenced by pubertal development and individual characteristics as well as by family and peers.

SEXUAL ACTIVITY IN MIDLIFE

- Postmenopausal physical changes can lead to painful intercourse.
- Some women show a decline in sexual interest and capacity for orgasm whereas others show the opposite pattern.

SEXUAL ACTIVITY IN LATER LIFE

- Sexual activity can have physical, psychological, and emotional benefits for older individuals.
- Interest in sexual activity remains fairly high throughout adulthood, declining gradually in the later years.
- Sexual interest and activity are greater for older men than for older women. One reason for decreased sexual activity, especially for women, is the lack of a partner.
- Physical changes, illness, disability, and psychosocial factors influence sexual behavior in older women.
- Sexuality may be enhanced through counseling, changes in societal attitudes, and greater opportunities for intimate contact.

Key Terms

vulva *110*
mons pubis *110*
labia majora *110*
labia minora *110*
clitoris *110*
vagina *110*
sexual response cycle *110*
vasocongestion *110*
orgasmic platform *110*

sexual double standard *111*
inhibited sexual desire *113*
sexual arousal disorder *113*
female orgasmic disorder *113*
dyspareunia *113*
vaginismus *113*
lesbian *115*
gay man *115*
bisexual *115*

asexual *115*
transgender *115*
asexuality *116*
heterosexism *116*
homophobia *116*
cybersex *119*
hook-up *120*
friends with benefits *120*
sexual agency *121*

What Do You Think?

1. Why do you think women generally have less permissive attitudes toward sexual behavior than men do?
2. Why do you think that society holds negative attitudes toward gay men and lesbians?
3. If you were to design a school-based or community-based sex education program, what would you include?
4. What is your position on programs that provide contraceptives to teenagers?

If You Want to Learn More

Carpenter, L. & DeLamater, J. (2012). *Sex for life: From virginity to Viagra, how sexuality changes throughout our lives.* New York: New York University Press.

Castañeda, D. (Ed.) (2013). *The essential handbook of women's sexuality.* Santa Barbara, CA: ABC-CLIO.

Egan, D. (2013). *Becoming sexual: A critical appraisal of the sexualization of girls.* Cambridge, UK: Polity Press.

Erickson-Schroth, L. (2014). *Trans bodies, trans selves: A resource for the transgender community.* New York: Oxford University Press.

Kimmel, M. (2014). *Sexualities: Identities, behaviors, and society.* New York: Oxford University Press.

Melancon, T. & Braxton, J. (Eds.). (2015). *Black female sexualities.* Rutgers, NJ: Rutgers University Press.

Natterson, C. & Masse, J. (2013). *The care and keeping of you 2: The body book for older girls.* Middleton, WI: American Girl.

Orenstein, P. (2016). *Girls and sex: Navigating the complicated new landscape.* New York: Harper.

Rathus, S.A. et al. (2013). *Human sexuality in a world of diversity* (9th ed.). Upper Saddle River, NJ: Prentice Hall.

Richards, C. & Barker, M.-J. (2015). *The Palgrave handbook of the psychology of sexuality and gender.* New York: Palgrave Macmillan.

Rutter, V. & Schwartz, P. (2012). *The gender of sexuality: Exploring sexual possibilities* (2nd ed.). Lanham, MD: Rowman & Littlefield.

Shifren, J.L. et al. (2013). *Sexuality in midlife and beyond.* Cambridge, MA: Harvard University Press.

Tolman, D.L. & Diamond, L.M. (2013). *APA handbook of sexuality and psychology.* Washington, DC: American Psychological Association.

Wade, L. (2017). *American hookup: The new culture of sex on campus.* New York: W.W. Norton.

Websites

Disability

Disabled People's International
http://www.dpi.org

Sexual Minorities

American Civil Liberties Union—LGBT Rights
http://www.aclu.org/lgbt-rights
http://lgbt.foundation/get-support/
http://pride-institute.com/programs/?gclid=CPKoy5jyutACFdccgQodpZQDtQ

7 CHAPTER

Reproductive System and Childbearing

She was placed on my chest and I began to cry from the overwhelming sense of emotions I felt. I was feeling so many things simultaneously: relief, love, excitement, awe, astonishment, pride, and achievement. It was truly a momentous occasion, very surreal and very beautiful. When I looked deeply into my newborn daughter's eyes for the very first time, I kissed her softly and whispered: "Hi, baby, welcome to the world, we've been waiting for you." (Boston Women's Health Book Collective, 2008, p. 182)

Giving birth to a child can be one of the major events of a woman's life. Childbirth typically (although not exclusively) occurs during late adolescence and young adulthood. In this chapter, we focus on women's reproductive system functioning throughout the life span, including menstruation, contraception, abortion, pregnancy, and childbirth. We conclude with an exploration of reproductive functioning in midlife and beyond, looking at menopause and hormone replacement therapy.

MENSTRUATION

The menstrual cycle involves the release of a mature egg or ovum from its surrounding capsule or follicle. The cycle, which occurs in four phases, averages 28 days in length. (*Menstruation* is derived from the Latin word for *month*.) The menstrual cycle is governed by a feedback loop involving two brain structures—the hypothalamus and the pituitary gland—and the ovaries and uterus (Donatelle, 2017; Norman, 2014). In this section, we explore the biological, psychological, and cultural aspects of menstruation.

The Menstrual Cycle

In the *follicular* phase of the menstrual cycle, days 4 to 14, low levels of estrogen and progesterone cause the hypothalamus to stimulate the pituitary gland to secrete follicle-stimulating hormone (FSH). This causes the ovaries to increase estrogen production and bring several follicles and their eggs to maturity. Estrogen stimulates development of the endometrium (uterine lining) in order to receive a fertilized egg. Estrogen also signals the pituitary to stop producing FSH and to start producing luteinizing hormone (LH). The LH suppresses development of all but one follicle and egg.

In the second or *ovulatory* phase, about day 14, the LH level spikes, causing rupture of the follicle and release of the egg near a fallopian tube. This is called **ovulation**. A woman is most likely to become pregnant on the three days before or on the day of ovulation (Office on Women's Health, 2017). During ovulation, some women experience *mittelschmerz* ("middle pain") on the side of the abdomen where the egg has been released.

During the *luteal* phase, LH stimulates the follicle to form a yellowish group of cells called the *corpus luteum* ("yellow body"), which produces large amounts of progesterone and estrogen. These hormones, which reach their peak around day 20 or 21 of the cycle, cause the endometrium to secrete nourishing substances in the event the egg is fertilized and implanted in the uterine lining. If fertilization does not occur, high progesterone levels cause the hypothalamus to stop the pituitary's production of LH. This causes decomposition of the corpus luteum and a sharp drop in levels of estrogen and progesterone through day 28.

The fourth phase, *menstruation* (days 1 to 4), occurs when the low levels of estrogen and progesterone can no longer maintain the uterine lining, which is shed and exits through the cervix (the lower end of the uterus) and vagina as menstrual flow. The low hormone levels trigger the beginning of another cycle. Should the egg be fertilized, however, the hormone levels remain high, and a new cycle does not occur (Donatelle, 2017).

Menstrual Pain

Menstrual pain, or **dysmenorrhea**, includes painful abdominal cramps and lower back pain during menstruation. About 55 to 73 percent of adolescent girls and women report experiencing menstrual pain each month (Harel, 2008). Women who report higher levels of menstrual pain and discomfort are also more likely to report high levels of psychological stress in their lives, and poorer health. They are also more likely to smoke and to consume alcohol (Harel, 2008; Hirokawa, 2011; Miller, 2010).

The cause of menstrual discomfort is thought to be **prostaglandins**, *hormonelike chemicals secreted by the uterine lining and other tissues as menstruation approaches.* These substances cause uterine contractions, decreased blood flow, and increased sensitivity to pain, which lead to cramping. Women who suffer from severe menstrual pain often have unusually high levels of prostaglandins (Pruthi, 2010). Over-the-counter antiprostaglandin drugs such as ibuprofen and naproxen help relieve menstrual pain in many women (Donatelle, 2017). Oral contraceptive pills also provide relief (Jones, 2011). A warm bath or heating pad may be beneficial as well. Also helpful is a low-fat vegan diet, which includes whole grains, legumes, vegetables, and fruits, but no eggs or dairy products (Harel, 2008; Northrup, 2010; Physicians Committee, 2007).

Attitudes Toward Menstruation

On a recent TV show, the plot involved a man intent on killing a group of female medical students. He wore a T-shirt that read "Don't trust anybody who bleeds for five days and doesn't die." That chilling statement said volumes about a mind-set going back millennia.

(Pam, a 49-year-old school teacher)

Throughout history, menstruation has had "bad press." Menstrual blood has been viewed as having magical and often poisonous powers. Menstruating women have been isolated and forbidden to prepare food or to engage in sexual activity (Dunnavant & Roberts, 2013; Goldenberg et al., 2013; Newton, 2016). Menstrual myths and taboos still exist, although in a somewhat less extreme form. For example, some adolescent girls and women believe that menstruating women should not exercise, swim, or wash their hair (Chrisler, 2008). In addition, many euphemistic terms are used to avoid the word *menstruation*: "period," "that time of the month," "I've got my friend," "she's on the rag," "the curse," "Aunt FLO is visiting" (Jackson & Joffe Falmagne, 2013; Thornton, 2013). Have you heard or used other expressions? How many are positive? Many Americans believe that a woman cannot function normally when menstruating, but there is little evidence that athletic performance, academic performance, problem solving, memory, political and religious beliefs, or creative thinking show meaningful fluctuations over the menstrual cycle (Chrisler et al., 2015; Grose & Grabe, 2014; Harris & Mickes, 2014).

Still, negative attitudes toward the menstruating woman remain strong. In one study (Forbes et al., 2003), for example, college men and women both perceived a menstruating woman, compared to the "average woman," as being more irritable, angry, and sad, and as less energized and less sexy. Men, but not women, also saw her as annoying, unreasonable, "spacey," less nurturing, less reliable and dependable, less creative and intellectually curious, and more disagreeable and spiteful than other women. Women found some redeeming features in the menstruating woman, viewing her as more maternal, strong, and trustworthy than the average woman.

Menstrual Joy

Despite the prevalence of negative attitudes toward menstruation, some women experience their menstrual periods as self-affirming, creative, and pleasurable, and as signifying femininity and fertility (Ussher, 2014). Negative expectations about menstruation may influence many women to focus more on its associated unpleasant symptoms. But what would happen if menstruation were portrayed in a more positive light? Researchers (Aubeeluck & Maguire, 2002; Chrisler et al., 1994) studied the effects of presenting positive and negative views on women's reported responses to menstruation. The researchers administered both the Menstrual Joy Questionnaire (MJQ) and the Menstrual Distress Questionnaire (MDQ) to college women. The MJQ lists positive feelings that might be experienced before or during menstruation, such as self-confidence, creativity, and power. The MDQ lists negative feelings that might occur at these times, such as irritability, anxiety, and fatigue. The researchers found that women who completed the MJQ before they were given the MDQ reported less menstrual distress and more favorable attitudes toward menstruation than those who received the questionnaires in reverse order. It appears that the way menstruation is portrayed can affect the way women react to their menstrual cycles (Barnack-Tavlaris, 2015).

Interestingly, the findings that menstruation actually has some positive aspects did not generate a lot of media publicity or subsequent research. According to Margaret Matlin (2003), this illustrates the **women-as-problem bias**, that is, *psychologists' preference for studying negative aspects of women's lives rather than positive ones.*

Premenstrual Syndrome

For me, menstrual distress is very real. Every month, the week before my period started, I became a different person. I felt such rage and could not control it. My husband and

*children suffered verbal and physical abuse for years. I thought I was going insane. In the last
3 years, I have been taking medication and am doing better. I feel like I can take back my life.*

(Sharah, 35 years old)

For most women, mild-to-moderate physical and emotional fluctuations are part of the normal menstrual cycle experience. Women may experience breast tenderness, bloating, anxiety, or irritability that may be annoying but does not disrupt their daily lives (Chrisler & Gorman, 2015; Donatelle, 2017). A small minority of women experience *symptoms so severe that their normal functioning is impaired for a week each month preceding menstruation*, as illustrated in Sharah's comments. These women are considered to suffer from **premenstrual syndrome (PMS)** (Donatelle, 2017). Although the prevalence of PMS does not appear to be dependent on cultural or ethnic differences (Casper & Yonkers, 2010; Miller, 2010), it is not experienced the same way around the world. For example, women in China are much more likely to report temperature changes than emotional changes (Chrisler & Gorman, 2015).

WHAT IS PMS?   For years, controversy has swirled around the validity of PMS as a disorder because scientists have not agreed upon its definition. Since 1987, the American Psychiatric Association has included PMS in its diagnostic handbook, labeling its most severe form **Premenstrual Dysphoric Disorder (PMDD)**. To be diagnosed with PMDD, *a woman must experience at least five symptoms during the week before her menstrual period. One of these must be related to mood, including depression, anxiety, mood swings, or anger/irritability. The symptoms must interfere markedly with work or social relationships and must be present only in the premenstrual phase of the cycle* (Chrisler & Gorman, 2015). About 3 to 9 percent of women of reproductive age meet these strict criteria although 12 to 18 percent have symptoms sufficient to cause monthly distress and impairment (Kiesner, 2009; Potter et al., 2009). Some theorists feel that the diagnosis of PMDD validates the experiences of a group of women and is thus empowering (Chen, 2009). But others object to treating normal reproductive system functioning in women as a disease. Some feminist psychologists believe that classifying PMDD as a psychiatric disorder stigmatizes women as mentally ill, undermines their self-esteem, and feeds into socially constructed stereotypes about women (Enns, 2015; Ussher, 2013).

For example, a widely held stereotype in North America is that women experience negative moods before their menstrual periods (Ussher, 2014). Thus, if a woman feels anxious, sad, irritable, or moody and believes she is in the premenstrual phase of her cycle, she may attribute her feelings to PMS. Differences in the life circumstances of individual women may also influence their experiences with menstrual symptoms. For example, women with high levels of stress and with a history of early-life emotional or physical abuse report increased severity of symptoms before and during their menstrual periods (Bertone-Johnson et al., 2014; Gollenberg et al., 2010; Sadler et al., 2010). Genetic factors appear to be involved as well (Chrisler & Rose, 2011).

TREATING PMS.   Whether PMS/PMDD is a mental disorder or not, it is important to give help to women who seek it. Some women report that dietary changes or progesterone supplements provide some relief, but these approaches may be effective for only a small subset of women (Miller, 2010). Taking vitamins E and B and calcium with vitamin D reduces the symptoms of PMS in many women (Miller, 2010; O'Grady & Lori, 2009). Antidepressants, including Prozac and Paxil, that raise levels of serotonin in the brain relieve emotional and often physical symptoms of PMS. Exercise also helps to reduce symptoms (American College of Obstetricians and Gynecologists, 2015; Chrisler & Gorman, 2015; Van den Akker, 2012).

CONTRACEPTION

The typical American woman spends five years pregnant (or trying to be) and the next 25–30 years until menopause trying to avoid an unintended pregnancy (Guttmacher Institute, 2015). In this section, we look at the use of contraception, starting with the teen years.

Contraception in Adolescence

Girls make the decision [to use condoms] because males don't really care if you have a condom or not. . . . Just as long as he gets to [do] it. . . . He doesn't get pregnant.

(A sexually active teenage girl, in Denner & Coyle, 2006, p. 290)

The use of contraceptives, both condoms and long-acting methods such as intrauterine devices (IUDs) and implants, has increased among sexually active adolescents, especially girls, in recent years, due in part to the growing awareness of the danger of AIDS and other sexually transmitted infections (STIs) (Kann et al., 2016; Romero et al., 2015). In one study, a large majority of teenagers—nearly 60 percent of girls and 80 percent of boys—said they had used a condom the last time they had intercourse, compared with well under half of single adults (Harden, 2014). Still, a substantial number of adolescents do not use contraceptives consistently (Pazol et al., 2015b). Unfortunately, a sexually active teen who does not use contraception has an 85-percent chance of becoming pregnant within a year (Guttmacher Institute, 2015).

Many adolescent girls and women resist initiating use of condoms or other contraceptives. Why is this? Some women do not have enough power and control in their relationship with a male partner to be able to persuade him to wear a condom, particularly if he is reluctant to do so (Brody et al., 2017). In some cases, an abusive male may deliberately interfere with the adolescent girl or woman's attempt to use birth control methods, in order to promote a pregnancy unwanted by the woman (Miller et al., 2010). Women and girls may also reject condom use because they believe it diminishes sexual pleasure, disrupts intimacy, and suggests that the woman does not trust her partner (Barber et al., 2015; Peasant et al., 2015). For others, taking control of a sexual situation—even if just to introduce a condom—may disrupt their feminine sexual identity and threaten potential rewards they expect in the form of love and protection (Gavey & McPhillips, 1999). Other factors that contribute to lack of contraceptive use in women include reluctance to acknowledge one's own sexual activity, a sense of invincibility ("*I* won't get pregnant"), misconceptions regarding use of contraception, and cost (Barber et al., 2013; Sweeney & Raley, 2014).

Which individuals are most likely to practice contraception? The older teenagers are when they begin sexual activity, the more likely they are to use contraception (Magnusson et al., 2012). Other factors associated with contraceptive use in high school and college students include being in a committed relationship, having high educational aspirations and achievement, having knowledge about sex and contraception, desiring to avoid STIs and pregnancy, being minimal users of alcohol and drugs, having good communication and a supportive relationship with parents who monitor their activities, discussing contraceptive use with parents and with one's partner, having supportive friends who use contraceptives, waiting a longer time between the start of a relationship and having sex with that partner, and having high self-esteem and feelings of control over one's life (England, 2016; Richards et al., 2008; Temple-Smith et al., 2016; Van Home et al., 2009; Widman et al., 2014).

Teenagers who attend schools that distribute condoms, compared to teens in schools that don't, are more likely to delay initiation of sexual intercourse, have fewer sexual partners, and increased condom use (Boonstra, 2015). They are also less likely to get pregnant (Blank et al., 2010). Unfortunately, however, few high schools in the United States make contraceptives available (Boonstra, 2015).

Methods of Contraception

The one totally foolproof method of contraception is abstinence. Today, increasing numbers of teenagers are pledging not to have sex before marriage. However, a majority of those who take this virginity pledge do not live up to their vows (Paik et al., 2016). Moreover, those teenagers who have taken a virginity pledge are *less* likely to use contraception when they do engage in sexual activity (Bearman, 2004; Landor & Simons, 2014). In addition, sex education programs based on abstinence are generally ineffective; they do not delay the onset of sexual activity nor decrease the number of teenagers having sex and becoming pregnant (Lamb, 2010; Paik et al., 2016; Rutter & Schwartz, 2012). In fact, there is evidence that such programs are linked to an *increase* in STIs and teen pregnancies (Guttmacher Institute, 2016a).

A wide variety of contraceptive choices are available in addition to abstinence (see Table 7.1). The methods most commonly used by U.S. women are the pill and tubal ligation (used by 26 percent and 25 percent of women, respectively), the male condom (15 percent), and long-acting reversible contraceptives—IUDs or contraceptive implants (12 percent; Daniels et al., 2015). As women's reproductive goals change during their childbearing years, the type of contraception they choose also changes. Birth control pills are most often used by women in their teens and 20s, by unmarried women, and by those with some college education. Tubal ligation is more commonly used by women who are over 34, who have two or more children, or who have no more than a high school education. Tubal ligation for women is far more common than vasectomy is for their male sexual partners. This is especially the case for lower-income and ethnic minority women (Guttmacher Institute, 2015). Of all methods, the condom is the only one providing any protection against STIs (Curtis et al., 2016). Unfortunately, many women have difficulty preventing unintended pregnancy because they cannot afford the more effective prescription methods of contraception (Sweeney & Raley, 2014). Not surprisingly, uninsured women are less likely than insured women to use

TABLE 7.1   Effectiveness Rates of Contraceptive Methods

| Method | Effectiveness Percentage | | Disadvantages |
	Correct Use	Typical Use	
Birth control pills	99.7	91.0	Risk of blood clots in smokers over 35
Condom (sheath placed over penis)	98.0	82.0	Need to put on before intercourse; may lessen male's sensations; may tear or slip off
Injection	99.7	94.0	Menstrual bleeding
Diaphragm (cup placed in vagina)	94.0	88.0	Need to insert before intercourse; unreliable without spermicide
Essure (microcoil inserted in fallopian tubes)	99.8	99.8	Possible cramps
Hormonal vaginal ring (placed in vagina)	99.7	91.0	May slip out; must change monthly
Implants	99.9	99.9	Irregular menstrual periods
Intrauterine device (placed in uterus)	99.4	99.2	Heavy menstrual flow; cramps; inflammation
Rhythm method (fertility awareness)	95.0	76.0	High failure rate
Skin patch	99.7	91.0	Risk of blood clots in smokers over age 35
Spermicide	82.0	72.0	Need to insert before intercourse; not reliable when used alone
Sponge (placed in vagina)	91.0	88.0	Need to insert before intercourse; high failure rate; vaginal infection
Tubal ligation (cutting and tying fallopian tubes)	99.5	99.5	Slight surgical risk; not usually reversible
Vasectomy (cutting and tying sperm-carrying ducts)	99.9	99.8	Slight surgical risk; not usually reversible
Withdrawal (of penis before ejaculation)	96.0	78.0	High failure rate

Sources: Curtis et al. (2016); Donatelle (2017); Rathus et al. (2013).

contraceptives. One in ten women who has not used contraception regularly in the past year reports that difficulty in accessing methods was responsible for their nonuse (Frost et al., 2008).

In addition to these methods, emergency contraception, the so-called morning after pill (or "Plan B"), has been available in the United States since 2009. This method is typically used when regular contraception ("Plan A") either fails or is skipped (Bertotti, 2013). Plan B involves taking high doses of birth control pills within 72 hours of having sex, and then again 12 hours later. A newer version of Plan B, named Ella, is effective up to five days after sex (American Academy of Pediatrics, 2012). These procedures work by delaying ovulation or blocking fertilization of the egg. They do not affect a pre-existing pregnancy. About one in nine sexually active U.S. women has used emergency contraception at least once, with the rates being highest among young, unmarried women (Daniels et al., 2013). Contrary to popular belief, providing emergency contraception in advance to teenagers does not result in riskier sex practices or switching to less reliable contraceptive methods (Meyer et al., 2011). In the United States, one type of Plan B can be purchased over the counter (Guttmacher Institute, 2016d). Do you think Plan B should be available without prescription for all adolescents? Why or why not?

ABORTION

Abortion is one of the most commonly performed medical procedures and also one of the most controversial. The debate over abortion centers around two opposing views: abortion as a right and a means for attaining individual freedom and equity for women versus abortion as a threat to morality, the family, and society. These differing attitudes toward abortion in turn stem from different socially constructed beliefs, attitudes, and values about gender roles and female sexuality (Camosy, 2015; Pollitt, 2014; Rhode et al., 2014; Schoen, 2015). Currently, nearly all countries in the global North and in central and eastern Asia have liberal abortion laws, whereas countries in the global South either prohibit abortion or allow it only to save a woman's life (Finer & Fine, 2013).

The 1973 landmark Supreme Court decision in *Roe v. Wade* gave women the legal right to terminate pregnancy by abortion during the first trimester (three months) of pregnancy. The Court allowed individual states to set conditions for second-trimester abortions and ruled third-trimester abortions illegal except when the mother's life was endangered (Boonstra & Nash, 2014; Reingold & Gostlin, 2016). Since then, over 1,000 restrictions on abortion have been enacted by the states. For example, as of this writing, three-fourths of the states in the United States require parental consent or notification for minors seeking abortion (Institute for Women's Policy Research, 2015). The U.S. Congress has barred the use of federal Medicaid funds to pay for abortion except when the mother's life is endangered or in cases of rape or incest. Because poor families rely on Medicaid for health care and few have private health insurance, low-income women are less able to afford abortion (Guttmacher Institute, 2016c). Medicaid covers abortion in 17 states in the U.S., as of this writing (Guttmacher Institute, 2016c).

Nationwide polls conducted 40 years after the *Roe v. Wade* ruling have found that public opinion has shifted away from general acceptance of legal abortion toward a more ambivalent acceptance, favoring choice but only under certain conditions (Pew Research Center, 2013b). However, two-thirds of college students (both women and men) now believe that abortion should be legal, up from 58 percent in 2005 (Panetta Institute, 2012).

Incidence

Nearly half of the pregnancies among American women are unplanned, and four in ten of these are terminated by abortion (Guttmacher Institute, 2016b). In 2012, slightly under 700,000 abortions were performed in the United States (Centers for Disease Control and Prevention, 2015a). Not surprisingly, over 90 percent of abortions take place within the first trimester (Pazol et al., 2015a). In recent years, the abortion rate has steadily been declining, especially among teens (Pew Research Center, 2016b).

Three-fourths of women undergoing abortions are under 30. Four out of five are unmarried, over half are already mothers, and close to half have had a previous abortion. White women account for nearly 40 percent of all abortions, but their abortion *rate* is below that of women of color. Black women are more than three times as likely as White women to have an abortion and Latinas are twice as likely (Guttmacher Institute, 2016b; Pazol et al., 2015b). Why are abortion rates higher for women of color? Research suggests that they are more likely than White women to become pregnant unwillingly. Cultural pressures may disadvantage ethnic minority women in negotiating sexual and contraceptive choices with their male partners (Stevens & Galvao, 2007). In addition, poor women are more likely to get abortions than women above the poverty line. Their unintended pregnancy rates are higher than those of other women, most likely because they have less access to the most reliable forms of birth control (Guttmacher Institute, 2016a, b).

Abortion rates are similar in countries where it is legal and in those where it is outlawed (Burn, 2011). This suggests that banning abortion does not deter women who seek the procedure. In addition, although abortion is safe in countries where it is legal, it is more dangerous in nations where it is illegal and is often performed under unsafe conditions (Poltera, 2011; Sedgh et al., 2012).

Methods

The most common method of abortion is **vacuum aspiration**, in which *the contents of the uterus are removed by suction* (Pazol et al., 2015a). Although most American women prefer this surgical procedure, those up to eight weeks pregnant can choose to take certain drugs to induce abortion. Women take mifepristone, the pill formerly known as RU-486, and one to three days later take the drug misoprostol. This procedure, known as a medical abortion, is highly effective when used within the first ten weeks of pregnancy and is extremely safe (Upadhyay, 2016). Women who choose medical abortion prefer its privacy, sense of empowerment, naturalness, and avoidance of surgery (Feminist Women's Health Center, 2009; Upadhyay & Murthy, 2010). Currently, more than half of the early abortions in France, Scotland, and Sweden, and at least 25 percent in the United States, are carried out with pills rather than surgically (Pazol et al., 2015b; Tavernise, 2016).

Consequences of Abortion

Abortion is one of the safest medical procedures available. The risk of death from childbirth (less than 1 in 10,000) is 14 times higher than the risk of death from legal abortion performed within the first 12 weeks (Reingold & Gostlin, 2016). What about the psychological consequences of abortion? Because abortion is a planned response to an unwanted pregnancy, the woman may experience positive emotions to it, such as feelings of relief or of having made a good decision. On the other hand, negative emotions such as anxiety, regret, or guilt may also arise because of moral and social sanctions against abortion. Brenda Major and her colleagues (Major et al., 2009) found that a woman's reaction to abortion is affected by her particular circumstances, including her coping skills and the degree of social support she has. For example, a woman is more likely to experience postabortion stress if she has little social support from her partner, family, and friends; if she has poorer coping skills; if she blames herself for the pregnancy; and/or if she has a prior history of mental health problems. The most negative feelings occur *before* the abortion. Although some women report mild distress afterward—guilt, anxiety, and regret—the strongest feeling is one of relief (Mollen, 2014). A recent study found that more than 95 percent of women felt that abortion was the right decision, both after the abortion and three years later (Rocca et al., 2015). Research on the long-term psychological aftereffects of abortion has found no link between abortion and subsequent poor mental health (Biggs et al., 2016; Cohen, 2013; Foster et al., 2015; Munk-Olsen et al., 2011; Quinley et al., 2014).

When women seek but are *denied* abortions (as was the case in some eastern European countries), their children are more likely to feel neglected or rejected, to drop out of school, and to have social problems at work and with friends than children of mothers who did not seek abortion (David & Lee, 2001). This may be related to the fact that women who do not terminate their unintended pregnancies tend to have poorer mental health in later life than other women (Herd et al., 2016).

So far in this chapter, we have focused on the reproductive lives of young women in the United States and other Western nations. Let us now examine the reproductive lives of women in developing countries.

WOMEN'S REPRODUCTIVE LIVES AROUND THE WORLD

In order for women throughout the world to best fulfill their future roles as mothers, workers, and leaders, they need improved access to education and to reproductive health services. How are their reproductive health needs currently being met? (We look at education in Chapter 9.) Researchers have gathered information on this question from virtually all countries around the globe (Cherif, 2015; Cortez et al., 2015; Eswaran, 2014; Guttmacher Institute, 2010; Raj & Boehmer, 2013).

Key Findings

- Up to 60 percent of adolescent births throughout the world are unplanned.
- Contraceptive use by married and unmarried women is greater than in the past, but in most of the world is still low. In most Latin American and Caribbean countries, for example, 30–50 percent of young unmarried women do not use contraceptives. In sub-Saharan Africa, these figures range from 25 to 60 percent.
- Adolescent childbearing is declining in countries where it had been common, as access to education increases and the advantages of delayed childbearing are recognized. Still, in much of South Asia and sub-Saharan Africa, between 45 and 70 percent of women marry before age 18, and as many as one in ten women has their first child before age 16, when pregnancy and childbirth are risky for both mother and child.
- STIs that threaten the lives and health of young women and their newborns are on the rise, particularly in the developing world (see Chapter 12).
- Sexual relationships that result from force, coercion, and abuse; cultural practices such as female genital cutting; and sexual exploitation of young girls and adolescents for commercial gain endanger the reproductive and mental health of young women (see Chapter 14).

Who Is at Risk?

In most countries, the poorest young women are at greatest risk of poor sexual and reproductive health. In developing countries of South Asia and sub-Saharan Africa, they are more likely than wealthier women to be married and to have a child by age 18, and are less likely to use contraceptives or use maternal health services (Cortez et al., 2015; Raj & Boehmer, 2013).

PREGNANCY

For much of history, a woman's life was dominated by pregnancy and childbirth. A hundred years ago, death associated with pregnancy and childbirth was a serious threat for women around the globe. In the twentieth century, the risk dropped significantly for women in developed nations.

However, complications of pregnancy remain the number one cause of death and disability of young women in less developed parts of the world (Raj & Boehmer, 2013). For example, the maternal mortality rate is nearly 100 times higher for sub-Saharan Africa than for industrialized nations (1 maternal death for every 39 live births in sub-Saharan Africa versus 1 in 3,800 in industrialized nations) (Eswaran, 2014). Even within the same geographic area, striking differences exist. Haitian women, for instance, are nearly five times more likely to die in pregnancy than Dominican women, who live on the same island. And the maternal mortality rate for Russian women is more than 10 times higher than that of their Finnish neighbors (Burn, 2011). Women at greatest risk around the world are those who are young and poor, live in rural or poor urban areas, and are members of minority groups (Save the Children, 2015). For example, Black women in the United States are almost four times more likely to die of pregnancy complications than are White women (Logsdon-Conradsen, 2011). In Canada, Native women are at greater risk than White women (Maine & Chavkin, 2002). A key factor in these differences in maternal mortality is access to good-quality health care. Black Americans receive poorer health care than White Americans, even when they are of the same socioeconomic status (Saftlas et al., 2000). In developing countries, the low social status of women hampers their access to existing health care services (Bohren et al., 2015; Cohen, 2010). Women's lack of power in families and communities gives them little say over decisions to seek care that could save their lives (UNIFEM, 2008). For example, even where low-cost transportation has been arranged by charitable organizations to increase access to emergency facilities, some husbands refuse to spend scarce resources on their wives, even though they would do so for themselves or their sons (Liljestrand & Gryboski, 2002). For those women in poor countries who do receive childbirth care, many experience care that is abusive, neglectful, and disrespectful (Bohren et al., 2015).

The good news is that global maternal mortality fell 44 percent between 1990 and 2015, with the greatest reduction in East Asia (Alkema et al., 2016).

In the past several decades, the advent of the birth control pill, widespread contraceptive use, and legalized abortion have allowed individuals to plan and control the size of their families. The marvels of modern technology make it possible to monitor pregnancy virtually from the moment of conception and render it possible for infertile couples to bear children (Watt, 2016). In this section, we explore pregnancy, miscarriage and stillbirth, and pregnancy in teenagers.

Pregnancy: Physical and Psychological Changes

Pregnancy begins when an egg and a sperm cell unite in a fallopian tube. The fertilized egg begins to divide as it travels toward the uterus, a three- or four-day journey. When it arrives, it implants itself into the thick lining of the uterus. Pregnancy typically lasts 40 weeks and is divided into three trimesters of three months each. A missed menstrual period is often the first indication of pregnancy although simple tests that are available in any drugstore can detect pregnancy within days after conception (Simkin et al., 2016).

PHYSICAL CHANGES.   During pregnancy, the blood volume in the body doubles and the breasts generally increase two bra sizes. The most dramatic change occurs in the uterus, which grows from less than two ounces to almost two pounds, not including the placenta or the baby. Early signs of pregnancy include breast tenderness, more frequent urination, fatigue, and nausea. Nausea and vomiting are usually confined to the first trimester, and despite being called "morning sickness," they can occur anytime during the day (Mayo Clinic, 2013c). Claire and Judith can vouch for the value of eating crackers or toast slowly in the morning before getting up. Ginger and vitamin B6 are also good for reducing nausea (American Pregnancy Association, 2017; McParlin et al., 2016). Food aversions and cravings may also develop (Simkin et al., 2016). For example, Claire couldn't stand coffee or onions, which she normally loved. Many women describe the second trimester as the easiest stage of pregnancy. During this phase, most of the nausea and fatigue disappear. By the end of the fifth month, women begin to feel fetal movements ("quickening"). During the third trimester, weight gain and protrusion of the abdomen become quite noticeable. Some of the activities of daily living, such as tying one's shoes, may become a challenge. The expanding uterus exerts increasing pressure on the other internal organs, which may lead to shortness of breath, heartburn, and a need for frequent urination (Simkin et al., 2016).

In the past, pregnancy was viewed as an illness, but that is less true today. Most women feel that their pregnancy is a normal and healthy—if somewhat inconvenient—experience. Regular exercise along with good nutrition reduce or eliminate many discomforts (Donatelle, 2017; Simkin et al., 2016). Claire played pool well into her first pregnancy, until her bulging abdomen made it too difficult to bend over the pool table. During her pregnancy with her second child, a summer baby, she swam until the day she gave birth.

PSYCHOLOGICAL CHANGES.   A woman's feelings during pregnancy vary tremendously depending on such factors as her economic circumstances, her desire to be pregnant, her physical condition, and her childhood experiences (Simkin et al., 2016). At each stage, women sometimes feel positive and sometimes negative. Feelings of being more sensual, potent, creative, and loving may occur. Negative feelings include loss of individuality, worries about whether the baby will be normal, distress at gaining weight and looking awkward, concerns about changes in the couple's relationship, and anxieties about coping with the responsibilities of parenting (Barnes, 2014; Solomon, 2015; Sundstrom, 2015).

REACTIONS TO PREGNANT WOMEN.   A pregnant woman is subjected to heightened scrutiny and elicits a variety of reactions from those around her (Fox & Neiterman, 2015). Many women have had the experience of having their pregnant abdomen patted by people who would not consider such a gesture with a nonpregnant woman (Zimmerman, 2009). Pregnant women may also be targets of hostility and perceived as undependable and underperforming (Byron & Roscigno, 2014; Gatrell, 2014). Even when viewed as equally qualified, dependable, committed, and fit for the position, a pregnant applicant receives lower hiring recommendations than a nonpregnant candidate from both female and male raters (Cunningham & Macan, 2007; Masser et al., 2007). Discrimination toward pregnant working women is, unfortunately, all too common. Many have been denied training opportunities, experienced criticism of their performance, had their work hours reduced, or been dismissed without good reason after announcing their pregnancy (Byron & Roscigno, 2014; A.B. Fox et al., 2015; Greenhouse, 2014).

WOMEN WITH DISABILITIES.   Women with disabilities are sometimes discouraged from getting pregnant, under the misconception that they cannot have a safe pregnancy, have a healthy baby, and be a good mother (Maxwell et al., 2007; Meekosha, 2010). Depending on the nature of the disability, some women may in fact have special considerations to discuss with their health care providers. For these women, as with any other woman, regular prenatal care and a birth plan are important to ensure favorable pregnancy, birth, and postbirth outcomes.

Miscarriage and Stillbirth

Miscarriage is the *spontaneous loss of a pregnancy before the 20th week of gestation.* At least one in seven known pregnancies results in miscarriage (American College of Obstetricians and Gynecologists, 2015). However, the actual rate may be considerably higher because many very early pregnancies are lost before a woman realizes that she is pregnant (Mayo Clinic, 2013b). *Pregnancy loss at 20 weeks or later* is called **stillbirth**. About one in every 160 pregnancies in the U.S. ends in a stillbirth (Centers for Disease Control and Prevention, 2015e).

Most early miscarriages are a result of major genetic defects in the embryo or fetus. Others are caused by hormonal imbalances in the mother, structural problems in the uterus or cervix, or diseases of the immune system. Following one miscarriage, a woman's chances of having a subsequent normal pregnancy remain quite high. Even after three miscarriages, her chances of maintaining the next pregnancy are still about 60 percent (Mayo Clinic, 2013b).

Until recently, it was assumed that miscarriages and stillbirths were not very stressful to the parents because the embryo or fetus was not yet a "real child." Well-meaning friends and relatives, even to this day, say things such as "It was meant to be" or "You can always have another child." Worse yet, others may say nothing, as though the event had not happened (Keitel et al., 2017; Saint Louis, 2015). But, in fact, parents start anticipating the birth of their child very early in pregnancy, so a miscarriage or stillbirth produces grieving and a sense of loss (Gold et al., 2016; Jaffe, 2014; Leis-Newman, 2012). In addition, women may feel guilty and somehow responsible for the pregnancy loss. They may also feel angry and jealous toward other pregnant women. These feelings may be mingled with anxiety about the possibility of problems occurring in a future pregnancy (Flenady et al., 2014). Women who have been struggling for years with infertility problems and women who have delayed parenthood into their 30s may be especially devastated when they experience a miscarriage. Fathers grieve too, of course, but their grief is typically of shorter duration and less intense than that of mothers (Crawley et al., 2013; Wenzel, 2014).

Listening and responding supportively to the grieving parents can be very helpful (Campbell-Jackson & Horsch, 2014). Speaking with others who have been through the same experience is often beneficial for the parents. For example, when Claire's daughter Andi miscarried during her first pregnancy at age 39, she found it comforting to talk to her cousin, who had had two consecutive miscarriages before giving birth to two healthy babies.

Teenage Pregnancy

About 553,000 American girls aged 15 to 19 become pregnant each year, and most of these pregnancies are unplanned (Guttmacher Institute, 2016b). Substantial ethnic disparities exist among birth rates for adolescents. In 2012, the birth rate per 1,000 females, ages 15–19, was 7 for Asian Americans, 21 for Whites, 27 for Native Americans, 32 for Blacks, and 35 for Latinas. Since 1990, the birth rate for U.S. teens has declined, reaching a 70-year low in 2009 (Cox et al., 2014; Hamilton et al., 2016). The decrease has occurred for all ethnic groups (Finer & Zolna, 2016). Among those teens who have had babies, however, the proportion who are unmarried has jumped from 15 percent in 1960 to 89 percent in 2015 (Hamilton et al., 2016). The decrease in teenage births is not a result of abortion, which has declined among teenagers starting in the 1990s. Rather, young people are delaying sex until they are older; having sex less frequently; using birth control, especially condoms, more often and more responsibly; and choosing more effective contraceptive methods, such as long-lasting hormonal implants and IUDs (Boonstra, 2014; Pew Research Center, 2016b; Richards, 2016; Romero et al., 2015). The most recent drop is also attributed, in part, to the economic recession.

Despite the decline in births among American teenagers, the United States still has one of the highest teen pregnancy rates among industrialized nations. The U.S. rate is twice that of Canada, France, and Sweden, at least four times the rates of Japan and the Netherlands, and six times the rate of Germany and Switzerland (Sedgh et al., 2015). What could account for this big difference? Are U.S. teenagers more sexually active? Do they begin having sex at an earlier age? Research has found that levels of sexual activity and the age at which teenagers initiated sex do not, in fact, vary appreciably across the countries. The major reason that teen pregnancy is higher in the United States is that teens' use of contraceptives is higher in other countries, where teenage sexual activity is more accepted and contraceptive services are much more widely available (Kumar & Brown, 2016; Sedgh et al., 2015).

Interestingly, although the percentage of all births to unwed mothers reached a near all-time high of 40 percent in 2014, more than four in five of these mothers were not teenagers, but rather were 20 or older (Hamilton et al., 2016). As we shall see in Chapter 8, more single women in their 30s and 40s are choosing to have children. And many co-habiting couples are having children as well, as the stigma of having a child out of wedlock declines (Monte & Ellis, 2014; Sweeney & Raley, 2014).

CONSEQUENCES OF TEENAGE PREGNANCY.   The consequences of unplanned teenage pregnancy are often adverse for both mother and child (Fox & Barfield, 2016; Romero et al., 2015). Even before pregnancy, teenage mothers are likely to live in poverty and to suffer from a lack of psychological and social support (Mollborn, 2016). In addition, they typically drop out of school, have less stable employment patterns, and are more likely to be on public aid. Their marriages are less apt to be stable, they are more depressed, and they are more likely to have additional children out of wedlock (Assini-Meytin & Green, 2015; Coyne et al., 2013; Gibb et al., 2015; U.S.

Department of Health and Human Services, 2013). The impact of early childbearing continues well into adulthood for both women and men. At midlife, compared to delayed childbearers, teenage mothers have less schooling, less prestigious, lower-paying occupations, more unstable marriages, and poorer physical health (Assini-Meytin & Green, 2015; Taylor, 2009).

Children born to teenagers have an increased risk of prematurity, birth complications, or death during infancy (Fox & Barfield, 2016). This may result partly because the mothers' bodies are not yet mature and partly from inadequate prenatal care. Pregnant teenagers and teenage mothers also are more likely than other women to engage in behaviors that put their unborn babies and young infants at risk. For example, these women are more likely to drink and smoke during pregnancy (Fox & Barfield, 2016). In addition, they are less empathic, less cognitively stimulating, and less sensitive in their interactions with their infants (Jacobs et al., 2016). The children of young mothers are more apt to have emotional, behavioral, and cognitive difficulties, most likely as a result of their impoverished caregiving environment (Coyne et al., 2013; Tang et al., 2016), and they are more likely to be abused or neglected (Goerge et al., 2008; Jacobs et al., 2016). In adolescence, children of teenagers show higher rates of school failure, delinquency, substance abuse, and earlier sexual activity and pregnancy than children born to older mothers (Centers for Disease Control and Prevention, 2011; Coyne et al., 2013; Maynard & Hoffman, 2008).

SUPPORT FOR PREGNANT TEENAGERS.   Support programs for pregnant teenagers have met with some success in improving the lives of teenage parents and their children (Barnet, 2012; Cherry et al., 2009; Seitz, & Apfel, 2010). Programs include one or more of the following components: family planning services, child care provisions, education about parenting and job skills, and welfare reform incentives. Teenage mothers who participate in comprehensive programs have fewer children in the long run and are more likely to complete high school and become economically self-sufficient. Their children are healthier, suffer less abuse, have fewer developmental problems, and do better in school (Schellenbach et al., 2010; Seitz & Apfel, 2010).

PREVENTING TEENAGE PREGNANCY.   Programs aimed at preventing teen pregnancy have taken various approaches: providing knowledge of sexuality and contraception, teaching abstinence, building decision-making job and social skills, enhancing gender and ethnic pride, and discussing life options (Oringanje et al., 2009; Suellentrop, 2011). Programs that combine elements of these approaches are the most successful in delaying sexual activity, increasing contraceptive use, and reducing pregnancy (Drew, 2011; Suellentrop, 2011). Although an overwhelming majority of American parents favor sex education in school, there is considerable debate on what should be taught, when, and by whom. In recent years, many school-based programs focused only on abstinence because the schools were prohibited from mentioning contraception in order to receive federal funding (Lewin, 2010; Carr & Packham, 2016). Unfortunately, as we saw earlier, this approach has little effect on reducing sexual activity or pregnancy (Silk & Romero, 2014). Now read What You Can Do 7.1 to learn some ways you can help increase reproductive choices in girls and women.

WHAT YOU CAN DO 7.1
Help Increase Reproductive Choices of Girls and Women

1. Volunteer at a family planning clinic.
2. Work with a campus or community organization to create a program designed to help young women develop the skills to request that male sexual partners use condoms.

Present your program at residence hall and sorority meetings, or to at-risk teen girls.

_____

Source: Burn (2011).

CHILDBIRTH

The birth of one's first child can be a physically and psychologically transforming experience (Pruthi, 2010; also see the vignette at the beginning of the chapter). In Chapter 8, we will examine some of the psychological aspects involved in making the transition to motherhood. In this section, we focus on the biological aspects of childbirth. We also examine postpartum distress, infertility, and assisted reproductive technology.

Stages of Childbirth

In the first stage, the cervix becomes dilated to 10 centimeters (about 4 inches) in diameter, a process that may last from a few hours to a day or more. The *cervix* also *becomes flatter and thinner*, a process known as **effacement**. In the second stage, which lasts from a few minutes to several hours, uterine contractions move the baby through the vagina. At the end of this stage, the woman often feels the urge to push, and usually within minutes (sometimes hours), the baby is born. During the third stage, which lasts from five to thirty minutes, the placenta detaches from the uterine wall and is expelled. Progesterone and estrogen levels drop dramatically during the second and third stages (Simkin et al., 2016).

Methods of Childbirth

Throughout most of the twentieth century, and into the twenty-first, women have given birth in hospitals, attended by obstetricians using surgical instruments and anesthetics. Although use of these medical procedures has saved lives and reduced pain, it has also depersonalized childbearing. Feminists argue that it has taken from women control over their own bodies and, through drugs, denied many women the experience of giving birth (Finerman et al., 2015; Phipps, 2014; Prescott & Kline, 2013; Shaw, 2013).

One example of the medicalization of the birth process is the **cesarean section** (or C-section). *Incisions are made in the abdomen and uterus and the baby is surgically removed*. C-sections are performed if vaginal delivery is expected to be difficult or threatens the health of the mother or baby—as when the mother's pelvis is small or misshapen, the baby is very large, or the baby is not in the normal birth position. But more pregnant women in the United States, Canada, and other industrialized nations are choosing to deliver this way even when there is no medical need (Ajeet & Nandkishore, 2013; D'Alton & Hehir, 2015; King, 2014). In the United States, the rate of C-sections rose from 5 percent in 1970 to a record high of 33 percent of all births in 2011 (Morris, 2013). This increase in unnecessary C-sections may be driven in part by busy mothers wanting to schedule their deliveries, or avoid the weight gain of the last month of pregnancy, as well as by obstetricians seeking to avoid potential malpractice suits (Kozhimannil et al., 2014).

Another example of the medicalization of childbirth is the induction of labor for practical (rather than medical) reasons, such as the convenience of the doctor, hospital, or parents. Although the procedure is relatively safe, it may increase the risk of C-sections, especially in first-time mothers, because the cervix may not dilate quickly enough (Bonsack et al., 2014). In the United States, the rate of labor-induced births is causing some experts to speak out against the practice (Simkin et al., 2016).

Parents can now choose among more family-centered approaches to childbearing. The most popular method in the United States is prepared child birth, or the **Lamaze method**. *Prelabor classes are conducted to teach the mother to control her pain through relaxation, breathing techniques, and focusing exercises*. A labor coach (usually the husband or partner) provides moral support and coaches techniques of breathing and relaxation during childbirth. Others also may serve as a labor coach: a woman's mother, sister, friend, or *an experienced and knowledgeable female labor and birth coach* known as a **doula** (Hartocollis, 2015; Hunter & Hurst, 2016). *Doula* comes from the Greek word meaning "woman who serves." The continuous labor support provided by doulas has been shown to reduce C-section rates, decrease the need for pain medication, decrease the length of labor, increase maternal satisfaction, and improve breastfeeding success.

Home birth also has increased in recent years, providing mothers with familiar settings and enhancing the feeling that the woman and her family are in control (Burcher & Gabriel, 2016; Lewis, 2015; Likis, 2014). More women are also choosing to deliver in homelike birthing centers outside a hospital. Family members and friends may be present during labor and delivery. Many hospitals now provide family-friendly birthing rooms (Finerman et al., 2015; MacDorman et al., 2013; Romano, 2013). Other aspects of woman-empowering birth, include minimizing the use of anesthesia, using the more natural (and gravity-assisted) sitting position to give birth, and eliminating practices such as enemas, shaving of the genital area, and performing an episiotomy, an incision that widens the vaginal opening to allow passage of the baby's head (Finerman et al., 2015; Leap & Hunter, 2016).

Using certified nurse-midwives for prenatal care and delivery has also become increasingly popular in Canada, Europe, and the United States (Mortenson, 2011b; Shaw, 2013). Certified nurse-midwives now perform about 12 percent of vaginal deliveries (*Essential Facts*, 2016). Prematurity and mortality rates are lower and birth weights are higher for infants delivered by nurse-midwives than for those delivered by physicians, even though nurse-midwives tend to serve traditionally higher-risk women such as teenage mothers and those with lower income and less education (Lydon-Rochelle, 2004; Potera, 2013). Women using midwives are also less likely to request pain-reducing medication, more likely to have a vaginal delivery, and more likely to breastfeed (Johantgen et al., 2012; Snowden et al., 2015). The most likely explanation for this is that nurse-midwives, compared to physicians, spend more time with patients during prenatal visits, provide more patient education and counseling, and are with their patients throughout labor and delivery (Pergament, 2012; Shaw, 2013). In developing nations, an increase in the number of midwives in recent years has been linked to lower maternal mortality rates (UNFPA, 2014).

Childbearing After 35

Although 75 percent of mothers of newborns in the United States are 20–34 years old, a growing number of women are having babies at age 35 and older. In 2015, 15 percent of babies had a mother who was at least 35, and 3 percent (over 117,000) were born to women aged 40 and over (Hamilton et al., 2016). In 2014, over 9 percent of U.S. first-time births were to women 35 and over, a record high (Mathews et al., 2016). In large part, this increase is due to the growing number of highly educated women who delay childbearing during the early years of their careers (Pew Research Center, 2015a).

Over 8,400 women between ages 45 and 54 gave birth in 2015, a record high (Hamilton et al., 2016). But because fertility begins to decline after age 32, older women have a harder time conceiving. By age 45, very few women can conceive using their own eggs, as an increasing number of them become abnormal (American Society for Reproductive Medicine, 2014). Women over 35 have more miscarriages; more preterm, low-birth-weight, and stillborn babies; higher levels of complications during pregnancy; and more chromosomal abnormalities (such as Down syndrome), and are more likely to have C-sections than younger women (Mayo Clinic, 2013a; Schimmel et al., 2015). The good news is that almost all older mothers, like their younger counterparts, have healthy babies and that infant mortality rates are comparable for the two groups (Blomberg et al., 2014; Islam & Bakheit, 2014; Li et al., 2014; Mathews & Hamilton, 2016; Walker et al., 2016).

You may be surprised to learn that about half of the pregnancies of women over 40 are unintended—a rate second only to teenagers. During perimenopause, the years prior to the end of menstruation, women may grow lax about birth control because they think there is little risk of pregnancy and may believe they have reached menopause. However, a woman's menstrual cycle becomes less regular in perimenopause and she may go several months without a period before having one (North American Menopause Society, 2012).

To find out more about individual women's experiences with pregnancy and childbirth, try Get Involved 7.1.

Childbearing in the Later Years

An amusing comic strip several years ago featured an elderly couple sitting in rocking chairs. The woman, knitting a tiny sweater, was obviously pregnant. Looking at her husband with an irritated expression on her face, she exclaimed "You and your 'once more for old times' sake!'" The humor of the situation was based on the then impossibility of an elderly woman's becoming pregnant. But this is no longer a laughing matter.

GET INVOLVED 7.1
Pregnancy and Childbirth Experiences

1. Briefly interview two women in their 20s, two middle-aged women, and two older women about their experiences with pregnancy and childbirth. It will be helpful, but not essential, if you know your respondents fairly well. You may interview your sisters, cousins, friends, mother, aunts, grandmothers, and so on. Keep a record of your respondents' comments.

2. Compare and contrast the responses of the women in the three age groups.

WHAT DOES IT MEAN?

1. In what ways are the pregnancy experiences of the three groups of women different? In what ways are they alike?

2. In what ways are the childbirth experiences of the three groups different? In what ways are they alike?

3. What social and historical conditions may have influenced the pregnancy and childbirth experiences of these three generations of women?

In 2007, Frieda Birnbaum gave birth to healthy twin boys. News of the event spread like wildfire around the globe. What made this birth so special? Frieda Birnbaum was 60 years old (Saraceno, 2015). Her husband's sperm fertilized a young woman's donor eggs in a test tube, and the resulting embryos were implanted in Birnbaum's hormonally readied uterus. Most fertility clinics set an age limit of 50 to 55 for a woman seeking **in vitro fertilization** (IVF), but Birnbaum lied about her age. Recent successes in transplanting frozen ovarian tissue and in freezing eggs and embryos have made it possible for women to bear children well into their postmenopausal years (Kort et al., 2012).

Controversy swirls around the issue of whether postmenopausal women should be denied help in becoming pregnant (Bayer & Thornton, 2012; Ellin, 2016b; Ethics Committee, 2013; Munson, 2014). Those who support this view cite several reasons: (1) Such pregnancies risk the mother's health; (2) an older mother is less likely than a younger one to live long enough to raise her child to adulthood; (3) it is unnatural and a perverse use of technology that has been widely accepted for younger women for nearly 40 years.

These arguments have been rebutted by others (Ethics Committee, 2013) who claim that (1) the complications that could affect the older mother's health also occur in younger women, although less frequently, and are treatable; (2) any responsible mother, regardless of age, should make provisions for the care of her child in the event that she dies before the child is grown. Some younger women with severe medical conditions have babies. Should they also be barred from reproducing? (3) If the reproductive technology exists, why shouldn't an older woman take advantage of it? Should older women be denied other medical advances such as coronary bypass surgery? (Claire's mother-in-law had this procedure when she was in her early 80s and lived another 20 years in robust health. She did not, however, contemplate having another child.)

Some scholars believe that both age discrimination and gender discrimination are at the root of society's discomfort about older women's having babies (Deech & Smajdor, 2007). Think of people's reactions to the news of men becoming fathers in their 60s and beyond: comedian Charlie Chaplin, actor Tony Randall, singer Rod Stewart, and former U.S. senator Strom Thurmond, to mention but a few. Rather than disapproval, there is acceptance and even admiration of the sexual prowess of these older men.

Postpartum Distress

During the postpartum period, the first weeks after birth, many women experience some psychological distress. The mildest and most common form, called **maternity blues** or baby blues, is experienced by up to 75 percent of new mothers. *This mood state, characterized by crying, anxiety, and irritability, typically begins three to four days after childbirth and lasts for a few days or weeks.* Maternity blues are more common following a first birth and may reflect the mother's adjustment to the stresses of new parenthood (Grussu & Quatraro, 2013; Puryear, 2014).

One out of eight women has *severe feelings of depression that last for weeks or months after delivery*. These changes, called **postpartum depression**, are characterized by anxiety or panic attacks, loss of interest in daily activities, despair, feelings of worthlessness and guilt, sleep and appetite disturbances, fatigue, difficulty in concentrating, and thoughts of harming oneself or the baby (National Institutes of Health, 2013b). The peak period for experiencing postpartum depression is the first six months after the birth, although some cases actually start during pregnancy (O'Hara & McCabe, 2014; Siu et al., 2016). One or 2 in 1,000 women experiences postpartum psychosis, a serious condition that often includes delusions, hallucinations, and thoughts (or deeds) of hurting oneself or the infant (Belluck, 2014). Andrea Yates, convicted of drowning her five young children in the bathtub, suffered from postpartum psychosis. She explained that Satan told her this was the only way to save the children, because she was a bad mother (Vallance, 2011).

Women are more likely to develop postpartum depression if they are young, poor, less educated, or first-time mothers. Risk factors also include a history of mental illness, previous depression, marital difficulties or other stressful life events, and lack of support from family and friends (Ayers et al., 2016; Ganann et al., 2016; Grekin & O'Hara, 2014; Hahn-Holbrook & Haselton, 2014; Katon et al., 2014; Kerstis et al., 2016; Stewart & Vigod, 2016). In interviews with 35 British and American mothers with postpartum depression, Natasha Mauthner (2002) found that many of the women held idealized cultural constructions of the "perfect mother" that contrasted sharply with their perception that they were not measuring up. It is unclear whether the drastic drop in levels of estrogen and progesterone after birth also plays a role because symptoms of postpartum depression also occur in mothers of newly adopted children (Beck, 2014; Garfield et al., 2014).

Social support, various psychological interventions, and medications play an important role in reducing the risk of postpartum depression (Bornstein, 2014; Guille et al., 2013; Zhang & Jin, 2014). Although support and therapy clearly help prevent and treat postpartum depression many mothers, unfortunately, do not seek help (Bornstein, 2014), and many obstetrician-gynecologists do not recognize its symptoms (Poleshuck & Woods, 2014).

Infertility and Assisted Reproductive Technology

Infertility is *the failure to conceive a child after a year of trying* (Jin, 2015). About one in ten Americans in their reproductive years experiences infertility, and the likelihood of being infertile increases with age for both women and men. In 40 percent of the cases, the difficulty is traced to the woman, in 40 percent of the cases, the problem originates with the man, and in the remaining cases, the origin is combined or unknown (Centers for Disease Control and Prevention, 2015b, f). Causes of infertility in women include blockage of the fallopian tubes, failure of the ovaries to produce eggs, uterine fibroids, and **endometriosis**, *the presence of uterine lining tissue in abnormal locations*. A leading cause of infertility in women is polycystic ovary syndrome (PCOS), in which high levels of the hormone testosterone interfere with ovulation. Clues that a woman may have PCOS are the presence of facial hair, acne, obesity, and infrequent or irregular periods (Joham et al., 2015). Lifestyle factors also play a role in infertility. If a woman is obese, has an eating disorder, or is a heavy smoker, or if she or her partner drink heavily, the risk of infertility increases (Jin, 2015; McCartney & Marshall, 2016).

The number of infertile couples using assisted reproductive technologies is on the rise in the United States (Sunderam et al., 2015). In fact, these procedures now account for 1.5 percent of all U.S. births (Brody, 2016b; Myers, 2015). In the majority of those cases, couples use IVF in which *the couple's own sperm and egg are fertilized in a glass laboratory dish ("in vitro" means "in glass") and the resulting embryo is transferred into the woman's uterus* (Centers for Disease Control and Prevention, 2013b). Louise Brown, born in England in 1978 as a result of IVF, was the first of these so-called test-tube babies, now numbering over 5 million strong worldwide (Lewin, 2014). In over 20 percent of infertility treatments, the couple's frozen embryos are used (See In the News 7.1), and in 25 percent, fresh or frozen donor eggs are used (Centers for Disease Control and Prevention, 2013b). In one recent medical breakthrough, a woman gave birth using an ovary that had been removed and frozen in childhood prior to cancer treatment, and later reimplanted into her adult body (De Freytas-Tamura, 2016).

IN THE NEWS 7.1
Frozen Embryos: Controversial Adoption Option

The popularity of in vitro fertilization as a means for infertile couples to have a baby has resulted in hundreds of thousands of unused human embryos frozen in storage. What do couples do with their leftover embryos? Some dispose of them or donate them to science. Others donate them to another family, a practice called embryo adoption (Lewin, 2015). As you can imagine, this practice often raises legal, religious, and ethical questions (Greely, 2016). For example, what happens when couples disagree about donating their embryos? Should prospective adopters be screened in the same way that is required for families adopting an already existing child? To further muddy the waters, there are no nationwide laws governing embryo adoption, and only 10 states, as of this writing, have enacted laws to deal with the practice (Hanson, 2015). If you and your spouse/partner someday create frozen embryos, how would you feel about donating some of them for adoption?

Donated eggs are typically used for older women who do not produce eggs or whose eggs are damaged. Older women who use donor eggs from young women can have successful pregnancies at least until their mid-50s (Jackson et al., 2015; Yeh et al., 2014). In the United States, egg selling is big business. So-called Ivy League eggs are in great demand, and ads in campus newspapers offer tens of thousands of dollars for the eggs of college women (Baylis, 2015).

The "success rate," that is, the percentage of cycles in which a live birth results, is about 30 percent for freshly fertilized embryos from the woman's own eggs, 34 percent for IVF, 50 percent for freshly fertilized embryos from donor eggs, and 34 percent from the couples' frozen embryos (Centers for Disease Control and Prevention, 2013b, 2015b). Babies born after fertility treatments have higher rates of stillbirth, prematurity, low birth weight, and birth defects, although most are healthy (Jackson et al., 2015). Nearly half are multiple births (Sunderam et al., 2015). In addition, the treatments are expensive. For example, the average cost of a single IVF effort in the United States ranges from $12,000 and up, but insurance usually covers little or nothing of the procedure (Brezina, 2015).

Another approach to infertility, **surrogate motherhood**, involves *paying a woman who agrees to become pregnant and deliver a child for a couple.* Twenty years ago, the surrogate mother was almost always the baby's biological mother. Her egg was fertilized through artificial insemination by sperm from the man of the couple who hired the surrogate. In most surrogate pregnancies today, however, the couple's own embryo is carried by the surrogate mother, who is thus biologically unrelated to the baby (Almeling, 2015). In a few instances, women have served as surrogates for their daughters or daughters-in-law who were unable to carry pregnancies to term, thus giving birth to their own grandchildren (Dell'Antonia, 2015). Close to 2,000 infants are born through surrogacy every year in the United States (Lewin, 2014). This practice raises a number of social, legal, and financial questions (Lam, 2015; Robertson, 2016; Sarojini & Marwah, 2014). Can a contract signed before a baby's conception be legally binding after birth? Who are the legal parents? Should the surrogate mother be paid for her services? Some critics are concerned about the potential economic exploitation of poor women as surrogate mothers or as egg donors (Bromfield, 2016; Leve, 2013; Rotabi & Bromfield, 2016). Yet overall, surrogacy appears to be a positive experience for surrogate mothers. Most surrogates are married, often have completed a family of their own, enjoy being pregnant, and find it rewarding to help an infertile couple become parents. They generally have a good relationship with the commissioning couple and have few problems handing over the baby, and many maintain contact with the couple and the child (Bromfield, 2016; Lewin, 2014).

In addition, fears about the impact of surrogacy on the well-being of children and families appear to be unfounded (Golombok, 2013; Jadva & Imrie, 2014). In fact, mothers of children born via a surrogacy arrangement show more warmth toward their babies and are more emotionally involved than in families where the child is conceived naturally. Both the commissioning mother and father have better parenting skills than do the parents in nonsurrogate families, and the babies themselves show no differences in their temperament and behavior, when compared with nonsurrogate babies. Nor do there seem to be problems when the surrogate mothers hand over the babies to the mothers who have commissioned the surrogacy.

Whereas some couples wish to have children but cannot, others make a choice not to have children. For a fuller discussion of this issue, see Learn About the Research 7.1.

LEARN ABOUT THE RESEARCH 7.1
Childfree by Choice

At a certain point, we had decided we weren't going to have kids . . . My mom was kind of hopeful that I would change my mind. She would say things like "Well, when you're done with your education, we'll talk about it again." There was a lot of resistance, people saying "Oh, you wouldn't want a baby? But they're so cute." The people who've just recently had kids say things like "Oh, it's awesome. It's the greatest gift. You're really missing out."

(Tara, age 27, in Scott, 2009, p. 63)

More than at any other time in history, women and men in the industrialized world are deciding not to have children (Teitelbaum & Winter, 2014). Europe's population has been falling since 1998 as the birth rate there has continued to decline. Between 10 and 20 percent of western European women who are now in their 40s have no children (Miettinen et al., 2015). Similarly, in 2014, one in six U.S. women between ages 40 and 50 had no children (Centers for Disease Control and Prevention, 2016c). Although some of these women ultimately will have a child, most will not (U.S. Census Bureau, 2015a).

The decision to have few or no children is facilitated by the availability and legality of effective forms of birth control, the feminist view that women have a right to control their lives, and the wider participation of women in the labor force (Bianchi et al., 2014; Peterson, 2016). Moreover, as the world population moves increasingly from small-scale farming to urbanization, children are no longer an economic asset to their parents, but an expensive economic liability (Angier, 2013; Social Trends Institute, 2011). However, the decision not

to have children—to be childless or "childfree"—goes against the traditional gender norms of almost all cultures. Women who make this choice are often perceived negatively (Bays 2016; Daum, 2015; Morison et al., 2015). They are criticized as shallow, deviant, cold, self-indulging, immature, materialistic, irresponsible, unfeminine and unfulfilled (Ashburn-Nardo, 2016; Moore & Geist-Martin, 2013; Peterson & Engwall, 2013).They may be marginalized, pitied, given unsolicited advice, and pressured by others to have children (Doyle et al., 2012; Lee & Zvonkovic, 2014).

Why do women choose not to have children? The reasons are many. Some women want autonomy, economic independence, and increased career prospects. Other women simply do not enjoy children, believe that they would not make good parents, or want a flexible lifestyle that would be hampered by children. Still others perceive motherhood to be a sacrifice and a burden, involving loss of time, energy, leisure and, identity (Allen & Wiles, 2014). Some wish to reduce their carbon footprint on the environment (Moore & Geist-Martin, 2013). In addition, adults today view children as less central to marital happiness than was the case in the past. Only 41 percent of adults in the United States now believe that children are important to a happy marriage, down from 65 percent in 1990 (Livingston & Cohn, 2010). Consistent with this finding, couples who have never had children report greater emotional well-being than parents, even empty nesters (Glass et al., 2016). In addition, women who have never had children report higher levels of autonomy and self-realization than women with children (Read & Grundy, 2011).

WHAT DOES IT MEAN?

1. Are the terms *childless* and *childfree* exact synonyms? In what ways do they differ in meaning?

2. In what way could a mother's dissatisfaction or ambivalence about parenting influence

her daughter's decision about whether to have children?

3. What can be done to increase society's acceptance of women who decide not to have children?

REPRODUCTIVE FUNCTIONING IN MIDLIFE AND BEYOND

Menopause is a normal and natural part of aging, and each woman experiences it in her own way. The decline in hormone levels that occurs during menopause sometimes is treated medically with hormone replacement therapy. In this section, we examine both of these topics.

Menopause

Menopause is the *cessation of menstrual periods for a full year*. For most women in industrialized nations, menopause occurs between the ages of 48 and 52, with an average age of 51, while in developing nations, the average age is 48 (Sapre & Thakur, 2014). Smokers reach menopause up to two years earlier than nonsmokers (Pru, 2014). Compared with White women, menopause occurs somewhat earlier in Black and Latina women and somewhat later in Asian American women (Forman et al., 2013). Menopause occurs because of the decline in the number of ovarian follicles (egg-producing cells), which results in a decline in the production of both estrogen and progesterone. Some estrogen continues to be produced after menopause by the adrenal glands and fat cells (Sommer, 2013). *The five to seven years preceding the beginning of menopause*, known as the **perimenopause**, are marked by increasing irregularity of the menstrual cycle and variations in the amount of menstrual flow (Derry & Dillaway, 2013). As we shall see, the way in which a woman experiences menopause reflects a host of physiological, psychological, and cultural factors (Derry & Dillaway, 2013; Reid & Magee, 2015).

PHYSICAL SYMPTOMS.   The frequency and severity of physical symptoms associated with menopause vary widely among women. In North America, the most commonly reported symptom is the **hot flash**, *a sudden feeling of heat that spreads over the body with mild or profuse sweating, which usually lasts one to five minutes and may occur several times daily*. In Europe and the United States, up to 80 percent of menopausal women experience hot flashes. Some women will have hot flashes for a few months, some for a few years, and some not at all (Al-Safi & Santoro, 2014; Richard-Davis & Manson, 2015; Sussman et al., 2015). Black women experience the symptoms for the longest duration, while Asian-American women have the shortest duration (Avis et al., 2015; Parker-Pope, 2016; Richard-Davis & Manson, 2015). Hot flashes at night (sometimes called *night sweats*) can interfere with the sleep of some menopausal women, but most women find them to be only a minor inconvenience.

Loss of estrogen also causes thinning of the vaginal lining and decreased vaginal lubrication. These changes can lead to painful sexual intercourse and also make the vagina more prone to infection. Headaches and joint and muscle pains are other physical symptoms that are occasionally reported (Buster, 2013; Newhart, 2013; Sommer, 2013). Women who smoke experience more severe symptoms (Im et al., 2014). The most serious physical consequence of menopause, osteoporosis, is discussed in Chapter 12.

Women in different ethnic and cultural groups vary in the kinds and degrees of menopausal symptoms they report. For example, hot flashes are most prevalent in Black, women, followed by White and Latina women, and are least common in Asian American women (Im et al., 2014).

PSYCHOLOGICAL REACTIONS.   Women between the ages of 40 and 59 have higher rates of depression than either younger or older women (Pratt & Brody, 2014). While some scholars attribute this finding to the hormonal fluctuations of menopause, there is scant evidence linking depression, irritability, or mood swings with hormone levels during menopause (Freeman, 2015). Some women may feel irritable or tired, but these feelings may be linked to disruptions in sleep caused by hot flashes (North American Menopause Society, 2011). In fact, the majority of postmenopausal women report that the happiest and most fulfilling time of their lives was between the ages of 50 and 65 (North American Menopause Society, 2008).

Even if some women do show heightened psychological distress during the menopausal years, this cannot be attributed solely to biological processes. Stressful life events that occur in middle age (see Chapters 8 and 11) may be largely responsible for increased distress. For one thing, midlife women are confronting their own aging during this time, including changes in their appearance, sexuality, health status, and physical functioning (Kurpius et al., 2017). In addition, they are often juggling multiple family and employment roles. Stressful changes in the family may include the illness or death of a spouse or partner, divorce or separation, difficult teenagers, children who are preparing to leave home, and/or aging parents who require care (Etaugh, 2017; Seib et al., 2015; Sharifi et al., 2014).

ATTITUDES TOWARD MENOPAUSE.   Popular images and stereotypes of menopausal women are overwhelmingly negative in North America, especially among younger, premenopausal women (Ussher et al., 2015). Menopause continues to be described in the medical literature by a long list of negative symptoms and terms such as "hormone deficiency" and "ovarian failure." The popular press reinforces the notion of menopause as a condition of disease and deterioration that requires treatment by drugs (Derry & Dillaway, 2013; Newhart, 2013; van de Wiel, 2014).

Many women, however, view menopause as a positive life transition (McCloskey, 2012; Morrison et al., 2014). In fact, most middle-aged American women minimize the significance of menopause as only a temporary inconvenience. Many look forward to menopause as marking the end of menstruation and childbearing (Pearce et al., 2014; Stauss, 2013). In one survey, the majority of postmenopausal women reported feeling "only relief" when their menstrual periods stopped whereas only 2 percent said they experienced "only regret".

Not surprisingly, women express more positive attitudes toward menopause when it is described as a normal life transition than when it is described as a medical problem (Ayers et al., 2010). Similarly, a woman who expects menopause to be unpleasant is apt to focus on its negative aspects. For example, women with more negative attitudes toward menopause are more likely to report vaginal dryness, headaches, and irritability (Ayers et al., 2010), and greater symptom intensity.

Attitudes toward menopause also differ according to a woman's ethnic and cultural backgrounds. Studies of Asian American, Black, Latina, and White women found that Black women reported the most positive attitudes toward menopause whereas Asian American women were least positive (Dillaway et al., 2008; Wroolie & Holcomb, 2010). Across ethnic groups, better educated women held more positive views.

What are women's experiences with and attitudes toward menopause in non-Western societies?

 MENOPAUSE IN NON-WESTERN CULTURES.   Women in non-Western cultures often have menopausal experiences and attitudes very different from those reported by Western women, indicating that menopausal symptoms are at least in part socially constructed (Mackey et al., 2014; Morrison et al., 2014). For example, Chinese, Mayan, Japanese, and Indonesian women are much less likely than women in Western cultures to report hot flashes or other physical symptoms (Dillaway, 2015). Women of high social castes in India, and Lakota Sioux and Navajo women in the United States report very few negative symptoms, and for them, menopause is in fact an eagerly anticipated event. Why might that be? When these women reach menopause, they are freed from menstrual taboos, treated with increased respect and authority, and able to participate more fully in society (Chrisler & Versace, 2011; Ryle, 2016). No wonder they experience few negative menopausal symptoms! In Western cultures, on the other hand, aging does not confer higher status on a woman but rather lowers it. It is thus not surprising that there are more complaints about "symptoms" in such a youth-oriented culture.

Hormone Replacement Therapy

Hormone replacement therapy (HRT) is *a medical treatment that replaces hormones in women whose levels drop after menopause.* Women who have had their uterus removed can take estrogen alone whereas those who still have their uterus are advised to take a combination of estrogen and synthetic progesterone (progestin) in order to be protected against uterine cancer (Jacob, 2016).

The combined estrogen–progestin pill relieves the menopausal symptoms of hot flashes, night sweats, insomnia, and vaginal dryness. It also helps prevent osteoporosis and reduces the risk of colon cancer and heart disease, especially if started early in menopause. However, it also increases the risk of heart disease, stroke, breast and ovarian cancer, gallbladder disease, and urinary incontinence, particularly among women who began HRT 10–15 years after menopause (Hodis et al., 2016; Jacob, 2016; Richard-Davis & Manson, 2015).

Which women should use HRT after menopause? That decision must be based on each woman's evaluation of the benefits and risks to herself (see Table 7.2) given her personal and family medical history. Some women whose quality of life suffers because of extreme hot flashes or vaginal atrophy elect to use HRT. However, they are now advised to take the lowest dose that provides relief, and for the shortest time possible. Women should definitely *not* use hormones if they have a history of, or are at a higher risk for, heart disease, stroke, or breast cancer (Manson & Kaunitz, 2016).

ALTERNATIVES TO STANDARD HRT.   An alternative approach to standard HRT is the use of synthetic estrogens that have some of the benefits but fewer of the risks of natural estrogen. One such hormone, raloxifene, also *reduces* the risk of breast cancer and bone loss. Antidepressants such as paroxetine and cognitive behavioral therapy also reduce the discomfort of hot flashes and night sweats (Jacob, 2016; Manson & Kaunitz, 2016).

Lifestyle modifications, including engaging in regular exercise or yoga, may be beneficial in reducing menopausal symptoms. Limiting or eliminating caffeine, alcohol, and smoking reduces the frequency of hot flashes (Derry & Dillaway, 2013). Consuming foods and herbs that contain estrogen-like substances, such as soy products, flaxseed, and black cohosh, may be helpful as well, although the evidence is mixed (Bailey T.G. et al., 2016; Dvornyk, 2013; Lethalon et al., 2013). Known as **phyto-estrogens**, these *plant foods do not contain estrogen but affect the body in a similar manner.* Phyto-estrogens are many times weaker than pharmaceutical estrogens and may not alleviate severe menopausal symptoms or provide the same benefits against osteoporosis that estrogen provides (Dvornyk, 2013).

TABLE 7.2   Benefits and Risks of Combined HRT

Benefits	Risks (greater when HRT started 10–15 years after menopause)
Ends hot flashes	Increases risk of heart attack and stroke
Relieves vaginal dryness and atrophy	Increases risk of uterine cancer if estrogen is taken without progesterone
Delays bone loss	
Increases bone density	Increases risk of gallbladder disease
Decreases risk of colon cancer	Increases risk and severity of breast cancer
May delay cognitive decline if given at menopause	Increases risk of urinary incontinence

Sources: Bhupathiraju et al., 2016; Fischer et al., 2014; Harman, 2014; Reid & Magee, 2015.

Summary

MENSTRUATION

- The menstrual cycle is regulated by hormones, brain structures, and reproductive organs.
- Attitudes toward menstruation remain somewhat negative, despite evidence that physical and psychological performances do not change meaningfully over the menstrual cycle.
- Some women experience menstrual joy, a feeling of heightened creativity and energy.
- A small minority of women experience the symptoms of premenstrual syndrome (PMS).

CONTRACEPTION

- Contraceptive use has increased among adolescents, but many use contraceptives sporadically or not at all.
- The type of contraception chosen by women changes as their reproductive goals change.

ABORTION

- Most abortions occur within the first trimester by means of the vacuum aspiration method.
- Early abortion is physically safe and generally has no negative psychological aftereffects.

WOMEN'S REPRODUCTIVE LIVES AROUND THE WORLD

- Many women worldwide marry and bear children at a young age.
- STIs are increasing in the developing world.
- Practices such as female genital mutilation and sexual exploitation for money endanger the health of young women.
- The poorest women are at greatest risk.

PREGNANCY

- Physical effects of pregnancy include nausea, fatigue, and weight gain.
- Women have both positive and negative feelings during pregnancy.
- People may react negatively to a pregnant woman.
- Most miscarriages result from genetic defects in the embryo or fetus.
- The teenage pregnancy rate is higher in the United States than in most industrialized nations, but the teenage birth rate is declining, probably due to increased condom use.
- Teen pregnancy has serious economic, social, and medical costs.
- Programs stressing a combination of abstinence, contraception, and life skills can delay sexual activity and reduce pregnancy rates.

CHILDBIRTH

- The three stages of childbirth are dilation of the cervix, birth of the baby, and expulsion of the placenta.
- Rates of cesarean delivery and induction of labor are high in the United States.
- Family-centered approaches to childbearing include the Lamaze method, home birth, birthing rooms and centers, and use of midwives or doulas.
- Older women have more difficulty conceiving but generally have healthy babies.
- Many women experience maternity blues shortly after giving birth. A small percentage of women experience the more severe postpartum depression and postpartum psychosis.
- Increasing numbers of infertile couples are trying reproductive technologies, such as in vitro fertilization, frozen embryos, donor eggs, and surrogate motherhood.

REPRODUCTIVE FUNCTIONING IN MIDLIFE AND BEYOND

- Menopause, caused by a decrease in estrogen production, causes hot flashes and vaginal dryness but is not linked to heightened psychological distress.
- Menopausal experiences and attitudes differ across ethnic and cultural groups.
- Middle-aged women usually have positive attitudes toward menopause.
- Benefits of hormone replacement therapy (HRT) include decrease in menopausal symptoms and decrease in the risk of osteoporosis and colon cancer.
- Risks of HRT include increased risk of heart attack, stroke, breast and ovarian cancer, gall bladder disease, and urinary incontinence.
- Alternatives to HRT include synthetic estrogens and phyto-estrogens.

Key Terms

ovulation *129*

dysmenorrhea *129*

prostaglandins *129*

women-as-problem bias *130*

premenstrual syndrome (PMS) *131*

premenstrual dysphoric disorder (PMDD) *131*

vacuum aspiration *135*

miscarriage *138*

stillbirth *138*

effacement *141*

cesarean section *141*

Lamaze method *141*

doula *141*

in vitro fertilization *143*

maternity blues *143*

postpartum depression *144*

infertility *144*

endometriosis *144*

surrogate motherhood *145*

menopause *147*

perimenopause *147*

hot flash *147*

hormone replacement therapy *149*

phyto-estrogens *149*

What Do You Think?

1. If a friend of yours unexpectedly became pregnant, what factors might influence her decision about whether or not to terminate the pregnancy?

2. Why do you think that even though many college students have heard about the risks of sexually transmitted diseases, including HIV infection, they fail to use condoms regularly or to engage in other self-protecting behaviors? What actions could be taken to make more of your friends engage in "safer sex" practices?

3. Do you favor or oppose school-based education programs that provide contraceptives to teenagers? Support your answer.

4. Who is the baby's real mother—the surrogate mother who conceived and carried the baby or the wife of the man who fathers the baby? Is motherhood primarily a biological or psychological concept? Explain your answers.

5. Should women in their 50s and 60s have babies? Why or why not?

6. In your opinion, why do young women have more negative views of menopause than middle-aged women?

If You Want to Learn More

Barnes, D. (2014). *Women's reproductive mental health across the life span*. New York: Springer.

Camosy, C. (2015). *Beyond the abortion wars: A way forward for a new generation*. Cambridge, UK: Wm. B. Eerdmans.

Daum, M. (2015). *Selfish, shallow and self-absorbed: Sixteen writers on the decision not to have kids*. New York: Picador.

Erdmans, M.P. & Black, T. (2015). *On becoming a teen mom: Life before pregnancy*. Berkeley, CA: University of California Press.

Fahs, B. (2016). *Out for blood: Essays on menstruation and resistance*. Albany, NY: State University of New York, Albany.

Faubion, S. (2016). *Mayo Clinic: The menopause solution*. New York: Time Inc. Books.

Jensen, J.R. (2015). *Mayo Clinic guide to fertility and conception*. Rochester, MN: Mayo Clinic.

Kleiman, K. & Raskin, V.D. (2013). *This isn't what I expected: Postpartum depression* (2nd ed.). Cambridge, MA: DaCapo Lifelong Books.

Lehmann-Haupt, R. (2015). *In her own sweet time: Egg freezing and the new frontier of family*. San Francisco, CA: Nothing But The Truth LLC.

McHugh, M.C. & Chrisler, J.C. (Eds.). (2015). *The wrong prescription for women*. Santa Barbara, CA: Praeger.

Pearce, L.H. (2015). *Moon time: Harness the ever-changing energy of your menstrual cycle* (2nd ed.). Author.

Schoen, J. (2015). *Abortion after Roe*. Raleigh, NC: University of North Carolina Press.

Simkin, P. (2013). *The birth partner: A complete guide to childbirth for dads, doulas, and all other birth companions*. Cambridge, MA: Harvard Common Press.

Simkin, P. et al. (2016). *Pregnancy, childbirth, and the newborn* (4th ed.). Minnetonka, MN: Meadowbrook.

Websites

Sexuality and Reproductive Health
About Go Ask Alice!
http://www.goaskalice.columbia.edu/

Contraception
About Go Ask Alice!
http://www.goaskalice.columbia.edu/
Planned Parenthood: Your Contraceptive Choices
http://www.plannedparenthood.org/pp2/portal/
medicalinfo/birthcontrol/

Pregnancy and Childbirth
Reproductive Health
http://www.cdc.gov/reproductivehealth/index.htm
http://www.mayoclinic.org/healthy-lifestyle/
pregnancy-week-by-week/in-depth/hiv-20049471

Childbirth
http://www.childbirth.org
Pregnancy & Child Health Resource Centers
http://www.mayoclinic.com/findinformation/
healthylivingcenter/index.cfm

Infertility
Infertility Resources
http://www.ihr.com/infertility

Menopause
North American Menopause Society
http://www.menopause org

Relationships

A middle-aged lesbian couple had been together for 15 years when their daughter was born. To celebrate the joyous occasion, they held a naming ceremony for their friends. The nonbiological mother held the baby and presented her with her full name consisting of her given name and each parent's surname. Then each parent lit a candle and made a wish for their baby girl. Following this, they expressed their feelings for one another and for their new family. (Muzio, 1996)

Last Sunday, Ashley and I went over to my mom's house and we made applesauce together. It was really fun because it was all three of us and I used to do that with my mom when I was a kid . . . And we were just working together doing all the different parts of the applesauce and conversing. We were all acting like friends, but at the same time there was that bond there—that grandmom, mom, daughter thing. It was neat. (Denise, age 38, in Fingerman, 2003, p. 66)

These vignettes portray women's experiences with interpersonal relationships in different parts of the life cycle. In this chapter, we explore the nature of women's close relationships—including friendships, romantic relationships, marriage and other long-term relationships, unattached lifestyles, and motherhood. We end the chapter by examining women's relationships in the later years with their siblings, adult children, grandchildren, and parents.

FRIENDSHIPS

Close relationships are essential to good mental health and well-being. Friends, in particular, are a major source of support and self-esteem throughout an individual's life (Castañeda & Burns-Glover, 2008). Let's take a closer look at gender differences in friendships, starting in adolescence and moving through the adult life span.

Friendship in Adolescence

Starting in childhood and throughout life, a person's closest friends tend to be people of the same gender (Gillespie et al., 2015; Hartl et al., 2015). Even though romantic attachments increase during adolescence, in general, most teenagers around the world still choose members of their own gender as friends and as best friends (Furman & Rose, 2015; Mehta & Strough, 2010; Pinquart & Silbereisen, 2010). Starting in early adolescence, girls report higher levels of affection nurturance, trust, security, and closeness than do boys (McGuire & Leaper, 2016; Rose et al., 2016).

Intimacy, the sharing of thoughts and feelings with someone else, is a key characteristic of adolescent friendships, especially those of girls (Schneider, 2016). Girls show greater increases in intimacy from early to late adolescence, they report more self-disclosure and emotional support, and they spend more time with their friends than do boys (Rose et al., 2016; Rueger et al., 2008).

Girls tend to have close, intimate, one-on-one friendships characterized by self-disclosure and emotional support. In the words of one adolescent girl,

> I've had a best friend for about five years now, and she pretty much knows everything about me. I'd probably turn to her for all of my problems because she's always helped me out and always gave me the right answers for everything.

(Commonwealth Fund, 1997, p. 19)

Boys are more likely to have larger, less intimate friendship groups that focus on shared group activities, mostly sports and competitive games (Blakemore et al., 2009; Furman & Rose, 2015).

Studies of ethnically and socioeconomically diverse adolescents have found friendship patterns that differ somewhat from those commonly seen among White, middle-class adolescents (Rubin et al., 2010). For example, Julia Duff (1996) found that 95 percent of middle-class White girls reported competition as an aspect of their friendships, whereas only 38 percent of low-income girls of color did so. Similarly, White girls were five times as likely to report feeling "used" by a close friend and were nearly three times as likely to indicate that jealousy was an issue.

Friendship in Adulthood

Although both women and men highly value their friendships, women's friendships, as in adolescence, are more intimate and emotionally supportive than men's (Whitbourne et al., 2009). This greater desire for intimacy may lead young women to hold higher expectations and standards for their same-sex friends than young men do (Felmlee et al., 2012). Women and men achieve closeness with their friends somewhat differently. Women are described as operating "face to face," by sharing thoughts and feelings, whereas men develop closeness "side by side," by sharing activities (Ryle, 2016).

The emotional support shown in heterosexual female friendships is a particularly important quality of sexual minorities' friendships as well. The reinforcement and empathy that are part of close relationships in this "family of choice" can help sexual minority individuals cope with prejudice from the broader society and support the development of a positive sexual identity (Nelson, 2013; Rose & Hospital, 2015).

How can one account for gender differences in emotional intimacy and expressiveness in friendships? Consistent with the general assumption that gender is socially constructed, experiences and attitudes shape orientations toward friendship. As we saw in Chapter 4, parents are more likely to encourage emotional expression in their daughters and discourage it in their sons, and females and males carry these messages into their peer relationships. Furthermore, because emotional expression is viewed as a feminine trait and many males think of gay men as having feminine traits, males might associate emotional closeness between males with homosexuality. This perceived connection can be threatening and might steer boys and men away from expressing emotions to their male friends (Castañeda & Burns-Glover, 2008).

Although most research on adolescent and adult friendship has focused on same-sex friends, some recent studies have examined cross-sex friendships (Akbulut & Weger, 2016; Bleske-Rechek et al., 2012; Etaugh et al., 2017; Gillespie et al., 2015; Procsalet et al., 2015). These friendships are similar in many ways to same-sex friendships but also offer some unique benefits. Female–male friends provide each other with insider perspectives and other-sex companionship and also sensitize each other to gender differences in communication style. Men report more cross-sex friendships than do women (Gillespie et al., 2014). In addition, feminine men have more cross-sex friendships than masculine men, and masculine women have more cross-sex friendships than feminine women.

Friendship in Later Life

Friends provide the emotional support and companionship that sustain women as they meet the challenges, changes, and losses of later life (Blieszner, 2014; Gillespie et al., 2014). Because many married women eventually lose their spouses through death or divorce, most women grow old in the company of other women (Etaugh, 2017). In later life, women are more engaged with friendships and social networks than are men and are more likely to both give and receive emotional support (Arber, 2004; Canetto, 2003). Older women's close friends tend to be about the same age and socioeconomic status, have the same social and ethnic backgrounds, and live close to each other (Rawlins, 2004). Friendships among older women enhance physical and mental health and contribute to continued psychological growth (Blieszner, 2014; Moremen, 2008). Long-term friends contribute to a sense of continuity and connection with the past. Over time, friends can come to be considered as family, further increasing one's sense of connectedness (Hall, 2007).

Social class influences the way in which friendships are made and maintained. Older middle-class women often make friends through membership in an association. The main basis of such friendships is shared interest of the group and its activities. Working-class and poor women are more likely to choose relatives as close friends and to provide practical assistance to each other, including helping one another with transportation, shopping, and running errands (Moremen, 2008; Sanchez-Hucles, 2003).

For many sexual minority individuals, friendships function as an extended family of choice (Travis & Kimmel, 2014). Many midlife and older lesbians who came out during a period that was more hostile toward sexual minorities than is true today were not accepted by their families. For them, and for other sexual minority individuals who have been rejected by their families of origin, friendships serve this familial role (Barrett et al., 2015; Fredriksen-Goldsen et al., 2014; Gabrielson & Holston, 2014: Rose & Hospital, 2015; Traies, 2016). And because many lesbians have not married or created a traditional family, these social networks of friends can be an important source of support to midlife and older women (Rose & Hospital, 2015).

ROMANTIC RELATIONSHIPS

The process of looking for a suitable partner preoccupies many individuals during their teen and young adult years. In this section, we look at some features of this process. What qualities do women and men look for in a potential partner? How do they act in dating situations? How do they gauge their partner's interest in having sex?

Desirable Qualities in a Partner

What qualities do individuals look for in a romantic partner or mate? Both in heterosexual and same-sex relationships, people are often attracted to those whom they perceive as loving, supportive, warm, kind, agreeable, and intelligent (Boxer et al., 2015; Felmlee et al., 2010). Women prefer men who display ambition, but who also exhibit emotional stability and a desire for home and children. Although both sexes also value physical attractiveness, men put more emphasis on looks than women do, whereas women put a higher priority on status and resources (Boxer et al., 2015; Fales et al., 2016; Meltzer et al., 2014; Wang & Parker, 2014; Zell et al., 2015). In online profiles, for example, women are more likely to offer physical attractiveness and ask for financial stability whereas men are more apt to ask for physical attractiveness and offer financial security (Conkle, 2010; Glasser et al., 2009; Alterovitz & Mendelsohn, 2009). Not surprisingly, women are more likely than men to misrepresent their weight in online profiles, and men are more likely to misrepresent their financial assets (de Backer et al., 2008; Hall et al., 2010). Lesbians are less likely than heterosexual females to offer attractiveness as an attribute, perhaps because they are less likely to base their relationships on physical appearance (Kimmel, 2002; Smith & Stillman, 2002).

This great value placed on physical appearance has unfortunate consequences for heterosexual women. Not only can it contribute to a distorted body image and eating disorders (see Chapters 4 and 13), but it also denigrates women by placing more importance on superficial characteristics than on behaviors and accomplishments. Best-selling books such on the topic of looking younger play on women's fears of losing not only their sexual allure, but their edge in the workforce as well. Emphasis on physical appearance has a particularly negative impact on women with disabilities. These women are less likely than able-bodied women to be perceived as attractive and desirable and may even evoke reactions of repulsion and rejection. Not surprisingly, the resulting poor self-image and fear of rejection can lead women with disabilities to avoid social and intimate relationships (Banks, 2010; Nosek, 2010).

Given the double standard of aging (see Chapter 2), it is not surprising that body dissatisfaction is high in midlife women, especially those who place great importance on their appearance (Ginsberg et al., 2016; K. Jackson et al., 2014; Kilpela et al., 2015; McHugh & Interligi, 2014; Robert-McComb & Massey-Stokes, 2014). One study, for example, found that over 75 percent of U.S. women ages 50 and over were dissatisfied with their bodies (Runfola et al., 2013). Midlife women are more dissatisfied with their appearance than midlife men (Krekula, 2016). Consequently, they are more likely than men to diet and to use age concealment techniques, such as liposuction, breast and face lifts, tummy tucks, and injectable wrinkle fillers such as Botox (American Society of Plastic Surgeons, 2015; Chrisler et al., 2016; Katz & Gish, 2015; Markey & Markey, 2014). In addition, the demand for cosmetic genital surgery is increasing in the United States and western Europe, as more women seek to have "designer vaginas" (Goodman, 2011; Sharp et al., 2015). Even young mothers are increasingly getting "mommy makeovers"—including a breast lift, tummy tuck, and liposuction—intended to reduce postpartum stretch marks and abdominal fat (Matarasso & Smith, 2015). Moreover, women feel pressured to seek out surgery at younger ages than a decade ago (American Society of Plastic Surgeons, 2015). Whereas the vast majority of cosmetic surgeries are performed on White women, ethnic minority women are increasingly seeking these procedures (American Society of Plastic Surgeons, 2015). The good news is that as women move into their 50s and beyond, many become more satisfied with and accepting of their bodies (Jankowski et al., 2016; Tiggemann & McCourt, 2013).

The results reported in this section were based on U.S. samples. What do females and males in other cultures look for in a romantic partner or prospective mate?

David Buss (1994) and his colleagues studied the characteristics that adults in 37 cultures prefer in potential mates. In all cultures, men valued physical attractiveness more highly than did women. They also preferred younger mates and mates with domestic skills. Women in 36 of 37 cultures, however, valued "good earning capacity" more than men did and they preferred older mates. Still, there was a great degree of consistency in the preferences of women and men. Both ranked "kind and understanding" as most important, followed by "intelligent," "exciting personality," and "healthy." Despite these overall similarities, cultural differences occurred on almost all items. The largest cultural difference was found for chastity, which was considered to be unimportant by northern Europeans, but very important in China, India, and Iran. What might account for these cultural differences? Alice Eagly and her colleagues (Wood & Eagly, 2010) reexamined the 37 cultures as well as a subset of 9 of these cultures. They found that women's preference for older mates with resources and men's preference for younger women with domestic skills and intact virginity were most pronounced in societies in which women's status was low. These differences decreased as societies became more egalitarian. In other words, gender differences in the characteristics that people prefer in mates reflect the extent to which women and men occupy different roles in a given society.

Perception of Sexual Interest

How do young adults determine sexual interest of their partners? In heterosexual relationships, both males and females interpret certain nonsexual behaviors as cues that one's partner is interested in sex. For example, some young adults assume that how much a partner spends on a date influences how far things go sexually (Basow & Minieri, 2011).

In general, men are more likely than women to perceive sexual interest in nonsexual behaviors. For example, college men are more likely than college women to misperceive flirting (Henningsen, 2004), friendliness (Farris et al., 2008), or even a brief conversation (Henningsen et al., 2006; Levesque et al., 2006) as indicating sexual interest. Explanations of these gender differences range from differential socialization to greater readiness toward sexual arousal and mating in men (Perilloux et al., 2012). Whatever the cause, can you identify problems stemming from the cues men use to perceive sexual interest? Unfortunately, the sexual meaning men give to many nonsexual behaviors can lead to a misunderstanding of women's desires and to possible sexual aggression.

Dating

Almost all of the research on dating has focused on able-bodied women and men. Persons with disabilities face other issues in dating relationships. To examine some of the issues for women with disabilities, see Learn About the Research 8.1.

ONSET OF DATING.   The mixed-gender friendship and peer groups that start to form during early adolescence are central to the emergence of dating and romantic relationships that begin to blossom at this time (Kreager, Molloy, et al., 2016). Dating not only serves as a courting ritual that can lead to serious commitment and marriage, but also as an opportunity for sexual experimentation, enhancement of a teenager's social status and popularity, and development of a sense of identity (Furman & Rose, 2015; Norona et al., 2017).

Over the last several decades, the age when U.S. adolescents start dating has decreased. Many girls now begin to date at age 12 or 13, and many boys at 13 or 14. Some girls report dating as early as age 8, with parents as chaperones (Myers & Raymond, 2010). About one-quarter of 12-year-olds have been involved in a romantic relationship, compared to 70 percent of 18-year-olds (Connolly & McIsaac, 2009).

Many of the factors that are related to the initiation of sexual activity (see Chapter 6) are also related to the age at onset of dating. For example, Black teenagers begin both dating and sexual activity earlier than White and Latina/o adolescents. Other factors related to early dating include early age at puberty, associating with older peers, and belonging to a divorced or stepparent family (Connolly & McIsaac, 2009).

LEARN ABOUT THE RESEARCH 8.1
Dating Issues for Women With Physical Disabilities

Because previous research had shown that women with physical disabilities were considered asexual and not acceptable as romantic partners, Margaret Nosek and her colleagues examined dating issues experienced by women with and without disabilities. Their national sample included 475 women with disabilities (average age, 41.5) and 425 able-bodied women (average age, 38). These women responded to mailed questionnaires.

The researchers found that women who were disabled before their first date began dating approximately two-and-one-half years later than able-bodied women. However, there was no difference in the percentage of women with or without disabilities who had ever had sex with a man, although somewhat fewer women with disabilities reported having had sex with a woman.

Compared to able-bodied women, the women with disabilities were less satisfied about their dating frequency and perceived more problems trying to attract dating partners. They were also more concerned about both physical obstacles in the environment and societal barriers to dating, including people's assumptions that women with disabilities were uninterested in or unable to have sexual intimacy. Last, women with disabilities experienced more personal barriers to dating, such as pressure from family members not to date and low frequency of getting out of the house to socialize.

Based on these findings, the researchers suggest several interventions that might improve the dating experiences of women with disabilities. Some of these are (1) removal of physical barriers in public places, (2) educating the public about disability and sexuality, and (3) educating families about the appropriateness of dating for women with disabilities.

WHAT DOES IT MEAN?

1. What specific strategies could be used to educate the public about disability and sexuality and to change families' feelings about the appropriateness of dating? What solutions other than those presented here might improve the dating situation for women with disabilities?

2. This investigation focused on women only. Do you think men with disabilities experience similar problems? Explain your answer.

Source: Nosek et al. (2001).

Young people usually bring to their early dating encounters a set of beliefs regarding how they should behave in order to appeal to the other gender and maintain the relationship. The advice passed along to girls by girlfriends, mothers, older siblings, and the media frequently includes such helpful hints as massaging the boy's ego, bringing up subjects that he enjoys talking about, admiring his accomplishments (but not mentioning yours), and being understanding, but not too assertive or confrontational. A boy, on the other hand, learns to "take care" of a girl he dates by making the arrangements, being chivalrous (opening the door, helping her put her coat on), paying for the date, and taking her home (Boynton, 2003; Rose, 2000). Notice how traditionally gender-typed these dating expectations are.

DATING SCRIPTS. Suzanna Rose and Irene Hanson Frieze (1993) first explored this subject in greater detail by studying the expected **dating scripts** and actual dating behaviors of college students on a first date. A dating script is a *culturally developed sequence of expected events that guides an individual's behavior while on a date*. (The task the researchers used is described in Get Involved 8.1. Try it with some of your friends.) Students' expected dating behaviors and their actual behaviors were very similar. Some aspects of the dating script were the same for females and males. These included worrying about one's appearance, talking, going to a show, eating, and kissing goodnight. Many of the elements of the date, however, were strongly gender-stereotypical. Males were the initiators. They asked for and planned the date, drove the car and opened doors, and started sexual interaction. Females, on the other hand, reacted to what men did: being picked up, having doors opened, and responding to sexual overtures. They also focused more on the private domain, such as concern about appearance and enjoying the date (Rose & Frieze, 1993).

GET INVOLVED 8.1
Dating Scripts of Women and Men

Complete the following task from the study by Rose and Frieze (1993, p. 502). Then ask two unmarried female and two unmarried male undergraduates to do the same.

From the perspective of your own gender, list the actions that a woman (use the word "man" *for male participants) would typically do as she (he) prepared for a first date with someone new, then met her (his) date, spent time during the date, and ended the date. Include at least 20 actions or events that would occur in a routine first date, putting them in the order in which they would occur.*

WHAT DOES IT MEAN?

1. What elements of a dating script were shared by your female and male respondents?
2. In what ways were the dating scripts gender-stereotypical?
3. How do your results compare to those of Rose and Frieze (1993) described in the text?
4. Based on your knowledge of gender stereotypes, gender-related attitudes, and socialization experiences, what might account for the differences in the dating scripts of females and males?
5. Do you think that the degree of traditional gender-stereotypical behavior in dating scripts would be the same on a fifth date as on a first date? Explain your answer.

More recent research has confirmed that these dating scripts continue to operate in the twenty-first century (Eaton & Rose, 2011; Lamont, 2014; Paynter & Leaper, 2016) although after six months of dating, three-quarters of women and men report sharing expenses (Frederick et al., 2013). Dating scripts of lesbians and gay males are similar in many respects to those of heterosexuals, but they are not as strongly gender-typed (Rose & Zand, 2002).

Dating scripts reflect not only the stereotype of the communal female and the agentic male but also suggest that heterosexual romantic relationships are characterized by a power imbalance between women and men (Simpson et al., 2014). Does research support this assumption of greater male power? Studies of late adolescents and young adults find that some dating couples view their relationships as egalitarian, at least in terms of certain types of power, whereas others perceive a power imbalance (Galliher et al., 1999). When there is inequality, the male is far more likely to be the dominant partner, consistent with males' greater power in society (Bentley et al., 2007).

RECENT TRENDS IN DATING. As more individuals remain single for longer periods of time, or become single as a result of divorce, elaborate partnering "markets" have developed in major cities. Edward Laumann and his colleagues (2004) interviewed over 2,000 adults in four Chicago neighborhoods, including those with largely Black, Latino/a, or gay populations. They found that the partnering markets operate differently for women and men. Women, for example, were less likely than men to meet a partner through institutions such as work or church as they got older, in part because men in their 40s often sought women who were at least five to eight years younger. Neighborhoods and cultures also influenced the ways in which people found partners. In Latino/a neighborhoods, for example, family, friends, and the church played a more important role in meeting partners than in other areas. Young, upper-income individuals on the city's north side were more apt to find partners at school or work. Gay men were more likely to look for short-term relationships whereas lesbians usually sought long-term partners.

A more modern way to meet a potential partner is to visit online dating sites. Specialized sites for singles of various ages, religions, ethnicities, sexual orientation, and disabilities have proliferated in recent years (Finkel et al., 2012). For example, Tinder, the world's most popular dating app, has updated its options to allow users to choose transgender or gender nonconforming identities (Stack, 2016). One in ten Americans has used an online dating site or mobile dating app (Smith & Duggan,

2013). Over 20 percent of straight couples and nearly 70 percent of same-sex couples have met online (Ansari & Klinenberg, 2015). Online dating has shed its image as a last resort for losers or a meeting ground for casual sex, as word spreads of successful long-term relationships that began online (Smith & Duggan, 2013). Not surprisingly, traditional dating scripts still apply, at least in the sense that men usually send the first e-mail message and often do not respond when a woman does so (Harmon, 2003). Still another recent dating phenomenon is speed-dating, in which 10–12 couples sit around a room, exchanging information with potential dates in six- to eight-minute segments (Conkle, 2010; Tidwell et al., 2013).

Not only are there more single Americans than ever before, but more of them are middle-aged or older. Many older singles are either dating or looking for someone to date (Arndt, 2014; McWilliams & Barrett, 2013). Interestingly, some older women (like most men) prefer to date younger individuals. Older singles have more realistic dating expectations than younger ones. Most do not expect or want dating to lead to marriage and this is especially true for women (Brown & Shinohara, 2013). Instead, they are looking for someone to talk to and do things with. And, like their younger single counterparts, many older adults are looking for partners or companions online (McWilliams & Barrett, 2013).

COMMITTED RELATIONSHIPS

Committed relationships can take several different forms. Among heterosexuals, the most common type of committed relationship by far is marriage. Cohabitation (i.e., living together) has increased in recent years, often as a prelude to marriage. Lesbians and gay men also form committed relationships, and are able to legally marry in the United States and many other countries. In this section, we examine these forms of committed relationships.

Marriage

Although nearly all Americans hold marriage as an ideal, powerful social and cultural forces have made marriage increasingly optional in the twenty-first century (Coontz, 2016; Sawhill, 2014). Most women view marriage positively, although some variation occurs across ethnic groups. Latinas place a higher value on marriage than other groups (Darghouth et al., 2015; Sweeney & Raley 2014), which might reflect the strong value placed on family in Latina/o culture. Black women show less interest in marriage than do women of other ethnic groups, perhaps because they see marriage as less important to their individual success (Kaufman & Goldscheider, 2007). In addition, some college-educated Black women are concerned about a shortage of eligible Black men who meet their expectations for a marital partner, in part because college-going rates are higher in Black women than men (Ford, 2012). Just half of college-educated Black women marry a college-educated man, compared to 84 percent of White women with a college education (Rodrigue & Reeves, 2015).

MARRIAGE RATES.   High marriage rates indicate the continuing value placed on marriage in society. In 2011, 90 percent of White, 85 percent of Latina, and 68 percent of Black individuals, 46 years or older, were married or had been married at some point (Bureau of Labor Statistics, 2013a). College-educated individuals are more likely to be married than those with a high school diploma (Bureau of Labor Statistics, 2013a). The median age at first marriage has been increasing. In 2014, it was 27 for women and 29 for men, an increase of approximately six years since 1970 (Hymowitz et al., 2013; U.S. Census Bureau, 2015b). This increase in age of marriage is due in part to changes in economic conditions, leading both women and men to desire some degree of financial security before embarking on a long-term commitment. In addition, as more women pursue higher education and careers, they tend to marry later. Women with disabilities are less likely to marry and are more likely to marry later in life than men with disabilities or able-bodied women (Lu, 2016; Olkin, 2013). The vast majority of Americans marry individuals of their own race. However, during the past 25 years, the number of interracial marriages has increased, comprising 4 percent of all married heterosexual couples in 2012 (Vespa et al., 2013).

MARITAL SATISFACTION.   Couples who report high levels of marital satisfaction use active, problem-focused coping strategies; hold similar attitudes, goals, and values; and communicate well with each other (Cavanaugh & Blanchard-Fields, 2015; Grieger, 2017). Women are more involved than men in maintaining such communication, consistent with the social construction of females as concerned about the feelings of others and more emotionally adept (Loscocco & Walzer, 2013). For example, stressed wives provide better support to their spouses than do stressed husbands (Bodenmann et al., 2015). Wives also tend to be happier and more satisfied when their husbands are emotionally engaged and spend time with them and when they perceive that they and their spouses contribute equally to the marriage (Chong & Mickelson, 2016; DeMaris, 2010). A husband's marital satisfaction is related to that of his wife: When she is happy, so is he (Carr et al., 2014).

One of the biggest determinants of marital satisfaction is the presence of children. Marital satisfaction declines over time for women and men whether or not they have a child (Hirschberger et al., 2009; Johnson, 2016; Mitnick et al., 2009). Couples who become parents, however, show steeper declines in satisfaction than those who do not (Mollen, 2014; Peterson, 2016). When children leave home, couples experience an increase in marital satisfaction (Bookwala, 2012). What do you think accounts for these changes?

Most studies show that men report greater marital satisfaction than women (Ploubidis et al., 2015). It is clear, however, that marriage provides women and men with many benefits. Both married women and men are happier than their unmarried counterparts, a relationship found around the globe (Chen & Feeley, 2014; Helliwell & Grover, 2015; J. B. Jackson et al., 2014). Moreover, married individuals, especially those in good relationships, are mentally and physically healthier and better able to deal with stress (Birmingham et al., 2015; Chopik & O'Brien, 2017). However, this "marriage benefit" is smaller for women than for men (Robles, 2014). People in strained, unhappy relationships usually have poorer health than happily married individuals. Furthermore, marital stress affects women's health and sense of well-being more than men's (Liu & Waite, 2014; South & Krueger, 2013).

Why are people in good marriages happier and healthier than single individuals? One obvious answer is the care and support they receive from their spouses, although women provide more care and support than they receive. Second, married couples often benefit financially because they have a combined household and, frequently, two incomes. Third, spouses tend to encourage health-promoting behaviors in one another (Gomez et al., 2016; Lin & Brown, 2012; T.W. Smith et al., 2014). It is also possible, of course, that individuals with positive personality traits and healthier lifestyles are more likely to attract a mate in the first place.

Cohabitation

Cohabitation, *the state in which an unmarried couple lives together*, has dramatically increased in the United States over the last several decades. An estimated 50 percent or more of couples in the United States live together before marriage, with a higher incidence occurring among those with less education (Copen et al., 2013; Yarrow, 2015). Cohabitation is even more common in Europe (Comerford, 2011).

Many adolescents view living together as a way to test compatibility before marriage, and for many couples, cohabitation indeed serves as a trial marriage (Bianchi et al., 2014; Vespa, 2014). For some couples, however, especially divorced or widowed persons, cohabitation is seen as an alternative to marriage that is driven by finances, convenience, and housing considerations (Bianchi et al., 2014; Vespa, 2014).

Despite its popularity, not all people are in favor of cohabitation. Not surprisingly, middle-aged and older adults are more opposed than are young adults (Elias et al., 2015). Traditionally religious individuals also are less willing to cohabit (Jose et al., 2010; Stanley et al., 2011), perhaps because cohabitation is counter to the teachings of many religions. Furthermore, individuals who hold more liberal sexual views and less traditional gender and political attitudes have more positive views of cohabitation (Hardie & Lucas, 2010; Jose et al., 2010). Clearly, this lifestyle is inconsistent with traditional views about premarital chastity for women and is less likely than marriage to enable fulfillment of traditional gender roles.

Cohabiters report lower levels of affection and higher levels of conflict than couples who married without previously cohabiting (Brown et al., 2014). Interestingly, even after marriage, individuals who previously lived with each other have lower marital satisfaction, have higher levels of domestic violence, and are more likely to get divorced than married couples who had not lived together before marriage (Jose et al., 2010; Kuperberg, 2014; Patterson et al., 2014). This does not necessarily mean that cohabitation fosters marital instability. Rather, these findings could result from a **selection effect** whereby *the attitudes of individuals who cohabit are more accepting of divorce and less committed to marriage than the attitudes of noncohabiters* (Kuperberg, 2014). Age is another confounding factor. People are younger when they first live together than when they marry, and younger adults are less likely to remain in committed relationships (Kuperberg, 2014).

Living Apart Together

An emerging type of socially accepted, noncohabiting intimate relationship in Western countries is **living apart together (LAT)**, in which *two individuals consider themselves a couple but do not share the same residence* (Duncan et al., 2014). LAT relationships combine intimacy and commitment with personal autonomy and independence. For some couples, especially younger adults, LAT is a transitional step between singlehood and cohabitation or marriage. For middle-aged and older couples, on the other hand, the decision to live apart may involve factors such as not wanting to repeat a mistake (following divorce), or wishing to maintain one's own household and financial independence (Carter et al., 2016).

Lesbian Relationships

Contrary to popular stereotypes, lesbians are as likely as heterosexual women to be part of a couple and are more likely than gay men to be in a lasting monogamous relationship (Fisher et al., 2016; Potarca et al., 2015). According to U.S. Census data, for example, more same-sex households consist of two women than two men (U.S. Census Bureau, 2016a).

Lesbian relationships tend to be egalitarian, with household activities and other relationship behaviors determined through negotiation and based more on individual skills and interests than on rigid gendered conceptions of appropriate behaviors. In fact, lesbian relationships are characterized by more equality of power and a more equal division of paid and unpaid labor than are either heterosexual or gay relationships (Burns-Glover & Kasibhatla, 2013; Goldberg, 2017; Jaspers & Verbakel, 2013; Kelly & Hauck, 2015; Rith & Diamond, 2013). Interestingly, bisexual women who have had relationships with partners of both genders report more conflicts over power in their heterosexual than in their same-sex relationships, in part because of dissatisfaction with the power balance in heterosexual relationships (Weinberg et al., 1994).

Many lesbians are involved in sexually exclusive relationships (Cohen & Byers, 2014; Goldberg, 2017). They engage in considerable nongenital physical expression, such as hugging and cuddling, and are as satisfied with their sexual relationships as are heterosexual and gay couples (Rose & Eaton, 2013).

Although lesbians are generally satisfied with their relationships, lesbian couples experience a variety of unique stressors. First, conflicts can arise if one partner's lesbian identity is critical to her self-concept, while her partner's self-concept is based primarily on her profession or ethnicity (Rith & Diamond, 2013). Second, lesbians must cope with the frequent lack of societal acceptance of their relationship (Gonzales, 2014). Third, lesbian couples frequently face economic difficulties, in part because their income is based on the earnings of two women and women tend to earn less than men (see Chapter 10), and because many lesbian couples are denied domestic partner insurance and Social Security benefits typically awarded to married individuals (Goldberg, 2017).

Lesbian couples are more likely than gay men to be in a lasting, monogamous relationship.

On a more positive note, lesbians show higher levels of emotional closeness over time than either heterosexual couples or gay men (Rith & Diamond, 2013). In addition, lesbian couples report feeling less lonely than heterosexual married women (Grossman et al., 2013). Some writers suggest that lesbian couples are advantaged compared with heterosexual wives because they are more likely to share similar life expectancy, to be less threatened by changes in physical appearance, and to have accumulated their own financial resources through employment (Huyck, 1995).

Aging sexual minority women must confront the triple obstacles of sexism, ageism, and homophobia (Allen & Roberto, 2016; Clay, 2014b). Older lesbians who faced prejudice and discrimination during more hostile times often hid their identities and their relationships with other women (Rose & Hospital, 2015; Traies, 2016). Even now, because of social constraints, they may not openly acknowledge the nature of their relationship. Unfortunately, this secrecy has led to the near invisibility of the older lesbian and gay population, and to their reduced access to health services.

As is true for heterosexuals, being in a committed relationship increases life satisfaction for older lesbians (Grossman et al., 2013; Traies, 2016). Moreover, after spending many years coping with the social stigma of their sexual orientation, lesbians and gay men have developed the inner resilience and social networks that may make them better prepared than heterosexuals to cope with the stigma of aging (de Vries 2014; Orel and Fruhauf, 2015; Traies, 2016).

SINGLE WOMEN

When people marry, they don't always live happily ever after. Some divorce, others lose their spouses or same-sex partners through death. A small percentage of women never marry at all. In this section, we examine women who are divorced, never married, widowed, or who have lost a same-sex partner.

Divorced Women

Couples do not walk down the aisle with expectations of splitting up. Nevertheless, approximately 40 percent of all American marriages end in divorce, although divorce rates have decreased somewhat in recent years (C.C. Miller, 2014a). Although first marriages that end in divorce last for about eight years, marriages can dissolve at any point in the life cycle (U.S. Census Bureau, 2015b) and for numerous reasons—including incompatibility, communication problems, infidelity, substance abuse, and physical violence.

Although divorce occurs throughout the population, divorce rates differ depending on one's ethnic group, educational level, and age at marriage. African Americans are the most likely to divorce, followed by Latinos/as, Whites and then Asian Americans (Kreider & Ellis, 2011). College-educated individuals are less likely to divorce than those without college degrees (C.C. Miller, 2014a). In addition, as the age of marriage rises through the late 20s, the divorce rate falls and then levels off (C.C. Miller, 2014a).

Women with disabilities are more likely than able-bodied women or men with disabilities to be divorced (Olkin, 2008). Not surprisingly, both financial pressure and interpersonal problems can be contributing factors. If the spouse with a disability is unable to continue working, or if the able-bodied partner must quit work to care for her or his spouse, the couple might experience considerable financial strain. In addition, psychological reactions, such as anger or moodiness, on the part of either spouse or stress stemming from an overload of responsibilities for the able-bodied partner can damage the quality of the relationship. Consistent with the social construction of females as caregivers, wives are less likely than husbands to leave a spouse who has a disability (Etaugh, 2017).

EFFECTS OF DIVORCE ON WOMEN AND THEIR CHILDREN.   Although divorced mothers view themselves as better parents than do mothers in high-conflict marriages, single parenting after a divorce can be highly stressful (Hetherington & Kelly, 2002). The breakup of a marriage produces numerous stressors for custodial parents and their children. Not only must both deal with strong emotional reactions, such as grief, anger, and guilt, but also with those of their children. Daily routines and household responsibilities often involve major adjustments. Financial pressures can require the mother to begin or extend her employment, there can be major modifications in household responsibilities, and the family might have to change residence.

Given these and other stressors associated with parental divorce, children tend to experience a variety of emotional, academic, and behavioral problems in the immediate aftermath (Amato & Anthony, 2014; Hetherington, 2004; Hetherington & Kelly, 2002; Potter, 2010), but most rebound within two years. As adults, they are as psychologically healthy as children who grew up in two-parent homes (Beckmeyer et al., 2014). In fact, research comparing children from divorced and nondivorced families finds that differences are very small and that children in conflict-ridden intact families experience lower levels of psychological well-being than do children in divorced families (Amato & Anthony, 2014; Lansford, 2009). Moreover, children in joint-custody arrangements following divorce are as well adjusted as children in two-parent families (Bauserman, 2002).

Divorced women also experience initial problems followed by satisfactory adjustment. Immediately following the breakup, it is common for divorced women to experience higher levels of depression and distress than married women. These negative reactions are greatest in the first few years after the divorce. Most women are resilient in the face of divorce, however, and any negative reactions decrease over time, with few long-term effects on psychological adjustment (Hetherington & Kelly, 2002; Perrig-Chiello et al., 2015; Sbarra et al., 2015). Even if divorced women remarry, they are somewhat more likely to have chronic physical health problems than women who have been continuously married (Cornwell & Waite, 2009). Ethnicity also can affect a woman's adjustment to divorce. For example, studies suggest that Latinas experience more distress than White women, perhaps due to the strong emphasis on marriage in Hispanic culture (Pew Research Center, 2007a). However, Black mothers show a greater sense of personal mastery following divorce than White mothers (McKelvey & McKenry, 2000), possibly because African American culture provides these women with greater coping skills to deal with the adversities of divorce.

Many women experience a decline in family income after divorce, which places them in a significantly worse financial situation than divorced men (Demo & Fine, 2017; Rhode et al., 2014). Divorced mothers are twice as likely as divorced fathers to live in poverty. Many mothers receive irregular or incomplete child support payments and a substantial minority receives nothing (Demo & Fine, 2017). Not surprisingly, divorced women with low income and low occupational status are at greater risk for distress and depression (Etaugh, 2008).

Despite the problems resulting from a breakup, divorce can represent a positive means of reacting to a neglectful, conflict-ridden, or abusive relationship, and women do not feel more upset after a divorce than they did in their high-conflict marriages and are happier after divorce than they were during the last year of their marriage (Bourassa et al., 2015). Further, divorced women are likely to be less depressed than women in unhappy marriages (Hetherington & Kelly, 2002).

In addition to relief from leaving a conflict-laden marriage, many women report a variety of positive psychological outcomes—greater feelings of independence and freedom, the ability to meet the challenges of living without a spouse and functioning as a single parent, which can produce a new sense of competence (Hetherington & Kelly, 2002). In fact, divorced women are more likely than divorced men to say that they do not want to remarry (Livingston, 2014).

COPING WITH DIVORCE.   What factors help women cope with the strains of divorce? Employment is one factor that can facilitate adjustment (Amato, 2000). It provides an identity outside of women's marital role, is an avenue for productivity and income, and is a source of positive distraction and social support for divorced women. A divorced teacher stated, "Work filled my time and diverted my mind . . . It kept my mind off things for a while" (Bisagni & Eckenrode, 1995, p. 581). And a clerical worker noted, "My coworkers really do care. Like when I was going through the divorce, they really wanted to know if I was okay, without trying to pry. . . . if I couldn't talk to my coworkers, I probably would've gone to professional help a lot longer" (Bisagni & Eckenrode, 1995, p. 580).

Social support from family and friends is also vitally important in helping divorced women cope. Women who have a social network of friends and relatives to help them deal with the ramifications of divorce are less depressed and show more positive adjustment in the years following the marital breakup (Demo & Fine, 2017; Krumrei et al., 2007). Having a new partner is another source of support that can have beneficial effects in postdivorce adjustment (Demo & Fine, 2017).

Never-Married Women

Although some women become single at least for a period of time as a result of the end of a marriage, some never marry. Approximately 4 percent of women and 4.5 percent of men in the United States aged 65 and over have never married (Kincel, 2014). Women with disabilities are more likely to remain single than able-bodied women or men with disabilities (Olkin, 2008).

Although marriage is still viewed as the expected lifestyle, today there is more freedom in, acceptance of, and support for single lifestyles than in the past in both the United States and Canada (Wang & Parker, 2014). In one survey, 83 percent of American women and 73 percent of men said a woman can lead a complete and happy life if she is single (Pew Research Center, 2007b). Still, single women continue to be portrayed negatively in the media and are widely perceived as odd, social outcasts, or selfish, commitment-phobic career women who lead barren, disappointing lives (DePaolo, 2015). How do never-married heterosexual women feel about being single? Evidence shows that some are ambivalent about their marital status. On the one hand, they miss the benefits of steady companionship and feel sad about growing old alone, but at the same time, they enjoy their freedom, independence, and opportunities for personal growth (Bay-Cheng & Goodkind, 2016; DePaolo, 2015; Moore & Radtke, 2015; Sharp & Ganong, 2011). Increasing numbers of single women are signing up for housewarming and birthday registries, having decided not to wait for marriage to request the china, crystal, and appliances they wish to own (Zernike, 2003). Some are not only purchasing a home instead of renting but are also buying a second, vacation home (Cohen et al., 2003). Websites, such as SingleEdition.com, celebrate singlehood and offer shopping, financial, and other advice to singles (Newman, 2007).

The absence of a marital partner does not mean that single women are lacking social relationships. As we have seen, some date or are in committed romantic relationships, and many have strong ties to their extended families, network of friends, and community (DePaolo, 2015; North, 2015). Moreover, an increasing number of middle-aged never-married women are choosing to become mothers via adoption or sperm donation (Goldberg & Scheid, 2015; Patterson et al., 2014). In the words of one woman, "It would be nice to be in a relationship, but I don't really need that. My life is fine the way it is. And my life is full of love" (Boston Women's Health Book Collective, 1998, p. 187).

One disadvantage of being a single woman in midlife is that single women, more than their married sisters, are expected to, and in fact do, provide caregiving for aging parents, even at the expense of their own careers (Yorgason & Stott, 2017). On the plus side, never-married women typically have developed skills in independent living and in building support systems that stand them in good stead as they get older (Connidis, 2010). Compared with married women, the never-married older woman is better educated, has a higher income, and is less likely to be depressed (Dykstra & Hagestad, 2007; Etaugh, 2008; Wang & Parker, 2014). Never-married older women also have fewer chronic health problems than those who are divorced or widowed (Hughes & Waite, 2009). Single older women have also learned to cope in their earlier years with the "stigma" of not being married and so are better able to deal with the effects of ageism in their later years. Most older, single women are satisfied with their lives and seem at least as happy as married women (Newtson & Keith, 2001).

Widowed Women

Despite the increasing divorce rate, most marriages are terminated not by divorce, but by the death of a spouse. Around the world, women are more likely to become widowed than men, because women not only have a longer life expectancy but also tend to marry men older than themselves (Humble & Price, 2017; Kincel, 2014). In the United States, women 65 years and older are three times as likely as men of the same age to be widowed: 40 percent versus 13 percent (U.S. Census Bureau, 2015b).

Remarriage rates are much higher for widowers than for men who have lost a spouse through death or divorce than for women who have lost a spouse (Federal Interagency Forum, 2016; Schimmele & Wu, 2016). Consequently, older women are nearly twice as likely as older men to live alone (Donatelle, 2017).

One obvious reason for the much lower remarriage rate of women is that unmarried older women greatly outnumber unmarried older men. For instance, unmarried women aged 65 and over in the United States outnumber unmarried men in that age category by more than two to one (U.S. Census Bureau, 2015b). Furthermore, because men tend to marry women younger than themselves, the pool of potential mates expands for an older man but shrinks for an older woman. In addition, widowed women are much less interested than widowed men in forming a new relationship. They value their independence and are not eager to resume the domestic responsibilities of a long-term relationship. Many do not relish the idea of becoming a caregiver for an older man, having, in some cases, already experienced the stresses of caring for a terminally ill partner (Connidis, 2010; Koren, 2016; Sweeney, 2010). Widowers, on the other hand, typically want someone to organize their households and social lives and provide companionship (Olson, 2006).

> *Four months after her husband of 42 years died, Verna hit an emotional low. "I told myself I have two choices. I can sit home, mourn, complain and cry, or make a new life in which I would learn to smile and be happy again in my own activities such as volunteering and starting a social life with new friends who aren't couples."*

(Arney, 2001, p. A8)

REACTION AND ADJUSTMENT TO WIDOWHOOD.   Widowhood is one of the most stressful of all life events. The surviving spouse must not only cope with the loss of one's life partner but also adjust to a new status as a widowed person (Naef, 2013). During the first year after their husbands' deaths, widows show poorer mental and physical health than longer-term widows. Women who provided long-term care to their spouses prior to their deaths are more likely to be depressed than those who provided care on a short-term basis or not at all (Keene & Prokos, 2008). Most older widowed individuals adjust to their spouses' deaths within two to four years, although feelings of loneliness, yearning, missing their partner, and lowered life satisfaction remain for extended periods of time (Naef, 2013; Sullivan & Fenelon, 2013). As many as 10 to 20 percent of widows, however, experience long-term problems, including clinical depression, abuse of alcohol and prescription drugs, and increased susceptibility to physical illness. Among these are women with a prior history of depression, those whose marriages were less satisfactory, those whose husbands' deaths followed the deaths of other close relatives and friends, and those who depended on their husbands for most social contacts (Etaugh, 2008).

Other factors—age; the degree of forewarning of the spouse's death; and financial, social, and personal resources—also affect a woman's reaction to widowhood (Holden et al., 2010; Sullivan & Fenelon, 2013). Studies comparing the mental and physical health of older widows and older married women have not generally found any differences between these groups (Etaugh, 2008). Younger widows, on the other hand, initially experience greater difficulties in coping with their situation (Michael et al., 2003). One reason for the greater distress experienced by young widows may be the greater likelihood that the husband's death was unexpected. Although younger individuals experience greater distress following their partners' deaths, the length of recovery is greater for older people (Michael et al., 2003).

Widowhood often results in a substantial reduction in financial resources for women, not only because the husband's income or pension ceases, but also because considerable expenses may have been incurred during the husband's final illness (DiGiacomo et al., 2013). Loneliness is another problem faced by widows (Murray, 2016; Naef et al., 2013). About 70 percent of older widows live alone. Having the social support of family, friends, and neighbors to stave off loneliness helps to alleviate the psychological and physical effects of loss-related stress (Bookwala et al., 2014; Merz & Gierveld, 2016; Powers et al., 2013). Interestingly, research has found more loneliness among women who have lived with a spouse for many years than among women who live alone (Etaugh, 2008).

The death of a spouse takes a heavier toll on men than on women. Widowed men suffer more psychological depression, psychiatric disorders, and physical illnesses, and have higher death rates and suicide rates than widowed women (Kuther, 2017; Jadhav & Weir, 2017). This may be due to the fact that women are more apt than men to admit a need for social support, to benefit from that support, and to have broad social networks with relatives and friends, including other widows (Kemper, 2013; Sullivan & Fenelon, 2013; Wong & Waite, 2015).

The experiences of widowhood were vividly portrayed in a longitudinal study of over 4,300 older Australian widows by Susan Feldman and her colleagues (2000). The widows not only had to cope with bereavement and loss but also the challenges of daily life, including financial and social matters. Another common theme was the need to keep busy. Relationships to family, friends, neighbors, and social groups became especially important. Many women displayed an attitude of courage, strength, and resilience as they coped with the challenges of their new life. In the words of one woman, who had been widowed for four years,

> *I felt desolate and despairing [when he died] . . . I have managed to survive and lead a comfortable and quite interesting (albeit at times a rather lonely) life. I am pleased that I have adjusted, and I handle all of my affairs. I shall never get over the loss, but I have lived to see the day.*

> (Feldman et al., 2000, p. 164)

Widows learn to enjoy living alone and derive a sense of independence and competence from learning new, and some traditionally masculine, tasks (Moss & Moss, 2014; Murray, 2016). Moreover, the realization that they have withstood an event that seemed insurmountable enhances their self-esteem (Smoski et al., 2015).

 Keep in mind that this knowledge of widows has been obtained primarily from older women, most of whom had traditional marriages. When the young women of today become widows, they will be more likely to have had a different set of life experiences than the current population of widows, including a college education and a job or career that may better prepare them for a healthy adjustment to widowhood (Carr & Pudrovska, 2012; Etaugh, 2008). It is also important to note that much of the research on widowhood has been done in Western nations. In many parts of the world, losing one's husband involves more than dealing with grief and changed financial circumstances. In parts of Africa, the Middle East, and Asia, widows can suffer discrimination, sexual assault, and seizure of their property and children (Gorney, 2017). We will discuss these circumstances in greater detail in Chapter 10.

Women Who Have Lost a Same-Sex Partner

Lesbians and gay men may encounter unique problems when their partner dies. They may not be eligible for survivor benefits, and in the absence of a will, they may have no claim to the partner's estate that they have helped to build (Goldberg, 2017). *Loss of a same-sex partner is especially stressful if the relationship was not publicly acknowledged and given legitimacy*, a concept called **disenfranchised grief** (Allen & Roberto, 2016; Barrett et al., 2015; Murray, 2017). Even when the relationship is open, friends, family, and work colleagues may not comprehend the severity and nature of the loss (Fenge, 2014; Jenkins et al., 2014).

MOTHERHOOD

One of the most intimate relationships a woman can experience is her relationship with her child. Consistent with the assumption that motherhood serves as a major source of fulfillment for women, many women view having a child as a higher priority than having a good marriage (Pew Research Center, 2010). In the words of one mother, "For the first time I cared about somebody else more than myself, and I would do anything to nurture and protect her" (Boston Women's Health Book Collective, 1992, p. 488).

Although "the joy of having children" is by far the most important reason parents give for having children (Livingston & Cohen, 2010), this does not mean that parenting leads exclusively to positive emotions. Instead, mothers experience a swirl of opposing feelings. Motherhood can bring a great sense of love, connection, and joy accompanied by a tremendous burden of responsibility, exhaustion, and guilt (Deaton & Stone, 2014; Nelson et al., 2013; Wang, 2013). As one woman said, "The first month was awful. I loved my baby but felt apprehensive about my ability to satisfy this totally dependent tiny creature. Every time she cried I could feel myself tense up and panic" (Boston Women's Health Book Collective, 1998, p. 511). Motherhood can produce an expansion of personal identity as well as the loss of self. Mothers can feel exhilarated by their new role yet resent or mourn the loss of other aspects of their lives that might now diminish, such as involvement in work or community activities (Donath , 2015; Pew Research Center, 2015b). For many professional women, becoming pregnant for the first time leads to a restructuring of their professional identity to include identity as a working mother (Ladge et al., 2011). In addition, as we have seen, the transition to parenthood often has a negative impact on marital satisfaction (Ploubidis et al., 2015).

Stereotypes of Mothers

The "good mother" is socially constructed as a warm, forgiving, generous, nurturing person who is easily able to meet all her children's needs and who puts their needs before her own (Athan & Reel, 2015; Elliott et al., 2015; Jacobs & Gerson, 2016; Lowe, 2016). Unfortunately, no mother is able to consistently meet either her own standards or the standards of others, and all mothers suffer at least occasional feelings of inadequacy and guilt because of this idealized image (McKenzie-Mohr & LaFrance, 2014; Henderson et al., 2016). One mother complained, "I didn't know how to change a diaper any more than my husband did. In fact, I may have been more nervous about it, since I was 'supposed' to know how" (Boston Women's Health Book Collective, 1998, p. 511). Popular magazines and books do little to dispel this notion. One study examined the degree to which five current popular childrearing books portrayed the "new image" of the involved father (Schmitz, 2016). Only 10 percent of articles challenged the notion of the mother as the primary caregiver.

The good mother image can also lead people to blame mothers for their children's problems (Athan & Reel, 2015; O'Reilly, 2014) because the social construction of the mother role, more than the father role, assumes an all-knowing, self-sacrificing, always-caring parent. This may explain why a man who harms or even kills his own children receives relatively little media coverage, whereas when Andrea Yates drowned her five children (see Chapter 7), she received international attention

(Barash, 2002). Moreover, media speculate that the mothers are the culprits when mothers of murdered or missing children do not act exactly as the public thinks they should. The tears of Patsy Ramsey, mother of murdered JonBenét Ramsey, were labeled "an act," whereas Kate McCann was criticized for seeming too cool and composed about the disappearance of her young daughter in 2007 (Yabroff, 2007).

The good mother stereotype illustrates the **motherhood mandate**, *the societal belief that women should have children and that they should be physically available at all times to tend to their young children's needs* (Damaske et al., 2013; Wolf, 2016). This view of motherhood has persisted in North America into the twenty-first century, despite the dramatic increase in the employment of mothers in recent decades. The media glorify middle-class mothers who leave the workplace to become full-time homemakers (Jacobs & Gerson, 2016) and increasingly portray working mothers as struggling to meet the demands of work and family (Motro & Vanneman, 2015). Susan Douglas (2010) has criticized this "new momism," in which the mother is expected to devote every waking moment to raising the perfect child. Is such intensive mothering really needed for positive child outcomes? See In the News 8.1.

IN THE NEWS 8.1
Does Intensive Mothering Lead to Positive Child Outcomes?

Recent research by Melissa Milkie and her colleagues (2015) challenges the commonly held belief that more maternal time spent with children leads to better outcomes. They examined the relationship of mothers' time spent with their 3-to-11-year-old children and the children's behaviors, emotions, and school performance. The researchers studied these individuals again when the children were 12-to-18-year-olds. They separately examined whether a mother's time was "accessible" (present, but not involved in the child's activity) or engaged (involved in the child's activity). No relationship was found between either of those types of time and most of the child outcomes. The only exception was that "engaged" time with adolescents was linked to less delinquent behavior. These findings held across different levels of mothers' education and family income. What effect do you think these findings will have on the view that "intensive mothering" is the hallmark of a good mother?

In addition to communal qualities, numerous demographic characteristics are included in the societal image of the good mother (O'Reilly, 2014). She is expected to be middle class, heterosexual, married, not too old, and also to have a job that does not prevent her from spending "adequate" time with her children. The more a mother deviates from this image, the more devalued she is and the less likely her own mothering practices and experiences are seen as valid (Breheny & Stephens, 2009). As one example, women receiving public assistance who stay home with their children are criticized for *not* working (Macdonald, 2010).

While many working mothers struggle to balance intensive mothering expectations with their employment role (Schulte, 2014), this may be more characteristic of White women. Middle-class Black working mothers are more likely than their White counterparts to embrace what Dawn Dow (2016) calls **integrated motherhood**. *They feel an obligation to work outside the home and be financially self-reliant, and are comfortable with kin and community members as child care givers.* Being employed is viewed as the normal and natural choice, which demonstrates their commitment to family.

See What You Can Do 8.1 to help address issues related to parenting and work–family balancing.

Single Mothers

In the last several decades, there has been a significant increase in the percentage of single-parent, mother-headed families. The proportion of infants born to unmarried women rose to 40 percent in 2015 (Hamilton et al., 2016). Although many single mothers are in their 20s and have no more than a

WHAT <u>YOU</u> CAN DO 8.1
Help Address Issues of Parenting and Work–Family Balancing

Join, volunteer, or attend an event sponsored by the National Association of Mothers' Centers (motherscenters.org). Through its public policy initiative entitled MOTHERS (Mothers Ought to Have Equal Rights), it addresses many areas related to parenting, maternal health, child development, and work–family integration.

TABLE 8.1   Poverty Status of Single-Parent Families in 2012

Ethnicity	Single-Mother Families % Below the Poverty Level	Single-Father Families % Below the Poverty Level
All ethnic groups	35	16
Black	43	22
Latina/o	43	20
White	27	15
Asian	19	13

Source: Vespa et al., 2013.

high school education, an increasing number of unmarried mothers are in their 30s, 40s, and 50s and are college-educated. This is the group of women we discussed earlier in the section on "never-married women," who are choosing in early middle age to become mothers via adoption or sperm donation (Boyd et al., 2015; Patterson et al., 2015). Whereas in 1970 approximately 12 percent of families were maintained by a mother only, this figure increased to 27 percent in 2012, including 55 percent of Black, 26 percent of Latina, 18 percent of White, and 12 percent of Asian families. By comparison, only 4 percent of households are maintained by a single father (U.S. Census Bureau, 2015b). Who are these single mothers? Nearly two-thirds are White, and most have one or two children. About one in three of these women is cohabitating; the large majority, however, are heading a single-parent household.

Nearly 40 percent of all households below the poverty line are headed by single mothers (Vespa et al., 2013). As Table 8.1 shows, about one-third of female-headed families with dependent children live in poverty, and this number is significantly greater among Black and Latina families than White families. Note that single-father families of all ethnicities are much less likely to be poor, another illustration of the intersection of gender, class, and ethnicity (Kramer et al., 2016). *The increasing percentage of women living below the poverty line* is referred to as the **feminization of poverty** and is found across affluent Western democracies (Bullock, 2013; Spade & Valentine, 2016).

How do women cope with the responsibilities of single motherhood? One important factor is social support from family and friends (Hartwig, 2016; Hudson et al., 2016). This support can be both emotional and instrumental, such as helping when there is an emergency, assisting with transportation to and from day care, and caring for a child while the mother is at work.

Several strengths of Black families and communities can help Black single mothers cope more effectively. Because Blacks have a long history of maternal employment, single mothers have numerous role models for managing the stressors of coordinating these roles. **Extended families**, in which *at least one other adult family member resides in the same household as the mother and her children*, and **augmented families,** in which *adult nonrelatives live with the mother and her children*, are family structures in the Black community that can be helpful to single mothers (Belgrave & Allison, 2010; Jacobson, 2013; Nelson, 2013). These families offer additional role models for the children and provide substitute caregivers when the mother is at work or is tending to other responsibilities outside of the home. Because extended families are frequently involved in childrearing in Latina/o and Native American as well as Black families (Birditt & Fingerman, 2013; Gerstel, 2011; Sarche & Whitesell, 2012), they can be helpful to single mothers in these communities as well.

Lesbian Mothers

Until quite recently, most Americans viewed families from a heterosexual perspective. Now, however, a majority say their definition of family includes same-sex couples with children, as well as married same-sex couples (Powell et al., 2010). Nearly half of LBT women and 20 percent of gay men have a child in the household (Goldberg, 2017). Many of their children were born into previous heterosexual marriages (Traies, 2016). However, a growing number of lesbians choose to have children after they have identified as lesbians, by means of donor sperm, maternal surrogacy, or adoption (Abelsohn et al., 2013; Angier, 2014; Glazer, 2014; Yeshua et al., 2015).

Numerous studies have found that lesbian mothers are similar to heterosexual mothers in self-esteem and psychological adjustment (Goldberg, 2017). This similarity between lesbian and heterosexual mothers is particularly noteworthy considering that lesbian mothers face stressors such as social disapproval not experienced by heterosexual mothers (Titlestad & Pooley, 2013). In addition, some lesbians face rejection by their families of origin when they decide to parent (Goldberg, 2017).

Although lesbian women do not differ from heterosexual women in nurturance or commitment to their children, they do raise their daughters and sons in a less gender-stereotypic manner (Goldberg, 2017; Tasker, 2010). As models of gender-related behavior, they are less traditional than heterosexual mothers (Kenschaft & Clark, 2016). For example, partners are more likely to equally share financial and family responsibilities and be involved in feminist activities. Lesbian mothers are also less likely to purchase gender-stereotyped toys for their children and have less traditional gender-related expectations for their daughters and sons.

Research on lesbian donor insemination families shows that the quality of children's relationship with the social mother is comparable to that with the biological mother (Vanfraussen et al., 2003). Moreover, unlike fathers in heterosexual families, the social mother is as involved in the child's activities as is the biological mother.

Just as the research on lesbian mothers finds few differences from heterosexual mothers, scores of studies show few differences between children raised by lesbian mothers and those raised by heterosexual mothers. Reviews of this research conclude that children from lesbian and heterosexual families do just as well in psychological well-being, self-esteem, social and behavioral adjustments, and cognitive functioning (Bos et al., 2016; Fedewa et al., 2015; Golombok et al., 2014; Moore & Stambolis-Ruhstorfer, 2013). Similar results are found for the adjustment of children born to gay fathers through surrogacy (Golombok et al., 2014). Since lesbian mothers raise their children in a less gender-stereotypic manner than heterosexual parents, their children, especially daughters, are less likely to have stereotyped notions of masculine and feminine behavior (Goldberg & Garcia, 2016). These children are more tolerant of gender nonconformity and other forms of diversity in peers (Goldberg, 2014; Mortenson, 2011a), and are more likely to aspire to occupations that cross traditional gender lines (Fulcher et al., 2008). Also, adult children of same-sex parents, like those of heterosexual parents, have a gender identity and sex-typed behaviors and preferences consistent with their biological sex. They are not more likely than the adult children of heterosexual parents to have a lesbian, gay, or bisexual orientation (Fedewa et al., 2015; Goldberg, 2017). See Learn About the Research 8.2 to examine the psychological and social outcomes of adults raised by lesbian mothers.

Mothers With Disabilities

Women with disabilities are viewed as less able both physically and psychologically to cope with the demands of pregnancy, childbirth, and childrearing (Filax & Taylor, 2014; Pebdani et al., 2014; Tarasoff, 2015). However, there is no evidence that mothers with disabilities are less capable parents than able-bodied women. In fact, studies have demonstrated the ingenuity of mothers with disabilities in developing their own adaptive methods of baby care and mothering (Miles-Cohen & Signore,

LEARN ABOUT THE RESEARCH 8.2
Adult Children of Lesbian Mothers

Most of the research on the effects of lesbian mothers on children has focused on school-age children. Susan Golombok and her colleagues expanded on this research by comparing the experiences of young adults who had been raised by lesbian mothers, those raised by single heterosexual mothers, and those raised in two-parent heterosexual families. The researchers restricted the heterosexual single-mother sample to adults whose mothers had been single for some period while raising them in order to compare two groups of children whose mothers differed in sexual orientation, but not in the presence of a man in the household. There were similar numbers of female and male children in each family type. Mothers and their young adult children were given standardized interviews and completed questionnaires.

Psychological adjustment was similar among the three groups of adult children. The few differences found pointed to more positive family relationships and greater psychological well-being among young adults raised in mother-headed homes. Moreover, adults raised by lesbian mothers were no more likely than those in heterosexual families to have experienced same-gender sexual attraction. All of the respondents in the three groups had also experienced at least one heterosexual relationship. The finding that all but one of the young adults raised by lesbian mothers identified themselves as heterosexuals suggests that being raised by same-sex parents does not lead to a lesbian or gay sexual identity.

WHAT DOES IT MEAN?

1. Do you think that the results would have been different if the sample consisted of gay fathers and single heterosexual fathers instead of lesbian mothers and single heterosexual mothers? Explain your answer.

2. Prepare an argument in support of or in opposition to lesbian motherhood. Refer to the findings of this study, other materials from this chapter, theories of gender typing (see Chapter 3), and any other information that you believe is relevant.

3. Do you think that adults raised by lesbian mothers versus those reared by heterosexual mothers differ in the way they raise their own children? Explain your answer.

Source: Golombok & Badger (2010).

2016; Wolowicz-Ruszkowska, 2015). Through the Looking Glass is a nonprofit organization that provides services and training to prospective and new parents with disabilities (lookingglass.org).

The "Empty Nest" Period

Since my boys left, I have started dedicating my time to worthy causes that I enjoy. I volunteer at the hospital, spend a few hours a week at a retirement home, and I joined a women's group. My husband and I also are planning a vacation. We haven't done that—just the two of us—in a long time. These changes are good for me. Sure I still miss the boys, but they're growing up now. It's part of life, so you make the best of it.

(a 55-year-old woman)

Motherhood, as we have seen, is an important aspect of identity for most women. How do mothers experience the **empty nest period**, that is, *the period of a parent's life when children no longer live in the parents' home?* Most women react quite positively and seek opportunities to pursue new careers, further their education, or provide service to their communities (Etaugh, 2017; Kemper, 2013). And because children can be a source of tension in any marriage, couples often report higher marital satisfaction once their children have left home (Bookwala, 2012).

The empty nest period is not experienced the same way by all women. Women who are reluctant to let go of their parenting role may perceive this period as stressful and as a time of loss

(Better, 2014). However, mothers who are employed during the childrearing years establish an identity in addition to their motherhood role, and this can ease the difficulty of relinquishing parenting responsibilities.

Of course, mothers do not stop being parents when their children move out, but rather remain involved in their children's lives in somewhat different ways. Although their contacts are generally less frequent, they continue to offer advice and encouragement and often provide financial assistance (Davidson, 2014; Seltzer & Bianchi, 2013). Although most mothers experience the departure of their children at some point during midlife, there are variations in children's age of departure, and an increasing number who do not leave or who return home for some period of time after leaving because of personal or financial reasons (Davidson, 2014). This is especially true for sons (Fry, 2016). For the first time in the modern era, half of all young adults in their 20s and 30s live with their parents. The steady rise in the number of young adults living at home appears to be driven by several factors, including declining employment opportunities, an increase in college attendance, and later age at marriage (Fry, 2016). Parents' reaction to their children's return is related to the degree to which the return signals continued dependence on the parents. The greater the children's financial dependency and the lower their educational attainment and self esteem, the less statisfied parents are with the living arrangement. These findings suggest that parents are most satisfied with the parent–child relationship when they perceive their children as assuming the normative roles of adulthood (Etaugh, 2017; Sechrist et al., 2014). To find out more about experiences during the empty nest period, try Get Involved 8.2.

RELATIONSHIPS IN THE LATER YEARS

As women get older, they experience several changes in their family relationships. Earlier in the chapter, we saw that marriages may end as a result of divorce or a spouse's death. Bonds with siblings often become stronger as one gets older. In addition, new life enters the family in the form of grandchildren and great-grandchildren. Role reversal often occurs as aging women become caregivers for their even older parents. In this section, we will explore these changes.

GET INVOLVED 8.2
Women's Experiences During the Empty Nest Period

Interview two midlife women whose children have left home. Choose any women available to you, such as relatives, neighbors, classmates, and the like. However, if possible, select one woman whose last child left home within the year and another whose children have been gone for several years. Ask each to (1) identify any positive and/or negative experiences; (2) indicate any changes in her employment role (e.g., started a new job, increased her work hours), community service, and/or leisure activities as a result of her children's departure; and (3) indicate whether she perceives these changes as primarily positive or primarily negative.

WHAT DOES IT MEAN?

1. How would you characterize the experiences of your two interviewees? Did they mention more positive or negative experiences? How do their experiences compare to the empty nest experiences in the text?

2. What changes, if any, did they make in their life roles? How did they feel about these changes?

3. Were there any differences in the experiences of the woman whose last child recently left home and the woman whose children left years earlier? If yes, how do you explain these differences?

4. Do you think the empty nest experiences of these midlife women will differ from the future experiences of today's young adults? Why or why not?

Siblings

Sisters and brothers play a unique role in the lives of older people, drawing on the shared experiences of childhood and most of the life span (Dunn, 2014). Feelings of closeness and compatibility among siblings increase throughout the course of adulthood and are generally strong in later life (Conger & Little, 2010; Mikkelson, 2014). Types of sibling support vary across ethnic groups, with Blacks and Latinas/os relying more on siblings for practical assistance than do their White counterparts (Bedford, 1995; Conger & Little, 2010). Relationships with sisters are emotionally closer than those with brothers, and the bond between sisters is particularly close (Conger & Little, 2010; Feinberg et al., 2012; Mikkelson, 2014). Older adults who have close relationships with their siblings have better mental health and are less lonely than those who do not (Bedford & Avioli, 2012; Feinberg et al., 2012; Mikkelson, 2014). Older rural women have higher life satisfaction if they simply have a sister living nearby, regardless of the amount of contact they have (Bedford, 1995).

The closeness of the sibling bond in later life is illustrated in the following comment:

> I have two sisters who live upstairs. People are always surprised that we get along so well, living in the same house. My sisters never go out without coming by to ask me if they can get me anything. We weren't always like that. We were too busy with our own lives. Now we try hard to help each other.
>
> (a 70-year-old widow, in Doress-Worters & Siegal, 1994, p. 134)

Adult Children

Women are described as the family **kinkeepers**, *those who maintain the bonds between and within generations* (McCann, 2012). Their adult children are more apt to confide in them than their fathers (Miller-Day et al., 2014; Sarkisian & Gerstel, 2008). Adult daughters maintain closer ties to their parents than do sons, and unmarried daughters tend to have more intense ties to their parents than married daughters (Fingerman & Birditt, 2011; Sarkisian & Gerstel, 2008). During adolescence, the mother–daughter relationship is often characterized by both closeness and emotional conflict. Closeness typically increases once the daughter leaves home to attend college. Adult daughters continue to have more harmonious relationships and more frequent contact with their mothers than with their fathers (Sechrist et al., 2014). The close ties between grown daughters and their mothers, as shown in surveys of older women and their middle-aged daughters (Fingerman, 2003; Lefkowitz & Fingerman 2003; Sechrist et al., 2012), are characterized by satisfying interactions, a history of little conflict, few control issues, relatively equal exchange of resources, and many opportunities for informal contact. In the words of four mothers:

> She has been awfully good to me in every way, when I'm sick and when I'm well, when I'm in a good humor and when I'm in a bad humor.

> I can reason with [my daughter] and she understands me. We just sit down and talk it over. We never have an argument. Not that we're perfect, but it's just not necessary.

> We go for lunch. We go shopping . . . I may go three or four days or a week and not see her, but we talk. I feel like that starts my day. (all three quotes from Blieszner et al., 1996, pp. 13–18)

> She tells me about her work and sometimes her problems, which includes me in her world. It makes me happy. (Fingerman, 2003, p. 60)

Although some older Americans live with their adult children, they strongly prefer living alone in their own home even when in declining health (Stepler, 2016). Approximately half of older parents do, however, have an adult child living within 10 miles (Zhang et al., 2013). Older women who live alone report high levels of psychological well-being and appear to be doing as well as, or even better than, older women who live with a spouse (Michael et al., 2001). Informal and formal caregiving systems in the community contribute to this well-being by enabling older persons to remain at home longer. When the informal system of family, friends, and neighbors cannot meet their needs, older individuals turn to the services of organizations and professionals, such as Meals on Wheels, van service for the disabled, home aides, and visiting nurses (OWL, 2006).

About eight in ten older men, but only six in ten older women, in the U.S. reside with others, often a spouse or adult child (Stepler, 2016). Living with or close to an adult child is more prevalent among ethnic minority older people than among Whites in the United States, and this living arrangement is also common in developing countries, as we shall see below (Pew Research Center, 2010; Seltzer & Bianchi, 2013).

In the United States, one-third of older Asian American, Black, and Latina women, compared with only one-sixth of White women, live with their children and other relatives (Federal Interagency Forum, 2016). As we saw earlier, older ethnic minority women play key roles in their family networks by providing economic, social, and emotional support to their adult children and grandchildren. Black households are often organized around women, with older women at the center. Males are more directly involved in Latina/o and Native American households and families. Still, women in these groups enjoy greater prestige, respect, and domestic authority as they grow older (Armstrong, 2001; Padgett, 1999).

Let's take a closer look at the living arrangements of older women and men in other countries.

Living Arrangements of Older Women and Men

Over two-thirds of all U.S. adults aged 65 and over who live by themselves are women (Humble & Price, 2017). Figures for Canada, Great Britain, and most other Western nations are similar to those for the United States. In most Asian countries, however, the situation is quite different. About 75 percent of older women and men live with relatives, many of them in three-generation households (Koropeckyj-Cox & Call, 2007; Ofstedal et al., 2003). Multigenerational families also remain common in the southern European countries of Italy, Greece, and Spain (Billari & Liefbroer, 2008) and in rural parts of eastern Europe, including Russia, Poland, and Romania. Even so, older women in these countries are more likely than older men to live alone (Mercer et al., 2001).

In developing countries, older adults often live with their adult children (Ruggles & Heggeness, 2008). It is traditional for an older woman to live with her eldest son in some African countries and in several Asian nations, including China, India, Pakistan, and Bangladesh (Arnett, 2008; U.S. Census Bureau, International Database, 1997, 1995). We shall see, in Chapter 14, that these Asian countries place a much higher value on sons than daughters, resulting in abortion of female fetuses and greater neglect of female children. Can you see the link between these practices and the sons' obligation to care for parents in their old age?

Grandchildren

The greatest gift I ever received was my grandmother. My grandmother has been the backbone of my life since I was 18 months old, when I began living with her. My grandmother put her life on hold so that I could become the best I could be.

(Sharoia Taylor, age 16, in AARP, 2004, p. 11)

The stereotyped portrayal of a grandmother is often that of an older, white-haired woman providing treats for her young grandchildren. However, grandmothers do not fit into any one pattern. Although nearly 90 percent of Americans over age 65 are grandparents (Seltzer & Yahirun, 2013), some people become grandparents much earlier. About half of women experience this event before age 50, and some spend half of their lives as grandmothers (Etaugh, 2017). Nowadays, many middle-aged grandmothers are in the labor force and may also have responsibilities of caring for their older parents (Holstein, 2015). Thus, they may have less time to devote to grandparenting activities. On the other hand, more grandmothers are taking on the responsibility of raising their grandchildren, as we will see later in the chapter. Grandmothers' involvement with their grandchildren depends on a number of factors, including geographical distance, the grandmother's relationship with her grandchild's parents, the grandmother's physical and mental health, and the mother's employment status (Meyers, 2014; Turner, 2012).

Earlier in the chapter, we noted that the ties between family generations are maintained largely by women. One example of this is that grandmothers tend to have warmer relationships with their grandchildren, especially their granddaughters, than do grandfathers (Bates & Taylor, 2013; Scherrer, 2016). They are also more likely to be actively involved in caring for their grandchildren (Craig & Jenkins, 2016). The maternal grandmother often has the most contact and the closest relationship with grandchildren (Hayslip & Page, 2013; Luong et al., 2015). Children living with a single mother tend to be especially close to their maternal grandmother (Bridges et al., 2007). Moreover, strong relationships with maternal grandmothers may help grandchildren adjust to the divorce of their parents (Henderson et al., 2009).

In some parts of the world, the presence of a grandmother may literally spell the difference between life and death for her grandchildren.

 ## Grandmothers: The Difference Between Life and Death

According to researchers (Coall & Hertwig, 2011; Maklakov & Lummaa, 2013; Sear & Mace, 2008), grandmothers have helped ensure the survival and fitness of their grandchildren since pre-historic times. These women, no longer reproductively active themselves, are able to invest their energies in providing for the physical and psychological health of grandchildren and other young relatives. Kristen Hawkes (2010) studied the present-day Hadza hunter-gatherers of northern Tanzania and found that older women gather more edible plant foods than any other members of the group. Nursing Hadza women, unable to provide for their older children while tending their infants, rely not on their mates but on these postmenopausal women relatives—their mothers, aunts, or older cousins—to make sure that the older children are well fed. The presence or absence of a grandmother often makes the difference between life or death for grandchildren in other subsistence cultures as well (Coall & Hertwig, 2011). Anthropologists Rebecca Sear and Ruth Mace (2008) found that in rural Gambia, the presence of a maternal grandmother increased the survival rate of her toddler grandchildren. However, the presence of a paternal grandmother (the father's mother) made no difference in the children's survival. Even more surprisingly, the presence of the father didn't either! Similar results have been found in parts of rural India and Japan as well (Angier, 2002). Why do you think the role of the maternal grandmother is especially important?

PROVIDING CARE AND SUPPORT FOR GRANDCHILDREN.   During their grandchildren's infancy and childhood, many grandparents in the United States and other nations provide the children's parents with considerable emotional support, information, help with child care and household chores, and, to a lesser degree, financial support (Geurts et al., 2015; Meyers, 2014). For example, almost one-third of all preschoolers whose mothers work or are in school are looked after by their grandparents, usually a grandmother (Seltzer & Yahirun, 2013). Some baby-boomer grandmothers (such as Claire and her sister) are retiring or taking time off from their careers to become nannies for their grandchildren (Alexander, 2004). Others combine full-time employment with caring for grandchildren (Meyers, 2014). The grandmother's role in lending economic, social, and emotional support for her children and grandchildren is more active in many ethnic minority groups than among Whites. For example, Black and Latina/o grandparents are more likely than White grandparents to care for their grandchildren while the children's parents are at work (AARP, 2012). Native American, Latina, and Black grandmothers are significant figures in the stability and continuity of the family (Barnett et al., 2016; Mollborn, 2016; Turner, 2012; Zeiders et al., 2015). In one study of low-income multiracial Hawaiian children who had an absent or incapacitated parent, the nurturance and guidance of grandparents was a key factor in the children's well-being as they grew to adulthood (Werner, 2010; Werner & Smith, 2001). Similarly, close, supportive relationships with grandparents are linked with better social and cognitive development in children raised in both two-parent and single-parent families (Barnett et al., 2010; Bertera & Crewe, 2013).

For some children, grandparents are part of the family household. In the United States, the number of children living in homes with grandparents has more than doubled since 1970 to 7.1 million in 2012, including 14 percent of Asian American and Black children, 12 percent of Latina/o children, and 7 percent of White children (Ellis & Simmons, 2014). Some of the increase results from an uncertain economy and the growing number of single mothers, which has sent young adults and their children back to the parental nest. In other cases, older adults are moving in with their adult children's families when they can no longer live on their own. New immigrants with a tradition of multigenerational households have also swelled the number of such living arrangements (Seltzer & Yahirun, 2013). The arrangement benefits all parties. Grandparents and their grandchildren are able to interact on a daily basis. The grandparents often assume some parenting responsibilities, which makes it possible for young single mothers to stay in school (Gordon et al., 2004; Navarro, 2006).

RAISING GRANDCHILDREN. Increasing numbers of grandparents now find themselves raising their grandchildren on their own. Of the 7.1 million grandparents living in a household with a grandchild, close to 40 percent *are raising their grandchildren without a parent present*. Nearly two-thirds of these **skip-generation parents** are grandmothers (U.S. Census Bureau, 2015b). Grandparents become full-time caregivers for their grandchildren for a number of reasons: parental illness, child abuse or neglect, substance abuse, psychological or financial problems, divorce, incarceration, and military deployment (Bailey et al., 2013; Hadfield, 2014; Pittman, 2014). In some developing countries, parents migrate to urban areas to work, while grandparents remain behind and raise the grandchildren (Schatz & Gilbert, 2014). The AIDS epidemic has also increased the number of grandparents who are raising grandchildren in many nations, including the United States (Hadfield, 2014; Mhaka-Mutepfa et al., 2014). Children reared by their grandparents fare well relative to children in families with one biological parent. They also show little difference in health and academic performance relative to children raised in traditional families (Thomas et al., 2000).

The belief that caregiving grandmothers are primarily poor ethnic women of color is a myth. Parenting grandmothers can be found across racial and socioeconomic lines (Dunifon, 2013). Over half of the grandparents raising grandchildren are White, 24 percent are Black, 18 percent are Latina/o, 3 percent are Asian American, and 2 percent are Native American (Dunifon, 2013). Black women who are raising their grandchildren, compared to White women, report feeling less burdened and more satisfied in their caregiving role, even though they are generally in poorer health, dealing with more difficult situations, and dealing with them more often alone (Chen et al., 2014; Pruchno, 1999).

Rearing a grandchild is full of both rewards and challenges (Mhaka-Mutepfa et al., 2014; Sampson & Hertlein, 2015). Although parenting a grandchild is an emotionally fulfilling experience, there are psychological, health, and economic costs. A grandmother raising the young child of her troubled adult daughter may concurrently feel ashamed of her daughter; anxious about her own future, health, and finances; angry at the loss of retirement leisure; and guilt about her own parenting skills (Erbert & Alemán, 2008; Smith & Cichy, 2015). Moreover, grandparents primarily responsible for rearing grandchildren are more likely than other grandparents to suffer from a variety of health problems, including depression, diabetes, high blood pressure, heart disease, and a decline in self-rated physical and emotional health. Furthermore, they tend to delay seeking help for their own medical problems (Chen et al., 2014; Hadfield, 2014; Schatz & Gilbert, 2014; Trail Ross et al., 2015; Woods, 2014).

Grandparents raising grandchildren are often stymied by existing laws that give them no legal status unless they gain custody of the grandchild or become the child's foster parents. Each of these procedures involves considerable time, effort, and expense. Yet, without custody or foster parent rights, grandparents may encounter difficulties in obtaining the child's medical records, enrolling the child in school, or becoming eligible for certain forms of financial assistance (Dolbin-McNab & Hayslip, 2015). In most instances, grandchildren are ineligible for coverage under grandparents' medical insurance, even if the grandparents have custody (Ellin, 2004). Grandparents often are restricted from applying for other formal support programs, such as child welfare (TANF) and nutrition assistance (SNAP; Collins et al., 2016). Consequently, many grandparent caregivers face significant financial challenges (Haberken et al., 2013; Hadfield, 2014).

Parents

Although more women are becoming caregivers of their grandchildren, others are providing care for their aging parents, spouses, or other relatives (National Alliance for Caregiving and AARP, 2015; Rhode et al., 2014). Nearly half of all caregivers of the older people are daughters. Daughters-in-law and granddaughters play a substantial role as well (National Alliance for Caregiving and AARP, 2015).

The older caregiver may herself have some health problems which can be increased by the stresses of caregiving (Humble & Price, 2017). The sight of her parent becoming more frail and dependent may conjure up a frightening and saddening vision of what is in store for her (Yorgason & Stott, 2017). Older daughters sometimes feel angry and guilty at the sacrifices involved in looking after a parent (Brody, 2013b).

> *My grandmother lived to be almost one-hundred-and-two years old, and my mother cared for her until she was ninety-seven and had to go into a nursing home. Now my mother obviously feels it is her turn, which it is. I am the real problem here, for I have led a very active life and cannot seem to adjust to this demanding and devastating situation. I am almost overcome with the inevitable guilt at my resentment and anger.*
>
> (a 72-year-old woman, in Doress-Worters & Siegal, 1994, p. 208)

Ethnic minority groups provide more care for aging family members than Whites do, possibly as a result of strong cultural norms of filial responsibility among these groups, as well as financial considerations (Ellis & Simmons, 2014; Herrera et al., 2011; Piercy, 2014; Seltzer & Bianchi, 2013). Among Latinos/as, 21 percent care for older relatives, compared to 20 percent of Blacks and Asian Americans, and 17 percent of Whites (National Alliance for Caregiving and AARP, 2015).

We have been discussing older women's relationships with family and friends. To explore this topic on a more personal level, try Get Involved 8.3.

GET INVOLVED 8.3
Interview With Older Women: Reflections on Relationships

Interview two women aged 65 or older. It is helpful, but not essential, if you know your respondents fairly well. You may interview your mother, grandmothers, great-aunts, great-grandmothers, and so on. Keep a record of your respondents' answers to the questions given here. Compare and contrast the responses of the two women.

1. What is one of the nicest things to happen to you recently?

2. How would you describe your relationship with your children?

3. Do you have any sisters and brothers? How would you describe your relationship with them?

4. What do you like about being a grandparent? (if applicable)

5. What types of activities do (did) you enjoy with your grandchildren?

6. Tell me about your best friends and the kinds of things you enjoy doing together.

7. What do you like about your current living situation?

8. What do you dislike about it?

9. How do you feel about the life you've led?

10. As an experienced woman, what tidbit of wisdom could you pass on to me?

WHAT DOES IT MEAN?

1. How would you characterize the relationships of your interviewees with their adult children? Do they appear to be closer to their daughters than to their sons? If so, why?

2. What kinds of relationships do your interviewees have with their grandchildren, if applicable? Have either or both participated in child care activities with their grandchildren? How do their experiences compare to those reported in the text?

3. Were there any differences in the relationships of these women with their sisters as compared to their brothers? If yes, how do you explain these differences?

4. How does the discussion in this chapter help you understand your respondents' attitudes toward their current living situation and toward nursing homes?

Summary

FRIENDSHIPS

- Girls' friendships are more intimate than those of boys. Girls tend to have a few close friendships whereas boys have larger, less intimate friendship groups.
- Both college women and men like to talk to their friends about the other gender. However, women's conversations more than men's focus on interpersonal issues.
- Emotional closeness is important to the friendships of both heterosexual and lesbian women but is more central to women's than men's friendships.
- Gender socialization and heterosexual males' perceived connection between emotional closeness and homosexuality are two explanations for the gender difference.
- Friendships among older women enhance physical and mental health.

ROMANTIC RELATIONSHIPS

- Heterosexual women are more likely than heterosexual men to value a romantic partner's financial stability and less likely to place importance on physical attractiveness. Similarly, lesbian women put less emphasis on physical attractiveness than gay men do.
- Heterosexual and gay men put more emphasis on the physical attractiveness of a potential partner than heterosexual and lesbian women.
- Middle-aged women are more likely than middle-aged men to be dissatisfied with their appearance.

- Romantic relationships are commonly characterized by traditional gender-related behaviors and roles. When there is a power imbalance, the male is generally viewed as the more powerful partner.
- The age when adolescents start to date has decreased.
- Many dating behaviors are strongly gender-stereotypical.
- Men are more likely than women to perceive nonsexual behaviors, such as a female asking out a male, as indicative of sexual interest.
- Current dating trends include development of urban "partnering markets," online dating services, speed-dating, and dating among older singles.

COMMITTED RELATIONSHIPS

- Most women and men marry, but the age of marriage has gone up in recent years.
- High levels of marital satisfaction are related to problem-focused coping strategies, similarity of goals, values, and attitudes, and good communication.
- Marital satisfaction decreases when children are born and increases when they leave home.
- Women and men who are married are happier and healthier than their unmarried counterparts.
- More men than women are married in later life.
- Cohabiters who do not intend to marry tend to be less satisfied with their relationships than married individuals.

- Married couples who previously cohabited are more likely to get divorced. This might be accounted for by a selection effect.
- Most lesbians are in committed, egalitarian, sexually exclusive relationships. Although many experience stressors not encountered by heterosexuals, they are similar to their heterosexual counterparts in their relationship satisfaction.
- Older lesbians in committed relationships provide each other with a mutual support system and shared economic benefits.

SINGLE WOMEN

- About 40 percent of U.S. marriages end in divorce.
- Divorce is associated with stressors for both women and their children.
- Despite initial emotional problems, both women and children tend to effectively adjust.
- Divorced women are generally less depressed than those in unhappy marriages.
- Employment and social support help women cope during the postdivorce period.
- Single women report mixed feelings about being unattached. Some regret the absence of a steady partner, some are satisfied living alone, and some become involved in romantic relationships. Many are highly involved in social networks of relatives, friends, and neighbors.
- Single women have skills in independent living and in building support systems.
- Women are more likely than men to be widowed but are much less likely to remarry.
- Reaction to widowhood depends on several factors including age, degree of forewarning of the spouse's death, and financial and social resources.
- Loss of a same-sex partner may be very stressful.

MOTHERHOOD

- The good mother stereotype can lead to mothers being blamed and mothers' self-blame if something goes wrong or if the mothers deviate from the ideal stereotype.
- Many single mothers face financial problems. Social support, as well as extended and augmented families, can help single mothers cope.
- Lesbian and heterosexual mothers are similar in mothering style and adjustment. Children reared in lesbian and heterosexual families are similar in their psychological and social adjustment and their sexual orientation.
- Most women report positive feelings about the "empty nest" period. Women who were employed during the childrearing years find it easier to relinquish the parental role.

RELATIONSHIPS IN THE LATER YEARS

- Feelings of closeness among siblings increase during adulthood, and the sister–sister bond is especially strong.
- Older women generally have positive relationships with their adult daughters.
- Unmarried older adults, most of whom are women, prefer living alone. Living with an adult child is the least popular choice, especially among Whites.
- The closeness of the grandparent–grandchild relationship depends on many factors.
- More grandparents than ever live in multigeneration households, particularly in ethnic minority groups.
- Increasing numbers of grandmothers are rearing their grandchildren.
- Growing numbers of older adults, especially women, are caregivers of their parents.

Key Terms

dating scripts *158*
cohabitation *161*
selection effect *162*
living apart together *162*
disenfranchised grief *168*

motherhood mandate *169*
integrated motherhood *169*
feminization of poverty *170*
extended families *170*
augmented families *170*

empty nest period   *172*
kinkeepers *174*
skip-generation parents *177*

What Do You Think?

1. The text discusses several negative consequences of the strong emphasis placed by men on a romantic partner's appearance. What kind of societal changes might contribute to a de-emphasis on physical attractiveness in romantic attraction?

2. Letitia Peplau (1998) contends that research on lesbian and gay couples can help dispel biased stereotypes. What are some common stereotypes about lesbian couples? How can scientific research be made public and accessible so that these stereotypes can be altered? Do you think there should be an attempt to eradicate these stereotypes as well as other unfavorable attitudes? Explain your answer.

3. Gail Collins (2009) and Amy Richards (2008) contend that there has been a resurgence of praise for women who give up their careers for full-time motherhood. Do you agree? If so, how can society reconcile the contradictory assumptions that full-time motherhood is desirable for middle-class mothers, but that poor mothers should combine employment with parenthood? How do you think people react to middle-class mothers who choose to continue their employment? How do they react to fathers who opt for full-time parenting? Explain your answers.

4. What are the advantages and disadvantages of grandparents rearing their grandchildren?

5. Are older widows better off living alone? With family members? In a retirement community? Why?

6. More single women are deliberately choosing to have and rear children on their own. Are they being selfish? Explain your answer.

If You Want to Know More

Baker, M. & Elizabeth, V. (2014). *Marriage in an age of cohabitation: How and when people tie the knot in the 21st century*. New York: Oxford University Press.

Bookwala, J. (2016). *Couple relationships in the middle and later years: Their nature, complexity, and role in health and illness*. Washington, D.C.: American Psychological Association.

DePaulo, B. (2011). *Singlism: What it is, why it matters, and how to stop it*. DoubleDoor Books.

deToledo, S. & Brown, D.E. (2013). *Grandparents as parents: A survival guide for raising a second family*. New York: Guilford.

Dixon, P. (2017). *African American relationships, marriages, and families* (2nd ed.). New York: Routledge.

Fentiman, L.C. (2017). *Blaming mothers: American law and the risks to human health*. New York: New York University Press.

Golombok, S. (2015). *Modern families: Parents and children in new family forms*. Cambridge, UK: Cambridge University Press.

Lamanna, M.A. & Riedmann, A. (2014). *Marriages, families, and relationships: Making choices in a diverse society* (2nd ed.). Stamford, CT: Cengage Learning.

Marze, E.H. (2013). *Widowhood*. Mustang, OK: Tate.

Mezey, M.J. (2015). *LGBT families*. Thousand Oaks, CA: Sage.

Nielsen, L. (2012). *Father-daughter-relationships: Contemporary research and issues*. New York: Routledge.

Strong, B. & Cohen, T.F. (2013). *The marriage and family experience: Intimate relationships in a changing society*. Stamford, CT: Cengage Learning Systems.

Traister, R. (2016). *All the single ladies: Unmarried women and the rise of an independent nation*. New York: Simon & Schuster.

Willie, C.V. & Reddick, R.J. (2010). *A new look at Black families*. Lanham, MD: Rowman & Littlefield.

Websites

Lesbian Mothers
http://www.lesbian.org/lesbian-moms/
http://www.lifewithroozle.com/2013/05/11/lesbian-motherhood/

Living Arrangements
Senior Living Alternatives
http://www.senioralternatives.com/

Parents with Disabilities
http://www.ncd.gov/publications/2012/Sep272012/Ch13
http://www.disabledparentrights.org

Caregiving
National Alliance for Caregiving
http://www.caregiving.org

Grandparents
http://www.aarp.org/relationships/grandparenting/
http://www.grandparents.com/gp/home/index.html
http://www.aarp.org/relationships/friends-family/info-08-2011/grandfamilies-guide-getting-started.html

9 CHAPTER

Education and Achievement

If we're going to out-innovate and out-educate the rest of the world, we've got to open doors for everyone. We need all hands on deck, and that means clearing hurdles for women and girls as they navigate careers in science, technology, engineering and math (Michelle Obama, First Lady of the United States, White House Briefing Room, 2011).

In this chapter, we first examine females' educational goals, attainments, and college experiences. Next, we explore young women's career aspirations, issues related to career counseling, and women's plans regarding coordination of their careers with family life. Finally, we turn to influences on their career choices.

WOMEN'S EDUCATIONAL GOALS, ATTAINMENTS, AND CAMPUS EXPERIENCES

As we discuss in more detail in Chapter 10, men earn higher salaries than women and are more likely to hold leadership positions in domains such as politics, and professions (U.S. Census Bureau, 2015b). Do these discrepancies indicate, as some have suggested, that women, compared to men, place a lower value on education and have a lower level of educational attainments? In this section, we examine women's educational goals, attainments, and experiences on the college campus.

Educational Goals

Across ethnicities and around the world, adolescent girls endorse higher educational and occupational goals than do boys (Massey et al., 2008; OECD, 2015; Perry & Vance, 2010; Rivers & Barnett, 2013; Wang & Pomerantz, 2009). For example, Judith Kleinfeld (2009) interviewed high school seniors, differing in ethnicity and social class, about their future plans. Regardless of social class, female students were more apt than males to have well-developed plans to attend college, based on their view that education is a crucial investment toward pursuing an occupation that would allow them to contribute to society. Middle-class males, in contrast, saw college as just the expected path, which would provide a job with a good income. Most working-class males did not view college as necessary for their future success and did not plan on attending.

Let us now look at how women's educational goals translate into educational attainments.

Educational Attainments

In the United States, 93 percent of females and 90 percent of males graduate from high school (U.S. Census Bureau, 2015b). Until the mid-1980s, men earned the majority of bachelor's degrees each year, but since 1985, women have surpassed men (Snyder & Dillow, 2015). Some critics view this situation as a "boy crisis" in education. For more on this issue, see Learn About the Research 9.1.

You can see in Table 9.1 that within each ethnic group, women obtain the majority of associate's, bachelor's, master's, and doctoral degrees. Asian American, Black, and Latina women earn half or more of professional (e.g., medical, dental, law) degrees. Both doctoral and professional levels of education have experienced a dramatic change in the participation of women in the past few decades. For example, in 1965, women obtained only 12 percent of doctoral and 4 percent of professional degrees (U.S. Census Bureau, 2003), compared to the 2011–2012 figures of 51 percent and 49 percent, respectively. Today, women earn more than three-fourths of degrees in veterinary medicine and nearly two-thirds of degrees in pharmacy, formerly male-dominated fields. They also earn nearly half of law and medical degrees (Snyder & Dillow, 2015).

This high level of educational attainments by women is, unfortunately, more true of able-bodied women than of women with disabilities. Women with disabilities also have less education than men with disabilities and are less likely to graduate from high school or attend college (Beckles & Truman, 2011; Nosek, 2010). Furthermore, they are less likely than males with disabilities to receive occupationally oriented vocational training that can provide them with the skills needed in the job market (Schur, 2004). Not only must students with disabilities cope with physical barriers in educational settings (e.g., access to buildings, availability of appropriate instructional materials), but they also must contend with isolation, prejudice, and discrimination (Nosek, 2010; Olkin, 2010).

So far, we have been discussing educational attainments of girls and women in the United States. In developing societies, many girls are unable to attend school at all, or attend for just a few years before they drop out (Burn, 2011; Henderson & Jeydel, 2010). We turn now to look at the education of girls around the world.

Educating Girls Worldwide: Gender Gaps and Gains

What is the state of education for girls around the world? Studies in developing and developed nations report both good news and bad news. The good news is that between 1990 and 2011, access to education improved worldwide. For example, nearly two-thirds of countries studied now have no gender gap at the primary school level (United Nations News Center, 2013).

The bad news is that several countries still have serious gender gaps, with millions of fewer girls than boys in primary school. Gender disparities are greatest in South Asia and in northern sub-Saharan Africa (United Nations News Center, 2013). In most countries, girls from poor families are less likely to attend school than those from wealthier households (UNICEF, 2014; Unterhalter

LEARN ABOUT THE RESEARCH 9.1
Is There a "Boy Crisis" in Education?

Girls, nowadays, are more likely than boys to do well in school, graduate high school, and get college degrees. Some critics in the United States, Canada, Europe, and Australia suggest that as girls have progressed, boys have fallen behind (Anderson, 2014; Thompson & Armato, 2012). A few even claim that there is a "boy crisis" or a "war against boys" in which resources have been lavished on female students at the expense of male students (Anderson, 2014; Rosin, 2012; Sommers, 2013). Some colleges are pushing hard to recruit more male students, even going so far as giving men "special consideration." Some outstanding female applicants are being denied entrance to top colleges, whereas males with lesser credentials are admitted (Kahlenberg, 2011; Lewin, 2011).

Two studies (AAUW, 2008; Mead, 2006), however, cast serious doubt on the existence of a boy crisis in education. The studies used data from a survey of student achievement in the United States as well as SAT and ACT college entrance exam scores, and other measures of educational achievement. Both studies find that, in the words of study-author Sara Mead, "the real story is not bad news about boys doing worse; it's good news about girls doing better" (Mead, 2006, p. 3). Boys actually are scoring higher on standardized tests and achieving more than ever before. But girls have improved their performance even more. The

same is true of college enrollments, which are on the rise for both sexes. Once again, women's enrollment rates are increasing faster than men's.

Some groups of boys *are* falling behind, particularly African American and Latino boys and boys from low-income families (Kenschaft & Clark, 2016). The gender gap is greatest among low-income students of all races but disappears among students whose families are at the top of the economic ladder (AAUW, 2008; King, 2010; Mead, 2006). In fact, high-income men of all races are slightly *more* likely than high-income women to be in college (King, 2010). The results from these studies and from those done in other countries suggest that social class is a better predictor of school success than is gender (OECD, 2015). Several writers note that the educational crisis among low-income, ethnic minority boys will not be solved by blaming the preponderance of female teachers at the lower grades, or educational reforms that allegedly favor girls' learning styles. These reforms, including better trained teachers and a more co-operative, group-oriented, and hands-on learning approach, help both boys and girls learn (Kimmel, 2008). In addition, teaching boys skills that will better prepare them for classroom success will help them in learning to pay attention, listening, and cooperating with peers (Brown, 2006; DiPrete & Buchmann, 2013; Jacobson, 2006).

WHAT DOES IT MEAN?

1. Why do you think women's college-going rates are exceeding those of men?
2. Sara Mead, author of one of the studies discussed here, states that "the idea that women might actually surpass men in some areas . . . seems hard for many people to swallow. Thus, boys are routinely characterized

as falling behind even as they improve in absolute terms" (2006, p. 3). Do you agree or disagree with this statement? Support your answer.
3. What can be done to ensure that all students have the education and opportunities they need to realize their potential?

et al., 2014). Increasing numbers of unmarried girls are dropping out of school because of unplanned pregnancy or forced early marriage, which remains widespread in South Asia and sub-Saharan Africa (Unterhalter et al., 2014). School policies often require the expulsion of pregnant girls. Another reason that girls leave school earlier than boys is to work the land. In Africa, girls and women do the vast majority of the agricultural work, although they own just a small fraction of the farmland (UNIFEM, 2010). Moreover, the AIDS epidemic in Africa is forcing many girls to leave school to support the family and care for the sick (see Chapter 12).

Sadly, attacks against girls in school or those seeking access to education are on the rise, despite legal protections of gender equality. A recent United Nations report found that many attacks on schools in at least 70 countries between 2009 and 2014 were directed at girls, parents, and teachers who were pushing for gender equality in education (UN Human Rights Council, 2015). The report highlights already known horrific incidents including the Taliban's assault on a Pakistani school that killed

TABLE 9.1   Degrees Conferred by Ethnicity and Gender, 2011–2012

Type of Degree	Asian Americans		Blacks		Latinas/os		Native Americans		Whites	
	Women	Men	Women	Men	Women	Men	Women	Men	Women	Men
Associate's	58%	42%	67%	33%	62%	38%	63%	37%	60%	40%
Bachelor's	54	46	66	34	60	40	61	39	56	44
Master's	54	46	71	29	63	37	65	35	61	39
Doctorate	56	44	65	35	54	46	54	46	51	49
Professional	56	44	61	39	51	49	49	51	46	54

Source: Snyder and Dillow (2015).

132 children, the abduction of nearly 300 Nigerian school girls by the radical Islamist group Boko Haram, numerous acts of poisoning and acid attacks on school girls in Afghanistan, and the shooting of Malala Yousafzai, an educational activist described in more detail in In the News 9.1.

IN THE NEWS 9.1
Malala Yousafzai, a Powerful Voice for Girls' Education

Malala Yousafzai is an example of what we hope will be women's future worldwide, while also illustrating the challenges facing women in developing nations. Malala, from the Swat valley of Pakistan, became known at age 11 for her blog describing her struggles to get an education under the repressive Taliban regime. In an attempt to silence her, a Taliban gunman horrifically wounded and nearly killed her as she returned from school when she was 15. Nine months later, she defiantly addressed the United Nations, saying, "The power of education frightens them [the extremists]. The power of the voice of women frightens them . . . They thought that the bullet would silence us. But they failed." To this day, Malala Yousafzai continues her crusade on behalf of education for girls. In 2014, at age 17, she became the youngest person ever to receive the Nobel Peace Prize (Walsh, 2014).

Educating girls has many benefits. The more years of education, the less likely they are to marry early, and the fewer, healthier, and better educated are their subsequent children. Empowering women through literacy also enhances their voice in family affairs and reduces gender inequality in other areas. How can girls' enrollment in school be increased? Strategies (Kenschaft & Clark, 2016; Kristof & WuDunn, 2009; Unterhalter et al., 2014) include the following:

- Build more schools, especially in rural areas of developing countries.
- Lower families' costs of educating daughters by providing stipends or even free lunch.
- Educate parents about the importance of educating daughters as well as sons.
- Provide programs to prevent teenage pregnancy.
- Encourage teen mothers to stay in school.
- Attach day-care centers to schools to look after young children, allowing their older sisters to attend school.
- Provide toilets and menstrual supplies at schools.
- Provide flexible school hours.
- Recruit more female teachers.

Now read What <u>You</u> Can Do 9.1 to learn how you can help promote educational opportunities of girls worldwide.

Malala Yousafzai, a powerful activist for girls' education, won the Nobel Prize at age 17.

WHAT YOU CAN DO 9.1
Promote Education of Girls Worldwide

A number of organizations are devoted to helping girls in developing countries obtain an education. Two of them are Girls Global Education Fund (ggef.org) and Camfed International (us.camfed.org). Contact one of these organizations and see how you can help.

Campus Climate

Julie Zeigler arrived at Duke University in 2003 to work on a doctorate in physics. Instead, she left in 2004 with only a master's because of a hostile atmosphere towards women that female graduate students and faculty say has existed for years. These women report that male physicists have kissed and grabbed them, ignored them, refused to take them seriously and greeted their comments and questions with hostility.

(Wilson, 2004)

The gender biases in elementary and high school (Chapter 4) continue into college and graduate school. Female students often experience a **chilly climate** in the classroom and elsewhere on campus, in which *faculty members, staff, or students display different expectations for women students, or single them out or ignore them* (E. Pollack, 2015; Thompson & Armato, 2012). Some faculty members use sexist language, tell sexist jokes, suggest that women are less able to learn the material, ignore women's comments, or focus on women's appearance and sexuality rather than their intellectual competence. Eventually, this chilly atmosphere can negatively affect women's feelings of self-worth and confidence. The impact may be even greater for ethnic minority women, sexual minority women, and women with disabilities. These women may be the target of blatant sexist, racist, homophobic, and other prejudicial acts, such as placing signs on residence hall room doors that bar members of certain groups. Or they may experience more *subtle forms of humiliation and bias* called **microaggressions**. These can include sexual or racist humor, social exclusion, or making assumptions about abilities on the basics of race or sex (Comas-Diaz, 2013a; Corbett & Hill, 2015; Kaskan & Ho, 2016).

The chilly climate for women is another reflection of the gender inequality of power in North American society. Sexist treatment of women on campus, whether blatant or subtle, reflects a greater value attached to males and serves to maintain an already existing power imbalance. Furthermore, this treatment reinforces constructions of women as inferior or less valued than men.

THE ACADEMIC ENVIRONMENT FOR WOMEN OF COLOR.   Some women of color experience primarily White campuses as occasionally unwelcoming and unsupportive (Blume et al., 2012; Vaccaro & Camba-Kelsay, 2016; Winkle-Wagner, 2015). Some Black and Latina female students have reported instances in which they were ignored, devalued, and assumed to be less intelligent by their peers or professors (Crisp et al., 2015; Figueroa & Hurtado, 2013; Winkle-Wagner, 2015; Zambrana & MacDonald, 2009). The only Black female in a business class with White male students commented that when the class made a group presentation, "I was kind of ignored . . . whenever there was a question or something like that . . . It is hard to feel competent with them like that" (Winkle-Wagner, 2009; p. 117). For women of color majoring in sciences, mentoring by, and informal interactions with, a predominantly White male science faculty is severely lacking (Bowen, 2012).

Stereotype threat (discussed in Chapter 5 in relation to women) can also seriously affect the educational experience of students of color. According to this view, students of color must deal with the possibility that their poor performance will confirm the inferiority of their ethnic group. This concern may have a negative impact on students' class participation. A Black woman, one of three in a large chemistry lecture course of mostly White students, explained why she did not ask questions in class: "It's kind of like you're that black girl from the inner city school, of course you're going to need help . . . It's kind of like being afraid to raise your hand because you might be 'the dumb one'" (Lindemann et al., 2016, pp. 233–234).

In addition, disciplinary practices are often harsher for Black students than for White ones. On some measures, this racial disparity is even greater for girls than for boys. Some Black female students express the view that they are over-disciplined because they are perceived as "can't be trusted . . . loud and rowdy, ghetto and stuff like that" (Crenshaw, 2015, p. 31).

Another problem for some students of color is that they experience the individualism prominent in academic life as inconsistent with the collectivistic values of their culture. The individualistic value system of Western, primarily North American and European, cultures emphasizes personal achievement, independence, and individual uniqueness. The collectivistic values of Asian, Native American, and Latina/o cultures, on the other hand, stress the importance of the group, including the family, the community, and the work team. The competitive style of college education can be uncomfortable for these students (Jacob, 2012; Robinson-Wood, 2017). As one Native American college senior stated, "When I was a child I was taught certain things, 'don't stand up to your elders,' 'don't question authority,' 'life is precious,' 'the earth is precious,' 'take it slowly,' 'enjoy it.' And then you go to college and you learn all these other things and it never fits" (Canabal, 1995, p. 456).

Although the clash between individualism and collectivism can produce conflicts for some students, Angela Lew and her colleagues (Lew et al., 1998) note that these value systems can coexist. These researchers found that some Asian American students adopted both sets of values, viewing individual achievement as a way to fulfill both personal and family goals. Similarly, Native American students are more likely than White students to endorse a combination of communal and individualistic goals (J.S. Smith et al., 2014). Lew and her associates suggest that internalization of both value systems can help the student to function effectively in two different cultural environments. Of course, it may be easier for some students than for others to integrate and reconcile the disparate sets of values.

On the positive side, a number of factors are associated with academic success of ethnic minority students. These include positive interactions with peers and faculty mentors, engagement in ethnic minority student organizations and cultural activities, and warm, caring parental support (Crisp et al., 2015; Winkle-Wagner, 2015).

THE ACADEMIC ENVIRONMENT FOR WORKING-CLASS AND POOR WOMEN.   Research on working-class and poor women's adjustment to college life is very limited. We do know that both female and male students who struggle economically often find college to be a mystifying and hostile place, full of cultural codes they have not been exposed to and academic challenges for which they may have been poorly prepared (Harris & Gonzalez, 2012; Pappano, 2015). Studies (Davis, 2010; LePage-Lees, 1997) of students from working-class or poor families found that many felt they had to hide their backgrounds from others in order to achieve during undergraduate and graduate school. These students also felt that other students were better prepared and more intelligent. In one recent study, a female graduate student from a working-class background noted: "The daily traumas of [social] class are just ignored . . . It is a big part of my life that won't be acknowledged" (Gerbrandt & Kurtz, 2015, p. 161).

Low-income women with young children who decide to improve their lives through higher education face numerous challenges as they cope with limited finance, child care responsibilities, and juggling job and school schedules (Gault et al., 2014a; Institute for Women's Policy Research, 2016b). The story of Pauline illustrates the obstacles and the ultimate benefits. This Black woman attended college at age 17 but dropped out after falling in love. After having three children, she was deserted by the children's father. Once her youngest child was in child care, she began community college as a welfare recipient. Pauline successfully overcame several obstacles, completed college, and found a job in her town's school department (Kates, 1996, p. 550).

SINGLE-SEX EDUCATION.   Given the existence of an uncomfortable climate on some mixed-gender campuses, it is not surprising that scholars have been studying the benefits of single-sex high school and college environments for women's academic and personal development. The 44 women's colleges operating today in the United States are among the more ethnically and socioeconomically diverse liberal arts colleges, providing generous financial aid packages to underserved groups of women (Sax et al., 2015b; Women's College Coalition, 2014). Women's high schools and colleges provide more leadership opportunities for women students, higher achievement expectations for them, and more female role models within the faculty and administration (Mansfield, 2011; Women's College Coalition, 2008). Students at women's colleges have higher career goals, participate more actively in class, collaborate more frequently with other students, both in and out of class, and report higher levels of support than women at co-educational schools (Kinzie et al., 2007; Massey et al., 2008). Other benefits of women's high schools and colleges are the greater likelihood of close student–faculty relations, increased self-confidence and self-

Some educators believe that women's colleges provide a more effective educational environment for female students.

esteem, and less sexism (Mansfield, 2011; Pankake, 2011). Also, women's college graduates are more likely than graduates of mixed-gender institutions to pursue male-dominated fields, such as the physical sciences and mathematics, to reach high levels of achievement in their careers and, for both reasons, to earn higher salaries (Sax et al., 2015b). Recent research has questioned the validity of some of these conclusions, however (Pahlke & Hyde, 2016; Signorella et al., 2013). A major reason is that single-sex and co-ed institutions differ in many ways beyond their gender composition. Women's colleges in the U.S. are generally more selective and draw students from higher socioeconomic levels than co-educational schools. Pre-existing differences between the women in the two types of colleges could account for differences in academic achievement and attitudes. When pre-existing differences are controlled, studies find that single-sex schooling (both for females and for males) is not more effective than co-educational schooling at improving students' achievements or attitudes (Pahlke & Hyde, 2016; Signorella et al., 2013). Still, some scholars argue that women's colleges provide subtle benefits which can be more difficult to measure. For example, women's colleges may be better at addressing certain challenges and opportunities that are more salient for women, and may provide support for women to realize their potential in ways that co-ed colleges can miss (Allen, 2016).

Use the survey in Get Involved 9.1 to assess the academic climate on your campus.

WOMEN'S WORK-RELATED GOALS

In an address to the graduating class of a women's college, feminist author Gloria Steinem noted a major difference between the goals of her generation of female college graduates in 1956 and those of young women today: "I thought we had to marry what we wished to become. Now you are becoming the men you once would have wanted to marry" (Goldberg, 1999, p. G3). This quote suggests that college women are striving for, and attaining, high-achievement goals and are no longer living vicariously through the accomplishments of their husbands. In the following section, we discuss women's career aspirations and some differences in the career goals of females and males.

GET INVOLVED 9.1
Does Your Campus Have a Hospitable Environment for Women?

Answer the questions presented here and ask three female students the same questions. If possible, select interviewees who vary in ethnicity, physical ability/disability, and/or sexual orientation.

1. Did you ever hear a professor tell a sexist or racist "joke" during or outside of class?

2. Did you ever hear a professor make a derogatory comment about a student's gender, ethnicity, physical disability, or sexual orientation? If yes, indicate the nature of that comment.

3. Do you feel that women and men receive the same degree of encouragement and support from their instructors? If not, explain.

4. Do you feel that women of color, women with disabilities, and sexual minority women receive the same degree of encouragement and support from their instructors as White, able-bodied, heterosexual women? If not, explain.

WHAT DOES IT MEAN?

1. Did you find any evidence of bias against women based on sex, ethnicity, disability, or sexual orientation? If yes, do you think these experiences affect the education process of students who are targets of these behaviors? Why or why not?

2. Did you find any evidence of differential support for students because of their gender, ethnicity, physical ability, or sexual orientation? If yes, do you think this can affect the educational process of students who receive less support? Explain.

Career Aspirations

There are few differences in the career aspirations of women with and without disabilities (DeLoach, 1989) and among women of different ethnicities (Fouad & Byars-Winston, 2005). However, there is some evidence that Black college women expect success more than White women do (Ganong et al., 1996). In addition, Asian American college women are more likely than White college women to aspire toward male-dominated and more prestigious occupations (Lee & Zhou, 2015). One explanation is that although Asian culture values traditional gender roles, Asian American families encourage their children to pursue prestigious occupations associated with social status and security (Ghosh, 2014).

As we have seen, high school girls and college women generally have higher educational and career aspirations than their male counterparts (Perry & Vance, 2010; Snyder & Dillow, 2015). In fact, a recent survey by the Pew Research Center revealed that more young women (66 percent) than young men (59 percent) say that being successful in a high-paying career is either "one of the most important things" or "very important" in their lives, a significant shift from 15 years ago (Lips, 2016). Some women, however, lower their aspirations during high school and college; major in less prestigious, often female-dominated, career fields; and, therefore, eventually end up in lower-level careers (Betz, 2008; Frome et al., 2008; Paludi, 2008a). Let us take a closer look at factors that influence young women's career aspirations.

Women are more likely to seek and earn degrees in academic disciplines that focus on helping people, such as education, psychology, and health sciences (Butler, 2014; Liben & Bigler, 2014) (see Table 9.2). Interestingly, girls who believe in the altruistic value of math and science have more interest in, and more positive attitudes toward, these fields than do other girls (Weisgram & Bigler, 2006). What might account for this? One explanation is that, as we saw in Chapter 4, girls are socialized toward communal behaviors. Consistent with the social construction of women as caring and nurturant, they are encouraged to develop a strong interest in and concern for other people, and as a consequence, they develop career and life goals that focus on communion and caregiving (Evans & Diekman, 2009).

Table 9.2 also shows that relatively few female students aspire toward the high-paying fields of computer and information sciences, engineering, and physical sciences. Even those qualified college women who major in these science and engineering areas are more likely than college men

TABLE 9.2   Bachelor's, Master's, and Doctoral Degrees, 2011–2012, in Selected Fields by Gender

Educational Field	Bachelor's Degree		Master's Degree		Doctorate	
	Women	Men	Women	Men	Women	Men
Biological/life sciences	59%	41%	57%	43%	53%	47%
Business and management	48	52	46	54	42	58
Computer and information sciences	18	82	28	72	22	78
Education	79	21	81	19	68	32
Engineering	19	81	23	77	22	78
English	68	32	60	40	62	38
Health professions	85	15	81	19	58	42
Mathematics	43	57	41	59	28	72
Physical sciences	40	60	38	62	33	67
Psychology	77	23	80	20	74	26
Social sciences and history	49	51	50	50	46	54
Visual and performing arts	61	39	58	42	54	46

Source: Snyder and Dillow, 2015.

to drop out of these programs or later leave the field (Di Bella & Crisp, 2016; National Science Foundation, 2015a, b; Seron et al., 2016). Moreover, whereas men tend to stick with their science and engineering studies if their grades are average, women do so only if they earn high grades (Hill et al., 2010).

What accounts for women's continued low participation rate in these academic areas? As we saw in Chapter 5, the possibility that females are less mathematically or scientifically skilled can be ruled out. We also noted in that chapter that parents and teachers are less likely to encourage the development of math or science skills in girls than boys. We saw that gender differences in attitudes toward and interest in science emerge early with girls becoming less confident of their ability to do math and science (LaCosse et al., 2016). In fact, many college women are perceived as "different" from individuals in science fields (Carli et al., 2010). In addition, stereotypes of scientists as "nerds" who are obsessed with technology, but who have little interest in people, conflict more with the gender roles of women than of men (Cheryan et al., 2013; Drury, 2016; Kanny et al., 2014; Master et al., 2016; Seron et al., 2016). So it is not surprising that women who are interested both in science and in helping others tend to avoid engineering in favor of the biological and medical sciences (Newcombe et al., 2009). Moreover, female students who do choose to major in math, science, or engineering report higher levels of discrimination than either women in female-dominated majors—such as arts, education, humanities, and social sciences—or men in any major (J. Steele et al., 2002). Additionally, women in the sciences report that they are not taken as seriously as men. Moreover, their work is not evaluated as highly as that of their male colleagues (Bilimoria et al., 2014; Grunspan et al., 2016; Knobloch-Westerwick et al., 2013; Reuben et al., 2014; Silbey, 2016). Such negative experiences may lead to expectations of discriminatory hiring and promotion practices in these fields, causing some women to reconsider their career choices (Fouad et al., 2011; Silbey, 2016). The dearth of female role models and insufficient faculty encouragement may be other factors that play an important role in steering women away from careers in the sciences (van den Brink & Stobbe, 2014; Young et al., 2013). Indeed, when bright female college students have female professors in math and science courses, they do better in their classes, have more positive feelings about women in science, and are more likely to major in science or math (Carrell et al., 2009; van den Brink & Stobbe, 2014; Young et al., 2013).

Career Counseling

During the 1950s and 1960s, women were largely invisible to career counselors because women were not viewed as interested in pursuing careers (Betz, 2008). Starting in the 1960s and 1970s, career counselors tended to steer girls and women toward traditionally female careers (Farmer, 2006). Although there is now much greater acceptance of females' pursuit of traditionally male occupations, some counselors, teachers, and parents continue to show gender-biased attitudes toward career choices. Many girls still are discouraged from taking advanced math and science courses or from choosing high-status professions dominated by males (Corbett & Hill, 2015). Gender bias also permeates vocational interest inventories and aptitude testing (Lonborg & Hackett, 2006).

What can career counselors do to support, encourage, and expand the career aspirations of young women? Nancy Betz (2008) suggests that counselors should help women in the following areas: (1) advocating for family-friendly work policies, such as flex time; (2) locating support systems and mentors; (3) encouraging husbands or partners to participate fully in housework and child care; (4) developing effective cognitive and behavioral coping strategies; and (5) obtaining necessary education, training, and job-hunting skills. Career counselors also need to become aware and understand that both women's and men's views and needs are shaped by culture, ethnicity, social class, sexual orientation, and ableness (Fouad & Ihle, 2017; Hook & Bowman, 2008).

Work–Family Expectations

My plan is to get a job after graduate school and hopefully marry. After a few years of establishing myself in my career, I plan to have two children. After a short maternity leave, I plan to work part time, and hope my husband will too, so one of us can always be home. When I told my boyfriend this, he said he hasn't even considered how to balance work and family, and he was astonished that my plans for the future are all mapped out.

(Erika, a 21-year-old college senior)

The vast majority of college women nowadays desire marriage, motherhood, and a career. For example, in Michele Hoffnung's (Hoffnung & Williams, 2013) longitudinal survey of senior women at five American colleges, 96 percent planned to have a career, 86 percent planned to marry, and 98 percent planned to have children. Sixteen years after college graduation, nearly two-thirds were balancing full-time career and family, a considerably higher percentage than women who had graduated from college 30 years earlier. If you are interested in both employment and parenthood, have you considered how you would like to combine these? Research shows that most college women, like Erika, want to work before they have children and interrupt their employment for some period during their children's early years (e.g., Bridges & Etaugh, 1996). The majority of male students, however, are like Erika's boyfriend and are much less likely to think about connections between career and family goals (Bass, 2015; Lucas-Thompson & Goldberg, 2015).

Although most college women want to interrupt their employment for childrearing, Black college women want to discontinue their employment for a shorter period of time than White women do. For example, Judith and Claire found that Black women want to return to employment when their first child is approximately 2 years old, whereas White women want to delay employment until their child is approximately 4 (Bridges & Etaugh, 1996).

Why do Black college women prefer an earlier return to employment after childbirth? For one thing, their own mothers returned to work sooner after childbirth than did mothers of White college women (Hoffnung, 2004). This finding is consistent with Black women's long history of combining the roles of mother and provider (Frevert et al., 2015). The earlier return to work of Black mothers may account for the fact that their college-going daughters are less likely than White college women to believe that continuous maternal employment produces negative outcomes for children, such as low self-esteem, feelings of neglect, and lack of maternal guidance (Bridges & Etaugh, 1996). Along these same lines, evidence suggests that college-educated Black women are more likely than their White counterparts to be encouraged by their parents to consider an occupation as essential to success (Higginbotham & Weber, 1996). Regardless of social class, Black women expect to work continuously and be primary breadwinners (Damaske, 2011). Together, this body of research indicates that employment may be a more integral aspect of Blacks' construction of women's roles than it is for Whites. (Remember the concept of integrated motherhood from Chapter 8?)

Some educated women of color face another role-related problem: finding an appropriate mate within one's ethnic group. For example, Black college women express the desire to marry a person of equal or greater educational and occupational status. However, because they earn a higher proportion of every type of higher education degree than Black men, they may be frustrated in this desire (Clarke et al., 2011).

Work–Family Outcomes

In the previous section, we saw that the great majority of college women expect to "have it all": career, marriage, and motherhood. How do these expectations relate to actual career and family outcomes? In order to explore this question, Michele Hoffnung (2004; Hoffnung & Williams, 2012) surveyed some women as college seniors and again 7 and 14 years later.

Career remained the major focus for the women throughout their 20s. Not quite half had married, and most had not yet started a family. Marital status was unrelated to educational attainment and career status 7 years out from college graduation. The few women who had become mothers, however, had fewer advanced degrees and lower career status than other women. They typically chose more traditional careers that took less time to train for, such as teacher or physical therapist. These women also held more traditional attitudes toward women's rights, roles, and responsibilities and were more likely to come from families with lower socioeconomic status.

In college, women of color had lower expectations for marriage than White women did, and in fact, they were less likely to be married 14 years later. Their educational attainments were equal to those of White women and their careers had somewhat higher status. They also were more likely than White women to continue full-time employment regardless of motherhood status (Hoffnung & Williams, 2012). These findings are consistent with research we looked at in the previous section suggesting that college-educated women of color have very high career motivation (Bridges & Etaugh, 1996; Damaske, 2011).

Salary Expectations

Consistent with a tendency to have less prestigious career aspirations than men do, women expect lower salaries in their jobs. However, even among students majoring in the same field, women have lower salary expectations than men (Taylor, 2007). What might account for this? One possibility is that women know that females earn lower salaries than males and base their own salary expectations accordingly (Williams et al., 2010). Another possibility is that women lower their salary expectations because they place importance on making accommodations in their jobs to fulfill their family obligations (Heckert, 2002). A third possibility is that women are more likely than men to underestimate their worth (Ellin, 2004) (see Chapter 10).

INFLUENCES ON WOMEN'S ACHIEVEMENT LEVEL AND CAREER DECISIONS

Although this chapter focuses on women's education and achievement, it is essential to note that achievement goals can be satisfied in diverse ways. Raising a well-adjusted and loving child, providing emotional and physical support to a spouse recovering from a stroke, and helping the homeless in one's community are only a few of the numerous forms achievement can take that are independent of education and occupation. However, despite the diversity of achievement directions, researchers have focused primarily on the traditional areas of education and occupation, and if one defines achievement in this manner, it appears that women have achieved less than men. As we noted at the beginning of this chapter, more men than women aspire to the most prestigious careers, and hold high positions within their occupational fields. Now we examine possible internal and external influences on women's achievement levels and occupational decisions. First, we look at their orientation to achievement in general and the personal traits that might be related to their career decision making. Then, we explore social and cultural influences on young women's educational and occupational pursuits.

Orientation to Achievement

For several decades, psychologists attempted to explain women's lower achievement compared to men's as due, in part, to their orientation to achievement.

ACHIEVEMENT MOTIVATION.   One explanation was that females' **achievement motivation**, that is, their *need to excel*, was lower than males'. However, early studies by David McClelland and others on which this conclusion was based used a male-biased theoretical framework (McClelland et al., 1953). Achievement was defined primarily in ways applicable to men's lives and emphasized competition and mastery in such areas as school, jobs, and sports. But as we have seen, achievement can also occur in other domains, such as the personal or interpersonal areas.

At the present time, researchers believe that women and men are similarly motivated to achieve (Hyde & Kling, 2001). However, gender socialization practices of families, peers, teachers, and others teach youngsters not only the importance of achievement but also the "gender-appropriate" direction it should take. For example, girls tend to learn that, if they have children, they should be the primary caregiver. Consequently, they may adjust their achievement goals in order to meet this expectation.

FEAR OF SUCCESS.   Another view of women's lower achievement in comparison to men's came from Matina Horner (1972), who proposed that women want to achieve but have a **fear of success**, that is, *a motive to avoid situations of high achievement.* Horner contended that women were concerned about the negative social consequences that can result from success, especially social rejection and loss of femininity. This suggestion might seem strange as you read this book in the twenty-first century. However, in the 1970s and 1980s, this idea was embraced by many scholars who studied females' fear of success.

To test her concept of the fear of success, Horner devised the following statement: *After first-term finals, Anne/John finds herself/himself at the top of her/his medical school class.* She asked college women to write a paragraph about Anne and college men to write about John. Approximately two-thirds of the women wrote negative stories with themes such as Anne's physical unattractiveness, her inability to have romantic relationships, rejection by her peers, and her decision to transfer into a less prestigious occupation. Most of the stories told by the men about John, on the other hand, reflected positive outcomes.

Although Horner believed these results indicated a motive to avoid success on the part of women, subsequent research points to a different conclusion. It now appears that these stories did not reflect women's fear of high-achieving situations in general, but rather their awareness of negative consequences that can occur when individuals violate gender stereotypes. Medicine, especially in the 1970s when Horner performed her study, was strongly dominated by men. Thus, it is likely that females' negative stories reflected their concern about the problems individuals face in gender-atypical occupations, rather than their desire to avoid a high level of achievement (Hyde & Kling, 2001). Later studies showed that both women and men wrote negative stories about a successful woman in medicine *and* a successful man in nursing (Batalha & Reynolds, 2013). Years of subsequent research on this topic have failed to find reliable gender differences in fear of success (Butler, 2014). Consequently, psychologists today do not believe that women's lower level of educational or occupational achievement can be accounted for by their fear of success.

ACHIEVEMENT ATTRIBUTIONS.   A third explanation given for gender differences in levels of achievement is that females and males make different **achievement attributions**, that is, *explanations about their good and poor performance.* In general, people are *more likely to attribute positive performance to their own internal traits, such as their ability or effort, whereas they tend to attribute negative performance to external causes, such as task difficulty or bad luck.* This **self-serving attributional bias**, like self-esteem (see Chapter 4), is linked to healthy psychological adjustment and happiness (Mezulis et al., 2004). In other words, taking responsibility for good performance (e.g., "I did well on the test because I know the material"), but attributing poor performance to external factors (e.g., "I failed the test because it was unfair"), enables a person to maintain a good self-image. On the other hand, the reverse pattern—blaming yourself for failure and not taking credit for your successes—could lead to an unwillingness to persevere in a challenging situation and to low self-esteem.

A meta-analysis by Amy Mezulis and her colleagues (2004) shows that females, but not males, show a marked decline in the self-serving attributional bias starting in early adolescence. (Reread the section on self-esteem in Chapter 4, and note the similar, and possibly related, decline.) These gender differences in attributions of performance are small, but fairly consistent (Butler, 2014), and are associated with the type of performance situation. For example, in male-stereotyped domains, such as mathematics, males attribute success to ability more than females do, but in female-stereotyped domains, such as languages or English, the reverse pattern occurs (Beyer, 1997; Wigfield et al., 2014). Similarly, women are more likely to blame their lack of ability for failing a math test than for failing a verbal test, whereas men show the reverse tendency (Kiefer & Shih, 2004).

ACHIEVEMENT SELF-CONFIDENCE.   Another internal barrier that has been used to explain women's lower achievement in comparison to men's is their lower self-confidence (Killelea, 2016). Many studies show that males are more self-confident in academic situations than females. For example, even though girls get higher grades in school than boys, they tend to underestimate their grades, as well as their overall intelligence, and class standing whereas boys tend to overestimate theirs (Buser et al., 2014; Butler, 2014; Mullainathan, 2014). Mary Crawford and Margo MacLeod (1990) also found that when asked why they don't participate in class discussion, college women's responses reflected questionable confidence in their abilities, such as "might appear unintelligent in the eyes of other students" and "ideas are not well enough formulated" (p. 116). Men's reasons, on the other hand, focused on external factors, as in "have not done the assigned reading" or participation might "negatively affect [their] grade" (p. 116). Men tend to display more confidence than women in performance-oriented settings (Kenschaft & Clark, 2016). Even when minimally prepared, men tend to believe they can "wing it" and get through successfully. But no matter how thoroughly prepared women are, they often feel unprepared. Successful men are sure they can obtain beneficial results, while successful women continue to express doubts about their capabilities and hold themselves to a higher standard (Butler, 2014; Hill et al., 2010). Gender identity, and not just gender, is a factor as well. Women with higher masculine gender identity show more confidence in their abilities than women with low masculine identity (Etaugh et al., 2016).

Females do not show lower levels of confidence in all situations, however. Studies indicate that females' confidence is lower than males' in male-linked tasks, such as mathematics, and spatial skills, but is higher in female-linked tasks, such as reading and English, arts and music, and social skills (Butler, 2014; Nix et al., 2015; Simpkins et al., 2015a, b; Wigfield et al., 2014). Research (Daubman & Sigall, 1997; Heatherington et al., 1993) suggests that in some situations, what appears to be lower self-confidence (e.g., publicly predicting lower grades for oneself) might really reflect women's desire to be liked or to protect others from negative feelings about themselves.

CONCLUSION.   Early conclusions that women have lower aspirations than men because they are not as highly motivated to excel and because they fear the negative consequences of success have not been supported. Although some evidence exists for gender differences in achievement attributions and self-confidence, these differences are not observed in all situations. Furthermore, as is the case with all types of psychological gender differences, the differences are small and do not apply to all females and males. Thus, most social scientists point to other factors to help explain different career aspirations and attainment levels of women and men.

Personal Characteristics

Are personal characteristics related to women's career aspirations? The answer is "yes." For example, women who work full time are more likely to support egalitarian roles for women than are women who work part time (Cunningham et al., 2005). Also, women who choose male-dominated careers are more likely than those who pick female-dominated careers to be competitive, autonomous, and instrumental and to have less traditional gender attitudes and more liberal social and political attitudes (Betz, 2008; Gianettoni & Guilley, 2015; Martin, 2008b).

Another factor related to career choice is the individual's **self-efficacy**, that is, *the belief that one can successfully perform the tasks involved in a particular domain.* Individuals with high self-efficacy for a particular field are more likely to aspire toward and succeed in that field as a career (Stern, 2008). For example, although females tend to have lower self-efficacy in mathematics and science than males (Petersen & Hyde, 2014) (see Chapter 5), those women who select and persist in careers in science or engineering have high self-efficacy for mathematics (Fouad & Ihle, 2017). Furthermore, females, compared to males, have higher self-efficacy for health-related professions and other female-dominated professions such as social work, health care, and teaching (Tellhed et al., 2017). These gender differences, in turn, correspond to differences in occupational choices.

Sexual Orientation

Many lesbians and bisexual women become aware of their sexual identity during late adolescence or adulthood (Tulloch & Kaufman, 2013), at the same time that they are selecting a career. The overlap of these two processes can influence career development (Hook & Bowman, 2008; Lyons et al.,

2010; Prince 2013). Sexual minority women might put career selection on hold as they explore their sexuality and intimate relationships (Bieschke & Toepfer-Hendey, 2006; Lyons et al., 2010). Also, as a result of coming out, many lose the family support that can be beneficial to the career-selection process.

In addition, lesbians' career choices might be directly affected by their perception of the occupational climate for lesbians and gay men. Whereas some sexual minority individuals select occupations they perceive as employing large numbers of lesbians and gay men in order to experience an environment in which there is safety in numbers, those who are closeted or anxious about their sexual identity might avoid these occupations (Hook & Bowman, 2008; Prince, 2013).

On the positive side, lesbians tend to be less traditional in their attitudes about gender than are heterosexual women. Consequently, they tend to consider a broader range of occupational options and are more likely to choose jobs in male-dominated fields (Peplau & Fingerhut, 2004). These jobs, as we shall see, pay more than jobs in the female-dominated areas.

Social and Cultural Factors

Although some individual characteristics are related to individuals' career choices, career decisions are made within a sociocultural context in which the attitudes of significant people and the values of one's culture contribute to career selection as well. Support and encouragement from parents are very important for women of all ethnicities (DeCuir-Gunby et al., 2013; Leaper & Brown, 2014; Raque-Bogdan et al., 2013). Parental support and availability influence career aspirations and achievements in Black (Hanson, 2007; Jackson & Dorsey, 2009; Winkle-Wagner, 2015), Native American (Juntunen et al., 2001), and Latina (Aguinaga & Gloria, 2015) women. High-achieving Black and White women report receiving considerable family support for pursuing highly prestigious careers and being strongly influenced by their families. For example, a Black female scientist commented, "I was always encouraged to do the things I wanted to do and was told by my grandmother that I could be whatever I wanted to be if I committed myself to it and did not lose my focus on the objective" (Hanson, 2007, p. 25). A same-sex parent often has the greatest effect on career expectations and outcome of adolescents (Schoon et al., 2007; Whiston & Keller, 2004). One longitudinal study of female high school seniors, for example, found that attachment to the mother contributed to high career aspirations five years later (O'Brien et al., 2000). Another longitudinal study showed that mothers' high expectations for their 10-year-old daughters predicted the latter's earnings in adulthood (Flouri & Hawkes, 2008). Among female college students, those with plans for a nontraditional career are more likely than other women to have a highly educated mother with a nontraditional career and parents who support their career choices (Schoon et al., 2007; Whiston & Keller, 2004).

In addition to social support, cultural values play a role in women's career development. According to McAdoo (in Higginbotham & Weber, 1996), many Black families believe that college education and professional attainments are family, as well as individual, goals. Moreover, there is evidence that high-achieving Black women who move up from their working-class backgrounds feel a sense of obligation to their families. In one study (Higginbotham & Weber, 1996), almost twice as many Black as White upwardly mobile women expressed this sense of familial debt. A Black occupational therapist said, "I know the struggle that my parents have had to get me where I am. . . . I feel it is my responsibility to give back some of that energy they have given to me" (p. 139).

Another cultural value shown by Black women is their concern for their communities. Many successful Black women are committed to ending both sexism and racism in the workplace and community (Jackson & Dorsey, 2009) and using their achievements to inspire and mentor other people of color (Osborne, 2008; Robinson & Nelson, 2010). As expressed by a high-ranking Black female city official, "Because I have more opportunities, I've got an obligation to give more back and to set a positive example for Black people and especially for Black women. I think we've got to do a tremendous job in building self-esteem and giving people the desire to achieve" (Higginbotham & Weber, 1996, p. 142). Similarly, many Latina adolescents from working-class families realize that their parents work long hours at multiple dead-end jobs. They aspire to fulfilling careers that will allow them to create better lives for themselves and their families, and that will also enable them to make a positive contribution to their community (Marlino & Wilson, 2006). Many high-achieving Latina women receive family encouragement and have a supportive social network. However, some experience a conflict between traditional cultural values that guide them toward family-oriented goals and other socialization factors that encourage high educational and career attainments (Aguinaga-Gloria, 2015; Tirado et al., 2015).

Conflicting values are also evident in the experiences of educated Native American women (McCloskey & Mintz, 2006). Although research on Native Americans' achievement goals is sparse, it suggests that family and community members sometimes try to discourage Native women from attending college. Consequently, those who persist in seeking a college education may feel they are betraying their heritage or community (James et al., 2013).

To more directly learn about family and cultural influences on women's career goals, perform the interviews described in Get Involved 9.2.

In addition to cultural variations across ethnic groups, values associated with social class can influence career decisions. According to Constance Flanagan (1993), working-class families, who hold more traditional gender attitudes than middle-class families, also see less value in academic achievement. Thus, working-class women who have an interest in school and a willingness to be independent of their families are likely to become invested in employment immediately after high school, whereas middle-class women with those attributes are apt to seek higher education.

Job-Related Characteristics

Individuals vary in the benefits they want from working in a particular job, and these benefits can play a role in guiding career selections. Research shows that college women and men differ little in the importance they place on pay, job qualities, or factors related to promotions and job perks (Heckert et al., 2002).

However, women and men differ in the importance they attach to other job-related attributes, which can account for some of the differences in their occupational choices. For high school and college students and successful women and men (Butler, 2014; Carli & Eagly, 2011; Greenhaus & Kossek, 2014; Parker & Wang, 2013), differences are generally consistent with

---

GET INVOLVED 9.2
Family and Cultural Values About Education and Career Goals

Interview two female students who vary in ethnicity. Select your interviewees from any two of the following ethnic groups: Asian American, Black, Latina, Native American, and White. Inform them you are exploring connections between women's family and cultural values and their education and career goals.

First, ask each respondent to indicate her college major, career goal, and expected educational attainment (i.e., highest educational degree). Second, ask her to evaluate the degree to which her family's values support her specific educational aspirations and career goals. Third, ask her to evaluate the degree to which her specific educational aspirations and career goals were influenced by her ethnic or national cultural values.

WHAT DOES IT MEAN?

1. Did you find any differences among respondents in the extent to which they received support from their families? If yes, refer to information presented in the text or to your own ideas and explain these differences.

2. Did your respondents report that their goals were influenced by their values? Is the information you obtained consistent with the material presented in the text? If not, explain the discrepancies.

gender roles and stereotypes. For example, males are somewhat more likely to value material success, earnings, promotions, freedom, risk taking, challenge, leadership, and power. Females are more apt to value interpersonal relationships, helping others, respecting colleagues, working with people, and striking a balance between professional achievement and personal relationships.

Another gender difference in job values is the greater emphasis women place on good, flexible working hours and ease of commuting, especially if they have children (Bass, 2015; Parker & Wang, 2013; Petersen & Hyde, 2014). This gender difference probably reflects women's belief that mothers should stay home and care for infants, a value that is expressed during many stages of females' lives. For example, twelfth-grade girls who place a high value on having a family-friendly job are more likely to change their career aspirations from male-dominated fields (e.g., science) to female-dominated occupations (Frome et al., 2008).

Regardless of the type of job, women's ratings of the importance of several job characteristics has been increasing in recent years. These include job security, power, prestige, feelings of accomplishment, task enjoyment, and using one's abilities. It is possible that as gender barriers to opportunity decline, women's aspirations rise to obtain previously unavailable job attributes (Konrad et al., 2000).

Summary

WOMEN'S EDUCATIONAL GOALS, ATTAINMENTS, AND CAMPUS EXPERIENCES

- Across ethnicities, adolescent girls endorse higher educational and occupational goals than do boys.
- Women obtain the majority of associate's, bachelor's, master's, and doctoral degrees, and half of all professional degrees.
- Worldwide, girls' access to education is improving, but several countries still have serious gender gaps.
- The campus climate can be problematic for some women. They may experience sexism in the classroom, and many perceive the academic environment as hostile and demeaning.
- Women of color, poor women, and women with disabilities experience additional problems on campus.

WOMEN'S WORK-RELATED GOALS

- College women generally aspire to less prestigious careers than college men. Few women decide to enter the physical sciences or engineering.
- Career counselors can do several things to support and expand women's career aspirations.
- Most college women envision their futures as involving employment, marriage, and motherhood. Many plan to interrupt their employment for childrearing.

- Women have lower salary expectations than men. Possible explanations are women's knowledge that females earn less than males, their willingness to accommodate their jobs to their family lives, and their belief that they deserve less.

INFLUENCES ON WOMEN'S ACHIEVEMENT LEVEL AND CAREER DECISIONS

- There is no evidence that women have less motivation to achieve than men do or that women stay away from high-achieving situations because they fear success.
- Gender differences in attributions for performance are very small and are more likely to occur when making attributions in gender-stereotypic domains.
- Women display less self-confidence than men, especially in relation to male-linked tasks and when estimates of one's performance are made publicly.
- Women with nontraditional gender-related traits or attitudes are more likely to aspire toward male-dominated careers.
- Women's feelings of self-efficacy for particular occupational fields are related to their aspirations for those fields.
- Career decisions of sexual minority individuals are sometimes influenced by their perceptions of the job climate for lesbians and gay men.

- Family support and family and cultural values can influence women's career development.
- Job-related characteristics valued more highly by males include a good salary, promotions, and opportunity for advancement.

- Characteristics valued more strongly by females are interpersonal relationships and helping others. However, women in male-dominated occupations highly value masculine-typed job qualities.

Key Terms

chilly climate *186*

microaggressions *186*

achievement motivation *193*

fear of success *194*

achievement attributions *194*

self-serving attributional bias *194*

self-efficacy *195*

What Do You Think?

1. Discuss your opinion about the relative advantages and disadvantages for women of attending a women's college versus a mixed-gender college.

2. This chapter discusses several issues faced by women of color and women with disabilities on college campuses. Select two or three of these concerns and suggest institutional procedures that could address these problems and improve the academic climate for these groups.

3. Many women who desire both employment and motherhood want to interrupt their employment for childrearing. What can explain this? As part of your answer, discuss the extent to which gender differences in power (see Chapter 1) and gender socialization (see Chapter 4) explain this.

4. The traditional conception of achievement as the attainment of high academic and occupational success has been criticized as reflecting the achievement domains of men more than of women. Do you agree with this criticism? Give a rationale for your answer. Also, if you agree, suggest other indices of success that would reflect women's achievement more accurately.

5. Discuss the relationship between gender stereotypes and common career choices of young women and men. Also, several changes have occurred in the educational attainments and career aspirations of women over time. Show how a changing social construction of gender has contributed to this.

If You Want to Learn More

Bilimoria, D. & Lord, L. (Eds.). (2014). *Women in STEM careers: International perspectives*. Northampton, MA: Edward Elgar Publishing.

Branch, E.H. (Ed.). (2016). *Pathways, potholes, and the persistence of women in the sciences: Reconsidering the pipeline*. Lanham, MD: Lexington.

DuQuaine-Watson, J. (2017). *Mothering by degrees: Single women and the pursuit of post-secondary education*. New Brunswick, NJ: Rutgers University Press.

Fitzgerald, T. (2013). *Women leaders in higher education*. London, UK: Society for Research in Higher Education.

Gill, J. et al. (2016). *A girl's education: Schooling and the formation of gender, identities, and future visions*. London, UK: Palgrave Macmillan.

Jackson, J.F.L. & O'Callaghan, E.M. (2014). *Measuring glass ceiling effects in higher education: Opportunities and challenges*. San Francisco, CA: Jossey-Bass.

Kay, K. & Shipman, C. (2014). *The confidence code: The science and art of self-assurance—What women should know*. New York: HarperCollins.

Kerr, B. & McKay, R. (2014). *Smart girls in the 21st century: Understanding talented girls and women*. Tucson, AZ: Great Potential Press.

Liben, L.S. & Bigler, R.S. (Eds.). (2014). *Advances in child development and behavior: The role of gender in educational contexts and outcomes*. Waltham, MA: Academic Press.

Marina, B.L.H. & Ross, S.N. (2016). *Beyond retention: Cultivating spaces of equity, justice, and fairness for women of color in U.S. higher education*. IAP—Information Age Publishing, Inc.

Marx, S. (Ed.). (2017). *Qualitative research in STEM: Studies of equity, access, and innovation*. Amazon Digital Services.

Patton, L.D. & Croom, N.N. (2016). *Critical perspectives on Black women and college success*. New York: Routledge.

Pomerantz, S. & Raby, R. (2017). *Smart girls: Success, school, and the myth of post-feminism*. Los Angeles, CA: University of California Press.

Rosser, S. (2012). *Breaking into the lab: Engineering progress for women in science*. New York: New York University Press.

Stacki, S.L. & Bailey, S. (2015). *Educating adolescent girls around the globe: Challenges and opportunities*. New York: Routledge.

Yousafzai, M. (2013). *I am Malala: The girl who stood up for education and was shot by the Taliban*. New York: Little, Brown & Co.

Websites

Education
American Association of University Women
http://www.aauw.org

Women with Disabilities
Disabled People's International
http://www.dpi.org

CHAPTER 10

Employment

When a man leaves, he is getting the golden parachute to enjoy the good life. When a woman leaves of her own accord, they say "Well, she couldn't take the pressure" . . . (John Challenger, chief executive of Challenger, Gray, & Christman, a Chicago firm that tracks chief executives, in Stanley, 2002)

A couple of times in my career, someone would tell me that I couldn't do something. I would just tell myself that I wasn't going to talk to that person anymore, and I went ahead and did it anyway . . . I tell other women that persistence pays, and that if you can't work through a problem, to go around it. (Christine King, chief of AMI Semiconductor, in King & Olsen, 2002)

I've never felt held back. Have I seen things on an institutional level? Yeah, it's out there. (Monica Karo, chief executive of OMD, United States, in Ember, 2016)

At the top of the industry is a closed loop of white guys talking to other white guys (Cindy Gallop, consultant, public speaker, and former advertising executive, in Ember, 2016)

For the first time, there was a line in the Senate women's bathroom (Amy Klobuchar, Democrat from Minnesota, 2013, in Lennon, 2013

In this chapter, we examine the nature of women's employment. We begin with an overview of how many women work, what kinds of jobs they have, the challenges they face in job advancement and becoming leaders, the salaries they receive, and their job satisfaction. We then focus on the status of older women workers. Next, we consider procedures and policies that can improve the work environment for women. Finally, we turn to retirement and economic issues facing older women.

In our exploration of these topics, we use the terms *employment* and *work* interchangeably, so it is important that we clarify their meaning. The term *work* refers to *activities that produce a good or a service*. Thus, it includes all sorts of behaviors, such as cooking dinner, mowing the lawn, writing a term paper, teaching a class, fixing a car, volunteering in a nursing home, or running a corporation. The kind of work that we cover in this chapter is employment, that is *work for pay*, a major focus of the lives of women (and men) in terms of both time and personal identity. However, our focus on paid employment does not imply that this form of work is more valuable than other types of productive activities. Society would not function without the unpaid labor that contributes to family and community life.

WOMEN'S EMPLOYMENT RATES AND OCCUPATIONAL CHOICES

What percentage of women are employed? What occupations do they choose? Let's discuss each of these issues.

Employment Rates

Women's labor force participation has increased dramatically in recent decades, especially among mothers of young children. Women now comprise nearly half of the workforce. Whereas in 1975 only 39 percent of married women with children under age 6 were in the labor force, by 2011 this number had increased to 64 percent (Bureau of Labor Statistics, 2015). Among mothers of children age 6–17, 79 percent of Black women, 77 percent of White women, 75 percent of Asian American women, and 70 percent of Latina women are employed (Bureau of Labor Statistics, 2013b). Women with disabilities have lower employment rates than either men with disabilities or able-bodied women, and many are employed in low-paying jobs (Bureau of Labor Statistics, 2015). Women with disabilities may confront several barriers in the workplace, including little or no accessible parking or public transportation nearby, inaccessible work environments, and a need for adaptations to workstations (Davidson et al., 2017; Schur et al., 2016).

What accounts for the influx of women into the workplace? Several factors have contributed. First, the women's movement provided encouragement for women to consider other role options in addition to the homemaker role. Second, women's current higher level of educational attainment (see Chapter 9) has better prepared them for careers that provide greater challenge, stimulation, and a sense of accomplishment. Women with higher levels of education are more likely to be employed and to return to work more rapidly after giving birth (Guendelman et al., 2014; Kenschaft & Clark, 2016). Third, many women must work for financial reasons (Trask, 2014). Today, few middle-class families can afford home ownership, adequate health insurance, and a middle-class lifestyle on one income. In working-class families, two incomes are often needed to remain above the poverty line (Coontz, 2016). Currently, mothers are either the solo or primary breadwinner in two-thirds of American families (W. Wang et al., 2013). Economic necessity is particularly great for women who are single heads of households, and these women comprise more than half of all families living in poverty in the United States (U.S. Census Bureau, 2015b). In 2014, 25 percent of all families with children were headed by an unmarried mother, and 78 percent of these mothers with school age children were employed (Bureau of Labor Statistics, 2015b). Unfortunately, for poor women who are heads of household, the employment opportunities are greatly limited, and numerous obstacles block the way to employment. Read Learn About the Research 10.1 for an exploration of employment issues for low-income mothers.

LEARN ABOUT THE RESEARCH 10.1
Job Retention and Advancement Among Low-Income Mothers

The passage of welfare reform programs in 1996 increased employment rates and reduced poverty rates among poor mothers. However, earning enough to support a family continues to be problematic for these women and their employment options remain limited. A low-wage earner who has left the welfare system may earn too much to be eligible for benefits such as Medicaid and food stamps, yet be too poor to afford health insurance or adequate food. Thus, many former welfare recipients are more financially strapped than before (Lee, 2007). In addition, much of the low-income work available occurs in evening or night shifts, creating scheduling and child care problems for families (Crosnoe & Cavanagh, 2010).

In order to understand influences on the job retention and advancement of poor mothers, Sunhwa Lee (2007) studied over 2,600 low-income mothers. Half of these women were White, 25 percent were Black, and nearly 20 percent were Latina.

Over half had never been married, and they had an average of two children.

Nearly 40 percent of the sample worked in service occupations, primarily food, health, and cleaning services. This figure is higher than the overall percentage of women in these occupations. Because these jobs are often of limited duration, pay low wages, provide little opportunity for advancement, and offer limited benefits, they do not readily lead to self-sufficiency.

The study found that having at least some college education, a regular source of child care, and employer-provided health insurance were critical factors for mothers' job retention and advancement. However, two-thirds of the women had neither any college education nor employer-provided health insurance. The author concluded by emphasizing the need for a more comprehensive support system for low-wage women workers to help them more successfully navigate the current employment environment (Lee, 2007).

WHAT DOES IT MEAN?

1. How can some of the problems raised by this study be addressed by government, the private sector, educational institutions, or other societal institutions? Be specific.

2. Most of the research on women's achievement and career aspirations has focused on middle-class women. Which factors examined in Chapter 9 are less relevant to the lives of poor women? Explain your answer.

Source: Lee (2007).

Occupational Segregation

The clustering of particular demographic groups in specific jobs is called **occupational segregation** (Richardsen et al., 2016). The 20 occupations with the lowest percentage of women are clustered in four major groups, sometimes called "hard hat" occupations: construction; installation, maintenance, and repair; production; and transportation and material moving. The 20 occupations with the greatest concentration of women are similarly clustered in just a few groups, principally health care, office and administrative work, teaching, and caring for young children (Hegewisch & Hartmann, 2014a, b).

Occupational segregation has declined considerably in the past 40 years (Hegewisch & Hartmann, 2014a, b). Women have increased their numbers in both managerial and professional jobs, and now hold half of these positions (Bureau of Labor Statistics, 2016). However, women and ethnic minorities in managerial positions tend to be concentrated in positions with lower pay and less authority and are more likely to manage workers of their own sex and ethnicity (International Labour Organization, 2015; U.S. Department of Commerce, 2011). This *restriction of women to only certain types of management experience*, the so-called **glass wall**, makes it more difficult for women to rise to the top of the organization (International Labour Organization, 2015). Moreover, significant differences still remain in the types of occupations pursued by women and men. In 2015, women accounted for over 95 percent of all kindergarten teachers and dental assistants and 92 percent of registered nurses, but only 20 percent of computer programmers and 7 percent of civil engineers. In addition, although more women have entered the relatively high-paying skilled trades (e.g., as carpenters, plumbers, and electricians), they still comprise less than 3 percent of these workers. Women remain segregated in so-called pink-collar fields. About 30 percent of female employees work in just 10 occupations. Most of these are low-status, low-paying service jobs such as secretary, cashier, restaurant server, nursing aide, home health worker, and cook (Bureau of Labor Statistics, 2016). Thus, the workplace continues to be characterized by significant sex segregation, with men tending to dominate the most high-paying and prestigious occupations such as medicine, engineering, and banking (Bureau of Labor Statistics, 2016). This situation persists all around the globe (Thompson & Armato, 2012).

Furthermore, more employers today are cutting costs by hiring part-time or temporary workers, who are paid less and have minimal or no benefits. Women are more likely than men to hold these jobs, whose flexibility may fit well with a woman's family obligations.

The workplace is segregated not only by gender but also by ethnicity. White and Asian American women are more likely than Black and Latina women to hold high-status and high-paying managerial or professional jobs and Black and Latina women are more likely than White women to hold service jobs (Bureau of Labor Statistics, 2016). Immigrant women, regardless of ethnicity, also tend to be employed in low-paying, low-status occupations such as nanny, housekeeper, and farm worker. Their employment, especially in the first two of these jobs, has played a critical role in allowing middle- and upper-income women to participate in the workforce (Milkman, 2016).

GENDER DIFFERENCES IN LEADERSHIP AND JOB ADVANCEMENT

Nearly half of all law school graduates and nearly half of the new associates in law firms are women. Yet, women represent only 15 percent of equity partners and 5 percent of managing partners at law firms.

(Lennon, 2013)

Women account for only 26 percent of guests on major TV networks' Sunday morning news shows. They likewise constitute only 27 percent of opinion writers at the USA's three most prestigious newspapers (the New York Times, Wall Street Journal, and Washington Post).
The vast majority in both cases are White men.

(Women's Media Center, 2014, 2015)

Businesses with women on their boards outperform companies with all-male boards by 26 percent.

(Lennon, 2013)

Leadership Positions

First, some good news. Within the past few years, the U.S. government has registered some historic firsts: first woman House speaker (Nancy Pelosi); first woman to be a presidential candidate (Hillary Clinton); first Republican woman to run for vice president (Sarah Palin); first Supreme Court to have three female justices (Ruth Bader Ginsburg, Sonia Sotomayor, and Elena Kagan).

But the picture isn't all rosy. In virtually every nation, women are less likely than men to hold positions of authority. Elsesser, 2016; Glassdoor Economic Research, 2016; Nicolson, 2015; Tutchell & Edmonds, 2015). For example, although 50 percent of managers in the United States are women, women become scarcer the higher one goes in an organization (ILO, 2015). Women constitute only 8 percent of Fortune 500 chief executive officers, 17 of board directors of these companies,

20 percent of U.S senators, 12 percent of state governors, and 27 percent of college and university presidents. The situation for women of color is even worse (AAUW, 2016; American Council on Education, 2016; Center for American Women and Politics, 2015; Verveer & Azzarelli, 2015). Although the United States has yet to elect a woman as president, 73 other countries such as Pakistan (Benazir Bhutto), Israel (Golda Meir), India (Indira Gandhi), and Great Britain (Margaret Thatcher) have been elevating women to the role of chief executive for decades (Bisom-Rapp & Sargeant, 2016; Martin & Borrelli, 2016). In the twenty-first century alone, several women have risen to lead their countries. These include Ellen Johnson Sirleaf of Liberia, Africa's first female president; Michelle Bachelet of Chile, the first woman to lead a major Latin American country; Dilma Rousseff, Brazil's first woman president; Angela Merkel, the first female chancellor of Germany, and Theresa May, the second female prime minister of the United Kingdom. In 2016, out of 192 member countries of the United Nations, 10 had female presidents (including one chancellor), 6 had women prime ministers, and 3 had queens (Catalyst, 2016). Out of 193 countries, the United States ranks 101st—slightly worse than the United Arab Emirates—in women's participation in the lower or single legislative body of the country. Women make up just 19 percent of the U.S. House of Representatives. Iceland is near the top of the list, with 48 percent, whereas Qatar is at the bottom with no women (Inter-Parliamentary Union, 2017). Even in female-dominated fields, such as nursing, social work, and education, *men are likely to earn more and get promoted faster*, a phenomenon known as the **glass escalator** (Elsesser, 2015). For example, nearly 80 percent of grade school teachers are women, but nearly 50 percent of school superintendents are men (U.S. Census Bureau, 2015b). While being a **token** (i.e., *a sole representative of one's group*) thus clearly benefits men, it often is disadvantageous for women. The token woman in a male-dominated workplace is often perceived negatively, excessively scrutinized, treated unfairly, and isolated (Cain & Leahey, 2014; Combs & Milosevic, 2016).

The **glass ceiling**, which refers to *invisible but powerful barriers that prevent women from advancing beyond a certain level*, is a global phenomenon (Punnett, 2016). One variation on this concept is the "stained glass ceiling" for female clergy. Another is the "concrete ceiling" for ethnic minority women, in reference to the difficulties these women face in moving into higher positions because of the intersecting effects of sexism and racism (Jackson & O'Callaghan, 2014). Women who do pass through the glass ceiling are more likely than men to be assigned to a **glass cliff** position, which involves *leading a unit that is in crisis and has a high risk of failure* (Elsesser, 2015; Huston, 2014, Trop, 2014). There is also a **sticky floor** in traditional women's jobs, meaning *women have little or no job ladder, or path, to higher positions* (Ahmad & Naseer, 2015). Clerical work and the garment industry are examples of occupations with little room for growth. Furthermore, some women experience a **maternal wall**, in which they *get less desirable assignments, lower salaries, and more limited advancement opportunities once they become mothers* (Dworkin et al., 2015; Fuegen & Biernat, 2013). Fatherhood, however, has no such effect on men.

Even the best and brightest women find progress to be frustratingly slow. For example, a recent study of the careers of high-potential graduates from elite MBA programs found that women lagged behind men in advancement and compensation, starting from their first job, and were less satisfied with their careers (Carter & Silva, 2010).

Barriers That Hinder Women's Advancement

What prevents women from reaching positions of leadership? We now turn to the role of mentors, social networks, and discrimination.

MENTORS AND SOCIAL NETWORKS. A **mentor** *is a senior-level person who takes an active role in the career planning and development of junior employees*. Mentors help their mentees develop appropriate skills, learn the informal organizational structure, meet key people, and have access to opportunities that enable them to advance. Consequently, mentoring has positive effects on job satisfaction, promotion, and career success (Ehrich & Kimber, 2016; van den Brink & Stobbe, 2014). This is especially true for women with male mentors (Kulik et al., 2016).

Since she became the first female chancellor of Germany in 2005, Angela Merkel has widely been considered the most powerful woman in world politics. More women around the world are assuming positions of political power, although their numbers remain small.

Women employees may have difficulty in identifying an appropriate mentor. The limited number of women in senior-level positions, especially in male-dominated fields, makes it hard for a woman to find a female mentor (Richardsen et al., 2016). In addition, men may be reluctant to mentor young women for a variety of reasons, including fear of gossip about an affair or a possible sexual harassment suit (Elsesser, 2015; Rhode et al., 2014).

A second vehicle for advancement that is limited for women and people of color is access to informal social networks (AAUW, 2016). These networks can provide information about job opportunities, informal workplace norms and behaviors, and opportunities to meet important members of the organization (Bruckmüller et al., 2013). Furthermore, they offer social support and can serve as an important step in developing a mentoring relationship with a senior-level person. However, male reluctance to deal with women means women experience "micro-inequities" such as not being invited to informal social events (e.g., golf outings, after-hours drinking group, strip club) or being excluded from informal communication networks (Combs & Milosevic, 2016; Elsesser, 2015; Powell & Sang, 2015; van den Brink & Stobbe, 2014). Such social opportunities are especially likely to be lacking for women who work in male-dominated occupations. Women with child care responsibilities right after work also are limited in opportunities for after-hours socializing. One way for women to become part of a network is to become involved in local or national women's organizations such as the National Association for Female Executives, the American Association of University Women (AAUW), or the Association of Women in Science (Cahusac & Kanji, 2014; Cain & Leahey, 2014; Marina et al., 2015; Miles-Cohen et al., 2010).

DISCRIMINATION.   Another factor limiting the job advancement of women is sex discrimination, that is, unfavorable treatment based on gender. Such discrimination occurs despite the existence of laws that prohibit using gender (as well as ethnicity, national origin, or age) as a determinant in hiring or in other employment decisions (The last remaining legal barrier to women's full participation in the U.S. military was removed recently. See In the News 10.1) (Blossfield et al., 2015; Sheltzer & Smith, 2015; Thomas, 2016).

IN THE NEWS 10.1
U.S. Opens All Combat Roles to Women

In a groundbreaking decision, the U.S. military, at the end of 2015, opened all combat positions to women, with no exceptions. The decision overturned a long-standing rule that barred women from combat roles, even though women had in fact been serving in such roles in Iraq and Afghanistan (Rosenberg & Philips, 2015). Women in the military welcomed the ruling, which not only acknowledges the service they were already performing, but also will aid in their career advancement. As of this writing, legislation is moving through the U.S. Congress that would require women to register for the draft, as men now do (Steinhauer, 2016). Some conservative senators strongly object to this legislation which, said one, would "forcibly conscript young girls in[to] combat" (Steinhauer, 2016, p. A10). How do you feel about drafting women into the military?

One factor that influences evaluation of job applicants is the gender dominance of the occupations, with neither sex favored for female-dominated jobs but males favored for male-dominated jobs (Koch et al., 2015). Moreover, gender discrimination in hiring is most likely to occur when little information is provided about the candidate's qualifications. In this case, the applicant's gender is highly salient and can give rise to stereotyped impressions and decisions. However, when the applicant's academic and employment records are presented, these materials strongly influence the evaluator's impressions, especially for highly competent candidates (Reuben et al., 2014).

Discrimination also operates after the point of hiring. Recently settled and ongoing lawsuits against major corporations and brokerage firms including Wal-Mart, Morgan Stanley, Merrill Lynch, Boeing, Sterling Jewelers, and Novartis reveal major sex and ethnic inequities in pay and promotion (AAUW, 2016; Antilla, 2014; Rhode et al., 2014; Rivers & Barnett, 2014). For example, brokerage firms have been found to take away women's clients and commissions, give them pay cuts and demotions following maternity leave, and assign lucrative accounts to male cronies (Anderson, 2007). A more subtle form of discrimination is **patronizing behavior**, in which *supervisors give subordinates considerable praise while withholding valued resources such as raises and promotions*. Such behavior has a more negative effect on the performance of female workers than male workers (Catalyst, 2015; Fiske, 2010; Sue, 2010). A recent meta-analysis documenting the phenomenon of patronizing behavior found that women, compared to men, received slightly better performance evaluations, yet lower ratings on promotion potential (Roth et al., 2012). Another study found that White men received higher raises than women and ethnic minorities with the same performance evaluation scores doing the same job (Castilla, 2015). Another subtle form of discrimination is **managerial derailment** (Bono et al., 2016). When female and male managers show equal levels of poor interpersonal skills, supervisors evaluate the women more negatively and give them less mentoring.

Gender discrimination is alive and well in higher education as well. For example, college students in online courses give better evaluations to instructors they think are men—even when the instructor is actually a woman (MacNell et al., 2014). Students also are much more likely to evaluate male faculty as "brilliant" or "genius" whereas female faculty are more often viewed as "bossy" or "annoying" (Storage et al., 2016). Among faculty with children, women are less likely than men to be granted tenure (Catalyst, 2015). In addition, the more prestigious the university, the fewer women it has on the faculty and in tenured positions (Clauset et al., 2015). Those women who do get hired at major research universities often experience discrimination. For example, studies at the Massachusetts Institute of Technology (MIT), a top science and engineering university, found that women were disadvantaged not only in promotions and salary but also in research grants, appointments to important committees, types of teaching assignments, and even in the size of their research laboratories. As discussed in Chapter 9, these "micro-inequities," or microaggressions, are subtle forms of marginalization that accumulate over time to create an unfair and hostile environment for women (Corbett & Hill, 2015; E. Pollack, 2015). MIT responded by instituting several steps to improve the status of women faculty. By 2011, the number of women in science and engineering had doubled, pay and other resources were more equitably distributed, and more women were serving in senior leadership positions, including MIT's first woman president. The downside has been a growing perception on campus that correcting earlier biases has meant hiring less qualified women. In addition, letters of recommendation for tenure written for male faculty focus on their intellect, whereas those written for women emphasize their temperament (MIT, 2011). It is not surprising, perhaps, that women are more likely than men to leave academe, a phenomenon referred to as the "leaky pipeline" (Hormes, 2016).

Experiences of gender discrimination at work are related to more negative relationships with supervisors, and coworkers, along with lower levels of organizational commitment and job satisfaction (Bernstein & Russo, 2008; Settles et al., 2013). For women, perceiving and experiencing discrimination are associated with negative psychological symptoms, such as increased anxiety and depression, and lowered self-esteem. Among men, however, the perception and experience of discrimination are unrelated to well-being (Combs & Milosevic, 2016; Schmitt et al., 2002).

Let's now look at three factors that help explain why women experience discrimination in the workplace: stereotypes, ingroup favoritism, and perceived threat.

STEREOTYPES.   One important factor is the operation of gender stereotypes. The successful manager is seen as having male gender-stereotypic traits, such as ambition, decisiveness, self-reliance, ability to handle stress, and strong commitment to the work role. This "think manager–think male" mindset leads to the conclusion that a woman is less qualified (Cuadrado et al., 2015; Eagly et al., 2014; Hoobler et al., 2014). Across a wide variety of settings, women are presumed to be less competent than men and less motivated to hold leadership positions (Berkery et al., 2013; Hoobler et al., 2014; Richardsen et al., 2016). Reviews of studies in the United States, Europe, and Asia reveal that individuals in these nations, especially men, perceive men to be more qualified managers (Punnett, 2016; Tati et al., 2012). When female managers do succeed, their success is devalued or is attributed to external factors rather than to the woman's competence. They are often viewed as violating gender stereotypes that require women to be communal. As a consequence, people, especially males, often dislike and dismiss the contributions of highly competent women who speak and act decisively and assertively (Chin, 2016; Eagly, 2013b; Elsesser, 2015; Newton-Small, 2016; Williams & Tiedens, 2016). In one study of highly achieving women and men with overall positive performance evaluations, the reviews of women included less constructive and more personal criticism. The word "abrasive" was used 17 times to describe 13 different women, but never appeared in men's reviews (Snyder, 2014). In another study of women in leadership positions in the technology industry, 84 percent had been told they were "too aggressive" (Vassallo, 2015). Women are especially likely to be evaluated negatively when they adopt less pleasant aspects of masculine style of leadership, that is, an autocratic, angry, punitive, nonparticipative approach (Rhode et al., 2014; Salerno & Peter-Hagene, 2015). In the words of a male corporate vice president, "With a male executive there's no expectation to be nice. He has more permission to be an ass. But when women speak their minds, they're seen as harsh" (Banerjee, 2001). In order to be influential, women therefore must combine agentic qualities such as competence and directness with communal qualities such as friendliness and warmth but not emotionality (Eagly et al., 2014; Smith et al., 2016; Williams & Dempsey, 2014).

Racial stereotypes also include attributes that are viewed as not conducive to leadership. For example, Blacks are stereotyped as antagonistic, Latinos/as as unambitious, and Asian Americans as unassertive (Eagly & Chin, 2010). These stereotypes constitute an additional barrier confronting ethnic minority women who aspire to leadership roles.

Unfavorable gender stereotypes of women are most likely to operate when the evaluators are men (Basow, 2013; Koch et al., 2015). Given that more than half of all managers and administrators are men and that men dominate higher-level management and professional positions, many female workers are evaluated by men and, therefore, face the possibility of similar stereotype-based judgments and decisions. Negative gender stereotypes also are more likely to operate when women perform in a male domain. In such settings, women are less likely than men to be selected as leaders, be promoted, receive positive evaluations for their leadership, or be liked (Bohnet, 2016; Eagly et al., 2014; Paustian-Underdahl et al., 2014; Settles et al., 2013). Even a small mistake can be damaging to their status (Elsesser, 2015). You may have heard the saying that women or ethnic minorities must be "twice as good" as men or White individuals to receive the same level of respect or status. (Interestingly, a biography of Condoleeza Rice, the first Black female U.S. secretary of state, has this exact title [Mabry, 2007].) This concept that *standards are higher for groups stereotyped as less competent, known as the* **shifting standards hypothesis**, has in fact been supported in a series of studies by Monica Biernat and her colleagues (Fuegen & Biernat, 2013).

The operation of negative stereotyping when women work in male-related jobs or use masculine styles is clearly illustrated by the experience of Ann Hopkins (see Chapter 2). Hopkins, a high-performing manager, was denied promotion to partner because her employers claimed she was not sufficiently feminine. Apparently Ann Hopkins was punished for her masculine style in a male-dominated field (Scheiber, 2015). Recent studies of women and men working in the fields of science, engineering, and technology portray a pervasive macho culture where women are outsiders (Herman et al., 2013; Hewlett et al., 2008). The study reported that the culture within these fields is at best unsupportive and at worst hostile to women. The statistics in the report by Sylvia Hewlett and her colleagues paint a grim picture: Nearly two-thirds of the women said they experienced sexual harassment on the job; over half said that in order to succeed, they had to "act like a man"; half of the women engineers lacked a mentor; and 40 percent of technology workers said they needed to be available 24/7, hours that put greater strain on working mothers than on working fathers. Given such a culture, it is not surprising that by age 40, half of the women respondents had left science, engineering, and technology for other fields, a rate twice that of their male colleagues.

INGROUP FAVORITISM.   Ingroup favoritism (i.e., liking those who resemble us) can reinforce biases that stem from cultural stereotypes (Dworkin et al., 2015; Holgersson, 2013; van den Brink & Stobbe, 2014). Differences between White male managers and females or people of color can create tension that managers attempt to avoid. In one study, nearly two in three senior men said they were hesitant to initiate one-on-one contact with promising women employees. Women of color are especially likely to experience exclusion. Nearly half of Black women, compared to one-third of White women, report a lack of senior-level support in advancing their careers (Rhode, 2016). Ingroup favoritism also emerges in allocating work and client development opportunities. One survey of recent business school graduates, for example, found that men were given assignments with greater responsibility, budgets, and visibility than were comparable women (Rhode, 2016).

PERCEIVED THREAT.   A third factor influencing discrimination in the workplace is the perception of threat. Some White male managers view the career progression of women or people of color as a direct threat to their own advancement (Metz & Kulik, 2014). In one study, male managers were more likely to perceive women as a threat when their department contained more female managers (Beaton et al., 1996). As you might expect, women view women's gains in power more positively than men do (Kehn & Ruthig, 2013). Similarly, current progress toward gender equality seems more substantial to men than to women (Eibach & Ehrlinger, 2010). Not surprisingly, groups that are disadvantaged by the present hierarchy are more likely to approve of social change and also view such change as occurring more slowly (Anderson, 2014).

What do all of the barriers against the advancement of women have in common? Consistent with one of the major themes of this book, these obstacles are clear reflections of power differences in the workplace. Men have higher status and more resources; that is, they have higher organizational power. Although there has been progress in recent years, men continue to have the ability to control opportunities and decisions that have major impact on women (Richardsen et al., 2016; Stainback et al., 2016). On the positive side, however, as more and more women and people of color enter higher-status occupations and gradually advance within these fields, they will acquire greater organizational resources, thus contributing to a reduction in this power inequality. In addition, exposure to female leaders helps to reduce bias. Just as we saw with respect to the hiring process, bias is greatest when individuals think abstractly about women leaders, but is minimized in evaluations of actual women leaders (Elsesser, 2015).

Women as Leaders

Women share their power more; men guard their power (Michael Genovese, Institute for Leadership Studies, Loyola Marymount University, in Miller, 2016b, p. 11).

We have seen that women face more barriers to becoming leaders than men do, especially in male-dominated fields (Carli & Eagly, 2011). How do women and men actually behave once they attain these positions? In other words, what are their leadership styles? And are women and men equally effective as leaders?

(Alice Eagly et al., 2014) has identified three types of leadership styles: **transformational**, **transactional**, and **laissez-faire**. Transformational leaders *set high standards and serve as role models by mentoring and empowering their subordinates.* They focus on the success of the group and the organization's. Transactional leaders *clarify workers' responsibilities, monitor their work, reward them for meeting objectives, and correct their mistakes.* They focus on the individual power of the leader. Laissez-faire leaders *take little responsibility for managing.*

Studies indicate that women are more transformational and that men are more transactional (Basow, 2013; Eagly, 2013b). Male managers are less likely than female managers to reward good performance and are more likely to pay attention to workers' mistakes, wait until problems become severe before attending to them, and be absent and uninvolved in critical times.

Recent research shows that women's more transformational style and greater use of rewards for good performance are linked to higher ratings of leadership effectiveness (De Mascia, 2015). For example, a five-year study of the leadership skills of over 2,400 female and male managers found that female managers were rated significantly better than their male counterparts by their supervisors, themselves, and the people who worked for them (Pfaff et al., 2013). These differences extended both to the communal skills of communication, feedback, and empowerment and to agentic skills such as decisiveness, planning, and setting standards. Moreover, work teams with more women outperform teams with more men (Woolley et al., 2015) and companies with more women board directors have better performance than those with the fewest women (Catalyst, 2013). In certain organizations highly dominated by men, such as the military, however, male leaders still tend to be perceived as more effective. And interestingly, across all types of organizations, men rate themselves as more effective leaders than women rate themselves (Paustian-Underdahl et al., 2014). How might this finding be related to the research on achievement self-confidence of women and men that we examined in Chapter 9?

GENDER DIFFERENCES IN SALARIES

Women, want to earn more than men? Here's how: Be an office clerk, data entry keyer, baker, or a wholesale and retail buyer (except farm products)! . . . Otherwise, forget it.

This clearly fictitious job ad is based on real data released recently by the Bureau of Labor Statistics on the salaries of hundreds of jobs (Institute for Women's Policy Research, 2016a). In the jobs mentioned here, women earned slightly more than men, on average. In all other occupations, women earned less.

In this section, we look at the gender gap in salaries and explore reasons for this difference.

Comparative Salaries

Although the earnings gap between women and men in the United States has declined over the last few decades, in 2015, women still earned only 80 cents for each dollar men earned (AAUW, 2017). Similar gender gaps in salary exist worldwide. In the United States, men who worked full time in 2014 earned a median annual salary of $50,383 compared with $39,521 for women (Institute for Women's Policy Research, 2016a). Full-time employed women of color fare even more poorly than White women, except for Asian American women who earn 90 percent of what White men earn, compared to 78 percent for White women. Black women earn 61 percent of what White men earn, Native American Women earn 59 percent, and Latinas earn just 51 percent (Institute for Women's Policy Research, 2016a). Similarly, women with disabilities have lower earnings than either their male counterparts or able-bodied women (AAUW, 2016; Institute for Women's Policy

Research, 2016a). In addition, the gender gap in pay increases with age. In 2014, full-time women workers aged 65 and older earned 74 percent of the weekly salary of men in the same age group. Women aged 20 to 24, on the other hand, were paid 90 percent of the weekly wages of men of comparable age (AAUW, 2016; Bureau of Labor Statistics, 2015; Pew Research Center, 2013a). Why are older women's earnings depressed? For one thing, older women have spent less time in the labor force than younger women. Also, some started working when employers were free to discriminate in pay between women and men doing the same work. Even now, more than 50 years after the passage of the 1963 Federal Equal Pay Act, the legacy of once-legal salary discrimination remains.

In the typical two-parent family, women provide nearly 40 percent of their families' incomes, and low-income families are even more dependent upon women's earnings (Joint Economic Committee, 2016). Thus, the gender gap in wages has important implications for families. Not only is it detrimental to the financial well-being of many families, both two-parent and single-parent, but it also places more women than men at risk of poverty (Hartmann et al., 2014).

To get a more detailed picture of the gender gap, let's examine wage differentials within selected occupations. In 2012, the ratio of female-to-male-earnings was 70 percent for financial managers, 80 percent for lawyers, 79 percent for scientists, and 84 percent for computer programmers (Institute for Women's Policy Research, 2016a). Even in occupations that employ primarily women, women's salaries are lower than men's. In 2014, female nurses earned 90 percent as much as male nurses, and female high school teachers earned 88 percent of what male teachers earned (Institute for Women's Policy Research, 2016a).

The cumulative effect of the gender pay gap is far from trivial. For the average college-educated woman born in the late 1950s, the wage gap translated into nearly $800,000 by the time she reached age 59 (Joint Economic Committee, 2016). For poor, single mothers, the earnings gap poses additional problems. Many employed unmarried women do not earn enough to support their families (AAUW, 2017). Analyses indicate that if single mothers were paid the same as men with comparable education and work hours, the poverty rate for their families would be reduced substantially (Joint Economic Committee, 2016). Not surprisingly, most studies show that women believe their salaries are not commensurate with the value of their work or their abilities and experience. Regardless of their age, ethnicity, occupation, or income, nine out of ten say that equal pay for equal work is a priority (AAUW, 2011).

Reasons for Differences in Salaries

Several factors have been offered as explanations of the pay differential. In considering these reasons, keep in mind the societal power differential in the workplace.

GENDER DIFFERENCES IN INVESTMENTS IN THE JOB.   According to the **human capital perspective**, *salaries reflect investments of human capital (e.g., education and work experience). Because of their family responsibilities, women, relative to men, reduce their investment in their education and jobs and so are paid less* (Blau & Kahn, 2016). Does the evidence support this viewpoint?

Let's look first at the influence of education. If educational differences could explain salary differences, females and males with comparable levels of education should earn similar wages. The reality is that at every level of educational attainment, from high school to master's degree, Asian, Black, Latina, and White women earn less than men in the same ethnic group (Bureau of Labor Statistics, 2013b). It is disheartening that male high school graduates earn more than women with an associate's degree and that the average salary of women with a college degree is $16,000 less than that of male college graduates (AAUW, 2017).

What about investment of time on the job? Women spend an average of 35.6 hours per week at work compared to men's 40.6 hours (Bureau of Labor Statistics, 2013b), and time at work does play some role in the wage gap (Rhode et al., 2014). Another indicator of time investment is the interruption of employment. Because of their childbearing, childrearing, and eldercare responsibilities, women are more likely than men to temporarily leave employment (Blau & Kahn, 2016; Evers & Sieverding, 2014). However, employment interruptions are becoming less common because there is a greater dependence on two incomes, thus shortening parental leaves, and also because women are having fewer children. Currently, nearly six in ten American women return to work within one year of giving birth to their first child. In addition, professional and managerial occupations increasingly expect workers to be continuously available and to work long hours (a concept called "overwork"). Men are more likely than women to hold such jobs (thus working more hours), perhaps reflecting cultural pressures on women to be the primary caregivers (Cha & Weeden, 2014).

So, do differences in investment help explain pay differences? Studies have found that human capital factors such as differences in educational background and time commitment explain only a portion of the gender wage gap (Lips, 2013; Tharenou, 2013). Let's look at other possible factors.

OCCUPATIONAL SEGREGATION. A major factor contributing to both gender and ethnic differences in pay is the difference in jobs held by women and men and by individuals in different ethnic groups (AAUW, 2017; Boushey, 2009; Hegewisch & Hartmann, 2014a). We saw earlier in this chapter that women and people of color are less likely than White men to attain higher-level, higher-paying positions. Women tend to be congregated in female-dominated occupations, and these occupations are at the low end of the salary scale. Moreover, the greater the number of women in an occupation, the lower the wages (Hegewisch & Hartmann, 2014). As an example, child care workers earn a lower hourly wage than janitors, car washers, or parking lot attendants (Bureau of Labor Statistics, 2013b). Two-thirds of minimum-wage workers in the U.S. are women, as are nearly 70 percent of tipped workers, whose federal minimum wage is only $2.13 an hour (O'Neill, 2015).

Why do occupations employing mostly women pay less than those employing mostly men? One answer is that women's occupations are devalued relative to men's (Rhode et al., 2014). In Chapter 3, we saw that people more highly value males and male-related attributes. In the workplace, this value difference gets translated into employers' higher evaluation of male-dominated jobs and job-related skills associated with men. For example, an Illinois job evaluation study found that registered nurses deserved higher pay than electricians, but in fact were paid $11,000 less per year. In California, although children's social workers (mostly women) were found to merit pay equal to that of probation officers (mostly men), they actually earned $20,000 less (Rhode et al., 2014).

SALARY NEGOTIATIONS. Another reason for the gender gap in salaries is that women are less likely than men to initiate salary negotiations and are more willing to accept whatever salary is offered by their employers (Bear & Babcock, 2012; Stuhlmacher & Linnabery, 2013; Lipman, 2015). For example, in Linda Babcock's survey of Carnegie Mellon graduates who had master's degrees, it found that only 7 percent of the women but 57 percent of the men had negotiated their salaries. Moreover, those who negotiated raised their salaries by an average of about $4,000 (Babcock & Laschever, 2008). By failing to negotiate for their starting salary, women can lose half a million dollars or more by the time they retire (Babcock & Laschever, 2008). Even when women do negotiate, a starting salary or a raise, men receive more than women do (Mazei et al., 2015).

Why are women less likely to bargain when setting their starting salaries or raises? When they do negotiate, why do they settle for less? One factor is that women are generally less comfortable than men with self-promotion. Starting in childhood, boys are encouraged to talk about their achievements, whereas girls are taught to be polite, compliant, and modest, and not to brag (Mazei et al., 2015; Smith & Huntoon, 2014). This makes some women feel that negotiating brands them as overly aggressive and pushy, thereby violating gender norms (Amanatullah & Tinsley, 2013; Bowles, 2013). Indeed, women who initiate salary negotiations are judged more harshly than men who do so (Stuhlmacher & Linnabery, 2013). In addition, women are more likely to believe that employers will notice and reward good performance without being asked (Fogg, 2003; Katz & Andronici, 2006). Another factor is that women often underestimate their worth whereas men may overestimate theirs (Hurst et al., 2016). For example, one study found that men typically applied for promotion if they met only 60 percent of the qualifications, whereas women typically applied only when they believed they met 100 percent of the qualifications (Kay & Shipman, 2014). Men's tendency to overestimate their value may be driven both by their higher self-confidence level, and a sense of entitlement that is culturally supported (Lips, 2016). (Remember the concept of male hegemony that we discussed in Chapter 1?) For tips on negotiating your salary, see What You Can Do 10.1.

WHAT **YOU** CAN DO 10.1
Effectively Negotiate Your Salary

1. Find out salary information for comparable jobs by using Websites, contacting professional associations, talking to colleagues, using your college's placement office.

2. Assess the value of your skills and work experience using the same resources mentioned in item 1.

3. During negotiations, indicate that salary is important to you.

4. Negotiate things other than salary: benefits, perks, job title, responsibilities, and so on.

5. Be persistent and willing to compromise. If the hiring individual says "no," don't simply accept this. Ask "How close can you come to my offer?"

6. Role-play salary negotiations with experienced colleagues, or job counselors at your college.

Sources: Babcock and Laschever (2008); Rapley (2016).

WAGE DISCRIMINATION.   One key factor in the gender gap in salaries is **wage discrimination**, *differential payment for work that has equal or substantially similar value to the employer* (Goldin, 2014). Unequal pay scales were once considered justifiable by employers on the basis that women work only for "extras" or "pocket money" or that women can function with less money than men can (Paludi, Martin, Paludi et al., 2010). Since passage of the 1963 Federal Equal Pay Act, however, unequal pay for equal work has been illegal. Nevertheless, because wage discrimination laws are poorly enforced, equal pay legislation has not guaranteed equality (AAUW, 2017). It should not be surprising, therefore, that thousands of women have filed discrimination claims (Rhode et al., 2014), and settlements have been made for women employed in a range of occupations. Still, only a small fraction of individuals who have experienced unfair treatment take legal action. Reasons for not pursuing such actions include costly legal fees, low probability of winning, and concerns about reputation and blacklisting (Rhode et al., 2014).

Another troubling finding is that *women with children earn significantly less than childless women, even when they have comparable education, work experience, and job characteristics.* This phenomenon, known as the **motherhood wage penalty** or maternal wall, is a 4–10 percent reduction in salary per child in the United States and much of Europe (AAUW, 2017; Budig et al., 2016; Joint Economic Committee, 2016; Kahn et al., 2014). This motherhood penalty is even larger among low-paid women workers (Lips, 2016). In contrast, men with children enjoy a **fatherhood wage premium**, *earning more than men without children* (Budig, 2014; Bullock, 2013; Kenschaft & Clark, 2016). What can account for the motherhood penalty? One possibility is that mothers may be less productive on the job than nonmothers because the latter can spend more of their nonemployment time in refreshing leisure, rather than in exhausting housework and child care. Alternatively, employers may discriminate against mothers in terms of job placement, promotion, or pay levels within jobs (Budig, 2014; Tutchell & Edmonds, 2015). In support of this view, even outstanding employees who are mothers are perceived as less professionally competent than those who have no children (Lips, 2016). They are also viewed as less competent, less committed, and less available for work than employed fathers and are held to higher performance and punctuality standards (Dworkin et al., 2015; Rivers & Barnett, 2013; Williams et al., 2016). Once again, as we saw in Chapter 2, social roles influence gender stereotypes.

We now look at the wages and working conditions for women in developing nations.

Girls and Women in the Global Factory

What are wages and working conditions like for women in developing nations?

The fact that women's work worldwide is frequently unpaid or underpaid is closely linked to women's lower power and status (Spade & Valentine, 2016). In many developing countries in Africa, Central America, and Asia, thousands of women and girls as young as 8 work for low wages

GET INVOLVED 10.1
Gender-Based Treatment in the Workplace

Interview two employed women. If possible, select full-time employees, but if they are not available, include any working women, including students with part-time jobs. Ask each respondent to discuss her experiences with the following: (1) discrimination in salary, (2) discrimination in promotion, (3) gender stereotyping by coworkers or supervisors, and (4) any other types of gender-based unfair treatment.

WHAT DOES IT MEAN?

1. Compare the reported experiences of your respondents with the information reported in the chapter. Describe both the differences and similarities between your findings and the material presented in the text. Give possible reasons for the differences, if any.

2. What kinds of changes do you think could be instituted so that the specific problems your respondents identified would be eliminated or greatly reduced?

15 or more hours a day, every day, in **sweatshops**—*businesses that violate safety, wage, and child labor laws* (Burn, 2011; Kristof & WuDunn, 2009). Health problems are common in these factories due to harsh working conditions such as poor ventilation, exposure to chemicals, and repetitive motion. Most of the clothes, shoes, toys, and electronics purchased by North Americans were likely manufactured by women working in sweatshops in nations such as Bangladesh, Burma, China, the Dominican Republic, Haiti, Honduras, Indonesia, Guatemala, Malaysia, Mexico, Nicaragua, the Philippines, and Vietnam (Burn, 2011; Lorber, 2010). In El Salvador, for example, the young female workers are paid an average of 94 cents for each $165 jacket that they sew for North Face (Burn, 2011). In addition, thousands of women and girls are trafficked from poor countries to wealthy ones, where they are forced to work against their will in factories, in restaurants, on farms, and in people's homes (Peters, 2015; Trask, 2014). These women laborers seldom question their working conditions, having grown up in male-dominated households where they have learned to be subservient and dutiful (Freeman, 2010). In addition, they are often unaware of their rights and afraid of losing their jobs if they assert themselves (Henderson & Jeydel, 2010; Motlagh & Taylor, 2013). The efforts of the International Labour Organization, along with women's increasing union membership and the work of women activists around the world, have produced some progress in passing laws to improve women's work conditions, producing greater implementation of these laws, and educating women about their rights (Burn, 2011).

Now that you are familiar with some of the problems experienced by women in the workplace, perform the interviews in Get Involved 10.1 to gain firsthand knowledge about women's experiences with wage or promotion discrimination, and with other forms of gender-biased treatment.

WOMEN'S JOB SATISFACTION

Earlier in this chapter, we saw that women and men congregate in different jobs and that the most prestigious occupations employ more men than women. We also noted that women's job levels and salaries are generally lower than men's. Do these gender differences in occupational dimensions correspond to differences in job satisfaction?

Gender Differences in Satisfaction

Research generally finds either no gender differences in overall job satisfaction or higher satisfaction in women (van der Heijden et al., 2013; Zou, 2015). *Situations in which women are as satisfied as men with their jobs despite having lower pay and status* have been labeled the **paradox of the contented female worker** (Zou, 2015). In such cases, women may be comparing themselves to other

Many of the clothes, shoes, toys, and electronics purchased by North Americans are manufactured by women working in Asian or Latin American sweatshops.

women rather than to men, which is more likely to occur in a female-dominated work setting. They also may either deny that they are being treated unfairly or justify their unequal pay (Lips, 2016). The fact that women are often as satisfied as men suggests that many extrinsic factors such as job and salary level contribute to their overall job satisfaction. Indeed, women are more likely than men to value intrinsic and interpersonal rewards such as social support from peers and supervisors (Kulik et al., 2016; Kuther, 2017; Zou, 2015). Ellen Auster (2001) and Wendy Campione (2008) have identified a number of other factors that are associated with women's midcareer satisfaction:

1. Having children, which seems to serve as a counterbalance to work pressures (see Chapter 11);
2. For ethnic minority women, developing a broad social network that crosses racial/ethnic boundaries;
3. Having employment gaps (e.g., parental leave) that are voluntary and supported by the organization;
4. Using flexible options, such as job sharing and flextime (see Chapter 11);
5. Having mentors in one's career;
6. Networking (i.e., developing relationships that have the potential to assist in one's career);
7. Having balanced proportions of women and men within one's work unit;
8. Experiencing lower levels of sex bias and discrimination;
9. Having family-friendly organizational policies such as parental leave, day care, and fitness activities (see Chapter 11);
10. Having opportunities for autonomy, creativity, training, development, and advancement within the context of job security;
11. Having lower stress levels;
12. Having a recent meaningful promotion;
13. Being in a supervisory capacity.

Job Satisfaction of Sexual Minorities

Increasing numbers of organizations and nearly half of states in the U.S. have adopted antidiscrimination policies that include sexual orientation (Colgan & Rumens, 2015; Scheiber, 2015). Unfortunately, many lesbian, gay, bisexual, and transgender employees continue to experience workplace discrimination based on their sexual orientation. Such discrimination is related to lower levels of job satisfaction and organizational commitment and higher levels of psychological distress, absenteeism, and job turnover (Brenner et al., 2010; Fassinger et al., 2010). Thus, the decision of whether or not to come out is a major concern for sexual minority workers, who fear that sexual identity disclosure might precipitate workplace discrimination (Colgan & Rumens, 2015; Goldberg, 2017). In one survey, 90 percent of transgender individuals said they faced harassment, mistreatment, or discrimination on the job. The worst off were Black and Latina trans women, particularly those lacking the financial means to alter their physical appearance as much as they would like ("The Struggle," 2015). Sexual minority women of color experience an extra burden because they risk adding homophobia to the gender or ethnic prejudice which they might already experience Sadly, sexual minority employees have been fired or passed over for promotion because of their sexual identity (Eckholm, 2015), and it is legal to do so in much of the United States (Institute for Women's Policy Research, 2015; Meyer, 2016; Woodruff-Burton, 2016). Given the possible risks of coming out in the workplace, it is not surprising that lesbian and gay employees are less likely to disclose their sexual orientation in workplaces in which they have observed or experienced discrimination related to sexual orientation (Chung et al., 2012; Mohr & Fassinger, 2012).

THE OLDER WOMAN WORKER

After Helen Martinez's children were grown, she worked as an executive secretary with a large corporation for several years. Helen decided to retire when her husband did. When he died eight years later, Helen found that her Social Security benefits and the income from her pension were barely enough to support her. At the age of 70, she went back to work half-time for her old firm. Now 79, she does not plan to retire again unless forced to by poor health.

Brenda Milner, at age 93, has been a dedicated neuroscientist for more than 60 years. Her many accomplishments include her groundbreaking research on the localization of memory in the brain. Milner, a professor at McGill University's Montreal Neurological Institute, continues to work five days a week teaching medical students and doing research on brain activity.

("Milner Awarded," 2014)

Helen Martinez is typical of many women workers who enter or reenter the labor force in later life. Brenda Milner, on the other hand, represents older women workers who have been employed continuously throughout their adult lives. In this section, we examine the varying experiences of older women workers.

Employment Rates

Labor force participation of middle-aged and older women has increased sharply over the past 50 years (Brown et al., 2016). Over two-thirds of women aged 55 to 61 are now in the labor force. Between the ages of 65 and 89, one woman in four is employed. During the same 50-year period, by contrast, men have been retiring earlier. By 2011, only 75 percent of 55-to-61-year-old men were in the workforce, compared to 90 percent in 1963. Similarly, the participation rate of men aged 65 and over dropped from 43 to 37 percent (Federal Interagency Forum, 2016). As a consequence of these changes, which hold across all ethnic groups, the proportion of paid women workers aged 55 and over is higher than ever before (Women's Bureau, 2013).

Why Do Older Women Work?

Older women work for most of the same reasons as younger women. Economic necessity is a key factor at all ages. Some women want to make up for opportunities missed when they were raising children. Others desire to remain in career positions they worked hard to attain (Denmark et al., 2015). In fact, a recent Pew Research Center survey found that among middle-aged and older workers, women and men were equally likely to rate career success as an important outcome for them. This marked a shift from 15 years earlier, when more men than women endorsed this outcome (Lips, 2016). In addition, feeling challenged and productive and meeting new coworkers and friends give women a sense of personal satisfaction and recognition outside the family (Etaugh, 2008; Span, 2016). Healthier, better educated women are more likely than other older women to work (Hartmann & Hayes, 2013; Humble & Price, 2017). In turn, active involvement in work and outside interests in women's later years appear to promote physical and psychological well-being. Work-centered women broaden their interests as they grow older and become more satisfied with their lives. Employed older women have higher morale than women retirees, whereas women who have never been employed outside the home have the lowest.

Entering the Workforce in Later Life

Many older women have been employed throughout adulthood. For some—working-class women, women of color, and single women—economic necessity has been the driving force. But for many women, a more typical pattern has been movement in and out of the labor force in response to changing family roles and responsibilities. Some women, for example, decide to reenter the labor force after their children are grown, or following divorce or the death of their spouses (Duberley et al., 2014; Etaugh, 2013a). The recent economic recession also has pulled older women in the employment either because their husbands have lost their jobs or because they are concerned about their retirement security (Etaugh, 2013a). The prospects of entering or reentering the labor force after 25 or 30 years may be daunting to some women who wonder if they have the skills to be hired. Older women should not overlook the wealth of relevant experience they have accumulated through their homemaking, childrearing, and volunteer activities.

Age Discrimination in the Workplace

Earlier in the chapter, we discussed gender discrimination in employment. As women get older, they, like men, also confront age discrimination in the workplace (Cohen, 2016; Holstein, 2015; Olen, 2014). The reasons for age discrimination and the age range during which it occurs differ for women and men. Women's complaints filed with the Equal Employment Opportunity Commission primarily concern hiring, promotion, wages, and fringe benefits. Men more often file on the basis of job termination and involuntary retirement (Etaugh, 2008).

Women also experience age discrimination at a younger age than men (Rife, 2001). This is another example of the double standard of aging discussed in Chapter 2. Women are seen as becoming older at an earlier age than men (Holstein, 2015). Society's emphasis on youthful sexual attractiveness for women and the stereotype of older women as powerless, weak, sick, helpless, and unproductive create obstacles for older women who are seeking employment or who wish to remain employed. In addition, age discrimination is associated with higher psychological distress and lower positive well-being, especially for women (Kuther, 2017).

CHANGING THE WORKPLACE

We have seen that women continue to be more heavily concentrated in lower-status occupations, to have limited opportunities for advancement, to earn lower salaries than men, and to be targets of biased behavior. What can be done to continue improvements in the work environment that have begun during the last few decades?

Organizational Procedures and Policies

PAY EQUITY. We have seen that equal pay legislation has not eliminated the gender or ethnicity wage gaps. As long as women and men or Whites and people of color are segregated in different occupations, it is legal to pay them different wages. One way of narrowing these earnings gaps is **pay equity**, *pay policies based on workers' worth and not their gender or ethnicity* (AAUW, 2011). Pay equity would require that employees in different jobs that are similar in skill, effort, and responsibility receive comparable wages.

AFFIRMATIVE ACTION.   Think of what affirmative action means to you. To what extent do you characterize affirmative action as a set of procedures that ensures equitable treatment of underrepresented individuals or, alternatively, as a policy that fosters preferential treatment and reverse discrimination? Affirmative action goals and procedures are highly misunderstood. Let's examine the legal conception of affirmative action as well as typical misconceptions of its meaning.

Affirmative action in employment refers to *positive steps taken by an employer that facilitate the recruitment and advancement of historically underrepresented workers in order to ensure equal opportunity for all* (Crosby et al., 2013). To achieve equity, these procedures involve weighing candidates' qualifications as well as group membership. Is this definition consistent with your conception of affirmative action?

Perceptions of affirmative action are often unfavorable (Crosby et al., 2013). Both women and men view the beneficiaries of affirmative action as less competent employees who are less entitled to their positions (Iyer, 2009). Thus, according to Jennifer Eberhardt and Susan Fiske (1998), men and women think that affirmative action results in reverse discrimination that hurts qualified White males in favor of unqualified women or people of color. Contrary to these misperceptions, Eberhardt and Fiske claim that the recruitment and promotion of unqualified individuals and the reliance on group membership only, without consideration of qualifications, are highly unusual and illegal practices. Furthermore, the U.S. Department of Labor (n.d.) reports that accusations of reverse discrimination comprised less than 2 percent of the 3,000 discrimination cases filed in federal courts between 1990 and 1994 and that few of these were upheld as legitimate claims.

Despite criticisms of its practices, affirmative action has played an important role in reducing gender inequity in the workplace (Crosby et al., 2013), and there is evidence that it has done so without negatively affecting performance, productivity, or company profits (Iyer, 2009). Its success in bringing more women into the workplace and increasing the gender similarity in occupations, job levels, and salaries is likely to result in even further reductions in gender imbalances in the future.

What kind of actions would be most effective in improving the workplace for women? The exercise in Get Involved 10.2 explores this issue.

OTHER ORGANIZATIONAL PROCEDURES.   Improvements for women and other underrepresented groups must also involve changes in the workplace itself. It is essential for employers to develop a work environment that values diversity and to back up this attitudinal climate with well-publicized antidiscrimination policies. Managers and other workers can be sensitized about both subtle and blatant forms of prejudice and discrimination in the work environment and can learn that the employer will not tolerate any form of discrimination. This can be accomplished through workshops aimed at increasing awareness of how stereotypes operate in evaluating and treating less powerful individuals, including women, people of color, sexual minorities, and people with disabilities (Rhode et al., 2014; Slaughter, 2015).

Another strategy is for organizations to identify employees with high potential, including women and people of color, and provide them with career development opportunities, such as specialized training, employer-sponsored networks, and job assignments that expand their experience and organizational visibility (Barnett & Rivers, 2013). Equally important is that senior management clearly communicate throughout the organization its firm commitment to a diverse workforce.

In order to facilitate reporting of complaints, organizations should also make use of clear, well-publicized procedures for filing and evaluating claims of discrimination. Organizations that enact such procedures and ensure that claims can be filed without fear of recrimination produce more favorable work environments for women (Rhode et al., 2014).

Strategies for Women

Although organizational efforts have more far-reaching effects, there are several actions that women can take as they either prepare themselves for employment or attempt to improve their own situation in the workplace (Barnett & Rivers, 2013; Verveer & Azzarelli, 2015). Women can benefit from workshops or work-related social networks that arm them with information that can help them better understand and fight against discriminatory practices in the workplace.

GET INVOLVED 10.2
Ways to Make the Workplace Better for Women

Following are six factors that can improve women's opportunities and experiences at work. Indicate how important you think each would be to making the workplace better for women in the future by rank ordering these from 1 to 6. Give 1 to the factor you think would be most beneficial to improving future conditions for women, give a 2 to the factor you consider would be next most helpful, and so on. Also, ask a woman who differs from you in ethnicity to do the same.

__1. Women's hard work

__2. Efforts of feminists to improve conditions for women

__3. Women's past contributions that demonstrate their value as workers

__4. Laws that make it less likely for employers to discriminate

__5. Greater number of women who know how to succeed in the workplace

__6. A workplace that is more responsive to women's needs

WHAT DOES IT MEAN?

Factors 1, 3, and 5 (set A) point to actions on the part of working women. Factors 2, 4, and 6 (set B) reflect adaptations resulting from political/social activism, legal mandates, and adaptations within the workplace. Determine the number of items in each set that you included among your top three items. Do the same for your other respondent.

Carol Konek and her colleagues asked a large number of career women to rank these influences and found that these women ranked the items in set A higher than those in set B. The researchers interpreted this as an emphasis on individualism, a belief that one's success is due to one's own efforts.

1. Did your answers match the responses of the study's respondents? If yes, was the reason the same? That is, do you value self-reliance and hard work more than external changes that provide increased opportunities?

2. Make the same comparison for your other respondent. Do her answers reflect an emphasis on individualism?

3. Did you notice any differences between the answers given by you and your other respondent? If yes, is it possible that these differences reflect a different emphasis on individualism versus collectivism?

Source: Based on Konek et al. (1994).

A useful strategy for women who experience discrimination is to join together with others who are experiencing similar inequities. Reporting a shared problem can, in some situations, receive both attention and a commitment to institutional change. Remember how a collective effort by women at MIT led to improvements in salary, research money, and laboratories.

RETIREMENT

Much of what is known about the effects of retirement is based on studies of men, despite the steady increase in women in the workplace over the past 70 years. This bias reflects the assumption that retirement is a less critical event for women than for men because of women's lesser participation in the labor force and their greater involvement in family roles. But nearly half of workers now are women, and retirement has equally important consequences for them (Bureau of Labor Statistics, 2013b; Price & Nesteruk, 2015). In this section, we examine factors that influence women's decision to retire, their adjustment to retirement, and their leisure pursuits in retirement. Conduct the interviews in Get Involved 10.3 to learn about the work and retirement experiences of individual older women.

The Retirement Decision

The decision to retire depends upon many factors including health, income, occupational characteristics, and marital and family situations (Wang & Shi, 2014). When men retire, they are leaving

GET INVOLVED 10.3
Interview With Older Women: Work and Retirement

Interview two women, aged 65 or older. It is helpful, but not essential, to know your interviewees fairly well. You may interview your mother, grandmothers, great-aunts, great-grandmothers, and so on. Keep a record of your interviewees' responses to the following questions. Compare and contrast the responses of the two women.

1. (If employed) How are things going in your job?

2. Have you reached most of the goals you set for yourself in your life?

3. When do you plan on retiring? (or when did you retire?)

4. What are some of the day-to-day activities that you look forward to after retirement (or that you've enjoyed since retirement)?

5. How will (did) retirement change you and your lifestyle?

6. How will you adjust (or how have you adjusted) to these changes?

7. In general, how would you describe your current financial situation?

8. What do you think of the Social Security system?

WHAT DOES IT MEAN?

1. How do the work and/or retirement experiences of these women compare with the experiences of older women reported in this book?

2. Are the financial situations of your respondents similar or different to those of older women described in the text? In what ways?

---

a role that has typically dominated their adult years. They are more likely than women to retire for involuntary reasons, such as mandatory retirement or poor health. Women, on the other hand, are more apt to retire for voluntary, family-related reasons, such as the retirement of one's husband or the ill health of a relative (Loretto & Vickerstaff, 2013; Szinosvacz, 2012; Wickrama & O'Neal, 2013).

Compared to men, women arrive at the threshold of retirement with a different work and family history, less planning for retirement, and fewer financial resources (Duberley et al., 2014). As noted earlier, women typically experience greater job discontinuity. They may have had fewer opportunities to obtain personal career goals and may therefore be more reluctant to retire. Given their more discontinuous employment history and their employment in lower-paid jobs, women are not as likely as men to be covered by pension plans, and their Social Security benefits are lower (Fischer & Hayes, 2013). Many older women workers with low salaries choose to continue to work as long as they can. These women may not be able to afford the luxury of retirement because of economic pressures, such as inadequate retirement income or sudden loss of a spouse (Duberley et al., 2014; Span, 2016). Unmarried women are more apt than married women to report plans for postponed retirement or plans not to retire at all (Szinovacz et al., 2012). A growing number of women continue to work after their husbands retire (Rosen, 2016).

In addition, women and men who have strong work identities have more negative attitudes toward retiring than those with weaker work identities (Frieze et al., 2011). Highly educated, professional women and those who are self-employed, who presumably have strong work identities, are less likely than other women to retire early (Wang & Shi, 2014). Martha Graham, for example, danced until age 76 and then kept choreographing for another 20 years. Georgia O'Keeffe continued to paint into her 90s (Springen & Siebert, 2005). Older professional women do not often make systematic plans for their retirement, nor do they wish to do so (Etaugh, 2017). Working-class women and men, on the other hand, are more likely to view retirement as a welcome relief from exhausting or boring labor, and desire to retire earlier than other workers (Solem et al., 2016; Shultz & Wang, 2011).

We have seen why some women may delay their retirement. Why do others retire early? Poor health is one of the major determinants of early retirement (Humble & Price, 2017;

Wang & Shi, 2014). Because aging Black women and men tend to be in poorer health than aging Whites, they are likely to retire earlier (Wang, 2012). Health is a more important factor in the retirement decision for men than for women, among both Blacks and Whites (Etaugh, 2008). This gender difference may result from the fact that, unlike married men, married women in poor health may withdraw early from the labor force or do not enter it in the first place. Early withdrawal or nonparticipation in the workforce is enabled by having a provider husband and by societal expectations that employment is optional for women.

Women's role as primary caregiver is another factor contributing to their early retirement. Women provide the majority of unpaid home care to frail older individuals (Duberley et al., 2014). Eldercare responsibilities often result in increased tardiness and absenteeism at work, as well as health problems for the caregiver. Because most businesses do not offer work flexibility to workers who care for older relatives, women caregivers reduce their hours or take time off without pay. Others are forced to retire earlier than planned (Etaugh, 2013a; Wang & Shi, 2014). Early retirement due to ill health or to providing care for others is associated with poorer mental health for both women and men (Vo et al., 2015).

Some women, of course, simply want to retire, whether to spend more time with a partner, grandchildren, or friends; to start one's own business; to pursue lifelong interests; or to develop new ones (Cohen, 2014; Loretto & Vickerstaff, 2013).

> *I haven't regretted retiring. I didn't quit my job through any dissatisfaction with the job or the people but I just felt that my life needed a change. I noticed that after working an eight-hour day I didn't have much steam left for a social life and fun. It's been pleasant spending these years doing what I want to do because I spent so many years accommodating myself to other people's needs and plans.*

> (a woman in her 70s, in Doress-Worters & Siegal, 1994, p. 183)

Adjustment to Retirement

Retirement has long been seen as an individual—primarily male—transition. But now, couples must increasingly deal with two retirements (Bernard, 2014) Phyllis Moen and her colleagues (2001) found that retirement generally was a happy time for couples. But the transition to retirement, defined as *the first two years after leaving a job*, often was a time of marital conflict. Wives and husbands who retired at the same time were happier than couples in which the spouses retired at different times. Marital conflict was highest when husbands retired first, perhaps because of discomfort with the role reversal of a working wife and a stay-at-home husband. Not only does the situation pose a potential threat to the husband's role as provider, but it can also lead to disagreements over the division of household chores (Szinovacz et al., 2012).

Although both genders typically adjust well to retirement, women may take longer to get adjusted (Etaugh, 2008). Newly retired women report lower morale and greater depression than newly retired men (Coursolle et al., 2010; Moen et al., 2001). Men seem to enjoy the freedom from work pressure when they retire whereas women appear to experience the retirement transition as a loss of roles. Because women are not under the same socially prescribed pressures to be employed as are men, those who *do* work, whether out of financial need or commitment to their job, may find it more difficult to stop working (Szinovacz, 1991).

For both men and women, a high level of life satisfaction in retirement is generally associated with having good health, adequate income, and active participation in leisure pursuits (Heo et al., 2014; Wang & Shi, 2014). Lower income and poorer health may account for the fact that Black retirees have lower levels of life satisfaction than White retirees (Kim & Moen, 2001). Marital status also contributes to retirement satisfaction. Married people have more positive retirement attitudes and higher retirement satisfaction than unmarried retirees (Wang et al., 2011). Retired women, particularly unmarried ones, are more involved with friends, family, organizations, and volunteer work than are retired men or lifelong homemakers (Etaugh, 2013a; McDonald & Mair, 2010).

For women who have never married, retirement can represent an especially significant transition. Although work assumes a greater importance in their lives than in the lives of never-married men and other women, most never-married women appear to be satisfied with retirement. Still, many pursue second careers after retirement, or continue to work part time (Etaugh, 2013a).

We shall see in Chapter 11 that multiple roles often have positive consequences for women who are employed. What is the effect of multiple role identities among older retired women? Pamela Adelmann (1993) compared Black and White women aged 60 and over who considered themselves retired only, homemakers only, or both. Women who called themselves both retired and homemakers had higher self-esteem and lower depression than women who identified with only one role, especially the homemaker role. Apparently, multiple-role identities continue to benefit women even after retirement.

Leisure Activities in Retirement

Leisure or free time in later life is a fairly recent social phenomenon. In 1900, the average work week was over 70 hours. Most adults died by their mid-40s, and worked until their death. Until the Social Security Act of 1935, retirement was not a reality for most Americans. The economic safety net provided by Social Security, along with increased life expectancy, has given older Americans the opportunity for retirement and, consequently, an increased amount of free time (Lemme, 2006; Shultz & Wang, 2011).

GENDER DIFFERENCES.   Women and men, regardless of age, vary in the nature of leisure activities they prefer. Older women are more likely than older men to participate in social activities, domestic crafts (e.g., baking, quilting), and reading. Older males are more likely to engage in outdoor activities (e.g. fishing, hunting) and spectator sports (Mock et al., 2012; Shaw et al., 2010). In retirement, women are more apt than men to integrate their spheres of leisure activities, bringing together their worlds of friends, home, and hobbies (Hanson & Wapner, 1994).

Much of the research on leisure activities for older people has focused on middle-class Whites and often has been studied from a male perspective. Little is known about the context and meanings of leisure for aging, usually poor, minority women. Katherine Allen and Victoria Chin-Sang interviewed 30 retired Black women. Work had largely dominated the lives of these women. Most of them had worked in domestic and service jobs. When asked how their experience of leisure had changed since retirement, most women replied that they had none in the past. The women considered leisure time in older age to be time to relax or to work with and for others. The church and the senior center provided important contexts for their leisure activities (Allen & Chin-Sang, 1990). A more recent study comparing older Latina and White women found similar patterns of leisure activity in the two groups, with the exception that Latinas used computers less and were more likely to be caregivers (Herrera et al., 2011).

FACTORS AFFECTING LEISURE ACTIVITY.   For look at the relationship between age and leisure activity, try the exercise in Get Involved 10.4.

Variables affecting leisure involvement include the amount of free time, transportation, information on and availability of leisure programs, and health status (Cavanaugh & Blanchard-Fields, 2015). Caring for ill family members, a responsibility usually assumed by women, can severely curtail the amount of available free time. Women may also be more affected than men by the lack of transportation services, lack of information about programs, and physical difficulties (Britain et al., 2011; Nilsson et al., 2015). Because those over 85 (a majority of them women) are the fastest growing segment of the population, greater emphasis will need to be given to providing leisure services for older people who are physically impaired (Leitner & Leitner, 2004).

VARIETIES OF LEISURE ACTIVITY.   There are many paths to fulfilling leisure activities for women in later life. Some older women devote themselves to pursuits that they had little time for in their younger years. Think of Grandma Moses, for example, who took up painting late in life and became

GET INVOLVED 10.4
Leisure Activities of Older and Young Women

1. Make three columns with the following headings:

Young Women's Current Activities	Older Women's Current Activities	Older Women's Past Activities

2. Briefly interview three young adult females about their current leisure activities. List the most common activities in the first column.

3. Briefly interview three women aged 65 or older about their current leisure activities and about their leisure activities when they were in their early 20s. List their most common current activities in the second column, and their most common leisure activities when they were young adults in the third column.

WHAT DOES IT MEAN?

1. How do the leisure activities of the older women compare with the leisure activities of older women reported in this book?

2. How similar are the current leisure activities of the older women to those when they were young women?

3. Are the leisure activities of the older women when they were young adults more similar to their current activities, or to the activities of the young adult females you interviewed? In what way?

4. Based on this exercise, would you predict that young women's leisure activities in later life would be more similar to their present activities or to those of today's older women? Explain your answer.

Source: Adapted from Leitner and Leitner (2012). Reprinted with permission from Haworth Press.

---

an internationally acclaimed artist. Then there are the increasing number of older adults who are taking college courses and participating in elderhostels and Lifelong Learning Institutes (Rohlinger & Gentile, 2015). Some older women join civic-minded social clubs, such as the Red Hat Society. Other older women and men do volunteer work in a wide variety of community settings: schools, hospitals, museums, churches, and service organizations, including the Peace Corps (Kulik, 2010; Price & Nesteruk, 2011). Devotion to volunteering remains strong well into old age (Cavanaugh & Blanchard-Fields, 2015; Moen & Flood, 2013). Volunteer service provides a number of benefits for the older people, including increased life satisfaction (Bowen et al., 2011; Charlesworth et al., 2016) and psychological well-being, and is associated with increased longevity (Rogers et al., 2016). In one study, for example, older African American women who volunteered as tutors in elementary schools showed improved physical activity, social interaction, and cognitive stimulation compared to a control group of nonvolunteers (Fried et al., 2004).

Whatever a woman's situation as she ages, there is usually some way in which she can serve as an **advocate**, *a person who plays an active role in making changes in her life, in the lives of others, and in society* (McHugh, 2012). For example, women can and do join and actively participate in any number of organizations that advocate for the rights of older persons or specifically for older women. AARP (formerly the American Association of Retired Persons), with over 24 million members, is a powerful advocacy group. The Gray Panthers, a smaller, more activist group, was founded by Maggie Kuhn following her forced retirement at age 65. The Older Women's League (OWL) focuses on social policies affecting midlife and older women (van Mens-Verhulst & Radtke, 2013). Another advocacy organization, the Raging Grannies, consists of groups of feisty older women who dress as "grannies" while altering the words of traditional songs to communicate political messages at organized protests (Sawchuk, 2009). Some older women have been political and social activists for most of their lives and do not let their age slow them down. For example, Doris "Granny D" Haddock walked across the United States when she was 90 to raise awareness of finance reform. In 2004, at age 93, she undertook a 15,000 mile road trip to encourage working women to vote (Bridges et al., 2003/2004). Then there are sisters Carrie and Mary Dann, elders of the western Shoshone nation, who, well into their 70s, continued their 30-year fight to keep the U.S. government from seizing tribal lands (Bridges et al., 2003/2004).

Becoming an activist can transform the life of an older woman. Take the case of Rosemary Bizzell, a widow and grandmother of eight. Prior to joining OWL, she had never been involved in community affairs. Within three years, she had risen to prominence in the city council and in state government. In her words,

> My self-image as an older woman has improved tremendously in spite of much rejection in job hunting. Apparently I was supposed to count my blessings and not expect to advance. Well, becoming involved in OWL has certainly challenged me. I cannot thank the OWL enough for opening up a whole new world for older women. I am proud of the opportunity to be part of it.
>
> (Doress-Worters & Siegal, 1994, p. 436)

ECONOMIC ISSUES IN LATER LIFE

> After I've paid the rent, I pay the phone bill. . . . Then there's my health. My doctor refused Medicaid—after 15 years—and now I have to pay him $27 out of every check. Then it takes $2.50 to do the laundry—you've got to keep your linens clean. I try to buy the cheapest things. I always make my own milk from powder. I only buy bread and chicken, and those no-name paper articles, but it still adds up. If I need clothes, I go across the street to the thrift shop. I watch for yard sales—if you see something for half a buck, there's a Christmas present. . . . But the last two weeks of the month are always hard. You just can't make it. I'm down to my last $10, and I've got more than two weeks to go.
>
> (a woman in her 70s, cited in Doress-Worters & Siegal, 1994, pp. 191–192)

At every age, women are more likely to live in poverty than men, and poverty rates are higher for ethnic minority women than for their White counterparts (National Women's Law Center, 2016). But financial insecurity can be an even greater problem for older women, who are nearly twice as likely as older men to live in poverty (Bisom-Rapp & Sargeant, 2016; Kincel, 2014). In this section, we examine reasons for the precarious financial condition of many older women. We then turn to actions that young women can take to ensure a more secure financial future when they retire.

Poverty

What factors account for the relatively high poverty rates of older women? Their lower lifetime earnings and reduced time in the labor force adversely affect eligibility and benefits from Social Security and pensions (DeNavas-Walt et al., 2013; Lips, 2016). Women are also less likely to have accumulated income from savings and investments. The net result is that the income gap between women and men increases in retirement. U.S. women aged 65 and older have an average income of only a little more than half that of men the same age and are 80 percent more likely to be poor (Joint Economic Commttee, 2016).

Another factor associated with poverty is marital status (Bullock, 2013). Nearly 20 percent of single older women in the United States who live alone live in poverty and are poorer than their counterparts in other industrialized nations (Fleck, 2007; Hayes et al., 2010). Women who are widowed or divorced are worse off financially than other older women (Bisom-Rapp & Sargeant, 2016; Brown et al., 2016). Among married women, only 5 percent are below the poverty line (Institute for Women's Policy Research, 2015). But a married woman is just a heartbeat away from widowhood. The income from a husband's pension is usually reduced considerably or eliminated when he dies, greatly increasing his widow's risk of plunging into poverty. Because women usually marry older men and outlive them, there is a high likelihood that they will live alone on a meager income as they grow older. The costs of a husband's illness and burial may seriously deplete the couple's savings, leaving the widow in a precarious economic state (Canetto, 2003). The longer an older woman lives, the further her assets must stretch. This situation helps explain why the very oldest women have the highest poverty rates (Holstein, 2015; Society of Actuaries, 2010). Figure 10.1 illustrates older women are more likely to be poor than older men across ethnic groups (Seltzer & Yahirun, 2013).

For a closer look at the economic status of older women in other parts of the world, read.

Economic Status of Older Women Worldwide

In richer (i.e., developed) countries, older people can more easily afford to retire because of Social Security systems or pensions. In the United States, for example, only about one in four women aged 65 to 69 is in the labor force (Federal Interagency Forum, 2016). However, these retirement benefits are often inadequate for women because they penalize the female-dominated activities of homemaker, part-time employee, domestic worker, and agricultural worker. In several countries, even women who have worked for much of their adult lives receive smaller pensions than men. In one study, women's benefits as a proportion of men's were 64 percent in the United States, 77 percent in France and Switzerland, and 85 percent in Sweden. However, at least five developed countries provide equal benefits for women and men: Australia, New Zealand, Great Britain, Germany, and the Netherlands (Mercer et al., 2001).

In developing nations, the economic situation for older women is much starker than in developed countries. Social Security and pension plans are often nonexistent. Therefore, older women and men must continue working. In Rwanda, for example, nearly three-quarters of women between ages 65 and 69 remain economically active (Kinsella & Velkoff, 2001). The low status of women in developing countries can have devastating effects in later life. For example, in most of sub-Saharan Africa, women do not have land rights or property rights. A husband typically allocates his wife a plot of land to work on to produce food for the family. But if he dies, she no longer has the right to that land or even to the family's house. The land and house are taken over by the husband's family, and she often is evicted and left destitute (Gorney, 2017).

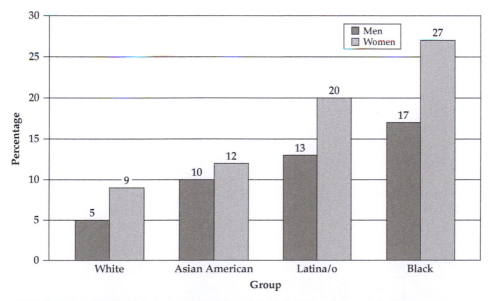

FIGURE 10.1 Percentage of Older Black, Latina/o, Asian American, Native American and White Women and Men Below the Poverty Level, 2015.
Source: National Women's Law Center (2016).

Retirement Income: Planning Ahead

Young women often find it hard to visualize their retirement years. However, information in this chapter makes it clear that women must take steps early in their adult life to make plans to improve their financial security in retirement. Until fairly recently, retirement planning and money management were often done by husbands (Wasik, 2017). As a result, many women of all ages have relatively little understanding of what retirement planning entails. It is never too early to start thinking about the issues involved. See What You Can Do 10.2 for guidelines on how to start planning for retirement *now*.

First, you need to know that a secure retirement is based on a three-legged stool consisting of Social Security, pension income, and savings and investments. As we have seen, all three are linked to a woman's lifetime earnings, work history, and marital status (Brown et al., 2016).

SOCIAL SECURITY.   Social Security benefits are the major source of income for most older women, especially those who are poor. Social Security provides nearly half of the income for unmarried women 65 years and older (Poterba, 2014) and keeps over two-thirds of unmarried older women from sinking into poverty. Almost 30 percent of all older women rely on Social Security as their *only* source of income (Fischer & Hayes, 2013). But heavy reliance on Social Security can be a financial nightmare. For example, the average Social Security benefit for retired women workers in 2014 was $13,824 a year, only slightly above the federal poverty threshold for older adults (Brown et al., 2016).

The Social Security system was designed to serve the typical family of the mid-1930s, which included a breadwinner father, a homemaker mother, and children. Most of today's families do not fit that mold because the majority of women are in the labor force. Women's different work patterns mean that they are disadvantaged by a Social Security system designed to reward male work histories that often include many uninterrupted years in relatively high-paying jobs (Brown et al., 2016).

Ethnic minority women, who tend to be concentrated in lower-paying jobs and to have higher unemployment rates, receive even lower benefits than White women (Fischer & Hayes, 2013). Because they are more likely than White women to be employed "off the books" where benefits do not accrue, their benefits are the lowest of all, whereas those of White men are the highest. Moreover, many women apply for their benefits early, at age 62, because they need the income. But doing so reduces their benefits (Holstein, 2015).

Spousal Benefits.   A lifelong homemaker has no Social Security protection in her own name. She is eligible to receive a spousal benefit equal to half of her husband's benefit if they have been

---

WHAT <u>YOU</u> CAN DO 10.2
Start Planning for Retirement

1. Establish your own savings and checking accounts.

2. Learn about your job benefits, such as health insurance, pension plan, and Social Security.

3. Minimize your credit card debt.

4. Set up an emergency fund worth three to six months' salary.

5. Learn about financial planning by taking a course or finding a financial advisor.

6. Consider setting up an IRA (individual retirement account).

7. Participate in employer-sponsored retirement plans, such as a 401(k).

8. Carry enough insurance to cover loss of life, health, home, and earning power.

9. Make a will.

10. Set up a **durable power of attorney**, *a document that authorizes someone to manage your financial affairs should you become incompetent.*

Sources: Collinson, 2015; MetLife (2010); Orman (2010).

married for at least 10 years. A divorced woman is also eligible to receive half of her ex-husband's benefit if they were married for at least 10 years. If she remarries, she forfeits her right to her former husband's benefit. A widow becomes eligible to receive a portion of her husband's benefit at age 60, but she must wait until age 65 for full benefits (Social Security Administration, 2016). Cohabiting couples receive no Social Security benefits as a family unit. Beginning in 2013, however, married same-sex couples now receive Social Security benefits (Center for Community Change and Older Women's Economic Security Task Force, 2013).

Dual Entitlement.   Married women who are wage earners have **dual entitlement** but are, in effect, penalized as well. *They qualify for Social Security benefits based on both their own and their husbands' work histories.* But they receive only the higher of the two benefits to which they are entitled. Most dually entitled women draw benefits based on their husbands' work records because the husbands' benefits are greater than theirs. These women would have been entitled to these benefits even if they had never worked a day in their lives! Thus, the Social Security contributions that married women make as workers seem unnecessary and unfair (Hartmann, 2014).

PENSION INCOME.   The second leg of the retirement stool—private pensions—can be an important source of income for women. Women are less likely than men to receive income from traditional pension plans, and if they do have pension income, it is smaller than men's (Joint Economic Committee, 2016). Ethnic minority and less educated women are less likely than White and better educated women to receive pension benefits (U.S. Department of Labor, 2015). Why are women less likely to have pension income? First, they are more likely to work at jobs that have little or no pension coverage, such as service jobs, non-union jobs, small businesses, and part-time or temporary work (Brown, 2016; WISER, 2015). Also, some do not meet the minimum time requirements required for eligibility because they more often move in and out of the workforce to care for children and other family members (Joint Economic Committee, 2016).

SAVINGS AND INVESTMENTS.   The third leg of the retirement stool is income from savings and investments. Today's older women have little income from savings, and their lower earnings leave them with few resources to invest (Brown et al., 2016).

Women who do invest generally are more cautious investors than men (Brown, 2016). They are more wary of risk (Carr & Steele, 2010), and so are more likely to invest in conservative options such as bonds, certificates of deposit, and money-market accounts that pay lower returns than stocks. Although women tend to take fewer risks in the stock market, they do as well as or better than men. Why? Women trade less, and those who trade less do better (Kristof, 2016).

Summary

WOMEN'S EMPLOYMENT RATES AND OCCUPATIONAL CHOICES

- More than 60 percent of women 16 years and older, including those who are married and have young children, are employed. Economic necessity is a major reason for women's employment.
- Although the last several decades have seen a decrease, gender and ethnic segregation in the workplace continue to be highly prevalent. The most prestigious occupations are dominated by White men.

GENDER DIFFERENCES IN LEADERSHIP AND JOB ADVANCEMENT

- Women and people of color are less likely than White males to attain high positions in their occupations.
- Barriers that hinder women's advancement include the glass ceiling, shorter job ladders, limited availability of mentors, exclusion from informal social networks, and discrimination.
- Discriminatory treatment is due, in part, to the operation of gender stereotypes, ingroup favoritism, and White males' perception of threat.

- Women are presumed to be less capable lead-ers than men. Males often express dislike for highly competent and agentic women.
- As leaders, women tend to be more transfor-mational and less transactional than men.

GENDER DIFFERENCES IN SALARIES

- Women earn 80 percent of what men earn. The gender discrepancy is even greater between women of color and White men. These income differences result from several factors, including gender differences in job investments, in occupations, in job levels, and in salary negotiation, as well as discrimination.
- Women generally believe their salaries are not commensurate with their work value, ability, and experience.
- In many developing countries, girls and women work in sweatshops for low wages.

WOMEN'S JOB SATISFACTION

- Women are as satisfied as or more satisfied than men with their jobs.
- One factor contributing to job satisfaction for sexual minorities is the organizational climate for lesbian, gay, bisexual, and transgender workers.

THE OLDER WOMAN WORKER

- Increased numbers of middle-aged and older women are in the labor force. Economic necessity is a key reason.
- Employment among older women promotes physical and psychological well-being.
- Women face age discrimination in the work-place at a younger age than men.

CHANGING THE WORKPLACE

- Organizational strategies that can improve the workplace for women and people of color include implementation of pay equity,

establishment of clearly defined affirmative action policies and procedures, and mainte-nance of an organizational environment char-acterized by sensitivity to diversity.

RETIREMENT

- Women's retirement decisions depend on many factors.
- Women earning low wages tend to delay retire-ment, as do professional and self-employed women. Older women with caregiving respon-sibilities tend to retire early.
- The decision to retire is influenced by indi-vidual, family, economic, and occupational factors.
- The transition to retirement is a time of marital conflict, especially when husbands retire first.
- Satisfaction in retirement is associated with hav-ing good health, adequate income, a high activ-ity level, and contact with friends and relatives.
- Older women and men differ in the nature of their preferred leisure activities.

ECONOMIC ISSUES IN LATER LIFE

- Older women, especially minorities, are more likely than older men to be poor or near-poor.
- The poverty rate is greater for very old women and for unmarried women.
- Because women, compared with men, spend less continuous time in the workforce, and are in more low-paying jobs, their eligibil-ity for and benefits from Social Security and pensions suffer. Women also have less income from savings and investments than do men.
- In developing nations, retirement benefits often do not exist, and many women must work in later life.
- Preretirement planning in young adulthood can improve women's financial security during later life.

Key Terms

What Do You Think?

1. What kinds of rewards, other than financial, are provided by employment? How does gender socialization affect the particular values women attach to work? Explain your answers.

2. Why do you think many people have negative impressions, including misconceptions, of affirmative action? Incorporate information about stereotypes, gender socialization, gender differences in power, and/or any other material related to this course.

3. This chapter discussed several procedures for improving the workplace for women and people of color. What other actions can be undertaken by employers or individuals in these groups to decrease gender and ethnicity inequities in the work environment?

4. How might greater gender equity in the workplace change the current social construction of gender?

Would this, in turn, influence the gender acquisition of gender-related traits, behaviors, roles, and/or career goals of future generations of females? Explain your answers.

5. Given the substantial influx of women into the labor force in the past several decades, the proportion of retired working women to lifelong homemakers will continue to increase among older women. What are the implications of this?

6. What can be done to help ease the "feminization of poverty"?

7. What are some implications of the older woman's greater economic insecurity?

8. What is meant by the statement that older minority women are in "triple jeopardy"? Provide and discuss examples.

If You Want to Learn More

Bennett, J. (2016). *Feminist fight club: An office survival manual (for a sexist workplace)*. New York: HarperCollins.

Bisom-Rapp, S. & Sargeant, M. (2016). *Lifetime disadvantage, discrimination and the gendered workforce*. Cambridge, UK: Cambridge University Press.

Brzezinski, M. (2012). *Knowing your value: Women, money, and getting what you're worth*. New York: Weinstein Publishing.

Bullock, H.E. (2013). *Women and poverty: Psychology, public policy, and social justice*. Chichester, UK: Wiley-Blackwell.

Chin, J.L. & Trimble, J.E. (2015). *Diversity and leadership*. Thousand Oaks, CA: Sage.

Colgan, F. & Rumens, N. (Eds.). (2015). *Sexual orientation at work: Contemporary issues and perspectives*. New York: Routledge.

Connerly, M.L. & Wu, J. (Eds.). (2015). *Handbook on well-being of working women*. New York: Springer.

Goodman, J. et al. (Eds.). (2013). *Global perspectives on gender and work: Readings and interpretations*. Lanham, MD: Rowman & Littlefield.

Karsten, M.F. (2016). *Gender, race, and ethnicity in the workplace: Emerging issues and enduring challenges*. Santa Barbara, CA: Praeger.

Lublin, J.S. (2016). *Earning it: Hard-won lessons from trailblazing women at the top of the business world*. New York: HarperBusiness.

Nicolson, P. (2015). *Gender, power, and organization: A psychological perspective on life at work*. New York: Routledge.

Patton, W. (Ed.). (2013). *Conceptualising women's working lives: Moving the boundaries of discourse*. Rotterdam: Sense.

Sandberg, S. (2013). *Women, work, and the will to lead*. New York: Knopf Doubleday.

Solotoff, L. & Kramer, H.S. (2014). *Sex discrimination and sexual harassment in the workplace*. New York: Law Journal Press.

Verveer, M. & Azzarelli, K.K. (2015). *Fast forward: How women can achieve purpose and power*. Boston, MA: Houghton Mifflin Harcourt.

Williams, J.C. & Dempsey, R. (2014). *What works for women at work: Four patterns working women need to know*. New York: New York University Press.

Websites

Women in the Workplace
Women's Bureau of the U.S. Department of Labor
http://www.dol.gov/wb/

Lesbians in the Workplace
Human Rights Campaign: Workplace
http://www.hrc.org/issues/workplace.asp

Pay Equity
AFL-CIO: Working Women Working Together
http://www.aflcio.org/women

Retirement and Economic Issues
AARP (formerly, the American Association of
Retired Persons)
http://www.aarp.org
Gender and the Social Security System
http://www.socialsecuritymatters.org/

CHAPTER 11

Balancing Family and Work

My daughter was less than 1 year old when I started working as an assistant professor of psychology and my son was born two years later. Although I adored my children, and got enormous satisfaction from my career, juggling the two roles was often stressful. To this day, I can vividly recall the anxiety that erupted when my daughter or son woke up too sick to go to their caregiver's home or when both were of school age and school was canceled because of snow (a frequent occurrence in our New England community). I was plagued by worry that my commitment to my children was preventing me from devoting sufficient time and energy to my career and that my employment was somehow hurting my children. Interestingly, however, I don't recall ever feeling that my husband's job was damaging our children or that being a father was hindering his job advancement. (Judith Bridges)

Historically, women and men had different roles within the family. Men were the economic providers and women the caregivers and homemakers. However, the traditional family consisting of a provider-father, a stay-at-home mother, and their children is relatively rare today. Whereas 57 percent of U.S. children in 1960 were raised in this type of household, fewer than one in four children in married-couple heterosexual families now has a stay-at-home mother (Spade & Valentine, 2016).

As we saw in Chapter 10, the majority of women, including married women with children, are now employed. Not only are more married women working, but they are also working longer hours than women did a generation ago, in a "culture of overwork" that increasingly prizes total availability at all times (Boushey 2016; Slaughter, 2015). Women now constitute nearly half of the American labor force, a trend fueled by the recent recession, which resulted in more men than women losing their jobs. As a result, four out of five couples are now dual-earner couples. The women in these couples contribute nearly half of the family income. For poorer families, those in the lowest 20 percent of income, women's wages are particularly important, with more than two-thirds of women bringing in as much or more than their husbands (Fredrickson, 2015). As a consequence of this major transformation in women's roles, today's young women are involved in a challenging balancing act between the demands of completing their education, beginning their work lives, finding a partner, and having children. Some women postpone or even forego marriage and/or children in favor of work or career, others leave the workplace or choose part-time employment while their children are young, and still others combine family and full-time careers (Cram et al., 2016). Women balance these roles of worker, wife, and mother in different combinations over the course of their lives (Pew Research Center, 2015c). Stories in high-profile media have been asserting that highly educated mothers are "opting out" of careers to stay home with their children. In Learn About the Research 11.1, we examine the evidence for and against this assertion.

This chapter explores issues related to the coordination of women's multiple responsibilities in the domestic and employment domains. We begin with a look at perceptions of and attitudes toward their family and employment roles. Then we examine the impact of women's employment on the division of labor in the home as well as the challenges, costs, and benefits of balancing family and work. We explore employer resources that facilitate this coordination and consider strategies women use to manage family and work responsibilities. We conclude with a discussion of midlife transitions in family and work roles.

WOMEN'S FAMILY AND EMPLOYMENT ROLES: PERCEPTIONS AND ATTITUDES

Although the traditional view of the male provider–female homemaker was once seen as the expected and desirable family type, most adults today do not perceive it as ideal (Donnelly et al., 2016). Let us examine how working and stay-at-home mothers are perceived. We'll then look at factors that influence attitudes toward women's multiple roles.

Perceptions of Working and Stay-at-Home Mothers

Remember from Chapter 2 that, according to social role theory, women are assumed to be higher than men in warmth and nurturance, whereas men are assumed to be higher than women in agency and competence. Consistent with social role theory, mothers who go back to work or school immediately after childbirth or following a brief maternity leave are viewed as less warm and communal than mothers who cut back to part-time work or school or stay at home (Bridges & Etaugh, 1995; Coleman & Franiuk, 2011; Etaugh & Folger, 1998; Etaugh & Moss, 2001; Mottarella et al., 2009).

In addition, mothers who are employed full time are judged more harshly than nonmothers who are employed full time, especially by men (Kiser, 2015). They are viewed as both less nurturing *and* less professionally competent (Etaugh & Folger, 1998; Livengood, 2010; Okimoto & Heilman, 2012). Along the same lines, mothers are judged as less likely to be hired than are nonmothers with the same credentials (an example of the "maternal wall"). Fathers, on the other hand, are judged to be as hirable as nonfathers (Fuegen et al., 2004).

LEARN ABOUT THE RESEARCH 11.1
Are Women "Opting Out" of Careers?

Some headlines in national media such as the *New York Times* and the *Wall Street Journal* claim that mothers are increasingly opting out of their careers to stay home with their children. How accurate is this assertion?

Studies based on large, representative samples show that women are, in fact, *not* opting out, and that working mothers are more likely than ever to pursue jobs and careers while raising their families (Lips, 2016). Highly educated mothers aged 25–45 are as likely to be in the labor force as women without children, a trend that started in the mid-1980s and continues to this day (Percheski, 2008). Only two groups of women are opting out in any meaningful numbers. The larger group consists of mothers whose earnings are so low that they cannot afford child care. This group tends to be younger, less educated, and Latina or foreign born. The other group consists of women whose husbands earn extremely high salaries (Hersch, 2013; Lips, 2016). Given this evidence, what might account for the myth that the best and brightest American women are dropping out of the workplace? Harvard economist Claudia Goldin (2006) suggests that some people find it hard to believe that women can both contribute to their profession and participate meaningfully in raising children. The social construction of women as the primary caregivers seems to take precedence over the evidence that most women today intend to combine family and employment, and in fact are doing so.

WHAT DOES IT MEAN?

1. How does the debate on whether women are opting out of the workforce illustrate how different research methods can lead to very different conclusions?

2. During an economic recession, women and men with and without children are more likely to leave the labor force. Why has the focus been largely on *mothers* who leave the workforce?

3. What social and economic conditions of the past few decades have led to an increase in the percentage of women who are combining work and family roles?

Attitudes Toward Married Women's Employment: A Cross-Cultural Perspective

What are the attitudes toward maternal employment in other industrialized nations? Judith Treas and Eric Widmer (2000) examined attitudes toward married women's employment in 23 largely Western and industrial countries. Recall from Chapter 3 that almost everyone agreed that married women should work, preferably full time, before they had children. Support for full-time work was almost as high after children were grown. However, mothers of preschoolers were expected either to stay home or work only part time. Those with school-age children were expected to work only part time. Despite this general consensus, nations also showed some difference in attitudes. Basically, three different nation clusters were identified: the "work-oriented," "family accommodating," and "motherhood-centered." The work-oriented cluster consisted of Canada, East Germany, Israel, the Netherlands, Norway, Sweden, and the United States. Whatever the life-course stage, this cluster's respondents were the least likely to recommend that married women stay home. Unlike other clusters, they favored part-time employment for mothers of preschoolers. These countries had more egalitarian gender-role attitudes than the other nations in the study and perceived fewer conflicts between women's work and family roles. The "family accommodating" cluster (Australia, Austria, Great Britain, Italy, Japan, New Zealand, Northern Ireland, Russia, and West Germany) put less emphasis on maternal employment. They expected mothers to stay at home with preschoolers and work only part time not only when their children reached school age, but even after they were grown. The "motherhood centered" cluster (Bulgaria, the Czech Republic, Hungary, Ireland,

Poland, Slovenia, and Spain) endorsed full-time employment before and after marriage, but staying at home with preschoolers and, even to some extent, with school-age children. Not surprisingly, this group had the most traditional gender-role attitudes.

Factors Influencing Attitudes Toward Women's Multiple Roles

Among all U.S adults, nearly three in four now approve of mothers working when their children are young, compared to fewer than half of adults in 1977 (Donnelly et al, 2016). What are some of the variables that are associated with attitudes toward women's multiple roles? One factor is age. Younger adults (ages 18–29) are more likely than older adults to favorably view the employment of mothers with young children (Newton-Small, 2016; Wang et al., 2013). The large majority of today's young adults—both women and men—support working mothers (Donnelly et al., 2016) and desire an egalitarian gender-role relationship with their future spouse (Sells & Ganong, 2016).

Ethnicity also plays a role in attitudes toward working mothers. Historically, poor and working-class women of color have been in the labor force in order to help support their families (Pedulla & Thebaud, 2015). Thus, it is not surprising that, as we saw in Chapter 9, Black female college students plan to return to work sooner than White female students following a child's birth (Bridges & Etaugh, 1996). Still, a sizable minority of Black and Latina/o adults, especially recent immigrants, believe that men should maintain the primary financial responsibility for their families. Possibly, this belief is an attempt to maintain male dignity in a society that makes it difficult for ethnic minority men to fulfill their provider role responsibility (Goldberg & Lucas-Thompson, 2014).

Gender, as you might expect, also influences attitudes toward women's family and work roles. Women are less likely than men (55 percent versus 65 percent) to agree that children are better off when a parent stays home with them (Cohn & Caumont, 2014). But most men and women say that person should be the mother (Parker & Wang, 2013). Still, attitudes toward working mothers and stay-at-home fathers are changing and currently appear to depend less on the parent's gender than on the specific circumstances and pressures of individual families. (See In the News 11.1.)

IN THE NEWS 11.1
Shifting Attitudes on Who Works and Who Stays Home

Most U.S. parents of young children—70 percent of mothers and 93 percent of fathers—work, but the view that mothers should be caregivers and that fathers should be breadwinners has been slow to change (C.C. Miller, 2015a). New research (Jacobs & Gerson, 2016), however, shows a shift in attitudes, as Americans acknowledge that job conditions and family circumstances may be more important than gender in determining who stays home and who works. The study found that under a variety of circumstances, up to 92 percent of Americans endorsed mothers working and up to 77 percent favored fathers staying home. The conditions most likely to earn support for mothers to work were if they were satisfied with their job and child care arrangements, and their families needed their income. This was especially true for single mothers. The conditions most likely to gain support for fathers staying home were the opposite: they were not satisfied with their job and child care arrangements, and their families did not need their incomes. Although the American public seems to be showing more flexibility in its views of women's and men's work and family roles, it is clear that women still have greater latitude than men to assume nontraditional responsibilities. Why do you think that is?

Another key factor that influences views on working mothers is the employment history of one's own mother. Women and men whose mothers worked all or most of the time while they were growing up are more likely than those whose mothers worked little or not at all to be accepting of working mothers (Donnelly et al., 2016). Working women's grown-up daughters are even more likely than their grown-up sons to strongly agree with this statement. Thus, consistent with the assumption that gender is constructed in part from interpersonal experiences, it seems that positive experiences with an employed mother early in their childhood lead women to view the

GET INVOLVED 11.1
How Do College Students Evaluate Mothers Who Are Full-Time Students?

For this activity, based on a study by Karen Mottarella and her colleagues (2009), ask four traditional-aged (18–21-year-old) female students to read a brief description of a mother and indicate their impression of her on rating scales. Give two participants description A, followed by the rating scales, and two participants description B, followed by the same scales.

Description A: Emily is a 31-year-old married mother. She was a full-time college student before her child was born and returned to school full time at the end of her six-week maternity leave.

Description B: Emily is a 31-year-old married mother. She was a full-time college student before her child was born and returned to school full time when her child was in first grade.

Now indicate how much you like and respect Emily by completing the following two rating scales:

like her very little	1 2 3 4 5 6 7	like her very much
respect her very little	1 2 3 4 5 6 7	respect her very much

WHAT DOES IT MEAN?

Calculate the average rating for each respondent. A high score reflects a positive evaluation of the mother and a low score shows a negative evaluation. Next, average the responses given by the two respondents who read the description of the mother who stayed in school (description A) and average the scores of the two who read the paragraph about the mother who interrupted her education (description B).

1. Similar to studies in the text, this study found that mothers who take a brief maternity leave are more negatively evaluated than those who interrupt their education. Did you find the same results? If yes, give reasons for this finding.

2. Describe socialization experiences that might influence young women's personal beliefs about a brief maternity leave versus interrupted employment or education.

3. This study and others presented in the text examined attitudes of traditional-aged college students. Do you think that older women would have different impressions? Explain your answer.

Source: Based on Mottarella et al. (2009).

---

combination of motherhood and employment as acceptable female role choices that are not harmful to children (Goldberg & Lucas-Thompson, 2014). Try the Get Involved 11.1 activity to examine attitudes toward mothers who are in school full time.

DIVISION OF FAMILY LABOR

Increasing numbers of women and men have substantial household and child care obligations along with major work responsibilities. Moreover, a majority of unmarried young adults say they would like a relationship with a future spouse or partner in which all work and family responsibilities were shared equally (Pedulla & Thebaud, 2015). Do these ideal views reflect the current realities of work and family roles in the lives of women and men? Do the husbands of employed women contribute more to child care or housekeeping labor than the husbands of nonemployed women? Has this changed over time? Are women and men satisfied with this division of labor? We now explore these questions and others related to the division of family responsibilities.

Housework and Child Care

Studies published in the 1970s and the 1980s showed that husbands increased their household labor very little when their wives were employed. Although husbands have increased their housework participation somewhat since then and wives have reduced theirs, men's contribution to household labor worldwide still does not equal that of women (Baxter & Tai, 2016; Dotti Sani, 2016; Doucet & Lee, 2014; Institute for Women's Policy Research, 2015; C.C. Miller, 2016a; Sabattini & Crosby, 2016).

In 1965, American women did 32 hours of housework a week, compared to 4 hours for men. By 2011, women averaged 18 hours and men averaged 10 hours (Parker & Wang, 2013). The division of housework between women and men is more egalitarian in countries with progressive gender ideologies (Treas & Tai, 2016). For example, women in Japan, which has relatively traditional gender attitudes, perform 90 percent of the housework, compared to 67 percent in Denmark and Sweden, where gender ideologies are more egalitarian (Baxter & Tai, 2016). Employed women of all ethnicities in the U.S. perform a disproportionate share of household and child care responsibilities (Sayer & Fine, 2011). Women still assume the main responsibility for traditional female chores such as cooking, cleaning, and laundry, whereas men have more responsibility for traditional male chores such as yard work, repairs, and car maintenance (Baxter & Tai, 2016). Note that the tasks done by women are repetitive and never-ending while those by men are done only periodically.

Regardless of their employment role, and across ethnicities, social classes, and nations, women continue to perform most child care activities, including feeding and bathing young children, attending school conferences and sports events, helping with homework, disciplining, organizing leisure activities, taking children to the doctor, and providing or arranging for substitute care when there is a school vacation or when a child is sick (Bornstein et al., 2016; Kotila et al., 2013; Parke, 2013; Pew Research Center, 2015c; Shulevitz, 2015; Sullivan, 2013; Taylor et al., 2015; Yavorsky et al., 2015). Fathers, on the other hand, tend to focus more on play activities with their infants and young children (Parke, 2013). In lesbian families, couples are more likely to share both child care and household tasks (Kenschaft & Clark, 2016; Moore & Stambolis-Ruhstorfer, 2013).

Because employed women perform the bulk of child care and housework duties, it is no surprise that one of their major concerns is simply finding the time to adequately fulfill all their responsibilities (Schulte, 2014; Shulevitz, 2015). Another primary issue is arranging for good child care. "I honestly do think that if Lizzie hadn't been there to take care of her then things would have been different because I don't think I would have been able to leave her with somebody I didn't know" (Leach et al., 2006, p. 483). "Once I found child care, I could then structure my work around it." (Doherty & Lassig, 2013, p. 89) Comments like these illustrate the central importance of child care for employed women. Not surprisingly, worries about child care can lead to high levels of stress for employed mothers (Leach et al., 2006; Press et al., 2006).

Caring for Aging Parents

Increasing numbers of midlife women are part of the "sandwich generation," caring simultaneously for their children and their aging parents (and in some cases, grandparents) who need assistance with daily activities such as cooking, bathing, financial matters, transportation to doctors, and shopping. Although men also provide assistance, especially to their own parents, women perform the bulk of eldercare both in the United States and in other nations (Alzheimer's Association, 2014; Boyczuk & Fletcher, 2016; MetLife, 2011; Mitchell, 2014; Piercy, 2014). Some women will spend more years providing care to an older parent than they devoted to childrearing (Span, 2015).

The average female caregiver is 49 and married, and works outside the home. We saw in Chapter 8 that she is likely to be a daughter, daughter-in-law, or granddaughter (MetLife, 2011; National Alliance for Caregiving and AARP, 2015). The financial impact of caring for older relatives is considerable. More than one-third of employed caregivers have reported rearranging work schedules, decreasing working hours, or taking an unpaid leave. Still others pass up promotions, quit their jobs, or retire early (Cohen, 2017; Pew Research Center, 2013a). The same pattern is also found in other nations. For example, European and Australian women who provide extensive care for older relatives are also more likely to cease employment than women who are not providing such care (Austen & Ong, 2010; Masuy, 2009). Taking time out of the labor force for caregiving places a strain on women's income (MetLife, 2011). In addition, caregivers of older parents may also have less time for family and friends, further increasing emotional strain (MetLife, 2011). No wonder caregivers of older relatives are more likely than noncaregivers to show higher levels of depression, anxiety, hostility, stress, exhaustion, and family tension (Kemper, 2013; National Alliance for Caregiving and AARP, 2015; Reinhard et al., 2015).

Leisure Time

With all the time women are spending on child care, eldercare, and employment, it is no surprise that employed mothers have less leisure time than either employed fathers (Parker & Wang, 2013; W. Wang, 2013), nonemployed mothers (Cohn & Caumont, 2014), or childless women (Kuykendall et al., 2015). Feminists point out that the concept of leisure is different for women and men, with women experiencing less time for leisure in their lives than men. A common focus of women's leisure, according to this perspective, is the combining of family obligations with leisure opportunities. A woman may perceive the family's leisure as her leisure and vice versa. The home is the most common place in which women's leisure occurs. In this way, leisure can sometimes be combined with household chores. Women often multitask and may, for example, engage in a leisure activity, such as watching television, while at the same time doing housework, such as cooking or mending. Thus, much of women's leisure time may be fragmented rather than occurring in large blocks of time (Offer, 2016; Ryle, 2016; Spade & Valentine, 2016). Even after retirement, women have less time for leisure than men because they continue to remain more occupied with domestic chores and family responsibilities. For example, we saw in Chapter 8 that many older women have caregiving responsibilities for grandchildren, ailing spouses, or parents. Still, older women are more involved than older men in volunteer work, organized groups, and attendance at various events (Antonucci et al., 2014).

Women's Perceptions of the Division of Family Labor

Although women perform about two-thirds of the total household labor, only a small percentage rate their division of labor as unfair (Perales et al., 2015; Sardadvar, 2011). What might account for this apparent paradox between women's heavier workload and their satisfaction with the allocation of domestic responsibilities? Possibly, women's gender socialization has led them to believe that both childrearing and household work are in women's domain. This construction of the female role may produce no discrepancy between what they expect and what they experience. Moreover, pressures to adhere to their socially prescribed maternal role make it difficult for some women to relinquish caregiving duties to their spouses or partners (Kenney & Bogle, 2009; Mannino & Deutsch, 2007). Additionally, some women, especially those holding traditional gender ideologies, might compare their own household responsibility to that of other women, rather than to their husbands' responsibility, and, therefore, not see themselves as unfairly burdened (Kornrich & Eger, 2016).

For those women who feel that the division of domestic labor is unfair, the perceived inequity does not stem from the amount of time they spend on household tasks, but from their *share* of the total time spent by the couple. For married women around the globe, the more time wives spent relative to their husbands', the more likely they were to view the allocation of family responsibilities as unfair (Jansen et al., 2016). On the other hand, the more a wife believes she matters to her husband, the more likely she is to report that the division of housework is fair, regardless of the share of housework she performs (Kawamura & Brown, 2007).

Explanations of the Division of Family Labor

What accounts for women's disproportionate share of child care and housekeeping duties? At least three explanations have been offered.

TIME AVAILABILITY.   One explanation for the unequal division of household labor is that domestic responsibilities are allocated on the basis of each spouse's time availability (Baxter & Tai, 2016). Consistent with this view, full-time homemakers, who have more time available, spend more time in household tasks than do employed women (Burn, 2011; Treas & Lui, 2013). Furthermore, the more hours women and men spend in paid work, the less time they expend in housework (Poortman & Van der Lippe, 2009).

However, some patterns of domestic involvement are inconsistent with this explanation. For example, even when comparing spouses with comparable work hours, mothers spend more time than fathers caring for their children and doing household tasks (Baxter & Tai, 2016). Thus, although time availability plays some role, it alone cannot explain the allocation of domestic responsibilities.

RELATIVE POWER.   Another possible explanation is that women's disproportionate share of household labor results from their lower degree of marital power (Zilanawala, 2016). According to this view, power in marriage depends, in part, on work-related resources, such as income. The more resources one partner has in relation to the other, the greater that partner's influence (i.e., power) over the other. Because people tend to dislike household chores, the person with greater power will limit engagement in these tasks. Does research support this view? Evidence indicates that it may not be the *difference* in husbands' and wives' income that explains women's participation in household labor, but rather how much she earns herself (Gupta, 2007). For every $7,500 in additional income, a woman's share of housework declines by one hour per week. Yet, even when women bring greater work resources to the marriage, men retain higher status and power. For example, Veronica Tichenor (2005) found that even when wives earned significantly more than their husbands, neither husbands nor wives evaluated her career as more important than his. Furthermore, despite their lower income, husbands maintained greater financial decision-making power. Thus, even when men have fewer occupational resources than their wives, they apparently maintain other forms of power.

GENDER ATTITUDES.   A third explanation for the division of household labor is that the unequal distribution reflects spouses' beliefs about appropriate gender roles (Powell & Greenhaus, 2010). According to this view, many couples have internalized the traditional gender beliefs that managing children and the home is primarily the wife's responsibility and that husbands should be the main financial providers. Thus, they may feel uncomfortable if they deviate from these strong societal norms (Baxter & Tai, 2016).

Consistent with this explanation, men who have nontraditional attitudes about family roles spend more time doing housework than those with traditional views (Lachance-Grzela & Bouchard, 2010), whereas women with nontraditional beliefs spend less time in household labor than women who have traditional attitudes (Davis & Greenstein, 2009). Moreover, college students with traditional gender-role attitudes find it more acceptable for a man to contribute less to household chores (Swearingen-Hilker & Yoder, 2002).

FAMILY–WORK COORDINATION

Balancing Family and Work: Costs and Benefits

What kind of costs and benefits might stem from juggling family and work roles? Consider these questions, then try Get Involved 11.2 to explore your personal expectations of this issue. When Judith and Claire (Bridges & Etaugh, 1996) asked White and Black college women to respond to the items presented in Get Involved 11.2, they found that these students estimated that the benefits would be greater than the costs (70 percent versus 55 percent). Although both White and Black students had similarly viewed the probability of benefits, White students estimated a higher likelihood of negative outcomes from working during motherhood than did Black students. The long history of Black women's employment (Abrams et al., 2016) may contribute to their more positive attitude toward maternal employment. These different views held by Black and White women show that these attitudes are socially constructed from individuals' experiences and do not simply arise from one's gender.

In actuality, the effects of performing family and work roles are complex and encompass both positive and negative aspects. Because of this, it is important to examine women's actual experiences associated with these roles as well as explanations of these outcomes.

COSTS.   As might be expected, many employed women, especially mothers, experience **role strain**, that is, *stress stemming from one's roles* (Perrone et al., 2009). In the words of one employed mother

GET INVOLVED 11.2
What Psychological Experiences Do You Think You Will Have If You Combine Employment and Parenthood?

Pretend that you have two children and a spouse/partner employed full time outside of the home. Given these circumstances, think about the experience you might have if you, also, were employed full time outside the home throughout your child-rearing years. For each of the following possible consequences of employment during parenthood, estimate the probability, from 0 percent to 100 percent, that you would experience that outcome.

_1. higher self-esteem

_2. more guilt feelings

_3. greater feeling of missing out on your children's developmental progress (e.g., first steps)

_4. greater self-fulfillment

_5. greater number of conflicting demands

_6. greater intellectual stimulation

_7. more resentment from spouse/partner

_8. more anxiety about your child

_9. more mental exhaustion

_10. greater degree of pride

_11. more social stimulation

_12. more irritability

_13. more conflict with your spouse/partner

_14. more approval from other people

WHAT DOES IT MEAN?

Items 2, 3, 5, 7, 8, 9, 12, and 13 are possible costs and items 1, 4, 6, 10, 11, and 14 are possible benefits of employment for mothers. For each of these two sets of outcomes, calculate the average probability that you reported. First, add up the eight probabilities you specified for the costs and divide that total by 8. Then, sum the probabilities you estimated for the six benefits and divide that total by 6. After calculating your averages, read the text's presentation of the findings of this study.

1. Compare your expectations to those reported in the text. Are they similar? If not, can you think of reasons for any observed differences?

2. Do you think your expectations will influence your decision about the timing of your employment and childbearing?

3. Do you think your answers would have differed if you were the other gender? Refer to material on gender attitudes and gender socialization to explain your answer.

Source: Based on Bridges and Etaugh (1996).

of an infant, "Everything was a compromise. When I went to work, I felt like I should be at home. And when I was at home, I thought [about that] I left in the middle [of] all of these management meetings. And everybody's looking around like, 'Where's she going?'" (Hattery, 2001, p. 58). Role strain can stem from **role overload**, *role demands that exceed one's available time and/or energy*, and/or **interrole conflict**, *incompatible demands stemming from two or more roles* (Kinnunen et al., 2013; Nelson & Lyubomirsky, 2015). Role overload can occur, for example, when, after 9 hours of work and commuting, a mother does her family's laundry, cooks dinner, washes the dishes, and supervises her children's homework. Interrole conflict, on the other hand, would occur if a mother wants to attend her child's band concert at school but has an important business meeting scheduled for the same time. Women in two-career families often experience the dual pressures of performing well in fast-paced demanding careers and performing well in their roles as mothers, increasing their risk of stress and exhaustion. The more role strain women experience, the greater their depression and stress and the lower their job and life satisfaction (Baxter & Tai, 2016).

What produces role strain? According to the **scarcity hypothesis**, *excessive role responsibilities deplete the individual's limited supply of time and energy and, consequently, can lead to stress.* When individuals have more responsibilities than they have time or energy for handling them, or when they are overwhelmed by conflicts between their role responsibilities, they can experience frustration, fatigue, or other indications of stress (Kinnunen et al., 2013; Zimmerman & Hammer, 2010).

Experiences related to family–work balancing can be influenced by numerous factors, not the least of which is the presence of children. The wife and worker roles alone are not related to role overload or conflict. It is the addition of the caregiver role to the worker role that creates women's role strain (Brough & O'Driscoll, 2015). Having a child, particularly one who is young, disabled, or difficult, is particularly likely to increase role strain (Martinengo et al., 2010; Michel et al., 2011; Rabins, 2016).

Employed married women are more likely than employed married men to experience both role overload and interrole conflict and this gender difference holds across ethnic groups (Baxer & Tai, 2016). The social construction of women as the major caregivers and homemakers and the construction of men as the primary providers means that women's employment is seen as *addition to* their family role, whereas men's employment is viewed as *part of* their family role (Damaske, 2011).

In addition to role strain, sexual minority role jugglers must face other problems as well. For example, their coworkers and/or supervisors might disapprove of their sexual orientation, making the work environment uncomfortable. Furthermore, the lack of insurance benefits available for many sexual minority families can produce economic pressures (Harley & Teaster, 2016).

BENEFITS.   Juggling family and work can lead to role overload and interrole conflict, but it can also bring numerous rewards, including higher self-esteem, better physical and mental health, greater respect from others, and greater economic security (Frech & Damaske, 2012; Kim & Wickrama, 2014; Nelson & Lyubomirsky, 2015). Indeed, even though employed mothers are more likely than unemployed mothers to report they "always feel rushed," they are also more likely to say that they get "a great deal" or "a very great deal" of satisfaction from their family lives (Cherlin & Krishnamurthy, 2004). Employed women with nontraditional gender attitudes are more likely than those with traditional attitudes to report benefits from working (Marshall & Barnett, 1993).

The benefits of multiple role coordination are explained by the **enhancement hypothesis** (Sumra & Schillaci, 2015; Williams et al., 2016). According to this perspective, *each additional role provides a new source of self-esteem, social approval, social status, and other benefits.* Successfully applying the different skills required by different roles can lead to achievements in many areas. Consequently, family–work balancers can develop competence in numerous domains and experience greater personal pride and fulfillment.

Aside from any rewards associated with managing several roles, women can benefit by using one role to buffer strains associated with another (Kinnunen et al., 2013; diScalea et al., 2012); that is, positive events in one role can reduce the psychological impact of negative events in another role. A 35-year-old professional woman describes it like this: "Sometimes I have a really rough day at work and then I come home and these two little kids run to the door. My older daughter says 'I'm really glad you got picked to be my mother.' Then, I forget the day at work" (Crosby, 1991, p. 103). Similarly, women who enjoy their jobs are more likely to show warm and consistent parenting (Cooklin et al., 2014).

Faye Crosby and Laura Sabattini (2006) discuss three reasons why buffering helps psychological well-being. First, involvement in more than one role allows the family–work juggler to distance herself from the problems in one role while she engages in another role. For instance, a mother who is upset about her child's school performance can put that worry aside while she focuses on her job responsibilities.

Second, challenges in one role help put into perspective worries associated with another role. For example, a woman who is bothered about conflicts with her coworkers might view this problem as less important when faced with her husband's serious illness. When his health improves, she might continue to view the interpersonal tension at work as minor.

Third, positive events in one role can bolster self-esteem that has been damaged by negative events in another role. Thus, the disappointment of not receiving a promotion at work can be eased by a mother's feelings of competence as she helps her child successfully cope with a bully at school.

In addition to immediate benefits earned while juggling family and work roles, there is evidence of long-term positive outcomes. Longitudinal follow-up of women who graduated from college in the 1960s found that those who combined family and employment roles in early adulthood had more positive role experiences in middle age and experienced greater midlife well-being than did other women (Vandewater et al., 1997).

Effects of Mothers' Employment

What are the effects of maternal employment on a woman's children and on her spouse or partner? Let us now examine these questions.

EFFECTS ON CHILDREN.   Nearly two in three first-time mothers now return to work within a year after giving birth (U.S. Census Bureau, 2016b). As a result, nearly three-fourths of infants and preschool children in the United States spend time in the care of nonparental caregivers (Child Trends, 2016). Indeed, access to child care is a key factor in women's decision to work (Herbst & Barnow, 2008).

Decades of research have demonstrated that high-quality day care, as measured by characteristics such as appropriate group size, favorable staff-to-child ratio, teacher training, and caregivers' commitment to children, does not adversely affect children's social, academic, or emotional development (Bassok et al., 2016; Brooks-Gunn et al., 2010; Burchinal et al., 2015; Lombardi & Coley, 2014; Phillips, 2015; Pingault et al., 2015). In fact, high-quality child care provides significant academic, socioemotional, and behavioral benefits to children, especially those from economically disadvantaged homes (Bassok et al., 2016; Burchinal et al., 2015; Lee et al., 2014; Li et al., 2013; Miller et al., 2014; Neuman, 2014; Watamura et al., 2011). Long-term benefits for children from low-income families include higher rates of educational attainment and employment, higher earnings, delayed childbearing, and lower rates of criminal offenses in adulthood (Campbell et al., 2012; Chase-Lansdale & Brooks-Gunn, 2014; Peters et al., 2010).

Maternal employment provides other benefits as well. For example, research has found that preschoolers with employed mothers were more prosocial, less anxious, and less hyperactive than children whose mothers were not employed (Lucas-Thompson, 2010). Girls and boys whose mothers are employed develop less stereotypical attitudes about gender roles than children with nonemployed mothers (Davis & Greenstein, 2009; Goldberg & Lucas-Thompson, 2008). Because employment is seen as an agentic role and because maternal employment frequently leads to nonstereotypical structuring of household responsibilities among parents, employed mothers often serve as less traditional role models than do full-time homemakers. So it is not surprising that children with employed mothers have more egalitarian views toward sharing household and child care tasks than students with nonemployed mothers (Cunningham, 2001; Halpern & Perry-Jenkins, 2016; Riggio & Desrochers, 2006; Treas & Tai, 2007). Moreover, sons of employed women, compared to sons of nonemployed women, perceive females as more competent, and view men as warmer and more expressive (Parke & Buriel, 2006) and spend more time on housework and childcare (C.C. Miller, 2015a). In addition, daughters of working mothers show greater self-efficacy than daughters of nonemployed mothers (Dunifon et al., 2013; Liben & Bigler, 2014; C.C. Miller, 2015a). Research in Asia, Europe, and North America finds that adult daughters of employed women, compared to daughters of nonemployed women, are more highly educated, and are more likely to be employed and to hold supervisory positions (C.C. Miller, 2015a; McGinn et al., 2015). Moreover, the great majority of young adults (almost 8 of 10) who grew up with employed mothers are pleased with their mother's working (Gerson, 2010). And today's school-age children find it equally acceptable for both mothers and fathers to work full time (Sinno & Killen, 2009).

Our exploration of the benefits that can result from maternal employment does not imply that full-time homemaking is detrimental to children's development. What is important is the consistency between a mother's role (employed or not employed) and her belief about the value of maternal employment for her family and herself. Mothers whose roles match their own attitudes are likely to be more effective parents. A mother who is dissatisfied with her role is less likely to display the type of positive parenting characteristics that can lead to good outcomes for her children (Goldberg & Lucas-Thompson, 2008; Lawson et al., 2014; Lerner et al., 2002).

Interestingly, most research on the effects of parental employment on children has focused on maternal employment. The social construction of gender leads us to conceptualize parenting as part of women's role and to frame child care as a women's issue rather than as a family issue (Newcombe, 2007).

EFFECTS ON THE RELATIONSHIP WITH THE SPOUSE/PARTNER.   Because employment of wives and mothers represents a departure from traditional gender roles, does it have implications for the woman's relationship with her spouse or partner? The comprehensive National Survey of Families and Households found that women's employment does not affect the likelihood of divorce among couples who are happily married. However, it is a factor in ending unhappy marriages (Shellenbarger, 2008). Can you think of a reason for this? According to the economic opportunity hypothesis, employment gives women the resources to leave an unhappy marriage (Ozcan & Breen, 2012). How about the alternative hypothesis that a woman's employment *causes* a rift in the marital relationship? Let us examine some of the research that relates women's employment to the marital satisfaction of both wives and husbands.

Women's feelings about their marriages are related, in part, to the consistency between their roles and their gender-related attitudes. Maureen Perry-Jenkins and her colleagues (1992) found that employed women who were uncomfortable about their work role experienced less marital satisfaction than those who wanted to work outside the home, and were less satisfied than full-time homemakers. It appears that positive outcomes can result from either full-time homemaking or from combining family and work. What is more important than the actual roles is the attitude toward those roles.

Studies of the relationship between women's employment and wives' and husbands' sexual satisfaction show parallel findings. Janet Hyde and her colleagues (2001) found that both women and men reported greater sexual satisfaction when they had more rewarding work experiences. This could be because positive experiences in the workplace help couples more fully enjoy their sexual relationship or because a satisfactory sex life contributes to enjoyment on the job. Or, it may be that neither domain influences the other, but that well-adjusted adults lead lives that are satisfying in many domains, including work and sexual relationships.

Solutions to Family–Work Balancing Challenges

As we have seen, the numerous rewards that can result from combining family and work roles do not eliminate the challenges family-work jugglers face in managing their roles. What approaches can help reduce these challenges?

PARENTAL LEAVE.   Although some young college women would like to discontinue their employment for some period of time after the birth of a baby, most women do not follow that pattern. In 2014, 57 percent of married women with infants 1 year or under were employed (Bureau of Labor Statistics, 2015).

The high employment rate of mothers with infants points to the importance of adequate parental leave policies that provide sufficient time to adjust to parenthood and allow biological mothers to recuperate from the physical and psychological stresses of pregnancy and birth (Gault et al., 2014b). Incredibly, the United States is one of the few countries in the world without a national policy requiring paid parental leave. As of this writing, only a small percentage of states provide even partial wage replacement to workers who take parental leave (Gault et al. 2014b; C.C. Miller, 2015a). Why do you think the United States lags so far behind other nations in providing paid parental leave?

Of the 178 countries providing paid leaves, including many developing nations in Africa, Asia, and Latin America, 98 offer at least 14 weeks of paid leave (Blau & Kahn, 2016). Sweden provides the most fully paid leave, over 15 months (Sholar, 2016). Five other countries offer at least six months at full pay: Canada, Finland, Greece, Japan, and Norway (Burn, 2011). The United States offers the briefest leave of any industrialized nation (12 weeks) and is among only three countries with an unpaid leave, the others being Liberia, Papua New Guinea, and Swaziland (Williams & Dempsey, 2014).

The only federal law mandating parental leave in the United States is the Family and Medical Leave Act, which is applicable only to workplaces with 50 or more employees, thus covering only about

60 percent of the workforce. The act allows workers (women and men) who have been employed for a year in those companies to take up to 12 weeks of *unpaid* leave for medical conditions or family responsibilities, including the birth or adoption of a child"(Gault et al., 2014b). As of this writing, only a small percentage of states provide even partial wage replacement of workers who take parental leave (Gault et al., 2014b; C.C. Miller, 2015b). Why do you think the United States lags so far behind other nations in providing paid parental leave? Many women take shorter leaves than they would like to take because their families cannot afford the loss of their income. Not surprisingly, women with the lowest incomes return to work most quickly (Dagher et al., 2014). Low-income Native American and Asian American women take the shortest leaves of any ethnic group (Fredrickson, 2015).

Nowadays, four out of five first-time mothers work until 1 month or less before giving birth. Over two-thirds return to work within 6 months and four in five return within a year. Women with higher levels of education work later into their pregnancies, return to work more rapidly after giving birth, and are more likely to return to work full time than women with less education (Guendelman et al., 2014; Laughlin, 2011). Other factors associated with women's earlier planned return to work after childbirth include having more positive attitudes about combining employment and parenting and perceiving one's employer as supportive of employees' family needs (Russell & Banks, 2011). The belief that the employer is sensitive to work–family issues likely contributes to a greater comfort at work and an expectation that family responsibilities will be accommodated.

How does parental leave affect women's employment? The evidence suggests that using family leave may, in fact, be harmful to the work lives of both men and women. Mothers who take time off after giving birth are more likely to experience negative career consequences than those who do not (Blau & Kahn, 2016). Men who take leave for childbirth or care of a sick parent are viewed as less committed to the organization than men who do not take leave, as are women who take leave for the same reason (Rhode et al., 2014; Williams et al., 2013). Stay-at-home fathers often find a stigma attached to their decision, especially when they return to the workforce after a period at home. As a result, fathers are much less likely than mothers to use family-friendly benefits (Bartel et al., 2015; C.C. Miller, 2015b; Rehel, 2014). As long as workplace norms penalize individuals who use such benefits, workers will be reluctant to take advantage of them (Berdahl & Moon, 2013; Sabattini & Crosby, 2016; Sprung et al., 2015).

"FAMILY-FRIENDLY" WORKPLACE POLICIES. Employers can play a key role in helping parents coordinate their family and work roles by being supportive and providing a family-friendly culture (Butts et al., 2013; Moen et al., 2016; Sabattini & Crosby, 2016). One way to do this is by offering paid family leave, discussed earlier. Unfortunately, just 12 percent of workers in the United States private sector have access to paid family leaves, many of them in white-collar technology companies trying to attract and retain young skilled workers (Miller & Streitfeld, 2015).

A second family-friendly benefit is flexible work hours (Butts et al., 2013). **Flextime**, *flexible work scheduling that allows the employee to choose the arrival and departure time within a set of possible options offered by the employer*, can enable parents to better accommodate their work hours to their children's regular child care or school schedules and to deal with unforeseen and unscheduled family demands. One recent poll of over 1,000 organizations found that one-third of them offered flextime and 10 percent offered compressed work weeks (Galinsky et al., 2010). Flexible benefits such as these are associated with increased employee retention and engagement, reduced work–family conflict, lower absenteeism, greater job satisfaction, and higher productivity (Kelly et al., 2014; Kulow, 2012; Richardsen et al., 2016), benefitting both employees and employers. Unfortunately, the low-wage jobs held by many women offer highly inflexible hours, and unpredictable schedules are commonplace (Jacobs & Padavic, 2015). (See Learn About the Research 11.2.)

A third option that helps many workers is telecommuting. The increasing use of technology in the labor force makes this option to work from home attractive to certain types of workers. As with flextime, telecommuting is linked to greater job satisfaction, increased performance, and reduced work–family conflict (Butts et al., 2013; Matos & Galinsky, 2015).

Fourth, employer help with child care would ease a major burden faced by employed parents. Child care assistance programs can include referral services and day care subsidies as well as on-site day care and backup day care when families have emergencies. Given that child care is one

LEARN ABOUT THE RESEARCH 11.2
Work-Hours Dilemmas of Low-Wage Women Workers

Research on women's experiences with work schedules and flexibility often focuses on professional women in high-paying careers, despite women's far greater prevalence in low-wage jobs. Anna Jacobs and Irene Padavic (2015) studied how work-on-demand and other aspects of low-wage part-time labor limit women's ability to make ends meet. They interviewed 17 primarily young women—Asian, Black, Latina, and White—who worked as servers, fast-food employees, clerks, and cashiers. All of the women reported experiencing unpredictable schedules and too few hours to make ends meet. Many also reported working unpaid hours (e.g., employers extending unpaid breaks or pressuring them to work off the clock). Many also had employers curtail their hours to control or punish them for infractions (e.g., coming in late). These scheduling dilemmas had two major effects on the employees' relationships and families. One was the inability to schedule regular time with partners or to attend to children's emergencies. The second was a lack of money needed to maintain relationships with partners and to provide for their children.

WHAT DOES IT MEAN?

1. What solutions might be effective in easing the dilemmas of these low-wage workers?

2. In what ways are the scheduling problems of low-wage and professional women similar? In what ways are they different?

---

of employed parents' greatest worries, it is not surprising that workers who have child care benefits show greater commitment to their employers (Hipp et al., 2016; Matos & Galinsky, 2014).

Finally, eldercare services would help many of the millions of workers who provide care for older relatives. Fewer than half of companies in the United States provide such benefits, but more are doing so than in the past (Matos & Galinsky, 2014; Sprung et al., 2015).

Unfortunately, the family-friendly benefits mentioned above are offered primarily by large companies, yet the majority of workers are employed by small companies. Furthermore, companies that employ better educated, highly skilled workers are more likely to offer these benefits than companies with a primarily unskilled labor force (Milkman, 2016; Miller & Streitfeld, 2015; O'Connor et al., 2014). Interestingly, employers with more women and minorities in top-level positions offer more family-friendly benefits (Matos & Galinsky, 2014).

SUPPORT FROM OTHER PEOPLE.   Enlisting the aid of others to help with domestic duties can be effective for some family–work jugglers (Haslam et al., 2015). Families who have the financial resources can purchase services such as housecleaning and meal preparation, although women still remain responsible for arranging the execution and management of these services (Wolf, 2016). Other women rely on the assistance of friends, family, and neighbors (Allen et al., 2014; Cheung & Halpern, 2010). Women's well-being is positively related to having a supportive spouse who participates in child care and housework (Edwards, 2007; Lee et al., 2014). Keep in mind, however, that support from husbands or male partners is frequently construed as "help," not as a shared responsibility, underscoring the social construction of different and unequal roles for women and men.

PERSONAL COPING STRATEGIES.   Unfortunately, some women receive no support from others, or the help they do receive is insufficient. Under these circumstances, women use several personal strategies to manage their numerous role responsibilities. Active, problem-focused coping aimed at solving the stressful situation is more beneficial than simply avoiding or complaining about the situation (Kinnunen et al., 2013). For example, some women negotiate with their employers about reduced hours. Women who reduce their work hours as a means of coping with family and work responsibilities report both benefits and costs. They experience greater satisfaction at home and less work–family conflict than women employed full time. However, they also report less career opportunity and work success (Hewlett, 2007; Reid, 2015). Erin Reid (2015) found that women are more likely than men to formally request reduced work hours. Men who want to increase family time, on the other hand, are more likely to lighten their work load informally, without asking for permission. For example, they may cover for each other, or reduce travel time by lining up local clients. The outcome? Individuals (mostly women) who specifically request a lighter load receive lower performance reviews than those (mostly men) who discreetly limit their work schedules (Reid, 2015).

Another strategy for women is to change their expectations of their responsibilities (Kinnunen et al., 2013). They might, for example, relax their standards for housecleaning or accept the possibility that a promotion might take longer to achieve. Many employed women utilize this strategy to some extent. As we saw earlier in this chapter, for example, employed mothers spend fewer hours doing housework than do stay-at-home mothers.

A third approach women use to coordinate family and work roles is to cut back on other activities such as sleep and leisure pursuits in order to handle all role responsibilities (Higgins et al., 2010; Martino, 2015). This approach can be difficult and exhausting, and women who use it are sometimes referred to as "supermoms." A fourth strategy used by some college-educated women is to devote themselves to their careers and then take time off to be stay-at-home mothers while their children are young. This option, however, is seldom realistic for single mothers or for women whose husbands do not earn a sizable income (Lips, 2016). The exercise in Get Involved 11.3 will help you gain firsthand information about women's experiences in balancing family and work roles. Then see What <u>You</u> Can Do 11.1 to become an advocate for family-friendly work policies.

MIDLIFE TRANSITIONS IN FAMILY AND WORK ROLES

Many women who currently are in their middle adult years go through a process of life review, that is, an intensive self-evaluation of numerous aspects of their lives (Etaugh, 2017). They reexamine their family and occupational values and goals, evaluate their accomplishments, and sometimes consider new career directions. Some make transitions to different jobs during their middle adult years whereas others begin their paid work role at this point in their lives.

Because of the many societal gender-role messages encountered by the current cohort of midlife women, some have followed traditional roles early in adulthood and continued these roles at midlife whereas others began their adult lives committed to traditional roles but made changes

---

GET INVOLVED 11.3
Women's Experiences in Coordinating Family and Work Roles

Interview two employed mothers who have children under 6 years of age. Ask each to talk about the following experiences: (1) time problems, if any, in performing all of their responsibilities; (2) conflicts, if any, between demands from different roles; (3) problems, if any, in arranging for child care; (4) psychological benefits they receive from their mother role; (5) psychological benefits they receive from their worker role; (6) personal coping strategies and/or employment benefits that have helped them deal with any time problems, conflicts, or child care difficulties; and (7) additional employer benefits they would find beneficial.

WHAT DOES IT MEAN?

1. What new information did you learn from these mothers' experiences that you did not learn from the text?
2. Did the responses of these women enhance your understanding of the costs and benefits of balancing motherhood and employment? Explain your answer.
3. Which solution do you think is the most effective for dealing with family–work balancing? Explain your answer.
4. Which family–work balancing hypothesis best accounts for these mothers' experiences? Explain your answer.

WHAT YOU CAN DO 11.1
Advocate for Family-Friendly Work Policies

Contact or join MomsRising (momsrising.org), a grassroots campaign devoted to making employment policies more family friendly (e.g., paid family leave, paid sick days, increased support for high-quality child care). Make a presentation on this topic to a class, residence hall meeting, or campus organization.

_____

Source: Kinser (2010).

in their middle adult years. Still others departed from traditional expectations by committing themselves to careers in early adulthood. Because each of these patterns of choices can be fulfilling, many women are satisfied with their life paths and, therefore, make no changes at midlife (Etaugh, 2017).

Given changing societal standards about appropriate roles for women, it is not surprising that one characteristic theme in the life reviews of midlife women today has been the search for an independent identity. Ravenna Helson (1992) has noted that for many women, the need to rewrite the life story in middle age is related to the lessening of the dependence and restriction associated with marriage and motherhood as children grow up. Thus, many heterosexual women attempt to affirm their own being, independent of their husbands, through graduate education, beginning a career, or switching careers (Newton et al., 2012). Sexual minority women, however, generally do not experience major transitions at midlife. Many are not mothers and have not experienced the role constraints characteristic of traditional heterosexual marriages. Therefore, they are not aiming to redefine themselves as separate from significant others. Furthermore, they already have a strong sense of self due to years of defining themselves independently of others' expectations and fighting hostility directed toward sexual minorities, and most have considered work an important part of their identity throughout their adult lives (Etaugh, 2017).

Satisfaction With Life Roles

For both young and midlife women, paid work is a significant predictor of psychological and physical well-being (Bericat, 2016; Bertrand, 2013). Middle-aged women who are involved in either beginning or building their career are both psychologically and physically healthier than women who are maintaining or reducing their career involvement (Etaugh, 2017). Women who have attained the occupational goals they set for themselves in young adulthood also have a greater sense of life purpose and are less depressed in midlife than those who fall short of their expectations (Carr, 1997). Furthermore, satisfaction with work predicts a general sense of well-being: The more satisfied women are with their jobs, the better they feel in general (Vandewater et al., 1997).

For other women, being a full-time homemaker can be as satisfying as combining a career and family or having a career but no spouse or children (Bertrand, 2013). Midlife homemakers whose life goal was a domestic role have a comparable sense of purpose in life to women who aspired toward and achieved an occupational role. Not surprisingly, however, women who are involuntarily out of the workforce, due to forced early retirement or layoff, are not as satisfied with midlife as women with a chosen role (Etaugh, 2013a). Thus, there are multiple routes to well-being in midlife, and it appears that a key factor influencing midlife role evaluation is not a woman's *role* per se but fulfillment of her *preferred role* (Bertrand, 2013).

Regrets About Life Direction

Although some midlife women are satisfied with traditional roles, others are distressed about missed educational or occupational opportunities (Newton et al., 2012). Some middle-class women, who as young adults devoted themselves solely to marriage and motherhood, voice regrets in midlife about their earlier traditional decisions. Abigail Stewart and Elizabeth Vandewater (1999) examined regrets experienced by women who graduated from college in the mid-1960s. These women reported disappointments about not pursuing a more prestigious career, marrying before establishing a career, and not returning to work after having children. The women who made changes based on these regrets experienced greater psychological well-being at midlife than those who had regrets but did nothing to alter their life direction.

Why did some women have regrets but not act on them? Interestingly, it was not external constraints, such as the number of children they had, that seemed to prevent these women from making goal-related changes. Instead, it was the tendency to ruminate on negative life events and engage in self-pity. Thus, these women seem to have been constrained by personality characteristics rather than external obstacles.

Making Changes

Pursuing a new direction at midlife involves making significant changes in one's life role during the middle adulthood years (Etaugh, 2017). A midlife woman who chooses to switch direction at this point must be willing to leave one long-term role (e.g., full-time homemaking or career) that has been a significant part of her identity and proceed down a new and unfamiliar path. In so doing, she is leaving a role to which she has devoted considerable time and energy during her adult years. What are the psychological experiences of women who begin a work role or alter occupational directions in midlife?

Let's take another look at Stewart and Vandewater's (1999) women college graduates who made major work-related changes in midlife. After an earlier full-time commitment to the traditional roles of wife and mother or to traditional female jobs, such as elementary or secondary school teacher, these women decided to follow a new career interest or return to an earlier interest that they had never pursued. What precipitated their new directions? For many, the women's movement made a strong impact on their midlife development by raising their awareness of the increasing possibilities open for women and, consequently, changing the way they constructed the female role. As they described it, "[The] women's movement taught me that I could be a doer and not a helper" and "[The] women's movement and political activism of the '60s led me to law school" (p. 404). These women were happy about the changes they made and felt a sense of accomplishment and pride, despite the fact that making these significant life changes was often difficult.

Midlife Transitions: A Cautionary Note

We saw in Chapter 1 that generalization based on one type of respondent can lead to false conclusions about individuals who are not represented in the sample. For at least two reasons, the research findings presented here are relevant to a specific group of midlife women and should not be extended to other women. First, the respondents in these studies were primarily White, highly educated, middle-class women. The midlife experiences of ethnic minority, less educated, and poor women are vastly different (Allen & Walker, 2009). For example, many of them have been both breadwinners and caregivers throughout their adult lives. They have not had the luxury of being able to choose one role or the other. Large variations in the options available to different groups of women can affect their aspirations and opportunities during early adulthood and at midlife. For example, poor women may feel so constrained by poverty that significant change and growth at midlife appears outside the realm of possibility.

Second, the midlife experiences discussed here must be placed in historical context. As social constructions of gender have evolved over time, women have experienced differing perceptions of their options. Women examined in the studies reported here were in their middle adult years in the late twentieth and early twenty-first centuries. Consequently, the gender-based social climate that shaped their development was different from the societal attitudes influencing the lives of future generations of midlife women. For example, today's midlife women were exposed to both traditional and flexible gender-role expectations at different points in their lives. Thus, it is likely that they experienced more regrets about previous traditional choices than future generations of midlife women will. Because there are greater options for young women today than there were when current midlife women were making life choices, fewer young women today may feel the need to make significant revisions in their life paths during middle age (Etaugh, 2017). Today's older women have also experienced different constructions of women's roles than have current midlife women. Because they were in midlife before the major societal role changes discussed here, they did not experience the career and role opportunities encountered by today's midlife women and, consequently, were not faced with decisions about major role changes.

Summary

WOMEN'S FAMILY AND EMPLOYMENT ROLES: PERCEPTIONS AND ATTITUDES

- Four out of five U.S. couples are dual-earner couples.
- The two groups of mothers who tend to opt out of the labor force are poor single women and women with high-earning husbands.
- Most North Americans now approve of employment among mothers of young children.
- Mothers who continue full-time employment after childbirth are evaluated more negatively than those who stay home or work part time.

DIVISION OF FAMILY LABOR

- Women perform most of the child care and housekeeping duties in the family even if they are employed. This pattern exists across ethnic groups, and around the world.
- Women provide the majority of care for aging parents and other older relatives.
- Much of women's leisure time is fragmented into small blocks of time.
- Women tend to be satisfied with the division of labor, although they perform the greater share.
- One reason may be that women have been socialized to view household duties as their domain. They might also view their obligations as fair compared to those of other women.
- Explanations for the unequal division of labor focus on time availability, relative power, and gender attitudes.

FAMILY–WORK COORDINATION

- Women across ethnic groups experience role strain as well as numerous benefits from multiple role juggling.

- Role strain can be explained by the scarcity hypothesis; benefits, such as self-esteem and approval from others, can be explained by the enhancement hypothesis.
- Another benefit of engaging in both family and work roles is that one role can buffer strains associated with the other.
- High-quality day care, even during infancy, does not hinder the child's social, academic, or emotional development. Furthermore, it can help improve school performance and reduce the social problems of children from low-income homes.
- Children with employed mothers have less stereotypical attitudes about gender roles than children of full-time homemakers.
- Positive psychological feelings, good parenting, and marital satisfaction are more likely when a woman feels comfortable about her role, whether as a full-time homemaker or employed wife and mother.
- The United States is one of the few countries that do not have federal legislation mandating paid parental leave.
- Women take shorter parental leaves if they are more highly educated, have nontraditional attitudes toward combining employment and parenting, and perceive their employers as family friendly.
- Employer resources, such as flextime, telecommuting, and child care assistance, and husbands' participation in family responsibilities and provision of emotional support can help women more effectively manage their multiple demands.
- Personal adjustments, such as altering one's role definitions, changing one's perceptions of responsibilities, and attempting to perform all role duties, are types of strategies women use to balance their family and work roles.

MIDLIFE TRANSITIONS IN FAMILY AND WORK ROLES

- Many women go through a life review during their middle adult years.
- Because those who are in midlife at the beginning of the twenty-first century were exposed to traditional gender-role expectations during their early years and to flexible gender roles later, many women now seek an identity independent of their husbands'.
- Some midlife women are satisfied with either the career or traditional paths they have followed.
- Other women experience regrets about previous traditional role choices, and some of these women choose to make significant changes in their life direction.

Key Terms

role strain *238*
role overload *239*

interrole conflict *239*
scarcity hypothesis *239*

enhancement hypothesis *240*
flextime *243*

What Do You Think?

1. Use any theory of gender typing (see Chapter 3) to explain the current division of household labor as presented in the text. Would this theory predict a greater equality of child care and household responsibilities in the future? Explain your answer.
2. Recall that women seem to be satisfied with an unequal division of household labor. Do you agree with the explanations given in the text? Are there other factors that can account for this phenomenon? Explain your answer.
3. Explain why young Black women, compared to White women, desire an earlier return to employment after they have children. Refer to material in previous chapters and any other information that addresses the question.
4. Women experience more role strain than men. Do you think this will change in the future? Explain your answer.
5. Does any of the material in this chapter have public policy implications related to parental leave? That is, does it point to the need for new parental leave legislation? Explain your answer.
6. Discuss the origins and implications of the widespread conceptualization of parenting as a female role. What benefits to mothers, fathers, and children would stem from a more inclusive view of parenting?

If You Want to Learn More

Boushey, H. (2016). *Finding time: The economics of work-life conflict.* Cambridge, MA: Harvard University Press.

Ecklund, E. & Lincoln, A.E. (2016). *Failing families, failing science: Work-family conflict in academic science.* New York: New York University Press.

Friedman, S.D. (2014). *Leading the life you want: Skills for integrating work and life.* Cambridge, MA: Harvard University Business School.

Grzywacz, J.G. & Demerouti, E. (2013). *New frontiers in work and family research.* New York: Psychology Press.

Hampson, S.C. (2017). *The balance gap: Working mothers and the limits of the law.* Stanford, CA: Stanford University Press.

Jones, B.D. (2012). *Women who opt out: The debate over working mothers and work-family balance.* New York: New York University Press.

Jones, F., Burke, R., & Westman, M. (Eds.). (2013). *Work–life balance: A psychological perspective.* New York: Psychology Pres.

Korabik, K. & Aycan, Z. (Eds.). (2017). *The work-family interface in global context.* New York: Routledge.

Kunin, M.M. (2012). *The new feminist agenda: Defining the next revolution for women, work, and family.* White River Junction, VT: Chelsea Green.

Liss, M. & Shiffrin, H. (2014). *Balancing the big stuff: Finding happiness in work, family, and life.* Lanham, MD: Rowman & Littlefield.

Meyers, M.H. (2014). Grandmothers at work: Juggling families and jobs. New York: New York University Press.

Mills, M. (2014). *Gender and the work-family experience: An intersection of two domains.* New York: Springer.

O'Brien, M. & Wall, K. (Eds.). (2016). *Comparative perspectives on work-life balance and gender equality: Fathers on leave alone.* New York: Springer Open.

Paludi, M.A. (Ed.). (2014). *Women, work, and family: How companies thrive with a 21st-century multicultural workforce.* Santa Barbara. CA: ABC-CLIO.

Schulte, B. (2014). *Overwhelmed: Work, love, and play when no one has the time.* New York: Sarah Crichton Books.

Slaughter, A.-M. (2015). *Unfinished business: Women men work family.* New York: Random House.

Websites

Family–Work Coordination

Catalyst
http://www.catalystwomen.org/
Institute for Women's Policy Research
http://www.iwpr.org/
Work and Family: National Partnership for
Women and Family
http://www.nationalpartnership.org/

Work and Family Connection
http://www.workfamily.com
Sloan Work and Family Research Network
http://www.bc.edu/wfnetwork

CHAPTER **12**

Physical Health

Several years ago, Dr. Annette Stanton, a professor of psychology at the University of Kansas, attended a university reception with a colleague. She reacted strongly when her colleague referred to a recent study concerning the connection between heart disease and caffeine consumption, which had received a great deal of media coverage. "I guess our hearts are safe if we have a cup of coffee," he said. "Your heart may be safe; I have no idea about the safety of my heart! That study was conducted on over 45,000 men," retorted Dr. Stanton. (adapted from Stanton, 1995, p. 3)

Physical health is not just a biological phenomenon, but a psychosocial one as well. It involves both individual behaviors and lifestyles and societal systems. There is a growing realization that women's health and health care are linked to inequalities in assessment, treatment, and access to care, and lack of research on health topics relevant to women in general and to ethnic minority women (Grigg & Kirkland, 2016; Hoffman et al., 2017) in particular. As a result, gender-sensitive and feminist health care has been increasingly moving into the mainstream of health policy (Palley, 2014; Sammarco, 2017).

A **feminist health care model** contrasts with the long-standing biomedical model, which views medical personnel as having power and control over patients, and which focuses on pathology rather than normalcy and wellness (Low & Bailey, 2017). The feminist model *supports egalitarian relationships between women and their health care providers, acknowledges that a woman is an expert on her own body, and does not view normal bodily functions and changes as diseases. In addition, the feminist framework rejects androcentric (male-based) models of health, challenges the "medicalizing" of women's health, and recognizes the broader psychosocial contexts of women's lives.* (The new view of women's sexual problems discussed in Chapter 6 is an example of a feminist approach to health.)

In this chapter, we examine issues in women's health and health care. We start by focusing on health services. Next, we turn to sexually transmitted infections, including AIDS, which has become the scourge of adolescent and young women worldwide. We then explore disorders that tend to affect women in the middle and later years: reproductive system disorders, osteoporosis, heart disease, breast cancer, and lung cancer. We continue with a discussion of women's health later in life. We close by focusing on ways to promote good health.

HEALTH SERVICES

Until the 1990s, little was known about many aspects of women's health. Women were routinely excluded as research participants in large studies designed to examine risk factors and potential treatments for various diseases, as shown in the chapter-opening vignette (Sagon, 2017). Even the first clinical trials to examine the effects of estrogen on heart disease were conducted solely on men! Scientists gave two principal reasons for confining medical experiments to men. First, women's monthly hormonal fluctuations "complicated" research results. Second, potential ethical and legal problems might arise from experimenting on women who would later bear children (Klein et al., 2015, Rabin, 2014a). The "male as normative" assumption (see Chapter 2) played a role as well (Kenschaft & Clark, 2016).

The growing recognition that women have a number of poorly understood medical problems and that diseases sometimes affect women and men in radically different ways has increasingly led health researchers to include women in their studies (Clayton & Collins, 2014; Elahi et al., 2016; "Why Science," 2015). Under the leadership of the first woman director of the National Institutes of Health, Bernadine Healy, the federal government established an Office of Research on Women's Health, and the National Institutes of Health mandated the inclusion of women in federally funded medical research (Hegarty et al., 2013). However, although more women are being studied, many medical studies still exclude or underrepresent them. For example, men continue to be the focus for much of the research on the leading cause of death among both women and men: heart disease (Gupta et al., 2013; Hayes et al., 2015; Horton, 2014; Nolan & Nguyen, 2013). In another glaring instance, recent research on the effects of alcohol on flibanserin, the drug to treat low sexual desire in women, was conducted almost solely on men ("A Pill to Boost," 2015). Studies include relatively few older women, even though heart disease is common in this group (Dodd et al., 2011; Kitzman & Rich, 2010). In addition, women, older people, and ethnic minorities are underrepresented in medical research including studies on three leading causes of cancer death: lung, breast, and colorectal cancers (Denson & Mahipal, 2014; Jenkins & Miller, 2016). Other health issues of ethnic minority women and poor rural women (Leach et al., 2011; Plank-Bazinet et al., 2016) have also not been sufficiently explored.

Moreover, medical researchers often ignore the requirement that they analyze their data to see if women and men respond differently to a given treatment (Jenkins & Miller, 2016). In addition, women are still underrepresented in studies to establish standard doses of new medications (Rodriguez et al., 2015). This omission can have serious consequences because women, especially older women, may have adverse effects from unnecessarily high drug doses, which have been established using male body weight as the standard (Rabin, 2014b).

In addition, gender biases still exist within the health care delivery system, leading to differences in the way health professionals interact with women and men and to differences in the care women and men receive (Grigg & Kirkland, 2016; Horton, 2014). In this section, we examine issues of gender discrimination in health services.

The Physician–Patient Relationship

Sexism in the physician–patient interaction is well documented (Chrisler et al., 2016; Edwards, 2013). Feminist analyses describe the interaction between female patients and male physicians as paternalistic, with women patients treated as subordinates. Male physicians frequently trivialize women's experiences by interrupting female patients and making jokes in response to their concerns. Physicians may belittle women's health complaints by attributing them to psychosomatic factors. For example, women's pain reports are taken less seriously than men's, and they receive less aggressive treatment for it. Women's pain reports are more likely to be dismissed as "emotional" and thus not "real" (Edwards, 2013). This stereotype may account for the fact that women consistently receive more prescriptions for tranquilizers, antidepressants, and anti-anxiety drugs than men (Kantor et al., 2015; Moore & Mattison, 2016; National Center for Health Statistics, 2015).

Sexist views of women are perpetuated in medical journal advertisements and medical textbooks as well. For example, anatomy and physical diagnosis textbooks have considerably fewer illustrations of women than men, and most of these are in the sections on reproduction (Mendelson, in Levison & Straumanis, 2002). Men are overrepresented in cardiovascular drug ads in medical journals, even though heart disease is the number one killer of both women and men (Cambronero-Saiz et al., 2013). In addition, the women in these ads are predominantly White, even though the rate of heart disease for African American is higher than for White women (Ahmed et al., 2004). Moreover, most men physicians depicted in medical journal ads are in paid productive roles shown in the home or in social contacts (Cambronero-Saiz et al., 2013).

A nationwide survey of women's health (Commission on Women's Health, 2003) found that women were twice as likely as men to report negative feelings about the patient–physician relationship. One in four women (compared to one in eight men) reported that they were "talked down to" by a physician. Moreover, 17 percent of women (compared to 7 percent of men) have been told that a medical condition they felt they had was "all in their head." Female physicians are more likely than male physicians to establish interpersonal rapport with their patients and to provide them with information about required tests and preventive services (DaSilva et al., 2013; Grant & Denmon, 2012; Reid et al., 2010). They also spend more time with their patients and tend to focus on them as people rather than on the procedures they need (Carrard & Mast, 2015; Hall et al., 20??). Moreover, women with heart disease risk factors and patients with diabetes and other medical conditions receive higher quality care from female physicians than from male physicians (Carvajal, 2011; Grant & Denmon, 2012; Parks & Redberg, 2016). Patients of female physicians report a greater willingness to reveal personal problems such as family violence or sexual abuse (Clancy, 2000). Not surprisingly, both women and men express more satisfaction with women physicians (Carrard & Mast, 2015; Janssen & Lagro-Janssen, 2012; Marks et al., 2015).

Type and Quality of Care

Discrimination based on gender affects not only interpersonal aspects of health care but also the type and quality of care that women receive. When one looks at medical conditions that affect both women and men, women often receive less adequate care even when the severity of the condition is the same for both (Chrisler et al., 2016). As we shall see later in this chapter, women with heart disease receive less aggressive treatment than men (McDaniel, 2014). Women are also not as likely as men to receive kidney dialysis, a kidney transplant, or knee replacement surgery (Borkhoff et al., 2008).

Biases exist even in childhood. For example, girls who are growing too slowly are referred to specialists only half as often as boys (Grimberg et al., 2005). Although it is true that boys tend to suffer greater social consequences if they are short, slow growth may be a sign of underlying disease. The failure of doctors to send small girls for closer examination can mean that serious problems go undetected.

Ageism presents older women with a double whammy. For one thing, health care professionals often emphasize older women's dependence, reinforcing women's perceptions of low self-efficacy and decreasing their active health care behaviors (Alexander et al., 2017, p. 279). Older patients of both sexes are more likely than younger patients to be addressed with less respect and patience, given less precise information, and asked fewer open-ended questions (Holstein, 2015). Moreover, older women are less likely than younger women to receive Pap smears, mammograms, or tests for colon cancer ("QuickStats," 2008; Yankaskas et al., 2010). In addition, physicians often attribute an older woman's chronic ailments to natural aging, and consequently, they are less apt to treat her for these conditions. For example, despite the fact that urinary incontinence and arthritis, which affect more women than men, can be treated effectively using medical or behavioral means, many health professionals dismiss it as an inevitable part of the aging process (Lachs, 2010; Pruthi, 2010).

Ethnicity, Poverty, and Health Care

Low-income individuals are more likely than others to have poor health (Chetty et al., 2016). Women of color are more likely than White women to have low income and to be uninsured. Latinas have the highest uninsurance rate of any group of women, followed by Native American women (Kogan et al., 2010; Moonesinghe et al., 2011). Because the lack of health insurance is often a financial barrier to seeking preventive health care, women of color and poor women are less likely to get the medical care they need (Pickett & Wilkinson, 2015; Rauscher et al., 2012; Weitz, 2010). In particular, women of color have often lacked access to preventive health care services such as Pap smears, mammograms, and cholesterol screening (Chen et al., 2012; Low Dog & Maizes, 2010). Furthermore, experiences with prejudice or culturally inappropriate health care cause many women of color to visit the doctor less frequently than White women do and to forego or delay follow-up and treatment after a medical test indicates an abnormality (Oyserman et al., 2014; Sewell, 2015; Tejeda et al., 2013). Immigrant women, in addition to facing the obstacles just mentioned, must often contend with language barriers (Genoff et al., 2016). In the words of one lower-income Latina woman, "They don't understand my language, my culture, my issues" (Clemetson, 2002, p. A12).

The good news is that the number of poor and ethnic minority women receiving mammograms and Pap smears has risen substantially during the past two decades (U.S. Department of Health & Human Services, 2013). The bad news is that even when their insurance and income are the same, racial and ethnic minorities in the United States often receive health care of lower quality than Whites (Klonoff, 2014; Paradies et al., 2014). In addition, poor women receiving Medicaid assistance have different reproductive health benefits than women with employment-based health insurance. Poor women on Medicaid receive mandated coverage of contraceptives, while until the recently passed Affordable Care Act working- and middle-class women often lacked much coverage. On the other hand, working- and middle-class women often have mandated coverage for infertility treatments, which Medicaid does not cover. The result is a policy that discourages poor women from having children (Lott & Bullock, 2001).

White women use prescription medications at a somewhat higher level than women of color (U.S. Department of Health & Human Services, 2013). One possible reason for this is that ethnic minority women may be more likely to encounter special difficulties procuring and using medications. Language differences and cultural differences in perceptions of illness can make communicating with the doctor especially problematic for immigrant women and men, resulting in greater difficulty following a prescribed regimen (Flores, 2006; Groh, 2009).

Women With Disabilities and Health Care

About 20 percent of all women in the United States have some level of disability. Native American and Black women have the highest incidence of severe disability, followed by White women, Latinas, and Asian American Women (Groh, 2009). Women with disabilities are faced with several barriers to health, including limited information, lack of transportation, physical inaccessibility to medical offices and equipment, and discrimination by health care providers, who may focus on the women's disability, rather than on basic routine health care needs (Alexander et al., 2017, Rios et al., 2016; UNAIDS, 2014a). Women with disabilities are more likely than other women to be poor, which further limits access to needed medical care (UNAIDS, 2014a).

Sexual Minority Women and Health Care

Sexual minority women may be at increased risk for certain health problems (Boehmer & Elk, 2015; Rosario et al., 2014). For one thing, they are at greater risk of breast and ovarian cancers because they are less likely than heterosexual women to experience the protective hormonal changes associated with pregnancy, and because they are more likely to smoke, consume alcohol, and be overweight (Cochran et al., 2016; Fredricksen-Goldsen et al., 2014).

The social stigma attached to sexual minority status also contributes health risks for lesbian, bisexual, and transgender women by reducing access to health care (Brotman et al., 2014; Erdley et al., 2014; Sabin et al., 2015; UNAIDS, 2014a).

Many sexual minority women avoid going to the doctor for routine checkups because they feel uncomfortable talking about issues that may reveal their sexual orientation and consequently elicit negative reactions from the physicians, many of whom lack expertise in LGBT health (Institute for Womens Policy Research, 2015; Orel, 2014). In the words of a physician who specializes in care of LGBT individuals, "Imagine if you're a masculine looking trans man, and you're going to the gynecologist. You go to the front desk and you have to out yourself. Everyone can hear what's going on. You just want to run out the door" (Grady, 2016a, p. A10). LBT women may also limit their visits to doctors because they are less likely to have health insurance as same-sex partners often cannot share spousal benefits (Lamm & Eckstein, 2015). Even for those who do have coverage, managed health care plans often limit women's ability to choose lesbian-friendly health care providers. The reduced access to health care that results from fear of discrimination and from financial barriers elevates health risks for lesbians, bisexuals, and transgender women (Allen & Roberto, 2016; Dahlhamer et al., 2016; Institute for Women's Policy Research, 2015; Orel, 2014; Rowan & Giunta, 2016). Transgender individuals have the greatest difficulty with accessing health care. They are more likely than other sexual minorities to be denied care or receive inferior care ("Access," 2015; Buchholz, 2015; Clay, 2014b; Ellin, 2016a; Schuster et al., 2016). Organizations that can help locate health professionals who are sensitive to the needs of female sexual minorities are listed in the Websites at the end of this chapter.

Health Insurance

What kinds of insurance programs are available to U.S. adults and how do they affect women? These programs can be grouped into government plans (Medicare, Medicaid, Affordable Care Act), and private plans (fee-for-service and managed care).

GOVERNMENT PLANS. **Medicare** is the *federal program designed to provide medical care for those who are over 65 or permanently disabled, regardless of income.* Medicare covers less than half of medical costs and it does not cover most long-term care or home and supportive care. These limitations affect women disproportionately because they not only have more medical concerns but also have more complex medical conditions than men. In addition, some physicians do not accept Medicare patients because the reimbursement is low (AARP, 2006; Alexander et al., 2013; Donatelle, 2017).

Medicaid is a *combined state and federal program designed to provide medical care for the needy of any age* (Iglehart, 2010). As with Medicare, many health care providers refuse to see Medicaid recipients because of low reimbursement rates. These patients have to rely on clinics and emergency rooms. Individuals with high medical bills who do not qualify for Medicaid *ultimately become eligible once they have depleted most of their financial resources and assets.* This process, called **spending down**, is most common among residents of nursing homes, most of whom are women (O'Brien, 2005).

Women rely more heavily than men on both Medicaid and Medicare because they are more likely to be poor and because they live longer (U.S. Department of Health and Human Services, 2013). Moreover, women are less likely than men to have insurance through their own employers because they are more likely to work in temporary or part-time jobs or in occupations that do not provide health insurance benefits (Meyer & Herd, 2007). A woman who is covered under a spouse's plan risks losing coverage in the event of divorce, the spouse's death, or his retirement (Office on Women's Health, 2007).

The newest government health plan is the Affordable Care Act. For details, see In the News 12.1.

IN THE NEWS 12.1
Women and the Affordable Care Act

The Affordable Care Act (ACA) has changed the face of health care in the United States since it began in 2013, providing treatment and coverage to millions of the uninsured while transforming the insurance and hospital industries. The number of uninsured Americans has dropped by half, with 20 million more people gaining coverage (Pear, 2015; E. Rosenthal, 2016). Immigrants, the poor, and ethnic minorities make up the majority of those now covered (Tavernise & Gebeloff, 2016). The health of those covered already is improving compared to that of individuals without coverage (Sommers, 2016). One important benefit for women under the ACA is that health insurance plans are now required to cover key preventive health care services for women without charging co-pays or deductibles. These include contraceptive care, tests for sexually transmitted infections, well-woman preventive care, maternity and newborn care, and screening and counseling for intimate partner violence. Moreover, insurance companies can no longer charge women more than men for the same insurance plan. In addition, medical eligibility has been expanded to many more low-income women, whether or not they have children (Pearson, 2013; Politi, 2016; Salganicoff & Sobel, 2016; Simmons, 2016). As of this writing, however, the new U.S. president is proposing changes to the ACA that would limit or eliminate health care for many, especially those with lower incomes (Goodnough & Abelson, 2017).

PRIVATE INSURANCE PLANS.   Most Americans are covered by private health insurance provided by their own employers or the employer of a family member. One of the two types of private plans is **fee-for-service insurance**. *The insurer pays part of the cost (usually 80 percent) for specified services, including hospitalization (up to a certain limit) and diagnostic services, but not preventive care.* The second type of private insurance is **managed care**, which has become the leading means of financing health care (Donatelle, 2017). Managed care *provides services to members for a flat fee and emphasizes preventive care and early detection of disease more than fee-for-service plans do.* Health maintenance organizations (HMOs) and preferred provider organizations (PPOs) are the most common types of managed care (Donatelle, 2017). Providing inexpensive screening procedures such as mammograms and Pap tests makes the services affordable for many women. However, managed care often limits access to specialists and reduces treatment options for many women, particularly older women who frequently have many chronic ailments requiring treatment by different specialists. Limited finances often prevent older women from seeing the physicians or purchasing the medications not covered by their managed care insurance (Older Women's League, 2004). Moreover, women enrolled in HMOs are more likely than those not in HMOs to report not getting needed care and being less satisfied with their physicians (Davis et al., 2000).

Older women may view health and health care differently than younger women. To compare how these two groups view health issues, try Get Involved 12.1.

GET INVOLVED 12.1
What Women Say About Their Health

Answer the following questions and ask two young adult women and two women aged 65 or older to answer the same questions.

1. Whom would you trust more to be your doctor, a woman or a man, or would you trust them equally?

2. Which presents the more serious risk: heart disease or breast cancer?

3. How would you describe your health: excellent, good, fair, or poor?

4. In general, who has more health problems: men or women?

5. Who handles being sick better: women or men?

6. Whose complaints do doctors take more seriously: men's, women's? Or do they give equal consideration to both?

7. How often do doctors talk down to you: most of the time, some of the time, hardly ever, or never?

8. Where do you get most of your medical information: doctors, television, newspapers and magazines, or the Internet?

WHAT DOES IT MEAN?

1. How do the responses of the older women compare with the information presented in the chapter?

2. How do the responses of the older women compare with the responses of your college-age friends? How can age account for these differences?

3. Can you think of any factors other than age that might account for any differences between the responses of the two groups of women?

Source: Elder (1997).

SEXUALLY TRANSMITTED INFECTIONS (STIs)

Sexually transmitted infections (STIs) have reached epidemic proportions around the world (Marks et al., 2015; World Health Organization, 2015a). Of the more than 19 million new cases of STIs diagnosed in the United States each year, nearly half occur in teens and young adults (Centers for Disease Control and Prevention, 2014). Four in ten sexually active American teenage girls are infected (Office of Adolescent Health, 2016). Yet two-thirds of adolescent girls do not discuss STIs with their health care providers (Kaiser Family Foundation, 2014). We will first give an overview of STIs (see Table 12.1) and then turn to AIDS, the most life-threatening of the STIs.

Overview of STIs

If untreated, STIs can have serious consequences. For example, chlamydia, the most commonly reported STI in the United States today, can lead to chronic pain, pelvic inflammatory disease, and infertility (Torrone et al., 2014). In addition, the human papillomavirus (HPV), found in nearly half of young American women, increases the risk of cervical cancer (American Cancer Society, 2016a; Markowitz et al., 2016). People with syphilis, gonorrhea, chlamydia, or herpes are more likely than others to become infected with the AIDS virus, in part because they have open sores that allow the virus to enter the body (Rogstad, 2011).

STIs have a disproportionate impact on women. They are transmitted more easily to women than to men and are more difficult to diagnose in women (Institute for Women's Policy Research, 2015). In addition, women may be at high risk of STIs because of social and cultural norms that dictate that women do not decline sexual intercourse with their partners or insist on the use of condoms (UNAIDS, 2014a, b). Factors that enhance a woman's risk for contracting STIs include being

TABLE 12.1   Major Sexually Transmitted Infections (STIs)

STI	Mode of Transmission	Symptoms	Treatment
Chlamydia	Sexual contact; from mother to baby during birth	Painful urination and intercourse, vaginal discharge; often no symptoms	Antibiotics, e.g., doxycycline, azithromycin
Genital herpes	Sexual contact; most contagious during active outbreaks	Painful blisters near vagina, buttocks; often no symptoms	No cure. Antiviral drugs help healing
Gonorrhea	Sexual contact; from mother to baby during birth	Vaginal discharge, painful urination, bleeding between periods; often no symptoms	Antibiotics, e.g., cephalosporins
Hepatitis B	Sexual contact	Jaundice, loss of appetite	Interferon; preventive vaccine
HIV/AIDS	Sexual contact; infected blood transfusions; from mother to baby during birth or breastfeeding	Flu; weight loss; fatigue; opportunistic infections such as thrush, shingles, herpes	No cure. Antiretroviral drugs delay progress of the disease
HPV/Genital warts	Sexual contact	Painless warts in vagina; often no symptoms	No cure. Wart removal by laser or burning; preventive vaccine
Syphilis	Sexual contact when sores are present; mother to fetus	Initially, hard, painless chancre (sore)	Penicillin
Trichomoniasis	Sexual contact	Yellow odorous vaginal discharge; itching, burning in vulva	Antibiotics, e.g., metronidazole

Sources: Donatelle (2017); Jones (2016); Rathus et al. (2013); Workowski and Bolan (2015).

under 25, using condoms inconsistently, being sexually active at an early age, and having sex frequently and with multiple partners (Centers for Disease Control and Prevention, 2014; Workowski & Bolan, 2015). Because the risk of woman-to-woman sexual transmission of STIs is small, the prevalence of STIs in lesbians and bisexual women is fairly low but is not zero (Chan et al., 2014; Tat et al., 2015).

One factor behind the rapid increase in STIs is that the majority of American women have relatively little knowledge of STIs and even less concern about contracting one (Friedman & Bloodgood, 2010). For more on this subject, see Learn About the Research 12.1.

AIDS

Acquired immunodeficiency syndrome (AIDS), *caused by the human immunodeficiency virus (HIV)*, is the most devastating of all the STIs. For women aged 15-44, HIV/AIDS is the leading cause of death worldwide (World Health Organization, 2015a). Although the overall number of AIDS cases in the United States began to drop in the mid-1990s, cases of HIV infection and AIDS among individuals of color have continued to increase. Women—particularly women of color—are the fastest-growing group of Americans infected with HIV. Heterosexual sex has become the leading method of transmission for women both in the United States and abroad (Bradley et al., 2014; Haley & Justman, 2013).

LEARN ABOUT THE RESEARCH 12.1
Knowledge and Communication About STIs

In 2007–2008, individual interviews were conducted in 10 metropolitan areas with Black, Latina, and White females of ages 15–25 to determine their knowledge of and communication about STIs (Friedman & Bloodgood, 2010). Most of the young women were not knowledgeable about chlamydia, its asymptomatic nature, its potential to cause infertility, or its screening. One in five thought the Pap test screened for all STIs. Moreover, most felt uncomfortable discussing STIs with parents, partners, or friends. Nearly one in three had never discussed STIs with a health care provider, mentioning barriers such as having a male provider, feeling rushed during the visit, or having their mothers present.

WHAT DOES IT MEAN?

1. What actions can be taken to better educate women about STIs? What should school children be taught on this topic?

2. What can be done to increase communication between a young woman and her reproductive health care provider?

Women accounted for 20 percent of new HIV infections in the United States in 2010 (Kaiser Family Foundation, 2014). Although many are young, low-income women of color who live in urban areas, the incidence of HIV-infected rural White women is also on the rise (Rural Center for AIDS/STD Prevention, 2009). Black women, who constitute just 13 percent of American women, make up nearly two-thirds of women with AIDS in the United States (Kaiser Family Foundation, 2014). In 2011, their HIV rate was 20 times higher than that of Whites and nearly 5 times higher than that of Latinas (U.S. Department of Health and Human Services, 2013). Why are Black women at heightened risk for AIDS? Poverty, inadequate access to HIV prevention services, and a dearth of information about safe sex are major reasons (Centers for Disease Control and Prevention, 2014). In addition, the lower number of economically viable and available Black men may lead Black women to take more sexual risks in order to attract and keep a partner (El-Bassel et al., 2009). Moreover, low-income women may be economically dependent on a partner and thus not in a position to negotiate safer sex (Watkins-Hayes, 2014).

Women, especially Black women, are sicker at the time of diagnosis with HIV or AIDS and die more quickly than men with the disease (Alexander et al., 2013; Rubin, Colen, et al., 2009). Why are women often diagnosed at a later stage of HIV than men? For one thing, women are generally viewed as being at low risk for the disease and so they and their physicians may overlook signs of HIV infection that they exhibit. Second, women usually serve as caregivers for family members and, increasingly, as breadwinners. As a result, they may delay seeking health care for themselves until they are very ill. Finally, as noted earlier, many HIV-infected women live in poverty and fewer have access to health care (El-Bassel et al., 2009; M. Hoffman et al., 2017).

Decisions about childbearing can be difficult for HIV-infected women (Sandelowski et al., 2009). Without any intervention, the chances of passing the virus to their children are 25 percent (Wilson, 2011). In industrialized countries, an infected woman who takes antiretroviral drugs during pregnancy, has a cesarean delivery, avoids breastfeeding, and whose newborn is given antiretroviral drugs has only about a 1- to 2-percent chance of infecting her child (Kaiser Family Foundation, 2014). But in developing countries, complex antiretroviral drug regimens are often unavailable, and avoidance of breastfeeding is not a realistic option for most women. Consequently, many women with HIV must wrestle with the fact that their children may be infected and may also be motherless at a young age. It is helpful for HIV-infected women to share dilemmas such as this in a support group or HIV workshop (Rural Center for AIDS/STD Prevention, 2009). Many of these women feel isolated and have not disclosed their illness out of fear of rejection and ostracism (Rural Center for AIDS/STD Prevention, 2009). Often, a support group may be a woman's first opportunity to meet other women with HIV or AIDS and to receive help in locating government-subsidized sources of anti-HIV medication (Cowley & Murr, 2004).

The best way to prevent HIV infection is to practice "safer sex," that is, avoid unprotected sex with multiple partners and always use latex or polyurethane condoms during sexual intercourse (Johnston et al., 2015b; Workowski & Bolan, 2015). The good news is that, in recent years, American teenagers have shown improvement in these HIV-related sexual risk behaviors (Gavin et al., 2009). Unfortunately, many young people, including college students, still fail to engage in safer sex practices. Factors underlying these risky sexual behaviors include a perceived low risk of infection and negative attitudes toward condom use (Rathus et al., 2013). Let us now take a closer look at the worldwide AIDS epidemic.

 THE GLOBAL AIDS EPIDEMIC.   Nearly 37 million people worldwide, more than half of them women, are infected with HIV (Grady, 2016b). Sub-Saharan Africa, with 10 percent of the world's population but over two-thirds of the world's HIV/AIDS sufferers, is the most severely affected region. There, nearly 60 percent of those infected are women (UNAIDS, 2014a, b).

Adolescent girls and young women of childbearing age in Africa are two to five times more likely to develop HIV/AIDS than their male counterparts for a variety of biological, social, and economic reasons (UNAIDS, 2014a, b). Many adolescent girls marry older men, who have likely had several previous sexual partners. At the same time, cultural resistance to condom use is high. Moreover, many adolescents in sub-Saharan Africa have limited knowledge of how to protect themselves from HIV infection (Icheku, 2016; UNAIDS, 2014a, b). These factors result in high rates of STIs, which increase chances of HIV transmission. In addition, poverty, economic dependency, and low status render women powerless to protect themselves against unsafe or unwanted sex. Sadly, the proportion of infected women has rapidly expanded in other parts of the world as well, particularly eastern Europe and central and Southeast Asia (UNAIDS, 2014a, b). In countries such as India, where the vast majority of females with HIV are infected by their husbands, women are unable to negotiate condom use without risking reprisals (Kenschaft & Clark, 2016). Women who contract HIV from their husbands may be blamed and stigmatized (Asiedu & Myers-Bowman, 2014). Even those girls and women who do not contract HIV are deeply affected by the epidemic, because the burden of caring for the sick usually falls on them. Girls are often withdrawn from school to care for ailing parents or younger siblings, or to earn an income (Henderson & Jeydel, 2010; Mukherjee et al., 2010).

Several developing countries have had some recent success in slowing the spread of HIV through AIDS education and condom promotion, and in providing greater access to HIV treatment for those who are infected (UNAIDS, 2014a, b).

AIDS IN OLDER WOMEN.   Whatever a woman's age, if she is sexually active, she is at risk for contracting sexually transmitted diseases, including HIV. Today, about 6 percent of the new cases of HIV/AIDS in U.S. women are diagnosed among women aged 55 and older, and this number is growing (National Center for Health Statistics, 2014). In the mid-1980s, most AIDS cases among women in that age group were caused by blood transfusions. Now, heterosexual contact is the leading cause (Kaiser Family Foundation, 2014). One factor increasing older women's risk during heterosexual contact is the thinning of the vaginal tissues and the decrease in lubrication after menopause, which can cause small skin tears or abrasions during intercourse, thus increasing the chance of HIV entering the bloodstream. Another factor in the rise of HIV in older people is the increase in sexual activity fueled by Viagra, but without a corresponding increase in condom use (Greene et al., 2013). Many of today's aging baby boomers grew up before the HIV epidemic and didn't learn how to negotiate condom use with their partners. The result is that most sexually active older singles report having unprotected sex (Centers for Disease Control and Prevention, 2013a; UNAIDS, 2014a, b).

Older women who have HIV infection may have a harder time than infected younger women in obtaining a correct diagnosis and treatment. Because older women are generally viewed as sexually disinterested and inactive, they are less likely to be given information about safer sex practices (Johnson, 2013; Spring, 2015). Moreover, physicians do not expect to see AIDS in older women, and therefore, they are more likely to make a late diagnosis or a misdiagnosis. Also, women of this age group are less likely to think of themselves as being at risk for AIDS, and so they may not think to ask for an HIV test (Beaulaurier et al., 2014; National Institute on Aging, 2015; Watkins-Hayes, 2014). Failure to diagnose HIV early can have serious consequences at any age because it is harder to arrest the disease when it becomes more advanced. But older adults with HIV are even more likely to deteriorate rapidly because their already weakened immune system does not respond as well to antiretroviral therapy (UNAIDS, 2014a, b).

HIV infection takes an enormous emotional toll on older women, many of whom live alone and are already trying to cope with physical, economic, and personal losses. Whereas today's younger women are used to talking more freely about sexual problems, this is difficult for many older women. They feel ashamed and may suffer alone, avoiding telling friends and family (Centers for Disease Control and Prevention, 2013a; Durvasula, 2014). Many older women with HIV, however, are learning to adjust to their condition and report using strategies to "live well" within the context of the disease (Durvasula, 2014; Psaros et al., 2014).

REPRODUCTIVE SYSTEM DISORDERS

STIs are not the only diseases that can affect the reproductive system. We now turn to other disorders including benign (noncancerous) conditions such as endometriosis and fibroid tumors, as well as various cancers.

Benign Conditions

Endometriosis is a chronic and sometimes painful condition in which the *lining of the uterus (endometrium) migrates and grows on pelvic structures, such as the ovaries, fallopian tubes, and bladder.* This condition affects 6–10 percent of women of reproductive age in the United States each year. Endometriosis can cause pelvic and menstrual pain and heavy bleeding. Severe endometriosis is a major cause of infertility (Brown & Farquhar, 2015; Ellin, 2015; Young et al., 2013).

Up to two out of three women will develop **uterine fibroid tumors**, which are *noncancerous growths of the uterus*, at some time in their lives. Fibroids are not dangerous, but they can cause severe pelvic and menstrual pain, heavy bleeding, and possibly infertility and miscarriage. They occur more often in Black women than in White women (Chabbert-Buffet et al., 2014; Mayo Clinic, 2014).

Cancers

Endometrial (uterine) cancer is the most common cancer of the female reproductive tract and is often characterized by vaginal bleeding. Risk factors include estrogen replacement therapy (without use of progestin), obesity, early menarche, late menopause, and never having children (American Cancer Society, 2015). Although it is more common in White women than in Black women, Black women are more likely to die from it (Singh et al., 2017b). Because most cases are detected early, this is one of the most curable cancers of the reproductive system, with a 5-year survival rate of over 90 percent for localized uterine cancer (American Cancer Society, 2015).

Cancer of the **cervix**, *the lower end of the uterus*, is the third most common cancer of the female genital system, after uterine and ovarian cancers (American Cancer Society, 2016a). In the United States, more than 90 percent of those who have developed cervical cancer have a 5-year survival rate if the cancer is detected in its earliest stages (American Cancer Society, 2014). Black, Latina, and Native American women, however, have a much higher death rate, probably because their more limited access to medical care prevents early diagnosis and treatment (Beavis et al., 2017; Benard et al., 2014). Factors that increase the risk of cervical cancer include smoking, being overweight, early age at first intercourse, multiple sex partners, extended use of oral contraceptives, and infection with HPV, the common virus that causes genital warts (American Cancer Society, 2014). The **Pap smear**, *an inexpensive and effective screening technique*, has been used for several decades to identify precancerous changes in the cervix. Over the past 50 years, the test has slashed cervical cancer deaths by 70 percent and saved thousands of lives (Saslow, 2012). In the United States, of those women who develop cervical cancer, about half have never had a Pap smear (Chen et al., 2012). Women should start getting an annual Pap test by age 21 or 3 years after the onset of sexual activity, whichever comes first. If a woman aged 30 or older has had three normal test results in a row, the interval can be increased to every 2 to 3 years (Beavis et al., 2017; Benard et al., 2014). Unfortunately, only slightly more than 80 percent of women have Pap smears at least once every 5 years. Women who are poor, uninsured, less educated, and older are least likely to get regular Pap tests (Beavis et al., 2017; Benard et al., 2014). The good news is that the HPV vaccine developed in 2006 could drastically reduce the incidence of cervical cancer worldwide over the next several decades (Daley et al., 2016). It has already reduced the prevalence of HPV in U.S. teen girls by over 50 percent. However, only about four in ten girls have received the recommended three doses of the vaccine (Viens et al., 2016). One reason is the relatively high cost of the vaccine. Another is that some parents fear that giving their daughters the preventive vaccine might send the subtle message that premarital sex is acceptable (Holman et al., 2014; McKeever et al., 2015). What is your view on this issue?

Ovarian cancer is a major killer of women, causing more deaths than any other cancer of the female reproductive system. It is a so-called silent killer because its symptoms usually do not appear until the cancer is in an advanced stage (Wardle et al., 2015). For all types of ovarian cancer, the 5-year survival rate is 46 percent. Risk factors include having immediate family members with ovarian, breast, or colon cancer; having early menarche and late menopause; using hormone replacement therapy; being obese; and smoking. However, bearing children, breastfeeding, being physically active, taking birth control pills, and eating a low-fat diet are protective factors (American Cancer Society, 2016a; Rebbek et al., 2015). Early symptoms of ovarian cancer include bloating, pelvic or abdominal pain, difficulty eating or feeling full quickly, and frequent or urgent urination. Women with these symptoms for more than a few weeks are advised to see their doctors (American Cancer Society, 2014). The tests used most often for detecting ovarian cancer are a blood test for the CA-125 tumor marker followed by a transvaginal ultrasound. However, these tests have not lowered ovarian cancer deaths in women with average risk (American Cancer Society, 2014).

Hysterectomy

Each year, over 600,000 women in the United States undergo a **hysterectomy**, the *removal of the uterus*. By age 60, more than one in four American women have had their uterus removed, one of the highest rates in the world (Alexander et al., 2013). For years, many critics have questioned the high rate of hysterectomy in this country. Although removal of the uterus is considered appropriate in cases of cancer of the uterus, cervix, or ovaries, these situations account for only a small fraction of the total hysterectomies performed in the United States. Endometriosis, uterine fibroid tumors, heavy menstrual bleeding, and chronic pelvic pain are other common reasons for hysterectomy (Office on Women's Health, 2014). Because Black women are more likely than White women to have fibroid tumors, their hysterectomy rates are also higher (Stewart et al., 2013).

What is the psychological impact of a hysterectomy? Jean Elson (2004) interviewed 44 women, ages 24 to 69, whose uterus had been removed for benign conditions. All the women reflected on their gender identity following surgery. Their reactions ranged all the way from "Now I feel like a fake woman" to "I have always been . . . the same person" (Ayoub, 2004, p. A18). Most of the women missed the potential to have children. This was true whether or not they already had children and even if they never intended to have them (Ayoub, 2004). In spite of feelings of loss, however, many women view their hysterectomy positively as relieving chronic pain and enabling them to regain control over their bodies (Markovic et al., 2008).

Another common practice, which has been heavily criticized, is the removal of the ovaries along with the uterus, even when the ovaries are normal and healthy. Physicians who carry out such surgery contend that when a women is in her mid-40s or older, the ovaries' major function is over and that removing them forestalls the possibility of ovarian cancer (Parker et al., 2013). Can you see the sexist bias in this argument? Could one not equally argue that the prostate and testes of middle-aged men should be removed to prevent cancer of these organs? Recent evidence (Parker et al., 2013) shows that women who keep their ovaries actually live *longer* than those whose ovaries are removed during a hysterectomy. This is due largely to the heart-protective effects of estrogen.

OSTEOPOROSIS

Osteoporosis is an *excessive loss of bone tissue in older adults, which results in the bones becoming thinner, brittle, and more porous.* Osteoporosis affects about 10 million Americans, 80 percent of them women (Kling et al., 2014; National Osteoporosis Foundation, 2014). But the seeds of osteoporosis are sown in adolescence, when bone building is most rapid (Zumwalt & Dowling, 2014). By their middle to late 20s, women reach their peak bone mass. Around age 30, gradual bone loss begins. The rate of bone loss accelerates sharply for 5 to 7 years after the onset of menopause, as estrogen levels drop (National Osteoporosis Foundation, 2014). Each year, 1.5 million fractures related to osteoporosis occur in the United States. Half of all women over 50 years of age will have a fracture during their lifetime because of osteoporosis. These fractures can be crippling and painful and can cause permanent loss of mobility. As many as one in three patients with a hip fracture dies of complications such as blood clots and pneumonia (National Osteoporosis Foundation, 2014).

Risk Factors

Some women are more likely to develop osteoporosis than others. For a list of risk factors, see Table 12.2. Postmenopausal women with one or more of these risk factors, and all women over 65, should consider getting a bone density test, which can detect even a small loss of bone mass (National Osteoporosis Foundation, 2014).

TABLE 12.2   Risk Factors for Osteoporosis

Biological Factors
- Gender: women's risk is greater because their bones are smaller and lighter
- Age: after age 30, bone loss begins
- Menopause: drop in estrogen levels increases bone loss
- Thin, small-framed body
- Ethnicity: White and Asian women, who have lower bone density, are at greater risk
- Family history of osteoporosis or older relatives with fractures

Lifestyle Factors
- Diet low in calcium and vitamin D
- High intake of sodium, animal protein, caffeine
- Lack of physical activity
- Smoking
- Alcohol intake of two or more drinks a day

Medical Factors
- Rheumatoid arthritis, diabetes, celiac disease, lactose intolerance
- Eating disorders
- Certain medications: diuretics, steroids, anticonvulsants

Sources: National Osteoporosis Foundation (2014); North American Menopause Society, 2014.

Prevention and Treatment

A look at Table 12.2 suggests several ways to build and keep as much bone as possible. Increasing calcium and vitamin D intake during childhood, adolescence, and young adulthood is the most effective way of building denser bones and reducing risk of bone fracture (National Osteoporosis Foundation, 2014). In order to suppress bone loss, experts recommend consumption of 1,300 milligrams of calcium per day for adolescents, 1,000 milligrams for women aged 19 to 50, and 1,200 milligrams for postmenopausal women. Good sources of calcium include low-fat and nonfat milk, cheese, and yogurt; tofu and other soy products; dark-green leafy vegetables such as kale and spinach; almonds; and canned sardines and salmon (Brody, 2016b).

Unfortunately, most adolescents and women consume far less calcium than they should (National Institutes of Health, 2013c). Calcium supplements are good additional sources, especially those containing calcium carbonate (found in Tums and Rolaids) or calcium citrate (found in Citracal). Calcium cannot be absorbed without vitamin D. In order to keep bones strong, women under age 50 need 400–800 international units per day of vitamin D, and older women need 800–1,000 international units (National Osteoporosis Foundation, 2014). Milk fortified with vitamin D and sunlight are two of its best sources. Still, most adults may need dietary supplements in order to prevent vitamin D deficiency (National Osteoporosis Foundation, 2014).

Diet is only part of the equation, however. Exercise is very important in increasing bone mass during adolescence and young adulthood and in slowing bone loss after menopause. The exercise should be weightbearing, such as brisk walking, low-impact aerobics, or lifting weights. Even everyday activities such as climbing stairs, walking the dog, doing yard work, dancing, or playing with children can be beneficial. It is never too late to start exercising and a little bit of physical activity is better than none (Donatelle, 2017). Not only decreasing or eliminating smoking and decreasing consumption of alcohol and most sources of caffeine (except for green tea) are good for strong bones, but they may also confer many other health benefits, as we shall see later in the chapter (Conforti et al., 2012).

Estrogen helps build and maintain strong bones. Estrogen replacement therapy starting in perimenopause and continuing after menopause slows bone loss, increases bone mass, and reduces the incidence of fractures (National Osteoporosis Foundation, 2014). However, because hormone replacement therapy is now known to increase the risk of heart attack, stroke, and breast cancer (see Chapter 7), it is no longer considered an option for preventing osteoporosis. Fortunately, other medications can help a woman strengthen her bones. Drugs called bisphosphonates (sold as Fosamax, Actonel, Reclast, and Boniva) decrease the risk of hip and spinal fractures. **Raloxifene**, a *synthetic estrogen* marketed as Evista, decreases bone loss in postmenopausal women and reduces the risk of spinal fractures and also breast cancer (National Osteoporosis Foundation, 2014).

HEART DISEASE

Heart disease is the leading cause of death for both women and men around the world. More women in the United States die of heart disease than from all forms of cancer combined, including breast cancer. Specifically, over one in three women will eventually die from heart disease compared to only one in thirty from breast cancer (American Heart Association, 2015). Yet many women are not aware of the risks of heart disease (Garcia et al., 2016) and perceive breast cancer as a far greater threat to their health. Although awareness that heart disease is the top killer of women has grown since the late 1990s, awareness of risk factors for the disease remains low, particularly for women under age 55 and for ethnic minority women (American Heart Association, 2015; Koniak-Griffin & Brecht, 2015; Ramachandran et al., 2016).

Gender Differences

Important gender differences in heart disease affect the onset, diagnosis, and treatment of the disease in women and men (McDaniel, 2014). Heart disease in women becomes apparent about 10 years later than in men. Illness and death from heart disease increase dramatically in women after menopause, partly due to declining levels of heart-protective estrogen (Bertone-Johnson et al., 2015). By her 70s, a woman has a greater risk of heart attack and heart disease than a man her age (Pruthi, 2010). Women are more likely than men to die after a heart attack. If they survive, they are more likely to have a second attack (Texas Heart Institute, 2015). Because women are older than men when they develop heart disease, their prognosis is poorer. But women are more likely than men to die after treatment for heart disease, even when they are equally old and ill (American Heart Association, 2015).

Risk Factors

Some risk factors for heart disease are unchangeable. In addition to gender and age, these include income level, ethnicity, and family history. Women from low-income households are more likely to have heart attacks and to die from them (American Heart Association, 2015). Because Black and Native American women are disproportionately represented at the low end of the income scale, this may partly explain why they are more likely to die from heart disease than are White women (Mehta et al., 2016). The risk of heart disease and stroke also increases if close family members have had these diseases (National Heart, Lung, and Blood Institute, 2014).

Major risk factors over which women have control include physical inactivity, smoking, being overweight, having a poor diet, and using hormone replacement therapy (Brody, 2015; Yu et al., 2016). Women who have none of these factors have a much lower risk of heart disease than other women. Even young women, who have a low rate of heart disease, should begin controlling these risk factors early in life (American Heart Association, 2015).

Inactivity is a major risk factor in heart disease and stroke. Sedentary women are much more likely to die from cardiovascular disease than women who are very active. Women benefit from vigorous exercise such as aerobics, running, biking, or swimming for at least 30 minutes, most days of the week. But even moderate everyday activities such as a brisk walk, gardening, household chores, and climbing stairs provide health benefits (Ekelund et al., 2015; Reynolds, 2015). Unfortunately, more than 40 percent of American women are sedentary or do not engage in any regular physical activity. In addition, women become even less active as they get older, when they most need the cardiovascular benefits of exercise (National Center for Health Statistics, 2014).

High blood pressure (hypertension) is another major risk factor for heart attack and the most important risk factor for stroke (Bushnell et al., 2014; Centers for Disease Control and Prevention, 2017). The incidence of high blood pressure increases with age, especially among Black women. Reducing intake of salt and red and processed meats, losing weight (if overweight), exercising, eating a fiber-rich diet, and taking medication (if needed) can bring high blood pressure under control and reduce risk of stroke (Brody, 2016c). Best of all, eating of dark chocolate lowers blood pressure and reduces the risk of stroke and heart disease (Kwok et al., 2015). Who says if it's good for you it must taste bad?

Women with *diabetes* are more likely to have a heart attack or stroke than are nondiabetic women. Diabetes may be delayed by controlling blood sugar, eating less saturated fat, not smoking, limiting alcohol consumption, and staying physically active (Mehta et al., 2016). Being *overweight* also increases the risk of heart attack, stroke, high blood pressure, high cholesterol levels, and diabetes (Mehta et al., 2016).

Smoking also is a powerful risk factor for heart disease and stroke in women (American Heart Association, 2015). Smoking is especially harmful in women because it decreases estrogen's protective effects and can cause menopause to occur about two years early. The vast majority of women who develop heart disease before age 50 are smokers. The good news is that quitting smoking may cut heart attack risk to that of a nonsmoker within 8 years (Ahmed et al., 2013).

Diet is important in reducing the risk of heart disease and stroke. A heart-healthy diet—sometimes called "the Mediterranean diet"—is rich in vegetables and fruits (especially blueberries and strawberries), whole grains, nuts, soy, monounsaturated oils (olive, canola), and protein derived from fish, beans, low-fat or nonfat dairy products, lean meats, and poultry (Rehm et al., 2016; Yu et al., 2016; Zong et al., 2016). Drinking coffee (in moderation) and green tea appear to protect against heart disease as well (Ding et al., 2013; "Green Tea," 2012). In addition, women who consume one glass of red wine per day are less likely to suffer a heart attack or stroke than women who drink more than that or who do not drink (Gepner et al., 2015; Gonçalves et al., 2015; Kadlecova et al., 2015). Moreover, one baby aspirin (81 mg) per day lowers the risk of both heart disease and cancer in women (Parekh et al., 2013).

Hormones also affect heart disease. *Birth control pills* decrease women's risk of heart disease and stroke (Hannaford, 2010). As noted in Chapter 7, however, *hormone replacement therapy* increases the risk of heart disease if not started early in menopause.

Men and women with aspects of so-called Type A personality—particularly anger and hostility—are more prone to develop heart disease (Donatelle, 2017). Depression is another risk factor for developing heart disease and dying from it (Clay, 2014a; Galatzer-Levy & Bonanno, 2014; Shah et al., 2013). Because women are more likely than men to be depressed (see Chapter 13), this factor increases women's risk. Social factors play a role in heart disease as well. For example, loneliness and low levels of social support are associated with an increased risk of heart disease for women, but not for men (Czajkowski et al., 2012; Thurston & Kubzansky, 2009). In addition, women who are divorced, widowed, or unhappily married have a higher risk of heart disease than women who are satisfied with their marriages (Orth-Gomér, 2009; Troxel et al., 2005). Stress and experiencing discrimination also increase women's risk of heart disease (Kershaw et al., 2016; Nabi et al., 2013).

Diagnosis and Treatment

The management, diagnosis, and treatment of heart disease in women are poorly understood and often carried out in an inconsistent manner. The result is that women receive poorer care (American Heart Association, 2015; Horton, 2014; McDaniel, 2014). Women with heart disease often do not receive the aggressive treatment from physicians that men do (Haskell et al., 2014; Worrall-Carter, 2016). For one thing, physicians often miss the signs of heart disease and heart attack in women because women are less likely to show the "classic" male symptom of crushing chest pain and are more apt than men to show symptoms such as nausea; dizziness; shortness of breath; profuse sweating; chest pressure, burning, or heaviness; extreme fatigue; sleep disturbance; back or abdominal pain; heartburn; heart palpitations; or just an odd, unwell feeling. Women may be misdiagnosed as simply suffering from indigestion, muscle pain, stress, or anxiety (DeVon et al., 2016; Chrisler et al., 2016, Mehta et al., 2016). In addition, many health care providers do not take heart disease risk in women seriously (Brody, 2015). In one recent study of physicians, women at risk of developing heart disease were more likely than men to be assigned to a low-risk category. They also were less likely to be advised about ways to help prevent heart attacks (Leifheit-Limson et al., 2015). Even when women experience the classic symptoms of chest pain, they are more likely than men to delay getting medical care. Women with heart attack symptoms are also more likely to delay going to the hospital if they lack adequate medical insurance. Sometimes, women ignore the symptoms because they do not want to trouble family members (Moser et al., 2012) or be perceived as hypochondriacs (Mehta et al., 2016).

But even when women do call 9-1-1 after experiencing heart attack symptoms, they are much less likely than men to receive prompt medical care, losing precious minutes before the onset of treatment (Concannon et al., 2009).

Women heart patients also are less likely to be treated by a specialist and are less likely to receive cholesterol-lowering drugs, devices such as stents (to open clogged arteries), and treatments such as coronary bypass surgery, cardiac resynchronization therapy, pacemakers, and implantable defibrillators. And in the critical hours following a heart attack, fewer women are given clot-dissolving drugs (American Heart Association, 2015; McDaniel, 2014; Herz et al., 2015), and they wait longer than men to receive an emergency angioplasty to open blocked arteries ("Women and Heart Health," 2005). Moreover, they are less often given aspirin, which aids in dissolving blood clots, or beta-blockers, which protect against future heart attacks (Garcia et al., 2016). Women also get fewer

WHAT <u>YOU</u> CAN DO 12.1
Ways to Promote Your Heart Health

- Don't smoke
- Eat balanced, healthful meals
- Get active: exercise 3–4 times a week
- Drink in moderation
- Manage your blood pressure

- Get enough sleep
- Know your family history

Source: American Heart Association (2015).

referrals for cardiac rehabilitation programs following heart attacks, even though they benefit from therapy at least as much as men do (Garcia et al., 2016). Even if they are referred, women are more likely than men to experience various barriers to participation in cardiac rehabilitation (Supervia et al., 2017). Because women are poorer and are older when they have a heart attack, they are less likely to have access to a car to transport them to the rehab site. Moreover, they are more often family caregivers, leaving less time to look after their own health (Mehta et al., 2016). In addition, women more often have other medical conditions, such as osteoporosis and urinary incontinence, which can serve as deterrents to exercise in rehab programs because of fear of falling and leakage accidents, respectively (Grace et al., 2009). Finally, women are often underrepresented in studies designed to test the effectiveness of cardiac rehabilitation programs (American Heart Association, 2015).

Psychological Impact

The psychosocial health of women following a heart attack or coronary bypass surgery is worse than that of men (Jacobs et al., 2017; Oertelt-Prigione & Regitz-Zagrosek, 2012; Xu et al., 2015). Women are more anxious and depressed, return to work less often, take longer to recuperate physically, and resume their sex lives later than men. In spite of their poorer health, women resume household activities sooner than men and are more likely to feel guilty that they cannot quickly resume the chores they once did (Prentice, 2008; Stevens & Thomas, 2012). Women's poorer psychosocial functioning after heart attack and heart surgery can take a toll on their well-being, productivity, and quality of life (Husser & Roberto, 2009). In addition, the greater depression experienced by women after heart attack or heart surgery is associated with a greater risk of death and of second heart attack. Health care providers need to become aware of the potential difficulties faced by women with heart disease and to take steps to enhance the recovery of their female patients (Mehta et al., 2016).

BREAST CANCER

As we noted earlier, women fear breast cancer more than any other disease including heart disease, the top killer of women. Yet breast cancer is not even the number one cancer killer of women. That dubious distinction belongs to lung cancer (American Cancer Society, 2013). One out of every eight women will develop breast cancer at some time in her life. Although this statistic sounds frightening, it represents a lifetime risk (American Cancer Society, 2016a).

The majority of women in whom breast cancer is diagnosed—80 percent—do not die of the disease. Moreover, the death rate from breast cancer has been dropping in recent years as a result of earlier detection, improved treatments, and a decrease in the use of hormones to treat menopause (American Cancer Society, 2016a). The 5-year survival rate for women with localized breast cancer is 99 percent. Even if the cancer has spread to lymph nodes, 85 percent of women will be alive 5 years later. If it invades bones or other organs, the rate drops to 25 percent (American Cancer Society, 2016a).

Why is the prospect of getting breast cancer so terrifying? The extensive publicity given to the disease in recent years in order to stimulate research and raise women's awareness has created the misleading impression that breast cancer is more common and more deadly than it actually is (Berry et al., 2015). In addition, breast cancer kills more women ages 35 to 54 than any other disease. The untimely deaths of these relatively young women may trigger greater alarm than the heart attack deaths of a far greater number of women later in life (Herscher, 2015).

Risk Factors

Age, as we have just seen, is the greatest risk factor for breast cancer. Four in five breast cancers are diagnosed in women over 50 and the average age when diagnosed is 61 (American Cancer Society, 2016a).

Ethnicity and *social class* are also risk factors. Black women are as likely as White women to get breast cancer overall, but are far more likely to die from it (DeSantis et al., 2015; George et al., 2015). One reason is that Black women are poorer. Low-income women, regardless of race, tend to delay breast cancer screening, follow-up, and treatment, receive lower quality of care, and are more likely to die of breast cancer than other women (American Cancer Society, 2013; Nonzee et al., 2015). But in addition, the tumors of Black women appear to be faster growing and more malignant (American Cancer Society, 2015–2016).

Family history of breast cancer—especially in one's mother, sister, or daughter—is another risk factor, accounting for 5 to 10 percent of breast cancers. A small percentage of women with a family history of breast cancer have unusually high risk—50 to 85 percent—as a result of inheriting one of two breast cancer genes, BRCA1 and BRCA2 (Rebbek et al., 2015). Inherited breast cancer occurs at younger ages, is more likely to affect both breasts, and often appears in multiple family members, including men, over several generations. The genes are more common in Jewish women of eastern European origin than in other groups (Hartmann & Lindor, 2016). Some women who have a high genetic risk of breast cancer, such as actor and filmmaker Angelina Jolie Pitt, choose to have both breasts removed, along with their ovaries and fallopian tubes, as a preventive measure which greatly reduces their risk of breast and ovarian cancers (Belluck, 2015; Hartmann & Lindor, 2016; Jolie Pitt, 2015).

Age, ethnicity, and family history are risk factors women cannot change. Other factors over which they have little or no control include *early age at menarche, late age at menopause, late age at first birth* (after 30), and *having no or few children*. All these events lengthen the amount of time women's breast tissue is exposed to high levels of estrogen, which can stimulate growth of breast cancer cells (American Cancer Society, 2016a).

Women can reduce their risk of breast cancer by making certain lifestyle choices. One of these choices is *not smoking* (Spring et al., 2015). Another is cutting down on alcohol or avoiding it altogether, as even one drink per day increases the risk of developing breast cancer (American Cancer Society, 2016a). Red wine may be an exception to this link, however (Liu et al., 2015).

The same diet recommended for heart health, one that is high in vegetables, fruits, whole grains, and legumes and low in red meat and processed foods, is also linked to a reduction in breast and other cancers (American Cancer Society, 2016c; Aune et al., 2016). Drinking green tea also reduces breast cancer risk (Love, 2010). Being overweight is a risk factor (American Cancer Society, 2010). Body fat produces estrogen, which can help breast cancer grow. Engaging in *physical activity* reduces breast cancer risk, most likely because it reduces body fat. Recent use of *birth control pills* or *hormone replacement therapy* increases risk of breast cancer (American Cancer Society, 2016a; Liu et al., 2015; Port, 2015). To assess your risk of breast cancer, try Get Involved 12.2.

Detection

The American Cancer Society no longer recommends that women aged 20 and older do a monthly breast self-examination since research has found that doing so does not increase detection or survival outcomes (American Cancer Society, 2015–2016). Instead, it and other organizations advocate breast self-awareness, which involves knowing the look, feel, and shape of your breasts, and reporting changes to your doctor. New guidelines also no longer recommend that women have an annual clinical breast exam by a health professional.

GET INVOLVED 12.2
Assessing Your Risk of Breast Cancer

Put a check mark next to each risk factor listed here. The total number of checks gives a general indication of your relative risk. Remember that some women have many risk factors but never get breast cancer. Others have few or no factors but do get the disease.

After you assess your relative risk, give the questionnaire to female friends and relatives, including both young and older women.

BREAST CANCER RISK FACTORS

- Increasing age
- BRCA1 or BRCA2 gene mutation
- Family history of breast cancer
- High breast density
- Personal history of breast, uterine, colon, or ovarian cancers
- Menopause after age 55
- Not having children
- Having first child after age 35

- Never breastfeeding
- Being overweight after menopause
- More than one alcoholic drink per day
- Smoking
- Sedentary lifestyle
- Younger than 12 at first period
- Recent postmenopausal hormone replacement therapy
- Recent oral contraceptive use

Total: _____

WHAT DOES IT MEAN?

1. How did breast cancer risk vary with the age of your respondents?
2. What advice can you give to your respondents who have moderate to high risk of breast cancer?

_____

Sources: American Cancer Society (2016c); Rice et al. (2016).

A **mammogram**, *a low-dose X-ray picture of the breast*, detects small suspicious lumps up to 2 years before they are large enough to be felt. Most health organizations recommend a yearly mammogram for women, starting at age 40, although the American Cancer Society recently recommended a starting age of 45 (Grady, 2015). Nationwide, the number of women who are screened has increased since 1990. Now, two-thirds of women aged 40 and over have had a mammogram in the last 2 years (American Cancer Society, 2015–2016). However, women with low income or less education, who have more limited access to affordable health care, are less likely to be screened (Wardle et al., 2015). In addition, older women are screened less often than those in midlife (American Cancer Society, 2015–2016). Some women avoid mammograms because they fear the pain or discomfort of the procedure itself, or believe they are at low risk for the disease, whereas others fear receiving a breast cancer diagnosis (Wardle et al., 2015).

Mammograms are less effective at detecting tumors in dense young breast tissue. Women with dense breast tissue and those with high risk of breast cancer are encouraged to use ultrasound, digital mammograms, or magnetic resonance imaging (MRI) to help detect early breast cancer (American Cancer Society, 2015–2016; Slanetz et al., 2015).

Treatment

When breast cancer is diagnosed, several treatment options are available. For many years, the standard treatment was **radical mastectomy**, *the removal of the breast, underlying chest wall, and underarm lymph nodes*. Because of disfigurement and side effects, it is rarely done now. **Modified radical mastectomy** involves *removal of the breast and underarm lymph nodes* and **simple mastectomy** involves *removal of the breast only*. In **lumpectomy**, also known as partial mastectomy or breast-conserving surgery, only *the lump and some* *surrounding tissue are removed.* Lumpectomy is almost always followed by several weeks of radiation. For small tumors in the early stages of disease, lumpectomy followed by radiation is as effective in terms of 20-year survival as mastectomy (Port, 2015). Black women are less likely than White women to receive radiation after lumpectomy. It is unclear whether this disparity occurs because fewer Black women are offered the therapy, because they are more likely to decline it, or because they are unable to complete the entire treatment due to other barriers (Hampton, 2008). In addition, older and poorer women are less likely to receive appropriate treatment for breast cancer (Boehmer & Bowen, 2010).

Chemotherapy may be used to kill cancer cells that the surgeon was not able to remove. Other drugs that cut rates of breast cancer occurrence include the estrogen blockers raloxifene and tamoxifen and drugs called aromatase inhibitors. Another drug, Herceptin, shrinks tumors in women who have a certain type of fast-growing cancer or whose advanced breast cancer is not responsive to other treatments (American Cancer Society, 2016c).

Psychological Impact

The diagnosis of breast cancer and the surgery that often follows cause fatigue, depression, anxiety, and anger in many women (National Cancer Institute, 2014; Reyes-Gibby et al., 2012). If the cancer recurs at some point after treatment, women may experience even higher levels of distress. Concerns about bodily appearance can be substantial for women who have had breast surgery (Brunet et al., 2013; Ussher et al., 2013).

Individual differences in reactions to breast cancer vary considerably. Young women appear to be affected more negatively than middle-aged or older women. They are more likely to have to deal with disruptions in family life and careers, as well as problems with fertility and sexual functioning. Consequently, they show greater declines in social functioning, mental health, and quality of life (Champion et al., 2014). Women of color are more likely than White women to use certain coping strategies that are positive (e.g., positive reappraisal) and those that are negative (e.g., emotional suppression) (Yoo et al., 2014). But regardless of age or ethnicity, women with a "fighting spirit," sense of control, positive thinking, and higher levels of hostility and those who voice their fears and anxieties survive breast cancer longer than those who show passive acceptance, stoicism, emotional inhibition, feelings of hopelessness, or denial of facts about the cancer (Astin et al., 2013).

Support groups are important in helping women cope with cancer (Stringer, 2014). David Spiegel (2011) and his colleagues found that among breast cancer patients who had a poor prognosis, those who were randomly assigned to attend weekly group therapy sessions lived longer than women in the control group. Similarly, Barbara Andersen and her colleagues (2008) found that after 11 years, women with breast cancer who participated in a group-based psychological intervention program were 45 percent less likely to have had their cancer return and 56 percent less likely to have died of the disease. Moreover, cancer patients who have friends, close relatives, and adult children live longer than patients who lack these sources of social support (Gomez et al., 2016; Lutgendorf & Anderson, 2015). Although social support does not always improve survival rates, it can enhance quality of life, mood, energy levels, and tolerance of chemotherapy and reduce depression and pain (Janz et al., 2014; Spiegel, 2011). Psychosocial interventions that focus on reducing stress, increasing knowledge, and improving coping skills give survivors of breast and other cancers a greater sense of control, improved body image and sexual functioning, reduced distress, and greater adherence to their prescribed course of therapy (Cramer et al., 2012; Faller et al., 2013; Greenlee et al., 2014).

LUNG CANCER

Lung cancer is the leading cause of cancer deaths in women, killing more women each year than breast, uterine, and ovarian cancers combined (American Cancer Society, 2016a).

Risk Factors

Although fewer men have been dying of lung cancer in the past several years, women have shown the opposite trend. Women's lung cancer death rates began to increase in the mid-twentieth century, finally leveling off in 2003. This increase is most likely linked to women's increased cigarette smoking during these years because cigarette smoking is responsible for more than 80 percent of lung cancer cases (Henley et al., 2014; May, 2014). Other risk factors include exposure to second-hand smoke, asbestos, and radon (American Cancer Society, 2016a).

Lung cancer develops differently in women and men. For example, women are at greater risk than men for developing lung cancer among individuals who have never smoked. Women also tend to develop lung cancer at younger ages than men. Although the reasons for these differences are not completely understood, one factor may be women's high levels of naturally occurring estrogen (Honma et al., 2015).

Detection and Treatment

Women are more likely than men to be diagnosed with lung cancer at an earlier stage. Early detection is difficult, however, because symptoms, such as persistent coughing, chest pain, and voice hoarseness, do not appear until the disease has reached an advanced stage. Treatment typically includes surgery, followed by radiation and chemotherapy. Women with lung cancer tend to survive longer than men at all stages of the disease (North & Christiani, 2013). Sadly, however, the 5-year survival rate for women with lung cancer is only 17 percent, compared with a nearly 90-percent survival rate for breast cancer (American Cancer Society, 2016a).

PHYSICAL HEALTH IN LATER LIFE

In this section, we examine factors contributing to women's health in later life. We also explore gender differences in **mortality** (*death rates*) and in **morbidity** (*illness*), look at disability in old age, and, finally, discuss the conditions that promote good health.

Gender Differences in Mortality

Women are sicker; men die quicker. This old saying sums up what is often referred to as the **gender paradox**: *women live longer than men, but in poorer health* (Short et al., 2013). Women outlive men in all but a few countries that are ravaged by war, disease, and extreme poverty (U.S. Department of Health and Human Services, 2013).

The female–male mortality gap begins before birth. Although as many as 170 males are conceived for every 100 females, the rate of miscarriage and stillbirth is higher for males. Although in most nations about 105 live males are born for every 100 live females, more male babies die in infancy and thereafter throughout life (Centers for Disease Control and Prevention, 2016a). Starting at age 35, women outnumber men in the United States (U.S. Census Bureau, 2008) and by age 100, women outnumber men by more than four to one (Kincel, 2014; Xu, 2016).

In 1900, life expectancy in the United States was 51 years for women and 48 years for men. Since then, the gender gap has widened. Life expectancy at birth now is about 81 for women and 76 for men. The gender gap exists for all ethnicities. For example, White women tend to outlive White men by 5 years (81.2 versus 76.5) and Black women, on average, outlive Black men by nearly 7 years (78.1 versus 71) (National Center for Health Statistics, 2015; Xu et al., 2016). Why do women outlive men? Some explanations focus on biological factors, others on lifestyle behavioral differences.

BIOLOGY.   One biological factor proposed to account for gender differences in mortality is that male fetuses are attacked by their mothers' immune systems because of male proteins that are foreign to the mothers' bodies. Another is the slower maturation of male fetuses, possibly making them more vulnerable (DiPietro, 2015). An additional biological explanation is that females' second X chromosome protects them against certain lethal diseases—such as hemophilia and some forms of muscular dystrophy—that are more apt to occur in individuals (i.e., males) who have only one X chromosome (Maklakov & Lummaa, 2013). Another biological reason for women's greater longevity involves their higher estrogen levels, which seem to provide protection against fatal conditions such as heart disease (Regan & Partridge, 2013). In addition, women have a lower rate of metabolism, which is linked to greater longevity. There also is evidence that women's immune systems are more robust than men's, making men more susceptible to contracting certain fatal diseases (Short et al., 2013).

LIFESTYLE BEHAVIORS.   One lifestyle factor accounting for the gender gap in mortality is that males are more likely than females to engage in potentially risky behaviors such as smoking, drinking, violence, and reckless driving. They also may be exposed to more hazardous workplace conditions and are more likely to be injured at work (Humble & Price, 2017; Centers for Disease and Control and Prevention, 2016d; Mata et al., 2016b; National Center for Health Statistics, 2016). Table 12.3 shows that accidents and unintentional injuries are the third leading cause of death of males, but the sixth leading cause for females. Men are twice as likely as women to die of cirrhosis, caused largely by excessive drinking. In addition, homicide claims the lives of four times as many men as women (National Center for Health Statistics, 2016).

SMOKING.   As women's lifestyles have become more similar to men's, so have some of their health behaviors. For example, although the frequency of men's smoking has declined over the past 40 years, that of women increased from the 1930s through the 1990s before starting to decline. Tobacco use remains high among women aged 18–24 (Jamal et al., 2015). About one in six women in the United States currently smokes, close to the rate for men (Centers for Disease Control and Prevention, 2016b). The prevalence of smoking varies widely across educational levels and ethnic groups. For example, fewer than one in ten college graduates smokes, compared with one in four who has not completed high school (Centers for Disease Control and Prevention, 2016b). Among women, Asian Americans have the lowest rates of smoking followed by Latinas, Blacks, Whites, and Native Americans (Spring et al., 2015).

The result of women's increase in smoking and men's decrease, as we have seen, is that smoking-related deaths from lung cancer have declined for men but have soared for women (Schroeder, 2013; Thun et al., 2013), surpassing breast cancer as the leading cause of cancer deaths among women. Smoking is also a key factor in the rise of chronic lung disease, heart disease, and stroke as a cause of death in women (Bushnell et al., 2014; Jha et al., 2013).

In the United States, and in half of the 151 countries recently surveyed by the World Health Organization, teenage girls are as likely or nearly as likely to smoke as boys (National Center for Health Statistics, 2015; World Health Organization, 2015a). Teenage girls are drawn to smoking for many

TABLE 12.3   Ten Leading Causes of Death for Females and Males in 2014

Rank	Women	Men
1	Heart disease	Heart disease
2	Cancer	Cancer
3	Chronic lung disease (asthma, bronchitis)	Unintentional injuries
4	Cerebrovascular diseases (stroke)	Chronic lung disease (asthma, bronchitis)
5	Alzheimer's disease	Cerebrovascular diseases (stroke)
6	Unintentional injuries	Diabetes
7	Diabetes	Suicide
8	Pneumonia and influenza	Alzheimer's disease
9	Kidney disease	Pneumonia and influenza
10	Septicemia (infection of the blood)	Chronic liver disease and cirrhosis

Source: National Center for Health Statistics (2016).

reasons, including an attempt to express independence, curb appetite, reduce stress, and display "adult" behavior (Karpf, 2015). Young women, especially women of color, are heavily targeted by the tobacco industry, which has intentionally designed cigarette ads to promote smoking in women (Centers for Disease Control and Prevention, 2016b; World Health Organization, 2015b). In response to one advertiser's slogan, "You've come a long way, baby," Claire reminds her students, "Yes, your rates of lung disease are getting closer to men's." The good news is that the younger you are when you stop smoking, the greater your chance of living a long, healthy life (Jha et al., 2013).

Another behavioral difference contributing to women's longevity is that women make greater use of preventive health services and are more likely to seek medical treatment when they are ill (National Center for Health Statistics, 2015). This may help explain why women live longer than men after the diagnosis of a potentially fatal disease. Women's greater tendency to visit the doctor's office suggests that they are more health conscious than men. Women generally know more than men about health, do more to prevent illness, are more likely to look up health information on the Internet, are more aware of symptoms, are more likely to talk about their health concerns, and ask doctors more questions during visits (Fox & Duggan, 2013; Manierre, 2015). On the other hand, women's competing work and family demands, life stressors, and social factors such as poverty and violence can make it difficult for them to make their own health needs a high priority (Poleshuck & Woods, 2014).

Women also outlive men because of their more extensive social support networks involving family, friends, and formal organizational memberships. Involvement in social relationships is related to living longer, perhaps because social ties reduce the impact of life stresses or convince individuals to increase their health-producing behaviors (Shor et al., 2013; Trudel-Fitzgerald, 2016).

Cultural, Social Class, and Ethnic Differences

Women live longer than men regardless of nationality, social class, and ethnic membership. Nevertheless, there are differences in longevity among women across cultures, social classes, and ethnic groups. Let us examine these factors.

HEALTH REPORT CARD FOR WOMEN AROUND THE WORLD.   Women outlive men in almost every nation, by an average of almost 5 years. In 2011, women's life expectancy at birth was more than 80 years in 52 countries, but under 60 years in sub-Saharan Africa (World Health Organization, 2015a). Longevity has increased for both sexes in almost all nations, with the exception of some African countries that have been devastated by HIV/AIDS (World Health Organization, 2015a). Death in childbirth partially accounts for the smaller female advantage in longevity in developing countries, mostly in sub-Saharan Africa and South Asia (Kassebaum et al., 2014; World Health Organization, 2015a). In many of these countries, women often delay seeking health care because of their limited time and access to money, their restricted mobility, and the need to get their husbands' permission to seek care. In some countries, however, the smaller difference is also a result of female infanticide and neglect of female children (see Chapter 14). Access to better health care helps account for the larger longevity differences between females and males in developed countries (Sen, 2010).

SOCIAL CLASS.   Around the world, women and men with higher incomes and more education have longer life expectancies and better health (Chetty et al., 2016; Dorling, 2015; Neumayer & Plümper, 2016; Underwood, 2014). Some of this difference can be accounted for by the higher incidence in lower-income populations of risk factors such as smoking, unhealthy diet, obesity, high blood pressure, physical inactivity, more limited access to medical care and adequate food, and higher levels of stress resulting from financial difficulties, job loss, and discrimination rooted in racist or social class bias. The combination of all these factors shortens life expectancy and increases rates of illness and disease (Ruiz & Brondolo, 2016; Underwood, 2014; Zajakova, 2014).

ETHNICITY.   Health risks and mortality rates for women vary by ethnic group (see Table 12.4). Mortality rates from all of the major causes of death (except car accidents, chronic lung disease, and suicide) are higher for Black women than for White women. White women are less likely than women in other ethnic groups to die of diabetes. Asian American women, compared to White women, have lower mortality rates from heart disease; stroke; lung, breast, and cervical cancers; cirrhosis; and chronic lung disease. Black women have the shortest life expectancy of any group and Asian Americans the longest (Heron, 2010). Differences in mortality rates for women of different ethnic groups are related to their economic status throughout their lives. Blacks and Native Americans, for example, have high mortality rates and low lifetime family incomes, whereas Asian Americans have some of the highest family incomes and lower mortality rates (Meyer & Herd, 2007). Racial discrimination is an additional stressor linked to poor health outcomes among Black and Native American individuals (Espey et al., 2014; Fuller-Rowell et al., 2012).

Gender Differences in Illness

Although they live longer than men, women suffer from more chronic health conditions. This is true in every country in which these statistics have been gathered, including developing nations (Alberts et al., 2014; Karvonen-Gutierrez, 2015). Women have higher rates of asthma, chronic fatigue syndrome, fibromyalgia, thyroid conditions, migraine headaches, anemia, urinary incontinence, and more than 80 autoimmune disorders such as rheumatoid arthritis, multiple sclerosis, and lupus (Mallampalli et al., 2013; U.S. Department of Commerce, 2011). American women are less likely than their male counterparts to rate their health as excellent and more likely to describe it as good or fair (Adams et al., 2008; "QuickStats," 2011).

Women and men actually spend about the same number of years in good health and free of disability. It is only because women live longer than men that they spend more years with chronic, often disabling, illnesses (Friedman et al., 2016). Keep in mind that a person may have one or more chronic diseases without being disabled. The key issue is whether the chronic condition restricts daily life or reduces the ability to take care of oneself (Bjorklund & Bee, 2014).

Disability

The degree of disability resulting from chronic conditions is assessed by measuring how well individuals can carry out two groups of activities: (1) **activities of daily living (ADLs)**, which include *basic self-caring activities such as eating, bathing, toileting, walking, and getting in and out of a bed or chair*; and (2) **instrumental activities of daily living (IADLs)**, which *go beyond personal care to include preparing meals, doing housework, shopping, doing laundry, attending social activities, using the telephone, taking medications, and managing money* (Federal Interagency Forum, 2016). As you might expect,

TABLE 12.4   Leading Causes of Death for Females by Ethnicity, 2014

Rank	White	Black	Native American	Asian/Pacific Islander	Latina
1	Heart disease	Heart disease	Cancer	Cancer	Cancer
2	Cancer	Cancer	Heart disease	Heart disease	Heart disease
3	Chronic lung disease	Stroke	Unintentional injuries	Stroke	Stroke
4	Stroke	Diabetes	Chronic liver disease	Alzheimer's disease	Diabetes
5	Alzheimer's disease	Chronic lung disease	Diabetes	Diabetes	Unintentional injuries

Note: Native American includes American Indian and Alaska Native females.
Source: National Center for Health Statistics (2016).

the chances of developing a disability increase with age (Brown, 2014). Older women are more likely than older men to have functional limitations that affect both ADLs and IADLs (National Center for Health Statistics, 2015).

Native American women are more likely than other women to report chronic and/or disabling conditions, followed by African American, Latina, and White women. Asian American women are least likely to suffer from disabilities (U.S. Department of Health and Human Services, 2013). Life satisfaction is often lower for women who have disabilities than for other women. They are more likely to be depressed, to have elevated stress levels, and to rate their health as only fair or poor (Bericat, 2016; Nosek, 2010). But chronic illness need not prevent a woman from enjoying her life. In the Women's Health and Aging Study, 35 percent of women with moderate to severe disabilities reported a high sense of happiness and personal mastery and low levels of anxiety and depression (Unger & Seeman, 2000).

PROMOTING GOOD HEALTH

Aging is not a disease but a natural process in a woman's life cycle. Throughout life, women can take active steps to maintain good health and decrease the impact of any health problems that develop. Lifestyle choices involving physical activity, good nutrition, not smoking, and moderate alcohol use can promote longevity and good health (Aichele et al., 2016).

In this section, we examine practices that promote good health. For a closer look at some of these factors in older women, see Learn About the Research 12.2.

Physical Activity and Exercise

It's never too late. I'm 81 years old and look what I did. I didn't sit in my rocking chair and say "I got a pain here and a pain there, and I can't do anything." I get out there and I work out the pain (Flo Meiler, heptathlete; Jimenez, 2015).

LEARN ABOUT THE RESEARCH 12.2
Good Health Habits and Longevity

The relationship between good health habits and longevity was demonstrated dramatically in a large-scale longitudinal investigation conducted in California. At the beginning of the study, the researchers asked nearly 7,000 randomly chosen adults about their health practices. In a follow-up study done 18 years later, five good health behaviors were found to predict lower rates of death among the participants: keeping physically active, not smoking, drinking moderately, maintaining normal weight, and sleeping seven to eight hours a night. The most unexpected finding was that being involved in close relationships was as powerful a predictor of life expectancy as good health practices. Individuals who followed the greatest number of good health practices and who were most involved in social networks were least likely to die or develop disabilities over the 18 years of the study (Housman & Doorman, 2005). Recent studies in Europe and the United States (Berstad et al., 2016; Liu et al., 2016; Muller et al., 2016; Petersen et al., 2015) have found strikingly similar results.

Other longitudinal studies suggest that both leisure activities and productive activities such as volunteering may be just as important as physical activity in helping older people live longer (Nilsson et al., 2015; Paggi et al., 2016; Rogers et al., 2016).

WHAT DOES IT MEAN?

1. In this chapter, we learned that women are more health conscious than men. Why do you think that is?
2. Young adults are less likely to engage in good health practices than are older adults. What might account for this difference?
3. How can more young adults be encouraged to develop good health habits?
4. Why do you think leisure and productive activities increase longevity?

PHYSICAL BENEFITS.   The numerous health benefits of physical activity have been well documented. Regular physical exercise controls weight gain and is linked to improved overall health, quality of life, and increased longevity (Ekelund et al., 2015; Seguin et al., 2014; U.S. Department of Health and Human Services, 2013). More specifically, physical activity is associated with decreased incidence of heart disease; stroke; many types of cancer; hypertension; diabetes; respiratory and kidney diseases; osteoporosis; and physical disability (Carroll, 2016; Moore et al., 2016; Notthoff & Carstensen, 2014; Pahor et al., 2014).

In the later years, physical activity helps maintain the muscle strength, balance, and flexibility needed to perform activities of daily living, provide mobility, and decrease falls (Guo et al., 2013; Hafner, 2014; Robertson & Gillespie, 2013).

PSYCHOLOGICAL BENEFITS.   Regular exercise promotes a sense of well-being, feelings of accomplishment, happiness, and increased self-esteem. It also decreases tension, anxiety, depression, and anger (Allerhand et al., 2014; Bergouignan et al., 2016; Carroll, 2016; Langguth et al., 2016; Mammen & Faulkner, 2013). Furthermore, physically active older adults outperform sedentary older people on tests of memory, reaction time, reasoning, attention, planning ability, mental speed, and mental flexibility. They are also less likely to develop dementia. These findings suggest that regular participation in exercise improves cognitive functioning in later life (Ferencz et al., 2014; Gill & Seitz, 2015; Prakash et al., 2015; Raji et al., 2016; Rao et al., 2014). An alternative explanation, of course, is that smart people may exercise more because they are aware of its benefits!

FACTORS LINKED TO WOMEN'S ACTIVITY LEVELS.   Although inactivity increases with age for both sexes, women of all ages are less apt to exercise than men (National Center for Health Statistics, 2015). The proportion of American women who say they never exercise almost doubles with age, from 36 percent for those under 25 to 65 percent for those 75 and older.

White women are more likely to exercise on a regular basis than women of other ethnicities, with Black women exercising least (Centers for Disease Control and Prevention, 2016d ; U.S. Department of Health and Human Services, 2013). Much of this ethnic difference may be accounted for by differences in educational and income levels. Ethnic minority women are more likely to live in poverty and have lower income and educational levels than White women. Their neighborhoods often lack adequate and safe facilities that enable and promote physical activity (Watson et al., 2016; Wineman et al., 2014). The proportion of women who engage in exercise rises as educational and income levels increase (Fakhouri et al., 2014; Marks et al., 2015; National Center for Health Statistics, 2015).

Several barriers prevent individuals with disabilities from engaging in proper amounts of physical activity. These include limitations resulting from the disability itself, lack of transportation to exercise facilities, the perception (or reality) that these facilities are not disability friendly, and social attitudes that people with disabilities cannot or do not need to exercise (Ansehl et al., 2010; Rolfe et al., 2009).

One explanation for the low levels of physical activity among older women is the stereotype that exercise is increasingly seen as inappropriate as a person ages. This stereotype applies even more strongly to women than to men because of the societal expectation that, at all ages, women are less physically active than men (Marks et al., 2015). In addition, the social construction of gender dictates that women are the primary caregivers and managers of home and family. Taking time away from domestic responsibilities to indulge in personal leisure may cause some women to feel selfish, guilty, or overwhelmed (Beydoun et al., 2014). In addition, the caregiving duties that many older women perform may make them too tired to be physically active.

Older women must not only overcome sexist and ageist views about appropriate physical activity in later life but must also combat chronic health problems that inhibit many older people from exercising. Arthritic pain and urinary incontinence, chronic conditions that are more prevalent in older women than in older men, may serve as deterrents to physical activity. Other barriers include the absence of a companion and the lack of convenient transportation to a safe and affordable exercise facility (Britain et al., 2011; Justine et al., 2013). In addition, some women feel that they are too sick or too old to improve their physical condition, or fear that exercise may lead to injury (Ansehl et al., 2010; Bird et al., 2009; Stephan et al., 2010). Unfortunately, older people are less likely than younger individuals to receive exercise counseling from their physicians (Barnes & Schoenborn, 2012). Moreover, the issue of attractive exercise programming for older women has been largely overlooked by exercise specialists, yet another example of the relative invisibility and lack of power of older women (Travis & Compton, 2001).

Nutrition

Good nutrition is a key factor in promoting health and improving cognitive function. Regardless of age, a healthful diet includes lots of vegetables, fruits, and whole grains; moderate amounts of protein; and sparing use of red and processed meat, fats, oil, and sugar (Aune et al., 2016; Brody, 2016b; Valls-Pedret et al., 2015; Zong et al., 2016).

But a woman's nutritional needs also vary over her life span. During puberty, for example, calorie requirements rise to at least 2,200 per day for the average girl, and more if she is physically active. Calcium intake is especially important to ensure maximum bone growth. Pregnant women need about 300 extra calories a day. By menopause, women need only about two-thirds of the calories required when they were 20 (Cespedes, 2015).

Many older women who live independently do not consume sufficient amounts of one or more essential nutrients. The reasons for this include difficulty getting to stores, insufficient income to buy wholesome foods, medications that interfere with absorption of nutrients, chronic conditions that restrict people to bland diets low in certain nutrients, problems with chewing, and loss of appetite. Poor appetite can result from illness, inactivity, diminished senses of taste and smell, depression, or eating alone (Brody, 2001; Wellman et al., 2007). Adequate intake of calcium and vitamin D is very important for older women in order to minimize the onset and severity of osteoporosis (Brody, 2013a). But few women consume the 1,200 milligrams of calcium and the 800 units of vitamin D recommended during the menopausal and postmenopausal years (Brody, 2013a).

Summary

HEALTH SERVICES

- A feminist health care model supports egalitarian relationships between women and health care providers, acknowledges women's expertise on their own bodies, and rejects the "medicalizing" of women's health.
- Women are increasingly being included in health research. Unfortunately, they continue to be treated with less respect within the health care system and receive poorer medical care than men.
- Women of color are more likely than White women to be poor, uninsured, and lack medical care.
- Sexual minority women may have elevated health risks, in part due to reduced access to health care.
- Women rely more heavily than men on Medicare and Medicaid.

- Managed care insurance plans have both advantages and disadvantages for women.

SEXUALLY TRANSMITTED INFECTIONS (STIs)

- Sexually transmitted infections (STIs) are transmitted more easily to women than to men and are harder to diagnose in women.
- Women, especially those of color, are the fastest-growing group of Americans with HIV.
- HIV infection in older women is less often diagnosed and treated correctly than in younger women.

REPRODUCTIVE SYSTEM DISORDERS

- Benign disorders of the reproductive system include endometriosis and fibroid tumors.
- Uterine and cervical cancers have higher survival rates than ovarian cancer.

- The Pap smear is an effective screening device for cervical cancer.
- American women have one of the highest hysterectomy rates in the world.

OSTEOPOROSIS

- Osteoporosis, the loss of bone tissue, increases after menopause and can lead to disabling and even fatal fractures.
- Building and maintaining bone mass is enhanced by increasing calcium intake; decreasing use of alcohol, caffeine, and tobacco; increasing physical activity; and taking estrogen or certain medications.

HEART DISEASE

- Heart disease, the leading killer of women, increases dramatically after menopause.
- Women develop heart disease later than men and are twice as likely to die of it.
- Risk factors for heart disease include gender, age, ethnicity, family history, smoking, physical inactivity, high cholesterol levels, high blood pressure, diabetes, and being overweight.
- Women with heart disease receive less aggressive treatment than men.

BREAST CANCER

- One in eight women will develop breast cancer, but survival rates have been increasing.

- Risk factors include age, ethnicity, family history, drinking, smoking, weight gain, and inactivity.
- Many women do not perform monthly breast self-exams or get regular mammograms.
- For small early tumors, lumpectomy with radiation is as effective as mastectomy.
- Support groups help women cope with cancer.

LUNG CANCER

- Lung cancer is the leading cause of cancer deaths in women.
- The increase in lung cancer deaths in women is likely linked to an increase in smoking.
- Lung cancer develops differently in women and men, and women survive longer with the disease.

PHYSICAL HEALTH IN LATER LIFE

- At every age, women report more illness and use of health care services than men, yet women consistently outlive men.
- Both biological factors and lifestyle differences are responsible for women's greater longevity.
- Health risks and mortality rates for women differ by social class and ethnic group.
- Older women are more likely than older men to have some difficulty with various activities of daily living.

PROMOTING GOOD HEALTH

- Practices that promote good health include physical activity and good nutrition.

Key Terms

feminist health care model *252*
Medicare *255*
Medicaid *255*
spending down *256*
fee-for-service insurance *256*
managed care *256*
acquired immunodeficiency syndrome (AIDS) *258*
endometriosis *261*

uterine fibroid tumors *261*
cervix *261*
Pap smear *261*
hysterectomy *262*
osteoporosis *263*
raloxifene *264*
mammogram *269*
radical mastectomy *269*
modified radical mastectomy *269*

simple mastectomy *269*
lumpectomy *269*
mortality *271*
morbidity *271*
gender paradox *271*
activities of daily living (ADLs) *274*
instrumental activities of daily living (IADLs) *274*

What Do You Think?

1. Why do you think women's heart disease risks were largely ignored until fairly recently? What actions can individuals take to help improve this situation? What actions can members of the medical community take?

2. How can knowledge of risk factors for diseases in older White women and older women of color help individuals in prevention and early detection of these diseases? How can high risk factors be reduced for both groups?

3. Why do you think there is a difference between mammogram screening rates for women who differ in socioeconomic status? What actions could be taken to change these disparities?

4. Of the health conditions mentioned in this chapter, which ones can you prevent? Which ones can you delay? What actions can you take now to protect yourself from these problems? Which of these are you currently doing, and why?

If You Want to Learn More

Alexander, L.L. et al. (2017). *New dimensions in women's health* (7th ed.). Burlington, MA: Jones & Bartlett.

Barr, D.A. (2014). *Health disparities in the United States: Social class, race, ethnicity, and health* (2nd ed.). Baltimore, MD: Johns Hopkins University Press.

Boyd-Judson, L. & James, P. (2014). *Women's global health: Norms and state policies.* Lanham, MD: Rowman & Littlefield.

Buehler, A.E. (2016). *Rethinking women's health: A guide to wellness.* Metro-Jackson, MI: Sartoris Literary Group.

Clark, R., Maupin, R., & Hayes, J. (2012). *A women's guide to living with HIV infection.* Baltimore, MD: Johns Hopkins Press.

Donatelle, R.J. (2017). *Access to health* (15th ed.). Boston, MA: Pearson.

Dworkin, S. & Gandhi, M. (2017). *Women's empowerment and global health: A twenty-first-century agenda.* Oakland, CA: University of California Press.

Gurr, B. (2015). *Reproductive justice: The politics of health care of Native American women.* New Brunswick, NJ: Rutgers University Press.

Harvey, V.L. et al. (Eds.). (2014). *Health care disparities and the LGBT population.* Lanham, MD: Rowman & Littlefield.

Kolander, C. & Ballard, D. (2013). *Contemporary women's health: Issues for today and the future.* New York: McGraw-Hill.

LaVeist, T.A. & Isaac, L.A. (Eds.). (2014). *Race, ethnicity, and health: A public health reader* (2nd ed.). San Francisco, CA: Jossey-Bass.

Liamputtong, P. (2016). *Children and young people living with HIV/AIDS: A cross-cultural perspective.* Switzerland: Springer International Publishing.

Maizes, V. & Low Dog, T. (Eds.). (2015). *Integrative women's health* (2nd ed.). New York: Oxford University Press.

Navia, N. & Nurgul, K. (2015). *Heart disease in women.* Philadelphia, PA: Jay Pee Medical Inc.

Nelson, J. (2015). *More than medicine: A history of the feminist women's health movement.* New York: New York University.

Port, E. (2015). *The new generation breast cancer book.* New York: Penguin Random House.

Sammarco, J. (2017). *Women's health issues across the life cycle: A quality of life perspective.* Burlington, MA: Jones & Bartlett Learning.

Schuiling, K.D. & Likis, F.E. (2017). *Women's gynecological health* (3rd ed.). Burlington, MA: Jones & Bartlett.

Spiers, M.V. & Geller, P.A. (2013). *Women's health psychology.* Hoboken, NJ: Wiley.

Youngkin, E.Q. & Davis, M.S. (2012). *Women's health: A primary care clinical guide* (4th ed.). Boston, MA: Pearson.

Websites

Health Care and Health Issues: General

The New York Times articles on women's health and excerpts from the *Harvard Guide to Women's Health* and the *American Medical Women's Association Women's Complete Health Book*
http://topics.nytimes.com/topics/reference/timestopics/subjects/w/women/index.html
Iris Cantor Women's Health Center

http://www.cornellwomenshealth.com
The Society for Women's Health Research
http://www.womenshealthresearch.org/
http://www.fda.gov/womens/tttc.html
http://www.nwhn.org/
http://www.cdc.gov/women/
http://www.womenshealth.gov
http://www.fda.gov/ForConsumers/ByAudience/

ForWomen/
http://iwhc.org
http://www.healthywomen.org/about-us

Disability
Disabled People's International
http://www.dpi.org
National Organization on Disability
http://www.nod.org
American Association of People With Disabilities
http://www.aapd.com

Heart Disease
American Heart Association
http://www.heart.org/HEARTORG/

Cancer
American Cancer Society
http://www.cancer.org
National Ovarian Cancer Coalition (NOCC)
http://www.ovarian.org
Susan G. Komen for the Cure

http://www.komen.org
Foundation for Women's Cancer
http://www.foundationforwomenscancer.org/

Arthritis
Arthritis Foundation
http://www.arthritis.org
National Institute of Arthritis and Musculoskeletal
and Skin Diseases
http://www.niams.nih.gov

Diabetes
American Association of Diabetes Educators
http://diabeteseducator.org
National Institute of Diabetes and Digestive and
Kidney Diseases
http://www2.niddk.nih.gov/

Sexual Minority Health
Gay and Lesbian Medical Association
http://www.glma.org
LinksGayandLesbianHealth.htm

Mental Health

I was diagnosed with anorexia nervosa in my sophomore year of high school. I was always the bigger one of my friends and my boyfriend at the time would always tell me he liked the fact that I was chubby. I would see all the stick-skinny models and actresses on TV and feel completely disgusted with myself. At one point during my fight with anorexia, I weighed about 35 pounds less than what was healthy for my height and I was very sick. It is so scary to look in a mirror and see fat when you are actually skin and bones. It ruined my relationship with so many loved ones and I still don't have regular menstrual cycles. (Stephanie, college junior, age 20)

It happened one Saturday night [at] a Greek restaurant . . . Suddenly I began to feel as if the walls were edging in. My palms grew damp, my heart drummed, my stomach churned. I had only one thought: If you don't get out of this restaurant immediately, you are going to faint or die. I mumbled that I didn't feel well and raced for the door . . . I began to avoid restaurants, but then my panic [appeared] in other venues . . . My world shrank to a thin corridor of safe places. (Anndee Hochman, 2004, pp. 99–100)

I have known suicidal depression . . . It is a state of cold, agitated horror and relentless despair. The things that you love most in life leach away. Everything is an effort, all day and throughout the night. There is no hope, no point, no nothing . . . There is no way out and an endless road ahead. (Kay Redfield Jamison, 2014, p. A19).

Overall, rates of mental illness are almost identical for women and men. There are, however, striking gender differences in the prevalence of specific mental disorders. Females have higher rates of eating disorders, depression, and anxiety disorders. Males are more likely to have impulse-control, antisocial, and substance abuse disorders (Eaton et al., 2012; Pine & Fox, 2015; U.S. Department of Health and Human Services, 2013). In this chapter, we focus not only on pathology but also on mental *health* and the factors that promote it. We begin the chapter by looking at two key factors that are associated with good mental health: social support and optimism. We then explore mental health in childhood and adolescence, followed by a discussion of eating disorders and substance abuse. Next, we explore anxiety disorders, depression, and suicide. We then discuss mental health issues of sexual minority women and of older women. We close with a look at the diagnosis and treatment of psychological disorders.

FACTORS PROMOTING MENTAL HEALTH

Social Support

A substantial body of research indicates that both receiving and giving social support play an important role in maintaining good physical and mental health and helping people cope with stressful life events (Bookwala et al., 2014; Cohen et al., 2014; Holt-Lunstad et al., 2015; Miller, 2014; Shor et al., 2013; Yang et al., 2016). This association is especially strong for females. For example, girls are more likely than boys to seek social support following stressful events, and this support appears to play a more protective role for girls than for boys (Eschenbeck et al., 2007; Jackson & Warren, 2000; Rose & Rudolph, 2006). Similarly, studies have found that women who feel more loved and supported by their friends, relatives, and children are at less risk for major depression. Among men, however, level of social support is less strongly related to the risk of depression (Wareham et al., 2007).

TEND AND BEFRIEND.   Women also use social support as a coping aid more readily than men do. Shelley Taylor (2010; Taylor & Master, 2011) and her colleagues have proposed that women often respond to stress by tending to themselves and their children and by forming ties with others (the "tend and befriend" response). Men, in contrast, are more likely to show aggression or escape. This so-called fight or flight response was proposed by psychologists 60 years ago to explain how both men and women react to stress. That view, however, was heavily based on studies of males (Goode, 2000) and was just assumed to apply to females (yet another example of the "male as normative"). But Taylor and her colleagues found many studies that supported their model. For example, Rena Repetti's research (cited in Taylor et al., 2000) showed that mothers returning home after a stressful day at the office were more caring and nurturant toward their children, while stressed fathers were more likely to withdraw from their families or incite conflict. What stimulates these different behaviors in females and males? Taylor and her colleagues suggest that hormonal differences are partly responsible, but they and others are quick to reject the idea that gender stereotypes are biologically hard-wired. Alice Eagly (cited in Goode, 2000), for example, points out that the gender difference could be a result of cultural conditioning that prepares females from an early age for the role of caregiver and nurturer.

Optimism: "The Power of Positive Thinking"

Question: "Do you know the difference between an optimist and a pessimist?"
Answer: The first one sees the glass as half full, while the second sees it as half empty.

You may have heard this saying before, but did you also know that optimism can actually be good for your health? An optimistic outlook—the expectation that good rather than bad things will happen—has been linked to a variety of positive mental and physical health outcomes, including longer life (Anthony et al., 2016; Galatzer-Levy & Bonanno, 2014; Kim et al., 2017; Lawrence et al., 2015). Pessimism, on the other hand, is associated with poorer health outcomes and higher mortality (Marks et al., 2015; Olson et al., 2014; Pankalainen et al., 2016). What accounts for the beneficial effects of optimism? One reason is that optimists are more likely than others to deal actively with or find solutions to problems (Lee & Mason, 2013). Another reason is that optimism appears to protect women from some of the health risks associated with depression (Galatzer-Levy & Bonanno, 2014).

MENTAL HEALTH IN CHILDHOOD AND ADOLESCENCE

Compared to boys, girls show fewer serious emotional and behavioural problems in childhood. Girls, however, are more likely than boys to first manifest psychological difficulties during the adolescent years (Hayden & Mash, 2014; Pine & Fox, 2015; "QuickStats," 2015). Stress levels increase for both genders during these years. However, the patterns of stress girls encounter may leave them more vulnerable to emotional disorders, such as anxiety and depression, than do those experienced by boys (Alloy et al., 2016; Hayden & Mash, 2014). We shall explore these stresses later in the chapter.

Internalizing Disorders in Girls

Adjustment problems that are more common in girls and women, such as depression, anxiety, and social withdrawal, are often labeled "internalizing problems" (Russo, 2010). Later in the chapter, we discuss these disorders in greater detail. Internalizing disorders are harder to detect and thus are more often overlooked than the externalizing problems shown by boys and men: aggression, conduct disorders, antisocial behaviors, and attention deficit hyperactivity disorder (Perou et al., 2013; Pine & Fox, 2015; Piotrowska et al., 2015). Early socialization of girls and boys into gender-typed behaviors may be responsible for these differences in the expression of distress (Hayden & Mash, 2014).

Externalizing Disorders in Girls

Boys are more likely than girls to show externalizing behavior such as hyperactivity and aggression (National Center for Health Statistics, 2014). Unfortunately, girls with externalizing disturbances are rarely studied because of the notion that these are "male" problems (Brennan & Shaw, 2013; Hayden & Mash, 2014; Portnoy et al., 2014). This stereotype of the masculine nature of externalizing disorders persists despite the fact that the percentage of violent crimes committed by teenage girls, such as aggravated assault, is on the increase (Russell et al., 2014). Girls who show externalizing problems exhibit deficits in social, emotional, and communication skills and elevated rates of substance use, depression, anxiety, and risky sexual behavior (Brennan & Shaw, 2013; Obradović & Hipwell, 2010). Moreover, these girls are more likely to have difficulties as adults. For example, longitudinal studies in Sweden (Wangby et al., 1999), New Zealand (Fergusson & Woodward, 2000), Canada (Serbin et al., 2004), and the United States (Hinshaw et al., 2012; Miller et al., 2013) found that girls with externalizing problems in childhood and early adolescence were at greater risk of all types of maladjustment in late adolescence and adulthood than were those without such problems. They had higher rates of educational failure, juvenile crime, substance abuse, mental health problems, suicide attempts, poor decision making, pregnancy, and poor parenting skills. On the other hand, there was little or no relationship between having internalizing problems during adolescence and later maladjustment (Wangby et al., 1999).

EATING DISORDERS

The prevalence of eating disorders among women has increased dramatically around the world over the past few decades (Gerbasi et al., 2014; Pike & Dunne, 2015), paralleling the increase in girls' and women's body dissatisfaction that we discussed in Chapter 4. In this section, we examine types of eating disorders, their likely causes, and their treatment.

Types of Eating Disorders

Three major types of eating disorders have been identified. They are anorexia nervosa, bulimia nervosa, and binge eating disorder. Stephanie, one of Claire's students, described her battle with anorexia in the first vignette at the beginning of this chapter.

ANOREXIA NERVOSA.   The defining characteristics of **anorexia nervosa** are *a significantly low body weight, intense fear of gaining weight, a distorted body image (feeling fat even when too thin)*. Anorexic individuals diet, fast, and exercise excessively in order to lose weight (American Psychiatric Association, 2013). Unlike "normal" dieters, anorexics may lose 25 percent of their original body weight. Many of them share self-starvation tips and "thinspiration" messages on so-called pro-ana Websites (Chang & Bazarova, 2016; Ghaznavi & Taylor, 2015; Arseniev-Koehler et al., 2016; Perloff, 2014; Yom-Tov & Boyd, 2014). Unfortunately, dramatic weight loss can cause osteoporosis, fertility problems, hormone abnormalities, cardiovascular problems (including dangerously low blood pressure), and damage to vital organs (Campbell & Peebles, 2014). Anorexic individuals have a nearly 10-fold greater risk of death from all causes and a 57-fold greater risk of death by suicide than their peers (Button et al., 2009; Mehler & Brown, 2015).

Girls and women account for more than 95 percent of cases of anorexia nervosa. About 1 percent of female adolescents and young adults suffer from the disorder in the United States and western Europe (DeBate et al., 2010). However, many more girls and young women show poor eating behaviors characteristic of anorexia (Smink et al., 2014). While anorexia is often thought of as a White, middle- or upper-class disease, its incidence is increasing among women of color and poor women (Dohm et al., 2010; Franko et al., 2007). Although the peak period for anorexia is adolescence (Maine & Kelly, 2016), females can become anorexic at virtually any age. Increasing numbers of girls as young as 6 have been diagnosed (Donatelle, 2017). In addition, a growing number of women in midlife and beyond are developing or continuing to have eating disorders. Many of these women have likely been overly concerned with weight and body image throughout their lives (Ackard et al., 2014; Maine & Kelly, 2016; Mangweth-Matzek et al., 2014). The midlife trigger for the eating disorder may be the changes in shape and weight that typically occur during menopause. Fear of aging, losing a spouse, dealing with a troubled child, or even having a child leave for college also can set off eating problems (Maine & Kelly, 2016; Mangweth-Matzek et al., 2013).

Young women with physical disabilities also have an elevated risk of developing symptoms of eating disorders. These women may be more vulnerable because their disabilities often involve body-image disturbances, they feel lack of control resulting from needing assistance from others, and they may focus on weight maintenance to sustain mobility (Gross et al., 2000).

BULIMIA NERVOSA.   The primary features of **bulimia nervosa** are *recurrent episodes of uncontrolled binge eating, followed by purging activities aimed at controlling body weight.* Purging activities include self-induced vomiting, exercise, extreme dieting or fasting, and the abuse of laxatives, diuretics, or enemas (American Psychiatric Association, 2013). One young woman, bulimic since the age of 9, graphically describes her binge–purge cycles:

> *At my lunch break, I would eat a quarter-pounder with cheese, large fries, and a cherry pie. Then I would throw up in the antiseptic-scented bathroom, wash my face, and go back on the floor, glassy-eyed and hyper. After work, I would buy a quarter-pounder with cheese, large fries, and a cherry pie, eat it on the way home from work, throw up at home with the bathtub running, eat dinner, throw up, go out with friends, eat, throw up, go home, pass out.*

(Hornbacher, 1998, p. 91)

Individuals with bulimia seem to be driven by an intense fear of weight gain and a distorted perception of body size similar to that seen in anorexics. Unlike anorexics, however, bulimics often maintain normal weight (Golden et al., 2015). Although usually not life-threatening, bulimia can cause gastrointestinal problems, as well as extensive tooth decay because of gastric acid in the vomited food. Bulimia may also result in an imbalance of electrolytes, the chemicals necessary for the normal functioning of the heart (Mehler, 2011).

As with anorexia nervosa, young women account for more than 90 percent of the cases of bulimia. Across the United States and western Europe, about 1 percent of females in late adolescence and early adulthood have bulimia (DeBate et al., 2010).

BINGE EATING DISORDER.   This disorder is characterized by recurrent binge eating in the absence of compensatory weight-control efforts. It is the most common of the eating disorders, has a later onset, and is often associated with obesity (DeBate et al., 2010). Although sex differences are less pronounced for this disorder, the female-to-male ratio is still 3:1 (Maine et al., 2010).

Causes of Eating Disorders

Biological, psychological, and cultural factors all seem to play a part in the development of eating disorders (Steinhausen et al., 2015). Let us consider each of these in turn.

BIOLOGICAL FACTORS.   One line of biological evidence comes from comparing identical twins (who share the same genetic material) with fraternal twins (who share only half). An identical twin is much more likely than a fraternal twin to develop an eating disorder if her co-twin also has the disorder (Zerwas & Claydon, 2014). This is especially true for anorexia nervosa (Wade et al., 2013). In addition, anorexics are more likely than controls to have a mother or sister with the disorder (Steinhausen et al., 2015). While this research suggests the existence of a genetic predisposition toward eating disorders, these findings could also reflect identical twins' highly similar social and cultural environments. Another biological consideration is that anorexics have disturbances in their levels of serotonin, a mood- and appetite-regulating chemical in the brain. However, these chemical imbalances may result *from* the eating disorder rather than cause it (Smolak & Thompson, 2009).

PSYCHOLOGICAL FACTORS.   Certain psychological characteristics also put young women at higher risk for eating disorders. These include low self-esteem, high levels of anxiety, depression, perfectionism, conscientiousness, competitiveness, obsessive-compulsive thoughts and behaviors, difficulty in separating from parents, strong need for approval from others, and perceived lack of control in one's life (Keel & Forney, 2013; Keski-Rahkonen et al., 2014; Liechty & Lee, 2013; Parisi et al., 2017; Zerwas & Claydon, 2014). Eating disorders may also reflect family problems (Holtom-Viesel & Allan, 2014). For example, parents of anorexics are overly nurturant and overprotective and place undue emphasis on achievement and appearance (Sim et al., 2009). Parents of bulimics tend to be highly critical and controlling, overprotective, and low in nurturance and support (Salafia et al., 2008). Another risk factor for eating disorders is sexual or physical abuse (Castellini et al., 2013; Madowitz et al., 2015).

CULTURAL FACTORS.   Feminist scholars view eating disorders as drastic attempts to attain the reed-thin ideal of beauty that has been socially constructed by a patriarchal society (Murnen & Smolak, 2013; van Amsterdam, 2013). The impact of the media in transmitting this message is illustrated dramatically in Anne Becker's (2007) study of adolescent girls living in Fiji, a small nation in the Pacific Ocean.

Just as television was introduced in 1995, only 3 percent of girls reported they vomited to control their weight. In 1998, 15 percent reported the behavior. Similarly, 29 percent scored highly on a test of eating-disorder risk in 1998 compared with just 13 percent in 1995. The more television the girls watched, the more likely they were to diet and to report feeling "too big or fat." Several girls mentioned that they wanted to look like the Western women they saw on television shows (Becker et al., 2007). The study does not conclusively prove that television helps cause eating disorders. Still, Becker notes that the increases are dramatic in a culture that traditionally has equated a robust, nicely rounded body with health and that considers considerable weight loss ("going thin") a sign of illness.

In North America, the effect of cultural pressures to be thin is perhaps seen most vividly among girls and young women who are involved in sports. The incidence of disordered eating among female athletes is far greater than among the general population of girls and young women (Tan et al., 2016). *The combination of low energy with or without disordered eating accompanied by amenorrhea (lack of menstruation) and premature bone loss, or osteoporosis* (discussed in Chapter 12), is sometimes called the **female athlete triad** (Kransdorf et al., 2013). The prevalence of this condition appears to have grown along with girls' participation in dance and performance sports such as gymnastics, distance running, diving, cheerleading, and figure skating, activities that favor a lean body shape (Javed et al., 2013; Tan et al., 2016). Varsity athletes, especially those competing at highly competitive levels, are at greatest risk (Varnes et al., 2013; Berz & McCambridge, 2016). Claire's student Betsy, who spent several years at a strict elite ballet academy, described the pressure to stay thin:

> *Standing at the barre, the ballet master would poke and pull at your body. The professionals would stand outside between rehearsals always holding a cigarette. All the young students concluded that smoking, in replacement of food, made you thinner. Although I never started smoking, I started consuming orange juice . . . and that's all. At slumber parties on the weekends, I made sure that my friends thought I loved food, and saw me devour the pizza. I also made sure that they didn't see me get rid of it in the bathroom afterward.*

Treatment of Eating Disorders

Eating disorders are difficult to cure. Cognitive behavioral therapy, which helps people to change both their behaviors and the way they think about themselves and others, seems to be the most effective therapy for bulimia and binge eating disorder (Hay, 2013; Hoek, 2015; Parisi et al., 2017; Waller et al., 2014). Antidepressants may also be of use in treating bulimia (Campbell & Peebles, 2014; Hay, 2013). Family therapy, which elicits the parents' aid in getting the client to eat and then gradually returns control of eating to the client, shows promise in the treatment of anorexia in adolescents (Brauhardt et al., 2014; Couturier et al., 2013; Dole, 2017). Cognitive behavioral therapy also may be helpful in improving outcomes and preventing relapse (Galsworthy-Francis & Allan, 2014). Antidepressants sometimes help prevent relapse once the anorexic client returns to normal. They are not effective in reversing anorexic symptoms, however (Sargent et al., 2009).

Anorexia is particularly resistant to a wide range of interventions (Foerde et al., 2015). While long-term outcomes vary by study, typically fewer than half of the clients fully recover, 20 to 30 percent show some improvement, 10 to 20 percent remain chronically ill, and 5 to 10 percent die from their illness (Galsworthy-Francis & Allan, 2014; Keski-Rahkonen et al., 2014). Treatment for bulimia tends to be more successful. About three-fourths of women diagnosed as bulimic show full recovery 20 years later, while 5 percent still have an eating disorder (Keel et al., 2010). Binge eating disorder has a more favorable prognosis than either anorexia or bulimia, with a recovery rate of about 80 percent 5 years after treatment and a low relapse rate (Mehler, 2011).

SUBSTANCE USE AND ABUSE

Until recently, substance use was considered primarily a male problem, and much of the research dealing with abuse of alcohol and other drugs was carried out on males. This oversight has led to inadequate diagnosis and treatment of women with substance abuse disorders. In this section, we concentrate on substance abuse issues in women.

Alcohol

INCIDENCE.   Starting in adolescence and into old age, females around the world are less likely than males to use alcohol and to be heavy drinkers (Delker et al., 2016; Hughes et al., 2016; Centers for Disease Control and Prevention, 2016d; U.S. Department of Health and Human Services, 2013). Over their lifetime about 8 to 10 percent of women and 15 to 20 percent of men will develop alcohol problems, a male-to-female ratio of over 2:1 (Butler, 2008). *However, while women's alcoholism starts later than men's alcoholism, it progresses more quickly*, a pattern called **telescoping**. White women have higher rates of alcohol use than women in other ethnic groups; they are followed by Native American women, Black women, and Latinas. Asian American women have the lowest rates of alcohol use (U.S. Department of Health and Human Services, 2010).

Problem drinking in young women has reached an alarming rate both in the United States and abroad (Davoren et al., 2016; Hoeppner et al., 2013). For example, U.S. college women are now almost as likely as college men to engage in **binge drinking**, defined as *having five drinks in a row for men or four in a row for women during a two-hour period* (U.S. Department of Health and Human Services, 2013). Heavy drinking is especially prevalent among sorority women and fraternity men (Mignon et al., 2009) and others whose peers drink heavily. Sadly, the gender gap in drinking has disappeared among young adolescents: Female high schoolers are more likely to be current drinkers than male high school students (36 versus 34 percent) and females are almost as likely to binge drink (17 versus 19 percent) (Centers for Disease Control and Prevention, 2016c). One possible explanation is an increase in alcohol advertising targeting teenage girls. In the past few years, advertising for low-alcohol drinks such as wine coolers and alcoholic iced teas has increased in national magazines, especially in those read primarily by adolescent girls (Center on Alcohol Marketing and Youth, 2010).

HEALTH CONSEQUENCES.   Women have more body fat, less water, and less of the enzyme that breaks down alcohol than men do. As a result, they have higher levels of alcohol in their blood even when they consume the same amount of alcohol per unit of body weight (Hughes et al., 2016). For example, 3 ounces of alcohol consumed by a 120-pound woman has a greater effect on her than the equivalent 6 ounces of alcohol consumed by a 240-pound man has on him. As women age, they have even greater physiological susceptibility to alcohol's effect and, thus, experience impairment or intoxication after fewer drinks. Another consequence is that women develop cirrhosis of the liver, hepatitis, heart disease, and brain damage at lower levels of alcohol intake than men. Prolonged heavy drinking also increases the risk of breast cancer, osteoporosis, and infertility (National Institute on Alcohol Abuse and Alcoholism, 2015).

Drinking alcohol during pregnancy can lead to fetal alcohol spectrum disorder (FASD). The most severe form of the disorder is **fetal alcohol syndrome (FAS)**, *a disorder characterized by mental retardation, growth deficiencies, facial deformities, and social, emotional, learning, and behavioral problems* (Centers for Disease Control and Prevention, 2015d). FAS is the leading preventable cause of mental retardation in the United States. Even light drinkers risk having children with FASD (Green et al., 2016). Unfortunately, more than half of the women of childbearing age drink occasionally, and 12 percent report that they binge drink at least once a month, potentially exposing fetuses early in the first trimester before the women realizes she is pregnant (Green et al., 2016). Even more alarming, 10 percent of women who *know* they are pregnant drink occasionally, and 3 percent have engaged in binge drinking within the last month (Tan et al., 2015). A recent government warning about drinking generated some unexpected reactions. For details, read In the News 13.1.

IN THE NEWS 13.1
CDC Advice on Women and Alcohol is Criticized

A seemingly well-meaning warning from the Centers for Disease Control and Prevention (Green et al., 2016) about the risks of drinking and pregnancy has set off a firestorm of criticism. The report advises women to stop drinking if they are trying to get pregnant or even if they are not using contraception when having sex. The report also notes that drinking can make women more vulnerable to violence and sexually transmitted infections. But several commenters see a double standard, pointing out that there was no report warning men that drinking could lead to violence or STIs (Aubrey, 2016). Still others viewed the report as a condescending and patronizing statement, giving the impression that women are incapable of making responsible choices about their reproductive health (Brice, 2016). Some writers accuse the report of victim-blaming by saying that women should avoid drinking in order to not become the subject of unwanted sexual attention and possible rape (Fox, 2016). What is your view of the CDC's advice?

RISK FACTORS.   Children of alcoholic parents or siblings have increased rates of alcoholism. Genetic factors appear to play about as strong a role for daughters as for sons (Velasquez et al., 2015; Vogeltanz-Holm et al., 2013). Adolescents whose parents and peers consume alcohol and tolerate its use are more likely to start drinking at an early age, which places them at higher risk for later alcohol-related problems (Brown & Rinelli, 2010). Divorced and single women are more likely than married or widowed women to drink heavily and to have alcohol-related problems. Women who are depressed and anxious and report stressful life events such as physical or sexual abuse also are more likely to be heavy drinkers (Velasquez et al., 2015; Vogeltanz-Holm et al., 2013).

TREATMENT.   Society has set up several double standards for women and men. The double standard of aging was described in Chapter 2 and the double standard of sexuality was discussed in Chapter 6. There is also a double standard with regard to drinking. Heavy drinking in men is often expected and seen as normal, whereas heavy drinking in women is strongly criticized. As a result, women tend to hide or deny their alcohol use, making them less likely to seek help and to be more seriously ill before the disease is diagnosed (Velasquez et al., 2015; Vogeltanz-Holm et al., 2013). Moreover, physicians are less likely to counsel female patients than male patients on alcohol or drug use (McKnight-Eily et al., 2014). Alcohol problems in older women often are mistaken for other aging-related conditions, and thus are missed and untreated by health care providers (National Institute on Alcohol Abuse and Alcoholism, 2015). Twelve-step alcoholism treatment programs such as Alcoholics Anonymous have been criticized for being based exclusively on research with alcoholic men. Alternative programs, such as Women for Sobriety and the Women Recovery Group, focus on the special issues and needs of women with drinking and substance abuse problems (Greenfield, 2016; Vogeltanz-Holm et al., 2013). These programs have shown some success in treating alcohol disorders in women. However, treatment options for older women remain limited (Epstein et al., 2007).

Illegal Substances

INCIDENCE.   Use of illegal substances such as marijuana, cocaine, heroin, hallucinogens, and steroids varies by gender and ethnic group. Among women, use is highest among Native Americans, followed by White, Latina, Black, and Asian American women. Regardless of ethnicity, however, males generally have higher rates of illegal drug use than females, both in adolescence and in adulthood. Males also use illegal drugs more heavily than females do (Kann et al., 2016; Miech et al., 2016; U.S. Department of Health and Human Services, 2013; Johnston et al., 2011). A possible reason for the gender gap is that drug use among girls and women is less acceptable in society. Recently, however, 8th- and 10th-grade girls have shown higher rates of drug use than males for some drugs, including inhalants, amphetamines, and tranquilizers (Johnston et al., 2015a).

   Typically, individuals who use illegal substances use more than one substance and also use or abuse alcohol. In girls and women, the problem is compounded because they are more likely than men to both use and misuse prescription drugs, such as tranquilizers, antidepressants, and sleeping pills (Merline et al., 2004; Smith, 2011).

TREATMENT.   As with treatment for alcohol problems, women in drug abuse treatment programs have different needs than men in treatment. Consequently, a successful program often depends on meeting these different needs (Kissin et al., 2014; Velasquez et al., 2017). Data comparing outcomes from women-only versus mixed-gender treatments show some advantages for the women-only programs (Velasquez et al., 2017).

ANXIETY DISORDERS AND DEPRESSION

More than one in four Americans will have an anxiety disorder in their lifetime and nearly one in five will develop major depression (Bourne, 2010; Kessler et al., 2005). Women are at greater risk than men for both disorders in virtually every nation studied (Freeman & Freeman, 2014; Seedat et al., 2009). In this section, we first review anxiety disorders. We then turn to depression and its all-too-frequent outcome: suicide.

Anxiety Disorders

Almost everyone feels anxious now and again. When you have to give a speech in class, for instance, it is normal to feel anxious. But when anxiety is irrational, excessive, and persists over several months, it is called an anxiety disorder. Most anxiety disorders occur twice as frequently in women as in men (Anxiety and Depression Association of America, 2016). What might account for this? One view is that girls are socialized to adopt a feminine gender role, which supports fearful negative responses to adversity that contribute to an increased risk for anxiety. In addition, affiliation is emphasized more in raising girls, leaving them more vulnerable in the face of relationship stresses (Hodgson et al., 2016).

Generalized anxiety disorder is characterized by *excessive worry and anxiety about a variety of life situations or events.* Many people experience physical symptoms as well. It is one of the most common anxiety disorders, with about 7 percent of women developing it at some time in their lives (Yonkers et al., 2016). The difference between ordinary worrying and generalized anxiety disorder is that the level of concern is excessive, resulting in distress and interfering with everyday functioning.

Panic disorder is marked by *sudden unpredictable attacks of intense anxiety accompanied by a pounding heart, dizziness, sweating, shortness of breath, and trembling.* A person having an attack has a sense of impending doom, losing control, or dying (National Institute of Mental Health, 2013). Women are twice as likely as men to develop this disorder at some time (Johnson et al., 2017). As shown in the second vignette at the beginning of the chapter, panic disorder can lead to **agoraphobia**, a *fear of being in public places where escape might be difficult if one were suddenly incapacitated* (*agora* is the Greek word for marketplace) (Yonkers et al., 2016). Agoraphobia will be experienced by about 7 percent of women and 4 percent of men during their lifetime (Russo & Tartaro, 2008).

Agoraphobia is just one of a group of anxiety disorders known as a **specific phobia**, a *fear of a specific object, such as a spider, or a specific situation, such as being in public places, or flying.* About 12 percent of women experience a specific phobia in any given year (Yonkers et al., 2016). Specific phobias usually start in childhood. Social construction of gender-specific attitudes and behaviors may account for the higher prevalence of these phobias in females than in males. Expression of fear and anxiety is more socially acceptable in girls and women than in boys and men, who are discouraged from displaying these emotions (McHugh, 2008).

Depression

> *I have been immobilized, unable to formulate thought or action. Can't get out of bed most of the time. I feel terrible—hopeless, joyless, exhausted, lost.*
>
> (Sondra, age 48, cited in "Depression & Women," 2003, p. 1)

INCIDENCE. **Depression** is *characterized by prolonged sadness or irritability and loss of pleasure in most activities, often accompanied by fatigue and feelings of worthlessness* (Ali, 2017). Higher rates of depression among females first appear in early adolescence and continue into adulthood (Hyde, 2014, Rohde et al., 2013). As many as one in five adolescents has experienced an episode of depression (Nock et al., 2014). Women with disabilities have higher rates of depression than able-bodied women (Brown, 2014), and ethnic minority women have higher rates than White women (Anderson & Mayes, 2010). Across many nations, cultures, and ethnicities, women are about twice as likely as men to suffer from depression (Avenevoli et al., 2015; Centers for Disease Control & Prevention, 2016d). Moreover, women are more likely than men to suffer from an anxiety disorder along with their depression (Hilt & Nolen-Hoeksema, 2014).

What are the stresses of adolescence that are linked to higher rates of depression in girls than in boys? Lisa Flook (2011) and Karen Rudolph (2009) and her colleagues found that girls experience considerable stress from relationship problems, including fights with peers, siblings, or friends. Because girls have closer, more intimate relationships with family and friends than boys do, disruptions and conflicts in these relationships can lead to depression and distress (Hamilton et al., 2015; Rudolph & Flynn, 2014). Just being in a romantic relationship is associated with depression in early adolescent girls (Hammer & Silveira, 2014). Another stressor linked to girls' depression is concern about weight and body image (Dole, 2017). In addition, adolescent girls are more likely than adolescent boys to be victims of cyberbullying (see Chapter 14), which is linked to depression (Mojtabai et al., 2016).

THEORIES. Many theories have been offered to explain the gender difference in depression. Gender differences in help-seeking behavior or willingness to report symptoms have been ruled out as possible reasons (Urbancic, 2009). One explanation is biological, linking depression to hormonal changes that occur during the menstrual cycle, the postpartum period, and menopause (Hilt & Nolen-Hoeksema, 2014). As we saw in Chapter 7, however, menopause is not associated with an increase in depression. In Chapter 7, we also noted that direct relationships between menstrual and postpartum hormonal changes and depression are weak, temporary, and far from universal (Hilt & Nolen-Hoeksema, 2014). One biological factor that *is* strongly linked to depression is having a low level of the neurochemical serotonin (Kelly & Dinan, 2016). Women produce less serotonin than men do, which makes them more susceptible to depression (Gressier et al., 2016).

A second explanation for the gender difference in depression is that girls and women are more likely than boys and men to experience stresses that are linked to depression (Hilt & Nolen-Hoeksema, 2014). We have seen that relationship stresses are linked to increased depression for adolescent girls. In addition, women are more likely than men to have low social status, undergo economic hardship, face sexism, gendered racism, and discrimination in the workplace and elsewhere, experience marital and family strains, and be subjected to intimate partner violence, sexual abuse, and sexual harassment (Carr et al., 2014; Hilt & Nolen-Hoeksema, 2014; Mickelson & Hazlett, 2014; Schmitt et al., 2014).

A third proposed explanation is that the feminine role makes women more vulnerable to depression by making them feel helpless and powerless to control aspects of their lives (Hammen et al., 2014). Females are expected to be less competent and more in need of help than males. Their efforts and achievements are more likely to be ignored or devalued. The sense that one's actions do not count can lead to a feeling of "learned helplessness," which in turn is linked to depression. In support of this view, girls and women with more masculine behavior traits are less likely to experience depression than those with more feminine traits (Lengua & Stormshok, 2000; Vafei et al., 2016).

A fourth theory known as *silencing the self* (Ali et al., 2017; Jack, 2012) is based on the assumption that women are socialized to place a high value on establishing and maintaining close relationships. According to this view, women defer to the needs of others, censor their self-expression, repress anger, and restrict their own initiatives, which increase their vulnerability to depression.

Susan Nolen-Hoeksema (Hilt & Nolen-Hoeksema, 2014) has proposed a fifth theory based on the way that females and males respond when they are depressed. She has found that when adolescent girls and women are depressed, they *focus on their inner feelings and try over and over again to analyze the causes and consequences of their depression*. This so-called **ruminative style** may be accompanied by **corumination**, which involves *extensively discussing one's problems with another person* (Hammer & Silveira, 2014). Both rumination and corumination lead to more severe and longer-lasting depressed moods. Adolescent boys and men, on the other hand, tend to engage in activities to distract themselves when they are depressed (Hamilton et al., 2015; Nolen-Hoeksema, 2014). Try Get Involved 13.1 to see whether you find differences in the way women and men respond when they are depressed.

These explanations of depression are not mutually exclusive. Indeed, several of these factors most likely are involved (Hamilton et al., 2015; Ussher, 2010). For example, one large-scale study of adults suggests that women are more likely than men to get caught in a cycle of despair and passivity because of a lower sense of control over important areas of life, compounded by more chronic strain caused by women's lesser social power. In the study, chronic strain led to more rumination, which in turn increased feelings of powerlessness and depression (Nolen-Hoeksema et al., 1999).

GET INVOLVED 13.1
How Do Women and Men Respond to Depression?

For this activity, ask one young adult woman, one young adult man, one middle-aged woman, and one middle-aged man to complete the following survey.

WHAT DO YOU DO WHEN YOU'RE FEELING DEPRESSED?

Instructions: Everyone gets depressed—sad, blue, down in the dumps—some of the time. People deal with being depressed in many different ways. For each item, please circle the number that best describes what you *generally* do when you are *depressed*. Choose the most accurate response for *you*, not what you think "most people" would say or do. There are no right or wrong answers.

	Never or Almost Never	Sometimes	Often	Always or Almost Always
1. I try to figure out why I am depressed	1	2	3	4
2. I avoid thinking of reasons why I am depressed	1	2	3	4
3. I think about how sad I feel	1	2	3	4
4. I do something fun with a friend	1	2	3	4
5. I wonder why I have problems that others do not	1	2	3	4
6. I think about all my short-comings, faults, and mistakes	1	2	3	4
7. I think of something to make myself feel better	1	2	3	4
8. I go to a favorite place to distract myself	1	2	3	4
9. I think about why I can't handle things better	1	2	3	4
10. I do something that made me feel better before	1	2	3	4

WHAT DOES IT MEAN?

Before adding up each respondent's scores for the ten items, reverse the points for items 2, 4, 7, 8, and 10. That is, for a rating of 1 (never or almost never), give 4 points; for a rating of 2, give 3 points, and so on. Then sum the points for the ten items for each respondent. Higher scores reflect greater rumination.

1. Are there differences between your female and male respondents in how they react when they are depressed? If so, how do you account for differences?

2. Did your young adults respond differently from your middle-aged adults? Account for any differences.

3. Did your results support Susan Nolen-Hoeksema's findings regarding how women and men respond when they are depressed? Account for any differences.

Source: Adapted from Butler and Nolen-Hoeksema (1994).

DEPRESSION IN LATER LIFE.   Clinical depression affects approximately 10 percent of older men and 16 percent of older women in the United States (Federal Interagency Forum on Aging-Related Statistics, 2012). Higher rates of depression are found among medically ill, unmarried, socially isolated, homebound, or functionally impaired older adults (Blazer & Hybels, 2014; Fiske et al., 2009; Schwarzbach et al., 2014). Interestingly, having an ill spouse is linked to depression for women, but not for men (Ayotte et al., 2010). Depression, in turn, can contribute to heart disease and earlier onset of death (Clay, 2014a; Shah et al., 2014).

These statistics may be underestimates, however, because many depressed older people are undiagnosed and untreated (Ghio et al., 2014; Park & Unützer, 2011). Studies of older adults who committed suicide have found that the majority had visited a doctor within a month before their deaths (Morichi et al., 2015). Unfortunately, even when older patients clearly are depressed, most physicians do not adequately diagnose or treat the condition (America Psychological Association, 2014). Older adults do not always experience the classic symptoms of depression, such as sleeplessness, fatigue, low energy, loss of appetite, guilt feelings, and depressed mood, but rather may show anxiety, confusion, and physical complaints (Blazer & Hybels, 2014; Fiske et al., 2009). Sometimes, these symptoms are side effects of medications taken for other health conditions, and changing the medication removes the symptoms. Some symptoms, such as irritability and fault finding, or pessimism and little hope for the future, may be dismissed as typical personality changes that accompany aging. Even the classic symptoms of low energy, loss of appetite, or loss of interest in former sources of enjoyment may be viewed incorrectly by doctors as a "normal" consequence of medical, financial, or family difficulties or the losses that come with age (Chrisler et al., 2016; Olthoff, 2013). While it is true that health problems among older adults may contribute to symptoms of depression, most older people confront their problems without becoming clinically depressed. In fact, older adults have a lower prevalence of depression than younger individuals (Morichi et al., 2015).

Depression is highly treatable in older adults. Unfortunately, older adults are less likely than younger and middle-aged adults to receive mental health services (American Psychiatric Association, 2013).

Suicide

INCIDENCE.   Across all ages and ethnic groups in the United States, boys and men are nearly four times as likely as women to commit suicide, whereas girls and women are two to three times more likely than men to attempt it. Among women, Native American women have the highest suicide rates and Black women have the lowest. Older White males have the highest rate of all (Curtin et al., 2016; Kann et al., 2016). This group, probably the most privileged earlier in life, experiences the greatest loss of status in old age, contributing to ill health and depression (Roark, 2009). The lower suicide rates among Black women, on the other hand, are thought to be related to the protective factors of extended family and community networks and religious faith (Goldston et al., 2008). For a look at global gender differences in suicide, see the next section.

GENDER DIFFERENCES IN SUICIDE ACROSS CULTURES.   In most countries, men are more likely than women to commit suicide. In high-income industrialized nations, the male-to-female suicide ratio is about 3.5:1. In low- and middle-income countries, women's rates are higher and men's rates are lower, resulting in a lower male-to-female ratio of 1.6:1 (World Health Organization, 2014b). In industrialized nations, the male-to-female suicide ratio ranges from a low of 2.3:1 in Norway to a high of 4.5:1 in the Russian Federation. The ratio for the United States is 3.7:1. Worldwide, higher divorce rates are associated with higher suicide rates. Interestingly, this association is stronger for men than for women (Stack & Scourfield, 2013), in line with findings that marriage seems more beneficial for men than for women (see Chapter 8). Across cultures, unemployment is also more strongly associated with suicide among men than among women (Haw et al., 2015). For women, suicide is more closely linked to their social and economic status. In nations where women's status is low, such as China, India, the Pacific Island countries, and parts of Turkey, their suicide rates are higher than that of boys and men (Milner & DeLeo, 2010; World Health Organization, 2014b). One of the differences between women's suicides in the West and in developing countries is the method used. Women in Western countries usually swallow pills or slash their wrists, which are treatable events. In Asia, however, women ingest highly lethal insecticides, hang themselves, or set themselves on fire (Milner & DeLeo, 2010; Raj et al., 2008).

Why are young Asian women committing suicide at such a high rate? A major factor seems to be cultural and gender conflicts that are made more intense as these traditional agricultural societies are transforming themselves into industrial societies. Many girls are still forbidden to go to school or to work and they are forced into arranged marriages, which may be abusive or unhappy (Kristof & WuDunn, 2009; Raj et al., 2008). At the same time, they are exposed through movies and television to a more prosperous, egalitarian life, which is denied to them. Such lack of control of one's life may lead to despair and suicide (Frantz, 2000; Milner & DeLeo, 2010).

Maggie Kuhn, who founded the Gray Panthers after her forced retirement at age 65, illustrates the active role older women can play as advocates for social change.

SUICIDE IN ADOLESCENCE AND YOUNG ADULTHOOD. Nearly half of all suicides among females occur between the ages of 15 and 44. Suicide is the fourth leading cause of death for women of these ages and the second leading cause of death for those 10 to 24 years old (Sullivan et al., 2015). Risk factors for suicide in both sexes include depression, exposure to suicide or suicide attempts by family or friends, stressful life events such as interpersonal loss or disciplinary crises, substance or alcohol abuse, and having guns in the home (Donatelle, 2017; Franklin et al., 2017; Tingley, 2013). Social factors are more strongly associated with having suicidal thoughts for girls than for boys. In particular, girls who are socially isolated from peers are more likely to think about suicide than are girls with strong social networks (Bearman & Moody, 2004).

SUICIDE IN LATER LIFE. Risk factors associated with suicide in older people are the death of a loved one; physical illness; uncontrollable pain; the specter of dying a prolonged death that harms family members emotionally and financially; fear of institutionalization; social isolation; loneliness; elder abuse; and major changes in social roles, such as retirement. As in adolescence, those who abuse alcohol and other drugs, are depressed, or suffer from other mental disorders are also at high risk (Conwell et al., 2010; Franklin et al., 2017; Nock et al., 2014; Olthoff, 2013).

On a positive note, remember that most older people with health and other problems cope well with the changes of later life and do not become depressed or suicidal (Schaupp & Ting, 2017). Many continue to lead active and productive lives. In the words of Maggie Kuhn, an older woman activist,

> *Old age is not a disaster. It is a triumph over disappointment, failure, loss, illness. When we reach this point in life, we have great experience with failure. I always know that if one of the things that I've initiated falters and fails, it won't be the end. I'll find a way to learn from it and begin again.*

(Kuhn, 1991, p. 214)

MENTAL HEALTH OF SEXUAL MINORITY WOMEN

Until 1973, the American Psychiatric Association classified homosexuality as a mental disorder (Baams et al., 2015; Hottes et al., 2015; McCarthy & Fisher, 2014; Mustanski et al., 2016). It took nearly another 30 years for the American Psychological Association to adopt guidelines for psychotherapy with gay, lesbian, and bisexual clients ("Guidelines," 2000), and 15 more years to issue guidelines for psychological practice with transgender individuals (American Psychological Association, 2015a). These guidelines urge psychologists to understand how prejudice, discrimination, and violence pose risks to the mental health and well-being of lesbian, gay, bisexual, and transgender (LGBT) clients. Let us look at stress-related difficulties faced by the LGBT community and some helpful coping mechanisms.

Stresses and Problems

In Chapter 6, we discussed the widespread nature of prejudice and discrimination against LGBT individuals. Such homophobia can cause considerable stress in the lives of sexual minorities and increase their risk of physical and psychological problems (American Psychological Association, 2016; Gonzales, 2014; Mayer et al., 2014; Ngamake et al., 2016; Rosario et al., 2014; Sabin et al., 2015).

Compared to heterosexual teens, lesbian, gay, and bisexual adolescents have higher rates of substance abuse, poor school adjustment, truancy, running away from home, risky sexual behavior, conflicts with the law, depression, and suicidal thoughts (Collier et al., 2013; Kann et al., 2016; Kerr et al., 2014; Mustanski & Liu, 2013; Whitaker et al., 2015). In adulthood, sexual minorities report higher rates of alcohol and substance abuse than heterosexuals (Austin et al., 2016; Clay, 2014b; Cochran et al., 2015; Katz, 2016; Medley et al., 2016; Przedworski et al., 2014). They also show poorer mental health, and higher rates of anxiety disorder, depression, suicide attempts, and suicide (Duncan & Hatzenbuehler, 2014; Hottes et al., 2015; Katz, 2016; Medley et al., 2016; Mustanski et al., 2016). Bisexual and transgender individuals show particularly high rates of mood and anxiety disorders and of substance and alcohol abuse (Cochran et al., 2016; Miller & Grollman, 2015; Newcomb et al., 2014; Robles et al., 2016; Talley et al., 2014).

Coping Mechanisms

On a more positive note, many sexual minority individuals develop effective coping responses that are linked to good mental health. These include accepting one's sexual orientation, having a good social support network, being in a satisfying relationship, and actively participating in the lesbian and gay community (Graham & Barnow, 2013; Mason et al., 2015; Tabaac et al., 2015; Poteat et al., 2015). Having family and friends who acknowledge and support their sexual identity is another key factor linked to the well-being of LGBT individuals (Denes & Afifi, 2014; Follins et al., 2014; McConnell et al., 2015). LGBT individuals are also more likely than heterosexuals to seek psychological counseling (Robinson-Wood, 2017). However, sexual minorities may be especially vulnerable to misdiagnosis and other forms of bias, which can serve as a barrier to seeking treatment (Robinson-Wood, 2017). Not surprisingly, sexual minority individuals are more likely to seek counseling from therapists who have been trained to work with their needs and issues (Spengler & Ægisdóttir, 2015).

MENTAL HEALTH OF OLDER WOMEN

As my hair grays, my skin wrinkles, and my fat redistributes, I can't take it all too sorrowfully. I have had a productive youth and have accomplished enough during it to provide a dozen people with material for my birthday roast. Milestone birthdays of middle age are wonderful when you have made positive choices, managed the unexpected, learned from the storms and sorrows, but still find yourself emotionally and physically whole.

(Pam, on the occasion of her 50th birthday)

In this section, we look at the mental health of women as they get older. First we focus on gender differences. We then concentrate on the vital older woman.

Gender Differences

The psychological health of women tends to improve as they get older (Barrett & Toothman, 2016; Kemper, 2013). For example, older women show fewer negative emotions, less depression, greater well-being, and more emotional control than younger women. Still, older women, compared to older men, are more depressed (Hilt & Nolen-Hoeksema, 2014; Hyde, 2014) and report more stress, worry, and sadness, more frequent negative emotions, poorer mental health, and a lower sense of well-being (George, 2010; Pratt & Brody, 2014). However, gender differences in depression decline or even disappear by age 85 because men's depression rates increase after age 60, while those of women remain the same or decrease (Cong & Pei, 2017). Similarly, rates of frequent anxiety decline as women age, but this is not the case for men (Federal Interagency Forum on Aging-Related Statistics, 2012; O'Brien & Whitbourne, 2015). In addition, the gender difference in self-esteem that emerges in adolescence (boys' is higher) narrows and disappears in old age (Bleidorn et al., 2016; Orth & Robins, 2014).

The Vital Older Woman

In my sixties, I found my first taste of freedom. My earlier life was spent living according to other people's expectations of me: my parents, my husband, my family. When your family doesn't need you anymore, that's frightening, but freeing. There's time to explore and contemplate what you've learned so far. And there's a duty to send out some of those messages so that other people can benefit from all the difficult lessons you've learned. (Anna Kainen, 1995, age 82, writer)

Women, speak out. Stand up for what you believe. Go back to that teenage person you were, who wanted something very badly, then go out and get it. This is a time in your life when there's nothing and no one standing in your way. (Elizabeth Watson, 1995, age 82, theologian and environmental activist)

We have examined a number of challenges faced by many older women: declining health, financial problems, and the loss of loved ones. But this does not mean that the later years of a woman's life are filled with frustration and despair. Many older women cope successfully with the challenges that old age brings. They don't just *endure* old age; they *enjoy* it.

Most older women maintain a positive outlook and high levels of life satisfaction (Majerovitz, 2006). In some cases, positive changes in family or work situations occur as a result of women's actions. In other cases, stress relief comes about through role changes and the passage of time. Finally, some women continue to lead lives that have always been relatively satisfying (Antonucci et al., 2010; Etaugh, 2017). Key components of a satisfying life for older women include caring family and friends, independence, meaningful activities, good health, a sense of purpose, spirituality, and generativity (i.e., a concern for younger generations) (Burton-Jeangross & Zimmermann-Sloutskis, 2016; Chew-Graham & Ray, 2016; Troutman Jordan et al., 2013; Versey et al., 2013; Windsor et al., 2015). Older Black women express significantly more contentment with their lives than older White women, even though Blacks are more disadvantaged socioeconomically and perceive their health as worse than Whites do (Nguyen et al., 2013). How can we explain this? Many aging ethnic minority women are able to draw on psychological, social, and cultural strengths that ease their transition to old age. They have spent their lives marshaling scarce resources to cope with everyday demands, and these coping strategies pay off later on as self-reliance. Strengths also arise from family, church, community networks, and shared ethnic identity (Antonucci et al., 2010a; Mattis, 2002; Yoon & Lee, 2004). In addition, White women may have expectations of life in the later years that are unrealistically high.

See What <u>You</u> Can Do 13.1 for ways to manage stress and promote mental health. Practice these methods yourself and share with others.

DIAGNOSIS AND TREATMENT OF PSYCHOLOGICAL DISORDERS

The diagnosis and treatment of psychological disorders in women have often been topics of controversy. Feminist researchers and theorists point out that diagnosis and treatment are conducted by a predominantly male psychiatric culture, using a medical model of psychological illness and viewing many aspects of female behavior as pathological (L. Brown, 2016). In recent times, gender bias has become more covert, but still remains a powerful force in psychological practice (American Psychological Association, 2007). Let's take a closer look at diagnosis and treatment of women's psychological disorders.

Gender Bias in Diagnosis

Is there a double standard of mental health for women and men? In a classic study, Inge Broverman and her colleagues (1970) reported that mental health professionals gave similar descriptions for a "healthy" adult (gender unspecified) and a "healthy" male. A "healthy" woman, however, was seen as less healthy in several ways: more submissive, more excitable in minor crises, more emotional, more illogical, more easily hurt, more sneaky, and less independent. Over the years, other researchers have found that gender bias in diagnosis remains alive and well. A later study, for example, found that counselors-in-training continue to have different standards of mental health for women and men, and that "healthy women" are viewed differently than "healthy adults" (Seem & Clark, 2006).

Although gender bias has become more covert, it still exists. For example, disorders that conform to gender stereotypes (e.g., anxiety in women, antisocial behavior in men) may be overdiagnosed and overtreated (Russo & Tartaro, 2008). One meta-analysis of 42 studies, for example, found that professionals were more likely to diagnose and treat anxiety when it occurred in women and were more likely to diagnose and treat antisocial behavior when it occurred in men. By the same token, misdiagnosis can occur when a client's problem behaviors are inconsistent with societal expectations, such as when a woman exhibits antisocial symptoms (American Psychological Association, 2007). A volatile, angry, difficult female client may be given a diagnosis of borderline personality disorder, whereas a man's anger may be considered to be related simply to situational factors, such as "having a bad day" (Swartz, 2013; Ussher, 2013). For more about gender biases in diagnosis, see Learn About the Research 13.1.

Gender Bias in Psychotherapy

Gender bias also exists in psychotherapy. One classic study (American Psychological Association, 1975) documented bias in the form of fostering traditional gender roles (e.g., "be a better wife"),

---

WHAT <u>YOU</u> CAN DO 13.1
Ways to Manage Stress and Promote Good Mental Health

- Identify the major stressors in your life.
- Think of ways you can reduce these stresses and take appropriate actions.
- Learn to delegate and share.
- Learn to say "no."
- Communicate with support groups: friends, family, and counselors.
- Use meditation, yoga, or prayer.
- Use visualization to imagine yourself in a peaceful, relaxing place.

- Exercise.
- Spend time with a pet.
- Get a massage.
- Make time for activities you enjoy: hiking, gardening, reading, and so on.

Sources: Alexander et al. (2017) and Donatelle (2017).

LEARN ABOUT THE RESEARCH 13.1
What Is "Normal"? Gender Biases in Diagnosis

Some psychologists (e.g., Worell & Johnson, 2001) argue that the definitions of "normal" that guide psychological diagnoses are socially constructed by the dominant cultural group (i.e., White heterosexual males) and reflect stereotypical notions of gender, race/ethnicity, and sexuality. To test this view, Jill Cermele and her colleagues (2001) analyzed the depiction of women and men in the Casebook that accompanies the **Diagnostic and Statistical Manual of Mental Disorders, IV,** the *standard classification system used in the United States.* The researchers found that the Casebook (Spitzer et al., 1994), which provides case studies to guide the clinician, does indeed contain stereotyped descriptions of women and men. Men's personality traits were much more likely to be described in positive ways (e.g., charming, friendly, engaging) than in negative ways, whereas females were more often described negatively (e.g., frightened, sad, helpless). In addition, there were more than three times as many negative physical descriptions of women (e.g., disheveled, pale, obese) than of men, who were more often described positively (e.g., tall, handsome, healthy). Women were also more apt to be infantilized (e.g., described as tiny, childlike, frail, and girlish). In addition, they were more often referred to in terms of sexual behavior (e.g., seductive, flirtatious), even when these behaviors had nothing to do with the diagnosis.

WHAT DOES IT MEAN?

1. How might constructing women as different from men influence clinicians in diagnosing mental illness?

2. What can psychologists do to address biases in their notions of what constitutes normalcy and mental illness?

---

telling sexist jokes, not taking violence against women seriously, and seducing female clients (American Psychological Association, 1975). In another study (Fowers et al., 1996), over 200 clinical psychologists were asked to recommend strategies that would best help hypothetical females and males with identically described problems. The psychologists indicated that male clients could best be helped by increasing their instrumental (traditionally masculine) actions, whereas females could benefit more by enhancing their expressive (traditionally feminine) behaviors. Moreover, therapists are more likely to see women's emotional problems as internally caused (intrapsychic) than they are to regard men's emotional problems in this way, and they may fail to perceive the external stresses of women's lives (Russo & Tartaro, 2008; Worell, 2001).

Some therapists expect a more positive outcome with male clients than with female clients. These therapists may have even lower expectations of outcomes for ethnic minority women, sexual minority women, and women with disabilities (American Psychological Association, 2007). In order to increase the likelihood of positive outcomes when working with women clients, therapists need to understand the challenges, strengths, intersecting identities, and social contexts of these clients (Nutt & Brooks, 2008).

Therapy Issues for Women of Color, Poor Women, and Immigrant Women

Women of color, poor women, and immigrant women face a number of external stresses that can cause or intensify mental health problems: racism, poverty, culturally approved subordinate status, and living in contexts of violence and chronic strain (American Psychological Association, 2016; Mizock & Kaschak, 2015; Schmitt et al., 2014). Unfortunately, these women confront several obstacles that limit their access to psychological help. For one thing, cultural challenges pressure many women of color to be "strong," or to "save face," and not discuss problems outside the family (Chaney et al., 2012: Comas-Diaz, 2013a; Kim et al., 2017). Moreover, financial constraints, lack of insurance, and time and transportation problems prevent many poor and ethnic minority women from seeking help (Sue & Sue, 2015; Villatoro et al., 2014). In addition, people of color, immigrant women, and those from low-income backgrounds are underrepresented in the mental health professions so that members of these groups often have a therapist who does not know their culture or speak their language (Blume, 2016; Comas-Diaz, 2013b; Espin & Dottolo, 2015; Robinson-Wood, 2017). Nonminority providers may apply racial stereotypes to their minority patients instead of seeing them as individuals. Moreover, they can be insensitive to the social and economic conditions in which women of color, poor women, and immigrant women live (Goodman et al., 2013; Lee, 2013; Ladany & Krikorian, 2013). One reason for this is that clinical psychology literature does not contain adequate coverage of ethnically diverse populations (Clay, 2015; Espin & Dottolo, 2015; Trotman & Tirrell, 2015). Information about the mental health problems of Native Americans is especially limited, reflecting their social marginalization (Comas-Diaz, 2013a).

Types of Therapy

TRADITIONAL THERAPIES.   Traditional psychotherapies are based on a medical model in which emotional pain is viewed as a "disease," which must be "treated" by an expert. This leads to a therapeutic relationship marked by an imbalance of power between therapist (often male) and patient (often female). In addition, the individual's emotional problems are seen as having internal, not external, causes. The goal of therapy is to promote the person's adjustment to existing social conditions (Brown, 2010).

FEMINIST THERAPIES.   **Feminist therapy**, on the other hand, *emphasizes the role of social, political, and economic stresses facing women as a major source of their psychological problems* (L. Brown, 2016; Robinson-Wood, 2017). Feminist therapists focus on issues of oppression, such as sexism, racism, classism, ableism, and heterosexism. A key goal of feminist therapy is to empower clients in all spheres of life: physical, psychological, social, and spiritual (L. Brown, 2016). Clients are encouraged to become psychologically and economically independent and to try to change a sexist society rather than adjust to it. Another principle of feminist therapy is that therapists should not be more powerful than their clients but should build egalitarian, respectful, and collaborative relationships with them (L. Brown, 2016; Friedlander et al., 2017; Roffman, 2008). One vehicle for doing so is **counselor self-disclosure**, *the imparting of personal information about the life experiences of the therapist to the client* (L. Brown, 2016; Moore, 2010). In addition, feminist therapy stresses awareness of possible identity differences between client and therapist in terms of culture, class, sexual orientation, religion, and so on (Ballou et al., 2017; Friedlander et al., 2017). Feminist therapy is a philosophy underlying therapy rather than a specific therapeutic technique, and it can be integrated with other treatment approaches (Enns, 2017).

Summary

FACTORS PROMOTING MENTAL HEALTH

- Social support enhances mental health.
- Females seek and use social support more than males do.
- In reaction to stress, women more often show the "tend and befriend" response, whereas men are more likely to exhibit "fight or flight" behavior.
- Optimism is linked to positive mental and physical health.

MENTAL HEALTH IN CHILDHOOD AND ADOLESCENCE

- Stress levels increase for girls and boys during adolescence. Much of girls' stress stems from relationship problems and is linked to higher rates of depression.
- Externalizing problems in girls are less common than internalizing problems, but are more likely to be associated with adult maladjustment.

EATING DISORDERS

- Anorexia nervosa is marked by severe weight loss and fear of being overweight.
- Bulimia nervosa is characterized by cycles of binging and purging.
- Biological, psychological, and cultural factors are involved in these disorders, which occur most often in adolescent girls.

SUBSTANCE USE AND ABUSE

- Women are less likely to be heavy drinkers than men, but binge drinking is on the increase in college women.
- Women's alcoholism starts later than men's, progresses more quickly, and is diagnosed at a more advanced stage.
- Drinking in pregnancy can cause FASD.
- Females are less likely than males to use most illegal drugs.

ANXIETY DISORDERS AND DEPRESSION

- Anxiety disorders are more common in women than men. These include panic disorders and specific phobias.
- Depression is twice as common in women as in men. Possible explanations for this difference include biological factors, stressful life events, learned helplessness, self-silencing, and women's ruminative style in responding to depression.

MENTAL HEALTH OF SEXUAL MINORITY WOMEN

- Homophobia can cause considerable stress in the lives of lesbians, gays, bisexuals, and transgender individuals, resulting in a variety of psychological problems.

- Effective coping mechanisms include accepting one's sexual orientation, having social support and a satisfying relationship, and participating in the LGBT community.

MENTAL HEALTH OF OLDER WOMEN

- The psychological health of women improves as they get older.
- Older women who cope successfully with aging tend to integrate agency and communion.
- Some older women continue their careers; others become volunteers or advocates for social causes.

DIAGNOSIS AND TREATMENT OF PSYCHOLOGICAL DISORDERS

- Gender bias exists in diagnosis and treatment of psychological disorders.
- Women of color face external stresses, which can intensify mental health problems and prevent them from seeking help.
- Traditional psychotherapies are marked by a power imbalance between therapist and client, and focus on internal causes of emotional problems.
- Feminist therapy is nonsexist, encourages equal power between therapist and client, and focuses on societal causes of women's problems.

Key Terms

What Do You Think?

1. If you become aware that a friend of yours has an eating disorder, what steps could you take to try to help?
2. Why do you think that society is less tolerant of drinking in women than in men?
3. In your opinion, why are women more likely than men to suffer from anxiety disorders and depression?
4. Why do you think that U.S. males are more likely to commit suicide than females, whereas females are more likely to attempt it?
5. How might stereotypes about women and men affect the way psychotherapists work with female and male clients?

If You Want to Learn More

Barnes, D.L. (Ed.). (2014). *Women's reproductive mental health across the lifespan.* New York: Springer.

Beauchamp, T.P. & Hinshaw, S.P. (2013). *Child and adolescent psychopathology.* Hoboken, NJ: Wiley.

Choate, L.H. (2013). *Eating disorders and obesity: A counselor's guide to prevention and treatment.* Alexandria, VA: American Counseling Association.

Comas-Diaz, L. & Greene, B. (Eds.). (2013). *Psychological health of women: Intersections, challenges, and opportunities.* Santa Barbara, CA: ABC-CLIO.

Enns, C.Z. & Williams, E.N. (Eds.). (2013). *The Oxford handbook of feminist multicultural counseling psychology.* New York: Oxford University Press.

Enns, C.Z., Rice, J.K., & Nutt, R.L. (2015). *Psychological practice with women: Guidelines, diversity, and empowerment.* Washington, D.C.: American Psychological Association.

Glaser, G. (2014). *Her best kept secret: Why women drink and how they can regain control.* New York: Simon & Schuster.

Kopala, M. & Keital, M. (2017). *Handbook of counseling women* (2nd ed.). Thousand Oaks, CA: Sage.

Orel, N.A. & Fruehauf, C.A. (Eds.). (2014). *The lives of LGBT older adults: Understanding challenges and resilience.* Washington, D.C.: American Psychological Association.

Reel, J.J. (2013). *Eating disorders: An encyclopedia of causes, treatments, and prevention.* Santa Barbara, CA: ABC-CLIO.

Robinson-Wood, T. (2017). *The convergence of race, ethnicity, and gender: Multiple identities in counseling.* Thousand Oaks, CA: Sage.

Singh, A.E. & Dickey, L.M. (Eds.). (2017). *Affirmative counseling and psychological practice with transgender and gender nonconforming clients.* Washington, D.C.: American Psychological Association.

Websites

Mental Health
Mental Health Net: Self-Help Resources Index
http://www.mentalhelp.net/articles/psychological-self-tools-online-self-help-book/
National Mental Health Association
http://www.nmha.org
Suicide Prevention Action Network
http://www.spanusa.org

Eating Disorders
http://www.mirror-mirror.org/

National Eating Disorders Association (NEDA)
http://nationaleatingdisorders.org/
http://www.anad.org

Alcohol and Substance Abuse
National Institute on Drug Abuse
http://www.nida.nih.gov

Vital Older Women
Older Women's League (OWL)
http://www.owl-national.org/
Center for Healthy Aging
http://www.ncoa.org/center-for-healthy-aging

Violence Against Girls and Women

Ana Redmond, an expert coder, began a technology career for an exciting challenge and a chance to change the world. But over the years, she encountered a work environment that was hostile and unwelcoming to women. In her words, "It was like they were trying to push me out at every stage . . . They just kept asking me to prove myself over and over again." She was often passed up for no apparent reason, and her projects often were taken away or given to others. In 2011, after 15 years, she left the field. (Lien, 2015).

I suffered at home for over 20 years watching my father try to kill my mother. It was unbelievably frightening to me, and I feel it's taken a terrible toll on me, which is still going on. I'm talking about depression, relationship problems, you name it, my life feels like a mess. Living in that situation was horrific. I used to see the carving knife on the landing, and my father would chase my mother upstairs with it. I would hide her in my bedroom and put the chest of drawers against the door, and I'd tell her to get into my bed. Then I'd go out of my bedroom to take the knife off him. That happened dozens and dozens of times in my life. It's beyond words to describe this situation. My father never actually killed my mother, but the constant threat was almost as bad because I never knew what he'd do. I felt I could never go out—that I had to stay at home with my mother because who knew what would happen if I went out and left her alone. To put this on a child destroys you. (Susan, mid-30s, in Russell, 2001, p. 132)

Harassment and violence are serious public health problems that transcend demographic, social, and national boundaries. In this chapter, we focus on harassment and violence experienced by girls and women in personal relationships, at school, and on the job. We start by exploring sexual harassment at school and in the workplace and then focus on stalking. We then turn to a bleak aspect of childhood for all too many girls: sexual abuse and others forms of violence and neglect. Next, we look at the disturbing violent side of some relationships, with an examination of dating violence, rape (including acquaintance rape), and intimate partner violence. We conclude with an examination of elder abuse.

SEXUAL HARASSMENT AT SCHOOL

Sexual harassment in an educational setting includes *unwelcome verbal or physical behavior of a sexual nature when (a) submission to or rejection of the behavior forms the basis for decisions about the student (e.g., admission, grades); or (b) the behavior creates an intimidating, hostile, or offensive study environment.* Sexual harassment at school unfortunately is widespread in the United States and elsewhere (Leaper & Brown, 2014; National Center for Education Statistics, 2016). In most cases, boys harass girls, rather than the other way around. Ethnic minority girls, girls with advanced pubertal status, students with disabilities, and lesbian, gay, bisexual, and transgender students are more likely to be sexually harassed than their peers (Centers for Disease Control and Prevention, 2016d; Paludi, 2015; Petersen & Hyde, 2013; Poteat et al., 2014; Van De Griend & Messias, 2014). Sexual harassment by peers is much more common than sexual harassment committed by teachers, but students are more distressed when the harasser is a teacher (Rosenthal et al., 2016; Timmerman, 2003). Sadly, the Internet has become a venue for sexually harassing others. (See In the News 14.1.)

IN THE NEWS 14.1
Sexual Harassment in the Digital Age: Cyberbullying and Gendertrolling

The Internet has given rise to a new form of sexual harassment called cyberbullying or cyber-harassment, which includes name-calling, shaming, rumors, and unwelcome comments, jokes, or pictures. It can be particularly cruel, since the harassment may be anonymous, can quickly reach wide audiences, and can occur at any time (Rice et al., 2015). Cyberbullying is more likely than other forms of bullying to be linked to outcomes such as depression, suicidal thoughts, and suicide (Rice et al., 2015; Sales, 2016). An estimated 10 to 40 percent of individuals report being cyberbullied, with females and sexual minorities more likely to be victims (Kowalski et al., 2014; Rice et al., 2015). In the AAUW (2011) survey described in this chapter, 36 percent of girls and 24 percent of boys reported being harassed online. Many of them had also been harassed in person. These "mixed" incidents had the greatest emotional impact (Mitchell et al., 2016). Females are more likely than males to perpetrate cyber-harassment in early-to-mid-adolescence, while males are more likely to do so in late adolescence (Barlett & Coyne, 2014). Gendertrolling is a particularly misogynistic (i.e. woman-hating) form of cyber-harassment (see In the News 5.1). It is aggressive, threatening, and violent, mostly perpetrated by men (sometimes in a coordinated attack by many people), that aims to publicly shame women over a long period of time (Fichman & Sanfilippo, 2016; Mantilla, 2015). Can you think of ways to combat cyber-harassment?

Elementary and Secondary School

Reports of student sexual harassment are on the rise among middle and high school students. In one survey (AAUW, 2011), about half of the girls said they had received sexual comments or

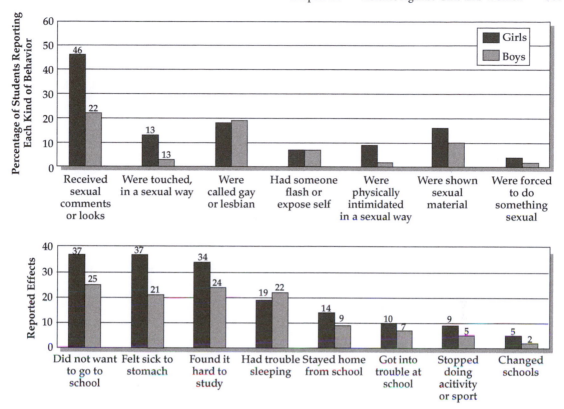

FIGURE 14.1 Percentage of Middle and High School Students Who Reported Experiencing Unwelcomed Sexual Behavior at School and Its Effects.
Source: American Association of University Women (AAUW, 2011).

looks either in person or electronically (see Figure 14.1). Over 1 in 10 reported being touched, grabbed, or pinched in a sexual way. Girls, more than boys, said they were upset after being harassed. More than one-third of the girls reported that the unwanted activity made them not want to go to school. Girls who are harassed are also more likely to experience academic difficulties, physical symptoms (e.g., headache, digestive upset), interpersonal relationship problems, and negative psychological outcomes such as disordered eating, and feeling self-conscious, embarrassed, anxious, afraid, less confident, and unpopular (Leaper & Brown, 2014; Petersen & Hyde, 2014; Poteat et al., 2014). Sadly, teachers often do not intervene, even when they are aware of serious incidents of sexual harassment. Instead of considering sexual harassment to be serious misconduct, school authorities too often treat it as harmless instances of "boys will be boys" (Troop-Gordon, 2015).

Just as disturbing is the finding that harassment has damaging effects even on those who do not directly experience it, by creating a school climate that appears to tolerate harassment. Those girls and boys who perceived that sexual harassment was accepted at school also felt unsafe at school, tended to withdraw from school, and had lower self-esteem (Paludi, 2015). Later in the chapter, we shall examine a closely related phenomenon, organizational tolerance of harassment, which has a similar chilling effect on women in the workplace.

The College Campus

Although sexual harassment in an educational setting was legally defined earlier in the chapter, there are wide variations in people's conceptions of harassing behaviors. Before reading this section,

GET INVOLVED 14.1
What Constitutes Sexual Harassment on Campus?

Check each of the following items that you believe is a form of sexual harassment if experienced by a student. Then ask one female student and one male student to do the same.

_____ comments on personal appearance by a student

_____ comments on personal appearance by a professor

_____ unwanted letters or phone calls of a sexual nature from a student

_____ unwanted letters or phone calls of a sexual nature from a faculty member

_____ unwanted sexually suggestive looks or gestures from a student

_____ unwanted sexually suggestive looks or gestures from a faculty member

_____ offensive sexually suggestive stories or jokes told by a student

_____ offensive sexually suggestive stories or jokes told by a faculty member

_____ inappropriate staring by a student that causes discomfort

_____ inappropriate staring by a faculty member that causes discomfort

_____ unwelcome seductive remarks or questions by a student

_____ unwelcome seductive remarks or questions by a faculty member

_____ unwanted pressure for dates by a student

_____ unwanted pressure for dates by a faculty member

_____ unwanted leaning, touching, or pinching by a student

_____ unwanted leaning, touching, or pinching by a faculty member

_____ unwanted pressure for sexual favors by a student

_____ unwanted pressure for sexual favors by a faculty member

_____ nonforced sexual relationship between a faculty member and a student

_____ nonforced sexual relationship between two students

_____ forced sexual intercourse by a student

_____ forced sexual intercourse by a faculty member

WHAT DOES IT MEAN?

Separately sum the behaviors you classified as sexual harassment if performed by a student and those seen as sexual harassment if performed by a faculty member. Do the same for each of your respondents.

1. Compare the number of behaviors seen as harassment if performed by a student to those if performed by a faculty member. Is there a difference in your answers or in those of your respondents? Explain any differences

you found. Are these differences consistent with the evidence presented in the text?

2. Is there any difference in the number of behaviors seen as harassment by your female and male respondents? If yes, does it match the difference presented in the text? What might explain this?

_____

Source: Based on Shepela and Levesque (1998).

perform the exercise in Get Involved 14.1 to examine the behaviors and situations that you and your acquaintances classify as sexual harassment.

Research shows that there are gender differences in the tendency to classify behaviors such as those listed in Get Involved 14.1 as sexual harassment. Women perceive more situations as harassing than men do (Lundy-Wagner & Winkle-Wagner, 2013), and they are harsher in their judgments of the harasser (Sigal et al., 2005). Whether an individual perceives a behavior as harassment also depends, in part, on the role relationship between the harasser and the target. When students are targets, behaviors are more likely to be seen as harassment if they are performed by a professor than by another student (e.g., Bursik, 1992). Did you find these two patterns when you performed the Get Involved activity?

The questions in Get Involved 14.1 raise two controversial issues related to power. One is whether sexual harassment, by definition, is restricted to behaviors performed by a person with authority (e.g., a professor) over a target (e.g., a student). The other is whether a sexual relationship between individuals who differ in power, as in a professor–student relationship, constitutes sexual harassment even if the student gives consent. In the first issue, the crucial criteria are (1) the target perceives the behavior as unwelcome, and (2) the unwanted behavior creates a hostile or an offensive atmosphere for the target. If these conditions are met, it is not necessary that the perpetrator have power over the target (DeSouza & Chien, 2010).

There is greater controversy surrounding the second issue. Does a romantic relationship between a professor and student constitute sexual harassment, regardless of whether it is consensual? One view is that as long as the student is an adult and expresses willingness to enter into a sexual relationship with a professor, that relationship is acceptable (Kipnis, 2015). Another perspective is that whenever a formal power differential between two people is present, a sexual relationship involves some degree of coercion because the target is not really in a position to freely consent or refuse. According to this viewpoint, *any* sexual behavior directed at a student by a professor is harassment (DeSouza & Chien, 2010). Some schools have gone so far as to forbid any consensual sexual relationship between students and faculty, whereas others merely suggest that such relationships are a bad idea (Chappell, 2015). What is the policy at your school?

INCIDENCE OF SEXUAL HARASSMENT.   The frequency of sexual harassment on college campuses is hard to assess for a number of reasons. Not only do few students submit formal complaints of harassment, but surveys of harassment experiences also show that the incidence varies from campus to campus. Also, the frequency of sexual harassment varies according to the specific type of unwanted conduct and the nature of the power relationship between the harasser and the target (Paludi, 2016). Despite these problems, however, one can draw certain conclusions from surveys. First, women are more likely than men to be sexually harassed. Second, women are more likely to experience subtle forms of harassment, such as unwanted sexually suggestive jokes or body language, than they are to encounter more blatant forms, such as unwanted sexual advances, although the latter do occur (Rosenthal et al., 2016). Third, students are more likely to experience unwanted sexual behaviors by other students than by faculty or staff members (Lundy-Wagner & Winkle-Wagner, 2013). Fourth, the incidence of sexual harassment is higher for certain groups of women students: those who are poor, are socially isolated, have disabilities, are ethnic or sexual minorities, or are majors in male-dominated fields such as engineering (Kosciw et al., 2014). Fifth, sexually harassing events are more distressing for women than for men (Leaper & Bigler, 2013). Sixth, women who identify as feminists are more likely to confront their harassers (Ayres et al., 2009).

RESPONSES TO SEXUAL HARASSMENT.   What do college students do when they experience sexual harassment? The most common response is to ignore the behavior (Swim et al., 2010a). Avoidance of the harasser and talking to others about the harassment are other common reactions. Few file a formal complaint (Hill & Silva, 2005). Unfortunately, this lack of formal response hinders attempts to reduce the frequency of harassment. See What You Can Do 14.1 for actions you can take to reduce sexual harassment on campus.

SEXUAL HARASSMENT IN THE WORKPLACE

Analogous to the definition of sexual harassment in academic settings, the legal definition of **sexual harassment in the workplace** is *unwelcome verbal or physical behavior when (a) submission to or rejection of the behavior forms the basis for work-related decisions* (**quid pro quo harassment**)*, or (b) the behavior creates an intimidating, hostile, or offensive work environment* (**hostile environment**) (Maass et al., 2013; Paludi, 2015). Examples of quid pro quo harassment would be the offer of a promotion in exchange for sex and the threat of a layoff if sex were refused. The hostile environment form of harassment is illustrated by the experience of Ana Redmond, the computer coder described in the vignette at the beginning of the chapter. In Louise Fitzgerald's widely used three-part model of sexual harassment, *quid pro quo* harassment is labeled **sexual coercion** (Fitzgerald et al., 2001). She divides the *hostile environment* category into two types of behavior: **Gender harassment** is insulting, hostile, and degrading behavior, but not for the purpose of sexual activity (i.e., "the put down"); **unwanted sexual attention** is unwelcome and offensive behavior of a sexual nature (i.e., "the come on") (Buchanan & Harrell, 2014).

WHAT YOU CAN DO 14.1
Reducing Sexual Harassment on Campus

There are several actions students can take to ensure that a campus environment is free of sexual harassment. Here is a sampling of what you can do:

1. Find out whether your campus has policies and procedures for dealing with sexual harassment.
2. Establish a Sexual Harassment Awareness Week during which campuswide activities related to sexual harassment take place.

These events can include activities such as plays, movies, and group discussions about sexual harassment.

3. Establish a peer educators program. Peer educators can provide both information to the campus community at large and support to those who have been harassed.

_____

Source: Based on Paludi (2008a).

Incidence

How common is sexual harassment in the workplace? Studies conducted around the world have concluded that a large proportion of women experience some form of sexual harassment at work (Cunningham et al., 2014; Sojo et al., 2016; Spade & Valentine, 2016). Most commonly, harassment takes the form of sexual remarks and jokes (Holland & Cortina, 2016). Although sexual coercion is relatively rare, it does occur. Frequently, the victims are relatively uneducated, and desperately in need of work. Several particularly disturbing cases have involved immigrant farm workers in the United States who were forced to have sex with their supervisors or risked being fired, being deported, being given more physically demanding work, or receiving a cut in pay (Deitch, 2015; Institute for Women's Policy Research, 2015; Padilla & Bacon, 2016).

Although any woman in any work situation might experience harassment, there are certain factors associated with the greater likelihood of its occurrence. We now turn to an examination of these.

OCCUPATIONAL CHARACTERISTICS RELATED TO SEXUAL HARASSMENT.   Sexual harassment is more common in male-dominated blue-collar occupations, such as auto work, manufacturing, firefighting, law enforcement, coal mining, construction, trades, and transit, than in other male-dominated, female-dominated, or gender-balanced jobs (Ainsworth et al., 2014; Brunner & Dever, 2014; Denissen & Saguy, 2014; Kelly et al., 2015).

Women in these jobs have been subjected to isolation, work sabotage, severe verbal abuse, physical violence, and intentional exposure to hazardous work conditions (Kelly et al., 2015; Nixon, 2014). For example, women officers in the New Jersey State Police Department in the early 2000s reported deer testicles put in one officer's locker, nails in another's tires, and an obscene valentine from yet another's commanding officer (Schuppe, 2007). Similarly, women in the building trades have reported sledgehammers dropped on them, being thrown off scaffolding, and having obscenities written on their equipment (Eisenberg, 2010).

Another historically male-dominated field associated with a high incidence of sexual harassment and sexual abuse is the military (Kintzle et al., 2015; Rock et al., 2014; Skaune, 2016). In one glaring recent example, 62 women recruits at Lackland Air Force Base were sexually assaulted by 32 training instructors over a 4-year period. Research shows that, overall, about one in three women among all branches of the U.S military has been sexually assaulted, twice as high as the civilian rate ("Sexual Assaults," 2013). Similarly, more than one in four women in the Canadian military have been sexually assaulted (Austen, 2016). In 2015 alone, over 6,000 U.S. servicewomen reported being sexually assaulted by fellow troops. These figures are undoubtedly low, given that an estimated 70–75 percent of military rapes go unreported in the U.S. and Canada (Austen, 2016; Department of Defense, 2015). Many women do not report the incidents because they fear ostracism, humiliation, and reprisals (Risen, 2013). Sadly, these concerns are well founded, as there is a high incidence of retribution against those who report sex crimes in the military (Hallett, 2015).

Sexual harassment is not confined to male-dominated occupations, however. As one example: tipped restaurant workers, many of them women, are vulnerable to harassing behaviors from customers, co-workers, and managers, which they must tolerate in order to make a living (Jayaraman, 2015).

WHO IS HARASSED?   Sexual harassment tends to target certain groups more than others. Women are far more likely than men to be targets and are more likely to report finding these experiences distressing (Sears et al., 2011). Women are more apt to feel frightened and degraded, whereas men more often feel flattered by these behaviors (Holland & Cortina, 2016). Younger or unmarried women are more likely than older or married females to be harassed (Clancy et al., 2014; Holland & Cortina, 2016; Maass et al., 2013), possibly because they are seen as more powerless and vulnerable than their older or married counterparts. Sexual minority women are another group at higher risk (Martin-Storey, 2015; Woodruffe-Burton, 2016). If their sexual identity is not known, they are seen as single women and their risk goes up for that reason. Alternatively, if they are open about their identity, anti-gay prejudice can increase the likelihood that they will be harassed.

In addition, *women of color are more likely to experience sexual harassment than are White women*, a phenomenon called **racialized sexual harassment**. Such harassment is more likely to occur in blue-collar and other male-dominated settings (Corbett & Hill, 2015). When Janice Yoder and Patricia Aniakudo interviewed Black female firefighters, they found that nearly all the women received unwanted sexual behaviors including teasing and jokes, suggestive looks, touching, and pressure for dates. The women also reported isolation, lack of support, hostility, and hypercritical training, as well as racism. Consider one woman's experience: "I'd walk in and everything would get quiet. I'd go to eat; everybody leaves the room . . . I've been on the job now 7 years, and there're still guys that don't talk to me" (Yoder & Aniakudo, 1999, p. 141). Another woman noted that in her first day on the job, her White male captain told her: "I don't like you. Number one, cuz you're Black. And number two, cuz you're a woman" (Yoder & Aniakudo, 1999, p. 140). Susan Martin (2010) found similar instances of isolation and harassment of Black female police officers: "I was at the precinct 10 days before I knew I had a partner 'cause . . . [the men] called in sick" (p. 266); "There was a cutout arrow taped to the window [of my patrol car]. The word 'N____' was written on the arrow pointing to my seat" (p. 268).

CHARACTERISTICS OF OFFENDERS.   The picture that emerges from research on harassers is that the way these men construct gender might serve as a foundation for their harassing behaviors. Specifically, harassers tend to have negative attitudes toward women, hold traditional gender attitudes, perceive sexual relationships as manipulative and exploitative, and have high levels of hostile sexism (Combs & Milosevic, 2016; Holland & Cortina, 2016; Maass et al., 2013). That is, the most likely offenders appear to be traditional men who do not view women as equals.

Consequences

Across ethnic groups, and around the world, sexual harassment is associated with psychological and physical consequences for women, including decreased self-esteem, lowered life satisfaction, anger, fear, depression, anxiety, post-traumatic stress disorder, interpersonal difficulties, headaches, gastrointestinal problems, sleep disturbances, high blood pressure, disordered eating, substance abuse, and sexual problems. Additionally, women can experience undesirable job-related outcomes, including reduced job satisfaction, decreased morale, increased absenteeism, and a decline in organizational commitment (Holland & Cortina, 2016; Maass et al., 2013; Nielsen et al., 2015; Robinson et al., 2014; Sojo et al., 2016; Van De Griend & Messias, 2014). Even if a woman has not experienced sexual harassment herself, just working in an organizational environment that is hostile toward women or overhearing a sexist or uncivil remark made to someone else can have negative effects on her job satisfaction and sense of well-being (Feldblum & Lipnic, 2016). As you might expect, the more frequent and ongoing the sexual harassment, the more distressing it is.

In addition, women who experience unwelcome sexual behaviors have negative psychological and physical reactions, whether or not they label their experience as harassment. Women might not realize certain behaviors fit the definition of *harassment* or, alternatively, they might want to avoid the label of victim. Whatever the case, it is the experiencing of these behaviors, and not the labeling of them as harassment, that leads to unpleasant psychological and physical outcomes (Holland & Cortina, 2016).

Explanations

Why does sexual harassment in the workplace occur? According to **sex-role spillover theory** (Burn, 2011), *in occupations with few women, men's traditional gender roles spill over into the workplace and influence their interactions with female workers.* The high incidence of sexual harassment among blue-collar workers supports this theory and points to the importance of an employment context in which male-related physical attributes are very prominent (Ainsworth et al., 2014; Denissen & Saguy, 2014). In this type of situation, harassment reflects a restrictive construction of gender that results in viewing women not as competent workers but as targets of male–female interactions.

The **power theory** of sexual harassment states that *sexual harassment is an abuse of power to gain sexual favors or to reinforce men's sense of power and privilege in the workplace.* Men generally have more power in the workplace, and some men abuse this power for sexual ends (McLaughlin et al., 2012). Consistent with this theory, power increases the erroneous perception that one's subordinates have a sexual interest in the powerful person (Kunstman & Maner, 2011). The male-dominated blue-collar occupations and the military, where sexual harassment is most frequent, provide a good example of power theory. Men in these occupations hold most of the power for several reasons. First, men historically view the blue-collar and military workplaces as their own territory. Second, they are in the majority. Third, they view the few women who enter these occupations as being on probation. Fourth, the generally male supervisors support male workers' power. Fifth, men's overall greater physical strength, which symbolizes their masculinity, is an important attribute for many of these jobs. Sixth, men have higher status in society in general (Ainsworth et al., 2014; Bergmann, 2011; Crawley, 2011).

These factors not only maintain a power imbalance in which men are more likely to harass, but also contribute to an **organizational tolerance** in which *the negative effects of sexual harassment tend to be minimized and complaints about harassment are not taken seriously* (Sojo et al., 2016).

Women's Responses

> *After we, a mostly female staff, facilitated the removal of our harassing principal, we had a long group lunch together. We all shared our personal experiences with that man. The shocking thing was that most of the staff had been targeted at one time or another over an 18-year period, and that each of us thought we were the only one and that it was our fault.*
>
> (Holly, a 50-year-old school teacher)

How do women respond to sexual harassment? Louise Fitzgerald and her colleagues (2001) classify responses to sexual harassment as either internally focused or externally focused. **Internally focused responses** are *responses that attempt to manage the emotions and cognitions associated with the incident(s).* Examples include ignoring the situation, minimizing the event, or blaming oneself. **Externally focused responses**, on the other hand, are *responses that attempt to solve the problem.* Examples are avoiding the harasser, asking him to stop, or seeking organizational assistance. Filing a complaint or lawsuit are rare responses (Feldblum & Lipnic, 2016).

Most women who are sexually harassed do not confront the perpetrator or report the event, as in Holly's example at the beginning of this section. Why is this? Major barriers to reporting include guilt, shame, embarrassment, desire to maintain harmony in the workplace, and fear of retaliation from the perpetrator (Holland & Cortina, 2016; Van De Griend & Messias, 2014). These fears are often justified. Women who report their harassment often experience negative outcomes, such as lowered job evaluations, humiliation, and both physical and psychological health problems (Van De Griend & Messias, 2014; Sojo et al., 2016).

Latina women are more likely than White women to avoid or not report the harasser. This may stem from several elements in Hispanic culture, including respect for individuals of higher status, emphasis on harmonious in-group relations, and a greater adherence to traditional gender roles, which fosters more tolerance of sexual harassment and discourages women from discussing sexual topics (Holland & Cortina, 2016).

STALKING

Like sexual harassment, stalking is a crime of power and control.

What Is Stalking?

Stalking can be described as *unwanted and repeated actions toward an individual that induce fear or concern for safety* (Owens, 2016). Stalking behaviors include attempts to contact the individual and/or place the person under surveillance (e.g., following the person, waiting outside or driving by the person's home or workplace). The most common forms of stalking are unwanted phone calls, letters, and electronic messages (Fisher et al., 2014).

Perpetrators, Victims, and Effects

The overwhelming majority of stalkers are male, and the majority of their victims are female, including up to 15 percent of U.S. women each year (Breiding et al., 2014). Nearly two-thirds report being stalked by current or former partners (Breiding et al., 2014; Edwards & Gidycz, 2014; National Center for Victims of Crime, 2015). The unpredictable nature of stalking, combined with fear of violence, can produce harmful psychological effects such as anxiety, depression, fear, extreme stress, and symptoms of post-traumatic stress disorder (PTSD), as well as physical consequences such as nausea, headaches, and sleep disruption (Diette et al., 2014; Kuehner et al., 2012). Some victims feel compelled to change jobs or schools, move to a new residence, or seek counseling. One in four victims considers suicide (Martin, 2008a). As is true for most forms of harassment and violence, many stalking victims do not report their experiences to the police (Institute for Women's Policy Research, 2015).

VIOLENCE AGAINST GIRLS

> *Violence against women is a problem that encompasses physical and sexual abuse perpetrated against a woman or female child by persons known or unknown to her . . . At least one woman in three globally is beaten, coerced into sex, or otherwise abused in her lifetime. . . . Because women represent 85% of the victims of incidents of nonfatal intimate assaults that occur each year in the U.S. . . . violence is a women's health concern, a human rights issue, and a major public health problem.*

> (Herrera et al., 2006, p. 458)

Tragically, both girls and women are victims of violence around the globe and often face multiple types of abuse (Ellis & Thiara, 2014; Kuklanz & McIntosh, 2015; UN Women, 2014; World Health Organization, 2014a). In this section, we focus on two forms of violence that are especially likely to be perpetrated against girls: child sexual abuse, and infanticide or neglect.

Child Sexual Abuse

Sexual abuse of children is viewed by many as among the most heinous of crimes (Rathus et al., 2013). Although definitions vary, a typical definition of **child sexual abuse** *includes both contact and* *noncontact sexual experiences in which the victim is below the age of consent and the abuser is significantly older or in a position of power over the child* (Whealin & Barnett, 2015). Sexually suggestive language or exhibitionism are examples of noncontact experience, whereas contact abuse may range from kissing, fondling, and sexual touching to oral sex and vaginal or anal intercourse. The most recent development in child sexual abuse is exploitation through the Internet. Children may be propositioned online for sexual activity, may be exposed to various forms of sexually explicit material, or may experience online harassment (Kloess et al., 2014).

Incest, a form of child abuse, may be defined narrowly as *sexual contact between a child and a close relative or other family member.* Incest may be particularly devastating emotionally to a child. It involves a loss of trust in and deep sense of betrayal by the abuser and perhaps other family members—especially the mother—whom the child may perceive as failing to provide protection (Rathus et al., 2013). Victims often blame themselves for allowing the incident to occur.

The most frequently reported and publicized type of incest is between a daughter and her father or stepfather, but surveys indicate that brother–sister incest is at least twice as common (Stroebel et al., 2013). Sibling incest is highly underreported, perhaps because it is sometimes viewed as "sexual curiosity" rather than as sexual abuse (Monahan, 2010; Thompson, 2009).

INCIDENCE.   The incidence of child sexual abuse is difficult to pinpoint precisely. In the United States, approximately 14 percent of girls and 6 percent of boys have experienced *substantiated* sexual abuse (Finkelhor et al., 2015). Around the world, 18–20 percent of girls and 8–10 percent of boys are sexually abused (Collin-Vézina et al., 2013). Because many cases of abuse are never reported, these figures are unfortunately quite conservative (Finkelhor et al., 2013). Asian American, Black, Latina, Native American, and White women report similar rates of child sexual abuse (Elliott & Urquiza, 2006; White & Frabutt, 2006). Children with disabilities are more likely to be sexually and physically abused than able-bodied children (McEachern, 2012; Martinello, 2014). Also, lesbian and bisexual women report a higher incidence of childhood sexual abuse than do heterosexual women (Hequembourg et al., 2013).

For both females and males, most sexual abuse is committed by a family member or a family friend, takes place at home, and occurs more than once. The large majority of cases involve a female victim and a male perpetrator (Singh & Sikes, 2014; Whealin & Barnett, 2015), a blatant illustration of the power differential between females and males. The recent scandal involving the cover-up of child sexual abuse of children by Catholic clergy illustrates how abusers may be shielded by powerful social institutions (Whittier, 2016).

Few children tell anyone about being sexually abused. Girls are more likely than boys to confide in others about the experience, especially a friend or a parent, usually the mother (Bottoms et al., 2016; Hunter, 2009; Reitsema & Grietens, 2016). Why do so few children talk about being sexually abused? For one thing, they are relatively powerless and may fear retaliation from the abuser. Second, the offender is often a trusted and beloved adult whom the youngster may be reluctant to accuse. In addition, the child may feel embarrassed, humiliated, and responsible for encouraging or allowing the abuse to occur (Deblinger et al., 2015; McElvaney et al., 2014; Tener & Murphy, 2014). Claire knows this from personal experience. As she walked home from school one day at age 12, a nicely dressed man who introduced himself as a doctor began chatting with her about the possibility of baby-sitting for his two young sons. He became increasingly graphic about the details of bathing them. When they reached her apartment building, he began fondling her breasts ("My boys don't have anything like this") until she broke away and ran upstairs, flushed with shame and guilt. It was days before she was able to tell her best friend and weeks before she told her mother. Until writing this book, she had told no one else, and even decades after the incident, it was difficult for her to write these words.

CONSEQUENCES.   Sexual abuse can result in devastating consequences for children, not only in the short term, but throughout their adult lives (Collin-Vézina et al., 2013; Maniglio, 2012; Ogle et al.,

2013). Girls are more likely than boys to be sexually abused and they are more adversely affected by it (Australian Institute of Family Studies, 2013; Whealin et al., 2007). Sexually abused children are more likely than other children to be depressed, anxious, or angry; have behavioral, social, sexual, and school problems; show aggression and bullying; feel ashamed; have low self-esteem; and show symptoms of PTSD including fears, nightmares, and sleep disturbances, and "flashbacks" of the traumatic event (Blanchard-Dallaire & Hebert, 2014; Maniglio, 2014).

Adolescents who were sexually abused in childhood show earlier sexual activity, have more sex partners, and are more likely to engage in risky sexual behaviors and to become pregnant (Ryan et al., 2015). They are also more likely than other teenagers to have eating disorders, be depressed, use drugs and alcohol, begin drug use at an early age, and try to injure themselves or commit suicide (Collin-Vézina et al., 2013; Miller et al., 2013).

In adulthood, victims of child sexual abuse continue to be more anxious, depressed, and angry; have relationship and marital problems and impaired self-concept; feel isolated, stigmatized, and distrustful; have sexual and substance-abuse problems; have medical problems such as chronic pain, headaches, and neurological, musculoskeletal, and gastrointestinal problems; and show more PTSD, suicidal, and self-injurious behavior. They are also more likely to have experienced further sexual assault or physical abuse as adults (Beach et al., 2013; Bryan et al., 2016; Bryant-Davis & Bellette, 2013; Cashmore & Shackel, 2013; Fagundes & Way, 2014; Hillberg et al., 2011; Lacelle et al., 2012). The effects of sexual abuse are greatest when the abuser was someone close to the child; the abuse was frequent, severe, and continued over a long period of time; force was used; vaginal, oral, or anal penetration occurred; and little social support was available after disclosure of the abuse.

The good news is that anywhere between 10 and 50 percent of survivors of child sexual abuse show great resilience and retain normal levels of functioning. Protective factors associated with resilience are education, interpersonal and emotional competence, control beliefs, active coping, optimism, social attachment, external attribution of blame, and support from the family and wider social environment (Domhardt et al., 2015).

TREATMENT. Healing from childhood incest and other forms of sexual abuse is a long and arduous process. Group or individual psychotherapy helps adult survivors break their silence, gain perspective and realize they are not alone, and relinquish feelings of responsibility for the abuse. We now examine three of these practices in greater detail: infanticide and neglect of girls, female genital mutilation/cutting, and human trafficking (Harvey & Taylor, 2010). Ultimately, therapy can improve survivors' self-esteem and their ability to have intimate relationships.

Therapy programs for sexually abused children and adolescents are also available (Capella et al., 2016). A comprehensive approach is usually recommended. This may involve play therapy or art therapy for very young children; group therapy for adolescents; individual therapy for the child and each parent; marital therapy for the parents; and family therapy (Rathus et al., 2013). Cognitive behavioral therapy that specifically focuses on the abuse appears more effective than other treatments.

PREVENTION. Increasing numbers of schools are offering sexual-abuse prevention programs (Barron et al., 2015). In these programs, children are taught to distinguish between "good" touching (such as an affectionate pat on the back) and "bad" touching, to say "no," to leave risky situations, and to tell a trusted adult about "secrets" concerning touching (Eckenrode, 2011). Children who participate in comprehensive school-based programs are more likely to use effective strategies such as refusing, running away, or yelling when confronted by a potential abuser, and they are more apt to report incidents to adults (Gidycz et al., 2011; Rathus et al., 2013).

In addition, all 50 states have enacted laws designed to inform communities of the presence of known sex offenders who have been released from prison. These laws are collectively referred to as Megan's Law, after a 7-year-old girl who was raped and murdered in 1994 by a male neighbor who had recently completed a prison sentence for child sexual abuse (Smith & Li-Ching, 2011).

Global Violence Against Girls

Sadly, cultural attitudes that devalue females in many parts of the world lead to practices that have harmful and even deadly effects on female infants and girls.

 INFANTCIDE AND NEGLECT.   Women around the world normally give birth to about 105 boys for every 100 girls. In some parts of rural China, the sex ratio is as high as 140 boys for every 100 girls (Zhou & Wang, 2015). In India, the ratio is 115 boys for every 100 girls, and in rural areas, as in China, the sex ratio is even more skewed. An estimated 100 million girls and women who should be alive in these two countries today are simply "missing" (Ghosh & Sharma, 2012; Kenschaft & Clark, 2016). In societies where the preference for sons is strong, such as China, India, and Pakistan, discrimination and abuse toward female children can take extreme forms such as infanticide, in which the newborn girl is suffocated, drowned, poisoned, or abandoned (Porter, 2014; Sammarco, 2017). In addition, girls in India, Pakistan, and China are often victims of neglect, not fed as well, vaccinated as often, or taken to the doctor as quickly when ill (Jayachandran & Pande, 2014; Priya et al., 2014). Poor families in China and India often view their daughters as a burden, leading them to abandon or sell them into unwanted marriages (Buckley & Barry, 2015; Silvestri & Crowther-Dowey, 2016). With the advent of ultrasound, abortion rates of female fetuses have soared in India, Korea, and rural China, even though elective-sex abortions are now illegal in these countries (Agrawal 2012; Chen et al., 2013).

The extreme preference for sons in these countries stems from the tradition that sons, not daughters, care for aging parents, perform religious rituals, and carry on the family name and occupation (Barot, 2012; Priya et al., 2014). In China, the pressure for sons is intensified by family planning laws that, until recently, limited couples to one child (Zhou & Wang, 2015). In India, a girl is viewed as a burden who requires a costly dowry when she marries, leaving her parents in debt. If her dowry is deemed insufficient, the husband's family may resort to "bride burning," a hideous form of domestic violence in which the woman is doused with kerosene and set on fire (Dyson, 2012; Kristof & WuDunn, 2009).

What are the consequences of having a disproportionate number of males in the population? The surplus of unattached men has already triggered sex-related crimes such as rape, prostitution, abduction of women, and forced marriages in India and China (Shelley, 2010). Other violent crimes and social disorder also have increased (Barot, 2012; Dyson, 2012).

 FEMALE GENITAL MUTILATION/CUTTING.   **Female genital mutilation/cutting** (FGM/C), *the surgical removal of parts of the external female genitalia*, is a major source of reproductive health problems for girls and women in 29 African and Middle Eastern countries, as well as for immigrants of those nations who live in Europe, Australia, and North America (Turkewitz, 2015b; UNICEF, 2016). An estimated 3 million girls and women per year undergo this procedure, usually in early childhood or adolescence. The mildest and most common form of FGM/C involves removing the clitoris, but usually both the clitoris and labia minora are removed. The most extreme form, known as **infibulation** or pharaonic circumcision, consists of *removing the clitoris, labia minora, and the inner two-thirds of the labia majora, which are then sewn together*. A tiny pencil-sized hole is left for the passage of urine and menstrual flow (Burrage 2015; Icheku, 2016). The procedure is usually performed by women, often using crude, unsterilized instruments and without anesthesia. Resulting medical problems range from pain and infection to long-term difficulties with urination, menstruation, sexual intercourse, fertility, and childbirth (Burrage, 2015; Population Reference Bureau, 2014).

Why does this practice persist when it is so obviously harmful to women? Girls in these cultures are considered unmarriageable without undergoing FGM/C (Cloward, 2016). Some people mistakenly believe that the Islamic religion requires it. Others argue that eliminating the source of women's sexual sensations ensures female chastity (Berg & Denison, 2013; Burrage, 2015; Eswaran, 2014; Launius & Hassel, 2015). The practice is banned in the United States, and it is condemned by the United Nations and World Health Organization. Women's organizations in Africa are actively involved in efforts to eradicate FGM/C, which is now outlawed in most African nations although it is still practiced (UNICEF, 2016a).

HUMAN TRAFFICKING.   Nearly 1 million women and girls worldwide are lured into leaving their homeland each year and forced into prostitution or menial work in other nations (Trask, 2014). Many are duped with the promise of good jobs as nannies, models, or exotic dancers in wealthier countries, only to find themselves bound by contracts that immediately place them in enormous debt. Some are forced into unpaid and often inhumane servitude as domestics or child laborers (Dragiewicz, 2015; Gozdziak, 2014; Peters, 2015). But most are forced into sex work in order to pay off their debt (Burn, 2011). Countries that are poor, have high unemployment, and lack women's rights show the most **human trafficking**, defined as *the practice of buying and selling people for profit*. Heavy trafficking occurs in Asia, Africa, central and eastern Europe, Latin America, and the Middle East (Henderson & Jeydel, 2010; Silvestri & Crowther-Dowey, 2015; United Nations, 2015). Sex trafficking is not just a problem of poor countries, however. Primary destinations for trafficked individuals often are relatively prosperous nations, including those in western Europe and North America (Trask, 2014; Weitzer, 2015). The United States, for example, has become a major importer of sex slaves with an estimated 30,000 to 50,000 in captivity at any given time, many from Thailand, Malaysia, Mexico, Russia, and Ukraine (Pearce et al., 2011; Suchland, 2015). Sadly, the typical age of trafficking victims is dropping. It is not uncommon to find pre-teenage girls caught in the tragic net of sexual slavery (Shelley, 2010). One reason is that men who seek out prostitutes are looking for young girls in order to minimize their risk of exposure to HIV (Trask, 2014).

DATING VIOLENCE

A darker and rarely mentioned side of dating relationships is physical aggression toward a dating partner. Dating violence cuts across socioeconomic boundaries and is occurring with alarming frequency.

Incidence

The most rigorous studies show that anywhere from 6 to 30 percent of adolescents report having had at least one experience of physical aggression in a dating relationship, ranging from being hit, shoved, and slapped to being punched, choked, threatened with a weapon, and forced to engage in sexual activity (Coker et al., 2014; Espelage et al., 2014). Sexual minority students are more likely to report dating violence than are heterosexual students (Edwards et al., 2015). Females typically engage in milder forms of aggression, such as psychological abuse and slapping, whereas males engage in more serious acts of violence (Spencer et al., 2015; Vagi et al., 2015; Ybarra et al., 2016). In some studies, females are more likely than males to report being recipients of dating violence, while in others, perhaps surprisingly, males are more likely to report being the victims (e.g., Coker et al., 2014; Espelage et al., 2014).

One possible explanation of these latter findings is that females underreport aggression and/or that males overreport it. Males might overreport their victimization in order to rationalize their own aggression (e.g., "She hits me, so I hit her back"). Another possibility is that females *are* actually more aggressive in their dating relationships, using aggression as self-defense or in retaliation for emotional hurt from their partner (Leisring, 2013).

Who Engages in Dating Violence?

Certain factors increase the likelihood of dating violence. One of the strongest predictors is being the recipient of dating violence (Dardis et al., 2015; Kaukinen, 2014). This finding supports the self-defense explanation. Believing that physical violence is justifiable is another strong predictor. (Interestingly, both genders are more accepting of dating violence in females.) Holding traditional gender-role attitudes is also linked to dating violence for both sexes (Dardis et al., 2013). In addition, dating violence is more prevalent among individuals who were abused as children and who were exposed to family or community violence (Coker et al., 2014; Foshee et al., 2015; Karlsson et al., 2016; Kaukinen, 2014).

Female victims of dating violence are more likely than nonvictims to show risky sexual behavior, depression, low self-esteem, attempted suicide, disordered eating behavior, substance abuse, and binge drinking (Bonomi et al., 2013; Exner-Cortens et al., 2013; Kaukinen, 2014; Vagi et al., 2015). These findings suggest that teen dating violence can lead to a host of negative health consequences. Other warning signals that a young couple's relationship may turn violent include possessiveness, controlling behavior, low relationship satisfaction, unpredictable mood swings, humiliating one's partner, and antisocial behavior (Dardis et al., 2015; Kaukinen, 2014). Sadly, these factors continue to be involved in violent adult relationships, as we shall see later in the chapter. The fact that young women who experience dating violence in high school are at greater risk for sexual victimization during the college years and beyond highlights the need to implement programs early in the teen years to curtail such violence (Bowen & Walker, 2015; Spivak et al., 2014; Temple et al., 2013). High school interventions such as the Safe Dates, Fourth R, and It's Your Game programs increase knowledge of dating violence and decrease tolerance of this behavior, but do not reduce its incidence (De La Rue et al., 2016; Peskin et al., 2014).

RAPE

During spring break of my senior year in high school, I went to San Padre Island with my girlfriends. One night, we went to a bar and somehow got split up. I had no money and didn't know the way back. Some guys said they'd take a cab with me. They got off at their hotel and told me to come to their room while they called my friends. I was scared to go in but I did. One big guy started to force himself on me. I fought him off and he finally stopped. He didn't actually rape me but he violated my body and my trust. He walked me to my hotel acting like nothing had happened. I never told anyone what went on. I felt people would blame me for losing my friends at the bar and being stupid.

(Melinda, a 20-year-old college junior)

The definition of **rape** varies across states. However, the new (2013) federal definition is "The penetration, no matter how slight, of the vagina or anus with any body part or object, or oral penetration by a sex organ of another person, without the consent of the victim" (Chokshi, 2014). Unlike the old definition, the new one includes oral and anal assault and rape of men. The term "sexual assault" is increasingly used to represent this broader spectrum of sexually violating acts, up to and including rape (Gidycz & Johnson, 2017). The incident described earlier by Melinda fits the definition of an attempted rape. First, she clearly communicated her nonconsent and, second, the size differential between her and the perpetrator provided him with the physical force necessary to proceed against her will.

Incidence

In the United States, one out of five women has been a victim of rape or attempted rape. Nearly half of these victims are under 18 and four in five are under 35 (Donde, 2015). Sexual minority women are more likely than heterosexual women to experience sexual violence (Gidycz & Johnson, 2017). Women with disabilities also have an elevated risk of being sexually assaulted (Linton & Rueda, 2015). One of the difficulties in obtaining a "true" rate of rape is that the measurement of sexual victimization is not consistent (Johnson et al., 2015). For example, studies have found that behaviorally specific questions (e.g., "Has anyone ever put his penis in your vagina by using force or threatening to harm you?") yield more rape disclosures than more broadly worded questions (Cook et al., 2011).

Few studies have included large numbers of people of color. Furthermore, methodological problems, such as ethnic differences in willingness to report rape, make ethnic comparisons difficult (Koss et al., 2011). Given these limitations, the available evidence suggests that the rape rate is highest among Native American and multiracial women, followed by Blacks, Whites, Latinas, and Asian Americans, who have the lowest rate (Breiding et al., 2014). In addition, women who live in lower-income households and in rural areas are more likely than other women to be sexually assaulted (Planty et al., 2013; Rennison, 2014).

Acquaintance Rape

Often he would rape me while I was still sleeping in my bedroom. I would wake with him inside me. He wouldn't stop even after I asked him to.

(Peacock, 1998, p. 229)

Many people view "real rape" as being attacked violently by a stranger in a dark alley. But, in fact, about 9 out of 10 cases of rape are **acquaintance rape**, in which *the perpetrator and victim know each other* (Flores, 2015; Moor, 2016). Although marital rape has been illegal in the United States since 1993, an estimated 10–14 percent of women each year are raped by their husbands (Clinton-Sherrod & Walters, 2014). The reported frequency of such sexual aggression is highest in Black couples, followed by Latina/o and White couples (Ramisetty-Mikler et al., 2007). The majority of states treat marital rape more leniently than other sexual assaults. Sadly, the psychological consequences of marital rape are more severe than those resulting from other types of sexual assault (Rhode et al., 2014).

Although a large proportion of women have had incidents consistent with the legal definition, most do not label their experience as rape, especially if they are raped by an acquaintance (Cleere & Lynn, 2013; Kelley & Gidycz, 2015; Moor, 2016). Why is this? One view is that the woman blames herself for the experience, and also feels responsible for protecting her partner. She therefore reframes the situation as being not violent or abusive (Edwards et al., 2014). In addition, many women (as well as men) are not aware of the broad range of behaviors that constitute rape. When the assault involves a boyfriend, if the act involves oral or manual sex, if the woman is verbally rather than physically coerced, or if she is intoxicated she is less likely to label the situation as rape, probably because this scenario deviates from the typical view of "real rape" (Johnstone, 2016; Kelley & Gidycz, 2015; Wilson & Miller, 2016).

Victims of rape are less likely to report incidents to the police than victims of other violent crimes. At least two-thirds of all instances of rape are not reported to formal authorities (Paul et al., 2013; U.S. Department of Justice, 2012). Ethnic minority women have especially low rates of reporting sexual assault (Gidycz & Johnson, 2017). In addition, like Melinda in the vignette opening this section, women are even less likely to report acquaintance rape than rape committed by strangers. Why is this? Few crimes elicit as much skepticism and victim-blaming as do allegations of rape (McHugh et al., 2013). Fear of receiving negative responses from legal authorities and being labeled as promiscuous or a troublemaker may discourage sexual assault victims from reporting their experience. In addition, victims may blame themselves for getting into a dangerous situation or for not communicating their intentions more clearly (Cleere & Lynn, 2013; Sabina & Ho, 2014). Fear of reprisal from the perpetrator may also be a factor (Cohn et al., 2013).

Factors Associated With Acquaintance Rape

What accounts for the high incidence of acquaintance rape?

SEXUAL SCRIPT.   Some psychologists (e.g., Cooper et al., 2013) contend that the social construction of the roles of men and women in male–female sexual situations provides a social context in which acquaintance rape can occur. This traditional **sexual script** is *a socialized set of expected behaviors characterized by an aggressive male who initiates and pushes for sexual activity and a gatekeeping female* *who sets the limits.* Interpreting roles in this sexual script can lead to rape for a number of reasons. First, some men take the initiator role to the extreme and engage in sexual aggression. Second, as discussed in Chapter 8, men frequently infer sexual interest when it is not intended (Perilloux & Kurzban, 2015), which can fuel their sexual aggressiveness (Sanchez et al., 2012). Third, the differing roles within the sexual script can set the framework for misunderstanding because the male assumes the female will attempt to limit sexual activity as part of her role (McHugh et al., 2013). If a woman does not resist a man's sexual advances, both women and men assume that she is agreeing to have sex (Jozkowski et al., 2014). But if she says "no," a man may misinterpret this response as token resistance that really means "yes," leading him to disregard her objections to sex (McHugh et al., 2013). Research indicates that, in fact, a large majority of women who say "no" really do mean "no" (Muehlenhard, 2011). Thus, all refusals should be taken seriously. Recently, most sexual assault prevention programs have shifted from a "no means no" policy to one that promotes the concept that giving explicit permission (i.e., "yes means yes") is the clearest way of communicating one's intention to participate in sexual activity (Bennett, 2016; Oliver, 2016).

CHARACTERISTICS OF SEXUALLY AGGRESSIVE MEN.   Around the world, sexually aggressive men are more likely than nonaggressive men to have witnessed or experienced family violence, hold stereotypical attitudes about gender roles, feel hostility toward women, be high in the need to dominate, and be physically aggressive in other situations. They are also more likely to believe in **rape myths** (Finley, 2016; Fox & Potocki, 2015; Gidycz & Johnson, 2017; Greathouse et al., 2015; Hayes et al., 2016; Wegner et al., 2015). These are *false beliefs about rape that are widely held and that serve to justify male sexual aggression against women.* Prevalent rape myths include beliefs that forced sex by an intimate partner is not really rape; that women lead men on and therefore deserve to be raped; that women often make false accusations of rape; and that women secretly want to be raped and can prevent it if they really want to (Hackett et al., 2016; Spade & Valentine, 2016).

As might be expected, men tend to endorse these myths more than women do (Emmers-Sommer, 2014; Fox & Potocki, 2016; Germain, 2016). Moreover, college men who participate in athletics or belong to fraternities are more likely to have rape-supportive attitudes than other college men (Hayes et al., 2016; Martin, 2016; McMahon, 2015). Among both women and men, rape myth acceptance is associated with greater sexism, racism, homophobia, ageism, and classism, less education and religious intolerance (Abeid et al., 2015; Angelene et al., 2012). To get firsthand knowledge about rape myth acceptance, try Get Involved 14.2. Then, to learn more about attitudes toward rape victims in other cultures, read on.

 GLOBAL ATTITUDES TOWARD WOMEN WHO EXPERIENCE RAPE   How are rape victims viewed in cultures outside the United States? Madhabika Nayak and her colleagues (2003) and researchers led by Colleen Ward (cited in Best, 2001) examined cross-cultural attitudes toward rape victims by interviewing university students from 17 countries. Relatively favorable attitudes were found in the United Kingdom, the United States, Germany, and New Zealand, whereas less favorable views were expressed in Turkey, Mexico, Zimbabwe, India, Japan, Kuwait, and Malaysia. Having read Chapters 2 and 3 about cross-cultural differences in gender-role attitudes, can you see a recurring pattern in these findings regarding attitudes toward rape victims? In the countries with more egalitarian views of women, attitudes toward rape victims are more positive, whereas rape victims are more likely to be stigmatized in countries where women's status is much lower than that of men. Some Middle Eastern and South Asian cultures have social and legal customs that sanction severe punishment of women in response to infractions of family "honor" (Payton, 2014; Kenschaft & Clark, 2016). For example, victims of rape may be subjected to severe punishments, including imprisonment, public flogging, and being stoned to death (Worth, 2010). Little distinction is made between forced and consensual sex. Men are rarely convicted in rape cases, but girls and women who report a rape are often charged with adultery, which is considered a crime more serious than murder (Burn, 2011). Each year, hundreds of girls or women die of "honor killings," often by male members of their own families, for perceived breaches of chastity. In Turkey, a girl who has allegedly dishonored the family may be pressured to commit suicide, in order to spare her family from having to murder her (Gill & Brah, 2014).

GET INVOLVED 14.2
Gender and Rape Myths

Ask two female and two male acquaintances to indicate their degree of agreement with each of the following four statements about rape, from *strongly disagree* (1) to *strongly agree* (7). If possible, select participants from different ethnic groups.

_____**1.** Women often provoke rape.
_____**2.** Women enjoy rape.
_____**3.** Women frequently falsely claim that they have been raped.
_____**4.** Only men who are psychologically disturbed engage in rape.

WHAT DOES IT MEAN?

Sum the four ratings for each respondent. The scores can range from 4 to 28, with higher scores reflecting greater acceptance of rape myths. After scoring each person's answers, average the scores of the two females and those of the two males.

1. Did your male respondents express greater acceptance of rape myths than your female respondents did? If yes, explain. If no, indicate possible reasons why your respondents did not reflect the typically found gender difference.

2. If you tested men of different ethnicities, did you note any difference in their scores?

If yes, is this difference consistent with that presented in the text? Was there a difference between women respondents of different ethnicities?

3. Which of these four statements received the greatest degree of agreement from your respondents and which received the least agreement? Give possible reasons for these findings.

4. What do you think influences the development of these rape myths?

5. How do you think rape myth acceptance can be reduced?

CHARACTERISTICS OF SURVIVORS.   Any woman can be sexually assaulted, but some are especially vulnerable, such as adolescents and young women, those with disabilities, Black and Native American women, sexual minorities, poor and homeless women, and those living in war zones (Basile et al., 2016; Everfi, 2015; Krahn et al., 2015; Montgomery et al., 2015). Moreover, as we saw earlier in this chapter, women who are raped are more likely than nonvictimized women to have been sexually abused in childhood and/or adolescence (Collin-Vézina et al., 2013; Montgomery et al., 2015), possibly because early victimization can contribute to feelings of self-blame and powerlessness. Victims of intimate partner violence are also more likely than other women to suffer forced sexual activity.

ALCOHOL CONSUMPTION.   There is considerable evidence that alcohol consumption by the perpetrator and the victim increases the risk of rape or attempted rape. In part, this is because alcohol impairs the perpetrator's judgment and lowers the victim's resistance. Furthermore, when men drink, they may be more likely to misperceive women's behavior as a sign of sexual interest (Abbey et al., 2014; Cowley, 2014).

Effects of Rape

The psychological impact of rape can be profound. Whether they are victims of acquaintance rape or stranger rape, survivors may be plagued by anxiety, self-blame, shame, humiliation, powerlessness, lowered self-esteem depression, and suicidal thoughts (Donatelle, 2017; Gidycz & Johnson, 2017). Some symptoms, such as self-blame and powerlessness, may be more common among acquaintance victims. As shown in one college student's emotional reaction to rape by her resident advisor, "I wouldn't even admit it to myself until about 4 months later when the guilt and fear that had been eating at me became too much to hide and I came very close to a complete nervous breakdown. I tried to kill myself, but fortunately I chickened out at the last minute" (Warshaw, 1988, pp. 67–68). Women with a prior history of emotional and behavioral problems have greater difficulty than other women in recovering from rape (Campbell et al., 2009). In addition, women who blame themselves for being sexually assaulted show poor recovery (Martin et al., 2011). Women who are victims of multiple sexual assaults also have more severe physical and emotional consequences than women who experience a single rape (Lundberg-Love & Waits, 2010).

Some rape survivors also develop physical health problems, such as chronic headaches, pain, fatigue, and sleep disturbances (Stöckl & Penhale, 2015). Some may experience sexual problems, including diminished sexual activity, interest, and enjoyment (Alexander et al., 2017). Others abuse drugs and alcohol or attempt suicide (Campbell et al., 2009). Often, rape survivors undergo a "second rape," which refers to further victimization at the hands of insensitive medical, legal, and mental health personnel (Relyea & Ullman, 2015; Smith & Freyd, 2014). Placing unnecessary blame on rape survivors adds to the trauma of the original sexual assault and may hamper recovery. Moreover, the trauma of rape can disrupt women's employment in several ways, including time off, diminished performance, and inability to work (Loya, 2014, 2015).

Despite the many negative effects of rape, many survivors report positive life changes following sexual assault that help them cope with the event. For a closer look, see Learn About the Research 14.1. In addition, cognitive processing therapy and prolonged exposure therapy have been effective in helping women recover from sexual violence (Castillo, 2014).

Rape Prevention

Many rape education programs exist, most of them focusing on changing attitudes such as rape myths or increasing women's self-protection (McHugh et al., 2013; Montgomery et al., 2015). Although education can help women learn how to communicate better with male partners or how to avoid high-risk situations, it is basically men's behaviors that must be changed if rape is to be

LEARN ABOUT THE RESEARCH 14.1
Positive Life Changes Following Sexual Assault

In the aftermath of traumatic events, some individuals may experience positive as well as negative life changes as a of trying to come to terms with these events (Campbell et al., 2009; Martin et al., 2011; Vishnevsky et al., 2010; Wadsworth, 2010). Patricia Frazier and her colleagues (2005; Frazier & Kaler, 2006) conducted a longitudinal study of 171 women who experienced sexual assault, in order to assess factors that best predicted positive life changes during the women's recovery process. Positive life change was measured by asking participants to rate the extent to which specific aspects of their lives had changed since the assault. Items dealt with one's self (e.g., "My ability to take care of myself"); relationships (e.g., "My relationships with family"); life philosophy or spirituality (e.g., "My sense of purpose in life"); and empathy (e.g., "My concern for others in

my similar situation"). Participants rated each item on a 5-point scale ranging from "much worse now" to "much better now." The participants, who were between 16 and 52 years old (mean age, 27), filled out questionnaires at 2 weeks, 2 months, 6 months, and 1 year after the assault.

One factor that strongly related to positive change was social support, which, as we have seen, is related to good mental health. A second factor related to positive change, called "approach coping," involved viewing the stressful event differently and expressing emotions about it (as opposed to avoiding people and acting as if nothing had happened). In addition, those who showed positive life changes relied on their religious faith to cope, and perceived that they had control over their recovery process.

WHAT DOES IT MEAN?

1. Based on these results, what suggestions could you offer to a friend of yours who has just experienced sexual assault?

2. Do you think that these results would be similar for men who are survivors of sexual assault? Explain your answer.

prevented. Because attitudes supportive of rape and the sexual script are learned at a young age, rape education programs should begin early.

In addition to rape education, institutions must develop effective procedures for dealing with complaints. Women who report a rape must be assured that their claims will be fairly investigated and that if guilt is determined, the perpetrators will receive appropriate sanctions. Currently, there are about 1,200 rape crisis centers in the United States. These centers partner with other community agencies to provide comprehensive services, including counseling and medical advocacy, to rape survivors and their families (Shaw & Campbell, 2014).

Theories of Rape

How can rape be explained? Our examination focuses on three theories that posit different mechanisms to account for rape.

EVOLUTIONARY THEORY. **Evolutionary theory** applies the principles of natural selection and its goal of reproductive survival to understand social behavior, including rape. According to this theory, *rape evolved because it was a strategy males could use to ensure their genes would be passed on to future generations.* From an evolutionary view, it is to males' reproductive advantage to mate often and with numerous partners (Kenschaft & Clark, 2016). To support this view, evolutionary theorists note that forced copulations have been observed in a variety of animal species and that females of child-bearing age are the most likely rape victims (Thornhill & Palmer, 2000).

Critics, however, contend that it is not appropriate to draw conclusions about rape by observing nonhuman species because human behavior is more complexly determined (Butler, 2008; Travis, 2003). Others question the theory's view that frequent copulation with multiple partners is reproductively effective for men. Natalie Angier (1999) argues that a continuous relationship with one woman might be as reproductively successful as promiscuous mating. Others note that rape victims include females too young or old to reproduce (Turchik et al., 2016). Furthermore, the fact that some men rape wives and partners with whom they also have had consensual sex and that most men do not rape are not consistent with this assumption that the purpose of rape is reproduction (de Waal, 2002; Rutter & Schwartz, 2012). Finally, evolutionary theorists ignore instances of rape that are inconsistent with the theory, such as same-sex rape or rape in the context of war (Rhode et al., 2014).

FEMINIST THEORY. A different perspective is offered by **feminist theory**, *which contends that rape is rooted in the longstanding and pervasive power imbalance between women and men* (Bahun & Rajan, 2015; Belknap, 2015). Men have greater legal, economic, and political power, which provides them with more power in interpersonal situations. Men use rape as one mechanism to control women and maintain their dominance.

Support for feminist theory at the societal level is provided by evidence that cultural areas with greater gender equality in economic, legal, and political power have lower rape rates than do those with less gender equality (Turchik et al., 2016). Moreover, a man's endorsement of male dominance and restricted rights for women is strongly connected to his acceptance of rape myths (Ahrens et al., 2008).

SOCIAL LEARNING THEORY. **Social learning theory** provides a third perspective to the phenomenon of rape. As discussed in Chapter 3, this theory *contends that social behaviors are learned through observation and reinforcement. This includes learning both attitudes supportive of rape and sexually aggressive behaviors* (Turchik et al., 2016). The theory assumes, for example, that men can develop attitudes supportive of rape or sexually aggressive behaviors via media depictions of sexuality and violence. The theory further holds that men's sexual aggressiveness can be reinforced by the widespread acceptance of rape myths, which blame the victim and excuse the perpetrator, and by the traditional sexual script, which encourages males to be aggressive and women to be passive in sexual situations (Belknap, 2015).

Both of these assumptions have received some support from research. Consistent with the hypothesized influence of observational learning, for example, studies have shown that experience with pornography is related to greater sexual aggressiveness (Cooper et al., 2013). However, this relationship could reflect either an effect of pornography on sexual aggressiveness or the possibility that sexually aggressive men choose to view violent pornography. In support of the importance of reinforcement, men who more strongly accept rape myths tend to be more sexually aggressive (Tharp et al., 2012).

INTIMATE PARTNER VIOLENCE

I have had glasses thrown at me. I have been kicked in the abdomen, kicked off the bed, and hit while lying on the floor—while I was pregnant. I have been whipped, kicked, and thrown, picked up and thrown down again. (Boston Women's Health Book Collective, 1998, p. 162)

I was pretty much in a cage . . . He didn't let me use the phone . . . didn't let me go out . . . took away all of my freedom. (Zink & Sill, 2004, p. 33)

Intimate partner violence refers to *physical and psychological abuse committed by an intimate partner, that is, a spouse, romantic partner, or a former spouse/partner* (Hardesty & Crossman, 2015; Khaw, 2017). It is a major social and public health problem with significant costs to women across all cultures, ethnicities, income levels, and sexual orientations (World Health Organization, 2014a). Intimate partner violence ranges from the relatively mild **common (or situational) couple violence**, which consists of *minor acts of aggression such as pushing, slapping, and shoving*, that is rooted in a particular situation to **intimate terrorism**, *the systematic use of violence, threats, and isolation to dominate and control a partner* (Leone et al., 2014). As with dating violence, women are equally or somewhat more likely than men to engage in common couple violence, often in self-defense (Fanslow et al., 2015; Hamburger & Larsen, 2015; Silvestri & Crowther-Dowey, 2016). The vast majority of acts of intimate terrorism, illustrated by the opening vignette of this section, are perpetuated by men (Hamby, 2014; Zweig et al., 2014). Psychological abuse, illustrated in the second vignette, includes overt attempts to dominate, isolate, control, and undermine self-esteem (Sylvestri & Crowther-Dowey, 2016; Watkins et al., 2014). Psychological abuse may be just as damaging as physical violence because it involves emotional humiliation and the destruction of one's identity (Belknap & Sharma, 2014; Khaw, 2017).

Incidence

Like rape, intimate partner violence is an underreported crime, but it is estimated that nearly one in three women is assaulted by her male partner in the United States and globally during her lifetime (Breiding et al., 2014; World Health Organization, 2013). Nearly 40 percent of all murders of women around the world are committed by intimate partners, compared to only 6 percent of men's murders (UN Women, 2015; World Health Organization, 2013). In one study, about half of women seeking health care at emergency departments or primary care clinics reported having experienced physical and/or emotional abuse at some point in their lives. One in four reported severe physical or sexual abuse. Only one-quarter of the women had ever been asked about abuse by a health care provider. Most, however, said they would reveal abuse if asked in a nonhurried, concerned manner (Kramer et al., 2004). Similar results have been reported on college campuses (Sutherland et al., 2016). Sadly, many doctors say that they don't ask such questions because of a lack of time, training, and easy access to services that help these patients (Marcus, 2008).

Violence in LGBT relationships occurs at least as often, and perhaps more often, as in heterosexual couples (Brown & Herman, 2015; Hellemans et al., 2015; Martin-Storey, 2015), with transgender individuals experiencing the highest rates (Langenderfer-Magruder et al., 2016). Similar to violence in heterosexual relationships, this abuse can be both physical and emotional (Badenes-Ribera et al., 2016; Menning & Holtzman, 2014).

Role of Disability, Social Class, and Ethnicity

Disability, poverty, and ethnicity are all factors in intimate partner violence, once again demonstrating the influence of intersectionality (Cheng & Lom, 2016; Krahn et al., 2015). Women with disabilities experience abuse at a higher rate than able-bodied women, and their abusive relationships continue for a longer period of time (Robinson-Whelen et al., 2014; Scherer et al., 2016; UNAIDS, 2014a, b). They are also abused by a greater number of people, including health care providers or attendants, in addition to partners or family members (Alexander et al., 2017). Poorer women, ethnic minorities, and those with less education report the highest rates of physical abuse (Farber & Miller-Cribbs, 2014; Stockman et al., 2015). Black women are more likely than White women to be victims of domestic violence (Breiding et al., 2014). They are less likely than their White counterparts to seek formal help (i.e., police, social service agencies) but are more apt to seek help from informal sources, such as family, friends, and clergy (Anyikwa, 2015).

The Asian American community has the lowest reported rates of intimate partner violence of any other ethnic group (Breiding et al., 2014), but this could be an underestimate of its actual occurrence. Asian Americans emphasize the family over the individual, the strong value placed on the male as the authority in the family, and the belief that family affairs must be kept private. These reasons may keep Asian American women from seeking assistance for their abuse (Le & Dinh, 2015).

Studies of domestic violence among Latinas/os in the United States have produced a mixed picture, although often their rates are between those of Blacks and Whites (Reingle et al., 2014). Methodological problems, such as lumping together all Latina/o subgroups and not considering the influence of acculturation into U.S. society, may be responsible for these inconsistencies.

Native American and Alaska Native women have the highest rate of intimate partner violence (Crossland et al., 2013). This may be related to both alcohol abuse and patriarchal beliefs introduced by the Westernization of native peoples (Robinson-Wood, 2017). In addition, the forced removal from homes and disrupted family structures that resulted from European colonization may make native women particularly vulnerable to violence (Peters, 2015).

Intimate Partner Violence Around the World

Sadly, violence against women by their male partners occurs in all countries, (Khaw, 2017). Data from Australia, the United States, Canada, Israel, and South Africa, for example, show that 40 to 70 percent of female murder victims are killed by their partners (Burn, 2011; Kirk & Okazawa-Rey, 2013; "Violence Against Women," 2009). In addition, thousands of women each year are victims of dowry-related killings or are disfigured with fire or acid by rejected suitors in Bangladesh, Colombia, India, Nigeria, and Pakistan (Burn, 2011; Furr, 2014; Kirk & Okazawa-Rey, 2013). In sub-Saharan Africa and in the patriarchal societies of the Middle East and South Asia, both men and women often consider wife beating to be justified under certain circumstances, such as disobeying one's husband and neglecting one's children (Khaw, 2017; Waltermaurer, 2012). Furthermore, they blame women for the beating, believe that women benefit from the violence, and oppose assistance for battered women from governmental agencies (Btoush & Haj-Yahia, 2008).

Immigrant and ethnic minority women may be at greater risk of experiencing intimate partner violence. Institutional discrimination, lack of knowledge of services, and cultural differences can prevent women who experience such violence from seeking help (World Health Organization, 2014a). Even when they do, the criminal justice system may take crimes of violence against ethnic minority or immigrant women less seriously than those committed against ethnic majority women. For example, the longstanding ill treatment of the Roma (formerly called Gypsy) people in many European countries has made Roma women reluctant to report crimes of violence to the police (Sorde et al., 2014).

Risk Factors

The need for power and control and the belief that men have the right to punish their female partners play an important role in men's intimate partner violence (Westmarland, 2015). Alcohol and drug abuse by batterers in both heterosexual and same-sex relationships are also common (Lechtenberg & Stith, 2017; Nowotny & Graves, 2013; Reingle et al., 2014). Violent husbands are more likely than other husbands to display poor problem-solving and communication skills, high levels of anger and hostility, antisocial behavior, and low self-esteem. Occupational, economic, and marital stresses are also associated with intimate partner violence (Hardesty & Crossman, 2015; Stover & Kiselica, 2015; Westmarland, 2015). Not surprisingly, male batterers and abused women are more likely than other men and women to have witnessed violence between their parents or experienced physical or sexual abuse in childhood (Murphy et al., 2014; Williams et al., 2014). This does not mean that all adults with a history of violence will be involved in an abusive relationship, or that all those involved in domestic violence have a history of family battering (Tharp et al., 2012). However, these findings do suggest that observing a parent commit violence gives boys the message that violence is a means for handling anger and conflict and influences the development of negative attitudes toward women. For women, the early experience of family violence can provide a similar message that aggression is a "normal" aspect of close relationships.

Effects of Intimate Partner Violence

The effects of abuse include a wide variety of long-term physical and psychological problems and reduced economic well-being (Hughes & Brush 2015; Moulding, 2016). Health problems include physical injuries and reproductive difficulties. Abused women may also suffer psychological problems such as lower self-esteem, depression, anxiety, drug and alcohol abuse, sexual risk-taking behavior, eating disorders, PTSD, and suicide attempts (Alvarez-Segura et al., 2014; Breiding et al., 2014; Watkins et al., 2014). Moreover, the health problems caused by physical and psychological abuse may keep women from obtaining or keeping employment, which can keep them financially dependent on the abuser (Adams et al., 2012; Loya, 2014). Children who observe parental violence also suffer psychological trauma (Hardesty & Crossman, 2014; Holmes et al., 2014; Jouriles & McDonald, 2015), as illustrated by Susan's anguished comments at the beginning of the chapter.

Leaving the Abusive Relationship

Many people wonder why abused women don't leave their abuser. Two major barriers to leaving are financial dependence and fear of retaliation (Khaw, 2017; Stöckl & Penhale, 2015). Abusers can interpret women's attempt to leave as a loss of control and their violence can accelerate. As one abused woman reported, "The very first time that I attempted to leave he tried to choke me with the sheets to the point where I turned blue" (Sorenson, 1996, p. 129). Many older women have stayed in abusive marriages because they were socialized to remain with their husbands regardless of circumstances (Roberto et al., 2014). Women with disabilities may also be more likely than other women to stay in an abusive relationship, especially if their job or transportation opportunities are limited, or if their only alternative living arrangement is in an institution (Olkin, 2008). Other women stay because cultural or religious beliefs forbid divorce or are more accepting of intimate partner violence (Williams et al., 2014). Immigrant women may be reluctant to inform authorities about domestic violence because of fear of deportation, discrimination, and anti-immigrant sentiment (Alexander et al., 2017; Reina et al., 2013).

Theories of Intimate Partner Violence

Two theories presented as explanations of rape are also useful in understanding intimate partner violence. As discussed previously, feminist theory emphasizes gender power imbalance as a destructive factor in men's interactions with women. When applied to intimate partner violence, it contends that men use violence against women as a means to maintain their power and status (Keating, 2015; Khaw, 2017; McPhail, 2016). Social learning theory posits that domestic violence is a learned behavior that can develop from observing violence within the family and from receiving reinforcement for aggressive acts (Hamby & Grych, 2016).

Interventions

In the past 30 years, a body of laws and policies has developed nationally and globally concerning domestic violence. These include mandatory arrest of the abuser and orders of protection that prohibit the abuser from coming near or contacting the woman (Hardesty & Crossman, 2014: Khaw, 2017). The development of shelters, transitional housing programs, and other services for abused women have been other key interventions (Enns, 2014; Khaw, 2017). Various psychotherapies are useful tools for helping to re-empower the survivor of abuse (Hackett et al., 2016). Programs also have been designed to treat the abuser either alone or with his or her partner. They deal with attitudes toward women and toward violence against women, as well as anger management (Cooper et al., 2013; Gondolf, 2015). Unfortunately, the effects of such programs in preventing further violence are modest (Cooper et al., 2013; Radatz & Wright, 2016).

ELDER ABUSE

A nursing home worker pushes, slaps, and throws food at four different residents (Payne, 2011).

A crack-addicted man physically batters his elderly aunts if they do not give him money for his next fix. Eventually, they lose their savings and their home and are reduced to begging in the streets. (Kleinfield, 2004)

Elder abuse refers to *physical, psychological, financial, and neglectful acts that harm the health or welfare of an older adult, and that occur within a relationship of trust* (Hildreth, 2011; Lachs & Pillemer, 2015) (see Table 14.1). Abuse of older people is a significant public health problem. An estimated 1 in ten older people in the United States experience moderate to severe abuse each year (Humble & Price, 2017; Lachs & Pillemer, 2015). Older Blacks have the highest rates of reported abuse. Latinos/as and Asian Americans are the least likely to report abuse, which may result in part from language barriers and from a reluctance to bring dishonor upon the family (Humble & Price, 2017). Neglect, psychological abuse, and financial exploitation are the most commonly reported types of abuse (Dong, 2015). Sadly, a substantial number of older women have experienced more than one type of abuse (Fisher et al., 2011).

All states now have laws against elder mistreatment, with most mandating that abuse be reported. Yet studies estimate that the majority of cases are not reported (Amstadter et al., 2011; Phelan, 2013). One obstacle is denial of the problem. In addition, older persons themselves may lack the opportunity or the physical and mental abilities to report abuse. They often fear not being believed, reprisal, abandonment, and institutionalization. Also, victimized older people may wish to protect the abuser, who is most often a family member (Burnes et al., 2014; Humble & Price, 2017).

TABLE 14.1   Types of Elder Abuse

Type of Abuse	Description
Physical and sexual abuse	Inflicting physical pain, sexually molesting, or confining the person against her or his will
Psychological abuse	Threatening, humiliating, insulting, and/or intimidating the person; forcing the person to do degrading things; treating the person like a child
Financial abuse	Destroying property or possessions, stealing the person's money, denying the person access to his or her money
Neglect	Depriving the person of items needed for daily living (food, warmth, shelter, glasses, dentures, money), inattention, isolation

Source: Humble and Price, 2017.

Elder Abuse: A Global Perspective

Unfortunately, elder abuse exists around the world. The highest prevalence has been reported in China (36 percent) and Nigeria (30 percent), followed by Israel (18 percent), India (14 percent), Europe (11 percent), the United States (10 percent), and Canada (4 percent; Pillemer et al., 2015). Among European countries, the prevalence rate is 2 percent in Nordic countries, 10 percent in Germany, and 12 percent in Italy (Garre-Olmo et al., 2009). Although forms of abuse vary across countries, the most common victims are the older poor, widows, and childless older women. In Austria, India, Japan, Korea, Lebanon, and Taiwan, older women report that family conflict and jealousy lead to neglect and abuse by their daughters-in-law (Phelan, 2013). In Hong Kong, Kenya, and Brazil, one serious form of abuse is the practice of abandoning older family members in hospitals, especially during times of drought, poor crop yields, or even holidays. A common theme across many cultures is a pervasive lack of respect for older people, whether in health, governmental, and commercial institutions or in personal interactions (Phelan, 2013).

Who Is Abused and Who Abuses?

As with any form of abuse, the perpetrators and victims of elder abuse may be of either sex. However, the typical victim of elder abuse is a woman over age 75, usually widowed or divorced. She often lives at home with adult caregivers but is isolated and fearful. Frequently, she is physically and/or mentally frail and may suffer from cognitive impairments (Humble & Price, 2017; Roberto et al., 2015). Most elder abuse is committed by family members, including adult children and spouses. Paid household workers or caregivers may be abusive as well, as shown in the vignettes at the beginning of this section. The typical abuser is a middle-aged son of the victim, who may have mental, alcohol, or drug problems. Often, the abuser is the caregiver of the victim and may also be financially dependent upon the victim (Burnes et al., 2014; Roberto et al., 2015).

The stress of providing care for an ill relative may contribute to the problem of elder abuse because the caregiver may be unprepared, unable, or unwilling to provide the necessary care (Humble & Price, 2017) and may express frustration by becoming abusive. However, one must be careful not to simply "blame the victim" for being abused. (Notice the parallel with inappropriately blaming a woman who has been raped.) The feminist perspective puts elder abuse in a larger social context. From this point of view, elder abuse is part of a spectrum of male violence against women (Phelan, 2013) that reflects a social context in which men wield more power and dominance over women.

What Can Be Done?

Some of the options that are available to the younger abused woman—deciding to leave a relationship or going to a shelter—are impractical or virtually impossible for most abused older people (Pillemer et al., 2016). Awareness of the problem is the first step. One encouraging sign is that elder abuse is now a major global concern for international agencies such as the United Nations and the World Health Organization (Phelan, 2013). Education and training are essential to alert the general public and professional service providers to the prevalence of elder abuse and neglect (National Center for Injury Prevention & Control, 2016). Professionals must learn to recognize the symptoms of abuse, understand the victim's denial, and strengthen the victim's resolve to end the abuse. The public should be encouraged to report any known or suspected case of abuse (Mustafa & Kingston, 2014; Pillemer et al., 2015). New laws have been passed in recent years governing the treatment of victims, which focus on the need for safety, assistance in accessing the courts, and information about the progress of the proceedings. Support groups for victims help validate the victims' experiences and provide a sense of empowerment that may enable them to change the power structure of the abusive relationship (Roberto, 2016).

What can you do? See What <u>You</u> Can Do 14.2 for ways in which you can work to combat violence against women.

Summary

SEXUAL HARASSMENT AT SCHOOL

- Reports of sexual harassment are increasing among middle and senior high school students.
- Girls are more likely than boys to be sexually harassed by their schoolmates and they are more upset by it.
- Schools are now legally obligated to protect students from severe and pervasive harassment by other students.
- More female than male students experience sexual harassment on campus. Most incidents involve subtle forms of harassment, and most are perpetrated by other students.
- Ethnic and sexual minority students are more likely to experience harassment than are other students.

SEXUAL HARASSMENT IN THE WORKPLACE

- It is estimated that a large proportion of employed women will experience sexual harassment. Sexist remarks and jokes are common forms of harassment; sexual coercion is relatively rare.
- Women in blue-collar occupations and the military are more likely to be targets of harassment than other women.
- This might be due to the high prevalence of both the male gender stereotype and male-related physical traits in these fields.
- According to sex-role spillover theory, sexual harassment occurs because men respond to females in the workplace as women rather than as workers. Power theory states that harassment is used by more powerful individuals either to gain sexual favors or to reinforce their position of greater power.
- Most targets of sexual harassment use informal strategies for dealing with the harassment, such as ignoring it or asking the harasser to stop. They rarely file formal complaints or seek legal redress.
- Numerous negative outcomes can stem from sexual harassment.

STALKING

- Stalking refers to unwanted and repeated actions toward an individual that induce fear or concern for safety.
- Most stalkers are male and most victims are female.
- Stalking can produce harmful psychological effects.

VIOLENCE AGAINST GIRLS

- The incidence of child sexual abuse may run as high as one in five girls and one in ten boys. Most abuse is committed by a relative or family friend (usually male).
- Sexual abuse can have a devastating impact on the physical and mental health of children, both immediately and in the long term.
- School-based sexual-abuse prevention programs may help children avoid and report abuse. Psychotherapy can help abused children and women heal.

- Countries with strong preferences for boys show elevated rates of abortion, infanticide, and neglect of female children.
- Female genital mutilation/cutting can cause severe medical problems. Some cultures practice it, believing it will ensure chastity.
- Many girls and young women around the world have been lured into sexual slavery.

DATING VIOLENCE

- Substantial numbers of teenagers experience violence in their dating relationships. More males than females report being victims of such violence.

RAPE

- An estimated one in five women experience rape or attempted rape, much of it perpetrated by acquaintances.
- Physical aggressiveness, hostility toward women, gender-stereotypical attitudes, and a history of family violence differentiate sexually aggressive men from other men.
- Alcohol consumption increases the risk of sexual coercion and rape.
- Rape victims can experience a variety of emotional and health problems.
- Evolutionary, feminist, and social learning theories attempt to account for rape. Although some support for all three has been reported, there are many criticisms of evolutionary theory.

INTIMATE PARTNER VIOLENCE

- Nearly one in three women in the United States and globally is a victim of intimate partner violence each year.

- Intimate partner violence occurs in sexual minority and heterosexual relationships and across ethnic groups, although it is more frequent among Blacks than Whites.
- Major risk factors for both perpetrators and victims of intimate partner violence are a history of family violence and alcohol and drug abuse.
- Numerous physical and psychological problems can result from victimization, including physical injuries, reproductive difficulties, lower self-esteem, anxiety, and depression.
- Financial problems and fear of the perpetrator are the primary reasons for remaining in an abusive relationship.
- Feminist and social learning theories help explain intimate partner violence.

ELDER ABUSE

- Elder abuse can have physical, psychological, financial, and neglect dimensions. An estimated one in ten older adults in the United States are affected, but few cases are reported.
- Rates and forms of elder abuse vary across nations.
- The typical victim is a woman age 75 or older, who lives with a caregiver. The typical abuser is a middle-aged son who has mental, alcohol, or drug problems.
- The following are essential in order to combat elder abuse: educating professionals and the public; reporting abuse cases; passing victims' rights laws; and forming support groups.

Key Terms

sexual harassment in an educational setting *302*
sexual harassment in the workplace *305*
quid pro quo harassment *305*
hostile environment *305*
sexual coercion *305*
gender harassment *305*
unwanted sexual attention *305*
racialized sexual harassment *307*
sex-role spillover theory *308*

power theory *308*
organizational tolerance *308*
internally focused responses *308*
externally focused responses *308*
stalking *309*
child sexual abuse *309*
incest *310*
female genital cutting *312*
infibulation *312*
human trafficking *313*
rape *314*

acquaintance rape *315*
sexual script *315*
rape myths *316*
evolutionary theory *319*
feminist theory *319*
social learning theory *319*
intimate partner violence *320*
common couple violence *320*
intimate terrorism *320*
elder abuse *323*

What Do You Think?

1. Some people have criticized the recent U.S. Supreme Court ruling that obligates schools to protect students from severe and pervasive sexual harassment by other students. Some argue that sexual taunting and even touching are normal rites of adolescence. Others contend that even such apparently innocent gestures as the exchange of Valentine's Day cards by first graders will now be classified as sexual harassment and thus forbidden. What is your position on this issue, and why?

2. Which of the recommended procedures for reducing sexual harassment on campus do you think would be particularly effective at your school? Can you think of other activities that might be beneficial on your campus?

3. Why are family members often the perpetrators of child sexual abuse? What actions can be taken to prevent such behaviors?

4. Using either the feminist or social learning theory as a framework, discuss societal changes that might lead to a reduction in both rape and intimate partner violence.

5. How can public awareness of elder abuse be increased?

If You Want to Learn More

Bryant-Davis, T. (2014). *Surviving sexual violence: A guide to recovery and empowerment.* Lanham, MD: Rowman & Littlefield.

Dragiewicz, M. (2015). *Global human trafficking: Critical issues and contexts.* New York: Routledge.

Gartner, R. & McCarthy, B. (Eds.). (2014). *The Oxford handbook of gender, sex, and crime.* New York: Oxford University Press.

Harding, K. (2015). *Asking for it: The alarming rise of rape culture—and what we can do about it.* Boston, MA: Da Capo Press.

Hepburn, S. & Simon, R. (2013). *Human trafficking around the world: Hidden in plain sight.* New York: Columbia University Press.

Messinger, A.M. (2017). *LGBTQ intimate partner violence: Lessons for policy, practice, and research.* Oakland, CA: University of California Press.

Messner, M.A. et al. (Eds.). (2015). *Some men: Feminist allies and the movement to end violence against women.* New York: Oxford University Press.

Paludi, M.A. (Ed.). (2016). *Campus action against sexual assault: Needs, policies, procedures, and training programs.* Santa Barbara, CA: Praeger.

Paludi, M.A., Martin, J.L., & Finerman, S. (Eds.). (2015). *Sexual harassment in education and work settings: Current research and best practices for prevention.* Santa Barbara, CA: ABC-CLIO.

Samuels, O. (2016). *A beginner's guide to sexual harassment at work.* Amazon Digital Services.

Sigal, J.A. & Denmark, F.L. (Eds.). (2013). *Violence against girls and women: International perspectives.* Santa Barbara, CA: ABC-CLIO.

Spitzberg, B.H. & Cupach, W.R. (2014). *The dark side of relationship pursuit: From attraction to obsession and stalking.* New York: Routledge.

Strauss, S. (2012). *Sexual harassment and bullying: A guide to keeping kids safe and holding schools accountable.* Lanham, MD: Rowman & Littlefield.

Wooten, S. & Mitchell. R. (2015). *The crisis of campus sexual violence: Critical perspectives on prevention and response.* New York: Routledge.

Websites

Education

American Association of University Women
http://www.aauw.org

Sexual Harassment

https://www.unh.edu/sharpp/helping-friend
http://www.novabucks.org/otherinformation/sexualharassment/

Violence Against Girls

Abuse/Incest Support
http://www.siawso.org/

Rape

National Clearinghouse on Marital and Date Rape
http://www.ncmdr.org/

Intimate Partner Violence

American Bar Association Commission on Domestic Violence
http://www.americanbar.org/groups/domestic_violence.html
National Center for Injury Prevention and Control
http://www.cdc.gov/ncipc

Family Violence Prevention Fund
http://endabuse.org
Same-Sex Domestic Violence
http://www.rainbowdomesticviolence.itgo.com/
State Reporting Requirements
http://endabuse.org/statereport/list.php3
Stop Abuse for Everyone (SAFE)
http://www.safe4all.org

U.S. Department of Justice
http://www.ovw.usdoj.gov/

Elder Abuse
National Center on Elder Abuse (NECA)
http://www.ncea.aoa.gov/ncearoot/Main_Site/
index.aspx

CHAPTER 15

A Feminist Future
Goals, Actions, and Beliefs

It has become customary for the three of us [friends taking Claire's Psychology of Women course] to discuss women's issues at a local coffee shop on Tuesday evenings, not just among ourselves, but our friends as well . . . I have never taken a class that has caused me to engage in so much conversation outside of the classroom. The biggest success of your class is that regardless of how people feel about a certain issue, your class is causing people to talk and more people are becoming aware of issues that wouldn't be discussed otherwise . . . I feel that my eyes have been opened to a world of issues that have always been right in front of me. (Julie, a 22-year-old senior)

We saw in Chapter 1 that science is not value free, and as the experience of Julie and her friends illustrates, neither is teaching. "The process of education is political" (Wyche & Crosby, 1996, p. 5); that is, both subject matter and teaching methods are influenced by the value system of the instructor and the academic community. Applying this to the field of psychology, Kimberly Kinsler and Sue Rosenberg Zalk (1996) contend that "the greatest value of psychology lies in the field's ability to reveal the psychological processes perpetuating social injustices and to correct the social systems that have an unjust impact on the quality of people's lives" (p. 35). Given this political dimension of teaching, we end this textbook with a look at feminist goals for the future.

In Chapter 1, we presented three feminist themes that have recurred throughout this book: the intersectionality and diversity of women's lives and experiences, gender differences in power, and the social construction of gender. In this chapter, we return to these themes and translate them into goals for the future, consider actions for achieving these aims, and, because these goals have their roots in feminist thought, explore the prevalence of feminist beliefs among North American women.

FEMINIST GOALS

Based on the themes in this book, we have chosen four feminist goals for the future. Do you have others that you would add?

Goal One: Gender Equality in Organizational Power

Despite legislation that prohibits gender discrimination in employment (Title VII of the Civil Rights Act of 1964) and educational programs (Title IX, 1972), gender differences in organizational and interpersonal power continue to limit women's advancement in the workplace. Antidiscrimination legislation alone cannot change attitudes, and discriminatory policies are hard to monitor. Therefore, as has been noted throughout this text, men, especially White men, continue to have greater access to economic and political resources than women do (Launius & Hassel, 2015). They continue to greatly outnumber women at high levels of management and in political office and own most of the wealth (Chapter 10).

To combat this inequity, we choose as our first goal for the future greater equality of organizational power. A strong commitment from an organization's top management can help create a culture that promotes the advancement of young women (Catalyst, 2013). As more and more women attain levels of power currently held by men, gender equality will begin to affect other areas. Women's accessibility to important mentors and social networks will increase, providing even more promotion opportunities for women. And because job level is one factor determining salaries, women's wages will rise and become more similar to those of men. The close association between sexual harassment and the power imbalance also suggests that a greater power equality will mean less harassment of women.

Goal Two: Gender Equality in Relationship Power

In addition to greater organizational power, men continue to hold more interpersonal power relative to women. For instance, they tend to have more control over a couple's activities on dates and more influence in marriage (Chapter 8). A second goal, therefore, is greater equality in relationship power. Women would benefit by having a greater voice in dating decision making and a more balanced division of household labor. The latter, in turn, could reduce women's role overload and interrole conflict. Furthermore, because both rape and domestic violence are due, at least in part, to male dominance, shared interpersonal power would go a long way in reducing intimate violence against women.

Goal Three: Gender Equality in Power for All Groups of Women

Women are disadvantaged due not only to the gender inequality of power, but also to differences within genders that add extra burdens to the lives of many women. White women are advantaged compared to women of color; middle-class women have more power than working-class or poor women; heterosexual women are privileged in comparison to lesbian, bisexual, and transgender women; able-bodied women are more advantaged than women with disabilities; and younger women have more power than their older counterparts. We have seen that ethnic minority women and women with disabilities experience even greater wage inequities than White and able-bodied women (Chapter 10). Furthermore, women of color and sexual minority women experience more job discrimination and sexual harassment than White and heterosexual women (Chapters 10 and 14). Thus, a third power goal is to ensure that increases in female power benefit all women, regardless of ethnicity, class, ableness, sexual orientation, or age (Sprague, 2016).

Goal Four: Greater Flexibility in the Social Construction of Gender

We have noted throughout the text that gender is socially constructed and that most gender behaviors and roles—such as career choice (Chapter 9), friendship behaviors (Chapter 8), and contribution to household labor (Chapter 11)—are shaped by interpersonal, societal, and cultural expectations and are not constrained by biological sex. In examining some of the mechanisms that influence this construction of gender, we explored stereotypes that reflect societal gender expectations (Chapter 3), theoretical perspectives about the mechanisms whereby children learn the behaviors and roles expected for their gender (Chapter 3), and parental shaping of the behaviors and interests of girls and boys (Chapter 4). We saw that it is not the biological nature of females and males that serves as the major foundation for people's view of gender or their gender-related activities and preferences, but their conception of what it means to be a female or a male in society today.

Additionally, we have seen that the imbalance of power also guides the social construction of gender (Spade & Valentine, 2016). People with more power, who are in dominant positions, are likely to acquire and use different traits and behaviors than people in subordinate positions. Individuals in high-status positions are more likely to display independence, a male gender-related trait that is difficult to embrace if one lacks access to necessary resources in the home, workplace, or social environment. People lacking powerful resources, on the other hand, are more likely to rely instead on emotional connections between people and, consequently, to develop female gender-related traits, such as compassion. Thus, females' and males' development of gender-related traits, behaviors, and roles is constructed via stereotype-based expectations; socialization by parents, peers, and others; and hierarchical status within society.

Unfortunately, a rigid construction of gender is damaging to human potential (Sprague, 2016). It hinders development of individuals' unique talents and interests by guiding them in directions dictated by the social constructs of their biological sex. Judith recalls her days as a new bride when she refused to allow her husband to share the housecleaning, although both she and her husband were employed full time. Her insistence was based on her traditional conception of the "wife" role, a perception that was constructed from television and magazine images and from the roles of many married couples at that time (the 1960s). Her "wife role" behaviors were not based on her own interests, her time availability, or her husband's desires, but solely on her construction of this role from the societal images and social behaviors she observed around her.

A fourth goal for women, then, is greater flexibility in the construction of gender. Flexibility can lead to an expansion in career options, more flexible decisions about work and family dilemmas, greater sexual equality, and numerous other reductions in gender-constrained behaviors that limit choices made by both women and men. Flexibility of gender-related behaviors and roles also has the potential to reduce the prevalence of sexual harassment and acquaintance rape (Chapter 14), both of which are fostered, at least in part, by traditional constructions of the behaviors of men and women. Further, it can enhance communication within heterosexual couples by freeing each partner from constraints expected for her or his gender.

ACTIONS TO ACHIEVE THESE GOALS

Research and Teaching

Research and teaching about the psychology of women can play a significant role in achieving feminist goals for several reasons. First, greater knowledge of gender differences in interpersonal and societal power can help clarify the role that power imbalance plays in women's lives. Understanding the extent to which male power influences rape and battering (Chapter 14), serves as the basis for the division of household labor (Chapter 11), and contributes to wage inequities (Chapter 10) means that both female and male students will be aware of the prevalence of male power. A reduction in male privilege cannot occur until people recognize that it exists (Hidalgo, 2011; Launius & Hassel, 2015). Exposure to this issue within the classroom can increase awareness that can spark the motivation and action necessary for change. The more we (psychologists and students) understand the dynamics and the effects of power differentials, the better armed we are to reduce privilege and its negative consequences for the less powerful.

Second, research and teaching about the psychology of women enlighten people about the way they construct gender in their lives. Scientific investigation gives people a better understanding of the influences on this construction and of the effects their personal images of gender have on their experiences as females or males. Similarly, exploration of these issues in the classroom has the potential to transform. As both women and men learn about the social basis for gender behaviors and roles, they might feel freer to experiment and to make choices that are less traditional but more personally appropriate (Paludi et al., 2008c).

Third, research and teaching about the experiences of diverse women can dispel myths and stereotypes that distort individuals' understanding and reduce tolerance. These activities also foster greater understanding, appreciation, and celebration of people's similarities and differences and can empower all females, not only those in the most privileged group. Although recent years have brought a greater inclusion of underrepresented groups in both research and educational curricula to achieve these diversity goals, the field must continue to expand the diversity of its research participants. A more representative body of knowledge can ensure that researchers, instructors, and students do not generalize from one narrow group of females, carrying the implicit message that people in this group are "normal" and any discrepant behaviors, attitudes, or roles on the part of other individuals are "abnormal" (Brabeck, 2016; Sprague, 2016; Yoder, 2015).

Consideration of diverse women's experiences must include a broader scope of topics as well. Research and teaching must address previously underexamined issues, such as employment obstacles for poor women, dating concerns of women with disabilities, experiences of lesbian mothers, outcomes of living in an extended family, and achievement goals of working-class and poor young women. A broader conceptualization of research and teaching topics not only facilitates understanding, but can also inform policy interventions. For example, although company-supplied day care might ease the work–family burden of women in white-collar and professional jobs, free temporary child care might be a better resource for women in poverty who are seeking job training. Similarly, principles guiding custody decisions for divorced heterosexual women might not apply to divorced lesbian, bisexual, or transgender women. It is only through an examination of questions relevant to all types of women that societal interventions can best address the diversity of women's needs.

Although there is less information available about ethnic minority women, working-class and poor women, women with disabilities, sexual minority women, and older women, it is essential that psychologists incorporate the knowledge base that does exist into their teaching (Basow, 2010a; Sprague, 2016). This diversity focus in their teaching will better prepare students to function in a culturally pluralistic and global society. Focusing on diversity also helps demonstrate to students how culture, marginalization, and privilege have formed their own experiences (Brabeck, 2016).

Socialization of Children

Another approach to developing greater flexibility in gender construction is the feminist socialization of children. Parents can bring up their children so that preferences and skills, rather than gender, are the defining characteristics that guide development. How can this be achieved? Read Learn About the Research 15.1 to examine a feminist perspective on this topic.

What would be the outcomes of gender-flexible upbringing? First, it would expand the range of activities, behaviors, and roles from which the child and, later, the adult could choose.

LEARN ABOUT THE RESEARCH 15.1
Why and How Should We Raise Feminist Children?

What does it mean to raise a feminist child? One answer is the elimination of all gender-related traits, behaviors, and roles, that is, raising children so that gender is irrelevant. However, this probably would not be possible. Children are exposed to influences beyond the home. Consequently, even if parents were to treat their daughters and sons identically, these children would continue to be exposed to other people for whom gender was important.

Instead, feminists such as Christy Spears Brown (2014), Jo Paoletti (2013), and Melissa Atkins Wardy (2014) advocate raising children to be gender flexible, that is, to select activities and behaviors on the basis of "individual likes and skills rather than gender stereotypes." They note

that because much gender learning takes place during the preschool years, several actions by the parents can play an important role. One is role modeling. For example, maternal employment and nontraditional division of household labor by parents can help develop less stereotypic expectations and behaviors in children. Furthermore, the kinds of activities and goals encouraged by the parents can be instrumental. As examples, discouragement of gender stereotypic activities, toys, and future aspirations can be effective. Also, Brown and Wardy note that limiting the amount of television children can watch might be beneficial because there is some evidence that children who watch less television have less stereotypic conceptions of gender.

WHAT DOES IT MEAN?

1. Do you think that the development of gender flexibility is a positive goal? Explain your answer.

2. Brown and Wardy suggest it might not be possible to eliminate all gender-stereotypic influences on children. Do you agree or disagree? Explain your answer.

3. Regardless of your own opinion about gender flexibility, use the knowledge you have gained from this course to suggest other factors besides parental behaviors that might facilitate its development in children and adolescents.

Instead of assuming, for example, that men make dating decisions, pay for dates, and initiate sex (Chapter 8), whichever dating partner was more comfortable with these behaviors could select them. Furthermore, these might vary depending on the circumstances. This, in turn, could lead to more egalitarian relationships because decision making and instrumental behaviors would not be relegated specifically to men. Similarly, women and men would make occupational choices on the basis of skills, interests, and personal needs without consideration of the gender appropriateness of the field (Chapter 10), a process that might lead to greater occupational prestige and salaries for women and to greater job satisfaction for both genders.

Second, given the higher status of the male role in North American society, gender flexibility would lead boys to develop a greater understanding and respect for behaviors and roles traditionally associated with females. If boys observe their fathers and other influential adult men performing traditional female behaviors, such as washing the dishes and caring for young children, and if boys are required to perform these chores, they will be more apt to view the traditional female role as worthy and dignified. The far-reaching implications are, of course, that when these boys grow up to be men, the values instilled in them in childhood will influence their own involvement in traditional female activities and increase their respect for others who perform such activities. This greater respect could, in turn, carry over to the workplace, where more familiarity with family-related activities might encourage the initiation and support of additional family-friendly policies.

Third, gender flexibility would minimize the extent to which people view and evaluate others on the basis of a rigid construction of gender. For example, girls who play sports would receive the same degree of encouragement as sports-oriented boys (Chapter 4) and women in blue-collar trades would be accepted rather than harassed by their coworkers (Chapter 14). People would evaluate mothers who voluntarily stay home to care for their children or those who elect to work full time in the same way as they would evaluate fathers in these roles. They would have the same reaction to women and men who are fiercely independent and to those who are highly dependent. That is, if children were brought up with a feminist perspective of equality, their impressions of others would be influenced by their behaviors and roles rather than by the perceived suitability of those behaviors for individuals of one gender or the other, and the choice of roles, for everyone, would be limitless.

Institutional Procedures

Another route for attaining feminist goals is for institutions to initiate practices that reduce gender inequality and that create hospitable environments for both women and men. In Chapters 10 and 11, we examined organizational procedures that improve working conditions for women (e.g., pay equity, affirmative action) or that facilitate balancing of family and work (e.g., flextime, child care assistance programs). Institutional initiatives can enhance the quality of life for women in other ways as well. Raising public awareness of women's issues on a community-wide basis, with stakeholders including educators, religious organizations, media, and health care institutions among others, is critical (Launius & Hassel, 2015; Sen, 2017). For example, Bonnie Fisher and her colleagues (Fisher et al., 2010) propose several college campus interventions that can lower the risk of sexual victimization and assist women who have experienced it.

First, Fisher and her associates emphasize the importance of education in changing the traditional culture of the campus. They suggest that the curriculum should include an examination and reconceptualization of gender roles, prevention of substance abuse, and exploration of rape myths. This type of curriculum would expose students to problems inherent in traditional gender-related behaviors and roles, would make them more sensitive to the experiences and pressures of the other gender, and would make them aware of the nature of and influences on violence against women.

Second, the researchers state that female students must be protected against sexual predators. This can include measures such as escort services, key cards at residence halls, call boxes, extra lighting, and self-defense training.

Third, Fisher and her colleagues address ways that counseling and health care services on campus can more effectively treat women who have been victimized. They stress the importance of campus policy and health care providers having adequate training in treating the physical and mental health problems that arise from sexual victimization. These campus personnel must be sensitive to victims' needs and be able to offer effective medical treatment as well as appropriate referrals for psychological counseling or legal assistance.

Individual Actions

Many women seek to achieve success and better their own lives through individual efforts. In fact, consistent with a traditional North American value system that applauds individualism, many American women place greater emphasis on their own hard work in improving their lives than on women's collective efforts (Kelly, 2015; Trask, 2014). These women believe that women's personal effort and success today, more than changes in organizational or governmental policies and practices, will lead to better opportunities for future generations of women, and they are willing to work hard, assert their rights, seek out opportunities for advancement, and make sacrifices if necessary. This is the approach sometimes called "neoliberalism" (see Chapter 1).

Collective Action

Contrary to the individual approach, many feminists contend that collective action is necessary in order to achieve significant improvement in women's lives (Armstrong, 2014; Wallace, 2015). This does not imply that women should not work hard to attain personal goals. However, it does mean that women, both individually and in groups, should strive to empower all women, not just themselves; they should advocate for social change, not just personal betterment. Furthermore, these collective efforts should address the concerns of diverse groups of women.

One woman who has made a difference in the lives of many other women is Catherine Hamlin, an Australian-born surgeon who has spent over 40 years in Ethiopia repairing fistulas, which are seriously ripped tissues resulting from female genital cutting. She and her husband founded a fistula hospital, which has treated thousands of women.

Three other wonderful examples of women who have made a difference are the winners of the Nobel Peace Prize in 2011. Ellen Johnson Sirleaf, Africa's first woman to win a free presidential election, has worked for peace and reconciliation in her country, Liberia. Leymah Gbowee helped end a 14-year civil war in Liberia, organizing Christian and Muslim women into a peace movement. The third Nobel awardee, Tawakkol Karman, is a Yemeni journalist, activist, and politician who has fought human rights violations (Comas-Diaz, 2012).

Girls and women also work together in groups, taking up the banner of collective activism to advocate for social change. They are fighting for issues such as immigrant rights, protections against violence, increased spending on education, and taking on corporate sexist practices (Armstrong, 2014; Taft, 2010). As one example, Native American women have led a tribal grassroots movement to increase the safety of Native women through the passage and 2013 reauthorization of the Violence Against Women Act and the Tribal Law and Order Act (Agtuca & Sayneyah, 2014). Another group using collective activism is India's Gulabi Gang, rural women in pink saris who use civil disobedience techniques to fight political corruption and an entrenched patriarchal system that condones domestic violence and rape. They have helped to release wrongly imprisoned women and regain pensions for widows (Fontanella-Khan, 2013). Or take the example of a group of girls, ages 13 to 16, who protested against Abercrombie and Fitch (A&F) tee shirts printed with demeaning slogans such as "Who needs a brain when you have these?" The girls worked with the Women and Girls Foundation of Southern Pennsylvania to organize a "girlcott" of A&F that drew national media attention and led A&F to withdraw the shirts from stores (APA Task Force, 2007). See What You Can Do 15.1 for ways you can become an advocate for change.

Liberian President Ellen Johnson Sirleaf (right), Yemeni human rights activist Tawakkol Karman (center), and Liberian activist Leymah Gbowee (left) were jointly awarded the 2011 Nobel Peace Prize for advancing freedom and women's rights in their countries.

WHAT YOU CAN DO 15.1
Become an Advocate

1. Volunteer to help a woman's organization in your community.
2. Go to Amnesty International's Website, http://www.amnesty.org, and take action

   to support a currently imprisoned women's rights activist.
3. Participate in hashtag activism.

FEMINIST MOVEMENTS IN THE UNITED STATES.   The feminist movement in the United States, a collective movement aimed at enhancing women's lives, was focused initially on the needs of White, middle-class, heterosexual, able-bodied women and has been criticized for failing to deal with unique problems faced by women of color, poor and working-class women, sexual minority women, and women with disabilities (Higgins, 2016; Trask, 2014; Vasiljevic et al., 2017). In the words of a Black college instructor and administrator, "Until very recently I did not call myself a feminist . . . even academic feminism did not include me until the 1980s. Feminism in the United States was pretty monolithic, pretty homogeneous . . . and so until recently, America did not embrace my experiences" (Kmiec et al., 1996, p. 58).

Although all women have certain experiences in common by virtue of their gender, other factors like racism, classism, ageism, heterosexism, and ableism contribute to double and triple jeopardies experienced by women who are not in the privileged group (Hill Collins & Bilge, 2016). Fortunately, the efforts of women of color, poor women, older women, sexual minority women, and women with disabilities have gradually expanded the feminist movement's perspective, and participation by previously excluded groups has increased (Spade & Valentine, 2016). This expansion of goals and inclusive participation must continue to grow. Attempts to achieve gender equality should concurrently strive to eradicate inequalities based on ethnicity, class, sexual orientation, ableness, and age. Only the collective efforts of diverse groups of women working together for the elimination of all types of power inequality can provide a brighter future for all girls and women.

 WOMEN'S MOVEMENTS WORLDWIDE.   Until recently, feminist academics from the Western world focused on the largely middle-class women's movements in the United States and Europe. However, women in the non-Western world, many of them poor, also have had their own long history of battling for women's rights. Because cultures differ, the struggle does not always focus on the same set of issues that have mobilized Western feminists (Armstrong, 2014; Baksh & Harcourt, 2015; Enns, 2015). In addition to women's movements that exist in individual countries, there is also an international women's movement, known as transnational feminism (Baksh & Harcourt, 2015). This movement advocates for political and social equality across nations, while at the same time recognizing the diversity of women's lives and cultures. The transnational feminist movement is working to challenge violence against women, expand the education of girls, support women's reproductive and sexual freedom, increase women's political power, and champion women's access to health care and economic independence (Armstrong, 2014; Baksh & Harcourt, 2015; Spade & Valentine, 2016; Trask, 2014). The United Nations has attempted to play a leadership role in this effort. In 1979, it issued a treaty known as the Convention on the Elimination of All Forms of Discrimination Against Women. Out of 193 nations, only 7 have not ratified the treaty. The nonratifying countries are Iran, Sudan, South Sudan, Somalia, two small Pacific islands—and the United States (Feminist Majority Foundation, 2014). Why do you think the United States is the only developed nation to not ratify the treaty?

Given that some women ascribe to beliefs in equality but are not oriented toward working for change for others, how can these women's motivation for social activism be enhanced? Communication with other women, learning about the experiences and problems of other women, and exposure to varied situations that involve gender discrimination can broaden one's understanding of women's issues and encourage greater involvement in advocating for women's rights (Kirk & Okazawa-Rey, 2013). Taking women's studies courses, experiencing discrimination firsthand, and having a mother who is a feminist also are linked to students' participation in collective action (Liss et al., 2004).

The Internet has revolutionized the way women organize and act collectively. To learn more about how the Internet has affected women's activism, read In the News 15.1.

IN THE NEWS 15.1
The Internet Revolutionizes Women's Activism

The Internet has revolutionized the way women organize and act collectively. The use of e-mail, Websites, Listservs, search engines, and social media has improved communication for all groups, but it has been especially important in linking women's groups, which tend to be small and often isolated from each other (Anid et al., 2016; Baer, 2016; Baksh & Harcourt, 2015; Scharff et al., 2016). Media campaigns that originate in particular cultural contexts may go viral online, as in the recent example of the SlutWalk protest against sexual violence (Mendes, 2015). Girls, many of them bloggers and avid users of social media, are increasingly involved in feminist activism online and in their communities (Keller, 2016). One example of the effectiveness of social media in advancing feminist objectives was initiated by 14-year-old Julia Bluhm, who started an online petition requesting that *Seventeen* magazine stop using Photoshopped images of women and girls. She argued that such images can lead girls to develop unhealthy body images and disordered eating behaviors. The petition gathered over 80,000 signatures, received intense media coverage, and resulted in a pledge by *Seventeen* magazine to never change girls' body or face shapes when retouching images (Homayoun, 2013). Have you ever signed a petition that advocated for a feminist cause?

Do feminist goals presented here for the future coincide with your perspectives and those of your acquaintances? Try Get Involved 15.1 to explore students' fantasies about their ideal futures.

GET INVOLVED 15.1
A Perfect Future Day

Imagine what you would like your life to be like 10 years in the future. Write a paragraph describing what your ideal typical day would be like. Also, ask one same-gender and two other-gender students to perform the same exercise.

WHAT DOES IT MEAN?

Read through the four descriptions and record similarities and differences about the following: (1) marital status, (2) presence of children, (3) if married or in a long-term partnership, family responsibilities of each spouse, (4) employment status, (5) if employed, gender dominance of the occupation, and (6) leisure activities.

1. Do the descriptions written by the women differ from those written by the men in relation to these or any other topics? If yes, use information learned in this course to explain these differences.

2. Are there any current gender-based expectations about interpersonal or societal roles and behaviors that might hinder your own ideal life from becoming a reality? If yes, what kinds of changes do you think would reduce this impediment? Would you be interested in working for this change?

_____

Source: Based on Kerr (1999).

FEMINIST BELIEFS

We began the text with a discussion of the meaning of feminism, and now we come full circle, back to this topic. Because the goals we have presented and many of the actions taken to achieve these goals are rooted in a feminist perspective, it is important to explore the prevalence and accuracy of feminist beliefs.

Although most North Americans believe that feminism has had a positive impact on women's attainment of greater economic, political, and legal opportunities, a relatively small number have argued that feminists are the root of numerous personal and social problems and are responsible for the decline of the "traditional" North American family (Anderson, 2014; Faludi, 2007). Many feminists are, indeed, disturbed about the subordination of women within *patriarchal* families where husbands hold the power and dictate the activities of wives and children (Coontz, 2016; Kirk & Okazawa-Rey, 2013), but they are supportive of egalitarian families in which husbands and wives share power and respect. It is untrue to say that most feminists oppose the notion of the family—they oppose the notion of an unequal family.

Another accusation made by some antifeminists is that feminists hate men. While it is true that many feminists object to male power that has oppressed women in the workplace, government, education, and the home (Launius & Hassel, 2015), an objection to male *privilege* should not be confused with an objection to men per se.

Sadly, these antifeminist beliefs not only dangerously distort the truth but also discredit feminist ideology. Given that most North Americans are strongly profamily and that males have high status and respect within society, the depiction of feminists as antifamily male-bashers sets them up for ridicule and makes it easier to dismiss their beliefs as extremist (Tomlinson, 2010). What are your thoughts on feminism? Perform Get Involved 15.2 to reassess your views.

Feminist Identification

Although support for the women's movement has increased steadily since the mid-1970s, the proportion of American women who identify themselves as feminists remains low (Redford et al., 2016; Rhode et al., 2014).

According to nationwide polls and studies of college students (Duncan, 2010; Fitz et al., 2012), only about 25 to 30 percent of American women label themselves as feminists, and the percentage of men is even lower. Furthermore, college women of color and working-class White women are less likely than middle-class White college women to label themselves as feminists (Aronson, 2003; Myaskovsky & Wittig, 1997). As stated earlier, the feminist movement has been dominated by White women, and some women of color feel that feminists do not have an interest in their unique experiences and concerns (Bryant-Davis & Comas-Diaz, 2016). Some women of color, therefore, have embraced women of color feminism or mujerista psychology forms of feminism that, as we saw in Chapter 1, addresses racism and other issues of importance to ethnic minority females. Another problem for some women of color is the perception of conflict between the values embraced by their ethnic group and values associated with feminist ideology. For example, Latina women may feel torn between the more patriarchal belief system of their cultures and the feminist value of egalitarianism (Bryant-Davis & Comas-Diaz, 2016).

Interestingly, many women who reject the feminist label support the goals of feminism (Charter, 2015; Fitz et al., 2012; Redford et al., 2016; Rhode et al., 2014). Alyssa Zucker (Bay-Cheng & Zucker, 2007) refers to this group of women as "egalitarians." How can these discrepancies between a feminist identification and views about feminist goals be explained? First, women may be concerned about negative images that some people attach to feminism and feminists. At a personal level, they might want to avoid a negative self-image, which they believe would result from identifying themselves with a term that has negative connotations. At a public level, they might fear the social disapproval that could follow from their identification as a feminist (Moradi et al., 2012; Radke et al., 2016; Swirsky & Angelone, 2014, 2015). One negative image, that of feminists as anti-male, was illustrated in Chapter 1 by a student's definition of feminist as "a big, bra-burning

GET INVOLVED 15.2
How Do You View Feminism?

Answer the following questions without looking back at the answers you gave in Chapter 1. First, indicate which of the following categories best characterizes your identity as a feminist.

  a. consider myself a feminist and am currently involved in the women's movement
  b. consider myself a feminist but am not involved in the women's movement
  c. do not consider myself a feminist but agree with at least some of the objectives of feminism
  d. do not consider myself a feminist and disagree with the objectives of feminism.

Second, on a scale from 1 (strongly disagree) to 6 (strongly agree), indicate the extent to which you disagree or agree with each of the following statements.

  1. Women should be considered as seriously as men as candidates for the presidency of the United States.

  2. Although women can be good leaders, men make better leaders.
  3. A woman should have the same job opportunities as a man.
  4. Men should respect women more than they currently do.
  5. Many women in the workforce are taking jobs away from men who need the jobs more.
  6. Doctors need to take women's health concerns more seriously.
  7. Women have been treated unfairly on the basis of their gender throughout most of human history.
  8. Women are already given equal opportunities with men in all important sectors of their lives.
  9. Women in the United States are treated as second-class citizens.
  10. Women can best overcome discrimination by doing the best they can at their jobs, not by wasting time with political activity.

WHAT DOES IT MEAN?

Before computing your score for the 10 items, reverse the points for statements 2, 5, 8, and 10. That is, for a rating of "1" (strongly disagree), give 6 points, for a rating of "2," give 5 points, and so on. Then sum the points for the 10 items. Note that higher scores reflect greater agreement with feminist beliefs.

  1. Compare your feminist identification (Part I) here with your feminist identification at the

beginning of the course (see Get Involved 1.1). If there has been a change, explain why.

  2. Compare your feminist beliefs at the two points in time. If there has been a change, explain why. What specific course material, if any, contributed to this change?

_____

Source: Based on Morgan (1996).

man-hater" (Anderson, 2014). Still others equate feminism with being unfeminine and physically unattractive, using terms such as "militant," "violent," "fat," and "butch" (Leaper & Arias, 2011; Radke et al., 2016). Given the perception that feminists are overly masculine, it is not surprising that women who rate themselves high in femininity are more likely to reject the "feminist" label than women who rate themselves high in masculinity (Toller et al., 2004). Along these same lines, college students respond more favorably to a profeminist message when it is presented by a feminine-appearing speaker than by a masculine-appearing speaker (Bullock & Fernald, 2003), a phenomenon referred to as "feminism lite."

A second reason that some women refuse to identify as feminists despite their agreement with many feminist goals is that they believe that gender equality has already been achieved (Radke et al., 2016; Swirsky & Angelone, 2014, 2015). Illustrating this view, college women who believe that women are disadvantaged relative to men are more likely to participate in activities that enhance the status of women (e.g., talking about women's issues with others, attending talks on women's issues, joining protests). Women who perceive fewer gender differences in social conditions are less likely to be involved in activism (Foster, 1999).

A third reason some women do not label themselves as feminists is because they associate feminism with collective political activism, whereas they personally favor individual actions in everyday life as a way to achieve feminist goals. Recent research (Radke et al., 2016; Redford et al., 2016; Rhode et al., 2014) does, in fact, show that women who label themselves as feminists are more likely to engage in increased activism on behalf of women.

Today, the increased visibility of feminism within popular media cultures means that more teens are hearing about feminism and perhaps will adopt a feminist identity in the company of influential celebrities such as Beyoncé, Lorde, and Emma Watson (Hamad & Taylor, 2015).

Emergence of Feminist Beliefs

During this class, I feel my eyes have been opened to what not just women in general, but ethnic, young, old, and disabled women go through every day. . . . Before I took this class, I thought I was aware of all the issues women face. Boy, was I wrong! (Shawna, a 21-year-old senior)

Before this course, I thought some women made too big a deal over women's rights issues. My eyes have been so opened, and now I am extremely sensitized to gender issues in society. I actively try to educate people on gender inequality of power and social construction of gender. I am really going to try to raise very gender-flexible children. In a way, I feel like I stepped out of the dark into the light. (Jessica, a 25-year-old senior)

One important route to feminist consciousness is enrollment in women's studies courses (Leaper & Arias, 2011; Marine & Lewis, 2014). Women's studies programs (some are now called gender studies) have proliferated since the early 1970s, and courses in these areas are a common feature on many college and university campuses around the world (Launius & Hassel, 2015; Norcross et al., 2016). These courses help foster feminist goals by providing students with the knowledge to transform society (Berger & Radeloff, 2015; Henry, 2014). Similar to the experiences of Shawna and Jessica (section-opening vignettes), and Julie (chapter-opening vignette), studies have shown that women's studies courses are instrumental in decreasing gender-stereotypic attitudes (Bryant, 2003; Case, 2007) and increasing commitment to feminism and social justice (Nelson et al., 2008; Swirsky & Angelone, 2015; Yoder, 2015). Furthermore, women's studies and gender studies courses can encourage activism. Students who take such courses, compared to those who do not, become more active in feminist activities and make more changes in their own roles and/or ways of interacting with others. Moreover, these changes last over time (Kirkup et al., 2015; Stake, 2007). Exposure to feminism in other ways can also give rise to feminist identity. For example, feminists are more likely than other women to have a feminist mother or sister (Nelson et al., 2008) or a mother who encourages pursuit of both feminine and masculine domains (Colaner & Rittenour, 2015). But even simply reading a paragraph containing positive statements about feminists increases the likelihood that women will identify themselves as feminist (Roy et al., 2007).

A second route toward feminism involves personal experiences women have that make them painfully aware that they live in a sexist society. For example, experiencing sexual harassment or rape is associated with increased support for feminism and women's rights activism (Ayres et al., 2009; Marine & Lewis, 2014; Nelson et al., 2008; Swirsky & Angelone, 2015). For some women, social or historical events such as the *Roe v. Wade* Supreme Court decision on abortion rights, attending NOW (National Organization for Women) meetings, or reading Betty Friedan's book *The Feminine Mystique* (1963) shaped their feminist identity (Coontz, 2011).

Whatever a woman's route to feminism, studies show that women who identify as feminists have greater psychological well-being than other women (Kinsaul et al., 2014; Matheson & Foster, 2013; Zucker & Bay-Cheng, 2010). They also show greater resilience in the face of negative experiences such as sexual harassment (Holland et al., 2015). This may result from a sense of greater independence and personal empowerment on the part of feminist women.

To assess your own involvement in feminist activism, try Get Involved 15.3.

Men and Feminism

Various men's movements have developed in recent years, partly as a response to the women's movement. The mythopoetic movement started by Robert Bly (1990) emphasizes men reconnecting with each other through rituals and retreats. Two religiously based movements of the late 1990s are the Promise Keepers, a Christian fundamentalist group, and the Million Man March, a Black men's group. Both of these movements seek to bring men back into the family, certainly a desirable objective. However, the underlying theme is a return to the traditional roles of men as leaders and women as followers (Kimmel et al., 2001).

Other men work within a feminist framework as part of the profeminist movement, which supports equality of women and men in all spheres of life, both professional and personal, and is redefining traditional ideas about manhood and fatherhood (Farr, 2013; Kimball et al., 2013; Messner et al., 2015; Okun, 2014; Van Der Gaag, 2014). Since the 1970s profeminist men have initiated a number of organizations including the National Organization for Men Against Sexism (Kimmel, 2011), as

GET INVOLVED 15.3
How Involved in Feminist Activism Are You?

Check each of the following nine activities you engaged in during the six months before the beginning of this semester. Then check each activity you engaged in during this semester.

Before

___ kept informed on women's rights issues
___ talked with others to influence their attitudes about women's rights issues
___ signed a petition related to women's rights
___ attended a march, rally, or protest related to women's rights
___ wrote letters to politicians or newspapers about women's rights issues
___ contributed money to a women's rights cause or to politicians who supported such causes
___ circulated a petition about a women's rights cause
___ worked for a phone bank, letter writing campaign, or political campaign in the cause of women's rights
___ participated in online hashtag activity related to women's rights

During

___
___
___
___
___
___
___
___
___

WHAT DOES IT MEAN?

1. Has there been an increase in your feminist activities due to this course? If yes, indicate some of the information you learned that contributed to this change.
2. Which of the following types of activities do you believe is the preferable route toward increased rights and opportunities for women: individual effort alone or individual effort combined with collective action? Explain your answer.

Source: Based on Stake et al. (1994); Wallace (2015).

well as programs such as One in Four Men Against Sexual Assault, Men Stopping Violence, and Men Can Stop Rape, which focus on preventing violence against women (Okun, 2014; Pease, 2016; Thompson & Armato, 2012). The Global MenEngage alliance is a network of over 400 organizations, as well as individuals, working with men and boys to achieve gender equality, end violence, and promote women's empowerment (UN Women, 2014). One of the most successful profeminist organizations is the White Ribbon Campaign, which began in Canada in 1991 in response to the mass killing of 14 women engineering students at the University of Montreal by a deranged man. The campaign, whose slogan is "Men, working to end men's violence against women," has now spread to over 60 countries (Decker, 2014).

POSTSCRIPT

We end this exploration of women's lives with two cautionary notes. First, when thinking about the material in this text, keep in mind that the knowledge individuals have about the psychology of women is situated in a particular time in history. It is strongly connected to existing societal attitudes and to current political, economic, and legal events. As a result of economic and attitudinal changes in the last decades of the twentieth century and the first two decades of the twenty-first century, for example, a major concern for many married mothers today is the balancing of work and family. However, this issue would have been largely irrelevant to stay-at-home mothers in the 1960s. We can expect that some of the information presented here will become obsolete over time. In fact, if women are successful in their efforts, if legislative initiatives and workplace policies address gender inequities in power and opportunities, and if gender roles become more flexible, some current problems, such as wage differentials and sexual harassment, will, we hope, be eliminated.

Second, as discussed in Chapter 1, teaching does not take place in an ideological vacuum. Even if not explicitly stated, a particular set of values underlies all scholarly research, textbooks, and course content, and this book is no exception. Our (authors of this text) feminist values served as the basis for our examination of the lives of girls and women. Regardless of your own commitment to these beliefs, we hope your exploration of the psychology of women has been an enriching experience and that you have achieved an increased understanding of the negative effects of male privilege, a greater appreciation of women's intersecting identities and diversity, and a greater awareness of the role that interpersonal and societal forces play in shaping gender-based attitudes, behaviors, and goals. And, we sincerely hope you apply what you have learned from this text and course to other academic interests, career pursuits, your own experiences, and perhaps to societal change.

Summary

FEMINIST GOALS

- Greater gender equality of organizational and interpersonal power would benefit women in several ways by increasing opportunities in the workplace, giving women a greater voice in dating relationships, creating a more equitable division of household labor, and reducing intimate violence. It is essential that increases in women's power benefit all women, regardless of ethnicity, class, disability/ability, sexual orientation, or age.
- The benefits of a flexible construction of gender include behavior and role choices that reflect individual preferences instead of social expectations, as well as a reduction in sexual harassment and acquaintance rape.

ACTIONS TO ACHIEVE THESE GOALS

- Several actions can facilitate the achievement of these goals including a diversity-oriented psychology of women that can inform about the role of male privilege and the constraints of rigid gender roles, and enhance one's understanding of diversity and increase tolerance.
- Raising gender-flexible children would free people to make personally appropriate choices, rather than those based on gender-role expectations. Additionally, it would help foster greater appreciation of women's traditional roles and lessen the tendency to evaluate others on the basis of their conformity to gender expectations.

- Interventions by societal institutions, as well as the media, can address violence against women.
- Some women believe that they can enhance their own lives more through their individual efforts than as a result of collective action.
- Many feminists believe that improvement of the lives of women requires collective action. However, the feminist movement has been focused more on the lives of privileged women than on those who experience double and triple jeopardies stemming from racism, classism, ageism, homophobia, and/or ableism.

FEMINIST BELIEFS

- North Americans have mixed views about the value of feminism. Some believe it has helped women. Others believe that feminists are responsible for many personal and social problems.
- Only 25 percent of U.S. women label themselves as feminists. Some of the women who do not identify themselves as feminists

support the goals of feminism. Reasons for this discrepancy include negative images of feminists, the assumption that women have already attained power equality, and the belief that feminism implies collective action.
- Women's studies courses tend to decrease students' gender-stereotypic attitudes and increase their commitment to feminism and activism.
- Various profeminist men's movement's have developed in recent years, including Global MenEngage, the National Organization for Men against Sexism, and the White Ribbon campaign.

POSTSCRIPT

- Current knowledge about women's lives is situated in this historical period.
- This textbook is grounded in feminist values that emphasize women's intersecting identities and diversity, the importance of empowering girls and women, and the critical role of interpersonal and social forces in constructing gender.

What Do You Think?

1. The text presented greater equality of power and greater flexibility in the construction of gender as beneficial to girls and women. Do you think there are any disadvantages for females associated with these goals? In what ways would these goals benefit males? In what ways might they be detrimental to males?
2. Which one or more of the various strategies for improving women's lives do you think would be most effective? Explain your answer.

If You Want to Learn More

Armstrong, S. (2014). *Uprising: A new age is dawning for every woman's daughter*. New York: St. Martin's Press.

Baksh, R. & Harcourt, W. (2015). *The Oxford handbook of transnational feminist movements*. New York: Oxford University Press.

Bates, L. (2016). *Everyday feminism*. New York: St. Martin's Press.

Chesler, E. & McGovern, T. (2016). *Women and girls rising: Progress and resistance around the world*. New York: Routledge.

Cobble, D.S., Gordon, L., & Henry, A. (2014). *Feminism unfinished: A short, surprising history of American women's movements*. New York: W.W. Norton.

Fraser, T. & Hagel, C. (2016). *Girl positive: Supporting girls to shape a new world*. Canada: Random House Canada.

Marso, L.J. (2016). *Fifty-one key feminist thinkers*. New York: Routledge.

Martin, J., Nickels, A.E., & Sharp-Grier, M. (2016). *Feminist pedagogy, practice, and activism: Improving lives for girls and women*. New York: Routledge.

McCann, C. & Kim, S. (2017). *Feminist theory reader: Local and global perspectives*. New York: Routledge.

Okun, R.A. (Ed.). (2014). *Voice male: The untold story of the pro-feminist men's movement*. Northampton, MA: Interlink.

Ortenblad, A., Marling, R., & Vasiljevic, S. (Eds.). (2017). *Gender equality in a global perspective*. New York: Routledge.

Ross, M.E. (2015). *She takes a stand: 16 fearless women who have changed the world*. Chicago: Chicago Review Press.

Scharff, C. et al., (2016). *Digital feminism: Transnational activism in German protest cultures*. New York: Routledge.

van der Gaag, N. (2014). *Feminism and men*. London: Zed Books.

Zheng, J. (2016). *New feminism in China: Young middle-class Chinese women in Shanghai*. New York: Springer.

Zoepf, K. (2016). *Excellent daughters: The secret lives of young women who are transforming the Arab world*. New York: Penguin Press.

Websites

Feminism

feminist.com http://www.feminist.com/
http://www.theestablishment.com/aboutus/
http://everydayfeminism.com
https://femwoc.com
http://feministing.com
https://femsplain.com
http://www.global-briefing.org/2015/01/feminism-is-men-too/

Advocating for Change

http://therepresentationproject.org
http://sparksummit.org
http://iknowpolitics.org/sites/default/files/feminist_advocacy_guide_awid_2.pdf

REFERENCES

A pill to boost female libido. (2015, June 22). *New York Times,* p. A22.

AARP. (2004, Winter). *The GIC Voice,* p. 11.

AARP. (2006). *Medicare at 40: Past accomplishments and future challenges.* Washington, DC: Author.

AARP. (2012). *Insights and spending habits of modern grandparents.* Washington, DC: Author.

AAUW. (2008). *Where the girls are: The facts about gender equity in education.* Washington, DC: Author.

AAUW. (2010). *Why so few? Women in science, technology, engineering, and mathematics.* Washington, DC: Author.

AAUW (2011) *Crossing the line: Sexual harassment at school.* Washington DC: Author.

AAUW. (2014, Winter). Coming out at work. *AAUW Outlook,* 6–9.

AAUW. (2016). *Barriers and bias: The status of women in leadership.* Washington, DC: Author.

AAUW (2017, Spring). *The simple truth about the gender pay gap.* Washington, DC: Author.

Abbey, A. et al. (2014). Review of survey and experimental research that examines the relationship between alcohol consumption and men's sexual aggression perpetration. *Trauma, Violence, & Abuse, 15,* 265–282.

Abbey, A. D., Jacques-Tiura, A. J., & Parkhill, M. R. (2010). Sexual assault among diverse populations of women: Common ground, distinctive features, and unanswered questions. In H. Landrine & N. F. Russo (Eds.), *Handbook of diversity in feminist psychology* (pp. 391–425). New York: Springer.

Abdessamad, H. M. et al. (2013). Attitudes and knowledge among obstetrician-gynecologists regarding lesbian patients and their health. *Journal of Women's Health, 22,* 85–93.

Abeid, M. et al. (2015). Knowledge and attitude towards rape and child sexual abuse—a community-based cross-sectional study in rural Tanzania. *BMC Public Health, 15,* 1–13.

Abelsohn, K. A. et al. (2014). Celebrating the "other" parent: Mental health and wellness of expecting lesbian, bisexual, and queer non-birth parents. *Journal of Gay & Lesbian Mental Health, 17,* 387–405.

Abortion. (2010, March 7). *Gallup.* Retrieved from gallup.com/poll/1576/abortion.aspx

Abraczinskas, M. et al. (2012). The relation between parental influence, body image, and eating behaviors in a nonclinical female sample. *Body Image, 9,* 93–100.

Abrams, J. A. et al. (2016). Distant but relative: Similarities and differences in gender role beliefs among African American and Vietnamese American women. *Cultural Diversity and Ethnic Minority Psychology, 22,* 256–267.

Access to transgender medical care. (2015, December 9). *New York Times,* p. A30.

Ackard, D. M. et al. (2014). Poor outcome and death among youth, young adults, and midlife adults with eating disorders: An investigation of risk factors by age at assessment. *Journal of Eating Disorders, 47,* 825–835.

Acosta, R. V. & Carpenter, L. J. (2014). *Women in intercollegiate sport: A longitudinal, national study: Thirty-seven-year update.* West Brookfield, MA: Acosta/Carpenter.

Adams, A.E. et al. (2012). The impact of intimate partner violence on low-income women's economic well-being: The mediating role of job stability. *Violence Against Women, 18,* 1345–1367.

Adams, H. L. & Phillips, L. (2009). Ethnic related variations from the Cass Model of Homosexual Identity formation: The experiences of two-spirit, lesbian and gay Native American. *Journal of Homosexuality, 56,* 959–976.

Adams, P. F., Lucas, J. W., & Barnes, P. M. (2008). *Summary health statistics for the U.S. Population: National Health Interview Survey, 2006.* NCHS Vital Health Statistics, 10(236). Washington, DC: U.S. Government Printing Office.

Adams, R. & Moulton Belec, H. (2014, Fall). Contraception doesn't equal abortion: How birth control works. *AAUW Outlook,* 11–16.

Adelman, R. D. (2014). Care of the aging parent: From evidence to action. *Journal of the American Medical Association, 311,* 1052–1060.

Adelmann, P. K. (1993). Psychological well-being and homemaker vs. Retiree identity among older women. *Sex Roles, 29,* 195–212.

Agonito, J. (2016). *Brave Hearts: Indian women of the Plains.* Lanham, MD: TwoDot/Rowman & Littlefield.

Agrawal, S. (2012). The sociocultural context of family size preference, ideal sex composition, and induced abortion in India: Findings from India's National Family Health Surveys. *Health Care for Women International, 33,* 986–1019.

Agronin, M.E. (2014). Sexuality and aging. In Y. Binik & K. Hall (Eds.). *Principles and practice of sex therapy* (pp. 525–539). New York: Guilford.

Agtuca, J. & Sahneyah, D. (2014). *Safety for Native women; VAWA and American Indian tribes.* Lame Deer, MT: National Indigenous Women's Resource Center.

Aguinaga, A. & Gloria, A. M. (2015). The effects of generational status and university environment on Latina/o undergraduates' persistence decisions. *Journal of Diversity in Higher Education, 8,* 15–29.

Ahmad, M. & Naseer, H. (2015). Gender bias at workplace: Through sticky floor and glass ceiling: A comparative study of private and public organizations of Islamabad. *International Journal of Management and Business Research, 5,* 249–260.

Ahmed, S. et al. (2013). *Smokers who quit cut heart disease risk faster than previous estimates.* Paper presented at the annual meeting of the American Heart Association, Dallas, TX.

Ahmed, S. B. et al. (2004). Gender bias in cardiovascular advertisements. *Journal of Evaluation in Clinical Practice, 10,* 531.

Aichele, S. et al. (2016). Think fast, feel fine, live long: A 29-year study of cognition, health and survival in middle-aged and older adults. *Psychological Science,* doi: 10.1177/0956797615626906

Ainsworth, S. et al. (2014). Women constructing masculinity in voluntary firefighting. *Gender, Work and Organization, 21,* 46–47.

Ajeet, A. & Nandkishore, K. (2013). The boom in unnecessary caesarean surgeries is jeopardizing women's health. *Health Care for Women International, 34,* 513–521.

Akbulut, V. & Weger, H. (2016). Predicting responses to bids for sexual and romantic escalation in cross-sex friendships. *Journal of Social Psychology, 156,* 98–114.

Alberts, S.C. et al. (2014). The male-female health-survival paradox: A comparative perspective on sex differences in aging and mortality. In M Weinstein & M. Lane (Eds.). *Sociality, hierarchy, health: Comparative biodemography: A collection of papers.* (Paper 15). Washington, DC: National Academies Press.

Alcohol and pregnancy. (2016). Atlanta, GA: Centers for Disease Control and Prevention.

Alexander, K. (2004, April 13). Grandma finds a job, looking after junior. *New York Times,* p. E2.

Alexander, L.L. et al. (2017). *New dimensions of women's health* (7th ed.). Sudbury, MA: Jones and Bartlett.

Alfieri, T., Ruble, D. N., & Higgins, E. T. (1996). Gender stereotypes during adolescence: Developmental changes and the transition to junior high school. *Developmental Psychology, 32,* 1129–1137.

Ali, A. et al. (2017). Women and depressive disorders. In M. Kopala & M. Keitel (Eds.), *Handbook of counseling women* (2nd ed., pp. 435–448). Thousand Oaks, CA: Sage.

Alkema, L. et al. (2016). Global, regional, and national levels and trends in maternal mortality between 1990 and 2015, with scenario-based projections to 2030: A systematic analysis by the UN Maternal Mortality Estimation Inter-Agency Group. *The Lancet, 387,* 462–474.

Allen, J. (2016, May). Why women's colleges are still needed. *University Business.* Retrieved from universitybusiness.com/article/why-womens-colleges-are-still-needed

Allen, K. R. & Chin-Sang, V. (1990). A lifetime of work: The context and meanings of leisure for aging black women. *Gerontologist, 30,* 734–740.

Allen, K. R. & Roberto, K. A. (2016). Family relationships of older LGBT adults. In D. A. Harley & P. B. Teaster (Eds.), *Handbook of LGBT elders: An interdisciplinary approach to principles, practices, and policies* (pp. 43–64). Switzerland: Springer International Publishing.

Allen, K. R. & Walker, A. J. (2009). Theorizing about families and aging from a feminist perspective. In V. Bengtson, M. Silverstein, N. M. Putney, & D. Gans (Eds.), *Handbook of theories of aging* (2nd ed., pp. 517–528). New York: Springer.

Allen, R. E. & Wiles, J. L. (2014). How older people position their late-life childlessness: A qualitative study. *Journal of Marriage and Family, 75,* 206–220.

Allen, T. D. et al. (2014). Work-family boundary dynamics. *The Annual Review of Organizational Psychology And Organizational Behavior, 1,* 99–121.

Allerhand, M. et al. (2014). The dynamic relationship between cognitive function and positive well-being in older people: A prospective study using the English longitudinal study of aging. *Psychology and Aging, 29,* 306–318.

Allison, C. M. & Hyde, J. S. (2013). Early menarche: Confluence of biological and contextual factors. *Sex Roles, 68,* 55–64.

Allison, D. C. (2016). *Black women's portrayals on reality television: The new Sapphire.* New York: Lexington Books.

Alloy, L. B. et al. (2016). Pubertal development, emotional, regulatory styles, and the emergence of sex differences in internalizing disorders and symptoms in adolescence. *Clinical Psychological Science, 4,* 867–881.

Almeling, R. (2015). Reproduction. *Annual Review of Sociology, 41,* 423–442.

Almy, B. et al. (2015). Perceptions of siblings' sexual activity predict sexual attitudes among at-risk adolescents. *Journal of Developmental and Behavioral Pediatrics, 36,* 258–266.

Al-Safi, Z.A. & Santoro, N. (2014). Menopausal hormone therapy and menopausal symptoms. *Fertility and Sterility, 101,* 905–915.

Alteri, R. et al. (2013). *Breast cancer basic facts & figures 2013–2014.* Atlanta, GA: American Cancer Society, Inc.

Alterovitz, S. S. & Mendelsohn, G. A. (2009). Partner preferences across the life span: Online dating by older adults. *Psychology and Aging, 24,* 513–517.

Altmaier, E. M. et al. (2013). Health, psychology, social class, and counseling. In W. M. Liu (Ed.), *Oxford handbook of social class in counseling.* New York: Oxford University Press.

Altuntug, K. et al. (2014). An investigation of sexual/reproductive health issues in women with physical disability. *Sexuality & Disability, 32,* 221–229.

Alvarez-Segura, M. et al. (2014). Are women with a history of abuse more vulnerable to perinatal depressive symptoms? A systematic review. *Archives of Women's Mental Health, 17,* 343–357.

Alvy, L. (2013). Do lesbian women have a better body image? Comparisons with heterosexual women and model of lesbian-specific factors. *Body Image, 9,* 524–534.

Alzheimer's Association. (2014). *2014 Alzheimer's Disease facts and figures.* New York: Author.

Amato, P. R. (2000). The consequences of divorce for adults and children. *Journal of Marriage and the Family, 62,* 1269–1287.

Amato, P. R. & Anthony, C. J. (2014).Estimating the effects of parental divorce and death with fixed effects models. *Journal of Marriage and Family, 76,* 370–386.

Ambady, N. & Weisbuch, M. (2010). Nonverbal behavior. In S. T. Fiske, D. T. Gilbert, & G. Lindzey (Eds.), *Handbook of social psychology* (5th ed., Vol. 1, pp. 464–497). Hoboken, NJ: Wiley.

American Academy of Pediatrics. (2012). Emergency contraception. *Pediatrics, 130,* 1174–1182.

American Cancer Society. (2013). *Menopausal hormone therapy and cancer risk.* Atlanta, GA.

American Cancer Society. (2014). *Ovarian cancer.* Atlanta, GA: Author.

American Cancer Society. (2015). *Endometrial (uterine) cancer.* Atlanta, GA: Author.

American Cancer Society. (2015–2016). *Breast cancer facts and figures 2015–2016.* Atlanta, GA: Author.

American Cancer Society. (2016a). *Cancer facts and figures 2016.* Atlanta, GA: Author.

American Cancer Society. (2016b). *Reach to recovery.* Atlanta, GA: Author.

American Cancer Society. (2016c). Treating breast cancer. Atlanta, GA: Author.

American College of Obstetricians and Gynecologists. (2014). Female age-related fertility decline. *Fertility and Sterility, 101,* 633–634.

American College of Obstetricians and Gynecologists. (2015). *Frequently asked questions.* Retrieved from acog.org

American Council on Education. (2016). *Pipelines, pathways, and institutional leadership: An update on the status of women in higher education.* Washington, DC: Author.

American Heart Association. (2014). *Go red for women 2014 fact sheet.* Washington, DC: Author.

American Heart Association. (2015). *Cardiovascular disease: Women's No. 1 health threat.* Washington DC: Author.

Amato, P. R. & Anthony, C. J. (2014).Estimating the effects of parental divorce and death with fixed effects models. *Journal of Marriage and Family, 76,* 370–386.

American Pregnancy Association (2017). *Morning sickness.* Irving TX: Author.

American Psychiatric Association. (1994). *Diagnostic and statistical manual of mental disorders* (4th ed.). Washington, DC: Author.

American Psychiatric Association. (2013). *Diagnostic and statistical manual of mental orders* (5th ed.). Arlington, VA: Author.

American Psychological Association. (1975). Report of the task force on sex bias and sex-role stereotyping in psychotherapeutic practice. *American Psychologist, 30,* 1169–1175.

American Psychological Association. (2002). *Developing adolescents: A reference for professionals.* Washington, DC: Author.

American Psychological Association. (2004). Guidelines for psychological practice with older adults. *American Psychologist, 59,* 236–260.

American Psychological Association. (2007). Guidelines for psychological practice with girls and women. *American Psychologist, 62,* 949–979.

American Psychological Association. (2010). *Publication manual of the American Psychological Association* (6th ed.). Washington, DC: Author.

American Psychological Association. (2012). Guidelines for psychological practice with lesbian, gay, and bisexual clients. *American Psychologist, 67,* 10–42.

American Psychological Association. (2014). Guidelines for psychological practice with older adults. *American Psychologist, 69,* 34–65.

American Psychological Association. (2015a). Guidelines for psychological practice with transgender and gender nonconforming people. *American Psychologist, 70,* 832–864.

American Psychological Association. (2015b). *Mental and behavioral health and older Americans.* Washington, DC: Author.

American Psychological Association. (2016). *Discrimination linked to increased stress, poorer health, American Psychological Association survey finds.* Washington, DC: Author.

American Society for Reproductive Medicine. (2014). Female age-related fertility decline. *Fertility and Sterility, 101,* 633–634.

American Society of Plastic Surgeons. (2015). *Plastic surgery statistics report.* Arlington Hts. IL: Author.

Andersen, B. L. et al. (2008). Psychologic intervention improves survival in breast cancer patients. *Cancer, 113,* 3450–3458.

Anderson, E. R. & Mayes, L. C. (2010). Race/ethnicity and internalizing disorders in youth: A review. *Clinical Psychology Review, 30,* 338–348.

Anderson, J. (2007, April 25). Morgan Stanley to settle sex bias suit. *New York Times,* pp. C1, C18.

Anderson, K. J. (2014). *Modern misogyny: Anti-feminism in a postfeminist era.* New York: Oxford University Press.

Anderson, M.D. (2015, May 15). Black girls should matter too. *Atlantic*. Retrieved from theatlantic.com/education/archive/2015/05/black-girls-should…/392879

Anderson, S. J. & Johnson, J. T. (2003). The who and when of "gender-blind" attitudes: Predictors of gender- role egalitarianism in two different domains. *Sex Roles, 49,* 527–532.

Andre, S. et al. (2013). Support for traditional female roles across 32 countries: Female labour market participation, policy models and gender differences. *Comparative Sociology, 12,* 447–476.

Andreescu, T., Gallian, J. A., Kane, J. M., & Mertz, J. E. (2008). Cross-cultural analysis of students with exceptional talent in mathematical problem solving. *Notices of the American Mathematical Society, 55,* 1248–1260.

Andrew, R. et al. (2016). Predictors and health-related outcomes of positive body image in adolescent girls: A prospective study. *Developmental Psychology, 52,* 463–474.

Andrews, N. C. Z. et al. (2016). Development of expectancies about own-and other-gender group interactions and their school-related consequences. *Child Development, 87,* 1423–1435.

Angelone, D. J. et al. (2012). Predicting perceptions of date rape: An examination of perpetrator motivation, relationship length, and gender role beliefs. *Journal of Interpersonal Violence, 27,* 2582–2602.

Angier, N. (1999, February 21). Men, women, sex and Darwin. *New York Times Magazine*, pp. 48–53.

Angier, N. (2001, April 10). A lifetime later, still in love with the lab. *New York Times*, pp. D1, D6.

Angier, N. (2002, November 5). The importance of grandma. *New York Times*, pp. D1, D4.

Angier, N. (2007, April 10). Birds do it. Bees do it. People seek the keys to it. *New York Times*, pp. D1, D4.

Angier, N. (2013, November 26). The changing American family. *New York Times*, pp. D1, D3–4.

Anid, N. et al. (2016). *The Internet of women: Accelerating cultural change.* Delft, The Netherlands: River Press.

Annis, A. H. (2016, Winter-Spring). Which way is feminism leaning? A critique of Sandberg's "Feminist Manifesto". *Feminist Collections, 37,* pp. 3–5.

Ansari, A. & Klinenberg, E. (2015, June 14). How to make online dating work. *New York Times*, pp. SR6, 7.

Ansehl, A., Katz, M. B., & Murthy, P. (2010). Society, exercise, and women. In P. Murthy & C. L. Smith (Eds.), *Women's global health and human rights* (pp. 451–460). Sudbury, MA: Jones and Bartlett.

Anthony, E. G. et al. (2016). Optimism and mortality in older men and women: The Rancho Bernardo study. *Journal of Aging Research*, doi:10.1155/2015/5155104.

Antilla, S. (2014, March, 28). Women charge bias and harassment in suit against Sterling Jewelers. *New York Times*, p. B1.

Antonucci, T. et al. (2014). Social capital and gender: Critical influences and living arrangements and care. *Oxford handbook of clinical geropsychology* (pp. 104–124). New York: Oxford University Press.

Anxiety and Depression Association of America. (2016). *Living with anxiety: Women.* Silver Spring, MD: Author.

Anyikwa, V. A. (2015). The intersections of race and gender in help-seeking strategies among a battered sample of low-income African-American women. *Journal of Human Behavior in the Social Environment, 25,* 948–959.

APA Task Force on the Sexualization of Girls. (2007). *Report on the APA task force on the sexualization of girls.* Washington, DC: American Psychological Association.

Arber, S. (2004). Gender, marital status, and ageing: Linking material, health, and social resources. *Journal of Aging Studies, 18,* 91–108.

Archer, S. L. (1992). A feminist's approach to identity research. In G. R. Adams, T. P. Gullotta & R. Montemayor (Eds.), *Adolescent identity formation* (pp. 25–49). Newberry Park, CA: Sage.

Arendt, C. E. & Buzzarell, P.M. (2017) Gender equality in the United States. In A. Ortenblad et al. (Eds.). *Gender equality in a global perspective* (pp. 177–198). New York: Routledge.

Arias, B. J. et al. (2013). Voices of healing and recovery from childhood sexual abuse. *Journal of Child Sexual Abuse, 7,* 822–841.

Armstrong, E. A. et al. (2012). Accounting for women's orgasm and sexual enjoyment in college hookups and relationships. *American Sociological Review, 77,* 435–462.

Armstrong, M. J. (2001). Ethnic minority women as they age. In J. D. Garner & S. O. Mercer (Eds.), *Women as they age* (2nd ed., pp. 97–114). New York: Haworth.

Armstrong, S. (2014). *Uprising: A new age is dawning for every mother's daughter.* New York: St. Martin's Press.

Arndt, B. (2014, February 18). Love across the ages in online dating. *The Sydney Morning Herald*, pp. 1–4.

Arnett, J. J. (2008). The neglected 95%: Why American psychology needs to become less American. *American Psychologist, 63,* 602–614.

Arney, H. T. (2001, May 23). Friends, active social life help turn widow's life around. *Peoria Times-Observer*, p. A8.

Aronson, P. (2003). Feminists or "postfeminists"? Young women's attitudes toward feminism and gender relations. *Gender & Society, 17,* 903–922.

Aronson, P. (2008). The markers and meanings of growing up: Contemporary young women's transition from adolescence to adulthood. *Gender & Society, 22,* 56–82.

Arseniev-Koehler, A. et al. (2016). #Proana: Pro-eating disorder socialization on Twitter. *Journal of Adolescent Health, 58,* 659–664.

Årseth, A. K., Kroger, J., Martinussen, M., & Bakken, G. (2009). Intimacy status, attachment, separation-individuation patterns, and identity status in female university students. *Journal of Social and Personal Relationships, 26,* 697–712.

Article on body image in women's tennis was offensive. (2015, July 19). *New York Times*, p. SP4.

Asa, C. et al. (2015). Childhood exposure to intimate partner violence and adult mental health problems: Relationship with gender and age of exposure. *Journal of Family Violence, 30,* 875–886.

Ashburn-Nardo, L. (2016). Parenthood as a moral imperative? Moral outrage and stigmatization of voluntarily childfree women and men. *Sex Roles*, doi:10.1007/s11199-016-0606-1.

Asher, S. R. et al. (2014). Children as friends. In G. B. Melton & A. Ben-Arieh (Eds.), *Sage handbook of child research* (pp. 169–194). *Thousand Oaks, CA: Sage.*

Ashley, W. (2014).The angry black woman: The impact of pejorative stereotypes on psychotherapy with black women. *Social Work in Public Health, 29,* 27–34.

Asiedu, G. B. & Myers-Bowman, K.S. (2014). Gender differences in the experiences of HIV/AIDS-related stigma: A qualitative study in Ghana. *Health Care for Women International, 35,* 703–727.

Assini-Meytin, L. C. & Green, K. M. (2015). Long-term consequences of adolescent parenthood among African-American urban youth: A propensity score matching approach. *Journal of Adolescent Health, 56,* 529–535.

Astin, J. A. et al. (2013). Psychological control and morbidity/mortality in breast cancer patients: A 20-year follow-up study. *Behavioral Medicine, 39,* 7–10.

Athan, A. & Reel, H. L. (2015). Maternal psychology: Reflections on the 20th anniversary of deconstructing developmental psychology. *Feminism & Psychology, 25,* 311–325.

Athenstaedt, U., Haas, E., & Schwab, S. (2004). Gender role self-concept and gender-typed communication behavior in mixed-sex and same-sex dyads. *Sex Roles, 50,* 37–52.

Aubeeluck, A. & Maguire, M. (2002). The menstrual joy questionnaire alone can positively prime reporting of menstrual attitudes and symptoms. *Psychology of Women Quarterly, 26,* 160–162.

Aubrey, A. (2016, February 4). Women blast CDC's advice to use birth control if drinking alcohol. Retrieved from npr.org/sections/health-shots/2016/02/04/465607147/women-blast-cdcs-advice-to-use-birth-control-if-drinking-alcohol

Aubrey, J. S. & Frisby, C. M. (2011). Sexual objectification in music videos: A content analysis comparing gender and genre. *Mass Communication and Society, 14,* 475–501.

Aune, D. et al. (2016). Whole grain consumption and risk of cardiovascular disease, cancer, and all cause and cause specific mortality: A systematic review and dose-response meta-analysis of prospective studies. *BMJ, 353,* 2716.

Austen, I. (2016, November, 29). High rates of sex assault seen in Canada military. *New York Times*, pA7.

Austen, S. & Ong, R. (2010). The employment transitions of mid-life women: Health and care effects. *Ageing and Society, 30,* 207–227.

Auster, E. R. (2001). Professional women's midcareer satisfaction: Toward an explanatory framework. *Sex Roles, 44,* 719–750.

Austin, A. et al. (2016). Adverse childhood experiences related to poor adult health among lesbian, gay, and bisexual individuals. *AJPH, 106,* 314–320.

Australian Institute of Family Studies. (2013). The long-term effects of child sexual abuse. CFCA Paper No. 11.

Avenevoli, S. et al. (2015). Major depression in the national comorbidity survey: Adolescent supplement: Prevalence, correlates, and treatment. *Journal of the American Academy of Child & Adolescent Psychiatry, 54,* 37–44.

Avis, N. E. et al. (2015). Duration of menopausal vasomotor symptoms over the menopause transition. *JAMA Internal Medicine, 175,* 531–539.

Ayers, B., Forshaw, M., & Hunter, M. S. (2010). The impact of attitudes towards the menopause on women's symptom experience: A systematic review. *Maturitas, 65,* 28–36.

Ayers, S. et al. (2016). The aetiology of post-traumatic stress following childbirth: A meta-analysis and theoretical framework. *Psychology Medicine, 46,* 1121–1134.

Ayotte, B. J., Yang, F. M., & Jones, R. N. (2010). Physical health and depression: A dyadic study of chronic health conditions and depressive symptomatology in older adult couples. *Journal of Gerontology: Psychological Sciences, 65B,* 438–448.

Ayoub, N. C. (2004, April 2). Nota bene. *Chronicle of Higher Education,* p. A18.

Ayres, M. M., Friedman, C. K., & Leaper, C. (2009). Individual and situational factors related to young women's likelihood of confronting sexism in their everyday lives. *Sex Roles, 61,* 449–460.

Azar, B. (2011, January). Meet your 2011 president. *Monitor on Psychology,* pp. 64–66.

Aznar, A. & Tenenbaum, H. R. (2015). Gender and age differences in parent-child emotion talk. *British Journal of Developmental Psychology, 33,* 148–155.

Baams, L. et al (2015). Minority stress and mechanisms of risk for depression and suicidal ideation among gay, lesbian, and bisexual youth. *Developmental Psychology,* 51, 688–696.

Babcock, L. & Laschever, S. (2008). *Ask for it: How women can use the power of negotiation to get what they really want.* New York: Bantam.

Badenes-Ribera, L. et al. (2016). Intimate-partner violence in self-identified lesbians: A systematic review of its prevalence and correlates. *Trauma, Violence, and Abuse, 17,* 284–297.

Badger, K., Craft, R. C., & Jensen, L. (1998). Age and gender differences in value orientation among American adolescents. *Adolescence, 33,* 591–596.

Baer, H. (2016). Redoing feminism: Digital activism, body politics, and neoliberalism. *Feminist Media Studies, 16,* 17–34.

Bagès, C. et al. (2016). Virtues of a hardworking role model to improve girls' mathematics performance. *Psychology of Women Quarterly, 40,* 55–64.

Bahun, S. & Rajan, V. G. J. (2015). *Violence and gender in the globalized world: The intimate and the extimate.* Burlington, VT: Ashgate Publishing.

Bailey, J. M. et al. (2016). Sexual orientation, controversy, and science. *Psychological Science in the Public Interest, 17,* 45–101.

Bailey, S. J. et al. (2013). "How can you retire when you still got a kid in school?": Economics of raising grandchildren in rural areas. *Marriage & Family Review, 49,* 1–3.

Bailey, T. G. et al. (2016). Exercise training reduces the frequency of menopausal hot flushes by improving thermoregulatory control. *Menopause, 23,* 708–718.

Bair-Merritt, M. H., Crowne, S. S., Thompson, D. A., Sibinga, E., Trent, M., & Campbell, J. (2010). Why do women use intimate partner violence? A systematic review of women's motivations. *Trauma, Violence & Abuse, 11,* 178–189.

Baird, C., Pancari, J. V., Lutz, P. J., & Baird, T. (2009). Addiction disorders. In J. C. Urbancic & C. J. Groh (Eds.), *Women's mental health: A clinical guide for primary care providers* (pp. 125–179). Philadelphia, PA: Lippincott Williams & Wilkins.

Baker, A. C. et al. (2016). Confronting barriers to critical discussions about sexualization with adolescent girls. *Social Work, 61,* 79–81.

Baker, J. (2015). Conceptions and dimensions of social equality. In C. Fourie et al. (Eds.), *Social equality: On what it means to be equals* (pp. 65–86). New York: Oxford University Press.

Baker, L. (2010). In women's voices. In M. A. Paludi (Ed.), *Feminism and women's rights worldwide: Feminism as human rights* (Vol. 2, pp. 251–252). Santa Barbara, CA: Praeger.

Bakirci, K. (2011). Sexual orientation-based violence: Outside United States. In M. Z. Stange, C. K. Oyster, & J. E. Sloan (Eds.), *Encyclopedia of women in today's world.* Newberry Park, CA: Sage.

Bakker, M. P., Ormel, J., Verhulst, F. C., & Oldehinkel, A. J. (2010). Peer stressors and gender differences in adolescents' mental health: The TRAILS study. *Journal of Adolescent Health, 46,* 444–450.

Baksh, R. & Harcourt. (2015). *The Oxford handbook of transnational feminist movements.* New York: Oxford University Press.

Baldissera, V. D. et al. (2012). Improvement of older women's sexuality through emancipatory education. *Health Care for Women International, 33,* 956–972.

Baldwin, R. C. & Garner, J. (2016). Anxiety and depression in women in old age. In D. J. Castle & K. M. Abel (Eds.), *Comprehensive women's mental health* (pp. 247–267). Cambridge UK: Cambridge University Press.

Ball, L. C. et al. (2013a). Beyond gender differences: Using tests of equivalence to evaluate gender similarities. *Psychology of Women, 37,* 145–154.

Ball, L. C. et al. (2013b). Using psychology's feminist voices in the classroom. *Psychology of Women Quarterly, 37,* 261–266.

Ballou, M. & Hill, M. (2008). The context of therapy: Theory. In M. Ballou, M. Hill, & C. West (Eds.), *Feminist therapy theory and practice: A contemporary perspective* (pp. 1–8). New York: Springer.

Ballou, M. et al. (2017). The evolution of feminist psychology: Integrating feminism and multiculturalism in counseling women. In M. Kopala & M. Keitel (Eds.), *Handbook of counseling women* (2nd ed., pp. 74–88). Thousand Oaks, CA: Sage.

Banerjee, N. (2001, August 10). Some "bullies" seek ways to soften up. *New York Times,* pp. C1, C2.

Banks, A. & Gartrell, N. K. (1995). Hormones and sexual orientation: A questionable link. *Journal of Homosexuality, 28,* 247–268.

Banks, M. E. (2010). Feminist psychology and women with disabilities: An emerging alliance. *Psychology of Women Quarterly, 34,* 431–442.

Barash, D. P. (2002, May 24). Evolution, males, and violence. *Chronicle of Higher Education,* pp. B7–B9.

Barash, D. P. & Lipton, J. E. (2002). *Gender gap: The biology of male-female differences.* New York: Transaction.

Barber, J. et al. (2015). Black-white differences in attitudes related to pregnancy. *Demography, 52,* 751–786.

Barlett, C. P. & Coyne, S. M. (2014). A meta-analysis of cyberbullying behavior: The moderating role of age. *Aggressive Behavior, 40,* 474–488.

Barnack-Tavlaris, J. (2015). The medicalization of the menstrual cycle: Menstruation as a disorder. In M.C. McHugh & J.C. Chrisler (Eds.) *The wrong prescription for women* (pp. 61–76). Santa Barbara, CA: Praeger.

Barnes, D. L. (2014). The psychological gestation of motherhood. In D. Barnes (Ed.), *Women's reproductive and mental health across the lifespan* (pp. 75–90). New York: Springer.

Barnes, P. M. & Schoenborn, C. A. (2012). *Trends in adults receiving a recommendation for exercise or other physical activity from a physician or other health professional.* NCHS Data Brief No. 86. Hyattsville, MD: National Center for Health Statistics.

Barnet, B. (2012). Supporting adolescent mothers: A journey through policies, programs, and research. *American Journal of Public Health, 102,* 2201–2203.

Barnett, M. A., Scaramella, L. V., Neppl, T. K., Ontai, L. L., & Conger, R. D. (2010). Grandmother involvement as a protective factor for early childhood social adjustment. *Journal of Family Psychology, 24,* 635–645.

Barnett, M. A. et al. (2016). Grandmother involvement in Mexican American families: Implications for transborder relationships and maternal psychological distress. *Journal of Family Issues, 37,* 1945–1967.

Barnett Kissin, W. et al. (2014). Women's employment outcomes following gender-sensitive substance abuse treatment. *Journal of Drug Issues, 10,* 1–14.

Barot, S. (2010, Spring). Past due: Emergency contraception in U.S. reproductive health programs overseas. *Guttmacher Policy Review, 13*(2), 8–11.

Barot, S. (2012. Spring). A problem-and-solution mismatch: Son preference and sex-selective abortion bans. *Guttmacher Policy Review, 15,* 18–22.

Barrett, A. E. & Naiman-Sessions, M. (2016). 'It's our turn to play': Performance of girlhood as a collective response to gendered ageism. *Ageing & Society, 36,* 764–784.

Barrett, A. E. & Toothman, E. L. (2016). Explaining age differences in women's emotional well-being: The role of subjective experiences of aging. *Journal of Women & Aging, 28,* 285–296.

Barrett, C. et al. (2015). Understanding the experiences and needs of lesbian, gay, bisexual, and trans Australians living with dementia, and their partners. *Australasian Journal of Ageing, 34,* (Supp 2), 34–38

Barretto, M. & Ellemers, N.(2013). Sexism in contemporary societies: how it is expressed, perceived, confirmed, and resisted. In M. K. Ryan & N. R. Branscombe (Eds.). *Sage handbook of gender and psychology* (pp. 289–305). Los Angeles, CA: Sage.

Barron, I. G. et al. (2015). School-based child sexual abuse prevention programs: Moving toward resiliency-informed evaluation. *Journal of Child Sexual Abuse, 24,* 77–96.

Barry, E. & Feit, C. (2016, July 25). Mortal to divine and back: India's transgender goddesses. *New York Times,* p. A24.

Bartel, A. et al. (2015). *Paid family leave, father' leave-taking, and leave-sharing in dual-earner households.* Cambridge, MA: National Bureau of Economic Research.

Bartini, M. (2006). Gender role flexibility in early adolescence: Developmental change in attitudes, self-perception, and behaviors. *Sex Roles, 55,* 233–245.

Bartlett, J. (2016, September 25). Longing for the male gaze. *New York Times,* p. SR9.

Bartlett, T. (2009, November 27). The puzzle of boys: Scholars and others debate what it means to grow up male in America. *Chronicle of Higher Education,* pp. B7–B9.

Barton, L. (2005, January 5). Celebrities distort girls' search for ideal shape. *Guardian (London),* p. 7.

Basile, K. C. (2015). A comprehensive approach to sexual violence prevention. *New England Journal of Medicine, 372,* 2350–2351.

Basile, K. C. et al. (2016). Disability and risk of recent sexual violence in the United States. *AJPH, 106,* 928–933.

Basow, S. A. (2010a). Changes in psychology of women and psychology of gender textbooks (1975–2010). *Sex Roles, 62,* 151–152.

Basow, S. A. (2010b). Women in education: Students and professors worldwide. In M. A. Paludi (Ed.), *Feminism and women's rights worldwide* (Vol. 1, pp. 43–62). Santa Barbara, CA: Praeger.

Basow, S. A. (2013). Women in management: Does Manager equal male? In M. A. Paludi (Ed.), *Women and management: Global issues and promising solutions* (pp. 3–20). Santa Barbara, CA: ABC-CLIO.

Basow, S. A. & Minieri, A. (2011). "You owe me a date": Effects of date cost, who pays, participant gender, and rape myth beliefs on perceptions of rape. *Journal of Interpersonal Violence, 26,* 479–449.

Bass, B. C. (2015). Preparing for parenthood? Gender, aspirations, and the reproduction of labor market inequality. *Gender & Society, 29,* 362–385.

Bassok, D. et al. (2016). Within- and between-sector quality differences in early childhood education and care. *Child and Development, 87,* 1627–1645.

Batalha, L. & Reynolds, K. J. (2013) Gender and personality: Beyond gender stereotypes to social identity and the dynamics of social change. In M. K. Ryan & N. R. Branscombe (Eds.). *Sage hand-book of gender and psychology* (pp165–182). Los Angeles, CA: Sage.

Bates, L. (2016). *Everyday sexism: The project that inspired a worldwide movement.* New York: St. Martin's Press.

Bates, J. S. & Taylor, S. C. (2013). Taking stock of theory in grandparent studies. In M. A. Fine & F. D. Fincham (Eds.), *Handbook of family theories: A content-based approach* (pp. 51–70). New York: Routledge.

Bauer, P. J., Liebl, M., & Stennes, L. (1998). Pretty is to dress as brave is to suitcoat: Gender-based property-to-property inferences by 4-year-old children. *Merrill-Palmer Quarterly, 44,* 355–377.

Baumann, S. & Ho, L. (2014). Cultural schemas for racial identity in Canadian television advertising. *Canadian Review of Sociology, 51,* 152–169.

Bauserman, R. (2002). Child adjustment in joint-custody versus sole-custody arrangements: A meta-analytic review. *Journal of Family Psychology, 16,* 91–102.

Baxter, J. & Tai, T. (2016). Inequalities in unpaid work: A cross-national comparison. In M. L. Connerley & J. Wu (Eds.), *Handbook on well-being of working women* (pp. 653–660). Dordrecht, Netherlands: Springer.

Bay-Cheng, L. Y. (2015). The agency line: A neoliberal metric for appraising young women's sexuality. *Sex Roles, 73,* 279–291.

Bay-Cheng, L. Y. & Goodkind, S. A. (2016). Sex and the single (neoliberal) girl: Perspectives on being single among socioeconomically diverse young women. *Sex Roles, 74,* 181–194.

Bay-Cheng, L. Y. & Zucker, A. N. (2007). Feminism between the sheets: Sexual attitudes among feminists, nonfeminists, and egalitarians. *Psychology of Women Quarterly, 31,* 157–163.

Bayer, S. R. & Thornton, K. (2012). Medical ethics in reproductive medicine. In S. R. Bayer & M. M. Alper (Eds.), *The Boston IVF handbook of infertility: A practical guide for practitioners who care for infertile couples* (pp. 162–168). Boca Raton, FL: CRC Press.

Baylis, F. (2015). Human embryos for reproduction and research. In J. D. Arras & E. Fenton (Eds.), *The Routledge companion to bioethics* (pp. 357–359). New York: Routledge.

Bays, A. (2016). Perceptions, emotions, and behaviors toward women based on parental status. *Sex Roles,* doi: 10.1007/s11199-016-0655-5.

Beach, S. R. H. et al. (2013). Impact of child sex abuse on adult psychopathology: A genetically and epigenetically informed investigation. *Journal of Family Psychology, 27,* 3–11.

Beane, C. et al. (2014). *Closing the leadership gap: How educators can help girls lead.* Washington, DC: National Education Association.

Bear, J. B. & Babcock, L. (2012). Negotiation topic as a moderator of gender differences in negotiation. *Psychological Science, 23,* 743–744.

Bearman, P. (2004, March). *Rules, behaviors, and networks that influence STD prevention among adolescents.* Paper presented at the meeting of the National STD Prevention Conference, Philadelphia.

Bearman, P. S. & Moody, J. (2004). Suicide and friendships among American adolescents. *American Journal of Public Health, 94,* 89–96.

Beaton, A. M., Tougas, F., & Joly, S. (1996). Neosexism among male managers: Is it a matter of numbers? *Journal of Applied Social Psychology, 26,* 2189–2203.

Beaulaurier, R. et al. (2014). Attitudes and stereotypes regarding older women and HIV risk. *Journal of Women and Aging, 26,* 352–368.

Beavis, A. L. et al. (2017, January 23). Hysterectomy-corrected cervical cancer mortality rates reveal a large racial disparity in the United States. *Cancer, 123,* 1044–1050.

Beck, J. (2014). *Postpartum depression can happen to any parent.* Retrieved October 20, 2014, from HYPERLINK "http://www.theatlantic.com" \h www.theatlantic.com

Becker, A. E., Fay, K., Gilman, S. E., & Striegel-Moore, R. (2007). Facets of acculturation and their diverse relations to body shape concern in Fiji. *International Journal of Eating Disorders, 40,* 42–50.

Becker, C. B. et al. (2014). Can we reduce eating disorder risk factors in female college athletes? A randomized exploratory investigation of two peer-led interventions. *Body Image, 9,* 31–42.

Becker, J. C. & Sibley, C. G. (2013). Sexism. In T. D. Nelson (Ed.), *Handbook of prejudice, stereotyping, and discrimination* (pp. 315–336). New York: Psychology Press.

Becker, M. et al. (2014). Sexual orientation, psychological well-being, and mental health: A longitudinal analysis from adolescence to young adulthood. *Psychology of Sexual Orientation and Gender Diversity, 1,* 132–145.

Beckles, G. L. & Truman, B. I. (2011, January 14). Education and income—United States, 2005 and 2009. *Morbidity and Mortality Weekly Report, 60*(Suppl.), 13–17.

Beckmeyer, J. J. et al. (2014). Postdivorce coparenting typologies and children's adjustment. *Family Relations, 63,* 526–535.

Bedford, V. H. (1995). Sibling relationships in middle and old age. In R. Blieszner & V. H. Bedford (Eds.), *Handbook of aging and the family* (pp. 201–222). Westport, CT: Greenwood.

Bedford, V. H. & Avioli, P. S. (2012). Sibling relationships from midlife to old age. In R. Blieszner & V. H. Bedford (Eds.), *Handbook of families and aging* (pp. 125–152). Santa Barbara. CA: ABC-CLIO.

Bekker, M. H. J. & van Assen, M. A. L. M. (2008). Autonomy-connectedness and gender. *Sex Roles, 59,* 532–544.

Belec, H. (2015, Fall). Princess of geek: What attracts women to science? *AAUW Outlook,* 18–21.

Belgrave, F. Z. & Allison, K. W. (2010). *African American psychology: From Africa to America* (2nd ed.). Thousand Oaks, CA: Sage.

Belknap, J. (2015). The invisible women: Gender, crime, and justice. Stamford, CT: Cengage.

Belknap, J. & Sharma, N. (2014). The significant frequency and impact of stealth (nonviolent) gender-based abuse among college women. *Trauma, Violence, & Abuse, 15,* 181–190.

Bell, L. C. (2004). Psychoanalytic theories of gender. In A. H. Eagly, A. E. Beall, & R. J. Sternberg (Eds.), *The psychology of gender* (pp. 145–168). New York: Guilford.

Belluck, P. (2014, June 16). "Thinking of ways to harm her:' New finding on timing and range of maternal mental illness. *New York Times,* pp. A1, A14.

Belluck, P. (2015, March 25). Experts back actress in choices for cancer prevention. *New York Times,* p. A3.

Belluck, P. (2016, January 27). Panel urges screening for maternal depression. *New York Times,* pp. A1, A13.

Beltz, A. M. et al. (2014). Modeling pubertal timing and tempo and examining links to behavioral problems. *Developmental Psychology, 50,* 2715–2726.

Bem, S. L. (1974). The measurement of psychological androgyny. *Journal of Consulting and Clinical Psychology, 42,* 155–162.

Bem, S. L. (1993). *The lenses of gender: Transforming the debate on sexual inequality.* New Haven, CT: Yale University Press.

Bem, S. L. (1998). *An unconventional family.* New Haven, CT: Yale University Press.

Benard, V. B. et al. (2014). Vital signs: Cervical cancer incidence, mortality, and screening—United States, 2007–2012. *Morbidity and Mortality Weekly Report, 63,* 1–5.

Benenson, J. F., Morash, D., & Petrakos, H. (1998). Gender differences in emotional closeness between preschool children and their mothers. *Sex Roles, 38,* 975–985.

Bennett, J. (2009, April 6). Tales of a modern diva. *Newsweek,* pp. 42–43.

Bennett, J. (2016, January 10). Sex, with a syllabus. *New York Times,* pp. SR1, SR7.

Bennett, J. & Yabroff, J. (2008). Revenge of the nerdette. *Newsweek,* pp. 44–45.

Bentley, C. G. et al. (2007). Associations among aspects of interpersonal power and relationship functioning in adolescent romantic couples. *Sex Roles, 57,* 483–495.

Berdahl, J. L. (2007). The sexual harassment of uppity women. *Journal of Applied Psychology, 92,* 425–437.

Berdahl, J. L. & Moon, S. H. (2013). Workplace mistreatment of middle class workers based on sex, parenthood, and caregiving. *Journal of Social Issues, 2,* 341–366.

Berdahl, J. L. & Raver, J. L. (2011). Sexual harassment. *APA Handbook of Industrial and Organizational Psychology, 3,* 641–669.

Berg, R. C. & Denison, E. (2013). A tradition in transition: Factors perpetuating and hindering the continuance of female genital mutilation/cutting (FGM/C) summarized in a systematic review. *Health Care for Women International, 34,* 837–859.

Berge, J. M. et al. (2014). Parent-adolescent conversations about eating, physical activity and weight: Prevalence across sociodemographic characteristics and associations with adolescent weight and weight-related behaviors. *Journal of Behavioral Medicine, 38,* 122–135.

Berge, J. M. et al. (2016). Do parents or siblings engage in more negative weight-based talk with children and what does it sound like? A mixed-methods study. *Body Image, 18,* 27–33.

Berger, M. & Radeloff, C. (2015). *Transforming scholarship: Why women's and gender studies students are changing the world and themselves.* New York: Routledge.

Bergmann, B. R. (2011). Sex segregation in the blue-collar occupations: Women's choices or unremedied discrimination? Comment on England. *Gender & Society, 25,* 88–93.

Bergouignan, A. et al. (2016). Effect of frequent interruptions of prolonged sitting on self-perceived levels of energy, mood, food cravings, and cognitive function *International Journal of Behavioral Nutrition and Physical Activity, 13,* 113.

Bericat, E. (2016). The subjective well-being of working women in Europe. In M. L. Connerly & J. Wu (Eds.), *Handbook on well-being of working women* (pp. 633–648). Dordrecht, Netherlands: Springer.

Berk, L. E. (2013). *Child development* (9th ed.). Boston, MA: Allyn & Bacon.

Berkery, E. et al. (2013). Beyond gender role stereotypes and requisite managerial characteristics: From communal to androgynous, the changing views of women. *Gender in Management: An International Journal, 28,* 278–298.

Bernard, T. (2014, March 22). Coping when not entering retirement together. *New York Times,* p. B1.

Bernstein, B. L. & Russo, N. F. (2008). Explaining too few women in STEM careers: A psychosocial perspective. In M. A. Paludi (Ed.), *The psychology of women at work: Challenges and solutions for our female workforce: Obstacles and the identity juggle* (Vol. 2, pp. 1–33). Westport, CT: Praeger.

Berry, T. R. et al. (2015). Women's perceptions of heart disease and breast cancer and the association with media representations of the diseases. *Journal of Public Health,* doi:10.1093/pubmed/fdv177.

Bersamin, M. M. et al. (2014). Risky business: Is there an association between casual sex and mental health among emerging adults? *Journal of Sex Research, 51,* 43–51.

Berstad, P. et al. (2016). Lifestyle changes at middle age and mortality: A population-based prospective cohort study. *Journal of Epidemiology and Community Health,* doi.10.1136/jech-2015-206760.

Bertera, E. M. & Crewe, S. E. (2013). Parenthood in the twenty-first century: African American grandparents as surrogate parents. *Journal of Human Behavior in the Social Environment, 23,* 178–192.

Bertone-Johnson, E. R. & Manson, J. E. (2015). Early menopause and subsequent cardiovascular disease. *Menopause, 22,* 1–3.

Bertone-Johnson, E. R. et al. (2014). Early life emotional, physical, and sexual abuse and the development of premenstrual syndrome: A longitudinal study. *Journal of Women's Health, 23,* 729–739.

Bertotti, A. M. (2013). Gendered divisions of fertility work: Socioeconomic predictions of female versus male sterilization. *Journal of Marriage and Family, 75,* 13–25.

Bertrand, M. (2013). Work on women's work is never done: Career, family, and the well-being of college-educated women. *American Economic Review: Papers & Proceedings 2013, 103,* 244–250.

Berz, K. & McCambridge, T. (2016). Amenorrhea in the female athlete: What to do and when to worry. *Pediatric Annals, 45,* e97–e102.

Bessenoff, G. R. & Del Priore, R. E. (2007). Women, weight, and age: Social comparison to magazine images across the lifespan. *Sex Roles, 56,* 215–222.

Best, D. L. (2001). Cross-cultural gender roles. In J. Worell (Ed.), *Encyclopedia of women and gender* (pp. 279–290). San Diego, CA: Academic Press.

Best, D. L. (2009). Another view of the gender-status relation. *Sex Roles, 61,* 341–351.

Best, D. L. (2010). Gender. In M. H. Bornstein (Ed.), *Handbook of cultural developmental science* (pp. 209–222). New York: Psychology Press.

Best, D. L. & Thomas, J. J. (2004). Cultural diversity and cross-cultural perspectives. In A. H. Eagly, A. E. Beall, & R. J. Sternberg (Eds.), *The psychology of gender* (pp. 296–327). New York: Guilford.

Better, N. M. (2014, October 12). The empty-nest book hatchery. *New York Times,* p. ST2.

Betz, D. E. et al. (2013). Gender stereotype threat among women and girls. In M. K. Ryan & N. R. Branscombe (Eds.) *Sage handbook of gender and psychology* (pp. 428–449). Los Angeles: Sage .

Betz, N. E. (2008). Women's career development. In F. L. Denmark & M. A. Paludi (Eds.), *Psychology of women: A handbook of issues and theories* (2nd ed., pp. 717–752). Westport, CT: Praeger.

Beumont, P. (2005, January 9). Alexander the Turkey? *Observer (London),* p. 22.

Beydoun, M. A. et al. (2014). Epidemiologic studies of modifiable factors associated with cognition and dementia: Systematic review and meta-analysis. *BMC Public Health, 2,* 1–24.

Beyer, S. (1997, June). *Gender differences in causal attributions of imagined performance on English, history, and math exams.* Paper presented at the meeting of the American Psychological Society, Washington, DC.

Beyers, W. & Seiffge-Krenke, I. (2010). Does identity precede intimacy? Testing Erikson's theory on romantic development in emerging adults of the 21st century. *Journal of Adolescent Research, 25,* 387–415.

Bhupathiraju, S. N. et al. (2016). Exogenous hormone use: Oral contraceptives, postmenopausal hormone therapy, and health outcomes in the Nurses' Health Study. *AJPH, 106,* 1631–1637.

Bian, L. et al. (2017). Gender stereotypes about intellectual ability emerge early and influence children's interests. *Science, 355,* 389–391.

Bianchi, S. M. (2014). A demographic perspective on family change. *Journal of Family Theory & Review, 6,* 35–44.

Bianchi, S. M., Hotz, V. J., McGarry, K., & Seltzer, J. A. (2008). Intergenerational ties: Theories, trends, and challenges. In A. Booth, A. C. Crouter, S. M. Bianchi, & J. A. Seltzer (Eds.), *Intergenerational caregiving* (pp. 3–43). Washington, DC: Urban Institute Press.

Bianchi, S. M. et al. (2014). Gender and time allocation of cohabiting and married women and men in France, Italy, and the United States. *Demographic Research, 31,* 183–216.

Bieschke, K. J. & Toepfer-Hendey, E. (2006). Career counseling with lesbian clients. In W. B. Walsh & M. J. Heppner (Eds.), *Handbook of career counseling for women* (2nd ed., pp. 351–386). Mahwah, NJ: Erlbaum.

Biggs, M.A. et al. (2017). Women's mental health and well-being after receiving or being denied an abortion: A prospective longitudinal cohort study. *JAMA Psychiatry,74,* 169–178.

Bilefsky, D. (2016, April 7). British group says model for Gucci is 'unhealthily thin.' *New York Times,* p. A4.

Bilimoria, D. & Lord, L. (2014). Women in STEM careers: An international perspective. *North Hampton, MA: Edward Elgar Publishing.*

Bilimoria, D. et al. (2014). An introduction to women in STEM careers: International perspectives on increasing workforce participation, advancement, and leadership. In D. Bilimoria & L. Lord (Eds.), *Women in STEM careers: International perspectives on increasing workforce participation, advancement, and leadership* (pp. 3–15). North Hampton, MA: Edward Elgar Publishing.

Billari, F. C. & Liefbroer, A. C. (2008). Intergenerational ties: What can be gained from an international perspective? In A. Booth, A. C. Crouter, S. M. Bianchi, & J. A. Seltzer (Eds.), *Intergenerational caregiving* (pp. 53–66). Washington, DC: Urban Institute Press.

Billings, A. C. et al. (2014). (Re)calling London: The gender frame agenda within NBC's primetime broadcast of the 2012 Olympiad. *Journalism & Mass Communication Quarterly, 9,* 38–58.

Binder, E. F. et al. (2008). Effects of exercise training on frailty in community-dwelling older adults: Results of a randomized, controlled trial. *Journal of the American Geriatrics Society, 50,* 1921–1928.

Birchler, G. & Fals-Stewart, W. (1998). Marriage and divorce. In M. Hersen & V. B. Van Hasselt (Eds.), *Handbook of clinical geropsychology* (pp. 449–467). New York: Plenum.

Bird, S. et al. (2009). The influence of the built environment and other factors on the physical activity of older women from different ethnic communities. *Journal of Women & Aging, 21,* 33–47.

Birditt, R. S. & Fingerman, K. (2013). Parent child and intergenerational relationships in adulthood. In M. A. Fine & F. D. Fincham (Eds.), *Handbook of family theories: A content-based approach* (pp. 71–86). New York: Routledge.

Birkett, M. et al. (2015). Does it get better? A longitudinal analysis of psychological distress and victimization in lesbian, gay, bisexual, transgender, and questioning youth. *Journal of Adolescent Health, 56,* 280–285.

Birmingham, W. C. et al. (2015). It's complicated: Marital ambivalence on ambulatory blood pressure and daily interpersonal functioning. *Annals of Behavioral Medicine, 49,* 743–753.

Bisagni, G. M. & Eckenrode, J. (1995). The role of work identity in women's adjustment to divorce. *American Journal of Orthopsychiatry, 65,* 574–583.

Bisom-Rapp, S. & Sargeant, M. (2016). *Lifetime disadvantage, discrimination and the gendered workforce.* New York: Cambridge University Press.

Bjorklund, B. R. & Bee, H. L. (2014). *The journey of adulthood* (8th ed.). Upper Saddle River, NJ: Prentice Hall.

Black, K. A., Marola, J. A., Littman, A. I., Chrisler, J. C., & Neace, W. P. (2009). Gender and form of cereal box characters: Different medium, same disparity. *Sex Roles, 60,* 882–889.

Blackwell, G. L. (2010, Winter). A little help along the way. *American Association of Univeristy Women Outlook, 104*(1), 16–19.

Blakemore, J. E. O. (2003). Children's beliefs about violating gender norms: Boys shouldn't look like girls, and girls shouldn't act like boys. *Sex Roles, 48,* 411–419.

Blakemore, J. E. O. & Centers, R. E. (2005). Characteristics of boys' and girls' toys. *Sex Roles, 53,* 619–633.

Blakemore, J. E. O. & Hill, C. A. (2008). The child gender socialization scale: A measure to compare traditional and feminist parents. *Sex Roles, 58,* 192–207.

Blakemore, J. E. O., Berenbaum, S. A., & Liben, L. S. (2009). *Gender development.* New York: Psychology Press.

Blanchard-Dallaire, C. & Hebert, M. (2014). Social relationships in sexually abused children: Self-reports and teachers' evaluations. *Journal of Child Sexual Abuse, 23,* 326–344.

Blank, L., Baxter, S. K., Payne, N., Guillaume, L. R., & Pilgrim, H. (2010). Systematic review and narrative synthesis of the effectiveness of contraceptive service interventions for young people, delivered in educational settings. *Journal of Pediatric and Adolescent Gynecology, 23,* 341–351.

Blau, F. D. & Kahn, L. M. (2016). *The gender wage gap: Extent, trends, and explanations.* Cambridge, MA: National Bureau of Economic Research.

Blazer, D. & Hybels, C. (2014). Depression in labor life. In I. H. Gotlib & C. L. Hammen (Eds.), *Handbook of depression* (pp. 429–447). New York: Guilford.

Bleidorn, W. et al. (2016). Age and gender differences in self-esteem—A cross-cultural window. *Journal of Personality and Social Psychology, 111,* 396–410.

Bleske-Rechek, A. et al. (2012). Benefit or burden? Attraction in cross-sex friendship. *Journal of Social and Personal Relationships, 29*, 569–596.

Blieszner, R. (2014, Spring). The worth of friendship: Can friends keep us happy and healthy? *Generations, 38*, 24–30.

Blieszner, R., Vista, P. M., & Mancine, J. A. (1996). Diversity and dynamics in late-life mother-daughter relationships. *Journal of Women and Aging, 8* (3/4), 5–24.

Block, J. D. (2008). *Sex over 50*. New York: Penguin.

Blomberg, M. et al. (2014). Impact of maternal age on obstetric and neonatal outcome with emphasis on primiparous adolescents and older women: A Swedish medical birth register study. *BMJ Open, 4*, e005840.

Blossfield, H. P. et al. (2015). *Gender, education and employment: An international comparison of school-to-work transitions* (eduLIFE lifelong learning series). Northampton, MA: Elgar Publishing.

Blume, A. W. (2016). Advances in substance abuse prevention and treatment interventions among racial, ethnic, and sexual minority populations. *Alcohol Research: Current Reviews, 38*, 47–53.

Blume, A. W. et al. (2012). The relationships of microaggressions with alcohol use and anxiety among ethnic minority college students in a historically White institution. *Cultural Diversity and Ethnic Minority Psychology, 18*, 45–54.

Bly, R. (1990). *Iron John*. Reading, MA: Addison-Wesley.

Bobel, C. (2010). *New blood: Third-wave feminism and the politics of menstruation*. Piscataway, NJ: Rutgers University Press.

Bobo, M., Hildreth, B. L., & Durodoye, B. (1998). Changing patterns in career choices among African-American, Hispanic, and Anglo children. *Professional School Counseling, 1*, 37–42.

Bodenmann, G. et al. (2015). Effects of stress on the social support provided by men and women in intimate relationships. *Psychological Sciences, 26*, 1584–1594.

Boehmer, U., & Bowen, D. J. (2010). Breast and cervical cancer among diverse women. In H. Landrine & N. F. Russo (Eds.), Handbook of diversity in feminist psychology (pp. 311–333). New York: Springer.

Boehmer, U. & Elk, R. (2015). *Cancer and the LGBT community: Unique perspectives from risk to survivorship*. New York: Springer.

Bohnet, I. (2016). *What works: Gender by design*. Cambridge, MA: Harvard University Press.

Bohren, M. A. (2015). The mistreatment of women during childbirth in health facilities globally: A mixed-methods systematic review. *PLoS Medicine,12*, e1001847.

Boiche, J. et al. (2014). Social antecedents and consequences of gender-sport stereotypes during adolescence. *Psychology of Women Quarterly, 38*, 259–274.

Bono, J. et al. (2016). Dropped on the way to the top: Gender and managerial derailment. *Personnel Psychology*, doi:10.1111/peps.12184.

Bonomi, A. E. et al. (2013). History of dating violence and the association with late adolescent health. *BMC Public Health, 13*, 821.

Bonsack, C. F. et al. (2014). Induction of labor: Update and review. *Journal of Midwifery & Women's Health, 59*, 606–615.

Book, A. S. et al. (2001) Relationship between testosterone and aggression: A meta-analysis. *Aggression and Violent Behavior, 6*, 579–599.

Bookwala, J. (2012). Marriage and other partnerships in middle and late adulthood. In R. Blieszner & V. H. Bedford (Eds.), *Handbook of families and aging* (2nd ed., pp. 91–124). Santa Barbara, CA: ABC-CLIO.

Bookwala, J. et al. (2014). Benefits of having friends in older ages: Differential effects of informal social activities on well-being. *Health Psychology, 33*, 505–515.

Boonstra, H. D. (2014). What is behind the declines in teen pregnancy rates? *Guttmacher Policy Review, 17*, 15–21.

Boonstra, H. D. (2015). Meeting the sexual and reproductive health needs of adolescents in school-based health centers. *Guttmacher Policy Review, 18*, 1–8.

Boonstra, H. D. & Nash, E. (2014). A surge of state abortion restrictions puts providers—and the women they serve—in the crosshairs. *Guttmacher Policy Review, 17*, 9–15.

Bordo, S. (2004). *Unbearable weight: Feminism, Western culture and the body*. Berkeley, CA: University of California Press.

Borkhoff, C. M., Hawker, G. A., Kreder, H. J., Glazier, R. H., Mahomed, N. N., & Wright, J. G. (2008). The effect of patients' sex on physicians' recommendations for total knee arthroplasty. *Canadian Medical Association Journal, 178*, 681–687.

Bornstein, D. (2014, October 19). Treating depression before it's postpartum. *New York Times*, p. SR9.

Bornstein, M. H. (2013). Parenting, gender, culture, time. *Gender and parenthood: Biological and social scientific perspectives* (pp. 191–119). New York: Columbia University Press.

Bornstein, M. H. et al. (2008). Mother-child emotional availability in ecological perspective: Three countries, two regions, two genders. *Developmental Psychology, 44*, 666–680.

Bornstein, M. H. et al. (2016). Gender in low- and middle-income countries. *Monographs of the Society for Research in Child Development*, 81.

Boroughs, M. S., Krawczyk, R., & Thompson, J. K. (2010). Body dysmorphic disorder among diverse racial/ethnic and sexual orientation groups: Prevalence estimates and associated factors. *Sex Roles , 63*, 725–737.

Bos, H. et al. (2016). Same-sex and different-sex parent households and child health outcomes: Findings from the national survey of children's health. *Journal of Developmental & Behavioral Pediatrics, 37*, 179–187.

Bosacki, S. L., & Moore, C. (2004). Preschoolers' understanding of simple and complex emotions: Links with gender and language. *Sex Roles, 50*, 659–675.

Bosson, J. K. et al (2013). Precarious manhood. In M. K. Ryan & N. R. Branscombe (Eds.). *Sage handbook of gender and development* (pp. 115–130). Los Angeles, CA: Sage.

Bosson, J. K. & Michniewicz, K. S. (2013). Gender dichotomization at the level of ingroup identity: What it is, and why men use it more than women. *Journal of Personality and Social Psychology, 105*, 425–442.

Boushey, H. (2016). *Finding time: The economics of work-life conflict*. Cambridge, MA: Harvard University Press.

Boushey, H. & Ansel, B. (2016). *Overworked America: The economic causes and consequences of long work hours*. Washington, DC: Washington Center for Equitable Growth.

Boston Women's Health Book Collective. (2011). *Our bodies, ourselves for the new century: A book by and for women*. New York: Touchstone.

Boston Women's Health Book Collective. (2008). *Our bodies ourselves: Pregnancy and birth*. New York: Touchstone.

Bottoms, B. L. et al. (2016). Abuse characteristics and individual differences related to disclosing sexual, physical, and emotional abuse and witnessed domestic violence. *Journal of Interpersonal Violence, 31*, 1308–1339.

Bou-Franch, P. (Ed.). (2016). *Exploring language aggression against women*. Philadelphia: John Benjamins.

Boucher, K. L. (2015). Forecasting the experience of stereotype threat for others. *Journal of Experimental Social Psychology, 58*, 56–62.

Bourassa, K. J. et al. (2015). Women in very low quality marriages gain life satisfaction following divorce. *Journal of Family Psychology, 29*, 490–499.

Bourne, E. J. (2010). *The anxiety and phobia workbook* (5th ed.). Oakland, CA: New Harbinger.

Bowen, C. E., Noack, M. G., & Staudinger, U. M. (2011). Aging in the work context. In K. W. Schaie & S. L. Willis (Eds.), *Handbook of the psychology of aging* (7th ed., pp. 279–294). San Diego, CA: Academic Press.

Bowen, D. (2012). Visibly invisible: the burden of race and gender for female students of color striving for an academic career in sciences. In G. G. Muhs & Y. F. Niemann (Eds.), *Presumed incompetent: The intersections of race and class for women in academia* (pp. 166–932). Logan, UT: Utah State University.

Bowen, E. & Walker, K. (2015). *The psychology of violence in adolescent romantic relationships*. New York: Macmillan.

Bowles, H. R. (2013).Psychological perspectives on gender in negotiation. In M.K. Ryan & N.R. Branscombe (Eds.). *Sage handbook of gender and psychology* (pp. 465–483). Los Angeles, CA: Sage.

Bowman, C. P. (2014). Women's masturbation: Experiences of sexual empowerment in a primarily sex-positive sample. *Psychology of Women Quarterly, 38,* 363–378.

Boxer, C. F. et al. (2013). Measuring mate preferences: A replication and extension. *Journal of Family Issues, 36,* 136–187.

Boxer, C. F. et al. (2015). Measuring rate preferences: A replication and extension. *Journal of Family Issues, 36,* 163–187.

Boyczuk, A. & Fletcher, P. (2016). The ebbs and flows: Stresses of sandwich generation generation caregivers. *Journal of Adult Development, 23,* 51–61.

Boyd, S. D. et al. (2015). *Autonomous motherhood?: A socio-legal study of choice and constraint.* Toronto: University of Toronto Press.

Boynton, P. (2003). Abiding by the rules: Instructing women in relationships. *Feminism & Psychology, 13,* 237–245.

Brabeck, M. M. (2016). Building on the feminist legacy of *PWQ. Psychology of Women Quarterly, 40,* 7–9.

Bradley, H. et al. (2014). Vital signs: HIV diagnosis, care, and treatment among persons living with HIV-United States, 2011. *Morbidity and Mortality Weekly Report, 63,* 1113–1117.

Branch, J. (2015, July 28). Dutee Chand, female sprinter with high testosterone level, wins right to compete. *New York Times,* p. A1.

Brandt, M. J. (2011). Sexism and gender inequality across 57 societies. *Psychological Science, 22,* 1413–1418.

Brauhardt, A. et al. (2014). The therapeutic process in psychological treatments for eating disorders: A systematic review. *International Journal of Eating Disorders, 47,* 565–584.

Braveman, P. A., Cubbin, C., Egerter, S., Williams, D. R., & Pamuk, E. (2010). Socioeconomic disparities in health in the United States: What the pattern tells us. *American Journal of Public Health, 100,* S186–S196.

Breheny, M. & Stephens, C. (2009). A life of ease and immorality: Health professionals' constructions of mothering on welfare. *Journal of Community & Applied Social Psychology, 19,* 257–270.

Breiding, M. J. et al. (2014). Prevalence and characteristics of sexual violence, stalking, and intimate partner violence victimization—National Intimate Partner and Sexual Violence Survey, United States, 2011. *MMWR Surveillance Summaries, 63.*

Brennan, L. M & Shaw, D. S. (2013). Revisiting data related to the age of onset and developmental course of female conduct problems. *Clinical Child and Family Psychology Review, 16,* 35–58.

Brescoll, V. & LaFrance, M. (2004). The correlates and consequences of newspaper reports of research on sex differences. *Psychological Science, 15,* 515–520.

Brewer, L. C. et al. (2014). African American women's perceptions and attitudes regarding participation in medical research: The Mayo Clinic/ the links, incorporated partnership. *Journal of Women's Health, 23,* 681–687.

Brezina, P.R. (2015). Fertility treatment in the United States: The case for increased access to care. *Journal of Fertilization: In Vitro—IVF—Worldwide, Reproductive Medicine, Genetics, & Stem Cell Biology, 3,* e112.

Brice, A. (2016, February 18). Is CDC's alcohol warning paternalistic? Some women think so. *Berkeley News.* Retrieved from news.berkeley.edu/2016/02/18/is-cdc-warning-paternalistic

Bridges, J. S. & Etaugh, C. (1995). College students' perceptions of mothers: Effects of maternal employment-childrearing pattern and motive for employment. *Sex Roles, 32,* 735–751.

Bridges, J. S. & Etaugh, C. (1996). Black and white college women's maternal employment outcome expectations and their desired timing of maternal employment. *Sex Roles, 35,* 543–562.

Bridges, J. S. & Orza, A. M. (1993). Effects of maternal employment-childrearing pattern on college students' perceptions of a mother and her child. *Psychology of Women Quarterly, 17,* 103–117.

Bridges, J. S. & Orza, A. M. (1996). Black and white employed mothers' role experiences. *Sex Roles, 35,* 377–385.

Bridges, L. J., Roe, A. E. C., Dunn, J., & O'Connor, T. G. (2007). Children's perspectives on their relationships with grandparents following parental separation: A longitudinal study. *Social Development, 16,* 539–554.

Bridges, M. (2003/2004, Winter). Poverty up, women still down. *Ms.,* p. 16.

Bridges, S. K., Lease, S. H., & Ellison, C. R. (2000, August). *Predicting women's sexual satisfaction: Implications for the new millennium.* Paper presented at the meeting of the American Psychological Association, Washington, DC.

Brinkmann, A. O. (2009). Androgen physiology: Receptor and metabolic disorders. In R. McLachlan (Ed.), *Endocrinology of male reproduction.* South Dartmouth, MA: MDText.com, Inc. Retrieved from http://www.endotext.org/male/male3/male frame3.htm

Brisolara, S. et al. (Eds.). (2014) *Feminist evaluation and research: Theory and practice,.* New York: Guilford

Britain, D. R., Gyurcsik, N. C., McElroy, M., & Hillard, S. A. (2011). General and arthritis-specific barriers to moderate physical activity in women with arthritis. *Women's Health Issues, 21,* 57–63.

Britsch, B., Callahan, N., & Peterson, K. (2010, Winter). The power of partnerships. *AAUW Outlook, 104*(1), 12–15.

Broadbridge, A. & Hearn, J. (2008). Gender and management: New directions in research and continuing patterns in practice. *British Journal of Management, 19,* S38–S49.

Brody, J. E. (2001, August 21). Nutrition a key to better health for elderly. *New York Times,* p. D8.

Brody, J. E. (2009, March 31). A dip in the sex drive, tied to menopause. *New York Times,* p. D7.

Brody, J. E. (2013a, April 8). Thinking twice about calcium supplements. *New York Times,* p. D3.

Brody, J. E. (2013b, September 17). When parents need nurturing: Navigating care for the aging presents many challenges. *New York Times,* pp. D6.

Brody, J. E. (2014, January 25). Infertility issue is little understood. *New York Times,* p. D7.

Brody, J. E. (2015, April 11). The No. 1 killer of women, too. *New York Times,* p. D7.

Brody, J. E. (2016a, June 14). A deeper understanding of gender. *New York Times,* p. D5.

Brody, J. E. (2016b, January 19). Guidelines, if not clarity, for U.S. diets. *New York Times,* p. D5.

Brody, J. E. (2016c, August 2). Rediscovering the kitchen for heart health. *New York Times,* p. D5.

Brody, J. E. (2016d, October 11). Some IVF experts discourage multiple births. *New York Times,* p. D7.

Brody, L. R. et al. (2016). Gender and emotion: Theory, findings, and context. In L. F. Barrett et al. (Eds.), *Handbook of emotions* (4th ed., pp. 369–392). New York: Guilford.

Brody, L. R. & Hall, J. A. (2008). Gender and emotion in context. In M. Lewis & J. M. Haviland-Jones (Eds.), *Handbook of emotions* (3rd ed., pp. 395–408). New York: Guilford.

Brody, L. R. et al. (2017). Gender roles in women with HIV: Intersection with psychological and physical health outcomes. In S. Dworkin & M. Gandhi (Eds.), *Women's empowerment and global health: A twenty-first-century agenda* (pp. 138–158). Oakland, CA: University of California Press.

Bromfield, N. F. (2016). "Surrogacy has been one of the most rewarding experiences in my life": A content analysis of blogs by U.S. commercial gestational surrogates. *Project Muse, 9,* 192–217.

Brooks-Gunn, J., Han, W. -J., & Waldfogel, J. (2010). First-year maternal employment and child development in the first 7 years. *Monographs of the Society for Research in Child Development, 75*(2, Serial No. 296), 1–147.

Brotman, S. et al. (2014). Access and equity in the design and delivery of health and social care to LGBTQ older adults: A Canadian perspective. In N. A. Orel & C. A. Fruhauf (Eds.), *The lives of LGBT older adults: Understanding challenges and resilience* (pp. 111–140). Washington, DC: American Psychological Association.

Brough, P. & O'Driscoll, M. P. (2015). Integrating work and personal life. In R. J. Burke & K. M Paige (Eds.), *Flourishing in life, work, and careers: Individual wellbeing and career experiences* (pp. 377–393). Northampton, MA: Edward Elgar.

Broverman, I. K., Broverman, D. M., Clarkson, F. E., Rosenkrantz, P. S., & Vogel, S. R. (1970). Sex-role stereotypes and clinical judgements of mental health. *Journal of Consulting Psychology, 34,* 1–7.

Brown, C. S. (2014). *Parenting beyond pink and blue: How to raise your kids free of gender stereotypes.* New York: Random House.

Brown, C. S. & Leaper, C. (2010). Latina and European American girls' experiences with academic sexism and their self-concepts in mathematics and science during adolescence. *Sex Roles, 63,* 860–870.

Brown, D. et al. (2013). The effectiveness of group treatment for female adult incest survivors. *Treatment of sexually abused children and adult survivors, 22,* 143–152.

Brown, J. & Farquhar, C. (2015). Endometriosis: An overview of Cochrane Reviews. *Cochrane Database of Systematic Reviews, Issue 3,* Article No. 009590.

Brown, J. E. et al. (2016). *Shortchanged in retirement: Continuing challenges to women's financial future.* Washington, DC: National Institute on Retirement Security.

Brown, L. (2016). *Supervision essentials for the feminist psychology model of supervision.* Washington, DC: American Psychological Association.

Brown, L. M. (2006, Spring). What about the boys? *Feminist Psychologist,* p. 5.

Brown, R. (2014). Psychological distress and the intersection of gender and physical disability: Considering gender and disability-related risk factors. *Sex Roles, 71,* 171–181.

Brown, S. L. et al. (2013). Dating relationships in older adulthood: A national portrait. *Journal of Marriage and Family, 75,* 1194–1202.

Brown, S. L. et al. (2014). *Relationship quality among cohabiting versus married couples.* National Center for Family & Marriage Research: Bowling Green State University.

Brown, S. L., & Rinelli, L. N. (2010). Family structure, family processes, and adolescent smoking and drinking. *Journal of Research on Adolescence, 20,* 259–273.

Brown, S. L. & Shinohara, S. K. (2013). Dating relationships in older adulthood: A national portrait. *Journal of Marriage and Family, 75,* 1195–1202.

Brown, T. N. T. & Herman, J. L. (2015). *Intimate partner violence and sexual abuse among LGBT people: A review of existing research.* Los Angeles, CA: Williams Institute, UCLA School of Law.

Brownstein, A. (2015, Spring/Summer). Women get in the game. *AAUW Outlook,* 14–17.

Bruce, T. (2016). New rules for new times: sportswomen and media representation in the third wave. *Sex Roles, 74,* 361–376.

Bruckmüller, S. et al. (2013). Ceilings, cliffs, and labyrinths: Exploring metaphors for workplace gender discrimination (Eds.). *Sage handbook of gender and psychology* (pp. 450–464). Los Angeles, CA: Sage.

Brunet, J. et al. (2013). Surviving breast cancer: Women's experiences with their changed bodies. *Body Image, 10,* 344–351.

Brunner, L. K. & Dever, M. (2014). Work, bodies and boundaries: Talking sexual harassment in the New Economy. *Gender, Work, and Organization, 21,* 459–464.

Bryan, A. E. B. et al. (2016). Longitudinal change in women's sexual victimization experiences as a function of alcohol consumption and sexual victimization history: A latent transition analysis. *Psychology of Violence, 6,* 271–279.

Bryant, A. N. (2003). Changes in attitudes toward women's roles: Predicting gender-role traditionalism among college students. *Sex Roles, 48,* 131–142.

Bryant-Davis, T. & Bellette, N. (2013). Restoring sexuality: Women's sexuality in the aftermath of trauma. In D. Castaneda (Ed.), *The essential handbook of women's sexuality* (pp. 277–292). Santa Barbara, CA: Praeger.

Bryant-Davis, T. & Comes-Diaz, L. (2016). *Womanist and mujerista psychologies: Voices of fire, acts of courage.* Washington, DC: American Psychological Association.

Btoush, R. & Haj-Yahia, M. M. (2008). Attitudes of Jordanian society toward wife abuse. *Journal of Interpersonal Violence, 23,* 1531–1554.

Bucchianeri, M. M. et al. (2016). Body dissatisfaction: Do associations with disordered eating and psychological well-being differ across race/ethnicity in adolescent girls and boys? *Cultural Diversity and Ethnic Minority Psychology, 22,* 137–146.

Buchanan, N. T. & Harrell, Z. A. (2014). Surviving sexual harassment: Coping with recognizing and preventing unwanted sexual harassment in the workplace. In T. Bryant-Davis (Ed.), *Surviving sexual violence: A guide to recovery and empowerment* (pp. 7–22). Lanham, MD: Rowman & Littlefield.

Buchanan, N. T. et al. (2013). Exploring gender differences in body image, eating pathology and sexual harassment. *Body Image, 10,* 352–360.

Buchholz, L. (2015). Transgender care moves into the mainstream. *Journal of the American Medical Association, 314,* 1785–1787.

Buchmann, C., DiPrete, T. A., & McDaniel, A. (2008). Gender inequalities in education. *Annual Review of Sociology, 34,* 319–337.

Buckley, C. (2015, December 10). Transgender, and embraced on red carpet. *New York Times,* pp. C1–2.

Buckley, C. & Barry, E. (2015, August 3). Rohingya women flee violence only to be sold into marriage. *New York Times,* pp. A1, A8.

Budig, M. J. (2014). The fatherhood bonus & the motherhood penalty: Parenthood and the gender pay gap. *Third Way,* 5–6.

Budig, M. J. & Hodges, M. J. (2010). Differences in disadvantage: Variation in the motherhood penalty across white women's earnings distribution. *American Sociological Review, 75,* 705–727.

Budig, M. J. et al. (2016). Work-family policy trade-offs for mothers? Unpacking the cross-national variation in motherhood earnings penalties. *Work and Occupations, 43,* 119–177.

Bugental, D. B. & Hehman, J. A. (2007). Ageism: A review of research and policy implications. *Social Issues and Policy Review, 1,* 173–216.

Bukowski, W. M. et al. (2016). Androgyny in liking and in being liked are antecedent to well-being in pre-adolescent boys and girls. *Sex Roles,* doi:10.1007/s11199-016-0638-6.

Buller, D. J. (2009). Four fallacies of pop evolutionary psychology. *Scientific American, 300,* 74–81.

Bullock, H. E. (2013). *Women in poverty: Psychology, public policy, and social justice.* Sussex, UK: Wiley.

Bullock, H. E. & Fernald, J. L. (2003). "Feminism?" Feminist identification, speaker appearance, and perceptions of feminist and antifeminist messengers. *Psychology of Women Quarterly, 27,* 291–299.

Bullock, H. E., Lott, B., & Wyche, K. F. (2010). "Making room at the table": Gender, ethnic, and class inequities. In H. Landrine & N. F. Russo (Eds.), *Handbook of diversity in feminist psychology* (pp. 479–499). New York: Springer.

Burcher, P. & Gabriel, J. (2016). There is no place like home: Why women are choosing home birth in the era of "homelike" hospitals. *Project Muse, 9,* 149–165.

Burchinal, M. et al. (2015). Early child care and education. In R. M. Lerner et al. (Eds.), *Handbook of child psychology and developmental science* (pp. 223–267). Hoboken, NJ: Wiley.

Bureau of Labor Statistics (2013a). *Marriage and divorce: Patterns by gender, race, and educational attainment.* Washington, DC: Author.

Bureau of Labor Statistics (2013b). *Women in the labor force: A databook.* Washington, DC: Author.

Bureau of Labor Statistics (2014). *Employment characteristics of families—2014.* Washington, DC: Author.

Bureau of Labor Statistics (2015). *Women in the labor force: A databook.* Washington, DC: Author.

Bureau of Labor Statistics (2016). *Labor force statistics from the current population survey.* Washington, DC: Author.

Burleson, W. E. (2016). *Bisexuality: An invisible community among LGBT elders.* Switzerland: Springer International.

Burn, S. M. (2011). *Women across cultures: A global perspective* (3rd ed.). New York: McGraw-Hill.

Burnes, D. P. R. et al. (2014). Elder abuse and neglect risk alleviation in protective services. *Journal of Interpersonal Violence, 29,* 2091–2113.

Burnett, V. (2016, June 23). Bathroom debates a town's acceptance of a third gender. *New York Times,* pp. A4, A16.

Burns-Glover, A. L. & Kasibhatla , B. S.(2013). Tensions and intersections: Motherhood, work and sexuality in U.S. and India contexts. In D. Castaneda (Ed.). *The essential handbook of women's sexuality* (vol. 1) (pp. 93–112). Santa Barbara, CA: Praeger.

Burrage, H. (2015). *Eradicating female genital mutilation: A UK perspective*. Burlington, VT: Ashgate Publishing.

Bursik, K. (1992). Perceptions of sexual harassment in an academic context. *Sex Roles, 27,* 401–412.

Burton-Jeangros, C. et al. (2016). Life and satisfaction trajectories of elderly women living in Switzerland: An age—period—cohort analysis. *Ageing & Society, 36,* 106–132.

Buser, T. et al. (2014). Gender competitiveness and career choices. *Quarterly Journal of Economics, 129,* 1409–1447.

Bushnell, C. et al. (2014). Guidelines for the prevention of stroke in women: A statement for healthcare professionals from the American Heart Association American Stroke Association. *Stroke, 45,* 1545–1588.

Buss, D. M. (1994). *The evolution of desire: Strategies of human mating.* New York: Basic Books.

Bussey, K (2013). Gender development. In M.K. Ryan & N.R Branscombe (Eds.). *Sage handbook of gender and psychology* (pp. 81–99). Los Angeles,CA: Sage.

Buster, J. E. (2013). Managing female sexual dysfunction. *Fertility and Sterility, 100,* 905–913.

Butler, B. J. (2008). Psychiatric disorders in women. In A. L. Clouse & K. Sherif (Eds.), *Women's health in clinical practice: A handbook for primary care* (pp. 317–354). Totowa, NJ: Humana Press.

Butler, L. D. & Nolen-Hoeksema, S. (1994). Gender differences in responses to depressed mood in a college sample. *Sex Roles, 30,* 331–346.

Butler, R. (2014). Motivation in educational contexts: Does gender matter? In L. S. Liben & R. S. Bigler (Eds.), *The role of gender in educational contexts and outcomes* (pp. 1–41). San Diego, CA: Academic Press.

Button, D. M. & Worthen, M. G. F. (2014). General strain theory for LGBQ and SSB youth: The importance of intersectionality in the future of feminist criminology. *Feminist Criminology, 9,* 270–297.

Button, E. J., Chadalavada, B., & Palmer, R. L. (2009). Mortality and predictors of death in a cohort of patients presenting to an eating disorders service. *International Journal of Eating Disorders, 43,* 387–392.

Butts, M. M. et al. (2013). How important are work-family support policies? A meta-analytic investigation of their effects on employee outcomes. *Journal of Applied Psychology, 98,* 1–25.

Butts, S. F. & Seifer, D. B. (2010). Racial and ethnic differences in reproductive potential across the life cycle. *Fertility and Sterility, 93,* 681–690.

Byrd-Craven, J. & Geary, D.C. (2013). An evolutionary understanding of sex differences. In M.K. Ryan & N.R. Branscombe (Eds.). *Sage handbook of gender and psychology* (pp. 100–114). LosAngeles, CA: Sage

Byron, R. A. & Roscigno, V. J. (2014). Relational power, legitimation, and pregnancy discrimination. *Gender & Society, 28,* 435.

Cacchioni, T. (2015). *Big pharma, women, and the labour of love.* Toronto, Canada: University of Toronto Press.

Cahusac, E. & Kanji, S. (2014). Giving up: How gendered organizational cultures push mothers out. *Gender, Work & Organization, 21,* 57–58.

Cain, C. L. et al. (2014). Cultural correlates of gender integration in science. *Gender, Work & Organization, 21,* 1–3.

Cain, C. L. & Leahey, E. (2014). Cultural correlates of gender integration in science. *Gender, Work & Organization, 21,* 516–530.

Calabrese, S. K. et al. (2015). Exploring discrimination and mental health disparities faced by black sexual minority women using a minority stress framework. *Psychology of Women Quarterly, 39,* 287–304.

Calvert, S. & Wartella, E. (2014). Children and electronic media. In E. T. Gershoff & R. S. Mistry (Eds.), *Societal contexts of child development: Pathways of influence and implications for practice and policy* (pp. 175–18). New York: Oxford University Press.

Calvert, S. L., Kondla, T. A., Ertel, K. A., & Meisel, D. S. (2001). Young adults' perceptions and memories of a television woman hero. *Sex Roles, 45,* 31–52.

Calzo, J. et al. (2016). Gender conformity, use of laxatives, and muscle-building products in adolescents and young adults. *Pediatrics, 138 (2).* e20154073.

Cambronero-Saiz, B. (2013). Gender policies and advertising and market practices that affect women's health. *Global Health Action, 6,* doi:10.3402/gha.v6i0.20372.

Cambronero-Saiz, B. et al. (2012).quality of pharmaceutical advertising and gender bias in medical journals (1998–2008): A review of the scientific literature. *Gac. Sanit., 26,* 469–476.

Cameron, D. (2007). *The myth of Mars and Venus: Do men and women really speak different languages?* Oxford, UK: Oxford University Press.

Camosy, C. C. (2015). *Beyond the abortion wars: A way forward for a new generation.* Grand Rapids, MI: Eerdmans.

Campbell, F. A. et al. (2012). Adult outcomes as a function of an early childhood educational program: An Abecedarian Project follow-up. *Developmental Psychology, 48,* 1033–1043.

Campbell, K. & Peebles, R. (2014). Eating disorders in children and adolescents: State of the art review. *Pediatrics, 134,* 582–592.

Campbell, R., Dworkin, E. & Cabral, G. (2009). An ecological model of the impact of sexual assault on women's mental health. *Trauma, Violence, and Abuse, 10,* 225–246.

Campbell-Jackson, L. & Horsch, A. (2014). The psychological impact of stillbirth on women: A systematic review. *Illness, Crisis & Loss, 22,* 237–256.

Campione, W. (2008). Employed women's well-being: The global and daily impact of work. *Journal of Family and Economic Issues, 29,* 346–361.

Canabal, M. E. (1995). Native Americans in higher education. *College Student Journal, 29,* 455–457.

Canetto, S. S. (2003). Older adulthood. In L. Slater, J. H. Daniel, & A. E. Banks (Eds.), *The complete guide to mental health for women* (pp. 56–64). Boston, MA: Beacon Press.

Cann, A. & Vann, E. D. (1995). Implications of sex and gender differences for self: Perceived advantages and disadvantages of being the other gender. *Sex Roles, 33,* 531–541.

Cantor, D. et al. (2015). *Report on the AAU campus climate survey on sexual assault and sexual misconduct.* Rockville, MD: Westat.

Capella, C. et al. (2016). Winning a race: Narratives of healing and psychotherapy in children and adolescents who have been sexually abused. *Journal of Child Sexual Abuse, 25,* 73–92.

Capodilupo, C. M. & Forsyth, J. M. (2014). Eating disorders, body image, and vice. In M. L. Miville & A. D. Ferguson (Eds.), *Handbook of race- ethnicity, and gender in psychology* (pp. 343–360). New York: Springer.

Caprara, G. V., Barbaranelli, C., & Pastorelli, C. (2001). Prosocial behavior and aggression in childhood and pre-adolescence. In A. C. Bohart & D. J. Stipek (Eds.), *Constructive and destructive behavior: Implications for family, school, and society* (pp. 187–203). Washington, DC: American Psychological Association.

Carbin, M. & Edenheim, S. (2013). The intersectional turn in feminist theory: A dream of a common language? *European Journal of Women's Studies, 20,* 233–248.

Carli, L. L. (2010). Gender and group behavior. In J. C. Chrisler & D. R. McCreary (Eds.), *Handbook of gender research in psychology* (Vol. 2, pp. 337–358). New York: Springer.

Carli, L.L. (2013). Gendered communication and social influence. In M. K. Ryan & N. R. Branscombe (Eds.). *Sage handbook of gender and psychology* (pp199–215). Los Angeles, CA: Sage.

Carli, L.L. & Eagly, A. H. (2011). Gender and leadership. In A. Bryman & D. L. Collinson (Eds.), *The Sage handbook of leadership* (pp. 103–117). Thousand Oaks, CA: Sage.

Carlson, D. L. et al. (2014). Neighborhoods and racial/ethnic disparities in adolescent sexual risk behavior. *Journal of Youth and Adolescence, 43,* 1536–1549.

Carlsson J. et al. (2015). Identity development in the late twenties: A never-ending story. *Developmental Psychology, 51,* 334–345.

Carothers, B. J. & Reis, H. T. (2013). Men and women are from Earth: Examining the latent structure of gender. *Journal of Personality and Social Psychology, 104,* 385–407.

Carr, C. L. (2007). Where have all the tomboys gone? Women's accounts of gender in adolescence. *Sex Roles, 56,* 439–448.

Carr, D. & Pudrovska, T. (2012). Divorce and motherhood in later life. In R. Blieszner & V. H. Bedford (Eds.), *Handbook of families and aging* (pp. 489–514). Santa Barbara, CA: ABC-CLIO.

Carr, D. et al. (2014). Happy marriage, happy life? Marital quality and subjective well-being in later life. *Journal of Marriage and Family, 76,* 930–948.

Carr, E. R. et al. (2014). Understanding the link between multiple oppressions and depression among African American women: The role of internalization. *Psychology of Women Quarterly, 38,* 233, 245.

Carr, J. B. & Packham,, A. (2016).The effects of state-mandated abstinence-based sex education on teen health outcomes. *Health Economics, 26.* 403–420.

Carrard, V. & Mast, M. (2015). Gender in patient-physician interactions. In K. Faniko et al. (Eds.), *Gender and social hierarchies: Perspectives from social psychology* (pp. 58–72.). New York: Routledge.

Carre, J. M. & Olmstead, N. (2015). Social neuroendocrinology of human aggression: Examining the role of competition-induced dynamics. *Neuroscience, 286,* 171–186.

Carrell, S. E., Page, M. E., & West, J. E. (2009). *Sex and science: How professor gender gap perpetuates the gender gap.* Cambridge, MA: National Bureau of Economic Research.

Carroll, A. E. (2016, June 21). Closest thing to a wonder drug? Try exercise. *New York Times,* p. A3.

Carter, J. et al. (2016). Sex, love and security: Accounts of distance and commitment in living apart together relationships. *Sociology, 50,* 576–593.

Carter, J. C. et al. (2010). Maintenance treatment for anorexia nervosa: A comparison of cognitive behavior therapy and treatment as usual. *International Journal of Eating Disorders, 42,* 202–207.

Carter, J.S. et al. (2009). The interaction of race and gender: Changing gender-role attitudes, 1974–2006. *Social Science Quarterly, 90,* 196–211.

Carter, N. M. & Silva, C. (2010). *Pipeline's broken promise.* New York: Catalyst.

Carvajal, D. (2011, March 7). The changing face of medical care. *New York Times.* Retrieved from nytimes.com/2011/03/08/world/europe/08iht-ffdocs08.html?_r=1& amp=&pagewanted=all

Case, A. & Paxson, C. (2013). HIV risk and adolescent behaviors in Africa. *American Economic Review 103,* 433–438.

Case, K. A. (2007). Raising male privilege awareness and reducing sexism: An evaluation of diversity courses. *Psychology of Women Quarterly, 31,* 426–435.

Cash, T. F., Morrow, J. A., Hrabosky, J. I., & Perry, A. A. (2004). How has body image changed? A cross-sectional investigation of college women and men from 1983 to 2001. *Journal of Consulting and Clinical Psychology, 72,* 1081–1089.

Cashdan, E. (1998). Smiles, speech, and body posture: How women and men display sociometric status and power. *Journal of Nonverbal Behavior, 22,* 209–228.

Cashmore, J. & Shackel, R. (2013). The long-term effects of child sexual abuse. *Child Family Community Australia Information Exchange,* 1–2.

Casper, R. F. & Yonkers, K. A. (2010). *Epidemiology and pathogenesis of premenstrual syndrome and premenstrual dysphoric disorder.* Retrieved from uptodate.com/contents/epidemiology-and-pathogenesis-of-premenstrual-syndrome-and-premenstrual-dysphoric-disorder?source=see_link

Cassidy, A. et al. (2013). High anthocyanin intake is associated with a reduced risk of myocardial infarction in young and middle-aged women. *Circulation, 127,* 188–196.

Castañeda, D. (2008). Gender issues among Latinas. In J. C. Chrisler, C. Golden, & P. D. Rozee (Eds.), *Lectures on the psychology of women* (pp. 250–267). New York: McGraw-Hill.

Castañeda, D. & Burns-Glover, A. L. (2008). Women's friendships and romantic relationships. In F. L. Denmark & M. A. Paludi (Eds.), *Psychology of women: A handbook of issues and theories* (2nd ed., pp. 332–350). Westport, CT: Praeger.

Castellini, G. et al. (2013). Childhood sexual abuse moderates the relationship between sexual functioning and eating disorder psychology in anorexia nervosa and bulimia: A 1-year follow-up study. *Journal of Sexual Medicine, 10,* 2190–2200.

Castilla, E. J. (2015). Accounting for the gap: A firm study manipulating organizational accountability and transparency in pay decisions. *Organization Science, 26,* 311–333.

Castillo, D. T. (2014). Cognitive and behavioral treatments for sexual violence. In T. Bryant-Davis (Ed.), *Surviving sexual violence: A guide to recovery and empowerment* (pp. 91–111). Lanham, MD: Rowman & Littlefield.

Castro Baker, A. et al. (2016). Confronting barriers to critical discussions about sexualization with adolescent girls. *Social Work, 61,* 79–81.

Catalyst. (2013). *Why diversity matters.* New York: Author.

Catalyst. (2015). *Women in academia.* New York: Author.

Catalyst. (2016). *Catalyst quick take: Women in government.* New York: Author.

Cavanaugh, J. C. & Blanchard-Fields, F. (2015). *Adult development and aging* (7th ed.). Belmont, CA: Wadsworth.

Cavazos-Rehg, P. A. et al. (2010). Understanding adolescent parenthood from a multisystemic perspective. *Journal of Adolescent Health, 46,* 525–531.

Ceci, S. et al. (2014). Women in academic science: A changing landscape. *Psychological Science in the Public Interest, 15,* 75–141.

Center for American Progress/Work Life Law. (2010). *The three faces of work-family conflict: The poor, the professionals, and the missing middle.* Washington/San Francisco, DC/CA: Author.

Center for American Women and Politics. (2014). Women in the U.S. Congress 2015. Rutgers, NJ: Author.

Center on Alcohol Marketing and Youth. (2010). *Youth exposure to alcohol advertising in national magazines, 2001–2008.* Baltimore, MD: Johns Hopkins University.

Center for Community Change & Older Women's Economic Security Task Force. (2013).*Expanding social Security benefits for financially vulnerable populations.* Washington, DC: Authors.

Centers for Disease Control and Prevention. (2000). *All the stages of our lives.* Atlanta, GA: Author.

Centers for Disease Control and Prevention. (2011). Vital signs: Teen pregnancy—United States, 1991–2009. *Morbidity and Mortality Weekly Report, 60,* 414–420.

Centers for Disease Control and Prevention. (2013a). *HIV among older Americans.* Atlanta, GA: Author.

Centers for Disease Control and Prevention. (2013b). *National ART success rates.* Atlanta, GA: Author.

Centers for Disease and Control and Prevention. (2014). *Sexually transmitted disease surveillance 2013.* Atlanta: Author.

Centers for Disease Control and Prevention. (2015a). *Abortion Surveillance—United States, 2012.* Atlanta, GA: Author.

Centers for Disease Control and Prevention. (2015b). *2012 ART fertility success rates.* Atlanta, GA: Author.

Centers for Disease Control and Prevention. (2015c). *Current cigarette smoking among adults—United States, 2005–2014.* Atlanta, GA: Author.

Centers for Disease Control and Prevention. (2015d). *Facts about FASDs.* Atlanta, GA: Author.

Centers for Disease Control and Prevention. (2015e). *Facts about stillbirth.* Atlanta, GA: Author.

Centers for Disease Control and Prevention. (2015f). *Infertility FAQS.* Atlanta, GA: Author.

Centers for Disease Control and Prevention. (2016a). *Quickstats: Death rates for children and adolescents aged 1–14 years, by sex—United States, 1999–2014.* Atlanta, GA: Author.

Centers for Disease Control and Prevention. (2016b). *Tobacco industry marketing.* Atlanta, GA: Author.

Centers for Disease Control and Prevention. (2016c). *Quarterly provisional estimates—Natality.* Atlanta, GA: Author.

Centers for Disease Control and Prevention. (2016d). *Youth risk behavior surveillance—United States, 2015.* Atlanta, GA: Author.

Centers for Disease Control and Prevention. (2017). *High blood pressure.* Atlanta, GA: Author.

Cerankowski, K. & Milks, M. (Eds.), (2014). *Asexualities: Feminist and queer perspectives*. New York: Routledge.

Cermele, J. A., Daniels, S., & Anderson, K. L. (2001). Defining normal: Constructions of race and gender in the *DSM-IV* casebook. *Feminism & Psychology*, 11, 229–247.

Cespedes, A. (2015). *Daily recommended caloric intake for women*. Retrieved from livestrong.com

Cha, Y. & Weeden, K. A. (2014). Overwork and the slow convergence in the gender gap in wages. *American Sociological Review*. 79, 457–484.

Chabbert-Buffet, N. (2014). Fibroid growth and medical options for treatment. *Fertility and Sterility*. 102, 630–639.

Chambers, P., Allan, G., Phillipson, C., & Ray, M. (2009). *Family practices in later life*. Bristol, UK: Policy Press.

Champion, V. L. et al. (2014). Comparison of younger and older breast cancer survivors and age-matched controls on specific and overall quality of life domains. *Cancer, 120*, 2237–2246.

Chan, S. K. et al. (2014). Likely female-to-female sexual transmission of HIV—Texas, 2012. *Morbidity and Mortality Weekly Report, 63*, 209–212.

Chaney, C. et al. (2012). An exploration of financial coping strategies for college-educated African American women: A research note. *Black Women, Gender, and Families, 6*(2), 75–94.

Chang, J. T. et al. (2004). Interventions for the prevention of falls in older adults: Systematic review and meta-analysis of randomised clinical trials. *British Medical Journal, 328*, 680–683.

Chang, P. F. & Bazarova, N. N. (2016). Managing stigma: Exploring disclosure-response patterns in pro-anorexic websites. *Health Communication, 31*, 217–229.

Chaplin, T. M. (2015). Gender and emotion expression: A developmental contextual perspective. *Emotion Review, 7*, 14–21.

Chappell, B. (2015, February 5). Harvard bans sexual relationships between professors and Students. *NPR*. Retrieved from npr.org/sections/thetwo-way/2015/02/05/384080539/harvard-bans-sexual-relationships-between-professors-and-students

Charlesworth, G. et al. (2016). The impact of volunteering on the volunteer: Findings from a Peer-support programme for family carers of people with dementia. *Health & Social Care In the Community*, doi,10.11111/hsc.12341.

Charter, M. L. (2015). Feminist self-identification among social work students. *Journal of Social Work and Education, 51*, 72–89.

Chase-Lansdale, P. L. & Brooks-Gunn, J. (2014). Two-generation programs in the twenty-first century. HYPERLINK "http://www.futureofthechildren.org" \h *www.futureofthechildren.org. 24*, 13–14.

Chen, F. et al. (2014). Race/ethnic differentials in the health consequences of caring for grandchildren for grandparents. *The Journals of Gerontology Series B: Psychological Sciences and Social Studies, 70*, 793–803.

Chen, H.-Y. et al. (2012). Cervical cancer screening in the United states, 1993–2010: Characteristics of women who are never screened. *Women's Health, 21*, 1132–1138.

Chen, I. (2009). A clash of science and politics over PMS. *New York Times*. Retrieved from nytimes.com

Chen, Y. & Feeley, T. H. (2014). Social support, social strain, loneliness, and well-being among older adults: An analysis of the health and retirement study. *Journal of Social and Personal Relationships, 31*, 141–161.

Chen, Y. et al. (2013). Prenatal sex selection and missing girls in china: Evidence from the diffusion of diagnostic ultrasound. *The Journal of Human Resources, 48*, 36–70.

Cheng, J. K. & Sue, S. (2016). Addressing cultural and minority issues in the acceptance and mindfulness movement. In A. Masuda (Ed.). *Mindfulness and acceptance in multicultural competency* (pp. 21–38). Oakland, CA: Harbinger.

Cheng, T. C. & Lom C. C. (2016). Racial disparities in intimate partner violence examined through the multiple disadvantage model. *Journal of Interpersonal Violence, 31*, 2026–2051.

Cherif, F. M. (2015). *Myths about women's rights: How, where, and why rights advance*. New York: Oxford University Press.

Cherlin, A. J. & Krishnamurthy, P. (2004, May 9). What works for mom. *New York Times*, p. WK13.

Cherry, A. L., Byers, L., & Dillon, M. (2009). A global perspective on teen pregnancy. In J. E. Ehiri (Ed.), *Maternal and child health: Global challenges, programs, and policies* (pp. 375–397). New York: Springer.

Cheryan, S. et al. (2013). The stereotypical computer scientist: Gendered media representations as a barrier to inclusion for women. *Sex Roles, 69*, 58–71.

Cheryan, S. et al. (2015). Enduring influence of stereotypical computer science role models on women's academic aspirations. *Psychology of Women Quarterly, 37*, 72–79.

Chetty, R. et al. (2016). The association between income and life expectancy in the United States, 2001–2014. *Journal of the American Medical Association, 315*, 1750–1766.

Cheung, F. M. & Halpern, D. F. (2010). Women at the top: Powerful leaders define success as work + family in a culture of gender. *American Psychologist, 65*, 182–193.

Chew-Graham, C.A. & Ray, M. (2016). *Mental health and older people: A guide for primary care physicians*. New York: Springer.

Chin, L. (2016). Unequal egalitarianism. *Gender in Management: An International Journal, 31*, 19–42.

Chisholm, J. & Greene, B. (2008). Women of color: Perspectives on "multiple identities" in psychological theory, research, and practice. In F. L. Denmark & M. A. Paludi (Eds.), *Psychology of women: A handbook of issues and theories* (2nd ed., pp. 40–69). Westport, CT: Praeger.

Choksi, M. (2013, December 19). The ties that bind transgendered communities. *New York Times*, pC1.

Chopik, W. J. & O'Brien E. (2017). Happy you, healthy me? Having a happy partner is independently associated with better health in one self. *Health Psychology, 36*, 21–30.

Chithambo, T. P. & Huey, S. J. (2013). Black/white differences in perceived weight and attractiveness among overweight women. *Journal of Obesity*, doi: 10.1155/2013/320326.

Chodorow, N. J. (1994). *Femininities, masculinities, sexualities: Freud and beyond*. Lexington, KY: University of Kentucky Press.

Chong, A. & Mickelson, K. D. (2016). Perceived fairness and relationship satisfaction during the transition to parenthood: The mediating role of spousal support. *Journal of Family Issues, 37*, 3–28.

Chrisler, J. C. (2007). Body image issues of women over 50. In V. Muhlbauer & J. C. Chrisler (Eds.), *Women over 50: Psychological perspectives* (pp. 6–25). New York: Springer.

Chrisler, J. C. (2008). The menstrual cycle in a biopsychosocial context. In F. L. Denmark & M. A. Paludi (Eds.), *Psychology of women: A handbook of issues and theories* (2nd ed., pp. 400–439). Westport, CT: Praeger.

Chrisler, J. C. (2013). The American Psychological Association's committee on women in psychology: 40 years of contributions to the transformation of psychology. *Psychology of Women Quarterly, 37*, 444–454.

Chrisler, J. C. & Clapp, S. K. (2008). When the boss is a woman. In M. A. Paludi (Ed.), *The psychology of women at work: Challenges and solutions for our female workforce: Career liberation, history, and the new millennium* (Vol. 1, pp. 39–65). Westport, CT: Praeger.

Chrisler, J. C., & Garrett, C. (2010). Women's reproductive rights: An international perspective. In M. A. Paludi (Ed.), *Feminism and women's rights worldwide: Feminism as human rights* (Vol. 2, pp. 129–146). Santa Barbara, CA: Praeger

Chrisler, J. C. & Gorman, J. A. (2015). The medicalization of women's moods: Premenstrual syndrome and premenstrual dysphoric disorder. In M. C. McHugh & J. C. Chrisler (Eds.). *The wrong prescription for women* (pp. 77–98). Santa Barbara, CA: Praeger.

Chrisler, J. C., & Versace, J. (2011). Menopause, social aspects of. In M. Z. Stange, C. K. Oyster, & J. E. Sloan (Eds.), *Encyclopedia of women in today's world* (Vol. 2, pp. 925–927). Newberry Park, CA: Sage.

Chrisler, J. C., Johnston, I. K., Champagne, N. M., & Preston, K. E. (1994). Menstrual joy: The construct and its consequences. *Psychology of Women Quarterly, 18*, 347–387.

Chrisler, J. C. et al. (2014). Ambivalent sexism and attitudes toward women in different stages of reproductive life: A semantic, cross-cultural approach. *Health Care for Women International, 35*, 634–657, 9–30.

Chrisler, J. C. et al. (2015). Older women, power, and the body. In V. Muhlbauer et al. (Eds.), *Women and aging: An international, intersectional power perspective* (pp. 9–30). Switzerland: Springer International Publishing.

Chrisler, J. C. et al. (2016). Ageism can be hazardous to women's health: Ageism, sexism, and Stereotypes of older women in the healthcare system. *Journal of Social Issues, 72*, 86–104.

Christmas, G. (2013). "It's a . . . does it matter?" Theorising "boy or girl" binary classifications, intersexuality and medical practice in New Zealand. *Women's Studies Journal, 27*, 25–35.

Christopher, B. & Coyne, S. M. (2014). A meta-analysis of sex differences in cyber-bullying behavior: The moderating role of age. *Aggressive Behavior, 40*, 474–488.

Chung, Y. B. et al. (2012). Sexual orientation and sexual identity: Theory, research and practice. In N.A. Fouad et al. (Eds.). *APA handbook of counseling psychology: Theories, research, and methods* (pp423–451). Washington, DC: American Psychological Association

Cichy, K. E., Lefkowitz, E. S., & Fingerman, K. L. (2007). Generational differences in gender attitudes between parents and grown offspring. *Sex Roles, 57*, 825–836.

Cillessen, A. et al. (2014). Aggressive effects of prioritizing popularity in early adolescence. *Aggressive Behavior, 40*, 204–213.

Clancy, C. M. (2000). Gender issues in women's health care. In M. B. Goldman & M. C. Hatch (Eds.), *Women & health* (pp. 50–64). New York: Academic Press.

Clancy, K. B. et al. (2014). Survey of academic field experiences (SAFE): Trainees report harassment and assault. Retrieved July 17, 2015, from journals.plos.org/plosone/

Clark, R. A. (1998). A comparison of topics and objectives in a cross section of young men's and women's everyday conversations. In D. J. Canary & K. Dindia (Eds.), *Sex differences and similarities in communication: Critical essays and empirical investigations of sex and gender in interaction* (pp. 303–319). Mahwah, NJ: Erlbaum.

Clarke, A. Y., Adams, J., & Steinmetz, G. (2011). *The inequalities of love: College-educated Black women and the barriers to romance and family.* Durham, NC: Duke University Press.

Clarke, P. & Ayres, I. (2014). The Chastain effect: Using Title IX to measure the causal effect of participating in high school sports on adult women's social lives. *Journal of Socio-Economics.* Retrieved from ssrn.com/abstracts2366906

Clarke, P. J., O'Malley, P. M., Johnston, L. D., Schulenberg, J. E., & Lantz, P. (2009). Differential trends in weight-related health behaviors among American young adults by gender, race/ ethnicity, and socioeconomic status: 1984–2006. *American Journal of Public Health, 99*, 1893–1901.

Clauset, A. et al. (2015). Systematic inequality and hierarchy in faculty hiring networks. *Science Advances, 1*(1). e1400005.

Clay, R. A. (2014a). Depression's toll on the heart. *Monitor on Psychology, 45*, 24.

Clay, R. A. (2014b). Double-whammy discrimination. *Monitor on Psychology, 45*, 1–4.

Clay, R. A. (2015). Eliminating class bias: An APA committee is working to help psychologists be more sensitive in their work with people living in poverty. *Monitor on Psychology*, 80–83.

Clayton, J. A. & Collins, F. S. (2014). Policy: NIH to balance sex in cell and animal studies. *Nature News*, 1–8.

Clayton, S., Garcia, A. L., & Crosby, F. J. (2010). Women in the workplace: Acknowledging difference in experience and policy. In H. Landrine & N. F. Russo (Eds.), *Handbook of diversity in feminist psychology* (pp. 559–581). New York: Springer.

Clearfield, M. W. & Nelson, N. M. (2006). Sex differences in mothers' speech and play behavior with 6-, 9-, and 14-month-old infants. *Sex Roles, 54*, 127–137.

Cleere, C. & Lynn, S. J. (2013). Acknowledged versus unacknowledged sexual assault among college women. *Journal of International Violence, 28*, 2593–2611.

Clemetson, L. (2002, October 7). A neighborhood clinic helps fill the gap for Latinos without health care. *New York Times*, p. A12.

Clinical Trends. (2013). *Child care.* Bethesda, MD: Author.

Clinton-Sherrod, A. W. & Walters, J. H. (2014). Marital rape and "sexual" violation by intimate partners. In T. Bryant-Davis (Ed.), *Surviving sexual violence: A guide to recovery and Empowerment* (pp. 48–58). Lanham, MD: Rowman & Littlefield.

Cloward, K. (2016). When norms collide. *Learning responses to activism against female genital mutilation and early menarche.* New York: Oxford University Press.

Coall, D. A. & Hertwig, R. (2011). Grandparental involvement: A relic of the past or a resource for the future? *Current Directions in Psychological Science , 20*, 93–98.

Cochran, S. D. et al. (2015). Mortality risks among persons reporting same-sex sexual 'partners: Evidence from the 2008 General Social Survey—National death index data set. *Research and Practice, 105*, 358–359.

Cochran, S. D. et al. (2016). Sexual orientation and all-cause mortality among US adults aged 18 to 59 years, 2001–2011. *AJPH, 106*, 918.

Cohen, D. (Ed.). (2010). *Oxford textbook of women and mental health.* Oxford, UK: Oxford University Press.

Cohen, J. & Byers, E. S. (2014). Beyond lesbian bed death: Enhancing our understanding of the sexuality of sexual-minority women in relationships. *Journal of Sex Research, 51*, 893–903.

Cohen, L. (2014). *Imagining women's careers. Oxford University Press.*

Cohen, P. (2016, January, 2). Over 50, female and jobless even as others return to work. *New York Times*, pp. A1, B4.

Cohen, P. (2017, January 25). Care chasm causes women to forgo jobs. *New York Times*, pA1.

Cohen, P. et al. (2003). Variations in patterns of developmental transitions in the emerging adulthood period. *Developmental Psychology, 39*, 657–669.

Cohen, S. et al. (2014). Does hugging provide stress-buffering social support? A study of susceptibility to upper respiratory infection and illness. *Psychological Science*, 1–13.

Cohen, S. A. (2010). Family planning and safe motherhood: Dollars and sense. *Guttmacher Policy Review, 13*(2), 12–16.

Cohen, S. A. (2013). Still true: Abortion does not increase women's risk of mental health problems. *Guttmacher Policy Review. 16*, 13–18.

Cohn, A. M. et al. (2013). Correlates of reasons for not reporting rape to police: Results from a national telephone household probability sample of women with forcible or drug-or-alcohol facilitated/ incapacitated rape. *Journal of Interpersonal Violence. 28*, 455–473.

Cohn, D. & Caumont, A. (2014). *7 key findings about stay-at-home moms.* Washington, DC: Pew Research Center.

Coker, A. L. et al. (2014). Dating violence victimization and perpetration rates among high school students. *Violence Against Women, 20*, 1220–1238.

Colaner, C. W. & Rittenour, C. E. (2015). "Feminism begins at home": The influence of mother gender socialization on daughter career and motherhood aspirations as channeled through daughter feminist identification. *Communication Quarterly, 63*, 81–98.

Cole, E. R. (2009). Intersectionality and research in psychology. *American Psychologist, 64*, 170–180.

Cole, E. R. (2013). Knowing then, understanding now: Different strokes for different folks: Jo Ann E. Gardner and Charles W. Thomas in conversation with T. George Harris. *Association for Psychological Science, 26*, 27–28.

Coleman, J. M. & Franiuk, R. (2011). Perceptions of mothers and fathers who take temporary work leave. *Sex Roles, 64*, 311–323.

Colgan, F. (2015). Organisational life within a UK "good practice employer": Experiences of black and minority ethnic and disabled LGBT employees. *Sexual orientation at work: Contemporary Issues and perspectives* (pp. 104–121). New York: Routledge.

Colgan, F. & Rumens, N. (2015). *Sexual orientation at work: Contemporary issues and perspectives.* New York: Routledge.

Collier, K. L. et al. (2013). Sexual orientation and gender identity/ expression related peer victimization in adolescence: A systematic review of associated psychological and health outcomes. *Journal of Sex Research, 50*, 299–317.

Collin-Vézina, D. et al. (2013). Lessons learned from child sexual abuse research: Prevalence, outcomes, and preventive strategies. *Child and Adolescent Psychiatry and Mental Health, 7*.

Collins, S. M. et al. (2016). Concerns and supports of grandfamilies using formal services: Do they have the help they need? *Grandfamilies: The Contemporary Journal of Research, Practice, and Policy, 3* (1),1–35.

Collinson, C. (2015). *Fifteen facts about women's retirement outlook . . . and seven steps to improve it.* Los Angeles, CA: Transamerica Center for Retirement Studies.

Comas-Diaz, L. (2012, Winter). International women as peacemakers. *The Feminist Psychologist*, p. 13.

Comas-Diaz, L. (2013a). Adult women of color: Coping with developmental issues. In L. Comas-Diaz & B. Greene. (Eds.), *Psychological health of women of color: Intersections, challenges, and opportunities* (pp. 57–80). Santa Barbara, CA: ABC-CLIO.

Comas-Diaz, L. (2013b). Culturally competent psychological interventions with women of color. In L. Comas-Diaz & B. Greene (Eds.), *Psychological health of women of color: Intersections, challenges, and opportunities* (pp. 373–408). Santa Barbara, CA: ABC-CL10.

Combs, G. & Milosevic, I. (2016). Workplace discrimination and the well-being of minority women: Overview, prospects, and implications. In M. Connerley & J, Wu (Eds.), *Handbook on well-being of working women* (pp. 24–31). Dordrecht, Netherlands: Springer.

Comerford, L. (2011). Partner rights. In M. Z. Stange, C. K. Oyster, & J. E. Sloan (Eds.), *Encyclopedia of women in today's world*. Newberry Park, CA: Sage.

Commission on Women's Health. (2003). *The Commonwealth Fund Survey of women's health*. New York: Commonwealth Fund.

Commonwealth Fund. (1997). *In their own words: Adolescent girls discuss health and health care issues*. New York: Author.

Compitello, V. (2017). Through the eye of a needle: The emerging adolescent. In M. Kopala & M. Keitel (Eds.), *Handbook of counseling women* (2nd ed., pp. 155–169). Thousand Oaks, CA: Sage.

Condis, M. (2015). Applying for the position of princess: Race, labor and the privileging of whiteness in disney princess line. In M. Forman-Brunell & R. C. Hains (Eds.), *Princess cultures: Mediating girls' imaginations and identities* (pp. 25–44). New York: Peter Lang.

Conforti, A. S. et al. (2012). Yerba mate (ilex paraguariensis) consumption is associated with higher bone mineral density in postmenopausal women, *Bone, 50*, 9–13.

Cong, Z. & Pei, Y. (2017). Older women's mental health. In K.A. Kendall-Tackett & L.M. Ruglass (Eds.). *Women's mental health across the lifespan* (pp. 59–82).New York: Routledge.

Conger, K. J. & Little, W. M. (2010). Sibling relationships during the transition to adulthood. *Child Development Perspectives, 4*, 87–94.

Conkle, A. (2010, February). Modern love: Scientific insights from 21st century dating. *Association for Psychological Science Observer, 23*, 12–16.

Connolly, J. A. & McIsaac, C. (2009). Romantic relationships in adolescence. In R. M. Lerner & L. Steinberg (Eds.), *Handbook of adolescent psychology* (3rd ed., Vol. 2, pp. 104–151). Hoboken, NJ: Wiley.

Conwell, Y., Duberstein, P. R., Hirsch, J. K., Conner, K. R., Eberly, S., & Caine, E. D. (2010). Health status and suicide in the second half of life. *International Journal of Geriatric Psychiatry, 25*, 371–379.

Cook, A. & Glass, C. (2013). Above the glass ceiling: When are women and racial/ethnic minorities promoted to CEO? *Strategic Management Journal, 35*, 1080–1089.

Cooklin, A. R. et al. (2014). Mothers' work-family conflict and enrichment: Associations with Parenting quality and couple relationship. *Child: Care, Health, and Development, 41*, 266–277.

Cooky C. et al. (2013) Women play sport, but not on TV. *Communication & Sport, 1*, 1–28.

Cooky, C. et al. (2015). "It's dude time!": A quarter century of excluding women's sports in televised news and highlight shows. *Communication & Sport, 3*, 261–287.

Coontz, S. (2011). *A strange stirring: "The feminine mystique" and American women at the dawn of the 1960's*. New York: Basic Books.

Coontz, S. (2013, June 2). The triumph of the working mother. *New York Times*, p. SR11.

Coontz, S. (2016). The way we never were: *American families and the nostalgia trap* (2nd ed.). New York: Basic Books.

Cooper, C. R. et al. (2014). Indigenous, immigrant, second class, and gender identities on their pathway to school. In K. C. McLean & M. Syed (Eds.), *The Oxford handbook of identity development* (pp. 299–318). New York: Oxford University Press.

Cooper, L. B. et al. (2013). Reducing gender-based violence. In M. K. Ryan & N. R. Branscombe (Eds.) *Sage handbook of gender and psychology*. Los Angeles, CA: Sage.

Copen, C. E. et al. (2013). *First premarital cohabitation in the United States: Data from the 2006–2010 National Survey of Family Growth*. Hyattsville, MD: National Center for Health Statistics.

Copen, C. E. et al. (2016). *Sexual behavior, sexual attraction, and sexual orientation among adults aged 18–44 in the United States: Data from the 2011–2013 National Survey of Family Growth*. Hyattsville, MD: National Center for Health Statistics.

Corbett, C. & Hill, C. (2015). *Solving the equation: The variables for women's success in engineering and computing*. Washington, DC: AAUW.

Cornwell, E. Y. & Waite, L. J. (2009). Social disconnectedness, perceived isolation, and health among older adults. *Journal of Health and Social Behavior, 50*, 31–48.

Cortez, R. et al. (2015). Socioeconomic differences in adolescent sexual and reproductive health: Marriage. Washington DC: World Bank.

Cote, L. R. & Bornstein, M. H. (2009). Child and mother play in three U.S. cultural groups: Comparisons and associations. *Journal of Family Psychology, 23*, 355–363.

Coursolle, K. M., Sweeney, M. M., Raymo, J. M., & Ho, J.-H. (2010). The association between retirement and emotional well-being: Does prior work-family conflict matter? *Journal of Gerontology: Social Sciences, 65B*, 609–620.

Courtney-Long, E. A. et al. (2015). Prevalence of disability and disability type among adults—United States 2013. *Mortality and Morbidity Weekly Report, 64*, 777–782.

Couturier, J. et al. (2013). Efficacy of family-based treatment for adolescents with eating disorders: A systematic review and meta-analysis. *International Journal of Eating Disorders, 46*, 3–11.

Cowley, A. D. (2014). "Let's get drunk and have sex": The complex relationship of alcohol, gender, and seual victimization. *Journal of Interpersonal Violence, 29*, 1258–1278.

Cowley, G. & Murr, A. (2004, December 6). The new face of AIDS. *Newsweek*, pp. 76–79.

Cox, S. et al. (2014). Vital signs: Births to teens aged 15–17 years—United States 1991–2012. *Mortality and Morbidity Weekly Report, 63*, 1–2.

Coyne, C. A. et al. (2013). The association between teenage motherhood and poor offspring outcomes: A national cohort study across 30 years. *Twin Research and Human Genetics, 16*, 679–689.

Coyne, S. et al. (2016). Pretty as a princess: Longitudinal effects of engagement with Disney princesses on gender stereotypes, body esteem, and prosocial behavior in children. *Child Development, 87*, 1909–1925.

Coyne, S. M., Archer, J., & Eslea, M. (2006). "We're not friends anymore! unless . . .": The frequency and harmfulness of indirect, relational, and social aggression. *Aggressive Behavior, 32*, 294–307.

Cragun, R. T. & Sumerau, J. E. (2015). The last bastion of sexual and gender prejudice? Sexualities, race, gender, religiosity, and spirituality in the examination of prejudice toward sexual and gender minorities. *Journal of Sex Research, 52*, 821–834.

Craig, L. & Jenkins, B. (2016). The composition of parents' and grandparents' child-care time: gender and generational patterns in activity, multi-tasking and co-presence. *Ageing & Society, 36*, 785–810.

Craig, L. & Sawrikar, P. (2009). Work and family: How does the (gender) balance change as children grow? *Gender, Work & Organization, 16*, 687–709.

Craig, S. L. & Keane, G. (2014). The mental health of multiethnic lesbian and bisexual adolescent females: The role of self-efficacy, stress, and behavioral risks. *Journal of Gay & Lesbian Mental Health, 18*, 1–2.

Cram, B. et al. (2016). Social costs: The career-family tradeoff. In M. Connerley & J. Wu (Eds.), *Handbook on well-being of working women* (pp. 473–487). New York: Springer.

Cramer, H. et al. (2012). Mindfulness-based stress reduction for breast cancer—a systematic review and meta-analysis. *Current Oncology, 19*, e343–e352.

Crawford, J. T. et al. (2016). Right-wing authoritarianism predicts prejudice equally toward "gay men and lesbians" and "homosexuals". *Journal of Personality and Social Psychology, 111*, e31–e35.

Crawford, M. (2013). Meaning-making and feminist practice. *Psychology of Women Quarterly, 37*, 256–260.

Crawford, M. B. & DeLisi, L. E. (2016). Issues related to sex differences in antipsychotic treatment. *Current Opinion in Psychology, 29*, 211–217.

Crawford, M. & MacLeod, M. (1990). Gender in the college classroom: An assessment of the "chilly climate" for women. *Sex Roles, 23*, 101–122.

Crawley, R. et al. (2013). Recovering from stillbirth: The effects of making and sharing memories on maternal mental health. *Journal of Reproductive and Infant Psychology, 31*, 195–207.

Crawley, S. L. (2011). Visible bodies, vicarious masculinity, and "the gender revolution": Comment on England. *Gender & Society, 25*, 108–112.

Creighton, S. M. et al. (2014). Childhood surgery for ambiguous genitalia: Glimpses of practice changes of more the same? *Psychology & Sexuality, 5*, 34–43.

Crenshaw, K. (2015). *Black girls matter: Pushed out, overpoliced and underprotected.* New York: Center for Intersectionality and Social Policy Studies.

Crick, N. R., Murray-Close, D., Marks, P. E., & Mohajeri-Nelson, N. (2009). Aggression and peer relationships in school-age children: Relational and physical aggression in group and dyadic contexts. In K. H. Rubin, W. M. Bukowski, & B. Laursen (Eds.), *Handbook of peer interactions, relationships, and groups* (pp. 287–302). New York: Guilford.

Crisp, G. et al. (2015). Undergraduate latina/o students: A systematic review of research identifying factors contributing to academic success outcomes. *Review of Educational Research, 85*, 249–274.

Cristidis, P. et al. (2016). Latest class of psychologists in more diverse. *Monitor on Psychology*, 24.

Crittenden, A. (2014, March 30). On top of everything else. *New York Times*, p. 15.

Crockett, L. J. (1991). Sex roles and sex-typing in adolescence. In R. M. Lerner, A. C. Petersen, & J. Brooks-Gunn (Eds.), *Encyclopedia of adolescence* (Vol. 2, pp. 1007–1017). New York: Garland.

Croft, A. et al. (2014). The second shift reflected in the second generation: Do parents' gender roles at home predict children's aspirations. *Psychological Science, 25*, 1418–1428.

Crosby, F. J. (1991). *Juggling: The unexpected advantages of balancing career and home for women and their families.* New York: Free Press.

Crosby, F. J. et al. (2013). Affirmative action and gender equality. In M.K. Ryan & N.R. Branscombe (Eds.). *Sage handbook of gender and psychology.* Los Angeles, CA: Sage.

Crosby, F. J. & Sabattini, L. (2006). Family and work balance. In J. Worell & C. D. Goodheart (Eds.), *Handbook of girls' and women's psychological health: Gender and well-being across the lifespan* (pp. 350–358). New York: Oxford University Press.

Crosnoe, R. & Cavanagh, S. E. (2010). Families with children and adolescents: A review, critique, and future agenda. *Journal of Marriage and Family, 72*, 594–611.

Crossland, C. et al. (2013). NIJ's program of research on violence against American Indian and Alaska Native women. *Violence Against Women, 19*, 771–772.

Crowley, K., Callanan, M. A., Tenenbaum, H. R., & Allen, E. (2001). Parents explain more often to boys than to girls during shared scientific thinking. *Psychological Science, 12*, 258–261.

Cruikshank, M. (2013). *Learning to be old: Gender, culture, and aging.* Lanham, MD: Rowman & Littlefield.

Cuadrado, I. et al. (2015). Gender-typing of leadership: Evaluations of real and ideal managers. *Scandinavian Journal of Psychology, 56*, 236–244.

Cuklanz, L. & Moorti, S. (2015). Television's new feminism: Primetime representations of women and victimization. In Dines & J. M. Humez (Eds.), *Gender, race, and class in media* (4th ed., pp. 175–186). Thousand Oaks, CA: Sage.

Cundiff, J.L. (2012). Is mainstream psychological research "womanless" and "raceless"? An updated analysis. *Sex Roles, 67*, 158–173.

Cunningham, B. C. et al. (2015). *Stats in brief: Gender differences in science, technology, and engineering, and mathematics (STEM) interest, credits earned, and NAEP performance in the 12th grade.* Washington, DC: National Center for Education Statistics.

Cunningham, G. B. (2008). Creating and sustaining gender diversity in sport organizations. *Sex Roles, 58*, 136–145.

Cunningham, G. B. et al. (2014). Interpersonal mistreatment of women in the workplace. *Sex Roles, 71*, 1–6.

Cunningham, J. & Macan, T. (2007). Effects of applicant pregnancy on hiring decisions and interview ratings. *Sex Roles, 57*, 497–508.

Cunningham, M. (2008). Changing attitudes toward the male breadwinner, female homemaker family model: Influences of women's employment and education over the lifecourse. *Social Forces, 87*, 299–322.

Cunningham, M., Beutel, A. M., Barber, J. S., & Thornton, A. (2005). Reciprocal relationships between attitudes about gender and social contexts during young adulthood. *Social Science Research, 34*, 862–892.

Curtin, S. C. et al. (2016). Suicide rates for females and males by race and ethnicity: United States, 1999 and 2014. *National Center for Health Statistics* Data Brief # 241.

Curtis, K.M. et al. (2016). U.S. selected practice recommendations for contraceptive use, 2016. *Morbidity and Mortality Weekly Reports, 65*, 1–66.

Curtis ,L. & Rybczynski. K. (2015). Are female baby boomers ready for retirement? *Population Change and Lifecourse Strategic Knowledge Center Discussion Paper Series, 3*, 1–26.

Czajkowski, S. M., Arteaga, S., & Burg, M. M. (2012). Social support and coronary heart disease. In R. Alan & J. Fisher (Eds.), *Heart and mind: The practice of cardiac psychology* (2nd ed., pp. 169–195). Washington, DC: American Psychological Association.

D'Alton, M. E. & Hehir, M. P. (2015). Cesarean delivery rates revisiting a 3-decades-old dogma. *Journal of the American Medical Association, 314*, 2238–2264.

D'Haese, L. et al. (2016). The relationship between childhood gender nonconformity and experiencing diverse types of homophobic violence. *Journal of Interpersonal Violence, 31*, 1634–1660.

Daar, J. F. & Brzyski, R. G. (2009, October 21). Genetic screening of sperm and oocyte donors: Ethical and policy implications. *Journal of the American Medical Association, 302*, 1702–1704.

Dagher, R. K. et al. (2014). Maternal depression, pregnancy intention, and return to paid work after childbirth. *Women's Health Issues*, 24, e297–e303.

Dahlhamer, J. M. et al. (2016). Barriers to health care among adults identifying as sexual minorities: A US national study. *American Journal of Public Research, 106*, 1116.

Daley, E. et al. (2016). The feminization of HPV: Reversing gender biases in US human papillomavirus vaccine policy. *American Journal of Public Health Perspectives, 106*, 983–984.

Damaske, S. (2011). *For the family? How class and gender shape women's work.* New York: Oxford University Press.

Damaske, S. et al. (2013). Work, family, and accounts of mothers' lives using discourse to navigate intensive mothering ideals. *Sociology Compass, 7*, 436–444.

Daniels, E. A. (2009). Sex objects, athletes, and sexy athletes: How media representations of women athletes can impact adolescent girls and college women. *Journal of Adolescent Research, 24*, 399–422.

Daniels, E. A. & La Voi, N. M. (2013). Athletics as solution and problem : Sports participation for girls and the sexualization of female athletes. In E. L. Zurbriggen & T. A. Roberts (Eds.). *The sexualization of girls and girlhood : Causes, consequences and resistance.* (pp. 63–83). New York: Oxford University Press.

Daniels, K. et al. (2013). *Use of emergency contraception among women aged 15–44: United States, 2006–2010.* Washington, DC: U.S. Department of Health and Human Services.

Daniels, K. et al. (2015). Current contraceptive use and variation by selected characteristics among women aged 15–44: United States, 2011–2013. *National Health Statistics Report, 86*, 1–6.

Dannels, E. A. & Gilen, M. M. (2014). Body image and identity: A call for new research. In K. C. McLean & M. Syed (Eds.), *Oxford handbook of identity development* (pp. 299–318). New York: Oxford University Press.

Dardenne, B., Dumont, M., & Bollier, T. (2007). Insidious dangers of benevolent sexism: Consequences for women's performance. *Journal of Personality and Social Psychology, 93*, 764–779.

Dardis, C. M. et al. (2014). An examination of the factors related to dating violence perpetration among young men and women and associated theoretical explanations: A review of the literature. *Trauma, Violence & Abuse, 16*, 136–152.

Darghouth, S. et al. (2015). Does marriage matter? Marital status, family processes, and psychological distress among Latino men and women. *Hispanic Journal of Behavioral Sciences, 37*, 482–502.

Daris, L. S. et al. (2015). Microaggressions in the workplace: Recommendations for best practices. In M. Paludi et al. (Eds.), *Sexual harassment in education and work settings: Current research and best practices for prevention* (pp. 135–156). Santa Barbara, CA: ABC-CLIO.

Das, M. (2011). Gender role portrayals in Indian television ads. *Sex Roles, 64*, 208–222.

DaSilva, R.B. et al. ((2013). Female doctors better than male doctors, but males are more productive. *Review of Epidemiology and Public Health, 61*, s210-s211.

Dasgupta, N. et al. (2015). Female peers in small work groups enhance women's motivation, verbal participation, and career aspirations in engineering. *PNAS*, 112, 4988–4993.

Daubman, K. A. & Sigall, H. (1997). Gender differences in perceptions of how others are affected by self-disclosure of achievement. *Sex Roles, 37*, 73–89.

Daum, M. (2015). *Selfish, shallow and self-absorbed: Sixteen writers on the decision not to have kids*. New York: Picador.

David, H. P. & Lee, E. (2001). Abortion and its health effects. In J. Worell (Ed.), *Encyclopedia of women and gender* (pp. 1–14). San Diego, CA: Academic Press.

Davids, C. M. & Green, M. A. (2011). A preliminary investigation of body dissatisfaction and eating disorder symptomatology with bisexual individuals, *Sex Roles, 65*, 533–547.

Davidson, A. (2014). It's official: The boomerang kids won't leave. *New York Times Magazine, 46*, 22–30.

Davidson, M. M. et al. (2017). The ecology of women's career barriers: Creating social justice through systemwide intervention. In M. Kopala & M. Keitel (Eds.), *Handbook of counseling women* (2nd ed., pp. 137–152). Thousand Oaks, CA: Sage.

Davies, E. et al. (2013). Is timing everything? A meeting report of the Society for Women's Health research roundtable on menopausal hormone therapy. *Journal of Women's Health, 22*, 303–304.

Davis, J. (2010). *The First Generation student experience: Implications for campus practice and strategies for persistence and success*. Sterling, VA: Stylus.

Davis, K., Collins, K. S., & Schoen, C. (2000). Women's health and managed care. In M. B. Goldman & M. Hatch (Eds.), *Women and health* (pp. 55–63). New York: Academic Press.

Davis, K. K. & Tuggle, C. A. (2012). A gender analysis of NBC's coverage of the 2008 Summer Olympics. *Electronic News, 6*, 51–66.

Davis, P. J. (1999). Gender differences in autobiographical memory for childhood emotional experiences. *Journal of Personality and Social Psychology, 76*, 498–510.

Davis, S. N. & Greenstein, T. N. (2009). Gender ideology: Components, predictors, and consequences. *Annual Review of Sociology, 35*, 87–105.

Davis, S. N. & Wills, J. B. (2014). Theoretical explanations amid social change: A content analysis of housework research (1975–2012). *Journal of Family Issues*, 35, 808–824.

Davoren, M. P. et al. (2016). Alcohol consumption among university students in Ireland and the United Kingdom from 2002 to 2014: A systematic review. *BMC Public Health, 16*, 1–11.

de Backer, C., Braeckman, J., & Farinpour, L. (2008). Mating intelligence in personal ads. In G. Geher & G. Miller (Eds.), *Mating intelligence: Sex, relationships, and the mind's reproductive system* (pp. 77–101). New York: Taylor & Francis.

Deech, R., & Smajdor, A. (2007). *From IVF to immortality: Controversy in the era of reproductive technology*. Oxford, UK: Oxford University Press.

De Guzman, N. & Nishina, A. (2014). A longitudinal study of body dissatisfaction and pubertal timing in an ethnically diverse adolescent sample. *Body Image, 11*, 68–71.

De La Rue, L. et al. (2016). A meta-analysis of school-based interventions aimed to prevent or Reduce violence in teen dating relationships. *Review of Educational Research*, doi: 10.3102/0034654316632061.

De Lisi, R. & Soundranayagam, L. (1990). The conceptual structure of sex role stereotypes in college students. *Sex Roles, 23*, 593–611.

De Mascia, S. (2015). Are women better leaders than men? *Human Resource Management International Digest, 23*, 1–4.

de Vries, B. (2014). Stigma and LGBT aging: Negative and positive marginality. In N. A. Orel & C. A. Fruhauf (Eds.), *The lives of LGBT older adults: Understanding challenges and resilience*. Washington, DC: American Psychological Association.

de Waal, F. B. M. (2002). Evolutionary psychology: The wheat and the chaff. *Current Directions in Psychological Science, 11*, 187–191.

Deardorff, M. D. & Dahl, J. G. (2016). *Pregnancy discrimination and the American worker*. New York: Palgrave Macmillan.

Deaton, A. & Stone, A. A. (2014). Evaluative and hedonic well-being among those with and without children at home. *PNAS, 11*, 1328–1333.

DeBate, R., Blunt, H., & Becker, M. A. (2010). Eating disorders. In B. L. Levin & M. A. Becker (Eds.), *A public health perspective of women's mental health* (pp. 121–142). New York: Springer.

DeBlaere, C. et al. (2014). The protective power of collective action for sexual minority women of color: An investigation of multiple discrimination experiences and psychological distress. *Psychology of Women Quarterly, 38*, 20–32.

Deblinger, E. et al. (2015). *Child sexual abuse: A primer for treating children*. New York: Oxford University Press.

Decker, D. (2014, Fall). In the aftermath of Isla Vista. *Ms. Magazine*, 27–29.

DeCuir-Gunby, J. T. et al. (2013). Exploring career trajectories for women of color in engineering: The experiences of African American and Latina engineering professionals. *Journal of Women and Minorities in Science and Engineering, 19*, 209–225.

DeFrancisco, V.P. et al. (2014) *Gender in communication: A critical introduction*. Thousand Oaks, CA: Sage.

DeFreytas-Tamura, K. (2016, December 16). Woman gives birth using ovary frozen since childhood. *New York Times*, p. A4.

Deitch, C. (2015). Sexual harassment of low-wage immigrant workers in the United States. In M. A. Paludi & J. L. Martin (Eds.), *Sexual harassment in education and work settings: Current research and best practices for prevention* (pp. 157–176). Santa Barbara, CA: Praeger.

del Rio, M. & Strasser, K. (2013). Preschool children's beliefs about gender differences in academic skills. *Sex Roles, 68*, 231–238.

DeLamater, J. & Koepsel, E. (2015). Relationships and sexual expression later in life: A biopsychosocial perspective. *Sexual and Relationship Therapy, 30*, 37–59.

Delker, E. et al. (2016). Alcohol consumption in demographic subpopulations. *Alcohol Research: Current Review, 38*, 7–15.

Dell'Antonia, K.J. (2015. February 23). Grandmother, surrogate mother. *New York Times*, p. B4.

DeLoach, C. P. (1989). Gender, career choice and occupational outcomes among college alumni with disabilities. *Journal of Applied Rehabilitation Counseling, 20*, 8–12.

DeLoache, J. S., Simcock, G., & Macari, S. (2007). Planes, trains, automobiles—and tea sets: Extremely intense interests in very young children. *Developmental Psychology, 43*, 1579–1586.

Del Rio, M. F. & Strasser, K. (2013). Preschool children's beliefs about gender differences in academic skills. *Sex Roles, 68*, 2 31–238.

DeMaris, A. (2010). The 20-year trajectory of marital quality in enduring marriages: Does equity matter? *Journal of Social and Personal Relationships, 27*, 449–471.

DeMello, M. (2014). *Body studies: An introduction*. New York: Routledge.

DeMello, M. (2014). *Body studies: An introduction*. New York: Routledge.

Demo, D. H. & Fine, M. (2017). Divorce: Variation and fluidity. In C. A. Price et al. (Eds.), *Families & change: Coping with stressful events and transitions* (pp. 139–160) Thousand Oaks, CA: Sage.

DeNavas-Walt, C. et al. (2013). *Income, poverty, and health insurance coverage in the United States*. Current Population Reports P60–235. Washington, DC: U.S. Census Bureau.

Denes, A. & Afifi, T. D. (2014). Coming out again: Exploring GLBQ individuals' communication with their parents after the first coming out. *Journal of GLBT Family Studies, 10*, 298–325.

Denissen, A. M. & Saguy, A. C. (2014). Gendered homophobia and the contradictions of workplace discrimination for women in the building trades. *Gender & Society, 28*, 381.

Denmark, F. L., Rabinowitz, V., & Sechzer, J. (2000). *Engendering psychology.* Needham Heights, MA: Allyn & Bacon.

Denmark, F. L. et al. (2015). Older women, leadership, and encore careers. In V. Muhlbauer et al. (Eds.), *Women and aging: An international, intersectional power perspective* (pp. 71–88). Switzerland: Springer International Publishing.

Denner, J. & Coyle, K. (2006). Condom use among sexually active Latina girls in alternative high schools. In B. J. R. Leadbeater & N. Way (Eds.), *Urban girls revisited: Building strengths* (pp. 281–300). New York: New York University Press.

Denner, J. et al. (2013). Computing goals, values, and expectations: Results from an after-school program for girls. *Journal of Women and Minorities in Science and Engineering, 18*, 199–213.

Denny, K. E. (2011). Gender in context, content, and approach: Comparing gender messages in girl scout and boy scout handbooks. *Gender and Society, 25*, 27–47.

Denson, A. C. & Mahipal, A. (2014). Participation of the elderly population in clinical trials: Barriers and solutions. *Cancer Central, 21*, 209–214.

DePaolo, B. (2011). *Singlism: What it is, why it matters, and how to stop it.* DoubleDoor Books.

DePaolo, B. (2015). *How we live now: Redefining home and family in the 21st century.* Hillsboro, OR: Atria Press.

Department of Defense. (2015). *Department of Defense annual report on sexual assault in the U.S. military: Fiscal year 2015.* Washington, DC: Author.

Depression & women. (2003, August). *National Women's Health Report, 25*, 1–4.

DeRose, L. M. & Brooks-Gunn, J. (2006). Transition into adolescence: The role of pubertal processes. In L. Balter & C. S. Tamis-LeMonda (Eds.), *Child psychology: A handbook of contemporary issues* (2nd ed., pp. 385–414). New York: Taylor & Francis.

Derry, P. S. & Dillaway, H. (2013). Rethinking menopause. In M. V. Spiers et al. (Eds.), *Women's health psychology* (pp. 440–466). Hoboken, NJ: Wiley.

DeSantis, C. E. et al. (2015). Breast cancer statistics, 2015: Convergence of incidence rates between black and white women. *CA Cancer Journal for Clinicians, 64 (1)*, 1–74.

Desmond, R. & Danilewicz, A. (2010). Women are on, but not in, the news: Gender roles in local television news. *Sex Roles, 62*, 822–829.

DeSouza, E. & Chien, J. (2010). Frequency rates and consequences of peer sexual harassment: Comparing U.S. and international students. In M. Paludi (Ed.), *Feminism and women's rights worldwide* (Vol. 2, pp. 195–208). Santa Barbara, CA: Praeger.

DeSouza, E. R. (2008). Workplace incivility, sexual harassment, and racial micro-aggression: The interface of three literatures. In M. A. Paludi (Ed.), *The psychology of women at work: Challenges and solutions for our female workforce: Obstacles and the identity juggle* (Vol. 2, pp. 65–84). Westport, CT: Praeger.

Deval, P. (2015). *American Indian women.* New York: Abbeville Press.

DeVon, H. A. et al. (2016). A review of the literature on cardiac symptoms in older and younger women. *Journal of Obstetric, Gynecologic, and Neonatal Nursing, 45*, 426–437.

DeWitt, A. L. et al. (2013). Parental role portrayals in twentieth century children's picture books: More egalitarian or ongoing stereotyping? *Sex Roles, 69*, 89–106.

Dey, J. (2014). Beyond the numbers: How has labor force participation among young moms and dads changed? A comparison of two cohorts. *Bureau of Labor Statistics, 3*, 1–9.

Di Bella, L. & Crisp, R. J. (2016). Women's adaptation to STEM domains promotes resilience and a lesser reliance on heuristic thinking. *Group Processes & Intergroup Relations, 19*, 184–201.

Di Scalea, T. L. et al. (2012). Role, stress, role reward, and mental health in a multiethnic sample of midlife women: Results from the Study of Women's Health Across the Nation (SWAN). *Journal of Women's Health, 21*, 481–489.

Diamond, L. M. (2008). Female bisexuality from adolescence to adulthood: Results from a 10-year longitudinal study. *Developmental Psychology, 44*, 5–14.

Diamond, L. M. & Dickenson, J. A. (2012). The neuroimaging of love and desire: Review and future directions. *Clinical Neuropsychiatry, 9*, 39–46.

Diamond, M. (2009). Clinical implications of the organizational and activational effects of hormones. *Hormones and Behavior, 55*, 621–632.

Diehl, W. (2013). Yes, I really am bisexual. Deal with it. *The New York Times*, p. ST6.

Dick, P. (2013). The politics of experience: A discursive psychology approach to understanding different accounts of sexism in the workplace. *Human Relations, 66*, 645–669.

Diekman, A. B. & Eagly, A. H. (1997, May). *Past, present, and future: Perceptions of change in women and men.* Paper presented at the meeting of the Midwestern Psychological Association, Chicago.

Diemer, M. A. et al. (2013). Best practices in conceptualizing and measuring social class in psychology research. *Analyses of Social Issues and Public Policy, 13*, 77–113.

Diette, T. M. et al. (2014). Stalking: Does it leave a psychological footprint? *Social Science Quarterly, 95*, 563–580.

DiGiacomo, M. et al. (2013). An integrative and socio-cultural perspective of health, wealth, and adjustment in widowhood. *Health Care for Women International, 34*, 1067–1083.

Dillaway, H. (2015). Menopause: Deficiency disease or normal reproductive transition? In M.C. McHugh & J. Chrisler (Eds.) *The wrong prescription for women* (pp.99–122). Santa Barbara, CA: Praeger.

Dillaway, H., Byrnes, M., Miller, S., & Rehan, S. (2008). Talking "among us": How women from different racial-ethnic groups define and discuss menopause. *Health Care for Women International, 29*, 766–781.

Dines, G. (2015). Growing up female in a celebrity-based pop culture. In G. Dines & J. M. Humez (Eds.), *Gender, race, and class in media: A critical reader* (4th ed., pp. 433–440). Thousand Oaks, CA: Sage.

Ding, M. et al. (2013). Long-term coffee consumption and risk of cardiovascular heart disease: A systematic review and a dose-response meta-analysis of prospective cohort studies. *Circulation, 129*, 643–659.

DiPietro, J. R. (2015). Studies in fetal behavior: Revisited, renewed, and reimagined. *Monographs of the Society for Research and Child Development, 80*, 59–60.

DiPrete, T. A. & Buchmann, C. (2013). *The rise of women: The growing gender gap in education and what it means for American schools.* New York: Russell Sage Foundation.

diScalea, T.L. et al. (2012). Role stress, role reward, and and mental health in a multiethnic sample of midlife women: Results from the Study of Women's Health Across the Nation (SWAN). *Journal of Women's Health, 21*, 481–489.

Dodd, K. S. et al. (2011). Exclusion of older adults and women from recent trials of acute coronary syndromes. *Journal of the American Geriatrics Society, 59*, 506–511.

Dodge, B. et al. (2016) Attitudes towards bisexual men and women among a nationally representative probability sample of adults in the United States. *PLoS One*, 11,e0164430.

Doey, L. et al. (2014). Bashful boys and coy girls: A review of gender differences in childhood shyness. *Sex Roles, 70*, 255–266.

Doherty, C. (2017). Counseling young adult women. In M. Kopala & M. Keitel (Eds.), *Handbook of counseling women* (2nd ed., pp. 182–191). Thousand Oaks, CA: Sage.

Doherty, C. & Lassig, C. J. (2013). Workable solutions: The intersubjective careers of women with families. In W. Patton (Ed.), *Conceptualising women's working lives: Moving the boundaries of discourse* (pp. 83–104). Rotterdam: Sense Publishers.

Dohm, F.-A., Brown, M., Cachelin, F. M., & Striegel-Moore, R. H. (2010). Ethnicity, disordered eating, and body image. In H. Landrine & N. F. Russo (Eds.), *Hand-book of diversity in feminist psychology* (pp. 285–309). New York: Springer.

Dohnt, H. & Tiggemann, M. (2006). The contribution of peer and media influences to the development of body satisfaction and self-esteem in young girls: A prospective study. *Developmental Psychology, 42*, 929–936.

Dolbin-MacNab, M. & Hayslip B. (2015). Grandparents raising grandchildren In J. A. Arditti (Ed.), *Family problems: Stress, risk, and resilience* (pp. 133–149). Malden, MA: Wiley.

Dole, T.R. (2017). Mental health of women: A focus on adolescent girls. In K.A. Kendall-Tackett & L.M. Ruglass (Eds.). *Women's mental health across the lifespan: Challenges, needs, and strengths* (pp. 3–16). New York: Routledge.

Doll, G. M. (2013). Sexuality in nursing homes: Practice and policy. *Journal of Gerontological Nursing, 39*, 30–37.

Domhardt, M. et al. (2015). Resilience in survivors of child sexual abuse: A systematic review of the literature. *Trauma, Violence & Abuse, 16*, 476–493.

Don't accept a diminished sex life as a "side effect" of illness. (2016, July). *Harvard Women's Health Watch*, p. 8.

Donatelle, R. (2017). *Access to health* (15th ed.). Boston: Pearson.

Donath, O. (2015). Regretting motherhood: A sociopolitical analysis. *Signs: Journal of Women in Culture and Society, 40*, 343–367.

Donde, S. (2015). College women's attributions of blame for experiences of sexual assault. *Journal of Interpersonal Violence, 10*, 1–19.

Dong, X. Q. (2015). Elder abuse: Systematic review and implications for practice. *Journal of the American Geriatric Society, 63*, 214–238.

Donnelly, K. & Twenge, J. M. (2016). Masculine and feminine traits on the Bem Sex-Role Inventory, 1993–2012: A cross-temporal meta-analysis. *Sex Roles*, doi:10.1007/s11199-016-0625-y.

Donnelly, K. et al. (2016). Attitudes toward women's work and family roles in the United States, 1976–2013. *Psychology of Women Quarterly, 40*, 41–54.

Doress-Worters, P. B. & Siegal, D. L. (1994). *The new ourselves growing older*. New York: Simon & Schuster.

Döring, N. (2000). Feminist views of cybersex: Victimization, liberation, and empowerment. *Cyberpsychology & Behavior, 3*, 863–884.

Döring, N. M. (2009). The Internet's impact on sexuality: A critical review of 15 years of research. *Computers in Human Behavior, 25*, 1089–1101.

Dorling, D. (2015). The mother of underlying causes—economic ranking and health inequality. *Social Science and Medicine, 128*, 327–330.

Dotti Sani, G. M. (2016). Undoing gender in housework? Participation in domestic chores by Italian fathers and children of different ages. *Sex Roles, 74*, 411–421.

Doucet, A. & Lee, R. (2014). Fathering, feminism(s), gender, and sexualities: Connections, tensions, and new pathways. *Journal of Family Theory & Review, 6*, 355–373.

Dougherty, C. & Isaac, M. (2016, March 14). SXSW takes a day to discuss online harassment of women in gaming. *New York Times*, p. B4.

Douglas, S. J. (2010). *Enlightened sexism: The seductive message that feminism's work is done*. New York: Times Books.

Dow, D. M. (2016). Integrated motherhood: Beyond hegemonic ideologies of motherhood. *Journal of Marriage and Family, 78*, 180–196.

Doyle, J. et al. (2012). A phenomenological exploration of the child-free choice in a sample of Australian women. *Journal of Health Psychology, 18*, 397–407.

Dragiewicz, M. (2015). *Global human trafficking critical issues and contexts*. New York: Routledge.

Drew, P. (2011). Sex education, comprehensive. In M. Z. Stange, C. K. Oyster, & J. E. Sloan (Eds.), *Encyclopedia of women in today's world* (Vol. 3, pp. 1299–1301). Newberry Park, CA: Sage.

Drury, M. (2016). Still alone at the table? Women working in technology organizations. In M. Connerley & J. Wu (Eds.), *Handbook on well-being of working women* (pp. 297–315). Dordrecht, Netherlands: Springer.

Duberley, J. et al. (2014). Exploring women's retirement: Continuity, context and career transition. *Gender, Work & Organization, 21*, 71–90.

Duffy, J., Wareham, S., & Walsh, M. (2004). Psychological consequences for high school students of having been sexually harassed. *Sex Roles, 50*, 811–821.

Duggan, M. (2015). *Gamers and gaming*. Washington, DC: Pew Research Center.

Dumith, S. C. et al. (2011). Physical activity change during adolescence: A systematic review and a pooled analysis. *International Journal of Epidemiology, 40*, 685–698.

Duncan, D. T. & Hatzenbuehler, M. L. (2014). Lesbian, gay, bisexual, and transgender hate crimes and suicidality among a population-based sample of sexual-minority adolescents in Boston. *AJPH, 104*, 272–273.

Duncan, L. E. (2010). Women's relationship to feminism: Effects of generation and feminist self-labeling. *Psychology of Women Quarterly, 34*, 498–507.

Duncan, S. et al. (2014). Practices and perceptions of living apart together. *Family Science, 5*, 1–10.

Dunifon, R. (2013). The influence of grandparents in the lives of children and adolescents. *Child Development Perspectives, 7*, 55–60.

Dunifon, R. et al. (2013). *The effect of maternal employment on children's academic performance*. Cambridge, MA: National Bureau of Economic Research.

Dunn, J. E. (2014). Siblings. In J. E. Grusec & P. D. Hastings (Eds.), *Handbook of socialization* (2nd ed., pp. 182–201). New York: Guilford.

Dunnavant, N. C. & Roberts, T. A. (2013). Restriction and renewal, pollution and power, constraint and community: The paradoxes of religious women's experiences of menstruation. *Sex Roles, 68*, 121–131.

DuQuaine-Watson, J. (2017). *Mothering by degrees: Single women and the pursuit of post-secondary education*. New Brunswick, NJ: Rutgers University Press.

Durvasula, R. (2014). HIV/AIDS in older women: Unique challenges, unmet needs. *Behavioral Medicine, 40*, 85–98.

Dvorak, P. (2016, August 8). Women make history and their husbands get the credit. How infuriating is that? *Washington Post*. Retrieved from washingtonpost.com/local/women-make-history-and-their-husbands-get-the-credit-how-infuriating-is-that/2016/08/08/192df022-5d70-11e6-af8e-54aa2e849447_story.html

Dvornyk, V. (2013). *Current topics in menopause*. Bentham Science Publishers.

Dworkin, T. M. et al. (2015). Still seeking pathways for women to organizational leadership. *UCLA Women's Law Journal*. Paper No. 1278.

Dye, H. (2016). Are there differences in gender, race, and age regarding body dissatisfaction? *Journal of Human Behavior in the Social Environment, 26*, 499–508.

Dyson, T. (2012). Causes and consequences of skewed sex ratios. *American Review of Sociology, 38*, 443–461.

Eagan, K. et al. (2013). *The American freshman: National norms, Fall 2013*. Los Angeles: Higher Education Research Institute, UCLA.

Eagly, A. H. (2013a). The science and politics of comparing women and men: A reconsideration. In M. K. Ryan & N. R. Branscombe (Eds.). *Sage handbook of gender and psychology* (pp. 11–28). Los Angeles, CA: Sage.

Eagly, A. H. (2013b). *Women as leaders*. Presented at research symposium, Gender & Work: Challenging Conventional Wisdom. Cambridge MA: Harvard Business School.

Eagly, A. H. & Carli, L. L. (1981). Sex of researchers and sex-typed communications as determinants of sex differences in influenceability: A meta-analysis of social influence studies. *Psychological Bulletin, 90*, 1–20.

Eagly, A. H. & Carli, L. L. (2007). *Through the labyrinth: The truth about how women become leaders*. Boston, MA: Harvard Business School Press.

Eagly, A. H. & Chin, J. L. (2010). Diversity and leadership in a changing world. *American Psychologist, 65*, 216–224.

Eagly, A. H. & Riger, S. (2014). Feminism and psychology: Critiques of methods and epistemology. *American Psychologist, 69*, 685–702.

Eagly, A. H. & Sczesny, S. (2009). Stereotypes about women, men, and leaders: Have times changed? In M. Barreto, M. K. Ryan, & M. T. Schmitt (Eds.), *The glass ceiling in the 21st century: Understanding barriers to gender equality* (pp. 19–47). Washington, DC: American Psychological Association.

Eagly, A. H. & Wood, W. (2013). Feminism and evolutionary psychology: moving forward. *Sex Roles, 69*, 549–556.

Eagly, A. H., Wood, W., & Johannesen-Schmidt, M. (2004). Social role theory of sex differences and similarities: Implications for the partner preferences of women and men. In A. H. Eagly, A. E. Beall, & R. J. Sternberg (Eds.), *The psychology of gender* (pp. 269–295). New York: Guilford.

Eagly, A. H. et al. (2012). Feminism and psychology: Analysis of a half-century of research on women and gender. *American Psychologist, 67*, 211–230.

Eagly, A. H. et al. (2014). Female advantage: revisited. In S. Kumra et al. (Eds.), *The Oxford handbook of gender in organizations* (pp. 153–174). New York: Oxford University Press.

Eaton, A. A. & Rose, S. (2011). Has dating become more egalitarian? A 35-year review using Sex Roles. *Sex Roles, 64,* 843–862.

Eaton, D. K., et al. (2010). Youth risk behavior surveillance—United States, 2009. *Morbidity and Mortality Weekly Report,* 59(SS–5), 1–142.

Eaton, N. R. et al. (2012). An invariant dimension liability model of gender differences in mental disorder prevalence: Evidence from a national sample. *Journal of Abnormal Psychology, 121,* 282–288.

Ebadi, S. (2016). *Until we are free: My fight for human rights in Iran.* New York: Random House.

Eberhardt, J. L. & Fiske, S. T. (1998). Affirmative action in theory and practice: Issues of power, ambiguity, and gender versus race. In D. L. Anselmi & A. L. Law (Eds.). *Questions of gender: Perspectives and paradoxes* (pp. 629–641). Boston: McGraw-Hill.

Eccles, J. S., Freedman-Doan, C., Frome, P., Jacobs, J., & Yoon, K. S. (2000). Gender-role socialization in the family: A longitudinal approach. In T. Eckes & H. M. Trautner (Eds.), *The developmental social psychology of gender* (pp. 333–360). Mahwah, NJ: Erlbaum.

Eccles, J. S. & Roeser, R. W. (1999). School and community influences on human development. In M. H. Bornstein & M. E. Lamb (Eds.), *Developmental psychology: An advanced textbook* (4th ed., pp. 503–554). Mahwah, NJ: Erlbaum.

Eckenrode, J. (2011). Primary prevention of child abuse and maltreatment. In M. P. Koss, J. W. White, & A. E. Kazdin (Eds.), *Violence against women and children: Navigating solutions* (Vol. 2, pp. 71–92). Washington, DC: American Psychological Association.

Eckert, P. & McConnell-Ginet, S. (2003). *Language and gender.* Cambridge, MA: Cambridge University Press.

Eckholm, E. (2015, June 27). Next fight for gay rights: Bias in jobs and housing. *New York Times,* pp. A1, A20.

Edwards, C. P., Knoche, L., & Kumru, A. (2001). Play patterns and gender. In J. Worell (Ed.), *Encyclopedia of women and gender* (pp. 809–815). San Diego, CA: Academic Press.

Edwards, K. M. & Gidycz, C.A (2014). In their own words: A content-analytic study of college women's resistance to sexual assault. *Journal of Interpersonal Violence, 29,* 2527–2547.

Edwards, K. M. et al. (2015). Physical dating violence, and unwanted pursuit victimization: A comparison of incidence rates among sexual-minority and heterosexual college students. *Journal of Interpersonal Violence, 30,* 580–600.

Edwards, K. M. & Gidycz, C. A. (2014) Stalking and psychological distress following the termination of an abusive dating relationship: A prospective analysis. *Violence against Women, 20,* 1383–1397.

Edwards, L. (2013, March 17). The gender gap in pain. *New York Times,* p. SR8.

Edwards, M. R. (2007). An examination of employed mothers' work-family narratives and perceptions of husbands' support. *Marriage & Family Review, 42,* 59–89.

Ehrich, L. C. & Kimber, M. (2016). The purpose and place of mentoring for women managers in organisations: An Australian perspective. In M. L. Connerley & J. Wu (Eds.), *Handbook on well-being of working women* (pp. 225–236). Dordrecht: Springer.

Eisenberg, M. (2015). A content analysis of weight stigmatization in popular television programming for adolescents. *International Journal of Eating Disorders, 48,* 759–766.

Eisenberg, M. E., Neumark-Sztainer, D., & Story, M. (2003). Associations of weight-based teasing and emotional well-being among adolescents. *Archives of Pediatrics and Adolescent Medicine, 157,* 733–738.

Eisenberg, N., Fabes, R. A., & Spinrad, T. L. (2006). Prosocial development. In W. Damon, R. M. Lerner (Series Eds.), & N. Eisenberg (Vol. Ed.), *Handbook of child psychology: Vol. 3. Social, emotional, and personality development* (6th ed., pp. 646–718). Hoboken, NJ: Wiley.

Eisenberg, N., Morris, A. S., McDaniel, B., & Spinrad, T. L. (2009). Moral cognitions and prosocial responding in adolescence. In R. M. Lerner & L. Steinberg (Eds.), *Handbook of adolescent psychology* (3rd ed., Vol. 1, pp. 229–265). Hoboken, NJ: Wiley.

Eisenberg, N., Spinrad, T. L., & Sadovsky, A. (2008). Empathy-related responding in children. In M. Killen & J. G. Smetana (Eds.), *Handbook of moral development* (pp. 517–549). Mahwah, NJ: Erlbaum.

Eisenberg, S. (2010). Marking gender boundaries: Porn, piss, power tools. In J. Goodman (Ed.), *Global perspectives on gender & work* (pp. 417–431). Lanham, MD: Rowman & Littlefield.

Ekelund, U. et al. (2015). Physical activity and all-cause mortality across levels of overall and abdominal adiposity in European men and women: The European prospective investigation into cancer and nutrition study (EPIC). *American Journal of Clinical Nutrition, 101,* 613–621.

El-Bassel, N., Caldeira, N. A., Ruglass, L. M., & Gilbert, L. (2009). Addressing the unique needs of African-American women in HIV prevention. *American Journal of Public Health, 99,* 996–1001.

Elahi, M. et al. (2016). The Food and Drug Administration office of women's health: Impact of science on regulatory policy: An update. *Journal of Women's Health, 25,* 222–234.

Elder, J. (1997, June 22). Poll finds women are the healthsavvier sex, and the warier. *New York Times,* p. WH8.

Eleuteri, S. et al. (2014). Questionnaires and scales for the evaluation of the online seual activities: A review of 20 years of research. *Cyberpsychology: Journal of Psychosocial Research on Cyberspace, 8,* 1–10.

Elias, V. L. et al. (2015). Long-term changes in attitudes toward premarital sex in the United States: Reexamining the role of cohort replacement. *Journal of Sex Research, 52,* 129–139.

Ellin, A. (2004, October 17). Helping grandparents help the grandkids. *New York Times,* p. BU9.

Ellin, A. (2015, March 31). Young, suffering and ignored: Endometriosis is often misdiagnosed as period pain. *New York Times,* p. D6.

Ellin, A. (2016a, February 16). Patients facing barriers in care. *New York Times,* pp. D1, D6.

Ellin, A. (2016b, August 6). Single, 54, and a new dad: Why some families start late. *New York Times,* p. B5.

Elliott, K. & Urquiza, A. (2006). Ethnicity, culture, and child maltreatment. *Journal of Social Issues, 62,* 787–809.

Elliott, S. et al. (2015). Being a good mom: Low-income, black single mothers negotiate intensive mothering. *Journal of Family Issues, 36,* 351–370.

Ellis, J. et al. (2016). Women 1.5 times more likely to leave STEM pipeline after calculus compared to men: Lack of mathematical confidence a potential culprit. *PLoS One 11* (7), e1057447.

Ellis, J. & Thiara, R. K. (2014). *Preventing violence against women and girls: Educational work with children and young people.* Chicago, IL: Policy Press.

Ellis, J. et al. (2016). Women 1.5 times more likely to leave STEM pipeline after calculus compared to men: Lack of mathematical confidence a potential culprit. *PLOS ONE,11* 7: e0157447.

Ellis, L. et al. (2008). *Sex differences: Summarizing more than a century of scientific research.* New York: Taylor & Francis Group.

Ellis, R. R. & Simmons, T. (2014). *Coresident grandparents and their grandchildren: 2012.* Washington, DC: U.S. Department of Commerce.

Else-Quest, N. M. (2014). Robust but plastic: Gender differences in emotional responses to sexual debut. *Journal of Sex Research, 51,* 473–476.

Else-Quest, N. M., Hyde, J. S., Goldsmith, H. H., & Van Hulle, C. A. (2006). Gender differences in temperament: A meta-analysis. *Psychological Bulletin, 132,* 33–72.

Else-Quest, N. M. et al. (2013). Math and science attitudes and achievement at the intersection of gender and ethnicity. *Psychology of Women Quarterly, 37,* 293–309.

Elsesser, K. (2015). *Sex and the office: Women, men, and the sex partition that's dividing the workplace.* Lanham, MD: Rowman & Littlefield.

Elson, J. (2004). *Am I still a woman?* Philadelphia, PA: Temple University Press.

Eltahawy, M. (2014, November 17). Fighting female genital mutilation. *New York Times,* p. A25.

Ember, S. (2016, May 2). It's a 'Mad Men' world: Women in advertising say they still feel pressure to be one of the guys. *New York Time*, pp. B1, B6.

Emmers-Sommer, T. (2014). Adversarial sexual attitudes toward women: The relationships with gender and traditionalism. *Sexuality & Culture, 18,* 804–817.

Emont, J. (2015, December 23). Transgender Muslims find a home for prayer. *New York Times*, p. A8.

Endendijk, J. J. et al. (2016). Gender differences in child aggression: Relations with gender-differentiated parenting and parents' gender-role stereotypes. *Child Development*, doi: 10.1111/cdev.12589.

Engeln-Maddox, R. et al. (2011). Tests of objectification theory in gay, lesbian, and heterosexual community samples: Mixed evidence for proposed pathways. *Sex Roles, 65,* 518–532.

England, D. E., Descartes, L., & Collier-Meek, M. A. (2011). Gender role portrayal and the Disney princesses. *Sex Roles, 64,* 555–567.

England, P. (2016). Sometimes the social becomes personal: Gender, class, and sexualities. *American Sociological Review,* 81, 4–28.

England, P., Schafer, E. F., & Fogarty, A. C. K. (2007). Hooking up and forming romantic relationships on today's college campuses. In M. Kimmel (Ed.), *The gendered society reader* (pp. 531–547). New York: Oxford University Press.

Enns, C. Z. (2014). Feminist counseling as a pathway to recovery. In T. Bryant-Davis (Ed.), *Surviving sexual violence: A guide to recovery and empowerment* (pp. 160–178). Lanham, MD: Rowman & Littlefield.

Enns, C. Z. (2015). Toward a transnational psychology of women: APA pre-conference summit. *Feminist Psychology,* 27.

Enns, C. Z. (2017). Contemporary adaptations of traditional approaches to counseling women. In M. Kopala & M. Keitel (Eds.), *Handbook of counseling women* (2nd ed., pp. 51–62). Thousand Oaks, CA: Sage.

Epstein, E. E., Fischer-Elber, K., & Al-Otaiba, Z. (2007). Women, aging, and alcohol use disorders. *Journal of Women and Aging,* *19,* 31–48.

Epstein, M. & Ward, M. W. (2011). Exploring parent-adolescent communication about gender: Results from adolescent and emerging adult samples. *Sex Roles,* 65, 108–118.

Equity in Business Leadership. (2014). *Lesbian, gay, bisexual & transgender workplace issues.* Retrieved May 15, 2014, from "http://www.catalyst.org" \h www.catalyst.org

Erbert, L. A. & Alemán, M. W. (2008). Taking the grand out of grandparent: Dialectical tensions in grandparent perceptions of surrogate parenting. *Journal of Social and Personal Relationships,* *25,* 671–695.

Erdley, S. D. et al. (2014). Breaking barriers and building bridges: Understanding the pervasive needs of older LGBT adults and the value of social work in health care. *Journal of Gerontological Social Work,* 57, 362–385.

Erikson, E. H. (1968). *Identity: Youth and crisis.* New York: Norton.

Erikson, E. H. (1980). *Identity and the life cycle.* New York: Norton.

Erkut, S. & García Coll, C. (2013). Girls of color: Strengths and challenges of growing up in this time and place. In L. Comas-Diaz & B. Greene (Eds.), *Psychological health of women of color: Intersections, challenges and opportunities* (pp. 23–38). Santa Barbara, CA: ABC-CLIO.

Eschenbeck, H., Kohlmann, C. W., & Lohaus, A. (2007). Gender differences in coping strategies in children and adolescents. *Journal of Individual Differences, 28,* 18–26.

Espelage, D.L. et al. (2014). Bullying, sexual, and dating violence trajectories from early to late adolescence. Report to the National Institute of Justice, Washington, DC.

Espey, D. K. (2014). Leading causes of death and all-cause mortality in American Indians and Alaska Natives. *AJPH, 104,* S303.

Espey, D. L. et al. (2014). *Bullying, sexual, and dating violence trajectories from early to late adolescence.* Washington, DC: U.S. Department of Justice.

Espin, O. M. & Dottolo. A. L. (Eds.). (2015). *Gendered journeys: Women, migration, and feminist psychology.* New York: Palgrave Macmillan.

Essential facts about midwives. (2016). Silver Springs, MD: American College of Nurse-Midwives.

Eswaran, M. (2014). *Why gender matters in economics.* Princeton, NJ: Princeton University Press.

Etaugh, C. (2008). Women in the middle and later years. In F. L. Denmark & M. A. Paludi (Eds.), *Psychology of women: A handbook of issues and theories* (3rd ed., pp. 271–302). Westport, CT: Praeger.

Etaugh, C. (2013a). Midlife career transitions for women. In W. Patton (Ed.), *Conceptualising women's working lives: Moving the boundaries of our discourse* (pp. 105–117). Rotterdam, Netherlands: Sense Publishers.

Etaugh, C. (2013b). Women and sexuality in the middle and later years. In D. Castaneda (Ed.), *An essential handbook of women's sexuality* (pp. 125–139). Westport: Praeger.

Etaugh, C. (2016). Psychology of gender: History and development of the field. In N. Naples (Ed.), *The Wiley-Blackwell encyclopedia of gender and sexuality studies,* vol IV (pp. 1944–1955). Oxford: Wiley-Blackwell.

Etaugh, C. (2017). Midlife transitions. In Travis, C. B. & White, A. W. (Eds.), *APA handbook of the psychology of women* (pp. xxx–xxx). Washington, DC: American Psychological Association.

Etaugh, C. & Conrad, M. (2004, July). *Perceptions of parents choosing traditional or nontraditional roles and surnames.* Poster presented at the meeting of the American Psychological Association, Honolulu, HI.

Etaugh, C. & Duits, T. (1990). Development of gender discrimination: Role of stereotypic and counter-stereotypic gender cues. *Sex Roles, 23,* 215–222.

Etaugh, C. & Folger, D. (1998). Perceptions of parents whose work and parenting behaviors deviate from role expectations. *Sex Roles, 39,* 215–223.

Etaugh, C. & Fulton, A. (1995, June). *Perceptions of unmarried adults: Gender and sexual orientation (not social attractiveness) matter.* Paper presented at the meeting of the American Psychological Association, New York.

Etaugh, C. & Geraghty, C. (2014, August). *Women's changing leadership roles and recognition: Comparing APA and APS.* Poster presented at the annual meeting of the American Psychological Association, Washington, DC.

Etaugh, C. & Liss, M. B. (1992). Home, school, and playroom: Training grounds for adult gender roles. *Sex Roles, 26,* 129–146.

Etaugh, C. & Moss, C. (2001). Attitudes of employed women toward parents who choose full-time or part-time employment following their child's birth. *Sex Roles, 44,* 611–619.

Etaugh, C. & Nekolny, K. (1990). Effects of employment status and marital status on perceptions of mothers. *Sex Roles, 23,* 273–280.

Etaugh, C. & O'Brien, E. (2003, April). *Perceptions of parents' gender roles by preschoolers in traditional and egalitarian families.* Paper presented at the meeting of the Society for Research in Child Development, Tampa, FL.

Etaugh, C. & Poertner, P. (1991). Effects of occupational prestige, employment status, and mental status on perceptions of mothers. *Sex Roles, 24,* 345–353.

Etaugh, C. & Poertner, P. (1992). Perceptions of women: Influence of performance, marital, and parental variables. *Sex Roles, 26,* 311–321.

Etaugh, C. & Rathus, S. (1995). *The world of children.* Fort Worth, TX: Harcourt Brace.

Etaugh, C. & Roe, L. (2002, June). *"What's in a name?" Surname choice affects perceptions of women and men.* Poster presented at the meeting of the American Psychological Society, New Orleans.

Etaugh, C. & Worell, J. (2012). Contemporary feminism for gender researchers: Not just "our bodies, our cells". *Psychology of Women Quarterly, 36,* 419–422.

Etaugh, C. et al. (2013, May). *Gender-typing and gender representations in children's picture books: The new millennium.* Paper presented at the annual meeting of the Midwestern Psychological Association, Chicago.

Etaugh, C. et al. (2016, May). *College students' self-efficacy beliefs: Both gender and gender identity matter.* Paper presented at the annual meeting of the Midwestern Psychological Association Meeting, Chicago.

Etaugh, C. et al. (2017, April) *Gender differences in current and previous same-and other-sex friendships*. Poster presented at the annual meeting of the Midwestern Psychological Association, Chicago.

Etaugh, C., Bridges, J. S., Cummings-Hill, M., & Cohen, J. (1999). "Names can never hurt me?" The effects of surname use on perceptions of married women. *Psychology of Women Quarterly, 23,* 819–823.

Etaugh, C., Grinnell, K., & Etaugh, A. (1989). Development of gender labeling: Effect of age of pictured children. *Sex Roles, 21,* 769–773.

Etaugh, C., Knoblauch, S., & Schwartz, N. (2010, April). *Women over 40: Invisible in psychology of women/gender textbooks?* Poster presented at the annual meeting of the Midwestern Psychological Association, Chicago, IL.

Etaugh, C., Levine, D., & Mennella, A. (1984). Development of sex biases in children: Forty years later. *Sex Roles, 10,* 913–924.

Etaugh, C., Roe, L., & Zurek, R. (2003, July). *From "frogs and snails" to "Mr. Mom": Stereotypes of boys and men in children's books*. Poster presented at the European Congress of Psychology, Vienna.

Etaugh, C., Campbell, P., Schwartz, N., Zurek, R., & Pasdach, T. (2007, May). *Four decades of gender stereotypes in children's picture books: Different patterns for children and adults*. Poster presented at the annual meeting of the Midwestern Psychological Association, Chicago, IL.

Etekal, I. & Ladd, G.W. (2015). Costs and benefits of children's physical and relational aggression trajectories on peer rejection, acceptance, and friendships: Variations by aggression subtype, gender, and age. *Child Development. 86,* 614–631.

Ethics Committee of the American Society for Reproductive Medicine. Oocyte or embryo donation to women of advanced age: A committee opinion. Birmingham, AL: American Society for Reproductive Medicine.

Evans, C. D. & Diekman, A. B. (2009). On motivated role selection: Gender beliefs, distant goals, and career interest. *Psychology of Women Quarterly, 33,* 235–249.

Evans, E. H. et al. (2013). Body dissatisfaction and disordered eating attitudes in 7-to 11-year-old girls: Testing a sociocultural model. *Body Image, 10,* 8–15.

Evans, M. (2014). *The Sage handbook of feminist theory*. Thousand Oaks, CA: Sage.

Everbach, T. (2013). Women's (mis)representation in news media. In C. L. Armstrong (Ed.), *Media disparity: A gender battleground* (pp. 15–26). Lanham, MD: Lexington Books.

Everfi (2015, Winter). *Sexual victimization and social norms on the college campus*. Washington, DC: Author.

Evers, A. & Sieverding, M. (2014). Why do highly qualified women (still) earn less? Gender differences in long-term predictors of career success. *Psychology of Women Quarterly, 38,* 93–106.

Ewing Lee, E. A. & Troop-Gordon, W. (2011). Peer processes and gender role development: Changes in gender atypicality related to negative peer treatment and children's friendships. *Sex Roles, 64,* 90–102.

Exner-Cortens, D., et al. (2013). Longitudinal associations between teen dating violence victimization and adverse health outcomes. *Pediatrics, 131,* 71–78.

Expósito, F., Herrera, M. C., Moya, M., & Glick, P. (2010). Don't rock the boat: Women's benevolent sexism predicts fears of marital violence. *Psychology of Women Quarterly, 34,* 36–42.

Eynon, N., Yamin, C., Ben-Sira, D., & Sagiv, M. (2009). Optimal health and function among the elderly: Lessening severity of ADL disability. *European Review of Aging and Physical Activity, 6,* 55–61.

Ezzedeen, S. R. (2015). Portrayals of career women in Hollywood films: implications for the glass ceiling's persistence. *Gender in Management: An International Journal, 30,* 239–264.

Fabes, R. A. & Martin, C. L. (2003). *Exploring child development* (2nd ed.). Boston, MA: Allyn & Bacon.

Fagundes, C. P. & Way, B. (2014). Early-life stress and adult inflammation. *Current Directions in Psychological Science, 23,* 277–283.

Fahs, B. (2016). *Out for blood: Essays on menstruation and resistance*. Albany, NY: State University of New York, Albany.

Fairclough, K. (2014). Nothing less than perfect. Female celebrity ageing and hyper-scrutiny in the gossip industry. In D. Jermyn (Ed.), *Female celebrity and aging: Back in the spotlight* (pp. 103–116). New York: Routledge.

Fakhouri, T. H. I. et al. (2014). *Physical activity in U.S. youth aged 12–15 years, 2012*. U.S. Department of Health and Human Services. Data Brief #141.

Fales, M. R. et al. (2016). Mating markets and bargaining hands: Mate preferences for attractiveness and resources in two national U.S. studies. *Personality and Individual Differences, 88,* 78–87.

Faller, H. et al. (2013). Effects of psycho-oncologic interventions on emotional distress and quality of life in adult patients with cancer: Systematic review and meta-analysis. *Journal of Clinical Oncology, 31,* 782–793.

Faller, K. C. (2011). Victim services for child abuse. In M. P. Koss, J. W. White & A. E. Kazdin (Eds.), *Violence against women and children: Navigating solutions* (Vol. 2, pp. 11–26). Washington, DC: American Psychological Association.

Faludi, S. (2007). *The terror dream: Fear and fantasy in post-9/11 America*. New York: Metropolitan Books.

Fanslow, J. L. et al. (2015). Hitting back: Women's use of physical violence against violent male partners, in the context of a violent episode. *Journal of Interpersonal Violence, 30,* 2963–2979.

Farber, N. & Miller-Cribbs, J. E. (2014). Violence in the lives of rural, southern, and poor white women. *Violence Against Women, 20,* 517–538.

Farcia, J. R. et al. (2013, February). Sexual hook-up culture. *Monitor on Psychology,* 62–67.

Fardouly, J. & Vartanian, L. R. (2016). Social media and body image concerns: Current research and future directions. *Current Opinion in Psychology, 9,* 1–5.

Fardouly, J. et al. (2015). The mediating role of appearance comparisons in the relationship between media usage and self-objectification in young women. *Psychology of Women Quarterly, 39,* 447–457.

Faris, R. & Felmlee, D. (2011). Status struggles: Network centrality and gender segregation in same-and cross-gender aggression. *American Sociological Review, 76,* 48–73.

Farkas, T. & Leaper, C. (2014). Is having an older sister or an older brother related to younger siblings' gender-typing? A meta-analysis. In P.J. Leman & H. Tenenbaum (Eds.), *Gender and development* (pp. 63–77). New York: Psychology Press.

Farmer, H. S. (2006). History of career counseling for women. In W. B. Walsh & M. J. Heppner (Eds.), *Handbook of career counseling for women* (2nd ed., pp. 1–44). Mahwah, NJ: Erlbaum.

Farr, D. (2013). Introduction: Special issue on men and masculinities in women's studies. *Women's Studies, 4,* 483–485.

Farris, C., Treat, T. A., Viken, R. J., & McFall, R. M. (2008). Perceptual mechanisms that characterize gender differences in decoding women's sexual intent. *Psychological Science, 19,* 348–354.

Fassinger, R. E. & Arseneau, J. R. (2008). Diverse women's sexualities. In F. L. Denmark & M. A. Paludi (Eds.), *Psychology of women: A handbook of issues and theories* (2nd ed., pp. 484–505). Westport, CT: Praeger.

Fausto-Sterling, A. (2012). *Sex/gender: Biology in a social war*. New York: Routledge.

Fawcett, B. (2016). Feminism and disability. In S. Wendt & N. Moulding (Eds.), *Contemporary feminisms in social work practice* (pp. 275–286). New York: Routledge.

February is black history month. (2004, February). *Women's Psych-E, 3*(2), 1.

Feder. E.K. (2014) *Making sense of intersex: Changing ethical perspectives in biomedicine*. Bloomington, IN: Indiana University Press.

Federal Interagency Forum on Aging-Related Statistics. (2012). *Older Americans 2012: Key indicators of well-being*. Washington, DC: Author.

Federal Interagency Forum on Age-Related Statistics (2016). *Older Americans: Key indicators of well-being*. Washington DC: Author.

Fedewa, A. L. et al. (2015). Children and adolescents with same-gender parents: A meta-analytic approach in assessing outcomes. *Journal of GLBT Family Studies, 11,* 1–34.

Feeney, B. C. & Collins, N. L. (2015). A new look at social support: A theoretical perspective on thriving through relationships. *Personality and Social Psychological Review, 19,* 133–147.

Feinberg, M.E. et al. (2012). The third rail of family systems: Sibling relationships, mental and behavioral health and preventive intervention in childhood and adolescence. *Clinical Child and Family Psychological Review, 15,* 43–57.

Feingold, A. (1993). Cognitive gender differences: A developmental perspective. *Sex Roles, 29,* 91–112.

Feldblum, C. R. & Lipnic, V. A. (2016). *Select Task Force on the Study of Harassment in the Workplace.* Washington, DC: U.S. Equal Employment Opportunity Commission.

Feldman, S., Byles, J. E., & Beaumont, R. (2000). "Is anybody listening?" The experiences of widowhood for older Australian women. *Journal of Women & Aging, 12,* 155–176.

Felmlee, D., Orzechowicz, D., & Fortes, C. (2010). Fairy tales: Attraction and stereotypes in same-gender relationships. *Sex Roles, 62,* 226–240.

Felmlee, D. et al. (2012). Gender rules: Same- and cross-gender friendship norms. *Sex Roles, 66,* 518–529.

Feminist Majority Foundation. (2014). *Ratifying CEDAW.* Arlington, VA: Author.

Feminist Women's Health Center. (2009). *The abortion pill: Medical abortion with mifepristone and misoprostol.* Yakima, WA: Author.

Fenge, L. (2014). Developing understanding of same-sex partner bereavement for older lesbian and gay people: Implications for social work practice. *Journal of Gerontological Social Work, 57,* 288–304.

Ferencz, B. et al. (2014). The benefits of staying active in old age: Physical activity counteracts the negative influence of PICALM, BINI, and CLU risk alleles on episodic memory functioning. *Psychology and Aging, 29,* 440–449.

Ferguson, C. J. et al. (2016). Violent video games don't increase hostility in teens, but they do stress girls out. *Psychiatric Quarterly, 87,* 49–56.

Fergusson, D. M. & Woodward, L. J. (2000). Educational, psychosocial, and sexual outcomes of girls with conduct problems in early adolescence. *Journal of Child Psychology and Psychiatry, 41,* 779–792.

Ferrari, G. et al. (2016). Domestic violence and mental health: A cross-sectional survey of women seeking help from domestic violence support services. *Global Health Action, 9,* doi:10.3402/gha.v9.29890e3

Few-Demo, A. L. (2014). Intersectionality as the "new" critical approach in feminist family studies: Evolving racial-ethnic feminisms and critical race theories. *Journal of Family Theory and Review, 6,* 169–183.

Fichman, P. & Sanfilippo, M. R. (2016). *Online trolling and its perpetrators: Under the cyberidge.* Lanham, MD: Rowman & Littlefield.

Field, D. & Weishaus, S. (1992). Marriage over half a century: A longitudinal study. In M. Bloom (Ed.), *Changing lives* (pp. 269–273). Columbia, SC: University of South Carolina Press.

Fielder, R. L. (2014). Sexual hookups and adverse health outcomes: A longitudinal study of first-year college women. *Journal of Sex Research, 51,* 131–144.

Fields, J. & Casper, L. M. (2001). *America's families and living arrangements: March 2000.* Current Population Reports, P20-537. Washington, DC: U.S. Census Bureau.

Figueroa, T. & Hurtado, S. (2013). *Underrepresented racial and/or ethnic minority (URM) graduate students in STEM disciplines: A critical approach to understanding graduate school experiences on obstacles in degree progression.* Los Angeles: Higher Education Research Institute, UCLA.

Fikkan, J. L. & Rothblum, E. D. (2012). Is fat a feminist issue? Exploring the gendered nature of weight bias. *Sex Roles, 66,* 575–592.

Filax, G. & Taylor, D. (2014). *Disabled mothers: Stories and scholarship by and about mothers with disabilities.* Bradford: Demeter Press.

Fileborn, B. et al. (2015). Sex, desire, and pleasure: Considering the experiences of older Australian women. *Sexual and Relationship Therapy, 30,* 117–130.

Findley, P. A. et al. (2016). Exploring the experiences of abuse of college students with disabilities. *Journal of Interpersonal Violence, 31,* 2801–2823.

Fine, C. (2010). *Delusions of gender: How our minds, society, and neurosexism create difference.* New York: W. W. Norton.

Fine, C. (2017). *Testoterone Rex: Myths of sex, science, and society.* New York: Norton.

Finer, L. & Fine, J. B. (2013). Abortion law around the world: Progress and pushback. *AJPH, 103,* 585–589.

Finer, L. B. & Zolna, M. R. (2016). Declines in unintended pregnancy in the United States 2008–2011. *New England Journal of Medicine, 374,* 843.

Finerman, R. D. et al. (2015). Pregnancy and birth as a medical crisis. In McHugh, M. & Chrisler, J. C. *The wrong prescription* (pp. 17–36). Santa Barbara, CA: Praeger.

Fingerman, K. L. (2003). *Mothers and adult daughters: Mixed emotions, enduring bonds.* Amherst, NY: Prometheus.

Fingerman, K. L. & Birditt, K. S. (2011). Relationships between adults and their aging parents. In K. W. Schaie & S. L. Willis (Eds.), *Handbook of the psychology of aging* (7th ed., pp. 219–232). San Diego, CA: Academic Press.

Fingerman, K. L., Miller, L., Birditt, K., & Zarit, S. (2009). Giving to the good and the needy: Parental support of grown children. *Journal of Marriage and Family, 71,* 1220–1233.

Fingerman, K. L., Pitzer, L. M., Chan, W., Birditt, K., Franks, M. M., & Zarit, S. (2010). Who gets what and why? Help middle-aged adults provide to parents and grown children. *Journal of Gerontology: Social Sciences, 66B,* 87–98.

Finkel, E. J. et al. (2012). Online dating: A critical analysis from the perspective of psychological science. *Psychological Science in the Public Interest, 13,* 3–66.

Finkelhor, D. et al. (2013). Prevalence of childhood exposure to violence, crime, and abuse: Results from the National survey of children's exposure to violence. *JAMA Pediatrics, 169,* 746–754.

Finley, L. L. (2016). *Domestic abuse and sexual assault in popular culture.* Santa Barbara, CA: Praeger.

Fischer, A. & Evers, C. (2013). The social basis of emotion in men and women. In M.K. Ryan & N.R. Branscombe (Eds.). *Sage handbook of gender and psychology* (pp. 183–198). Los Angeles, CA: Sage.

Fischer, A. & LaFrance, M. (2015). What drives the smile and the tear: Why women are more emotionally expressive than men. *Emotion Review, 7,* 22–29.

Fischer, A. R. & Holz, K. B. (2010). Testing a model of women's personal sense of justice, control, well-being, and distress in the context of sexist discrimination. *Psychology of Women Quarterly, 3,* 297–310.

Fischer, B. et al. (2014). Effects of hormone therapy on cognition and mood. *Fertility and Sterility, 101,* 898–899.

Fischer, J. & Hayes, J. (2013). *The importance of social security in the incomes of older Americans: Differences by gender, age, race/ethnicity, and marital status.* Washington, DC: Institute for Women's Policy Research.

Fischer, N. L. & Seidman, S. (Eds.). (2016). *Introducing the new sexuality studies* (3rd ed.). New York: Routledge.

Fisher, B. S., Daigle, L. E., & Cullen, F. T. (2010). *Unsafe in the ivory tower: The sexual victimization of college women.* Thousand Oaks, CA: Sage.

Fisher, B. S., Zink, T., & Regan, S. L. (2011). Abuses against older women: Prevalence and health effects. *Journal of Interpersonal Violence, 26,* 254–268.

Fisher, B. S. et al. (2014). Statewide estimates of stalking among high school students in Kentucky: Demographic profile and sex differences. *Violence Against Women, 20,* 1258–1279.

Fisher, L. L. (2010). *Sex, romance, and relationships: AARP survey of midlife and older adults.* Washington, DC: AARP.

Fisher, R. et al. (2016). *Joint filing by same-sex couples after Windsor: Characteristics of married tax filers in 2013 and 2014.* Washington, DC: U.S. Treasury Department.

Fisher-Thompson, D., Sausa, A. D., & Wright, T. F. (1995). Toy selection for children: Personality and toy request influences. *Sex Roles, 33,* 239–255.

Fiske, S. T. (2010). Venus and Mars or down to earth: Stereotypes and realities of gender differences. *Perspectives on Psychological Science, 5,* 688–692.

Fitz, C. C. et al. (2012). Not all nonlabelers are created equal: Distinguishing between quasi-feminists and neoliberals. *Psychology of Women Quarterly, 36,* 274–285.

Fitzgerald, L., Collinsworth, L. L., & Harned, M. S. (2001). Sexual harassment. In J. Worell (Ed.), *Encyclopedia of women and gender* (pp. 991–1004). San Diego, CA: Academic Press.

Fitzgerald, T. et al. (2016). *Lung cancer: A woman's health imperative.* Boston, MA: Brigham and Women's Hospital.

Fitzpatrick, M. J. & McPherson, B. J. (2010). Coloring within the lines: Gender stereotypes in contemporary coloring books. *Sex Roles, 62,* 127–137.

Fitzpatrick, T. R. (2009). The quality of dyadic relationships, leisure activities and health among older women. *Health Care for Women International, 30,* 1073–1092.

Fitzpatrick Bettencourt, K. E. et al. (2011). Older and younger adults' attitudes toward feminism: The influence of religiosity, political orientation, gender, education, and family. *Sex Roles, 64,* 863–874.

Fivush, R., Brotman, M. A., Buckner, J. P., & Goodman, S. H. (2000). Gender differences in parent-child emotion narratives. *Sex Roles, 42,* 233–253.

Flanagan, C. (1993). Gender and social class: Intersecting issues in women's achievement. *Educational Psychologist, 28,* 357–378.

Fleck, C. (2007, October). Women and a secure retirement: Two steps forward, one step back. *AARP Bulletin,* pp. 1–2.

Flenady, V. (2014). Meeting the needs of parents after a stillbirth or neonatal death. *Royal College of Obstetricians and Gynaecologists,* 121, 137–140.

Flook, L. (2011). Gender differences in adolescents' daily interpersonal events and well-being. *Child Development, 82,* 454–461.

Flore, P.C. & Wicherts, J.M. (2015) Does stereotype threat influence performance of girls in stereotyped domains? A meta-analysis. *Journal of School Psychology, 53,* 25–44.

Flores, G. (2006). Language barriers to health care in the United States. *New England Journal of Medicine, 355,* 229–231.

Flores, N. (2015). Campus sexual assault: Myths, facts, and controversies. In S. Tarrant (Ed.), *Sex and politics: In the streets and between the sheets in the 21st century* (pp. 289–306). New York: Routledge.

Flouri, E. & Hawkes, D. (2008). Ambitious mothers-successful daughters: Mothers' early expectations for children's education and children's earnings and sense of control in adulthood. *British Journal of Educational Psychology, 78,* 411–433.

Foegen, M. (2016). *Gender, race, and ethnicity in the workplace: Emerging issues and enduring challenges.* Santa Barbara, CA: Praeger.

Foerde, K. et al. (2015). Neural mechanisms supporting maladaptive food choices in anorexia nervosa. *Nature Neuroscience,18,* 1571–1573.

Fogg, P. (2003, April 18). The gap that won't go away: Women continue to lag behind men in pay; the reasons may have little to do with gender bias. *Chronicle of Higher Education,* pp. A12–A15.

Fogliati, V. J. (2013). Stereotype threat reduces motivation to improve: Effects of stereotype threat and feedback on women's intentions to improve mathematical ability. *Psychology of Women Quarterly, 37,* 310–324.

Follins, L. D. et al. (2014). Resilience in black lesbian, gay, bisexual, and transgender individuals: A critical review of the literature. *Journal of Gay & Lesbian Mental Health, 18,* 190–212.

Fontanella-Khan, A. (2013). *Pink sari revolution: A tale of women and power in the badlands of India.* New York: W. W. Norton.

Forbes, G. B. & Frederick, D. A. (2008). The UCLA Body Project II: Breast and body dissatisfaction among African, Asian, European, and Hispanic American college women. *Sex Roles, 58,* 449–457.

Forbes, G. B., Adams-Curtis, L. E., White, K. B., & Holmgren, K. M. (2003). The role of hostile and benevolent sexism in women's and men's perceptions of the menstruating woman. *Psychology of Women Quarterly, 27,* 58–63.

Forbes, G. B. et al. (2012). Body dissatisfaction and disordered eating in three cultures: Argentina, Brazil, and the United States. *Sex Roles, 66,* 677–694.

Ford, K.A. 2012). Thugs, nice guys, and players: Black college women's partner preferences and relationship expectations. *Black Women, Gender, and Families, 6,* 23–42.

Forman, M. R. et al. (2013). Life course origins of the ages at menarche and menopause. *Adolescent Health and Medical Therapy, 4,* 1–21.

Forney, K. J. et al. (2012). Influence of peer context on the relationship between body dissatisfaction and eating pathology in women and men. *International Journal of Eating Disorders, 45,* 982–989.

Forster, L. (2015). *Magazine movements: Women's culture, feminisms and media form.* New York: Bloomsbury Academic.

Fortenberry, J. D. (2013). Puberty and adolescent sexuality. *Hormones and Behavior, 64,* 280–287.

Fortenberry, J. D., Schick, V., Herbenick, D., Sanders, S. A., Dodge, B., & Reece, M. (2010). Sexual behaviors and condom use at last vaginal intercourse: A national sample of adolescents ages 14 to 17 years. *Journal of Sexual Medicine, 7,* 305–314.

Foshee, V. A. (2015). The process of adapting a universal dating abuse prevention program to adolescents exposed to domestic violence. *Journal of Interpersonal Violence, 30,* 2151–2173.

Foshee, V. A. et al. (2015). Shared longitudinal predictors of physical peer and dating violence. *Journal of Adolescent Health, 56,* 106–112.

Foster, D. G. et al. (2015). A comparison of depression and anxiety symptom trajectories between women who had an abortion and women denied one. *Psychological Medicine, 45,* 1–10.

Foster, M. D. (1999). Acting out against gender discrimination: The effects of different social identities. *Sex Roles, 40,* 167–186.

Fouad, N. & Ihle, K. (2017). Effective strategies for career counseling with women. N M. Kopala & M. Keitel (Eds.), *Handbook of counseling women* (2nd ed., pp. 317–339). Thousand Oaks, CA: Sage.

Fouad, N. et al. (2011). Resistance of women in engineering careers: A qualitative study of current and former female engineers. *Journal of Women and Minorities in Science and Engineering, 17,* 69–96.

Fowers, B. J., Applegate, B., Tredinnick, M., & Slusher, J. (1996). His and her individualisms? Sex bias and individualism in psychologists' responses to case vignettes. *Journal of Psychology, 130,* 159–174.

Fox, A. B. et al. (2015). Pregnant women at work: The role of stigma in predicting women's intended exit from the workforce. *Psychology of Women Quarterly, 39,* 226–242.

Fox, B. & Neiterman, E (2015). Embodied motherhood: Women's feelings about their postpartum bodies. *Gender & Society, 29,* 670–693.

Fox, J. (2015). Sexualized avatars lead to women's self-objectification and acceptance of rape myths. *Psychology of Women Quarterly, 39,* 349–362.

Fox, J. (2016). Decreasing unintended pregnancy opportunities created by the Affordable Care Act. *Journal of the American Medical Associatio,* doi:10.1001/jama.2016.8800.

Fox, J. & Potocki, B. (2016). Lifetime video game consumption, interpersonal aggression, hostile sexism, and rape myth acceptance: A cultivation perspective. *Journal of Interpersonal Violence, 31,*1912–1931.

Fox, M. (2016, February 4). CDC sets off firestorm by warning women about alcohol. NBC News. Retrieved from nbcnews. com/health/womens-health/cdc-sets-firestorm-warning-women-about-alcohol-n511136

Fox, S. & Duggan, M. (2013). *Health online 2013.* Washington, DC: Pew Research Center.

Foynes M.M. et al. (2013). Race and gender discrimination in the Marines. *Cultural Diversity and Ethnic Minority Psychology, 19,* 111–119.

Francisca del Rio, M. & Strasser, K. (2013). Preschool children's beliefs about gender.differences in academic skills. *Sex Roles. 68,* 231–238.

Frank, A. (1995). *The diary of a young girl: The definitive edition.* New York: Bantam Books.

Franklin, J.C. et al. (2017). Risk factors for suicidal thoughts and behaviors: A meta-analysis of 50 years of research. *Psychological Bulletin, 143*, 187–232.

Franko, D. L., Becker, A. E., Thomas, J. J., & Herzog, D. B. (2007). Cross-ethnic differences in eating disorder symptoms and related distress. *International Journal of Eating Disorders, 40*, 156–164.

Frazier, P. A. & Kaler, M. E. (2006). Assessing the validity of self-reported stress-related growth. *Journal of Consulting and Clinical Psychology, 74*, 859–869.

Frazier, P. A., Mortensen, H., & Steward, J. (2005). Coping strategies as mediators of the relations among perceived control and distress in sexual assault survivors. *Journal of Counseling Psychology, 52*, 267–278.

Frech, A. & Damaske, S. (2012). The relationships between mothers' work pathways and physical and mental health. *Journal of Health and Social Behavior, 53*, 396–412.

Frederick, D. et al. (2013, August 11). *Who pays for dates? Following versus challenging conventional gender norms.* Presented at the annual meeting of the American Sociological Association, New York.

Fredrickson, C. (2015). Under the bus: How working women are being run over. New York: New Press.

Fredriksen-Goldsen, K. I. et al. (2014). The health and well-being of LGBT older adults: Disparities, risk, and resilience across the life course. In N. A. Orel & C. A. Fruhauf (Eds.), *The lives of LGBT older adults: Understanding challenges and resilience* (pp. 25–53). Washington, DC: American Psychological Association.

Fredriksen-Goldsen, K. I. et al. (2013). Creating a vision for the future: Key competencies and strategies for culturally competent practice with lesbian, gay, bisexual, and transgender (LGBT) older adults in the health and human services. *Journal of Gerontological Social Work, 57*, 80–107.

Freedman, D.J. (2013). *The stressed sex:* Oxford University Press.

Freedman, V.A. et al. (2016). Disability-free life expectancy over 30 years: A growing female disadvantage in the U.S. population. *AJPH, 106*, 1079–1085.

Freeman, C. (2010). Myths of docile girls and matriarchs: Local profiles of global workers. In J. Goodman (Ed.), *Global perspectives on gender & work* (pp. 289–304). Lanham, MD: Rowman & Littlefield.

Freeman, D. & Freeman, J. (2014). The stressed sex? *The Psychologist, 27*, 84–87.

Freeman, E. W. (2015). Depression in the menopause transition: Risks in the changing hormone milieu as observed in the general population. *Women's Midlife Health, 1*, doi:10.1186/s40695-015-0002-y.

Freud, S. (1925/1989). Some psychological consequences of the anatomical distinction between the sexes. In P. Gay (Ed.), *The Freud reader* (pp. 670–678). New York: Norton.

Freud, S. (1938). The transformation of puberty. In A. A. Brill (Ed. and Trans.), *The basic writings of Sigmund Freud* (pp. 604–629). New York: Random House.

Frevert, T. K. et al. (2015). Exploring the double jeopardy effect: The importance of gender and race in work–family research. In M. Mills (Ed.), *Gender and the work-family experience: An intersection of two domains* (pp. 57–75). New York: Springer.

Frias-Navarro, D. et al. (2015). Etiology of homosexualtiy and attitudes toward same-sex parenting: A randomized study. *The Journal of Sex Research, 52*, 151–161.

Fried, L. P. et al. (2004, March). A social model for health promotion for an aging population: Initial evidence on the experience corps model. *Journal of Urban Health, 81*, 64–78.

Friedan, B. (1963). *The feminine mystique.* New York: Norton.

Friedlander, M. L. et al. (2017). Empowering female supervisees: A feminist, multicultural, and relational perspective. In M. Kopala & M. Keitel (Eds.), *Handbook of counseling women* (2nd ed., pp. 607–619). Thousand Oaks, CA: Sage.

Friedman, A. L. & Bloodgood, B. (2010). "Something we'd rather not talk about": Findings from CDC exploratory research on sexually transmitted disease communication with girls and women. *Journal of Women's Health, 19*, 1823–1831.

Friedman, R. A. (2015, August 23). How changeable is gender? *New York Times*, pp. SR1, SR4–5.

Frieze, I. H. & Li, M. Y. (2010). Gender, aggression, and prosocial behavior. In J. C. Chrisler & D. R. McCreary (Eds.), *Handbook of gender research in psychology* (Vol. 2, pp. 311–335). New York: Springer.

Frieze, I. H., Olson, J. E., & Murrell, A. L. (2011). Working beyond 65: Predictors of late retirement for women and men MBA's. *Journal of Women & Aging, 23*, 40–57.

Frieze, I. H. et al. (2003). Gender-role attitudes in university students in the United States, Slovenia, and Croatia. *Psychology of Women Quarterly, 27*, 256–261.

Frith, H. (2013). Labouring on orgasms: Embodiment, efficiency, entitlement and obligations in heterosex. *Culture, Health & Sexuality, 15*, 494–510.

Frome, P.M. et al. (2008). Is the desire for a family-flexible job keeping young women out of male-dominated occupations? In H.M. Watt & J.S. Eccles (Eds.). *Gender and occupational outcomes: Longitudinal assessments of individual, social, and cultural influences* (pp. 195–214). Washington, DC: American Psychological Association.

Frost, J. J., Darroch, J. E., & Remez, L. (2008). Improving contraceptive use in the United States. *In brief* (1). New York: Guttmacher Institute.

Fry, R. (2013). *A rising share of young adults live in their parents' home: A record 21.6 million in 2012.* Washington, DC: Pew Research Center.

Fry, R. (2016). *For the first time in modern era, living with parents edges out other living arrangements for 18-to 34-year-olds.* Washington, DC: Pew Research Center.

Fuegen, K. & Biernat. M. Gender-based standards of competence in parenting and wok roles. In M.K. Ryan & N.R. Branscombe (Eds.). *Sage handbook of gender and psychology* (pp.131–147). Los Angeles, CA: Sage. (2013).

Fuegen, K., Biernat, M., Haines, E., & Deaux, K. (2004). Mothers and fathers in the workplace: How gender and parental status influence judgments of job-related competence. *Journal of Social Issues, 60*, 737–754.

Fulcher, M. (2005, April). *Individual differences in children's occupational aspirations as a function of parental traditionality.* Poster presented at the meeting of the Society for Research in Child Development, Atlanta, GA.

Fulcher, M. (2011). Individual differences in children's occupational aspirations as a function of parental traditionality. *Sex Roles, 64*, 117–131.

Fulcher, M., Sutfin, E. L., & Patterson, C. J. (2008). Individual differences in gender development: Associations with parental sexual orientation, attitudes, and division of labor. *Sex Roles, 58*, 330–341.

Fuller-Rowell, T.E. et al. (2012). Poverty and health: The mediating role of perceived discrimination. *Psychological Science, 23*, 734–739.

Fuller-Rowell, T. E., & Doan, S. N. (2010). The social costs of academic success across ethnic groups. *Child Development, 81*, 1696–1713.

Furman, W. & Rose, A. J. (2015). Friendships, romantic relationships, and peer relationships. In R. M. Lerner (Ed.), *Handbook of child psychology and developmental science* (Vol. 3, pp. 1–43). New York: Wiley.

Furr, L. A. (2014). Facial disfigurement stigma: A study of victims of domestic assaults with fire in India. *Violence Against Women, 20*, 783–798.

Gabrielson, M. L. & Holston, E. C. (2014). Broadening definitions of family for older lesbians: Modifying the lubben social network scale. *Journal of Gerontological Social Work, 57*, 198–217.

Galatzer-Levy, I. R. & Bonanno, G. A. (2014). Optimism and death: Predicting the course and consequences of depression trajectories in response to heart attack. *Psychological Science, 25*, 2177–2188.

Galliher, R. V., Rostosky, S. S., Welsh, D. P., & Kawaguchi, M. C. (1999). Power and psychological well-being in late adolescent romantic relationships. *Sex Roles, 40*, 689–710.

Gallup. (2010, March 7). *Abortion.* Retrieved from gallup.com/poll/1576/abortion.aspx

Galsworthy-Francis, L. & Allan, S. (2014). Cognitive behavioural therapy for anorexia nervosa: A systematic review. *Clinical Psychology Review, 34*, 54–72.

Gammage, M. M. (2016). *Representations of black women in the media: The damnation of black womanhood.* New York: Routledge.

Ganann, R. et al. (2016). Predictors of postpartum depression among immigrant women in the year after childbirth. *Journal of Women's Health, 25*, 155–165.

Ganong, L. H., Coleman, M., Thompson, A., & Goodwin-Watkins, C. (1996). African American and European American college students' expectations for self and future partners. *Journal of Family Issues, 17*, 758–775.

Gao, G. (2015, June 29). *Most Americans now say learning their child is gay wouldn't upset them.* Washington, DC: Pew Research Center.

Garcia, J. et al. (2012). Sexual hookup culture: A review. *Review of General Psychology,16*, 161–176.

Garcia, M. et al. (2016). Cardiovascular disease in women: Clinical perspectives. *Cardiovascular Research, 118*, 1273–1293.

Garfield, C. F. et al. (2014). A longitudinal study of paternal mental health during transition to fatherhood as young adults. *Pediatrics, 133*, 836–847.

Garre-Olmo, J., Planas-Pujol, X., López-Pousa, S., Juvinyà, D., Vilà, A., & Vilalta-Franch, J. (2009). Prevalence and risk factors of suspected elder abuse subtypes in people aged 75 and older. *Journal of the American Geriatrics Society, 57*, 815–822.

Gatrell, C. L. (2014). *Maternal body work: How women managers and professionals negotiate pregnancy and new motherhood at work.* Thousand Oaks, CA: Sage.

Gaucher, D. et al. (2011). Evidence that gendered wording in job advertisements exists and sustains gender inequality. *Journal of Personality and Social Psychology, 101*, 109–128.

Gault, B. et al. (2014a). *College affordability for low-income adults: Improving returns on investment for families and society.* Institute for Women's Policy Research: Washington DC.

Gault, B. et al. (2014b). *Paid parental leave in the United States: What the data tell us about access, usage, and economic and health benefits.* Washington, D. C.: Institute for Women's Policy Research.

Gavey, N. (2012). Beyond empowerment? Sexuality in a sexist world. *Sex Roles, 66*, 718–724.

Gavey, N. & McPhillips, K. (1999). Subject to romance: Heterosexual passivity as an obstacle to women initiating condom use. *Psychology of Women Quarterly, 23*, 349–367.

Gavin, H. & Porter, T. (2014). *Female aggression.* Malden, MA: Wiley-Blackwell.

Gavin, L. et al. (2009). Sexual and reproductive health of persons aged 10–24 years—United States, 2002–2007. *Morbidity and Mortality Weekly Report, 58*(SS-6).

Geary, D. C. (2007). An evolutionary perspective on sex differences in mathematics and the sciences. In S. J. Ceci & W. M. Williams (Eds.), *Why aren't more women in science? Top researchers debate the evidence* (pp. 173–188). Washington, DC: American Psychological Association.

Geary, D. C. (2010). *Male, female: The evolution of human sex differences.* Washington, DC: American Psychological Association.

Gellad, W. F. et al. (2015). Evaluation of flibanserin: Science and advocacy at the FDA. *Journal of the American Medical Association, 314*, 869–870.

Gelman, S. A., Taylor, M. G., & Nguyen, S. P. (2004). *Mother-child conversations about gender.* Boston, MA: Blackwell Publishing.

The gender wage gap by occupation. (IWPR #C350a). (2010, April). Washington, DC: Institute for Women's Policy Research.

Genoff, M.C. et al. (2016). Navigating language barriers: A systematic review of patient navigators' impact on cancer screening for limited English proficient patients. *Journal of General Internal Medicine, 31*, 426–434.

George, L. K. (2010). Still happy after all these years: Research frontiers on subjective well-being in later life. *Journal of Gerontology: Social Sciences, 65B*, 331–339.

George, P. et al. (2015). Diagnosis and surgical delays in African American and white women with early-stage breast cancer. *Journal of Women's Health, 24*, 209–217.

Gepner, Y. et al. (2015). Two-year moderate alcohol intervention in adults with type 2 diabetes. *Journals of Internal Medicine,* doi:10.7326/m14-1650.

Gerbasi, M. E. et al. (2014). Globalization and eating disorder risk: Peer influence, perceived social norms, and adolescent disordered eating in Fiji. *International Journal of Eating Disorders, 47*, 727–737.

Gerbrandt, R. & Kurtz, L. (2015). Keeping up appearances: Working-class feminists speak out about the success model in academia. In D. King & C. J. Valentine (Eds.), *Letting go: Feminist and social justice insight and activism* (pp. 161–172). Nashville, TN: Vanderbilt University Press.

Gergen, K. J. et al. (2015). The promises of qualitative inquiry. *American Psychologist, 70*, 1–9.

Germain, L. J. (2016). *Campus sexual assault: How women respond.* Baltimore, MD: Johns Hopkins University Press.

Gerson, K. (2010). *The unfinished revolution: How a generation is shaping family, work, and gender in America.* New York: Oxford University Press.

Gerstel, N. (2011). Rethinking families and community: The color, class, and centrality of extended kin ties. *Sociological Forum, 26*, 1–20.

Geurts, T. et al. (2015). Child care by grandparents: changes between 1992 and 2006. *Ageing & Society, 35*, 1318–1334.

Ghaznavi, J. & Taylor, L. D. (2015). Bones, body parts, and se appeal: An analysis of #thinspiration images on popular social media. *Body Image, 14*, 54–61.

Ghio, L. et al. (2014). Unmet needs and research challenges for late-life mood disorders. *Aging Clinical and Experimental Research, 26*, 101–114.

Ghosh, A. (2014). *Asian parents and their college age children: Examining family influence on careers.* Milwaukee, WI: University of Wisconsin Milwaukee.

Ghosh, R. & Sharma, A. K. (2012). Missing female fetus: A micro level investigation of sex determination in a periurban area of Northern India. *Health Care for Women International, 33*, 1020–1034.

Gianettoni, L. & Guilley, E. (2015). Sexism and the gendering of professional aspirations. In K. Faniko et al. (Eds.), *Gender and social hierarchies: Perspectives from social psychology* (pp. 11–25). New York: Routledge.

Giang, V. (2015, June 29). Transgender is yesterday's news: How companies are grappling with the "no gender" society. *Fortune.* Retrieved from fortune.com/2015/06/29/gender-fluid-binary-companies

Gibb, S. J. et al. (2015). Early motherhood and long-term economic outcomes: Findings from a 30-year longitudinal study. *Journal of Research on Adolescence, 25*, 163–172.

Gibbons, J. L. (2000). Gender development in cross-cultural perspective. In T. Eckes & H. M. Trautner (Eds.), *The developmental social psychology of gender* (pp. 389–415). Mahwah, NJ: Erlbaum

Gibbs, J. C., Basinger, K. S., Grime, R. L., & Snarey, J. R. (2007). Moral judgment development across cultures: Revisiting Kohlberg's universality claims. *Developmental Review, 27*, 443–500.

Gidycz, C. A. & Johnson, S. M. (2017). Violence against women: Treatment considerations. In M. Kopala & M. Keitel (Eds.), *Handbook of counseling women* (2nd ed., pp. 91–106). Thousand Oaks, CA: Sage.

Gidycz, C. A., Orchowski, L. M., & Edwards, K. M. (2011). Primary prevention of sexual violence. In M. P. Koss, J. W. White, & A. E. Kazdin (Eds.), *Violence against women and children: Navigating solutions* (Vol. 2, pp. 159–180). Washington, DC: American Psychological Association.

Giesbrecht, N. (1998). Gender patterns of psychosocial development. *Sex Roles, 39*, 463–478.

Gilbert, L. A. (1994). Reclaiming and returning gender to context: Examples from studies of heterosexual dual-earner families. *Psychology of Women Quarterly, 18*, 539–558.

Gilbert, L. A. & Scher, M. (1999). *Gender and sex in counseling and psychotherapy.* Boston, MA: Allyn & Bacon.

Giles, J. W. & Heyman, G. D. (2005). Young children's beliefs about the relationship between gender and aggressive behavior. *Child Development, 76,* 107–121.

Gill, A.K. & Brah, A. (2014). Interrogating cultural narratives about "honour"-based violence. *European Journal of Women's Studies,* 21, 72–86.

Gill, S. S. et al. (2015). What older individuals can do to optimize cognitive outcomes. *Lifestyles and Cognitive Health, 314,* 1–4.

Gillam, K., & Wooden, S. R. (2011). Post-princess models of gender: The new man in Disney. In M. Kimmel & A. Aronson (Eds.), *The gendered society reader* (4th ed., pp. 471–478). New York: Oxford University Press.

Gillespie, B. J. (2016). Correlates of sex frequency and sexual satisfaction among partnered older adults. *Journal of Sex and Marital Therapy,* doi:10.1080/0092623X.2016.1176608.

Gillespie, B. J. et al. (2015). Close adult friendships, gender, and the life cycle. *Journal of Social and Personal Relationships, 32,* 709–736.

Gilligan, C. (1982). *In a different voice.* Cambridge, MA: Harvard University Press.

Gilligan, C. (2011). *Joining the resistance.* Cambridge, UK: Polity Press.

Gilligan, C. (2002). *Beyond pleasure.* New York: Knopf.

Gilpatric, K. (2010). Violent female action characters in contemporary American cinema. *Sex Roles, 62,* 734–746.

Ginsberg, R. L. & Gray, J. J. (2006). The differential depiction of female athletes in judged and non-judged sport magazines. *Body Image, 3,* 365–373.

Ginsberg, R. L. et al. (2016). Prevalence and correlates of body image dissatisfaction in postmenopausal women. *Women Health, 56,* 23–47.

Ginsberg, S. D. (2016). Depression, sex and gender roles in older adult populations: The international mobility in aging study (IMIAS). *PLOS ONE, 11,* 1–11.

Girard, A. L. & Senn, C. Y. (2008). The role of the new "date rape drugs" in attributions about date rape. *Journal of Interpersonal Violence, 23,* 3–20.

GLAAD. (2015–2016). *Where we are on TV.* New York: Author.

GLAAD. (2016). *Studio responsibility index 2016.* New York: Author.

Glass, J. et al. (2016). *CCF Brief: Parenting and happiness in 22 countries.* Austin, TX: Council on Contemporary Families.

Glass, V. Q. & Few-Demo, A. L. (2013). Complexities of informal social support arrangements for black lesbian couples. *Family Relations, 62,* 714–726.

Glassdoor Economic Research. (2016). *Which countries in Europe have the best gender equality in the workplace?* New York: Author.

Glasser, C. L., Robnett, B., & Feliciano, C. (2009). Internet daters' body type preferences: Race-ethnic and gender differences. *Sex Roles, 61,* 14–33.

Glazer, D. (2014). LGBT parenting: The kids are all right. *Journal of Gay & Lesbian Mental Health, 18,* 213–221.

Gleason, J. B. & Ely, R. (2002). Gender differences in language development. In A. McGillicuddy-DeLisi & R. DeLisi (Eds.), *Biology, society, and behavior: The development of sex differences in cognition. Advances in applied developmental psychology* (Vol. 21, pp. 127–154). Westport, CT: Ablex.

Glick, P. & Fiske, S. T. (2011). Ambivalent sexism revisited. *Psychology of Women Quarterly, 35,* 530–535.

Glick, P. et al. (2000). Beyond prejudice as simple antipathy: Hostile and benevolent sexism across cultures. *Journal of Personality and Social Psychology, 79,* 763–775.

Goble, P. et al. (2012). Children's gender-typed activity choices across preschool social contexts. *Sex Roles, 67,* 435–451.

Goerge, R. M., Harden, A., & Lee, B. J. (2008). Consequences of teen childbearing for child abuse, neglect, and foster care placement. In S. D. Hoffman & R. Maynard (Eds.), *Kids having kids: Economic costs and social consequences of teen pregnancy* (2nd ed., pp. 257–288). Washington, DC: Urban Institute Press.

Goff, P. A., Thomas, M. A., & Jackson, M. C. (2008). "Ain't I a woman?": Towards an intersectional approach to person perception and group-based harms. *Sex Roles, 59,* 392–403.

Gold, K. J. et al. (2016). Depression and posttraumatic stress symptoms after perinatal loss in a population-based sample. *Journal of Women's Health, 25,* 263–269.

Goldberg, A. E. (2013). "Doing" and "undoing" gender: The meaning and division of housework in same-sex couples. *Journal of Family Therapy & Review, 5,* 85–104.

Goldberg, A. E. (2017). LGBQ-parent families: Development and functioning in context. In C. A. Price et al. (Eds.), *Families & change: Coping with stressful events and transitions* (pp. 95–118). Thousand Oaks, CA: Sage.

Goldberg, A. E. & Garcia, R. L. (2016). Gender-typed behavior over time in children with lesbian, gay, and heterosexual parents. *Journal of Family Psychology, 30,* 854–865.

Goldberg, A. E. & Perry-Jenkins, M. (2007). The division of labor and perceptions of parental roles: Lesbian couples across the transition to parenthood. *Journal of Social and Personal Relationships, 24,* 297–318.

Goldberg, A. E. & Scheid, J. E. (2015). Why donor insemination and not adoption? Narratives of female-partnered and single mothers. *Family Relations, 64,* 726–742.

Goldberg, C. (1999, May 16). Wellesley grads find delicate balance. *Hartford Courant,* p. G3.

Goldberg, W. A. & Lucas-Thompson, R. (2008). Effects of maternal and paternal employment. In M. M. Haith & J. B. Benson (Eds.), *Encyclopedia of infant and early childhood development* (Vol. 2, pp. 268–279). San Diego, CA: Academic Press.

Goldberg, W. A. & Lucas-Thompson, R. G. (2014). College women miss the mark when estimating the impact of full-time maternal employment on children's achievement and behavior. *Psychology of Women Quarterly, 38,* 490–502.

Golden, C. (2014). A grand gender convergence: Its last chapter. *American Economic Review. 104,* 1091–1119.

Golden, N. H. et al. (2015). Update on the medical management of eating disorders in adolescents. *Journal of Adolescent Health, 56,* 370–375.

Goldenberg, J.L. et al. (2013). Monstrously mortal: Women's bodies, existential threat, and women's health risks. In M. K. Ryan & N. R. Branscombe (Eds.). *Sage handbook of gender and psychology* (pp. 397–411). Los Angeles, CA: Sage.

Goldin, C. (2006, March 15). Working it out. *New York Times,* p. A27.

Goldin, C. (2014). A grand gender convergence: Its last chapter. *American Economic Review, 104,* 1091–1119.

Goldner, M. & Drentea, P. (2009). Caring for the disabled: Applying different theoretical perspectives to understand racial and ethnic variations among families. *Marriage & Family Review, 45,* 499–518.

Goldston, D. B., Molock, S. D., Whitbeck, L. B., Murakami, J. L., Zayas, L. H., & Hall, G. C. N. (2008). Cultural considerations in adolescent suicide prevention and psychosocial treatment. *American Psychologist, 63,* 14–31.

Gollenberg, A. L. et al. (2010). Perceived stress and severity of perimenstrual symptoms: The biocycle study. *Journal of Women's Health, 19,* 959–967.

Golombok, S. (2013). Families created by reproductive donation: Issues and research. *Child Development Perspectives, 7,* 61–65.

Golombok, S. et al. (2017). Parenting and the adjustment of children born to gay fathers through surrogacy. *Child Development* doi:10,1111/cdev.12728

Golombok, S. & Badger, S. (2010). Children raised in mother-headed families from infancy: A follow-up of children of lesbian and single heterosexual mothers, at early adulthood. *Human Reproduction, 25,* 150–157.

Golombok, S., Rust, J., Zervoulis, K., Croudace, T., Golding, J., & Hines, M. (2008). Developmental trajectories of sex-typed behavior in boys and girls: A longitudinal general population study of children aged 2.5–8 years. *Child Development, 79,* 1583–1593.

Golombok, S. et al. (2014). Adoptive gay father families: Parent-child relationships and children's psychological adjustment. *Child Development, 85,* 456–468.

Gomez, S. L. et al. (2016). Effects of marital status and economic resources on survival after cancer: A population-based study. *Cancer, 122,* 1618–1625.

Gonçalves, A. et al. (2015). Alcohol consumption and risk of heart failure: The atherosclerosis risk in communities study. *European Heart Journal,* 1–14.

Gondolf, E. W. (2015). *Gender-based perspectives on batterer programs: Program leaders on history, approach, research, and development.* New York: Lexington Books.

Goñi-Legaz, S., Ollo-López, A., & Bayo-Moriones, A. (2010). The division of household labor in Spanish dual earner couples: Testing three theories. *Sex Roles, 63,* 515–529.

Gonzales, G. (2014). Same-sex marriage—A prescription for better health. *New England Journal of Medicine,* 1373–1376.

Good, C., Aronson, J., & Inzlicht, M. (2003). Improving adolescents' standardized test performance: An intervention to reduce the effects of stereotype threat. *Personality and Social Psychology Bulletin, 24,* 645–662.

Goode, E. (2000, May 19). Scientists find a particularly female response to stress. *New York Times,* p. A20.

Goodin, S. M. et al. (2011). "Putting on" sexiness: A content analysis of the presence of sexualizing characteristics in girls' clothing. *Sex Roles, 65,* 1–12.

Goodman, L. A. & Epstein, D. (2011). The justice system response to domestic violence. In M. P. Koss, J. W. White, & A. E. Kazdin (Eds.), *Violence against women and children: Navigating solutions* (Vol. 2, pp. 215–236). Washington, DC: American Psychological Association.

Goodman, L. A. et al. (2013). Poverty and mental health practice: Within and beyond the 50-minute hour. *Journal of Clinical Psychology, 69,* 182–190.

Goodman, M. P. (2011). Female genital cosmetic and plastic surgery: A review. *Journal of Sexual Medicine, 8,* 1813–1825.

Goodnough, A. & Abelson, R. (2017, March 8). Analysts say millions risk losing coverage in GOP health plan. *New York Times.* p. A15.

Gordon, R. A., Chase-Lansdale, P. L., & Brooks-Gunn, J. (2004). Extended households and the life course of young mothers: Understanding the associations using a sample of mothers with premature, low birth weight babies. *Child Development, 75,* 1013–1038.

Gorney, C. 2017, February). Life after loss. *National Geographic,* 78–103.

Gotlib, A. (2011). Computer games. In M. Z. Stange, C. K. Oyster, & J. E. Sloan (Eds.), *Encyclopedia of women in today's world* (Vol. 1, pp. 321–323). Newberry Park, CA: Sage.

Gould, H. N. et al. (2013). High levels of education and employment among women with Turner syndrome. *Journal of Women's Health, 22,* 230–235.

Gould, L. (1990). X: A fabulous child's story. In A. G. Halberstadt & S. L. Ellyson (Eds.), *Social psychology readings: A century of research* (pp. 251–257). Boston, MA: McGraw-Hill.

Gozdziak, E. M. (2014). Empirical vacuum: In search of research on human trafficking. In R. Gartner & B. McCarthy (Eds.), *The Oxford handbook of gender, sex, and crime* (pp. 613–634). New York: Oxford University Press.

Grabe, S. & Hyde, J. S. (2009). Body objectification, MTV, and psychological outcomes among female adolescents. *Journal of Applied Social Psychology, 39,* 2840–2858.

Graber, J. A. (2013). Pubertal timing and the development of psychopathology in adolescence and beyond. *Hormones and Behavior, 64,* 262–269.

Graber, J. A. & Brooks-Gunn, J. (2002). Adolescent girls' sexual development. In G. M. Wingood & R. J. DiClemente (Eds.), *Handbook of women's sexual and reproductive health* (pp. 21–42). New York: Kluwer Academic/Plenum.

Grace, S.L. et al. (2015, December 9). Cardiac rehabilitation program adherence and functional capacity among women: A randomized controlled trial. *Mayo Clinic Proceedings,* 1–9.

Grace, S. L., Gravely-Witte, S., Kayaniyil, S., Brual, J., Suskin, N., & Stewart, D. E. (2009). A multisite examination of sex differences in cardiac rehabilitation barriers by participation status. *Journal of Women's Health, 18,* 209–216.

Grady, D. (2015, October 20). New mammogram recommendations: A guide. *New York Times,* pB3.

Grady, D. (2016a, October 17). First, fighting cancer. Next, tackling issues of care for trans People. *New York Times,* p. A10.

Grady, D. (2016b, February 23). Vaginal ring with drug lowers HIV rates in African women. *New York Times,* pA6.

Graff, K. A. (2013). Low-cut shirts and high-heeled shoes: Increased sexualization across time in magazine depictions of girls. *Sex Roles. 69,* 571–582.

Graff, K. A. et al. (2012). Too sexualized to be taken seriously? Perceptions of a girl in childlike vs. sexualizing clothing. *Sex Roles, 66,* 764–775.

Graham, J. M. & Barnow, Z. B. (2013). Stress and social support in gay, lesbian, and heterosexual couples: Direct effects and buffering models. *Journal of Family Psychology, 27,* 569–578.

Granic, I. et al. (2014). The benefits of playing video games. *American Psychologist, 69,* 66–78.

Grant, L. & Denmon, A. (2012). Female physicians. In J. Kronenfeld et al. (Eds.) *Debates on U.S. health care* (pp. 415–432). Thousand Oaks, CA: Sage.

Grau, S. L. & Zotos, Y. C. (2016). Gender stereotypes in advertising: A review of current research. *International Journal of Advertising, 35,* 761–770.

Gray, J. (1992). *Men are from Mars, women are from Venus.* New York: HarperCollins.

Greathouse, S. M. et al. (2015). *A review of the literature on sexual assault perpetratorcharacteristics and behaviors.* Santa Monica, CA: Rand Corporation.

Greely, H. T. (2016). *The end of sex and the future of human reproduction.* Cambridge, MA: Harvard University Press.

Green tea may lower heart disease risk (2012, December). *Harvard Health Letter, 23,* 7.

Green, P. P. et al. (2016). Vital signs: Alcohol-exposed pregnancies—United States, 2011–2013. *Morbidity and Mortality Weekly Report, 65,* 91–97.

Greene, S. (2015). *The psychological development of girls and women: Rethinking change in time.* New York: Routledge.

Greene, M. et al. (2013). Management of human immunodeficiency virus infection in advanced age. *Journal of the American Medical Association, 309,* 1397–1398.

Greenspan, L. & Deardorff, J. (2014). *The new puberty: How to navigate early development in today's girls.* Emmaus, PA: Rodale.

Greenfield, S. F. (2016). *Treating women with substance use disorders: The women's recovery group manual.* New York: Guilford.

Greenhaus, J. H. & Kossek, E. E. (2014). The contemporary career: A work-home perspective. *Annual Review of Organizational Behavior, 1,* 361–388.

Greenhouse, S. (2014, July 15). Equal opportunity employment officials take new aim at pregnancy bias. *New York Times,* p. B4.

Greenlee, H. et al. (2014). Clinical practice guidelines on the use of integrative therapies as supportive care in patients treated for breast cancer. *JNCI Monographs, 50,* 346–358.

Greenwood, D. N. (2007). Are female action heroes risky role models? Character identification, idealization, and viewer aggression. *Sex Roles, 57,* 725–732.

Grekin, R. & O'Hara, M. W. (2014). Prevalence and risk factors of postpartum posttraumatic stress disorder: A meta-analysis. *Clinical Psychology Review, 34,* 389–401.

Gressier, F. et al. (2016). 5-HTTLPR and gender differences in affective disorders: *A systematic review. Journal of Affective Disorders, 190,* 193–207.

Grieger, I. (2017). Women in intimate relationships: Theory, research, and implications. In M. Kopala & M. Keitel (Eds.), *Handbook of counseling women* (2nd ed., pp. 352–369). Thousand Oaks, CA: Sage.

Grigg, A. J. & Kirkland, A. (2016). Health. In L. Disch & M. Hawkesworth (Eds.). *Oxford handbook of feminist theory* (pp. 326–345). New York: Oxford University Press.

Grijalva, E. et al. (2015). Gender differences in narcissism: A meta-analytic review. *Psychological Bulletin, 141,* 261–310.

Grimberg, A., Kutikov, J. K., & Cucchiara, A. J. (2005). Sex differences in patients referred for evaluation of poor growth. *Journal of Pediatrics, 146,* 212–216.

Grimes, S. M. (2015). Rescue the princess: The video game princess as prize, parody, and protagonist. *Princess cultures: Mediating girls' imaginations and identities* (pp. 65–88). New York: Peter Lang.

Grimmell, D. & Stern, G. S. (1992). The relationship between gender role ideals and psychological well-being. *Sex Roles, 27,* 487–497.

Grogan, S. (2017). *Body image: Understanding body dissatisfaction in men, women and children.* New York: Routledge.

Groh, C. J. (2009). Foundations of women's mental health. In J. C. Urbancic & C. J. Groh (Eds.), *Women's mental health: A clinical guide for primary care providers* (pp. 1–21). Philadelphia, PA: Lippincott Williams & Wilkins.

Groh, C. J., Urbancic, J. C., LaGore, S. M., & Whall, A. (2009). Mental health issues for older women. In J. C. Urbancic & C. J. Groh (Eds.), *Women's mental health: A clinical guide for primary care providers* (pp. 313–349). Philadelphia, PA: Lippincott Williams & Wilkins.

Grose, R. G. & Grabe, S. (2014). Sociocultural attitudes surrounding menstruation and alternative menstrual products: The explanatory role of self-objectification. *Health Care for Women International, 35,* 672–694.

Gross, S. M., Ireys, H. T., & Kinsman, S. L. (2000). Young women with physical disabilities: Risk factors for symptoms of eating disorders. *Developmental and Behavioral Pediatrics, 21,* 87–96.

Grossman, A. H., D'Augelli, A. R., & O'Connel, T. S. (2001). Being lesbian, gay, bisexual, and 60 or older in North America. *Journal of Gay & Lesbian Social Services, 13,* 23–40.

Grossman, A. H. et al. (2013). Sexual orientation and aging in Western society. In C. J. Patterson & A. R. D'Augelli (Eds.), *Handbook of psychology and sexual orientation* (pp. 132–150). New York: Oxford University Press.

Grossman, A. L. & Tucker, J. S. (1997). Gender differences and sexism in the knowledge and use of slang. *Sex Roles, 37,* 101–110.

Grumbein, A. & Goodman, J. R. (2013). The good, the bad, and the beautiful: How gender is represented on reality television. In C. L. Armstrong et al. (Eds.) *Media disparity: A gender battleground* (pp. 99–114). Lanham, MD: Lexington Books.

Grunspan, D. Z. et al. (2016). Males under-estimate academic performance of their female peers in undergraduate biology classrooms. *PLOS ONE,* 1–16.

Grussu, P. & Quatraro, R. M. (2013). Maternity blues in Italian primipara women: Symptoms and mood states in the first fifteen days after childbirth. *Health Care for Women International, 34,* 556–576.

Guastello, D. D. & Guastello, S. J. (2003). Androgyny, gender role behavior, and emotional intelligence among college students and their parents. *Sex Roles, 49,* 663–673.

Guendelman, S. et al. (2014). Work-family balance after childbirth: The association between employer-offered leave characteristics and maternity leave duration. *Maternal Child Health Journal, 18,* 200–208.

Guidelines for psychotherapy with lesbian, gay, and bisexual clients. (2000). *American Psychologist, 55,* 1440–1451.

Guille, C. et al. (2013). Management of postpartum depression. *Journal of Midwifery & Women's Health, 58,* 643–653.

Guimond, S. et al. (2013). The social psychology of gender across cultures. In M.K. Ryan & N.R. Branscombe (Eds.). *Sage handbook of psychology and gender* (pp. 216–233). Los Angeles, CA: Sage.

Guo, J. (2016, January 25). Researchers have found a major problem with "The Little Mermaid" and other Disney movies. *Washington Post.* Retrieved from washingtonpost.com/wonk/wp/2016/01/25/researchers_have_discovered_major_problem

Guo, J. et al. (2013). Interventions to reduce the number of falls among older adults with/without cognitive impairment: An exploratory meta-analysis. *Internal Geriatric Psychiatry, 29,* 661–669.

Gupta, A. et al. (2013). *Circulation: Cardiovascular quality and outcomes topic review.* Retrieved November 8, 2015, from circout-comes.ahajournals.org/content/circcvoq/5/3/e17.full.pdf

Gupta, S. (2007). Autonomy, dependence, or display? The relationship between married women's earnings and housework. *Journal of Marriage and Family, 69,* 399–417.

Gustines, G. G. (2015, December 24). Diversity comes to superheroes. *New York Times,* pp. D1, D8.

Guttmacher Institute. (2010). *Facts on satisfying the need for contraception in developing countries.* New York: Author.

Guttmacher Institute (2014). *American teens' sexual and reproductive health.* Washington, DC: Author.

Guttmacher Institute (2015). *Contraceptive use in the United States.* Washington, DC: Author.

Guttmacher Institute (2016a). *American teens' source of sexual health education.* Washington, DC: Author.

Guttmacher Institute (2016b). *Induced abortion in the United States.* Washington, DC: Author.

Guttmacher Institute (2016c). *State funding of abortion under Medicaid.* Washington, DC: Author.

Guttmacher Institute (2016d). *State policies in brief: Emergency contraception.* Washington, DC: Author.

Guttmacher Institute (2016e). *Unintended pregnancy in the United States.* Washington, DC: Author.

Guzmán, B. L. & Stritto, M. E. D. (2012). The role of socio-psychological determinants in the sexual behaviors of Latina early adolescents. *Sex Roles, 66,* 776–789.

Haberkern, K. et al. (2013). Gender differences in intergenerational care in European welfare states. *Ageing & Society, 35,* 298–320.

Hackett, S. et al. (2016). The therapeutic efficacy of domestic violence victim interventions. *Trauma, Violence, & Abuse, 17,* 123–132.

Hadfield, J. C. (2014). The health of grandparents raising grandchildren: A literature review. *Journal of Gerontological Nursing, 40,* 32–42.

Hafner, K. (2003, August 21). 3 women and 3 paths, 10 years later. *New York Times,* pp. E1, E7.

Hafner, K. (2014, November 4). Steps to avoid an accident. *New York Times,* p. D4.

Hahn-Holbrook, J. & Haselton, M. (2014). Is postpartum depression a disease of modern civilization. *Current Directions in Psychological Science, 23,* 395–400.

Haines, E. L. et al. (2016). The times they are a-changing . . . or are they not? A comparison of gender stereotypes, 1983–2014. *Psychology of Women Quarterly, 40,* 353–363.

Hains, R. C. (2014). *The princess problem: Guiding our girls through the princess-obsessed years.* Naperville, IL; Sourcebooks, Inc.

Haley, D. F. & Justman, J.E. (2013). The HIV epidemic among women in the United States: A persistent puzzle. *Journal of Women's Health, 22,* 715.

Halim, M. L. D. (2016). Princess and superheroes: Social-cognitive influences on early gender rigidity. *Child Development Perspectives, 10,* 155–160.

Hall, G. C. N. et al. (2016). On becoming multicultural in a mono-cultural research world: A conceptual approach to studying eth-nocultural diversity. *American Psychologist, 71,* 40–51.

Hall, J. A. (2006). How big are nonverbal sex difference? The case of smiling and nonverbal sensitivity. In K. Dindia & D. J. Canary (Eds.), *Sex differences and similarities in communication* (2nd ed., pp. 59–82). Mahwah, NJ: Erlbaum.

Hall, J. A. & Schmid Mast, M. (2008). Are women always more interpersonally sensitive than men? Impact of goals and content domain. *Personality and Social Psychology Bulletin, 34,* 144–155.

Hall, J.A. et al. (2014). Physician gender, physician patient-centered behavior, and patient satisfaction: A study in three practice settings within a hospital. *Patient Education Counseling, 95,* 313–318.

Hall, J. A., Park, N., Song, H., & Cody, M. J. (2010). Strategic misrepresentation in online dating: The effects of gender, self-monitoring, and personality traits. *Journal of Social and Personal Relationships, 27,* 117–135.

Hall, R. L. (2007). On the move: Exercise, leisure activities, and midlife women. In V. Muhlbauer & J. C. Chrisler (Eds.), *Women over 50: Psychological perspectives* (pp. 79–94). New York: Springer.

Hallett, S. (2015, Winter). Don't tell: Military rape survivors still face retaliation for reporting crimes. *Ms Magazine,* 10–12.

Halley, J. & Eshleman, A. (2016). *Seeing straight: An introduction to gender and sexual privilege.* Lanham, MD: Rowman & Littlefield.

Halpern, D. (2012). *Sex differences in cognitive ability* (4th ed.). New York: Psychology Press.

Halpern, D. F. & Cheung, F. M. (2008). *Women at the top: Powerful leaders tell us how to combine work and family.* Malden, MA: Wiley-Blackwell.

Halpern, D. F., Straight, C., & Stephenson, C. L. (2011). Beliefs about cognitive gender differences: Accurate for direction, underestimated for size. *Sex Roles, 64,* 336–347.

Halpern, H. P. & Perry-Jenkins, M. (2016). Parents' gender ideology and gendered behavior as predictors of children's gender-role attitudes: A longitudinal exploration. *Sex Roles, 74,* 527–542.

Hamad, H. & Taylor, A. (2015). Introduction: Feminism and contemporary celebrity culture. *Celebrity Studies, 6,* 124–127.

Hamberger, L. & Larsen, S. (2015). Men's and women's experience of intimate partner violence: A review of ten years of comparative studies in clinical samples; Part 1. *Journal of Family Violence, 30,* 699–717.

Hamby, S. (2014). Intimate partner and sexual violence research: Scientific progress, scientific challenges, and gender. *Trauma, Violence, & Abuse, 15,* 149–158.

Hamby, S. & Grych, J. (2016). The complex dynamics of victimization: Understanding differential vulnerability without blaming the victim. In C. Cuevas & C. Rennison (Eds.). *Wiley handbook on the psychology of violence* (pp. 66–85). Malden,,MA: Wiley.

Hamilton, B. E. et al. (2016). Births: Preliminary data for 2015. *National Vital Statistics Reports, 65*(3). Hyattsville, MD: National Center for Health Statistics.

Hamilton, J. L. et al. (2015). Stress and the development of cognitive vulnerabilities to depression explain sex differences in depressive symptoms during adolescence. *Clinical Psychological Science, 3,* 702–714.

Hamilton, M. C. (1991). Masculine bias in the attribution of personhood: People = male, male = people. *Psychology of Women Quarterly, 15,* 393–402.

Hammen, C. & Silveira, S. (2014). Child and adolescent depression. In E. J. Mash & R. A. Barkley (Eds.), *Child psychopathology* (pp. 225–263). New York: Guilford.

Hampson, E. & Moffat, S. D. (2004). The psychobiology of gender: Cognitive effects of reproductive hormones in the adult nervous system. In A. H. Eagly, A. E. Beall, & R. J. Sternberg (Eds.), *The psychology of gender* (pp. 38–64). New York: Guilford.

Hampton, T. (2008). Studies address racial and geographic disparities in breast cancer treatment. *Journal of the American Medical Society, 300,* 1641.

Hampton, T. (2010). Child marriage threatens girls' health. *Journal of the American Medical Association, 304,* 509–510.

Hancock, A. B. & Rubin, B. A. (2014). Influence of communication partner's gender on language. *Journal of Language and Social Psychology, 10,* 1–19.

Handwerk, B (2014). *Puberty is beginning earlier in girls, so what can parents do?* Retrieved December 26, 2014, from smithsonian.com

Hanley, S. & McLaren, S. (2015). Sense of belonging to layers of lesbian community weakens the link between body image dissatisfaction and depressive symptoms. *Psychology of Women Quarterly, 39,* 85–94.

Hans, A. (2015). *Disabilities, gender, and the trajectories of power.* Thousand Oaks, CA: Sage.

Hanson, A. G. (2015, December 18). *Frozen embryo donation and adoption: A new trend?* Retrieved from lawstreetmedia.com/issues/health-science/frozen -embryo-donation-adoption-new-trend

Hanson, K. & Wapner, S. (1994). Transition to retirement: Gender differences. *International Journal of Aging and Human Development, 39,* 189–208.

Hanson, S. L. (2007). Success in science among young African American women: The role of minority families. *Journal of Family Issues, 28,* 3–33.

Hant, M. A. (2011). Aging, attitudes toward. In M. Z. Stange, C. K. Oyster, & J. E. Sloan (Eds.), *Encyclopedia of women in today's world* (Vol. 1, pp. 46–48). Newberry Park, CA: Sage.

Harden, K. P. (2014). A sex-positive framework for research on adolescent sexuality. *Perspectives on Psychological Science, 9,* 455–469.

Hardesty, J. & Crossman, K. (2014). Intimate partner violence. In J. A. Arditti (Ed.), *Family problems: Stress, risk, and resilience* (pp. 213–227). Malden, MA: Wiley.

Hardie, J. H. & Lucas, A. (2010). Economic factors and relatiohship quality among young couples: Comparing cohabitation and marriage. *Journal of Marriage and Family, 72,* 1141–1154.

Harel, Z. (2008). Dysmenorrhea in adolescents. *Annals of the New York Academy of Sciences, 1135,* 185–195.

Hariri, S. et al. (2013). Population impact of HPV vaccines: Summary of early evidence. *Sciencedirect.com. 53,* 679–682.

Harley, D. A. & Teaster, P. B. (2016). *LGBT intersection of age and sexual identity in the workplace.* Switzerland: Springer International.

Harman, S. M. (2014). Menopausal hormone treatment cardiovascular disease: Another look at an unresolved conundrum. *Fertility and Sterility, 101,* 887–888.

Harmon, A. (2003, June 29). Online dating sheds its stigma as losers.com. *New York Times,* pp. YT1, YT21.

Harper, M. & Schoeman, W. J. (2003). Influences of gender as a basic-level category in person perception on the gender belief system. *Sex Roles, 49,* 517–526.

Harriger, J. A., Calogero, R. M., Witherington, D. C., & Smith, J. E. (2010). Body size stereotyping and internalization of the thin ideal in preschool girls. *Sex Roles, 63,* 609–620.

Harris, A. C. (1994). Ethnicity as a determinant of sex role identity: A replication study of item selection for the Bem Sex Role Inventory. *Sex Roles, 31,* 241–273.

Harris, A. P. & Gonzalez, C. G. (2012). Introduction. In G. Gutierrez y Muhs et al. (Eds.), *Presumed incompetent: The intersections of race and class for women in academia* (pp. 1–16). Boulder, CO: University Press of Colorado.

Harris, C. R. & Mickes, L. (2014). Corrigendum: Women can keep the vote: No evidence that hormonal changes during the menstrual cycle impact political and religious beliefs. *Psychological Science, 25,* 1969.

Harris, G. (2010a, August 14). F.D.A. approves 5-day emergency contraceptive. *New York Times,* p. A1.

Harris, G. (2010b, June 18). Panel recommends approval of after-sex pill to prevent pregnancy. *New York Times,* p. A14.

Harshman, M. (2014). *Women in need of reproductive health education.* Retrieved January 27, 2014, from health.harvard.edu/healthbeat

Hart, J. & Fellabaum, J. (2008). Analyzing campus climate studies: Seeking to define and understand. *Journal of Diversity in Higher Education, 1,* 222–234.

Hart, L. M. et al. (2015). Parents and prevention: A systematic review of interventions involving parents that aim to prevent body dissatisfaction or eating disorders. *International Journal of Eating Disorders, 48,* 157–169.

Harter, S. (1990). Adolescent self and identity development. In S. S. Feldman & G. R. Elliot (Eds.), *At the threshold: The developing adolescent* (pp. 352–387). Cambridge, MA: Harvard University Press.

Harter, S. (1998). The development of self-representations. In W. Damon (Series Ed.) & N. Eisenberg (Vol. Ed.), *Handbook of child psychology: Vol. 3. Social, emotional and personality development* (5th ed., pp. 553–617). New York: Wiley.

Harter, S. (1999). *The construction of the self: A developmental perspective.* New York: Guilford.

Hartl, A.C. et al. (2015). A survival analysis of adolescent friendships: The downside of dissimilarity. *Psychological Science, 26,*1304–1315.

Hartley, H. & Tiefer, L. (2003, Spring/Summer). Taking a biological turn: The push for a "female Viagra" and the push for medicalization of women's sexual problems. *Women's Studies Quarterly, 31,* 42–54.

Hartmann, H. (2014). *Enhancing social security for women and other vulnerable Americans: What the experts say.* Washington, DC: Institute for Women's Policy Research.

Hartmann, H. & Hayes, J. (2013). *How education pays off for older Americans.* Washington, DC: Institute for Women's Policy Research.

Hartmann, H. et al. (2014). How equal pay for working women would reduce poverty and grow the American economy. Washington. DC: Institute for Women's Policy Research.

Hartmann, L. C. & Lindor, N. M. (2016). The role of risk-reducing surgery in hereditary breast and ovarian cancer. *New England Journal of Medicine, 374,* 454–466.

Hartocollis, A. (2015, February 11). Doulas, a growing force in maternity culture, seek more recognition. *New York Times,* pp. A20–21.

Hartwig, E. K. (2016). Social networks: A village of support for single mothers. *Journal of Family Social Work, 19,* 22–37.

Harvard Women's Health Watch. (2014, October). Enjoying sex later in life, 4–5.

Harvey, A. & Fisher, S. (2015). "Everyone can make games!": The post-feminist context of women in digital game production. *Feminist Media Studies, 15,* 576–592.

Harvey, I. S. et al. (2013). Womanism, spirituality and self-health management behaviors of African American older women. *Women, Gender, and Families of Color, 1,* 59–84.

Harvey, S. T. & Taylor, J. E. (2010). A meta-analysis of the effects of psychotherapy with sexually abused children and adolescents. *Clinical Psychology Review, 30,* 517–535.

Hasinoff, A.A. (2016). How to have great sext: Consent advice in online sexting tips. *Communication and Critical/Cultural Studies, 13,* 58–74.

Haskell, S. G. et al. (2014). Sex differences in patient and provider response to elevated low-density lipoprotein cholesterol. *Women's Health Issues, 24,* 575–580.

Haslam, D. et al. (2015). Giving voice to working mothers: A consumer informed study to program design for working mothers. *Journal of Child & Family Studies, 24,* 2463–2473.

Hattery, A. (2001). *Women, work, and family: Balancing and weaving.* Thousand Oaks, CA: Sage.

Hausenblas, H. A. et al. (2013). Media effects of experimental presentation of the ideal physique on eating disorder symptoms: A meta-analysis of laboratory studies. *Clinical Psychology Review, 33,* 168–181.

Haw, C. et al. (2015). Economic recession and suicidal behaviour: Possible mechanisms and ameliorating factors. *International Journal of Social Psychiatry, 61,* 73–81.

Hawes, Z. et al. (2015). Effects of mental rotation training on children's spatial and mathematics performance: A randomized controlled study. *Trends in Neuroscience and Education, 4,* 60–68.

Hawes, Z. C., Wellings, K., & Stephenson, J. (2010). First heterosexual intercourse in the United Kingdom: A review of the literature. *Journal of Sex Research, 47,* 137–152.

Hawkes, K. (2010). How grandmother effects plus individual variation in frailty shape fertility and morality: Guidance from human-chimpanzee comparisons. *Proceedings of the National Academy of Sciences, 107,* 8977–8984.

Hawkesworth, M. (2016). *Embodied power: Demystifying disembodied politics.* New York: Routledge.

Hay, P. (2013). A systematic review of evidence for psychological treatments in eating disorders: 2005–2012. *International Journal of Eating Disorders, 46,* 462–469.

Hay, P. et al. (2014). Royal Australian and New Zealand College of Psychiatrists clinical practice guidelines for the treatment of eating disorders. *Australian and New Zealand Journal of Psychiatry, 48,* 1–62.

Hayden, E. & Mash, E. (2014). Child psychopathology: A developmental systems-perspective. In E. A. Mash & R. A. Barkley (Eds.), *Child psychopathology* (3rd ed., pp. 3–74). New York: Guilford.

Hayes, E. & Swim, K. K. (2013) African, Asian, Latina/o and European Americans' responses to popular measures of sexist beliefs: Some cautionary notes. *Psychology of Women Quarterly, 37,* 155–166.

Hayes, R. M. et al. (2016). It's her fault: Student acceptance of rape myths on two college campuses. *Violence Against Women, 22,* 1540–1555.

Hayes, S. N. et al. (2015). Taking a giant step toward women's heart health: Finding policy solutions to unanswered research questions. *Women's Health Issues, 25,* 429–432.

Hayes, J., Hartmann, H., & Lee, S. (2010). *Social security: Vital to retirement security for 35 million women and men* (IWPR #D487). Washington, DC: Institute for Women's Policy Research.

Hayfield, N. et al. (2014). Bisexual women's understandings of social marginalisation: 'The heterosexuals don't understand us but nor do the lesbians.' *Feminism & Psychology, 24,* 353–372.

Hayslip, B., Jr. & Kaminski, P. (Eds.). (2008). *Parenting the custodial grandchild: Implications for clinical practice.* New York: Springer.

Hayslip, B. & Page, K. S. (2012). Grandchildren: Grandchild and great grandchild relationships. In R. Blieszner & V. H. Bedford (Eds.), *Handbook of families and aging* (pp. 183–212). Santa Barbara, CA: ABC-CLIO.

Health Day. (2014). Heart failure therapy may benefit women more than men: But study finds they're less likely than males to receive pacemaker that synchronizes heartbeats. *MedlinePlus.* 1–2.

Heatherington, L. et al. (1993). Two investigations of "female modesty" in achievement situations. *Sex Roles, 29,* 739–754.

Heaverlo, C. A. et al. (2013). Stem development: Predictors for 6th-12th grade girls' interest and confidence in science and math. *Journal of Women and Minorities in Science and Engineering.* 121–142.

Heckert, T. M. et al. (2002). Gender differences in anticipated salary: Role of salary estimates for others, job characteristics, career paths, and job inputs. *Sex Roles, 47,* 139–151.

Heeter, C. (2016). Femininity. In B. Perron & M. Wolf (Eds.), *The Routledge companion to video game studies* (pp. 373–379). New York: Routledge.

Heflick, N. A. & Goldenberg, J. L. (2014). Seeing eye to body: The literal objectification of women. *Current Directions in Psychological Science, 23,* 225–229.

Hegarty, P. (2013). Androcentrism: Changing the landscape without leveling the playing field? In M. K. Ryan & N. R. Branscombe (Eds.). *Sage handbook of gender and psychology* (pp. 29–44). Los Angeles, CA: Sage.

Hegewisch, A. & Hartmann, H. (2014a). The gender wage gap: 2013 differences by race and ethnicity. Washington, DC: Institute for Women's Policy Research.

Hegewisch, A. & Hartmann, H. (2014b). Occupational segregation and the gender wage gap: A job half done. Washington, DC: Institute for Women's Policy Research.

Hei Li, R. Y. & Wong, W. I. (2016). Gender-typed play and social abilities in boys and girls: Are they related? *Sex Roles, 74,* 399–410.

Heiman, J. R. (2008). Treating low sexual desire—new findings for testosterone in women. *New England Journal of Medicine, 359,* 2047–2049.

Heinze, J. E. & Horn, S. S. (2014). Do adolescents' evaluations of exclusion differ based on gender expression and sexual orientation? *Journal of Social Issues, 70,* 63–80.

Hellemans, S. et al. (2015). Intimate partner violence victimization among non-heterosexuals: Prevalence and association with mental and sexual well-being. *Journal of Family Violence, 30,* 171–188.

Helliwell, J. F. & Grover, S. (2015). How's life at home? New evidence on marriage and the set point for happiness. The National Bureau of Economic Research. *NBER Working Paper No. 20794.*

Helms, J. E. (2017). Counseling Black women: Understanding the effects of multilevel invisibility. In M. Kopala & M. Keitel (Eds.), *Handbook of counseling women* (2nd ed., pp. 219–233). Thousand Oaks, CA: Sage.

Helson, R. (1992). Women's difficult times and the rewriting of the life story. *Psychology of Women Quarterly, 16,* 331–347.

Henderson, A. et al. (2016). The price mothers pay, even when they are not buying it: Mental health consequences of idealized motherhood. *Sex Roles, 74,* 512–526.

Henderson, C. E., Hayslip, B., Jr., Sanders, L. M., & Louden, L. (2009). Grandmother-grandchild relationship quality predicts psychological adjustment among youth from divorced families. *Journal of Family Issues, 30,* 1245–1264.

Henderson, D. & Tickamyer, A. (2009). The intersection of poverty discourses: Race, class, culture, and gender. In B. T. Dill & R. E. Zambrana (Eds.), *Emerging intersections: Race, class, and gender in theory, policy, and practice* (pp. 50–72). Piscataway, NJ: Rutgers University Press.

Henderson, S. L. & Jeydel, A. S. (2010). *Women and politics in a global world* (2nd ed.). New York: Oxford University Press.

Henig, R.M. (2017, January). Rethinking gender. *National Geographic,* pp. 48–73.

Henley, N. M. (1995). Body politics revisited: What do we know today? In P. J. Kalbfleisch & M. J. Cody (Eds.), *Gender, power, and communication in human relationships* (pp. 27–61). Hillsdale, NJ: Erlbaum.

Henley, S.J. et al. (2014). Lung cancer incidence trends among men and women—United States, 2005–2009. *Morbidity and Mortality Weekly Report, 63,* 1–5.

Henningsen, D. D. (2004). Flirting with meaning: An examination of miscommunication in flirting interactions. *Sex Roles, 50,* 481–489.

Henningsen, D. D., Henningsen, M. L. M., & Valde, K. S. (2006). Gender differences in perceptions of women's sexual interest during cross-sex interactions: An application and extension of cognitive valence theory. *Sex Roles, 54,* 821–829.

Henry, A. (2014). From a mindset to a movement: Feminism since 1990s. In D. C. Cobble et al. (Eds.), *Feminism unfinished: A short surprising history of American women's movements* (pp. 147–226). New York: W. W. Norton.

Hentges, B. & Case, K. (2013). Gender representations on Disney Channel, Cartoon Network, and Nickelodeon broadcasts in the United States. *Journal of Children and Media, 7,* 1–3.

Heo, J. et al. (2014). Weekend experiences and subjective well-being of retired older adults. *American Journal of Health Behavior, 4,* 598–604.

Hequembourg, A. L. et al. (2013). Sexual victimization and associated risks among lesbian and bisexual women. *Violence Against Women, 19,* 634–657.

Herbenick, D., Reece, M., Schick, V., Sanders, S. A., Dodge, B., & Fortenberry, J. D. (2010a). An event-level analysis of the sexual charateristics and composition among adults ages 18 to 59: Results from a national probability sample in the United States. *International Society for Sexual Medicine, 7,* 346–361.

Herbenick, D., Reece, M., Schick, V., Sanders, S. A., Dodge, B., & Fortenberry, J. D. (2010b). Sexual behavior in the United States: Results from a national probability sample of men and women ages 14–94. *International Society for Sexual Medicine, 7,* 255–265.

Herbenick, D., Reece, M., Schick, V., Sanders, S. A., Dodge, B., & Fortenberry, J. D. (2010c). Sexual behaviors, relationships, and perceived health status among adult women in the United States: Results from a national probability survey. *International Society for Sexual Medicine, 7,* 277–290.

Herbst, C. M. & Barnow, B. S. (2008). Close to home: A simultaneous equations model of the relationship between child care accessibility and female labor force participation. *Journal of Family and Economic Issues, 29,* 128–151.

Herd, P., House, J. S., & Schoeni, R. F. (2008). Income support policies and health among the elderly. In R. F. Schoeni, J. S. House, G. A. Kaplan, & H. Pollack (Eds.), *Making Americans healthier: Social and economic policy as health policy* (pp. 97–121). New York: Russell Sage Foundation.

Herd, P. et al. (2016). The implications of unintended pregnancies for mental health later in life. *American Journal of Public Health, 106,* 421–429.

Herek, G. M. (2013). The social psychology of sexual prejudice. In T. D. Nelson (Ed.), *Handbook of prejudice, stereotyping and discrimination* (pp. 356–384). New York: Psychology Press.

Herek, G. M. (2015). Beyond "homophobia": Thinking more clearly about prejudice, stigma, and sexual orientation. *American Journal of Orthopsychiatry, 85,* S29–37.

Herek, G. M. & McLemore, K. A. (2013). Sexual prejudice. *Annual Review of Psychology, 64,* 309–333.

Herman, C. et al. (2013). Women scientists and engineers in European companies: Putting motherhood under the microscope. *Gender, Work & Organization, 20,* 467–476.

Heron, M. (2016). Deaths: Leading causes for 2013. *National Vital Statistics Reports, 65* (2). Hyattsville, MD: National Center for Health Statistics.

Herrera, A. P. et al. (2011). Emotional and cognitive health correlates of leisure activities in older Latino and Caucasian women. *Psychology, Health & Medicine, 16,* 661–674.

Herrera, V. M., Koss, M. P., Bailey, J., Yuan, N. P., & Lichter, E. L. (2006). Survivors of male violence: Research and training initiatives to facilitate recovery from depression and posttraumatic stress disorder. In J. Worell & C. D. Goodheart (Eds.), *Handbook of girls' and women's psychological health: Gender and well-being across the lifespan* (pp. 455–466). New York: Oxford University Press.

Hersch, J. (2013). *Opting out among women with elite education.* Vanderbilt Law and Economics Research Paper, *13,* 30–33.

Herscher, E. (2015). *Breast cancer myths.* Retrieved October 21, 2015 from consumer.health.com

Hervick, A. L. et al. (2014). Raising sexual minority youths' health level by incorporating resiliences into health promotion efforts. *AJPH, 104,* 206–210.

Herz, N. D. et al. (2015). Sex differences in device therapy for heart failure: Utilization, outcomes, and adverse events. *Journal of Women's Health, 24,* 261–271.

Hesse-Biber, S. N. (2013). *Feminist research practice: Primer.* Thousand Oaks, CA: Sage.

Hesse-Biber, S. N. (2016). Qualitative or mixed research inquiry approaches: Some loose guidelines for publishing in Sex Roles. *Sex Roles, 74,* 6–9.

Hetherington, E. M. (2004, July). *Lessons learned and unlearned in thirty five years of studying families.* Paper presented at the meeting of the American Psychological Association, Honolulu.

Hetherington, E. M. & Kelly, J. (2002). *For better or for worse: Divorce reconsidered.* New York: Norton.

Hewlett, S. A. (2007). *Off-ramps and on-ramps: Keeping talented women on the road to success.* Boston, MA: Harvard Business School Press.

Hewlett, S. A., Luce, C. B., & Servon, L. J. (2008). Stopping the exodus of women in science. *Harvard Business Review, 86.* doi:10.1225/F0806A.

Hidalgo, T. R. (2011). Feminism, American. In M. Z. Stange, C. K. Oyster, & J. E. Sloan (Eds.), *Encyclopedia of women in today's world.* Newberry Park, CA: Sage.

Hideg, I. & Ferris, D. L. (2016). The compassionate sexist? How benevolent sexism promotes and undermines gender equality in the workplace. *Journal of Personality and Social Psychology, 111,* 706–727.

Higginbotham, E. & Weber, L. (1996). Moving up with kin and community: Upward social mobility for Black and White women. In E. N. Chow, D. Wilkinson, & M. B. Zinn (Eds.), *Race, class, & gender: Common bonds, different voices* (pp. 125–148). Thousand Oaks, CA: Sage.

Higgins, C. A., Duxbury, L. E., & Lyons, S. T. (2010). Coping with overload and stress: Men and women in dual-earner families. *Journal of Marriage and Family, 72,* 847–859.

Higgins, N. A. (2016). *Feminism: Reinventing the F-word.* Minneapolis: Lerner Publishing.

Hilbrecht, M., Zuzanek, J., & Mannell, R. C. (2008). Time use, time pressure, and gendered behavior in early and late adolescence. *Sex Roles, 58,* 342–357.

Hildreth, C. J. (2011). Elder abuse. *Journal of the American Medical Association, 306,* 568.

Hill, P. L. & Turiano, N. A. (2014). Purpose in life as a predictor of mortality across adulthood. *Psychological Science, 25,* 1482–1486.

Hill, S. A. (2009). Cultural images and the health of African American women. *Gender & Society, 23,* 733–746.

Hill Collins, P. & Bilge, S. (2016). *Intersectionality: Key concepts.* Cambridge, UK: Polity Press.

Hillberg, T., Hamilton-Giachritsis, C., & Dixon, L. (2011). Review of meta analyses on the association between child sexual abuse and adult mental health difficulties: A systematic approach. *Trauma, Violence, & Abuse, 12,* 38–49.

Hilliard, L. J. & Liben, L. S. (2010). Differing levels of gender salience in preschool classrooms: Effects on children's gender attitudes and intergroup bias. *Child Development, 81,* 1787–1798.

Hillman, J. (2012). *Sexuality and aging: Clinical perspectives.* New York: Springer.

Hilt, L. & Nolen-Hoeksema, S. (2014). Gender differences in depression. In I. H. Gotlib & C. L. Hammen (Eds.), *Handbook of depression* (pp. 335–373). New York: Guilford.

Hines, M. (2010). Gendered behavior across the lifespan. In M. Lamb & A. Freund (Eds.), *The handbook of life-span development: Social and emotional development* (Vol. 2, pp. 341–378). Hoboken, NJ: Wiley.

Hinshaw, S. (2009). *The triple bind: Saving our teenage girls from today's pressures.* New York: Ballantine.

Hinshaw, S. P. et al. (2012). Prospective follow-up of girls with attention- deficit/hyperactivity disorder into early adulthood: Continuing impairment includes elevated risk for suicide attempts and self-injury. *Journal of Consulting and Clinical Psychology, 80,* 1041–1051.

Hipp, L. et al. (2016). Who participates and who benefits from employer-provided child-care assistance? *Journal of Marriage and Family,* doi:10.1111/jomf.12359.

Hirschberger, G. S., Srivastava, S., Marsh, P., Cowan, C. P., & Cowan, P. A. (2009). Attachment, marital satisfaction, and divorce during the first fifteen years of parenthood. *Personal Relationships, 16,* 401–420.

Hoang, M. (2013). Bisexual women's sexuality. In D. Castaneda (Ed.). *The essential handbook of women's sexuality* (vol.2) (pp. 29–50). Santa Barbara, CA: Praeger.

Hobson, J. (2016). *Are all the women still white? Rethinking race, expanding feminisms.* New York: State University of New York Press.

Hockett, J. M. (2016). Rape myth consistency and gender differences in perceiving rape victims: A meta-analysis. *Violence Against Women, 22,* 139–167.

Hodgson, J. et al. (2016). Considering issues of gender and sexuality in the assessment of anxiety disorder. In V. Brabender & J. L. Mihura (Eds.), *Handbook of gender and sexuality in psychological assessment* (pp. 290–315). New York: Routledge.

Hodis, H. N., et al (2016). Vascular effects of early versus late postmenopausal treatment with estradiol. *New England Journal of Medicine, 374,* 1221–1222.

Hoeber, L. (2008). Gender equity for athletes: Multiple understandings of an organizational value. *Sex Roles, 58,* 58–71.

Hoek, H. W. (2015). New developments in the treatment of eating disorders. *Current Opinion in Psychology, 28,* 445–447.

Hoeppner, B. B. et al. (2013). Sex differences in college student adherence to NIAAA drinking guidelines. *Alcoholism: Clinical and Experimental Research, 37,* 1779–1786.

Hofferth, S. L. & Goldscheider, F. (2010). Family structure and the transition to early parenthood. *Demography, 47,* 415–437.

Hoffman, A. C. et al. (2017). Health counseling: Assessment and intervention. In M. Kopala & M. Keitel (Eds.), *Handbook of counseling women* (2nd ed., pp. 507–521). Thousand Oaks, CA: Sage.

Hoffman, M. et al. (2011). Nurture affects gender differences in spatial abilities. *PNAS, 108,* 14786–14788.

Hoffman, M. A. et al. (2017). Breaking through barriers: Psycheducation and interventions for sexually transmitted infections in women. In M. Kopala & M. Keitel (Eds.), *Handbook of counseling women* (2nd ed., pp. 576–590). Thousand Oaks, CA: Sage.

Hoffnung, M. & Williams, M.A. (2013).Balancing act: Career and family during college-educated women's 30s. *Sex Roles, 68,* 321–334

Hogg, M. A. (2010). Influence and leadership. In S. T. Fiske, D. T. Gilbert, & G. Lindzey (Eds.), *Handbook of social psychology* (5th ed., pp. 1166–1207). Hoboken, NJ: Wiley.

Holden, K. C. et al. (2010). *Psychological adjustment to widowhood: The role of income, wealth and time.* Madison, WI: Society of Actuaries and University of Wisconsin.

Holgersson, C. (2013). Recruiting managing directors: Doing homosociality. *Gender, Work & Organization, 20,* 454–466.

Holick, M. F. (2007). Vitamin D deficiency. *New England Journal of Medicine, 357,* 266–281.

Holland, G. & Tiggemann, M. (2016). A systematic review of the impact of the use of social networking sites on body image and disordered eating outcomes, *Body Image, 17,* 100–110.

Holland, K. J. & Cortina, L. M. (2016). Sexual harassment: Undermining the well-being of working women. In M. L. Connerley & J. Wu (Eds.), *Handbook on well-being of working women* (pp. 83–98). Dordrecht: Springer.

Holland, K. J. et al. (2015). Sexual harassment against men: Examining the roles of feminist activism, sexuality, and organizational context. *Psychology of Men & Masculinity, 17,* 17–29.

Hollenstein, T. & Lougheed, J. P. (2013). Beyond storm and stress: Typicality, transitions timing, and temperament to account for adolescent change, *American Psychologist, 68,* 444–445.

Hollis-Sawyer, L. & Dykema-Engblade, A. (2016). *Women and aging: An International perspective.* San Francisco: Academic Press.

Holloway, V. & Wylie, K. (2015). Sex drive and sexual desire. *Current Opinion in Psychology, 28,* 424–429.

Hollywood's gender gap *Time* (2015, October 6). Retrieved from time.com/4062700/Hollywood-gender-gap

Holman, D. M. et al. (2014). Barriers to human papillomavirus vaccination among US adolescents: A systematic review of the literature. *Journal of the American Medical Association, 168,* 1–3.

Holmes, M. R. et al. (2014). Lasting effect of intimate partner violence exposure during preschool on aggressive behavior and prosocial skills. *Journal of Interpersonal Violence,* 1–20.

Holt-Lunstad, J. et al. (2015). Loneliness and social isolation as risk factors for mortality: A meta-analytic review. *Perspectives on Psychological Science, 10,* 227–237.

Holstein, M.(2015). *Women in late life: Critical perspectives on gender and age.* New York: Rowman & Littlefield.

Holtom-Viesel, A. & Allan, S. (2014). A systematic review of the literature on family functioning across all eating disorder diagnoses in comparison to control families. *Clinical Psychology Review, 34,* 29–43.

Homayoun, A. (2013). *The myth of the perfect girl: Helping our daughters find authentic success and happiness in school and life.* New York: Penguin.

Honma, N. et al. (2015). Estogen and cancers of the colorectum, breast and lung in postmenopausal women. *Pathology International, 65,* 451–459.

Hoobler, J. M. et al. (2014). Women's managerial aspirations: An organizational development perspective. *Journal of Management, 40,* 703–730.

Hook, M. K. & Bowman, S. (2008). Working for a living: The vocational decision making of lesbians. *Journal of Lesbian Studies, 12,* 85–95.

hooks, b. (1990). Feminism: A transformational politic. In D. L. Rhode (Ed.), *Theoretical perspectives in sexual difference* (pp. 185–193). New Haven, CT: Yale University Press.

Hormes, J.M. (2016, Winter). When the glass ceiling is made of concrete: What causes the progressive nature of the "leaky pipeline" in academia? *Behavior Therapist, 39,* 303–311.

Hornbacher, M. (1998). *Wasted: A memoir of anorexia and bulimia.* New York: Harper Perennial.

Horner, M. S. (1972). Toward an understanding of achievement-related conflicts in women. *Journal of Social Issues, 28,* 157–176.

Horney, K. (1926/1974). The flight from womanhood: The masculinity-complex in women as viewed by men and women. In J. Strouse (Ed.), *Women and analysis: Dialogues on psychoanalytic views of femininity* (pp. 171–186). New York: Viking.

Horowitz, J. E., Galst, J. P., & Elster, N. (2010). *Ethical dilemmas in fertility counseling.* Washington, DC: American Psychological Association.

Horton, M. J. (2014). RX for the XX: Despite progress, there needs to be more health research on women. *Feminist.org.* 48–49.

Hottes, T. S. et al. (2015). Lifetime prevalence of suicide attempts among sexual minority adults by study sampling strategies: A systematic review and meta-analysis. *American Journal of Public Health Research, 106,* e1.

Houndmouth, J. & Leka, S. (2014). *Contemporary occupational health psychology.* Malden, MA: Wiley.

Housman, J. & Dorman, S. (2005). The Alameda County study: A systematic, chronological review. *American Journal of Health Education, 36,* 302–308.

Houvouras, S. & Carter, J. S. (2008). The F word: College students' definition of a feminist. *Sociological Forum, 23,* 234–256.

Hu, W. (2016, July 14). Too old for sex? A nursing home in the Bronx says no such thing. *New York Times,* pp. A15, A17.

Hudson, D. B. et al. (2016). Social support and psychosocial well-being among low-income, adolescent, African-American, first-time mothers. *Clinical Nurse Specialist, 30,* 150–158.

Hughes, A. K. et al. (2015). Sexual problems among older women by age and race. *Journal of Women's Health, 8,* 663–669.

Hughes, M. M. & Brush, L. D. (2015). The price of protection: A trajectory analysis of civil remedies for abuse and women's earnings. *American Sociological Review, 80,* 140–165.

Hughes, T. L. et al. (2016). The influence of gender and sexual orientation on alcohol and alcohol-related problems. *Alcohol Research: Current Review, 38,* 121–132.

Humble, A. M. & Price, C. A. (2017). Stress and coping later in life. In C. A. Price et al. (Eds.), *Families & change: Coping with stressful events and transitions* (pp. 119–128). Thousand Oaks, CA: Sage.

Hunt, K., Adamson, J., & Galdas, P. (2010). Gender and help-seeking: Towards gender-comparative studies. In E. Kuhlmann & E. Annandale (Eds.), *The Palgrave handbook of gender and healthcare* (pp. 207–221). New York: Palgrave Macmillan.

Hunter, C. A. & Kallio, A. (2016). *Understanding doulas and childbirth: Women, love, and advocacy.* London: Palgrave Macmillan.

Hunter , C. A. & Hurst, A (2016). *Understanding doulas and childbirth: Women, love, and advocacy.* New York: Palgrave Macmillan.

Hurd, L. C. (2011). *Facing age: Women growing older in an anti-aging culture.* Lanham, MD: Rowman & Littlefield.

Hurd, L. C. & Griffin, M. (2008). Visible and invisible ageing: Beauty work as a response to ageism. *Ageing and Society, 28,* 653–674.

Hurst, J. et al. (2016). Women managing women. *Gender in Management: An International Journal, 31,* 61–74.

Husser, E. K. & Roberto, K. A. (2009). Older women with cardiovascular disease: Perceptions of initial experiences and long-term influences on daily life. *Journal of Women & Aging, 21,* 3–18.

Hust, S. et al. (2013). Gendered sexual scripts in music lyrics and videos popular among adolescents. In R. Gartner & B. McCarthy (Eds.), *The Oxford handbook of gender, sex, and crime* (pp. 286–318). New York: Oxford University Press.

Hutfless, S. et al. (2013). Strategies to prevent weight gain in adults. A systematic review. *Monitor on Psychology.* e41–e5.

Hutton, A. (2016). Sexual violence against transgender college students. In M. A. Paludi (Ed.), *Campus action against sexual assault: Needs, policies, procedures, and training programs* (pp. 140–146). New York: Praeger.

Huxley, C. J. et al. (2015). An examination of the tripartite influence model of body image: Does women's sexual identity make a difference? *Psychology of Women Quarterly, 39,* 337–348.

Huyck, M. H. (1995). Marriage and close relationships of the marital kind. In R. Blieszner & V. H. Bedford (Eds.), *Handbook of aging and the family* (pp. 181–200). Westport, CT: Greenwood.

Hyde, J. S. (2014). Gender similarities and differences. *Annual Review of Psychology, 65,* 373–398.

Hyde, J. S. & Kling, K. C. (2001). Women, motivation, and achievement. *Psychology of Women Quarterly, 25,* 364–378.

Hyde, J. S. & Mertz, J. E. (2009). Gender, culture, and mathematics performance. *Proceedings of the National Academy of Sciences, 106,* 8801–8807.

Hymowitz, K. et al. (2013). *Knot yet: The benefits and costs of delayed marriage in America.* UVA: National Marriage Project.

Icheku, V. (2016). Impact of HIV-related stigma and discrimination on working women in sub-Sahara Africa. In M. L. Connerley & J. Wu (Eds.), *Handbook on well-being of working women* (pp. 781–792). Dordrecht, Netherlands: Springer.

Iglehart, J. (2010). Medicaid expansion offers solutions, challenges. *Health Affairs, 29,* 230–232.

Im, E.-O. et al. (2014). Ethnic differences in the clusters of menopausal symptoms. *Health Care for Women International, 35,* 549–565.

Imperato-McGinley, J. (2002). 5a-reductase-2 deficiency and complete androgen insensitivity: Lessons from nature. In S. A. Zderic, D. A. Canning, M. C. Carr, & H. M. Snyder (Eds.), *Pediatric gender assignment: A critical reappraisal* (pp. 121–134). New York: Plenum.

Impett, E. A., Henson, J. M., Breines, J. G., Schooler, D., & Tolman, D. L. (2011). Embodiment feels better: Girls' body objectification and well-being across adolescence. *Psychology of Women Quarterly, 35,* 46–58.

Ingolfsdottir, G. et al. (2014). Changes in body image and dieting among 16–19-year-old Icelandic students from 2000 to 2010. *Body Image, 11,* 364–369.

Inman, J. & Cardella, M. E. (2015, June). Gender bias in the purchase of STEM-related toys. Paper presented at the 2015 ASEE Annual conference and Exposition, Seattle, Washington.

Institute for Women's Policy Research. (2007, November). *The economic security of older women and men in the United States.* Washington, DC: Author.

Institute for Women's Policy Research. (2014). *The gender wage gap by occupation 2013 and by race and ethnicity.* Washington, DC: Author.

Institute for Women's Policy Research. (2015). *The status of women in the States 2015.* Washington, DC: Author.

Institute for Women's Policy Research. (2016a). The gender wage gap by occupation 2015 and by race and ethnicity. Washington, DC: Author.

Institute for Women's Policy Research. (2016b). *Mothers in college have declining access to on-campus child care.* Washington, DC: Author.

International Center for Research on Women (2013). *Masculinity, son preference, and intimate partner violence.* Washington, D.C: Author.

International Labour Organization. (2015). *Women in business and management: Gaining momentum.* Geneva, Switzerland: Author.

Inter-Parliamentary Union. (2011). *Women in national parliaments.* Geneva, Switzerland: Author.

Irni, A. (2016). Steroid provocations: On the maternality of politics in the history of sex hormones. *Journal of Women in Culture and Society, 41,* 507–529.

Irwin, N. (2015, May 15). Lessons from faking an 80-hour workweek. *New York Times,* p. A3.

Islam, M. M. & Bakheit, C. S. (2014). Advanced maternal age and risks for adverse pregnancy outcomes: A population-based study in Oman. *Health Care for Women International, 36,* 1081–1103.

Iyer, A. (2009). Increasing the representation and status of women in employment: The effectiveness of affirmative action. In M. Barreto, M. K. Ryan, & M. T. Schmitt (Eds.), *The glass ceiling in the 21st century: Understanding barriers to gender equality* (pp. 3–18). Washington, DC: American Psychological Association.

Jack, D. C. (2012). Reflections on the Silencing the Self Scale and its origins. *Psychology of Women Quarterly, 35,* 523–529.

Jackson, A. P., & Dorsey, M. R. (2009). *Achieving against the odds: African American professional women in higher education.* Bloomington, IN: AuthorHouse.

Jackson, J. B. et al. (2014). Gender differences in marital satisfaction: A meta-analysis. *Journal of Marriage and Family, 76,* 105–129.

Jackson, J., & O'Callaghan, E. (2014). *Measuring glass ceiling effects in higher education: Opportunities and challenges.* San Francisco, CA: Jossey-Bass.

Jackson, K. et al. (2014). Body image satisfaction and depression in midlife women: The study of women's health across the nation (SWAN). *Archives of Women's Mental Health, 17,* 177–187.

Jackson, S. (2015). Pregnancy outcomes in very advanced maternal age pregnancies: The impact of assisted reproductive technology. *Fertility and Sterility, 103,* 76–80.

Jackson, T. E. & Joffe Falmagne, R. (2013). Women wearing white: Discourses of menstruation and the experience of menarche. *Feminism & Psychology, 23,* 379–398.

Jackson, Y. & Warren, J. S. (2000). Appraisal, social support, and life events: Predicting outcome behavior in school-age children. *Child Development, 71,* 1441–1457.

Jacob, J. A. (2016). Can nonhormonal treatment dial down the heat during menopause? *Journal of the American Medical Association, 315,* 14–16.

Jacob, M. M. (2012). Native women maintaining their culture in the white academy. In G. G. Muhs & Y. F. Niemann (Eds.), *Presumed incompetent: The intersections of race and class for women in academia* (pp. 242–249). Logan: Utah State University.

Jacobs, A. W. & Padavic, I. (2015). Hours, scheduling, and flexibility for women in the US low-wage labour force. *Gender, Work and Organization, 22,* 67–86.

Jacobs, F. et al. (2016). Improving adolescent parenting: Results from a randomized controlled trial of a home visiting program for young families. *American Journal of Public Health, 106*, 342.

Jacobs, J. A. & Gerson, K. (2016). Unpacking Americans' views of the employment of mothers and fathers using national vignette survey data: SWS presidential address. *Gender & Society, 30*, 413–441.

Jacobs, S. C. et al. (2017). Women and heart disease: Information for counselors. In M. Kopala & M. Keitel (Eds.), *Handbook of counseling women* (2nd ed., pp. 539–558). Thousand Oaks, CA: Sage.

Jacobson, J. (2006, July 7). Report disputes notion that boys' academic performance is in decline. *Chronicle of Higher Education*, p. A35.

Jacobson, R. (2013, November 26). Simply deciding to be related: Circumstances can lead to friendships becoming something more. *New York Times.* p. D6.

Jadhav, A. & Weir, D. (2017). Widowhood and depression in a cross-national perspective: Evidence from the united States, Europe, Korea, and China. *Journals of Gerontology Series B : Psychological Science and Social Science* doi.org/10/1093/geronb/gbx021

Jadva, V. & Imrie, S. (2014). The significance of relatedness for surrogates and their families. In T. Freeman & S. Graham (Eds.) *Relatedness in assisted reproduction: Families, image, and identities* (pp. 162–177). Cambridge, UK: Cambridge University Press.

Jaffe, J. (2014). In D. Barnes (Ed.), The reproductive story: Dealing with miscarriage, stillbirth, or other perinatal demise. *Women's reproductive mental health across the lifespan* (pp. 59–176). New York: Springer.

Jaffee, S. & Hyde, J. S. (2000). Gender differences in moral orientation: A meta-analysis. *Psychological Bulletin, 126*, 703–726.

Jamal, A. et al. (2015). Current cigarette smoking among adults—United States, 2005–2014. *Morbidity and Mortality Weekly Reports, 64*, 1233–1240.

James, R. D. et al. (2013). Launching native health leaders: Reducing mistrust of research through student peer mentorship. *American Journal of Public Health, 103*, 2215–2219.

Jamison, K. R. (2014, August 16). To know suicide. *New York Times*, p. A19.

Jankowski, G. S. et al. (2016). Looking age-appropriate while growing old gracefully: A qualitative study of ageing and body image among older adults. *Journal of Health Psychology, 21*, 550–561.

Jansen, L. et al. (2016). Perceived fairness of the division of household labor: A comparative study in 29 countries. *International Journal of Comparative Sociology, 57*, 53–68.

Janssen, S. M. & Lagro-Janssen, A. L. (2012). Physician's gender, communication style, patient preferences and patient satisfaction in gynecology and obstetrics: A systematic review. *Patient and Educational Counseling, 89*, 221–226. NJ: Humana Press.

Janz, N. K. et al. (2014). Emotional well-being years post-treatment for breast cancer: Prospective, multi-ethnic, and population-based analysis. *Journal of Cancer Survival, 8*, 131–142.

Jason, S. et al. (2014). Pregnancy outcomes decline in recipients over age 44: An analysis of 27,959 fresh donor oocyte in vitro fertilization cycles from the Society for Assisted Reproductive Technology. *Fertility and Sterility, 101*, 1331–1336.

Jaspers, E. & Verbakel, E. (2013). The division of paid labor in same-sex couples in the Netherlands. *Sex Roles, 68*, 335–348.

Javed A. et al. (2013). Female athlete triad and its components: Toward improved screening and management. *Mayo Clinic, 88*, 996–1009.

Jayachandran, S. & Pande, R. (2014, August 10). The youngest are hungriest. *New York Times.* p. SR4.

Jayaraman, S. (2015, October 16). Why tipping is wrong. *New York Times*, p. A29.

Jellinek, R. D. et al. (2016). The impact of doll style of dress and familiarity on body dissatisfaction in 6-to-8-year-old girls. *Body Image, 18*, 78–85.

Jenkins, C. L. et al. (2014). Older lesbians and bereavement: Experiencing the loss of a partner. *Journal of Gerontological Social Work, 57*, 273–287.

Jenkins, M. R. & Miller, V. M. (2016). 21st century women's health: Refining with precision. *Mayo Clinic Proceedings, 91*, 695–700.

Jennings, K. M. et al. (2015). Binge eating among racial minority groups in the United States: An Integrative review. *Journal of the American Psychiatric Nursing Association, 21*, 117–125.

Jensen, R. (2015). Letting go of "normal" when "normal" is pathological, why feminism is a gift to man. In D. King & C. G. Valentine (Eds.), *Letting go: Feminist and social justice insight and activism* (pp. 57–68). Nashville, TN: Vanderbilt University Press.

Jetten, J. et al. (2013). Appraising gender discrimination as legitimate or illegitimate: Antecedents and consequences. In M. K. Ryan & N. R. Branscombe (Eds.). *Sage handbook of gender and psychology* (pp. 306–322). Los Angeles, CA: Sage

Jewkes, R. et al. (2013). Prevalence of and factors associated with non-partner rape perpetration: Findings from the UN multi-country cross-sectional study on men and violence in Asia and the Pacific. *The Lancet Global Health, 1*, 208–218.

Jha, P. et al. (2013). 21st-century hazards of smoking and benefits of cessation in the United States. *New England Journal of Medicine, 368*, 341–350.

Jimenez, A. (2015, August 16). Racing a clock while scoffing at time. *New York Times*, p. SP5.

Jin, J. (2015). Treatments for infertility. *Journal of the American Medical Association, 313*, 1–3.

Jirout, J. J. & Newcombe, N. S. (2015). Building blocks for developing spatial skills: Evidence from a large, representative U.S. sample. *Psychological Science, 26*, 302–310.

Joel, D. et al. (2015). Sex beyond the genitalia: The human brain mosaic. *PNAS, 112*, 15468–15473.

Joffe, H. V. et al. (2016). FDA approval of flibanserin—Treating hypoactive sexual disorder. *New England Journal of Medicine, 374*, 101–104.

Joham, A. E. et al. (2015). Prevalence of infertility and use of fertility treatment in women with Polycystic Ovary Syndrome: Data from a large community-based cohort study. *Journal of Women's Health, 24*, 299–307.

Johantgen, M. et al. (2012). Comparison of labor and delivery care provided by certified nurse-midwives and physicians: A systematic review, 1990-2008. *Women's Health Issues, 22*, e73–81.

Johnson, B. K. (2013). Sexually transmitted infections and older adults. *Journal of Gerontological Nursing, 39*, 53–60.

Johnson, D. & Scelfo, J. (2003, December 15). Sex, love and nursing homes. *Newsweek*, pp. 54–55.

Johnson, D. M. et al. (2017). Treatment of anxiety disorders. In M. Kopala & M. Keitel (Eds.), *Handbook of counseling women* (2nd ed., pp. 449–469). Thousand Oaks, CA: Sage.

Johnson, H. et al. (2015). *Critical issues on violence against women: International perspectives and promising strategies.* New York: Routledge.

Johnson, M. (2016). *Great myths of intimate relationships: Dating, sex, and marriage.* Malden, MA: Wiley.

Johnson, P. et al. (2014). *Sex-specific medical research: Why women's health can't wait.* Boston: Brigham and Women's Hospital.

Johnston, L. D. et al. (2015a). *Demographic subgroup trends among adolescents in the use of various licit and illicit drugs, 1975–2014* (Monitoring the Future occasional paper no. 83). Ann Arbor, MI: Institute for Social Research, University of Michigan.

Johnston, L. D. et al. (2015b). *HIV/AIDS: Risk & protective behaviors among adults ages 21 to 40 in the U.S., 2004–2014.* Ann Arbor, MI: Institute for Social Research, University of Michigan.

Johnston-Robledo, I. & Chrisler, J. C. (2013). The menstrual mark: Menstruation as social stigma. *Sex Roles, 68*, 9–18.

Johnstone, D. J. (2016). A listening guide analysis of women's experience of unacknowledged rape. *Psychology of Women Quarterly, 40*, 275–289.

Joint Economic Committee (2016, April). *Gender pay inequality: Consequences, for women, families and the economy.* Washington, DC: Author.

Jolie Pitt, A. (2015, March 24). Diary of a surgery. *New York Times*, p. A23.

Jonason, P. K. & Fisher, T. D. (2009). The power of prestige: Why young men report having more sex partners than young women. *Sex Roles, 60*, 151–159.

Jones, C. (2014). "I don't want to be a guinea pig": Recruiting older African Americans. *Journal of Gerontological Nursing, 40*, 3–4.

Jones, K. et al. (2014). Negative consequences of benevolent sexism on efficacy and performance. *Gender in Management: An International Journal, 29,* 171–189.

Jones K. (Ed.). (2016). *Sexually transmitted diseases sourcebook* (6th ed.). Aston, PA: Omnigraphics Inc.

Jones, R. & Malson, H. (2013). A critical exploration of lesbian perspectives on eating disorders. *Psychology & Sexuality, 4,* 62–74.

Jones, S. M. & Dindia, K. (2004). A meta-analytic perspective on sex equity in the classroom. *Review of Educational Research, 74,* 443–471.

Jordan, J. V. (2017). Relational-cultural therapy. In M. Kopala & M. Keitel (Eds.), *Handbook of counseling women* (2nd ed., pp. 63–73). Thousand Oaks, CA: Sage.

Jordan, J. V. (Ed.). (1997). *Women's growth in diversity: More writings from the Stone Center.* New York: Guilford.

Jordan-Young, R. M. (2010). *Brainstorm: The flaws in the science of sex differences.* Cambridge, MA: Harvard University Press.

Jose, A., O'Leary, D., & Moyer, A. (2010). Does premarital cohabitation predict subsequent marital stability and marital quality? A meta-analysis. *Journal of Marriage and Family, 72,* 105–116.

Joslyn, M. R. & Haider-Markel, D. P. (2016). Genetic attributions, immutability, and stereotypical judgments: An analysis of homosexuality. *Social Science Quarterly, 93,* 376–390.

Josselson, R. (1996). *Revising herself: The story of women's identity from college to midlife.* New York: Oxford University Press.

Jouriles, E. N. & McDonald, R. (2015). Intimate partner violence, coercive control, and child adjustment problems. *Journal of Interpersonal Violence, 30,* 459–474.

Jozkowski, K. N. et al. (2014). Gender differences in heterosexual college students' conceptualizations and indicators of sexual consent: Implications for contemporary sexual assault prevention education. *Journal of Sex Research, 51,* 904–916.

Juntunen, C. L., Barraclough, D. J., Broneck, C. L., Seibel, G. A., Winlow, S. A., & Morin, P. M. (2001). American Indian perspectives on the career journey. *Journal of Counseling Psychology, 48,* 274–285.

Justine, M. et al. (2013). Barriers to participation in physical activity and exercise among middle-aged and elderly individuals, *Singapore Medical Journal, 53,* 581–586.

Kadlekova, P. et al. (2015). Alcohol consumption at midlife and risk of stroke during 43 years of follow up. *Stroke,* doi:10.1161/STROKEAHA.114.006724.

Kaestle, C. E. (2016). Feminist perspectives advance four challenges to transform family studies. *Sex Roles, 75,* 71–77.

Kaestner, R. & Xu, X. (2010). Title IX, girls' sports participation, and adult female physical activity and weight. *Evaluation Review, 34,* 52–78.

Kahlenberg, R. (2011, March 17). Are admissions preferences for men OK? *Chronicle of Higher Education.* Retrieved from chronicle.com/blogs/innovations/are-admissions-preferences-for-men-okay/28909

Kahlenberg, S. G. & Hein, M. M. (2010). Progression on Nickelodeon? Gender-role stereotypes in toy commercials. *Sex Roles, 62,* 830–847.

Kahn, J. R. et al. (2014). The motherhood penalty at midlife: Long-term effects of children on women's careers. *Journal of Marriage and Family, 76,* 56–72.

Kainen, A. (1995). Only your regrets. In B. Benatovich (Ed.), *What we know so far: Wisdom among women.* New York: St. Martin's Griffin.

Kaiser Family Foundation. (2014). *Sexual health of adolescents and young adults in the United States.* Menlo Park, CA: Author.

Kaminski, M. J. & Magee, R. G. (2013). Does this book make me look fat? The effect of protagonist body weight and body esteem on female readers' body esteem. *Body Image, 10,* 255–258.

Kan, M. L., Cheng, Y. A., Landale, N. S., & McHale, S. M. (2010). Longitudinal predictors of change in number of sexual partners across adolescence and early adulthood. *Journal of Adolescent Health, 46,* 25–31.

Kane, E. W. (2006). "No way my boys are going to be like that!": Parents' responses to children's gender nonconformity. *Gender & Society, 20,* 149–176.

Kang, S. K. (2015). Multiple identities in social perception and interaction: Challenges and opportunities. *Annual Review of Psychology, 66,* 547–574.

Kann, L. et al. (2016, August 12). Sexual identity, sex of sexual contacts, and health-related behaviors among students in grades 9–12—United States and selected sites, 2015. *Morbidity and Mortality Weekly Reports, Surveillance Summaries, 65* (9).

Kanny, M. A. et al. (2014). Investigating forty years of stem research: How explanations for the gender gap have evolved over time. *Journal of Women and Minorities in Science and Engineering, 20,* 127–148.

Kantor, E. D. et al. (2015). Trends in prescription drug use among adults in the United States from 1999–2012. *Journal of the American Medical Association, 314,* 1818–1831.

Kanuha, V. K. (2013). "Relationships so loving and so hurtful": The constructed duality of sexual and racial/ethnic intimacy in the context of violence in Asian and Pacific Islander lesbian and and queer women's relationships. *Violence Against Women, 19,* 1175–1196.

Karazsia, B. T. et al. (2013). Thinking meta-theoretically about the role of internalization in the development of body dissatisfaction and body change behaviors. *Body Image, 10,* 433–441.

Karkazis, K. & Jordan-Young. (2015). Debating a testosterone "sex gap." Policies unfairly exclude some women athletes from competition. *Science, 348,* 858–860.

Karlsson, M. E. et al. (2016). Witnessing interpersonal violence and acceptance of dating violence as predictors for teen dating violence victimization. *Violence Against Women, 22,* 625–646.

Karpf, A. (2015, January, 4). The liberation of growing old. *The New York Times,* p. SR9.

Karpiak, C. P., Buchanan, J. P., Hosey, M., & Smith, A. (2007). University students from single-sex and coeducational high schools: Differences in majors and attitudes at a Catholic university. *Psychology of Women Quarterly, 31,* 282–289.

Karraker, A. & DeLamater, J. (2013). Past-year sexual activity among older married persons and their partners. *Journal of Marriage and Family, 75,* 142–163.

Karraker, K. & Hartley, J. (2007, March). *Mothers' toy choices for their male and female toddlers.* Poster presented at the meeting of the Society for Research in Child Development, Boston, MA.

Karraker, K. H., Vogel, D. A., & Lake, M. A. (1995). Parents' gender-stereotyped perceptions of newborns: The eye of the beholder revisited. *Sex Roles, 33,* 687–701.

Karvonen-Gutierrez, C. A. (2015). The importance of disability as a health issue for mid-life women. *Women's Midlife Health,* doi: 10.1186/s40695-015-0011-x.

Kasai, M. & Rooney, S. (2012). The choice before the choice: Partner selection is essential to reproductive justice. In J.C. Chrisler (Ed,). *Reproductive justice: A global concern* (pp. 11-28). Santa Barbara, CA: ABC-CLIO.

Kasardo, A. E. & McHugh, M. C. (2015) From fat-shaming to size acceptance: Challenging the medicalmanagement of fat women. In M. C. McHugh & J. C. Chrisler (Eds.). *The wrong prescription for women* (pp. 179–202). Santa Barbara, CA: ABC-CLIO.

Kashubeck-West, S. & Huang, H. (2013). Social class relations with body image and eating disorders. In W. M. Liu (Ed.), *The Oxford handbook of social class in counselling* (pp. 197–217). New York: Oxford University Press.

Kaskan, E. R. & Ho, I. K. (2016). Microaggressions and female athletes, *Sex Roles, 74,* 275–287.

Kassebaum, N. et al. (2014). Global, regional, and national levels and causes of maternal mortality during 1990–2013: A systematic analysis for the global burden of disease study 2013. *Lancet, 384,* 980–1004.

Kates, E. (1996). Educational pathways out of poverty: Responding to the realities of women's lives. *American Journal of Orthopsychiatry, 66,* 548–556.

Kates, E. (2007). *Low income women's access to education?: A case-study of welfare recipients in Boston.* Boston, MA: Center for Women in Politics and Public Policy.

Katon, W. et al. (2014). Predictors of postpartum depression. *Journal of Women's Health, 23,* 753–759.

Kattari, S. (2014). Sexual experiences of adults with physical disabilities negotiating with sexual partners. *Sexuality & Disability, 32,* 499–513.

Katz, D. S. & Andronici, J. F. (2006, Fall). No more excuses! *Ms.,* 63–64.

Katz, M. H. (2016). Health care for lesbian, gay, and bisexual people comes out of the closet. *JAMA Internal Medicine, 176,* 1352.

Katz, S. & Gish, J. (2015). Aging in the biosocial order: Repairing time and cosmetic rejuvenation in a medical spa clinic. *The Sociological Quarterly, 56,* 40–61.

Katz-Wise, S. L (2015). Sexual fluidity in young adult women and men: Associations with sexual orientation and sexual identity development. *Psychology & Sexuality, 6,* 189–208.

Katz-Wise, S. L. & Hyde, J. S. (2012). Victimization experiences of lesbian, gay, and bisexual individuals: A meta-analysis. *Journal of Sex Research, 49,* 142–167.

Kaukinen, C. (2014). Dating violence among college students: The risk and protective factors. *Trauma, Violence, & Abuse, 15,* 283–296.

Kawamura, S. & Brown, S. L. (2007, August). *Mattering and wives' perceived fairness of the division of household labor.* Paper presented at the meeting of the American Sociological Association, New York.

Kay, K. & Shipman, C. (2014). The confidence gap. *The Atlantic, 313* (4), 55–66.

Kazer, M. W. (2013). Sexuality in older adults: Changing misconceptions. *Journal of Gerontological Nursing, 39,* 2–3.

Keating, B. (2015). Violence against women: A disciplinary debate and challenge. *The Sociological Quarterly, 56,* 108–124.

Keel, P. K. & Forney, K. J. (2013). Psychological risk factors for eating disorders. *International Journal of Eating Disorders, 46,* 433–439.

Keel, P. K., Gravener, J. A., Joiner, T. E., Jr., & Haedt, A. A. (2010). Twenty-year follow-up of bulimia nervosa and related eating disorders not otherwise specified. *International Journal of Eating Disorders, 43,* 492–497.

Keene, J. R. & Prokos, A. H. (2008). Widowhood and the end of spousal care-giving: Relief or wear and tear? *Ageing and Society, 28,* 551–570.

Kehn, A. & Ruthig, J. C. (2013). Perceptions of gender discrimination across six decades: The moderating roles of gender and age. *Sex Roles, 69,* 289–296.

Keitel, M. et al. (2017). Infertility and recurrent miscarriage. In M. Kopala & M. Keitel (Eds.), *Handbook of counseling women* (2nd ed., pp. 591–604). Thousand Oaks, CA: Sage.

Kelley, E. L. & Gidycz, C.A. (2015). Labeling of sexual assault and its relationship with sexual functioning: The mediating role of coping. *Journal of Interpersonal Violence, 30,* 348–366.

Kelly, E. L. et al. (2014). Changing work and work-family conflict: Evidence from the work, family, and health network. *American Sociological Review, 79,* 485–516.

Kelly, J. & Dinan, T. G. (2016). Depression: Special issues in women. In D. J. Castle & K. M. Abel (Eds.), *Comprehensive women's mental health* (pp. 233–246). Cambridge UK: Cambridge University Press.

Kelly, K. et al. (2013). Willing, able, and unwanted: High school girls' potential selves in computing. *Journal of Women and Minorities in Science and Engineering, 19,* 67–85.

Kelly, K. et al. (2016). Life course and intergenerational continuity of intimate partner aggression and physical injury: A 20-year study. *Violence and Victims, 31,* 381–401.

Kelly, M. (2015). Feminist identity, collective action, and individual resistance among contemporary U.S. feminists. *Women's Studies International Forum, 48,* 81–92.

Kelly, M. & Hauck, E. (2015). Doing housework, redoing gender: Queer couples negotiate the household division of labor. *Journal of LGBT Family Studies, 11,* 438–464.

Kelly, M. et al. (2015). When working hard is not enough for female and racial/ethnic minority apprentices in the highway trades. *Sociological Forum, 30,* 415.

Kelly, S. M. (2012, May 1). *Half of tween girls are online gamers.* Retrieved from mashable.com/2012/05/01/tween-gamers/#d0cUhMR.PmqM

Keltner, D. & Lerner, J. S. (2010). Emotion. In S. T. Fiske, D. T. Gilbert, & G. Lindzey (Eds.), *Handbook of social psychology* (5th ed., Vol. 1, pp. 317–352). Hoboken, NJ: Wiley.

Kemper S. (2013). Gender and the psychology of aging. In M.K. Ryan & N.R. Branscombe (Eds.). *Sage handbook of gender and psychology* (pp.148–162). Los Angeles, CA: Sage.

Kenfield, S. A., Stampfer, M. J., Rosner, B. A., & Colditz, G. A. (2008). Smoking and smoking cessation in relation to mortality in women. *Journal of the American Medical Association, 299,* 2037–2047.

Kenney, C. T. & Bogle, R. (2009, May 2). *Mothers' gatekeeping of father involvement in married and cohabiting-couple families.* Paper presented at the annual meeting of the Population Association of America, Detroit, MI.

Kenschaft, L. & Clark, R. (2016). *Gender inequality in our changing world: A comparative approach.* New York: Routledge.

Kerr, B. (1999, March 5). When dreams differ: Male–female relations on campus. *Chronicle of Higher Education,* pp. 87, 88.

Kerr, D. et al. (2013). A comparison of lesbian, bisexual, and heterosexual college undergraduate women on selected mental health issues. *Journal of American College Health, 61,* 185–194.

Kerr, D. et al. (2014). Substance use of lesbian, gay, bisexual, and heterosexual college students. *American Journal of Health Behavior, 38,* 951–962.

Kershaw, K. N. et al. (2016). Self-reported experiences of discrimination and inflammation among men and women: The multi-ethnic study of atherosclerosis. *Health Psychology, 35,* 343–350.

Kersting, K. (2003, May). Cognitive sex differences: A "political minefield." *Monitor on Psychology, 34,* 54–55.

Kerstis, B. et al. (2016). Association between depressive symptoms and parental stress among Mothers and fathers in early parenthood: A Swedish cohort study. *Upsala Journal of Medical Sciences, 121,* 60–64.

Keski-Rahkonen, A. et al. (2014). Factors associated with recovery from anorexia nervosa: A population-based study. *International Journal of Eating Disorders, 47,* 117–123.

Kessler, R. C., Berglund, P., Demler, O., Jin, R., & Walters, E. E. (2005). Lifetime prevalence and age-of-onset distributions of DSM-IV disorders in the National Comorbidity Survey Replication. *Archives of General Psychiatry, 62,* 593–602.

Kether, J. (2016). *Girls' feminist blogging in a post-feminist age.* New York: Taylor & Francis.

Khaw, L. (2016). Stress and coping with intimate partner violence. In C. A. Price et al. (Eds.), *Families & change: Coping with stressful events and transitions* (pp. 249–268). Thousand Oaks, CA: Sage.

Kian, E. M. et al. (2013). A major boost for gender equality or more of the same? The television coverage of female athletes at the 2012 London Olympic Games. *The Journal of Popular Television, 1,* 143–149.

Kiang, L., Moreno, A. J., & Robinson, J. L. (2004). Maternal preconceptions about parenting predict child temperament, maternal sensitivity, and children's empathy. *Developmental Psychology, 40,* 1081–1092.

Kiefer, A. K. & Sekaquaptewa, D. (2007). Implicit stereotypes, gender identification, and math-related outcomes: A prospective study of female college students. *Psychological Science, 18,* 13–18.

Kiefer, A. K. & Shih, M. J. (2004, May). *Stereotype relevance and gender differences in performance attributions.* Poster presented at the meeting of American Psychological Society, Chicago.

Kiesner, J. (2009). Physical characteristics of the menstrual cycle and premenstrual depressive symptoms. *Psychological Science, 20,* 763–770.

Kilianski, S. E. (2003). Explaining heterosexual men's attitudes toward women and gay men: The theory of exclusively masculine identity. *Psychology of Men & Masculinity, 4,* 37–56.

Killelea, G. (2016). *The confidence effect: Every woman's guide to the attitude that attracts success.* New York: AMACOM.

Kilpela, L. S. et al. (2015). Body image in adult women: Moving beyond the younger years. *Advances in Eating Disorders: Theory, Research and Practice, 3,* 144–164.

Kim, E. (2014). Asexualities and disabilities in constructing sexual normalcy. In K. Cerankowski & M. Milks (Eds.), *Asexualities:*

Feminist and queer perspectives (pp. 249–282). New York: Routledge.

Kim, E.S. et al. (2017). Optimism and cause-specific mortality: A prospective cohort study. *American Journal of Epidemiology, 185,* 21–29.

Kim, J. & Wickrama, K. A. S. (2014). Mothers' working status and infant development: Mediational processes. *Journal of Family Issues, 35,* 1473–1496.

Kim, J. E. & Moen, P. (2001). Moving into retirement: Preparation and transitions in late midlife. In M. Lachman (Ed.), *Handbook of midlife development* (pp. 487–527). New York: Wiley.

Kim, S. C. et al. (2017). Counseling Eastern Asian American women. In M. Kopala & M. Keitel (Eds.), *Handbook of counseling women* (2nd ed., pp. 234–247). Thousand Oaks, CA: Sage.

Kimball, E. et al. (2013). Global efforts to engage men in preventing violence against women: An international survey. *Violence Against Women, 19,* 924–939.

Kimmel, D. G. (2002, August). *Ageism and implications for sexual orientation.* Paper presented at the American Psychological Association, Chicago.

Kimmel, M. (2008). A war against boys? In S. Coontz (Ed.), *American families: A multicultural reader* (2nd ed., pp. 387–393). New York: Taylor & Francis.

Kimmel, M. (2011). *Manhood in America: A cultural history* (3rd ed.). New York: Oxford University Press.

Kimmel, M. (2015). *Manhood in America.* New York: Routledge.

Kimura, D. (2007). "Underrepresentation" or misrepresentation? In S. J. Ceci & W. M. Williams (Eds.), *Why aren't more women in science? Top researchers debate the evidence* (pp. 39–46). Washington, DC: American Psychological Association.

Kincaid, C. et al. (2012). A review of parenting and adolescent sexual behavior: The moderating role of gender. *Clinical Psychology Review, 32,* 177–188.

Kincaid, E. A. (2013). Resistance refined, patriarchy defined: Carol Gilligan reflects on her journey from difference to resistance. *Sex Roles, 68,* 275–278.

Kincel, B. (2014). *The centenarian population: 2007–2011.* Washington, DC: U.S. Department of Commerce.

King, C. & Olsen, P. R. (2002, August 18). Follow the herd? Not her. *New York Times,* p. BU13.

King, M. M. et al. (2016). *Men set their their own sites high: Gender and self-citation across fields and over time.* Cornell University Library. Retrieved from arXiv:1607.00376

King, T. L. (2014). Reducing the cesarean rate: Our time is now. *Journal of Midwifery & Women's Health, 59,* 231–232.

Kinnunen, U. et al. (2013). Work-family interaction. In M. C. W. Peeters et al. (Eds.) *An introduction to contemporary work psychology* (pp. 267–290). Malden, MA: Wiley.

Kinsaul, J. A. E. et al. (2014). Empowerment, feminism, and self-efficacy: Relationships to body image and disordered eating. *Body Image, 11,* 63–67.

Kintzle, S. et al. (2015). Sexual trauma in the military: Exploring PTSD and mental health care utilization in female veterans. *Psychological Services, 12,* 394–401.

King, J. E. (2010). *Gender equity in higher education: 2010.* Washington, DC: American Council on Education.

King, L. A. & King, D. W. (1990). Abbreviated measures of sex role egalitarian attitudes. *Sex Roles, 23,* 659–673.

Kinsella, K. & Velkoff, V. A. (2001). *An aging world: 2001* (U.S. Census Bureau, Series P95/01-1). Washington, DC: U.S. Government Printing Office.

Kinser, A. E. (2010). *Motherhood and feminism.* Berkeley, CA: Seal Press.

Kinsey, A. C., Pomeroy, W. B., Martin, C. E., & Gebhard, P. H. (1953). *Sexual behavior in the human female.* Philadelphia, PA: Saunders.

Kinsler, K. & Zalk, S. R. (1996). Teaching is a political act: Contextualizing gender and ethnic voices. In K. F. Wyche & F. J. Crosby (Eds.), *Women's ethnicities: Journeys through psychology* (pp. 27–48). Boulder, CO: Westview.

Kinzie, J., Thomas, A. D., Palmer, M. M., Umbach, P. D., & Kuh, G. D. (2007). Women students at coeducational and women's colleges: How do their experiences compare? *Journal of College Student Development, 48,* 145–165.

Kipnis, L. (2015, February 27). Sexual paranoia strikes academe. *Chronicle of Higher Education.* Retrieved from chronicle.com/article/Sexual-Paranoia-Strikes/190351/

Kirk, G. & Okazawa-Rey, M. (2013). *Women's lives: Multicultural perspectives* (5th ed.). Mountain View, CA: Mayfield.

Kirkup, G. et al. (2015). The role of Women's/Gender Studies in the changing lives of British women. *Gender & Education, 27,* 430–444.

Kiser, A. I. T. (2015). Workplace and leadership perceptions between men and women. *Gender in Management: An International Journal, 30,* 598–612.

Kissin, W.B. et al. (2014). Gender-sensitive substance abuse treatment and arrest outcomes for women. *Journal of Substance Abuse Treatmet, 46,* 332–339.

Kite, M. E. (2001). Changing times, changing gender roles: Who do we want women and men to be? In R. K. Unger (Ed.), *Handbook of the psychology of women and gender* (pp. 215–227). New York: Wiley.

Kitzman, D. W. & Rich, M. W. (2010). Age disparities in heart failure research. *Journal of the American Medical Association, 304,* 1950–1951.

Klein, S. L. et al. (2015). Opinion: Sex inclusion in basic research drives discovery. *Proceedings of the National Academy of Sciences, 112,* 5257–5258.

Klein, S. L. (2016, Fall). Sex matters. *Hopkins Bloomberg Public Health.* Baltimore, MD: Johns Hopkins.

Kleinfeld, J. (2009). No map to manhood: Male and female mindsets behind the college gender gap. *Gender Issues, 26,* 171–182.

Kleinfeld, N.R. (2004, December 12). *Bowed by age, battered by an addicted nephew, and forced into begging and despair.* New York Times, pp.1, 56–57

Klimstra, T. A., Hale, W. W., III, Raaijmakers, Q. A. W., Branje, S. J. T., & Meeus, W. H. J. (2009). Maturation of personality in adolescence. *Journal of Personality and Social Psychology, 96,* 898–912.

Klimstra, T. A., Hale, W. W., III, Raaijmakers, Q. A. W., Branje, S. J. T., & Meeus, W. H. J. (2010). Identity formation in adolescence: Change or stability. *Journal of Youth and Adolescence, 39,* 150–162.

Kling, J. M et al. (2014). Osteoporosis prevention, screening, and treatment: A review. *Journal of Women's Health, 23,* 563–572.

Kling, K. C., Hyde, J. S., Showers, C. J., & Buswell, B. N. (1999). Gender differences in self-esteem: A meta-analysis. *Psychological Bulletin, 125,* 470–500.

Kloess, J. A. et al. (2014). Online child sexual exploitation: Prevalence, process, and offender characteristics. *Trauma, Violence, and Abuse, 15,* 126–139.

Klonoff, E. A. (2014). Introduction to the special section on discrimination. *Health Psychology, 33,* 1–2.

Kmiec, J., Crosby, J. F., & Worell, J. (1996). Walking the talk: On stage and behind the scenes. In K. F. Wyche & F. J. Crosby (Eds.), *Women's ethnicities: Journeys through psychology* (pp. 49–61). Boulder, CO: Westview.

Knobloch-Westerwick, S. et al. (2013). The Matilda Effect in science communication: An experiment on gender bias in publication quality perceptions and collaboration interest. *Science Communication, 10,* 1–23.

Koch, A. J. et al. (2015). A meta-analysis of gender stereotypes and bias in experimental simulations of employment decision making. *Journal of Applied Psychology, 100,* 128–161.

Koenig, A. M. & Eagly, A. H. (2014). Evidence for the social role theory of stereotype content: Observations of groups' roles shape stereotypes. *Journal of Personality and Social Psychology, 107,* 371–392.

Kogan, M. D. et al. (2010). Underinsurance among children in the United States. *New England Journal of Medicine, 363,* 841–851.

Kohlberg, L. (1966). A cognitive-developmental analysis of children's sex-role concepts and attitudes. In E. E. Maccoby (Ed.), *The development of sex differences* (pp. 82–173). Stanford, CA: Stanford University Press.

Kohlberg, L. & Puka, B. (1994). *Kohlberg's original study of moral development.* New York: Garland.

Kolata, G. & Moss, M. (2002, February 11). X-ray vision in hindsight: Science, politics and the mammogram. *New York Times,* p. A23.

Kolbert, E. (2014, May 26). No time: How did we get so busy? *The New Yorker,* p. 70.

Koniak-Griffin, D. & Brecht, M. L. (2015). Awareness of cardiovascular disease and preventive behaviors among overweight immigrant Latinas. *Journal of Cardiovascular Nursing, 30,* 447–455.

Konrad, A. M., Ritchie, J. E., Lieb, P., & Corrigall, E. (2000). Sex differences and similarities in job attribute preferences: A meta-analysis. *Psychological Bulletin, 126,* 593–641.

Koren, C. (2016). Men's vulnerability—women's resilience: From widowhood to late-life repartnering. *International Psychogeriatrics, 28,* 719–731.

Kornrich, S. & Eger, M. A. (2016). Family life in context: Men and women's perceptions of fairness and satisfaction across thirty countries. *Social Politics, 23,* 40–69.

Koropeckyj-Cox, T. & Call, V. R. (2007). Characteristics of older childless persons and parents: Cross-national comparisons. *Journal of Family Issues, 28,* 1362–1414.

Kort, D. et al. (2012). Pregnancy after age 50: Defining risks for mother and child. *American Journal of Perinatology, 4,* 245–250.

Kosciw, J. G., Diaz, E. M., & Greytak, E. A. (2014). *The 2013 national school climate survey: Key findings on the experiences of lesbian, gay, bisexual and transgender youth in our nation's schools.* New York: Gay, Lesbian and Straight Education Network.

Koss, M. P., White, J. W., & Kazdin, A. E. (2011). Violence against women and children: Perspectives and next steps. In M. P. Koss, J. W. White, & A. E. Kazdin (Eds.), *Violence against women and children: Navigating solutions* (Vol. 2, pp. 261–306). Washington, DC: American Psychological Association.

Kossek, E. E. & Lambert, S. J. (2005). *Work and life integration: Organizational, cultural, and individual perspectives.* Mahwah, NJ: Erlbaum.

Kossek, E. E. et al. (2012). Workplace social support and work-family conflict: A meta-analysis clarifying the influence of general and work-family-specific supervisor and organizational support. *Personnel Psychology, 64,* 289–313.

Kotila, L. E. et al. (2013). Time parenting activities in dual-earner families at the transition to parenthood. *Family Relations, 62,* 795–807.

Kowalski, R. M. et al. (2014). Bullying in digital age: A critical review and meta-analysis of cyberbullying research among youth. *Psychological Bulletin, 140,* 1073–1137.

Kozhimannil, K. B. et al. (2013). Doula care, birth outcomes, and costs among medicaid beneficiaries. *American Journal of Public Health, 103,* 113–114.

Kozhimannil. K. B. et al. (2014). Trends in childbirth before 39 weeks' gestation without medical indication. *Medical Care, 52,* 649–657.

Krahn, G. L. et al. (2015). Persons with disabilities as an unrecognized health disparity population. AJPH, *105,* Supplement 2, S198–206.

Kramer, A., Lorenzon, D., & Mueller, G. (2004, January/February). Prevalence of intimate partner violence and health implications for women using emergency departments and primary care clinics. *Women's Health Issues, 14,* 19–29.

Kramer, K. Z. et al. (2016). Comparison of poverty and income disparity of single mothers and fathers across three decades: 1990–2010. *Gender Issues, 33,* 22–41.

Kransdorf, L. N. et al. (2013). Everything in moderation: What the female athlete triad teaches us about energy balance. *Journal of Women's Health, 22,* 790–792.

Kraus, M. W., Côté, S., & Keltner, D. (2010). Social class, contextualism, and empathic accuracy. *Psychological Science, 21,* 1716–1723.

Kreager, D. A., Molloy, L.E., et al. (2016). Friends first? The peer network origins of adolescent dating. *Journal of Research on Adolescence,* 1–13.

Kreager, D. A., Staff, J. et al. (2016). The double standard at sexual debut: Gender, sexual behavior, and adolescent peer acceptance. *Sex Roles, 75,* 377–392.

Kreider, R. M. & Ellis, R. (2011). Number, timing, and duration of marriages and divorces: 2009. *Current Population Reports.* P70–125. Washington, DC: U.S. Census Bureau.

Krekula, C. (2016). Contextualizing older women's body images: Time dimensions, multiple reference groups, and age codings of appearance. *Journal of Women & Aging, 28,* 58–67.

Kreiger, T. C. (2005, April). *Gender-atypical behavior in young children and its relation to social adjustment.* Poster presented at the meeting of the Society for Research in Child Development, Atlanta, GA.

Kristof, N. (2014, February 6). At 90, this doctor is still calling. *New York Times,* p. A21.

Kristof, N. (2016, July 31). When women win, men win too. *New York Times,* p. SR9.

Kristof, N. D. & WuDunn, S. (2009). *Half the sky: Turning oppression into opportunity for women worldwide.* New York: Alfred A. Knopf.

Kromer, B. & Howard, D. (2013). *Labor force participation and work status of people 65 years and older.* Washington, DC: U.S Department of Commerce.

Krumrei, E., Coit, C., Martin, S., Fogo, W., & Mahoney, A. (2007). Post-divorce adjustment and social relationships: A meta-analytic review. *Journal of Divorce and Remarriage, 46,* 145–166.

Kuehner, C. et al. (2012). Mediating effects of stalking victimization on gender differences in mental health. *Journal of Interpersonal Violence, 27,* 199–221.

Kuhn, M. (1991). *No stone unturned.* New York: Ballatine Books.

Kuklanz, L. M. & McIntosh, H. (2015). *Documenting gendered violence: representatives, collaborations, and movements.* New York: Bloomsbury Academic.

Kulik, C. et al. (2016). In the company of women: The well-being consequences of working with (and for) other women, In M.L. Connerley & J. Wu (Eds.). *Handbook on well-being of working women* (pp, 189–208). New York: Springer.

Kulik, L. (2010). Women's experiences with volunteering: A comparative analysis by stages of the life cycle. *Journal of Applied Social Psychology, 40,* 360–388.

Kulow, M. D. (2012). Teaching disability employment discrimination law: Accommodating physical and mental disabilities. *Journal of Legal Studies Education, 29,* 334–362.

Kumar, N. & Brown, J.D. 2016). Access barriers to long-lasting reversible contraceptives for adolescents. *Journal of Adolescent Health, 59,* 248–253.

Kumra, S. & Simpson, R. (2014). *The Oxford handbook of gender in organizations.* New York: Oxford University Press.

Kunstman, J. W. & Maner, J. K. (2011). Sexual overperception: Power, mating motives, and biases in social judgment. *Journal of Personality and Social Psychology, 100,* 282–294.

Kuperberg, A. (2014). Age at coresidence, premarital cohabitation, and marriage dissolution: 1985–2009. *Journal of Marriage and Family, 76,* 352–369.

Kurpius, S. E. R. et al. (2017). Counseling women at midlife: A biopsychosocial perspective. In M. Kopala & M. Keitel (Eds.), *Handbook of counseling women* (2nd ed., pp. 192–203). Thousand Oaks, CA: Sage.

Kurtis, T. & Adams , G.2013). A cultural psychology of relationship: Toward a transnational feminist psychology.In M.K. Ryan & N.R. Branscombe (Eds.) *Sage handbook of gender and psychology* (pp. 251–269). Los Angeles, CA: Sage.

Kurz, T. & Donaghue, N. (2013). Gender and discourse. In M. K. Ryan & N. R. Branscombe (Eds.). *Sage handbook of gender and psychology* (pp. 61–78). Los Angeles, CA:Sage.

Kuther, T.L. (2017) *Lifespan development: Lives in context.* Los Angeles: Sage

Kuykendall, L. et al. (2015). Leisure engagement and subjective well-being: A meta-analysis. *Psychological Bulletin, 141,* 364–403.

Kuyper, L. (2015). Differences in workplace experiences between lesbian, gay, bisexual, and heterosexual employees in a representative population study. *Psychology of Sexual Orientation and Gender Diversity, 2,* 1–11.

Kwok, C. S. et al. (2015). Habitual chocolate consumption and risk of cardiovascular disease among healthy men and women. *Heart, 101,* 1279–1287.

Kwon, P. (2013). Resilience in lesbian, gay, and bisexual individuals. *Personality and Social Psychology Review, 17,* 371–383.

Lacelle, C. et al. (2012). Child sexual abuse and and women's sexual health: The contribution of CSA severity and exposure to multiple forms of childhood victimization. *Journal of Child Sexual Abuse, 21,* 571–592.

Lachance-Grzela, M. & Bouchard, G. (2010). Why do women do the lion's share of the housework? A decade of research. *Sex Roles, 63,* 767–780.

Lachs, M. S. & Pillemer, K. A. (2015). Elder abuse. *New England Journal of Medicine, 373,* 1947–1956.

LaCosse, J. et al. (2016). STEM stereotypic attribution bias among women in an unwelcoming science setting. *Psychology of Women Quarterly, 44,* 378–397.

Ladany, N. & Krikorian, M. (2013). Psychotherapy process and social class. In W. M. Liu (Ed.), *Oxford handbook of social class in counselling* (pp. 118–130). New York: Oxford University Press.

Ladge, J. J., Greenberg, D., & Clair, J. A. (2011). What to expect when she's expecting: Work family and identity integration challenges and opportunities of "soon-to-be" working professional mothers. In S. Kaiser, et al. (Eds.), *International perspectives on the work-life integration of professionals* (pp. 143–155). Berlin Heidelberg: Springer-Verlag.

LaFrance, M. (2001). Gender and social interaction. In R. K. Unger (Ed.), *Handbook of the psychology of women and gender* (pp. 245–255). New York: Wiley.

Lai, Y. & Hynie, M. (2011). A tale of two standards: An examination of young adults' endorsement of gendered and ageist sexual double standards. *Sex Roles, 64,* 360–371.

Lam, C. (2015). *New reproductive technologies and disembodiment: Material resolutions.* Burlington, VT: Ashgate.

Lamb, S. (2010). Toward a sexual ethics curriculum: Bringing philosophy and society to bear on individual development. *Harvard Educational Review, 80,* 81–105.

Lamm, L, & Eckstein, B. (2015). Lesbian, bisexual, and transgender health. In V. Maizes & T. Low Dog (Eds.). *Integrative women's health* (2nd ed.) (pp.737–753). New York: Oxford University Press.

Lamont, E. (2014). Negotiating courtship: Reconciling egalitarian ideals with traditional gender norms. *Gender & Society, 28,* 189–211.

Lancy, D. (2015). *The anthropology of childhood: Cherubs, chattel, changelings.* Cambridge: Cambridge University Press.

Landor, A. M. & Simons, L. G. (2014). Why virginity pledges succeed or fail: The moderating effect of religious commitment versus religious participation. *Journal of Child and Family Studies, 23,* 1102–1113.

Lapchick, R. (2016). *The 2015 racial and gender report card: College sports.* Orlando, FL: University of Central Florida.

Lapchick, R. (2017). *The 2016 racial and gender report card: College sports.* Orlando, FL: University of Central Florida.

Langenderfer-Magruder, L. et al. (2016). Experiences of intimate partner violence and subsequent police reporting lesbian, gay, bisexual, transgender, and queer adults in Colorado: Comparing rates of cisgender and transgender victimization. *Journal of Interpersonal Violence, 31,* 855–871.

Langguth, N. et al. (2016). Within-person link between depressed affect and moderate-to-vigorous physical activity in adolescence: An intensive longitudinal approach. *Applied Psychology: Health and Well-being, 8,* 44–63.

Lansford, J. E. (2009). Parental divorce and children's adjustment. *Perspectives on Psychological Science, 4,* 140–152.

Lapchick, R. (2016). *The 2016 racial and gender report card: College sport.* Orlando, FL: Institute for Diversity and Ethics in Sport.

Latif, E. Z. et al. (2013). Arriving at the diagnosis of female sexual dysfunction. *Fertility and Sterility, 100,* 898–904.

Latif, E. Z. & Diamond, M. P. (2013).Arriving at the diagnosis of female sexual dysfunction. *Fertility and Sterility, 100,* 898–904.

Laughlin, L. (2011). Maternity leave and employment patterns of first-time mothers:1961–2008. *Current Population Reports, P70–128.* Washington, DC: U.S. Department of Commerce.

Laumann, E. O. & Mahay, J. (2002). The social organization of women's sexuality. In G. M. Wingood & R. J. DiClemente (Eds.), *Handbook of women's sexual and reproductive health* (pp. 43–70). New York: Kluwer Academic/Plenum.

Laumann, E. O., Das, A., & Waite, L. J. (2008). Sexual dysfunction among older adults: Prevalence and risk factors from a nationally representative U.S. probability sample of men and women 57–85 years of age. *Journal of Sexual Medicine, 5,* 2300–2311.

Laumann, E. O., Leitsch, S. A., & Waite, L. J. (2008). Elder mistreatment in the United States: Prevalence estimates from a nationally representative study. *Journal of Gerontology, 63B,* S248–S254.

Laumann, E. O., Paik, A., & Rosen, R. C. (1999). Sexual dysfunction in the United States: Prevalence and predictors. *Journal of the American Medical Association, 281,* 537–544.

Laumann, E. O. et al. (2004). *The sexual organization of the city.* Chicago, IL: University of Chicago Press.

Launius, C. & Hassel, H. (2015). *Threshold concepts in women's and gender studies.* New York: Routledge.

Lauzen, M. M. (2015). *It's a man's (celluloid) world: On-screen representations of female characters in the top 100 films of 2014.* San Diego, CA: Center for the Study of Women in Television and Film, San Diego State University.

Lauzen, M. M. & Dozier, D. M. (2002). You look mahvelous: An examination of gender and appearance comments in the 1999–2000 prime-time season. *Sex Roles, 46,* 429–437.

Lauzen, M. M., Dozier, D. M., & Horan, N. (2008). Constructing gender stereotypes through social roles in prime-time television. *Journal of Broadcasting & Electronic Media, 52,* 200–214.

Lauzun, H. M. et al. (2012). Employing a conservation of resources framework to examine the interactive effects of work domain support and economic impact on work-family conflict. *The Psychologist-Manager Journal, 15,* 25–36.

Lavay, V. & Sand, E. (2015). On the origins of gender human capital gaps: Short and long term consequences of teachers' stereotypical biases. *NBER Working Paper Series.* Cambridge, MA: National Bureau of Economic Research.

Lawrence, E. M. et al. (2015). Happiness and longevity in the United States. *Social Science and Medicine, 145,* 115–119.

Laws, lies and the abortion debate. (2010, March 10). *New York Times,* p. A26.

Lawson, K. M. et al. (2014). Daily positive spillover and crossover from mothers' work to youth health. *Journal of Family Psychology, 28,* 897–907.

Lawton, C. A., Blakemore, J. E. O., & Vartanian, L. R. (2003). The new meaning of Ms.: Single, but too old for miss. *Psychology of Women Quarterly, 27,* 215–220.

Leach, C. R., Schoenberg, N. E., & Hatcher, J. (2011). Factors associated with participation in cancer prevention and control studies among rural Appalachian women. *Family & Community Health, 34,* 119–125.

Leach, P. et al. (2006). Child care before 6 months of age: A qualitative study of mothers' decisions and feelings about employment and non-maternal care. *Infant and Child Development, 15,* 471–502.

Leap, N. & Hunter, B. (2016). *Supporting women for labour and birth.* New York: Routledge.

Leaper, C. (2000). The social construction and socialization of gender during development. In P. H. Miller & E. K. Scholnick (Eds.), *Toward a feminist developmental psychology* (pp. 127–152). Florence, KY: Taylor & Francis/Routledge.

Leaper, C. (2004, July). Gender-related variations in affiliative and assertive speech: Meta-analyses. Paper presented at the American Psychological Association Convention, Honolulu.

Leaper, C. (2013). Gender development during childhood. In P.D. Zelazo (Ed.). *Oxford handbook of developmental psychology: Self and other* (vol.2) (pp. 327–377) New York: Oxford University Press.

Leaper, C. & Arias, D. M. (2011). College women's feminist identity: A multidimensional analysis with implications for coping with sexism. *Sex Roles, 64,* 475–490.

Leaper, C. & Ayers, M. M. (2007). A meta-analytic review of gender, variations in adults' language use: Talkativeness, affiliative speech, and assertive speech. *Personality and Social Psychology Review, 11,* 328–363.

Leaper, C. & Bigler, R. (2013). Gender. In M. K. Underwood & L. K. Rosen (Eds.). *Social development: Relationships in infancy, childhood, and adolescence* (pp. 289–315). New York: Guilford.

Leaper, C. & Brown, C. S. (2008). Perceived experiences with sexism among adolescent girls. *Child Development, 79,* 685–704.

Leaper, C. & Brown, C. S. (2014). Sexism in schools. *Advanced child development and behavior*, 47, 189–223.

Leaper, C. & Farkas, T. (2014). The socialization of gender during childhood and adolescence. In J. Grusec & P. Hastings (Eds.), *Handbook of socialization: Theory and research* (2nd ed., pp. 541–565). New York: Guilford.

Leaper, C. & Robnett, R. D. (2011). Women are more likely than men to use tentative language, aren't they? A meta-analysis testing for gender differences and moderators. *Psychology of Women Quarterly, 35,* 129–142.

Leaper, C. & Smith, T. E. (2004). A meta-analytic review of gender variations in children's language use: Talkativeness, affiliative speech, and assertive speech. *Developmental Psychology, 40,* 993–1027.

Leavell, A. S. & Tamis-LeMonda, C. S. (2013). Parenting in infancy and early childhood: A focus on gender socialization. In M. A. Fine & F. D. Fincham (Eds.), *Handbook of family theories: A context-based approach* (pp. 11–27). New York: Routledge.

Leavell, A. S. et al. (2012). African American, White, and Latino fathers' activities with their sons and daughters in early childhood. *Sex Roles, 66,* 52–65.

Lechtenberg, M. M. & Stith, S. M. (2017). Counseling women in violent relationships. In M. Kopala & M. Keitel (Eds.), *Handbook of counseling women* (2nd ed., pp. 107–119). Thousand Oaks, CA: Sage.

Lee, C. C. (2013). *Multicultural issues in counselling and new approaches.* Alexandria, VA: American Counselling Association.

Lee, G. & Mason, D. (2013). Optimism and coping strategies among Caucasian, Korean, and African American older women. *Health Care for Women International, 34,* 1084–1096.

Lee, J. (2008). "A kotex and a smile": Mothers and daughters at menarche. *Journal of Family Issues, 29,* 1325–1347.

Lee, J. & Zhou, M. (2015). *The Asian American achievement paradox.* New York: Russell Sage.

Lee, K. & Zvonkovic, A. M. (2014). Journeys to remain childless: A grounded theory examination of decision-making processes among voluntarily childless couples. *Journal of Social and Personal Relationships, 31,* 535–553.

Lee, N. et al. (2014). The impact of work–Family conflict and facilitation on women's perceptions of role balance. *Journal of Family Issues, 35,* 1252–1274.

Lee, R. et al. (2014). Head start participation and school readiness: Evidence from the early childhood longitudinal study-birth cohort. *Developmental Psychology, 50,* 202–215.

Lee, S. (2007). *Keeping moms on the job: The impacts of health insurance and child care on job retention and mobility among low-income mothers.* Washington, DC: Institute for Women's Policy Research.

Leeb, R. T. & Rejskind, F. G. (2004). Here's looking at you, kid! A longitudinal study of perceived gender differences in mutual gaze behavior in young infants. *Sex Roles, 50,* 1–14.

Lefkowitz, E.S. et al. (2014). How gendered attitudes relate to women's and men's sexual behaviors and beliefs. *Sexuality and Culture, 18,* 833–846.

Lehman, C. & Davis, L. (2014). *Strong at the heart: How it feels to heal from sexual abuse.* Arcata, CA: Sky Pilot Books.

Lehmann, R. et al. (2013). Age and gender differences in motivational manifestations of the Big Five from age 16 to 60. *Developmental Psychology, 49,* 365–383.

Lehr, S. (2001a). The anomalous female and the ubiquitous male. In S. Lehr (Ed.), *Beauty, brains, and brawn: The construction of gender in children's literature* (pp. 193–207). Portsmouth, NH: Heinemann.

Lehr, S. (Ed.). (2001b). *Beauty, brains, and brawn: The construction of gender in children's literature.* Portsmouth, NH: Heinemann.

Leifheit-Limson, E. C. et al. (2015). Sex differences in cardiac risk factors, perceived risk, and health care provider discussion of risk and risk modification among young patients with acute myocardial infarction. *Journal of the American Journal of Cardiology, 66,* 1949–1957.

Leis-Newman, E. (2012, June). Miscarriage and loss. *Monitor on Psychology,* pp. 62–63.

Leisring, P. A. (2013). Physical and emotional abuse in romantic relationships: Motivation for perpetration among college women. *Journal of Interpersonal Violence, 28,* 1437–1454.

Leitner, M. J. & Leitner, S. F. (2012). *Leisure in later life* (4th ed.). Urbana, IL: Sagamore.

Lemish, D. (2015). *Children and media: A global perspective.* New York: John Wiley.

Lengua, L. J. & Stormshok, E. A. (2000). Gender, gender roles, and personality: Gender differences in the prediction of coping and psychological symptoms. *Sex Roles, 42,* 787–819.

Lennon, T. (2013). *Benchmarking women's leadership in the United States.* Denver, CO: Colorado Women's College.

Leone, J. M. et al. (2014). Women's decisions to not seek formal help for partner violence: A comparison of intimate terrorism and situational couple violence. *Journal of Interpersonal Violence, 29,* 1850–1876.

Le, P. & Dinh, K. (2015). The intersection of gender and ethnicity: Asian-Pacific Islander American women. In C.Z. Enns et al. (Eds.). *Psychology practice with women: Guidelines, diversity, empowerment* (135–157). Washington, DC: APA Books.

LePage-Lees, P. (1997). Struggling with a nontraditional past: Academically successful women from disadvantaged backgrounds discuss their relationship with "disadvantage." *Psychology of Women Quarterly, 21,* 365–385.

Lepianka, D. (2015). How similar, how different? On Dutch media depictions of older and younger people. *Ageing & Society, 35,* 1095–1113.

Lerner, J. S., Castellino, D. R., Lolli, E., & Wan, S. (2002). Children, families and work: Research findings and implications for policies and programs. In R. M. Lerner, F. Jacobs, & D. Wertlieb (Eds.), *Handbook of applied developmental science* (Vol. 1, pp. 281–304). Thousand Oaks, CA: Sage.

Lethalon, S. et al. (2013). Phytoestrogens for vasomotor menopausal symptoms. *Cochrane Database for Systematic Reviews, 12,* 1–4.

LeVay, S. (2011). *Gay, straight, and the reason why: The scenario of sexual maturation.* New York: Oxford University Press.

Leve, M. (2013). Reproductive bodies and bits: Exploring dilemmas of egg donation neoliberalism. *Studies in Gender & Sexuality, 14,* 277–288.

Levesque, M. J., Nave, C. S., & Lowe, C. A. (2006). Toward and understanding of gender differences in inferring sexual interest. *Psychology of Women Quarterly, 30,* 150–158.

Levin, D. (2013, November 27). With glut of lonely men, china has approved outlet for unrequited lust. *New York Times,* p. A9.

Levine, S. C. et al. (2016). Sex differences in spatial cognition: Advancing the conversation. *Wiley Interdisciplinary Reviews: Cognitive Science, 7,* 127–155.

Levitt, H. M. & Ippolito, M. R. (2014). Being transgender: Navigating minority stressors and developing authentic self-presentation. *Psychology of Women Quarterly, 38,* 46–64.

Levy, B. (2009). Stereotype embodiment: A psychological approach to aging. *Current Directions in Psychological Science, 18,* 332–336.

Levy, B.R. et al. (2014). Subliminal strengthening: Improving elders' physical function over time through an implicit age-stereotype intervention. *Psychological Science, 25,* 2127–2135.

Lew, A. S., Allen, R., Papouchis, N., & Ritzler, B. (1998). Achievement orientation and fear of success in Asian American college students. *Journal of Clinical Psychology, 54,* 97–108.

Lewin, T. (2010, January 27). After long decline, teenage pregnancy rates rise. *New York Times,* p. A14.

Lewin, T. (2011, September 21). Universities seeking out students of means. *New York Times,* p. A21.

Lewin, T. (2014, September 18). Surrogates and couples face a maze of laws, state by state. *New York Times,* pp. A1, A20.

Lewin, T. (2015, June 17). Industry's growth leads to leftover embryos, and painful choices. *New York Times,* p. A1.

Lewis, R. (2015). As home births increase, recent studies illuminate controversies and complexities. *Journal of the American Medical Association, 313,* 553–555.

Li, R. Y. H. & Wong, W. I. (2016). Gender-typed play and social abilities in boys and girls: are they related? *Sex Roles, 74,* 399–410

Li, W. et al. (2013). Timing of high-quality child care and cognitive, language, and preacademic development. *Developmental Psychology, 49,* 1440–1451.

Li, Y. et al. (2014). The effect of maternal age and planned place of birth on intrapartum outcomes in healthy women with straightforward pregnancies: Secondary analysis of the birthplace national prospective cohort study. *BMJ Open, 4*, e004026.

Liben, L. S. (2016). We've come a long way, baby (but we're not there yet): Gender past, present, and future. *Child Development. 87*, 5–28.

Liben, L. S. & Bigler, R. S. (2014). *The role of gender in educational contexts and outcomes*. Amsterdam: Elsevier.

Liben, L. S. & Coyle, E. F. (2014). Developmental interventions to address the STEM gender gap: Exploring intended and unintended consequences. In L. Liben & R. Bigler (Eds.), *The role of gender in educational contexts and outcomes* (pp. 151–188). Amsterdam: Elsevier.

Liben, L. S. et al. (2002). The effects of sex steroids on spatial performance: A review and an experimental clinical investigation. *Developmental Psychology, 38*, 236–253.

Liechty, J. & Lee, M. (2013). Longitudinal predictors of dieting and disordered eating among young adults in the U.S. *International Journal of Eating Disorders, 46*, 790–800.

Lien, L., Haavet, O. R., & Dalgard, F. (2010). Do mental health and behavioural problems of early menarche persist into late adolescence? A three year follow-up study among adolescent girls in Oslo, Norway. *Social Science & Medicine, 71*, 529–533.

Lien, T. (2015, February 22). Why are women leaving the tech industry in droves? *LA Times*. Retrieved from latimes.com/business/la-fi-women-tech-20150222-story.html#page=1

Likis, F. E. (2014). Home birth: Moving toward shared goals. *Journal of Midwifery & Women's Health, 59*, 567–568.

Liljestrand, J. & Gryboski, K. (2002). Women at risk of maternal mortality. In E. Murphy (Ed.), *Reproductive health and rights: Reaching the hardly reached* (pp. 121–128). Washington, DC: Program for Appropriate Technology in Health.

Lin, I. F. & Brown, S. L. (2012). Unmarried boomers confront old age: A national portrait. *The Gerontologist, 52*, 153–165.

Lindau, S. T. & Gavrilova, N. (2010). Sex, health, and years of sexually active life gained due to good health: Evidence from two US population based cross sectional surveys of aging. *BMJ, 340*, c810.

Lindemann, D. et al. (2016). "I don't know why they make it so hard here": Institutional factors and undergraduate women's STEM participation. *International Journal of Gender, Science, and Technology, 8*, 222–238.

Lindner, K. (2004). Images of women in general interest and fashion magazine advertisements from 1955 to 2002. *Sex Roles, 51*, 409–421.

Lindsay, L. (2016). *Gender roles: A sociological perspective*. New York, Routledge.

Linn, M. C. & Petersen, A. C. (1985). Emergence and characterization of sex differences in spatial ability: A meta-analysis. *Child Development, 56*, 1479–1498.

Linton, K. F. & Rueda, H. A. (2015). Dating and sexuality among minority adolescents with disabilities: An application of sociocultural theory. *Journal of Human Behavior in the Social Environment, 25*, 77–89.

Lipka, M. (2015). *Where Europe stands on gay marriage and civil unions*. Washington, DC: Pew Research Center.

Lipman, J. (2015, August, 13). Let's expose the gender pay gap. *New York Times*. P. A19.

Lippa, R. A. (2008). Sex differences and sexual orientation differences in personality: Findings from the BBC Internet survey. *Archives of Sexual Behavior, 37*, 173–187.

Lips, H. M. (2010). Stalking a moving target: Thirty years of summarizing a changing field for changing students. *Sex Roles, 62*, 159–165.

Lips, H. M. (2013). The gender pay gap: Challenging the rationalizations: Perceived equity, discrimination, and the limits of human capital models. *Sex Roles, 68*, 189–185.

Lips, H. M. (2016). The gender pay gap and the well-being of working women. In M. L. Connerley & J. Wu (Eds.), *Handbook on well-being of working women* (pp. 141–155). Dordrecht: Springer.

Liss, M., Crawford, M., & Popp, D. (2004). Predictors and correlates of collective action. *Sex Roles, 50*, 771–779.

Liu, H. (2014). Bad marriage, broken heart? Age and gender differences in the link between marital quality and cardiovascular risks among older adults. *Journal of Health and Social Behavior, 55*, 403–423.

Liu, H. & Waite, L. (2014). Bad marriage, broken heart? Age and gender differences in the link between marital quality and cardiovascular risks among older adults. *Journal of Health and Social Behavior, 55*, 402–423.

Liu, W. M. (2013). Introduction to social class and classism in counseling psychology. In W. M. Liu (Ed.), *Oxford handbook of social class in counselling* (pp. 3–19). New York: Oxford University Press.

Liu, Y. et al. (2015). Links between alcohol consumption and breast cancer: A look at the Evidence. *Women's Health, 11*, 65–77.

Liu, Y. et al. (2016). Clustering of five health-related behaviors for chronic disease prevention among adults, United States, 2013. *Preventing Chronic Disease*, doi:10.5888/pcd13.160054.

Livengood, J. L. (2010). *Exploring predictors of preceptions of mothers and children in various work/family situations*. Unpublished master's thesis, Kansas State Univeristy, Manhattan, KS.

Livingston, G. (2014). *Four-in-ten couples are saying "I do," again.* Washington, DC: Pew Research Center.

Livingston, G. & Cohn, D. (2010). *The new demography of American motherhood*. Washington, DC: Pew Research Center.

Llorens, N. et al. (2016). A focus on the positive: Reasons for not engaging in physical aggression against a dating partner. *Journal of Family Violence, 31*, 75–83.

Logsdon-Conradsen, S. (2011). Pregnancy. In M. Z. Stange, C. K. Oyster, & J. E. Sloan (Eds.), *Encyclopedia of women in today's world*. Newberry Park, CA: Sage.

Lombardi, C. M. & Coley, R. L. (2014). Early maternal employment and children's school readiness in contemporary families. *Developmental Psychology, 50*, 2071–2084.

Lonborg, S. D. & Hackett, G. (2006). Career assessment and counseling for women. In W. B. Walsh & M. J. Heppner (Eds.), *Handbook of career counseling for women* (2nd ed., pp. 103–166). Mahwah, NJ: Erlbaum.

Lonsway, K. A. et al. (2013). Sexual harassment in law enforcement: Incidence, impact, and perception. *Police Quarterly, 16*, 177–210.

Loo, P. et al. (2017). Picture a woman: Counseling women living in poverty. In M. Kopala & M. Keitel (Eds.), *Handbook of counseling women* (2nd ed., pp. 120–136). Thousand Oaks, CA: Sage.

Lopez, I. & Legan, O. (2016). Controlling for class: Or the persistence of classism in psychology. In A. L. Hurst & S. K. Nenga (Eds.), *Working in class: How social class shapes our academic work* (pp. 23–34). Lanham, MD: Rowman & Littlefield.

Loretto, W. & Vickerstaff, A. (2013). The domestic and gendered context for retirement. *Human Relations, 66*, 65–86.

Loscocco, K & Walzer, S. (2013). Gender and the culture of heterosexual marriage in the United States. *Journal of Family Theory & Review, 5*, 1–14.

Lott, B. (2012). The social psychology of class and classism. *American Psychologist, 67*, 650–658.

Lott, B. & Bullock, H. (2010). Social class and women's lives. *Psychology of Women Quarterly, 3*, 421–422.

Lott, B. & Bullock, H. E. (2001, Summer). Who are the poor? *Journal of Social Issues, 57*, 189–206.

Lott, B. & Maluso, D. (2001). Gender development: Social learning. In J. Worell (Ed.), *Encyclopedia of women and gender* (pp. 537–549). San Diego, CA: Academic Press.

Lovas, G. S. (2005). Gender and patterns of emotional availability in mother-toddler and father-toddler dyads. *Infant Mental Health Journal, 26*, 327–353.

Love, S. M. (2010). *Dr. Susan Love's breast book* (5th ed). Philadelphia, PA: Da Capo Press.

Low, L. K. & Bailey, J. M. (2017). Women's health from a feminist perspective. In K. D. Schuiling & F. E. Likis (2017) *Women's gynecological health* (3rd ed., pp. 3–16). Burlington, MA: Jones & Bartlett.

Low Dog, T. & Maizes, V. (2010). Women's health: An epilogue. In V. Maizes & T. Low Dog (Eds.), *Integrative women's health* (pp. 660–670). New York: Oxford University Press.

Lowe, P. (2016). *Reproductive health and maternal sacrifice: Women, choice, and responsibility*. New York: Palgrave Macmillan.

Loya, R. M. (2014). The role of sexual violence in creating and maintaining economic insecurity among asset-poor women of color. *Violence Against Women, 20*, 1299–1320.

Loya, R. M. (2015). Rape as an economic crime: The impact of sexual violence on survivors' employment and economic well-being. *Journal of Interpersonal Violence, 30*, 2793–2813.

Lucas-Thompson, R. G. & Goldberg, W. A. (2015). Gender ideology and work-family plans. In M. Mills (Ed.), *Gender and the work-family experience: An intersection of two domains* (pp 3–20). New York: Springer.

Lum, A. (2015). *Transgenerational feminism and women's movements in post-1997 Hong Kong: Solidarity beyond the state*. Hong Kong: Hong Kong University.

Lummis, M. & Stevenson, H. W. (1990). Gender differences in beliefs and achievement: A cross-cultural study. *Developmental Psychology, 26*, 254–563.

Lundberg-Love, P. & Waits, B. (2010). Women and sexual violence: Emotional, physical, behavioral, and organizational responses. In M. A. Paludi (Ed.), *Feminism and women's rights worldwide: Mental and physical health* (Vol. 2, pp. 41–64). Santa Barbara, CA: Praeger.

Lundsberg, L. S. et al. (2014). Knowledge, attitudes, and practices regarding contraception and fertility: a population-based survey among reproductive age United States women. *Fertility and Sterility, 101*, 767–774.

Lundy-Wagner, V. & Winkle-Wagner, R. (2013). A harassing climate? Sexual harassment and campus racial climate research. *Journal of Diversity in Higher Education, 6*, 51–68.

Luong, G. et al. (2015). The multifaceted nature of late life socialization. In J. Grusec & M. Hastings (Eds.), *Handbook of socialization: Theory and research* (2nd ed., pp. 109–134). New York: Guilford.

Lutgendorf, S. K. & Anderson, B. L. (2015). Biobehavioral approaches to cancer progression and survival: Mechanisms and interventions. *American Psychologist, 70*, 186–197.

Lu, W. (2016, December 11) Dating with a disability. *New York Times*, p.ST15.

Lydon-Rochelle, M. T. (2004). Minimal intervention—nurse- midwives in the United States. *New England Journal of Medicine, 351*, 1929–1931.

Lynch, T. et al. (2016). Sexy, strong, and secondary: A content analysis of female characters in video games across 31 years. *Journal of Communication, 66*, 564–584.

Lyons, H. Z., Brenner, B. R., & Lipman, J. (2010). Patterns of career and identity interference for lesbian, gay, and bisexual young adults. *Journal of Homosexuality, 57*, 503–524.

Ma, Y. (2010). Model minority, model for whom? An investigation of Asian American students in science/engineering. *AAPI Nexus: Policy, Practice and Community, 8*(1), 43–74.

Mabry, M. (2007). *Twice as good: Condoleezza Rice and her path to power*. New York: Modern Times.

Maccoby, E. E. (1998). *The two sexes: Growing up apart, coming together*. Cambridge, MA: Harvard University Press.

Maccoby, E. E. & Jacklin, C. N. (1974). *The psychology of sex differences*. Stanford, CA: Stanford University Press.

Maass, A. et al. (2013). Sexual harassment: Motivations and consequences. In M. K. Ryan & N. R. Branscombe (Eds.), *Sage handbook of gender and psychology* (pp. 341–358). Los Angeles, CA: Sage.

MacDorman, M. F. et al. (2013). Recent trends in out-of-hospital births in the United States. *Journal of Midwifery & Women's Health, 58*, 494–501.

MacGeorge, E. L. et al. (2004). The myth of gender cultures: Similarities outweigh differences in men's and women's provision of and responses to supportive communication. *Sex Roles, 50*, 143–175.

Mackey, E. R. & La Greca, A. M. (2008). Does this make me look fat? Peer crowd and peer contributions to adolescent girls' weight control behaviors. *Journal of Youth and Adolescence, 37*, 1097–1110.

Mackey, S. et al. (2014). Knowledge, attitudes, and practices associated with menopause: A multi-ethnic, qualitative study in Singapore. *Health Care for Women International, 35*, 512–528.

MacNell, L. et al. (2014). What's in a name: Exposing gender bias in student ratings of teaching. *Innovative Higher Education, 40*, 291–303.

Madowitz, J. et al. (2015). The relationship between eating disorders and sexual trauma. *Eating and Weight Disorders, 3*, 281–293.

Mager, J. & Helgeson, J. G. (2011). Fifty years of advertising images: Some changing perspectives on role portrayals along with enduring consistencies. *Sex Roles, 64*, 238–252.

Maggio, R. (2015). *Unspinning the spin: The women's media center guide for fair and accurate language*. New York: Women's Media Center.

Magnusson, B.M. et al. (2012). Early age at first intercourse and subsequent gaps in contraceptive use. *Journal of Women's Health, 21*, 73–79.

Magnusson, E. & Marecek, J. (2012). *Gender and culture in psychology: Theories and practices*. Cambridge, UK: Cambridge University Press.

Maine, D. & Chavkin, W. (2002, Summer). Maternal mortality: Global similarities and differences. *Journal of the Medical Women's Association, 57*, 127–130.

Maine, M. & Kelly, J. (2016). *Pursuing perfection: Eating disorders, body myths, and women at midlife and beyond*. New York: Routledge.

Maine, M., McGilley, B. H., & Bunnell, D. (Eds.). (2010). *Treatment of eating disorders: Bridging the research-practice gap*. London, UK: Elsevier.

Mainiero, L. A., Gibson, D. E., & Sullivan, S. E. (2008). Retrospective analysis of gender differences in reaction to media coverage of crisis events: New insights on the justice and care orientations. *Sex Roles, 58*, 556–566.

Major, B., Appelbaum, M., Beckman, L., Dutton, M. A., Russo, N. F., & West, C. (2009). Abortion and mental health: Evaluating the evidence. *American Psychologist, 64*, 863–890.

Maklakov, A. A. & Lummaa, V. (2013). Evolution of sex differences in lifespan and aging: Causes and constraints. *Bioessays, 35*, 717–724.

Malanchuk, O. & Eccles, J. S. (2006). Self-esteem. In J. Worell & C. D. Goodheart (Eds.), *Handbook of girls' and women's psychological health: Gender and well-being across the life span* (pp. 149–156). New York: Oxford University Press.

Malcolmson, K. A. & Sinclair, L. (2007). The Ms. stereotype revisited: Implicit and explicit facets. *Psychology of Women Quarterly, 31*, 305–310.

Mallampalli, M. P. et al. (2013). Role of environment and sex differences in the development of autoimmune diseases: A roundtable meeting report. *Journal of Women's Health, 22*, 578.

Mammen, G. & Faulkner, G. (2013). Physical activity: The prevention of Depression? A systematic review of prospective studies. *Monitor on Psychology*, 649–657.

Maness, S. B. et al. (2016). Social determinants of health and adolescent pregnancy: An analysis of the National Longitudinal Study of Adolescent to Adult Health. *Journal of Adolescent Health, 58*, 636–643.

Mangweth-Matzek, B. et al. (2013). The menopausal transition—A possible window of vulnerability for eating pathology. *International Journal of Eating Disorders, 46*, 609–616.

Mangweth-Matzek, B. et al. (2014). Prevalence of eating disorders in middle-aged women. *International Journal of Eating Disorders, 47*, 320–324.

Manierre, M. J. (2015). Gaps in knowledge: Tracking and explaining gender differences in health information seeking. *Social Science & Medicine, 128*, 151–158.

Maniglio, R. (2012). Child sexual abuse in the etiology of anxiety disorders: A systematic review of reviews. *Trauma, Violence, and Abuse, 14*, 96–112.

Maniglio, R. (2014). Prevalence of sexual abuse among children with conduct disorder: A systematic review. *Clinical Child & Family Psychology Review, 17*, 268–282.

Manley, M. H. et al. (2015). Polyamory, monoamory, and sexual fluidity: A longitudinal study of identity and sexual trajectories. *Psychology of Sexual Orientation and Gender Diversity, 2*, 168–180.

Manning, W. D. et al. (2014). Child well-being in same-sex parent families: Review of research prepared for American Sociological Association amicus brief. *Population Research and Policy Review, 33*, 485–502.

Mannino, C. A. & Deutsch, F. M. (2007). Changing the division of household labor: A negotiated process between partners. *Sex Roles, 56*, 309–324.

Mansfield, K. C. (2011). Single-sex education. In M. Z. Stange, C. K. Oyster, & J. E. Sloan (Eds.), *Encyclopedia of women in today's world*. Newberry Park, CA: Sage.

Manson, J. E. & Kaunitz, A. M. (2016). Menopause management—Getting clinical care back on track. *New England Journal of Medicine, 374,* 803–805.

Mantilla, K. (2015). *Gendertrolling: How misogyny went viral.* Santa Barbara, CA: Praeger.

Manuel, T. & Zambrana, R. E. (2009). Exploring the intersections of race, ethnicity, and class on maternity leave decisions: Implications for public policy. In B. T. Dill & R. E. Zambrana (Eds.), *Emerging intersections: Race, class, and gender in theory, policy, and practice* (pp. 123–149). Piscataway, NJ: Rutgers University Press.

Marano, H. E. (1997, July 1). Puberty may start at 6 as hormones surge. *New York Times,* pp. B9, B12.

Marcus, E. N. (2008, May 20). Screening for abuse may be key to ending it. *New York Times,* p. F5.

Marecek, J. (2016). Invited reflections: Intersectionality theory and feminist psychology. *Psychology of Women Quarterly, 40,* 177–181.

Marecek, J., Crawford, M., & Popp, D. (2004). On the construction of gender, sex, and sexualities. In A. H. Eagly, A. E. Beall, & R. J. Sternberg (Eds.), *The psychology of gender* (2nd ed., pp. 192–216). New York: Guilford.

Margraf, J. et al. (2015). Pursuit of psychoplasty? Psychological health and aims of aesthetic surgery patients. *Clinical Psychological Science, 3,* 877–891.

Marecek, J. & Gavey, N. (2013). DSM-5 and beyond: A critical feminist engagement with psychodiagnosis. *Feminism & Psychology, 23,* 3–9.

Marina, B. et al. (2015). *Mentoring away the glass ceiling in academia: A cultured critique.* New York: Lexington Books.

Marine, S. B. & Lewis R. (2014). "I'm in this for real": Revisiting young women's feminist becoming. *Women's Studies International Forum, 47*(Part A), 11–22.

Markey, C. N. & Markey, P. M. (2009). Correlates of young women's interest in obtaining cosmetic surgery. *Sex Roles, 61,* 158–166.

Markey, C. N. & Markey, P. M. (2014). Gender, sexual orientation, and romantic partner influence on body image; An examination of heterosexual and lesbian women and their partners. *Journal of Social and Personal Relationships, 3,* 162–177.

Markovic, M., Manderson, L., & Warren, N. (2008). Pragmatic narratives of hysterectomy among Australian women. *Sex Roles, 58,* 467–476.

Markowitz, L.E. ret al. (2016). Prevalence of HPV after introduction of the vaccination program in the United States. *Pediatrics, 137,* e20151968.

Marks, D. F. et al. (2015). *Health psychology: Theory, research, and practice* (4th ed.). Thousand Oaks, CA: Sage.

Marlino, D. & Wilson, F. (2006). Career expectations and goals of Latina adolescents: Results from a nationwide study. In J. Denner & B. L. Guzmán (Eds.), *Latina girls: Voices of adolescent strength in the United States* (pp. 123–137). New York: New York University Press.

Marriage and the transition to parenthood. (2010). In T. N. Bradbury & B. R. Karney (Eds.), *Intimate relationships* (pp. 576–578). New York: W. W. Norton & Company, Inc.

Marshall, B. L. (2012). Medicalization and the refashioning of age-related limits on sexuality. *Journal of Sex Research, 49,* 337–343.

Marshall, N. L. & Barnett, R. C. (1993). Work-family strains and gains among two-earner couples. *Journal of Community Psychology, 21,* 64–78.

Martin, C. L. et al. (2013). The role of sex of peers and gender-typed activities in young children's peer affiliative networks: A longitudinal analysis of selection and influence. *Child Development, 84,* 921–937.

Martin, J. L. (2008a). Gendered violence on campus: Unpacking bullying, harassment, and stalking. In M. A. Paludi (Ed.), *Understanding and preventing campus violence* (pp. 3–26). Westport, CT: Praeger.

Martin, J. L. (2008b). Shifting the load: Personality factors and women in the workplace. In M. A. Paludi (Ed.), *The psychology of women at work: Challenges and solutions for our female workforce: Career liberation, history, and the new millennium* (Vol. 1, pp. 153–200). Westport, CT: Praeger.

Martin, J. L. (2010). Gender differences: The arguments regarding abilities. In M. A. Paludi (Ed.), *Feminism and women's rights worldwide* (Vol. 1, pp. 27–42). Santa Barbara, CA: Praeger.

Martin, J. M. & Borrelli, M. (2016). Learning what we know: The complexity of gender in U.S. and comparative executive studies. In J. M. Martin & M. Borrelli (Eds.), *The gendered executive: A comparative analysis of presidents, prime ministers, and chief executives* (pp. 1–24). Philadelphia, PA: Temple University Press.

Martin, K. A. & Kazyak, E. (2009). Hetero-romantic love and heterosexiness in children's G-rated films. *Gender & Society, 23,* 315–336.

Martin, K. A. & Luke, K. (2010). Gender differences in the ABC's of the birds and the bees: What mothers teach young children about sexuality and reproduction. *Sex Roles, 62,* 278–291.

Martin, L. Y. et al. (2016). A dual identity approach for conceptualizing and measuring children's gender identity. *Child Development,* doi:10.1111/cdev12568.

Martin, N., Williams, D. C., Harrison, K., & Ratan, R. A. (2009). A content analysis of female body imagery in video games. *Sex Roles, 61,* 824–836.

Martin, P. Y. (2016). The rape prone culture of academic contexts: Fraternities and athletics. *Gender & Society, 30,* 30–43.

Martinello, E. (2014). Reviewing strategies for risk reduction of sexual abuse of children with intellectual disabilities: A focus on early intervention. *Sexuality and Disability, 32,* 167–174.

Martino, S. (2015). Perfection in parenting may be the downfall of the supermom. *The Feminist Psychologist, 42,* 39–40.

Martin-Storey, A. (2015). Prevalence of dating violence among sexual minority youth: Variation across gender, sexual minority identity and gender of sexual partners. *Journal of Youth and Adolescence, 44,* 211–224.

Martin-Storey, A. (2016). Gender, sexuality, and gender nonconformity: Understanding variation in functioning. *Child Development Perspectives, 10,* 257–262.

Mason, J. E. (2014). Current recommendations: What is the clinician to do? *Fertility and Sterility, 101,* 916–917.

Mason, T. B. et al. (2015). External and internalized heterosexism among sexual minority women: The moderating roles of social constraints and collective self-esteem. *Psychology of Sexual Orientation and Gender Diversity, 2,* 313–320.

Masser, B., Grass, K., & Nesic, M. (2007). "We like you, but we don't want you"—the impact of pregnancy in the workplace. *Sex Roles, 57,* 703–712.

Massey, E. K., Gebhardt, W. A., & Garnefski, N. (2008). Adolescent goal content and pursuit: A review of the literature from the past 16 years. *Developmental Review, 28,* 421–460.

Massoni, K. (2004). Modeling work: Occupational messages in Seventeen magazine. *Gender & Society, 18,* 47–65.

Master, A. et al. (2016). Computing whether she belongs: Stereotypes undermine girls' interest and sense of belonging in computer science. *Journal of Educational Psychology, 108,* 424–437.

Masuy, A. J. (2009). Effect of caring for an older person on women's lifetime participation in work. *Ageing and Society, 29,* 745–763.

Mata, R. et al. (2016). Propensity for risk taking across the lifespan and around the globe. *Psychological Science, 27,* 231–243.

Matarasso, A. (2015). Strategies for aesthetic reshaping of the postpartum patient. *Plastic & Reconstructive Surgery, 136,* 245–257.

Matheson, K. & Foster, M. D. (2013). Coping with the stress of gender discrimination. In M. K. Ryan & N. R. Newcombe (Eds.). *Sage handbook of gender and psychology* (pp. 323–340). Los Angeles, CA: Sage.

Mathews, T. J. & Hamilton, B. E. (2016). *Mean age of mothers is on the rise: United States, 2000–2014.* NCHS Data Brief, No. 232. Atlanta, GA: National Center for Health Statistics.

Matlin, M. W. (2001, May). *Wise and wonderful . . . or wrinkled and wretched: How psychologists and the rest of the world view older women.* Invited address presented at the Midwestern Psychological Association, Chicago, IL.

Matlin, M. W. (2003). From menarche to menopause: Misconceptions about women's reproductive lives. *Psychology Science, 45,* 106–122.

Matos, K. & Galinsky, E. (2014). *2014 National study of employers*. New York: Families and Work Institute.

Matos, K. & Galinsky, E. (2015). Commentary on how effective is telecommuting? Assessing the status of our scientific findings. *Psychological Science in the Public Interest, 16*, 38–39.

Matthes, J. et al. (2016). Gender-role portrayals in television advertising across the globe. *Sex Roles, 75*, 314–327.

Maxwell, J., Belser, J. W., & David, D. (2007). *A health handbook for women with disabilities*. Berkeley, CA: Hesperian.

May, M. (2014). Attacking an epidemic: Despite a huge amount of funding and research, regional and individual differences in cancer trends make it a hard disease to wipe out. *Nature. 509*, 54–55.

May, V. (2015). *Pursuing intersectionality, unsettling dominant imaginaries*. New York: Routledge.

Mayer, K. H. et al. (2014). Promoting the successful development of sexual and gender minority youths. *American Journal of Public Health, 104*, 976–981.

Maynard, R. & Hoffman, S. D. (2008). The costs of adolescent childbearing. In S. D. Hoffman & R. Maynard (Eds.), *Kids having kids: Economic costs and social consequences of teen pregnancy* (2nd ed., pp. 359–402). Washington, DC: Urban Institute Press.

Mayo Clinic. (2013a). *Getting pregnant*. Rochester, MN: Author.

Mayo Clinic. (2013b). *Miscarriage*. Rochester, MN: Author.

Mayo Clinic. (2013c). *Morning sickness: Lifestyle and home remedies*. Rochester, MN: Author.

Mayo Clinic. (2014). *Uterine fibroids*. Rochester, MN: Author.

Mazei, J. et al. (2015). A meta-analysis on gender differences in negotiation outcomes and their moderators. *Psychological Bulletin, 141*, 85–104.

McAfee, T. & Burnette, D. (2014). The impact of smoking on women's health. *Journal of Women's Health, 23*, 881–885.

McBride, D. & Parry, J. (2016). *Women's rights in the USA* (5th ed.). New York: Routledge.

McCabe, M. P. & Goldhammer, D. L. (2012). Demographic and psychological factors related to sexual desire among heterosexual women in a relationship. *Journal of Sex Research, 49*, 78–87.

McCabe, S. E., Hughes, T. L., Bostwick, W. B., West, B. T., & Boyd, C. J. (2009). Sexual orientation, substance use behaviors and substance dependence in the United States. *Addiction, 104*, 1333–1345.

McCann, B. R. (2012). The persistence of gendered kin work in maintaining family ties: A review essay. *Journal of Family Theory and Review, 4*, 249–254.

McCann, C. R. & Kim, S.-K. (2017). Introduction: Feminist theory, local and global perspectives. In C. R. McCann & S.-K. Kim (Eds.), *Feminist theory reader: Local and global perspectives* (4th ed., pp. 1–8). New York: Routledge.

McCarthy, B. & Gartner, R. (2014). Introduction. In R. Gartner & B. McCarthy (Eds.), *The Oxford handbook of gender, sex, and crime* (pp. 1–18). New York: Oxford University Press.

McCarthy, M. A. & Fisher, C. M. (2014). Using the minority stress model to understand depression in lesbian, gay, bisexual, and transgender individuals in Nebraska. *Journal of Gay and & Lesbian Mental Health, 18*, 346–360.

McCartney, C. R. & Marshall, J. C. (2016). Polycystic ovary syndrome. *New England Journal of Medicine, 375*, 54–64.

McCleary-Skills, J. et al. (2015). Child marriage: A critical barrier to girls' schooling and gender equality in education. *The Review of Faith & International Affairs, 13*, 69–80.

McClelland, D. et al. (1953). *The achievement motive*. New York: Appleton-Century-Crofts.

McClelland, S. I. & Tolman, D. L. (2014). Adolescent sexuality. *Encyclopedia of Critical Psychology*, 40–47.

McCloskey, C. & Mintz, L. (2006). A culturally oriented approach for career counseling with Native American women. In W. B. Walsh & M. J. Heppner (Eds.), *Handbook of career counseling with women* (2nd ed., pp. 315–350). Mahwah, NJ: Erlbaum.

McCloskey, C.R. (2012) Changing focus: Women's menopausal journey. *Health Care for Women International ,33*, 540–559.

McConnell, E. A. et al. (2015). Typologies of social support and associations with mental health outcomes among LGBT youth. *LGBT Health, 2*, 1–2.

McDaniel, J. (2014). Heart disease: Lifesaving news for men and women. *AARP The Magazine, 29*, 32–76.

McDonald, S. & Mair, C. A. (2010). Social capital across the life course: Age and gendered patterns of network resources. *Sociological Forum, 25*, 335–359.

McEachern, A.G. (2012). Sexual abuse of individuals with disabilities: Prevention strategies for clinical practice. *Journal of Child Sexual Abuse, 21*, 386–398.

McElvaney, R. M. et al. (2014). To tell or not to tell? Factors influencing young people's informal disclosures of child sexual abuse. *Journal of Interpersonal Violence, 29*, 928–947.

McGinn, K. L. et al. (2015). Employment and gender inequality *Mum's the word! Cross-national relationships between maternal employment and gender inequalities at work and at home*. Working paper # 15–094. Cambridge, MA: Harvard Business School.

McGlone, M. S. & Aronson, J. (2006). Stereotype threat, identity salience, and spatial reasoning. *Journal of Applied Developmental Psychology, 27*, 486–493.

McGuire, J. E. & Leaper, C. (2016). Competition, coping, and closeness in young heterosexual adults' same-gender friendships. *Sex Roles, 74*, 422–435.

McHale, S. M., Bissell, J., & Kim, J.-Y. (2009). Sibling relationship, family, and genetic factors in sibling similarity in sexual risk. *Journal of Family Psychology, 23*, 562–572.

McHale, S. M., Crouter, A. C., & Tucker, C. J. (1999). Family context and gender role socialization in middle childhood comparing girls to boys and sisters to brothers. *Child Development, 70*, 990–1004.

McHale, S. M., Crouter, A. C., & Tucker, C. J. (2001). Free-time activities in middle childhood: Links with adjustment in early adolescence. *Child Development, 72*, 1764–1778.

McHugh, M. C. (2008). A feminist approach to agoraphobia: Challenging traditional views of women at home. In J. C. Chrisler, C. Golden, & P. D. Rozee (Eds.), *Lectures on the psychology of women* (pp. 392–417). New York: McGraw-Hill.

McHugh, M. C. (2012). Aging, agency, and activism: Older women as social change agents. *Women & Therapy, 35*, 279–295.

McHugh, M.C. et al. (2013). Constructing women as sexy: Implications for coercive sexuality and rape. In D. Castaneda (Ed.). *The essential handbook of women's sexuality*. Santa Barbara,CA: Praeger.

McHugh, M. C. (2015, Fall). Follow up on flibanserin—an ineffective drug with serious side effects. *Feminist Scholar, 42* (4), 23–24.

McHugh, M. C. & Interligi, C. (2015). Sexuality and older women: Desirability and desire. In V. Muhlbauer et al. (Eds.) *Women and aging: An international, intersectional power perspective* (pp. 89–116). New York: Springer.

McIntyre, M. H., & Edwards, C. P. (2009). The early development of gender differences *Annual Review of Anthropology, 38*, 83–97.

McKeever, A. E. et al. (2015). Human papillomavirus vaccination uptake and completion as a preventive health measure among female adolescents. *Nursing Outlook, 63*, 341–348.

McKelvey, M. W. & McKenry, P. C. (2000). The psychosocial well-being of Black and White mothers following marital dissolution. *Psychology of Women Quarterly, 24*, 4–14.

Mckenzie-Mohr, S. & LaFrance, N. M. (2014). Women counter-storying their lives. In S. McKenzie-Moore & N. M. LaFrance (Eds.) *Women voicing resistance: Discursive and narrative explorations* (pp. 1–15). New York: Routledge.

McKibbin, W. F., Shackelford, T. K., Goetz, A. T., & Starratt, V. G. (2008). Why do men rape? An evolutionary psychological perspective. *Review of General Psychology, 12*, 86–97.

McKnight-Eily, L. R. et al. (2014). Vital signs: Communication between health professionals and their patients about alcohol use—44 States and the District of Columbia, 2011. *Morbidity and Mortality Weekly Report. 63*, 1–7.

McLaughlin, H, et al .(2012) Sexual harassment, workplace authority and the paradox of power. *American Sociological Review, 77*, 625–647.

McMahon S. et al. (2015). Participation in high school sports and bystander intentions, efficacy to intervene, and rape myth beliefs. *Journal of interpersonal Violence, 30*, 2980–2998.

Mc Parlin, C. et al. (2016). Treatments for hyperemesis gravidarum and nausea and vomiting in pregnancy: A systematic review. *Journal of the American Medical Association, 316,* 1392–1401.

McPhail , B.A. (2016) Feminist framework plus: Knotting feminist theories of rape etiology into a comprehensive model. *Traiuma, Violence, and Abuse, 17,* 314–329.

McPherson, B. J., Fitzpatrick, M. J., Armenta, M. I., Dale, J. A., & Miller, T. E. (2007, August). *Coloring within the lines: Gender stereotypes in children's coloring books.* Poster presented at the annual meeting of the American Psychological Association, San Francisco, CA.

McRuer, R. & Mollow, A. (2012) *Sex and disability.* Raleigh, NC: Duke University Press.

McWilliams,S. & Barrett, A. (2013). Online dating in middle and later life: Gendered expectations and experiences. *Journal of Family Issues, 35,* 411–436.

Mead, S. (2006). *The evidence suggests otherwise: The truth about boys and girls.* Washington, DC: Education Sector.

Meadows, S. O. (2007). Evidence of parallel pathways: Gender similarity in the impact of social support on adolescent depression and delinquency. *Social Forces, 85,* 1143–1167.

Medley, G. et al. (2016). *Sexual orientation and estimates of adult substance use and mental health: Results from the 2015 National Survey on Drug Use and Health.* Washington, DC: Substance and Mental Health Services Administration.

Meekosha, H. (2010, Fall). The complex balancing act of choice, autonomy, valued life, and rights: Bringing a feminist disability perspective to bioethics. *International Journal of Feminist Approaches to Bioethics, 3,* 1–8.

Meem, D. T., Gibson, M. A., & Alexander, J. F. (2010). *Finding out: An introduction to LGBT studies.* Thousand Oaks, CA: Sage.

Mehler, P. S. (2011). Medical complications of bulimia nervosa and their treatments. *International Journal of Eating Disorders, 44,* 95–104.

Mehler, P. S. & Brown, C. (2015). Anorexia nervosa—medical complications. *Journal of Eating Disorders,* doi:10.1186/s40337-015-0040-8.

Mehta, C. M. & Strough, J. N. (2010). Gender segratation and gender-typing in adolescence. *Sex Roles, 63,* 251–263.

Mehta, L. S. et al. (2016). Acute myocardial infarction in women: A scientific statement from the American Heart Association. *Circulation, 133,* 1–17.

Meltzer, A. L. (2014). Sex differences in the implications of partner physical attractiveness for the trajectory of marital satisfaction. *Journal of Personality and Social Psychology, 106,* 418–428.

Mendes, K. (2015). *SlutWalk: Feminism, activism, and the media.* New York: Palgrave Macmillan.

Mendle, J. (2014). Beyond pubertal timing: New directions for studying individual differences in development. *Current Directions in Psychological Science, 23,* 215–219.

Mendle, J. et. al. (2016). Puberty, socioeconomic status, and depression in girls: Evidence for gene x environment interactions. *Clinical Psychological Science, 4,* 3–16.

Menning, C. L. & Holtzman, M. (2014). Processes and patterns in gay, lesbian, and bisexual assault: A multimethodological assessment. *Journal of Interpersonal Violence, 29,* 1071–1093.

Mercer, S. O., Garner, J. D., & Findley, J. (2001). Older women: A global view. In J. D. Garner & S. O. Mercer (Eds.), *Women as they age* (2nd ed., pp. 13–32). New York: Haworth.

Merline, A. C. et al. (2004). Substance use among adults 35 years of age: Prevalence, adulthood predictors, and impact of adolescent substance use. *American Journal of Public Health, 94,* 95–103.

Merry, S. (2016). *As Sally Field aged, her parts got less interesting—until 'Hello, my name is Doris.'* Retrieved March 17, 2016, from wapo.st/1vqialQ

Merz, E. A. & Gierveld, J. D. J. (2016). Childhood memories, family ties, sibling support and loneliness in ever-widowed older adults: Quantitative and qualitative results. *Ageing & Society, 36,* 534–561.

MetLife. (2010a). *The MetLife study of working caregivers and employer health care costs.* New York: Author.

MetLife. (2010b). *What today's woman needs to know and do: The new retirement journey.* New York: Author.

Messner, M. A., Duncan, M. C., & Jensen, K. (1993). Separating the men from the girls: The gendered language of televised sports. *Gender & Society, 7,* 121–137.

Messner, M. A. et al. (2015). *Some men: Feminist allies and the movement to end violence against women.* Oxford: Oxford University Press.

MetLife Mature Market Institute. (2013). *Metlife study of elder financial abuse: Crimes of occasion, depression, and predation against America's elders.* New York: Metlife.

Metz, I. & Kulik, C. T. (2014). The rocky climb: Women's and advancement in management. In S. Kumra et al. (Eds.), *The Oxford handbook of gender in organizations* (pp. 175–199). New York: Oxford University Press.

Meyer, I. H. (2016). The elusive promise of LGBT equality. *AJPH, 106,* 1356–1357.

Meyer, J. L., Gold, M. A., & Haggerty, C. L. (2011). Advance provision of emergency contraception among adolescent and young women: A systematic review of literature. *Journal of Pediatric and Adolescent Gynecology, 24,* 2–9.

Meyer, M. H. & Herd, P. (2007). *Market friendly or family friendly? The state and gender inequality in old age.* New York: Russell Sage Foundation.

Meyers, M. (2014). *Grandmothers at work: Juggling families' and jobs.* New York: New York University Press.

Mezulis, A. H., Abramson, L. Y., Hyde, J. S., & Hankin, B. L. (2004). Is there a universal positivity bias in attributions? A meta-analytic review of individual, developmental, and cultural differences in the self-serving attributional bias. *Psychological Bulletin, 130,* 711–747.

Mhaka-Mutepfa, M. et al. (2014). Grandparents fostering orphans: Influences of protective factors on their health and well-being. *Health Care for Women International, 35,* 1022–1039.

Michael, S. T., Crowther, M. R., Schmid, B., & Allen, R. S. (2003). Widowhood and spirituality: Coping responses. *Journal of Women & Aging, 15,* 145–166.

Michael, Y. L., Berkman, L. F., Colditz, G. A., & Kawachi, I. (2001). Living arrangements, social integration, and change in functional health status. *American Journal of Epidemiology, 153,* 123–131.

Michaud, S. L. & Warner, R. M. (1997). Gender differences in self-reported response to troubles talk. *Sex Roles, 37,* 527–540.

Mickelson, K. D. & Hazlett. (2014). "Why me?": Low-income women's poverty attributions, mental health, and social class perceptions. *Sex Roles, 71,* 319–332.

Miech, R. A. et al. (2016). *Monitoring the future national survey results on drug use, 1975–2015.* Ann Arbor, MI: University of Michigan.

Miettinen, A. et al. (2015). Increasing childlessness in Europe: Time trends and country differences. *Families and Societies: Working Paper Series, 33.*

Mikkelson, A. (2014). Adult sibling relationships. In K. W. Floyd & M. T. Morman (Eds.), *Widening the family circle: New research on family communication* (pp. 19–34). Thousand Oaks, CA: Sage.

Miles-Cohen, S. et al. (2016). *Eliminating inequities for women with disabilities: An agenda for health and wellness.* Washington, DC: American Psychological Association.

Miles-Cohen, S. E., Keita, G. P., Twose, G. H. J., & Houston, S. J. (2010). Beyond mentoring: Opening doors and systems. In C. A. Rayburn, F. L. Denmark, M. E. Reuder, & A. M. Austria (Eds.), *A handbook for women mentors: Transcending barriers of stereotype, race, and ethnicity* (pp. 233–248). Santa Barbara, CA: Praeger.

Miles-McLean, H. et al. (2015). "Stop looking at me!": Interpersonal sexual objectification as a source of insidious trauma. *Psychology of Women Quarterly, 39,* 363–374.

Milke, M. A., Raley, S. B., & Bianchi, S. M. (2009). Taking on the second shift: Time allocations and time pressures of U.S. parents with preschoolers. *Social Forces, 88,* 487–517.

Milkie, M. A. et al. (2015). Does the amount of time mothers spend with children and adolescents matter? *Journal of Marriage and Family, 77,* 3555–3572.

Milkman, R. (2016). *On gender, labor, and inequality.* Urbana, IL: University of Illinois Press.

Miller, A. (2014). Friends wanted: New research by psychologists uncovers the health risks of loneliness and the benefits of strong social connections. *Monitor on Psychology, 45,* 54.

Miller, A. B. et al. (2013). The relation between child maltreatment and adolescent suicidal behavior: A systematic review and critical examination of the literature. *Clinical Child and Family Psychology Review, 16,* 146–172.

Miller, C.C. (2014a, December 2) The divorce surge is over but the myth lives on. *New York Times,* p.A3.

Miller, C. C. (2014b, November 9). The leave seldom taken. *New York Times,* pp. BU1, BU6.

Miller, C. C. (2015a, May 17). Mounting evidence of advantages for children of working mothers. *New York Times,* p. SR5

Miller, C. C. (2015b, June 24). New momentum on paid leave, in business and politics. *New York Times,* p. B4.

Miller, C. C. (2016a, March 23). How society pays when women's work is unpaid. *New York Times,* p. A3.

Miller, C. C. (2016b, November 11). In substance and style, women govern differently. *New York Times,* p. B11.

Miller, C. C. & Streifield, D. (2015, April 2).Leaps in leave, if only parents would take it. *New York Times,* pp. A1–A3.

Miller, C. C. & Willis, D.(2015, June 28). Maiden names, on the rise again. *New York Times,* p. ST1.

Miller, D. (2010). Premenstrual syndrome. In V. Maizes & T. Low Dog (Eds.), *Integrative women's health* (pp. 165–187). New York: Oxford University Press.

Miller, D. I. & Eagly, A. H. (2015). Women's representation in science predicts national gender-science stereotypes: Evidence from 66 nations. *Journal of Educational Psychology, 107,* 631–644.

Miller, D. I. & Halpern, D. F. (2014). The new science of cognitive sex differences. *Trends in Cognitive Sciences, 18,* 37–46.

Miller, E. B. et al. (2014). Do the effects of head start vary by parental preacademic stimulation? *Child Development, 85,* 1385–1400.

Miller, E., Jordan, B., Levenson, R., & Silverman, J. G. (2010). Reproductive coercion: Connecting the dots between partner violence and unintended pregnancy. *Contraception, 81,* 457–459.

Miller, L. R. & Grollman, E. A. (2015). The social costs of gender nonconformity for ftransgender adults: Implications for discrimination and health. *Sociological Forum, 30,* 809–831.

Miller-Day, M. et al. (2014). Looking back and moving forward: Toward an understanding of mother-daughter and mother-son relationships. *Widening the family circle: New research on family communication* (pp. 1–18). Thousand Oaks, CA: Sage.

Mills, J. & Fuller-Tyszkiewicz, M. (2016). Fat talk and its relationship with body image disturbance. *Body Image,* doi:10.1016/j.bodyim. 2016.05.001.

Mills, M. & Taht, K. (2010). Nonstandard work schedules and partnership quality: Quantitative and qualitative findings. *Journal of Marriage and Family, 72,* 860–875.

Mills, M. B. (2016). Gendered divisions of labor. In J. Suchland (Ed.), *Economies of violence: Transnational feminism, post socialism, and the policies of sex trafficking* (pp. 283–303). Durham, NC: Duke University Press.

Milner awarded Kavli Prize. (2014, October). *APS Observer,* p. 7.

Milner, A. & Braddock, J. (2016). *Sex rejection in sports: Why separate is not equal.* Santa Barbara, CA: ABC-CLIO.

Milner, A. & DeLeo, D. (2010). Suicide research and prevention in developing countries in Asia and the Pacific. *Bulletin of the World Health Organization, 88,* 795–796.

Mindiola, T., Niemann, Y. F., & Rodríguez, N. (2002). *Brown-black relations and stereotypes.* Austin, TX: University of Texas Press.

Misa, T. J. (2010). *Gender codes: Women and men in the computing professions.* Hoboken, NJ: Wiley.

Mischner, I. H. S. et al. (2013). Thinking big: The effect of sexually objectifying music videos on bodily self-perception in young women. *Body Image, 10,* 26–34.

MIT. (2011). *A report on the status of women faculty in the schools of science and engineering at MIT, 2011.* Cambridge, MA: Author.

Mitchell, B. A. (2014). Generational juggling acts in midlife families: Gendered and ethnocultural intersections. *Journal of Women & Aging, 26,* 332–350.

Mitchell, K. J. et al. (2016). The role of technology in peer harassment: Does it amplify harm for youth. *Psychology of Violence, 6,* 193–204.

Mitchell, R. L. & Dezarn, L. (2014). Does knowing why someone is gay influence tolerance? Genetic, environmental, choice, and "reparative" explanations. *Sexuality & Culture, 18,* 994–1009.

Mizock, L. & Kaschak, E. (2015). Women with serious mental illness in therapy: Intersectional perspectives. *Women & Therapy, 38,* 6–13.

Mock, S. E. et al. (2012). Leisure and diversity in later life: Ethnicity, gender, and sexual orientation. *Leisure and Aging Theory and Practice,* 111–126.

Moe, A. (2009). Are males always better than females in mental rotation? Exploring a gender belief explanation. *Learning and Individual Differences, 19,* 21–27.

Moen, P. (2016). Women coming of age. *Sex Roles, 74,* 92–93.

Moen, P. & Flood, S. (2013). Limited engagements? Women's and men's work/volunteer time in the encore life course stage. *Social Problems, 60,* 1–22.

Moen, P., Kim, J. E., & Hofmeister, H. (2001). Couples' work/retirement transitions, gender, and mental quality. *Social Psychology Quarterly, 64,* 55–71.

Moen, P. et al. (2016). Does a flexibility/support organizational initiative improve high-tech employees' well-being? Evidence from the work, family, and health network. *American Sociological Review, 81,* 134–164.

Mohan, I. & Winifrid. (2015). Mental health consequences of violence against women and girls. *Psychiatry, Medicine and the Behavioural Sciences, 28,* 350–356.

Mohr, J. & Fassinger, R. (2013). Work, career, and sexual orientation. In C. J. Patterson & A. R. D'Augelli (Eds.), *Handbook of psychology and sexual orientation* (pp. 151–164). New York: Oxford University Press.

Moilanen, K. L. (2015). Predictors of latent growth in sexual risk taking in late adolescence and early adulthood. *The Journal of Sex Research, 52,* 83–97.

Mojtabai, R. et al. (2016). National trends in the prevalence and treatment of depression in adolescents and yung adults. *Pediatrics, 138,* e20161878

Mollborn, S. (2016). Teenage mothers today: What we know and how it matters. *Child Development Perspectives,* doi:10.1111/cdep.12205.

Mollen, D. (2013). Reproductive rights and informed consent: Toward a more inclusive discourse. *Analysis of Social Issues and Public Policy, 14,* 162–182.

Monahan, K. (2010). Themes of adult sibling sexual abuse survivors in later life: An initial exploration. *Clinical Social Work Journal, 38,* 361–369.

Mondschein, E. R., Adolph, K. E., & Tamis-LeMonda, C. S. (2000). Gender bias in mothers' expectations about infant crawling. *Journal of Experimental Child Psychology, 77,* 304–316.

Mongeau, P. A. et al. (2013). Identifying and explicating variation among friends with benefits relationships. *Journal of Sex Research, 50,* 37–47.

Monin, J. K., Clark, M. S., & Lemay, E. P. (2008). Communal responsiveness in relationships with female versus male family members. *Sex Roles, 59,* 176–188.

Monshouwer, K. et al. (2013). Possible mechanisms explaining the association between physical activity and mental health: Findings from the 2001 Dutch health behaviour in school-aged children survey. *Clinical Psychological Science, 1,* 67–74.

Monsour, M. (2012). Communicational cross-sex friendships across the life cycle: A review of the literature (pp. 375–414). *Communication Yearbook, 20.* New York: Routledge.

Montanoble, S. & Olivesi, A. (2016). *Gender testing in sport.: Ethics, cases, and controversies.* New York: Routledge.

Monte, L. M. & Ellis, R. R. (2014). Fertility of women in the United States: 2012. *Current Population Reports.* P 20–575. Washington, D.C.:U.S. Census Bureau

Montez, J. K. & Zajacova, A. (2014). Why is life expectancy declining among low-educated women in the United States? *American Journal of Public Health, 104,* e5–e7.

Montgomery, B. E. E. et al. (2015). Violence against women in selected areas of the United States. *American Journal of Public Health, 105,* 2156–2157.

Monto, M. A. & Carey, A. G. (2014). A new standard of sexual behavior? Are claims associated with the "hookup culture" supported by general social survey data? *Journal of Sex Research, 51,* 605–615.

Moonesinghe, R., Zhu, J., & Truman, B. I. (2011, January 14). Health insurance coverage—United States, 2004 and 2008. *Morbidity and Mortality Weekly Report, 60*(Suppl.), 35–37.

Moor, A. (2016). When does sexual coercion become rape? Common perceptions among students and implications for prevention. In M. A. Paludi (Ed.), *Campus action against sexual assault: Needs, procedures, policies, and training programs* (pp. 147–156). New York: Praeger.

Moore, A. (2010). From victim to empowered survivor: Feminist therapy with survivors of rape and sexual assault. In M. A. Paludi (Ed.), *Feminism and women's rights worldwide: Mental and physical health* (Vol. 2). Santa Barbara, CA: Praeger.

Moore, J. & Geist-Martin, P. (2013). In D. Castaneda (Ed.) *The essential sexuality of women* (pp.

Moore, J. A. & Radtke, H. L. (2015). Starting "real" life: Women negotiating a successful midlife single identity. *Psychology of Women Quarterly. 39,* 305–319.

Moore, M. R. & Stambolis-Ruhstorfer, M. (2013). LGBT sexuality and families at the start of the twenty-first century. *The Annual Review of Sociology, 39,* 491–507.

Moore, S. C. (2016). Association of leisure-time physical activity with risk of 26 types of cancer in 1.44 million adults. *JAMA Internal Medicine, 176,* 816–825.

Moore, S. E. H. (2008). Gender and the "new paradigm" of health. *Sociology Compass, 2,* 268–280.

Moore, S. R. et al. (2014). Pubertal timing and adolescent sexual behavior in girls. *Developmental Psychology, 50,* 1734–1745.

Moore, T. J. & Mattison, D. R. (2016). Adult utilization of psychiatric drugs and differences by sex, age, and race. *JAMA Internal Medicine* doi: 10.1001/jamainternmed.2016.7507

Moradi, B. et al. (2012). Disarming the threat to feminist identification: An application of personal construct theory to measurement and intervention. *Psychology of Women Quarterly, 36,* 197–209.

Moremen, R. D. (2008). Best friends: The role of confidantes in older women's health. *Journal of Women & Aging, 20,* 149–167.

Morgan, B. L. (1996). Putting the feminism into feminism scales: Introduction of a liberal feminist attitude and ideology scale (LFAIS). *Sex Roles, 34,* 359–390.

Morichi, V. et al. (2015). Diagnosing and treating depression in older and oldest old. *Current Pharmaceutical Design, 21,* 1690–1698.

Morison, T. et al. (2015). Stigma resistance in online childfree communities: The limitations of choice rhetoric. *Psychology of Women Quarterly, 10,* 1–15.

Morrill, M. (2014). Sibling sexual abuse: An exploratory study of long-term consequences for self-esteem and counseling considerations. *Journal of Family Violence, 29,* 205–213.

Morris, M. W. (2016). *Pushout: The criminalization of black girls in schools.* New York: The New Press.

Morris, T. (2013). *The c-section epidemic in America.* New York: New York University Press.

Morris, W. (2016, January 31). Women in love, then and now. *New York Times,* AR1, AR11.

Morrison, L.A. et al. (2014). Voices from the Hilo Women's Health Study: Talking story about menopause. *Health Care for Women International, 35,* 529–548.

Morrongiello, B. A. & Hogg, K. (2004). Mothers' reactions to children misbehaving in ways that can lead to injury: Implications for gender differences in children's risk taking and injuries. *Sex Roles, 50,* 103–118.

Mortenson, J. (2011a). Lesbian adoption. In M. Z. Stange, C. K. Oyster, & J. E. Sloan (Eds.), *Encyclopedia of women in today's world* (Vol. 2, pp. 839–842). Newberry Park, CA: Sage.

Mortenson, J. (2011b). Midwifery. In M. Z. Stange, C. K. Oyster, & J. E. Sloan (Eds.), *Encyclopedia of women in today's world* (Vol. 2, pp. 951–954). Newberry Park, CA: Sage.

Morton, T.A. (2013). An essential debate: Science, politics, difference and the gendered self. In M. K. Ryan & N. R. Branscombe (Eds.). *Sage handbook of gender and psychology* (pp. 378–393). Los Angeles, CA: Sage.

Moseley, R., et al. (Eds.) (2017). *Television for women: New directions.* New York: Routledge.

Moser, D. K., Dracup, K., & Wu, J. (2012). Cardiac denial and delay in treatment for myocardial infarction. In R. Alan & J. Fisher (Eds.), Heart and mind: The practice of cardiac psychology (2nd ed., pp. 305–326). Washington, DC: American Psychological Association.

Moss, M. S. & Moss, S. Z. (2014). Widowhood in old age: Viewed in a family context. *Journal of Aging Studies. 20,* 98–106.

Mostofsky, E. et al. (2016). Key findings on alcohol consumption and a variety of health outcomes from the Nurses' Health Study. *American Journal of Public Health, 106,* 1586–1591.

Motlagh, J. & Taylor, S. (2013). From the ashes of Rana Plaza. *Feminist.org. Summer 2013,* 26.

Motro, J. & Vanneman, R. (2015). The 1990s shift in the media portrayal of working mothers. *Sociological Forum. 30,* 1017–1037.

Mottarella, K. E., Fritzsche, B. A., Whitten, S. N., & Bedsole, D. (2009). Exploration of "good mother" stereotypes in the college environment. *Sex Roles, 60,* 223–231.

Motz, A. (2014). *Toxic couples: The psychology of domestic violence.* New York: Routledge.

Moulding, N. (2016). *Gendered violence, abuse, and mental health in everyday lives: Beyond trauma.* New York: Routledge.

Muehlenhard, C. L. (2011). Examining stereotypes about token resistance to sex. *Psychology of Women Quarterly, 35,* 676–683.

Muhlbauer, V. et al. (2015). *Women and aging: An international, intersectional power perspective.* New York: Springer.

Muhlig, Y. et al. (2016). Are bidirectional associations of obesity and depression already apparent in childhood and adolescence as based on high-quality studies? *Obesity Reviews, 17,* 235–249.

Mukherjee, J. S., Farmer, D. B., & Farmer, P. E. (2010). The AIDS pandemic and women's rights. In P. Murthy & C. L. Smith (Eds.), *Women's global health and human rights* (pp. 129–140). Sudbury, MA: Jones and Bartlett.

Mullainathan, S. (2014, May 11). A possible path to closing the pay gap. *New York Times.* p. BU6.

Muller, D. C. et al. (2016). Modifiable causes of premature death in middle-age in Western Europe: Results from the EPIC cohort study. *BMC Medicine, 14,* 1–13.

Mullis, I. V. S., Martin, M. O., Kennedy, A. M., & Foy, P. (2007). *IEA's progress in international reading literacy study in primary schools in 40 countries.* Boston, MA: Boston College.

Mullis, I. V. S. et al. (2012). *PIRLS 2011 international results in reading.* Chestnut Hill, MA: International Association for the Evaluation of Educational Achievement.

Mulvey, K. L. & Killen, M. (2015). Challenging gender stereotypes: Resistance and exclusion. *Clinical Development, 86,* 681–694.

Munk-Olsen, T., Laursen, T., Pedersen, C. B., Lidegaard, O., & Mortensen, P. B. (2011). Induced first-trimester abortion and risk of mental disorder. *New England Journal of Medicine, 364,* 332–339.

Munson, R. & Lague, I. (2016). *Intervention and reflection: Basic sources in bioethics* (10th ed.). Boston, MA: Cengage.

Murnen, S. K. et al. (2016). Boys act and girls appear: A content analysis of gender stereotypes associated with characters in children's popular culture. *Sex Roles, 74,* 78–91.

Murnen, S.K. & Smolak, L. (2013). "I'd rather be a famous fashion model than a famous scientist"" The rewards and costs of internalizing sexualization. In E.L. Zurbriggen & T.A. Roberts (Eds.). *The sexualization of girls and girlhood: Causes, consequences, and resistance* (pp. 235–256). New York: Oxford University Press.

Murphy, C. et al. (2014). Intimate partner violence: A biopsychosocial, social information processing perspective. In C. R. Agnew & C. S. South (Eds.), *Interpersonal relationships and health: social and clinical psychological mechanisms* (pp. 156–178). New York: Oxford University Press.

Murray, C. I. (2016). Death, dying, and grief in families. Physical and mental illness and family stress. In C. A. Price et al. (Eds.), *Families & change: Coping with stressful events and transitions* (pp. 359–380). Thousand Oaks, CA: Sage.

Murray, T. & Steil, J. (2000, August). *Construction of gender: Comparing children of traditional vs. egalitarian families.* Poster presented at the meeting of the American Psychological Association, Washington, DC.

Murray-Close, D. et al. (2016). Relational aggression: A developmental psychopathology perspective. In D. Ciccheti (Ed.), *Developmental psychopathology,* Vol IV, Article 13 (pp. 1–63). New York: John Wiley.

Mustafa, N. & Kingston, P. (2014). Elder abuse: A global epidemic. In N. A. Pachana & K. Laidlaw (Eds.), *Oxford handbook of clinical geropsychology* (pp. 571–583*).* New York: Oxford University Press.

Mustanski, B. & Liu, R. T. (2013). A longitudinal study of predictors of suicide attempts among lesbian, gay, bisexual, and transgender youth. *Archives of Sexual Behavior, 42,* 437–448.

Mustanski, B. et al. (2014). Envisioning an America without sexual orientation inequities in adolescent health. *AJPH, 104,* 218–225.

Mustanski, B. et al. (2016). The effects of cumulative victimization on mental health among lesbian, gay, bisexual, and transgender adolescents and young adults. *AJPH, 106,* 527–533.

Mustillo, S. et al. (2013). *Obesity, labeling, and psychological distress in late-childhood and adolescent black and white girls: The distal effects stigma.* Retrieved December 31, 2015, from journals.sagepub.com/

Muzio, C. (1996). Lesbians choosing children: Creating families, creating narratives. In J. Laird & R.-J. Green (Eds.), *Lesbians and gays in couples and families* (pp. 358–369). San Francisco, CA: Jossey-Bass.

Myaskovsky, L. & Wittig, M. A. (1997). Predictors of feminist social identity among college women. *Sex Roles, 37,* 861–883.

Myers, E. R. (2015). Repeated in vitro fertilization cycles for infertility. *Journal of the American Medical Association, 314,* 2627–2629.

Myers, K. & Raymond, L. (2010). Elementary school girls and heteronormativity: The girl project. *Gender & Society, 24,* 167–188.

Nabi, H. et al. (2013). Increased risk of coronary heart disease among individuals reporting adverse impact of stress on their health: The Whitehall II prospective cohort study. *European Heart Journal, 34,* 2697–2705.

Naef, R. et al. (2013). Characteristics of the bereavement experience of older persons after spousal loss: An integrative review. *International Journal of Nursing Studies, 50,* 1108–1121.

Naerde, A. et al. (2014). Normative development of physical aggression from 8 to 26 months, *Developmental Psychology, 50,* 1710–1720.

Nagoshi, J. et al. (2014). *Gender and sexual identity: Transcending feminist and queer theory.* New York: Springer.

Nash, I. (2015). The princess and the mean witch: Fantasies of the essential self. In M. Forman-Brunell & R. C. Hains (Eds.), *Princess cultures: Mediating girls' imaginations and identities* (pp. 3–24). New York: Peter Lang.

National Alliance for Caregiving and AARP. (2015). *Caregiving in the U.S.: 2015 report.* Bethesda, MD: National Alliance for Caregiving.

National Campaign to Prevent Teen Pregnancy. (2003). *With one voice 2003: America's adults and teens sound off about teen pregnancy.* Washington, DC: Author.

National Cancer Institute. (2014). *Feelings and cancer.* Bethesda, MD: Author.

National Center for Education Statistics (2016). *Student reports of bullying: Results from the 2015 school crime supplement to the National Crime Victimization Survey.* Washington DC: Author.

National Center for Health Statistics. (2015). *Health, United States: with special features on adults aged 55–64.* Hyattsville, MD: Author.

National Center for Health Statistics. (2016). Deaths: Leading causes for 2014. *National Vital Statistics Reports, 65* (5).

National Center for Injury Prevention and Control Division of Violence Prevention. (2013). *Understanding elder abuse.* Retrieved 2013, from HYPERLINK "http://www.cdc.gov/violenceprevention" \h www.cdc.gov/violenceprevention

National Center for Victims of Crime. (2015). *Stalking act sheet.* Washington, DC: Author.

National Coalition for Women and Girls in Education. (2012). *Title IX at 40.* Washington, DC: Author.

National Coalition of Anti-Violence Programs. (2016). *Lesbian, gay, bisexual, transgender, queer, and HIV-infected hate violence in 2015.* New York: Author.

National Council of Women's Organizations. (2013). Expanding social security benefits for financially vulnerable populations. *Center for Community Change & Older Women's Economic Security Task Force.*

National Heart, Lung, and Blood Institute. (2014). *Explore heart disease in women.* Washington, DC: Author.

National Institute of Mental Health. (2013). *Panic disorder: When fear overwhelms.* Bethesda, MD: Author.

National Institute on Aging. (2007). *Growing older in America: The health and retirement study.* Washington, DC: Author.

National Institute on Aging. (2015). *HIV, AIDS, and older people.* Gaithersburg, MD: Author.

National Institute on Alcohol Abuse and Alcoholism. (2015). *Alcohol: A women's health issue.* Rockville, MD: Author.

National Institute on Drug Abuse. (2009). *NIDA InfoFacts: Steroids (anabolic-androgenic).* Washington, DC: Author.

National Institutes of Health. (2013a). *Learning about Turner Syndrome.* Washington, DC: Author.

National Institutes of Health. (2013b). *Postpartum depression facts.* Washington, DC: Author.

National Institutes of Health. (2013c). *Strengthening knowledge and understanding of dietary supplements.* Washington DC: Author.

National Osteoporosis Foundation. (2014). *Clinician's guide to prevention and treatment of osteoporosis.* Washington, DC: Author.

National Science Foundation. (2015a). *Survey of earned doctorates.* Arlington, VA: Author.

National Science Foundation. (2015b). *Women, minorities, and persons with disabilities in science and engineering: 2015.* Arlington, VA: Author.

National Women's Law Center. (2016). *National snapshot: Poverty among women and families: 2015.* Washington, DC: Author.

Natsuaki, M. N. et al. (2014). Puberty, identity, and context: A biopsychological perspective on internalizing psychopathy in adolescent girls. In K. C. McLean & M. Syed (Eds.), *The Oxford handbook of identity development* (pp. 389–405). New York: Oxford University Press.

Navarro, M. (2002, May 16). Trying to get beyond the role of the maid. *New York Times,* pp. B1, B4.

Navarro, R. (2014). Children's preferences for gender-typed objects and colours: A commentary from gender research in Spain. *Escritos de Psicologia, 7,* 1–9.

Nayak, M. B., Byrne, C. A., Martin, M. K., & Abraham, A. G. (2003). Attitudes toward violence against women: A cross-nation study. *Sex Roles, 49,* 333–342.

Neff, K. D. & Terry-Schmitt, L. N. (2002). Youths' attributions for power-related gender attributes: Nature, nurture, or God? *Cognitive Development, 17,* 1185–1202.

Nelson, J. A. et al. (2008). Identity in action: Predictors of feminist self-identification and collective action. *Sex Roles, 58,* 721–728.

Nelson, M. K. (2013). Fictive kin, families we choose and voluntary kin: What does the discourse tell us? *Journal of Family Theory & Review. 5,* 259–281.

Nelson, S.K. et al. (2013). In defense of parenthood: Children are associated with more joy than misery. *Psychological Science, 24,* 3–10.

Nelson, S. K. & Lyubomirsky, S. (2015). Juggling family and career parents' pathways to abandoned and happy life. In R. J. Burke (Eds.) *Flourishing in life, work, and careers: Individual wellbeing and career experiences* (pp. 100–108). Northampton, MA: Edward Elgar.

Nelson, T. D. (2016). Ageism. In T. D. Nelson (Ed.), *Handbook of prejudice, stereotyping, and discrimination* (pp. 315–354). New York: Psychology Press.

Nesteruk, O. & Price, C. A. (2011). Retired women and volunteering: The good, the bad, and the unrecognized. *Journal of Women & Aging, 23,* 99–112.

Neuendorf, K. A., Gore, T. D., Dalessandro, A., Janstova, P., & Snyder-Suhy, S. (2010). Shaken and stirred: A content analysis of women's portrayals in James Bond films. *Sex Roles, 62,* 747–761.

Neuman, S. B. (2013). How can we change the odds for children at risk? In D.R. Reutzel (Ed.). *Handbook of research-based practice in early education* (pp. 3–14). New York: Guilford.

Neumayer, E. & Plümper, T. (2016). Inequalities of income and inequalities of longevity: A cross-country study. *AJPH, 106,* 160–165.

Newcomb, M. E. et al. (2014). Sexual orientation, gender and racial differences in illicit drug use in a sample of US high school students. *American Journal of Public Health, 104,* 304–310.

Newcombe, N. S. (2007). Taking science seriously: Straight thinking about spatial sex differences. In S. J. Ceci & W. M. Williams (Eds.), *Why aren't more women in science? Top researchers debate the evidence* (pp. 69–77). Washington, DC: American Psychological Association.

Newcombe, N. S. et al. (2009). Psychology's role in mathematics and science education. *American Psychologist, 64,* 538–550.

Newcombe, N. S. et al. (2013). *Spatial development.* New York: Oxford University Press.

Newhart, M. R. (2013). Menopause matters: The implications of menopause research for studies of midlife health. *Health Sociology Review, 22,* 365–376.

Newman, A. A. (2007, December 31). A guide to embracing life as a single (without the resignation, that is). *New York Times,* p. C4.

Newman, M. L., Groom, C. J., Handelman, L. D., & Pennebaker, J. W. (2008). Gender differences in language use: An analysis of 14,000 text samples. *Discourse Processes, 45,* 211–236.

Newton, N. et al. (2012). Women's regrets about their lives: Cohort differences in correlates and contents. *Sex Roles, 66,* 530–543.

Newton, V. L. (2016). *Everyday discourses of menstruation: Cultural and social perspectives.* London: Palgrave Macmillan.

Newton-Small, J. (2016). *Broad influence: How women are changing the way America works.* New York: Time Inc. Books.

Newtson, R. L. & Keith, P. M. (2001). Single women in later life. In J. M. Coyle (Ed.), *Handbook on women and aging* (pp. 385–399). Westport, CT: Greenwood.

Ngamake, S. T. et al. (2016). Discrimination and sexual minority mental health: Medication and moderation effects of coping. *Psychology of Sexual Orientation and Gender Diversity, 3,* 213–226.

Nguyen, A. W. et al. (2013). Health, disability, psychological well-being, and depressive symptoms among older African American women. *Women, Gender, and Families of Color, 1,* 105–123.

Nicholson, P. (2015). *Gender, power, and organization: A psychological perspective on life at work.* New York: Routledge.

Nielsen, M. B. et al. (2015). Post-traumatic stress disorder as a consequence of bullying at Work and at school: A literature review and meta-analysis. *Aggression and Violent Behavior, 21,* 17–24.

Niemann, Y. F., Jennings, L., Rozelle, R. M., Baxter, J. C., & Sullivan, E. (1994). Use of free responses and cluster analysis to determine stereotypes of eight groups. *Personality and Social Psychology Bulletin, 20,* 379–390.

Nilsson, I. et al. (2015). Leisure engagement: Medical conditions, mobility difficulties, and activity limitations—A later life perspective. *Journal of Aging Research,* doi:10.1155/2015/610154.

Nivette, A. E. et al. (2015). *Sex differences in aggression among children of low and high gender inequality backgrounds: A comparison of gender role and sexual selections.* Retrieved January 15, 2015, from web.a.ebscohost.com/ehost

Nix, S. et al. (2015). Perceived mathematical ability under challenge: A longitudinal perspective on sex segregation among STEM degree fields, *Frontiers, 10,* 1–29.

Nixon, R. (2014, September 20). Women allege harassment and abuse on forest service firefighting crews. *New York Times.* p. A14.

Nock, M. et al. (2014). Depression and suicide. In I. H. Gotlib & C. L. Hammen (Eds.), *Handbook of depression* (pp. 448–468). New York: Guilford.

Nolan, M. R. et al. (2013). Analysis and reporting of sex differences in phase III medical device clinical trials—How are we doing? *Journal of Women's Health, 22,* 399–401.

Nolen-Hoeksema, S., Larson, J., & Grayson, C. (1999). Explaining the gender difference in depressive symptoms. *Journal of Personality and Social Psychology, 77,* 1061–1072.

Nollan, J. (2015, March 1). Medicating women's feelings. *New York Times.* p. SR6.

Nonzee, N. J. et al. (2015). Delays in cancer care among low-income minorities despite access. *Journal of Women's Health, 24,* 506–514.

Norcross, J. C. et al. (2016). Undergraduate study in Psychology: Curriculum and assessment. *American Psychologist, 71,* 89–101.

Nordberg, J. (2014, October, 12). The underground girls of Kabul: In search of a hidden resistance in Afghanistan. *New York Times.* p. BR19.

Norman, R. (2014). The human menstrual cycle. In J. J. Robert-McComb et al. (Eds.), *The active female: Health issues throughout the lifespan* (pp. 61–66). New York: Springer.

Norona, J. C. et al. (2016). "I learned things that make me happy things that bring me down:" Lessons from romantic relationships in adolescence and emerging adulthood. *Journal of Adolescent Research,* doi: 10.1177./0743558415605166.

North, C.M. & Christiani, D.C. (2013). Women and lung cancer: What is new? *Seminars in Thoracic and Cardiovascular Surgery, 25* (2), 87–94.

North, M. S., & Fiske, S. (2015). Modern attitudes toward older adults in the aging world: A cross-cultural meta-analysis. *Psychological Bulletin, 141,* 993–1021.

North American Menopause Society. (2008, November). Super stats: 10 menopause-related facts & figures. *Menopause Flashes.* Retrieved from regardinghealth.com/nam/RHO/2008/11/Article.aspx?mkEMC=44420

North American Menopause Society. (2012). *The menopause guidebook.* Mayfield, OH: Author.

North American Menopause Society. (2014). What midlife women should know about osteoporosis risk and treatments. *The Journal of the North American Menopause Society, 21,* 1–2.

Northrup, C. (2010). *Women's bodies, women's wisdom.* New York: Bantam.

Norton, A. T. & Herek, G. M. (2013). Heterosexuals' attitudes toward transgender people: Findings from a national probability sample of U.S. adults. *Sex Roles. 68,* 738–753.

Nosek, M. A. et al. (2001). National study of women with physical disabilities: Final report. *Sexuality and Disability, 19,* 5–39.

Nosek, M. A. (2010). Feminism and disability: Synchronous agendas in conflict. In H. Landrine & N. F. Russo (Eds.), *Handbook of diversity in feminist psychology* (pp. 501–533). New York: Springer.

Notthoff, N. & Carstensen, L. L. (2014). Positive messaging promotes walking in older adults. *Psychology and Aging, 9,* 329–341.

Novotney, A. (2010, February). Members elect Vasquez as APA's next president. *Monitor on Psychology,* 60–61.

Nowotny, K. M. & Graves, L. J. (2013). Substance use and intimate partner violence victimization among white, African American, and Latina women. *Journal of Interpersonal Violence, 28,* 3301–3318.

Nutt, A. E. (2015). *Becoming Nicole: The transformation of an American family.* New York: Random House.

Nutt, R. L. & Brooks, G. R. (2008). Psychology of gender. In S. D. Brown & R. W. Lent (Eds.), *Handbook of counseling psychology* (4th ed., pp. 176–193). Hoboken, NJ: Wiley.

O'Brien, E. (2005). *Medicaid's coverage of nursing home costs: Asset shelter for the wealthy or essential safety net?* Washington, DC: Georgetown University Health Policy Institute. Retrieved from ltc.georgetown.edu/pdfs/nursinghomecosts.pdf

O'Brien, J. L. & Whitbourne, S. K. (2015). Clinical interventions to empower older women. In V, Muhlbauer et al. (Eds.). *Women and aging: An international, intersectional power perspective* (pp.). New York: Springer.

O'Brien, K., Friedman, S. C., Tipton, L. C., & Linn, S. G. (2000). Attachment, separation, and women's vocational development: A longitudinal analysis. *Journal of Counseling Psychology, 47,* 301–315.

O'Connor, R. et al. (2014). *Paid sick days access varies by race/ethnicity, sexual orientation, and job characteristics.* Washington, DC: Institute for Women's Policy Research.

O'Hara, M. W. & McCabe, J. E. (2014). Postpartum depression: Current status and future directions. *Annual Review of Clinical Psychology, 9,* 379–407.

O'Neill, T. (2015). *Wage gap denial: We can't believe we're still protesting this sh*t!* Ms Magazine.

O'Reilly, A. (2014). *Mothers, mothering and motherhood across cultural differences: A reader.* Bradford, ON: Demeter Press.

Oberwittler, D. & Kaseck, J. (2014). Honor killings. In R. Gartner & B. McCarthy (Eds.) *The Oxford handbook of gender, sex, and crime* (pp. 652–670). New York: Oxford University Press.

Obradović, J. & Hipwell, A. (2010). Psychopathology and social competence during the transition to adolescence: The role of family adversity and pubertal development. *Development and Psychopathology, 22,* 621–634.

O'Toole, C. J. (2004). The sexist inheritance of the disability movement. In B. G. Smith & B. Hutchison (Eds.), *Gendering disability* (pp. 294 –300). Piscataway, NJ: Rutgers University Press.

OECD Programme for International Student Assessment. (2009). *Equally prepared for life? How 15-year-old boys and girls perform in school.* Paris: Author.

OECD. (2015). *The ABC of gender equality in education: Aptitude, behavior, and confidence.* Paris: Author.

Oertelt-Prigione, S. & Regitz-Zagrosek, V. (2012). *Sex and gender aspects in clinical medicine.* New York: Springer.

Offer, S. (2016). Free time and emotional well-being: Do dual-earner mothers and fathers differ? *Gender & Society, 30,* 213–239.

Office of Adolescent Health. (2016). *Sexually transmitted diseases.* Rockville, MD: Author.

Office on Women's Health. (2007). *Frequently asked questions: Health insurance and women.* Washington, DC: Author. Retrieved from womenshealth.gov/faq/health-insurance-women.cfm

Office on Women's Health. (2009). *Action steps for improving women's mental health.* Washington, DC: Author.

Office on Women's Health. (2014). *Hysterectomy fact sheet.* Retrieved February 18, 2015, from "http://www.womenshealth.gov".

Office on Women's Health. (2017). *Menstruation and the menstrual cycle.* Washington, DC: Author.

Ofstedal, M. B., Reidy, E., & Knodel, J. (2003, November). *Gender differences in economic support and well-being of older Asians* (Report No. 03–540). Population Studies Center at the Institute for Social Research, University of Michigan.

Ogle, C. M. et al. (2013). The frequency and impact of exposure to potentially traumatic events over the life course. *Clinical Psychological Science, 1,* 426–434.

Okimoto, T. G. & Heilman, M. E. (2012). The "bad parent" assumption: How gender stereotypes affect reactions to working mothers. *Journal of Social Issues, 58,* 704–724.

Okun, R. A. (2014). *Voice male: The untold story of the nonfeminist men's movement.* Northampton, MA: Interlink.

Olen, H. (2014, March 25). Discriminate against the old? Even the old do it. *New York Times.* p. F4.

Oliver, H. (2014). It's all about shopping: The role of consumption in the feminization of journalism. In M. Evans et al. (Eds.), *The Sage handbook of feminist theory* (pp. 251–266). Thousand Oaks, CA: Sage.

Oliver, K. (2016). *Hunting girls: Sexual violence from the Hunger Games to campus rape.* New York: Columbia University Press.

Olkin, R. (2008). Women with disabilities. In J. C. Chrisler, C. Golden, & P. D. Rozee (Eds.), *Lectures on the psychology of women* (pp. 190–203). New York: McGraw-Hill.

Olkin, R. (2010). The three Rs of supervising graduate psychology students with disabilities: Reading, writing, and reasonable accommodations. *Women & Therapy, 33,* 73–84.

Olkin, R. (2013). Women's responses to disability. In M. V. Spiers et al. (Eds.), *Women's health psychology* (pp. 467–490). Hoboken, NJ: Wiley.

Olson, E. (2006, June 1). Widowers are eager for another whirl. *New York Times,* p. E2.

Olson, E. (2014). Differential trajectories of well-being in older adult women: The role of optimism. *The International Association of Applied Psychology, 6,* 362–380.

Olson, E. (2016, February 22). A lingerie brand offers real women as (role) models. *New York Times,* p. B3.

Olson, J. E. et al. (2007). Beliefs in equality for women and men as related to economic factors in Central and Eastern Europe and the United States. *Sex Roles, 56,* 297–308.

Olson, K. R. et al. (2016). Mental health of transgender children who are supported in their identities. *Pediatrics, 137,* e20153223.

Olthoff, J. K. (2013). Geropsychology, social class, and counselling. In W. M. Liu (Ed.), *The Oxford handbook of social class in counseling* (pp. 339–355). New York: Oxford University Press.

O'Neill, T. (2015, Spring) Wage gap denial: We can't believe we're still processing this sh*t!. *Ms.Magazine,* 40–42.

Ong, A. D. (2010). Pathways linking positive emotion and health in later life. *Current Directions in Psychological Science, 19,* 358–362.

Oram, S. et al. (2016). Human trafficking and health: A survey of male and female survivors in England. *AJPH,106,* 1073–1078.

Orel, N. A. (2014). *Investigating the needs and concerns of lesbian, gay, bisexual, and transgender older adults: The use of qualitative and quantitative methodology. Journal of Homosexuality, 61,* 53–78.

Orel, N. A. & Fruehauf, C. A. (2015). The intersection of culture, family, and individual aspects: A guiding model for LGBT older adults. In N. A. Orel & C. A. Fruehauf (Eds.), *The lives of LGBT older adults: Understanding challenges and resilience* (pp. 3–24). Washington, DC: American Psychological Association.

O'Reilly, A. (2014). *Mother, mothering, and motherhood across cultural differences: A reader.* Bradford, OH: Demeter Press.

Orenstein, P. (2007, July 15). Your gamete, myself. *New York Times,* pp. 34–41, 58, 63.

Orenstein, P. (2011). *Cinderella ate my daughter: Dispatches from the front lines of the new girlie-girl culture.* New York: Harper Collins.

Oringanje, C., Meremikwu, M. M., Eko, H., Esu, E., Meremikwu, A., & Ehiri, J. E. (2009). Interventions for preventing unintended pregnancies among adolescents. *Cochrane Database of Systematic Reviews.* (Art No. CD005215).

Orman, S. (2010). *Women and money: Owning the power to control your destiny.* New York: Spiegel & Grau.

Orth, U. & Robins, R. W. (2014). The development of self-esteem. *Current Directions in Psychological Science, 23,* 381–387.

Orth, U., Trzesniewski, K. H., & Robins, R. W. (2010). Self-esteem development from young adulthood to old age: A cohort-sequential longitudinal study. *Journal of Personality and Social Psychology, 98,* 645–658.

Orth-Gomér, K. (2009). Are social relations less health protective in women than in men? Social relations, gender, and cardiovascular health. *Journal of Social and Personal Relationships, 26,* 63–71.

Osborne, J. M. (2008). *The career development of Black female chief nurse executives.* FIU electronic theses and dissertations paper 208, Florida International University, Miami, FL.

Oshima, M. et al. (2014). The influence of childhood sexual abuse on adolescent outcomes: The roles of gender, poverty, and revictimization. *Journal of Child Sexual Abuse, 23,* 367–386.

Ostrov, J. M. & Godleski, S. A. (2010). Toward an integrated gender-linked model of aggression subtypes in early and middle childhood. *Psychological Review, 117,* 233–242.

Oswald, D. L. & Harvey, R. D. (2003). A Q-methodological study of women's subjective perspectives on mathematics. *Sex Roles, 49,* 133–142.

Otis, M. D., Riggle, E. D. B., & Rostosky, S. S. (2006). Impact of mental health on perceptions of relationship satisfaction and quality among female same-sex couples. *Journal of Lesbian Studies, 10,* 267–283.

Ovarian Cancer National Alliance. (2010). *About ovarian cancer.* Washington, DC: Author. Retrieved from ovariancancer.org/about-ovarian-cancer/3

Owen, J.J. et al. (2010). "Hooking up" among college students:Demographic and psychosocial correlates. *Archives of Sexual Behavior, 39,* 655–663.

Owen, R. & Spencer, R. M. C. (2013). Body ideals in women after viewing images of typical and healthy-weight models. *Body Image, 10,* 489–494.

Owens, J. G. (2016). Why definitions matter: Stalking victimization in the United States. *Journal of Interpersonal Violence, 31,* 2196–2226.

OWL. (2007). *Give 'em health revisited: Medicare for all.* Washington, DC: Author.

Oyserman, D. et al. (2014). Identity-based motivation: Implications for health and health disparities. *Journal of Social Issues, 70,* 206–225.

Ozcan, B. & Breen, R. (2012). Marital instability and female labor supply. *Annual Review of Sociology, 38,* 463–481.

Pacilli, M. et al. (2016). Exposure to sexualized advertisements disrupts children's math performance by reducing working memory. *Sex Roles, 74,* 389–398.

Padawer, R. (2016, July 3). Too fast to be female. *New York Times Magazine,* pp. 32–39, 49.

Padgett, D. (1999). Aging minority women. In L. A. Peplau, S. C. DeBro., R. C. Veniegas, & P. L. Taylor (Eds.), *Gender, culture and ethnicity: Current research about women and men* (pp. 173–181). Mountain View, CA: Mayfield.

Padilla, J. R. & Bacon, D. (2016, January 19). Protect female farmworkers. *New York Times,* A23.

Paek, H.-J., Nelson, M. R., & Vilela, A. M. (2011). Examination of gender-role portrayals in television adversiting across seven countries. *Sex Roles, 64,* 192–207.

Paggi, M. E. et al. (2016). The importance of leisure activities in the relationship between physical health and well-being in a lifespan sample. *Gerontology,* doi:10.1159/000444415.

Pahlke E. et al. (2014). Reasoning about single-sex schooling for girls among students, parents, and teachers. *Sex Roles, 71,* 261–271.

Pahlke, E. & Hyde, J. S. (2016). The debate over single-sex schooling. *Child Development Perspectives, 10,* 81–86.

Pahor, M. et al. (2014). Effect of structured physical activity on prevention of major mobility disability in older adults. *Journal of the American Medical Association, 311,* 2387–2396.

Paik, A. et al. (2016). Broken promises: Abstinence pledging and sexual and reproductive health. *Journal of Marriage and Family, 78,* 546–561.

Palley, H. (2014). *The politics of women's health care in the United States.* New York: Palgrave Macmillan.

Paludi, M. A. (2008a). Introduction. In M. A. Paludi (Ed.), *The psychology of women at work: Challenges and solutions for our female workforce* (Vol. 1, pp. xi–xviii). Westport, CT: Praeger.

Paludi, M. A. (2008b). *Understanding and preventing campus violence.* Westport, CT: Praeger.

Paludi, M. A. (2015). Sexual harassment of teenage girls. In M. A. Paludi et al. (Eds.) *Sexual harassment in education and work settings: Current research and best practices for prevention* (pp. 187–210). Santa Barbara, CA: ABC-CLIO.

Paludi, M. A. (2016). *Campus action against sexual assault: Needs, policies, procedures, and training programs.* New York: Praeger.

Paludi, M. A., Denmark, F. L., & DeFour, D. C. (2008). The psychology of women course as a "catalyst for change" for campus violence. In M. A. Paludi (Ed.), *Understanding and preventing campus violence* (pp. 103–111). Westport, CT: Praeger.

Paludi, M., Martin, J., Stern, T., & DeFour, D. C. (2010). Promises and pitfalls of mentoring women in business and academia. In C. A. Rayburn, F. L. Denmark, M. E. Reuder, & A. M. Austria (Eds.), *A handbook for women mentors: Transcending barriers of stereotype, race, and ethnicity* (pp. 79–108). Santa Barbara, CA: Praeger.

Paludi, M. A., Martin, J. L., Paludi, J. C., Boggess, S. M., Hicks, K., & Speach, L. (2010). Pay equity as justice: United States and international perspectives. In M. A. Paludi (Ed.), *Feminism and women's rights worldwide: Feminism as human rights* (Vol. 2, pp. 147–176). Santa Barbara, CA: Praeger.

Pan, G. (2008, Fall/Winter). The Internet and women: Shaping a new society. *AAUW Outlook,* 7–9.

Panetta Institute for Public Policy (2012). *2012 survey of America's college students. Washinton, DC: author*

Pankake, A. (2011). Women's colleges. In M. Z. Stange, C. K. Oyster, & J. E. Sloan (Eds.), *Encyclopedia of women in today's world* (Vol. 4, pp. 1566–1568). Newberry Park, CA: Sage.

Pankalainen, M. et al. (2016). Pessimism and risk of death from coronary heart disease amomg middle-aged and older Finns: An 11-year follow-up study. *BMC Public Health, 16,* 1124–1130.

Paoletti, J. B. (2013). *Pink and blue: Telling the boys from the girls in America.* Bloomington, IN: Indiana University Press.

Pappano, L. (2015, April 12). First Gens Unite. *New York Times,* pp. 18–21.

Paradies, Y. et al. (2014). A systematic review of the extent and measurement of healthcare provider racism. *Journal of General International Medicine, 29,* 364–387.

Parekh, A. K. et al. (2013). Aspirin in the secondary prevention of cardiovascular disease. *New England Journal of Medicine, 368,* 204–205.

Parisi, M. et al. (2017). Counseling women with eating disorders. In M. Kopala & M. Keitel (Eds.), *Handbook of counseling women* (2nd ed.). Thousand Oaks, CA: Sage.

Park, M. & Unützer, J. (2011). Geriatric depression in primary care. Psychiatric Clinic of North America, 34,469–487.

Parke, R. D. (2013). Gender differences and similarities in parental behavior. In W. B. Wilcox & K. K. Kline (Eds.), *Gender and parenthood: Biological and social scientific perspectives* (pp. 120–163). New York: Columbia University Press.

Parke, R. D. & Buriel, R. (2006). Socialization in the family: Ethnic and ecological perspectives. In W. Damon, R. M. Lerner (Series Eds.), & N. Eisenberg (Vol. Ed.), *Handbook of child psychology: Vol. 3. Social, emotional, and personality development* (6th ed., pp. 429–504). Hoboken, NJ: Wiley.

Parker, K. & Wang, W. (2013). *Modern parenthood: Roles of moms and dads converge as they balance work and family.* Washington, DC: Pew Research Center.

Parker, K. et al. (2014). Record share of Americans have never married; As values, economics and gender patterns change. Washington, DC: *Pew Research Center.*

Parker, W. et al. (2013). Long-term mortality associated with oophorectomy versus ovarian conservation in nurses' health study. *Obstetrics & Gynecology, 121,* 709–716.

Parker-Pope, T. (2008, June 23). Many normal-weight teens feel fat. *New York Times.* Retrieved from www.nytimes.com

Parker-Pope, T. (2011, March 28). An older generation falls prey to eating disorders. *New York Times,* p. D6.

Parker-Pope, T. (2008, October 27), Love, sex, and the changing landscape of infidelity. *New York Times,* p,D1

Parker-Pope, T. (2015, October 30). Breast cancer is on the rise among blacks: More deadly, and now parity with whites. *New York Times,* p. A3.

Parker-Pope, T. (2016, July 26). The unlucky super flashers. *New York Times,* p. D4.

Parkes, A., Henderson, M., Wight, D., & Nixon, C. (2011). Is parenting associated with teenagers' early sexual risk-taking, autonomy and relationship with sex partners? *Perspectives on Sexual and Reproductive Health, 43,* 30–40.

Parks, A. L. & Redberg, R. F. (2016). Women in medicine and patient outcomes: Equal rights for better work? *JAMA Internal Medicine* doi: 10.1001/jamainternmed.2016.7883

Parmley, M. & Cunningham, J. G. (2008). Children's gender-emotion stereotypes in the relationship of anger to sadness and fear. *Sex Roles, 58,* 358–370.

Pastrana, A. J. (2015). It takes a family: An examination of outness among black LGBT people in the United States. *Journal of Family Issues, 37,* 765–788.

Patterson, C. J. (2006). Children of lesbian and gay parents. *Current Directions in Psychological Science, 15,* 241–244.

Patterson, C. J. et al. (2014). Socialization in the context of family diversity. In J. D. Grusec & P. D. Hastings (Eds.) Handbook of socialization: Theory and research (2nd ed., pp. 202–227). New York: Guilford.

Paul, L. A. et al. (2013). College women's experiences with rape disclosure: A national study. *Violence Against Women, 19,* 486–502.

Pauletti, R. E. et al. (2016). Psychological androgyny and children's mental health. *Sex Roles,* doi: 10.1007/s11199-016-0627-9.

Paustian-Underdahl, S.C. et al. (2014). Gender and perceptions of leadership effectiveness: A meta-analysis of contextual moderators. *Journal of Applied Psychology, 99,* 1129–1145.

Payne, B.K. (2011). *Crime and elder abuse: An integrated perspective* (3rd ed.). Springfield, IL: Charles C. Thomas.

Paynter, A. & Leaper, C. (2016). Heterosexual dating double standards in undergraduate women and men. *Sex Roles, 75*, 393–406.

Payton, J. (2014). "Honor," collectivity, and agnation: Emerging risk factors in "honor"—based violence. *Journal of Interpersonal Violence, 29*, 2863–2883.

Pazol, K. et al. (2015a). Abortion surveillance—United States, 2012. *Morbidity and Mortality Weekly Report, 60*(SS10), 1–39.

Pazol, K. et al. (2015 b). Sporadic contraceptive use and nonuse: Age-specific prevalence and associated factors. *American Journal of Obstetrics and Gynecology, 212*, 324, e1–8.

Peacock, P. (1998). Marital rape. In R. K. Bergen (Ed.), *Issues in intimate violence* (pp. 225–235). Thousand Oaks, CA: Sage.

Pear, R. et al. (2015, June 26). If law is "here to stay", so are doubts about it. *New York Times*, pp. A1, A15.

Pearce, G. et al. (2014). Body image during the menopausal transition: A systematic scoping review. *Health Psychology Review, 8*, 473–489.

Pearce, S. C., Clifford, E. J., & Tandon, T. (2011). *Immigration and women: Understanding the American experience*. New York: New York University Press.

Pearsall, B. (2015, Fall). Engineering and computing's gender crisis. *AAUW Outlook*, 6–9.

Pearson, C. (2013, Spring). We've got you covered: 10 things women need to know about health reform. *Ms Magazine*, 39–42.

Peart, K. N. (2014). Science of baby-making still a mystery for many women. *Fertility & Sterility*, doi: 10.1016/j.fertnstert.2013.11.033.

Peasant, C. et al. (2015). Condom negotiation: Findings and future directions. *The Journal of Sex Research, 52*, 470–483.

Pease, B. (2016). Engaging in feminist social work: Theory, politics, and practice. In S. Wendt & N. Moulding (Eds.), *Contemporary feminisms in social work practice* (pp. 287–302). New York: Routledge.

Pebdani, R. et al. (2014). Personal experiences of pregnancy and fertility in individuals with spinal cord injury. *Sexuality & Disability. 32*, 65–74.

Pedulla, D. S. & Thebaud, S. (2015). Can we finish the revolution? Gender, work-family ideals, and institutional constraint. *American Sociological Review, 80*, 116–139.

Peeters, M. et al. (2013). *An introduction to contemporary work psychology*. Malden, MA: Wiley.

Pellegrini, A. D. (2001). A longitudinal study of heterosexual relationships, aggression, and sexual harassment during the transition from primary school through middle school. *Applied Developmental Psychology, 22*, 119–133.

Pennington, B. (2016, July 20). "Grandma": Little League thief. New York Times. p. B8.

Peplau, L. A. (1998). Lesbian and gay relationships. In D. L. Anselmi & A. L. Law (Eds.), *Questions of gender: Perspectives & paradoxes* (pp. 505–519). Boston: McGraw-Hill.

Peplau, L. A. (2002, August). *Venus and Mars in the laboratory: Current research on gender and sexuality*. Paper presented at the meeting of the American Psychological Association, Chicago, IL.

Peplau, L. A. & Fingerhut, A. W. (2004). The paradox of the lesbian worker. *Journal of Social Issues, 60*, 719–735.

Perales, F. et al. (2015). Gender, justice, and work: A distributive approach to perceptions of housework fairness. *Social Science Research, 51*, 51–63.

Percheski, C. (2008). Opting out? Cohort differences in professional women's employment rates from 1960–2005. *American Sociological Review, 73*, 497–517.

Pérez-Peña, R. (2015, September 22). 1 in 4 women experience sex assult on campus. *New York Times*, pp. A16.

Pergament, D. (2012, June 17). The midwife as status symbol. *New York Times*, p. ST12.

Pergament, D. (2013). *The allure of aging survey*. Retrieved January 13, 2015, from allure.com

Perilloux, C. & Kurzban, R. (2015). Do men overperceive women's sexual interest. *Psychological Science, 26*, 70–77.

Perilloux, C. et al. (2012). The misperception of sexual interest. *Psychological Science, 23*, 146–151.

Perloff, R. M. (2014). Social media effects on young women's body image concerns: Theoretical perspectives and an agenda for research. *Sex Roles, 71*, 363–377.

Perou, R. et al. (2013). Mental health surveillance among children: United States, 2005–2011. *Morbidity and Mortality Weekly Reports, 62* (02), 1–35.

Perrig-Chiello, P. et al. (2015). Patterns of psychological adaptation to divorce after a long-term marriage. *Journal of Social Personal Relationships, 32*, 386–405.

Perrone, K. M., Wright, S. L., & Jackson, Z. V. (2009). Traditional and nontraditional gender roles and work-family interface for men and women. *Journal of Career Development, 36*, 8–24.

Perry, J. & Vance, K. S. (2010). Possible selves among urban youths of color: An exploration of peer beliefs and gender differences. *Career Development Quarterly, 58*, 257–269.

Perry-Jenkins, F., Goldberg, A. E., Pierce, C. P., & Sayer, A. G. (2007). Shift work, role overload, and the transition to parenthood. *Journal of Marriage and Family, 69*, 123–138.

Perry-Jenkins, M. (2012). The changes to and consequences of "opting out" for low-wage new mothers. In B. D. Jones (Ed.), *Women who opt out: The debate over being mothers* (pp. 103–118). New York: New York University Press.

Perry-Jenkins, M. & Claxton, A. (2009). Feminist visions for rethinking work and family connections. In S. Lloyd, A. Few, & K. Allen (Eds.), *Handbook of family feminist studies* (pp. 121–133). Thousand Oaks, CA: Sage.

Perry-Jenkins, M., Seery, B., & Crouter, A. C. (1992). Linkages between women's provider-role attitudes, psychological well-being, and family relationships. *Psychology of Women Quarterly, 16*, 311–329.

Perry-Jenkins, M. et al. (2013). Family work through time and space: An ecological perspective. *Journal of Family Theory & Review, 5*, 105–123.

PerryUndem (2017). *The state of the union on gender equality, sexism. and women's rights*. Wahington, DC: Author.

Peskin, M. F. et al. (2014). Effects of the it's your game… Keep it real program on dating violence in ethnic-minority middle school youths: A group randomized trial. *AJPH*,104, 1471–1476.

Peters, A. W. (2015). *Responding to human trafficking: Sex, gender, and culture in the law*. Philadelphia: University of Pennsylvania Press.

Peters, R. D. et al. (2010). The better beginnings, better futures project: Findings from grade 3 to grade 9. *Monographs of the Society for Research in Child Development, 75*(3, Serial No. 297).

Peters, W. & Gray, J.S. (2014). Indigenous women and wisdom: An eternal chain of being. In T, Bryant-Davis et al. (Eds.). *Religion and spirituality for diverse women: Foundations of strength and resilience* (pp. 19–36). Santa Barbara, CA: ABC-CLIO.

Petersen, J. L. & Hyde, J. S. (2010). A meta-analytic review of research on gender differences in sexuality, 1993–2007. *Psychological Bulletin, 136*, 21–38.

Petersen, J. L. & Hyde, J. S. (2013). Peer sexual harassment and disordered eating in early adolescence. *Developmental Psychology, 49*, 184–195.

Petersen J. L. & Hyde, J. (2014). Gender-related academic and occupational interests and goals. In L. S. Liben & R. S. Bigler (Eds.), *The role of gender in educational contexts and outcomes* (pp. 43–76). Amsterdam: Elsevier.

Petersen, K. E. N. et al. (2015). The combined impact of adherence to five lifestyle factors on all-cause, cancer and cardiovascular mortality: A prospective cohort study among Danish men and women. *British Journal of Nutrition, 113*, 849–858.

Peterson, G. W. (2016). Conceptualizing parental stress with family stress theory. In C. A. Price Askeland & K. R. Bush (Eds.), *Families & change: Coping with stressful events and transitions* (pp. 53–78). Thousand Oaks, CA: Sage.

Peterson, H. & Engwall, K. (2013). Silent bodies: Childfree women's gendered and embodied experiences. *European Journal of Women's Studies, 20*, 376–389.

Pew Charitable Trusts. (2012). *Ups and downs: American's prospects for recovery after an Income loss*. New York: Author.

Pew Research Center. (2010). *The return of the multi-generational family*. Washington, DC: Author.

Pew Research Center. (2013a). *On pay gap, millennial women near parity—for now*. Washington, DC: Author.

Pew Research Center. (2013b). *Roe v. Wade at 40: Most oppose overturning abortion decision*. Washington, DC: Author.

Pew Research Center. (2013c). *A survey of LGBT Americans: Attitudes, experiences, and values in changing times.* Washington, DC: Author.

Pew Research Center. (2014). *Millennials in adulthood: Detached from institutions, networked with friends.* Washington, DC: Author.

Pew Research Center. (2015a). *Childlessness falls, family size grows among highly educated women.* Washington, DC: Author.

Pew Research Center. (2015b). *Parenting in America: Outlook, worries, aspirations are strongly linked to financial situation.* Washington, DC: Author.

Pew Research Center. (2015c). *Raising kids and running a household: How working parents share the load.* Washington, DC: Author.

Pew Research Center. (2016a). *Changing attitudes on gay marriage.* Washington, DC: Author.

Pew Research Center. (2016b). *Why is the teen birth rate falling?* Washington, DC: Author.

Pfaff, L. A. et al. (2013). Perceptions of women and men leaders following 360-degree feedback evaluations. *Performance Improvement Quarterly, 26,* 35–56.

Phelan, A. (Ed.). (2013). *International perspectives on elder abuse.* New York: Routledge.

Phillips, D. A. (2015). *"Facts, fantasies and the future of child care" revisited.* Retrieved March 2, 2015, from theguardian.com/observer

Phipps, A. (2014). *The policies of the body: Gender in a neoliberal and neoconservative age.* Cambridge: Polity Press.

Physicians Committee for Responsible Medicine. (2007). *Using foods against menstrual pain.* Washington, DC: Author.

Piatek-Jimenez, K et al. (2014). Equity in mathematics textbooks: A new look at an old issue. *Journal of Women and Minorities in Science and Engineering, 20,* 55–74.

Picho, K. et al. (2013). Exploring the moderating role of context on the mathematics performance of females under stereotype threat: A meta-analysis. *Journal of Social Psychology, 153,* 299–33.

Pickett, K. E. & Wilkinson, R. G. (2015). Income inequality and health: A causal review. *Social Science & Medicine, 28,* 316–326.

Pieper, L. (2016). *Sex testing: Gender policing in women's sports.* Urbana, IL: University of Illinois Press.

Piercy, K. W. (2014). Caring for older adults. In J. A. Arditti (Ed.), *Family problems: Stress, risk, and resilience* (pp. 150–166). West Sussex, UK: John Wiley.

Pike, K. M. & Dunne, P. E. (2015). The rise of eating disorders in Asia: A review. *Journal of Eating Disorders, 3,* doi:10.1186/s40337-015-00702.

Pillemer, K. et al. (2015). Elder abuse: Global situation, risk factors, and prevention strategies. *The Gerontologist, 56,* S194–S205.

Pine, D. S. & Fox, N. A. (2015). Childhood antecedents and risk for adult mental disorders. *Annual Review of Psychology,* 1–16.

Pingault, J. B. et al. (2015). Early non-parental care and social behavior in elementary school: Support for a social group adaptation. *Child Development, 8,* 1469–1488.

Pinquart, M. & Silbereisen, R. K. (2010). European Union. In M. H. Bornstein (Ed.), *Handbook of cultural developmental science* (pp. 341–358). New York: Psychology Press.

Pinsof, D. & Haselton, M. (2016). The political divide over same-sex marriage: Mating strategies in conflict? *Psychological Science, 37,* 435–442.

Piotrowska, P. J. et al. (2015). Socioeconomic status and antisocial behavior among children and adolescents: A systematic review and meta-analysis. *Clinical Psychology Review, 35,* 47–55.

Pittman, L. (2014). Doing what's right for the baby: Parental responses and custodial grandmothers' institutional decision making. *Women, Gender, and Families of Color, 2,* 32–56.

Plank-Bazinet, J. L. et al. (2016). A report of the women's health congress workshop on the health of women of color: A critical intersection at the corner of sex/gender and race/ethnicity. *Journal of Women's Health, 25,* 4–10.

Planty, M. et al. (2013). *Female victims of sexual violence, 1994–2010.* Washington, DC: U.S. Department of Justice.

Plec, E. (2011). Mankiller, Wilma. In M. Z. Stange, C. K. Oyster, & J. E. Sloan (Eds.), *Encyclopedia of women in today's world* (Vol. 2, pp. 893–894). Newberry Park, CA: Sage.

Ploubidis, G. B. et al. (2015). Life-course partnership status and biomarkers in midlife: Evidence from the 1958 British Cohort. *American Journal of Public Health, 105,* 1–3.

Plummer, S.-B. & Findley, P. A. (2012). Women with disabilities' experience with physical and sexual abuse: A review of the literature and implications for the field. *Trauma, Violence, & Abuse, 13,* 15–29.

Poleshuck, E. L. & Woods, J. (2014). Psychologists partnering with obstetricians and gynecologists: Meeting the need for patient-centered models of women's health care delivery. *American Psychologist, 69,* 344–354.

Politi, M. C. et al. (2016). Addressing challenges to implementation of the contraceptive coverage guarantee of the Affordable Care Act. *Journal of the American Medical Association, 315,* 653–654.

Polk, S. (2016, July 10). How Wall Street bro talk keeps women down. *New York Times,* p. SR2.

Pollack, A. (2014, August 31). New novartis drug effective in treating heart failure. *New York Times.* p. 4.

Pollack, A. (2015, June 1). The FDA is pressed on "women's Viagra". *New York Times,* pp. B1–2.

Pollack, E. (2015). *The only women in the room: Why science is still a boys' club.* Boston, MA: Beacon Press.

Pollitt, K. (2014). *PRO: Reclaiming abortion rights.* New York: Picador.

Pollock, R. S. et al. (2015). An investigation into the relationship between age and physiological function in highly active older adults. *Journal of Physiology, 593,* 657–680.

Poltera, J. (2011). Abortion, ethical issues of. In M. Z. Stange, C. K. Oyster, & J. E. Sloan (Eds.), *Encyclopedia of women in today's world* (Vol. 1, pp. 6–9). Newberry Park, CA: Sage.

Pomerleau, A., Bolduc, D., Malcuit, G., & Cossette, L. (1990). Pink or blue: Environmental gender stereotypes in the first two years of life. *Sex Roles, 22,* 359–367.

Poortman, A.-R. & Van der Lippe, T. (2009). Attitudes toward housework and child care and the gendered division of labor. *Journal of Marriage and Family, 71,* 526–541.

Popenoe, D. & Whitehead, B. D. (1999). *The state of our unions: The social health of marriage in America.* New Brunswick, NJ: National Marriage Project at Rutgers University.

Population Reference Bureau. (2014). *Female genital mutilation/cutting: Data and trends update 2014.* Retrieved 2014, from HYPERLINK "http://www.pbr.org" \h www.pbr.org

Port, E. (2015). *The new generation breast cancer book.* New York: Penguin Random House.

Porter, E. (2014, August 6). Reducing carbon by curbing population. *New York Times.* pp. B1, B5.

Porter, J. (2015, December 29). Lara Croft has company. *New York Times,* pp. C1, C5.

Portnoy, J. et al. (2014). Biological perspectives on sex differences in crime and antisocial behaviors in girls. In R. Gartner & B. McCarthy (Eds.), *The Oxford handbook of gender, sex, and crime* (pp. 260–285). New York: Oxford University Press.

Potarca, G. et al. (2015). Relationship preferences among gay and lesbian online daters: Individual and contextual influences. *Journal of Marriage and Family, 77,* 523–541.

Poteat, V. P. et al. (2014). Factors affecting academic achievement among sexual minority and gender-variant youth. In L. S. Liben & R. S. Bigler (Eds.) *The role of gender in educational contexts and outcomes* (pp. 261–300). Amsterdam: Elsevier.

Poteat, V. P. et al. (2015). Contextualizing gay-straight alliances: Student, Advisor, and structural factors related to positive youth development among members. *Child Development, 86,* 176–193.

Potera, C. (2013). Evidence supports midwife-led care models. *American Journal of Nursing, 113,* 11–15.

Poterba, J. (2014). Richard T. Ely Lecture: Retirement security in an aging population. *American Economic Review: Papers & Proceedings, 104,* 1–30.

Potter, D. (2010). Psychosocial well-being and the relationship between divorce and childrens' academic achievement. *Journal of Marriage and Family, 72,* 933–946.

Potter, J., Bouyer, J., Trussell, J., & Moreau, C. (2009). Premenstrual syndrome prevalence and fluctuation over time: Results from a French population-based survey. *Journal of Women's Health, 18,* 31–39.

Poulin, F. & Chan, A. (2010). Friendship stability and change in childhood and adolescence [Advance online publication]. *Developmental Review.*

Powell, A. & Sang, K. JC. (2015). Everyday experiences of sexism in male-dominated professions: A Bourdieusian perspective. *Sociology, 49*, 919–936.

Powell, B., Bolzendahl, C., Geist, C., & Steelman, L. C. (2010). *Counted out: Same-sex relations and Americans' definitions of family*. New York: Russell Sage.

Powell, G. (2014). Sex, gender, and leadership: What do four avenues of research tell us. In S. Kumra et al. (Eds.), *The Oxford handbook of gender in organizations* (pp. 224–268). New York: Oxford University Press.

Powell, G. N. & Greenhaus, J. H. (2010). Sex, gender, and decisions at the family → work interface. *Journal of Management, 36*, 1011–1039.

Powers, S. M. et al. (2013). Trajectories of social support and well-being across the first two years of widowhood. *Death Studies, 38*, 499–509.

Prakash, R. S. et al. (2015). Physical activity and cognitive vitality. *Annual Review of Psychology, 66*, 769–797.

Pratt, L. A. et al. (2015). *Depression in the U.S. household population, 2009–2012*. National Center for Health Statistics. Data Brief, No. 172.

Pratt, L. A. & Brody, D. J. (2014). *Depression in the U,S. household population, 2009–2012*. NCHS Data Brief No. 172. Hyattsville, MD: National Center for Health Statistics,

Pratto, F. & Walker, A. (2004). The bases of gendered power. In A. H. Eagly, A. E. Beall, & R. J. Sternberg (Eds.), *The psychology of gender* (pp. 242–268). New York: Guilford.

Prentice, K. (2008, February). When a caregiver needs care. *Heart Insight*, pp. 17–19.

Prescott, H. M. & Kline, W. (2013). Historical roots of women's health care. In M. V. Spier et al. (Eds.), *Women's health psychology* (pp. 3–24). Hoboken, NJ: Wiley.

Press, J., Fagan, J., & Bernd, E. (2006). Child care, work, and depressive symptoms among low-income mothers. *Journal of Family Issues, 27*, 609–632.

Price, C. A. & Nesteruk, O. (2015). What to expect when you retire: By women, for women. *Marriage and Family Review, 51*, 418–440.

Priebe, G. & Svedin, C. G. (2013). Operationalization of three dimensions of sexual orientation in a national survey of late adolescents. *Journal of Sex Research, 50*, 727–738.

Priess, H. A. & Lindberg, S. M. (2011). Gender intensification. In R. Levesque (Ed.), *Encyclopedia of adolescence* (pp. 1135–1142). New York: Springer.

Prince, J. P. (2012). Career development of lesbian, gay, bisexual, and transgender individuals. In S. D. Brown & R. W. Lent (Eds.) *Career development and counseling: Putting research and theory to work* (pp. 275–298). Hoboken, NJ: Wiley.

Pritchard, M. & Cramblitt, B. (2014). Media influence on drive for thinness and drive for muscularity. *Sex Roles, 71*, 208–218.

Priya, N. (2013). *Masculinity, son preference, and intimate partner violence*. Washington, DC: International Center for Research on Women.

Priya, N. et al. (2014). *Study on masculinity, intimate power violence and son preference in India*. New Delhi: International Center for Research on Women.

Procsal, A. D. et al. (2015). Cross-sex friendship and happiness. In M. Demir (Ed.), *Friendship and happiness: Across the lifespan and culture* (pp. 171–185). Dordrecht: Springer.

Pru, J. K. (2014). Genetic predisposition to ovotoxic effects of smoking may hasten time to menopause. *Menopause, 21*, 685–686.

Pruchno, R. A. (1999). Raising grandchildren: The experiences of Black and White grandmothers. *Gerontologist, 39*, 209–221.

Pruthi, S. (2010). *Women's health encyclopedia: An integrated approach to wellness for every season of a woman's life*. London, UK: Marshall Editions Ltd.

Przedworski, J. M. et al. (2014). Health and health risks among sexuall minority women: An examination of 3 subgroups. *AJPH, 104*, 1045–1047.

Psaros, C. et al. (2014). Reflections on living with HIV over time: Exploring the perspective of HIV-infected women over 50. *Aging & Mental Health, 19*, 1–3.

Punnett, B. J. (2016). Women in the workforce: A global snapshot. In M. L. Connerly & J. Wu (Eds.), *Handbook on well-being of working women* (pp. 579–586). Dordrecht, Netherlands: Springer.

Puryear, L. J. (2014). Postpartum adjustment: What is normal and what is not. In D. Barnes (Ed.) *Women's reproductive mental health across the lifespan* (pp. 109–122). New York: Springer.

Puts, D. A., McDaniel, M. A., Jordan, C. L., & Breedlove, S. M. (2008). Spatial ability and prenatal adrogens: Meta-analyses of congenital adrenal hyperplasia and digit ratio (2D:4D) studies. *Archives of Sexual Behavior, 37*, 100–111.

Quick, V. et al. (2013). Prospective predictors of body dissatisfaction in young adults: 10-year longitudinal findings. *Emerging Adulthood, 1*, 271–282.

QuickStats: Percentage of adults aged ≥25 years who reported regular leisure-time physical activity, by education level—National Health Interview Survey, United States, 1997 and 2007. (2009, March 20). *Morbidity and Mortality Weekly Report, 58*, 261.

QuickStats: Percentage of adults aged 25–44 years reporting fair or poor health, by sex—National Health Interview Survey, United States, 1999–2009. (2011, February 25). *Morbidity and Mortality Weekly Report, 60*, 216.

QuickStats: Percentage of children and adolescents aged 4–17 years with serious emotional or behavioral difficulties, by poverty status and sex—National Health Interview Survey, 2011–2014. (2015, November 27). *Morbidity and Mortality Weekly Report. 64*, 1303.

Quinlan, K., Bowleg, L., & Ritz, S. F. (2008). Virtually invisible women: Women with disabilities in mainstream psychological theory and research. *Review of Disability Studies: An International Journal, 4*, 4–17.

Quinley, K. E. et al. (2014). Psychological coping in the immediate post-abortion period. *Journal of Women's Health, 23*, 44–50.

Rabin, R. C. (2013). The drug-dose gender gap. *NewYorkTimes.com*. pp. 1–9.

Rabin, R. C. (2014a, September 24). Health researchers will get $10.1 million to counter gender bias in studies. *New York Times*. p. A16.

Rabin, R. C. (2014b, May 15). Labs are told to start including a neglected variable: Females. *New York Times*, pp. A1, A20.

Rabin, R. C. (2016, April 26). A baffling trend in surgery. *New York Times*, p. D4.

Rabins, P. R. (2016). Women as caregivers. In D. J. Castle & K. M Abel (Eds.), *Comprehensive women's mental health* (pp. 28030). Cambridge UK: Cambridge University Press.

Radatz, D. L. & Wright, E. M. (2016). Integrating the principles of effective intervention into batterer intervention programming: The case for moving toward more evidence-based programming. *Trauma, Violence & Abuse, 17*, 72–87.

Radke, H. R. M. et al. (2016). Barriers to women engaging in collective action to overcome sexism. *American Psychologist, 71*, 863–874.

Raffaelli, M., & Ontai, L. L. (2004). Gender socialization in Latino/a families: Results from two retrospective studies. *Sex Roles, 50*, 287–299.

Rahilly, E. P. (2015). The gender binary meets the gender-variant child: Parents' negotiations with childhood gender variance. *Gender & Society, 29*, 338–361.

Raillant-Clark, W. (2013). *Female doctors are better than male doctors, but males are more productive*. Retrieved July 17, 2015, from the umontreal.ca/en/

Raj, A. & Boehmer, U. (2013). Girl child marriage and its association with national rates of HIV, maternal health, and infant mortality across 97 countries. *Violence Against Women, 19*, 536–551.

Raj, A., Gomez, C., & Silverman, J. G. (2008). Driven to a fiery death—the tragedy of self-immolation in Afghanistan. *New England Journal of Medicine, 358*, 2201–2203.

Raji, C. A. (2016). Longitudinal relationships between caloric expenditure and gray matter in cardiovascular health study. *Journal of Alzheimer's Disease, 52*, 719–729.

Ramachandran, H.J. et al. (2016). Awareness, knowledge and healthy lifestyle behaviors related to coronary heart disease among women: An integrative review. *Heart & Lung: The Journal of Acute and Critical Care, 45*, 173–185.

Ramisetty-Mikler, S., Caetano, R., & McGrath, C. (2007). Sexual aggression among White, Black, and Hispanic couples in the U.S.: Alcohol use, physical assault and psychological aggression as its correlates. *American Journal of Drug and Alcohol Abuse, 33*, 31–43.

Rann, L. et al. (2014). Youth risk behavior surveillance: United States, 2013. *Morbidity and Mortality Weekly Report, 63,* 5–43.

Rao, A.K. et al. (2014). Systematic review of the effects of exercise on the activities of daily living in people with Alzheimer's disease. *Journal of Occupational Therapy, 68,* 50–56.

Rapley, T. (2016). *5 salary negotiation tips for women.* GoodCall. Retrieved from goodcall.com/career/salary-negotiation-tips-women

Raque-Bogdan, T. L. et al. (2013). Career-related parent support and career barriers: An investigation of contextual variables. *The Career Development Quarterly. 61,* 339–353.

Rathus, S et al. (2013). *Human sexuality in a world of diversity* (9th ed.). Boston: Pearson.

Räty, H. & Kasanen, K. (2010). A seven-year follow-up study on parents' expectations of their children's further education. *Journal of Applied Social Psychology, 40,* 2711–2735.

Rauscher, G. H. et al. (2012). Disparities in screening mammography services by race/ethnicity and health insurance. *Journal of Women's Health, 21,* 154–160.

Rauscher, L. & Cooky, C. (2016). Ready for anything the world gives her?: A critical look at sports-based positive youth development for girls. *Sex Roles, 74,* 288–298.

Rawlins, W. K. (2004). Friendships in later life. In J. F. Nussbaum & J. Coupland (Eds.), *Handbook of communication and aging research* (2nd ed., pp. 273–304). Mahwah, NJ: Erlbaum.

Read, S. & Grundy, E. (2011). Fertility history and quality of life in older women and men. *Ageing & Society, 31,* 125–145.

Rebbek, T. R. et al. (2015). *Association of type and location of BRCA1 and BRCA2 mutations with risk of breast and ovarian cancer.* Retrieved April 7, 2015, from jamanetwork.com

Record, K. L. & Austin, B. (2015). "Paris thin": A call to regulate life-threatening starvation of runway models in the US fashion industry. *AJPH, 106,* 206–206.

Redford, L. et al. (2016). Implicit and explicit evaluations of feminist prototypes predict feminist identity and behavior. *Group Processes & Intergroup Relations, 19,* 1–16.

Redshaw, M. et al. (2013). From antenatal to postnatal depression: Associated factors and mitigating influences. *Journal of Women's Health, 22,* 518–525.

Regan, J.C. & Partridge, L. (2013). Gender and longevity: Why do men die earlier than women?: Comparative and experimental evidence. *Best Practice and Research Clinical Endocrinology & Metabolism, 27,* 467–479.

Regan, P. C. & Cachelin, F. M. (2006). Binge eating and purging in a multi-ethnic community sample. *International Journal of Eating Disorders, 39,* 523–526.

Regnerus, M. & Uecker, J. (2011). *Premarital sex in America: How young Americans meet, mate and think about marrying.* New York: Oxford University Press.

Rehel, E. M. (2014). When dad stays home too: Paternity leave, gender, and parenting. *Gender & Society, 28,* 110–132.

Rehm, C. D. et al. (2016). Dietary intake among US adults, 1999–2012. *Journal of the American MedicalAssociation, 315,* 2542–2553.

Reichert, F. F., Barros, A. J. D., Domingues, M. R., & Hallal, P. C. (2007). The role of perceived personal barriers to engagement in leisure-time physical activity. *American Journal of Public Health, 97,* 515–519.

Reichert, T. et al. (2012). How sex in advertising varies by product category: An analysis of three decades of visual sexual imagery in magazine advertising> *Journal of Current Issues & Research in Advertising, 33,* 1–19.

Reichert, T. & Carpenter, C. (2004). An update on sex in magazine advertising: 1983–2003. *Journalism and Mass Communication Quarterly, 81,* 823–837.

Reid, E. (2015). *Embracing, passing, revealing, and the ideal worker image: How people navigate expected and experienced professional identities.* Retrieved April 20, 2015, from pubsonline.informs.org/journal/orsc

Reid, E. & Ely, R. (2015, May 31). The problem with work is overwork. *New York Times,* p. BU4.

Reid, P. T. & Kelly, E. (1994). Research on women of color: From ignorance to awareness. *Psychology of Women Quarterly, 18,* 477–486.

Reid, P. T., Cooper, S. M., & Banks, K. H. (2008). Girls to women: Developmental theory, research, and issues. In F. L. Denmark & M. A. Paludi (Eds.), *Psychology of women: A handbook of issues and theories* (2nd ed., pp. 237–270). Westport, CT: Praeger.

Reid, R. L. & Magee, B. A. (2015). Confronting the challenges of the menopausal transition. *Women's Midlife Health, 1,* 1–9.

Reid, R. O., Friedberg, M. W., Adams, J. L., McGlynn, E. A., & Mehrotra, A. (2010). Associations between physician characteristics and quality of care. *Archives of Internal Medicine, 170,* 1442–1449.

Reilly,D. & Neumann, D. (2013). Gender role differences in spatial ability: A meta-analytic review. *Sex Roles, 68,* 521–535.

Reilly, E. E. et al. (2014). Gender-based differential item functioning in common measures of body dissatisfaction. *Body Image, 11,* 206–209.

Reina, A. S. et al. (2013). "He said they'd deport me:" Factors influencing domestic violence help-seeking practices among latina immigrants. *Journal of Interpersonal Violence, 29,* 593–615.

Reiner, W. G. & Gearhart, J. P. (2004). Discordant sexual identity in some genetic males with cloacal exstrophy assigned to female sex at birth. *New England Journal of Medicine, 350,* 333–341.

Reingle, J. M. et al. (2014). On the pervasiveness of event-specific alcohol use, general substance use, and mental health problems as risk factors for intimate partner violence. *Journal of Interpersonal Violence, 29,* 2951–2970.

Reingold, R. B. & Gostlin, L. O. (2016). Women's health and abortion rights: Whole Women's Health v Hellerstedt. *Journal of the American Medical Association,* doi:10.1001/jama.2016.11074.

Reinhard, S. C. et al. (2015). *Valuing the invaluable: 2015 update.* Washington, DC: AARP Public Policy Institute.

Reitsema, A. M. & Grietens, H. (2016). Is anybody listening? The dialogical process of child sexual abuse disclosure reviewed. *Trauma, Violence, and Abuse, 17,* 330–340.

Relyea, M. & Ullman, S. E. (2015). Unsupported or turned against: Understanding how types of negative social reactions to sexual assault relate to post-assault outcomes. *Psychology of Women Quarterly, 39,* 37–52.

Rennison, C. M. (2014, December 22). Privilege, among rape victims. *New York Times,* p. A25.

Report of the Attorney General's National Task Force for Children Exposed to Violence. (2012). Washington, DC: Attorney General's Office.

Reuben, E. et al. (2014). How stereotypes impair women's careers in science. *PNAS, 111,* 4403–4408.

Revisiting our roots. (2010, Winter). *Psychology of Black Women Newsletter, 4–5,* 8. Retrieved from issuu.com/psychology_of_black_women/docs/winter_2010

Reyes-Gibby, C. C. et al. (2012). Depressive symptoms and health-related quality of life in breast cancer survivors. *Journal of Women's Health, 21,* 311- 318.

Reynolds, A. L. & Singh, A. A. (2017). Counseling issues for lesbian, bisexual, transgender, and queer women. In M. Kopala & M. Keitel (Eds.), *Handbook of counseling women* (2nd. ed., pp. 275–289). Thousand Oaks, CA: Sage.

Reynolds, G. (2015, April 21). The right dose of exercise for a longer life. *New York Times* p.D6.

Rhode, D. L. (2016). *Women and leadership.* New York: University Press.

Rhode, D. L. et al. (2014). *What women want: An agenda for the women's movement.* New York: Oxford University Press.

Rhodes, J. E., Davis, A. A., Prescott, L. R., & Spencer, R. (2007). Caring connections: Mentoring relationships in the lives of urban girls. In B. J. R. Leadbeater & N. Way (Eds.), *Urban girls revisited: Building strengths* (pp. 142–156). New York: New York University Press.

Ricciardelli, L. A., McCabe, M. P., Mussap, A. J., & Holt, K. E. (2009). Body image in preadolescent boys. In L. Smolak & J. K. Thompson (Eds.), *Body image, eating disorders, and obesity in youth: Assessment, prevention, and treatment* (pp. 77–96). Washington, DC: American Psychological Association.

Rice, C. (2014). *Becoming women: The embodied self in image culture.* Toronto: University of Toronto Press.

Rice, E. et al. (2015). Cyberbullying perpetration and victimization among middle-school students. *American Journal of Public Health, 105,* e66–e71.

Rice, L. & Bath, J. (2016). Hiring decisions: The effect of evaluator gender and gender stereotype characteristics on the evaluation of job applicants. *Gender Issues, 33,* 1–21.

Rice, M. S. et al. (2016). Breast cancer research in the Nurses' Health Studies: Exposures across the life course. *AJPH, 106,* 1592–1598.

Richard-Davis, G. & Manson, J. E. (2015). Vasomotor symptom duration in midlife women—Research overturn dogma. *JAMA Internal Medicine, 175,* 540–541.

Richards, C. (2016). Protecting and expanding access to birth control. *New England Journal of Medicine, 374,* 843–853.

Richards, C. & Barker, M.(2013). *Sexuality and gender for mental health professionals: A practical guide.* Thousand Oaks, CA: Sage.

Richards, J. E., Risser, J. M., Padgett, P. M., Rehman, H. U., Wolverton, M. L., & Arafat, R. R. (2008). Condom use among high-risk heterosexual women with concurrent sexual partnerships, Houston, Texas, USA. *International Journal of STD & AIDS, 19,* 768–771.

Richardsen, A. M. et al. (2016). Women and work stress: More and different? In M. L. Connerley & J. Wu (Eds.), *Handbook on well-being of working women* (pp. 123–138). Dordrecht: Springer.

Richardson, D. S. (2014). Everyday aggression takes many forms. *Psychological Science, 23,* 220–224.

Richardson, M. K. (2014). Menopause strategies: Finding lasting answers for symptoms and health: Eliminating hot flashes—still not a slam dunk! *The Journal of North American Menopause Services, 4,* 321–322.

Ridgeway, C. L. (2011). *Framed by gender: How gender inequality persists in the modern world.* New York: Oxford University Press.

Ridolfo, H. et al. (2013). Race and girls' self-evaluations: How mothering matters. *Sex Roles, 68,* 496–509.

Rife, J. C. (2001). Middle-aged and older women in the work force. In J. M. Coyle (Ed.), *Handbook on women and aging* (pp. 93–111). Westport, CT: Greenwood.

Riggio, H. R. & Desrochers, S. J. (2006). Relations with young adults' work and family expectations and self-efficacy. *American Behavioral Scientist, 49,* 1328–1353.

Rios, D. et al. (2016). Conducting accessible research: Including people with disabilities in public health, epidemiological, and outcome studies. *AJPH, 106,* 2137–2144.

Risen, J. (2013). Attacked at 19 by an Air Force trainer, and speaking out. *New York Times,* p. A1.

Rith, K. A. & Diamond, L. M. (2013). Same-sex relationships. In M. A. Fine & F. D. Fincham (Eds.), *Handbook of family theories: A content-based approach* (pp. 123–144). New York: Routledge.

Rivers, C. & Barnett,R.C. (2013). *The new soft war on women: How the myth of female ascendance is hurting women, men…and our economy.* New York: Penguin.

Robbins, C. L. & Padavic, I. (2007). Structural influences on racial and ethnic disparities in women's health care. *Sociology Compass, 1,* 682–700.

Robert-McComb, J. J. & Massey-Stokes, M. (2014). Body image concerns throughout the Lifespan. In J. J. McComb et al. (Eds.), *The active female: Health issues throughout the lifespan* (2nd ed., pp. 3–24). New York: Springer.

Roberto, K. A. (2016). The complexities of elder abuse. *American Psychologist, 71,* 302–311.

Roberto, K. A. et al. (2014). Abuse in later life. In J. A. Arditti (Ed.), *Family problems: stress, risk, and resilience* (pp. 228–248). Malden, MA: Wiley.

Robertson, J. A. (2016). Other women's wombs: Uterus transplants and gestational surrogacy. *Journal of Law and Biosciences, 3,* 68–86.

Robertson, M. C. & Gillespie, L. D. (2013). Fall prevention in community-dwelling older adults. *Journal of the American Medical Association, 309,* 1406–1407.

Robertson, T. (2017). *The convergence of race, ethnicity, and gender: Multiple identities in counseling.* Thousand Oaks, CA: Sage.

Robinson, G. & Nelson, B. M. (2010). Pursuing upward mobility: African American professional women reflect on their journey. *Journal of Black Studies, 40,* 1168–1188.

Robinson, J. D., Skill, T., & Turner, J. W. (2004). Media usage patterns and portrayals of seniors. In J. F. Nussbaum & J. Coupland (Eds.), *Handbook of communication and aging research* (2nd ed., pp. 423–450). Mahwah, NJ: Erlbaum.

Robinson, J. P. & Espelage, D. L. (2013). Peer victimization and sexual risk differences between lesbian, gay, bisexual, transgender, or questioning and nontransgender heterosexual youths in grades 7–12. *AJPH, 103,* 1810–1819.

Robinson, S. L. et al. (2014). Coworkers behaving badly: The impact of coworker deviant behavior upon individual employees. *Annual Review of Organizational Psychology and Organizational Behavior, 1,* 123–143.

Robinson-Cimpian, J. P. et al. (2014). Are schools shortchanging boys or girls? The answer rests on methods and assumptions: Reply to Card (2014) and Penner (2014). *Developmental Psychology, 50,* 1840–1844.

Robinson-Whelen, S. et al. (2014). A safety awareness program for women with diverse disabilities: A randomized controlled trial. *Violence Against Women, 20,* 846–868.

Robinson-Wood, T.L. (2017). *The convergence of race ethnicity and gender: Multiple identities in counseling* (5th ed.). Thousand Oaks, CA: Sage.

Robles, R. et al. (2016). Removing transgender identity from the classification of mental disorders: A Mexican field study for ICD-11. *The Lancet Psychiatry,* doi.org/10.1016/S2215-0366(16)30165-1.

Robles, T. F. (2014). Marital quality and health: implications for marriage in the 21st century. *Current Directions in Psychological Science, 23,* 427–432.

Robnett, R. (2016). Gender bias in STEM fields: Variation in prevalence and links to STEM self-concept. *Psychology of Women Quarterly, 40,* 65–79.

Robnett, R. D. et al. (2016). "She might be afraid of commitment": Perceptions of women who retain their surname after marriage. *Sex Roles, 75,* 1–14.

Rocca, C. H. et al. (2015). Decision rightness and emotional responses to abortion in the United States: A longitudinal study. *PLOS ONE, 10*(7), e0128832.

Roche, K. M. & Leventhal, T. (2009). Beyond neighborhood poverty: Family management, neighborhood disorder, and adolescents' early sexual onset. *Journal of Family Psychology, 23,* 819–827.

Rock, L. et al. (2014). *2014 Department of Defense report of friend groups on sexual assault prevention and response.* Washington DC: Department of Defense.

Rodero, E. et al. (2013). Male and female voices in commercials: Analysis of effectiveness, adequacy for the product, attention and recall. *Sex Roles, 68,* 349–362.

Rodrigue, E. & Reeves, R. V. (2015). *Single black female BA seeks educated husband: Race, assortative mating and inequality.* Retrieved April 14, 2015, from brookings.edu/blog/s/social-mobility-memos/posts

Rodriguez, M. et al. (2015). Is it time to integrate sex and gender into drug design and development? *Future Science, 7,* 557–559.

Roffman, E. (2008). Ethics and activism: Theory— identity politics, conscious acts, and ethical aspirations. In M. Ballou, M. Hill, & C. West (Eds.), *Feminist therapy theory and practice: A contemporary perspective* (pp. 109–125). New York: Springer.

Rogers, N. T. et al. (2016). Volunteering is associated with increased survival in able-bodied participants of the English Longitudinal Study of Aging. *Journal of Epidemiology and Community Health, 70,* 583–588.

Rohde, P. et al. (2013).Key characteristics of major depressive disorder occurring in childhood, adolescence, emerging adulthood, and adulthood. *Clinical Psychological Science, 1,* 41–53.

Rohde, P. et al. (2015). Development and predictive effects of eating disorder risk factors during adolescence: Implications for prevention efforts. *International Journal of Eating Disorders, 48,* 187–198.

Rohlinger, D. E. & Gentile, H. (2015). Letting go and having fun: Redefining aging in America. In D. King & C. G. Valentine (Eds.), *Letting go: Feminist and social justice insight and activism* (pp. 173–186). Nashville, TN: Vanderbilt University Press.

Rolfe, D. E., Yoshida, K., Renwick, R., & Bailey, C. (2009). Negotiating participation: How women living with disabilities address barriers to exercise. *Health Care for Women International, 30,* 743–766.

Romaine, S. (1999). *Communicating gender.* Mahwah, NJ: Erlbaum.

Romano, A. (2013). New opportunities for birth centers in a transforming health care system. *Journal of Midwifery & Women's Health, 8,* 5492–493.

Romero, L. et al. (2015). Vital signs: Trends in use of long-acting reversible contraception among teens aged 15–19 years seeking contraceptive services—United States, 2005–2013. *Centers for Disease Control and Prevention, 64,* 363–369.

Rosario, M. et al. (2014). Sexual orientation disparities in cancer-related risk behaviors of tobacco, alcohol, seual behaviors, and diet and physical activity: Pooled youth risk behavior surveys. *American Journal of Public Health, 104,* 245–246.

Rose, A. J., Swenson, L. P., & Waller, E. M. (2004). Overt and relational aggression and perceived popularity: Developmental differences in concurrent and prospective relations. *Developmental Psychology, 40,* 378–387.

Rose, A. J. et al. (2016). Girls' and boys' problem talk: Implications for emotional closeness in friendships. *Developmental Psychology, 52,* 629–639.

Rose, S. (2000, Summer). Heterosexism and the study of women's romantic and friend relationships. *Journal of Social Issues, 56,* 315–328.

Rose, S. & Frieze, I. H. (1993). Young singles' contemporary dating scripts. *Sex Roles, 28,* 499–509.

Rose, S. M. & Hospital, M. M. (2015). Lesbians over 60: Newer every day. In V. Muhlbauer et al. (Eds.), *Women and aging: An international, intersectional power perspective* (pp. 117–146). New York: Springer.

Rose, S. M. & Eaton, A. A. (2013). Lesbian love and relationships In D. Castaneda (Ed.). *An essential handbook of women's sexuality* (vol. 2, pp.3–28). Santa Barbara, CA: Praeger.

Rose, S. M. & Zand, D. (2002). Lesbian dating and courtship from young adulthood to midlife. In S. M. Rose (Ed.), *Lesbian love and relationships* (pp. 85–109). Binghamton, NY: Harrington Park Press.

Rosen, M. D. (2016, April). He wants to retire. She's not ready. What now? *AARP Bulletin,* pp. 18–20.

Rosenberg, M. & Philipps, D. (2015, December 3). All combat roles now open to women, defense secretary says. *New York Times.* pp. A1, A24.

Rosenthal, E. (2016, May 15). "Sorry, we don't take Obamacare". *New York Times,* pp. SR1, SR6.

Rosenthal, L. (2016). Incorporating intersectionality into psychology: An opportunity to promote social justice and equity. *American Psychologist, 71,* 474–485.

Rosenthal, M. N. et al. (2016). Still second class: Sexual harassment of graduate students. *Psychology of Women Quarterly, 40,* 364–377.

Rosin, H. (2012). *The end of men: And the rise of women.* New York: Riverhead & Banks.

Rosman, L. et al. (2014). Sexual health concerns in patients with cardiovascular disease. *Circulation, 129,* e313–e316.

Ross, J. M. & Babcock, J. C. (2010). Gender and intimate partner violence in the United States: Confronting the controversies. *Sex Roles, 62,* 194–200.

Rotabi, K. S. & Bromfield, N. F. (2016). *From intercountry adoption to global surrogacy: A human rights history and new fertility frontier.* New York: Routledge.

Roth, P.L. et al. (2012). A meta-analysis of gender group differences for measures of job performance in field studies. *Journal of Management, 38,* 7190739.

Rottenberg, C. (2013). The rise of neoliberal feminism. *Cultural Studies, 28,* 418–437.

Roughgarden, J. (2009). *Evolution's rainbow: Diversity, gender, and sexuality in nature and people.* Berkeley, CA: University of California Press.

Rowan, N. L. & Giunta, N. (2016). Lessons on health and social disparities from older lesbians with alcoholism and the role of interventions to promote culturally competent services. *Journal of Human Behavior in the Social Environment, 26,* 210–216.

Roy, R. E., Weibust, K. S., & Miller, C. T. (2007). Effects of stereotypes about feminists on feminist self-identification. *Psychology of Women Quarterly, 31,* 146–156.

Rubin, A. G., Gold, M. A., & Primack, B. A. (2009). Associations between depressive symptoms and sexual risk behaviors in a diverse sample of female adolescents. *Journal of Pediatric and Adolescent Gynecology, 23,* 306–312.

Rubin, J. D. (2016). #Gendertrolling: A (new) virtual iteration of everyday misogyny. *Sex Roles, 74,* 266–267.

Rubin, K. H., Cheah, C., & Menzer, M. M. (2010). Peers. In M. H. Bornstein (Ed.), *Handbook of cultural developmental science* (pp. 223–238). New York: Psychology Press.

Rubin, M. S., Colen, C. G., & Link, B. G. (2009). Examination of inequalities in HIV/AIDS mortality in the United States from a fundamental cause perspective. *American Journal of Public Health, 100,* 1053–1059.

Rudman, L. A. & Fairchild, K. (2007). The *F* word: Is feminism incompatible with beauty and romance? *Psychology of Women Quarterly, 31,* 125–136.

Rudolph, K. D. (2009). The interpersonal context of adolescent depression. In S. Nolen-Hoeksema & L. M. Hilt (Eds.), *Handbook of depression in adolescents* (pp. 377–418). New York: Taylor & Francis.

Rudolph, K. D. & Flynn, M. (2014). Depression in adolescent. In I. H. Gotlib & C. L. Hammen (Eds.), *Handbook of depression* (pp. 391–409). New York: Guilford.

Rudolph, K. D., Ladd, G., & Dinella, L. (2007). Gender differences in the interpersonal consequences on early-onset depressive symptoms. *Merrill-Palmer Quarterly, 53,* 461–488.

Rueger, S. Y., Malecki, C. K., & Demaray, M. K. (2008). Relationship between multiple sources of perceived social support and psychological and academic in early adolescence: Comparisons across gender. *Journal of Youth and Adolescence, 39,* 47–61.

Ruer, R. & Mollow, A. (Eds.). (2012). *Sex and disability.* Durham, NC: Duke University Press.

Ruggles, S. & Heggeness, M. (2008). Intergenerational coresidence in developing countries. *Population and Development Review, 34,* 253–281.

Ruiz, J. M. & Brondolo, E. (2016). Introduction to special issue disparities in cardiovascular health: Examining the contributions of social and behavioral factors. *Health Psychology, 35,* 309–312.

Runfola, C. D. et al. (2013). Characteristics of women with body size satisfaction at midlife: Results of the gender and body image (GABI) study. *Journal of Women & Aging, 25,* 287–304.

Rural Center for AIDS/STD Prevention. (2009). *Tearing down fences: HIV/STD prevention in rural America.* Bloomington, IN: Author.

Ruspini, E. (2011). Stereotypes of women. In M. Z. Stange, C. K. Oyster, & J. E. Sloan (Eds.), *Encyclopedia of women in today's world* (Vol. 3, pp. 1398–1401). Newberry Park, CA: Sage.

Russell, B. (Ed.). (2015). *Perceptions of female offenders: How stereotypes and social norms affect responses.* New York: springer.

Russell, D. E. H. (2001). Femicide: An international speakout. In D. E. H. Russell & R. A. Harmes (Eds.), *Femicide in global perspective* (pp. 128–137). New York: Teachers College Press.

Russell, S. T. & Seif, H. (2002). Bisexual female adolescents: A critical analysis of past research, and results from a national survey. *Journal of Bisexuality, 2,* 73–94.

Russey, M. A. et al. (2014). Developmental perspective: Sex differences in behavior from childhood to adulthood. In R. Gartner & B. McCarthy (Eds.), *The Oxford handbook of gender, sex, and crime* (pp. 286–318). New York: Oxford University Press.

Russo, N. F. & Tartaro, J. (2008). Women and mental health. In F. L. Denmark & M. A. Paludi (Eds.), *Psychology of women: A handbook of issues and theories* (2nd ed., pp. 440–483). Westport, CT: Praeger.

Rust, J. et al. (2000). The role of brothers and sisters in the development of preschool children. *Journal of Experimental Child Psychology, 77,* 292–303.

Rutter, V. & Schwartz, P. (2012). *The gender of sexuality: Exploring sexual possibilities* (2nd ed.). Lanham, MD: Rowman & Littlefield.

Ryan, P. et al. (2013). Agency, relationships, and sexuality. In P. Ryan & B. J. Coughlan (Eds.), *Ageing and older adult mental health: Issues and Implications for practice* (pp. 192–213). New York: Routledge.

Ryan, R. M. et al. (2015). Early childhood maltreatment and girls' sexual behavior: The mediating role of pubertal timing. *Journal of Adolescent Health, 57,* 342–347.

Ryle, R. (2016). *Questioning gender: A sociological exploration* (3rd ed.). Thousand Oaks, CA: Sage.

Sabattini, L. & Crosby, F. J. (2016). Work-life policies, programs, and practices: Helping women, men, and workplaces. In M. L. Connerley & J. Wu (Eds.), *Handbook on well-being of working women* (pp. 414–427). Dordrecht: Springer.

Sabin, J. A. et al. (2015). Health care providers' implicit and explicit attitudes toward lesbian women and gay men. *AJPH, 105,* 1831–1840.

Sabina, C. & Ho, L. Y. (2014). Campus and college victim responses to sexual assault and dating violence: Disclosure, service utilization, and service provision. *Trauma, Violence, & Abuse, 15,* 201–226.

Sabo, D. & Snyder, M. (2013). *Progress and promise: Title IX at 40 white paper.* Ann Arbor, MI: SHARP Center for Women and Girls.

Sadker, D. & Zittleman, K. (2009). *Still failing at fairness: How gender bias cheats girls and boys in school and what we can do about it.* New York: Scribner.

Sadker, M. & Sadker, D. (1994). *Failing at fairness: How America's schools cheat girls.* New York: Scribner.

Sadler, C. et al. (2010). Lifestyle factors, hormonal contraception, and premenstrual symptoms: The United Kingdom Southampton women's survey. *Journal of Women's Health, 19,* 391–396.

Saftlas, A. F. et al. (2000). Racial disparity in pregnancy-related mortality associated with live birth: Can established risk factors explain it? *American Journal of Epidemiology, 152,* 413–419.

Sagon, C. (2017, January-February). Medicine's gender issues. *AARP Bulletin,* pp. 24–27.

Saint Louis, C. (2015, June 23). All those what-ifs never get answered. *New York Times,* p. D2.

Sakaluk, J. K. & Milhausen, R. R. (2012). Factors influencing university students' explicit and implicit sexual double standards. *Journal of Sex Research, 49,* 843–862.

Salafia, E. H. B., Gondoli, D. M., Corning, A. F., Bucchianeri, M. M., & Godinez, N. M. (2008). Longitudinal examination of maternal psychological control and adolescents' self-competence as predictors of bulimic symptoms among boys and girls. *International Journal of Eating Disorders, 42,* 422–428.

Saleem, R. (2015). Global/international perspectives on the psychology of women: Calling for transnational feminist solidarity. *Feminist Psychology, 13.*

Salerno J. M. & Peter-Hagene, L. C. (2015). One angry woman: Anger expression increases influence for men, but decreases influence for women, during group deliberation. *Law and Human Behavior, 39,* 581–592.

Sales, N. J. (2016). *American girls: Social media and the secret lives of teenagers.* New York: Alfred Knopf.

Salganicoff, A. & Sobel, L. (2016). Women, private health insurance, and the Affordable Care Act. *Women's Health Issues, 26,* 2–5.

Sammarco, J. (2017). *Women's health issues across the life cycle: A quality of life perspective.* Burlington, MA: Jones and Bartlett Learning.

Sampson, D. & Hertlein, K. (2015). The experience of grandparents rearing grandchildren. *Grandfamilies: The Contemporary Journal of Research, Policy, and Practice, 2 (1),* Article 4, 1–24.

Sanchez, D.T. et al. (2012). Eroticizing inequality in the United States: The consequences and determinants of traditional gender role adherence in intimate relationships. *Journal of Sex Research, 49,* 168–183.

Sanchez-Hucles, J. V. (2003). Intimate relationships. In L. Slater, J. H. Daniel, & A. E. Banks (Eds.), *The complete guide to mental health for women* (pp. 104–120). Boston, MA: Beacon Press.

Sandberg, S. (2013). *Lean in: Women, work, and the will to lead.* New York: Knopf.

Sandelowski, M., Barroso, J., & Voils, C. I. (2009). Gender, race/ethnicity and social class in research reports on stigma in HIV-positive women. *Health Care for Women International, 30,* 273–288.

Sanders, A. R. et al. (2015). Genome-wide scan demonstrates significant linkage for male sexual orientation. *Psychological Medicine, 45,* 1379–1388.

Sani, G. M. D. (2014). Men's employment hours and time on domestic chores in European countries. *Journal of Family Issues, 35,* 1023–1047.

Sapre, S., & Thakur, R. (2014). Lifestyle and dietary factors determine age at natural menopause. *Journal of Midlife Health, 5,* 3–5.

Saraceno, J. (2015, January, February). Last chance babiew: Sure they do it—nut should they? *AARP Bulletin,* pp. 22–24.

Sarche, M. C. & Whitesell, N. R. (2012). Child development research in North American native communities—Looking back and moving forward: An introduction. *Child Development Perspectives, 6,* 42–48.

Sardavar, K. (2011). Household division of labor. In M. Z. Stange, C. K. Oyster, & J. E. Sloan (Eds.), *Encyclopedia of women in today's world* (Vol. 2, pp. 726–728). Newberry Park, CA: Sage.

Sargent, J., Stein, K., & Rosen, D. (2009). Eating disorders. In J. C. Urbancic & C. J. Groh (Eds.), *Women's mental health: A clinical guide for primary care providers* (pp. 180–224). Philadelphia, PA: Lippincott Williams & Wilkins.

Sargini, N. et al. (2014). *Reconfiguring reproduction: Feminist health perspectives on assisted reproductive technologies.* New York: Zubaan Banks.

Sarkisian, N. & Gerstel, N. (2008). Till marriage do us part: Adult children's relationships with their parents. *Journal of Marriage and Family, 70,* 360–376.

Sarno, E. L. et al. (2015). When identities collide: Conflicts in allegiances among LGB people of color. *Cultural Diversity and Ethnic Minority Psychology, 21,* 550–559.

Sarojini, N. & Marwah, V. (2014) (Eds.). *Reconfiguring reproduction: Feminist health perspectives on assisted reproductive technologies.* Chicago: University of Chicago Press.

Saslow, D. (2012). *Is a Pap test necessary every year?* Atlanta, GA: American Cancer Society.

Saunders, K. (2016). Women in the workplace: Feminism's potential impact. In M. L. Connerley & J. Wu (Eds.), *Handbook on well-being of working women* (pp. 565–573). Dordrecht: Springer.

Save the Children. (2015). *State of the world's mothers 2015: The urban disadvantage.* Fairfield, CT: Author.

Savin-Williams, R. C. (2006). Who's gay? Does it matter? *Current Directions in Psychological Science, 15,* 40–44.

Sawchuk, D. (2009). The raging grannies: Defying stereotypes and embracing aging through activism. *Journal of Women & Aging, 21,* 171–185.

Sawhill, I. (2014, September 14). Beyond marriage. *New York Times,* pp. SR1, SR9.

Sax, L. (2010). *Girls on the edge: The four factors driving the new crisis for girls: Sexual identity, the cyberbubble, obsessions, environmental toxins.* New York: Basic Books.

Sax, L. et al. (2015a). "But I'm not good at math": The changing salience of mathematical self-concept in shaping women's and men's STEM aspirations. *Research in Higher Education, 56,* 813–842.

Sax, L. et al. (2015b). *Who attends a women's college? Identifying unique characteristics and patterns of change, 1971–2011.* Retrieved 2015, from the ucla.edu

Sayer, L. & Fine, L. (2011). Racial-ethnic differences in U.S. married women's and men's housework. *Social Indicators Research, 101,* 259–265.

Sayer, L. C. (2005). Gender, time, and inequality: Trends in women's and men's paid work, unpaid work, and free time. *Social Forces, 84,* 285–303.

Sbarra, D. A. et al. (2015). Divorce and health: Beyond individual differences. *Current Directions in Psychological Science, 24,* 109–115.

Scharff, C. et al. (2016). *digital feminisms: Transnational activism in German protest cultures.* New York: Routledge .

Scharrer, E. (2013). Representations of gender in the media. In K.E. Dill (Ed.). *The Oxford handbook of media psychology* (pp. 267–273). New York: Oxford University Press.

Schatz, E. & Gilbert, L. (2014). "My legs affect me a lot. . . . I can no longer walk to the forest to fetch firewood": Challenges related to health and the performance of daily tasks for older women in a high HIV context. *Health Care for Women International, 35,* 771–788.

Schaupp, D. S. & Ting, L. (2017). Counseling women greater than 65 years of age. In M. Kopala & M. Keitel (Eds.), *Handbook of counseling women* (2nd ed., pp. 204–216). Thousand Oaks, CA: Sage.

Scheiber, N. (2015, July 18). U.S. agency rules for gays in workplace discrimination. *New York Times,* p.B1.

Schellenbach, C. J., Strader, K., Pernice-Duca, F., & Key-Carniak, M. (2010). Building strengths and resilience among at-risk mothers and their children: A community- based prevention partnership. In R. D. Peters, B. Leadbeater, & R. J. McMahon (Eds.), *Resilience in children, families, and communities: Linking context to practice and policy* (pp. 101–116). New York: Kluwer Academic/Plenum.

Scherer, H. L. et al. (2016). Intimate partner victimization among college students with and without disabilities: Prevalence of and relationship to emotional well-being. *Journal of Interpersonal Violence, 31,* 49–80.

Scherrer, K. S. (2016). Gay, lesbian, bisexual, and queer grandchildren's disclosure process with grandparents. *Journal of Family Issues, 37,* 739–764.

Schilt, K., & Westbrook, L. (2009). Doing gender, doing heteronormativity: "Gender normals," transgender people, and the social maintenance of heterosexuality. *Gender & Society,* 23, 440–464.

Schimmel, M. S. et al. (2015). The effects of maternal age and parity on maternal and neonatal outcome. *Archives of Gynecology and Obstetrics, 291,* 793–798.

Schimmele, C. M. & Wu, Z. (2016). Repartnering after union dissolution in later life. *Journal of Marriage and Family, 78,* 1013–1031.

Schmidt, F. & Hunter, J. (2014). *Methods of meta-analysis: concerning error and bias in research findings.* Thousand Oaks, CA: Sage.

Schmitt, M. T., Branscombe, N. R., Kobrynowicz, D., & Owen, S. (2002). Perceiving discrimination against one's gender group has different implications for well-being in women and men. *Personality and Social Psychology Bulletin, 28,* 197–210.

Schmitt, M. T. et al. (2014). The consequences of perceived discrimination for psychological well-being: A meta-analytic review. *Psychological Bulletin, 140,* 921–948.

Schmitz, R. M. (2016). Constructing men as fathers: A content analysis of formulations of fatherhood in parenting magazines. *Journal of Men's Studies, 24,* 3–23.

Schneider, B. (2016). *Childhood friendships and other relations: Friends and enemies.* New York: Routledge.

Schoen, J. (2015). *Abortion after Roe.* Raleigh, NC: University of North Carolina Press.

Schoon, I., Ross, A., & Martin, P. (2007). Science related careers: Aspirations and outcomes in two British cohort studies. *Equal Opportunities International, 26,* 129–143.

Schreier, H. M. C. & Chen, E. (2013). Socioeconomic status and the health of youth: A multilevel, multidomain approach to conceptualizing pathways. *Psychological Bulletin, 139,* 606–654.

Schroeder, S. A. (2013). New evidence that cigarette smoking remains the most important health hazard. *New England Journal of Medicine, 368,* 389–390.

Schuck, F. B. et al. (2016). Exercise as atreatment for depression: A meta-analysis adjusting for publication bias. *Journal of Psychiatric Research, 77,* 42–51.

Schuette, C. & Killen, M. (2009). Children's evaluations of genderstereotypic household activities in the family context. *Early Education and Development, 20,* 693–712.

Schuiling, K. D. & Low, L. K. (2017). Women's growth and development across the lifespan. In K. D. Schuiling & F. E. Likis (Eds.), Women's gynecological health (3rd ed., pp. 17–35). Burlington, MA: Jones & Bartlett.

Schulman, A. (2003). Female sexuality. In L. Slater, J. H. Daniel, & A. E. Banks (Eds.), *The complete guide to mental health for women* (pp. 82–91). Boston, MA: Beacon Press.

Schulte, B. (2014, March 30). Overwhelmed: Work, love, and play when no one has the time. *New York Times.* p. 15.

Schuppe, J. (2007). Women in the State Police: Trouble in the ranks. In P. S. Rothenberg (Ed.), *Race, class, and gender in the United States: An integrated study* (7th ed., pp. 274–277). New York: Worth.

Schur, L. (2004). Is there still a "double handicap"? Economic, social, and political disparities experienced by women with disabilities. In B. G. Smith & B. Hutchison (Eds.), *Gendering disability* (pp. 253–271). Piscataway, NJ: Rutgers University Press.

Schur, L. et al. (2016). Introduction to special issue on people with disabilities in the workplace. *International Journal of Human Resource Management, 27,* 1471–1476.

Schuster, M. A. et al. (2016). Beyond bathrooms—Meeting the needs of transgender people. *New England Journal of Medicine.* Retrieved from nejm.org/doi/full/10.1056/NEJMp1605912

Schwarzbach, M. et al. (2014). Social relations and depression in late life: A systematic review. *Geriatric Psychiatry, 29,* 1–21.

Scott, L. S. (2009). *Two is enough: A couple's guide to living childless by choice.* Berkeley, CA: Seal Press.

Sczesny, S. et al. (2016). Can gender-fair language reduce gender stereotyping and discrimination? *Frontiers in Psychology, 7,* Article 25, 1–11.

Sear, R. & Mace, R. (2008). Who keeps children alive? A review of the effects of kin on child survival. *Evolution and Human Behavior, 29,* 1–18.

Sechrist, J. et al. (2012). Aging parents and adult children: Determinants of relationship quality. In R. Blieszner & V. H. Bedford (Eds.), *Handbook of families and aging* (2nd ed., pp. 153–182). Santa Barbara, CA: ABC-CLIO.

Sechrist, J. et al. (2014). Perceptions of equity, balance of support exchange, and mother-adult child relations. *Journal of Marriage and Family, 76,* 285–299.

Sedgh, G. et al. (2012). Induced abortion: Incidence and trends worldwide from 1995 to 2008. The Lancet, 379, 625–632.

Sedgh, G. et al. (2015). Adolescent pregnancy, birth, and abortion rates across countries: Levels and recent trends. *Journal of Adolescent Health, 56,* 223–230.

Seedat, S. et al. (2009). Cross-national associations between gender and mental disorders in the World Health Organization world mental health surveys. *Archives of General Psychiatry, 66,* 785–795.

Seedyk, E. & deLaet, M. (2005). Women, games, and women's games. *Phi Kappa Phi Forum, 85*(2), 25–28.

Seem, S. R. & Clark, M. D. (2006). Healthy women, healthy men, and healthy adults: An evaluation of gender role stereotypes in the twenty-first century. *Sex Roles, 55,* 247–258.

Seguin, R. et al. (2014). Sedentary behavior and mortality in older women. *American Journal of Preventive Medicine, 46,* 122–135.

Seib, C. et al. (2015). Predictors of mental health in midlife and older Australian women: A multilevel investigation. *Health Care for Women International,* doi.1080/07399332.2015.1080262.

Seitz, V. & Apfel, N. (2010). Creating effective school-based interventions for pregnant teenagers. In R. D. Peters, B. Leadbeater, & R. J. McMahon (Eds.), *Resilience in children, families and communities: Linking context to practice and policy* (pp. 65–82). New York: Kluwer Academic/Plenum.

Sellers, S. A. (2008). *Native American women's studies: A primer.* New York: Peter Lang.

Sells, T. G. C. & Ganong, L. (2016). Emerging adults' expectations and preferences for gender role arrangements in long-term heterosexual relationships. *Sex Roles,* doi:10.1007/s11199-016-0658-2.

Seltzer, J. A. & Bianchi, S. M. (2013). Demographic change and parent-child relationships in adulthood. *The Annual Review of Sociology, 39,* 275–290.

Seltzer, J. A. & Yahirun, J. J. (2013). *Diversity in old age: The elderly in changing economic and family contexts.* New York: Russell Sage Foundation.

Sen, A. K. (2010). More than 100 million women are missing. In P. Murthy & C. L. Smith (Eds.), *Women's global health and human rights* (pp. 99–112). Sudbury, MA: Jones and Bartlett.

Sen, G. (2017). Introduction: Empowering women for health. In S. Dworkin & M. Gandhi (Eds.), *Women's empowerment and global health: A twenty-first-century agenda* (pp. 1–18). Oakland, CA: University of California Press.

Sengupta, S. (2015, March 10). U. N. reveals 'alarmingly high' levels of violence against women: Report finds 1 in 3 have been attacked. *New York Times,* p. A4.

Serbin, L. A., Powlishta, K. K., & Gulko, J. (1993). The development of sex-typing in middle childhood. *Monographs of the Society for Research in Child Development, 58,* 1–95. (Serial No. 232).

Serbin, L. A. et al. (2004). When aggressive girls become mothers: Problems in parenting, health, and development across two generations. In M. Putallaz & K. L. Bierman (Eds.), *Aggression, antisocial behavior, and violence among girls: A developmental perspective* (pp. 262–288). New York: Guilford.

Seron, C. et al. (2016). Persistence is cultural: Professional socialization and the reproduction of sex segregation. *Work and Occupation, 43,* 178–214.

Settles, I. H., Pratt-Hyatt, J. S., & Buchanan, N. T. (2008). Through the lens of race: Black and White women's perceptions of womanhood. *Psychology of Women Quarterly, 32,* 454–468.

Settles, I. H. et al. (2013). Derogation, discrimination, and (dis)satisfaction with jobs in science: A gendered analysis. *Psychology of Women Quarterly, 37,* 179–191.

Sewell, A. (2015). Disaggregating ethnoracial disparities in physician trust. *Social Science Research, 54,* 1–20.

Sexual assaults and military justice. (2013, March 12). *New York Times,* p. A24.

Shah, A. J. et al. (2014). Sex and age differences in the association of depression with obstructive coronary artery disease and adverse cardiovascular events. *Journal of the American Heart Association, 3,* e000741.

Shapiro, E. (2015). *Gender circuits: Bodies and identities in a technological age.* New York: Routledge.

Shapiro, G. (2014). Voluntary childlessness: A critical review of the literature. *Studies in the Maternal, 6,* 1–15.

Shapiro, J. R. et al. (2013). Are all interventions created equal? A multi-threat approach to tailoring stereotype threat interventions. *Journal of Personality and Social Psychology, 104,* 277–288.

Shapiro, J. R. et al. (2015). Stereotype threat. In T. D. Nelson (Ed.), *Handbook of prejudice, stereotyping, and discrimination* (pp. 87–106). New York: Psychology Press.

Sharifi, K. et al. (2014). Barriers to middle-aged women's mental health: qualitative study. *Iran Red Crescent Medical Journal, 16,* 1–8.

Sharp, E. A. & Ganong, L. (2011). "I'm a loser, I'm not married. Let's just all look at me": Ever-single women's perceptions of their social environment. *Journal of Family Issues, 32,* 956–980.

Sharp, G. et al. (2015). Predictors of consideration of labiaplasty: An extension of the tripartite influence model of beauty ideals. *Psychology of Women Quarterly, 39,* 182–193.

Sharpe, H. et al. (2013). Is fat talking a causal risk factor for body dissatisfaction? A systematic review and meta-analysis. *International Journal of Eating Disorders, 46,* 643–652.

Shaw, J. & Campbell, R. (2014). Rape crisis centers: serving survivors and their communities. In T. Bryant-Davis (Ed.), *Surviving sexual violence: A guide to recovery and empowerment* (pp. 112–128). Lanham, MD: Rowman & Littlefield.

Shaw, J. C. A. (2013). The medicalization of birth and midwifery as resistance. *Health Care for Women International, 34,* 522–536.

Sheehy, G. (2007). *Sex and the seasoned woman: Pursuing the passionate life.* New York: Ballantine.

Shellenbarger, S. (2008, March 20). In search of wedded bliss: What research can tell us. *Wall Street Journal,* p. D1.

Shelley, L. (2010). *Human trafficking: A global perspective.* Cambridge, UK: Cambridge University Press.

Sheltzer, J. M. & Smith, J.C. (2014). Elite male faculty in the life sciences employ fewer women. *Proceedings of the National Academy of Science, 111,* 10107–10112.

Shepela, S. T. & Levesque, L. L. (1998). Poisoned waters: Sexual harassment and the college climate. *Sex Roles, 38,* 589–611.

Sheppard, M. & Mayo, J. (2013). The social construction of gender and sexuality Learning from two-spirit traditions. *The Social Studies, 104,* 259–270.

Sherry, E et al. (2016). Images of sports women: A review. *Sex Roles, 74,* 299–309.

Shiraev, E. & Levy, D. (2013). *Cross-cultural psychology: Critical thinking and contemporary applications.* Boston, MA: Pearson.

Shields, S. A. (2013). Gender and emotion: What we think we know, what we need to know, and why it matters. *Psychology of Women Quarterly, 37,* 423–435.

Sholar, M. (2016). *Getting paid while taking time: The women's movement and the development of paid family leave policies in the United States.* Philadelphia, PA: Temple University Press.

Shor, E. et al. (2013). The strength of family ties: A meta-analysis and meta-regression of self-reported social support and mortality. *Social Networks, 35,* 626–638.

Short, S.E. et al. (2013). Sex, gender, genetics, and health. *American Journal of Public Health, 103* (Supp. 1), s93–s101.

Shufelt, C. et al. (2012). Red wine may decrease endogenous estrogen levels in premenopausal women, but does this protect against breast cancer? *Journal of Midwifery & Women's Health, 57,* 419–421.

Shulevitz, J. (2015, May 10). Mom: The designated worrier. *New York Times,* pp. SR1, SR6.

Shultz, K. S. & Wang, M. (2011). Psychological perspectives on the changing nature of retirement. *American Psychologist, 66,* 170–179.

Shutts, K. (2015). Young children's preferences: Gender, race, and social status. *Child Development Perspectives, 9,* 262–266.

Sices, L. et al. (2004). How do primary care physicians manage children with possible developmental delays? A national survey with an experimental design. *Pediatrics, 113,* 274–282.

Siebers, T. (2012). A sexual culture for disabled people. In R. McRuer & A Mollow (Eds.), *Sex and disability* (pp. 37–54). Raleigh, NC: Duke University.

Sigal, J. (2008). Stalking as a form of campus violence: Case studies. In M. A. Paludi (Ed.), *Understanding and preventing campus violence* (pp. 99–102). Westport, CT: Praeger.

Sigal, J. & Wnuk-Novitskie, D. (2010). Cross-cultural violence against women and girls: From dating to intimate partner violence. In M. A. Paludi (Ed.), *Feminism and women's rights worldwide: Mental and physical health* (Vol. 2, pp. 65–102). Santa Barbara, CA: Praeger.

Sigal, J. et al. (2005). Cross-cultural reactions to academic sexual harassment: Effects of individualist vs. collectivist culture and gender of participants. *Sex Roles, 52,* 201–215.

Sigal, J. A. & Denmark, F. L. (2013). Introduction. In J. A. Sigal & F. L. Denmark (Eds.), *Violence against women: International perspectives* (pp. 1–4). New York: Guilford.

Signorella, M. L. et al. (2013). A meta-analytic critique of Mael et al.'s review of single-sex schooling. *Sex Roles, 69,* 423–441.

Signorielli, N. & Bacue, A. (1999). Recognition and respect: A content analysis of prime-time television characters across the decades. *Sex Roles, 40,* 527–544.

Silbey, S. S. (2016). Why do so many women who study engineering leave the field? *Harvard Business Review.* Retrieved from hbr.org

Silk, J. & Romero, D. (2014). The role of parents and families in teen pregnancy prevention: An analysis of programs and policies. *Journal of Family Issues, 35,* 1339–1362.

Silvestri, M. & Crowther-Dowey, C. (2016). *Gender and crime: A human rights approach* (2nd ed.). Thousand Oaks, CA: Sage.

Sim, L. A., Homme, J. H., Lteif, A. N., Vande Voort, J. L., Schak, K. M., & Ellingson, J. (2009). Family functioning and maternal distress in adolescent girls with anorexia nervosa. *International Journal of Eating Disorders, 42,* 531–539.

Simkin, P. et al. (2016). *Pregnancy, childbirth, and the newborn* (5th ed.). Minnetonka, MN: Meadowbrook.

Simmons, A. et al. (2015). *The Affordable Care Act: Advancing the health of women and children.* Rockville, MD: U.S. Department of Health and Human Services.

Simmons, R. G. & Blyth, D. A. (1987). *Moving into adolescence: The impact of pubertal change and school context.* Hawthorne, NY: Aldine de Gruyter.

Simon, J. A. et al. (2014). Clarifying vaginal atrophy's impact on sex and relationships (CLOSER) survey: Emotional and physical impact of vaginal discomfort on North american postmenopausal women and their partners. *Menopause, 21,* 137–142.

Simon, S. S. et al. (2014). Cognitive behavioral therapies in older adults with depression and cognitive deficits: a systematic review. *Geriatric Psychiatry, 30,* 223–233.

Simons, R. L. (1996). The effect of divorce on adult and child adjustment. In R. L. Simons, et al. (Eds.), *Understanding differences between divorced and intact families: Stress, interaction, and child outcome* (pp. 3–20). Thousand Oaks, CA: Sage.

Simpkins, S. et al. (2015a). Families, schools, and developmental achievement-related motivations. In J. Grusec & P. Hastings (Eds.), *Handbook of socialization: Theory and research* (2nd ed., pp. 614–636). New York: Guilford.

Simpkins, S. et al. (2015b). The role of parents in the ontogeny of achievement-related motivation and behavioral choices. *Monographs of the Society for Research in Child Development, 80.*

Simpson, J. (2014). Power and social influence in relationships. In M. M. Kulincer & P. R. Shaver (Eds.), *APA handbook of personal-*

ity and social psychology (Vol. 3, pp. 393–420). Washington, DC: American Psychological Association.

Simpson, J. & Belsky, J. (2016). Attachment theory within a modern evolutionary framework: Theory, research, and clinical applications. *Handbook of attachment.* New York: Guilford.

Singer, B. & Deschamps, D. (2017). *LGBTQ Statistics: Lesbian, gay, bisexual, transgender and queer people by the numbers.* New York: New Press.

Singh, A. A. & Sikes, A. (2014). Understanding child sexual abuse: Prevalence, multicultural considerations and life span effects. In T. Bryant-Davis (Ed.), *Surviving sexual violence: A guide to recovery and empowerment* (pp. 77–90). Lanham, MD: Rowman & Littlefield.

Singh, A. A. et al. (2017). Counseling South Asian American women. In M. Kopala & M. Keitel (Eds.), *Handbook of counseling women* (2nd ed., pp. 248–260). Thousand Oaks, CA: Sage.

Singh, S.D. et al. (2017). Surveillance summary for cancer incidence and mortality—United states, 2013. *MMWR Surveillance Summaries, 66,* (SS-4). 1–36.

Sinno, S. M. & Killen, M. (2009). Moms at work and dads at home: Children's evaluations of parental roles. *Developmental Science, 13,* 16–29.

Sinozich, S. & Langton, L. (2014). *Rape and sexual assault victimization among college-age females, 1995–2013.* Washington, DC: U. S. Department of Justice.

Siu, A. L. U. et al. (2016). Screening for depression in adults; US preventive services task force recommendation statement. *Journal of the American Medical Association, 315,* 1–14.

Skaine, R. (2016). *Sexual assault in the U.S. military: The battle within America's Armed Forces.* Santa Barbara, CA: ABC-CLIO.

Skoe, E. E. A., Cumberland, A., Eisenberg, N., Hansen, K., & Perry, J. (2002). The influences of sex and gender-idle identity on moral cognition and prosocial personality traits. *Sex Roles, 46,* 295–309.

Skoog, T. & Stattin, H. (2014). Why and under what contextual conditions do early-maturing girls develop problem behaviors? *Child Development Perspectives, 8,* 158–162.

Skoog, T. et al. (2015). Understanding the link between pubertal timing in girls and the development of depressive symptoms: The role of sexual harassment. *Journal of Youth and Adolescence, 11,* 1–12.

Slanetz, P. et al. (2015). *Breast-density legislation: Practical considerations.* Retrieved February 18, 2015, from http://www.nejm.org/doi/full/10.1056/nejmp1413728.

Slaughter, A. M. (2015). *Unfinished business: Women, men, work, family.* New York: Random House. Smink, F. R. E. et al. (2014). Prevalence and severity of DSM-5 eating disorders in a community cohort of adolescents. *The International Journal of Eating Disorders, 47,* 610–619.

Slevin, K. F. (2010). "If I had lots of money . . . I'd have a body makeover:" Managing the aging body. *Social Forces, 88,* 1003–1020.

Smink, F. R. E. et al. (2014). Prevalence and severity of DSM-5 eating disorders in a community cohort of adolescents. *The International Journal of Eating Disorders, 47,* 610–619.

Smith, A. & Duggan, M. (2013). *Online dating & relationships.* Washington, DC: Pew Research Center.

Smith, C. A. & Stillman, S. (2002). What do women want? The effects of gender and sexual orientation on the desirability of physical attributes in the personal ads of women. *Sex Roles, 46,* 337–342.

Smith, C. P. & Freyd, J. J. (2014). Institutional betrayal. *American Psychologist, 69,* 575–587.

Smith, C. S. (2011). Psychotropic medications. In M. S. Stange, C. K. Oyster, & J. E. Sloan (Eds.), *Encyclopedia of women in today's world* (Vol. 3, pp. 1184–1185). Newberry Park, CA: Sage.

Smith, C. S., & Li-Ching, H. (2011). Megan's law. In M. Z. Stange, C. K. Oyster, & J. E. Sloan (Eds.), *Encyclopedia of women in today's world* (Vol. 2, pp. 920–922). Newberry Park, CA: Sage.

Smith, G., Mysak, K., & Michael, S. (2008). Sexual double standards and sexually transmitted illnesses: Social rejection and stigmatization of women. *Sex Roles, 58,* 391–401.

Smith, G. C. & Cichy, K. E. (2015). Impact of coping resources on the well-being of custodial grandmothers and grandchildren. *Family Relations, 64,* 378–392.

Smith, J. L. & Huntoon, M. (2014). Women's bragging rights: Overcoming modesty norms to facilitate women's self-promotion. *Psychology of Women Quarterly, 38,* 447–459.

Smith, J. S. et al. (2014). Giving back of giving up: Native American student experiences in science and engineering. *Clinical Diversity and Ethnic Minority Psychology, 20,* 413–429.

Smith, J. S. et al. (2016). Constrained by emotion: Women, leadership, and expressing emotion in the workplace. In M. L. Connerley & J. Wu (Eds.), *Handbook on well-being of working women* (pp. 209–220). Dordrecht, Netherlands: Springer.

Smith, S. L. et al. (2012). *Gender roles and occupations: A look at character attributes and job-related aspirations in film and television.* Retrieved from seejane.org

Smith, S. L. et al. (2015). *Inequality in 700 popular films: Examining portrayals of gender, race, & LGBT status from 2007 to 2014.* New York: The Harnisch Foundation.

Smith, S. L. et al. (2016a). *Inequality in 800 popular films: Examining portrayals of gender, race/ethnicity, LGBT, and disability from 2007–2015.* Los Angeles, CA: University of Southern California.

Smith, S. L. et al. (2016b). *The rare and ridiculed: Senior citizens in the top 100 films of 2015.* Los Angeles, CA: University of Southern California.

Smith, T. W. et al. (2014). On marriage and the heart: Models, methods, and mechanisms in the study of close relationships and cardiovascular disease. In C. R. Agnew & S. C. South (Eds.), *Interpersonal relationships and health: Social and clinical psychological mechanisms* (pp. 34–70). New York: Oxford University Press.

Smolak, L. & Munstertieger, B. F. (2002). The relationship of gender and voice to depression and eating disorders. *Psychology of Women Quarterly, 26,* 234–241.

Smolak, L. & Thompson, J. K. (Eds.). (2009). *Body image, eating disorders, and obesity in youth: Assessment, prevention, and treatment.* Washington, DC: American Psychological Association.

Smyth, M. & Jenness, V. (2014). Violence against sexual and gender minorities. In R. Gartner & B. McCarthy (Eds.), *The Oxford handbook of gender, sex, and crime* (pp. 403–423). New York: Oxford University Press.

Snell, M. B. (2002, November/December). Good going. *Sierra,* pp. 26–27.

Snowden, J. M. et al. (2015). Planned out-of-hospital birth and birth outcomes. *New England Journal of Medicine, 373,* 2642–2653.

Snyder, K. (2014). *The abrasiveness trap: High-achieving men and women are described differently in reviews.* Retrieved August 26, 2014, from fortune.com

Snyder, T. D. & Dillow, S. A. (2015). *Digest of education statistics 2015.* Washington, DC: National Center for Education Statistics.

Social Security Administration (2016). *What every woman should know* (SSA Publication No. 05-10127). Washington, DC: Author.

Social Trends Institute. (2011). *The empty cradle.* New York: Author.

Society of Actuaries. (2010). *Key findings and issues: The impact of retirement risk on women.* Schaumburg, IL: Author.

Sojo, V. E. et al. (2016). Harmful workplace experiences and women's occupational well-being: A meta-analysis. *Psychology of Women, 40,* 10–40.

Solem, P. E. et al. (2016). To leave or not to leave: Retirement intentions and retirement behaviour. *Ageing & Society, 36,* 259–281.

Solomon, A. (2015). *The newday demon: An atlas of depression.* New York: Scribner.

Solomon, C. (2005, July 17). Mean girls. *New York Times,* p. AR4.

Sommer, B.A. (2013). Menopause and women's sexuality. In D. Castaneda (Ed.). (pp. 113–124).

Sommers, B. D. et al. (2016). Changes in utilization and health among-low-income adults after Medicaid expansion expansion or expanded private insurance. *JAMA Internal Medicine* doi.10.1001/jamainternmed.2016.4419.

Sommers, C. H. (2013, February 3). The boys at the back. *New York Times,* p.SR1

Sontag, D. (2015, August 30). Once a pariah, now a transgender judge. *New York Times,* pp. Y1, Y18–19.

Sooryanarayana, R. et al. (2013). A review on the prevalence and measurement of elder abuse in the community. *Trauma, Violence, & Abuse, 14,* 316–325.

Soper, S. C. (2015, June 15). What's it like as a girl in the lab? *New York Times*, p. A31.

Sorde, T. et al. (2014). Solidarity networks that challenger racialized discourses: The case of Romani immigrant women in Spain. *European Journal of Women's Studies, 21*, 87–102.

Sorenson, S. B. (1996). Violence against women: Examining ethnic differences and commonalities. *Evaluation Review, 20*, 123–145.

South, S. C. & Krueger, R. F. (2013). Marital satisfaction and physical health: Evidence for an orchid effect. *Psychological Science, 20*, 1–6.

Spade, J. Z. & Valentine, C. G. (2016). *The kaleidoscope of gender: Prisms, patterns, and possibilities*. Thousand Oaks, CA: Sage Publications.

Span, P. (2015, December 8). Caregivers sometime give up one job for another. *New York Times*. p. D6.

Span, P. (2016, August 2). 65 is just a number. New York Times, p. D5.

Spearman, J. & Watt, H.M.G. (2013) women's aspirations toward STEM careers: A motivational analysis. In W. Patton (Ed.). *Conceptualising women's working lives: Moving the boundaries of discourse* (pp. 175–192). Sense Publishers.

Spellman, B. A. (2012). Introduction to the special section: Data, data, everywhere . . . especially in my file drawer. *Perspectives on Psychological Science, 7*, 58–59.

Spence, J. T. & Buckner, C. E. (2000). Instrumental and expressive traits, trait stereotypes, and sexist attitudes: What do they signify? *Psychology of Women Quarterly, 24*, 44–62.

Spence, J. T. & Helmreich, R. L. (1978). *Masculinity & femininity: Their psychological dimensions, correlates, & antecedents*. Austin, TX: University of Texas Press.

Spencer, R. A. et al. (2015). Patterns of dating violence perpetration and victimization in U.S. young adult males and females. *Journal of Interpersonal Violence, 10*, 1–22.

Spencer, S. J. & Loge, C. (2016). Stereotype threat. *Annual Review of Psychology, 67*, 1–14.

Spengler, E. S. & Ægisdóttir, S. (2015). Psychological help-seeking attitudes and intentions of lesbian, gay, and bisexual individuals: The role of sexual minority identity and perceived counselor sexual prejudice. *Psychology of Sexual Orientation and Gender Diversity, 2*, 482–491.

Spiegel, D. (2011). Mind matters in cancer survival. *Journal of the American Medical Association, 305*, 502.

Spiel, E. C. et al. (2012). Weight attitudes in 3-to-5-year-old children: Age differences and cross-sectional predictors. *Body Image, 9*, 524–527.

Spitzberg, B. H. &. Cupach, W. R. (2014). *The dark side of relationship pursuit: From attraction to obsession and stalking* (2nd ed.). New York: Routledge.

Spitzer, R. L. et al. (Eds.). (1994). *DSM-IV casebook*. Washington, DC: American Psychiatric Association.

Spivak, H. R. et al. (2014). CDC Grand Rounds: A public health approach to prevention of intimate partner violence. *Morbidity & Mortality Weekly Report, 63*, 38–41.

Sprague, J. (2016). *Feminist methodologies for critical researchers: Bridging differences*. Lanham, MD: Author.

Spring, B. et al. (2015). Fostering multiple healthy lifestyle behaviors for primary prevention of cancer. *American Psychologist, 70*, 75–90.

Spring, L. (2015). Older women and sexualtiy—are we still just talking lube? *Sexual and Relationship Therapy, 30*, 4–9.

Springen, K. & Seibert, S. (2005, January 17). Artful aging. *Newsweek*, pp. 57–65.

Sprung, J. M. et al. (2015). Family-friendly organizational policies, politics, and benefits through the gender lens. In M. Mills (Eds.), *Gender and the work-family experience: An intersection of two domains* (pp. 227–250). New York: Springer.

Spurgas, A. K. (2013). Interest, arousal, and shifting diagnoses of female sexual dysfunction, or: How women learn about desire. *Studies in Gender and Sexuality, 14*, 187–205.

Sroufe, L. A., Bennett, C., Englund, M., Urban, J., & Shulman, S. (1993). The significance of gender boundaries in preadolescence: Contemporary correlates and antecedents of boundary violation and maintenance. *Child Development, 64*, 455–466.

St. Rose, A. (2010, Winter). Why so few? Women in science, technology, engineering, and mathematics. *AAUW Outlook, 104*(1), 8–11.

Stack, L. (2016, November 20). Tinder swipes right for transgender. *New York Times*, pST10.

Stack, S. & Scourfield, J. (2013). Recency of divorce, depression, and suicide risk. *Journal of Family Issues, 36*, 695–715.

Stainback, K. et al. (2016). Women in power: Undoing or redoing the gendered organization? *Gender & Society, 30*, 109–135.

Stake, J. E. (1997). Integrating expressiveness and instrumentality in real-life settings: A new perspective on the benefits of androgyny. *Sex Roles, 37*, 541–564.

Stake, J. E. (2007). Predictors of change in feminist activism through women's and gender studies. *Sex Roles, 57*, 43–54.

Stake, J. E. & Rose, S. (1994). The long-term impact of women's studies on students' personal lives and political activism. *Psychology of Women Quarterly, 18*, 403–412.

Stake, J. E., Roades, L., Rose, S., Ellis, L., & West, C. (1994). The women's studies experience: Impetus for feminist activism. *Sex Roles, 18*, 17–24.

Stankiewicz, J. M. & Rosselli, F. (2008). Women as sex objects and victims in print advertisements. *Sex Roles, 58*, 579–589.

Stanley, A. (2002, January 13). For women, to soar is rare, to fall is human. *New York Times*, pp. BU1, BU10.

Stanley, S. M., Rhoades, G. K., & Fincham, F. D. (2011). Understanding romantic relationships among emerging adults: The significant roles of cohabitation and ambiguity. In F. D. Fincham & M. Cui (Eds.), *Romantic relationships in emerging adulthood* (pp. 234–251). New York: Cambridge University Press.

Stanton, A. L. (1995). Psychology of women's health: Barriers and pathways to knowledge. In A. L. Stanton & S. J. Gallant (Eds.), *The psychology of women's health: Progress and challenges in research and application* (pp. 3–21). Washington, DC: American Psychological Association.

Stearns, E. et al. (2016). Demographic characteristics of high school math and science teachers and girls' success in STEM. *Social Problems, 63*, 87–110.

Steele, C. M., Spencer, S. J., & Aronson, J. (2002). Contending with group image: The psychology of stereotype and social identity threat. In M. P. Zanna (Ed.), *Advances in experimental social psychology, 34*, 379–440.

Steele, J., James, J. B., & Barnett, R. C. (2002). Learning in a man's world: Examining the perceptions of undergraduate women in male-dominated academic areas. *Psychology of Women Quarterly, 26*, 46–50.

Stehle, M. (2016). *Awkward politics: Technologies of postfeminist activism*. Montreal: McGill-Queen's University Press.

Steinhauer, J. (2016, June 15). Senate votes to require women to register for the draft. *New York Times*, p. A10.

Steinhausen, H. C. et al. (2015). A nation-wide study of the family aggregation and risk factors in anorexia nervosa over three generations. *International Journal of Eating Disorders, 48*, 1–8.

Steinke, E. E. (2013). Sexuality and chronic illness. *Journal of Gerontological Nursing, 39*, 18–27.

Stephan, Y., Boiché, J., & Le Scanff, C. (2010). Motivation and physical activity behaviors among older women: A self-determination perspective. *Psychology of Women Quarterly, 3*, 339–348.

Stephenson, J. (2010). Human trafficking in Europe. *Journal of the American Medical Association, 304*, 513.

Stepler, R. (2016). *Smaller share of women ages 65 and older are living alone*. Washington, DC: Pew Research Center.

Stern, M. & Karraker, K. H. (1989). Sex stereotyping of infants: A review of gender labeling studies. *Sex Roles, 20*, 501–521.

Stevens, P., & Galvao, L. (2007). He won't use condoms: HIV-infected women's struggles in primary relationships with serodiscordant partners. *American Journal of Public Health, 97*, 1015–1022.

Stevens, S. & Thomas, S.P. (2012). Recovery of midlife women from myocardial infarction. *Health Care for Women International, 33*, 1096–1113.

Stevenson, M. R. (2015). The enigma of asexuality. *Psychology of Sexual Orientation and Gender Diversity, 2*, 207–208.

Stewart, A. J. & Vandewater, E.A. (1999). "If I had it to do over again...": midlife review, midcourse corrections, and women's well-being in midlife. *Journal of Personality and Social Psychology, 76*, 270–283.

Stewart, D. E. & Vigod, S. (2016). Postpartum depression. *New England Journal of Medicine, 375*, 2177–2186.

Stewart, E. A. et al. (2013). The burden of uterine fibroids for African-American women: Results of a national survey. *Journal of Women's Health, 22*, 807–816.

Stöckl, H. & Penhale, B. (2015). Intimate partner violence and its association with physical and mental health symptoms among older women in Germany. *Journal of Interpersonal Violence, 30*, 3089–3111.

Stockley, P. & Campbell, A. (2013). Female competition and aggression: Interdisciplinary perspectives. *Philosophical Transactions of the Royal Society B: Biological Sciences, 386*, 1–19.

Stockman, J. K. et al. (2015). Intimate partner violence and its health impact on disproportionately affected populations, including minorities and impoverished groups. *Journal of Women's Health, 24*, 62–79.

Stoet, G. & Geary, D. C. (2014). Sex differences in academic achievement are not related to political, economic, or social equality. *Intelligence, 48*, 137–151.

Stolberg, S. G. et al. (2016, May 22). A culture war on new front: The bathroom. *New York Times*, pp. A1, A16.

Stoner, C. C., Gallatti, N., Dugan, A. E., & Cole, P. M. (2005, April). *Anger expression, expressive language & gender in 18-month-olds.* Poster presented at the meeting of the Society for Research in Child Development, Atlanta, GA.

Storage, D. et al. (2016). The frequency of "Brilliant" and "Genius" in teaching evaluations predicts the representation of women and African Americans across fields. *PLOS ONE*, 1–12.

Stover, S. S. & Kiselica, A. (2015). Hostility and substance use in relation to intimate partner violence and parenting among fathers. *Aggressive Behavior, 41*, 205–213.

Strauss, J. R. et al. (2013). The baby boomers meet menopause: Fertility, attractiveness, and affective response to the menopausal transition. *Sex Roles, 68*, 77–90.

Strauss, J. R. (2015). Contextualizing the "student body": Is exposure to older students associated with body dissatisfaction in female early adolescents? *Psychology of Women Quarterly, 39*, 171–181.

Strauss, R. S. (2000). Childhood obesity and self-esteem. *Pediatrics, 105*(1), e15.

Stringer, H. (2014, November). Unlocking the emotions of cancer. *Monitor on Psychology, 45*, 34.

Stringer, H. (2016, April). Supporting opportunities for LGBT research. *Monitor on Psychology, 47*, 76.

Stroebel, S. S. et al. (2013). Brother-sister incest: Data from anonymous computer assisted self interviews. *Journal of Child Sexual Abuse, 22*, 255–276.

Stubbs, M. L. (2008). Cultural perceptions and practices around menarche and adolescent menstruation in the United States. *Annals of the New York Academy of Sciences, 1135*, 58–66.

Stubbs, M. L. & Johnston-Robledo, I. (2013). Kiddy thongs and menstrual pads: The sexualization of girls and early menstrual life. In E. L. Zurbriggen & T.-A. Roberts (Eds.) *The sexualization of girls and girlhood: Causes, consequences, and resistance* (pp.). New York: Oxford University Press.

Stuhlmacher, A. F. & Linna berry, E. (2013). Gender role negotiation: A social role analysis. In M'Olekalns & W. Adair (Eds.). *Handbook of research on negotiation research* (pp. 221–248). London, UK: Edward Elgar.

Suchert, V. et al. (2016). Screen time, weight status and the self-concept of physical attractiveness in adolescents. *Journal of Adolescents, 48*, 11–17.

Suchland, J. (2015). *Economies of violence: Transnational feminism, postsocialism, and the policies of sex trafficking.* Durham, NC: Duke University Press.

Sue, D. W. & Sue, D. (2015). *Counseling the culturally different: Theory and practice* (7th ed.). Malden, MA: Wiley.

Suellentrop, K. K. (2011). *What works 2011–2012: Curriculum-based programs that help prevent teen pregnancy.* Washington, DC: The National Campaign to Prevent Teen and Unplanned Pregnancy.

Sugarman, D.T., Livingston, E.H. (2013). US health compared with like countries. *Journal of the American Medical Association, 310*, 1996.

Sullivan, A. R. & Fenelon, A. (2013). Patterns of widowhood mortality. *Journal of Gerontology Series B: Psychological Sciences and Social Sciences, 69*, 53–62.

Sullivan, E. M. et al. (2015). Suicide trends among persons aged 10–24 years: United States, 1994–2012. *Morbidity and Mortality Weekly Report, 64*, 201–205.

Sullivan, O. (2013). What do we learn about gender by analyzing housework separately from child care? Some considerations from time-use evidence. *Journal of Family Theory & Review, 5*, 72–84.

Summers, A. & Miller, M.K. (2014). From damsels in distress to sexy superheroes. *Feminist Media Studies, 14*, 1028–1040.

Summers, C. H. (2013). *The war against boys: How misguided politics are harming our young men.* New York: Simon & Schuster.

Sumra, M. K. & Schillaci, M. (2015). Stress and the multiple-role woman: Taking a closer look at the "Superwoman." *PLOS ONE, 10*, 1–20.

Sunderam, S. et al. (2015). Assisted reproductive technology surveillance—United States, 2012. *MMWR Surveillance Summaries, 64*, 1–32.

Sundstrom, B. L. (2015). *Reproductive justice and women's voices: Health communication across the lifespan.* Lanham, MD: Lexington Books.

Sung, S. et al. (2016). Secure infant-mother attachment buffers the effect of early-life stress on age of menarche. *Psychological Science, 27*, 667–674.

Supervia , M. et al. (2017, March 13). Cardiac rehabilitation for women: A systematic review of barriers and solutions. *Mayo Clinic Proceedings*, doi:10.1016/j,mayocp.2017.01.007

Susman, E. J. & Rogol, A. (2004). Puberty and psychological development. In R. M. Lerner & L. Steinberg (Eds.), *Handbook of adolescent psychology* (2nd ed., pp. 15–44). Hoboken, NJ: Wiley.

Susskind, J. E., Hodges, C., Carter, B., & Witmack, C. (2005, April). *Cooties: Distinguishing gender-based in-group favoritism from out-group derogation.* Poster presented at the meeting of the Society for Research in Child Development, Atlanta, GA.

Sussman, M. et al. (2015). *Prevalence of menopausal symptoms among mid-life women: Findings from electronic medical records.* Retrieved November 8, 2015, from BMC Women's Health.

Sutherland, M. A. et al. (2016). Screening for intimate partner and sexual violence in college women: Missed opportunities. *Women's Health Issues, 26*, 217–224.

Swartz, S. (2013). Feminism and psychiatric diagnosis: Reflections of a feminist practitioner. *Feminism & Psychology, 23*, 41–48.

Swauger, M. (2010). Do (not) follow in my footsteps: How mothers influence working-class girls' aspirations. *Girlhood Studies 3*(2), 49–68.

Swearingen-Hilker, N. & Yoder, J. D. (2002). Understanding the context of unbalanced domestic contributions: The influence of perceiver's attitudes, target's gender, and presentational format. *Sex Roles, 46*, 91–98.

Sweeney, M. & Raley, R. K. (2014). Race, ethnicity, and the changing context of childbearing in the United States. *Annual Review of Sociology, 40*, 539–58.

Sweeney, M. M. (2010). Remarriage and stepfamilies: Strategic sites for family scholarship in the 21st century. *Journal of Marriage and Family, 72*, 667–684.

Swim, J. K., Becker, J. C., Lee, E., & Pruitt, E.-R. (2010b). Sexism reloaded: Worldwide evidence for its endorsement, expression, and emergence in multiple contexts. In H. Landrine & N. F. Russo (Eds.), *Handbook of diversity in feminist psychology* (pp. 137–171). New York: Springer.

Swim, J. K., Eyssell, K. M., Murdoch, E. Q., & Ferguson, M. J. (2010a). Self-silencing to sexism. *Society for the Psychological Study of Social Issues, 66*, 493–507.

Swirsky, J. M. & Angelone, D. J. (2014). Femi-Nazis and bra burning crazies: A qualitative evolution of contemporary beliefs about feminism. *Current Psychology, 3*, 229–245.

Swirsky, J. M. & Angelone, D. J. (2015). Equality, empowerment, and choice: What does feminism mean to contemporary women? *Journal of Gender Studies, 10*, 1–3.

Switzer, J. Y. (1990). The impact of generic word choices: An empirical investigation of age- and sex-related differences. *Sex Roles, 22,* 69–82.

Sybert, V. P. & McCauley, E. (2004). Turner's syndrome. *New England Journal of Medicine, 351,* 1227–1238.

Szinovacz, M. (1991). Women and retirement. In B. B. Hess & E. W. Markson (Eds.), *Growing old in America* (4th ed., pp. 293–303). New Brunswick, NJ: Transaction.

Szinovacz, M. E. et al. (2012). Families and retirement. In R. Blieszner & V. H. Bedford (Eds.), *Handbook of families and aging* (pp. 461–488). Santa Barbara, CA: ABC-CLIO.

Szymanski , D. M & Moffitt, L. B. (2012) Sexism and heterosexism (2012). In N. Fouad et al. (Eds.) *APA handbook of counseling psychology: Practice, interventions, and applications* (pp. 361–390). Washington, DC: American Psychological Association.

Tabaac, A. R. et al. (2015). Multiple mediational model of outness, social support, mental health, and wellness behavior in ethnically diverse lesbian, bisexual, and queer women. *LGBT Health, 2,* 243–249.

Tabuchi, H. (2015, October 29). A tiara? No thanks. *New York Times,* pp. B1, B8.

Taft, J. K. (2010). *Rebel girls: Youth activism & social change across the Americas.* New York: NYU Press.

Talley, A. E. et al. (2014). Explaining alcohol use behaviors among heterosexual and sexual minority adolescents: Interactions and with sex age, and race/ethnicity. *AJPH, 104,* 295–303.

Tan, C. H. et al. (2015). Alcohol use and binge drinking among women of childbearing age—United States, 2011–2013. *Morbidity and Mortality Weekly Report, 64,* 1042–1044.

Tan, J. O. A. et al. (2016). Understanding eating disorders in elite gymnastics: Ethical and conceptual challenges. *Clinics in Sports Medicine, 35,* 275–292.

Tang, C. (2014). Cohabitors' reasons for living together, satisfaction with sacrifices, and relationship quality. *Marriage & Family Review, 50,* 1–3.

Tang, S. et al. (2016). Adolescent pregnancy's intergenerational effects: Doed an adolescent mother's education have consequences for her children's achievement? *Journal of Research on Adolescence, 26,* 180–193.

Tarampi, M. R. et al. (2016). A tale of two types of perspective-taking: Sex differences in spatial ability. *Psychological Science, 27,* 1507–1516.

Tarasoff, L. A. (2015). Experiences of women with physical disabilities during the perinatal period: A review of the literature and recommendations to improve care. *Health Care for Women International, 36,* 88–107.

Tasker, F. (2010). Same-sex parenting and child development: Reviewing the contribution of parental gender. *Journal of Marriage and Family, 72,* 35–40.

Tat, S. A. et al. (2015). Women who have sex with women living in low- and middle-income countries: A systematic review of sexual health and risk behaviors, *LGBT Health, 2,* 91–104.

Tatangelo, G. et al. (2016). A systematic review of body dissatisfaction and sociocultural Messages related to the body image among preschool children. *Body Image,* doi:10.1016/j.bodyim.2016.06.003.

Tati, A. et al. (2012). An unrequited affinity between talent shortages and untapped female potential: The relevance of gender quotas for talent management in high growth potential economies of the Asia Pacific region. *International Business Review, 22,* 539–553.

Tavernise, S. (2015, November 10). Women's use of long-acting birth control methods is surging report finds. *New York Times,* p. D15.

Tavernise, S. (2016, March 31). New F.D.A. rules will ease access to abortion pill: A decades long debate. *New York Times,* pp. A1, A14.

Tavernise, S. & Gebeloff, R. (2016, April 18). Immigrants and minorities gain insurance. *New York Times,* pp. A1, A15.

Taylor, B. D. et al. (2015). What explains the gender gap in Schlepping? Testing various explanations for gender differences in household-serving travel. *Social Science Quarterly, 96,* 1493–1510.

Taylor, B. G. & Mumford, E. A. (2016). A national descriptive portrait of adolescent relationship abuse: Results from the National Survey on Teen Relationships and Intimate Violence. *Journal of Interpersonal Violence, 31,* 963–988.

Taylor, C. A. (2016). Relational by nature? Men and women do not differ in physiological response to social stressors faced by token women. *American Journal of Sociology, 122,* 49–89.

Taylor, D. (2007). Employment preferences and salary expectations of students in science and engineering. *BioScience, 57,* 175–185.

Taylor, J. L. (2009). Midlife impacts of adolescent parenthood. *Journal of Family Issues, 30,* 484–510.

Taylor, S. E. (2010). Health. In S. T. Fiske, D. T. Gilbert, & G. Lindzey (Eds.), *Handbook of social psychology* (5th ed., Vol. 1, pp. 698–723). Hoboken, NJ: John Wiley & Sons.

Taylor, S. E. & Master, S. L. (2011). Social responses to stress: The tend-and-befriend model. In R. J. Contrada & A. Baum (Eds.), *The handbook of stress science: Biology, psychology and health* (pp. 101–109). New York: Springer.

Taylor, S. E. et al. (2000). Biobehavioral responses to stress in females: Tend-and-befriend, not fight-or-flight. *Psychological Review, 107,* 411–429.

Taylor, U. Y. (2010). Black feminisms and human agency. In *No permanent waves: Recasting the history of U.S. feminism* (pp. 61–76). Piscataway, NJ: Rutgers University Press.

Teaster, P. B. et al. (2013). Elder abuse in aging families. In R. Blieszner & V. H. Bedford (Eds.), *Handbook of families and aging* (pp. 409–430). Santa Barbara, CA: Praeger.

Teig, S. & Susskind, J. E. (2008). Truck driver or nurse? The impact of gender roles and occupational status on children's occupational preferences. *Sex Roles, 58,* 848–863.

Teitelbaum, M. S. & Winter, J. M. (2014, April 6). Bye-bye, baby: Birthrates are falling around the world. And that's OK. *New York Times,* pp. SR1, SR8.

Tejeda, S. et al. (2013). Patient barriers to follow-up care for breast and cervical cancer abnormalities. *Journal of Women's Health, 22,* 507.

Tellhed, U. et al. (2017). Will I fit in and do well? The importance of social belongingness and self-efficacy for explaining gender differences in interest in STEM and HEED majors. *Sex Roles,* doi.10.1007/s11199-016-0694-y.

Temple, J. R. et al. (2013). *School-based dating violence prevention.* Retrieved February 28, 2015, from the Journal of Applied Research on Children.

Temple-Smith, M. et al. (2016). *Sexuality in adolescence: The digital generation adolescence and society.* New York: Routledge.

Tenenbaum, H. & May, D. (2013). Gender in parent-child relationships. In P. J. Leman & H. R. Tenenbaum (Eds.), *Gender and development* (pp. 1–19). New York: Psychology Press.

Tener, D. & Murphy, S. B. (2014). Adult disclosure of child sexual abuse: A literature review. *Trauma, Violence, & Abuse, 16,* 391–400.

Texas Heart Institute. (2015). *Women and heart disease.* Retrieved January 21, 2016, from the Texas Heart Institute.

Tharenou, P. (2013). The work of feminists is not yet done: The gender pay gap—a stubborn anachronism. *Sex Roles, 68,* 198–206.

Tharp, A.T. et al. (2012). A systematic qualitative review of risk and protective factors for sexual violence perpetration. *Trauma, Violence, & Abuse, 14,* 133–167.

The struggle for fairness for transgender workers. (2015, July 9). *New York Times,* p. A24.

Thielmann, I. et al. (2015). Now you see it, now you don't: Explaining inconsistent evidence on gender stereotyping of newborns. *European Journal of Social Psychology, 45,* 678–686.

Thogersen-Ntoumani, C. et al. (2016). "Mum's the word": Predictors and outcomes of weight concerns in pre-adolescent and early adolescent girls. *Body Image, 16,* 107–112.

Thomas, A. & Lou, C. (2015, July). New evidence on the relationship between academic ability and nonmarital teen childbearing. *Child Trends Research Brief,* 1–8. Bethesda,MD: Child Trends.

Thomas, A. J., Hacker, J. D., & Hoxha, D. (2011). Gendered racial identity of Black young women. *Sex Roles, 64,* 530–554.

Thomas, G. (2016). *Because of sex: One law, ten cases, and fifty years that changed American women's lives at work.* New York: St. Martin's Press.

Thomas, H. N. et al. (2014). Sexuality activity in midlife women: Importance of sex matters. *JAMA Internal Medicine, 174,* 631–633.

Thomas, J. L., Sperry, L., & Yarbrough, M. S. (2000). Grandparents as parents: Research findings and policy recommendations. *Child Psychiatry and Human Development, 31,* 3–22.

Thomas, H. N. et al. (2015). Correlates of sexual activity in midlife and older women. *Annals of Family Medicine, 13,* 336–342.

Thomas, H. N. & Thurston, RC. (2016). A biopsychosocial approach to

Thompson, K. M. (2009). Sibling incest: A model for group practice with adult female victims of brother-sister incest. *Journal of Family Violence, 24,* 531–537.

Thompson , M. E. & Armato, M. (2012). *Investigating gender: Deeloping a feminist, sociological imagination.* Cambridge: Polity Press

Thorne, B. (1993). *Gender play: Girls and boys in school.* New Brunswick, NJ: Rutgers University Press.

Thornhill, R. & Palmer, C. T. (2000). *A natural history of rape: Biological bases of sexual coercion.* Cambridge, MA: MIT Press.

Thornton, L. J. (2013). "Time of the month" on Twitter: Taboo, stereotype and bonding in a no-holds-barred public arena. *Sex Roles, 68,* 41–54.

Thorpe, R. et al. (2015). Old and desirable: Older women's accounts of ageing bodies in intimate relationships. *Sexual and Relationship Therapy, 30,* 156–166.

Thrane, C. (2000). Men, women, and leisure time: Scandinavian evidence of gender inequality. *Sport & Leisure Management, 22,* 109–122.

Thun, M. J. et al. (2013). 50-year trends in smoking-related mortality in the United States. *New England Journal of Medicine, 368,* 351–352.

Thurston, R. C. & Kubzansky, L. D. (2009). Women, loneliness, and incident coronary heart disease. *Psychosomatic Medicine, 71,* 836–842.

Tichenor, V. (2005). Maintaining men's dominance: Negotiating identity and power when she earns more. *Sex Roles, 53,* 191–205.

Tidwell, N. D. (2013). Perceived, not actual, similarity predicts initial attraction in a live romantic context: Evidence from the speed-dating paradigm. *Personal Relationships, 20,* 199–215.

Tiefer, L. (2014). New view campaign. Retrieved from newviewcampaign.org/

Tiggemann, M. & McCourt, A. (2013). Body appreciation in adult women: Relationships with age and body satisfaction. *Body Image, 10,* 624–627.

Tiggemann, M. & Slater, A. (2013). NetTweens: The internet, Facebook, and body image concern in adolescent girls. *International Journal of Eating Disorders, 46,* 630–633.

Tiggemann, M. & Slater, A. (2014a). Contemporary girlhood: Maternal reports on sexualized behaviour and appearance concern in 4–10 year-old girls. *Body Image, 11,* 396–403.

Tiggemann, M. & Slater, A. (2014b). NetTweens: The internet and body image concerns in preteenage girls. *Journal of Early Adolescence, 34,* 606–620.

Tiggemann, M. et al. (2013). Disclaimer labels on fashion magazine advertisements: Effects on social comparison and body dissatisfaction. *Body Image, 10,* 45–53.

Timmerman, G. (2003). Sexual harassment of adolescents perpetrated by teachers and by peers: An exploration of the dynamics of power, culture, and gender in secondary schools. *Sex Roles, 48,* 231–244.

Tingley, K. (2013). *I'm not ok.* Retrieved June 30, 2013, from New York Times Magazine.

Tirado, A. et al. (2015). Socio-cultural challenges for Latinas pursuing a college degree. *The Feminist Psychology, 5,* 42–45.

Titlestad, A. & Pooley, J. A. (2013). Resilience in same-sex parented families: The lived experience of adults with gay, lesbian, or bisexual parents. *Journal of GLBT Family Studies, 10,* 329–353.

Tobach, E. (2001). Development of sex and gender: Biochemistry, physiology, and experience. In J. Worell (Ed.), *Encyclopedia of women and gender* (pp. 315–332). San Diego, CA: Academic Press.

Todd, B. K. et al. (2016). Preferences for "gender-typed" toys in boys and girls aged 9 to 32 months. *Infant and Child Development,* doi:10.1002/icd.1986.

Toller, P. W., Suter, E. A., & Trautman, T. C. (2004). Gender role identity and attitudes toward feminism. *Sex Roles, 51,* 85–90.

Tolman, D. L. (2002). *Dilemmas of desire: Teenage girls talk about sexuality.* Cambridge, MA: Harvard University Press.

Tolman, D.L. (2012). Female adolescents, sexual empowerment, and desire: A missing discourse of gender equity. *SexRoles, 66,* 746–757.

Tolman, D. L. et al. (2015). Mobilizing metaphor: Considering complexities, contradictions, and contexts in adolescent girls' and young women's sexual agency. *Sex Roles, 73,* 298–310.

Tomlinson, B. (2010). *Feminism and affect at the scene of argument: Beyond the trope of the angry feminist.* Philadelphia, PA: Temple University Press.

Tomlinson, J. M. et al. (2014). The costs of being put on a pedestal: Effects of feeling over-idealized. *Journal of Social and Personal Relationships, 31,* 384–409.

Torpy, J. M. (2011). Generalized anxiety disorder. *Journal of the American Medical Association, 305,* 522.

Torre, E. D. (2013). The clitoris diaries: La donna clitoridea, feminine authenticity, and the phallic allegory of Carla Lonzi's radical feminism. *European Journal of Women's Studies, 21,* 219–232.

Torrone, E. et al. (2014). Prevalence of chlamydia trachomatis genital infection among persons aged 14–39 years—United States, 2007–2012. *Morbidity and Mortality Weekly Report, 63,* 834–837.

Tougas, F., Brown, R., Beaton, A. M., & Joly, S. (1995). Neosexism: Plus ça change, plus c'est pareil. *Personality and Social Psychology Bulletin, 21,* 842–849.

Traies, J. (2016). *The lives of older lesbians: Sexuality, identity & the life course.* New York: Palgrave Macmillan.

Trail Ross, M. E. et al. (2015). Psychological profile, salivary cortisol, C-reactive protein, and perceived health of grandmothers with child-rearing responsibility. *Journal of Family Issues, 36,* 1904–1927.

Traister, R. (2016). *All the single ladies: Unmarried women and the rise of an independent nation.* New York: Simon & Schuster.

Trask, B. S. (2014). *Women, work, and globalization.* New York: Routledge.

Trask, L. & Kimmel, D. (2014). Lesbian, gay, bisexual, and transgender aging: Considerations for interventions. In N. A. Pachana & K. Laidlaw (Eds.), *Oxford handbook of clinical geropsychology* (pp. 776–796). New York: Oxford University Press.

Travis, C. B. (2003). Theory and data on rape and evolution. In C. B. Travis (Ed.), *Evolution, gender, and rape* (pp. 207–220). Cambridge, MA: The MIT Press.

Travis, C. B. & Compton, J. D. (2001). Feminism and health in the decade of behavior. *Psychology of Women Quarterly, 25,* 312–323.

Treas, J. & Lui, J. (2013). Studying housework across nations. *Journal of Family Theory & Review, 5,* 135–149.

Treas, J. & Tai, T. (2016). Gender inequality in housework across 20 European nations: Lessons from gender stratification theories. *Sex Roles, 74,* 495–511.

Travis, L.A. & Kimmel, D.C. (2014). Lesbian, gay, bisexual, and transgender ageing. In N.A. Pachara & K. Laidlaw (Eds.). *Oxford handbook of clinical geropsychology* (pp.776–796). New York: Oxford University Press.

Treas, J. & Tai, T.-O. (2007, August). *Long apron strings of working mothers: Maternal employment, occupational attainments, and housework in cross-national perspective.* Paper presented at the meeting of the American Sociological Association, New York.

Treas, J. & Widmer, E. D. (2000). Married women's employment over the life course: Attitudes in cross-national perspective. *Social Forces, 78,* 1409–1436.

Trompeter, S. E. et al. (2012). Sexual activity and satisfaction in healthy community-dwelling older women. *American Journal of Medicine, 125,* 37–43.

Troop-Gordon, W. (2015). The role of the classroom teacher in the lives of children victimized by peers. *Child Development, 9,* 55–60.

Troop-Gordon, W. & Ranney, J. D. (2014). Popularity among same-sex and cross-sex peers: A process-oriented examination of links to aggressive behaviors and depressive affect. *Developmental Psychology, 50,* 1721–1733.

Trop, J. (2014). *Is Mary Barra standing on a "Glass Cliff?"* Retrieved April 29, 2014, from The New Yorker.

Trotman, F. & Tirrell, M. (2013). Older women of color: Considerations for mental health professionals. In L. Comas-Diaz & B. Greene (Eds.), *Psychological health of women of color:*

Intersections, challenges, and opportunities (pp. 81–100). Santa Barbara, CA: ABC-CLIO.

Troutman-Jordan, M. et al. (2013). An examination of successful aging among southern black and white older adults. *Journal of Gerontological Nursing, 39*, 42–52.

Troxel, W. M., Matthews, K. A., Gallo, L. C., & Kuller, L. H. (2005). Marital quality and occurrence of the metabolic syndrome in women. *Archives of Internal Medicine, 165*, 1022–1027.

Trudel-Fitzgerald, C. et al. (2016). Psychiatric, psychological, and social determinants of health in the Nurses' Health Study cohorts. *American Journal of Public Health, 106*, 1644–1649.

Tryon, G. S. (2017). Value choices and methodological issues in counseling research with women. In M. Kopala & M. Keitel (Eds.), *Handbook of counseling women* (2nd ed., pp. 620–630). Thousand Oaks, CA: Sage.

Tulloch, T. & Kaufman, M. (2013). Adolescent sexuality. *Pediatrics in Review, 34*, 39–34.

Turchik, J. A. & Hassija, C. M. (2014). Female seual victimization among college students: Assault severity, health risk behaviors, and sexual functioning. *Journal of Interpersonal Violence, 29*, 2439–2457.

Turchik, J. A. et al. (2016). An examination of the gender inclusiveness of current theories of sexual violence in adulthood: Recognizing male victims, female perpetrators, and same-sex violence. *Trauma, Violence, & Abuse, 17*, 133–148.

Turiel, E. (2006). The development of morality. In W. Damon, R. M. Lerner (Series Eds.), & N. Eisenberg (Vol. Ed.), *Handbook of child psychology: Vol. 3. Social, emotional, and personality development* (6th ed., pp. 789–857). Hoboken, NJ: Wiley.

Turk-Bicakci, L. & Berger, A. (2014). *Leaving STEM: STEM Ph.D. holders in non-STEM careers*. Washington, DC: American Institutes for Research.

Turkewitz, J. (2014, June 11). A fight as U.S. girls face genital cutting abroad. *New York Times*, pp. A1, A13.

Turkewitz, J. (2015a, January 3). After a spa day, looking years younger (O. K., they're only 7). *New York Times*, p. A10.

Turkewitz, J. (2015b, February 6). Effects of ancient custom present new challenge to U.S. doctors. *New York Times*, pp. A11, A15.

Turner de Tormes Eby, L. et al. (2013). An interdisciplinary meta-analysis of the potential antecedents, correlates, and consequences of protege perceptions of mentoring. *Psychological Bulletin, 139*, 441–476.

Turner, L. (2012). Constructing the grandmother-granddaughter relationship through communication: A review of the literature. I A. H. Deakins & R. B. Lockridge (Eds.). *Mothers and daughters: Complicated connections across cultures* (pp. 231–250). Lanham, MD: University Press of America.

Tutchell, E. & Edmonds, J. (2015). *Man-made: Why so few women are in positions of power*. Surrey, England: Gower Publishing.

Twenge, J. M. (1997). Changes in masculine and feminine traits over time: A meta-analysis. *Sex Roles, 36*, 305–325.

Twenge, J. M. (2001). Changes in women's assertiveness in response to status and roles: A cross-temporal meta-analysis, 1931–1993. *Journal of Personality and Social Psychology, 81*, 133–145.

Twenge, J. M. (2009). Status and gender: The paradox of progress in an age of narcissism. *Sex Roles, 61*, 338–340.

Twenge, J. M. & Crocker, J. (2002). Race and self-esteem: Meta-analyses comparing Whites, Blacks, Hispanics, Asians and American Indians and comment on Gray-Little and Hafdahl (2000). *Psychological Bulletin, 128*, 371–408.

Twenge, J. M. et al. (2015). Changes in American adults' sexual behavior and attitudes, 1972–2012. *Archives of Sex and Behavior, 44*, 2273–2285.

Tzuriel, D. & Egozi, G. (2010). Gender differences in spatial ability of young children: The effects of training and processing strategies. *Child Development, 81*, 1417–1430.

Ui, M. & Matsui, Y. (2008). Japanese adults' sex role attitudes and judgment criteria concerning gender equality: The diversity of gender egalitarianism. *Sex Roles, 58*, 412–422.

UN Women. (2014). *Expanding dialogue on gender equality, UN women at the MenEngage symposium in India*. New York: United Nations.

UNAIDS. (2014a). *The GAP Report*. Geneva, Switzerland: Author.

UNAIDS. (2014b). *UNAIDS report shows that 9 million of the 35 million people living with HIV today do not know that they have the virus*. Geneva, Switzerland: Author.

Underwood, E. (2014). Can disparities be deadly? Controversial research explores whether living in an unequal society can make people sick. *Sciencemag.org*. 344, 829–230.

Understanding and coping with sexual behavior problems in children. (2010). Los Angeles/Durham, CA/NC: National Child Traumatic Stress Network.

Unger, J. B. & Seeman, T. E. (2000). Successful aging. In M. B. Goldman & M. C. Hatch (Eds.), *Women & health* (pp. 1238–1251). New York: Academic Press.

UNICEF. (2014). *Child marriage is a violation of human rights, but is all too common*. New York: Author.

UNICEF. (2016a). *Female genital mutilation/ cutting: A global concern*. New York: Author.

UNICEF (2016b). *Harnessing the power and data for girls: Taking stock and looking ahead to 2030*. New York: Author.

UNIFEM. (2008). *Who answers to women? Gender and accountability*. New York: Author.

UNIFEM. (2010). *Gender justice: Key to achieving the millennium development goals*. New York: Author.

United Nations. (2014). *Global report on trafficking in persons*. Vienna, Austria: Author.

UN Human Rights Council. (2015). *Background paper on attacks against girls seeking to access education*. New York: Author.

United Nations News Center. (2013). *The millennium development goals report 2013*. Retrieved January, 2014, from un.org

United Nations News Center. (2015). *Global status report on violence prevention 2014*. Retrieved January, 2015, from "http://www.un.org".

United Nations Office on Drugs and Crime. (2009). *Trafficking in persons: Analysis on Europe*. Vienna: Author.

United Nations Population Fund. (2015). *The start of a movement: Girls rising up against FGM*. Retrieved February 6, 2015, "http://www.un.org".

Unützer, J. (2007). Late-life depression. *New England Journal of Medicine, 357*, 2269–2276.

U.S. Census Bureau. (2003). *Educational attainment in the United States: March 2001 and March 2002*. Current Population Reports. Washington, DC: Author.

U.S. Census Bureau. (2008, January 2). *Women's history month: March 2008* (CB08-FF.03). Washington, DC: Author.

U.S. Census Bureau. (2010). *Educational attainment in the United States: 2008*. Washington, DC: Author.

U.S. Census Bureau. (2013). *Frequently asked questions about same-sex couple households*. Retrieved August, 2013, from the U.S. Census Bureau.

U.S. Census Bureau. (2015a). *Updated tables on fertility*. CB15-TPS.33. Washington, DC: Author.

U.S. Census Bureau (2015b). *Statistical abstract of the United States*. Washington, D.C: Author.

U.S. Census Bureau. (2016a). *Characteristics of same-sex couple households: 2014*. Washington, DC: Author.

U.S. Census Bureau. (2016b). *Mother's Day: May 8, 2016*. (CB16-FF.09). Washington, DC: Author.

U.S. Census Bureau, International Database. (1997, 1995). Retrieved from census.gov/International/Aging Statistics.htm

U.S. Department of Commerce. (2011). *Women in America: Indicators of social and economic well-being*. Washington, DC: Author.

U.S. Department of Commerce. (2014). National grandparents day 2014: September 7. Washington, DC: U.S. Census Bureau News.

U.S. Department of Education. (2011a). *The condition of education 2011*. Washington, DC: Author.

U.S. Department of Education. (2011b). *The nation's report card: Writing 2011*. Washington, DC: Author.

U.S. Department of Education. (2016). *High-quality early learning settings depend on a high-quality workforce: Low compensation undermines quality*. Washington, DC: Author.

U.S. Department of Health and Human Services. (2013). *Women's Health USA 2013*. Rockville, MD: Author.

U.S. Department of Justice. (2012). *An updated definition of rape*. Washington, DC: Author.

U.S. Department of Labor. (n.d.). *Affirmative action at OFCCP: A sound policy and a good investment*. Employment Standards

Administration, Office of Federal Contract Compliance Programs. Washington, DC: Author.

U.S. Department of Labor (2015). *Older women workers and economic security*. Washington, DC:Author

Unterhalter, E. et al. (2014). *Reducing the gender gap in education*. Retrieved April 3, 2015, from blogs.worldbank.org/development-talk

Upadhyay, U. (2016). Comparison of outcomes before and after Ohio's law mandating use of the FDA-approved protocol for medication abortion: A retrospective cohort study. *PLOS Medicine, 13*(8). e1002110.

Ussher, J. M. et al. (2013). Diagnosing difficult women and pathologizing femininity: Gender bias in psychiatric nosology. *Feminism & Psychology, 23*, 63–69.

Ussher, J. M. (2014). Pathology or source of power? The construction and experience of premenstrual syndrome within two contrasting cases. *Feminism & Psychology, 24*, 332–351.

Ussher, J. M. (2015). Sex and the menopausal woman: A critical review and analysis. *Feminism & Psychology, 25*, 449–468.

Uttal, D. H. et al. (2013). The malleability of spatial skills: A meta-analysis of training studies. *Psychological Bulletin, 139*, 352–402.

Utter, J., Neumark-Sztainer, D., Wall, M., & Story, M. (2003). Reading magazine articles about dieting and associated weight control behaviors among adolescents. *Journal of Adolescent Health, 32*, 78–82.

Vaccaro & Camba-Kelsay (2016). *Centerin g women of color in academic counterspaces: A critical race analysis of teaching, learning, and classroom dynamics*. New York: Lexington Books.

Vacha-Haase, T. et al. (2014). Race-ethnicity and gender in older adults. In M. L. Miville & A. D. Ferguson (Eds.), *Handbook of race- ethnicity, and gender in psychology* (pp. 65–86). New York: Springer.

Vafei, A. et al. (2016). Depression, sex and gender roles in older adult populations: The International Mobility in Aging Study (IMIAS). *PLoS One ,11*, e1046867

Vagi, K. J. et al. (2015). Teen dating violence (physical and sexual) among US high school students: Findings from the 2013 National Youth Risk Behavior Survey. *JAMA Pediatrics, 169*, 474–482.

Valentine, C. G. (2015). Letting go feminism: Reconnecting self-care and social justice. In D. King & C. G. Valentine (Eds.), *Letting go: Feminist and social justice insight and activism* (pp. 1–14). Nashville, TN: Vanderbilt University Press.

Valla, J. & Williams, W. W. (2012). Increasing achievement and higher-education representation of underrepresented groups in science, technology, engineering and mathematical fields: A review of current K-12 intervention programs. *Journal of Women and Minorities in Science and Engineering, 18*, 21–53.

Valla, J. M. & Ceci, S. J. (2011). Can sex differences in science be tied to the long reach of prenatal hormones? Brain organization theory, digit ratio (2D/4D), and sex differences in preferences and cognition. *Perspectives on Psychological Science, 6*, 134–146.

Vallance, D. (2011). Yates, Andrea. In M. Z. Stange, C. K. Oyster, & J. E. Sloan (Eds.), *Encyclopedia of women in today's world* (Vol. 4, pp. 1599–1600). Newberry Park, CA: Sage.

Valls-Pedret, C. et al. (2015). Mediterranean diet and age-related cognitive declines: A randomized clinical trial. *JAMA International Medicine, 175*, 1094–1103.

van Amsterdam, N. (2013). Big fat inequalities, thin privilege: An intersectional perspective on 'body size.' *European Journal of Women's Studies, 20*, 155–169.

Van De Bongardt, D. et al. (2015). A meta-analysis of the relations between three types of peer norms and adolescent sexual behavior. *Personality and Social Psychology Review, 9*, 203–234.

Van De Griend, K. M. & Messias, D. K. (2014). Expanding the conceptualization of workplace violence: Implications for research, policy, and practice. *Sex Roles, 71*, 33–42.

van De Wiel, L. (2014). The time of the change: Menopause's medicalization and the gender politics of aging. *International Journal of Feminist Approaches to Bioethics, 7*, 74–98.

Van den Akker, O. (2012). *Reproductive health and psychology*. Malden, MA: Wiley.

Van den Berg, P., Neumark-Sztainer, D., Hannan, P. J., & Haines, J. (2007). Is dieting advice from magazines helpful or harmful? Five-year associations with weight-control behaviors and psychological outcomes in adolescents. *Pediatrics, 119*, e30–e37.

van den Brink, M. & Stobbe, L. (2014). Gender equality interventions in the STEM fields: Perceptions, successes and dilemmas. In D. Bilimoria & L. Lord (Eds.), *Women in STEM careers: International perspectives on increasing workforce participation, advancement, and leadership* (pp. 187–203). North Hampton, MA: Edward Elgar Publishing.

Van Der Gaag, N. (2014). *Feminism and men*. London: Zed Books.

Van der Heiden, B. et al. (2013). Individual characteristics and work-related outcomes. In M.C.W. Peters et al. (Eds.). *An introduction to contemporary work psychology*. (pp 243–266). Malden, MA: Wiley. (revision of ref, adding elements that had been omitted)

van der Heijden, B. et al. (2013). Individual characteristics and work-related outcomes. In M. E. W. Peters, J. de Jonge, & T. W. Taris (Eds.), *An introduction to contemporary work psychology* (pp. 243–266). Malden, MA: Wiley.

Van Home, B. S., Wiemann, C. M., Berenson, A. B., Horwitz, I. B., & Volk, R. J. (2009). Multilevel predictors of inconsistent condom use among adolescent mothers. *American Journal of Public Health, 99*, S417–S424.

van Oosten, J. M. F. et al. (2015). The influence of sexual music videos on adolescents' misogynistic beliefs: The role of video content, gender, and affective engagement. *Communication Research, 42*, 986–1008.

Van Mens-Verhulst, J. & Radtke, L. (2013). Women's identities and the third age: A feminist review of psychological knowledge. *Tijdschrift voor Genderstudies, 2*, 47–58.

Van Reijmersdal, E. A. et al. (2013). Why girls go pink: Game character identification and game-players' motivations. *Computers in Human Behavior, 29*, 2640–2649.

Vanfraussen, K., Ponjaert-Kristoffersen, I., & Brewaeys, A. (2003). Family functioning in lesbian families created by donor insemination. *American Journal of Orthopsychiatry, 73*, 78–90.

Varnes, J. R. et al. (2013). A systematic review of studies comparing body image concerns among female college athletes and non-athletes, 1997–2012. *Body Image, 10*, 421–432.

Varnes, J. R et al. (2015). Body esteem and self-objectification among collegiate female athletes: Does societal objectification make a difference? *Psychology of Women Quarterly, 39*, 95–108.

Vasiljevic, S. et al. (2017). Introducing different dimensions of gender equakity in a comparative perspective. In A. Ortenblad et al, (Eds.). *Gender equality in a global perspective* (pp.3–20). New York: Routledge.

Vasilyeva, M. (2010). Spatial development. In R. M. Lerner (Ed.), *The handbook of life-span development* (pp. 720–753). Hoboken, NJ: Wiley.

Vasquez, M. J. T. & de las Fuentes, C. (1999). American-born Asian, African, Latina, and American Indian adolescent girls: Challenges and strengths. In N. G. Johnson, M. C. Roberts, & J. Worell (Eds.), *Beyond appearance: A new look at adolescent girls* (pp. 151–173). Washington, DC: American Psychological Association.

Vassallo, T. et al. (2015). Women in tech. *Elephant in the Valley, 2*–15.

Velasquez, M. et al. (2015). *Women and drinking: Preventing alcohol-exposed pregnancies*. Ashland, OH: Hogrefe.

Velasquez, M. et al. (2017). Substance use disorders in women. In M. Kopala & M. Keitel (Eds.), *Handbook of counseling women* (2nd ed.). Thousand Oaks, CA: Sage.

Verdine, B. N. et al. (2014). Finding the missing piece: Blocks, puzzles, and shapes fuel school readiness. *Trends in Neuroscience and Education, 3*, 7–13.

Versey, H. S. et al. (2016). Successful aging in late midlife: The role of personality among college-educated women. *Journal of Adult Development, 20*, 63–75.

Verveer, M. & Azzarelli,K.K. (2015). *Fast forward: How women can achieve purpose and power*. Boston: Houghton Mifflin Harcourt.

Vespa, J. et al. (2013). *America's families and living arrangements: 2012.* P20–570. Washington, DC: U.S. Department of Commerce.

Vespa, J. (2014). Historical trends in the marital intentions of one-time serial cohabitors. *Journal of Marriage and Family, 76,* 207–217.

Viens, L. J. et al. (2016). Human papillomavirus-associated cancers—United States, 2008–2012. *Morbidity and Mortality Weekly Report, 65,* 661–666.

Villamor, E. & Jansen, E. C. (2016). Nutritional determinants of the timing of puberty. *Annual Review of Public Health, 37,* 33–46.

Villarosa, L. (2003, December 23). More teenagers say no to sex, but experts aren't sure why. *New York Times,* pp. D6, D8.

Villatoro, A.P. et al. (2014). Family cukture and mental health help-seeking and utility in a nationally representative sample of Latinos in the United States: The NLAAS. *American Journal of Orthopsychiatry, 84,* 353–363.

Vina, J. et al. (2013). Role of oestrogens on oxidative stress and inflammation in ageing. *Hormonal and Molecular Biology Clinical Investigation, 16,* 65–72.

Violence against women. (2009, April). Words to action: Newsletter on violence against women New York: United Nations.

Violence against women: An urgent public health priority. (2011). *Bulletin of the World Health Organization, 89,* 2–3.

Vishnevsky, T., Cann, A., Calhoun, L. G., Tedeschi, R. G., & Demakis, G. J. (2010). Gender differences in self-reported posttraumatic growth: A meta-analysis. *Psychology of Women Quarterly, 34,* 110–120.

Vo, K. et al. (2015). Retirement, age, gender and mental health: Findings from the 45 and up study. *Aging & Mental Health, 19,* 647–657.

Vogeltanz-Holm, N. et al. (2013). Alcohol use in women. In M. Spiers et al. (Eds.), *Women's health psychology* (pp. 91–122). New York: Wiley.

Voyer, D. (2011). Time limits and gender differences on paper-and-pencil tests of mental rotation: A meta-analysis. *Psychonomic Bulletin Review, 117,* 250–270.

Voyer, D. & Voyer, S. D. (2014). Gender differences in scholastic achievement: A meta-analysis. *Psychological Bulletin, 140,* 1174–1204.

Voyer, D., Voyer, S., & Bryden, M. P. (1995). Magnitude of sex differences in spatial abilities: A meta-analysis and consideration of critical variables. *Psychological Bulletin, 117,* 250–270.

Vrangalova, Z. & Savin-Williams, R. C. (2014). Psychological and physical health of mostly heterosexuals: A systematic review. *Journal of Sex Research, 51,* 410–445.

Wada, M. et al. (2014). Constructions of sexuality in later life: Analyses of Canadian magazine and newspaper portrayals of online dating. *Journal of Aging Studies, 32,* 40–49.

Wade, L. & Ferree, M. M. (2015). *Gender: Ideas, interactions, institutions.* New York: W. W. Norton.

Wade, T. D. et al. (2013). Genetic variants associated with disordered eating. *International Journal of Eating Disorders, 46,* 594–608.

Wadsworth, S. M. M. (2010). Family risk and resilience in the context of war and terrorism. *Journal of Marriage and Family, 72,* 537–556.

Wagner, L. (2014, November). Unlocking the emotions of cancer. *Monitor on Psychology,* 35–37.

Waits, B. L. & Lundberg-Love, P. (2008). The impact of campus violence on college students. In M. A. Paludi (Ed.), *Understanding and preventing campus violence* (pp. 51–70). Westport, CT: Praeger.

Walch, S. E. (2016). Discrimination, internalized homophobia, and concealment in sexual minority physical and mental health. *Psychology of Sexual Orientation and Gender Diversity, 3,* 37–48.

Waldron, J. C. et al. (2015). Sexual victimization history, depression, and task physiology revictimization: Results from a 6-month prospective pilot study. *Journal of Interpersonal Violence, 30,* 622–639.

Walker, K. F. et al. (2016). Randomized trial of labour induction in women 35 years of age or older. *New England Journal of Medicine, 374,* 813.

Walker, L. J. (2006). Gender and morality. In M. Killen & J. G. Smetana (Eds.), *Handbook of moral development* (pp. 93–115). Mahwah, NJ: Erlbaum.

Wallace, A. (2014). Unpacking the intersections of identity and politics and the politics of studying identity: A Black feminist theoretical and epistemological tool kit. In A. Jackson (Ed.), *Routledge international handbook of race, class, and gender* (pp. 10–18). New York: Routledge.

Wallace, R. (2015, Spring/Summer). Will the revolution be tweeted? *AAUW Outlook,* 1–2.

Waller, G. et al. (2014). Cognitive-behavioral therapy for bulimia nervosa and atypical bulimic nervosa: Effectiveness in clinical settings. International Journal of Eating Disorders, 47, 13–17.

Walsh, D. (2014, October 11, Two champions of children are given Nobel Peace Prize. *New York Times,* pA1.

Walsh, J. L., Ward, L. M., Caruthers, A., & Merriwether, A. (2011). Awkward or amazing: Gender and age trends in first intercourse experience. *Psychology of Women Quarterly, 35,* 59–71.

Waltermaurer, E. (2012). Public justification of intimate partner violence: A review of the literature. *Trauma, Violence, and Abuse, 13,*167–175.

Wang, M. (2012). *The Oxford handbook of retirement.* New York: Oxford University Press.

Wang, M. & Shi, J. (2014). Psychological research on retirement. *The Annual Review of Psychology, 65,* 209–233.

Wang, Q. & Pomerantz, E. M. (2009). The motivational landscape of early adolescence in the United States and China: A longitudinal investigation. *Child Development, 80,* 1272–1287.

Wang, U. M. et al. (2013). Weight status, quality of life, and cigarette smoking among adolescents in Washington state. *Quality of Life Research, 22,* 1577–1587.

Wang, W. (2013). Parents' time with kids more rewarding than paid work—and more exhausting. *Pew Research Social & Demographic Trends.* 1–12.

Wang, W. et al. (2013). *Breadwinner moms: Mothers are the sole or primary provider in four-in-ten households with children; Public conflicted about the growing trend.* Washington, DC: Pew Research Center.

Wang,W. & Parker, K. (2014) *Record share of Americans have never married.* Washington DC: Pew Research Center.

Wangby, M., Bergman, L. R., & Magnusson, D. (1999). Development of adjustment problems in girls: What syndromes emerge? *Child Development, 70,* 678–699.

Ward, L. M. & Harrison, K. (2005). The impact of media use on girls' beliefs about gender roles, their bodies, and sexual relationships: A research synthesis. In E. Cole & J. H. Daniel (Eds.), *Featuring females: Feminist analyses of media* (pp. 3–24). Washington, DC: American Psychological Association.

Wareham, S., Fowler, K., & Pike, A. (2007). Determinants of depression severity and duration in Canadian adults: The moderating effects of gender and social support. *Journal of Applied Social Psychology, 37,* 2951–2979.

Wardle, J. et al. (2015). Screening for prevention and early diagnosis of cancer. *American Psychologist, 70,* 119–133.

Ward, L.M. et al. (2016). Sexual media content and effects. *Oxford Research Encyclopedia of Communication.* doi:10.1093/acrefore/9780190228613.013.2

Wardy, M. A. (2014). *Redefining girly: How parents can fight the stereotyping and sexualizing of girlhood from birth to tween.* Chicago: Chicago Review Press.

Warren, C. S., Schoen, A., & Schafer, K. J. (2010). Media internalization and social comparison as predictors of eating pathology among Latino adolescents: The moderating effect of gender and generational status. *Sex Roles, 63,* 712–724.

Wasik, J.E. (2017, January 14). Death is inevitable. Financial turmoil afterward isn't. *New York times,* p.B3.

Warshaw, R. (1988). *I never called it rape: The Ms. report on recognizing, fighting, and surviving date and acquaintance rape.* New York: Harper & Row.

Wartl, A. C. et al. (2015). Survival analysis of adolescent friendships: The downside of dissimilarity. *Psychology Science, 26,* 1304–1315.

Wasylkiw, L. & Williamson, M. E. (2013). Actual reports and perceptions of body image concerns of young women and their friends. *Sex Roles, 68,* 239–251.

Watamura, S. E., Morrissey, T. W., Phillips, D. A., McCartney, K., & Bub, K. (2011). Double jeopardy: Poorer social-emotional outcomes for children in the NICHD SECCYD experiencing home and child-care environments that confer risk. *Child Development, 82,* 48–65.

Waterman, A. S. (1999). Identity, the identity statuses, and identity status development: A contemporary statement. *Developmental Review, 19,* 591–621.

Watkins, L. E. et al. (2014). The longitudinal impact of intimate partner aggression and relationship status on women's physical health and depression symptoms. *Journal of Family Psychology, 1,* 1–18.

Watkins-Hayes, C. (2014). Intersectionality and the sociology of HIV/AIDS: Past, present, and future research directions. *Annual Review of Psychology, 40,* 431–457.

Watson, K. B. et al. (2016). Physical activity among adults aged 50 years and older—United States, 2014. *Morbidity and Mortality Weekly Report, 65,* 954–958.

Watson, L. B. (2013). Racial identity buffers african American women from body image problems and disordered eating. *Psychology of Women Quarterly, 37,* 337–350.

Watson, L. B. (2015). Experiences of sexual objectification, minority stress, and disordered eating among sexual minority women. *Psychology of Women Quarterly, 39,* 458–470.

Watt, H. (2016). *The ethics of pregnancy, abortion and childbirth: Exploring moral choices in childbearing.* New York: Routledge.

Wave, L. J. et al. (2014). Sexual connectiveness at older age implications for health and well-being. In C. R. Agnew & S. C. South (Eds.), *Interpersonal relationships and health: Social and clinical psychological mechanisms* (pp. 202–231). New York: Oxford University Press.

Wayne, J. H. & Casper, W. J. (2016). Why having a family-supportive culture, not just policies, matters to male and female job seekers: An examination of work-family conflict, values, and Self-interest. *Sex Roles,* doi:10.1007/s11199-016-06457.

Weaver, H. N. (2009). The colonial context of violence: Reflections on violence in the lives of Native American women. *Journal of Interpersonal Violence, 24,* 1552–1563.

Webb, L. (2015). Shame transfigured: Slut-shaming from Rome to cyberspace. *First Monday, 20,* 1–22.

Webb, S. N. & Chonody, J. (2014). Heterosexual attitudes toward same-sex marriage: The influence of attitudes toward same-sex parenting. *Journal of GLBT Family Studies, 10,* 404–421.

Weber, D. et al. (2014). The changing face of cognitive gender differences in Europe. *Proceedings of the National Academy of Sciences, 111,* 11673–11678.

Wegner, R. et al. (2015). Sexual assault perpetrators' justifications for their actions: Relationships to rape supportive attitudes, incident characteristics, and future perpetration. *Violence Against Women, 21,* 1018–1037.

Weichold, K., Silbereisen, R. K., & Schmitt-Rodermund, E. (2003). Short-term and long-term consequences of early versus late physical maturation in adolescents. In C. Hayward (Ed.), *Gender differences at puberty* (pp. 241–276). Cambridge, MA: Cambridge University Press.

Weinberg, M. S., Williams, C. J., & Pryor, D. W. (1994). *Dual attraction: Understanding bisexuality.* New York: Oxford University Press.

Weiner, J. (2016, January 10). One day we can stop trying, right? *New York Times,* p. SR2.

Weir, K. (2015, November). Who are today's psychologists? *Monitor on Psychology,* 30–33.

Weisgram, E. S. & Bigler, R. S. (2006). Girls and science careers: The role of altruistic values and attitudes about scientific tasks. *Journal of Applied Developmental Psychology, 27,* 326–348.

Weisgram, E. S., Bigler, R. S., & Liben, L. S. (2010). Gender, values, and occupational interests among children, adolescents, and adults. *Child Development, 81,* 778–796.

Weisgram, E. et al. (2014). Pink gives permission: Exploring the roles of explicit gender labels and gender-typed colors on preschool children's toy preferences. *Journal of Applied Developmental Psychology, 35,* 401–409.

Weitz, R. (2010). *The sociology of health, illness, and health care: A critical approach.* Boston, MA: Wadsworth.

Weitzer, R. (2015). Human trafficking and contemporary slavery. *Annual Review of Sociology, 41,* 223–242.

Wellman, N. S., Kamp, B., Kirk-Sanchez, N. J., & Johnson, P. M. (2007). Eat better & move more: A community-based program designed to improve diets and increase physical activity among older Americans. *American Journal of Public Health, 97,* 710–717.

Welsh, A. (2010). On the perils of living dangerously in the slasher horror film: Gender differences in the association between sexual activity and survival. *Sex Roles, 62,* 762–773.

Wentzel, K. R., Filisetti, L., & Looney, L. (2007). Adolescent prosocial behavior: The role of self-processes and contextual cues. *Child Development, 78,* 895–910.

Wenzel. A. (2014). *Coping with infertility, miscarriage, and neonatal loss.* Washington, DC: American Psychological Association.

Werner, E. E. (2010). Resilience research: Past, present, and future. In R. D. Peters, B. Leadbeater, & R. J. McMahon (Eds.), *Resilience in children, families and communities: Linking context to practice and policy* (pp. 3–12). New York: Kluwer Academic/Plenum.

Werner, E. E. & Smith, R. S. (2001). *Journeys from childhood to midlife: Risk, resilience and recovery.* Ithaca, NY: Cornell University Press.

Wertheim, E. H., Paxton, S. J., & Blaney, S. (2009). Body image in girls. In L. Smolak & J. K. Thompson (Eds.), *Body image, eating disorders, and obesity in youth: Assessment, prevention, and treatment* (pp. 47–76). Washingt

Westmarland, N. (2015). *Violence against women: Criminological perspectives on men's violence.* New York: Routledge.

Westwood, S. (2016). *Aging, gender, and sexuality: Equality in later life.* New York: Routledge.

Whealin, J. & Barnett, E. (2015). *Child sexual abuse.* VA: National Center for PTSD.

Whealin, J. M., Zinzow, H. M., Salstrom, S. A., & Jackson, J. L. (2007). Sex differences in the experience of unwanted sexual attention and behaviors during childhood. *Journal of Child Sexual Abuse, 16,* 41–58.

Whiston, S. C. & Keller, B. K. (2004). The influences of the family of origin on career development: A review and analysis. *Counseling Psychologist, 32,* 493–568.

Whitaker, K. et al. (2015). School-based protective factors related to suicide for lesbian, gay, and bisexual adolescents. *Journal of Adolescent Health,58,* 63–68.

Whitbourne, S. K., Sneed, J. R., & Sayer, A. (2009). Psychosocial development from college through midlife: A 34-year sequential study. *Developmental Psychology, 45,* 1328–1340.

White, A. M. (Ed.). (2010). *African Americans doing feminism: Putting theory into everyday practice.* Albany, NY: SUNY Press.

White, C. N. & Warner, L. A. (2015). Influence of family and school-level factors age of sexual initiation. *The Journal of Adolescent Health, 56,* 231–237.

White, J. W. & Kowalski, R. M. (1994). Deconstructing the myth of the nonaggressive woman: A feminist analysis. *Psychology of Women Quarterly, 18,* 487–508.

Whitefield-Madrano A. (2016). *Face value: The hidden way beauty shapes women's lives.* New York: Simon & Schuster.

Whitehead, B. D. & Popenoe, D. (2008). *Life without children: The social retreat from children and how it is changing America.* Piscataway, NJ: The National Marriage Project, Rutgers.

Whitelock, C. F. et al. (2013). Overcoming trauma: Psychological and demographic characteristics of child sexual abuse survivors in adulthood. *Clinical Psychological Science, 20,* 1–12.

Whittier, N. (2016). Where are the children? Theorizing the missing piece in gendered sexual violence. *Gender & Society, 30,* 95–108.

WHO Women's Health. (2013). Media center women's health fact sheet No. 334. *WHO.* 1–9.

Why science needs female mice. (2015, July 19). *New York Times,* p. SR10.

Wickrama, K. A. S. & O'Neal, C. W. (2013). Marital functioning from middle to later years: A life course-stress process framework. *Journal of Family Theory & Review, 5,* 15–34.

Widman, L. et al. (2014). Sexual communication between early adolescents and their dating partners, parents, and best friends. *Journal of Sex Research, 51*, 731–741.

Wigfield, A. et al. (2014). Development of achievement motivation and engagement. In R. M Lerner & L. S. Liben (Eds.), *Handbook of child psychology and developmental science, vol. 3* (pp. 657–699). New York: Wiley.

Wilbourn, M. P. & Kee, D. W. (2010). Henry the nurse is a doctor too: Implicitly examining children's gender stereotypes for male and female occupational roles. *Sex Roles, 62*, 670–683.

Wilder, J. (2015). *Color stories: Black women and colorism in the 21st century.* Santa Barbara, CA: ABC-CLIO.

Wilkerson, A. (2014). Disability, sex, radicalism, and political agency. In K. Q. Hall (Ed.), *Feminist disability studies* (pp. 193–217). Bloomington, IN: Indiana University Press.

Williams, J. C. et al. (2013). Cultural schemas, social class, and the flexibility stigma. *Journal of Social Issues, 69*, 209–234.

Williams, J. C. et al. (2016). Beyond work-life "Integration." *Annual Review of Psychology, 67*, 515–539.

Williams, J. C. & Dempsey, R. (2014). *What works for women at work: Four patterns working women need to know.* New York: New York University Press.

Williams, J. E. & Best, D. L. (1990). *Measuring sex stereotypes: A multination study.* Newbury Park, CA: Sage.

Williams, M. J., Paluck, E. L., & Spencer-Rodgers, J. (2010). The masculinity of money: Automatic stereotypes predict gender differences in estimated salaries. *Psychology of Women Quarterly, 34*, 7–20.

Williams, M.J. & Tiedens, L.Z. (2016). The subtle suspension of backlash: A meta-analysis of penaltiesfor women's explicit and implicit dominance behavior. *Psychological Bulletin, 142*, 165–197.

Williams, S. L. et al. (2014). Intimate partner violence. In R. Gartner & B. McCarthy (Eds.), *Oxford handbook of gender, sex, and crime* (pp. 362–378). New York: Oxford University Press.

Williams, T. & Williams, K. (2010). Self-efficacy and performance in mathematics: Reciprocal determinism in 33 nations. *Journal of Educational Psychology, 102*, 453–466.

Wilson, J. (2011). Sexually transmitted infection in pregnancy. In K. E. Rogstad (Ed.), *ABC of sexually transmitted infections* (6th ed., pp. 59–63). New York: Wiley.

Wilson, L. C. & Miller, K. E. (2016). Meta-analysis of the prevalence of unacknowledged rape. *Trauma, Violence, & Abuse, 17*, 149–159.

Wilson, R. (2004, January 23). Louts in the lab. *Chronicle of Higher Education*, pp. A7–A9.

Windsor, T. D. et al. (2015). Sense of purpose as a psychological resource for aging well. *Developmental Psychology, 51*, 975–986.

Wineman, J.D. et al. (2014). Designing healthy neighborhoods: Contributions of the built environment to physical activity in Detroit. *Journal of Planning Education and Research, 34*, 180.

Winkle-Wagner, R. (2009). *The unchosen me: Race, gender, and identity among Black women in College.* Baltimore, MD: Johns Hopkins Press.

Winkle-Wagner, R. (2015). Having their lives narrowed down? The state of black women's college success. *Review of Educational Research, 85*, 171–204.

Winterich, J. A. (2003). Sex, menopause, and culture: Sexual orientation and the meaning of menopause for women's sex lives. *Gender & Society, 17*, 627–642.

WISER. (2006). *Social security reform.* Washington, DC: Author.

WISER. (2015). And. . . the pay gap's connected to the retirement gap! Washington, DC: Author.

Woertman, L. & van den Brink, F. (2012). Body image and female sexual functioning and behavior: A review. *Journal of Sex Research, 49*, 464–476.

Wohn, D.Y., (2011). Gender and race representation in casual games *Sex Roles.65*, 198–207.

Wolf, J. B. (2016). Framing mothers: Child-care research and the normalization of maternal care. *Signs: Journal of Women in Culture and Society, 41*, 627–651.

Wölfer, R. & Hewstone, M. (2015). Intra- versus intersex aggression: Testing theories of sex differences using aggression networks. *Psychological Science, 26*, 1285–1294.

Wolowicz-Ruszkowska, A. (2015). How Polish women with disabilities challenge the meaning of motherhood. *Psychology of Women Quarterly, 40*, 80–95.

Woman named Mohegan tribal chief. (2010, March 5). *Washington Times.* Retrieved from washingtontimes.com/news/2010/mar/05/woman-named-mohegan-chief/

Women and heart health: From prevention to intervention. (2005, February). *National Women's Health Report, 27*(1), 1–4.

Women can have multiple orgasms. (2007, April 10). *New York Times*, p. D6.

Women shirk cardiac rehab, study shows. (2016, March). *Harvard Women's Health Watch*, p.8.

Women's Bureau, U.S. Department of Labor (2013). *Older women and work.* Washington, DC: Author.

Women's College Coalition. (2008). What matters in college after college: A comparative alumnae research study. *West Hartford*, CT: Author.

Women's College Coalition. (2014). *The truth about women's colleges: comparative enrollment trends of women's colleges and private, co-educational colleges.* Decatur, GA: Wmen's College coalition.

Women's Media Center. (2014). *The status of women in the U.S. media 2014.* Washington, DC: Author.

Women's Media Center. (2015). *WMC divided 2015: The media gender gap.* Washington, DC: Author.

Women's rights are human rights: US ratification of the Convention on the Elimination of All Forms of Discrimination Against Women. (CEDAW). (2010). *Hearing before the Committee on the Judiciary, United States Senate. 111th Cong., 1.*

Women's Sports Foundation. (2016). *Beyond X's & O's: Gender bias and coaches of women's college sports.* New York: Author.

Wong, J. S. & Waite, L. J. (2015). Marriage, social networks, and health at ooder ages. *Journal of Population ageing, 8*, 7–25.

Wood, J. T. & Fixmer-Oraiz, N. (2017). *Gendered lives: Communication, gender, and culture.* (12th ed.). Boston, MA: Cengage.

Wood, W., & Eagly, A. H. (2010). Gender. In S. T. Fiske, D. T. Gilbert, & G. Lindzey (Eds.), *Handbook of social psychology* (5th ed., Vol. 1, pp. 629–667). Hoboken, NJ: Wiley.

Wood, W. & Eagly, A. H. (2015). Two traditions of research on gender identity. *Sex Roles*, 1–10.

Woodford, M. R. et al. (2014). Discrimination and mental health among sexual minority college students: The type and form of discrimination does matter. *Journal of Gay & Lesbian Mental Health, 18*, 142–163.

Woodhill, B. M. & Samuels, C. A. (2003). Positive and negative androgyny and their relationship with psychological health and well-being. *Sex Roles, 48*, 555–565.

Woodruffe-Burton, H. (2016). Countering heteronormativity: Lesbians and well-being in the workplace. In M. L. Connerley & J. Wu (Eds.), *Handbook on well-being of working women* (pp. 47–63). Dordrecht, Netherlands: Springer.

Woods, N. F. (2014). Grandmothering and health in midlife. *Menopause, 21*, 1032–1034.

Woolley, A. et al. (2015, January 18). Why some teams are smarter than others. *New York Times*, p. SB5.

Worell, J. (2001). Feminist interventions: Accountability beyond symptom reduction. *Psychology of Women Quarterly, 25*, 335–343.

Worell, J. & Etaugh, C. (1994). Transforming theory and research with women: Themes and variations. *Psychology of Women Quarterly, 18*, 443–450.

Worell, J. & Johnson, D. M. (2001). Feminist approaches to psychotherapy. In J. Worell (Ed.), *Encyclopedia of women and gender* (pp. 425–437). San Diego, CA: Academic Press.

World Health Organization. (2010). *Gender, women and primary health care renewal: A discussion paper.* Geneva, Switzerland: Author.

World Health Organization (2013). *World health statistics 2013.* Geneva, Switzerland: Author.

World Health Organization. (2014a). *Partner violence: Preventing and addressing intimate violence against migrant and ethnic minority women: The role of the health sector.* Geneva: Author.

World Health Organization. (2014b). *Preventing suicides: A global imperative.* Geneva: Author.

World Health Organization. (2015a). *Sexually transmitted infections (STIs).* Geneva: Author.

World Health Organization. (2015b). *WHO report on the global tobacco epidemic, 2015: Raising taxes on tobacco.* Geneva: Author.

Workowski, K.A. & Bolan, G.A.(2015). Sexually transmitted diseases treatment guidelines, 2015. *Morbidity and Mortality Weekly Reports, 64*(RR-03).

Worobey, J. & Worobey, H. S. (2014). Body-size stigmatization by preschool girls: In a doll's world, it is good to be "Barbie." *Body Image, 11,* 171–174.

Worrall-Carter, L. et al. (2016). Gender differences in presentation, coronary intervention, and outcomes of 28,985 acute coronary syndrome patients in Victoria, Australia. *Women's Health Issues, 26,* 14–20.

Worth, R. F. (2010, August 22). Crime (sex) and punishment (stoning). *New York Times,* pp. WK1, WK4.

Wrench, J. S. & Knapp, J. L. (2008). The effects of body image perceptions and sociocommunicative orientations on self-esteem, depression, and identification and involvement in the gay community. *Journal of Homosexuality, 55,* 471–503.

Wright, M. (2014). Transnational black feminisms, womenisms, and queen of color critiques. In M. Evans et al. (Eds.), *SAGE handbook of feminist theory* (pp. 327–342). Thousand Oaks, CA: Sage.

Wright, M. & Allbaugh, L. (2016). Promoting pathways to resilient outcomes for maltreated children. In C. Askeland Price & K. R. Bush (Eds.) *Families & change: Coping with stressful events and transitions* (pp. 223–248). Thousand Oaks, CA: Sage.

Wright, T. (2016). *Gender and sexuality in male-dominated occupations: women working in construction and transport.* New York: Palgrave Macmillan.

Wroolie, T. & Holcomb, M. (2010). Menopause. In B. L. Levin & M. A. Becker (Eds.), *A public health perspective of women's mental health* (pp. 143–164). New York: Springer.

Wuston, T. (2014, October 19). Are women better decision makers? *New York Times,* p. SR9.

Wyche, K. F. & Crosby, F. J. (Eds.). (1996). *Women's ethnicities: Journeys through psychology.* Boulder, CO: Westview.

Xie, Y. et al. (2015). STEM education. *Annual Review of Sociology, 41,* 331–357.

Xu, J. (2016). Mortality among centenarians in the United States, 2000–2014. *NCHS Data Brief, 233,* 1–3.

Xu, J. et al. (2016). Deaths: Final data for 2013. *National Vital Statistics Reports,64*(2). Hyattsville, MD: National Center for Health Statistics.

Xu, X. et al. (2015). Sex differences in perceived stress and early recovery in young and middle-aged patients with acute myocardial infarction. CHYPERLINK "http://circ.ahajournals.org" \h *irculation,* doi.org/10.1161/CIRCULATIONAHA.114.012826.

Yabroff, J. (2007, October 1). Mothers to blame. *Newsweek,* p. 86.

Yakushko, O. & Consoli, M. L. M. (2014). Politics and research of immigration: Implications for counseling and psychological scholarship and action. *Journal for Social Action in Counseling Psychology, 6,* 98–122.

Yang, C. et al. (2016). Social relationships and physiological determinants of longevity across the human lifespan, *PNAS, 113,* 578–583.

Yankaskas, B. C. et al. (2010). Barriers to adherence to screening mammography among women with disabilities. *American Journal of Public Health, 100,* 947–953.

Yarrow, A. L. (2015, February, 8). Falling marriage rates reveal economic fault lines. *New York Times,* p. ST15.

Yas, H. & Hamilton, C. (2013). Investigating the sexuality of disabled Japanese women: Six autobiographical accounts. *Women's Studies Journal, 27,* 44–53.

Yavorsky, J. E. et al. (2015). The production of inequality: The gender division of labor across the transition to parenthood. *Journal of Marriage and Family, 77,* 662–679.

Ybarra, M. L. et al. (2016). Lifetime prevalence rates and overlap of physical, psychological, and Sexual dating abuse perpetration and victimization in a national sample of youth. *Archives of Sexual Behavior.* doi:10.1007/s10508-016-0748-9.

Yeshua, A. et al. (2015). Female couples undergoing IVF with partner eggs (Co-IVF): Pathways to parenthood. *LGBT Health, 2,* 135.

Yoder, J. D. (2010). Does "making a difference" still make a difference? A textbook author's reflections. *Sex Roles, 62,* 173–178.

Yoder, J. D. (2015). Looking backward and moving forward: Our feminist imperative to do work that matters. *Psychology of Women Quarterly, 39,* 427–431.

Yoder, J. D. & Aniakudo, P. (1999). "Outsider within" the firehouse: Subordination and difference in the social interactions of African American women fire-fighters. In L. A. Peplau, S. C. DeBro., R. C. Veniegas, & P. L. Taylor (Eds.), *Gender, culture*

and ethnicity: Current research about women and men (pp. 135–152). Mountain View, CA: Mayfield.

Yoder, J. D., Tobias, A., & Snell, A. F. (2011). When declaring "I am a feminist" matters: Labeling is linked to activism. *Sex Roles, 64,* 9–18.

Yom-Tov, E. & Boyd, D. M. (2014). On the link between media coverage of anorexia and pro-anorexic practices on the web. *International Journal of Eating Disorders, 47,* 196–202.

Yonkers, K. A. et al. (2016). Anxiety disorders in women. In D. J. Castle & K. M. Abel (Eds.), *Comprehensive women's mental health* (pp. 220–232). Cambridge UK: Cambridge University Press.

Yoo, G. J. et al. (2014). Breast cancer and coping among women of color: A systematic review of the literature. *Support Care Cancer, 22,* 811–824.

Yorgason, J. & Stott, K. (2016). Physical and mental illness and family stress. In C. A. Price Askeland & K. R. Bush (Eds.), *Families & change: Coping with stressful events and transitions* (pp. 293–314). Thousand Oaks, CA: Sage.

Yost, M. R. & Chmielewski, J. F. (2013). Blurring the line between researcher and researched in interview studies: A feminist practice? *Psychology of Women Quarterly, 37,* 242–250.

Young, D.M. et al. (2013). The influence of female role models on women's implicit science cognitions, *Psychology of women Quarterly, 37,* 282–293.

Young, H. & Cochrane, B. (2015). Healthy aging for women. In E. Olshansky (Ed.), *Women's health and wellness across the lifespan* (pp. 95–122). Philadelphia: Wolters Kluwer Health.

Young, V. J. et al. (2013). The role of the peritoneum in the pathogenesis of endometriosis. *Europe PubMed Central, 19,* 558–569.

Yu, E. et al. (2016). Diet, lifestyle, biomarkers, genetic factors, and the risk of cardiovascular disease in the Nurses' Health Studies. *American Journal of Public Health, 106,* 1616–1623.

Yu, L. & Xie, D. (2010). Multidimensional gender identity and psychological adjustment in middle childhood: A study in China. *Sex Roles, 62,* 100–113.

Yücel, C. & Eroglu, K. (2013). Sexual problems in postmenopausal women and coping methods. *Sexual Disability, 31,* 217–228.

Zabin, L. S. & Cardona, K. M. (2002). Adolescent pregnancy. In G. M. Wingood & R. J. DiClemente (Eds.), *Handbook of women's sexual and reproductive health* (pp. 231–253). New York: Kluwer Academic/Plenum.

Zager, K. & Rubenstein, A. (2002). *The inside story on teen girls.* Washington, DC: American Psychological Association.

Zajakova, A. et al. (2014). Socioeconomic disparities among older adults and the implications for the retirement debate: A brief report. *Journals of Gerontology Series B: Psychological Science and Social Science 69,* 973–978.

Zambrana, R. E. & MacDonald, V.-M. (2009). Staggered inequalities in access to higher education by gender, race, and ethnicity. In B. T. Dill & R. E. Zambrana (Eds.), *Emerging intersections: Race, class, and gender in theory, policy, and practice* (pp. 73–100). Piscataway, NJ: Rutgers University Press.

Zeiders, K. H. et al. (2015). Grandmothers' familism values adolescent mothers' parenting efficacy, and children's well-being. *Journal of Family Psychology, 29,* 624–634.

Zeigler-Hill, V. & Noser, A. (2015). Will I ever think I'm thin enough? A moderated mediation study of women's contingent self-esteem, body image discrepancies, and disordered eating. *Psychology of Women Quarterly, 39,* 109–118.

Zell, E. et al. (2015). Evaluating gender similarities and differences using metasynthesis. *American Psychologist, 70,* 10–20.

Zerwas, S. & Claydon, E. (2014). Eating disorders during the lifespan: From menstruation to menopause. In D. Barnes (Ed.), *Women's reproductive mental health across the lifespan* (pp. 237–262). New York: Springer.

Zhang, S. et al. (2013). L'eggo my ego: Reducing the gender gap in math by unlinking the self from *performance. Self and Identity, 12,* 400–412.

Zhang, Y. et al. (2013). Moving considerations: A longitudinal analysis of parent-child residential proximity for older Americans. *Research on Aging, 35,* 663–687.

Zhang, Z. & Jin, S. (2014). The impact of social support on post-partum depression: The mediator role of self-efficacy. *Journal of Health Psychology, 21,* 720–726.

Zhou, X. & Wang, Y. (2015). The end of the one-child policy: Lasting implications for China. *Journal of the American Medical Association, 314,* 2619–2620.

Zilanawala, A. (2016). Women's time poverty and family structure: Differences by parenthood and employment. *Journal of Family Issues. 37,* 369–392.

Zimmerman, E. (2009, November 22). Expecting a baby, but not the stereotypes. *New York Times,* p. BU10.

Zimmerman, K. & Hammer, L. (2010). Where have we been and what lies ahead? In J. Joudmont & S. Leka (Eds.), *Contemporary occupational health psychology: Global perspectives on research and practice: Vol. 1* (pp. 272–295). Malden, MA: Wiley.

Zink, T. & Sill, M. (2004). Intimate partner violence and job instability. *Journal of the American Medical Women's Association, 59,* 32–35.

Zong, G. et al. (2016). Whole grain intake and mortality from all causes, cardiovascular disease, and cancer. *Epidemiology and Prevention, 133,* 2370–2380.

Zosuls, K. et al. (2014). Self-socialization of gender in African American, Dominican immigrant, and Mexican immigrant toddlers. *Child Development, 85,* 2202–2217.

Zou, M. (2015). Gender, work orientations and job satisfaction. *Work, Employment, and Society, 29,* 3–22.

Zucker, a. N. & Bay-Cheng, L. Y. (2010). Minding the gap between feminist identity and attitudes: The behavioral and ideological divide between feminists and non-feminists. *Journal of Personality, 75,* 1895–1924

Zucker, A. N. & Stewart, A. J. (2007). Growing up and growing older: Feminism as a context for women's lives. *Psychology of Women Quarterly, 31,* 137–145.

Zucker, K. J. (2001). Biological influences on psychosocial differentiation. In R. K. Unger (Ed.), *Handbook of the psychology of women and gender* (pp. 101–115). New York: Wiley.

Zucker, K. J. (2008). On the "natural history" of gender identity disorder in children. *Journal of American Academy of Child and Adolescent Psychiatry, 47,* 1361–1363.

Zuckerman, M. et al. (2016). When men and women differ in self-esteem and when they don't: A meta-analysis. *Journal of Research in Personality,* doi: http://dx.doi.org/10.1016/j.jrp.2016.07.007

Zulman, D. & Humphreys, K. (2014, May 23). You're never too old to be studied. *New York Times,* p. A19.

Zumwalt, M. & Dowling, B. (2014). Effects of the menstrual cycle on the acquisition of peak bone mass. In J. J. McComb et al. (Eds.), *The active female: Health issues throughout the lifespan* (2nd ed., pp. 81–92). New York: Springer.

Zweig, J. M. et al. (2014). Can Johnson's typology of adult partner violence apply to teen dating violence? *Journal of Marriage and Family, 76,* 808–825.

NAME INDEX

Page numbers in italics refer to figures. Page numbers in bold refer to tables.

SUBJECT INDEX

Page numbers in italics refer to figures. Page numbers in bold refer to tables.

PHOTO CREDITS